S0-AFI-310

To Jenny, Ben, Rebecca, and Zack

The book is done. Let's play.

Contents in Brief

Contents

Preface

If you walk down the aisle of the business section in your local bookstore (or surf the "Business" page at Amazon.com), you'll find hundreds of books that explain precisely what companies need to do to be successful. Unfortunately, these books tend to be faddish, changing every few years. Lately, the best-selling business books have emphasized technology, reengineering, and going global, whereas ten years ago the hot topics were joint ventures, mergers, and management buyouts.

One thing that hasn't changed, though, and never will, is the importance of good management. *Management* is getting work done through others. Organizations can't succeed for long without it. Well-managed companies are competitive because their work forces are smarter, better trained, more motivated, and more committed. Furthermore, good management leads to satisfied employees who, in turn, provide better service to customers. Because employees tend to treat customers the same way that their managers treat them, good management can improve customer satisfaction. Finally, research shows that companies that practice good management consistently have greater revenues and profits than companies that don't.

In writing *Management*, my goal was to write a textbook that students would enjoy, that students would refer to for practical, theory-driven advice, and that encouraged students to put theory-driven knowledge into practice for themselves. In short, the concepts that you, as students, will learn in this book can improve the performance of the organization and department where you work, can even help you solve job-related problems, and can improve your own job performance, even if you're not a manager.

So welcome to *Management*! Please take a few minutes to read the preface and familiarize yourself with the approach (combining theory with specific stories and examples), features, pedagogy, and end-of-chapter assignments in *Management*. This is time well spent. After all, along with your instructor, this book will be your primary learning tool.

Stories

Combining Theory with Specific Stories and Examples

Say "theory" to college students, and they assume that you're talking about complex, arcane ideas and terms that have nothing to do with the "real world," but that need to be memorized for tests and then forgotten after the final exam. However, as students, you needn't be wary of theoretical concepts. Theories are simply ideas. And good theories are simply good ideas that have been tested through rigorous scientific study and analysis.

Where textbooks go wrong is that they stop at theory and read like dictionaries. Or, they focus on theoretical issues related to research rather than practice. However, good management theories (i.e., good ideas) needn't be complex or arcane. In fact, the late Rensis Likert, of the University of Michigan, once said that there is nothing as practical as a good theory.

So, to provide you with practical, theory-driven advice and encourage you to put theory-driven knowledge into practice for yourselves, each chapter in this book contains 50 to 60 specific stories and examples that illustrate how managers are using management ideas in their organizations. Here's an example from Chapter 8 on global management to show you what I mean. One of the key issues in global management is successfully preparing employees for international assignments. In fact, the difficulty of adjusting to language, cultural, and social differences in another country is the primary reason that so many business people fail in international assignments. Consequently, you'll read this passage in Chapter 8.

> *For example, it is estimated that 10 percent to 45 percent of American expatriates sent abroad by their companies will return to the U.S. before they have successfully completed their international assignments. Of those who do complete their international assignments, as many as 30 percent to 50 percent are judged by their companies to be no better than marginally effective.*

This passage is fairly standard, research-based information. You'll find it in most textbooks. Is it important for you to know this information? You bet! Is it likely that you will find this and the thousands of other pieces of theory- and research-based facts throughout the book particularly compelling or interesting (and thus easier to learn)? Ah, there's the problem. However, what if we combine theory and research with specific, "real world" stories and examples that illustrate good or poor use of those theories? For instance, the passage below is also in Chapter 8, immediately following the research-based information about the difficulty of adjusting to foreign cultures.

> *In his book* Blunders in International Business, *David Ricks tells the story of an American couple in Asia. After a walk with their dog, the Americans had dinner at a local restaurant. Since the waiters and waitresses did not speak English, they ordered by pointing to items on the menu. Because their dog was hungry, they pointed to the dog and to the kitchen. The waiter had trouble understanding, but finally took the dog to the kitchen. The American couple assumed that this meant the dog could not be fed in the dining room, but was going to be fed in the kitchen. Unfortunately, to the couple's dismay, the waiter and the chef returned later to proudly show them how well they had cooked the poodle.*

After reading this passage, you will have a vivid understanding of what can go wrong if people don't receive cultural and language training before traveling or moving to another country. Why does this help you to learn? Because the first passage cites theory and research on the effectiveness of cross-cultural training, and the second brings the theory and research into the real world by illustrating what can go wrong if you don't get that cross-cultural training.

In short, both research and theory *and* stories and examples are important for effective learning. Therefore, this book contains thousands of specific examples and stories that apply management theories in interesting ways. So, to get more out of this book, read and understand the theoretical ideas. Then read the stories or examples to learn how those ideas should or should not be used in practice. You'll find that both the theories and the stories and examples are up to date.

A tremendous amount of time and thought went into planning this textbook. I reviewed over 25 top-selling texts in management, marketing, finance, statistics, and economics. I asked more than 200 students and dozens of professors what they specifically liked and disliked about their texts. And, I pulled some of my favorite books (many of which were not about business) from my bookshelf to figure out what made them great books. Only then did I create the plan and organization for *Management*. Take a few minutes now to familiarize yourself with its features. Doing so will help you get more out of the book and your management class.

Blast from the Past Nearly every management text contains the standard "history of management" chapter. However, after discussions with dozens of management professors, I learned that most of them struggled to teach it and that their students rarely saw its relevance. As a result, most of them no longer teach the history of management. So rather than write a chapter that professors wouldn't teach and that students wouldn't read, I decided instead to include a *Blast from the Past* historical feature in most of the chapters. The advantage of this approach is that you are exposed to management history in small bites, which is easier to consume than all at once. Also, since you come across the *Blast from the Past* in the normal course of reading a chapter, it's easier for you to see the link between historical management ideas and those you're studying today. The result, I hope, is that you will appreciate how yesterday's thinkers and pioneers paved the way for today's management theories and practice.

Back to the Future While appreciating history is important, given the pace of change in today's business world, it's also important to look ahead. Consequently, most chapters include a *Back to the Future* feature that focuses on management practices that are becoming or will likely become more important in the future. Not surprisingly, *Back to the Future* explores how technology is likely to change the way that companies manage themselves and their workers. However, this feature also explores the growing importance of Mother Nature as a corporate stakeholder and how tomorrow's organizations will be structured differently from today's. So, if you're interested in how management will change in the next few years, be sure to read the *Back to the Future* feature.

Been There, Done That My twin brother, who is a critical-care neurologist, likes to tease me by saying, "Those who can, do. Those who can't, teach." While I can't print my typical response here (ah, sibling rivalry), I do have to admit that he's partially right. We give special credibility to "experts" who can "walk their talk." For instance, in the last few years, I've had the opportunity to teach in Europe during the summer. Of course, I've also taken the opportunity to travel. But, if you know anything about Europe, you know that there are just too many places to see and not enough time or money to see them all. However, my wife and I started using travel guides written by Rick Steves, who hosts a PBS TV show called *Travels in Europe*. Steves' books provide daily itineraries for travel destinations that include specific advice on where to eat, where to stay, and what to do. My wife and I followed these plans and had a wonderful time in Europe for about half the price that most Americans pay. Why were we willing to trust his advice? His words explain it best. "I've spent twenty years exploring Europe through the back door. This book, which has evolved over twelve editions, is my report to you after a virtual lifetime in the travelers' school of hard knocks.

Experience is a great teacher. These are my notes, taken in the hope that you'll learn from my mistakes rather than your own and have the best possible trip." In other words, Rick Steves has visited every bed and breakfast, every restaurant, and every castle in his books. He figured out what worked for him, and shared that advice with others.

Most management problems work the same way. There's no point in starting from scratch when someone else has already faced the problem before. Who could be better to talk to about a problem than someone who has already "been there and done that"? So, if you want to learn about management from people who have faced and solved management problems firsthand, read the *Been There, Done That* interviews with experienced managers that you'll find in almost every chapter.

Personal Productivity Tips *PC Magazine* publishes a "road warrior's guide" to traveling with a laptop computer and doing business on the road. This guide discusses the importance of backup batteries, the necessity of toolkits for taking apart phone jacks in motel rooms (to rig a connection to your laptop modem at 3 a.m., so you can download that last killer slide for the 8 a.m. presentation), and many other things you'd never think of that could prevent computer-related disasters when you travel. Readers love the road warrior's guide because it's so helpful and useful. By contrast, most students believe that management theory is too abstract to be of any use to them. Therefore, to help you make the leap from management theory to management practice, you'll find three to four *Personal Productivity Tips* in each chapter. Located in the margins, *Personal Productivity Tips* are designed to give quick, useful, practical management advice that can make an immediate difference. So if you want to learn how to get a passport, how to encrypt computer files and e-mail (so that confidential company information remains confidential), how to use conflict to solve problems, how to create an electronic resume (and we don't mean using a word processor), or how to ask for a raise, and more, read the *Personal Productivity Tips* in the margins of each chapter.

What *Really* Works? Some studies show that two drinks a day increase life expectancy by decreasing your chances of having a heart attack. Yet other studies show that two drinks a day will shorten your life expectancy. For years, we've "buttered" our morning toast with margarine instead of butter, because margarine was supposed to be better for our health. However, new studies now show that the trans-fatty acids in margarine may be just as bad for our arteries as butter. Confusing scientific results like these frustrate ordinary people who want to "eat right" and "live right." It also makes many people question just how useful most scientific research really is.

Managers also have trouble figuring out what works, based on the scientific research published in journals like the *Academy of Management Journal*, the *Academy of Management Review*, the *Strategic Management Journal*, the *Journal of Applied Psychology*, and *Administrative Science Quarterly*. It's common for *The Wall Street Journal* to quote a management research article from one of these journals that says that total quality management is the best thing since sliced bread (without butter or margarine). Then, just six months later, *The Wall Street Journal* will quote a different article from the same journal that says that total quality management doesn't work. If management professors and researchers have trouble deciding what works and what doesn't, how can practicing managers know?

Thankfully, a research tool called *meta-analysis*, which is a study of studies, is helping management scholars understand how well their research supports management theories. Fortunately, meta-analysis is also useful for practicing managers, because it shows what works and the conditions under which management techniques may work better or worse in the "real world." Meta-analysis is based on the simple idea that if one study shows that a management technique doesn't work and another study shows that it does, an average of those results is probably the best estimate of how well that management practice works (or doesn't work). Plus, you don't need a Ph.D. to understand the statistics reported in a meta-analysis. In fact, one primary advantage of meta-analysis over traditional significance tests is that you can convert meta-analysis statistics into intuitive numbers that anyone can easily understand. Indeed, each meta-analysis reported in the *What Really Works?* sections of this text is accompanied by an easy-to-understand statistic called the *probability of success*. As its name suggests, the *probability of success* uses a bar graph and a percentage (0% to 100%) to indicate the likelihood that a management technique will actually work.

Of course, no idea or technique works every time and in every circumstance. However, in today's competitive, fast-changing, global marketplace, few managers can afford to overlook proven management strategies like those discussed in the *What Really Works?* feature of this book.

Pedagogy

Pedagogical features are meant to reinforce learning, but they don't have to be boring. Accordingly, the teaching tools used in *Management* will help students learn and will hold their interest, too.

Chapter Outline and Numbering System, Learning Objectives, and Section Reviews

Because of their busy schedules, very few students can read a chapter from beginning to end in one sitting. Typically, it takes students anywhere from two to five study sessions to completely read a chapter. Accordingly, at the beginning of each chapter, you'll find a detailed chapter outline in which each major part in the chapter is broken into numbered sections and subsections. For example, the outline for the first part of Chapter 3 on ethics and social responsibility looks like this:

What Is Ethical and Unethical Workplace Behavior?

1. Ethics and the Nature of Management Jobs
2. Workplace Deviance
3. U.S. Sentencing Commission Guidelines
   - 3.1 Who, What, and Why?
   - 3.2 Determining the Punishment

The numbered information contained in the chapter outline is then repeated in the chapter as learning objectives (at the beginning of major parts of the chapter) and as numbered headings and subheadings (throughout the chapter) to help students remember precisely where they are in terms of the chapter outline. Finally, instead of a big summary at the end of the chapter, students will find detailed reviews at the end of each section.

Together, the chapter outline, numbering system, learning objectives, section headings (which mark the beginning of a section), and section reviews (which mark the end of a section) allow students to break the chapter into smaller, self-contained segments that they can read in their entirety over multiple study sessions.

Furthermore, the numbered headings and outline should make it easier for instructors and students to know what is being assigned or discussed in class ("In section 3.1 of Chapter 3...").

Key Terms Key terms appear in boldface in the text, with definitions in the margins to make it easy for students to check their understanding. A complete alphabetical list of key terms appears at the end of each chapter as a study checklist, with page citations for easy reference.

What Would You Do? and What Really Happened? At the beginning of each chapter, there is an opening case called *What Would You Do?* in which a manager faces an interesting problem or situation related to the chapter's topics. Three to five teaser questions are usually posed at the end of the case, along with the general question "*If you were this manager, what would you do?*" Then at the end of each chapter, students find out the answers to these questions in a follow-up to the opening case called *What Really Happened?* Unlike most texts in which the follow-up to the opening case is typically very short, or is simply a technique for presenting more review questions, each *What Really Happened?* is typically a page or longer, answers each of the questions posed in the opening case, and provides enough information for students to understand how things turned out, what the companies did and why they did it, and whether it worked. Finally, each *What Really Happened?* shows how companies combined various ideas from the chapter to try to solve specific business problems.

End-of-Chapter Assignments

Most texts provide only two or three end-of-chapter assignments. By contrast, at the end of each chapter in *Management*, there are five assignments from which to choose. This gives instructors more choice in selecting just the right assignment for their classes. It also gives students a greater variety of activities, making it less likely that they'll repeat the same kind of assignment chapter after chapter.

What Would You Do-II? Similar to the case that opens the chapter, *What Would You Do-II?* is a case in which a manager faces an interesting problem or situation related to the chapter topics. Students are expected to analyze the case and suggest solutions. The *What Really Happened?* solutions for these cases appear in the instructor's manual.

Critical-Thinking Video Case The second case in each chapter is a video case, in which students read a short description of the company, view a short in-class video, and then answer several critical-thinking questions. All videos are part of South-Western's *Business Link* video series.

Management Decisions There are two *Management Decisions* in each chapter. Typically, these are somewhat shorter, more focused assignments, in which students must decide what to do and then answer several questions to explain their choices. For example, students must decide which of two employees deserves a promotion, what the company policy should be on personal use of e-mail, whether flexible work schedules are family-friendly or discriminatory toward workers who don't have children at home, and more. Also, one *Management Decision* in each chapter also includes Internet references and locations, so that students can gather additional information before deciding what to do.

Develop Your Management Potential These assignments have one purpose: to help students develop their present and future capabilities as managers. What students learn through these assignments is not traditional "book-learning" based on memorization and regurgitation, but practical knowledge and skills that help managers perform their jobs better. Assignments include interviewing managers, dealing with the press, visiting a charity or nonprofit, learning from failure, walking in someone else's shoes, 360-degree feedback, and more.

Supplements

Web Site A rich Web site at **http://williams.swcollege.com** complements this text with many extras for students and instructors. The student pages feature basic study aids, such as a tutorial on how to find things on the Internet, two Internet activities per chapter, one new *What Would You Do?* case per chapter, links to current articles related to chapter topics, links to the organizations cited in the text examples and cases, plus links to additional sites of interest. For each chapter, one Internet activity is aimed at beginning Web surfers, and the other leads more experienced Netizens in using the Web for business research. All *What Would You Do?* cases on the site focus on e-commerce, an important topic in management today.

The instructor's pages include links to the student materials, abstracts and discussion questions for the Internet articles, the *What Really Happened?* solutions to the e-commerce cases, plus solutions and implementation tips for the Internet activities.

Business Link Videos (ISBNs 0-538-88238-7, 0-538-88239-5, 0-538-86168-1). The *Business Link* video series is a set of video cases specifically created for use with South-Western Publishing Company's line of business texts. Each video runs approximately 10-15 minutes. The management videos were designed to cover the major topics in each chapter of this text.

The videos show real companies dealing with real management issues. Critical-thinking questions appear at appropriate points in the video, requiring students to think about the key issues. These questions, along with a brief case description, appear as the *Critical-Thinking Video Case* at the end of each text chapter. Solutions to the cases and run times appear in the instructor's manual.

Instructor's Manual (ISBN 0-538-86165-7). The instructor's manual offers comprehensive teaching outlines, annotated with teaching tips and prompts for when to show the transparencies and videos. The outlines cover the major topics of each chapter, including features, in a format that is easy to follow during class presentations.

Complete solutions to all end-of-chapter text activities appear in the manual, including the *What Really Happened?* follow-up to the *What Would You Do-II?* cases. An *Additional Learning Activities* section in each manual chapter provide ten discussion questions, with solutions, plus five group-based activities and Internet activities. Most of the Internet activities are based on an interesting and different style of Internet business magazine called *Fast Company*.

Supplements

Test Bank (ISBN 0-538-86166-5). The test bank contains 150 test questions for each chapter, for a total of 2,700 questions from which to choose. Each chapter offers 65 true-false, 70 multiple-choice, 10 short-answer, and 5 critical-thinking questions. Thorough solutions are provided for each question, including difficulty ratings and page references where the solutions appear in the text. A correlation table at the beginning of each test bank chapter makes it easy for instructors to select the appropriate mix of questions for their students.

A computerized version of the test bank is available upon request. *Thomson Learning Testing Tools* ***(ISBN 0-538-86167-3)*** allows instructors to create, edit, store, and print exams. The system is menu-driven with a desktop format to make the program quick and easy to use.

PowerPoint™ Slides (ISBN 0-538-86170-3). A rich set of PowerPoint slides, *with teaching notes,* will make class presentations easy and interesting! The approximately 30-50 colorful slides per chapter cover all key concepts, terms, features, and cases in the text. Animations and transitions add movement to many of the slides, allowing instructors to show one point at a time and adding a dynamic feel that will hold student interest throughout the presentation. Ample teaching notes offer additional insights and examples plus important points to cover in lectures.

Acetate Transparencies (ISBN 0-538-86169-X). For adopters without access to PowerPoint™, a set of over 100 transparencies are available upon request. These transparencies can supplement lectures by displaying the key illustrations from the text.

Student CD-ROM (ISBN 0-324-03715-5). The CD-ROM offers a new video case that explores the characteristics of learning organizations. It features Yahoo!, the zany company that leads the way for more traditional organizations on the Web, learning as it goes. Case questions are programmed to allow students to email their solutions directly to their instructors.

Also available on the CD-ROM are interactive quiz questions for each chapter plus complete business and management glossaries. The CD-ROM requires Internet Explorer or Netscape Navigator 3.0 or higher.

Student Study Guide (ISBN 0-538-86164-9). The study guide is designed to help students review the text's key concepts and prepare for tests. Each study guide chapter begins with questions that will help students approach the text's *What Would You Do?* opening case. A detailed chapter outline, containing the learning objectives, key term definitions, and major points in the chapter, serves as a useful review tool. After reading the chapter and reviewing the outline, students can test their understanding with multiple-choice, true-false, short-answer, and critical-thinking questions similar to those they might see on the tests. Solutions with text page references appear at the end of each study guide chapter.

Acknowledgments

Acknowledg-ments

Let's face it—writing a textbook is a long and lonely process. It's surely the most difficult (and rewarding) project I've ever tackled. And, as I sat in front of my computer with a rough outline on the left side of my desk, a two-foot stack of journal articles on the floor, and a blank screen in front of me, it was easy at times to feel isolated. But, as I found out, a book like this doesn't get done without the help of many other talented people.

First, I'd like to thank the outstanding team of supplement authors: Jennifer Dose, from the University of Minnesota, Morris, who wrote the fantastic student study guide; Nancy H. Leonard, from Lewis-Clark State College, who developed the great Web site for this text; Gerald W. Ramey, also of Lewis-Clark State College, who wrote parts of the instructor's manual; my friend and former colleague, Ken Eastman, of Oklahoma State University, for the superb PowerPoint slides; and David Leuser, of Plymouth State College, for the excellent test bank.

Secondly, I'd like to thank the world-class team at South-Western College Publishing for the outstanding support (and patience) they provided while I wrote this book. Executive Editor John Szilagyi was calm, collected, and continuously positive through the major ups and downs of this project. Rob Bloom, who was in charge of marketing the book, did an outstanding job of developing marketing themes and approaches. Kelly Keeler, who managed the production process, was consistently upbeat and positive with me when I deserved otherwise. Authors are prone to complain about their publishers. But that hasn't been my experience at all. Pure and simple, everyone at South-Western has been great to work with throughout the entire project. However, special thanks on this team go to Cinci Stowell, of Stowell Editorial Services, who was my developmental editor and with whom I had the most contact while writing the book. Cinci worked with reviewers, edited the manuscript, managed the development of supplements, provided superb feedback and guidance at every stage of the book, and nudged and prodded me to write faster, make improvements, and maintain the high quality standards that were set when I began writing. In fact, some of the better ideas for features and pedagogy were hers. Cinci, thanks for doing a great job.

I'd also like to thank an outstanding set of reviewers whose diligent and thoughtful comments improved this book in enormous ways.

Bruce R. Barringer
University of Central Florida

Gayle Baugh
University of West Florida

Diane P. Caggiano
Fitchburg State College

Nicolette DeVille Christensen
Guilford College

Kathy Daruty
Pierce College

Jennifer Dose
University of Minnesota, Morris

Charles R. Franz
University of Missouri-Columbia

Barry Allen Gold
Pace University

Jim Jawahar
Illinois State University

Paul N. Keaton
University of Wisconsin-La Crosse

Ellen Ernst Kossek
Michigan State University

Linda Livingstone
Baylor University

George Marron
Arizona State University

Robert McGowan
University of Denver

Acknowledgments

Sherry Moss
Florida International University

Stephanie Newport
Austin Peay State University

David M. Porter, Jr.
UCLA

Amit Shah
Frostburg State University

Thomas Shaughnessy
Illinois Central College

James O. Smith
East Carolina University

Gregory K. Stephens
Texas Christian University

Jennie Carter Thomas
Belmont University

James Thornton
Champlain College

Mary Jo Vaughan
Mercer University

Finally, my family deserves the greatest thanks of all for their love, patience, and support. Writing a textbook is an enormous project with incredible stresses and pressures on authors as well as their loved ones. However, throughout this project, my wife, Jenny, was unwavering in her support of my writing. She listened patiently, encouraged me when I was discouraged, read and commented on most of what I wrote, gave me the time to write, and took wonderful care of me and our children during this long process. My children, Benjamin, Rebecca, and Zack, also deserve special thanks for their patience and for understanding why Dad was locked away at the computer for all of this time. While writing this book has been the most rewarding professional experience of my career, it pleases me no end that my family is as excited as I am that it's done. So, to Jenny, Benjamin, Rebecca, and Zack. The book is done. Let's play.

Meet the Author: Chuck Williams, Texas Christian University

Chuck Williams is an Associate Professor of Management, Chair of the Management Department, and Interim Associate Dean at the M.J. Neeley School of Business at Texas Christian University. He received his B.A. in Psychology from Valparaiso University, and specialized in the areas of Organizational Behavior, Human Resources, and Strategic Management while earning his M.B.A and Ph.D. in Business Administration from Michigan State University. Previously, he taught at Michigan State University and was on the Faculty of Oklahoma State University.

His research interests include employee recruitment and turnover, performance appraisal, and employee training and goal-setting. Chuck has published research in the *Journal of Applied Psychology*, the *Academy of Management Journal*, *Human Resource Management Review*, *Personnel Psychology*, and the *Organizational Research Methods Journal*. He is a member of the *Journal of Management's* editorial board, and serves as a reviewer for numerous other academic journals. He is also the webmaster for the Research Methods Division of the Academy of Management (http://www.aom.pace.edu/rmd). Chuck was the 1997 co-recipient of the Society for Human Resource Management's Yoder-Heneman Research Award.

Chuck has consulted for a number of organizations: General Motors, IBM, JCPenney, Tandy Corporation, Trism Trucking, Central Bank and Trust, StuartBacon, the City of Fort Worth, the American Cancer Society, and others. He has taught in executive development programs at Oklahoma State University, The University of Oklahoma, and Texas Christian University.

Chuck teaches a number of different courses, but has been privileged to teach his favorite course, *Introduction to Management*, for nearly 20 years. His teaching philosophy is based on four principles: (1) courses should be engaging and interesting; (2) there's nothing as practical as a good theory; (3) students learn by doing; and (4) students learn when they are challenged. In 1995, the undergraduate students at TCU's Neeley School of Business named him instructor of the year. In 1997, he was a recipient of TCU's Dean's Teaching Award.

Part One

Introduction to Management

Chapter One

Chapter 1 Outline

Management

What Would **You** Do?

Headquarters, The Limited, Inc., Columbus, Ohio. It's late. You're tired. The comfort of your executive chair would lull you to sleep if you didn't have so much on your mind, like what kind of story *Forbes* magazine is going to print about your company. You just finished giving the *Forbes* reporter a tour of your retail empire at nearby City Center Mall, which serves as a testing ground for the new retail store ideas that have made you a billionaire in the last 15 years. The reporter visited each of your retail stores: Victoria's Secret (designer lingerie), Cacique (French lingerie), Bath & Body Works (toiletries for men and women), The Limited (the heart of your company, mainstream styles at good prices), Compagnie Internationale Expresse (trendier, European styles), Lerner New York (for cost-conscious buyers), Lane Bryant (fashionable clothes for larger women), Limited Too (sportswear for women), Abercrombie & Fitch (outdoors fashions), Structure (European clothes for men), and Henri Bendel (high-end women's fashion and accessories). Over the last five years, total corporate sales have grown by 40 percent. However, profits are flat. All that growth just to stay even with where the company was five years ago. Blaming someone other than yourself would be easy. After all, the entire retail industry has slumped, too. Kmart has closed stores, sold off its Price Warehouses, and canned its CEO. Sears has retrenched, too. So, it's understandable that The Limited, Inc. has struggled as well. But the slump has not hurt everyone. Other retailers have thrived during the industry downturn. Before, when faced with slower growth, you would come up with another idea for a new store to bolster sales. For example, Compagnie Internationale Expresse got its start as a set of goods on a table in a Chicago Limited store. Fifteen years later, sales totaled over $1.4 billion in 716 stores. This time, however, you just can't get by the idea that part of the problem is you. With over $7 billion in sales, you've slowly come to the conclusion that you can't run the company the way you did when you founded it or when you were achieving record growth. You pull your feet off the desktop, order a late dinner, and pull out your notepad. At the top of the page, you write "Back to Basics," and begin to list the key questions that you must answer if you're to successfully turn your company around. *What should you, the CEO, be responsible for at The Limited? Given these responsibilities, how should your role as CEO change? What should your middle managers be doing and how can you change the company to make sure they do it?* It's been a wild ride, and you have had success beyond anything you could imagine. But now, the money doesn't matter anymore. What keeps you going and motivated is how well you "play the game." Well, you're overdue for a big win. You write one more question on your notepad, *"What is good management?"* If you can't answer this question, maybe it's time to let someone else run the show. **If you were the CEO of The Limited, what would you do?**

Sources: L. Bird. "Limited to Shut 200 Stores, Change Express Managers," *The Wall Street Journal Interactive Edition*, 15 January, 1997. D. Machan, "Knowing Your Limits," *Forbes,* 5 June 1995, 128-132. B.D. Wolf, "Analysts Laud Limited Plan to Split into Three Companies," *Columbus Dispatch,* 29 March 1995.

The issues facing The Limited are fundamental to any organization: What is management and what do managers do? Good management is basic to starting a business, growing a business, and maintaining a business once it has achieved some measure of success.

This chapter begins by defining management and discussing the functions of management. Next, we look at what managers do by examining the four kinds of managers and reviewing the various roles that managers play. Third, we investigate what it takes to be a manager, by reviewing management skills, what companies look for in their managers, the most serious mistakes managers make, and what it is like to make the tough transition from being a worker to being a manager. We finish this chapter by examining the competitive advantage that companies gain from good management. In other words, we end the chapter by learning how to establish a competitive advantage through people.

What Is Management?

AT&T, the largest phone company in the world, spent nearly $350 million over a recent three-year period on "consulting and research services." Each year, the federal government spends more than $1.5 billion for similar services.[1] What AT&T and the federal government are really paying for is management advice. However, AT&T and the federal government aren't the only organizations in search of good management ideas. It's estimated that companies paid management consultants over $17 billion last year. Clearly, companies are looking for help with basic management issues, like how to make things happen, how to beat the competition, how to manage large-scale projects and processes, and how to effectively lead people. This textbook will help you understand some of the basic issues that management consultants help companies resolve (and, unlike AT&T and the federal government, this won't cost you millions of dollars).[2]

After reading these next two sections, you should be able to:

1 describe what **management is**.

2 explain the four **functions of management**.

1 Management Is . . .

Many of today's managers got their start welding on the factory floor, clearing dishes off tables, helping customers fit a suit, or wiping up a spill in aisle 3. Lots of you will start at the bottom and work your way up, too. There's no better way to get to know your competition, your customers, and your business. But whether you begin your career at the entry level or as a supervisor, your job is not to do the work, but to help others do their work. **Management** is getting work done through others. Pat Carrigan, a former elementary school principal who became a manager at a General Motors car parts plant, said, "I've never made a part in my life, and I don't really have any plans to make one. That's not my job. My job is to create an environment where people who do make them can make them right, can make them right the first time, can make them at a competitive cost, and can do so with

management
getting work done through others

efficiency
getting work done with a minimum of effort, expense, or waste

some sense of responsibility and pride in what they're doing. I don't have to know how to make a part to do any of those things."[3]

Pat Carrigan's description of managerial responsibilities indicates that managers also have to be concerned with efficiency and effectiveness in the work process. **Efficiency** is getting work done with a minimum of effort, expense, or waste. For example, at Springfield Remanufacturing Company, the machines are shut off for half an hour each week so that the 800 employees can break into small groups to study the company's weekly financial statements. With full information about the costs of labor, electricity, and raw materials, everyone at SRC can help increase efficiency by doing more with less cost and waste. For example, the workers learned that each sale of a rebuilt No. 466 crankshaft contributes $17.60 an hour toward paying overhead expenses. When they are able to rebuild these crankshafts quickly and efficiently, the additional inventory of finished crankshafts can generate as much as $170 a day that can be used to pay overhead costs, such as utility expenses or the salaries of scheduling and purchasing personnel. Countless small, efficiency-minded choices like that have helped SRC become one of the most profitable companies in its industry.

By itself, efficiency is not enough to ensure success. For years, Chrysler Motor Company watched its sales, market share, and profits shrink, despite being able to make a car for much less than either Ford or General Motors. It wasn't until Chrysler began producing award-winning car designs like the Dodge Stratus, Chrysler Concorde, Dodge Ram truck, and its completely redesigned, aerodynamic minivans that it began to regain market share and profitability. So, besides being concerned about efficiency, managers must also strive for **effectiveness**, which is accomplishing tasks that help fulfill organizational objectives.

Personal Productivity Tip

Do You Know How Efficient Your Business Is?

Many managers fail to keep track of one of the most important outcomes in business: efficiency. United Parcel Service, long regarded as the most efficient and productive company in the package shipping business, recently concluded that it had become much less efficient in the last few years. One clear indication: It took 8 separate phone calls to find a lost package! UPS's solution is to simply let customer service representatives directly contact drivers, thus reducing the process to a much more manageable four steps. If you want to improve how well your company is performing, keep close track of efficiency and productivity.

Source: R. Frank, "Efficient UPS Tries to Increase Efficiency," *The Wall Street Journal,* 24 May 1995, B1.

What Really Works

Meta-Analysis

Some studies show that two drinks a day increase life expectancy by decreasing your chances of having a heart attack. Yet other studies show that two drinks a day will shorten your life expectancy. For years, we've "buttered" our morning toast with margarine instead of butter because it was supposed to be better for our health. However, new studies now show that the trans-fatty acids in margarine may be just as bad for our arteries as butter. Confusing scientific results like these frustrate ordinary people who want to "eat right" and "live right." It also makes many people question just how useful most scientific research really is.

Managers also have trouble figuring out what works, based on the scientific research published in journals like the *Academy of Management Journal*, the *Academy of Management Review*, the *Strategic Management Journal*, the *Journal of Applied Psychology*, and *Administrative Science Quarterly*. It's common for *The Wall Street Journal* to quote a management research article from one of these journals that says that total quality management is the best thing since sliced bread (without butter or margarine). Then, just six months later, *The Wall Street Journal* will quote a different article from the same journal that says that total quality management doesn't work. If management professors and researchers have trouble deciding what works and what doesn't, how can practicing managers know?

meta-analysis
a study of studies, a statistical approach that provides the best scientific estimate of how well management theories and practices work

Thankfully, a research tool called **meta-analysis**, which is a study of studies, is helping management scholars understand how well their research supports management theories. However, meta-analysis is also useful for practicing managers, because it shows what works and the conditions under which management techniques may work better or worse in the "real world." Meta-analysis is based on the simple idea that if one study shows that a management technique doesn't work and another study shows that it does, an average of those results is probably the best estimate of how well that management practice works (or doesn't work). For example, medical researchers Richard Peto and Rory Collins averaged all of the different results from several hundred studies investigating the relationship between aspirin and heart attacks. Their analysis, based on more than 120,000 patients from numerous studies, showed that aspirin lowered the incidence of heart attacks by an average of 4 percent. Prior to this study, doctors prescribed aspirin as a preventive measure for only 38 percent of heart attack victims. Today, because of the meta-analysis results, doctors prescribe aspirin for 72 percent of heart attack victims.

Fortunately, you don't need a Ph.D. to understand the statistics reported in a meta-analysis. In fact, one primary advantage of meta-analysis over traditional significance tests is that you can convert meta-analysis statistics into intuitive numbers that anyone can easily understand.

Each meta-analysis reported in the "What Really Works?" section of each chapter is accompanied by an easy-to-understand statistic called the *probability of success.* As its name suggests, the *probability of success* shows how often a management technique will work.

For example, meta-analyses suggest that the best predictor of a job applicant's on-the-job performance is a test of general mental ability. In other words, smarter people tend to be better workers. The average correlation (one of those often-misunderstood statistics) between scores on general mental ability tests and job performance is .60. However, very few people understand what a correlation of .60 means. What most managers want to know is how often they will hire the right person if they choose job applicants based on general mental ability test scores. Likewise, they want to know how much of a difference a cognitive ability test makes when hiring new workers. The probability of success may be high, but if the difference isn't really that large, is it really worth a manager's time to have job applicants take a general mental ability test?

Well, our user-friendly statistics indicate that it's wise to have job applicants take a general mental ability test. In fact, the probability of success, shown in graphical form below, is 76 percent. This means that an employee hired on the basis of a good score on a general mental ability test stands a 76 percent chance of being a better performer than someone picked at random from the pool of all job applicants. So, chances are, you're going to be right much more often than you are wrong if you use a general mental ability test to make hiring decisions.

General Mental Ability

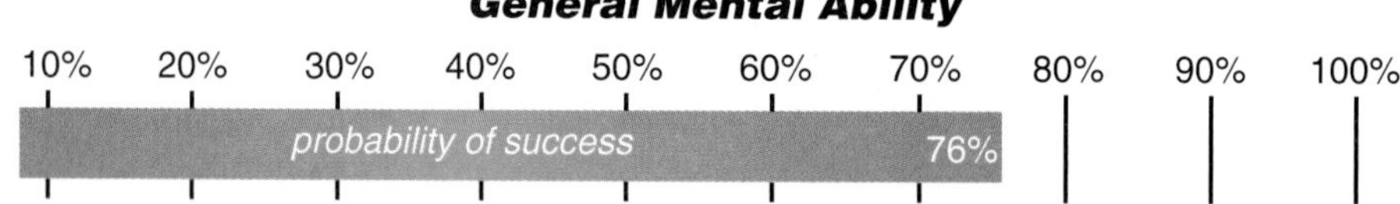

In summary, each "What Really Works?" section in this textbook is based on meta-analysis research, which provides the best scientific evidence that management professors and researchers have about what really works and what really doesn't work in management. An easy-to-understand index known as the "probability of success" will be used to indicate how well a management idea or strategy is likely to work in the workplace. Of course, no idea or technique works every time and in every circumstance. However, the management ideas and strategies discussed in the "What Really Works?" sections of this textbook can usually make a meaningful difference where you work. In today's competitive, fast-changing, global marketplace, few managers can afford to overlook proven management strategies like the ones discussed in "What Really Works?"

Sources: R.J. Grisson, "Probability of the Superior Outcome of One Treatment over Another," *Journal of Applied Psychology* 79 (1994): 314-316. J.E. Hunter & F.L. Schmidt, *Methods of Meta-analysis: Correcting Error and Bias in Research Findings* (Beverly Hills, CA: Sage, 1990).

effectiveness
accomplishing tasks that help fulfill organizational objectives

Review 1
Management Is . . .

Good management is working through others to accomplish tasks that help fulfill organizational objectives as efficiently as possible.

2 Management Functions

planning
determining organizational goals and the means for achieving them

organizing
deciding where decisions will be made, who will do what jobs and tasks, and who will work for whom

leading
inspiring and motivating workers to work hard to achieve organizational goals

controlling
monitoring progress toward goal achievement and taking corrective action when needed

Traditionally, a manager's job has been described according to the classical functions of management: planning, organizing, leading, and controlling. **Planning** is determining organizational goals and a means for achieving them. **Organizing** is deciding where decisions will be made, who will do what jobs and tasks, and who will work for whom in the company. **Leading** is inspiring and motivating workers to work hard to achieve organizational goals. **Controlling** is monitoring progress toward goal achievement and taking corrective action when progress isn't being made.

Studies indicate that managers who perform these management functions well are better managers. The more time that chief executive officers (CEOs) spend planning, the more profitable their companies are.[4] Over a 25-year period, AT&T found that employees with better planning and decision-making skills were more likely to be promoted into management jobs, to be successful as managers, and to be promoted into upper levels of management.[5]

The evidence is clear. Managers serve their companies well when they plan, organize, lead, and control. However, companies with familiar names like IBM, Hewlett-Packard, Digital Equipment Corporation, General Motors, and Sears are facing tremendous changes and are asking—if not demanding—that managers change the way they perform these functions. According to **Fortune** magazine, these changes are embodied in the difference between "old" management and "new" management. Old-style managers think of themselves as the "manager" or the "boss." New-style managers think of themselves as sponsors, team leaders, or internal consultants. Old-style managers follow the chain of command (reporting to the boss, who reports to the next boss at a higher managerial level, etc.), while new-style managers work with anyone who can help them accomplish their goals. Old-style managers make decisions by themselves. New-style managers ask others to participate in decisions. Old-style managers keep proprietary company information confidential. New-style managers share that information with others. Old-style managers demand long hours. New-style managers demand results.[6]

Such changes don't make the classical managerial functions obsolete. Indeed, managers are still responsible for performing the functions of management. For example, consider this description of a new-style manager and the people she works with (not the people who work for her, which is "old" management). The managerial functions represented by each action have been inserted in brackets.

> *Three years ago Ransom asked her workers at a 100-person plant in Fairfield, California, to redesign the plant's operations* [planning and organizing]. *As she watched, intervening only to answer the occasional question* [controlling], *a team of hourly workers established training programs, set work rules for absenteeism* [controlling], *and reorganized the once traditional factory into five customer-focused*

> *business units* [organizing and leading]. *As the workers took over managerial work* [decision making, organizing, and leading], *Ransom used her increasing free time to attend to the needs of customers and suppliers* [planning and controlling].[7]

As indicated within the brackets, Ransom and the members of her work group still perform the classical management functions. They just do them differently than old-style managers used to.

To reconcile the "new" with the "old," this textbook is organized around these four management functions (see Figure 1.1), which have evolved out of the traditional functions:

- Making Things Happen
- Meeting the Competition
- Organizing People, Projects, and Processes
- Leading

Note that these functions do not *replace* the classical functions of management; they *build* on them. For example, two of the four chapters under "Part

Figure 1.1 **Management Functions and Organization of the Textbook**

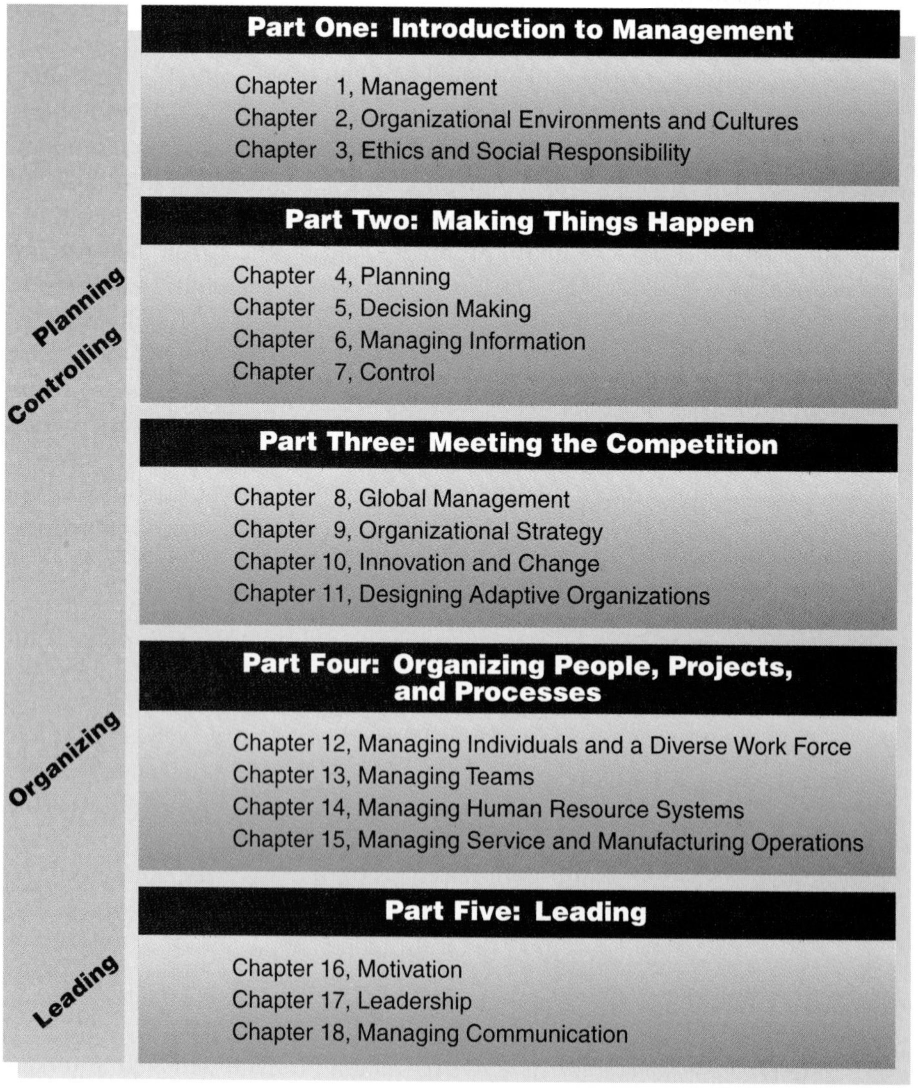

Part One: Introduction to Management

Chapter 1, Management
Chapter 2, Organizational Environments and Cultures
Chapter 3, Ethics and Social Responsibility

Part Two: Making Things Happen

Chapter 4, Planning
Chapter 5, Decision Making
Chapter 6, Managing Information
Chapter 7, Control

Part Three: Meeting the Competition

Chapter 8, Global Management
Chapter 9, Organizational Strategy
Chapter 10, Innovation and Change
Chapter 11, Designing Adaptive Organizations

Part Four: Organizing People, Projects, and Processes

Chapter 12, Managing Individuals and a Diverse Work Force
Chapter 13, Managing Teams
Chapter 14, Managing Human Resource Systems
Chapter 15, Managing Service and Manufacturing Operations

Part Five: Leading

Chapter 16, Motivation
Chapter 17, Leadership
Chapter 18, Managing Communication

2: Making Things Happen" are classical management functions (planning and controlling). Furthermore, two of the four classical functions of management, organizing and leading, remain as part of the "new" management functions. Finally, a brand new management function, "Meeting the Competition," has been added to reflect the importance of adapting and innovating to remain competitive in today's ever-changing and increasingly global marketplace.

Throughout this text, the major sections within a chapter will be numbered using a single digit: 1, 2, 3, and so on. Then the subsections will be consecutively numbered, beginning with the major section number. For example, "2.1" marks the first subsection under the second major section. This numbering system should help you easily see the relationships among topics and follow the topic sequence. It will also help your instructor refer to specific topics during class discussion.

Now let's take a close look at each of the management functions: **2.1** *Making Things Happen,* **2.2** *Meeting the Competition,* **2.3** *Organizing People, Projects, and Processes, and* **2.4** *Leading.*

2.1 *Making Things Happen*

For most of its existence, Lands' End, a successful catalog retailer, had been a small, informally run organization. Struggling under tremendous growth (revenues are now approximately $1 billion a year), founder Gary Comer looked outside the company to hire a new CEO to institute modern management methods. Comer hired William End (no relationship to the company name). End quickly introduced the latest management techniques: production teams, performance appraisal systems based on peer reviews (rather than supervisor-based reviews), and over 20 different training courses, such as effective communication. Although some of the techniques worked, others resulted in a large number of lost, late, or undelivered orders. Employees, many of whom had worked at the company since its inception, strongly resisted the changes. Furthermore, confusion resulted because too many changes were made in too little time. Supervisor Scott Jacobsen summed up the problems this way: "We spent so much time in meetings that we were getting away from the basic stuff of taking care of business."[8]

In his zeal to introduce the latest management techniques, End forgot that the most important management function is making things happen. To "make things happen," you must determine what you want to accomplish, plan how to achieve these goals, gather and manage the information needed to make good decisions, and control performance, so that you can take corrective action if performance falls short. In his estimation, company founder Gary Comer took corrective action when he fired William End for his failure to make things happen at Lands' End. In Chapters 4-7, you will learn more about how to make things happen.

2.2 *Meeting the Competition*

Microsoft was not in business 25 years ago. Yet now, because of its dominance of the software industry, *PC Magazine*, *Newsweek*, and *PC Week* are abuzz about possible antitrust action on the part of the federal government that would break Microsoft into several smaller, less-dominant companies.[9] Twenty years ago, these magazines said the same thing about IBM and its dominance of the computer industry. But because of stiff competition from Compaq, Dell, and dozens of other manufacturers of "IBM-compatible" computers, IBM lost more than $10 billion and saw its market share in personal computers drop from 80 percent to 8 percent by the early 1990s. Today, no one worries anymore about IBM dominating the computer industry. What made the difference in the fortunes of these two companies?

With free trade agreements that promote international competition, shorter product development cycles, and barriers to entry falling in most industries, market followers will continue to topple market leaders as companies are exposed to more competition than ever in the next decade. Companies that want to remain market leaders must consider the threat from international competitors, have a well-thought-out competitive strategy, be able to embrace change and foster new product and service ideas, and structure their organizations to quickly adapt to changing customers and competitors. Thus, "meeting the competition" is a critical management function in today's business world. In Chapters 8-11, you will learn some management skills for meeting the competition.

2.3
Organizing People, Projects, and Processes

In 1990, Ford Motor Company purchased Jaguar, a British automaker. Under Ford's guidance, Jaguar's new management laid off one-third of its employees and reorganized its North American operations into three smaller divisions. To emphasize its renewed commitment to customer satisfaction, Jaguar's new vice president of customer care met with Jaguar dealers to talk to them about working harder to please customers. But instead of lecturing the dealers, they lectured him. How could they take care of customers, they said, when Jaguar's management wasn't taking care of them, when all Jaguar's management did was put out recurring fires? The new vice president was surprised and admittedly not prepared for two days of "ranting" from Jaguar dealers.[10]

Like other managers who have tried to "reengineer" their companies, Jaguar's vice president of customer care found out that large-scale changes won't work without simultaneous consideration of people issues and work processes (how the work gets done).[11] Therefore, our next management function is "organizing people, projects, and processes." You will learn about this management function in Chapters 12-15.

2.4
Leading

In these litigious times, managers are sued for sexual harassment, wrongful discharge, and discrimination. They are shot at, lampooned in the funny pages (*Dilbert* is the fastest growing syndicated cartoon strip in years), and, in general, not accorded the respect they once had. In this decade of corporate layoffs, many would argue that managers are to be feared and disliked.

How is it, then, in this time of corporate distrust, that Mary Kay Ash, founder of Mary Kay cosmetics, and Herb Kelleher, founder of Southwest Airlines, are not only respected, but loved by the people they lead?[12] Gloria Mayfield, a former IBMer and a graduate of Harvard's MBA program, says, "I didn't see much recognition at IBM. At Mary Kay, if you do well, you know *for a fact* you'll get recognition. It's not influenced by politics." Mayfield goes on to say that "Mary Kay calls you her daughter and looks you dead in the eye. She makes you feel you can do anything. She's sincerely concerned about your welfare."[13]

At Southwest Airlines, pilots pitch in at the boarding gate, ticket agents help with the luggage, and employees in general do whatever needs to be done to keep customers happy. These positive attitudes help Southwest achieve the highest productivity in the industry, flying two-to-three times as many passengers per employee as its competitors at a cost that is 25 percent to 40 percent cheaper.[14] Kelleher, a notorious jokester and storyteller, draws exceptional effort from his troops by putting people first and by making work fun. When he finished negotiating a new contract with Southwest's flight attendants, he celebrated by leading the cafeteria crowd of Southwest workers in cheers. He has dressed up as Elvis, the Easter Bunny, and a boxer, complete with gloves and a silk robe, all to shape Southwest's corporate culture and win the hearts of his loyal work force.[15]

No one who has worked for an ordinary manager would ever deny the positive effects that inspirational leaders, such as Mary Kay and Herb Kelleher, bring to their companies. Thus, our last management function is "leading," which you will learn about in Chapters 16-18.

Review 2
Management Functions

Managerial jobs have traditionally been described according to the classical functions of management: planning, organizing, leading, and controlling. Although managers still perform these managerial functions, it's also true that companies and the managers who run them have undergone tremendous changes in the last decade. Accordingly, this text incorporates the classical functions of management into broader, updated management functions: making things happen; meeting the competition; organizing people, projects, and processes; and leading.

What Do Managers Do?

Not all managerial jobs are the same. The demands and requirements placed on the chief executive officer of General Motors are significantly different from those placed on the manager of your local Wendy's restaurant. After reading these next two sections, you should be able to:

3 describe different kinds of managers.

4 explain the major roles and subroles that managers perform in their jobs.

3 Kinds of Managers

As shown in Figure 1.2, there are four different kinds of managers with different jobs and responsibilities: **3.1** *Top Managers,* **3.2** *Middle Managers,* **3.3** *First-Line Managers, and* **3.4** *Team Leaders.*

Figure 1.2 **Jobs and Responsibilities of Four Kinds of Managers**

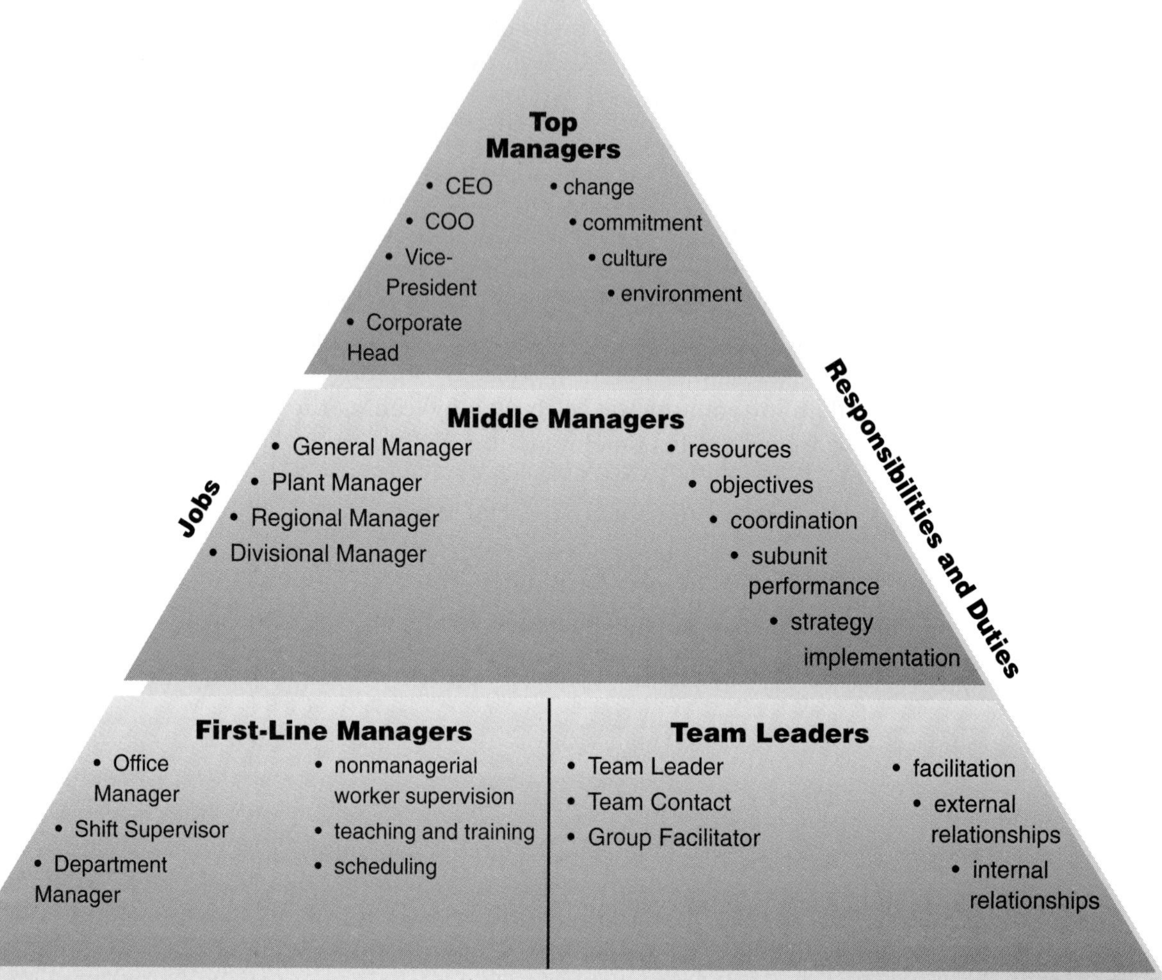

3.1 *Top Managers*

top managers
executives responsible for the overall direction of the organization

Top managers hold positions like chief executive officer (CEO) or chief operating officer (COO) and are responsible for the overall direction of the organization. Top managers have the following responsibilities.[16] First, they are responsible for creating a context for change. In fact, the CEOs of American Express, General Motors, Digital Equipment Corporation, Westinghouse, and Kodak were all fired within a year's time precisely because they had not moved fast enough to bring about significant changes in their companies. Creating a context for change also includes forming a long-range vision or mission for their companies. As one CEO said, "The CEO has to think about the future more than anyone."

Second, much more than used to be the case, top managers are responsible for helping employees develop a sense of commitment to the business. Stories abound at Southwest Airlines about CEO Herb Kelleher's willingness to listen to his employees. One such story has Kelleher out until four in the morning drinking in a bar with a Southwest mechanic. The point of the story is that Kelleher, supposedly the most important person in the company, was listening to the mechanic, supposedly one of the least important persons in the company, so he (Kelleher) could fix whatever was wrong.[17]

Third, top managers are responsible for creating a positive organizational culture through language and action. Top managers impart company values, strategies, and lessons through what they do and say to others, both inside and outside the company. One CEO said, "I write memos to the board and our operating committee. I'm sure they get the impression I dash them off, but usually they've been drafted ten or twenty times. The bigger you get, the more your ability to communicate becomes important. So what I write, I write very carefully. I labor over it."[18] David Glass, who became CEO of Wal-Mart when company founder Sam Walton passed away, continues to tell stories about how thrifty "Mr. Sam" was while running the company. However, Glass not only tells this story to emphasize Wal-Mart's thriftiness, but he and his top management team back it up by being thrifty themselves. For example, while visiting a local Wal-Mart (and Glass and his top executives spend two-to-three full days per week on the road visiting Wal-Mart stores), Glass and his managers stayed at a Super 8 hotel that cost $40 per room when they could have stayed at a nicer Holiday Inn, which was charging $75 per room.[19]

Finally, top managers are responsible for monitoring their business environments. This means that top managers must closely monitor customer needs, competitors' moves, and long-term business, economic, and social trends. Whenever he visits a Wal-Mart store, CEO David Glass always schedules a visit to the local competition, like Kmart or Target. And, like all of Wal-Mart's top executives, he always examines competitors' prices and is always on the lookout for good ideas that Wal-Mart might "borrow" for its own stores.[20]

3.2 *Middle Managers*

middle managers
managers responsible for setting objectives consistent with top management's goals, and planning and implementing subunit strategies for achieving these objectives

Middle managers hold positions like plant manager, regional manager, or divisional manager. They are responsible for setting objectives consistent with top management's goals and planning and implementing subunit strategies for achieving these objectives. One specific middle management responsibility is to plan and allocate resources to meet objectives. Another major responsibility is to coordinate and link groups, departments, and divisions within a company. Rather than calling the shots from company headquarters, each Monday morning in Bentonville, Arkansas, all of Wal-Mart's regional vice presidents, accompanied by merchandise buyers and personnel managers, board 15 company planes as they fly out to spend the next four days visiting the stores in each sales territory. The regional vice presidents then reconvene in Bentonville on Fridays and on Saturday mornings to share ideas and solve the problems they identified on their weekly trips.[21]

A third responsibility of middle management is to monitor and manage the performance of the subunits and individual managers who report to them. For example, one of the first things that Andy Wilson, a Wal-Mart regional vice president, will do when he visits a store in his territory is to find the store manager and then make a walking inspection of the store. On one inspection tour of a new store in his territory, Wilson was disappointed to find that products were not displayed according to headquarters' plans. Furthermore, because department managers had been slow to reorder products, many shelves were empty because replacement supplies had not yet

Middle managers set objectives, plan resources, coordinate groups, monitor performance, and implement changes and strategies. © David Joel/Tony Stone Images

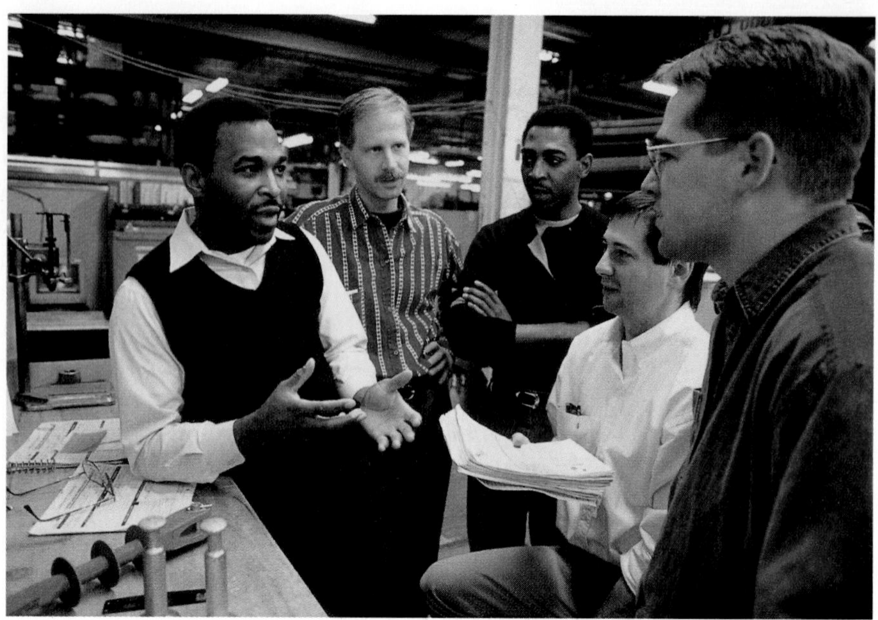

arrived from the Wal-Mart warehouses. Rather than waiting for the next truck shipment, Wilson told the department managers to correct the problem by arranging to transfer out-of-stock products from the nearest Wal-Mart store.[22]

Finally, middle managers are also responsible for implementing the changes or strategies generated by top managers. Since Wal-Mart competes by selling products at low prices—its advertising slogan is "always the low price"—Andy Wilson and the other regional vice presidents visit competitors' stores to check prices. At a Kmart that competes with one of his region's stores, Wilson found signs that compared the Kmart price for each product with Wal-Mart's price. Wilson filled a cart with these items, purchased them, and then took them back to the local Wal-Mart. When all the items were run through the Wal-Mart scanner, the bill was $20 lower than Kmart.[23] However, if the Kmart prices had been lower, Wilson and the local managers would have immediately cut Wal-Mart's prices.

3.3 *First-Line Managers*

first-line managers managers who train and supervise performance of nonmanagerial employees and who are directly responsible for producing the company's products or services

First-line managers hold positions like office manager, shift supervisor, or department manager. The primary responsibility of first-line managers is to manage the performance of entry-level employees, who are directly responsible for producing a company's goods and services. Thus, first-line managers are the only managers who don't supervise other managers. For example, DialAmerica Marketing is a large telemarketing company, one of those firms whose sales representatives always seem to call you at home during dinner or your favorite TV show. Working as a telemarketing representative can be a high-stress, thankless job. However, it is the job of each shift supervisor to encourage, monitor, and reward the performance of their telemarketing representatives. For example, during the evening shift, which is "prime time" because more Americans can be reached by phone then than at any other time of the day, shift supervisors listen in on telemarketing representatives' calls to customers. They also track each representative's sales on a blackboard and provide lots of encouragement and praise for achieving goals."[24]

First-line managers also spend time teaching entry-level employees how to do their jobs. Because telemarketing work is so stressful, most workers quit after three or four months on the job. In fact, any stay over three months is considered long-term employment. Because employee turnover is so high, DialAmerica's supervisors are constantly training new employees. This is one of the reasons that supervisors listen in on telemarketing representatives' phone calls: to observe their performance so that they can teach them how to make sales. For example, after listening in on one representative's calls, a supervisor called a representative in to encourage her not to rush through the prepared script that must be read to each customer.[25]

First-line managers also make detailed schedules and operating plans based on middle management's intermediate-range plans. In fact, contrary to the long-term plans of top managers (three-to-five years out), and the intermediate plans of middle managers (six-to-eighteen months out), first-line managers engage in plans and actions that typically produce results within two weeks.[26] For example, consider the job of nurse supervisor in charge of admissions in a nursing home. Each time someone new is admitted to the nursing home, this first-line supervisor must make sure that the admissions clerks and bookkeepers process the insurance and government papers, the dietary staff and rehabilitation workers put together a complete care plan, the social worker has obtained a complete medical and family history, and housekeeping has prepared and cleaned the new admission's room. Each of these activities must be performed no more than a week after being scheduled.[27]

3.4
Team Leaders

The fourth kind of manager is a team leader. This is a relatively new kind of management job that developed as companies shifted to self-managing teams, which, by definition, have no formal supervisor. In traditional management hierarchies, first-line managers are responsible for the performance of nonmanagerial employees and have the authority to hire and fire workers, make job assignments, and control resources. By contrast, team leaders have a much different role, because nearly all of the functions performed by first-line managers under traditional hierarchies are now performed by teams in this new structure. Instead of directing individuals' work, **team leaders** facilitate team activities toward goal accomplishment. For example, Hewlett-Packard advertises its team leader positions with an ad that says, "Job seeker must enjoy coaching, working with people, and bringing about improvement through hands-off guidance and leadership."[28] Team leaders who fail to understand this key difference often struggle in their roles. A team leader at Texas Instruments said, "I didn't buy into teams, partly because there was no clear plan on what I was supposed to do. . . . I never let the operators [team members] do any scheduling or any ordering of parts because that was mine. I figured as long as I had that, I had a job."[29]

team leaders
managers responsible for facilitating team activities toward goal accomplishment

Team leaders fulfill the following responsibilities.[30] First, team leaders are responsible for facilitating team performance. This doesn't mean team leaders are responsible for team performance. They aren't. The team is. Team leaders help their teams plan and schedule work, learn to solve problems, and work effectively with each other. Eric Doremus, a team leader whose team helped develop the B-2 bomber, said, "My most important task was not trying to figure out everybody's job. It was to help this team feel as if they owned the project by getting them whatever information, financial or otherwise, they needed. I knew that if we could all charge up the hill together, we would be successful."[31]

Second, team leaders are responsible for managing external relationships. Team leaders act as the bridge or liaison between their teams and other teams and other departments and divisions in a company. For example, if a member of Team A complains about the quality of Team B's work, the Team B leader is responsible for solving the problem by initiating a meeting with Team A's leader. Together, these team leaders are responsible for getting members of both teams to work together to solve the problem. If it's done right, the problem is solved without involving company management or blaming members of the other team.[32]

Third, team leaders are responsible for internal team relationships. Getting along with others is much more important in team structures, because team members can't get work done without the help of their teammates. And when conflicts arise on a six-, seven-, or eight-person team, the entire team suffers. So it is critical for team leaders to know how to help team members resolve conflicts. For example, at XEL Communications Corporation, the standard procedure is for a team leader to take the fighting team members to a conference room. The team leader attempts to mediate the disagreement, hearing each side, and encouraging the team members to agree to a practical solution.[33] Hewlett-Packard says that in extreme cases, team leaders can dissolve the team and reassign all team members to different teams.[34] Such instances, however, are rare.

Review 3
Kinds of Managers

There are four different kinds of managers. Top managers are responsible for creating a context for change, developing attitudes of commitment and ownership, creating a positive organizational culture through words and actions, and monitoring their company's business environments. Middle managers are responsible for planning and allocating resources, coordinating and linking groups and departments, monitoring and managing the performance of subunits and managers, and implementing the changes or strategies generated by top managers. First-line managers are responsible for managing the performance of nonmanagerial employees, teaching direct reports how to do their jobs, and making detailed schedules and operating plans based on middle management's intermediate-range plans. Team leaders are responsible for facilitating team performance, managing external relationships, and facilitating internal team relationships.

4 Managerial Roles

So far, we have described managerial work by focusing on the functions of management (making things happen; meeting the competition; organizing people, projects, and processes; and leading) and by examining the four kinds of managerial jobs (top managers, middle managers, first-line managers, and team leaders). Although these are valid and accurate ways of categorizing managerial work, if you followed managers around as they performed their jobs, you would probably not use the terms planning, organizing, leading, and controlling to describe what they do.

In fact, that's exactly the same conclusion that management researcher Henry Mintzberg came to when he followed five American CEOs around. Mintzberg spent a week "shadowing" each CEO and analyzing their mail, who they talked to, and what they did. Mintzberg concluded that managers fulfill three major roles while performing their jobs: [35]

1. interpersonal roles
2. informational roles
3. decisional roles

In other words, managers talk to people, gather and give information, and make decisions. Furthermore, as shown in Figure 1.3, these three major roles can be subdivided into ten subroles. Let's examine each major role— **4.1** *interpersonal,* **4.2** *informational, and* **4.3** *decisional roles—and their ten subroles.*

Figure 1.3 **Mintzbergs's Managerial Roles and Subroles**

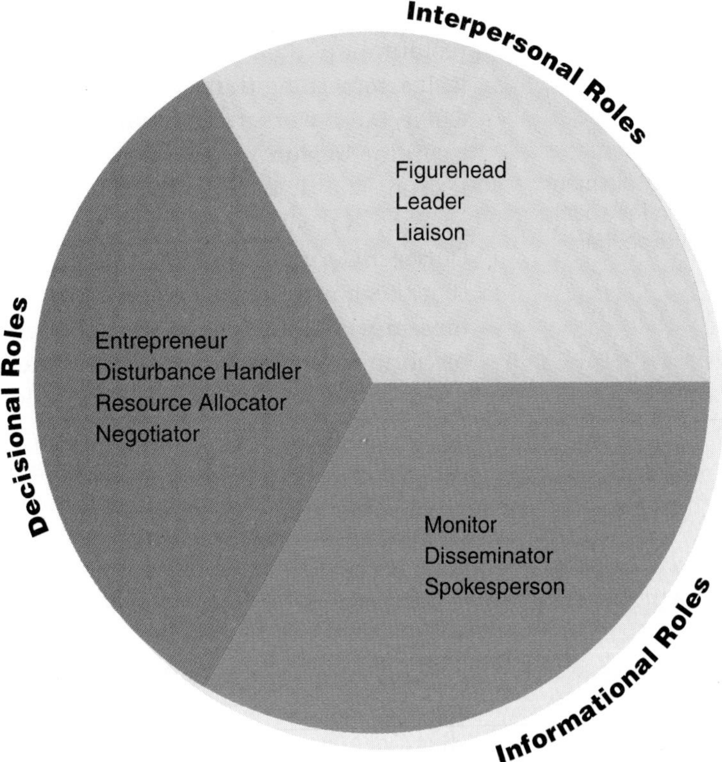

Source: Adapted from H. Mintzberg, *The Nature of Managerial Work* (New York: Harper & Row, 1973).

4.1 Interpersonal Roles

More than anything else, management jobs are people-intensive. Estimates vary with the level of management, but most managers spend between two-thirds and four-fifths of their time in face-to-face communication with others.[36] If you're a loner, or if you consider dealing with people to be a "pain," then you may not be cut out for management work. In fulfilling the interpersonal role of management, managers perform three interpersonal subroles: figurehead, leader, and liaison.

figurehead role
the interpersonal role managers play when they perform ceremonial duties

In the **figurehead role**, managers perform ceremonial duties, like greeting company visitors, making opening remarks when a new facility opens, or representing the company at a community luncheon to support local charities. Each time that Coca-Cola opens a new bottling plant somewhere around the world, Coke's CEO flies in on the Coke corporate jet for an opening celebration. For example, in Poland, Coke's CEO and Polish government officials christened Coke's new Warsaw bottling plant by drinking the first Coca-Colas produced by Polish workers. The Cokes were tied together with long red ribbons to symbolize cooperation between Coke and the Polish people.[37]

leader role
the interpersonal role managers play when they motivate and encourage workers to accomplish organizational objectives

In the **leader role**, managers motivate and encourage workers to accomplish organizational objectives. At Chiat/Day company, one of the world's leading advertising companies, managers found a mannequin arm and decided to turn it into a fun company award. Every month, one employee in Chiat/Day's New York office receives the "Right Arm Award" for outstanding performance, like pulling an all-nighter to meet a client's deadline. Right Arm Award winners also receive a gift certificate good for dinner for two at a restaurant of their choice. Says Chiat/Day's CEO, "We always have fun with it. It's something that everyone looks forward to."[38] The point? To motivate Chiat/Day's workers through frequent praise and recognition.

liaison role
the interpersonal role managers play when they deal with people outside their units

In the **liaison role**, managers deal with people outside their units. Studies consistently indicate that managers spend as much time with "outsiders" as they do with their own subordinates and their own bosses. When Chrysler Corporation was completely redesigning its minivans, it made sure that this happened by creating "Tech Clubs." Tech Clubs were regular meetings in which engineers and managers from all the platform teams (each platform team was responsible for the design and manufacture of a different car) met to share information and solutions and compare their progress. For example, the engineers and managers of the minivan platform team borrowed quality-assurance solutions from the LH Sedan platform team (Chrysler's full-size sedans), while learning how to do a more efficient job of stamping car body parts from the Ram Truck platform team.[39]

4.2 Informational Roles

While managers spend most of their time in face-to-face contact with others, most of that time is spent obtaining and sharing information. Indeed, Mintzberg found that the managers in his study spent 40 percent of their time giving and getting information from others. In this regard, management can be viewed as processing information, gathering information by scanning the business environment and listening to others in face-to-face conversations, and then sharing that information with people inside and outside the company. Mintzberg described three informational subroles: monitor, disseminator, and spokesman.

monitor role
the informational role managers play when they scan their environment for information

In the **monitor role**, managers scan their environment for information, actively contact others for information, and, because of their personal contacts, receive a great deal of unsolicited information. Besides receiving first-hand information, managers monitor their environment by reading local newspapers and *The Wall Street Journal* to keep track of customers, competitors, and technological changes that may affect their businesses. However, managers can now take advantage of electronic monitoring and distribution services that track the news wires (Associated Press, Reuters, etc.) for stories related to their businesses. These services literally deliver customized electronic newspapers to managers, including only the stories on topics the managers specify. One such company is Business Wire. Business Wire (http://www.businesswire.com) offers services like IndustryTrak, which monitors and distributes daily news headlines from 23 major industries; CompetitorTrak, which keeps round-the-clock track of new stories in categories chosen by each subscriber; and BW News Clips, a joint venture with DataTimes, that provides electronic news clips from more than 500 U.S. and foreign sources.[40]

disseminator role
the informational role managers play when they share information with others in their departments or companies

Because of their numerous personal contacts, and because of the access they have to subordinates, managers are often hubs for distribution of critical information. In the **disseminator role**, managers share the information they have collected with their subordinates and others in the company. Although there will never be a complete substitute for face-to-face dissemination of information, the primary method of communication in large companies like Intel, maker of Pentium Processors, and Microsoft, maker of Windows software, is e-mail. Intel's Chairman, Andy Grove, says that he may exchange as many as a half-dozen e-mail "volleys" (I send you an e-mail, and you send one back) with key managers each morning. Mike Murray, a top manager at Microsoft, estimates that he regularly spends two or three hours per day writing and responding to his e-mail—in other words, gathering and disseminating information.[41]

spokesman role
the informational role managers play when they share information with people outside their departments or companies

In contrast to the disseminator role, in which managers distribute information to employees inside the company, in the **spokesman role**, managers share information with people outside their departments and companies. One of the most common ways in which CEOs serve as spokespeople for their companies is at annual meetings with company shareholders or the board of directors. For example, at McDonald's recent shareholder meeting, Michael Quinlan, who had been CEO for 11 years, announced that Jack Greenberg would replace him as McDonald's new CEO. Quinlan will stay on as chairman of McDonald's board of directors.[42] Likewise, at Waste Management's recent shareholder meeting, interim CEO Robert Miller announced that the company would be cutting costs by laying off 1,200 workers.[43]

4.3
Decisional Roles

While managers spend most of their time in face-to-face contact with others, obtaining and sharing information, that time, according to Mintzberg, is not an end in itself. The time spent talking to and obtaining and sharing information with people inside and outside of the company is useful to managers because it helps them make good decisions. According to Mintzberg, managers engage in four decisional subroles: entrepreneur, disturbance handler, resource allocator, and negotiator.

entrepreneur role
the decisional role managers play when they adapt themselves, their subordinates, and their units to incremental change

In the **entrepreneur role**, managers adapt themselves, their subordinates, and their units to incremental change. Take the case of GTE Mobilnet, GTE's cellular phone division based in Atlanta. GTE Mobilnet set the

Back to the Future

Technology and Managerial Roles

Although managers' responsibilities have changed over the years, one constant remains: the long hours and incredibly fast pace of managerial work are spent dealing with people, acquiring information, sharing information, and making decisions. In the future, it is unlikely that these basic parts of managerial work will change. However, technology may change the way managers perform those roles. We can peer into that future by spending a day with Oracle Software's Regional Vice President for New York, Danny Turano.

Turano's basic tools are his cellular phone and palmtop computer. Obviously, there's nothing special about these tools; they're commonplace in many corporations. However, Turano uses them in ways that few managers do. For example, his palmtop computer contains his entire year's schedule, plus a database of 1,000 names, addresses, and phone numbers, and it has a wireless modem which allows him to receive e-mail wherever he is. Like most managers, Turano's long day begins early.

5:00 a.m. In his home office, while his wife and kids are still sleeping, Turano logs on to Oracle Mail, his company's internal e-mail system, to get a head start on the 100 e-mail messages he gets each day.

6:47 a.m. With traffic slowly approaching the Lincoln Tunnel, Turano uses his cell phone to confirm appointments and leave voice messages for people who sent him e-mail.

8:01 a.m. In his Manhattan office, he walks through the hallways, greeting co-workers and subordinates. After visiting with the troops, he and his assistant synchronize his schedule on their identical palmtop computers. Although they could quickly copy the files from his computer to hers, Turano and his assistant find it more useful to talk through the changes in his schedule together.

9:33 a.m. Stuck in cross-town traffic, Turano hops out of a cab and walks the rest of the way to his appointment. He calls his assistant to ask her to phone ahead to say that he'll be a few minutes late.

10:00 a.m. Turano can't find the person he's to meet for breakfast. He's about to phone his assistant to see if there's been a mix-up when he spots the person he's looking for, who has his own cell phone out ready to call Turano.

12:03 p.m. In another taxi, Turano uses his wireless modem to read and respond to e-mail in the back of the cab.

12:15 p.m. At lunch with a client, Turano's table is in the back of a restaurant. Neither his cell phone nor his wireless modem can pick up a signal. After 45 minutes of being out of "touch," he can't stand it any longer and uses a pay phone to call his assistant.

1:20 p.m. Back in a cab and on his palmtop to catch up on e-mail, he spots a message about possible changes with one of his biggest global accounts. He calls one of his key subordinates in Denver to talk strategy.

2:00 p.m. Turano returns to his office to catch part of a presentation. He stays long enough to voice his support for the proposed solutions.

3:30 p.m. Turano leaves the office with one of his sales support staff members. She's from England and misses her family. They walk to a nearby airline ticket office, and he gets her a round-trip ticket to England with his frequent flyer miles, of which he has over a million.

5:23 p.m. Turano is stuck in traffic on his way out of Manhattan. He checks his voice mail, hearing three messages that have come in since he left the office. He forwards one, replies to another, and calls back the third. He typically uses afternoon drive time to call associates and customers in California who are in the middle of their afternoons as he heads home from the office.

6:35 p.m. A 16-car accident makes him late for his dinner appointment, but he calls his assistant who notifies his dinner partner. At dinner, his palmtop beeps, indicating reception of an e-mail message from the United Kingdom. He replies before dinner is over.

8:45 p.m. Turano arrives home, kisses his wife, greets his kids, and checks his fax machine, voice mail, and e-mail for the last time that day.

Source: J. Young, "One Day on the Wire: A Road Warrior's Journal," *Forbes ASAP,* 28 August 1995, 102-104.

goal of becoming the top cellular phone network in terms of customer satisfaction. One of the hundreds of small steps that the company took to make customers more satisfied was to ship new cellular phones with already-charged batteries. "Instead of saying to the customer, 'Here's your phone, go home and charge it for eight hours before you use it," the salespeople were really happy to be able to promise a phone that would work right away." Why was this small step so important? Because when the average customer buys a cellular phone for the first time, they use it to call everybody they know. "You're never going to believe where I'm calling from . . . I'm at my daughter's soccer practice. Yeah, I just got a cellular phone. . . . " So by making this small change, GTE Mobilnet was able to satisfy customers and increase revenues.[44]

disturbance handler role
the decisional role managers play when they respond to severe problems that demand immediate action

By contrast, in the **disturbance handler role**, managers respond to pressures and problems so severe that they demand immediate attention and action. Managers often play the role of disturbance handler when the company board hires a new CEO, charged with turning around a failing company. When Compaq Computer posted its first quarterly loss, Compaq's board of directors got rid of the company founder and replaced him with a new CEO. When National Car Rental took a three-quarter of a million dollar loss in one quarter (a quarter is a three-month period), the company board hired a turnaround expert, someone who specializes in fixing failing companies. In both instances, the new CEOs of Compaq and National served as disturbance handlers, trimming company work forces, cutting costs, and moving quickly to turn around their companies.[45]

resource allocator role
the decisional role managers play when they decide who gets what resources

In the **resource allocator role**, managers decide who will get what resources and how many resources they get. When Scott Paper reported a loss of $300 million, its new CEO used a four-step plan to quiclky and dramatically change the allocation of resources: Step one, determine what business you're in. Scott Paper was already the largest paper tissue company in the world. Step two, keep those resources, sell off the other assets, like a coated-paper business and a power plant. Step three, make one-time major cuts. The first week on the job, he fired 9 of the 11 top managers at the company. The corporate headquarters, 750,000 square feet on 55 rolling acres, was gone, sold, replaced by a 30,000 square foot building, less than 5 percent of the size of the former headquarters. Of the headquarters staff, 71 percent were laid off, reducing the overall headcount 20 percent. Finally, step four, invest your resources in the right business strategy. While the overall headcount shrank by 20 percent, hiring in marketing grew because the CEO had determined that Scott had great products but lousy marketing of those products. So Scott Paper put its resources into developing a strong marketing strategy. Within a year, Scott emerged as a very different company, with a very different allocation of resources and record profits.[46]

negotiator role
the decisional role managers play when they negotiate schedules, projects, goals, outcomes, resources, and employee raises

In the **negotiator role**, managers negotiate schedules, projects, goals, outcomes, resources, and employee raises. For example, every three years the United Auto Workers labor union renegotiates its labor contract with the "Big Three" auto companies, Ford, Chrysler, and General Motors. For more than a decade, Peter J. Pestillo has been Ford's lead negotiator with the union. When some wondered whether Ford would survive financially, Pestillo convinced the union to help Ford cut costs by significantly reducing the number of union workers it employed. In return, Pestillo promised the union that remaining workers would be guaranteed higher pay through more scheduled overtime, for which workers are paid time-and-a-half after 40 hours and double time on Saturdays or Sundays.[47] These days, Pestillo and the UAW negotiate over whether the labor contract should have a guaranteed 2 percent annual wage increase or lump-sum bonuses based on company performance and profitability. Another issue is whether new workers should continue to be paid less than experienced autoworkers.[48] Negotiating is a basic part of managerial work.

Review 4
Managerial Roles

Managers perform interpersonal, informational, and decisional roles in their jobs. In fulfilling the interpersonal role, managers act as figureheads by performing ceremonial duties, as leaders by motivating and encouraging workers, and as liaisons by dealing with people outside their units. In performing their informational role, managers act as monitors by scanning their environment for information, as disseminators by sharing information with others in the company, and as spokesmen by sharing information with people outside their departments or companies. In fulfilling decisional roles, managers act as entrepreneurs by adapting their units to incremental change, as disturbance handlers by responding to larger problems that demand immediate action, as resource allocators by deciding who will get what resources and how many resources they will get, and as negotiators by bargaining with others about schedules, projects, goals, outcomes, and resources.

What Does It Take to Be a Manager?

I didn't have the slightest idea what my job was. I walked in giggling and laughing because I had been promoted and had no idea what principles or style to be guided by. After the first day I felt like I had run into a brick wall. (Sales Representative #1)

Suddenly, I found myself saying, boy, I can't be responsible for getting all that revenue. I don't have the time. Suddenly you've got to go from [taking care of] yourself and say now I'm the manager, and what does a manager do? It takes awhile thinking about it for it to really hit you . . . a manager gets things done through other people. That's a very, very hard transition to make.[49] (Sales Representative #2).

The above statements were made by two star sales representatives, who, on the basis of their superior performance, were promoted to the position of sales manager. Their comments clearly indicate that at first they did not feel confident about their ability to do their jobs as managers. Like most new managers, these sales managers were suddenly faced with the realization that the knowledge, skills, and abilities that led to success early in their careers (and which were probably responsible for their promotion into the ranks of management) would not necessarily help them succeed as managers. As sales representatives, they were only responsible for managing their own performance. But as sales managers, they were now directly responsible for supervising all of the sales representatives in their sales territories. Furthermore, they were now held directly accountable for whether those sales representatives achieved their sales goals.

If performance in nonmanagerial jobs doesn't necessarily prepare you for a managerial job, then what does it take to be a manager? After reading these next three sections, you should be able to:

5 explain what companies look for in managers.

6 discuss the top mistakes that managers make in their jobs.

7 describe the transition that employees go through when they are promoted to management.

5 What Companies Look for in Managers

Broadly speaking, when companies look for employees who would be good managers, they look for individuals who have technical skills, human skills, and conceptual skills, and are motivated to manage.[50] Figure 1.4 shows the relative importance of these four skills to the jobs of team leaders, first-line managers, middle managers, and top managers.

technical skills
the ability to apply the specialized procedures, techniques, and knowledge required to get the job done

Technical skills are the ability to apply the specialized procedures, techniques, and knowledge required to get the job done. For the sales managers described above, technical skills are the ability to find new sales prospects, develop accurate sales pitches based on customer needs, and close the sale. For a nurse supervisor, technical skills include being able to insert an IV or operate a "crash cart" if a patient goes into cardiac arrest.

Figure 1.4

Relative Importance of Managerial Skills to Different Managerial Jobs

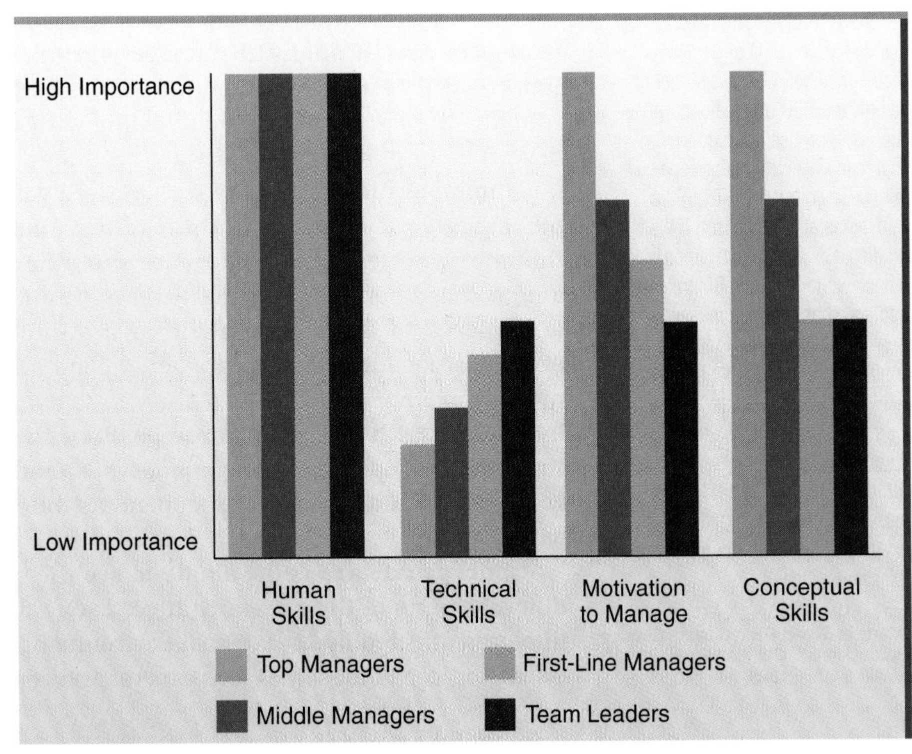

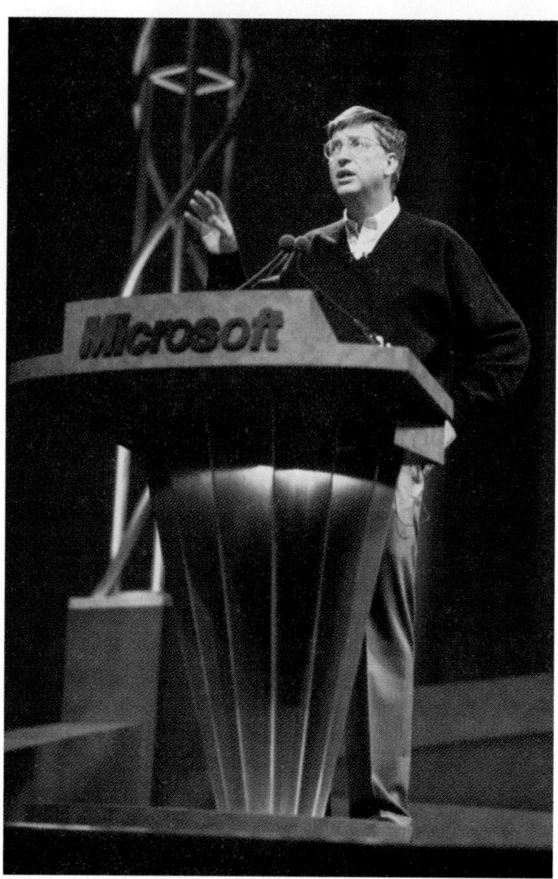

To be effective, CEOs, like Bill Gates of Microsoft, need human skills, conceptual skills, and motivation to manage. © Corbis/ Judy Griesedieck

human skill
the ability to work well with others

conceptual skill
the ability to see the organization as a whole, how the different parts affect each other, and how the company fits into or is affected by its environment

Personal Productivity Tip

Have You Trained Your Replacement?

Jack Welch, the CEO of General Electric, had heart bypass surgery. Anytime the CEO of a major corporation is ill or dies, it's big news. What made Welch's illness especially newsworthy was that GE had not designated a successor. If Welch had died, GE would have temporarily been without a CEO. But training a replacement isn't just an issue for top managers. According to Eugene Jennings, Professor Emeritus at Michigan State University, managers who haven't trained replacements will find it much harder to get promoted. So, if you want to increase your chances of getting that next promotion, begin training your replacement today.

Source: W.M. Carley, "CEO's Heart Surgery Is Giving GE a Case of Succession Jitters," *The Wall Street Journal*, 24 July 1995, A1.

Technical skills are most important for lower-level managers, because these managers supervise the workers who produce products or serve customers. Team leaders and first-line managers need technical knowledge and skills to train new employees and help employees solve problems. Technical knowledge and skills are also needed to troubleshoot problems that employees can't handle. Technical skills become less important as managers rise through the managerial ranks, but they are still important. Indeed, Bill Gates, founder and CEO of Microsoft Corporation, spends roughly 40 percent of his time dealing with the technical issues related to development of Microsoft software products.

Human skill is the ability to work well with others. Managers with "people" skills work effectively within groups, encourage others' to express their thoughts and feelings, are sensitive to others' needs and viewpoints, and are good listeners and communicators. Human skills are equally important at all levels of management, from first-line supervisors to CEOs. However, because lower-level managers spend much of their time solving technical problems, upper-level managers may actually spend more time dealing directly with people. On average, first-line managers spend 57% of their time with people, middle managers spend 63% of their time directly with people, and top managers spend as much as 78% of their time dealing with people.[51]

Conceptual skill is the ability to see the organization as whole, how the different parts of the company affect each other, and how the company fits into or is affected by its external environment, such as the local community, social and economic forces, customers, and competition. Good managers have to be able to recognize, understand, and reconcile multiple complex problems and perspectives. In other words, managers have to be smart! In fact, intelligence makes so much difference for managerial performance that managers with above-average intelligence typically outperform managers of average intelligence by approximately 48 percent.[52] Clearly, companies need to be careful to promote smart workers into management. Conceptual skill increases in importance as managers rise through the management hierarchy.

However, there is much more to good management than intelligence. For example, making the department genius a manager can be disastrous if that genius lacks technical skills, human skills, or one other factor known as the motivation to manage. **Motivation to manage** is an assessment of how motivated employees are to interact with superiors, participate in competitive situations, behave assertively toward others, tell others what to do, reward good behavior and punish poor behavior, perform actions that are highly visible to others, and handle and organize administrative tasks. Managers typically have a stronger motivation to manage than their subordinates, and managers at higher levels usually have stronger motivation to manage than managers at lower levels. Furthermore, managers with stronger motivation to manage are promoted faster, are rated by their employees as better managers, and earn more money than managers with a weak motivation to manage.[53]

motivation to manage
an assessment of how enthusiastic employees are about managing the work of others

Review 5
What Companies Look for in Managers

Companies do not want one-dimensional managers. They want managers with a balance of skills. They want managers who know their stuff (technical skills), are equally comfortable working with blue-collar and white-collar employees (human skills), are able to assess the complexities of today's competitive marketplace and position their companies for success (conceptual skills), and want to assume positions of leadership and power (motivation to manage). Technical skills are most important for lower-level managers, human skills are equally important at all levels of management, and conceptual skills and motivation to manage increase in importance as managers rise through the managerial ranks.

6 Mistakes Managers Make

Another way to understand what it takes to be a manager is to look at the mistakes managers make. In other words, we can learn just as much from what managers shouldn't do as we can from what they should do. Table 1.1 lists the top ten mistakes managers make.

Several studies of U.S. and British managers have compared "arrivers," managers who made it all the way to the top of their companies, to "derailers," managers who were successful early in their careers but were knocked off the "fast track" by the time they reached middle to upper levels of management.[54] The first result they found was that there were few differences between arrivers and derailers. For the most part, both groups were talented and both groups had weaknesses. But what distinguished derailers from

Table 1.1	Top Ten Mistakes That Managers Make
	1. Insensitive to others: abrasive, intimidating, bullying style. 2. Cold, aloof, arrogant. 3. Betrayal of trust. 4. Overly ambitious: thinking of next job, playing politics. 5. Specific performance problems with the business. 6. Overmanaging: unable to delegate or build a team. 7. Unable to staff effectively. 8. Unable to think strategically. 9. Unable to adapt to boss with different style. 10. Overdependent on advocate or mentor. Source: M.W. McCall, Jr. & M.M. Lombardo, "What Makes a Top Executive?" *Psychology Today,* February 1983, 26-31.

arrivers was that derailers possessed two or more "fatal flaws" with respect to the way that they managed people! By contrast, arrivers, who were by no means perfect, usually had no more than one fatal flaw, or they had found ways to minimize the effects of their flaws on the people with whom they work.

The number one mistake made by derailers was that they were insensitive to others by virtue of their abrasive, intimidating, and bullying management style. The authors of one study cited the manager who walked into his subordinate's office and interrupted a meeting by saying, "I need to see you." When the subordinate tried to explain that he wasn't available because he was in the middle of a meeting, the manager barked, "I don't give a damn. I said I wanted to see you now."[55] Not surprisingly, only 25 percent of derailers were rated by others as being good with people, compared to 75 percent of arrivers.

An intimidating management style may also have been partly responsible for Kmart's firing its former CEO, Joseph Antonini. According to *Forbes* magazine, Antonini publicly berated his senior corporate executives in front of Kmart store personnel, regularly using words like "stupid," "jerk," and "inept." He also told them they weren't worth the salary they were paid.[56] Even the U.S. Army recognizes the seriousness of managers being insensitive to others. For example, officers who have been promoted to the rank of general are officially sent to the Brigadier General Training Conference. Informally, however, the Army calls this "charm school." The basic goal of this training is simple: to encourage each new general to get in touch with and lose his or her "inner jerk." Says Lt. Col. Howard Olsen, who runs the training, "Each and every one of you has something that makes you a jerk. Some of you have more than one. I know. I've talked to you."[57]

The second mistake was that derailers were often cold, aloof, or arrogant. While this sounds like insensitivity to others, this has more to do with derailed managers being so smart, so expert in their areas of knowledge, that they treated others with contempt because they weren't experts, too. For example, the Ameritech phone company called in an industrial psychologist to counsel its vice-president of human resources because she had "been blamed for ruffling too many feathers at the regional telephone company."[58] Interviews with the vice-president's co-workers and subordinates revealed that everyone thought she was brilliant, that she was "smarter and faster than other people," that she "generates a lot of ideas," and that she "loves to deal with complex issues." Unfortunately, these smarts were accompanied by a cold, aloof, and arrogant management style. The people she worked with complained that she did "too much too fast," that she treats co-workers with "disdain," that she "impairs teamwork," that she "doesn't always show her warm side," and that she has "burned too many bridges."

The third and fourth mistakes made by derailers, betraying a trust and being overly ambitious, indicate a lack of concern for co-workers and subordinates. Betraying a trust doesn't mean being dishonest. Instead, it means making others look bad by not doing what you said you would do when you said you would do it. That mistake, in itself, is not fatal, because managers and their workers aren't machines. Tasks go undone in every company every single business day. There's always too much to do and not enough time, people, money, or resources to do it. The fatal betrayal of trust is failing to inform others when things would not be done on time. This failure to admit mistakes, to quickly inform others of the mistakes, to take responsibility for the mistakes, and then to fix the mistakes without blaming others clearly distinguished the behavior of derailers from arrivers.

The fourth mistake, mentioned above, was being overly political and ambitious. Managers who always have their eye on their next job rarely do more than establish superficial relationships with peers and co-workers. In their haste to gain credit for successes that would be noticed by upper management, they make the fatal mistake of treating people like they don't matter.

The fatal mistakes of being unable to delegate, to build a team, and to staff effectively indicate that many derailed managers were unable to make the most basic transition to managerial work: to quit being hands-on "doers" and get work done through others. Two things go wrong when managers make these mistakes. First, when managers meddle in decisions that their subordinates should be making, when they can't quit being doers, they alienate the people who work for them. Second, because they are trying to do their subordinates' jobs in addition to their own, managers who fail to delegate to their workers will not have enough time to do much of anything well. For example, before becoming president of Harvard University, Neil Rudenstine's management style had always been to take on more and more work himself. So when he became a university president, and the demands placed on him increased, he responded by working even longer hours, usually 12 to 14 hours a day. For example, on the day before Thanksgiving, normally a quiet day on college campuses as students travel home to be with their families, Dr. Rudenstine began his day with an 8 a.m. meeting with several deans, had lunch with visiting Russian dignitaries, attended a faculty meeting, and finished his day with a dormitory dinner and reception for students. He got home at 8:30 p.m., more than 12 hours after the start of his day. While it is the norm for university presidents to put in long hours, Dr. Rudenstine made it even tougher on himself by failing to delegate work to his associates. Figuring out how to solve the shortage of parking spaces on campus or arranging to have contractors fix leaky roofs are not good uses of a university president's time. Indeed, the combination of long hours and his inability to delegate led to mental and physical exhaustion and a physician-mandated leave of absence from his job as Harvard University president.[59]

Review 6
Top Mistakes Managers Make

Another way to understand what it takes to be a manager is to look at the top mistakes managers make. Five of the most important mistakes made by managers are being abrasive and intimidating; being cold, aloof, or arrogant; betraying trust; being overly ambitious; and failing to build a team and then delegate to that team.

7 The Transition to Management: The First Year

In her book *Becoming a Manager: Master of a New Identity*, Harvard Business School Professor Linda Hill followed the development of 19 people in their first year as managers. Two overall themes emerged from Dr. Hill's study. First, becoming a manager produced a profound psychological transition that changed the way these managers viewed themselves and others. Second, the only way to really learn how to manage was to be a manager. As shown in Table 1.2, a good way to appreciate the magnitude of the changes these managers experienced is to describe their thoughts, expectations, and realities as they evolved over the course of their first year in management.

Initially, the managers in Hill's study believed that their job was to exercise formal authority and to manage tasks — basically being the boss, telling others what to do, making decisions, and getting things done. One manager said, "Being the manager means running my own office, using my ideas and thoughts." Another said, "It's [the office] my baby. It's my job to make sure it works." In fact, most of the new managers were attracted to management positions because they wanted to be "in charge." Surprisingly, the new managers did not believe that their job was to manage people. The only two aspects of people management mentioned by the new managers were hiring and firing.

Table 1.2 **The Transition to Management: Initial Expectations, after Six Months, and after a Year**

Managers' Initial Expectations	*After Six Months as a Manager*	*After a Year as a Manager*
• Be the boss • Formal authority • Manage tasks • Job is not managing people	• Initial expectations were wrong • Fast pace • Heavy workload • Job is people development	• No longer "doers" • Communication, listening, & positive reinforcement • Job is to be problem-solver and trouble-shooter for subordinates.

Source: L.A. Hill, *Becoming a Manager: Mastery of a New Identity* (Boston, MA: Harvard Business School Press, 1992).

Been There, Done That

Travis Reynolds, A Brand New Manager

Travis Reynolds, 24, is a first-level manager for a financial services company offering insurance, 401Ks, retirement planning, and mutual funds to its customers. Travis has been a manager for nine months.

Q: What responsibilities do you have in your job?
A: My job is supervision, training, and running the office (expenses and personnel). I'm also in charge of how the office and sales associates use technology. I recruit new sales associates and spend a lot of time with them while they're still learning the job. I help them with their daily activities, such as seeing potential customers, preparing for sales calls, calling for appointments, and doing insurance and financial applications correctly. I assist them whenever they need help, explaining new products and sometimes going out on sales calls with them.

Q: What was your first month as a manager like?
A: (He laughs.) High stress! I set very high expectations for myself. Being a numbers-oriented person (Travis has a degree in finance), I was very frustrated. I was looking at and trying to make decisions by the numbers, and that doesn't work well when you're dealing with people.

Q: In retrospect, do you now know what you were doing wrong?
A: I didn't look at individual situations. I have a great manager who empowers me, but I wasn't empowering the associates who work for me. I came down on them like a "steel hammer" because they weren't meeting their numbers. I was very autocratic. There was a lot of conflict between the associates and me the first couple of months because of my management style. In fact, it was so bad that on my first day, during the morning sales meeting, one of the associates got up and left because he was so upset with the tough way in which I was running the meeting. It took me a long time to mend fences.

Q: Did you ever think about quitting?
A: No. I eventually learned a new system of managing. My senior managers advised me on ways to empower rather than being autocratic. They taught me how to be more people-oriented without losing track of the results and numbers that my department has to produce. You don't have to give up one for the other.

Q: What prompted you to change?
A: (He laughs again.) Well, that associate leaving my first meeting was a sign, wasn't it? It didn't happen immediately, though. It was still pretty rough around the office for several more months. In terms of dealing with people, I guess I had to learn the hard way. New associates were literally running away from me. The group would disburse when I came into the break room for some coffee. But even more serious than that, I noticed that they weren't coming to me for help. And you can't identify and solve problems unless your people bring them to you.

They taught me how to be more people-oriented without losing track of the results . . .

Q: Any idea why you were so tough on them and yourself at first?
A: I was trying to establish a difference between myself and the previous manager, who was very positive with the associates. As soon as I got the title, I felt like I had to prove my worth. Sales people are entrepreneurial. They come into this line of work to be their own boss. So when I played the role of the tough, controlling supervisor, I contradicted everything that attracted them to the job and our company. It's funny. I still have an e-mail from one of my bosses that said "Now that you've been promoted, don't get a big head." I still reread that occasionally to remind myself that the agents are my customers. I realize now that my job is to help them make sales.

Q: Would you recommend a management job to others?
A: Yes. I love it! I like interacting with people. I like watching them be successful. I can't take credit for it, but I like to see them be successful, especially when they turn it around. For example, I had an agent in my office two days ago who was making the very basic mistake of not setting up enough appointments. It was an issue of time management. In this job, we say that you have to dial 40 times to reach 15 prospects to set up 6 appointments. So I coached him on time management and phone calling skills. The next day, he made 52 calls, reached 18 prospects, and set up appointments with 9. That made me extremely happy. It was a baby step, but it was important. Going from one appointment a day to nine is a huge difference.

Personal Productivity Tip

Find Someone To Talk To

Management is inherently stressful, and managers need to be able to talk to someone about those stresses. In Boston, a dozen women in the health care field have been meeting monthly for two decades just to talk. They call themselves the "A-Team." They discuss how to handle nursing shortages, but they also talk about difficult management problems and how to solve them. The support they have provided to each other over the years has paid off. Nearly half now occupy top positions in their companies. When you become the boss (or if you already are), find someone to talk to about your job. It helps.

Source: A. Gabor, "Send in the A-Team," *Executive Female* 18 (1 May 1995): 35.

After six months, most of the new managers had come to the conclusion that their initial expectations about managerial work were wrong. Management wasn't being "the boss." It wasn't just about making decisions and telling others what to do. The first surprise to the new managers was the fast pace and heavy workload involved in being a manager. One manager stated, "This job is much harder than you think. It is 40 to 50 percent more work than being a producer! Who would have ever guessed?" The pace of managerial work was startling, too. Another manager said, "You have eight or nine people looking for your time . . . coming into and out of your office all day long." A somewhat frustrated manager declared that management was "a job that never ended," "a job you couldn't get your hands around."

Informal descriptions like this are consistent with studies that indicate that the average first-line manager spends no more than two minutes on a task before being interrupted by a request from a subordinate, a phone call, or an e-mail. The pace is somewhat less hurried for top managers, who spend an average of approximately nine minutes on a task before having to switch to another. In practice, this means that supervisors may perform thirty different tasks per hour, while top managers perform seven different task per hour, with each task typically different from the one that preceded it. A manager described this frenetic level of activity by saying, "The only time you are in control is when you shut your door, and then I feel I am not doing the job I'm supposed to be doing, which is being with the people."

The other major surprise after six months on the job was that the managers' expectations about what they should do as managers were very different from their subordinates' expectations. Initially, the managers defined their jobs as helping their subordinates perform their jobs well. For the managers, who still defined themselves as doers rather than managers, assisting their subordinates meant going out on sales calls or handling customer complaints. One manager said, "I like going out with the rep, who may need me to lend him my credibility as manager. I like the challenge, the joy in closing. I go out with the reps and we make the call and talk about the customer; it's fun." But when the managers "assisted" in this way, their subordinates were resentful and viewed their help as interference. What the subordinates wanted in the way of assistance was for their managers to solve problems that they couldn't solve. Once the managers realized this contradiction, they embraced their role as problem-solver and troubleshooter. Thus, they could help without interfering with their subordinates' jobs.

After a year on the job, most of the managers no longer thought of themselves as doers, but managers. In making the transition, they finally realized that people management was the most important part of their jobs. One manager summarized the lesson that had taken him a year to learn by saying, "As many demands as the manager has on his time, I think his primary responsibility is people development. Not production, but people development." Another indication of how much their views had changed was that most of the managers now regretted the rather heavy-handed approach they had used in their early attempts to manage their subordinates. "I wasn't good at managing . . . , so I was bossy like a first-grade teacher." "Now I see that I started out as a drill sergeant. I was inflexible, just a lot of how-to's."

By the end of the year, most of the managers had abandoned their authoritarian approach for one based on communication, listening, and positive reinforcement. One manager explained, "Last night at five I handed out an award in the boardroom just to the individual. It was the first time in his career that he had done [earned] $100,000, and I gave him a piece of glass [a small award] and said I'd heard a rumor that somebody here just crossed over $100,000 and I said congratulations, shook his hand, and walked away. It was not public in the sense that I gathered everybody around. But I knew and he did too."

Finally, after beginning their year as managers in frustration, the managers came to feel comfortable with their subordinates, with the demands of their jobs, and with their emerging managerial styles. While being managers had made them acutely aware of their limitations and their need to develop as people, it also provided them with an unexpected reward of the "thrill" of coaching and developing the people who worked for them. One manager said, "It gives me the best feeling to see somebody do something well after I have helped them. I get excited." Another stated, "I realize now that when I accepted the position of branch manager that it is truly an exciting vocation. It is truly awesome, even at this level; it can be terribly challenging and terribly exciting."

Review 7
The Transition to Management: The First Year

Managers often begin their jobs by using more formal authority and less people management. However, most managers find that being a manager has little to do with "bossing" their subordinates. After six months on the job, the managers were surprised at the fast pace, the heavy workload, and that "helping" their subordinates was viewed as interference. After a year on the job, most of the managers no longer thought of themselves as doers, but managers who get things done through others. And, because they finally realized that people management was the most important part of their job, most of them had abandoned their authoritarian approach for one based on communication, listening, and positive reinforcement.

Why Management Matters

If you walk down the aisle of the "business" section in your local bookstore, you'll find hundreds of books that explain precisely what companies need to do to be successful. Unfortunately, business books tend to be faddish, changing every few years. Lately, the best-selling business books have emphasized technology, reengineering, and going global, whereas ten years ago the hot topics were joint ventures, mergers, and management buyouts. One thing that hasn't changed, though, is the importance of good people and good management: Companies can't succeed for long without them.

After reading this section, you should be able to:

8 explain how and why companies can create competitive advantage through people.

8 Competitive Advantage Through People

Let's pretend that it's 20 years ago and you just inherited $5,000. However, you can't spend the money. The will stipulates that you have to invest the money in the stock market and you can't touch the stocks, win or lose, for 20 years. After that time, you can cash in your stocks and do what you want. If you had been really smart, or really lucky, you would have taken your $5,000, split it up, and invested $1000 in five companies: Plenum Publishing, Circuit City, Tyson Foods, Wal-Mart, and Southwest Airlines. If you had done that, your $1,000 investments would have grown to $156,890, $164,100, $181,180, $198,070, and $217,750, respectively, after 20 years. Your initial $5,000.00 investment would be worth a total of $917,990.00, for a spectacular return on investment of 18,359.80%.[60] In fact, no other combination of companies could produce as large a return, because these companies were the five top-performing companies in American business over the last two decades.

Naturally, you might wonder how these companies achieved their phenomenal success. Did they invent a new technology in a fast-growth business, did they have fewer competitors, or were they just lucky? Well, none is a high-technology company. Plenum is an old-fashioned book publisher. Circuit City sounds high-tech, but is just a retailer that happens to sell appliances, electronics, and computers. Tyson Foods raises and sells chickens. Wal-Mart is a discount retail chain. And Southwest Airlines is a no-frills, low-cost airline. Also, each of these companies achieved its success in highly competitive industries, which, by definition, are supposed to lower company profits, because companies have to either lower prices (and thus profits) or invest huge amounts of money in product innovation just to keep the customers they have.[61] So each of these companies should have found it enormously difficult to make above-average profits. Nonetheless, they did. Why? Because they effectively managed their people.

In his book, **Competitive Advantage Through People**, Stanford University business professor Jeffrey Pfeffer contends that what separated these companies from their competitors and made them top performers was the way they treated their work forces, in other words, management. Managers in

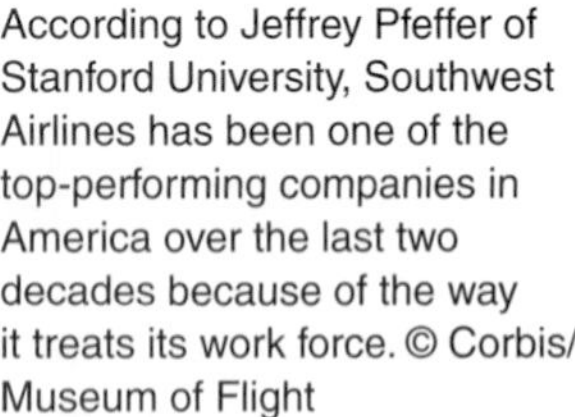

According to Jeffrey Pfeffer of Stanford University, Southwest Airlines has been one of the top-performing companies in America over the last two decades because of the way it treats its work force. © Corbis/ Museum of Flight

these companies used ideas like employee ownership, incentive pay, employee participation and empowerment, and the ten other techniques explained in Table 1.3 to develop work forces that were smarter, better trained, more motivated, and more committed than their competitors' work forces. And, as indicated by the phenomenal growth and return on investment earned by these five companies, smarter, better trained, and more committed work forces provide superior products and service to customers, who keep buying and who, by telling others about their positive experiences, bring in new customers.

Pfeffer also argues that companies that invest in their people will create long-lasting competitive advantages that are difficult for other companies to duplicate. Indeed, studies clearly demonstrate that sound management practices can produce substantial advantages in three critical areas of organizational performance: sales revenues, profits, and customer satisfaction. For example, a study of nearly 1,000 U.S. firms indicated that companies that use *just some* of the ideas shown in Table 1.3 had $27,044 more sales per employee and $3,814 more profit per employee than companies that didn't.[62] For a 100-person company, these differences amount to $2.7 million more in sales and nearly $400,000 more in annual profit! For a 1,000-person company, the difference grows to $27 million more in sales and $4 million more in annual profit!

Another study found that poorly performing companies that adopted management techniques as simple as setting expectations (setting goals, results, and schedules) coaching (informal, ongoing discussions between managers and subordinates about what is being done well and what could be done better), reviewing (annual, formal discussion about results), and rewarding (adjusting salaries and bonuses based on employee performance and results) were able to improve average return on investment from 5.1 percent to 19.7 percent and increase sales by $94,000 per employee![63] So, in addition to significantly improving the profitability of healthy companies, sound management practices can turn around failing companies.

Research also indicates that managers have an important effect on customer satisfaction. However, many people find this surprising. They don't understand how managers, who are largely responsible for what goes on inside the company, can affect what goes on outside the company. They wonder how managers, who often interact with customers under negative conditions (when customers are angry or dissatisfied), can actually improve customer satisfaction. It turns out that the way managers influence customer satisfaction is through employee satisfaction. When employees are satisfied with their jobs, their bosses, and the companies they work for, they provide much better service to customers.[64] In turn, customers are more satisfied, too.

Review 8
Competitive Advantage through People

Why does management matter? Well-managed companies are competitive because their work forces are smarter, better trained, more motivated, and more committed. Furthermore, companies that practice good management consistently have greater revenues and profits than companies that don't. Finally, good management matters because good management leads to satisfied employees who, in turn, provide better service to customers. Because employees tend to treat customers the same way that their managers treat them, good management can improve customer satisfaction.

Table 1.3

Competitive Advantage through People: 13 Practices

1. **Employment Security** - Employment security is the ultimate form of commitment that companies can make to their workers. Employees can innovate and increase company productivity without fearing the loss of their jobs.
2. **Selectivity in Recruiting** - If employees are the basis for a company's competitive advantage, and those employees have employment security, then the company needs to aggressively recruit and selectively screen applicants in order to hire the most talented employees available.
3. **High Wages** - High wages are needed to attract and retain talented workers. They also indicate that the organization values its workers.
4. **Incentive Pay** - Not only do talented employees need to be paid good wages to encourage them to join and stay with a company, but like company founders, shareholders, and managers, they need to share in the financial rewards when the company is successful.
5. **Employee Ownership** - Employees who own stock in their companies are more likely to take a long-run view of the business. They are also more likely to think like owners, thus minimizing potential conflicts between management, which represents company owners, and labor. With an investment in company stock, employees are owners, too.
6. **Information Sharing** - If employees are to make decisions that are good for the long-run health and success of the company, they need to be given information about costs, productivity, development times, and strategies that were previously known only by company managers.
7. **Participation and Empowerment** - Once employees possess critical information, they should be given the authority to act on their knowledge by making decisions in the long-run best interest of the company and its customers. Participation, empowerment, and autonomy allow employees who are closest to problems, production, and customers to make timely decisions. They also increase employee satisfaction and commitment.
8. **Self-Managed Teams** - Information sharing and participation and empowerment come together in the form of self-managed teams that are responsible for their own hiring, purchasing, job assignments, and production. Self-managed teams can often produce enormous increases in productivity.
9. **Training and Skill Development** - Like a high-tech company that spends millions of dollars to upgrade computers or research and development labs, a company whose competitive advantage is based on its people must invest in the training and skill development of its people.
10. **Cross-Utilization and Cross-Training** - Having workers perform multiple jobs makes work more interesting, forces companies to keep jobs relatively simple (as workers shift back and forth between different jobs), and promotes innovation as people new to a job may see problems or solutions that people who have been in jobs for years take for granted.
11. **Symbolic Egalitarianism** - This is a fancy term that indicates that the company treats everyone, no matter what his or her job is, as an equal. There are no reserved parking spaces. Everyone eats in the same cafeteria. The result: Much improved communication as managers and employees jointly focus on problems and solutions rather than pleasing upper management.
12. **Wage Compression** - If employees work in teams, and some members of the team are paid much more than other members, team members may focus more on the pay inequalities than on accomplishing their tasks. If employees are already well paid compared to other companies, and if pay is already closely linked to performance, then compressing pay, that is reducing large differences in pay between workers, may reduce competition between employees. It may also reduce gaming and politicking efforts to convince those in charge to increase wages.
13. **Promotion from Within** - Promotion from within encourages employees that companies have trained and developed to stay. It also ensures that the people in charge know the basics involved in running the company and competing within its industry.

Source: J. Pfeffer, "Producing Sustainable Competitive Advantage through the Effective Management of People," *Academy of Management Executive* 9 (1995): 55-72.

What**Really**Happened?

At the beginning of this chapter, you read about the issues facing Leslie Wexner and the company he founded, The Limited. As you'll see below, both Wexner and his company have undergone considerable changes. These changes are related to the basic issues in this chapter: "What is management?" and "What do managers do?" Find out what really happened at The Limited by reading the following answers to the chapter-opening case "What Would You Do?"

What should you, the CEO, be responsible for at The Limited?

In general, top managers are responsible for setting the long-term direction and monitoring the overall performance of their companies. With that in mind, founder and CEO Wexner announced that The Limited would be splitting into three different companies, each of which would issue its own publicly available stock. Said Wexner, "I believe there is always a better way to do things, and bold ideas that make business sense can lead us to someplace new." The first company, which includes Victoria's Secret stores and catalog, Bath & Body Works, and Cacique, will focus on lingerie and personal products. The second, which includes Compagnie Internationale Expresse, The Limited, Lane Bryant, and Lerner's, will focus on traditional women's fashions. The third company will try to grow the newest stores, Structure, Abercrombie & Fitch, The Limited Too, Henri Bendel, and Mast Industries, and will be responsible for developing new retail ideas.

Given these responsibilities, how should your role as CEO change?

Wexner now realizes that he can't run The Limited, which is now a multibillion dollar company, like he used to when it was a small business. Consequently, the most important lesson that he has learned is that he can't do everything himself. For instance, he used to go to Hong Kong three times a year to make judgments on sleeve lengths. But not anymore. Now, he will focus on the overall performance of the company and what he loves most and does best: creating, developing, and growing new retail concepts. Consequently, Wexner will limit most of his responsibility to the new-venture division. Wexner has also changed the number of people that he directly supervises. Just a few years ago, he had as many as 24 executives reporting directly to him. Not anymore. With The Limited now split into three different companies, he no longer oversees as many managers. Now, instead of 24 managers, only his finance executives and the top managers from the lingerie and women's fashion companies report directly to him.

What should your middle managers be doing and how can you change the company to make sure they do it?

Traditionally, middle managers have been responsible for planning and allocating resources, and for implementing the changes or strategies generated by top managers. By splitting the company into three parts, and by limiting his focus to the new-venture division, CEO Wexner has given his middle managers (and his top managers, too) much more discretion to fulfill their responsibilities. For example, Vice Chairman Michael Weiss, who is now responsible for the traditional women's apparel company, brought in Pamela McConathy Goodman to manage the Lerner's store division. She immediately canceled several million dollars of orders for clothes she thought were dull and boring. To improve Lerner's store image, she decided that all garment labels would read "Lerner New York," and that all shopping bags would be imprinted with a black and white graphic of the New York skyline. Likewise, Grace Nichols, head of Victoria's Secret, will decide how the stores will be run. Grace plans to add nearly 50 stores a year, bringing the total number of stores from 600 to nearly a thousand over the next eight years. Grace and her managers also have the discretion to do what they think will work. For example, Victoria's Secret stores play classical music to create an upscale atmosphere. Customers liked the music and began asking for it. Since 1989, 10 million tapes and CDs, recorded specially by the London Symphony Orchestra for Victoria's Secret, have been sold.

What is good management?

Leslie Wexner concluded that, "For me, the split-up is a matter of maturation and liberation." By splitting The Limited into three separate companies, by limiting his focus to the new-venture division, and by giving the managers in the other two companies much more control and responsibility for the success of their operations, Wexner has completed the classic transition from "doer" to "manager." "Doers" try to do everything themselves. "Managers" get work done through others.

Sources: L. Bird. "Limited to Shut 200 Stores, Change Express Managers," *The Wall Street Journal Interactive Edition*, 15 January, 1997. D. Machan, "Knowing Your Limits," *Forbes,* 5 June 1995, 128-132. B.D. Wolf, "Analysts Laud Limited Plan to Split into Three Companies," *Columbus Dispatch,* 29 March 1995.

conceptual skill p. 24

controlling p. 7

disseminator role p. 19

disturbance handler role p. 21

effectiveness p. 5

efficiency p. 5

entrepreneur role p. 20

figurehead role p. 18

first-line managers p. 14

human skill p. 24

leader role p. 18

leading p. 7

liaison role p. 18

management p. 4

meta-analysis p. 5

middle managers p. 13

monitor role p. 19

motivation to manage p. 25

negotiator role p. 21

organizing p. 7

planning p. 7

resource allocator role p. 21

spokesman role p. 19

team leaders p. 15

technical skills p. 23

top managers p. 12

What Would You Do-II?

Asian Regional Bank Headquarters, Singapore.

It's Sunday morning as you sit on the patio of your 14th floor condo, soaking up the sunshine and the view of the harbor while you read your copy of the *London Times*. As head of Asian futures market trading for your bank's regional headquarters in Singapore, you supervise 20 different traders who, by buying thousands of dollars worth of futures contracts, can take advantage of price differences between contracts traded in Osaka, Japan, and Singapore. Technically, what they trade doesn't really matter, because the traders make their money by buying something for 50 cents in Osaka and selling it for 50 and 3/8 cents in Singapore. By making volume purchases, that small price difference earns the bank profits.

Most of the people who work for you are professionals. The typical trader in your office was a finance major as an undergraduate and then attended one of the better graduate schools of business in Europe or the United States. Traders work long hours and must follow financial news around the world as it happens. Seventy-hour weeks are the norm. Furthermore, futures trading is an aggressive business and is not for the faint of heart. Millions can be won or lost in a very short time. This is why you're concerned about two of your employees, John and Mary. John is extremely talented, one of your best performers, but he is insensitive to others and does not have good interpersonal skills. Because of his capabilities and his sheer intelligence, John is impatient with co-workers who cannot keep up with his trading activity and strategies. Not only have you begun to get complaints about John from his co-workers, but you're also beginning to get complaints from traders outside the company.

In contrast, Mary is very easy to get along with. Charming is a word that is frequently used to describe her. While a fun person to be around, Mary's job performance is a problem. Frequently, you and other traders have to cover for mistakes she makes or for work that she did not get done on time. Usually, Mary seems to get by without getting in trouble. She has been careful to build alliances with important people in the company. She can often be found at higher-up social gatherings or at lunch with important company clients. However, you fear that her performance is putting you and the company at risk.

Unfortunately, you're not sure how to handle John or Mary. In fact, you've been avoiding them for the past few months, hoping that the problems would just take care of themselves. The problem is complicated because it's difficult to find good traders and then even more difficult to get them to locate overseas. Financial firms are in strong competition for trading talent, so it won't be easy to find good replacements.

Suddenly, the wind from the harbor blows the financial section of the *London Times* out of your hand. It sails off the patio and slowly begins its descent, alternately rising and falling with the wind gusting between the high-rise buildings that dominate the downtown skyline. A bad omen? You hope not as you watch the paper float away. **If you were the head of trading at Asian Regional Bank Headquarters in Singapore, what would you do?**

Critical-Thinking Video Case

A Management Success Story: Sunshine Cleaning Systems

Former professional baseball player, Larry Calufetti, founded Sunshine Cleaning Systems, a privately held company in Fort Lauderdale, Florida, in 1976. Today, Sunshine also has offices in Tampa, Orlando, and West Palm Beach, Florida. Sunshine is one of the largest contract cleaning companies in the state of Florida. Sunshine cleans entire facilities inside and out. Sunshine also specializes in cleaning windows, carpets, ceilings, and even construction sites. Customers include sports facilities, office buildings, stores, malls, the Orlando Convention Center, and the Fort Lauderdale Airport.

In this video, we learn how Larry Calufetti made the transition from professional baseball player and local collegiate baseball coach to founder, manager, and then CEO of Sunshine Cleaners. As you watch the video, consider the following critical thinking questions.

Critical-Thinking Questions

1. How does a person successfully change careers? What kind of changes do you think Larry experienced when he changed from being a professional baseball player to being a small business owner and manager?
2. How does a person's background contribute to starting and building a business? Is there anything in Larry's background that prepared him for success as a manager? If so, what?
3. How does the role of the founder change as the business grows? What kinds of tasks do you think Larry did when the business first started? As CEO of a company with over 400 people, is he likely to do things the same or differently now?

Management Decisions

Who Deserves the Promotion?

Frank, my first boss and long-time mentor, laughed when I asked him what he thought I should do. "You're the one who wanted to be an executive, hotshot. What do YOU think you should do?" "Seriously," he said, "I can't make this decision for you. Trust your instincts. But remember, you're going to have to live with the consequences of your decision for a long time."

Frank was right. Whoever I promoted was going to be working with me and supervising one of my units for at least three years. And whoever I didn't promote was going to be disappointed for a long time, too. But who deserved the promotion? Should it go to John? When I asked him why he wanted the promotion, he said he earned it by turning in three solid years of performance. Or should it go to Valerie? Valerie's teams had been top producers. When I asked her why she wanted the promotion, she said it was because she was getting burned out in her current job and needed a change. However, she also mentioned that management had been a long-time goal.

Questions

1. Who would you promote, John or Valerie? Why?
2. In order of importance, name three criteria that companies should use when deciding who to promote. Explain why each is important and why they can help companies make good promotion decisions.

Management Decisions

Settle this Bet

Your local professional baseball team has been sold to a new investment group. But because they paid so much money to get the team, and because the local TV contract doesn't provide much revenue (it's a small market like Minneapolis or St. Louis), the new owners have only so much money to spend to improve the team. They spent some of it resigning the team's all-star shortstop, who was about to go into free agency. Price: $5 million a year. Then the new general manager picked up a veteran first baseman with a lifetime .290 batting average. Price: $3 million a year. Fortunately, there's enough money left for one more big move. But the general manager, the ownership group, and the team's scouts cannot agree on what it should be.

The general manager wants to make Tony LaRussa the new team manager. LaRussa's Oakland A's teams have struggled the last few years, but prior to that he had been one of the best managers in baseball for nearly a decade, winning four division championships, three American League championships, and one World Series. However, the team scouts want to use the remaining money to hire Greg Maddux. Maddux has won three straight Cy Young awards for being the best pitcher in the National League. No one in baseball history has ever done that. The ownership group isn't really sure what to do, but wants to make a decision that is in the long-run best interest of the team.

Additional Internet Resources:

For a direct link to these Web sites, see Chapter 1 of the Web site for this textbook.

- **@BAT, The Official Site of Major League Baseball, (http://www.majorleaguebaseball.com/).** This site contains information about great moments in baseball, past award winners, the history of the all-star game, postseason history, franchise histories, baseball's all-time leaders, as well as links to all of the American and National League clubs. Click "National League," and then the team icons for the Atlanta Braves or St. Louis Cardinals to find out additional information about Greg Maddux and Tony LaRussa.
- **Official Home Page of the Atlanta Braves (http://www.atlantabraves.com/).** This site contains information for the press (the media center), and a game center, a team center, and something called Fan Clubhouse. Click on "Roster" to find additional information about pitcher Greg Maddux.
- **Official Home Page of the St. Louis Cardinals (http://www.stlcardinals.com/).** This site contains press releases, a roster, team and player statistics, trades, and much more. Search here for additional information about Manager Tony LaRussa.

Questions

1. If it was your money to spend, would you hire LaRussa as manager or sign Maddux to anchor your pitching staff? Explain your choice.
2. How much of a difference can a good manager make to the won-loss record of a team: a big difference, some difference, or no difference? Explain your answer.

Develop Your Management Potential

Interview Two Managers

Welcome to the first "Develop Your Managerial Potential" activity! These assignments have one purpose: To help you develop your present and future capabilities as a manager. What you will be learning through these assignments is not traditional "book-learning" based on memorization and regurgitation, but practical knowledge and skills that help managers perform their jobs better. Lessons from some of the assignments—for example, goal setting—can be used for immediate benefit. Other lessons will obviously take time to accomplish, but you can still benefit now by making specific plans for future improvement.

Step 1: Interview Two Practicing Managers

In her book *Becoming a Manager: Master of a New Identity*, Harvard Business School professor Linda Hill conducted extensive interviews with 19 people in their first year as managers. To learn firsthand what it's like to be a manager, interview two managers that you know, asking them some of the same questions, shown below, that Professor Hill asked her managers. Be sure to interview managers with different levels of experience. Interview one person with at least five years' experience as a manager and then interview another person with no more than two years' experience as a manager. Ask the managers these questions:

1. Briefly describe your current position and responsibilities.
2. What do your subordinates expect from you on the job?
3. What are the major stresses and challenges you face on job?
4. What, if anything, do you dislike about the job?
5. What do you like best about your job?
6. What are the critical differences between average managers and top-performing managers?
7. Think about the skills and knowledge that you need to be effective in your job. What are they and how did you acquire them?
8. What have been your biggest mistakes thus far? Could you have avoided them? If so, how?

Step 2: Prepare to Discuss Your Findings

Prepare to discuss your findings in class or write a report (if assigned by your instructor). What conclusions can you draw from your interview data?

Source: L.A. Hill, *Becoming a Manager: Mastery of a New Identity* (Boston, MA: Harvard Business School Press, 1992).

Chapter Two

Chapter 2 Outline

Organizational Environments and Cultures

What Would **You** Do?

All-World Travel, Amherst, Massachusetts. You can remember it like it was yesterday: the precise moment at which external forces began to permanently change the travel agency that you, Mary Martin, had founded 12 years ago. You can still hear your office assistant yell, "Oh my gosh. Mary! Come read this fax. I don't think it's good news . . ." Well, it wasn't. The fax announced that Delta Airlines was cutting its commission payments to travel agents. Instead of the traditional 10 percent commission on the price of a ticket, Delta was capping commissions to no more than $25 on one-way travel and $50 on round-trip travel. While this had little effect on the profits your travel agency made from leisure travelers (i.e., vacationers) who typically purchase lower-priced tickets, it had a significant effect on the commissions you earned from business travelers who commonly pay $1,000 and up when booking last-minute reservations. Now, instead of earning a $100 commission from a corporate traveler who spends $1,000 for a ticket, you only earn $50. At first, you were in denial. You couldn't believe it. You were sure the fax was a joke from one of your cross-town competitors. Then, when you realized it wasn't, you figured that given Delta's recent financial losses, the commission cap was just a temporary thing. You figured it would go away after a couple of months and that none of the other airlines would match the cuts. But, you were wrong. It got worse. American, Continental, Northwest, United, and USAir soon announced similar commission caps in the name of "competition" and "cost cutting." Unbelievably, events beyond your control continued to make things worse for your travel business. It was almost as if you were located in the Bermuda Triangle instead of Amherst, Massachusetts. The next threat to occur was that Wal-Mart, one of the business world's most-feared competitors, decided to enter the travel business. Wal-Mart isn't out to take over the travel industry. It just wants to offer one-stop shopping in its Super Wal-Mart stores. With the addition of travel services to regular department store items, groceries, eyeglasses and eye exams, haircuts, dry cleaning, and photo development, the average Wal-Mart shopper is now even less likely to make the extra trip required to get to All-World Travel, just four blocks away. Why do that when you can stop by Wal-Mart Travel while you're waiting for Wal-Mart Auto to finish changing your car's oil? Many of your friends in the business don't think Wal-Mart is a threat, but you started worrying about them when the Walt Disney Travel Company signed up as one of Wal-Mart Travel's first "suppliers." In fact, Disney hopes that Wal-Mart Travel will help it do a better job of reaching "rubber tire" customers, that is, lower-income customers who drive to Disney World and Disneyland. As if commission caps and the threat of Wal-Mart weren't enough, you've got technology and the Internet to worry about, too. Now instead of just competing with local travel agencies, you've also got to compete with Web-based travel agencies, like TRAVELOCITY (*http://www.travelocity.com*), Preview Travel (*http://www.vacations.com*), and Microsoft Expedia (*http://expedia.msn.com*) that are online, open 24 hours a day, and accessible from anywhere in the world. Furthermore, the Internet allows leisure and business travelers to bypass travel agents altogether by logging directly onto airlines' Web sites. American (*http://www.americanair.com/*), British Airways, (*http://www.british-airways.com/bans/checkin.htm*), Continental (*http://www.flycontinental.com/index.html*), Delta (*http://www.delta-air.com/index.html*), Northwest (*http://www.nwa.com*), Southwest (*http://www.iflyswa.com*), and United (*http://www.ual.com*) are just some of the major airlines from which travelers can purchase tickets, all without the help of a travel agent. The frustrating part is that after 12 years of success and growth, it's hard to understand why these things are happening to your business. For example, you'd like to know why the changes all seem to occur at once rather than gradually. Also, once external forces began to change things, it would have helped to be able to categorize the changes affecting your business. But even better than that, you'd like to know how to identify, make sense of, and react to the external threats and opportunities in your industry. Finally, you worry that these external changes will affect the positive atmosphere of your business. It's a fun place to work. And with just 20 employees, it feels like a close-knit family. Hopefully, that won't change, too. **If you were Mary Martin, founder and owner of All-World Travel, what would you do?**

Sources: S. Bittle, "Business Travel Buzzword: Intranet," *Travel Weekly*, 5 August 1996, 1-3. J. Dorsey, "Year of Caps: Survival of the Fittest," *Travel Weekly*, 8 February 1996, 1-2. P. Holley, "Agent of Change: Technology Transforms Travel Industry," *The Business Journal-Milwaukee*, 8 June 1996, 1-2. G. Marc, "Travel Planning in Cyberspace," *Fortune*, 9 September 1996, 187-188. M.A. Mitchell, "Rival Agents Shrug off In-Store Competition from Wal-Marts," *Travel Weekly*, 18 January 1996, 1-2. K. O'Meara, "Shifting Sands: Agents Adopt a Variety of Strategies to Cope with Airline Commission Caps," *Travel Weekly*, 29 August 1996, S84-88.

Travel agents are a frustrated group these days. Wherever they look, they see changes and forces beyond their control that threaten their traditional way of doing business. This chapter examines the internal and external forces that affect companies. We begin by explaining how the changes in external organizational environments affect companies. Next, we examine the two kinds of external organizational environments: the general environment that affects all organizations and the specific environment unique to each company. Then, we learn how managers make sense of their changing general and specific environments. The chapter finishes with a discussion of internal organizational environments by focusing on organizational culture.

External Environments

external environments all events outside a company that have the potential to influence or affect it

External environments are all the events outside a company that have the potential to influence or affect it. For example, several significant events have occurred in newspapers' external environments. With the arrival of network television in the 1950s and the introduction of cable television in the 1980s, newspapers have experienced a long-term decline in readership. More recently, the cost of newsprint, which represents 30 percent of the total cost of a newspaper, has risen by nearly a third. To reduce overall costs, newspapers have laid off workers and turned daily features like stock and mutual fund listings into weekly features to save paper. Also, a substantial portion of newspaper profit comes from classified advertisements. For example, a two-line advertisement running for 10 days (Lizard for sale! Call 555-1212 after 5 p.m.) costs between $20 and $25 in most local papers. Additional lines (Only to a loving family . . .) cost $10 and $15 each. However, anyone with Internet access can place free classified ads in Internet news groups like DFW.FORSALE in Dallas-Fort Worth, or NYC.FORSALE in New York City. Although fewer people will see the ad on the Internet, the ad can run free as long as you want. Eventually, Internet news groups like DFW.FORSALE could compete with newspapers' classified sections.

After reading the next four sections, you should be able to:

1. discuss how **changing environments** affect organizations.
2. describe the four components of the **general environment.**
3. explain the five components of the **specific environment.**
4. describe the process that companies use to **make sense of their changing environments.**

1 Changing Environments

Let's examine the three basic characteristics of changing external environments: **1.1** *environmental change,* **1.2** *environmental complexity,* **1.3** *environmental munificence, and* **1.4** *the uncertainty that environmental change, complexity, and munificence can create for organizational managers.*

1.1 Environmental Change

environmental change the rate at which a company's general and specific environments change

stable environment environment in which the rate of change is slow

dynamic environment environment in which the rate of change is fast

Environmental change is the rate at which a company's general and specific environments change. In **stable environments**, the rate of environmental change is slow. In **dynamic environments**, the rate of environmental change is fast. EA Sports is a company that competes in one of the most dynamic external environments, video games. Its best-selling products are sports games, like John Madden Football, NBA Basketball, NHL Hockey, PGA Tour Golf, and FIFA Soccer. EA Sports' business environment is dynamic because gaming technology changes so quickly. EA Sports produced its first product for the Atari 800, one of the earliest computers designed to play computer games. However, the more powerful Commodore 64 replaced the Atari 800, which was replaced by the Commodore Amiga, and then the 8-bit Nintendo, the 16-bit Sega Genesis, and now 32-bit and 64-bit Segas, Nintendos, Sony PlayStations, and desktop computers. With game development costs running around $1 million, if EA guesses wrong and develops games for computers that become obsolete, it could join the dozens of game companies that have already closed their doors.[1]

punctuated equilibrium theory theory that holds that companies go through long, simple periods of stability (equilibrium), followed by short periods of dynamic, fundamental change (revolution), and ending with a return to stability (new equilibrium)

While it would seem that companies would either be in stable external environments *or* dynamic external environments, recent research suggests that companies often experience both stable and dynamic external environments. According to **punctuated equilibrium theory**, companies go through long, simple periods of stability (equilibrium), followed by short, complex periods of dynamic, fundamental change (revolutionary periods), finishing with a return to stability (new equilibrium).[2]

As shown in Figure 2.1, one example of punctuated equilibrium is the U.S. airline industry. Twice in the last 20 years, the U.S. airline industry has experienced revolutionary periods. The first, from mid-1979 to mid-1982, occurred immediately after airline deregulation in 1978. Prior to deregulation, the federal government controlled where airlines could fly, when they could fly, and the number of flights they could have on a particular route. After deregulation, these choices were left to the airlines. The large financial losses during this period clearly indicate that the airlines had trouble adjusting to the intense competition that occurred after deregulation. However, by mid-1982, profits returned to the industry and held steady until mid-1989. Then, after experiencing record growth and profits, U.S. airlines lost billions of dollars between 1989 and 1993 as the industry went through dramatic changes. Key expenses, like jet fuel and employee salaries, which had held steady for years, suddenly increased. Furthermore, revenues, which had grown steadily year after year, suddenly dropped because of dramatic changes in the airlines' customer base. Business travelers, who typically pay full-priced fares, comprised more than half of all passengers during the 1980s. But now, the largest group is leisure travelers who, in contrast to

Figure 2.1 **Punctuated Equilibrium: U.S. Airline Profits from 1976 to 1996**

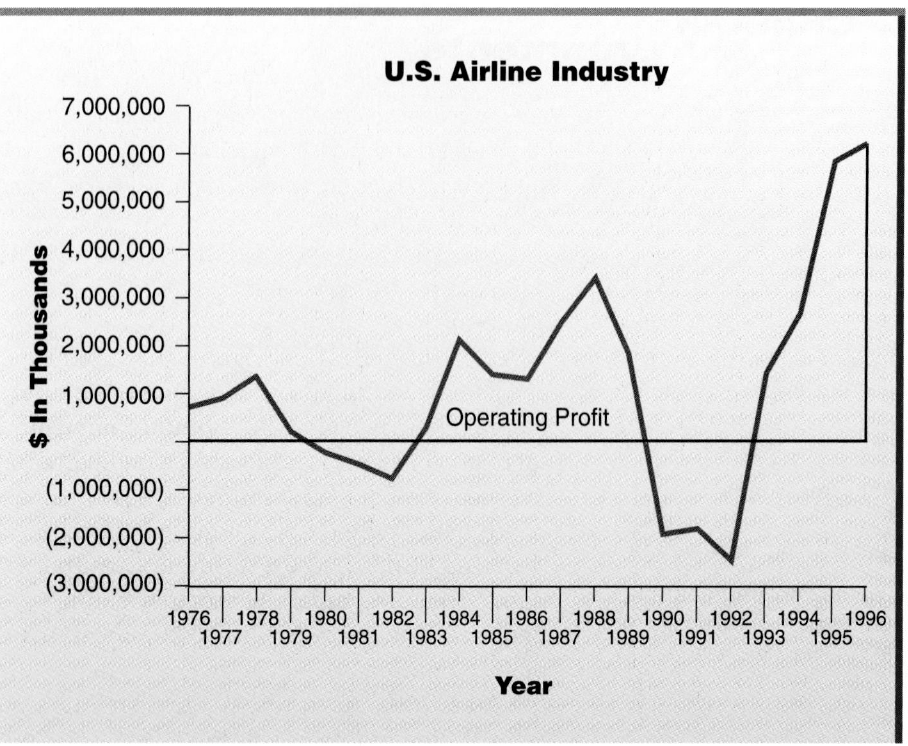

Source: Air Transport Association, [Online] Available http://www.airtransport.org/data/earnings.htm January 5, 1998.

business travelers, want the cheapest flights they can get.[3] With expenses suddenly up and revenues suddenly down, the airlines responded to these changes in their business environment by laying off 5–10 percent of their workers, canceling orders for new planes, and getting rid of routes that were not profitable. Starting in 1993, these changes helped profits return even stronger than before. Furthermore, the industry has again begun to stabilize, if not flourish, just as punctuated equilibrium theory predicts.[4]

1.2 *Environmental Complexity*

environmental complexity the number of external factors in the environment that affect organizations

simple environment an environment with few environmental factors

complex environment an environment with many environmental factors

Environmental complexity is the number of external factors in the environment that affect organizations. **Simple environments** have few environmental factors, whereas **complex environments** have many environmental factors. For example, the baking industry exists within a relatively simple external environment. Except for more efficient ovens (i.e., technology), bread is baked, wrapped, and delivered fresh to stores each day much as it always has been. Likewise, although some new breads have become popular, the white and wheat breads that customers bought 20 years ago are still today's best sellers. Baking bread is a highly competitive, but simple business environment that has experienced few changes.

By contrast, in recent years, cereal companies like Kellogg's, maker of Kellogg's Corn Flakes, Frosted Flakes, Sugar Pops, and other popular cereals, find themselves in a more complex environment in which three significant changes have occurred. The first significant change has been more competition. Twenty years ago, Kellogg's competed against just a few cereal companies, like General Mills and Post. Today, Kellogg's competes against those companies, plus a dozen more private-label store brands (IGA, Good Value, etc.).

The second significant change in the cereal industry has been significant price cuts. For years, Kellogg's made gross profits of 50 percent on a box of cereal. In other words, it only cost Kellogg's $2.50 to make a $5 box of cereal. Yet, with profits that high, private-label store brands could still make a profit of $1 per box by slashing the price to $3.50 per box of cereal.

The third significant change has been the entrance of Wal-Mart into the grocery business. Wal-Mart, much more than other national grocery chains, relies on cheaper private-label store brands, like its own Sam's Choice soft drinks and Old Roy dog food. Consumers like these products because they cost substantially less than brand-name products. However, Wal-Mart prefers private-label store brands because, even with their lower prices, the store makes a higher profit on these brands. So when Wal-Mart aggressively expanded into the grocery business in the last few years, Kellogg's saw its market share drop even more as Wal-Mart pushed cheaper private-label cereals. Together, these three changes have made Kellogg's external environment much more complex than it used to be.[5]

1.3 *Environmental Munificence*

environmental munificence
degree to which an organization's external environment has an abundance or scarcity of critical organizational resources

The third characteristic of external environments is environmental munificence. **Environmental munificence** is the degree to which an organization's external environment has an abundance or scarcity of critical organizational resources. For many companies, qualified employees are one of the scarcest resources around. While companies continue to lay off workers in particular industries or jobs, in today's economy good job applicants are hard to find. The reason is simple: Demand for job applicants exceeds the supply. In fact, the number of job openings at companies is five times greater than the number of layoffs.[6] Consequently, employers are having to work harder than ever before to find and attract skilled employees, especially in technological and professional jobs.

For example, Cisco Systems started a "Friends" program to help recruit more engineers. When potential job applicants visited Cisco's Internet home page to read about job openings, they would visit the "Friends" page **(http://www.cisco.com/friends/)**, where they would electronically submit their resumes. When this happened, an e-mail would automatically be forwarded to a Cisco employee who had volunteered to be a "Friend." That "Friend" would then call the job applicant within 24 hours. The program, which has been an overwhelming success, has helped Cisco solve the problem of job applicant scarcity. Cisco's CEO said, "Basically, over 60% of our hires are through that program. Before the Friends program, our Web site got 13,000 hits every seven weeks. Now it gets 54,000 hits. We are now hiring one out of every two or three we interview, where it used to be one in ten. We advertised the Cisco Friends program in local movie theaters and on a billboard at the San Jose airport. Since a lot of us in this industry are techies, we also put ads in places like the Dilbert Zone on the Internet *(http://www.unitedmedia.com/comics/dilbert/)*, which gets 228,000 hits every day—mostly from engineers."[7]

1.4
Uncertainty

uncertainty
extent to which managers can understand or predict which environmental changes and trends will affect their businesses

Figure 2.2 shows that environmental change, complexity, and resources (i.e., munificence) affect environmental **uncertainty**, which is how well managers can understand or predict the external changes and trends affecting their businesses. Starting at the left side of the figure, environmental uncertainty is lowest when there is little complexity and change, and resources are plentiful. In these environments, managers feel confident that they can understand and predict the external forces that affect their business. By contrast, the right side of the figure indicates that environmental uncertainty is highest when there is much complexity and change, and resources are scarce. In these environments, managers may not be at all confident that they can understand and predict the external forces affecting their businesses.

Review 1
Changing Environments

Environmental change, complexity, and munificence are the basic components of external environments. Environmental change is the rate at which conditions or events affecting a business change. Environmental complexity is the number of external factors in an external environment. Environmental munificence is the scarcity or abundance of resources available in the external environment. The greater the rate of environmental change and environmental complexity and the lower the environmental munificence, the less confident managers are that they can understand and predict the trends affecting their businesses. According to punctuated equilibrium theory, companies experience periods of stability followed by short periods of dynamic, fundamental change, followed by a return to periods of stability.

Figure 2.2 **Environmental Change, Complexity, & Munificence**

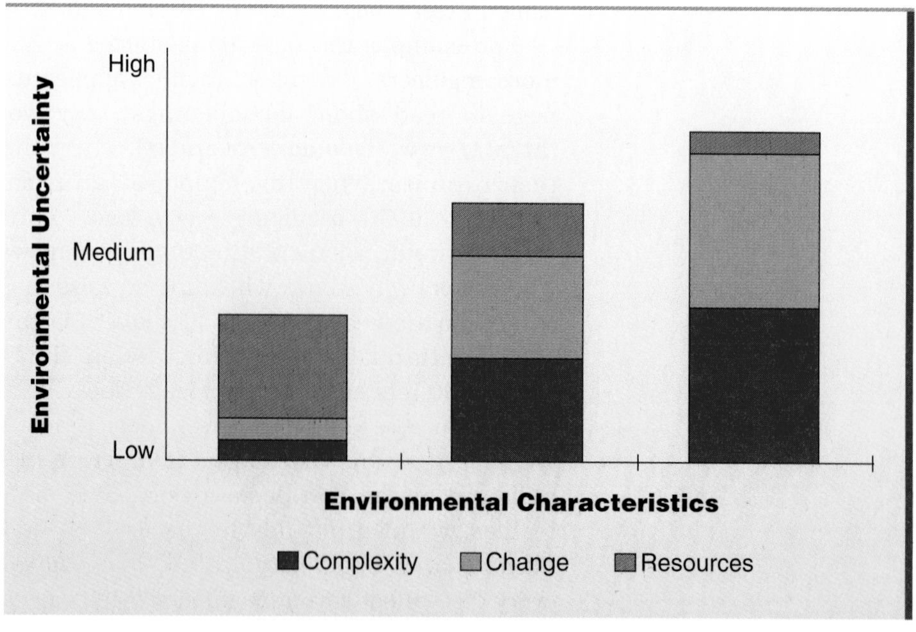

2 General Environment

general environment the economic, technological, sociocultural, and political trends that indirectly affect all organizations

specific environment the customer, competitor, supplier, industry regulation, and public pressure group trends that are unique to an industry and which directly affect how a company does business

Figure 2.3 shows the two kinds of external environments that influence organizations: the general environment and the specific environment. The **general environment** consists of the economy and the technological, sociocultural, and political/legal trends that indirectly affect all organizations. Changes in any sector of the general environment eventually affect most organizations. For example, most businesses benefit when the Federal Reserve lowers its prime lending rate, because banks and credit card companies will then lower the interest rates they charge for loans. Consumers, who can then borrow money more cheaply, will borrow more money to buy homes, cars, refrigerators, and large-screen TVs. By contrast, each organization has a **specific environment** that is unique to that firm's industry

Figure 2.3 **General and Specific Environments**

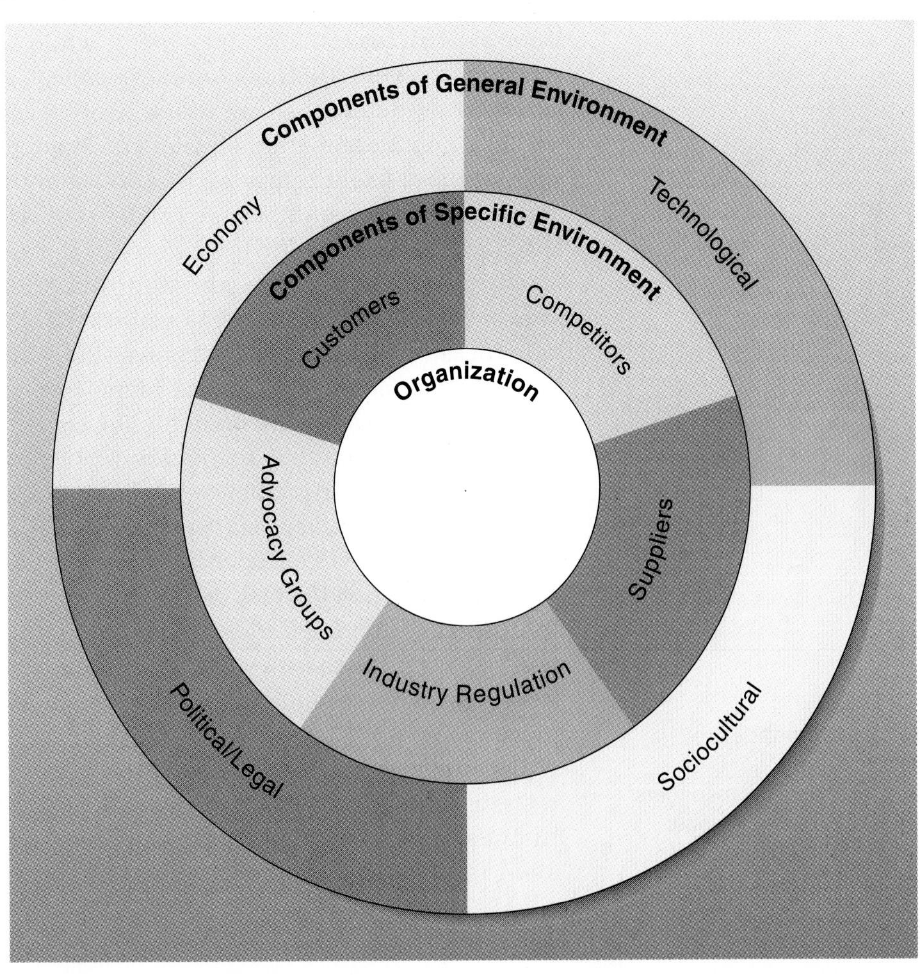

and directly affects the way it conducts day-to-day business. The specific environment, which will be discussed in detail in Section 3 of this chapter, includes customers, competitors, suppliers, industry regulation, and advocacy groups.

Let's take a closer look at the four components of the general environment: **2.1** *the economy, and the* **2.2** *technological,* **2.3** *sociocultural, and* **2.4** *political/legal trends that indirectly affect all organizations.*

2.1 *Economy*

The current state of a country's economy affects most organizations operating in it. A growing economy means that, in general, more people are working and therefore have relatively more money to spend. More products are being bought and sold than in a static or shrinking economy. While a growing economy doesn't mean that sales of an individual firm are necessarily growing, it does provide an environment favorable to business growth. On the other hand, a shrinking economy means that consumers have less money to spend. Also, relatively fewer products are being bought and sold. Thus, a shrinking economy makes growth for individual businesses more difficult.

For example, as I write this chapter, the United States is in its seventh straight year of economic expansion. Companies are reporting record profits. Inflation and interest rates are low. Job opportunities are at a 25-year high.[8] So, according to economic statistics, U.S. businesses are in a healthy, growing economy. In contrast, Japan is in its fifth straight year of economic recession. Japanese companies such as Mazda Motors are reporting regular, if not record, losses. Unemployment, while still low by U.S. standards, is growing. A record 160,000 Japanese college graduates were unable to find jobs after graduation. To cut costs, improve efficiency, and restore lost profitability, Japanese manufacturers cut 5 percent of manufacturing jobs last year, for an absolute loss of 740,000 manufacturing jobs.[9] According to economic statistics, Japanese businesses are currently in an unhealthy, shrinking economy.[10]

Of course, by the time you read this, the Japanese economy could be growing and the U.S. economy could be shrinking. Because the economy influences basic business decisions, like whether to hire more employees, expand production, or take out loans to purchase equipment, managers scan their economic environments for signs of change. Unfortunately, the economic statistics that managers rely on when making these decisions are notoriously poor predictors of *future* economic activity. A manager who decides to hire ten more employees because economic data suggest future growth could very well have to lay those newly hired workers off when the economic growth does not occur. In fact, a famous economic study found that at the beginning of a business quarter (a period of only three months), even the most accurate economic forecasters could not accurately predict whether economic activity would grow or shrink in that same quarter![11]

business confidence indices
indices that show managers' level of confidence about future business growth

Because economic statistics are such poor predictors, some managers try to predict future economic activity by keeping track of business confidence. **Business confidence indices** show how confident actual managers are about future business growth. For example, the Cahners Business Confidence Index is a monthly telephone survey of 400 senior business executives in the electronics, computer, construction, consumer goods, and manufacturing industries. Another widely cited measure is the U.S. Chamber of Commerce Business Confidence Index, which asks 7,000 small business owners to express their optimism (or pessimism) about future business sales and prospects. Managers often prefer business confidence indices to economic statistics, because they know that the level of confidence reported by real managers affects their business decisions. In other words, it's reasonable to expect managers to make decisions today that are in line with their expectations concerning the economy's future. So if Cahner's Business Confidence Index suddenly drops, managers would think hard about hiring new employees, or might stop plans to increase production for fear of being stuck with unsold inventory should the economy slow dramatically in the future.

Back to the Future

Technology, Customers, and Competitors

Ask any small business owner what his or her number one complaint is. The answer will be "I can't find the money I need to start or expand my business." Because of the historically high rate of small business failures, banks have been very cautious about lending to small businesses, that is, until Wells Fargo Bank started using computer technology to change the way it handled small business loans.

There are two sides to small business loans: (1) small businesses want the money fast; and (2) banks want to lend money that will be paid back. Wells Fargo accomplishes both using computers. The standard small business loan involves a lengthy loan application, multiple trips to the bank by the small business owner, and then a careful, thorough, and slow review process by the bank's loan committee, which, if the bank is customer-oriented, might meet weekly instead of monthly. Historically, banks have designed this slow, expensive process to please the banks rather than the small business owner.

Wells Fargo used technology to change three key factors in the small business loan application process. First, rather than using a committee to discuss each loan as it came in, Wells Fargo developed proprietary software called a loan scorecard. By gathering scorecard information on a large-enough number of small businesses, and then running that information through its in-house software programs, Wells Fargo could do a more accurate job of predicting which companies would pay back their loans and which wouldn't. So by developing and continuing to refine its own loan software, Wells Fargo decreased the loan default rate. Oh, and there was one unanticipated benefit: small businesses typically deposit $3 for every $1 they borrow. Consequently, Wells Fargo not only decreased its default rate, but also significantly increased the money in its banks from depositors.

Second, Wells Fargo purchased laptop computers for its loan officers and trained them how to use the scorecard software to approve loans without waiting for committee approval. This step allows loan officers to make on-the-spot decisions to accept or reject a small business's loan application. So, by combining the sales and loan processes, Wells Fargo could make speedier loan decisions at less cost. For example, it costs a traditional bank $1,700 to find a small business and then lend money to it. By contrast, by using technology, this process only costs Wells Fargo's $200.

Third, the combination of laptop computers and accurate loan software, which increases in accuracy as Wells Fargo's database increases in size, permits Wells Fargo, a California-based bank, to lend money to small businesses in new out-of-state markets like Florida and Texas. A stock market analyst who follows the banking industry says, "Wells Fargo is stealing all of this business and their competitors don't even know they are there." In fact, Wells Fargo enters new out-of-state markets by quickly qualifying approved small businesses for nearly instant loans of up to $50,000.

In summary, by paying attention to the customer, competitor, technology, economic, and supplier components in its business environment, Wells Fargo has expanded its business, increased its profitability, and better served its customers.

Source: G. Rifkin, "Loan Rangers," *Forbes ASAP*, 4 December 1995, 42-45.

2.2
Technological Component

Personal Productivity Tip

Computer Skills and Lifetime Earnings

Studies show that workers with basic computer skills earn 15 percent to 30 percent higher lifetime incomes than workers without them. Computers are becoming an integral part of managerial work. What should you do to learn about computers? Subscribe to *PC Magazine*, *PC World*, or *Mac World*. Take applied computer classes about word processing, spreadsheets, relational databases, and the Internet (File Transfer Protocol, World Wide Web, Telnet, E-mail, Usenet groups, FAQs). If these computer terms sound like a foreign language to you, start learning about computers now, or you may experience less job security and smaller lifetime income.

Source: J. Hearn & D. Lewis, "Keyboarding Course Work and Employment, Earnings, and Educational Attainment," *Journal of Education for Business* 68 (1993): 147.

Technology is the knowledge, tools, and techniques used to transform inputs (raw materials, information, etc.) into outputs (products and services). For example, the knowledge of authors, editors, and artists (technology) and the use of equipment like computers and printing presses (also technology) transformed paper, ink, and glue (raw material inputs) into this book (the finished product). In the case of a service company such as an airline, the technology would consist of equipment, like airplanes, repair tools, and computers, and the knowledge of mechanics, ticketers, and flight crews. The output would be the service of transporting people from one place to another.

Changes in technology can help companies provide better products or produce their products more efficiently. For example, advances in surgical techniques and imaging equipment have made open-heart surgery much faster and safer in recent years. While technological changes can benefit a business, they can also threaten it. For example, CD-ROM technology has allowed publishers of traditional print material, like books and encyclopedias, to cheaply add videos, sound, and animation to their products. Since the arrival of CD-ROM encyclopedias, sales of the paper version of Encyclopaedia Britannica are down by 30 percent. Rather than pay $1,500 for Britannica's 32-volume edition, consumers are buying CD-ROM encyclopedias that retail for less than $100.[12] Companies must embrace new technology and use it to improve products and services or decrease costs. If they don't, they will lose out to competitors who do. Chapter 11, on Organizational Change and Innovation, provides a more in-depth discussion of how technology affects a company's competitive advantage.

2.3
Sociocultural Component

technology
knowledge, tools, and techniques used to transform inputs (raw materials) into outputs (finished products or services)

The sociocultural component of the general environment refers to the demographic characteristics and general behavior, attitudes, and beliefs of people in a particular society. Sociocultural changes and trends influence organizations in two important ways.

First, changing demographic characteristics, such as the number of people with particular skills, or the growth or decline in particular population segments (single or married; old or young; men or women; or Caucasians, Hispanics, Blacks, or Asians; etc.) affects how companies run their businesses. For example, Figure 2.4 shows that married women with children are much more likely to work today than four decades ago. In 1960, only 18.6 percent of women with children under 6 years old and 39 percent of women with children between the ages of 6 and 17 worked. In 1996, those percentages had risen to 62.7 percent and 76.7 percent, respectively. Because of these changes, many more companies now offer child care as a benefit to attract and retain scarce, talented workers of both genders.[13] One example: At Chase Manhattan Bank, new mothers receive eight free weeks of care for new infants in the company's on-site child care center. However, 30 years from now, companies may find that elder care is a more important benefit than child care. Why? The number of people 55 or older who rely on their children for support, now estimated at 31 million, will double by 2025 to an estimated 63 million, and continue to double every 30 years after that. Contrast this with the fact that there were but eight million Americans who were 55 or older in 1890.[14]

Figure 2.4

Demographics: Percentage of Married Women with Children Who Work

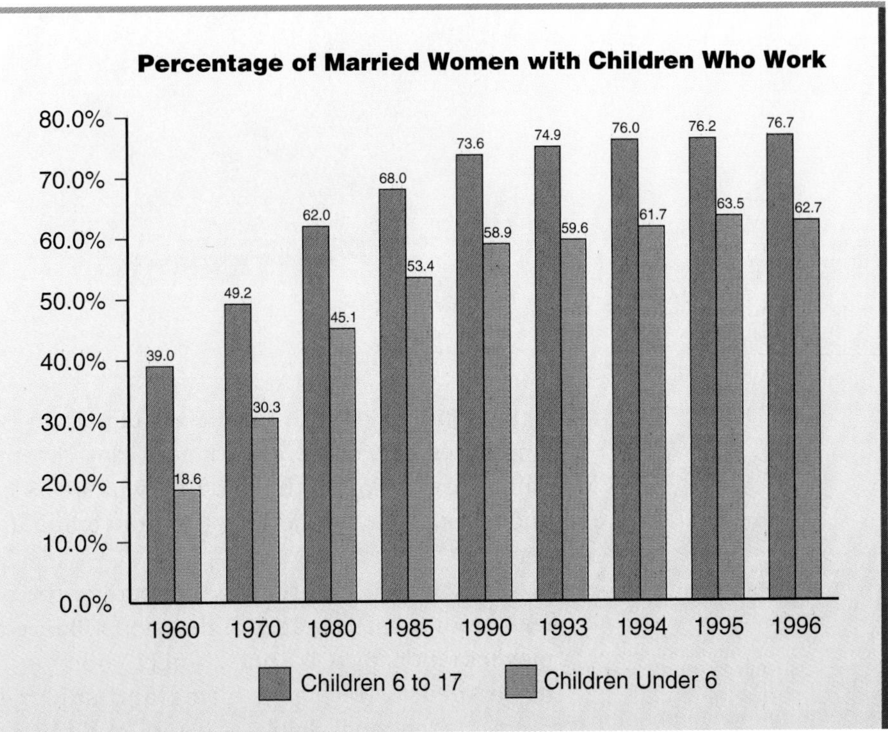

Source: U.S. Census Bureau, *Statistical Abstract of the United States, 1997.* "Employment Status of Women by Marital Status and Presence and Age of Children: 1960 to 1966," Table No. 631 (Washington, D.C.: U.S. Government Printing Office, 1997).

Second, sociocultural changes in behavior, attitudes, and beliefs also affect the demand for a business's products and services. One consequence of the large number of working women is that companies such as Avon and Tupperware now get more of their sales from rush-hour and lunchtime "parties" in workplaces than from "parties" in people's living rooms. Another is the increased sale of phone pagers (beepers) for teenagers. Working parents increasingly use beepers to keep track of their teenagers during after-school hours.[15]

2.4 *Political/Legal Component*

The political/legal component of the general environment includes the legislation, regulation, and court decisions that govern and regulate business behavior. Throughout the last decade, new legislation and regulation have placed additional responsibilities on companies. Unfortunately, many managers are unaware of these new responsibilities. For example, according to the 1991 Civil Rights Act, if an employee is sexually harassed by anyone at work (a supervisor, a co-worker, or even a customer), the company—not just the harasser—is potentially liable for damages, attorneys' fees, and back pay.[16] Under the Family Leave Act, employees who have been on the job one year are guaranteed 12 weeks of unpaid leave a year to tend to their own illnesses, or to their elderly parents, a newborn baby, or a newly adopted child. Employees are guaranteed the same job, pay, and benefits when they return to work.[17] Because of the 1990 Clean Air Act, companies

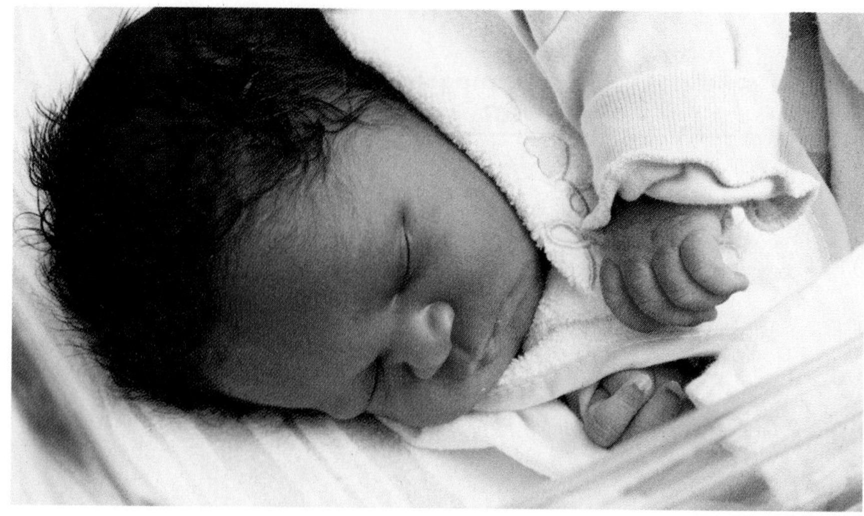

The Family Leave Act allows employees 12 weeks of unpaid leave a year to care for their newborn babies.
© PhotoDisc, Inc.

located in regions with high levels of polluted air must reduce the number of employees who drive to work each day by approximately 25 percent. Companies are exploring the possibility of sponsoring car pools or renting buses and vans, because the fines for noncompliance can be as high as $25,000 per day![18]

Many managers are also unaware of the potential legal risks associated with traditional managerial decisions like recruiting, hiring, and firing employees. Indeed, it is increasingly common for businesses and managers to be sued for negligent hiring and supervision, defamation, invasion of privacy, emotional distress, fraud, and misrepresentation during employee recruitment.[19] Likewise, there were few wrongful termination cases (i.e., unfairly firing employees) in 1975, but, today, there are more than 24,000 such cases in the U.S. court system.[20] One in four employers are eventually sued for wrongful termination. Employers lose 70 percent of these cases and a typical settlement payment to former employees will cost an average of $500,000 or more.[21]

Another area in which companies face potential legal risks these days is from customer-initiated lawsuits. For example, under product liability law, manufacturers can be liable for products made decades ago. Also, the law, as it is now written, does not consider whether manufactured products have been properly maintained and used. In one product liability case, a customer changed the product, did not follow the manufacturer's written instructions, and violated the manufacturer's warnings that were clearly marked on the product and in the instruction manual. Yet, despite the customer's negligence, the company was forced to recall the product (at tremendous expense) and pay damages of $6 million.[22] Why? Because product liability only requires plaintiffs to demonstrate that they were damaged by the manufacturer's product. In turn, under the concept of "strict liability," the burden of proof is shifted to the company, which must now prove that the product was safe.[23] So, once damages have been shown, the company is assumed guilty until it proves its innocence.

Not everyone agrees that companies face severe legal risks. Indeed, many believe that government should do more to regulate and restrict business behavior, and that it should be easier for average citizens to sue dishonest or negligent corporations. From a managerial perspective, the best medicine against legal risk is prevention. As a manager, it is your responsibility to educate yourself about the laws and regulations and potential lawsuits that could affect your business. Failure to do so may put you and your company at risk of sizable penalties, fines, or legal charges.

Review 2
General Environment

The general environment consists of economic, technological, sociocultural, and political/legal events and trends that affect all organizations. Because the economy influences basic business decisions, managers often use economic statistics and business confidence indices to predict future economic activity. Changes in technology, which is used to transform input into outputs, can be a benefit or a threat to a business. Sociocultural trends, like changing demographic characteristics, affect how companies run their businesses. Similarly, sociocultural changes in behavior, attitudes, and beliefs affect the demand for a business's products and services. Court decisions and revised federal and state laws have placed much larger political/legal responsibilities on companies. The best way to manage legal responsibilities is to educate managers and employees about laws and regulations and potential lawsuits that could affect a business.

3 Specific Environment

In contrast to general environments that indirectly influence organizations, changes in an organization's specific environment directly affect the way a company conducts its business. If customers decide to use another product, or a competitor cuts prices 10 percent, or a supplier can't deliver raw materials, or federal regulators specify that industry pollutants must be reduced, or environmental groups accuse your company of selling unsafe products, the impact on your business is immediate.

Let's examine how the **3.1** *customer,* **3.2** *competitor,* **3.3** *supplier,* **3.4** *industry regulation, and* **3.5** *advocacy group components of the specific environment affect businesses.*

3.1
Customer Component

Customers purchase products and services. Companies cannot exist without customer support. Therefore, monitoring customers' changing wants and needs is critical to business success. For example, while the 1980s were a decade of consumer materialism and instant gratification, the 1990s, by contrast, have been a time in which consumer tastes have shifted to value. Buying less, paying less, but getting better quality and durability when they buy have become more important to consumers in the 1990s. One clear example of this trend is that since 1990, automobile dealers have actually been selling more used cars than new cars. The reasons are simple. First, the average new car costs $20,450, whereas the average used car costs only $11,000. Second, because of leasing contracts that limit annual mileage on new cars, there are many more used cars on the market with low miles on them. Businesses have responded to these changes by creating used-car superstores like CarMax (created by electronics retailer Circuit City) and AutoNation and CarChoice (owned by Wayne Huizenga, who founded Block-Buster Video). In contrast to the small number of used cars offered at your local "mom and pop" used-car lot, these used-car superstores look like new-car dealerships and have 500 to 1,000 used cars on their lots, each sold with a used-car warranty.[24]

There are two basic strategies for monitoring customers: reactive and proactive. Reactive customer monitoring is identifying and addressing customer trends and problems after they occur. One reactive strategy is to identify customer concerns by listening closely to customer complaints. Not only does listening to complaints help identify problems, but the way in which companies respond to complaints indicates how closely they are attending to customer concerns. For example, companies that respond quickly to customer letters of complaint are viewed much more favorably than companies that are slow to respond or never respond. In particular, studies have shown that when a company's follow-up letter thanks customers for writing, offers a sincere, specific response to the customer's complaint (i.e., not a form letter, but an explanation of how the problem will be handled), and contains a small gift, coupons, or a refund to make up for the problem, customers will be much more likely to purchase products or services again from that company.[25]

Proactive monitoring of customers means trying to sense events, trends, and problems before they occur (or before customers complain). For example, Cotton Incorporated, the trade group that encourages consumers to purchase cotton clothing ("The look, the feel of cotton..."), publishes a quarterly newsletter called *Lifestyle Monitor* that reports the results of ongoing research. According to Cotton Inc.'s president and CEO, the research is an "early radar detection system" for changes in consumer attitudes and behavior regarding clothing, appearance, fashion, home furnishings, and other topics.[26] To illustrate, this research indicates that blue jeans continue to be as popular as ever. Eighty-five percent of respondents disagreed with a statement saying, "Jeans are in my past, not in my future." Furthermore, when women were asked whether "A good-looking man looks most sexy in denim jeans and a casual shirt, or a jacket and tie or slacks and a nice sweater?" 53 percent said denim jeans, 25 percent said slacks and a sweater, and 20 percent said a jacket and tie.[27]

3.2 *Competitor Component*

competitors
companies in the same industry that sell similar products or services to customers

Competitors are companies in the same industry that sell similar products or services to customers. GM, Ford, and Chrysler all compete for automobile customers. NBC, ABC, CBS, and Fox compete for TV viewers' attention. And McDonald's, Burger King, and Wendy's compete for fast-food customers' dollars. Often, the difference between business success and failure comes down to whether your company is doing a better job of satisfying customer wants and needs than your competitors. Consequently, companies need to keep close track of what their competitors are doing. To do this, managers perform what's called a **competitive analysis**, which is deciding who your competitors are, anticipating competitors' moves, and determining competitors' strengths and weaknesses.

competitive analysis
a process for monitoring competitors that involves identifying competitors, anticipating their moves, and determining their strengths and weaknesses

Surprisingly, because they tend to focus on only two or three well-known competitors with similar goals and resources, managers often do a poor job

PersonalProductivityTip

Improve Your Competitive IQ

Ninety percent of organizations do a poor job of gathering information about competitors. However, by using publicly available information, you can improve your competitive IQ. You can get information from government documents, public speeches, published writings, press releases, court transcripts, industry seminars, trade shows, and U.S. embassies (which write detailed economic, demographic, and political studies for each country). One example is the Foreign Broadcast Information Service, published by the U.S. State Department, which contains translations of worldwide radio and TV broadcasts. These public reports, which can be ordered by geographic area, provide a quick way to keep track of foreign markets and competition.

Source: B. Ettorre, "Managing Competitive Intelligence," *Management Review*, 1 October 1995, 15-19.

of identifying potential competitors.[28] For example, Coke and Pepsi undoubtedly spend more time keeping track of each other than they do Dr. Pepper or Snapple. Likewise, Bell-South, which provides local and long-distance phone service in the southeastern portion of the U.S., is expecting intense competition from MCI. MCI, which has been a long-distance phone service company, is spending $2 billion nationwide to enter the local phone service business and has made Atlanta, one of Bell-South's largest cities, one of its key markets. However, if Bell-South only worries about MCI, it will overlook the 55 other companies that are trying to take away its customers with lower-priced local phone service.[29]

The second mistake managers make when analyzing the competition is to underestimate potential competitors' capabilities. When this happens, managers don't take the steps they should to continue to improve their products or services. The result can be significant decreases in both market share and profits. For example, with software products like Internet Phone, it is possible to make free long-distance phone calls on the Internet. To use Internet Phone, you need an Internet service provider (typically $20-$30 a month) and a computer with a sound card, speakers, and a microphone. The sound quality using Internet Phone is only as good as AM radio (but it's getting better).[30] Yet, despite these limitations, the prospect of free long-distance calls (especially free international calls!) is leading many people and companies to try these products. However, because the number of Internet Phone users is still small, phone companies don't yet see Internet Phone as a competitive threat. Indeed, when a phone company manager was asked whether he was worried about the likes of Internet Phone, his response was: "Some people will use it. But it won't really affect our business."[31]

3.3 *Supplier Component*

suppliers
companies that provide material, human, financial, and informational resources to other companies

Suppliers are companies that provide material, human, financial, and informational resources to other companies. U.S. Steel buys iron ore from suppliers to make steel products. When IBM sells a mainframe computer, it

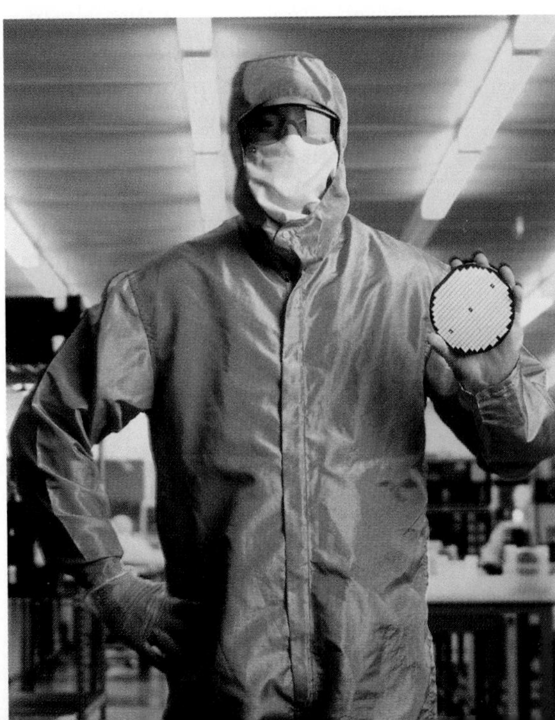

Many companies are highly dependent on their suppliers for key product components, such as computer chips.
© Alan Levenson/Tony Stone Images

also provides support staff, engineers, and other technical consultants to the company that bought the computer. If you're shopping for desks, chairs, and office supplies, chances are Office Depot will be glad to help your business open a revolving charge account to pay for your purchases. Or when a clothing manufacturing firm has spent $100,000 to purchase new high-pressure "water drills" to be used to cut shirt and pants patterns to precise sizes, the water drill manufacturer will, as part of the purchase, agree to train workers how to use the machinery.

supplier dependence degree to which a company relies on a supplier because of the importance of the supplier's product to the company and the difficulty of finding other sources of that product

A key factor influencing the relationship between companies and their suppliers is how dependent they are on each other.[32] **Supplier dependence** is the degree to which a company relies on a supplier because of the importance of the supplier's product to the company and the difficulty of finding other sources of that product. For example, until recently, manufacturers of IBM-compatible personal computers had one primary source for computer processor chips: Intel Corporation, maker of the Pentium chip. Because Intel controls 80 percent of this market, manufacturers like Compaq Computers had little choice but to buy their chips from Intel. However, two competitors now produce alternatives to the Pentium chip: Cyrix and AMD.[33] Now that they have a choice, computer manufacturers are somewhat less dependent on Intel.

buyer dependence degree to which a supplier relies on a buyer because of the importance of that buyer to the supplier and the difficulty of selling its products to other buyers

Buyer dependence is the degree to which a supplier relies on a buyer because of the importance of that buyer to the supplier and the difficulty of selling its products to other buyers. For example, because it believed that the clothes sold in its stores were too expensive, Wal-Mart's Canadian division sent letters to its clothing suppliers, demanding a "retroactive, nonnegotiable price rollback of between 4 and 10 percent." So if Wal-Mart had purchased $100,000 of goods from a supplier in the last six months, it expected to receive a refund from the supplier totaling between $4,000 and $10,000. The suppliers were furious, but had little choice since Wal-Mart was one of their largest customers. The suppliers claimed that Wal-Mart told them that if they did not pay the 4–10 percent "mark down allowance," their orders would be canceled and Wal-Mart would end their business relationship.[34]

opportunistic behavior transaction in which one party in the relationship benefits at the expense of the other

As Wal-Mart's demand indicates, greater buyer or seller dependence can lead to **opportunistic behavior,** in which one party benefits at the expense of the other. For example, because there are hundreds of small clothing manufacturers, but few department stores to buy those clothes, department stores often demand that clothing suppliers follow strict guidelines. And if they fail to follow those guidelines, the suppliers are punished. Ames Department Stores penalizes its suppliers $300 for incorrect labels, $500 for the wrong packing materials, and 5 percent of the total cost of an order if the shipment arrives late or early![35]

Opportunistic behavior between buyers and suppliers will never be completely eliminated. However, many companies believe that both buyers and suppliers can benefit by improving the buyer-supplier relationship. General Motors, for example, which has a long history of adversarial relationships with its suppliers, has recently begun its new "Ambassador Program." The Ambassador Program is designed to improve communication between GM and its suppliers by assigning a GM executive (but not the GM executive who makes purchases from the company) to meet regularly with the supplier to discuss problems or new ideas. In contrast to opportunistic behavior, buyer-supplier transactions like GM's Ambassador Program emphasize

relationship behavior mutually beneficial, long-term exchanges between buyers and suppliers

relationship behavior, which focuses on establishing a mutually beneficial, long-term relationship between buyers and suppliers. Like General Motors, the trend in the last decade is for companies to reduce the number of suppliers they deal with and to improve the relationships they have with remaining suppliers.[36]

3.4 *Industry Regulation Component*

industry regulation regulations and rules that govern the business practices and procedures of specific industries, businesses, and professions

In contrast to the political/legal component of the general environment that affects all businesses, the **industry regulation** component consists of regulations and rules that govern the business practices and procedures of specific industries, businesses, and professions. For example, if you buy two apple pies from a neighbor who makes a little extra money selling homemade baked goods, your neighbor could be fined. In most states, it is illegal to sell food from your home. State regulations typically require a business license plus a state certificate of inspection that indicates that the food is stored properly; insects have not infested the premises; ovens are state approved; electrical wiring, lighting, and smoke detectors are up to code; and so on.[37] Likewise, only the car industry is subject to CAFE regulations. In this case, CAFE doesn't mean restaurants. CAFE stands for the Corporate Average Fuel Economy regulations that require American auto manufacturers to sell cars that average 27.5 miles per gallon.[38]

Regulatory agencies affect businesses by creating and enforcing rules and regulations to protect consumers, workers, or society as a whole. For example, after seven years of planning, the Department of Health and Human Services issued rules and regulations regarding the quality of care to be provided in 17,000 nursing homes across the U.S. The law not only spelled out standards concerning health, safety, nutrition, and cleanliness, but it also authorized fines for nursing homes that fail to meet these standards. Punishments for minor violations begin at $50 but can go as high as $10,000 a day for serious violations. Furthermore, anyone who lets a nursing home know when the government will be making its surprise annual inspection can be fined $2,000.[39]

There are nearly 100 federal government agencies and regulatory commissions that can affect nearly any kind of business. Table 2.1 lists some of the most influential federal agencies and commissions.

Overall, the number of federal regulations has nearly tripled in the last 25 years. However, businesses are not just subject to federal regulations. They must also meet state, county, and city regulations, too. Surveys indicate that managers rank government regulation as one of the most demanding and frustrating parts of their jobs.[40]

3.5 *Advocacy Groups*

advocacy groups groups of concerned citizens who band together to try to influence the business practices of specific industries, businesses, and professions

Advocacy groups are groups of concerned citizens who band together to try to influence the business practices of specific industries, businesses, and professions. The members of a group generally share the same point of view on a particular issue. For example, environmental advocacy groups might try to get manufacturers to reduce smokestack pollution emissions. Unlike the industry regulation component of the specific environment, advocacy groups cannot force organizations to change their practices. However,

Table 2.1 **Federal Regulatory Agencies and Commissions**

Federal Agency	*Regulatory Responsibilities*
Consumer Product Safety Commission	Reduce risk of injuries and deaths associated with consumer products, set product safety standards, enforce product recalls, and provide consumer education
Environmental Protection Agency	Reduce and control pollution through research, monitoring, standard setting, and enforcement activities
Equal Employment Opportunity Commission	Promote fair hiring and promotion practices
Federal Communications Commission	Regulate interstate and international communications by radio, television, wire, satellite, and cable
Federal Reserve System	As nation's central bank, control interest rates and money supply, and monitor the U.S. banking system to produce a growing economy with stable prices
Federal Trade Commission	Restrict unfair methods of business competition and misleading advertising, and enforce consumer protection laws
Food and Drug Administration	Protect nation's health by making sure food, drugs, and cosmetics are safe
National Labor Relations Board	Monitor union elections and stop companies from engaging in unfair labor practices
Occupational Safety & Health Administration	Save lives, prevent injuries, and protect the health of workers
Securities and Exchange Commission	Protect investors in the bond and stock markets, guarantee access to information on publicly traded securities, and regulate firms that sell securities or give investment advice

they can use a number of techniques to try to influence companies: public communications, media advocacy, and product boycotts.

public communications an advocacy group tactic that relies on voluntary participation by the news media and the advertising industry to get an advocacy group's message out

The **public communications** approach relies on *voluntary* participation by the news media and the advertising industry to get an advocacy group's message out. For example, Project Lean, begun in 1987 by the Henry J. Kaiser Family Foundation, is a ten-year public information campaign that aims to reduce average dietary fat intake levels to 30 percent and to increase the availability of low-fat foods at restaurants, supermarkets, cafeterias, and schools.[41] To accomplish its goals, Project Lean makes heavy use of public service announcements on TV and radio (as part of their community service, TV and radio stations donate this time). It also maintains a consumer hotline, publishes a free newsletter, and works in conjunction with the American Dietetic Association, American Public Health Association, and the American Academy of Family Physicians to make Americans more aware of the dangers of eating a high-fat diet.

media advocacy an advocacy group tactic of framing issues as public issues, exposing questionable, exploitative, or unethical practices, and forcing media coverage by buying media time or creating controversy that is likely to receive extensive news coverage

In contrast to the public communications approach, media advocacy is a much more aggressive form of advocacy. A **media advocacy** approach typically involves framing issues as public issues (i.e., affecting everyone); exposing questionable, exploitative, or unethical practices; and forcing media coverage by buying media time or creating controversy that is likely to receive extensive news coverage. Millionaire Phillip Sokolof conducted one of the most famous media advocacy campaigns against McDonald's. Sokolof, who had once suffered a heart attack, took out full-page ads in 20 major newspapers to decry McDonald's "Poisoning of America." The ads stated, "McDonald's, your hamburgers still have too much fat and your french fries are cooked with beef tallow!" The ads also encouraged McDonald's to reduce fat levels in its hamburgers, cook French fries in vegetable oil, and use skim milk rather than 2 percent milk. By buying advertising in 20 major newspapers and picking on a well-known, respected company like McDonald's, Sokolof knew that press coverage would be guaranteed. Furthermore, he scheduled his press conference for noon, early enough to ensure that the story could be covered in time for the evening network news. Finally, he used Federal Express to send press releases and information packets to local TV stations throughout the U.S. Three weeks later, McDonald's and Wendy's announced that they would begin cooking French fries in vegetable oil instead of beef tallow.[42]

product boycott
an advocacy group tactic of protesting a company's actions by convincing consumers not to purchase its product or service

A **product boycott** is a tactic in which an advocacy group actively tries to convince consumers to not purchase a company's product or service. For example, when the French government made the controversial decision in 1995 to resume nuclear testing in the Pacific, French winemakers, who sell $7 billion of wine worldwide every year, feared a boycott. The general delegate of the French Federation of Exporters of Wines and Spirits said, "We are taking the threats of a boycott very seriously and we are very worried."[43] French winemakers were worried because boycotts can significantly reduce company sales and profits. When it was learned that Shell Oil was going to dispose of an old oil storage rig by letting it drop to the bottom of the North Sea, Greenpeace, an environmental advocacy group, complained to the press that this posed environmental hazards. Greenpeace members drew attention to this cause by boarding the barge that was taking the oil storage rig to sea. Customers in Denmark, Holland, and Germany boycotted and cut Shell's sales by 30 percent, costing the company millions in revenues and profit.[44]

Review 3
Specific Environment

The specific environment is made up of five components: customers, competitors, suppliers, industry regulators, and advocacy groups. Companies can monitor customers' needs by identifying customer problems after they occur or by anticipating problems before they occur. However, because they tend to focus on well-known competitors, managers often underestimate their competition or do a poor job of identifying future competitors. Since suppliers and buyers are very dependent on each other, that dependence sometimes leads to opportunistic behavior, in which one benefits at the expense of the other. Regulatory agencies affect businesses by creating rules and then enforcing them. Overall, the level of industry regulation has nearly tripled in the last 25 years. Advocacy groups cannot regulate organization practices. However, through public communications, media advocacy, and product boycotts, they try to convince companies to change their practices.

4 Making Sense of Changing Environments

In Chapter 1, you learned that managers are responsible for making sense of their business environments. However, our just-completed discussions of the general and specific environments indicate that making sense of business environments is not an easy task. Because external environments can be dynamic, confusing, and complex, managers use a three-step process to make sense of the changes in their external environments: **4.1** environmental scanning, **4.2** interpreting environmental factors, and **4.3** acting on threats and opportunities.

4.1 *Environmental Scanning*

environmental scanning searching the environment for important events or issues that might affect an organization

Environmental scanning is searching the environment for important events or issues that might affect an organization. Managers scan the environment to stay up-to-date on important factors in their industry. For example, a survey conducted by the International Hotel Association indicated that technology and prices were the most important trends being tracked and scanned by international hotel chain executives. In particular, they were looking for any information about the rates that competitors were charging for hotel rooms in particular international markets or on how to install and use global reservation systems.[45]

Managers also scan their environments to reduce uncertainty. For example, many mail-order, catalog, and Internet-based businesses were hurt when they didn't anticipate the Teamsters Union strike against United Parcel Service in 1997. Because they relied on UPS to deliver their products to customers, their sales dropped immediately when the strike began. However, some companies, like Amazon.com, the Internet-based bookseller (*http://www.amazon.com*), saw the strike coming. The weekend before the strike was announced, Amazon shifted its shipments to the U.S. Postal Service and Airborne Express.[46]

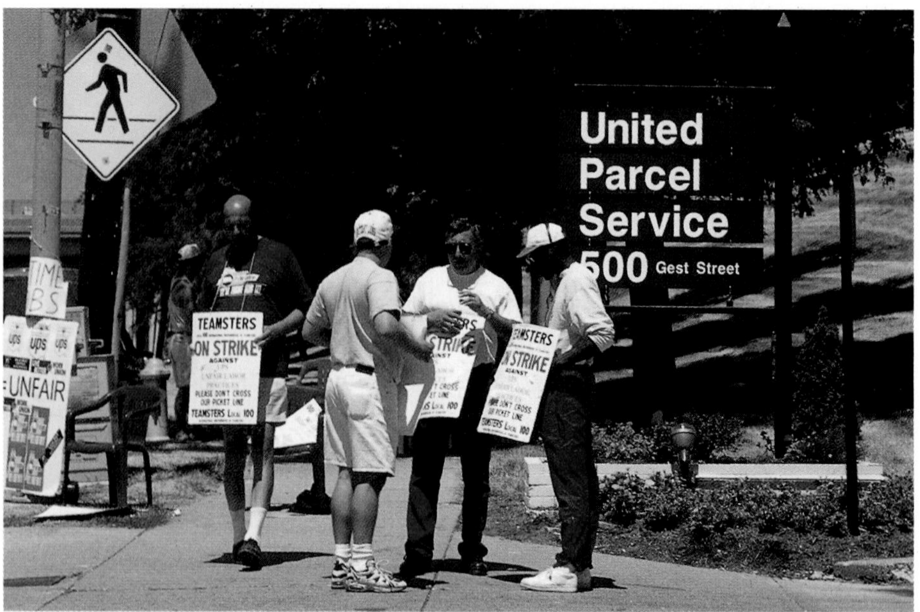

Managers scan the environment to identify potential threats to their company's operations, such as a strike that could hamper product delivery.
© SWCP/Cary Benbow

Personal Productivity Tip

Manage by Reading Around

Traditionally, managers have used personal contacts and newspapers to track changes that affect their businesses. However, Intel's Chairman, Andy Grove, says that the Internet, America Online, Prodigy, and CompuServe can help uncover trends. Grove conducts electronic keyword searches on news databases. Others track Internet discussion groups for mention of their company's products or services. Indeed, the public first learned that Intel's Pentium chips could produce wrong answers for basic math computations from an Internet discussion group. So get online, get connected, and do what Andy Grove calls "managing by reading around."

Source: A. Deutschman, "The Managing Wisdom of High-Tech Superstars," *Fortune*, 17 October 1994, 197-206.

Organizational strategies also affect environmental scanning. In other words, managers pay close attention to trends and events that are directly related to their company's ability to compete in the marketplace.[47] And by keeping their eyes and ears open, managers sometimes come across important information by accident. For example, Gary Costley, an employee of Kellogg's, was pulling into the parking lot at work when he noticed a crane on the loading dock of the General Foods' Post cereal plant across the street. He could see that the crane was unloading a special machine made by a German company for manufacturing cereal. This caught his attention, because Kellogg's was having trouble getting a similar machine from a French manufacturer to work. So he went to a store, purchased a camera and film, and stood across the street while taking pictures. A Post employee yelled, "Hey, you can't do that." Costley responded, "I'm standing on a public street taking photos. You shouldn't unload your machines in plain sight." The pictures helped convince Kellogg's management to buy the German machines and to not spend any more time or money to make the French machines work.[48]

Finally, environmental scanning is important because it contributes to organizational performance. Environmental scanning helps managers detect environmental changes and problems before they become organizational crises.[49] Furthermore, companies whose CEOs do more environmental scanning have higher profits.[50] CEOs in better-performing firms scan their firms' environments more frequently and scan more key factors in their environments in more depth and detail than do CEOs in poorer-performing firms.[51]

4.2 *Interpreting Environmental Factors*

After scanning, managers determine what environmental events and issues mean to the organization. Typically, managers either view environmental events and issues as threats or opportunities. When managers interpret environmental events as threats, they take steps to protect the company from further harm. For example, in France, the neighborhood boulangerie, boucherie, fromagerie, patisserie, and poissonnerie (bakery, butcher, cheese, pastry, and fish shops) have begun to go out of business in large numbers. Their existence is now threatened by the Carrefour, huge hypermarkets that are sometimes as large as three football fields. French shoppers load up on cartloads of groceries once a week at the Carrefour to save scarce time and money. One of the best buys is France's traditional loaf of bread, the baguette, which sells for about $1 at small bakeries but goes for 40 cents at the hypermarket. So with their businesses in decline, the neighborhood boulangerie, boucherie, fromagerie, patisserie, and poissonnerie have turned to the French government for help, asking it to enact laws limiting construction of new hypermarkets. They're also asking the French government to prevent hypermarkets from selling products below cost, a practice that hypermarkets say they don't use.[52]

By contrast, when managers interpret environmental events as opportunities, they will consider strategic alternatives for taking advantage of the event to improve company performance. In the snack business, Frito-Lay saw opportunities in the increasing demand for healthier snacks. By being quick to market with Baked Lays, Baked Tostitos, and Rold Gold Fat Free Pretzels, Frito-Lay captured a large share of the low-fat snack market.[53]

4.3 *Acting on Threats and Opportunities*

After scanning for information on environmental events and issues, and interpreting them as threats or opportunities, managers have to decide how to respond to these environmental factors. However, deciding what to do under conditions of uncertainty is difficult. Managers are never completely confident that they have all the information they need, or that they correctly understand the information they have.

cognitive maps graphic depictions of how managers believe environmental factors relate to possible organizational actions

Because it is impossible to comprehend all the factors and changes, managers rely on simplified models of external environments called cognitive maps. **Cognitive maps** summarize the perceived relationships between environmental factors and possible organizational actions. For example, the cognitive map shown in Figure 2.5 represents a small clothing store owner's interpretation of her business environment. The map shows three kinds of variables. The first, shown as rectangles, are environmental factors such as Wal-Mart or a large mall 20 minutes away. The second, shown in ovals, are potential actions that the store owner might take, such as a low-cost strategy; a good value, good service strategy; or a large selection of the latest fashions strategy. The third, shown as trapezoids, are company strengths, such as low employee turnover, and weaknesses, such as small size.

The arrows on the map indicate whether the manager believes there is a positive or negative relationship between variables. For example, the manager believes that a low-cost strategy wouldn't work, because Wal-Mart and Kmart are nearby. Offering a large selection of the latest fashions would not

Figure 2.5 **Cognitive Maps**

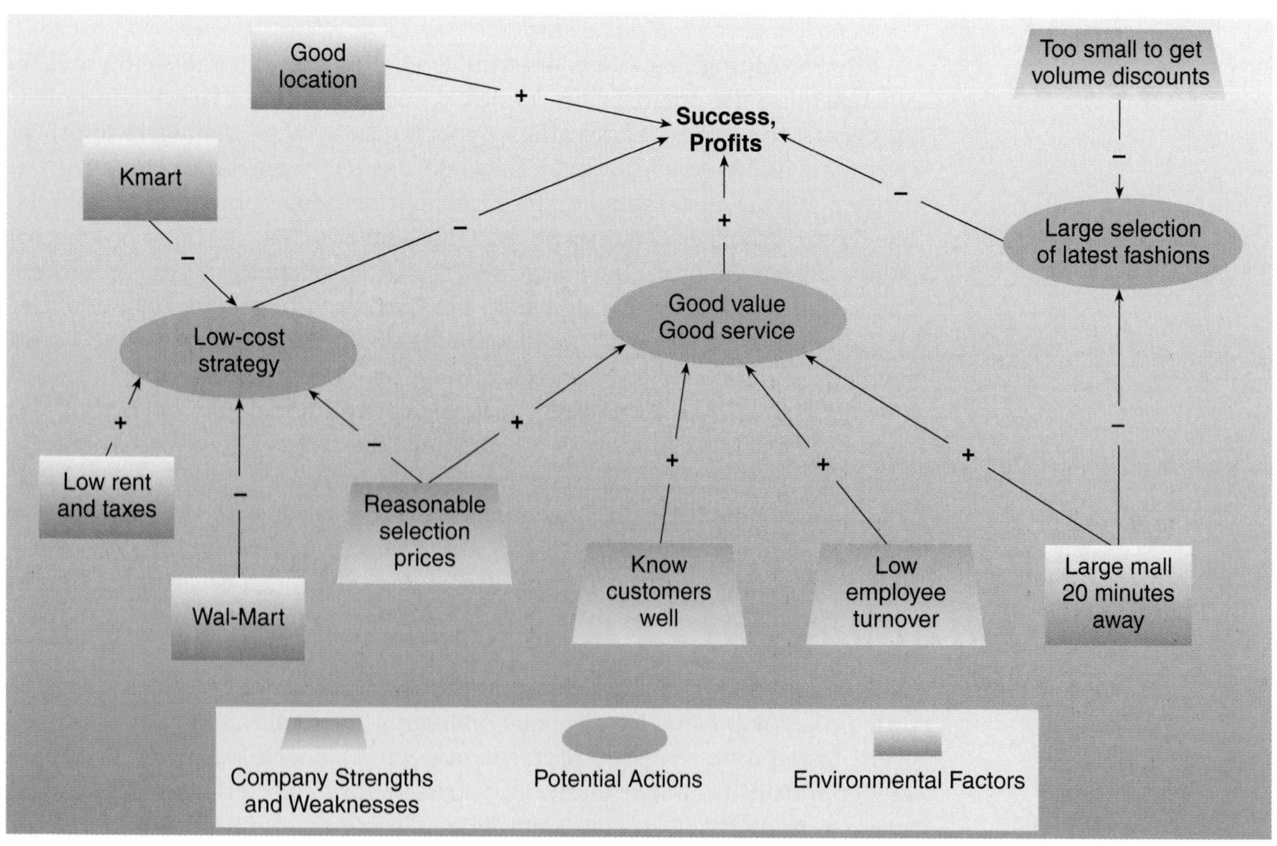

work either—not with the small size of the store and that large nearby mall. However, this manager believes that a good value, good service strategy would lead to success and profits, because of low employee turnover, knowing customers well, a reasonable selection of clothes at reasonable prices, and a good location.

In the end, managers must complete all three steps—environmental scanning, interpreting environmental factors, and acting on threats and opportunities—to make sense of changing external environments. Environmental scanning helps managers more accurately interpret their environments and take actions that improve company performance. Through scanning, managers keep tabs on what competitors are doing, identify market trends, and stay alert to current events that affect their company's operations. Armed with the environmental information they have gathered, managers can then take action to minimize the impact of threats and turn opportunities into increased profits.

Review 4
Making Sense of Changing Environments

Managers use a three-step process to make sense of external environments: environmental scanning, interpreting information, and action. Managers scan their environments based on their organizational strategies, their need for up-to-date information, and their need to reduce uncertainty. When managers identify environmental events as threats, they take steps to protect the company from harm. When managers identify environmental events as opportunities, they formulate alternatives for taking advantage of them to improve company performance. Using cognitive maps can help managers visually summarize the relationships between environmental factors and the actions they might take to deal with them.

Internal Environments

internal environment
the events and trends inside an organization that affect management, employees, and organizational culture

External environments are external trends and events that have the potential to affect companies. The **internal environment** consists of the trends and events within an organization that affect the management, employees, and organizational culture.

Since its inception, IBM's culture promised lifetime employment to its workers and corporate benevolence to the towns in which IBM plants and offices were located. For example, if you drive down Route 9 into Poughkeepsie, New York, you'll see the IBM Credit Union, the IBM Conference Center (a country club for IBM employees), and the schools and parks that were built with IBM donations and tax revenues. However, in the early 1990s, as IBM lost market share in the mainframe computer and personal computer businesses, it had to cut costs to minimize financial losses. Manufacturing plants were sold, the long-term research and development budget was cut, and the number of IBM employees was reduced by 40 percent. With such significant changes to the company's internal environment, one might expect that IBMers would have a different attitude about how their company should be run. However, a survey of 1,200 top managers indicated that 40 percent did not see "the need for change." In fact, many IBMers were angry at new CEO Louis Gerstner for introducing "unnecessary" changes.[54]

Clearly, CEO Gerstner was doing many things that he hoped would change IBM's internal environment by changing the attitudes and behaviors of IBM's managers and employees. However, Gerstner finally admitted that he was having trouble changing the most important part of IBM's internal environment: its culture. **Organizational culture** is the set of key values, beliefs, and attitudes shared by organizational members. Clearly, despite significant changes to its internal environment, many of the remaining employees at IBM were unwilling to reassess their own attitudes, or IBM's core values and beliefs.

organizational culture the values, beliefs, and attitudes shared by organizational members

After reading the next section, you should be able to:

5 Explain how **organizational cultures are created** and how they can help companies be **successful.**

5 Organizational Cultures: Creation, Success, and Change

Let's take a closer look at **5.1** *how organizational cultures are created and maintained,* **5.2** *the characteristics of successful organizational cultures, and* **5.3** *how companies can accomplish the difficult task of changing organizational cultures.*

5.1 *Creation and Maintenance of Organizational Cultures*

A primary source of organizational culture is the company founder. Founders like Thomas J. Watson (IBM), Sam Walton (Wal-Mart), Bill Gates (Microsoft), or Frederick Maytag (Maytag) create organizations in their own images that they imprint with their beliefs, attitudes, and values. For example, Thomas J. Watson, Sr., proclaimed that IBM's three basic beliefs were the pursuit of excellence, customer service, and showing "respect for the individual," meaning company employees. Microsoft employees share founder Bill Gates's intensity for staying ahead of software competitors. Says a Microsoft vice-president, "No matter how good your product, you are only 18 months away from failure."[55]

Founder Thomas J. Watson created IBM's culture around his beliefs in the pursuit of excellence, customer service, and respect for the individual. © Corbis Bettman

BLASTFROMTHEPASS

Capturing Corporate Culture by Writing Corporate History

Typically, the "Blast from the Past" features in this book will teach you something about the history of management ideas presented in a chapter. This time, however, instead of learning about the history of internal and external organizational environments, you will learn how companies are capturing their corporate cultures by writing their corporate histories. Three basic questions are relevant to the issue of cultures and corporate history: Why? How? and How much?

Why should a company capture its corporate culture by writing its corporate history? When it comes to corporate culture, history matters, because it helps employees and managers understand the key people, events, and changes that shaped a company. For example, McDonald's helps preserve its history and culture each year as it celebrates founder Ray Kroc's birthday by having McDonald's executives spend the day working in its restaurants. According to Kroc, this is to remind McDonald's managers that "if it's below [their] dignity to mop floors, clean toilets, and roll up [their] sleeves, then [they] are not going to succeed: [Their] attitude is wrong." McDonald's even created an exhibit called "Talk to Ray," in which, thanks to messages videotaped before his death, anyone can "ask" Ray questions about McDonald's values and history.

How does a company capture its history? According to Willa Baum, who directs the Regional Oral History Office at the University of California, Berkeley, "You start with who's alive and has a good memory, and then expand out. You want to have people who represent the workers and can talk about the progression and changes in the organization from their perspective." For example, Clarence Leis, who was the second manager of the very first Wal-Mart store, tells this story about Wal-Mart founder Sam Walton and how Wal-Mart developed its strategy of everyday low prices:

> *Rogers [the store in Rogers, Arkansas] had been open about a year, and everything was just piled up on tables, with no rhyme or reason whatsoever. Sam [Walton] asked me to kind of group the stuff by category or department, and that's when we began our department system. The thing I remember most, though, was the way we priced goods. Merchandise would come in and we would just lay it down on the floor and get out the invoice. Sam wouldn't let us hedge on a price at all. Say the list price was $1.98, but we had only paid 50 cents. Initially, I would say, 'Well, it's originally $1.98, so why don't we sell it for $1.25?' And he'd say 'No. We paid 50 cents for it. Mark it up 30 percent, and that's it. No matter what you pay for it, if we get a great deal, pass it on to the customer.' And of course that's what we did.*

What does it cost to capture a company's history? It depends on what kind and how extensive a history a company wants. Oral histories, in which videotaped interviews are recorded and edited together, much like a movie, can be expensive. For mid-sized companies, the cost of an oral history can run between $20,000 and $30,000. A rough estimate is approximately $1,000 an hour of filmed interviews. This includes the cost of interviewing, transcribing, editing, and indexing for research purposes. Written histories can also be expensive. A British firm, Royal Insurance, spent roughly half a million dollars for 50,000 copies of a full-color, 240-page book to celebrate its 150th year in business.

Many companies, however, consider the money well spent. Hamish MacGibbon, director of publisher James & James, which has published over 40 company histories, says, "It [a company history] is a way of engaging people in what the company is about and getting across certain messages. It says, 'This is why we're good at what we're doing, why we're a good company to trade with, invest in or work for, or why we're doing a good job for the community.' In short, it gets people involved in the culture of a company."

Sources: K.D. Conti, "Oral Histories: The Most Overlooked Public Relations Tool," *Communication World,* June-July 1995, 52-54. N. Hassell, "Trading on the Past," *Management Today,* March 1996, 81-82. M.A. Salva-Ramirez, "McDonald's: A Prime Example of Corporate Culture," *Public Relations Quarterly,* Winter 1995, 30-32. S. Walton & J. Huey, *Sam Walton: Made in America* (New York: Doubleday, 1992).

While company founders are instrumental in the creation of organizational cultures, founders retire, die, or choose to leave their companies. For example, neither Steve Wozniak, co-founder of Apple Computers, nor Mitch Kapor, founder of Lotus software, which created Lotus 1-2-3, one of the first and most successful spreadsheet programs, is still with the companies they created. Yet, they all still work in the computer industry. So when the founders are gone, how are the founders' values, attitudes, and beliefs sustained in the organizational culture? Answer: stories and heroes.

organizational stories stories told by organizational members to make sense of organizational events and changes, and to emphasize culturally consistent assumptions, decisions, and actions

Organizational members tell **stories** to make sense of organizational events and changes, and to emphasize culturally consistent assumptions, decisions, and actions.[56] For example, Mark McCormack, author of *What They Don't Teach You at Harvard Business School*, tells a story that made the rounds at Ford Motor Company.

> *Many years ago the Ford Motor Company went through a period in which the numbers people literally took over the company and were closing plants left and right in order to cut costs. They had already succeeded in shutting down plants in Massachusetts and Texas and seemed to be relishing their newfound power.*
>
> *Robert McNamara, who was president of Ford at the time, called a meeting of his top executives to discuss a recommendation he had received for the closing of yet another plant. Everyone was against it, but the predictions from the accountants were so glum that no one was willing to speak up.*
>
> *Finally, a salty Ford veteran by the name of Charlie Beacham said, "Why don't we close down all the plants and then we'll really start to save money?"*
>
> *Everyone cracked up. The decision was made to postpone any more closings for a while, and the bean counters went back to working for the company rather than running it."*[57]

In fact, Charlie Beacham's humorous comment, and the retelling of it in story form at Ford, was consistent with founder Henry Ford's belief that costs should not be cut for the sake of cutting costs (and making more profit), but to make cars more affordable for customers.[58]

organizational heroes people celebrated for their qualities and achievements within an organization

A second way in which organizational culture is sustained is by creating and celebrating heroes. By definition, **heroes** are organizational people admired for their qualities and achievements within the organization. For example, when Jack Welch became the CEO at General Electric Corporation, he tried to change the then-conservative corporate culture by encouraging managers and employees to be creative and innovative and to take risks. After a $20 million project failed, Welch rewarded the project manager with a bonus and a promotion. The members of the project team were rewarded with bonuses and videocassette recorders. Welch was not celebrating their failure. He was celebrating their willingness to take risks. In other words, he treated the manager and the project team as heroes for other GE employees to emulate.[59]

5.2 *Successful Organizational Cultures*

Preliminary research shows that organizational culture is related to organizational success. As shown in Figure 2.6, cultures based on adaptability, involvement, a clear mission, and consistency can help companies achieve higher sales growth, return on assets, profits, quality, and employee satisfaction.[60]

Adaptability is the ability to notice and respond to changes in the organization's environment. Previously, we discussed the difficulty that CEO Louis Gerstner was having trying to turn around IBM. Frustrated with his inability to change IBM culture, Gerstner eventually decreed that the core IBM beliefs set forth by founder Thomas J. Watson, Sr. (excellence, customer satisfaction, and respect for the individual) were to be replaced with the eight new

Figure 2.6 **Successful Organizational Cultures**

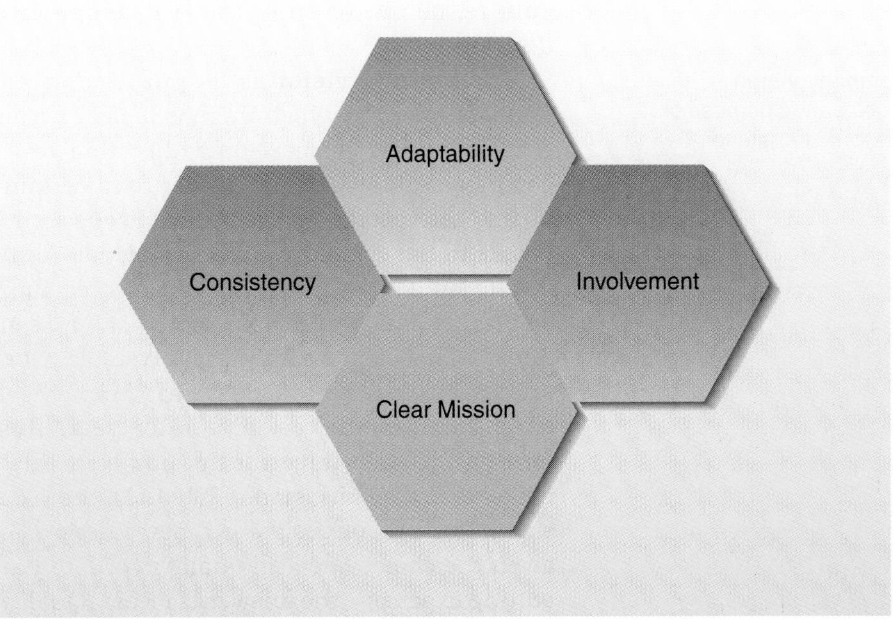

Source: D.R. Denison & A.K. Mishra, "Toward a Theory of Organizational Culture and Effectiveness, *Organization Science* 6 (1995): 204-223.

goals shown in Table 2.2. Instead of responding to his attempts to improve the company, many IBMers were shocked because Thomas J. Watson, Jr., who succeeded his father as IBM's CEO, once stated that IBM's success was dependent on its ability to change everything "except those basic beliefs."[61]

In cultures that promote higher levels of employee involvement in decision making, employees feel a greater sense of ownership and responsibility. For example, at Hewlett-Packard, managers and workers are given a high degree of autonomy, accountability, and responsibility. The company is organized into decentralized, focused teams that "own" their businesses. Each "business," like laser printers, calculators, or personal computers, makes its

Table 2.2 **IBM's New Cultural Principles**

1. The marketplace is the driving force behind everything we do.
2. At our core, we are a technology company with an overriding commitment to quality.
3. Our primary measures of success are customer satisfaction and shareholder value.
4. We operate as an entrepreneurial organization with a minimum of bureaucracy and a never-ending focus on productivity.
5. We never lose sight of our strategic vision.
6. We think and act with a sense of urgency.
7. Outstanding, dedicated people make it all happen, particularly when they work together as a team.
8. We are sensitive to the needs of all employees and to the communities in which we operate.

Source: L. Hays, "Gerstner Is Struggling as He Tries to Change Ingrained IBM Culture," *The Wall Street Journal,* 13 May 1994, A1.

own decisions. So when the video products division was deciding which computer chips to use in its products, it chose not to use H-P's own computer chips because they were too expensive. Instead, they purchased integrated circuits for half the price from one of the H-P computer chip division's competitors. Because involvement and participation are so central to H-P's culture, no one (even in the H-P computer chip division) questioned this decision.[62]

company vision
a company's purpose or reason for existence

A company's **vision** is its purpose or reason for existing. In organizational cultures in which there is a clear organizational vision, the organization's strategic purpose and direction are apparent to everyone in the company. And, when managers are uncertain about their business environments, the vision helps guide the discussions, decisions, and behavior of the people in the company. For example, at Ford Motor Company, the advertising slogan is "Quality is Job 1." However, this isn't just an ad slogan; this is a succinct, but powerful statement of Ford's strategic purpose and direction. Since "Job 1" is auto industry terminology for the first car rolling off an assembly line in a new model year, "Quality is Job 1" sends the message that every car, even the very first of the year, must meet Ford's high standards for quality. Most importantly, however, this slogan helps Ford employees make everyday decisions. Whether they're installing seats, testing new safety features, or designing a new interior, Ford employees know that when given the choice between quality work and acceptable work, or quality and cutting expenses, the answer is clear: "Quality is Job 1."[63]

Finally, in consistent organizational cultures, the company actively defines and teaches organizational values, beliefs, and attitudes. Consistent organizational cultures are also called strong cultures, because the core beliefs are widely shared and strongly held. The culture aboard nuclear submarines is an example of a highly consistent, extremely strong organizational culture. Because they are driven by nuclear power, the threat of a nuclear accident is real (though no accident has ever occurred on a U.S. nuclear submarine). Accordingly, two of the key cultural values are prevention and containment, that is, preventing and containing system failures that could lead to a nuclear spill or accident. Consequently, crew members spend three hours a day learning and practicing jobs outside of their responsibility. In theory, any crew member should know what to do in almost any situation to prevent a small problem from becoming a crisis. Another important cultural value is quiet. Unlike ships that engage in direct battles, submarines hide, trying to avoid detection. Since a sound can easily be heard hundreds of miles away, the dropping of a tool or slamming of a door can easily give away the submarine's position. Thus, every procedure, rule, and practice is designed to be done quietly.[64]

5.3
Changing Organizational Cultures

At the beginning of this section, we learned about the problems that CEO Louis Gerstner was having trying to change IBM's culture. However, managers can and do change organizational cultures. Indeed, thanks to Gerstner's prodding, IBM has returned to solid profitability by becoming more customer-oriented, faster at decision making, and quicker to apply the new technologies invented by its legendary research and development labs.[65] As IBM's experience demonstrates, changing organizational

Been There,

Bernie Marcus Discusses Home Depot's Organizational Culture

Bernie Marcus is one of the co-founders of Home Depot, the fastest growing and largest seller of hardware and home improvement products. Home Depot was founded in 1978.

Q. How do you perpetuate your corporate culture in light of Home Depot's rapid growth?
A. If you look at it in retrospect, 15 years ago we had virtually no people and today we have more than 60,000 employees. It goes back to the basics: hiring the right people, the folks in the store who will create the shopping environment. We want extroverts, people who like other people. We look for people with pleasing personalities and people who are highly motivated and want to learn. You have to be discerning in finding them. Typically, out of 8,000 applicants, we hire 200 people. With those numbers, you can be choosy. We look for quality in all ages and in all colors. We don't look for price; we pay people what they're worth. Just because two people have the same job description doesn't mean they get paid the same wages. An electrician with 25 years experience is going to get paid more than someone with one year of experience. One advantage of having someone with that much experience is that they train the others. So mixing the right combination of people has been one of our strengths.

"And we've always stuck by the idea that work should be fun."

Q. I've heard some people say that while Home Depot has a very progressive public image, in reality its corporate structure is quite bureaucratic. How accurate is that observation?
A. A bureaucracy is stifling. It means no growth, no future. However, I think from a business standpoint you can be as entrepreneurial as you want, but you have to run a business based on fundamentals. Arthur Blank [co-founder] and I are basically entrepreneurial, but we understand that we need to have strong fiscal controls. Having said that, we are constantly aware of the fact that if we stifle the entrepreneurial spirit, we will hurt the growth of the company, so in many cases we cut right through to the hands-on approach. We regularly visit the stores and talk with the employees directly. There are no memos being filtered up or down. It's our way of finding out what's really happening. Having a successful business isn't about continuing what you do right; it's about finding out what you do wrong and correcting those things. Even our board members are obligated to visit seven stores a quarter. They go into our stores as shoppers and then introduce themselves in the break rooms and talk with employees about anything they saw that was wrong. I don't think there's another company in the world that has board members who do that.

Q. Many people use the word "irreverent" to describe Home Depot's corporate culture. Do you agree?
A. I would agree it's irreverent compared to the norm. Everyone calls me and Arthur by our first names. In a company our size that's unheard of. Today I'm not wearing a shirt and tie. In most companies that would be irreverent. When I visit a store, I never wear a tie. So compared to the norm, yes, we probably could be called irreverent. We are nowhere near the norm.

Q. Has Home Depot's culture changed over the years?
A. The basic principles of the company have not changed. There have been embellishments to those principles as we've expanded. It's important to remember that we never envisioned what Home Depot has become. To be a $12 billion business in 15 years is one of the miracles of retailing. But as we've grown we've stuck to our basics: quality merchandise, tremendous service, tremendous value, and the most dedicated, experienced salespeople in America. Those things have not changed. And we've always stuck by the idea that work should be fun. To go to work everyday and not enjoy it would be total drudgery. So the atmosphere that we try to develop is one in which people can enjoy themselves. And I think that comes through on the floor of the store. You can't have people that are deadly serious; you aren't going to smile if you are having a miserable time. When I walk around, if I see sour faces, if someone can't take a joke, I know we have a leadership problem. So part of our philosophy is quite simply: Have fun.

Q. What communication techniques do you use to spread your corporate culture throughout the company?
A. We use as much direct communication as possible. We use satellite programs, which is the best thing we have now. We do have question and answer capabilities, but it's through the phone lines. Interactive capabilities are coming. We tell our people as much as possible. If there are questions, rumors, concerns or insecurities, we want to answer them right away. Sometimes we may use voice mail to do that. We say, "We've heard . . . Let me tell you exactly what is happening." I would say we have a well-informed group of folks that

know what we are doing. If we veer from what is expected, we communicate what we are doing as soon as possible.

Q. What's the biggest mistake you see companies make when it comes to corporate culture?
A. They become distant. They allow themselves to get caught in the corporate ivory tower. They lose a feel for what is happening out in the actual workings of the company. They become engrossed in who they are and the position they have achieved. It's the classic story of the company chairman who never goes on the factory floor. And this elitist mind set can happen at many levels. You can't enforce a corporate culture if you are so out of touch that you don't even know if it's effective or if it's changed.

Q. You're on the verge of significant international expansion. How will you spread your corporate culture to foreign operations?
A. I'm not sure it can be done. That's why when it comes to Mexico, we are not going to be betting the whole enchilada. We're not sure. Different people. Different culture. Different way of life. We're not sure it can happen. But we have moved into markets in the U.S. where we weren't sure the Home Depot culture would work and it did. People said it would never work in the northeast. They said people are tougher, too cynical. But we found people who are great, wonderful, excellent examples of the Home Depot kind of person.

Q. How do new employees pick up Home Depot's corporate culture?
A. You can't change someone's philosophy by putting out memos or showing them a video. What we do when we open a new store is make sure 15 to 30 percent of the staff is made up of seasoned employees. If it's a new store in an established market, our customers actually help spread the culture to new employees. We also take new hires and train them in our existing stores from three to nine months.

Source: J. Donner, "Bernard Marcus Talks about Corporate Culture," *Georgia Trend*, July 1994, 14-16. This interview was edited for inclusion in this textbook.

Done That

behavioral addition
the process of having managers and employees perform new behaviors that are central to and symbolic of the new organizational culture that a company wants to create

behavioral substitution
the process of having managers and employees perform new behaviors central to the "new" organizational culture in place of behaviors that were central to the "old" organizational culture

visible artifacts
visible signs of an organization's culture, such as the office design and layout, company dress codes, and company benefits and perks like stock options, personal parking spaces, or the private company dining room

culture just takes patience, vigilance, and a focus on changing the parts of an organizational culture that managers can control: behavior and symbolic artifacts.

One way of changing a corporate culture is to use behavioral addition or behavioral substitution to establish new patterns of behavior among managers and employees.[66] **Behavioral addition** is the process of having managers and employees perform a new behavior, while **behavioral substitution** is having managers and employees perform a new behavior in place of another behavior. The key in both instances is to choose behaviors that are central to and symbolic of the "old" culture you're changing and the "new" culture that you want to create. For example, when Jack Messman became CEO of Union Pacific Resources (an oil company), his most important goal was to transform UPR's culture. His first step was to change the most important behavior in the company: the approval of where and when to drill for oil wells. He says, "When I came here my predecessor approved every [oil] well. I haven't approved a well since I came here. The people who do the work ought to make the decisions."[67]

The second way in which managers can begin to change corporate culture is to change **visible artifacts** of their old culture, such as the office design and layout, company dress codes, and who benefits (or doesn't) from company benefits and perks like stock options, personal parking spaces, or the private company dining room. Besides changing who is responsible for oil drilling decisions at UPR, Jack Messman also implemented a "smart casual" dress code for every day of the week. And on Fridays, even blue jeans are acceptable, as long as employees are not scheduled to visit with customers. Messman is even planning to move the company headquarters, because the current headquarters, with its wood-paneled walls and plush carpeting, is no longer consistent with the new, informal culture.

Another company making sizable changes in visible corporate artifacts is Yellow Freight, a trucking company. The courtyard fountains, once a prominent sign of company success, are now viewed as a needless expense and have been turned off. Expensive paintings, once displayed in the headquarters lobby, have been replaced by pictures of trucks and freight terminals. The executive dining room, once reserved for senior managers, has been converted to a conference room that anyone can use for special occasions.[68]

Corporate cultures are very difficult to change. Consequently, there is no guarantee that behavioral substitution, behavioral addition, or changing visible cultural artifacts will change a company's organizational culture. However, these methods are some of the best tools that managers have for changing culture, because they send the clear message to managers and employees that "the accepted way of doing things" has changed.

Review 5
Organizational Cultures: Creation, Success, and Change

Organizational culture is the set of key values, beliefs, and attitudes shared by organizational members. Organizational cultures are often created by company founders, and then sustained through the telling of organizational stories and the celebration of organizational heroes. Adaptable cultures that promote employee involvement, that make clear the organization's strategic purpose and direction, and that actively define and teach organizational values and beliefs can help companies achieve higher sales growth, return on assets, profits, quality, and employee satisfaction. Behavioral substitution, behavioral addition, and changing visible artifacts are ways in which managers can begin to change their organizational cultures.

What**Really**Happened?

Many people believe that managers have total control over their organizations. If management wants something done, it happens. Yet, as you learned in the case of All-World Travel at the beginning of the chapter, managers cannot control all external factors. However, a lack of control isn't necessarily a bad thing. Companies can succeed by scanning their business environments for events and trends, interpreting what those changes mean, and then acting to adapt to those changes. Read the following answers to the opening case to find out how travel agencies are trying to make sense of the changes in their external environments:

The frustrating part is that after 12 years of success and growth, it's hard to understand why these things are happening to your business. For example, you'd like to know why the changes all seem to occur at once rather than gradually.

According to punctuated equilibrium theory, companies experience periods of stability followed by short periods of dynamic, fundamental change, followed by a return to periods of stability. Presently, travel agencies and the entire travel reservation business are in a period of dynamic fundamental change in which, it seems, significant changes occur on a weekly basis. For example, American Airlines' Sabre computer reservations systems now sell 1.6 million tickets a year directly to travelers without the help of a single travel agent. Another significant change is the use of e-mail to stay in contact with customers. Each Wednesday, American Airlines sends e-mail to the 250,000 customers of American's NetSaavers club (it's free), informing them of heavily discounted fares for flights leaving that Friday and Saturday of the same week. NetSaavers helps customers save a bundle, but it also helps American contact over a quarter million customers a week (with little effort and almost no cost), so that it can fill seats that would probably have gone empty. These changes, along with the hundreds of new travel-related Web sites that have been created in the last few years, are bringing dynamic, fundamental change to the way travel agents run their businesses.

Also, once external forces began to change things, it would have helped to be able to categorize the changes affecting your business.

Organizations are influenced by two kinds of external environments: the general environment, which consists of economic, technological, sociocultural, and political/legal events and trends, and the specific environment, which consists of customers, competitors, suppliers, industry regulators, and advocacy groups. Besides the technological changes described above, most of the changes affecting travel agents are occurring in the supplier, competitor, and customer components of their specific environment. These changes have had a direct and immediate impact on their businesses.

For example, suppliers (the airlines) and buyers (travel agencies) are very dependent on each other. Sometimes, that dependence leads to opportunistic behavior in which one benefits at the expense of the other. When the airlines capped ticket agent commissions at $25 for one-way travel and $50 for round-trip travel, they engaged in opportunistic behavior, in which they benefited at the expense of travel agencies. Indeed, after the commission caps were put in place, there was a 25 percent increase in the number of travel agencies that went out of business compared to the previous year and a 66 percent increase compared to two years earlier.

In terms of competition, the travel agency market is no longer a local market, but a national or international market. The entrance of Wal-Mart and Internet-based travel services means that the average travel agency has more serious competition than it had before.

As these changes reverberate through the travel industry, customers want lower costs. Corporate customers, in particular, want to use the Internet to reduce costs and increase compliance with corporate travel policies. For example, when Charles Schwab, an investment firm, linked its employees to an intranet travel service (a private Internet connection), the average cost to book a flight dropped from $36 to $8. The same intranet travel service also helped the company save money by only offering employees travel options that were consistent with company travel policies (e.g., approved carriers, no first-class tickets, corporate discounts, etc.).

But even better than that, you'd like to know how to identify, make sense of, and react to the external threats and opportunities in your industry.

Managers use a three-step process to make sense of external environments. First, they scan their environments based on their organizational strategies, their need for up-to-date information, or their need to reduce uncertainty. Second, when they identify environmental events as threats, they take steps to protect their companies from harm. And third, when they identify environmental events as opportunities, they formulate strategies to improve company performance.

In general, travel agency managers and owners have perceived the changes in their external environments as threats and have responded accordingly. For example, according to *Travel Weekly* magazine, nearly two thirds of travel agencies have cut costs since the airlines capped ticket commissions. However, agencies are now more likely to sell cruises, car rentals, and international flights on which they can make higher commissions. Furthermore, some travel agencies are viewing these changes as an opportunity to improve company performance. By buying large blocks of tickets from the airlines (at a discounted price), and then reselling them at regular prices, some travel agencies have been able to double the revenues they would have received under the new commission system. John Werner, who owns The Total Traveler in Hoffman Estates, Illinois, said, "After the initial shock wore off, I became even more positive about the business. The caps were enough to push the agency community to make changes that would have had to be made anyway."

Finally, you worry that these external changes will affect the positive atmosphere of your business. It's a fun place to work. And with just 20 employees, it feels like a close-knit family. Hopefully, that won't change, too.

The worry here is that the changes in a company's external environment will negatively affect its internal environment, the key part of which is an organization's culture. However, adaptable cultures that promote employee involvement, that make clear the organization's strategic purpose and direction, and that actively define and teach organizational values and beliefs can help companies adjust and adapt to significant changes in their external business environments.

Sources: S. Bittle, "Business Travel Buzzword: Intranet," *Travel Weekly*, 5 August 1996, 1-3. J. Dorsey, "Year of Caps: Survival of the Fittest," *Travel Weekly*, 8 February 1996, 1-2. P. Holley, "Agent of Change: Technology Transforms Travel Industry," *The Business Journal-Milwaukee*, 8 June 1996, 1-2. G. Marc, "Travel Planning in Cyberspace," *Fortune*, 9 September 1996, 187-188. M.A. Mitchell, "Rival Agents Shrug off In-Store Competition from Wal-Marts," *Travel Weekly*, 18 January 1996, 1-2. K. O'Meara, "Shifting Sands: Agents Adopt a Variety of Strategies to Cope with Airline Commission Caps," *Travel Weekly*, 29 August 1996, S84-88.

Key Terms

advocacy groups p. 57

behavioral addition p. 70

behavioral substitution p. 70

business confidence indices p. 48

buyer dependence p. 56

cognitive maps p. 62

company vision p. 68

competitive analysis p. 54

competitors p. 54

complex environment p. 44

dynamic environment p. 43

environmental change p. 43

environmental complexity p. 44

environmental munificence p. 45

environmental scanning p. 60

external environments p. 42

general environment p. 47

industry regulation p. 57

internal environment p. 63

media advocacy p. 58

opportunistic behavior p. 56

organizational culture p. 64

organizational heroes p. 66

organizational stories p. 66

product boycott p. 59

public communications p. 58

punctuated equilibrium theory p. 43
relationship behavior p. 56
simple environment p. 44
specific environment p. 48
stable environment p. 43
supplier dependence p. 56
suppliers p. 55
technology p. 50
uncertainty p. 46
visible artifacts p. 70

What Would You Do-II?

Anytown, USA

"You heard what?" "You heard me," said your assistant manager, "Home Depot is going to put up a store on the corner of Perkins and McElroy." "Nooooo." "Yes, they are." "We're toast." "No, even worse, we're dog meat."

Over the last decade, conversations like this have been repeated in hardware stores throughout the U.S. During that time, Home Depot, the orange-colored hardware superstore, grew from roughly 20 stores to nearly 300 stores. For do-it-yourselfers, a trip to Home Depot is a religious experience (Insert Tim-the-Toolman Taylor grunt here: "ahhhh-uhhhhh-ahhhh."). Unlike traditional, small-town hardware stores, Home Depots average more than 100,000 square feet of floor space. Its stores are stuffed from floor to ceiling (three stories high) with more than 50,000 items. Whether you're putting in a lawn sprinkler system, installing oak flooring in a family room, attaching a fluorescent street lamp to your garage to light your driveway, or getting flowers for your garden, you can find it at incredibly low prices at Home Depot.

To no one's surprise, competitors hate Home Depot almost as much as its customers love it. For example, only a year after building stores in the Detroit area, the Home Depot parking lots were twice as full as those of Hechinger Hardware, once a dominant player in the industry. In fact, Hechinger closed its stores in the Greensboro/Winston-Salem, North Carolina area after only two years of competition from Home Depot. Even Wal-Mart, the world's largest and most efficient retailer, expects to have below-average hardware, yard, and garden sales when there's a Home Depot in the neighborhood.

You own the "Hammer and Nail," a small hardware business, and compete with only four other hardware stores in your town. However, Home Depot is coming to town. How will you compete? Like most independent hardware stores, your store is only about 20,000 square feet compared to Home Depot's 100,000 square feet. With so little space, you can't stock as many different items. Furthermore, you won't be able to out-advertise Home Depot. You can only afford one full-page newspaper ad per month, whereas Home Depot usually runs several full-page newspaper ads per week.

Well, you're not sure how you'll do it. However, you've got a year to think, plan, and prepare. Your assistant, the one who brought you the bad news, said something about needing to look at how this changes your "specific business environment," whatever that is. Must be that management class she's enrolled in this semester.

If you were the owner of the Hammer and Nail, what would you do? (Hint: Use the five components of the specific environment to assess the business environment for small hardware stores.)

Sources: "Superstore Chain Home Depot Will Test a Novel Idea: Think Small," *Dow Jones NewsWires*, 13 May 1998. T. Ehrenfeld, "The Demise of Mom and Pop?" *Inc.*, 1 January 1995, 46. C. Gentry, "Spurned by Town Leaders, Home Depot Charms Public," *The Wall Street Journal Interactive Edition*, 13 May 1998. N. Gillespie, "One-Shop Stopping," *Reason*, 1 May 1995, 37. G. Johnson, "Making Hardware Easy: Male Traditions Aside, Big Chains and Local Stores are Retooling Their Operations to Attract Female Do-It-Yourselfers," *Los Angeles Times*, 15 October 1995, 1. R. La Franco, "Comeuppance?" *Forbes*, 4 December 1995, 74-76. C. Roush, "Shopper Survey Shows Strengths of Home Depot; But Service Seen as a Weak Point," *The Atlanta Journal and Constitution*, 9 August 1995, E/01.

Critical-Thinking Video Case

Health Care Environment: Central Michigan Community Hospital

Central Michigan Community Hospital is a nonprofit, regional health care center. It includes a full-service, 151-bed hospital, a medical staff of over 120 doctors, a walk-in urgent care center, wellness services, occupational medicine, home health care, and numerous other services. The hospital is riding a tidal wave of change in the health care environment. It is striving to meet the demands of patients, employers, insurance companies, and the state and federal governments to provide quality care at a competitive price.

In this video, we learn about the significant changes in Central Michigan Community Hospital's external environment and how it is responding to those changes. As you watch the video, consider the following critical-thinking questions.

Critical-Thinking Questions

1. Who are Central Michigan Community Hospital's customers?
2. How do technology, competition, and physicians influence Central Michigan Community Hospital?

Management Decisions

Can You Envision the Future?

The drive began with 1 minute and 45 seconds left in the game and the ball on your 20 yard line. Fifty-two yards later, the ball sits on your opponent's 28 yard line, and the New Orleans SuperDome clock shows just three seconds remaining in the game. Your opponent calls a time-out as you run onto the artificial turf, hoping that the two-minute wait will fry your nerves and shatter your confidence. There's plenty to be nervous about. If you make the 45-yard field goal, your team wins and you become an instant hero. Yet if you miss, they'll be questioning your parentage and your ability on the call-in sports-radio shows all week long.

The two minutes are up. Both teams take their formations: nine men on the line of scrimmage for your team; eleven on the line for the defense. The center squats, places both hands on the ball, and looks back between his legs to receive the snap count from your holder. "37, 48, hut, hut, HUT!" In one smooth motion perfected by hundreds of hours of practice, the ball flies 7 3/4 yards from the center to your holder, an all-pro tight end with the best pair of hands in football. He catches the ball, places it in an upright position, one end on the ground, the other topped by the index finger on his left hand. Less than a second has expired. Two seconds show on the clock as he rotates the ball 90 degrees with his right hand, turning the laces away from you toward the goal posts. You step, plant your front foot, lock your left knee, and whip your kicking leg soccer-style through the ball that clears the outstretched arms of diving defenders by inches. One second left. The crowd hushes as the ball climbs into the air. Just as the ball begins its descent, the gun fires, seemingly knocking the ball from its apex. No time left on the clock. The referees, positioned directly under the left and right ends of the goal post, wait. When the ball clears the uprights, the refs glance at each other to confirm the call before raising both arms into the air. It's good!

This football scenario you just read is real enough to happen. Sometimes it does happen. In reality, this football scenario is a visualization that field goal kickers use to mentally prepare themselves for game conditions. Each day, as part of their training, pro kickers turn out the lights, take the phone off the hook, and close their eyes to envision a scenario where they come into a game and kick the winning field goal. All kinds of athletes, Olympic divers, golfers, and baseball pitchers, also use visualization because it builds confidence.

To date, visualization has been used extensively with athletes and to help people deal with anxieties, like the fear of flying. However, cognitive psychologists have also determined that visualization helps people think in concrete terms, identify factors that they might have otherwise ignored, and be much more creative and innovative in their thinking. Consequently, studies have shown that managers can use visualization to identify environmental trends and to think of creative ways to deal with those changes.

To try visualization, turn off the radio and the TV. Take the phone off the hook. Read the following scenario to yourself. Turn off the lights. Set your alarm clock to go off in five minutes. (Even better, have a friend read it to you as you listen with your eyes closed.) Close your eyes and imagine this scenario for five minutes. When your alarm goes off, turn on the lights and immediately write down the first seven things you can remember.

> *It's the Thursday of the last week of December, five years from today. On Thursdays, you work at home, connecting to the bank's computer via your local Internet provider. With a cup of coffee in hand, the first thing you do is check the* Wall Street Journal. *Instead of walking out to the driveway, you reach for the computer mouse to double-click on the WSJ icon in the upper right-hand corner of your computer screen. Today's headline reads, "The Business Year in Review." As you read the article, you realize that you'd forgotten how much things had changed in banking over the last year. But the changes that have occurred to the banking industry since you took your job with Central Bank right out of college have been even more astounding. Changes in technology have changed the way banks interact with customers and have changed what customers want from banks. Banking itself has changed. It used to be that you just competed with other banks, but that's not so now. As business has become more global, banking regulations have changed, too. You consider yourself lucky. Rather than hiding its head in the sand, your bank embraced the changes, identifying and responding to them as quickly as possible. Scrolling down to the second page of the article, you find a secondary article called "The Top Ten Changes in Banking in the Last 5 Years." Laughing to yourself, you think, "Things would have been simpler if we'd seen these changes coming.*

For the next five minutes, envision how banking will have changed five years from now. Where and how will you get your money, apply for a loan, or check your monthly statement? How will technology affect banking? How will customers be different? Who will banks compete with? How will bank laws and regulations have changed?

When your alarm goes off, immediately write down the first seven changes that you envision for the banking industry five years from now.

Sources: W.P. Anthony, R.H. Bennett, III, E.N. Maddox, & W.J. Wheatley, "Picturing the Future: Using Mental Imagery to Enrich Strategic Environmental Assessment," *Academy of Management Executive* 7 (1993): 43-56. D. Bank, "Uneasy Banks Must Make a Deposit on On-Line Future — If Established Firms Don't Succeed Electronically, Software Giants May Leap In," *The Wall Street Journal*, 3 December 1997, B10. D. Foust, "Special Report: Annual Guide to Computers: Computer Banking: from In Line to Online: The Best Ways to Do Your Banking from Your Keyboard," *Business Week*, 6 November 1995,146. G. Hamel & C.K. Prahalad, "Seeing the Future First," *Fortune*, 5 September 1994, 64-70. A. Serwer, "The Competition Heats Up in Online Banking," *Fortune*, 26 June 1995, 18-19.

Management Decisions

Cultural Change: Evolution or Revolution?

Tandem Computer makes "fault tolerant" computers guaranteed to keep working during power outages, natural disasters, and catastrophic computer glitches that would easily shut down standard computers. Since 1974, Tandem has sold its computers at high prices and high profit margins to stock exchanges, phone companies, banks, airlines, and other companies whose businesses are dependent on uninterrupted computer service. Tandem computers are used in 75 percent of all ATM transactions, 66 percent of all credit card transactions, and 70 percent of electronic interchange networks (data sharing between companies).

Jimmy Treybig, Tandem's CEO, founded the company with $1 million in venture capital money from Thomas Perkins, who chairs Tandem's Board of Directors. That $1 million investment grew into a company with $2.1 billion in annual revenues. During its 20-year run of success, Treybig developed a patriarchal culture at Tandem. Once a week, at every Tandem facility, there was a "beer bust." Attendance wasn't mandatory, but most peopled wanted to attend. The point: not to promote drinking, but to get to know each other better and encourage informal communication, which is often lacking in corporate environments. Treybig's stated management philosophy was that:

> *(1) all people are good;*
> *(2) workers, management and company are all the same thing;*
> *(3) every single person in the company must understand the essence of the business;*
> *(4) every employee must benefit from the company's success;*
> *(5) you must create an environment where all the above can happen.*
>
> (Ward, 1995)

One symbol of this philosophy was that Tandem's sales representatives had one of the most generous compensation plans in the industry, earning $100,000 to $400,000 a year. In all, CEO Treybig was well liked and ran the company like an extended family.

Unfortunately, the party ended a few years ago. Customers began refusing to pay premium prices for Tandem's computers, especially since they used Tandem's proprietary software, Guardian, which was not compatible with other kinds of computers. In just three years, profits, which had been running between $100 million and $200 million annually, dropped to a loss of more than $500 million. Customers wanted Tandem to produce computers that run UNIX, an "open" operating system that runs on different kinds of computers, unlike Guardian, which runs only on Tandem computers.

The company's struggles have not only affected profits, but have also begun to affect Tandem's organizational culture. Said CEO Treybig, "Nothing is as fun as it used to be. My wife says I never use the word 'fun' anymore. In the 1980s you could just do a good job and make money. But nowadays, you have to be the best. I mean, every day you have to really worry about being successful. The bar for success is higher. It takes fun out of it" (Ward, 1995).

1. At critical times like this, CEOs have two basic choices: evolutionary change or revolutionary change. Explain which would be the best choice for returning Tandem to profitability? Why?
2. Either approach will affect Tandem's family-like culture. Depending on which you chose, explain three ways in which a company like Tandem could incrementally change its culture or change its culture in a revolutionary way.

Sources: R. Karpinski, "Tandem Slates Web Server Product Line," *Interactive Age*, 10 April 1995, 24. T.J. Peters & N.K. Austin, *A Passion for Excellence* (New York: Random House, 1985). E. Ramstad & L. Gomes, "Compaq to Acquire Tandem Computers," *The Wall Street Journal*, 24 June 1997, A3. J.E. Rigdon, "Cruel World: Cannibalism Is a Virtue in Computer Business, Tandem's CEO Learns," *The Wall Street Journal*, 24 August 1994, A1. J. Ward, "The Thrill Is Gone," *Financial World*, 11 April 1995, 32. A.L. Wilkins & N.J. Bristow, "For Successful Organization Culture, Honor Your Past," *Academy of Management Executive* 1 (1987): 221-229.

Develop Your Management Potential

Dealing with the Press

In this age of 24-hour cable news channels, tabloid news shows, and aggressive local and national news reporters intent on exposing corporate wrongdoing, one of the most important skills for a manager to learn is how to deal effectively with the press. Test your ability to deal effectively with the press by putting yourself in the following situations. To make the situation more realistic, read each scenario and then give yourself two minutes to write a response to each question.

Fatty Restaurant Food Contributes to Heart Attacks

Today, in the nation's capital, a public-interest group held a press conference to release the results of a study that found that the food sold in most Chinese restaurants is high in fat. The group claims that the most popular Chinese dishes, like orange chicken, pork fried rice, and Hunan beef, contain nearly as much fat as the food you get from fast-food chains like McDonald's, Wendy's, and Burger King. (Much of it is fried or is covered with heavy sauces.) Furthermore, the group says that customers who hope to keep their cholesterol and blood pressure low by eating Chinese food are just fooling themselves.

A TV reporter from Channel 5 called your Szechuan-style Chinese restaurant, "Szechuan," to get your response to this study. When she and the camera crew arrived, she asked you the following questions. (To simulate these conditions, give yourself only two minutes to write a response to each question.)

1. "A new study released today claims that food sold in Chinese restaurants is on average nearly as fattening as that sold at fast-food restaurants. How healthy is the food that you serve at Szechuan's?"
2. "Get the camera in close here (camera closes in to get the shot) because I want the audience at home to see that you don't provide any information on your menu about calories, calories from fat, or cholesterol. Without this information (camera pulls back to get a picture of you and the reporter), how can your customers know that the food that you serve is healthy for them?"
3. "These new studies were based on lunches and dinners sampled from Chinese restaurants across the nation. A local company, Huntington Labs, has agreed to test foods from local restaurants, so that we can provide accurate information to our viewers. Would you agree to let us sample the main dishes in your restaurant to test the level of calories, calories from fat, and cholesterol? Furthermore, can we take the cameras into your restaurant, so that we can get your customers' reactions to these studies?"

Hotel Customer Dies in Strange Accident

"Beep." You look at your watch. It's 4 A.M. This has been the longest night of your life. You've worked for the Hamada Jackson hotel for about a year as the late-night manager. The pay is OK, but the best part is that it's safe, really quiet, and you can study. Your college grades have gotten much better since you started, and it looks like you'll be able to make it into graduate school. But you didn't get any studying done tonight. Channel 8's news crew just left. They were monitoring the police scanner around 1:15 A.M., right after you called 911 in a panic. One of your responsibilities is to take a quick walk through the hallways a couple of times a night just to make sure everything is OK. When you made your 1 A.M. check, everything was quiet until you hit the last hallway on the west side of the hotel. As you came around the corner, you almost stepped on her. Somehow, in a freak accident, a young woman who, according to your records, had checked into the hotel at about 10:30, an hour before you came on duty, was dead on the floor. She was still soaking wet from the rain that had started that afternoon. You learned later that she had been electrocuted when she put her card-key in the lock of her metal door.

Much to your dismay, the Channel 8 news crew arrived 10 minutes after the cops and the emergency medical team. After videotaping the scene and the crews loading the body into the ambulance, they turned their attention, lights, and camera on you. (To simulate these conditions, give yourself only two minutes to write a response to each question.)

1. "Can you tell us what happened? The emergency medical team told us that the burns on her hands and the smell of smoke led them to believe that she was electrocuted in your hotel hallway. Can you tell us what happened and how someone could be electrocuted in this way?"
2. "What was the victim's name? How old was she? Where is she from? Do you know what she was doing while staying at the hotel?"
3. "The emergency medical team estimated the time of death to be between 10:30 and 11:00

P.M., which means that the body has been in the hallway for several hours. Does your hotel have a security force? Why wasn't somebody making periodic checks of the premises to make sure everything was safe? Also, does anybody on the staff have any medical training to deal with emergencies like choking, heart attacks, or things like this?"

Sources: P. Flanagan, "Ten Public Relations Pitfalls," *Management Review*, October 1995, 45-48. D. Gellene, "Sears Drops Car Repair Incentives: The Company Says 'Mistakes Have Been Made' in Its Aggressive Commission Program," *Los Angeles Times*, 23 June 1992, 1. P. Hertneky, "Mastering the Media: Press Handling for Restaurant Managers" *Restaurant Hospitality*, June 1995, 59-69. B. Horowitz, "Intel Needs Damage Control," *USA Today*, 13 December 1994. L. Koss-Feder, "Crisis Brings Media Scrutiny," *Hotel & Motel Management*, 14 August 1995, 5. "How to Get Your CEO in Print or in Front of TV Cameras in the Right Light," *PR News*, 21 April 1997.

Chapter Three

Chapter 3 Outline

Ethics and Social Responsibility

What Would **You** Do?

Walt Disney Headquarters, Orlando, Florida. As you turn right out of your driveway, heading toward the Orlando freeway, you begin to think about today's big meeting. Specifically, you wonder if your company is going to decide to extend full benefits (health insurance, life insurance, retirement accounts, etc.) to "domestic partners." Disney, like most companies, makes full benefits available to employees' spouses and families. However, for the last three years, company management has carefully considered the costs and benefits of offering full benefits to the same-sex partners of gay and lesbian employees. Other entertainment companies such as MCA/Universal, Paramount Pictures, Sony, and Warner Brothers already have domestic-partner policies in place. Disney is one of the last major entertainment corporations to not have such a policy. In the last few years, middle-level managers at Disney have been complaining that not having such a policy makes it difficult to attract and retain talented workers who can get better benefits elsewhere. Because of the potential controversy associated with domestic-partner benefits, Disney management has taken this decision very seriously. For example, when a division of Apple Computer, located in Williamson County, Texas, announced that it was implementing domestic-partner benefits, county officials decided *not* to grant Apple a previously promised tax break. The county later changed its mind. Likewise, when Lotus Software decided to offer domestic-partner benefits, customers returned computer disks with angry letters. And when clothing company Levi Strauss offered domestic-partner benefits, it was met by the threat of boycotts from numerous groups. However, Disney is also aware of arguments that offering full benefits to heterosexual workers and their spouses and families, while at the same time not offering the same benefits to homosexual workers and their partners and families, is viewed by some as a form of workplace discrimination. After three years of deliberation, the meeting to make the final decision is in 90 minutes

You grab a cup of coffee, shut your door, and start typing these questions on your laptop computer. What is the ethical thing to do in this situation? If Disney offers benefits to domestic partners, is it morally obligated to offer the same benefits to the live-in partners of unmarried, heterosexual employees? Who is interested in or affected by this decision, and how do we decide whose interests take precedence? Is it more socially responsible to offer benefits to domestic partners, or not to offer those benefits? No matter what we decide, this is an extremely difficult decision. **If you were making this decision for the Disney Corporation, what would you do?**

Sources: "Baptists Unresponsive to Disney Boycott," *The Providence Journal-Bulletin*, 2 May 1998. V. Griffith, "Welcome to Your Friendlier Company," *Financial Times*, 9 March 1998. D.J. Jefferson, "Family Matters: Gay Employees Win Benefits for Partners at More Corporations," *The Wall Street Journal*, 18 March 1994, A1. J. Mason, "Domestic-Partner Benefits," *Management Review*, 1 November 1995, 53-55. P. Perry, "Benefits for Nontraditional Partners," *Folio: The Magazine for Magazine Management*, 1 November 1995, 62-63. B. Svetkey, "Disney Catches Hell: Gay and Subliminal Messages at Mickey & Co. Bring on the Religious Right's Wrath," *Entertainment Weekly*, 15 December 1995, 42. C. Woodyard & D. Lee, "Disney to Give Benefits to Partners of Gay Workers," *Los Angeles Times*, 7 October 1995, p. 1.

Disney's domestic-partner dilemma is an example of the tough decisions that managers face about ethics and social responsibility. Unfortunately, one of the "real world" aspects of these decisions is that no matter what you decide, someone or some group will be unhappy with the decision. Another characteristic is that managers don't have the luxury of choosing theoretically optimal, win-win solutions that are obviously correct to everyone involved. In practice, solutions to ethics and social responsibility problems aren't optimal. Often, they are "make-do" or "do the least harm" kinds of solutions. Clear rights and wrongs rarely reveal themselves to managers charged with "doing the right thing." The business world is much messier than that.

We begin this chapter by examining ethical behavior in the workplace, and how the 1991 U.S. Sentencing Guidelines now make ethical behavior much more important for businesses. Second, we examine the influences on ethical decision making, and then review practical steps that managers can take to improve ethical decision making. We finish by reviewing to whom organizations are socially responsible, what organizations are socially responsible for, how they can respond to societal expectations for social responsibility, and whether social responsibility hurts or helps an organization's economic performance.

What Is Ethical and Unethical Workplace Behavior?

ethics
the set of moral principles or values that defines right and wrong for a person or group

Ethics is the set of moral principles or values that defines right and wrong for a person or group. Unfortunately, several studies have produced distressing results about the state of ethics in today's business world. First, in a series of in-depth interviews, 30 graduates of Harvard's MBA program indicated they had been pressured by their bosses to do "sleazy, unethical, or sometimes illegal" things.[1] They were asked to fake research results, to "recalculate" the numbers until they produced the "desired results," to ignore product safety defects, or to violate company policies. Yet, despite these pressures, these MBAs felt that most people in their companies were ethical. Second, in a study of 1,324 randomly selected workers, managers, and executives across multiple industries, 48 percent of respondents admitted to committing an unethical or illegal act in the past year! These acts included cheating on an expense account, discriminating against co-workers, forging signatures, paying or accepting kickbacks, and "looking the other way" when environmental laws were broken.[2] However, 60 percent said that business ethics could be improved through better communication and strong commitment from managers.

After reading the next three sections, you should be able to:

1. discuss how the **nature of a management job** creates the possibility for ethical abuses.
2. identify common kinds of **workplace deviance.**
3. describe the 1991 **U.S. Sentencing Commission Guidelines** and how its recommendations now make ethical behavior much more important for businesses.

Personal Productivity Tip

Build Up Your "Forget You Fund"

Mike Royko, a columnist for the *Chicago Tribune*, boiled business ethics down to two key ingredients. The first is your conscience. Royko says that if your parents didn't do their job, you won't have one. Ingredient number two is to get a "Forget You Fund." Basically, an FUF is three- to six-months' worth of paychecks in the bank. When your boss asks you do something that you cannot in good conscience do, quit! Royko said that an FUF takes the control that your boss and the company have over you and replaces it with your freedom to do what you think is right.

1 Ethics and the Nature of Management Jobs

ethical behavior
behavior that conforms to a society's accepted principles of right and wrong

Ethical behavior follows accepted principles of right and wrong. For example, Wal-Mart has very strict guidelines concerning its employees' ethical behavior. Any employee who accepts anything of value (dinner, free tickets to a sports event, a round of golf, etc.) from a company that Wal-Mart does business with will immediately be dismissed. Wal-Mart employees aren't even permitted to allow representatives from other companies to buy them a cup of coffee. Furthermore, to encourage employees to behave ethically, all of Wal-Mart's suppliers and vendors are required to do business with Wal-Mart employees in "glass rooms," visible to anyone who walks through the lobby at company headquarters. Finally, the walls in each of these glass rooms are covered with posters that say, "Any item received [from a supplier or vendor] will be returned to sender at their expense."[3]

Unethical management behavior occurs when managers personally violate accepted principles of right and wrong. The authority and power inherent in some management positions can tempt managers to engage in unethical practices. Since managers often control company resources, there is a risk that some managers will cross over the line from legitimate use of company resources to personal use of those resources. For example, treating a client to dinner is a common and legitimate business practice in many companies. But what about treating a client to a ski trip? Taking the company jet to attend a business meeting in San Diego is legitimate. But how about using the jet to come home to Chicago by way of Honolulu? Human resources can be misused as well. For example, using employees to do personal chores, like picking up the manager's dry cleaning, is unethical behavior.

Handling information is another area in which managers must be careful to behave ethically. Information is a key part of management work. Managers collect it, analyze it, act on it, and disseminate it. However, they are also expected to deal in truthful information and, when necessary, to keep confidential information confidential. Leaking company secrets to competitors,

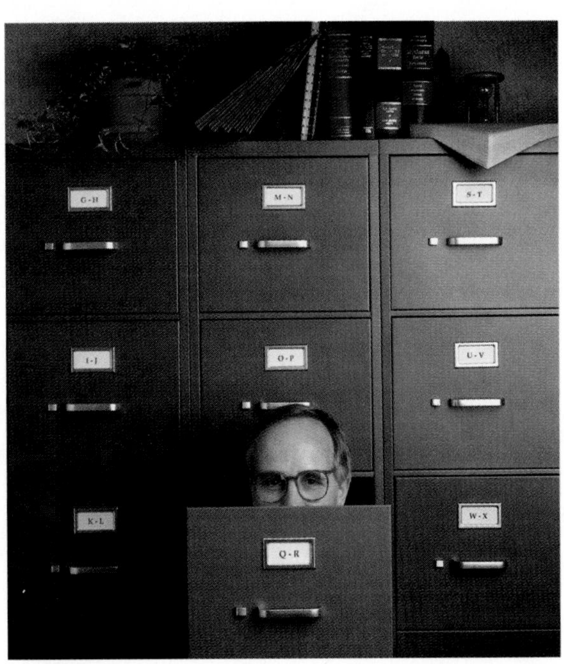

Managers are information brokers. They collect it, analyze it, act on it, and disseminate it.
© 1997 James Marvy/
The Stock Market

"doctoring" the numbers, wrongfully withholding information, or lying are some possible misuses of the information entrusted to managers. For example, in Hong Kong, "Ba dan" literally means white sheet. At Bausch & Lomb's Hong King division, managers used the term "Ba dan" to refer to the fake sales numbers they sent to company headquarters each month. To maintain its status as Bausch & Lomb's top international division, Hong Kong managers would fake the sales numbers for its Southeast Asian customers. Then, to make the fake numbers look like real sales, it would ship its product (glasses and contact lenses) to a phony customer warehouse.[4] Bausch & Lomb used company auditors plus its internal security department, which was run by ex-Secret Service agents and police officers, to set up "sting" operations to catch the employees who were running the "Ba dan" scam in Hong Kong.

A third area in which managers must be careful to engage in ethical behavior is the way in which they influence the behavior of others, especially those they supervise. Managerial work gives managers significant power to influence others. If managers tell employees to perform unethical acts (or face punishment), such as "faking the numbers to get results," then they are abusing their managerial power. This is sometimes called the "move it or lose it" syndrome. "Move it or lose it" managers tell employees, "Do it. You're paid to do it. If you can't do it, we'll find somebody who can."[5]

Not all unethical managerial influence is intentional, however. Sometimes managers unintentionally influence employees to act unethically by creating policies that inadvertently reward employees for unethical acts. For example, in an attempt to make its automotive repair shops more profitable, Sears restructured its incentive system. It paid mechanics and shop managers a commission depending on the number of batteries, shock absorbers, oil changes, or tune-ups they sold per work shift. However, this pay system put the workers' best interests (higher pay) directly in conflict with the interests of customers (honest repair work). What management was trying to accomplish was greater productivity, but instead, employees started selling unneeded parts and repair work. This practice became so widespread that customers and state agencies in more than 40 states accused Sears of cheating customers by selling unnecessary parts and repairs. Sears management has since ended the incentive program.[6]

Setting goals is another way that managers influence the behavior of their employees. If managers set unrealistic goals, the pressure to perform and to achieve these goals can influence employees to engage in unethical business behaviors. For example, at Bausch & Lomb, there was tremendous pressure to achieve double-digit increases in revenues each year. Said a former company president, "Once you signed up for your target number, you were expected to reach it," no excuses accepted. The pressure to make numbers was so great that Bausch & Lomb told its customers that they could buy Bausch & Lomb's best-selling glasses and contact lenses only if they also bought slow-selling products they didn't want. Furthermore, when competitors came out with disposable contact lenses, Bausch and Lomb simply took the regular contact lenses it had sold for 15 years and fraudulently repackaged them to consumers as the advanced, disposable contacts.[7] The company later settled a class-action lawsuit in which it agreed to pay $68 million to consumers who thought they were buying the better, newer contacts.[8] As a result of all of these problems, Bausch & Lomb has changed its compensation and reward systems to reward managers and employees for long-term rather than short-term performance.

Review 1
Ethics and the Nature of Management Jobs

Ethics is the set of moral principles or values that define right and wrong. Ethical behavior occurs when managers follow those principles and values. Because they set the standard for others in the workplace, managers can model ethical behavior by using resources for company and not personal business. Furthermore, managers can encourage ethical behavior by handling information in a confidential and honest fashion, by not using their authority to influence others to engage in unethical behavior, by not creating policies that unintentionally reward employees for unethical behavior, and by setting reasonable rather than unreasonable goals.

2 Workplace Deviance

Depending on which study you look at, one-third to three-quarters of all employees admit that they have stolen from their employers or committed computer fraud, embezzled funds, vandalized company property, sabotaged company projects, or been "sick" from work when they really weren't sick. Experts estimate that unethical behaviors like these, which researchers call "workplace deviance," may cost companies as much as $200 billion a year.[9]

workplace deviance
unethical behavior that violates organizational norms about right and wrong

More specifically, ***workplace deviance*** is unethical behavior that violates organizational norms about right and wrong. Figure 3.1 shows that workplace deviance can be categorized by how deviant the behavior is, from minor to serious, and by the target of the deviant behavior, either the organization or particular people in the workplace.[10] One kind of workplace deviance, called ***production deviance***, hurts the quality and quantity of work produced. Examples include leaving early, taking excessively long work breaks, purposely working slower, or intentionally wasting resources.

production deviance
unethical behavior that hurts the quality and quantity of work produced

property deviance
unethical behavior aimed at the organization's property

Property deviance is unethical behavior aimed at company property. Examples include sabotaging, stealing or damaging equipment or products, or overcharging for services and then pocketing the difference. For example, Cashway Building Centres in Port Hope, Ontario, Canada, conducted a routine corporate investigation for employee fraud. The investigation revealed that an employee, who had ostensibly written 50 refunds to customers, had really faked the refunds and pocketed the money for himself. The local managers in charge of the Port Hope store never suspected the loss, which totaled nearly $21,000, or nearly 2 percent of the store's annual sales.[11]

shrinkage
employee theft of company merchandise

Another common form of property deviance, called ***shrinkage***, is the theft of company merchandise by employees. For example, in Canada, while the average shoplifter makes off with $83 worth of goods per theft, the average employee who steals makes off with $203 per incident. Shrinkage costs Canadian companies nearly $2 billion a year.[12] In the U.S., employee shrinkage costs retailers nearly 1 percent of their sales—nearly $13 billion each year.[13]

political deviance
using one's influence to harm others in the company

While workplace and production deviance harm companies, political deviance and personal aggression are unethical behaviors that hurt particular people within companies. ***Political deviance*** is using one's influence to harm others in the company. Examples include making decisions based on favoritism rather than performance, spreading rumors about co-workers, or

Figure 3.1 **Types of Workplace Deviance**

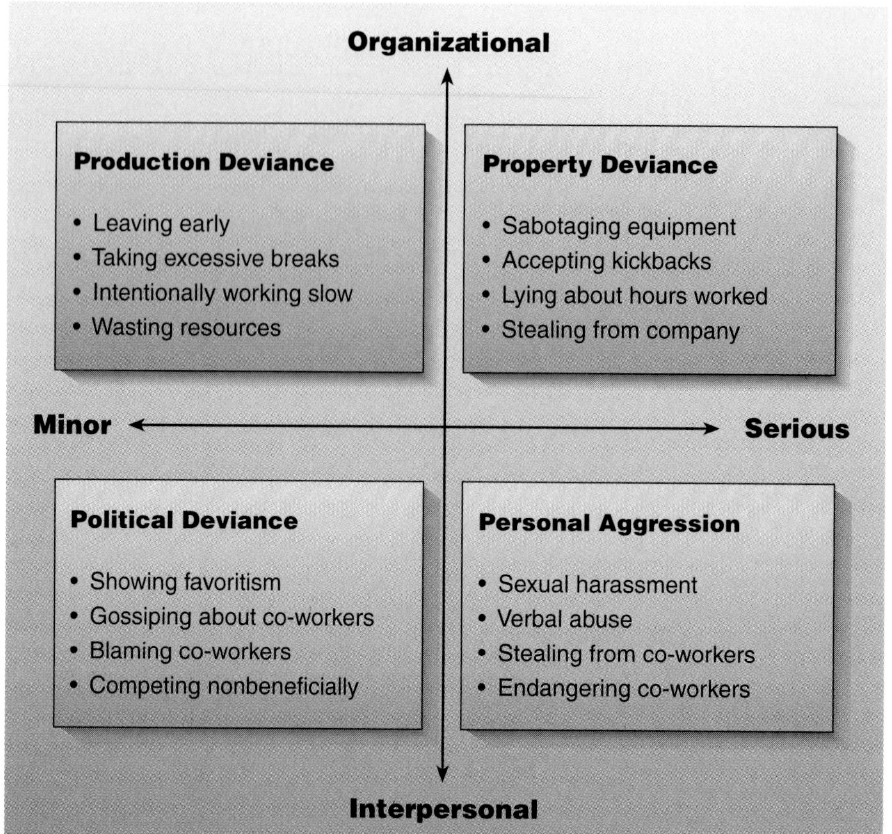

Source: S.L. Robinson & R.J. Bennett, "A Typology of Deviant Workplace Behaviors: A Multidimensional Scaling Study," *Academy of Management Journal* 38 (1995): 555-572.

personal aggression
hostile or aggressive behavior toward others

falsely blaming others for mistakes they didn't make. ***Personal aggression*** is hostile or aggressive behavior toward others. Examples include sexual harassment, verbal abuse, stealing from co-workers, or personally threatening co-workers. One of the fastest-growing kinds of personal aggression is workplace violence. In the 1980s, 7,600 U.S. workers were killed at work, making workplace homicide the third leading cause of death at work. Since 1992, more than 1,000 people per year, or roughly 3 people per day, have been killed at work. While many victims are police officers, security guards, or taxi drivers, store owners and company managers are the most often killed group.[14]

Review 2
Workplace Deviance

Workplace deviance is behavior that violates important organizational norms about right and wrong and harms the organization or its workers. Production deviance and property deviance harm the company, whereas political deviance and personal aggression harm individuals within the company.

3 U.S. Sentencing Commission Guidelines

A male supervisor is sexually harassing female co-workers. A sales representative offers a $10,000 kickback to persuade an indecisive customer to do business with his company. A company president secretly meets with her biggest competitor's CEO, and both agree not to compete in markets where the other has already established customers. Each of these behaviors is clearly unethical (and, in these cases, illegal, too). Historically, if management was unaware of such activities, the company could not be held responsible for an employee's unethical acts. However, under the 1991 U.S. Sentencing Commission Guidelines, companies can be prosecuted and *punished even if management didn't know about the unethical behavior.* Moreover, penalties can be substantial, with maximum fines approaching three hundred million dollars![15]

Let's examine **3.1** *who the guidelines apply to and what they cover, and* **3.2** *how, according to the guidelines, an organization can be punished for the unethical behavior of its managers and employees.*

3.1
Who, What, and Why?

Nearly all businesses, nonprofits, partnerships, labor unions, unincorporated organizations and associations, incorporated organizations, and even pension funds, trusts, and joint stock companies are covered by the guidelines. If your organization can be characterized as a business (remember, nonprofits count too), then it is subject to the guidelines.[16]

The guidelines cover federal laws such as invasion of privacy, price fixing, fraud, customs violations, antitrust violations, civil rights violations, theft, money laundering, conflict of interest, embezzlement, dealing in stolen goods, copyright infringements, extortion, and more. However, it's not enough to stay "within the law." The purpose of the guidelines is not just to punish companies *after* they or their employees break the law. The purpose is to encourage companies to take proactive steps that will discourage or prevent white-collar crime *before* it happens. The guidelines also give companies an incentive to cooperate with and disclose illegal activities to federal authorities.[17]

3.2
Determining the Punishment

The guidelines impose smaller fines on companies that take proactive steps to encourage ethical behavior or voluntarily disclose illegal activities to federal authorities. Essentially, the law uses a "carrot-and-stick" approach. The stick is the threat of heavy fines that can total millions of dollars. The carrot is greatly reduced fines, but only if the company has started an effective compliance program (discussed below) to encourage ethical behavior *before* the illegal activity occurs.[18] Understanding how a company's punishment is determined can help you understand the importance of establishing a compliance program.

The first step is computing the base fine by determining what level of offense has occurred. The level of the offense (i.e., the seriousness of the problem) is figured by examining the kind of crime, the loss incurred by the victims, and how much planning went into the crime. For example, committing simple fraud is a level 6 offense (there are 38 levels in all). But if the victims of that fraud lost more than $5 million, that level 6 offense becomes a level 22 offense. Moreover, anything beyond minimal planning to commit the fraud results in an increase of two levels to a level 24 offense. How much of a difference would this make to the company? Crimes at or below level 6 incur a base fine of $5,000, whereas the base fine for level 24 is $2.1 million. So the difference is $2.095 million! The base fine for level 38, the top-level offense, is an astounding $72.5 million!

After assessing a base fine, the judge computes a culpability score, which is a way of assigning blame to the company. Higher culpability scores suggest greater corporate responsibility in conducting, encouraging, or sanctioning illegal or unethical activity. The culpability score is a number ranging from a minimum of 0.05 to a maximum of 4.0. A company that already has a compliance program and voluntarily reports the offense to authorities will incur a culpability score of 0.05. By contrast, a company in which management secretly plans, approves, and participates in illegal or unethical activity will receive the maximum score of 4.0.

The culpability score is critical, because the total fine is computed by multiplying the base fine by the culpability score. Going back to our level 24 fraud offense, a company with a compliance program that turns itself in will only be fined $105,000 ($2,100,000 × 0.05). However, a company that secretly plans, approves, and participates in illegal activity will be fined $8.4 million ($2,100,000 × 4.0)! The difference is even more astronomical for level 38 offenses. The "good guys" are only fined $3.635 million, whereas the "bad guys" are fined a whopping $290 million! These differences clearly show the importance of having a compliance program in place.

Fortunately, for those who want to avoid paying these stiff fines, the 1991 U.S. Sentencing Guidelines are clear on the seven necessary components of an effective compliance program.[19] Table 3.1 lists those components.

Review 3
U.S. Sentencing Commission Guidelines

Under the 1991 U.S. Sentencing Commission Guidelines, companies can be prosecuted and fined up to three hundred million dollars for employees'

Table 3.1

Compliance Program Steps for the 1991 U.S. Sentencing Guidelines

1. Establish standards and procedures to meet the company's business needs.
2. Put upper-level managers in charge of the compliance program.
3. Don't delegate decision-making authority to employees who are likely to act illegally or unethically.
4. Use auditing, monitoring, and other methods to encourage employees to report violations.
5. Use company publications and training to inform employees about the company's compliance standards and procedures.
6. Enforce compliance standards by fairly and consistently disciplining violators.
7. After violations occur, find appropriate ways to improve the compliance program.

Source: D.R. Dalton, M.B. Metzger, & J.W. Hill, "The 'New' U.S. Sentencing Commission Guidelines: A Wake-up Call for Corporate America," *Academy of Management Executive* 8 (1994): 7-16.

illegal actions. Fines are computed by multiplying the base fine by a culpability score, which ranges from 0.05 to 4.0. Companies that establish compliance programs to encourage ethical behavior can reduce their culpability scores and their fines. Companies without compliance programs can pay fines four times larger than companies without established compliance programs. Compliance programs must establish standards and procedures, be run by top managers, encourage hiring and promotion of honest and ethical people, encourage employees to report violations, educate employees about compliance, punish violators, and find ways to improve the program after violations occur.

How Do You Make Ethical Decisions?

On a cold morning in the midst of a winter storm, schools were closed and most people had decided to stay home from work. However, Richard Addessi had already showered, shaved, and dressed for the office. Addessi, whose father worked at IBM for 36 years, was just four months short of his 30-year anniversary with the company. Addessi kissed his wife Joan goodbye, but before he could get to his car he fell dead on the garage floor of a sudden heart attack. Having begun work at IBM at the age of 18, he was just 48 years old.[20]

You're the vice-president in charge of benefits at IBM. Yes or no, given that he was four months short of full retirement, do you award full retirement benefits to Mr. Addessi's wife and daughters? If the answer is yes, they will receive his full retirement benefits of $1,800 a month and free lifetime medical coverage. If you say no, Mrs. Addessi and her daughters will only receive $340 a month. They will also have to pay $473 a month just to continue their current medical coverage. As the VP in charge of benefits at IBM, what would be the ethical thing to do?

After reading the next two sections, you should be able to:

4 describe what **influences ethical decision making.**

5 explain what **practical steps** managers can take **to improve ethical decision making.**

4 Influences on Ethical Decision Making

So, what did IBM decide to do? Since Richard Addessi was four months short of 30 years with the company, IBM officials felt they had no choice but to give Joan Addessi and her two daughters the smaller, partial retirement benefits. Do you think that IBM's decision was ethical? Probably many of you don't. You wonder how the company could be so heartless as to not give Richard Addessi's family the full benefits to which you believe they were entitled. Yet others might argue that IBM did the ethical thing by strictly following the rules laid out in its pension benefit plan. After all, being fair means applying the rules to everyone.

While some ethical issues are easily solved, for many there are no clearly right or wrong answers. The ethical answers that managers choose depend on **4.1** *the ethical intensity of the decision,* **4.2** *the moral development of the manager, and* **4.3** *the ethical principles used to solve the problem.*

4.1 Ethical Intensity of the Decision

Managers don't treat all ethical decisions the same. The manager who has to decide whether to deny or extend full benefits to Joan Addessi and her family is going to treat that decision much more seriously than the manager who has to deal with an assistant who has been taking computer diskettes home for personal use. The difference between these decisions is one of ***ethical intensity***, which is how concerned people are about an ethical issue. When addressing issues of high ethical intensity, managers are more aware of the impact their decisions have on others. They are more likely to view the decision as an ethical or moral decision rather than an economic decision. They are also more likely to worry about doing the "right thing."

ethical intensity the degree of concern people have about an ethical issue

Ethical intensity depends on six factors:[21]

- magnitude of consequences
- social consensus
- probability of effect
- temporal immediacy
- proximity of effect
- concentration of effect

Magnitude of consequences is the total harm or benefit derived from an ethical decision. The more people who are harmed, or the greater the harm to those people, the larger the consequences. ***Social consensus*** is agreement on whether behavior is bad or good. For example, other than the act of self-defense, most people agree that killing is wrong. However, people strongly disagree about whether abortions or the death penalty are wrong. ***Probability of effect*** is the chance that something will happen and then result in harm to others. For example, the probability of effect is strong for cigarettes. We know that cigarette smoking strongly increases the chances of heart attack, cancer, and emphysema. We also know that the nicotine in cigarettes is addictive, and that once you start, it's hard to stop. Consequently, smokers are very likely to contract one of these diseases.

magnitude of consequences the total harm or benefit derived from an ethical decision

social consensus agreement on whether behavior is bad or good

probability of effect the chance that something will happen and then result in harm to others

Temporal immediacy is the time between an act and the consequences the act produces. Temporal immediacy is stronger if a manager has to lay off workers next week as opposed to three months from now. ***Proximity of effect*** is the social, psychological, cultural, or physical distance of a decision maker to those affected by his or her decisions. In the previous example, proximity of effect would be greater for the manager who works with employees who are to be laid off than it would be for a staff person who works where no layoffs are occurring. Finally, whereas the magnitude of consequences is the total effect across all people, ***concentration of effect*** is how much an act affects the average person. Cheating 10 investors out of $10,000 apiece is a greater concentration of effect than cheating 100 investors out of $1,000 apiece.

temporal immediacy the time between an act and the consequences the act produces

proximity of effect the social, psychological, cultural, or physical distance between a decision maker and those affected by his or her decisions

concentration of effect the total harm or benefit that an act produces on the average person

Many people will likely feel IBM was wrong to deny full benefits to Joan Addessi. Why? Because IBM's decision met five of the six characteristics of ethical intensity. The difference in benefits ($23,000 per year) is likely to have serious consequences on the family. The decision is certain to affect them. It will affect them immediately. We can closely identify with Joan Addessi and her daughters (as opposed to IBM's faceless, nameless corporate identity). And, the decision will have a concentrated effect on the family in terms of their monthly benefits ($1,800 and free medical coverage if you award full benefits versus $340 a month and medical care that costs $473 per month if you don't).

The exception, as we will discuss below, is social consensus. Not everyone will agree that IBM's decision was unethical. The judgment also depends on your level of moral development and which ethical principles you use.

4.2
Moral Development

A friend of yours has given you the latest version of Microsoft Word. She stuffed the computer disks in your backpack with a note saying that you should install it on your computer and get it back to her in a couple of days. You're tempted. You have papers to write, notes to take, presentations to plan. Besides, all of your friends have the same version of Microsoft Word. They didn't pay for it either. Copying the software to your hard drive without buying your own copy clearly violates copyright laws. But no one would find out. Even if they do, Microsoft isn't going to come after you. Microsoft goes after the big fish, companies that illegally copy and distribute software to their workers. Your computer has booted up, and you've got your mouse in one hand and the installation disk in the other. What are you going to do?[22]

preconventional level of moral development first level of moral development in which people make decisions based on selfish reasons

conventional level of moral development second level of moral development in which people make decisions that conform to societal expectations

In part, according to Lawrence Kohlberg, the decision will be based on your level of moral development. Kohlberg identified three phases of moral development, with two stages in each phase (see Table 3.2).[23] At the ***preconventional level*** of moral development, people decide based on selfish reasons. For example, if you were in Stage 1, the punishment and obedience stage, your primary concern would be not to get in trouble. So, you wouldn't copy the software. Yet, in Stage 2, the instrumental exchange stage, you make decisions that advance your wants and needs. So, you copy the software.

People at the ***conventional level*** of moral development make decisions that conform to societal expectations. In Stage 3, the good boy—nice girl stage, you normally do what the other "good boys" and "nice girls" are doing. If everyone else is illegally copying software, you will, too. In the law and order stage, Stage 4, you do whatever the law permits, so you wouldn't copy the software.

Table 3.2 **Kohlberg's Stages of Moral Development**

Preconventional Level

Stage 1: Punishment and Obedience
Stage 2: Instrumental Exchange

Conventional Level

Stage 3: Good Boy—Nice Girl
Stage 4: Law and Order

Post Conventional Level

Stage 5: Legal Contract
Stage 6: Universal Principle

Source: W. Davidson III & D. Worrell, "Influencing Managers to Change Unpopular Corporate Behavior Through Boycotts and Divestitures," *Business & Society* 34 (1995): 171-196.

post conventional level of moral development
third level of moral development in which people make decisions based on internalized principles

People at the ***post conventional level*** of moral maturity always use internalized ethical principles to solve ethical dilemmas. In Stage 5, the legal contract stage, you would refuse to copy the software because, as a whole, society is better off when the rights of others—in this case, the rights of software authors and manufacturers—are not violated. In Stage 6, the universal principle stage, you might or might not copy the software, depending on your principles of right and wrong. Moreover, you will stick to your principles even if your decision conflicts with the law (Stage 4) or what others believe is best for society (Stage 5). For example, someone with socialist or communist beliefs would always choose to copy the software, because they view goods and services as owned by society rather than by individuals and corporations. (For information about the dos, don'ts, and legal issues concerning software piracy, see the Software Publisher's Association Web site at **http://www.spa.org**.)

principle of long-term self-interest
ethical principle that holds that you should never take any action that is not in your or your organization's long-term self-interest

Kohlberg originally predicted that people would progress sequentially from earlier stages to later stages. We now know that one's level of moral maturity can change, depending on individual and situational factors. As people age, become more educated, or deal with dilemmas high in ethical intensity, they are more likely to make ethical decisions using a higher level of moral maturity.

4.3 *Principles of Ethical Decision Making*

Personal Productivity Tip

Could You Tell Your Parents or the Public?

Besides the sleep test, managers also judge the ethics of what they're doing by trying to anticipate how others would view their actions. One manager said, "Ummm . . . This is going to sound trite. But if you can comfortably tell your parents, I think you are probably doing the right thing." Or, "Can you tell your grandfather about it and be proud?" Practicing managers were also aware of the importance of how their choices were viewed by the general public. Said one manager, "If you wouldn't share it with '60 Minutes' news cameras, don't do it."

Sources: J.L. Badaracco, Jr. & A.P. Webb, "Business Ethics: A View from the Trenches," *California Management Review* 37 (1995): 8-28.

Besides an issue's ethical intensity and a manager's level of moral maturity, the particular ethical principles that managers use will also affect how they solve ethical dilemmas. Unfortunately, there is no one "ideal principle" by which to make ethical business decisions.

According to Professor Larue Hosmer, a number of different ethical principles can be used to make business decisions: long-term self-interest, personal virtue, religious injunctions, government requirements, utilitarian benefits, individual rights, and distributive justice.[24] What these ethical principles have in common is that they encourage managers and employees to take others' interests into account when making ethical decisions. At the same time, however, these principles can lead to very different ethical actions. This is illustrated by using these principles to decide whether to award full benefits to Joan Addessi and her children.

According to the ***principle of long-term self-interest***, you should never take any action that is not in your or your organization's long-term self-interest. While it sounds as if the principle of self-interest promotes selfishness, it doesn't. What we do to maximize our long-term interests (save more, spend less, exercise every day, watch what we eat) is often very different from what we do to maximize short-term interests (max out our credit cards, be a couch potato, eat whatever we want). At any single time, IBM has nearly 1,000 employees who are just months away from retirement. Thus, because of the costs involved, it serves IBM's long-term interest to pay full benefits only after employees have put in their 30 years.

principle of personal virtue
ethical principle that holds that you should never do anything that is not honest, open, and truthful, and which you would not be glad to see reported in the newspapers or on TV

The ***principle of personal virtue*** holds that you should never do anything that is not honest, open, and truthful, and which you would not be glad to see reported in the newspapers or on TV. Using the principle of personal virtue, IBM should have quietly awarded Joan Addessi her husband's full benefits. Had it done so, it could have avoided the publication of an embarrassing *Wall Street Journal* article on this topic.

Personal Productivity Tip

The "Sleep Test"

Professors use fancy words like "utilitarian benefits" to describe ethical decision making. However, practicing managers refer to something much simpler, the "sleep test." "If I do this, can I sleep at night?" "Can I look at myself in the mirror in the morning?" "The bottom line is what you're comfortable with. I want . . . to be able to both meet my house payments, and have some dignity left." In short, if you're asked to do something that just "feels" wrong, sleep on it. If it still feels wrong in the morning, don't do it.

Sources: J.L. Badaracco, Jr. & A.P. Webb, "Business Ethics: A View from the Trenches," *California Management Review* 37 (1995): 8-28.

principle of religious injunctions
ethical principle that holds that you should never take any action that is not kind and that does not build a sense of community, a sense of everyone working together for a commonly accepted goal

principle of government requirements
ethical principle that holds that you should never take any action that violates the law, for the law represents the minimal moral standard

principle of utilitarian benefits
ethical principle that holds that you should never take any action that does not result in greater good for society. Instead, do whatever creates the greatest good for the greatest number

principle of individual rights
ethical principle that holds that you should never take any action that infringes on others' agreed-on rights

principle of distributive justice
ethical principle that holds that you should never take any action that harms the least among us: the poor, the uneducated, the unemployed

The ***principle of religious injunctions*** holds that you should never take an action that is unkind or that harms a sense of community, such as the positive feelings that come from working together to accomplish a commonly accepted goal. Using the principle of religious injunctions, IBM would have been concerned foremost with compassion and kindness. Thus, it would have awarded full benefits to Joan Addessi.

According to the ***principle of government requirements***, the law represents the minimal moral standards of society, so you should never take any action that violates the law. Using the principle of government requirements, IBM would deny full benefits to Joan Addessi because her husband did not work for the company for 30 years. Indeed, an IBM spokesperson stated that making exceptions would violate the federal Employee Retirement Income Security Act of 1974.

The ***principle of utilitarian benefits*** states that you should never take any action that does not result in greater good for society. In short, you should do whatever creates the greatest good for the greatest number. At first, this principle suggests that IBM should award full benefits to Joan Addessi. However, if IBM did this with any regularity, the costs would be enormous, profits would shrink, and IBM's stock price would drop, harming countless shareholders, many of whom rely on IBM stock dividends for retirement income. So, in this case, the principle does not lead to a clear choice.

The ***principle of individual rights*** holds that you should never take any action that infringes on others' agreed-on rights. Using the principle of individual rights, IBM would deny Joan Addessi full benefits. If it carefully followed the rules specified in its pension plan, and if it permitted Mrs. Addessi due process, meaning the right to appeal the decision, then IBM would not be violating Mrs. Addessi's rights. In fact, it could be argued that providing full benefits to Mrs. Addessi would violate the rights of employees who had to wait 30 years to receive full benefits.

Finally, the ***principle of distributive justice*** is that you should never take any action that harms the least among us in some way. This principle is designed to protect the poor, the uneducated, and the unemployed. While Joan Addessi could probably find a job, it's unlikely, after 20 years as a stay-at-home mom, that she could easily find one that would support herself and her daughters in the manner to which they were accustomed. Using the principle of distributive justice, IBM would award her full benefits.

As stated at the beginning of this chapter, one of the "real world" aspects of ethical decisions is that no matter *what* you decide, someone or some group will be unhappy with the decision. This corollary is also true: No matter *how* you decide, someone or some group will be unhappy. Consequently, despite the fact that all of these different ethical principles encourage managers to balance others' needs against their own, they can also lead to very different ethical actions. So, even when managers strive to be ethical, there are often no clear answers when it comes to doing "the" right thing.

Review 4
Influences on Ethical Decision Making

Three factors influence ethical decisions: the ethical intensity of the decision, the moral development of the manager, and the ethical principles used to solve the problem. Ethical intensity is strong when decisions have large, certain, immediate consequences, and when we are physically or psychologically close to those affected by the decision. There are three phases of moral maturity and two steps within each phase. At the preconventional level, decisions are made for selfish reasons. At the conventional level, decisions conform to societal expectations. At the post conventional level, internalized principles are used to make ethical decisions. Finally, managers can use a number of different principles when making ethical decisions: self-interest, personal virtue, religious injunctions, government requirements, utilitarian benefits, individual rights, and distributive justice.

5 Practical Steps to Ethical Decision Making

Managers can encourage more ethical decision making in their organizations by **5.1** *carefully selecting and hiring new employees,* **5.2** *establishing a specific code of ethics,* **5.3** *training employees how to make ethical decisions, and* **5.4** *creating an ethical climate.*

5.1 Selecting and Hiring Ethical Employees

If you found a wallet containing $50, would you return it with the money? *Reader's Digest* magazine examined this question by leaving 120 wallets in an unscientifically selected sample of three big cities, three large suburban areas, and three small towns.[25] Each wallet contained $50, a name, a local address, family pictures, notes, and coupons—in other words, what you'd find in most wallets. Overall, 67 percent of the wallets were returned with the $50. The wallets were more likely to be returned by women (72 percent) than by men (62 percent), and were more likely to be returned in small towns (80 percent) than in major cities (70 percent), suburbs (60 percent), or medium cities (57 percent).

As an employer, you can increase your chances of hiring the honest person who returns the wallet with the money if you give job applicants integrity tests. ***Overt integrity tests*** estimate employee honesty by directly asking job applicants what they think or feel about theft or about punishment of unethical behaviors.[26] For example, an employer might ask an applicant, "Do you think you would ever consider buying something from somebody if you knew the person had stolen the item?" or "Don't most people steal from their companies?" Surprisingly, because they believe that the world is basically dishonest and that dishonest behavior is normal, unethical people will usually answer yes to such questions.[27]

overt integrity test
written test that estimates employee honesty by directly asking job applicants what they think or feel about theft or about punishment of unethical behaviors

Personality-based integrity tests indirectly estimate employee honesty by measuring psychological traits such as dependability and conscientiousness. For example, prison inmates serving time for white-collar crimes (counterfeiting, embezzlement, and fraud) scored much lower than a comparison group of middle-level managers on scales measuring reliability, dependability, honesty, and being conscientious and rule-abiding.[28] These results show that companies can selectively hire and promote people who will be more ethical.[29] For more on integrity testing, see the "What Really Works?" feature in this chapter.

personality-based integrity test
written test that indirectly estimates employee honesty by measuring psychological traits such as dependability and conscientiousness

What Really Works

Integrity Tests

Under the 1991 U.S. Sentencing Commission Guidelines, unethical employee behavior can lead to multimillion dollar fines for corporations. Moreover, workplace deviance, like stealing, fraud, and vandalism, can cost companies an estimated $200 billion a year. One way to reduce workplace deviance and the chance of a large fine for unethical employee behavior is to use overt and personality-based integrity tests to screen job applicants.

One hundred eighty-one studies, with a combined total of 576,460 study participants, have examined how well job performance and various kinds of workplace deviance are predicted by integrity tests. Not only do these studies show that integrity tests can help companies reduce workplace deviance, but they have the added bonus of helping companies hire workers who are better performers in their jobs.

Workplace Deviance (Counterproductive Behaviors)

Compared to job applicants who score poorly, there is an 82 percent chance that job applicants who score well on overt integrity tests will participate in less illegal activity, unethical behavior, drug abuse, or workplace violence.

Overt Integrity Tests & Workplace Deviance

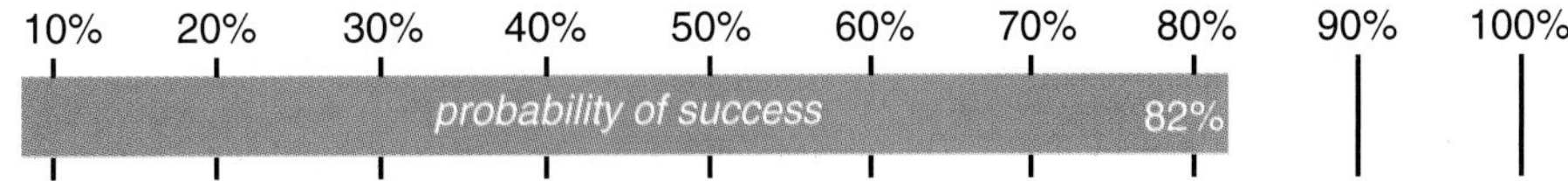

Personality-based integrity tests also do a good job of predicting who will engage in workplace deviance. Compared to job applicants who score poorly, there is a 68 percent chance that job applicants who score well on personality-based integrity tests will participate in less illegal activity, unethical behavior, excessive absences, drug abuse, or workplace violence.

Personality-Based Integrity Tests & Workplace Deviance

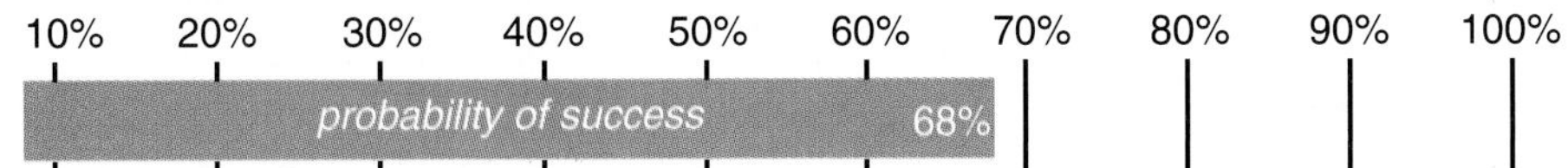

Job Performance

Integrity tests not only reduce unethical behavior and workplace deviance, but they also help companies hire better performers. Compared to employees who score poorly, there is a 69 percent chance that employees who score well on overt integrity tests will be better performers.

Overt Integrity Tests & Job Performance

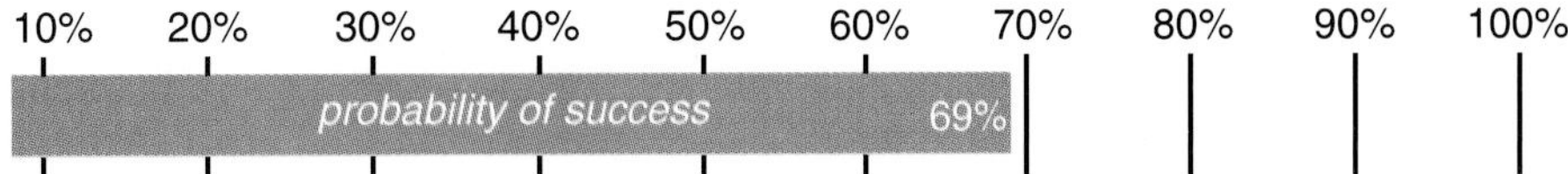

The figures are nearly identical for personality-based integrity tests. Compared to those who score poorly, there is a 70 percent chance that employees who score well on personality-based integrity tests will be better at their jobs.

Personality-Based Integrity Tests & Job Performance

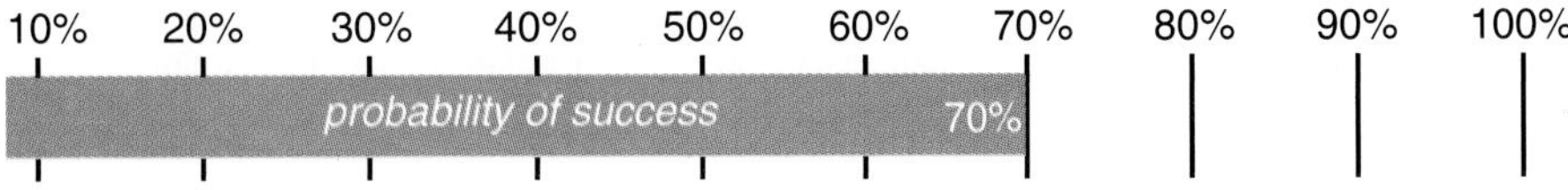

Theft

While integrity tests can help companies decrease most kinds of workplace deviance and increase employees' job performance, they have a smaller effect on a specific kind of workplace deviance: theft. Compared to employees that score poorly, there is a 57 percent chance that employees who score well on overt integrity tests will be less likely to steal. No theft data were available to assess personality-based integrity tests.

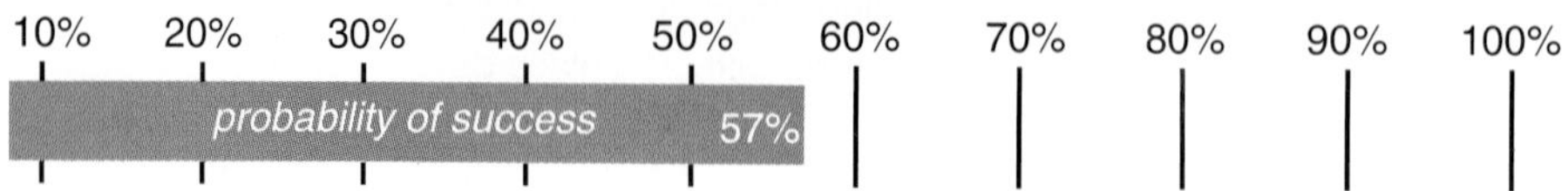

Source: D.S. Ones, C. Viswesvaran, & F.L. Schmidt, "Comprehensive Meta-Analysis of Integrity Test Validities: Findings and Implications for Personnel Selection and Theories of Job Performance," *Journal of Applied Psychology* 78 (1993): 679-703.

5.2 *Codes of Ethics*

As shown in Table 3.3, James Cash Penney, founder of the J.C. Penney Company, established one of the first modern codes of business conduct in 1913. Indeed, the last statement in the code encouraged Penney's employees to test their actions by asking, "Does it square with what is right and just?"

Today, nine out of ten large corporations have an ethics code in place. However, two things must happen if those codes are to encourage ethical decision making and behavior.[30] First, companies must communicate the codes to others both within and outside the company. An excellent example of a well-communicated code of ethics can be found at Northern Telecom's (NorTel) Internet site, at **http://www.nortel.com/cool/ethics/home.html**. With the click of a computer mouse, anyone inside or outside the company can obtain detailed information about the company's core values, specific ethical business practices, and much more.

Table 3.3 **J.C. Penney 1913 Code of Conduct**

The Penney Idea:
To serve the public as nearly as we can to its complete satisfaction.
To expect for the service we render a fair remuneration, and not all the profit the traffic will bear.
To do all in our power to pack the customer's dollar full of value, quality and satisfaction.
To continue to train ourselves and our associates so that the service we give will be more and more intelligently performed.
To improve constantly the human factor in our business.
To reward men and women in our organization through participation in what the business produces.
To test our every policy, method and act in this wise: Does it square with what is right and just?
— James Cash Penney, 1913

Source: J.C. Penney. [Online] Available **http://a.jcpenney.com/aboutjcp/pen_idea.htm**, January 18, 1996.

Second, in addition to general guidelines and ethics codes like "do unto others as you would have others do unto you," management must also develop practical ethical standards and procedures specific to the company's line of business. Visitors to NorTel's Internet site can instantly access references to 36 specific ethics codes, ranging from bribes and kickbacks to expense vouchers and illegal copying of software. For example, a NorTel employee who wants to learn more about the company's position on bribes and kickbacks would find the following information on NorTel's web site:

> *Under no circumstances is it acceptable to offer, give, solicit, or receive any form of bribe, kickback, or inducement. This principle applies to NorTel transactions everywhere in the world, even where the practice is widely considered* a way of doing business. *Under some statutes (such as the U.S. Foreign Corrupt Practices Act), these are criminal actions that can lead to prosecution.*

Specific codes of ethics such as these make it much easier for employees to decide what they should do when they want to do the "right thing."

5.3 *Ethics Training*

The first objective of ethics training is to develop employee awareness about ethics.[31] This means helping employees recognize what issues are ethical issues, and then avoid the rationalization of unethical behavior: "This isn't really illegal or immoral." "No one will ever find out." Two companies have created board games to improve awareness about ethical issues.[32] Citicorp Bank has a game called "The Work Ethic" in which players win or lose points, depending on their answers to legal, regulatory, policy-related, and judgmental questions. Aerospace company Martin Marietta's game, called "Gray Matters," is loosely based on the child's game "Chutes and Ladders." Players go up and down career ladders, depending on their answers to ethical questions.

The second objective for ethics training programs is to achieve credibility with employees. Not surprisingly, employees can be highly suspicious of management's reasons for offering ethics training. At NYNEX, the regional telephone company for the New York area, employees initially assumed that management instituted the program to get employees to "rat" on each other. So they labeled the program, "1-800-SNITCH."[33] One of the ways in which companies mistakenly hurt the credibility of their ethics programs is by having outside instructors and consultants conduct the classes. Employees often complain that outside instructors and consultants are teaching theory that has nothing to do with their jobs and the "real world." NYNEX, seeking to regain credibility with its workers, avoided this problem by having supervisors conduct 30-minute "tailgate" sessions in which they could literally begin the training by talking to their workers from atop a truck tailgate rather than a classroom.

The third objective of ethics training is to teach employees a practical model of ethical decision making. A basic model should help them think about the consequences their choices will have on others and consider how they will choose between different solutions. Table 3.4 presents a basic model of ethical decision making.

Personal Productivity Tip

Consider Ethics from the Start

Many jobs begin with a short honeymoon period in which you're excited and still relatively idealistic. This is a good time to write down your thoughts about the ethical aspects of the job. Start positive. Describe your ethical aspirations (i.e., satisfied customers) and what you will do to accomplish them (i.e., be completely honest). Then, go negative. Describe parts of the job in which you fear that your ethics may be compromised. Then describe unethical behaviors that people may perform on the job (so you can avoid them). Review these lists occasionally to determine if your ethics are what you wanted them to be.

Source: David M. Porter, Jr., The Anderson School, University of California, Los Angeles, from his review of this chapter, 22 January 1997.

Table 3.4

A Basic Model of Ethical Decision Making

1. Identify the problem.

What makes it an ethical problem? Think in terms of rights, obligations, fairness, relationships, and integrity. How would you define the problem if you stood on the other side of the fence?

2. Identify the constituents.

Who has been hurt? Who could be hurt? Who could be helped? Are they willing players, or are they victims? Can you negotiate with them?

3. Diagnose the situation.

How did it happen in the first place? What could have prevented it? Is it going to get worse or better? Can the damage now be undone?

4. Analyze your options.

Imagine the range of possibilities. Limit yourself to the two or three most manageable. What are the likely outcomes of each? What are the likely costs? Look to the company mission statement or code of ethics for guidance.

5. Make your choice.

What is your intention in making this decision? How does it compare with the probable results? Can you discuss the problem with the affected parties before you act? Could you disclose without qualm your decision to your boss, the CEO, the board of directors, your family or society as a whole?

6. Act.

Do what you have to do. Don't be afraid to admit errors. Be as bold in confronting a problem as you were in causing it.

Source: L.A. Berger, "Train All Employees to Solve Ethical Dilemmas," *Best's Review—Life-Health Insurance Edition* 95 (1995): 70-80.

5.4
Ethical Climate

In study after study in which researchers have asked, "What is the most important influence on your ethical behavior at work?" the answer comes back, "My manager." The first step in establishing an ethical climate is for managers to act ethically themselves. Managers who decline to accept lavish gifts from company suppliers; who only use the company phone, fax, and copier for business and not personal use; or who keep their promises to employees, suppliers, and customers encourage others to believe that ethical behavior is normal and acceptable.

A second step in establishing an ethical climate is for top management to be active in the company ethics program. For example, Thomas Russo heads the corporate advisory division in charge of ethical behavior at Lehman Brothers, a Wall Street investment firm. Russo is not just a middle-level manager reporting to upper management. As a top-level managing director, he runs the firm's general counsel (legal), credit, and corporate audit departments. He says, "Just three or four years ago, [Wall Street] wouldn't have put the emphasis on preventive steps. We are putting an [ethics] system into place to prevent problems."[34]

whistleblowing
reporting others' ethics violations to management or legal authorities

A third step is to put in place a reporting system that encourages managers and employees to report potential ethics violations. ***Whistleblowing***, that is, reporting others' ethics violations, is a difficult step for most people to take. Potential whistleblowers often fear that they will be punished rather than the ethics violators.[35] Managers who have been interviewed about whistleblowing have said, "In every organization, someone's been screwed for standing up." "If anything, I figured that by taking a strong stand I might get myself in trouble. People might look at me as a 'goody two shoes.' Someone might try to force me out." Today, however, many federal and state laws protect the rights of whistleblowers. In addition, some companies, like Northrup Grumman, a defense contractor, have made it easier to report possible violations by establishing anonymous toll-free corporate ethics hot lines. NorTel even publicizes which of its ethics hot lines don't have caller ID (so that they cannot identify the caller's phone number). However, the factor that does the most to discourage whistleblowers is lack of company action on their complaints.[36]

Thus, the final step in developing an ethical climate is for management to fairly and consistently punish those who violate the company's code of ethics. At Allied Security, which provides security guards to corporations, one of its guards reported a fire at a building he was guarding. He reduced the damage by quickly calling the local fire department. But when Allied's investigators conducted a routine investigation, they discovered that the guard, who had become a local hero for preventing the fire from spreading, had set the fire himself. Allied filed criminal arson charges against the employee and then reimbursed its customer for $50,000 in property damage.

Review 5
Practical Steps to Ethical Decision Making

Employers can increase the chances of hiring more ethical employees by administering overt integrity tests and personality-based integrity tests to all job applicants. Most large companies now have corporate codes of ethics. But for those codes to affect ethical decision making, they must be known both inside and outside the organization. In addition to offering general rules, ethics codes must also offer specific, practical advice. Ethics training seeks to make employees aware of ethical issues, to make ethics a serious, credible factor in organizational decisions, and to teach employees a practical model of ethical decision making. The most important factors in creating an ethical business climate are the personal examples set by company managers, involvement of management in the company ethics program, a reporting system that encourages whistleblowers to report potential ethics violations, and fair but consistent punishment of violators.

What Is Social Responsibility?

social responsibility
a business's obligation to pursue policies, make decisions, and take actions that benefit society

Social responsibility is a business's obligation to pursue policies, make decisions, and take actions that benefit society.[37] Unfortunately, because there are strong disagreements over to whom and for what in society organizations are responsible, it can be difficult for managers to know what is or will be perceived as socially responsible corporate behavior. For example, Gillette Corporation's use of rats and rabbits for product testing continues to draw protests from PETA (People for the Ethical Treatment of Animals, **http://www.peta-online.org/**) and from elementary school teachers who encourage their students to write directly to Gillette. In one such letter, a 13-year-old wrote, "Would you like it if someone put acids in your eyes and shoved cleaning materials down your throat?" In response to complaints, Gillette now spends about a million dollars a year on alternatives to animal testing. However, Gillette argues that eliminating animal testing altogether would be socially irresponsible, because it is critical to producing a safe product for its customers. Furthermore, if a product liability lawsuit were to be filed against the company, its best legal defense would be the scientific testing it performs on rats and rabbits.[38]

After reading the next four sections, you should be able to explain:

6 **to whom organizations are socially responsible**.

7 **for what organizations are socially responsible**.

8 how organizations can choose to **respond to societal demands for social responsibility**.

9 whether **social responsibility** hurts or helps an organization's **economic performance**.

6 To Whom Are Organizations Socially Responsible?

shareholder model
view of social responsibility which holds that an organization's overriding goal should be profit maximization for the benefit of shareholders

There are two perspectives on to whom organizations are socially responsible: the shareholder model and the stakeholder model. According to Nobel prize-winning economist Milton Friedman, the only social responsibility that organizations have is to satisfy their owners, that is, company shareholders. This view—called the ***shareholder model***—holds that the only social responsibility that businesses have is to maximize profits. By maximizing profit, the firm maximizes shareholder wealth and satisfaction. More specifically, as profits rise, the company stock owned by company shareholders generally increases in value. For example, the year after Microsoft released

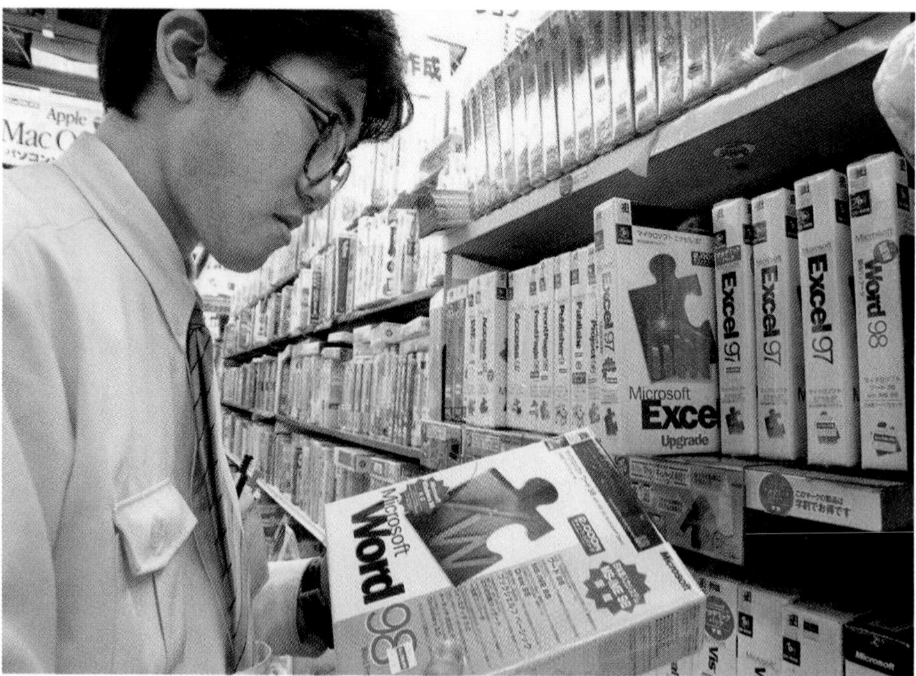

When successful products, such as Microsoft software, increase profits for a corporation, its stock prices tend to rise, increasing shareholders' wealth. © Corbis/AFP

its Windows 95 operating software, company earnings increased by 45 percent over the previous year. During this time, Microsoft's stock rebounded from a low of $58.25 to $90, increasing the wealth of Microsoft shareholders by 54.5 percent.

Friedman argues that it is socially irresponsible for companies to divert their time, money, and attention from maximizing profits to social causes and charitable organizations. The first problem he sees is that organizations cannot act effectively as moral agents for all company shareholders. While shareholders are likely to agree on investment issues concerning a company, it's highly unlikely that they possess common views on what social causes a company should or should not support. For example, after 25 years of support, AT&T announced that it would no longer provide cash grants to Planned Parenthood. An AT&T spokesperson said that "eighty percent of the decision to stop funding Planned Parenthood was based on its ever-increasing political nature, and its increasing attention to a very divisive issue [abortion]."[39] Rather than act as moral agents, Friedman argues that companies should maximize profits for shareholders. Shareholders can then use their time and increased wealth to contribute to the social causes, charities, or institutions they want, rather than those that companies want.

The second major problem, according to Friedman, is that the time, money, and attention diverted to social causes undermine market efficiency. In competitive markets, companies compete for raw materials, talented workers, customers, and investment funds. Spending money on social causes means there is less money to purchase quality materials or to hire talented workers who can produce a valuable product at a good price. If customers find the product less desirable, sales and profits will fall. If profits fall, stock prices will decrease and the company will have difficulty attracting investment funds that could be used to fund long-term growth. In the end, Friedman argues, diverting the firm's money, time, and resources to social causes hurts customers, suppliers, employees, and shareholders.

stakeholder model
theory of corporate responsibility which holds that management's most important responsibility, long-term survival, is achieved by satisfying the interests of multiple corporate stakeholders

stakeholders
persons or groups with a "stake" or legitimate interest in a company's actions

By contrast, under the ***stakeholder model***, management's most important responsibility is long-term survival (not just maximizing profits), which is achieved by satisfying the interests of multiple corporate stakeholders (not just shareholders). ***Stakeholders*** are people or groups with a legitimate interest in a company.[40] Since stakeholders are interested in and affected by the organization's actions, they have a "stake" in what those actions are. Consequently, stakeholder groups may try to influence the firm to act in their own interests. Figure 3.2 shows the various stakeholder groups that the organization must satisfy to assure long-term survival.

Been There,

Martin P. Connell, Chairperson of the Canadian Centre for Philanthropy

Martin P. Connell heads two organizations, Calmeadow, a charitable agency that lends funds in Canada, and Conwest Exploration Company Limited, a Toronto-based resource company with interests in oil and gas exploration and development, mining, and small-scale hydroelectric development. He is also Chairperson of the Canadian Centre for Philanthropy. As a businessperson and a philanthropist, he is uniquely qualified to speak about corporate social responsibility.

Q. How can corporations ensure that their involvement in the community is more effective?

A: Corporate giving is relatively small compared with individual giving, but it can set a campaign in motion. No fund-raiser who is trying to identify resources for initiatives at the community level would dream of not approaching a corporation for a leadership gift. That gift sends the signal that the community project is a good one and that it deserves broader support. Thereafter, it becomes easier to raise individual gifts. I believe the real force of corporate philanthropy is in its leadership role.

"I believe the real force of corporate philanthropy is in its leadership role."

Q. What are the greatest barriers to increasing corporate involvement in the community?

A. One of the barriers is the frustration of making the appropriate decision. Traditionally, when corporations would work in the community, it was with the "charitable elites": large institutions, hospitals, health-care institutions, scientific research groups in health care, universities and colleges, the United Way, the Salvation Army's Red Shield. That made it relatively straightforward. But now, with so much in the community being pushed down to the grassroots level, how do you sift through literally hundreds of applications that arrive on your doorstep and decide which ones add the most value to your community and reflect well on the corporation? These issues are difficult.

Q. How do we ensure that corporate investment in the community is sustainable?

A. Let me give you the example of the relationship that Calmeadow has with the Royal Bank in Nova Scotia. It is one example of a promising approach. Initially, it was a pilot project; then it became a long-term community-based loan fund. Now our hope is that it will become a sustainable institution. At the end of the cycle of support from the Royal Bank, this initiative should be up and running on its own, and won't need continual grant infusions. This is a paradigm we're starting to see in the philanthropic marketplace. How can we bring corporations into partnerships with charities and then create an exit point, three to five years down the road, so that the gift stops but the program doesn't?

Q. Like any other function in a corporation, community investment is becoming more accountable. What is the best way to prove there is a return on a corporation's investment?

A. Given that corporations are in the business of maximizing shareholder value and developing a healthy return on equity, I think the term "community investment" is a more thoughtful and appropriate term than "philanthropy." Once you start using the concept of investment, then you have to start considering the concepts of "due diligence" and "return on investment"—that is a healthy shift. One way to start is by raising the demands a corporation places on the charitable organizations it supports. You should expect organizations that are seeking funding to come back with objective studies that evaluate the success or failure of their initiatives. With charities now turning en masse to the corporate sector, they present a very challenging task for a corporation to make decisions about how to best allocate their resources. I think accountability is going to be the key issue over the next five years. Are charities giving value for money? Are they having the appropriate impact on the target group? Are they potentially sustainable with local and community resources? Are they well supported by the volunteer community?

Q. Don't you think that corporations already perceive that they are being asked to take on too much in terms of social responsibility?

A. Corporations should not be, and probably won't be, guilted into thinking they should be doing more. Nor should corporations feel they have to change their levels of giving unless they want to, or unless their shareholders want them to. However, those of us who have championed the model of a caring company would like to see corporations that are currently not giving, give 1 percent to achieve that goal. But that's only a part of our challenge. The issue, really, is how to apply resources more effectively.

Source: G.M. Khoury, "Corporate Responsibility & Community Service: An Interview with Martin P. Connell," *Canadian Business Review,* 1 July 1995. Martin Connell spoke recently in his offices in Toronto with George M. Khoury, Director, the Canadian Centre for Business in the Community. This interview was edited for inclusion in this text.

Done That

Being responsible to multiple stakeholders raises two basic questions. First, how does a company identify organizational stakeholders? Second, how does a company balance the needs of different stakeholders? Distinguishing between primary and secondary stakeholders can answer these questions.[41]

Figure 3.2 **Stakeholder Model of Corporate Social Responsibility**

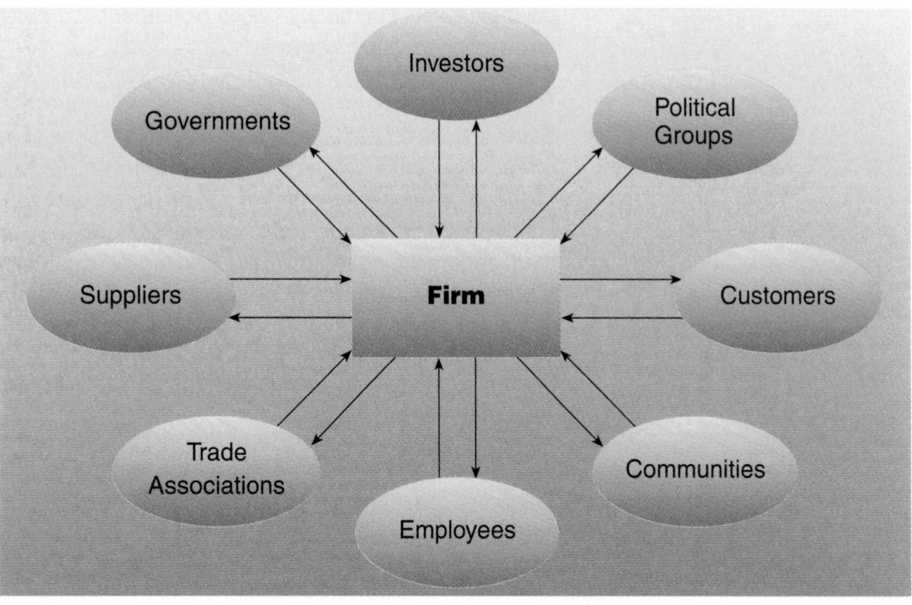

Source: T. Donaldson & L.E. Preston, "The Stakeholder Theory of the Corporation: Concepts, Evidence, and Implications," *Academy of Management Review* 20 (1995): 65-91.

primary stakeholder
any group on which an organization relies for its long-term survival

Some stakeholders are more important to the firm's survival than others. ***Primary stakeholders*** are groups, such as shareholders, employees, customers, suppliers, governments, and local communities, on which the organization depends for long-term survival. So when managers are struggling to balance the needs of different stakeholders, the stakeholder model suggests that the needs of primary stakeholders take precedence over the needs of secondary stakeholders. However, contrary to the shareholder model, no primary stakeholder group is more or less important than another, since all are critical to the firm's success and survival. So managers must try to satisfy the needs of all primary stakeholders. Table 3.5 displays a list of issues that organizations will probably have to address to keep their primary stakeholders satisfied.

Addressing the concerns of primary stakeholders is important, because if a stakeholder group becomes dissatisfied and terminates its relationship with the company, the company could be seriously harmed or go out of business. For example, when Kmart experienced financial troubles, it fell behind on payments to three major suppliers. These suppliers notified Kmart that they would not ship any more of their products to Kmart stores unless paid in cash before or at the time of delivery. The danger for Kmart was that this problem could spread to other stakeholder groups. On hearing that Kmart could not pay these suppliers, other Kmart suppliers might also demand to be paid in cash before delivery. With fewer products being delivered to stores, customers might quit shopping at Kmart if they couldn't find what they wanted. Either case could hurt Kmart's long-term business.[42]

secondary stakeholder
any group that can influence or be influenced by the company and can affect public perceptions about its socially responsible behavior

Secondary stakeholders, such as the media and special interest groups, can influence or be influenced by the company. Yet in contrast to primary stakeholders, they do not engage in regular transactions with the company and are not critical to its long-term survival. Consequently, meeting the needs of primary stakeholders is usually more important than meeting the needs of secondary stakeholders. While not critical to long-term

Table 3.5

Issues Important to Primary Stakeholders

Company

Company history, industry background, organization structure, economic performance, competitive environment, mission or purpose, corporate codes, stakeholder and social issues management systems.

Employees

Benefits, compensation and rewards, training and development, career planning, employee assistance programs, health promotion, absenteeism and turnover, leaves of absence, relationships with unions, dismissal and appeal, termination, layoffs, retirement and termination counseling, employment equity and discrimination, women in management and on the board, day care and family accommodation, employee communication, occupational health and safety, and part-time, temporary, or contract employees.

Shareholders

Shareholder communications and complaints, shareholder advocacy, shareholder rights, and other shareholder issues.

Customers

Customer communications, product safety, customer complaints, special customer services, and other customer issues.

Suppliers

Relative power, general policy, and other supplier issues.

Public Stakeholders

Public health, safety, and protection, conservation of energy and materials, environmental assessment of capital projects, other environmental issues, public policy involvement, community relations, social investment and donations.

Source: M.B.E. Clarkson, "A Stakeholder Framework for Analyzing and Evaluating Corporate Social Performance," *Academy of Management Review* 20 (1995): 92-117.

survival, secondary stakeholders are still important, because they can affect public perceptions and opinions about socially responsible behavior. For instance, most American kids in the 1960s and 1970s grew up eating tuna salad sandwiches, tuna casserole (with potato chips on top), and "Tuna Helper." However, by the mid-1980s, public perceptions about tuna fishermen and the tuna industry had turned negative, as environmental groups publicized the fact that approximately one hundred thousand dolphins were killed each year in the fishing nets used to catch tuna.[43] Consequently, many restaurants and schools protested by banning tuna from their menus.

So to whom are organizations socially responsible? Many, especially economists and financial analysts, continue to argue that organizations are only responsible to shareholders. However, since the Depression, when General Electric identified shareholders, employees, customers, and the general public as its stakeholders; since 1947, when Johnson & Johnson listed customers, employees, managers, and shareholders as its stakeholders; and since 1950, when Sears, Roebuck announced that its most important stakeholders were "customers, employees, community, and stockholders," top managers have increasingly come to believe that they and their companies must be socially responsible to their stakeholders.[44] Surveys show that as many as 80 percent of top-level managers believe that it is unethical to focus just on shareholders. Similarly, 29 states have changed their laws to allow company boards of directors to consider the needs of employees, creditors, suppliers, customers, and local communities, besides those of shareholders.[45] So while there is not complete agreement, a majority of

Back to the Future

Will Mother Nature Become a Corporate Stakeholder?

In a *Harvard Business Review* article entitled "It's Not Easy Being Green," authors Noah Walley and Bradley Whitehead commented on Texaco's plans to spend $1.5 billion a year to reduce pollution emissions. What bothered Walley and Bradley was that Texaco planned to spend $7.5 billion over five years, an amount three times larger than Texaco's book value (an accounting measure of a company's worth) and two times larger than the value of all of the company's assets. They asked, "Can anyone argue convincingly that an investment of this magnitude will yield a positive financial return to shareholders? We doubt it."

According to Professor Paul Shrivastava, there is one "person" who would argue that this is a smart investment. That "person" is Mother Nature. Shrivastava believes that in the future, companies will need to shift from the traditional industrial view of management to an ecocentric view. The industrial view emphasizes the production of products and services for customers and the creation of wealth for shareholders. Shrivastava argues that industrial management is based on anthropocentrism, which "asserts the separateness, uniqueness, primacy, and superiority of the human species." From an anthropocentric perspective, raw materials and natural resources are expendable. Further, there is no moral obligation to protect or sustain natural settings, wildlife, or resources.

By contrast, ecocentric management:

1. assumes that, along with customers, suppliers, and shareholders, Mother Nature is a primary corporate stakeholder.
2. strives for ecofriendly products through better design, packaging, and use of materials.
3. tries to minimize the use of virgin materials and maximize the use of recycled materials.
4. attempts to eliminate air- and water-based pollution.
5. tries to minimize the life-cycle cost of products and services: for example, after a product like a lawn mower "dies," there are collection, recycling, incineration, or landfill costs associated with full disposal of the product.

Shrivastava says that an industrial ecosystem is a good illustration of ecocentric management. Since one company's industrial waste can be another company's energy or raw material, industrial ecosystems are collections of companies that work together to minimize the use of virgin natural resources and overall waste and pollution. For example, instead of condensing its used steam into water and dumping it into the local water supply, a coal-fired power plant in Denmark sells its used steam as energy to an enzyme plant and an oil refinery. In return, the oil refinery sells treated waste water back to the electric plant, which then uses it in a cooling process. The refinery also sells the power plant desulfurized gas, which is emitted as oil is manufactured. The power plant sells surplus ash to a cement company, which mixes it into the cement it produces. In turn, the cement company sells low-grade cement to a wallboard plant, which uses the cement in place of virgin gypsum, which would otherwise have been mined from the earth. Together, these companies reduce landfill waste, airborne pollution, and water-based pollution. They also have successfully reduced the use of water and other virgin materials.

Will ecocentric management replace industrial management? Will Mother Nature become a primary corporate stakeholder? No one knows for sure. However, more than 800 companies have joined the Buy Recycled Business Alliance. Begun in 1993 by 25 blue-chip companies, ranging from American Airlines to Wal-Mart, the goal of the BRBA is to educate its members about recycling. In just the first year alone, the 25 founding companies purchased $10 billion in recycled goods. Membership is free and is open to any business. If you think ecocentric management might be part of your company's future, call the National Recycling Coalition (202-625-6406) for a membership kit and a 30-page guidebook on how to implement a recycling program and where to buy reusable and recycled goods.

Sources: D. Biddle, "Recycling for Profit: The New Green Business Frontier," *Harvard Business Review*, November-December 1993, 145-156. "Saving Cash with Second-Time-Around Goods," *Inc.* 16, no. 1 (May 1994): 162. P. Shrivastava, "Ecocentric Management for a Risk Society?" *Academy of Management Review* 20 (1995): 118-137.

opinion makers would make the case that companies must be socially responsible to their stakeholders.

Review 6
To Whom Are Organizations Socially Responsible?

Social responsibility is a business's obligation to benefit society. Who are organizations socially responsible to? According to the shareholder model, the only social responsibility that organizations have is to maximize shareholder wealth by maximizing company profits. According to the stakeholder model, companies must satisfy the needs and interests of multiple corporate stakeholders, not just shareholders. However, the needs of primary stakeholders, on which the organization relies for its existence, take precedence over those of secondary stakeholders.

7 For What Are Organizations Socially Responsible?

If organizations are to be socially responsible to stakeholders, just what are they to be socially responsible for? As illustrated in Figure 3.3, companies can best benefit their stakeholders by fulfilling their economic, legal, ethical, and discretionary responsibilities.[46] Figure 3.3 indicates that economic and legal responsibilities play a larger part in a company's social responsibility than do ethical and discretionary responsibilities. However, the relative importance of economic, legal, ethical, and discretionary responsibilities depends on the expectations that society has toward corporate social responsibility at a particular point in time.[47] A century ago, society expected businesses to meet their economic and legal responsibilities and little else. Today, however, when society judges whether businesses are socially re-

Figure 3.3 **Social Responsibilities**

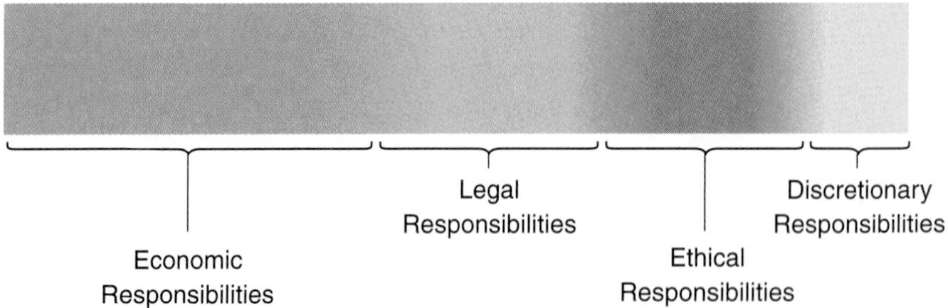

Source: A.B. Carroll, "A Three-Dimensional Conceptual Model of Corporate Performance," *Academy of Management Review* 4 (1979): 497-505.

sponsible, ethical and discretionary responsibilities are considerably more important than they used to be.

economic responsibility
the expectation that a company will make a profit by producing a valued product or service

Historically, ***economic responsibility***, making a profit by producing a product or service valued by society, has been a business's most basic social responsibility. Organizations that don't meet their financial and economic expectations come under tremendous pressure. For example, when Apple Computer reported a quarterly loss of $69 million on sales of more than $11 billion, an investor stood up at Apple's annual shareholder meeting and stated (to Apple's CEO, Michael Spindler), "You have mismanaged assets, you have wasted a valuable franchise, and you have brought a great company to its knees. Mr. Spindler, it is time to go."[48] One week later, Spindler was let go from his job as Apple's CEO.

legal responsibility
the expectation that a company will obey society's laws and regulations

Legal responsibility is the expectation that companies will obey a society's laws and regulations as they try to meet their economic responsibilities. For example, under the 1990 Clean Air Act, the smell of fresh baked bread is now illegal. Actually, it's not the smell that is illegal, but the ethanol that is emitted when baking bread.[49] Ethanol itself is nontoxic; however, it contributes to pollution, because it promotes the formation of the harmful atmospheric compound ozone. Consequently, to meet the law, large bakery plants may have to spend millions to purchase catalytic oxidizers that remove ethanol emissions.[50]

ethical responsibility
the expectation that a company will not violate accepted principles of right and wrong when conducting its business

Ethical responsibility is society's expectation that organizations will not violate accepted principles of right and wrong when conducting their business. Because different stakeholders may disagree about what is or is not ethical, meeting ethical responsibilities is more difficult than meeting economic or legal responsibilities. For example, several years ago a jury awarded an 81-year-old woman $2.9 million in punitive damages to compensate for the third-degree burns she suffered after spilling coffee in her lap while going through a McDonald's drive-through window.[51] Most Americans thought the verdict was ludicrous, that it was just another example of a money-hungry jury out to pick the pockets of a big company. Was it illegal for McDonald's to serve coffee at 180 degrees, on average 20 degrees hotter than other restaurants? No. But after receiving nearly 700 customer complaints about coffee burns, was it right for McDonald's to continue serving coffee at 180 degrees? After receiving 700 complaints, was it right for McDonald's not to warn customers about the danger of second- or third-degree burns (which can require skin-graft surgery)? McDonald's now has warning signs about hot beverages posted on its drive-through windows, and it has lowered the temperature of the hot drinks it sells.[52]

discretionary responsibilities
the expectation that a company will voluntarily serve a social role beyond its economic, legal, and ethical responsibilities

Discretionary responsibilities pertain to the social roles that businesses play in society beyond their economic, legal, and ethical responsibilities. For example, American Express and its cardholders have teamed up with the charitable organization Share Our Strength to fight hunger in America. Every time someone uses an American Express Card to make a purchase, American Express donates three cents to Share Our Strength.[53] While three cents doesn't seem like much, the hundreds of thousands of daily American Express transactions have produced $10.7 million in contributions in two years. Discretionary responsibilities are voluntary. Companies will not be considered unethical if they don't perform them. However, today, corporate stakeholders expect companies to do much more than in the past to meet their discretionary responsibilities.

BLASTFROMTHEPAST

100 Years of Corporate Philanthropy

Corporate philanthropy has changed tremendously in the last century. For example, in the 1800s, under the doctrine of *ultra vires* (behavior beyond the incidental powers of the firm), it was illegal for companies to make charitable contributions. By law, corporate funds could only be spent for "business-related" purposes. One of the first legal tests of *ultra vires* was the 1881 Old Colony Railroad case, in which the company financially supported a "world peace jubilee and international music festival."[54] The court ruled that contributing money to the music festival had damaged stockholders, because the festival was not business-related.

Fifteen years later, in 1896, courts broadened the definition of what was considered business-related. In Steinway v. Steinway & Sons et al. (1896), the court ruled that it was appropriate for the Steinway company to use its funds to build homes, churches, and schools for its employees. Though these acts clearly benefited local neighborhoods and towns, they were viewed as business-related, because they also benefited Steinway's employees. So by the late 1800s, providing social benefits to employees had become an acceptable and legal form of corporate philanthropy.

The next significant change occurred in 1917, during World War I. The Red Cross, with the support of President Woodrow Wilson, began its "Red Cross dividend" program, which used a creative work-around to avoid legal restrictions on corporate giving. Needing to raise $100 million to meet wartime needs, the Red Cross mailed a standard form letter, encouraging corporations to declare a special earnings dividend that would be paid directly to the Red Cross rather than to corporate shareholders. Interested companies then asked shareholders to vote on the special dividend. Freed from the legal restrictions that had previously prevented this kind of corporate giving, shareholders from more than 1,100 companies raised nearly $20 million by voting to declare Red Cross dividends. Contrary to negative public perceptions of businesses at the time, this indicated that companies and their shareholders were willing to make charitable contributions.

The next major change occurred from 1936 to 1945 as corporate giving increased by a factor of nine to $270 million a year (the equivalent of billions in today's dollars). Unlike the Red Cross dividend, most of these contributions were encouraged by the excess profits tax that, after a particular level, taxed 90 cents out of each extra dollar of profit. However, companies could avoid the excess profits tax by making donations to their local communities. While most companies gave because it was in their financial interest to do so, it's important to know that corporate giving dropped by only 19 percent the year that congress repealed the excess profits tax, and by only 11 percent two years following repeal. In other words, by the early 1950s, corporate philanthropy had become the right thing to do, even if companies did not receive a direct financial benefit.

In the late 1940s and early 1950s, another significant change in corporate philanthropy took place. The American Bar Association Committee on Business Corporations suggested that states change the basic legal definition of a corporation, so that companies could make donations without having to demonstrate business-relatedness. Within six years, 27 states had adopted the ABA recommendation to encourage corporate giving. Remaining states adopted the change after a 1953 U.S. Supreme Court ruling. The Supreme Court let stand a lower court's ruling that it was legal for A.P. Smith Manufacturing, a New Jersey company, to donate $1,500 to Princeton University, despite any obvious financial benefit to the company.

Today, with corporate giving and philanthropy legal for more than 40 years, U.S. companies donate approximately $6 billion a year to communities, causes, and charities.

Sources: L. Light & P. Eng, "Charity Cases: When Charity Doesn't Begin at Home," *Business Week*, 27 November 1995. M. Sharfman, "Changing Institutional Rules: The Evolution of Corporate Philanthropy: 1883-1953," *Business and Society* 33, no. 34 (December 1994): 236.

Review 7
For What Are Organizations Socially Responsible?

Companies can best benefit their stakeholders by fulfilling their economic, legal, ethical, and discretionary responsibilities. Being profitable, or meeting one's economic responsibility, is a business's most basic social responsibility. Legal responsibility consists of following a society's laws and regulations. Ethical responsibility means not violating accepted principles of right and wrong when doing business. Discretionary responsibilities are social responsibilities beyond basic economic, legal, and ethical responsibilities.

8 Responses to Demands for Social Responsibility

social responsiveness
the strategy chosen by a company to respond to stakeholders' economic, legal, ethical, or discretionary expectations concerning social responsibility

Social responsiveness is the strategy chosen by a company to respond to stakeholders' economic, legal, ethical, or discretionary expectations concerning social responsibility. A social responsibility problem exists whenever company actions do not meet stakeholder expectations. One model of social responsiveness, shown in Figure 3.4, identifies four strategies for responding to social responsibility problems: reactive, defensive, accommodative, and proactive. These strategies differ in the extent to which the company is willing to act to meet or exceed society's expectations.

reactive strategy
a social responsiveness strategy where a company chooses to do less than society expects and to deny responsibility for problems

A company using a ***reactive strategy*** will do less than society expects. It may deny responsibility for a problem or "fight all the way" any suggestions that the company should solve a problem. For example, *Consumer Reports* magazine came out with a report showing that the Suzuki Samurai would tip over when drivers changed lanes or went around corners at normal speeds. The Samurai, a four-wheel-drive vehicle, was easy to tip over because it was a lightweight vehicle with a high center of gravity and a narrow wheelbase. Rather than admit this safety problem, Suzuki Corporation immediately embarked on a multimillion dollar television advertising campaign to dispute *Consumer Reports'* findings.[55]

defensive strategy
a social responsiveness strategy where a company chooses to admit responsibility for a problem but do the least required to meet societal expectations

By contrast, a company using a ***defensive strategy*** would admit responsibility for a problem, but would do the least required to meet societal expectations. For example, if Suzuki had agreed to recall all of the Samurais so that it could fix the vehicles, it would have been using a defensive strategy. After a year of denying there was a problem (a reactive strategy), Suzuki did eventually adopt a defensive strategy. It announced that it would quit selling the Samurai and begin selling the Suzuki Sidekick. Because the Sidekick was shorter, heavier, and wider, it would not tip over at normal driving speeds.[56]

Figure 3.4 **Social Responsiveness**

Reaction	**Defense**	**Accommodation**	**Proaction**
Fight all the way	Do only what is required	Be progressive	Lead the industry

Withdrawal — Public Relations Approach — Legal Approach — Bargaining — Problem Solving

DO NOTHING ⟷ DO MUCH

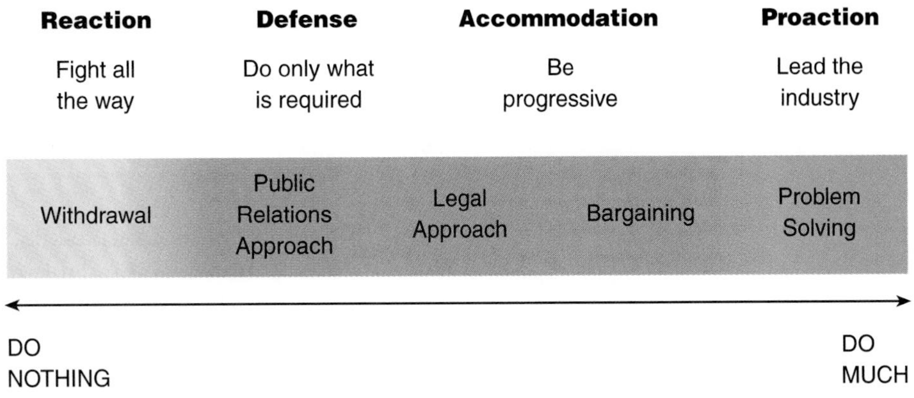

Source: Adapted from A.B. Carroll, "A Three-Dimensional Conceptual Model of Corporate Performance," *Academy of Management Review* 4 (1979): 497-505.

accommodative strategy a social responsiveness strategy where a company chooses to accept responsibility for a problem and do all that society expects to solve problems

A company using an ***accommodative strategy*** would accept responsibility for a problem and take a progressive approach by doing all that was expected to solve the problem. In contrast to Suzuki, Nissan Motors took an accommodative strategy when it voluntarily recalled 33,000 minivans that were prone to catch fire when the engine's fan belt broke. Nissan spent $45 million to fix the vans, installing a brand new heavy-duty cooling system with warning lights in each vehicle. However, it also reimbursed customers for 900 vans that were beyond repair. Then it destroyed the 900 vans, so that they could not be resold to unsuspecting used-car buyers. To maintain customers' goodwill, Nissan also made other major repairs on the vans, such as air conditioning or transmission repairs, for free.[57]

proactive strategy a social responsiveness strategy where a company anticipates responsibility for a problem before it occurs and would do more than society expects to address the problem

Finally, a company using a ***proactive strategy*** would anticipate responsibility for a problem before it occurred, do more than expected to address the problem, and lead the industry in its approach. For example, in 1990, McDonald's began its McRecycle USA program to increase its use of recycled materials in McDonald's restaurants. Of course, there's nothing proactive or leading edge about a company recycling program. Lots of companies have them. However, McDonald's discovered that it simply could not buy the recycled materials it needed. There just weren't enough recycled materials available at the time. McDonald's innovative solution was to take out full-page advertisements in newspapers around the country. These advertisements let recycling companies know that it was committed to spending $100 million a year to buy recycled products for its restaurants! In the advertisement, McDonald's listed a toll-free 800 phone number that potential suppliers could call to find out what materials the company needed. The ads were a phenomenal success. McDonald's now spends more than $250 million a year on recycled products in its playgrounds, floor and ceiling tiles, and paper products.[58]

Review 8
Responses to Demands for Social Responsibility

Social responsiveness is a company response to stakeholders' demands for socially responsible behavior. There are four social responsiveness strategies. When a company uses a reactive strategy, it denies responsibility for a problem. When it uses a defensive strategy, it takes responsibility for a problem, but does the minimum required to solve it. When a company uses an accommodative strategy, it accepts responsibility for problems and does all that society expects to solve them. Finally, when a company uses a proactive strategy, it does much more than expected to solve social responsibility problems.

9 Social Responsibility and Economic Performance

One question that managers often ask is, "Does it pay to be socially responsible?" While this is an understandable question, asking whether social responsibility pays is a bit like asking if giving to your favorite charity will help you get a better-paying job. The obvious answer is no. There is not an inherent relationship between social responsibility and economic performance. However, this doesn't stop supporters of corporate social responsibility from claiming a positive relationship. For example, one study shows that the Domini 400 Social Index, which is a stock fund consisting of 400 socially responsible companies, has out-performed the Standard and Poor's 500 (an index of 500 stocks representative of the entire economy) by nearly 5 percent. On the other hand, critics have plenty of facts to support their claim that social responsibility hurts economic performance. For example, another study of 42 socially responsible mutual funds found that the socially responsible companies under-performed the Standard and Poor's 500 by 8 percent.[59]

When it comes to social responsibility and economic performance, the first reality is that it can sometimes cost a company significantly if it chooses to be socially responsible. During the 1980s, American multinational corporations were under intense public pressure to withdraw their operations from South Africa. Political activists argued that if businesses withdrew from South Africa, the white-controlled government would be hurt economically. Thus, it would be more difficult for it to maintain its system of apartheid against black South Africans. Many companies chose to pull their businesses out of South Africa. Yet when they did, they paid a steep price, selling corporate land, buildings, and equipment at a fraction of their value. Furthermore, within days of announcing that they were leaving South Africa, their company stock price dropped an average of 5.5 percent.[60] Here, socially responsible behavior not only harmed the company financially, but harmed its shareholders financially, too. Nonetheless, hundreds of top managers still felt it was the right thing to do.

The second reality of social responsibility and economic performance is that sometimes it does pay to be socially responsible. A good example is Ben & Jerry's Homemade Ice Cream. Ben & Jerry's started in 1978 when founders Ben Cohen and Jerry Greenfield mailed away for a $5 course on how to make ice cream. Today, Ben & Jerry's is as well known for its super premium ice cream as it is for its reputation as a socially responsible company. Ben & Jerry's donates 7.5 percent of its pretax profits to social causes, donating more than $800,000 in 1993 to charitable groups supporting AIDS patients, the homeless, and the environment.[61] The company buys brownies from a bakery that employs homeless workers and blueberries from Native American Indian tribes. Moreover, customers buy Ben & Jerry's ice cream because it tastes great *and* because they want to support a socially responsible company. As Ben Cohen says, "We see ourselves as somewhat of a social service agency and somewhat of an ice cream company."[62]

The third reality of social responsibility and economic performance is that while socially responsible behavior may be "the right thing to do," it does not guarantee profitability. Socially responsible companies experience the same ups and downs in economic performance that traditional businesses do. For example, after a year in which neither market share nor profits grew and the company's stock dropped 72 percent in value, Ben Cohen announced that he was stepping aside as Ben & Jerry's CEO. A "professional manager" who is now charged with turning around the company's financial performance replaced him.

However, while Ben & Jerry's struggled, Seattle-based Starbucks Coffee, which markets itself as a socially responsible company, grew from 11 to more than 600 gourmet coffee shops nationwide. Starbucks pays its coffee shop workers much more than minimum wage, provides full health insurance coverage to anyone who works at least 20 hours a week, and gives

Starbucks Coffee implements its philosophy of social responsibility by taking good care of its employees and contributing generously to CARE, a relief agency that benefits coffee-growing regions.

employees with six or more months at the company the chance to participate in its "Bean Stock" stock options program. Besides taking good care of its employees, Starbucks also makes an annual six-figure charitable contribution to CARE, an international relief agency, for feeding, clothing, and educating the poor in the coffee-growing regions where it gets its coffee beans.[63]

In the end, if company management chooses a proactive or accommodative strategy toward social responsibility (rather than a defensive or reactive strategy), it should do so because it wants to benefit society and its corporate stakeholders, not because it expects a better financial return.

Review 9
Social Responsibility and Economic Performance

Does it pay to be socially responsible? Sometimes it costs and sometimes it pays. Overall, there is no clear relationship between social responsibility and economic performance. Consequently, managers should not expect an economic return from socially responsible corporate activities. If your company chooses to practice a proactive or accommodative social responsibility strategy, it should do so to better society and not to improve its financial performance.

WhatReallyHappened?

In the opening case, Disney faced an issue confronting many companies in the 90s: Should the company provide domestic-partner benefits to same-sex partners and unmarried, heterosexual partners? Here is what Disney decided to do.

What is the ethical thing to do in this situation?

Ethical behavior follows accepted standards of right and wrong. However, it's difficult to judge what's ethical in this instance, because there are no accepted standards when it comes to domestic-partner benefits. Lotus Software (now owned by IBM) was one of the first major corporations to offer domestic-partner benefits in 1991. Since then, an additional 400 U.S. companies have decided to offer domestic-partner benefits. Yet most companies still only offer medical benefits to married couples or to parents with children.

Three factors influence the ethical decisions that managers make: the ethical intensity of the decision, the moral development of the manager, and the ethical principles used to solve the problem. For example, the principle of self-interest holds that you should "never take any action that is not in the long-term self-interests of yourself and the organization to which you belong." In terms of self-interest, one of the biggest concerns that companies, including Disney, have had about domestic-partner benefits is the cost. Because of the increased chance of AIDS among male partners, they feared that the cost would be prohibitive. However, companies have found that roughly 80 percent of the couples who sign up for domestic-partner benefits are opposite-sex partners. Furthermore, nearly three-quarters of the same-sex partners are female rather than male. Finally, the Center for Disease Control estimates that the lifetime cost of treating AIDS, about $119,000, is much less than the cost of treating cancer, coronary bypass surgery, or premature birth, the latter of which can run as high as $1 million.

So what did Disney decide? Disney eventually decided to provide domestic-partner benefits to same-sex partners. A Disney spokesperson said, "We constantly review our benefits. We made this decision because it brings our health benefits in line with our corporate nondiscrimination policy." Analysts speculate that Disney started the program to help attract and retain talented workers who were leaving to get domestic-partner benefits at other entertainment companies.

If Disney offers benefits to domestic partners, is it morally obligated to offer the same benefits to the live-in partners of unmarried, heterosexual employees?

Disney decided not to offer domestic-partner benefits to unmarried, heterosexual couples, but declined to explain why. Was it unethical for them to exclude unmarried heterosexual couples? Maybe, but again we need to recognize that judgments about what is or is not ethical depend on the ethical intensity of the decision, one's moral development, and the ethical principles used to solve the problem.

For example, the principle of government requirements holds that you should "never take any action that violates the law, for the law represents the minimal moral standards of our society." While it's legal to offer domestic-partner benefits, Disney's refusal to give full benefits to single, heterosexual partners may lead to a discrimination charge on the basis of sexual orientation or marital status. On the other hand, Disney would likely argue that since state laws don't sanction homosexual marriage the way they do heterosexual marriage, it is simply making up for this disparity by offering the same benefits to homosexual partners (who can't legally marry) that it does to married heterosexual partners.

Who is interested in or affected by this decision, and how do we decide whose interests take precedence?

There are two views on this issue. The shareholder model says that Disney should only concern itself with what its shareholders think of domestic-partner programs. And if Disney can convince its shareholders that the costs are low and the benefits are high, then the shareholders would probably approve, because it will help the company be more profitable.

By contrast, the stakeholder model says that companies must satisfy the needs and interests of multiple corporate stakeholders. The problem for Disney is that as a highly visible entertainment company, it has to try to balance the needs of many different stakeholder groups. For example, prior to approving domestic-partner benefits, Rick Leed, a gay man who works for Disney and runs the production company that filmed the TV show "Home Improvement," said, "Disney is supposed to be a family company, yet they don't recognize my family." However, Rev. Louis Sheldon, who heads an advocacy group called the Traditional Values Coalition, stated, "With the understanding that the homosexual agenda has penetrated Hollywood, it should come as no surprise that Disney now supports anti-family values."

So if Disney is supposed to satisfy the needs of multiple stakeholders, and the stakeholders disagree, how does it decide whose wishes take precedence? The stakeholder model argues that the needs of primary stakeholders (customers, employees, suppliers, shareholders, etc.) on which the organization relies for its existence take precedence over those of secondary stakeholders (the press, advocacy groups). Does this mean that Disney can just ignore secondary stakeholders like the Traditional Value Coalition? No. In fact, Disney is very concerned about these groups and their perceptions of the company.

Is it more socially responsible to offer benefits to domestic partners or not to offer those benefits?

Social responsibility is a business's obligation to pursue policies, make decisions, and take actions that benefit society. Unfortunately, there is little agreement on what does or does not benefit society. For instance, is Disney benefiting society by giving more people good health insurance, life insurance, and retirement benefits, or is it harming society and undermining family values by giving full benefits to unmarried workers? Unfortunately, managers are not likely to find easy answers to these questions. Corporate social responsibility is one of the most difficult areas for companies to address. At a minimum, companies can begin to fulfill their social responsibility by trying to meet their economic, legal, ethical, and discretionary responsibilities.

Sources: "Baptists Unresponsive to Disney Boycott," *The Providence Journal-Bulletin*, 2 May 1998. V. Griffith, "Welcome to Your Friendlier Company," *Financial Times*, 9 March 1998. D.J. Jefferson, "Family Matters: Gay Employees Win Benefits for Partners at More Corporations," *The Wall Street Journal*, 18 March 1994, A1. J. Mason, "Domestic-Partner Benefits," *Management Review*, 1 November 1995, 53-55. P. Perry, "Benefits for Nontraditional Partners," *Folio: The Magazine for Magazine Management*, 1 November 1995, 62-63. B. Svetkey, "Disney Catches Hell: Gay and Subliminal Messages at Mickey & Co. Bring on the Religious Right's Wrath," *Entertainment Weekly*, 15 December 1995, 42. C. Woodyard & D. Lee, "Disney to Give Benefits to Partners of Gay Workers," *Los Angeles Times*, 7 October 1995, 1.

Key Terms

accommodative strategy p. 109

concentration of effect p. 90

conventional level of moral development p. 91

defensive strategy p. 109

discretionary responsibilities p. 107

economic responsibility p. 107

ethical behavior p. 83

ethical intensity p. 90

ethical responsibility p. 107

ethics p. 82

legal responsibility p. 107

magnitude of consequences p. 90

overt integrity test p. 94

personal aggression p. 86

personality-based integrity test p. 94

political deviance p. 85

post conventional level of moral development p. 92

preconventional level of moral development p. 91

primary stakeholder p. 103

principle of distributive justice p. 93

principle of government requirements p. 93

principle of individual rights p. 93

principle of long-term self-interest p. 92

principle of personal virtue p. 92

principle of religious injunctions p. 93

principle of utilitarian benefits p. 93

proactive strategy p. 109

probability of effect p. 90

production deviance p. 85

property deviance p. 85

proximity of effect p. 90

reactive strategy p. 109

secondary stakeholder p. 103

shareholder model p. 100

shrinkage p. 85

social consensus p. 90

social responsibility p. 99

social responsiveness p. 109

stakeholder model p. 101

stakeholders p. 101

temporal immediacy p. 90

whistleblowing p. 98

workplace deviance p. 85

What Would You Do-II?

***Anytown Daily Herald*, Anytown, USA**

You've been in editorial meetings all morning, trying to figure out whom the newspaper should endorse for mayor. It wasn't fun. The meeting lasted 90 minutes longer than planned, and half of your staff is angry about whom the paper is endorsing. But as the newspaper's publisher, you get the "big bucks" to make the tough calls. As you sit down at your desk, the computer monitor shows 13 new e-mails and the phone light is blinking. Let's see, Wednesday, 2:00 p.m. Your best guess is that it's got 10 messages on it. There's also a yellow Post-it note sitting in the middle of your keyboard that says "Rent-All just bought a year's worth of full-page ads! Can you believe it? This will really help with cash flow! Sarah."

Sarah is the *Herald's* new sales director. She's been working on the folks at Rent-All for three months. This is her first big new account since moving into the sales director job last year. Rent-All is one of those places where you can rent a TV, stereo, couch, or refrigerator for a small weekly payment. Since you're renting these products, you can bring them back whenever you want. However, if you make all of your weekly payments for a typical period of 18 months (the time period can vary), you own the product; hence the phrase "rent to own."

The problem is that you're not sure that you want Rent-All's business. Contrary to common belief, newspapers don't have to take a business's advertisement. For example, monthly revenues dropped about 2 percent after you decided to quit printing advertisements for topless bars and adult video stores. It was easy money, too, because the ads were guaranteed to run week after week, month after month. But since you believed that these businesses exploited women and were bad for the community, it was a simple decision to make. The *Daily Herald* just would not run those ads anymore.

You have a similar concern about Rent-All. Your editorial page writers have been complaining that Rent-All overcharges its customers, most of whom are poor and have bad credit records (which prevents them from buying appliances and refrigerators on credit at other stores). For example, Rent-All lists a purchase price of $290 for a small microwave oven. However, if you "rent to own" by making weekly payments for 18 months, the total cost of the microwave rises to $551. By contrast, the same microwave lists for $140 at a nearby discount store. Similarly, with 18 months of payments, you can "rent to own" a $299 television for $920, a $290 videocassette recorder for $1,004, and a $399 washer for $1,086. In each case, the cost of "renting to own" is two and a half to three and a half times the original purchase cost. Amazingly, the effective annual rate of interest on these products is 200 percent, 231 percent, and 171 percent, nearly ten times the maximum rates that state and federal laws permit for credit cards (usually 18 percent to 21 percent).

However, when you asked your business writers about the rent-to-own business, they said that the editorial page writers just don't understand the basics of the "rent-to-own" business. First, there's no such thing as interest payments or an annual rate of interest when you rent something. People who rent apartments don't pay interest; they just make a monthly payment. The same thing holds true for Rent-All's customers, who pay weekly or monthly fees when renting a big-screen TV, couch, or VCR. Second, customers have the option of buying, but don't have to buy. They can bring the product back whenever they want. For example, if that 32-inch TV isn't good enough for watching the Super Bowl, all they have to do is bring it back. As long as their weekly payments are up to date, they can sign a new rental agreement and have that 40-inch picture-in-picture TV in their living room that afternoon. Third, not every rented product comes back in great shape. They're often returned dented, torn, scratched, or just not working. Finally, on average, 12 out of 100 rented products are stolen and never come back to the store.

You're not sure whom to believe. Is Rent-All ripping off the poor, or is it providing a service to customers who, because of their poor credit records, wouldn't otherwise be able to purchase or "rent-to-own" TVs, refrigerators, washers, and dryers? One thing you do know is that the *Daily Herald* could use Rent-All's advertising revenues. The cost of newsprint has soared in the last 18 months, shrinking the *Herald's* profit margins from 8 percent to 1 percent. So as publisher, you've got your own profit pressures to consider. But in the end, you want to do the right thing, too. **If you were the publisher of the *Daily Herald*, what would you do?** (Hint: Use the information in Section 4, "Influences on Ethical Decision Making," to analyze the case and justify your answer.)

Critical-Thinking Video Case

Ethics in Business: The Bank of Alma

Bank of Alma is a community bank with branches in Alma, Michigan, and surrounding communities. Alma is a small, rural community. Bank of Alma emphasizes customer service and individual attention. Ethics are incredibly important in the banking industry, especially for small, community banks that rely on word-of-mouth endorsements from satisfied customers.

In this video, you learn how the Bank of Alma encourages and practices ethical behavior as it handles customers' checking and saving accounts, or when it makes decisions to approve or deny loans for home mortgages or small businesses. As you watch the video, consider the following critical-thinking question.

Critical-Thinking Question

1. What are the ethical issues for the Bank of Alma?

Management Decisions

Should Joe Camel Be Snuffed Out?

Chances are, you already know that Joe Camel is the cartoon character used by the R.J. Reynolds Tobacco Company to advertise Camel cigarettes. Joe wears sunglasses and a T-shirt underneath a dark blazer. In advertisements, he's always shown in the company of his admiring friends and attractive "Josephine Camels." The odds are also very good that children know who Joe Camel is. Studies published in the *Journal of the American Medical Association* indicate that 30 percent of 3-year-olds and 91 percent of 6-year-olds can accurately identify Joe Camel. (Author's note: Being a researcher and a parent, I was naturally suspicious of these results. So I showed Joe Camel's picture to my kids, then ages nine, five, and three. All three said, "Daddy, that's Joe Camel." My wife and I were shocked that they knew, especially since we don't smoke, most of our friends don't smoke, and no one in our immediate families smokes either.)

Critics claim that R.J. Reynolds is purposely using Joe Camel to market cigarettes to underage smokers (anyone 17 or under). After all, what better way to appeal to kids than through a cartoon character? For example, studies estimate that since R.J. Reynolds began using Joe Camel to advertise Camel cigarettes in 1988, the percentage of smokers under 18 who smoke Camels has risen from less than 1 percent to nearly 33 percent. It's also estimated that nearly one-quarter of Camel's sales are to underage smokers. Studies also show that kids smoke the most heavily advertised brands, and Camel has been the second most-advertised brand of cigarette since 1988.

R.J. Reynolds strongly denies that Joe Camel is being used to encourage children and teenagers to smoke. The company points out that Joe may be widely recognized by youngsters, but that brand names like Ford, Chevrolet, Coca-Cola, and McDonald's have much wider recognition among 3-to-6-year-olds than Joe Camel. The company also argues that recognition of Joe Camel and Camel cigarettes is not the same as forming an intention to smoke Camels. Reynolds executives cite studies that show that peer pressure and whether their parents smoke are the two largest factors influencing children's decision to smoke.

Additional Internet Resources

- **American Cancer Society: Frequently Asked Questions (http://www.cancer.org/smokeout/faq.html/).** This site contains information about smoking, children, teenagers, and cigarette advertising.
- **Welcome to the R.J. Reynolds Home Page (http://www.greensboro.com/rjrt/).** This site is the home page for R.J. Reynolds Corporation, manufacturer of Camel cigarettes. It contains information on smokers' rights and on steps that Reynolds is taking to prevent teens and children from starting to smoke.
- **INFACT's Tobacco Industry Campaign (http://www.boutell.com/infact/infact.html).** INFACT is an advocacy group against marketing cigarettes to children. This site contains INFACT's arguments and evidence that cigarette companies are purposely targeting cigarette advertising toward children.

Questions

1. Is it ethical or socially responsible for Reynolds to advertise cigarettes using a cartoon character like Joe Camel? Why or why not?
2. Reynolds is under extreme pressure from protest groups and the medical field to quit using Joe Camel for Camel cigarette advertising. However, Joe Camel is by far Reynolds's most successful advertising campaign. Should Reynolds keep Joe Camel around to advertise Camel cigarettes, or should Reynolds snuff Joe Camel out? If Reynolds cannot satisfy all of its stakeholders, which stakeholders should it try to please?

Sources: A.M. Freedman & S.L. Hang, "Marketing & Media: Reynolds Marketing Strategy Sought to Get Young Adults to Smoke Camels," *The Wall Street Journal*, 2 November 1995, B10. K. Goldman, "A Stable of Females Has Joined Joe Camel in Controversial Cigarette Ad Campaign," *The Wall Street Journal*, 18 February 1994, B1. L. Jones, "Surgeon General, AMA: Snuff Out 'Old Joe Camel,'" *American Medical News* 35, no. 2 (23 March 1992): 1. J. Perrone, "Tobacco Firm Attacks JAMA Ad Studies," *American Medical News* 35, no. 2 (2 March 1992): 3. B. Williams, "Burned by Image, Joe Camel Packs It in for Now," *News & Observer-Raleigh NC*, 26 October 1995.

Management Decisions

Speeding Tickets or a Poor Credit Record?

Who is the poorer risk for an insurance company: someone who has been caught speeding numerous times or someone who has a bad credit record? Logically, it should be the speeder, because everyone knows that "speed kills," that speeders are in more accidents themselves, and that speeders cause other drivers to have accidents. In fact, government studies confirm that speed is one of the major causes of fatal car accidents. Everyone knows this to be true!

Surprisingly, however, the speeder is less likely to file benefit claims with an insurance company than someone with a poor credit record. Why? It's not exactly clear. However, insurance executives suspect that people who are good with their money are reliable and conscientious about driving (except for speeding). On the other hand, they speculate that people with poor credit records may be more likely to file false claims. Keith Corley, a Farmers Insurance Group agent in Fort Worth, Texas, said, "When people have bad credit and need money, one way to solve their credit problems is to burn their house down."

Regardless of the reasons, auto insurers have found that adding credit record information to a standard auto insurance application helps them do a better job of screening good insurance risks, that is, identifying people who will pay their premiums each month and won't file claims for insurance benefits. For example, after examining the records of 60,000 customers, Allstate Insurance, one of the U.S.'s largest insurance companies, found that policyholders with poor credit records were 40 percent more expensive to insure than those with standard credit records. Specifically, Allstate paid out 80 cents in auto insurance benefits for each $1 in auto premiums for policyholders with good credit records and a couple of speeding tickets. By contrast, it paid out more than a $1 in auto insurance benefits for each $1 premium paid by policyholders with perfect driving records but bad credit records. "The data is absolutely overwhelming," says Steve Sheffey, Allstate associate counsel. "There is a very strong correlation between serious financial instability and future loss." Allstate believes that not issuing auto insurance to drivers with poor credit records will allow it to charge 5 percent less for auto coverage.

Critics charge that insurers, like Allstate, who use credit records when deciding whether to offer insurance coverage are simply discriminating against the poor and minorities. Studies show that credit problems are inversely related to one's level of income. For example, the Federal Reserve found that 20 percent of families with annual incomes less than $20,000 typically paid at least one monthly bill late compared to only 6 percent of households with incomes between $100,000 and $250,000. Others simply doubt that credit records are accurate predictors of insurance risk. Jane Danduran, president of Danduran and Associates Insurance Agency in Columbus, Ohio, said, "I don't think that someone who is having financial problems is necessarily a bad risk. I don't think that makes them a moral hazard."

Questions

1. Is it unethical or socially irresponsible for auto insurers to use credit records to screen applicants for auto insurance? Explain.
2. There is often disagreement about what companies should be socially responsible for. Explain what an insurance company's economic, legal, ethical, and discretionary responsibilities should be.

Sources: J. Barks, "Credit Reports Aid Underwriters, But Is It Worth the Controversy?" *Best's Review/Property-Casualty Insurance* 96 (1 August 1995): 44. K. Hoke, "Big Insurers Divide on Linking Auto Premiums to Credit History," *Business First-Columbus*, 8 January 1996. G. Sanders, "Arizona Probing Insurers on Redlining, Credit Checks," *Best's Review / Property-Casualty Insurance Edition*, 95 (1 January 1995): 12. L. Scism, "Turned Down: A Bad Credit Record Can Get You Rejected for Auto Insurance," *The Wall Street Journal*, 11 November 1995.

Develop Your Management Potential

It is only the farmer who faithfully plants seeds in the Spring, who reaps a harvest in the Autumn.

B.C. Forbes, Founder of *Forbes* Magazine

The purpose of these assignments is to develop your present and future capabilities as a manager. Since stakeholders increasingly expect companies to do more to fulfill their discretionary responsibilities, chances are you and your company will be expected to support your community in some significant way. To begin learning about community needs and corporate social responsibility, you are assigned to visit a local charity or nonprofit organization of your choosing, perhaps a hospital, the Red Cross, Goodwill, Planned Parenthood, a soup kitchen, or a homeless shelter. Talk to the people who work or volunteer there. Gather the information you need to answer the following questions. However, before making your visit, be sure to read the "*Been There, Done That*" interview with Martin Connell, who discusses corporate philanthropy.

Questions

1. What is the organization's mission?
2. Who does the organization serve and how does it serve them?
3. What percentage of the organization's donations is used for administrative purposes? What percentage is used to directly benefit those served by the organization? What is the ratio of volunteers to paid workers?
4. What job or task does the "typical" volunteer perform for the organization? How much time per week does the typical volunteer give to the organization? For what jobs do they need more volunteers?
5. How does the business community support the organization?
6. Why are you interested in the activities of this organization?

Part Two

Making Things Happen

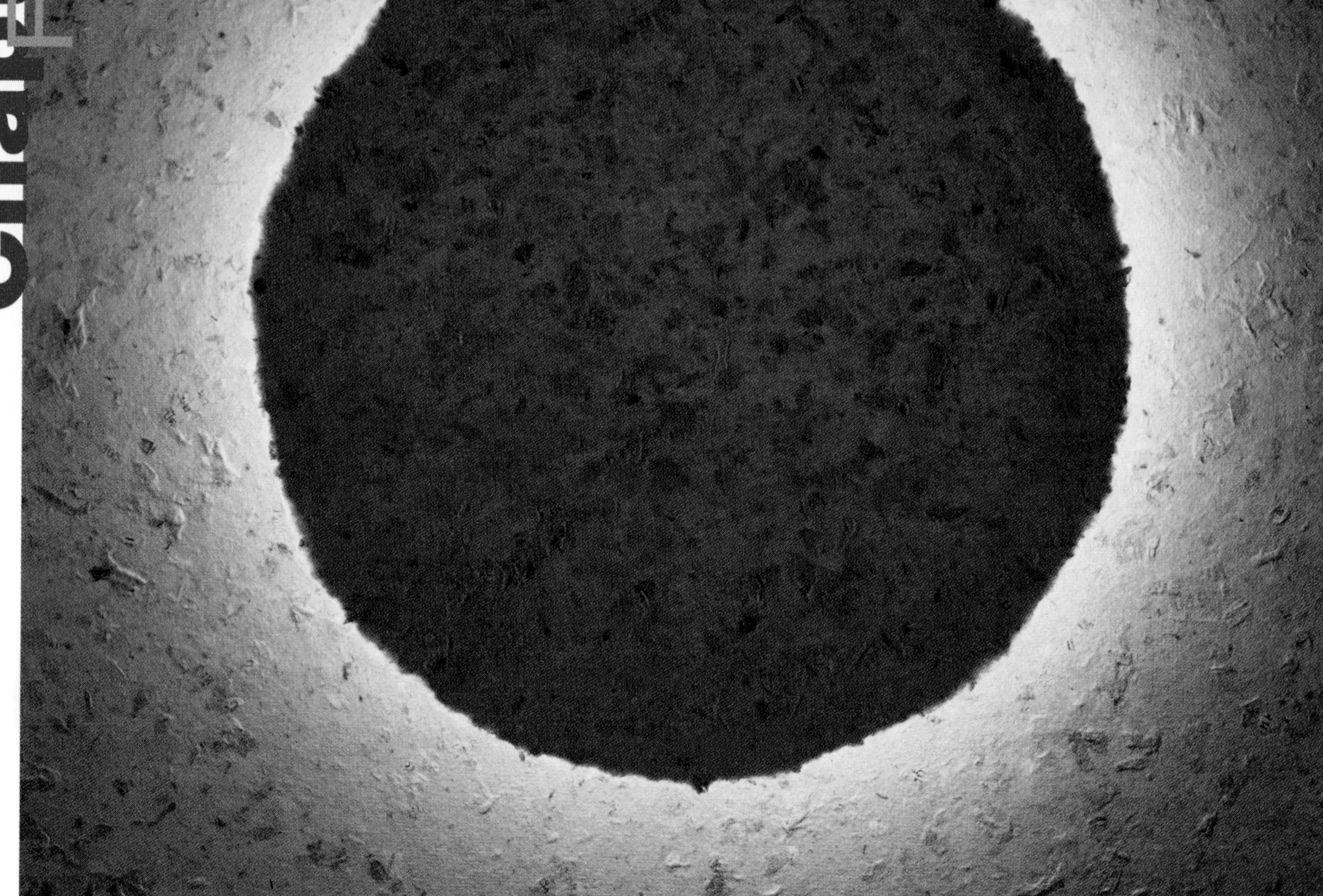

Chapter Four

Chapter 4 Outline

Planning

What Would **You** Do?

Tandy Center, Fort Worth, Texas. When a corporate headhunter contacted you about running Radio Shack, your initial response was, "Radio Shack? I thought that place died." Ironically, six months later, you're now Radio Shack's president, and it's your job to breathe life back into the company. But how? Begun in 1921 as a Boston-based mail-order company catering to ham-radio operators and electronics buffs, Radio Shack, "America's Technology Store," has always been the place to get parts to repair radios, TVs, or computers. Consistent with its roots, the first thing customers see today when they step into a Radio Shack store (and with more than 6,600 stores nationwide, there's always one nearby) is the hundreds of connectors, capacitors, and electrical components hanging from racks in small plastic bags. Furthermore, Radio Shack has a storied past as one of the first manufacturers of personal computers, initially selling more computers than either IBM or Apple. Like Henry Ford's well-known model-T, Radio Shack's best-known computer was the TRS-Model 80. Radio Shack also had one of the first truly portable computers. Author James Fallows fondly remembered the Radio Shack Model 100, which he called "the traveling journalist's best friend." He said, "While living in Japan, I went to the 1988 Summer Olympics at Seoul, where I saw reporters from around the world hammering away on outdated Model 100s of their own."[1] In its heyday, Radio Shack was the premiere electronics store in America. However, advances in competition and technology seemed to have passed Radio Shack by. Rather than conveying a commitment to modern technologies, the hundreds of electrical parts displayed in each store give the impression of a technician's supply store rather than a technology store for the average person. Furthermore, Radio Shack now competes with large, attractive computer stores like CompUSA, and electronics retailers like Best Buy and Circuit City. These stores offer the latest technology, better prices, and much better product selection. Even Tandy Corporation, Radio Shack's parent company, recognized the problem. But rather than changing Radio Shack, it created Computer City, now one of the largest computer retail chains. After your word processor finishes loading, you type "Radio Shack Master Plan" across the top of the page. But how to make a plan that works? Technological products change so quickly that you can't afford to lock yourself into an inflexible plan that will be obsolete within a few years. Plus, if the plan is going to work, it has to be something that all managers in the company, from top to bottom, can believe in and make happen. So what will the plan have to look like to accomplish that? Finally, you wonder, how did Radio Shack get in this mess in the first place? Even more important, if we get ourselves out of this mess, how can we make sure that we don't find ourselves in it again? **If you were the president of Radio Shack, what would you do?**

Sources: J. Fallows, "The Cutting Edge; Alas, Poor Kaypro . . . A Requiem for PCs Past," *Los Angeles Times*, 11 April 1994, 31. S. Hightower, "Radio Shack Marketing Blitz Aids 'Traumatized,'" *Marketing News*, 4 July 1994, 5. C. Miller, "Radio Shack Expands," *Marketing News*, 24 April 1995, 1. N. O'Leary, "Roberts' New Rule of Order: Demystify the Technology," *Brandweek*, 21 March 1994, 22. D. Olenick, "Back to the Future: Radio Shack Returns to Customer-Service Roots," *Home Furnishing News*, 18 September 1995, 1. B. Woods, "Radio Shack's Nationwide Computer, Electronics Repair," *Newsbytes News Network*, 17 February 1995.

As Radio Shack's troubles show, creating and executing a plan is one of the most important tasks a manager has. This chapter begins by examining the costs and benefits of planning. Next, you will learn how to make a plan that works. Then, you will look at the different kinds of plans that are used from the top to the bottom in most companies. Finally, you will investigate the different kinds of special-purpose plans that managers use today.

Planning

planning
choosing a goal and developing a strategy to achieve that goal

Planning is choosing a goal and developing a method or strategy to achieve that goal. When Boeing Corporation's passenger jet sales dropped by one-third, the company CEO decided that its manufacturing costs had to be cut by a whopping 25 percent. How did Boeing accomplish this ambitious goal? Planning. A key part of Boeing's plan was simplifying the enormously complex task of building jets, and a critical step in simplifying jet assembly was the company's use of "production kits." Production kits are like the plastic car models that kids assemble for fun. When you open the box, you find all of the parts and instructions on how to put them together. Boeing used this same idea to create production kits for key parts of their planes, so that workers wouldn't have to waste time searching for the parts they needed to start and finish their assembly work. Production kits have cut Boeing's inventory costs nearly in half, from $270 million to $130 million, in just its Sheet Metal Division alone.[2]

After reading these next two sections, you should be able to:

1. discuss the **costs and benefits of planning.**
2. describe **how to make a plan that works.**

Boeing simplified its jet-building process by creating "production kits" for key parts of its planes. © Matthew McVay/Tony Stone Images

1 Costs and Benefits of Planning

Are you one of those naturally organized people who always makes a daily to-do list, who always writes everything down so you won't forget, and who never misses a deadline because you keep track of everything with your handy time-management notebook? Or are you one of those flexible, creative, go-with-the-flow people who dislikes planning and organizing because it restricts your freedom, energy, and performance? Some people are natural planners. They love it and can only see the benefits of planning. However, others dislike planning, and can only see its disadvantages. It turns out that both views are correct. Planning has advantages and disadvantages.

Let's learn about **1.1** *the benefits and* **1.2** *the pitfalls of planning.*

1.1 *Benefits of Planning*

Planning has several important benefits: intensified effort, persistence, direction, and creation of task strategies.[3] First, managers and employees put forth greater effort when following a plan. Take two workers. Instruct one to "do his or her best" to increase production, and instruct the other to achieve a 2 percent increase in production each month. Research shows that the one with the specific plan will work harder.[4] For example, paper companies were having trouble getting a consistent supply of pulpwood, the basic ingredient used to make paper, from their suppliers. The problem wasn't too few trees. It was that the suppliers worked hard on some days and not so hard on others. However, when the paper companies asked their suppliers' saw hands (the folks who cut down trees) to meet a specific daily production goal and gave them a tally meter to keep track of the number of trees they had cut down, productivity soared.[5] In other words, planning encouraged the saw hands to work harder.

Second, planning leads to persistence, that is, working hard for long periods. In fact, planning encourages persistence even when there may be little chance of short-term success.[6] For example, few people know that Jimmy Johnson (now the coach of the Miami Dolphins), who coached the Dallas Cowboys to back-to-back Super Bowls, coached the Cowboys to a 1 and 15 record during his first year with the team. Says Johnson, "At times people looked at me like I was a crazy man because we had the worst team in the NFL. But I never wavered in my attitude." (Even fewer people know that Johnson was 0 and 10 in his first year as a high school coach.) Likewise, Mary Kay Ash overcame numerous professional and personal obstacles before founding Mary Kay Cosmetics. For example, in the early 1960s, after 11 years as head of sales for a company (which she won't name), she was replaced by her assistant, a man whom she had spent the past nine months training. Then, despite her proven track record and years of experience, the company paid him twice what they had been paying her. Frustrated, she quit to start her own company, only to have her 45-year-old husband suddenly die of a heart attack a month prior to the company's startup. Today, because of her persistence and hard work, Mary Kay Cosmetics has 475,000 sales representatives worldwide and is the leading cosmetics company in the U.S. with over $2 billion in annual sales.[7]

The third benefit of planning is direction. Plans encourage managers and employees to direct their persistent efforts *toward* activities that help

Personal Productivity Tip

What Happens When Our Plans Fail?

We make plans to achieve goals. But what happens when our plans fail? First, we change our action plans, trying to find something that works. If problems persist, we give ourselves longer to reach the goal, decrease the quality of the work we expect, or reduce the difficulty of the goal. If these don't work, the final step is abandoning our goals. Notice, however, that except for the last step, failure is a beginning, not an end. So why does planning work when our plans fail? Because, according to Nobel laureate Herbert Simon, the positive force of motivation begins with the negative feeling of dissatisfaction.

Source: G. Brin, "Ambition: How to Manage Success and Failure Throughout Our Lives," *Psychology Today* 25 (1992): 48-54.

accomplish their goals and *away* from activities that don't. For example, a large insurance company wanted to improve the way its managers gave employees performance evaluation feedback. To help managers improve, company trainers taught them 43 effective performance feedback behaviors. Examples included, "I will give my subordinate a clear understanding of the results I expect him or her to achieve," or, "During the performance appraisal interview, I will be very supportive, stressing good points before discussing needed improvement." However, during training, managers were instructed to choose just 12 behaviors (out of the 43) on which they wanted to make the most improvement. When subordinates rated their managers on the 43 effective feedback behaviors, it became clear that no matter which 12 behaviors different managers chose, they only improved on the 12 behaviors for which they had set improvement goals. Plans direct behavior toward activities that lead to goal accomplishment and away from those that don't.

The fourth benefit of planning is that it encourages the development of task strategies. After selecting a goal, it's natural to ask, "How can it be achieved?" For example, after several years of losses, Delta Airlines wanted to reduce its costs from 9.76 cents per seat-mile to 7.5 cents per seat-mile, or nearly $2 billion per year. After announcing this goal, Delta's CEO asked his top managers and the pilots' and attendants' unions for their ideas, stating, "We've set a cost-reduction goal, and everything . . . is open for negotiation."[8] What were their suggestions? Cut 10,000 jobs, but when possible, encourage voluntary leaving through financial severance or buyout packages. Another suggestion was to end Delta's prized decade-long marketing relationship with Walt Disney World in Florida. Delta was paying Disney $2 million a year to sponsor its Tomorrowland attraction at Disney World and to be known as the "Official Airline of Walt Disney World." Managers and employees also suggested that Delta could offset its costs per mile by growing its cargo business. Since Delta planes only used 40 percent of the cargo space available in the belly of each passenger jet, the company could increase revenue and decrease costs by selling that freight capacity to companies that might otherwise use United Parcel Service or Federal Express to ship goods.[9] As this example shows, planning not only encourages people to work harder, to work hard for extended periods, and to engage in behaviors directly related to goal accomplishment, it also encourages them to think of better ways to do their jobs.

Finally, perhaps the most compelling benefit of planning is that it has been proven to work for both companies and individuals. On average, companies with plans have larger profits and grow much faster than companies that don't.[10] The same holds true for individual managers and employees. There is no better way to improve the performance of the people who work in a company than to have them set goals and develop strategies for achieving those goals. For more on the benefits of planning, see the "What Really Works?" feature in this chapter.

1.2 *Planning Pitfalls*

Despite the significant benefits associated with planning, planning is not a cure-all. Plans won't fix all organizational problems. In fact, many management authors and consultants believe that planning can harm companies in several ways.[11]

The first pitfall of planning is that it can impede change and prevent or slow needed adaptation. Sometimes companies become so committed to achieving the goals set forth in their plans, or they can become so intent on following the strategies and tactics spelled out in them, that they fail to see that their plans aren't working or that their goals need to change. For example, since its founding, McDonald's has relied on a plan of aggressive growth that, at its peak, had the company opening a new McDonald's every 17 hours! This plan continues to serve the company well in foreign markets where there are fewer competitors and still room for expansion. However, in the U.S., there are so many McDonald's that each time the company puts up a new store, the revenues of nearby McDonald's restaurants typically drop between 6 percent and 20 percent. Yet, despite these results, McDonald's continued its growth plan, adding nearly 2,500 new stores in the last three years. Finally, because of complaints about falling sales from unhappy franchisers (who own and run most of its stores), the company has finally cut its growth rate by nearly two-thirds.[12]

The second pitfall of planning is that it can create a false sense of certainty. Planners sometimes feel that they know exactly what the future holds for their competitors, their suppliers, and their companies. However, all plans are based on assumptions. "The price of gasoline will increase by 4 percent per year." "Exports will continue to rise." For plans to work, the assumptions on which they are based must hold true. If the assumptions turn out to be false, then plans based on them are likely to fail. For example, as cell phones became cheaper and more reliable, Nokia, a Finland-based manufacturer of cell phones, experienced tremendous growth in its business. So when sales suddenly dropped by 25 percent, Nokia was caught off guard. Officially, company management blamed "logistical hiccups." However, *The Wall Street Journal* concluded that, ". . . Nokia didn't see it coming and didn't know how to handle it [the 25 percent drop in sales]."[13] Because Nokia assumed that its cellular phone sales would continue to grow, it bought parts at high prices and did a poor job of controlling its costs. When the assumption (i.e., continued growth) underlying its production plans turned out to be false, the result was a 30 percent decline in operating profits.

The third pitfall of planning is the detachment of planners. In theory, strategic planners and top-level managers are supposed to focus on the big picture and not concern themselves with the details of implementation, that is, carrying out the plan. According to management professor Henry Mintzberg, detachment leads planners to plan for things they don't understand.[14] Plans are not meant to be abstract theories. They are meant to be guidelines for action. Consequently, planners need to be familiar with the daily details of their businesses if they are to produce plans that can work.

For example, if you doubt that the "details" are important to good execution of a plan, imagine that you're about to have coronary bypass surgery to replace four clogged arteries. Rather than having an experienced cardiologist perform your surgery, you're going under the knife of a first-year medical intern. The intern is a fully qualified M.D. who clearly understands the theory and the plan behind bypass surgery, but has never performed such an operation. As you lie on the operating table, who is the last person you'd like to see as the anesthesia kicks in, the first-year intern who knows the plan but has never done a bypass, or the experienced cardiologist who has followed the plan hundreds of times? Planning works better when the people developing the plan are not detached from the process of executing the plan.

BLASTFROMTHEPAST

Pericles of Athens, 495? - 429 B.C., Founder of Planning?

Three key components of modern-day planning—vision, nondetachment, and flexibility—may have originated with Pericles of Athens, who led Greece until his death in 429 B.C. Pericles was elected general, or strategos, in 458 B.C. Unlike modern leaders who routinely serve two-, four-, or six-year terms, Pericles faced yearly elections. Nonetheless, he was elected to the position of strategos for 30 years. Generals in Pericles' time were not just military strategists and leaders. Like today's presidents and prime ministers, they were also responsible for managing foreign affairs and governing domestic affairs.

According to Pericles, a leader's primary responsibility was to have a vision and then share it effectively with others. In a speech to the people of Athens, obviously made during an election, Pericles described himself as "one who has at least as much ability as anyone else to see what ought to be done and explain what he sees." He went on to say that "a man who has the knowledge but lacks the power clearly to express it is no better off than if he never had any ideas at all."[15] In a time of monarchies and tyrannical rulers, Pericles' unique vision for Athens was democratic. Laws were made by the assembly, executed by the Council of 500, and applied, in courts of law, to citizens who broke them. Pericles' democratic vision was evident in his view of war. Most leaders of his day had little regard for the lives of troops, viewing them, like horses and carriages, as expendable resources to be used to obtain the objectives of war. By contrast, "His chief maxim of war was, never to venture a battle unless he was almost certain of victory, and not to lavish the blood of the citizens. He used to say frequently, that were it in his power, they should be immortal; that when trees were felled, they shoot to life again in a little time, but when men once die, they are lost for ever."[16]

Perhaps better than modern company planners, the Athenians understood that planners could not be effective unless they were close to the events they were planning. Consequently, Athenians expected candidates for the position of strategos to have demonstrated their capabilities as warriors in individual combat and as military leaders. Furthermore, strategos were expected to guide their troops from the front line where they could observe the battle, adapt plans, and, if necessary, demonstrate leadership by fighting alongside troops. Athenians understood that plans are not abstract theories, but guidelines for action. Planners detached from the events for which they are planning will, on average, be poor planners.

Finally, while Pericles may have been the founder of planning, he understood that plans were a means to an end and that good planning required the flexibility to abandon a plan should circumstance require doing so. Pericles is known for the statement "opportunity waits for no man." He realized that circumstances could change, and that unanticipated events could render plans useless. Thus, he placed as much importance on adapting plans as on creating them. Pericles maintained, "There is often no more logic in the course of events than there is in the plans of men; this is why we blame our luck when things happen in ways that we did not expect."

Sources: S. Cummings, "Pericles of Athens—Drawing from the Essence of Strategic Leadership," *Business Horizons* 38, no. 6 (1995): 22. "Pericles," *Compton's Encyclopedia*, 1 January 1994. C. Rollin, "Rollin's Ancient History: History of the Persians and Grecians," Sections XII - XIV and VIII – XI, *History of the World*, 1 January 1992. "Works of Thucydides," Books 1 and 2, *Monarch Notes*, 1 January 1963.

Review 1
Costs and Benefits of Planning

Planning is choosing a goal and developing a method to achieve that goal. Planning is one of the best ways to improve organizational and individual performance. It encourages people to work harder (intensified effort), to work hard for extended periods (persistence), to engage in behaviors directly related to goal accomplishment (directed behavior), and to think of better ways to do their jobs (task strategies). But most important, companies that plan have larger profits and faster growth than companies that don't plan. However, planning also has three potential pitfalls. Companies that are overly committed to their plans may be slow to adapt to changes in their environment. Planning is based on assumptions about the future, and when those assumptions are wrong, plans are likely to fail. Finally, planning can fail when planners are detached from the implementation of plans.

2 How to Make a Plan That Works

Planning is a double-edged sword. If done right, planning brings about tremendous increases in individual and organizational performance. But if done wrong, it can have just the opposite effect. In this section, you will learn how to make a plan that works.

As depicted in Figure 4.1, planning consists of **2.1** *setting goals,* **2.2** *developing commitment to the goals,* **2.3** *developing effective action plans,* **2.4** *tracking progress toward goal achievement, and* **2.5** *maintaining flexibility in planning.*

2.1 *Setting Goals*

Since planning is choosing a goal and developing a method or strategy to achieve that goal, the first step in planning is to set goals. To direct behavior and increase effort, goals need to be specific and challenging.[17] For example, deciding to "increase sales this year" won't direct and energize workers as much as deciding to "increase North American sales by 4 percent in the next six months." Likewise, choosing to "drop a few pounds" won't motivate you as much as choosing to "lose 15 pounds." Specific, challenging goals provide a target to aim for and a standard against which to measure success.

S.M.A.R.T. goals goals that are specific, measurable, attainable, realistic, and timely

One way of writing effective goals for yourself, your job, or your company is to use the S.M.A.R.T. guidelines. **S.M.A.R.T. goals** are **S**pecific, **M**easurable, **A**ttainable, **R**ealistic, and **T**imely.[18] Let's see how a heating, ventilation, and air conditioning (HVAC) company might use S.M.A.R.T. goals in its business.

The HVAC business is cyclical. It's extremely busy at the beginning of summer, when homeowners find that their air conditioning isn't working, and at the beginning of winter, when furnaces and heat pumps need repair. During these times, most HVAC companies have more business than they can handle. But at other times of year, business can be very slow. So a ***spe**cific* goal would be to increase sales by 50 percent during the fall and spring, when business is slower. This goal could be ***m**easured* by keeping track of the number of annual maintenance contracts sold to customers. This goal

Figure 4.1 **How to Make a Plan That Works**

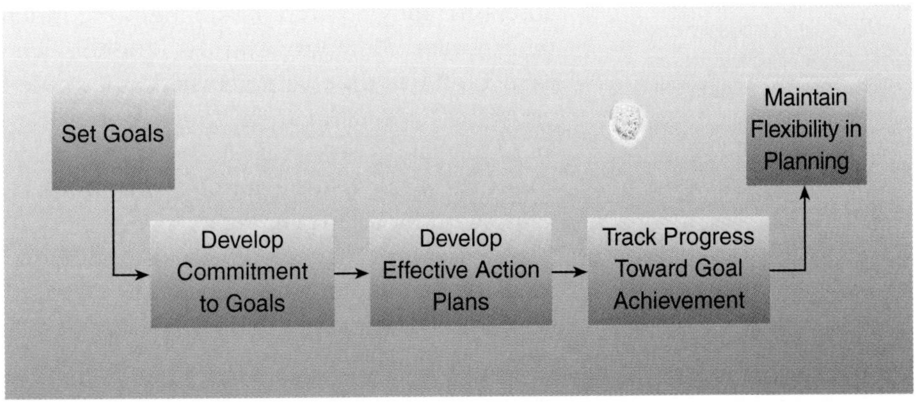

of increasing sales during the off seasons is ***a**ttainable*, because maintenance contracts typically include spring tune-ups (air-conditioning systems) and fall tune-ups (furnace or heating systems). Moreover, a 50 percent increase in sales during the slow seasons is ***r**ealistic*. Since customers want their furnaces and air conditioners to work the first time it gets cold (or hot) each year, they are likely to buy service contracts that ensure their equipment is in working order. Tune-up work can then be scheduled during the slow seasons, increasing sales at those times. Finally, this goal can be made ***t**imely* by asking the staff to push sales of maintenance contracts before Labor Day, the traditional end of summer, when people start thinking about the cold days ahead, and in March, when winter-weary people start longing for hot days in air-conditioned comfort. The result would be more work during the slow fall and spring seasons.

2.2 *Developing Commitment to Goals*

Just because a company sets a goal doesn't mean that people will try to accomplish it. If workers don't care about a goal, then the goal won't encourage them to work harder or smarter. Thus, the second step in planning is to develop commitment to goals.

goal commitment the determination to achieve a goal

Goal commitment is the determination to achieve a goal. Commitment to achieve a goal is not automatic. Managers and workers must choose to commit themselves to a goal. For example, Professor Edwin Locke, the foremost expert on how, why, and when goals work, tells a story about an overweight friend. After not seeing him for years, Locke ran into his friend, who had finally lost 75 pounds. Because of the change, he nearly walked by without recognizing him. Locke said, "So I asked him how he did it, knowing how hard it was for most people to lose so much weight." His friend responded, "Actually, it was quite simple. I simply decided that I *really wanted* to do it."[19] Said another way, goal commitment is really wanting to achieve a goal.

So how can managers bring about goal commitment? The most popular approach is to set goals participatively. Rather than assigning goals to workers ("Johnson, you've got 'til Tuesday of next week to redesign the flex capacitor so it gives us 10 percent more output"), managers and employees choose goals together. The goals are more likely to be realistic and attainable if employees participate in setting them. Also, people are more likely to strive for a goal they feel they have a reasonable chance of attaining. For example, would you be more likely to stick to an exercise program that required ½ hour per day or one that required 3 hours per day?

Another technique for gaining commitment to a goal is to make the goal public. For example, college students who publicly communicated their semester grade goals ("This semester, I'm shooting for a 3.5") to significant others (usually a parent or sibling) were much more committed to achieving their grades. More importantly, students who told others about their goals earned grades that were nearly a half-grade higher than students who did not tell others about their grade goals.[20] So, one way to increase commitment to goals is to "go public" by having individuals or work units tell others about their goals. For example, work units could post their goals on a bulletin board for all to see.

Another way to increase goal commitment is to obtain top management's support. Top management can show support for a plan or program by providing funds, speaking publicly about the plan, or participating in the plan

Personal Productivity Tip

Planning to Procrastinate?

Are you a great planner, but have trouble getting started or keeping on task? Some of the signs are a compulsion to organize files, long to-do lists, always getting up to get coffee, desk cleaning, etc. Here's the clincher. Do you use the computer—that supposedly productivity-enhancing machine—to play solitaire or surf the Internet? Congratulations, you're an official member of the procrastinators club! If you want your membership to expire, try these solutions. Put yourself on a schedule. Break big projects into bite-sized tasks. Finally, not all procrastination is bad. Some plans work out better when you've had longer to mull them over.

Sources: H. Lancaster, "Managing Your Career: Mend Procrastinating Ways before Your Job Stalls Out," *The Wall Street Journal Interactive Edition*, 7 May 1996.

itself. For example, when Chrysler Corporation decided to have small teams develop all of their new car designs, one way top management supported the change was to simply let the teams make all decisions without management interference. When it became clear that new car designs were theirs to make or break, the teams became, to use their own word, "passionate" about their work. Indeed, their level of passion and goal commitment helped reduce development time by one year, nearly 20 percent faster than before. Moreover, their commitment yielded a development cost of only $1 billion, which is just pennies compared to development costs at Ford ($3 billion) and GM/Saturn ($3.5 billion) for similar cars.[21]

2.3 Developing Effective Action Plans

action plan
the specific steps, people, and resources needed to accomplish a goal

The third step in planning is to develop effective action plans. An **action plan** lists the specific steps, people, resources, and time period for accomplishing a goal. For example, USAir, an east coast–based airline, announced a "Management Action Program" to significantly reduce costs and increase revenues. This program (i.e., plan) had three steps:

1. Cut all unprofitable routes.
2. Use technology to cut costs and increase efficiency.
3. Outsource any task that can be done better and cheaper by someone else.

Personal Productivity Tip

Are You an Owl or an Early Bird?

What time do you wake up on Saturday morning? Are you up and out of bed by 7:00 A.M., or are you up just in time to make it to the table for lunch? The term *morningness* describes a preference for morning activities. Studies show that morningness affects performance. Students with morning orientations get much better grades in 8:00 A.M. classes than do students with evening orientations (3.27 versus 2.78). So, to do a better job of achieving your goals, plan to do your most challenging work when you're at your peak energy levels and your routine work when your energy is low.

Sources: J.P. Guthrie, R.A. Ash, and V. Bendapudi, "Additional Evidence for a Measure of Morning," *Journal of Applied Psychology* 80 (1995): 186-190.

In step one, the company cut flights to money-losing destinations, such as Austin, TX, San Antonio, TX, Cincinnati, OH, and Albuquerque, NM. Today, USAir flies only 90 percent of the routes it once did. But, the routes it flies *are* profitable. Peter Haak, USAir's assistant vice president for schedules, said, "So we took seats out of the air, but we grew the revenue—a $211 million change in one quarter. That's really news." In step two, USAir installed an expensive computer-run, yield-management system called "Excalibur" to monitor how its prices compared to its competitors' prices. Excalibur helps USAir determine when to cut prices to stay competitive. Consequently, despite cutting prices, revenues are actually increasing, because USAir's jets now fly with fewer empty seats than previously. In step three, outsourcing, USAir is saving money by having outside companies handle cargo ($15 million saved), purchasing ($92 million saved), and crew scheduling ($40 million saved).[22] The only thing missing from USAir's plan was a specific goal and time period for accomplishing its cost savings. At Delta, the CEO gave the company three years to reduce its costs from 9.76 to 7.5 cents per seat-mile.[23]

2.4 Tracking Progress

proximal goals
short-term goals or subgoals

distal goals
long-term or primary goals

The fourth step in planning is to track progress toward goal achievement. There are two accepted methods of tracking progress. The first is to set proximal goals and distal goals. **Proximal goals** are short-term goals or subgoals, whereas **distal goals** are long-term or primary goals.[24] The idea behind setting proximal goals is that they may be more motivating and rewarding than waiting to achieve far-off distal goals. For example, a number of years ago Buick had a reputation for building unreliable cars. Since Buick management wanted to improve the quality of its cars, it set the specific, challenging goal of building its luxury sedan well enough to win *Consumer Reports* magazine's "well above average in reliability" rating. Because it normally takes several years of hard work to achieve such a turnaround in product quality, Buick managers and workers set proximal goals for improving its quality ratings each year. Indeed, whereas Buick's cars used to be rated by *Consumer Reports* magazine as well below average, in recent years the magazine and its readers have ranked Buicks as "above average in reliability." This is still short of the coveted "well above average" reliability rating, but in the short term, it indicates tremendous progress.[25]

The second method of tracking progress is to gather and provide performance feedback. Regular, frequent performance feedback allows workers and managers to track their progress toward goal achievement and make adjustments in effort, direction, and strategies.[26] For example, Figure 4.2 shows the result of providing feedback on safety behavior to the makeup and wrapping workers in a large bakery company. The company had a worker safety record that was 2½ times worse than the industry average. During the baseline period, workers in the wrapping department, who measure and mix ingredients, roll the bread dough, and place it into baking pans, performed their jobs safely about 70 percent of the time. The baseline safety record for workers in the makeup department, who bag and seal baked bread and assemble, pack, and tape cardboard cartons for shipping, was a bit better at 78 percent.

Figure 4.2 **Effects of Goal-Setting, Training, and Feedback on Safe Behavior in a Bread Factory**

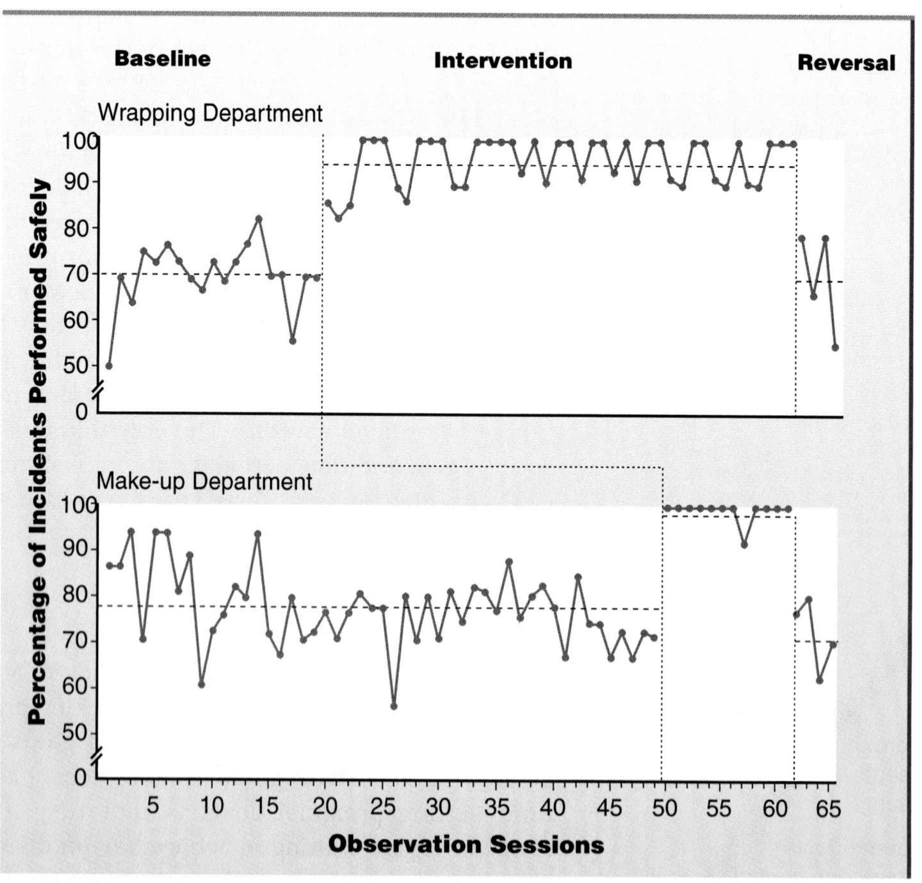

Source: J. Komaki, K.D. Barwick, & L.R. Scott, "A Behavioral Approach to Occupational Safety: Pinpointing and Reinforcing Safe Performance in a Food Manufacturing Plant," *Journal of Applied Psychology* 63 (1978): 434-445.

Yet, after the company gave workers 30 minutes of safety training, set a goal of 90 percent safe behavior, and then provided daily feedback (such as a chart similar to Figure 4.2), performance improved dramatically. During the intervention period, the percentage of safely performed behaviors rose to an average of 95.8 percent for wrapping workers and 99.3 percent for workers in the makeup department, and never fell below 83 percent. Thus, the combination of training, a challenging goal, and feedback led to a dramatic increase in performance.

However, the importance of feedback alone can be seen in the reversal stage, when the company quit posting daily feedback on safe behavior. Without daily feedback, the percentage of safely performed behavior returned to baseline levels, 70.8 percent for the wrapping department and 72.3 percent for the makeup department. For planning to be effective, workers need a specific, challenging goal and regular feedback to track their progress.

2.5 *Maintaining Flexibility*

Because action plans are sometimes poorly conceived and goals sometimes turn out to not be achievable, the last step in developing an effective plan is to maintain flexibility. For example, when fax machines were new and still too expensive to be found in many offices, Federal Express created Zap Mail. For $25 for the first five pages, and $1 a page beyond that, Federal Express would send a courier to your office to retrieve documents, fax those documents from its local office to the Federal Express office in the city you wanted, and then send a courier to deliver the faxed documents to whoever was to receive them. If delivery didn't occur within two hours, you got your money back. FedEx believed so strongly in Zap Mail that its ten-year investment plan specified that $1.2 billion was to be spent to launch satellites, build earth stations (to receive satellite transmissions), and to purchase high-speed fax machines. Unfortunately, two factors undermined FedEx's plan. Fax technology improved, and fax machines dropped significantly in price. So rather than pay Federal Express outlandish prices to fax documents, companies simply bought and installed inexpensive fax machines in their offices.[27]

When plans like Zap Mail fail, it's far better to scrap the plan and start over than it is to ride the failing plan into the ground. Federal Express management recognized its mistake and shut Zap Mail down, but not before taking a $190 million after-tax write-off. Having the flexibility (and the guts) to admit failure and move on is laudable. However, an even more desirable strategy is to build flexibility into planning from the start.

options-based planning maintaining planning flexibility by making small, simultaneous investments in many alternative plans

One method of maintaining flexibility while planning is to adopt an options-based approach.[28] The goal of **options-based planning** is to keep options open by making small, simultaneous investments in many options or plans. Then when one or a few of these plans emerge as likely winners, you invest even more in these plans while discontinuing or reducing investment in the others. In part, options-based planning is the opposite of traditional planning. For example, the purpose of an action plan is to commit people and resources to a particular course of action. However, the purpose of options-based planning is to leave those commitments open. Holding options open gives you choices and choices give you flexibility.

For example, in contrast to Federal Express, which invested more than $400 million in Zap Mail, MCI, the long distance company, began MCI Mail by investing just $40 million. Furthermore, unlike Zap Mail, which restricted the delivery of documents to just one method, MCI designed MCI Mail with many delivery options, such as regular document delivery (like Federal Express), plain text e-mail, fax transmission, and reception via computers, and the ability to retrieve messages or faxes from anywhere when using a computer connected to a modem. These options not only let MCI hedge its bets about what its customers wanted, but also allowed MCI to keep its options open about technology. Thus, when fax machines became cheap enough to be installed in most offices, MCI moved more investment into its e-mail option by developing one of the first international e-mail systems for companies and individuals. Later, when e-mail became commonplace because of the Internet, MCI moved more investment into its Internet option by offering direct Internet access to the same corporate and individual customers who once might have been MCI Mail customers. Small investments in multiple options are one way to maintain flexibility in planning.

learning-based planning learning better ways of achieving goals by continually testing, changing, and improving plans and strategies

Another method of maintaining flexibility while planning is to take a learning-based approach. In contrast to traditional planning, which assumes that initial action plans are correct and will lead to success, **learning-based planning** assumes that action plans need to be continually tested, changed, and improved as companies learn better ways of achieving goals.[29] Because the purpose is constant improvement, learning-based planning not only encourages flexibility in action plans, but it also encourages frequent reassessment and revision of organizational goals.

For example, Knight-Ridder Corporation, which owns the second-largest newspaper chain in the U.S., created project "25/43" to reverse the sharp decline in newspaper readership among people between the ages of 25 and 43. In contrast to traditional newspapers, where editors and reporters drive the newspaper's content and design, the first step in Knight-Ridder's learning-based planning was to ask readers what they wanted in their newspaper. The second step was to test those ideas and keep the ones that readers liked. Suggested changes included columns on environmental tips, shopping, parenting, high-tech, and fitness. Readers also insisted on shorter articles, the use of color, and better layouts and indexes, which made it easier to find what they were looking for. The third and final step, which is the key to learning-based planning, is that Knight-Ridder now regularly questions, experiments, and tests the changes it makes. Knight-Ridder's Vice President of News said,

> *Routinely now, our papers go to focus groups when they are going to try something new. Many of our editors have established a 25/43 goal, which means they conduct research, involve task forces from their newsrooms and other departments, assess the strengths and weaknesses of their papers, propose changes, and test some of these changes in the marketplace. It sounds so simple, but it is not the way the newspaper business tended to operate.*[30]

Review 2
How to Make a Plan That Works

There are five steps to making a plan that works: (1) Set S.M.A.R.T. goals—goals that are **S**pecific, **M**easurable, **A**ttainable, **R**ealistic, and **T**imely. (2) Develop commitment to the goal from the people who contribute to goal achievement. Managers can increase workers' goal commitment by encouraging worker participation in goal setting, making goals public, and getting top management to show their support for workers' goals. (3) Develop action plans for goal accomplishment. (4) Track progress toward goal achievement by setting both proximal and distal goals, and by providing workers regular performance feedback. (5) Maintain flexibility. Keeping options open through options-based planning and seeking continuous improvement through learning-based planning help organizations maintain flexibility as they plan.

Kinds of Plans

Chances are, you may have heard of Waste Management International, the largest garbage and recycling company in the U.S. But you're probably not familiar with United Waste Systems, a small garbage company only 3.6 percent the size of Waste Management. Yet, despite its smaller size, United Waste makes more profit per dollar of revenue than does Waste Management (a 24 percent operating margin versus 18 percent for Waste Management).[31]

What makes United Waste Systems more profitable than Waste Management? It has instituted successful planning processes at each level of the company. Beginning at the top, the company has a clear mission. Says CEO Bradley Jacobs, "We are not in medical waste. We are not in hazardous waste. We are not in incineration." What the company is in are rural areas, where, unlike giant Waste Management, it has little competition in the trash-pickup business. But once the trash is picked up, it's got to be delivered to a dump. Since competitors pay cities upwards of $45 per ton to empty their garbage trucks at municipally owned dumps, United's middle managers are in charge of a plan to find, buy, and run company-owned dump sites. Why? Because this lowers United's dumping costs to just $29 a ton. Finally, at lower levels, company managers and employees focus on plans to lower costs and increase productivity. For example, in Belchertown, Massachusetts, United has a one-truck, two-person crew pick up trash for the entire town on Wednesdays, Thursdays, and Fridays. The same route used to be covered by two trucks and two crews from another waste hauler.

After reading the next two sections, you should be able to:

3 discuss how companies can use **plans** at all management levels, **from top to bottom.**

4 describe the different kinds of **special-purpose plans** that companies use to plan for change, contingencies, and product development.

3 Planning from Top to Bottom

Planning works best when the goals and action plans at the bottom and middle of the organization support the goals and action plans at the top of the organization. In other words, planning works best when everybody pulls in the same direction. Figure 4.3 illustrates this planning continuity, beginning at the top with a clear definition of the company vision and ending at the bottom with the execution of operational plans.

Let's see how **3.1** *top managers create the organizational vision and mission,* **3.2** *middle managers develop tactical plans and use management by objectives to motivate employee efforts toward the overall vision and mission, and* **3.3** *first-level managers use operational, single-use, and standing plans to implement the tactical plans.*

Figure 4.3 **Planning from Top to Bottom**

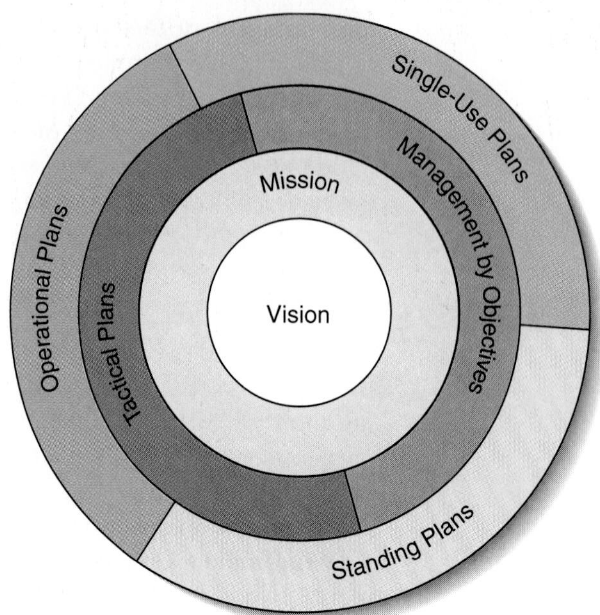

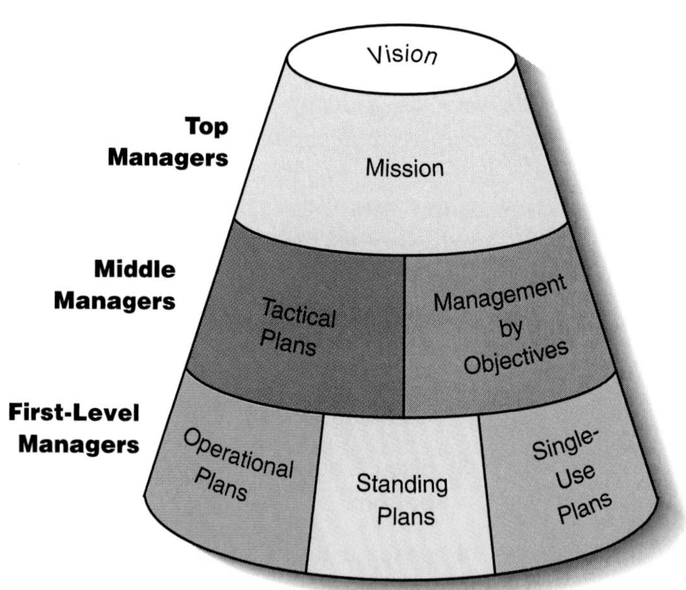

3.1
Starting at the Top

strategic plans
overall company plans that clarify how the company will serve customers and position itself against competitors over the next two to five years

vision
inspirational statement of an organization's enduring purpose

Top management is responsible for developing long-term **strategic plans** that make clear how the company will serve customers and position itself against competitors in the next two to five years. (The strategic planning and management process is reviewed in its entirety in Chapter 9.) Strategic planning begins with the creation of an organizational vision and an organizational mission.

A **vision** is a statement of a company's purpose or reason for existing.[32] Vision statements should be brief—no more than two sentences. They should also be enduring, inspirational, clear, and consistent with widely shared company beliefs and values. For example, Merck Corporation, a leading pharmaceutical firm, has a vision ". . . to provide society with superior products and services—innovations and solutions that improve the quality of life and satisfy customer needs—to provide employees with meaningful work and advancement opportunities and investors with a superior rate of return."[vi]. Merck's vision is enduring. It doesn't change if Merck uses natural or synthetic chemical compounds, or if its researchers use high-tech gene-splicing or low-tech petri dishes. The vision of "innovations and solutions that improve the quality of life," "meaningful work," and "superior rate of return" stays the same. Plus, the vision is clear and, inspirational. Other examples of organizational visions are Walt Disney Corporation's "to make people happy" and Schlage Lock Company's "to make the world more secure."[33]

mission
statement of a company's overall goal that unifies company-wide efforts toward its vision, stretches and challenges the organization, and possesses a finish line and a time frame

The **mission**, which flows from the vision, is a more specific goal that unifies company-wide efforts, stretches and challenges the organization, and possesses a finish line and a time frame. For example, in 1961, President John F. Kennedy established an organizational mission for NASA with this simple statement: "Achieving the goal, before this decade is out, of landing a man on the moon and returning him safely to earth."[34] NASA achieved this goal on July 20, 1969, when astronaut Neil Armstrong walked on the moon. Once a mission has been accomplished, a new one should be chosen. Again, however, the new mission must grow out of the organization's vision, which does not change over time. For example, NASA's vision statement is: "As explorers, pioneers, and innovators, we boldly expand frontiers in air and space to inspire and serve America, and to benefit the quality of life on earth." NASA used this vision to develop the three-part mission statement shown in Figure 4.4. Notice that for each

Planning works best when everyone pulls in the same direction.
© Ted Wood/Tony Stone Images

Figure 4.4 **NASA's Mission and Strategic Goals**

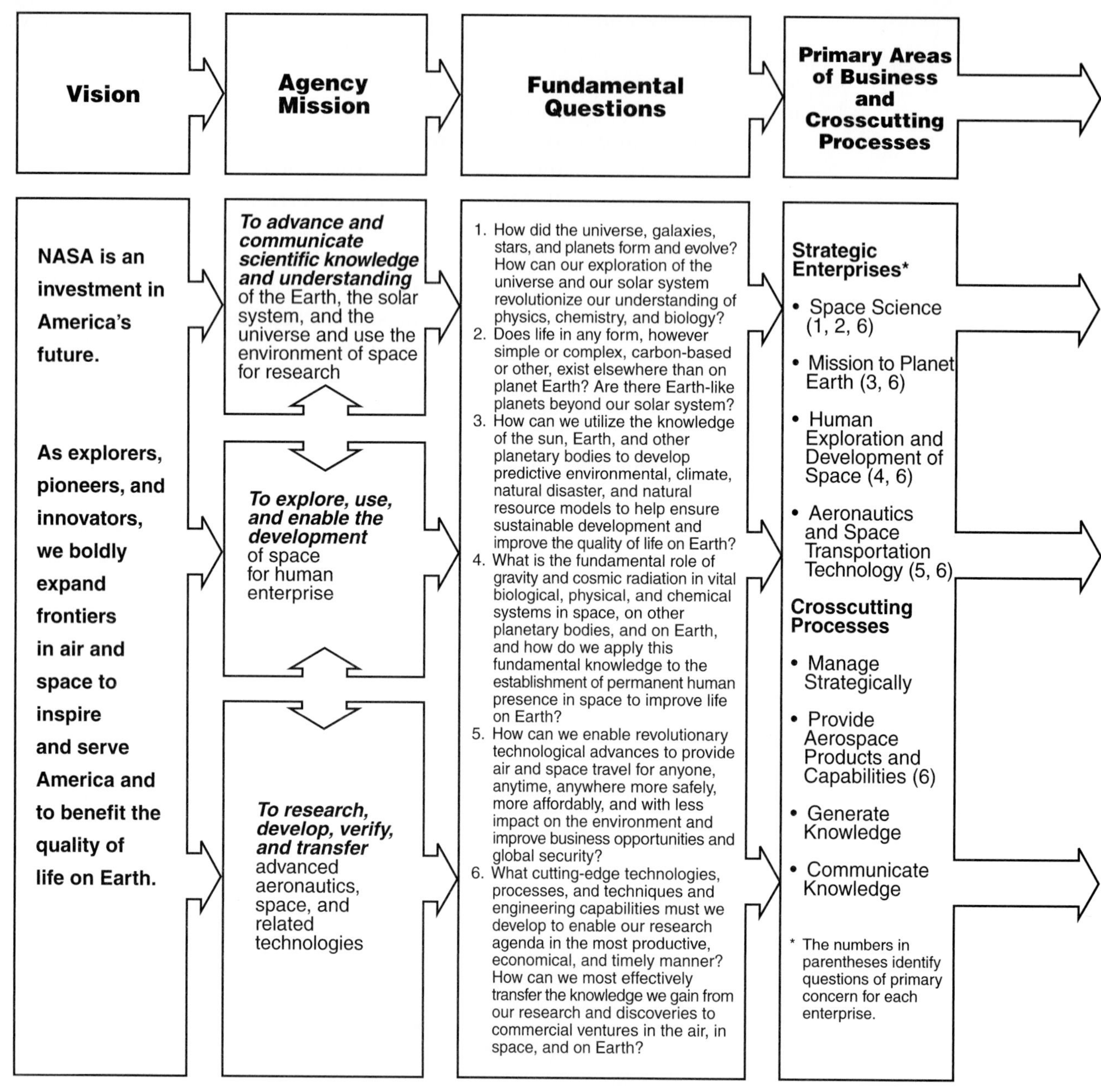

mission statement, NASA has created specific, challenging goals to be accomplished from 1998–2002, from 2003–2009, and from 2010–2023, and beyond.

targeting mission
mission stated as a clear, specific company goal at which to aim

Companies can set missions in four ways.[35] One is **targeting**, setting a clear, specific target and "aiming" right for it. Examples of targeting missions are Microsoft's "A computer on every desk and in every home" and Toyota's "Global Ten," which is short for Toyota's goal of a 10 percent share of the world automotive market.[36]

common-enemy mission
company goal of defeating a corporate rival

A second type of mission is the **common-enemy mission**, in which the company vows to defeat one of its corporate rivals. Pepsi's aspirations of beating Coke, Burger King's desire to defeat McDonald's, or Avis's hopes

<None><None>Figure 4.4 **NASA's Mission and Strategic Goals**

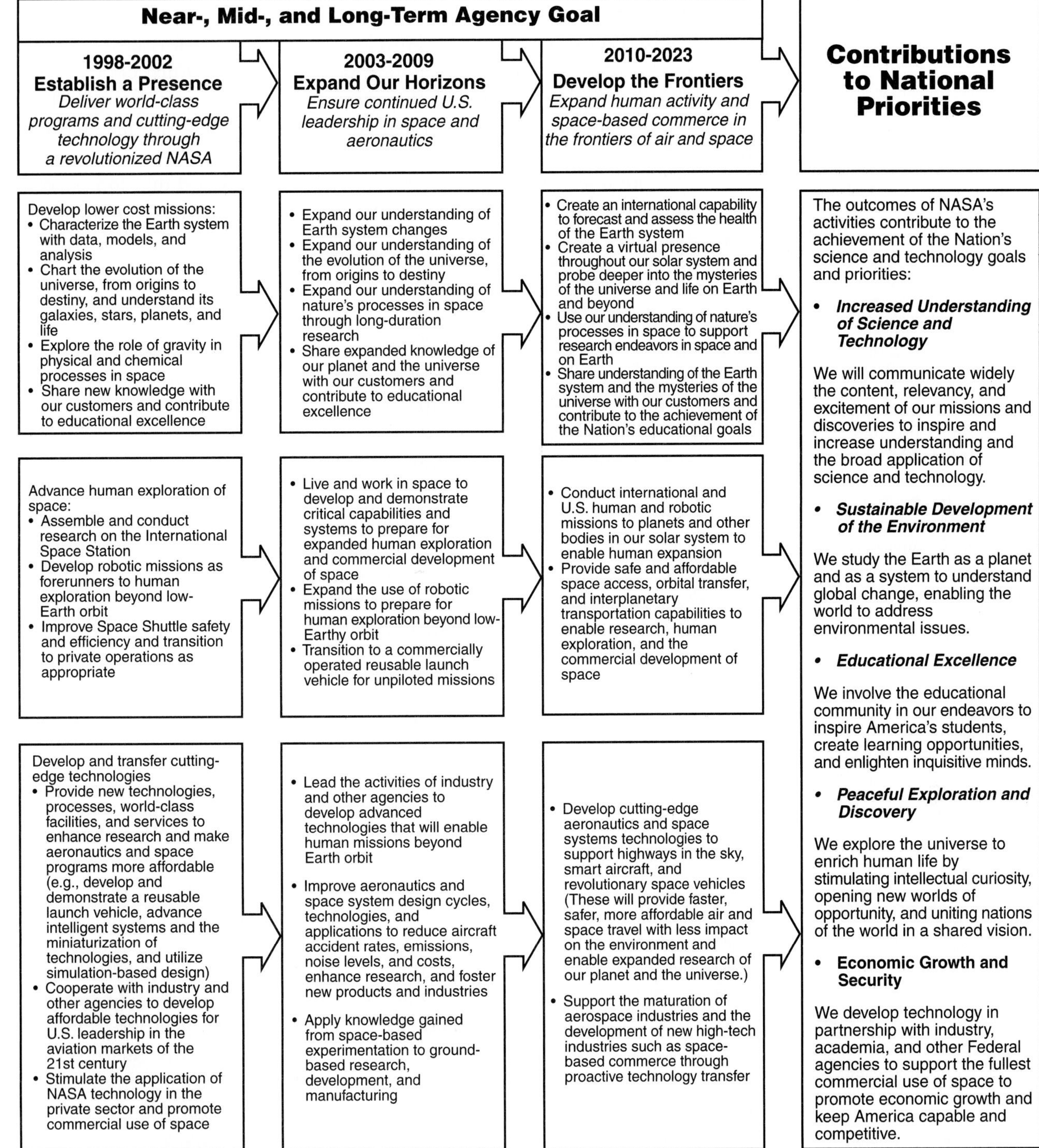

Source: "NASA's Strategic Management System Roadmap," [Online] Available *http://www.hq.nasa.gov/office/nsp/maps.htm,* 24 March 1998.

role-model mission
company goal of imitating the characteristics and practices of a successful company

("We're number two. We try harder.") to catch Hertz Rental Cars are all examples of common-enemy missions.

A third type of mission is the **role-model mission**. Here, rather than focusing on defeating specific competitors, as in the common-enemy mission, the company emulates the characteristics and practices of a successful company. For example, the CEO of Giro Sports Design vowed "to be a great company by the year 2000, to be to the cycling industry what Nike is to athletic shoes . . ."[37]

internal-transformation mission
company goal of remaining competitive by making dramatic changes in the company

A fourth type of mission is the **internal-transformation mission**, in which the company aims to achieve dramatic changes to remain competitive in its markets. Indeed, Ford Motor Company's transformation in the 1980s began with its mission to make "Quality Job 1." Ford cars at that time had a reputation for being the poorest-made cars in Detroit. More than a decade later, Ford now makes some of the highest-quality cars in the U.S.[38]

The bottom line is that developing a company vision and mission is critical to success. Studies consistently show that companies with more comprehensive mission statements do better financially than those with ambiguous missions or no mission at all.[39]

3.2
Bending in the Middle

tactical plans
plans created and implemented by middle managers that specify how the company will use resources, budgets, and people over the next six months to two years to accomplish specific goals within its mission

Middle management is responsible for developing and carrying out tactical plans to accomplish the organization's mission. **Tactical plans** specify how a company will use resources, budgets, and people to accomplish specific goals within its mission. Whereas strategic plans and objectives are used to focus company efforts over the next two to five years, tactical plans and objectives are used to direct behavior, efforts, and attention over the next six months to two years. For example, after three years of losses, Disneyland Europe managed to earn a profit in its fourth year of operation by making specific changes in its tactical plans that were not helping the company accomplish its mission "to make people happy." Management redesigned special package deals (for tickets, hotel, and food), because it realized that most families only wanted to spend two or three days at the park instead of five days or longer, which was the original tactical plan. Likewise, to increase attendance, Disney cut admission prices by 20 percent and hotel and food prices by 10 percent. Finally, management realized that it had miscalculated by "Europeanizing" park rides and shows. It turned out that European visitors wanted an "American experience." So instead of sit-down restaurants with waiters and servers, the emphasis is now on fast food and self-service. Rather than fine food and fine wines, restaurants serve hamburgers, brownies, stuffed potatoes, and carbonated beverages in disposable paper cups.[40]

management by objectives
a four-step process in which managers and employees discuss and select goals, develop tactical plans, and meet regularly to review progress toward goal accomplishment

Management by objectives (see the feature "What Really Works? Management by Objectives") is a management technique often used to develop and carry out tactical plans. **Management by objectives**, or MBO, is a four-step process in which managers and their employees (1) discuss possible goals, (2) participatively select goals that are challenging, attainable, and consistent with the company's overall goals, (3) jointly develop tactical plans that lead to accomplishment of tactical goals and objectives, and (4) meet regularly to review progress toward accomplishment of those goals. Lee Iacocca, the former CEO who brought Chrysler Corporation back from the verge of bankruptcy, credits MBO (though he called it a "quarterly review system") for his 30 years of extraordinary success as a manager. Iacocca said, "Over the years, I've regularly asked my key people—and I've had them ask *their* key people, and so on down the line—a few basic questions: 'What are your objectives for the next ninety days? What are your plans, your

Disneyland Europe adjusted its tactical plans to "make people happy" in Europe and finally earn a profit.
© Corbis/Dave G. Hauser

What Really Works

Management by Objectives

For years, both managers and management researchers have wondered how much of a difference planning made in terms of organizational performance, or whether it really made any difference at all. While proponents argued that planning encouraged workers to work hard, to persist in their efforts, to engage in behaviors directly related to goal accomplishment, and to develop better strategies for achieving goals, opponents argued that planning impeded organizational change and adaptation, created the illusion of managerial control, and artificially separated thinkers and doers.

Now, however, the results from 70 different organizations strongly support the effectiveness of management by objectives (i.e., short-term planning).

Management by Objectives (MBO)

Management by objectives is a process in which managers and subordinates at all levels in a company sit down together to jointly set goals, to share information and discuss strategies that could lead to goal achievement, and to meet regularly to review progress toward accomplishment of those goals. Thus, MBO is based on goals, participation, and feedback. On average, companies that effectively use MBO will outproduce those that don't use MBO by an incredible 44.6 percent! And in companies where top management is committed to MBO, that is, where objective-setting begins at the top, the average increase in performance is an even more astounding 56.5 percent. By contrast, when top management does not participate in or support MBO, the average increase in productivity drops to 6.1 percent. In all, though, there is a 97 percent chance that companies that use MBO will outperform those that don't! Thus, MBO can make a very big difference to the companies that use it.

MBO

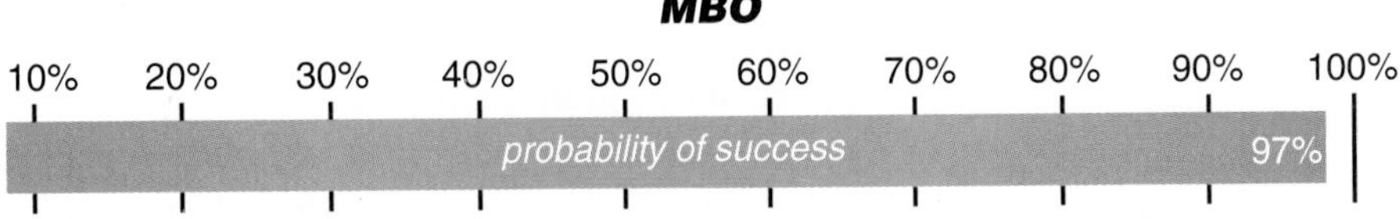

Sources: R. Rodgers & J.E. Hunter, "Impact of Management by Objectives on Organizational Productivity," *Journal of Applied Psychology* 76 (1991): 322-336.

priorities, your hopes? And how do you intend to go about achieving them?' "[41]

According to Iacocca, MBO (or his "quarterly review system") has the following advantages:

- *First, it allows a man to be his own boss and to set his own goals.*
- *Second, it makes him more productive and gets him motivated on his own.*
- *Third, it helps new ideas bubble to the top. The quarterly review forces managers to pause and consider what they've accomplished, what they expect to accomplish next, and how they intend to go about it.*
- *Another advantage . . .—especially in a big company—is that it keeps people from getting buried. It's very hard to get lost in the system if you're reviewed every quarter by your superior and, indirectly, by his boss and his boss's boss. This way good guys don't get passed over. And equally important, bad guys don't get to hide.*
- *Finally, and this is perhaps the most important of all, the quarterly review system forces a dialogue between a manager and his boss. In an ideal world, you wouldn't need to institute a special structure just to make sure that interaction takes place. But if a manager and his boss don't get along very well, at least four times a year they still have to sit down to decide what they're going to accomplish together in the months ahead. There's no way they can avoid this meeting, and over time, as they gradually come to know each other better, their working relationship usually improves.*[42]

When done right, MBO is an extremely effective method of tactical planning. However, MBO is not without disadvantages.[43] Some MBO programs involve excessive paperwork, requiring managers to file annual statements of plans and objectives, plus quarterly or semiannual written reviews assessing goal progress. Another difficulty is that managers are frequently reluctant to give employees feedback about their performance. A third disadvantage is that managers and employees sometimes have difficulty agreeing on goals. And when employees are forced to accept goals that they don't want, goal commitment and employee effort suffer. Last, because MBO focuses on quantitative, easily measured goals, employees may neglect important unmeasured parts of their jobs. In other words, if your job performance is judged only by whether you reduced costs by 3 percent or raised revenues by 5 percent, then you are unlikely to give high priority to the unmeasured, but still important parts of your job, like mentoring new employees or sharing new knowledge and skills with co-workers.

3.3

Finishing at the Bottom

operational plans
day-to-day plans, developed and implemented by lower-level managers, for producing or delivering the organization's products and services over a 30-day to 6-month period

Lower-level managers are responsible for developing and carrying out **operational plans**, which are the day-to-day plans for producing or delivering the organization's products and services. Operational plans direct the behavior, efforts, and priorities of operative employees for periods ranging from 30 days to six months. There are three kinds of operational plans: single-use plans, standing plans, and budgets.

single-use plans
plans that cover unique, one-time-only events

Single-use plans deal with unique, one-time-only events. For example, three huge U.S. companies recently decided to become smaller, either by splitting into separate, smaller companies, or by spinning off a large division.[44] ITT, a large conglomerate, split into a manufacturing company, an insurance company, and a hotel and gaming company. General Motors, the world's largest auto manufacturer, decided to spin off its Electronic Data Systems subsidiary, which is the world's largest computer services company. AT&T split into three companies: a phone company, a telecommunications equipment business, and a computer company. Although each company split up for strategic reasons, the actions taken to prepare for the split-ups were based on single-use plans. For example, EDS prepared for its split from General Motors by offering early retirement packages to 2,800 U.S. workers, taking a one-time pretax charge of over $500 million against earnings, and looking for "redundant facilities and assets" that it could close or sell prior to becoming an independent company.[45]

standing plans
plans used repeatedly to handle frequently recurring events

Unlike single-use plans that are created, carried out, and then never used again, **standing plans** save managers time, because they are created once and then used repeatedly to handle frequently recurring events. If you encounter a problem that you've seen before, someone in your company has probably written a standing plan that explains how to address it. There are three kinds of standing plans: policies, procedures, and rules and regulations.

policy
standing plan that indicates the general course of action that should be taken in response to a particular event or situation

Policies indicate the general course of action that company managers should take in response to a particular event or situation. A well-written policy will also specify why the policy exists and what outcome the policy is intended to produce. For example, because boxing is a "blood sport," the Nevada Athletic Commission has a policy that requires all boxers to be tested for HIV the first time they box in the state each year. If the test comes back positive, they ban the boxer from fighting. This policy exists to protect boxing opponents, referees, and courtside trainers and assistants from being exposed to HIV-infected blood during a fight.[46] Likewise, because of changes in environmental laws that restrict the use of coolants, like the Freon used in refrigerators and air conditioners, most appliance repair companies have policies similar to the following: "Refrigerant used in any type of air conditioning or refrigerating equipment shall be recovered for reuse or reclamation, or be properly disposed whenever it is removed from equipment."[47]

procedure
standing plan that indicates the specific steps that should be taken in response to a particular event

Procedures are more specific than policies, because they indicate the series of steps that should be taken in response to a particular event. For example, when a boxer's blood test comes back positive, the Nevada Athletic Commission follows a procedure that is designed to make sure that the test results were accurate. The procedure is to test the same blood sample three more times, with each subsequent test being more accurate (and expensive) than the one before it.

rules and regulations
standing plans that describe how a particular action should be performed, or what must happen or not

Rules and regulations are even more specific than procedures, because they specify what must happen or not happen. They describe precisely how a particular action should be performed. For instance, rules and regulations forbid many managers from writing job reference letters for employees who have worked at their firms. Companies insist on such rules because a negative reference letter may prompt a former employee to sue for defamation of character.[48]

One of the areas in which companies are struggling to create effective rules and regulations is the Internet. For example, a study by Nielsen Media Research found that of the 54 million "hits" to Penthouse Magazine's Web site during a two-month period, the most came from workers at IBM, Apple, Hewlett-Packard, and AT&T. When contacted by reporters about this study, Apple refused to comment, and IBM did not return reporters' calls. However, AT&T and Hewlett-Packard spokespeople indicated that employees caught "surfing" adult-oriented sites on company time could be fired. An HP spokesperson said, "We probably need to redouble our efforts to make clear what people can and cannot do with company equipment. But we won't watch over people's shoulders. There has to be a certain amount of trust."[49] In other words, given the easy, quick, and wide-open access to all kinds of material on the Internet, organizations need to make clear that it is against company rules and regulations to use company computers on company time to view adult-oriented content.

budgeting
quantitative planning through which managers decide how to allocate available money to best accomplish company goals

Budgets are the third kind of operational plan. **Budgeting** is quantitative planning, because it forces managers to decide how to allocate available money to best accomplish company goals. According to Jan King, author of *Business Plans to Game Plans*, "Money sends a clear message about your priorities. Budgets act as a language for communicating your goals to others." For example, Figure 4.5 shows the operating budget for the General Fund of the city of Austin, Texas. With nearly half this budget dedicated to public safety (49.3 percent), it's clear that keeping the city safe is the Austin city government's most important task.

One of the most difficult but important budgeting tasks for any manager is to produce a budget that is consistent with the company's mission and its

Figure 4.5 **Austin, Texas, Budget for General Fund Use**

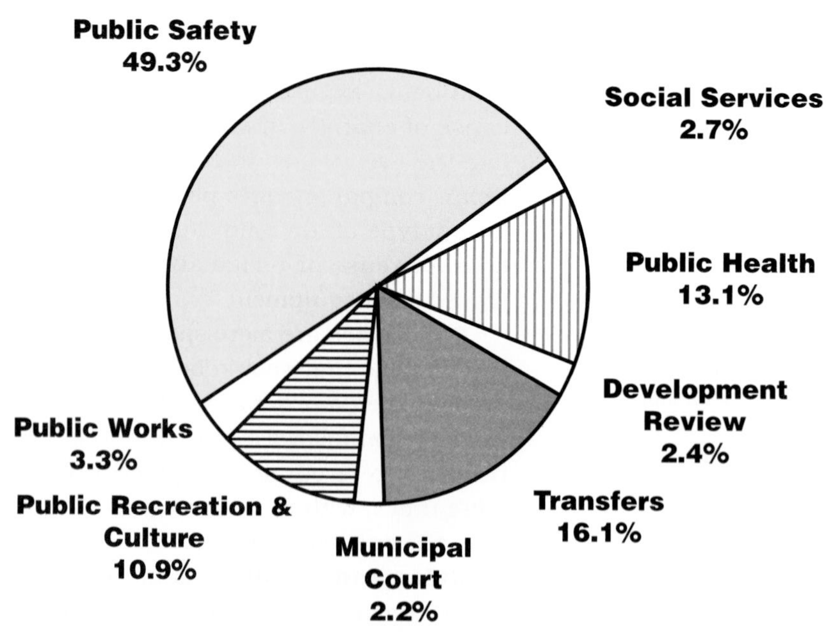

Source: City of Austin Financial and Administrative Services Department, "City of Austin: City Manager's Proposed Budget: Fiscal Year 1997-98, part 2," [Online] Available **http://www.ci.austin.tx.us/budgt2.htm,** 26 March 1998.

strategic and tactical objectives. Table 4.1 shows the change in NASA's budget from 1997 to 1998 for space shuttle operations. Notice that there is an overall decline in spending for shuttle operations. Importantly, these reductions are consistent with NASA's long-term goal of replacing government funding of the space-shuttle program with funds from private companies. (See Figure 4.4 to review NASA's strategic objectives.)

Review 3
Planning from Top to Bottom

Proper planning requires that the goals at the bottom and middle of the organization support the objectives at the top of the organization. Top management develops strategic plans that indicate how a company will serve customers and position itself against competitors over a two- to five-year period. Strategic planning starts with the creation of an organizational vision and mission. There are four kinds of organization missions: targeting, common enemy, role model, and internal transformation. Middle managers use techniques like management by objectives to develop tactical plans that direct behavior, efforts, and priorities over the next six months to two years. Finally, lower-level managers develop operational plans that guide daily activities in producing or delivering an organization's products and services. Operational plans typically span periods ranging from 30 days to six months. There are three kinds of operational plans: single-use plans, standing plans (policies, procedures, and rules and regulations), and budgets.

4 Special-Purpose Plans

You wouldn't use a hammer to flip your pancakes. You wouldn't hire a Ph.D. in archeology to install a new hard drive in your computer. And you wouldn't light an acetylene torch to make popcorn. Everyone knows that a

Table 4.1

1997–1998 Budget Changes for NASA's Space Shuttle Operations

Operations	1997	1998	Changes
Space shuttle	2,977.8	2,922.8	–50.0
Shuttle operations	***2,494.4***	***2,369.4***	***–120.0***
Orbiter and integration	463.1	502.9	44.8
Propulsion	1,136.7	1,061.8	–75.1
Mission and launch operations	894.4	804.7	–89.7
Safety and performance upgrades	***483.4***	***553.4***	***70.0***
Orbiter improvements	137.3	232.5	95.2
Propulsion upgrades	247.0	176.0	–71.0
Flight operations and launch site equipment	92.3	138.1	45.8
Construction of facilities	6.8	6.8	

Source: "Changes from FY 1997 Budget Estimate to FY 1998 Current Estimate," The NASA Homepage, [Online] Available **http://ifmp.nasa.gov/codeb/budget/fy99/summaries/FY_98_CHANGES.doc,** 25 March 1998.

big part of getting a job done right is to hire people who know what they're doing. Or, if you're brave enough to try to fix something on your own, the secret to getting something done right is to use the right tool.

Plans are like tools and technicians. If you use the wrong one, your plan will fail. But, if you use them for what they were intended, they'll serve you well.

Let's examine how companies use special-purpose plans to plan for **4.1** *change,* **4.2** *contingencies, and* **4.3** *product development. Make sure all the special-purpose plans reviewed in this section end up in your planning toolbox.*

4.1 Planning for Change

People are creatures of habit. It's extremely difficult to get them to change. Therefore, managers and employees are more comfortable trying to achieve small incremental improvements than overhauling the way they do business. They know that if they work a little harder, plan a bit smarter, and don't catch any unlucky breaks, they should be able to hit 3 percent, 4 percent, or 5 percent improvement goals year after year.

stretch goals
extremely ambitious goals that, initially, employees don't know how to accomplish

However, sometimes doing more of the same won't improve business performance sufficiently to achieve the company's mission. When this is the case, companies use stretch goals. **Stretch goals**, by definition, are extremely ambitious goals that you don't know how to reach.[50] The purpose of stretch goals is to achieve extraordinary improvements in company performance. Stretch goals are so demanding that they force managers and workers to throw away old comfortable solutions and adopt radical, never-used solutions. Steve Kerr, former dean of the University of Southern California's Business School, who is now General Electric's "Chief Learning Officer," illustrates the idea of stretch goals with this story:

> *You give a team an orange and say that each person must handle the orange—you can throw it to each other, do anything you want—but the orange has to end up in the hands of the person who started it. The group throws the orange back and forth, and you time it. The first time we did it, it took nine seconds. When asked to improve, they stood a little closer, threw it a little faster, and got it down to seven seconds. Then we said, "Many groups do this in less than a second, and it's possible to do it in less than half a second." In the third trial, the team did it in less than a second, by simply stacking up their hands. The guy with the orange dropped it, it went swoosh through everybody's hands, and he caught it at the bottom—that was it. It was a neat example of the power of a stretch goal.*[51]

benchmarking
the process of identifying outstanding practices, processes, and standards in other companies and adapting them to your company.

Since the first reaction to most stretch goals is, "You've got to be kidding," Kerr recommends setting "achievable" stretch goals. However, knowing what is too easy a goal (and thus not a stretch goal) and what is too difficult a goal (and thus not achievable) is difficult. One way companies choose a stretch goal of just the right difficulty is by benchmarking. **Benchmarking** is the process of identifying outstanding practices, processes, and standards in other companies and adapting them to your company.[52] For example, one of the biggest hassles associated with most hospital stays is the amount of paperwork and time it takes to complete the admission process. If you were a hospital administrator, who would you benchmark to learn how to streamline your slow, cumbersome admissions process? What business or company would know how to handle admissions-like situations and paperwork faster than your hospital? Well, many hospitals actually benchmark their admissions processes against Marriott Hotels. Think about it. Both admit people to rooms, typically for no more than a couple of nights, but longer if necessary. Both collect basic information, such as your name, address, phone number, and how payment will be made (a credit card for the hotel and a medical insurance card for the hospital). And both try to determine your preferences upon admission (smoking or nonsmoking room, the kind of room you desire, food preferences, etc.). The processes are nearly identical. Consequently, benchmarking helps employees realize that they can achieve extraordinary levels of performance; after all, it's being done at another company—in this case, Marriott.

Based on General Electric's experience, Kerr strongly recommends that companies not punish managers and workers when they fail to achieve stretch goals. Since the purpose of stretch goals is to achieve extraordinary improvements in performance, it is a mistake for companies to measure progress by assessing whether new levels of performance meet or fall short of the stretch goal. For example, Kerr would likely argue that it was wrong for Chrysler's board of directors to cut top management's annual bonuses by 18 percent because Chrysler failed to achieve stretch goals for improvements in car quality. Because of the inherent difficulty of stretch goals, companies need to assess progress by comparing new levels of performance to old levels. For example, though Chrysler's board punished top management by reducing its annual bonus, the punishment wasn't because quality didn't improve. Chrysler spokesperson Steve Harris said, "We just didn't reach the tough stretch goals we set," noting that Chrysler had made double-digit percentage improvements in quality in the last year.[53] What do you think? Did Chrysler managers fail because they didn't achieve their stretch goal? Or did they succeed because they achieved double-digit improvements in quality?

Been There,

Steve Kerr Discusses Stretch Goals at GE

Steve Kerr is the "Chief Learning Officer" of General Electric. Before coming to GE, he was a management professor and the dean of the University of Southern California's Business School. In this interview from Fortune Magazine, *he discusses the right and wrong ways of using stretch goals.*

Q: GE has been touting stretch targets for years, yet you say they can be destructive. What gives?

A: Most organizations don't have a clue about how to manage stretch goals. It's popular today for companies to ask their people to double sales or increase speed to market threefold. But then they don't provide their people with the knowledge, tools, and means to meet such ambitious goals. We all agree that generally you get more output by committing more input, but now corporate America seems to be trying to get more output just by demanding more output. Ask them to explain the incongruity, and they say, "We're smarter now. We're not going to give you more people, or money, or physical space; we're not going to give you more of any resource, so your solution is going to have to be to work smarter, get out of the box, and be creative."

"Stretch targets are an artificial stimulant for finding ways to work more efficiently."

Q: So what happens?
A: To meet stretch targets, people use the only resource that's not constrained, which is their personal time. I think that's immoral. People are under tremendous stress. And that's what I'm seeing all around this country, people working evenings, working Saturdays, working Sundays to achieve these stretch targets. Americans, in fact, now work longer days with fewer vacations than people in almost any other developed country. Therefore we have a moral obligation to try to give people the tools to meet tough goals. I think it's totally wrong if you don't give employees the tools to succeed, then punish them when they fail.

Q: Why bother with stretch targets in the first place if they're going to harm workers?
A: Well, if done right, a stretch target, which basically is an extremely ambitious goal, gets your people to perform in ways they never imagined possible. It's a goal that, by definition, you don't know how to reach. You might, for instance, ask people to cut costs by half or reduce product-development time from years to months. Stretch targets are an artificial stimulant for finding ways to work more efficiently. They force you to think "out of the box."

Q: What's the right approach?
A. No. 1, don't set goals that stress people crazily. No. 2, if you do set goals that stretch them or stress them crazily, don't punish failure. No. 3, if you're going to ask them to do what they have never done, give them whatever tools and help you can.

Q: But you can't really just pull a goal out of thin air.
A: No, of course not. You've got to find a middle ground. If you set easy goals, people may meet them but probably won't exceed them by very much. If you set extremely hard goals, people lose faith in them. Also, in this interdependent world of ours, you have to realize that when you set a stretch goal, it has implications for somebody else. Say I set a stretch goal for sales. You have been selling ten widgets a day, and now I want you to double it to 20. But you can't sell those extra widgets if manufacturing doesn't make them. So once we set that stretch goal, how many widgets should manufacturing build? If you don't make your numbers, you end up with that dreaded thing called inventory. It's hard not to get grouchy when manufacturing built stuff that didn't sell. That's a tough thing not to punish.

Q: What's the solution?
A: In this example, manufacturing and sales are going to have to communicate much more closely and adjust output as the year goes on.

Q: Should everyone be given the same stretch goals?
A: No, not at all. The danger is that you can end up hurting your best people. A golden rule of every work system is: Don't hurt the high performers. The folks in your best-performing business units may already be stretching themselves to the limit.

Q: What repercussions are there?
A: One issue is self-punishment. If you're truly setting stretch goals, by definition you can't have a high degree of success. For individuals who are high achievers, it's not their style to miss goals. So you end up making people who are winners feel as if they're losers.

Q: How do you know stretch goals are working?
A: You measure progress in three ways. One, you compare what you're doing now with your own past performance; two, you look for meaningful progress toward the stretch goal; and three, you benchmark competitors and see if you're doing at least as well as they are.

Q: And if it does work, what does the employee get out of it?
A: Money, for one thing. In a typical gain-sharing arrangement, you might split the incremental gain or savings sixty-forty or fifty-fifty. Say, if the people at a factory save $300,000, they get $150,000 and the company $150,000. Then there are the nonfinancial rewards. These may include increased job security and personal satisfaction.

Q: What are the most important things for managers to remember about stretch goals?
A: I think you absolutely have to honor the don't-punish-failure concept; stretch targets become a disaster without that. Also, you have to provide the right tools. Finally, you have to understand that stretch goals cannot be targets that you absolutely have to reach. Because if you absolutely need the results, let's face it, you're going to have to punish failure to reach it. On the other hand, there should never be excuses for failure to reach real goals like quarterly earnings or sales targets. Stretch goals are supplemental to those basic goals. All these points may not be rocket science, but you would be surprised how often managers violate them.

Source: S. Sherman, "Stretch Goals: The Dark Side of Asking for Miracles," *Fortune*, 13 November 1995.

4.2 *Planning for Contingencies*

General Motors once made six out of every ten cars sold in the U.S. Today, GM's market share has dropped nearly in half, to between 32 percent and 35 percent.[54] At one time, IBM made over 75 percent of all personal computers. Today, its market share is between 7 percent and 8 percent.[55] How could these companies, that once completely dominated their industries, fall so far so fast? Simply put, neither company anticipated nor was prepared for the tremendous changes that affected their industries (increased foreign competition, stagnant or falling prices, rapid introduction of new models and technology, etc.). General Motors did not realize that American auto buyers, in search of better quality, were quite willing to purchase German- and Japanese-made cars. IBM never envisioned that computer customers would risk their hard-earned money on "unproven IBM PC clones" when, after all, they could purchase a true IBM personal computer (rather than a "clone") for twice the money.

scenario planning
the process of developing plans to deal with several possible future events and trends that might affect the business

Scenario planning is the process of developing plans to deal with events and trends that might affect a business in the future. It helps managers answer "what if" questions and prepare responses should those "what if" scenarios actually occur. You probably do scenario planning often in your own life. Your plans could go something like this: "If I get the scholarship I applied for, I won't work this term. If I don't get it, I'll apply to work in the library."

Scenario planning was first used extensively in World War II when teams of U.S. and British military strategists created scenarios by assuming the role of enemy battle planners. Their job was to devise alternative strategies that enemy forces might use to attack Allied troops, and figure out the best way to defend against each strategy.[56] By anticipating possible enemy strategies and planning actions to counter each one, Allied commanders could be ready no matter which strategy the enemy actually employed.

Scenario planning can be broken down into seven steps:[57]

1. *Define the scope of the scenario.* The scope might include a time frame, assumptions about the product, and a geographic area in which the

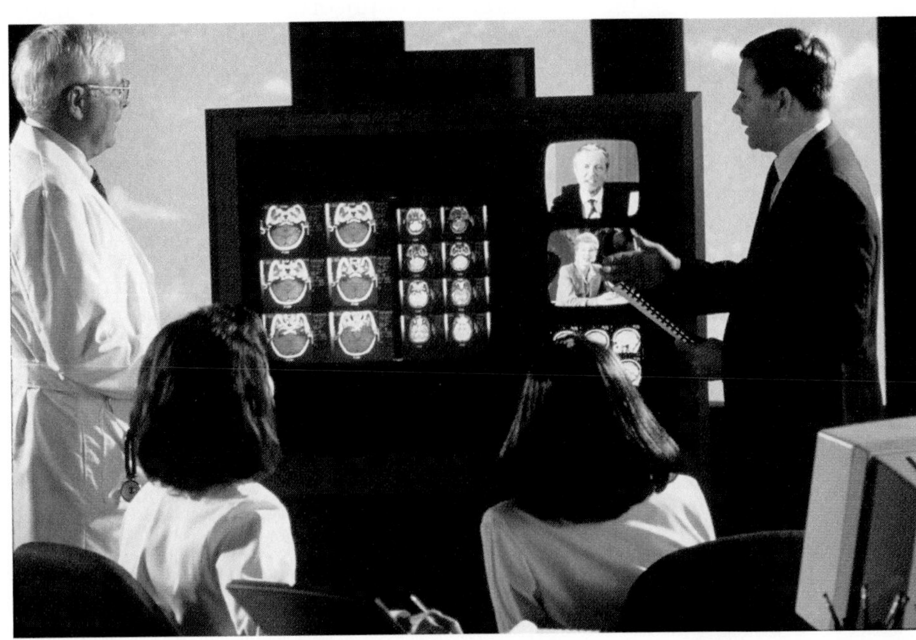

In making their scenario plans, hospitals may have to consider how advances in teleconferencing technology will affect the scope of their business.
© Jon Feingersh/The Stock Market

scenario is to take place. For example, a hospital might create a scenario like this:

> *Ten years from now, most hospital care (the product) will be short-term or outpatient treatment, and rather than just treating local community residents, our hospital will serve a wider geographic area, as doctors use the Internet and teleconferencing to offer medical analysis and treatment to patients who currently live too far away to be treated by hospital staff.*

2. *Identify the major stakeholders (customers, suppliers, competitors, government, etc.) and the roles you expect them to play in the scenario.* Today, HMOs, health maintenance organizations, are one of the leading suppliers of health care. HMOs have brought down the cost of medical care by only allowing patients to be treated by doctors who participate in their HMO and then by closely controlling the amount of money paid to those doctors. However, if the Internet and teleconferencing make it easier and economical for patients to receive medical advice and treatment from doctors and hospitals in other cities, then HMOs may have to allow patients to regularly receive treatment from doctors outside of their local HMOs.
3. *Identify basic political, economic, societal, technological, competitive, and legal trends that you expect to occur in the scenario. Explain how and why each trend will occur and what effects it will have.* For example, in the scenario described in step 1, use of the Internet and teleconferencing technology means that local hospitals will compete with each other *and* with distant hospitals and clinics. So a hospital in Indianapolis, Indiana, might find itself and its doctors competing with the renowned Mayo Clinic in Rochester, Minnesota. This might mean that local hospitals have to cut prices or develop particular specialties in order to attract patients.
4. *Identify key uncertainties and the likely outcomes associated with them.* One of the key uncertainties is how hospitals will change if they primarily provide short-term and outpatient care. Will they become much smaller? If so, will they need fewer doctors, nurses, and staffers? Will this make it easier or more difficult for hospitals to be profitable? Another set of uncertainties would be the legal questions surrounding "distant" care. Traditionally, medical care requires doctors to have face-to-face visits with their patients. However, with technology allowing doctors to recommend treatment without traditional face-to-face visits, would patients be more likely to sue if something went wrong? Would hospitals and doctors then deal with the threat of lawsuits by requiring patients to sign waivers in order to gain access to "distant" care?
5. *Using steps 1 through 4, put together your initial scenarios.* A common technique is to write scenarios that use different combinations of key uncertainties. Another is to create best-case and worst-case scenarios. A best-case scenario in this instance would be one in which your hospital wants to take the lead in using technology to provide "distant" care to patients. A worst-case scenario would be if your hospital was losing patients and revenues to another hospital that was aggressively using technology to provide "distant" care.

6. *Check for consistency and plausibility of facts and assumptions in each scenario.* The key here is to make sure that the scenario holds together as a whole. There shouldn't be any obviously inconsistent facts. For example, if the scenario states that the use of "distant" care will increase, it wouldn't make sense to also write that hospitals would be spending less money on technology when, in fact, they'd probably be spending much more. Before being used, each scenario should be read and checked by a number of people within an organization and industry.
7. *Write the final scenarios and conduct a series of planning sessions for management teams to develop contingency plans for each scenario.* For example, Figure 4.6 describes two scenarios developed and used by American Transitional Care, a company that offers low-cost, short-term hospitalization for patients in need of acute medical care.

Figure 4.6 **Scenarios Created by American Transitional Care**

American Transitional Care offers low-cost hospital care for patients in need of acute medical treatment. It created the following scenarios as part of its scenario planning process.

Scenario 1 - The Regulators Return

This scenario assumes strong economic growth, and increased regulation of health care. Fearful of spiraling medical costs, government planners put regulatory controls into effect for all medical treatment. Nonmedical decision makers, such as employers, HMOs, insurance companies, and government agencies, whose primary concern is cost containment, have much more say and influence on the kind, quality, and duration of health care. Medical providers who exceed the cost of treatments deemed acceptable by these groups are not reimbursed for their costs. Physician incomes begin to shrink. Older, more experienced physicians, frustrated by the changes, begin to retire in their early fifties. Consequently, physicians become less and less involved in most patients' medical decisions and treatment.

Scenario 2 - The Engine Slows

This scenario assumes slower economic growth. Because tax revenues have declined, the federal government places strong controls on what it is willing to pay for federal health care plans. With more employees out of work, and the cost of medical insurance rising, fewer people are covered by insurance plans. Accordingly, hospitals cut costs by consolidating and closing low-use departments and facilities. As the recession worsens, the federal government cuts federal health subsidies. Hospitals come under more cost pressures as improved drug treatments, less invasive surgical procedures, and coverage offered by insurance companies combine to reduce the number of people who need hospital-based treatment and the duration of hospital stays. Thus, faced by an increasing number of empty beds and more patients who can't pay for the beds that are occupied, hospitals are generally unprofitable. In many communities, local hospitals have to be closed to stem the loss of funds.

Source: R.D. Zentner & B.D. Gelb, "Scenarios: A Planning Tool for Health Care Organizations," *Hospital & Health Services Administration* 36 (1991): 211.

4.3 Planning for Product Development

Out of change and need to make a collect call? It used to be that your only option was to dial the operator, and hope that the operator did not connect the pay phone you were using to a small, regional company that charged five times as much for collect calls as for regular calls. But now that MCI has introduced 1-800-COLLECT, you're always guaranteed a lower price on a collect call, no matter where you are. Simple as it sounds now, 1-800-COLLECT was the first new product in over 100 years of collect phone calls. 1-800-COLLECT permitted MCI to triple its share of the collect-calling market in just nine months and substantially increase company earnings. Furthermore, by being first to market with a new product, MCI had the satisfaction of watching AT&T rush its imitation product, 1-800-OPERATOR, to market.[58]

Product development is an increasingly important competitive tool. Like MCI, companies that are first to market with new products or newly redesigned products that customers want can quickly increase market share, earn higher profits, and stay ahead of competitors who are forced to play catch-up.

aggregate product plans plans developed to manage and monitor all new products in development at any one time

The first step in effective product-development planning is to create an aggregate project plan.[59] Because very few companies can survive by relying on just one product, companies develop **aggregate product plans** to manage and monitor all new products in development at any one time. Aggregate product plans should indicate the resources (funds, equipment, facilities, materials, and employees) being used for each product, and how that product fits with the company's mission and strategic plan.

Back to the Future
Planning for Speed

Hewlett-Packard gets nearly 80 percent of its total revenue from products that are only two years old. To get new products to market this fast, HP relies on high-speed computers and software to design new products. Then, using a process called "stereo lithography," those same high-speed computers can be linked to machines that create plastic prototypes of new printers, calculators, and computers in just minutes. Likewise, it used to take HP nearly 20 days to design, build, and test the new circuit boards that go into those same printers, calculators, and computers. However, thanks again to computers and development software, HP engineers can now test new circuit boards in just three days.

Planning for speed is becoming a much more important part of overall company management. Traditionally, the term "time-to-market" was only used to describe how fast a company could take a new product idea, turn it into a product prototype, and then get the final product into the hands of consumers. Today, however, time-to-market also includes speed in engineering, production, sales response, and customer service. For example, Otis Elevators realized that building owners were pressuring architects to reduce the costs of new buildings. One way of doing that was to squeeze manufacturers like Otis Elevators to reduce the cost of their products (in this case, the high-speed elevators that go into new high-rise buildings). However, Otis knew that construction and design delays, not the cost of materials, actually represented the largest costs in building construction. Rather than reducing the price of its elevators, Otis realized that it could help architects achieve cost savings by increasing the speed with which they created and finalized building plans. So Otis installed computers in architects' offices to connect them directly to Otis engineers. If a hotel chain decided that it wanted eight elevators instead of six in its new 50-story hotel in Sydney, Australia, the architect would use the computer system to contact Otis engineers, who would then send the new elevator specifications back within hours. This simple change allowed architects to decrease costs by designing elevator subsystems 75 percent faster than before.

Sources: J. McLeod, "Thriving with a Rapid Product Turnover," *Electronics*, 13 March 1995, 15. R. Pawson, J.L. Bravard, & L. Cameron, "The Case for Expressive Systems," *Sloan Management Review*, Winter 1995, 41-48. J.T. Vesey, "The New Competitors: They Think in Terms of 'Speed-to-Market,'" *Academy of Management Executive* 5 (1991): 23-33.

More than anything else, aggregate product plans help companies avoid the classic mistake of having too many products in development at any one time. For example, in one subsidiary of an American firm, a product-development staff of 40 people was responsible for almost 140 projects. Not surprisingly, the subsidiary's managing director complained that "Nothing is getting done as well as we would like." And when asked if all 140 projects were equally important to the company, he replied, "We have no method of weighing the merits of one against another."[60] By contrast, after creating an aggregate product plan, a large manufacturer of scientific instruments and laboratory equipment reduced the number of products it planned to develop by nearly two-thirds. After topping out at a high of 30 products, it now has a much more manageable group of 11 products, all of which are consistent with the company's long-term strategic goals.

Besides keeping the overall set of products in balance and limited to a reasonable number, the second step is effective management of the product-development process itself. Four factors lead to a better, faster product-development process: cross-functional teams, internal and external communication, overlapping development phases, and frequent testing of product prototypes.[61]

Cross-functional teams, which are made up of individuals from different functional backgrounds (i.e., manufacturing, engineering, marketing), make better product-development decisions. The diversity of functional backgrounds means that cross-functional teams have a greater amount and variety of information, knowledge, and experience available as they develop new products. For example, one of the reasons that MCI could roll out 1-800-COLLECT in just 11 weeks was that it gave complete control of product development to a cross-functional team of specialists from marketing, engineering, MIS, and other functional areas.

Frequent *internal and external communication* is the second critical factor in the product-development process. Like cross-functional teams, frequent internal communication between product-development team members increases the amount of relevant information used to make decisions. It also builds group cohesion and reduces mistakes and misunderstandings that are commonplace in the product-development process. External communication with outsiders, such as customers and suppliers, broadens development team members' perspectives by helping them see their product and its uses through others' eyes. While communication with outsiders is typically beneficial, development teams may want to give more weight to what customers and suppliers do with new products (during product testing) than what they say they will do. For example, surveys and focus groups of fast-food restaurant customers usually result in the same conclusion: customers say they want healthier, low-fat food on the menu. However, Taco Bell's border lights, McDonald's McLean, Kentucky Fried Chicken's skinless chicken, and Pizza Hut's low-cal pizza all flopped and have been removed from restaurant menus. Not surprisingly, a National Restaurant Association study found a large difference between what people say they will eat (fruit, vegetables, etc.) and what they really eat (cheeseburgers and french fries).[62]

Overlapping development phases is the third critical factor when planning the product-development process. In contrast to a sequential design process, where each step (product plans and specs, product testing, product roll-out) must be completed before beginning the next step, overlapping development means multiple product-development steps and phases are

Figure 4.7 **Silicon Graphics: Overlapping Product-Development Phases for a New "Supercomputer" Server**

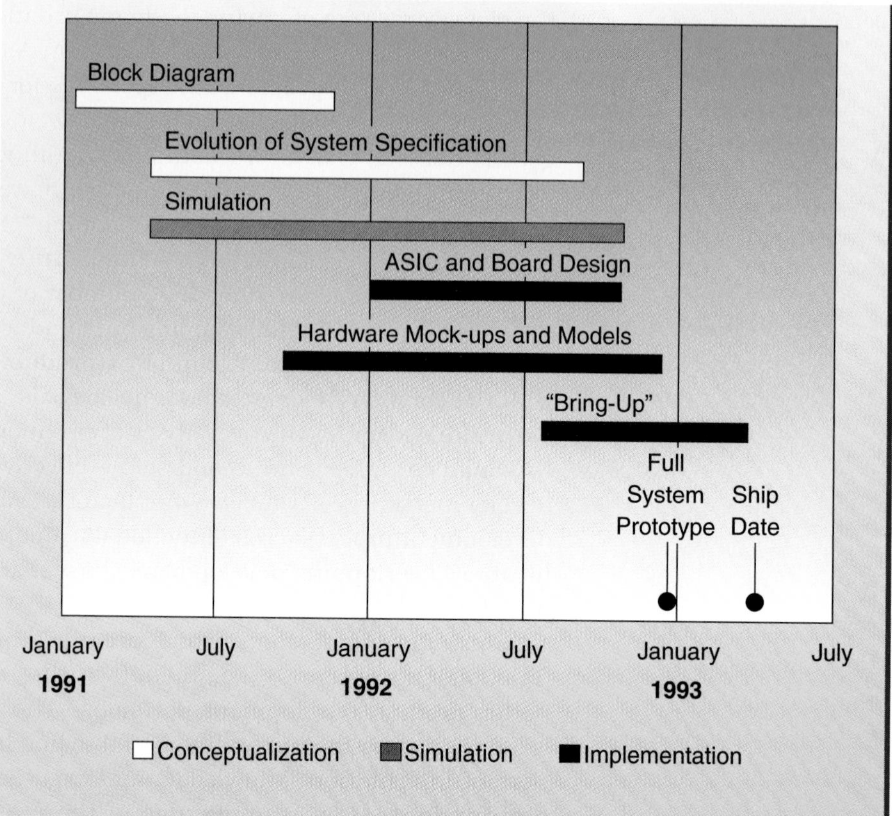

Source: M. Iansiti, "Shooting the Rapids: Managing Product Development in Turbulent Environments," *California Management Review* 38 (1995): 36-58.

started and completed at the same time. Figure 4.7 shows the development time line used by Silicon Graphics Incorporated to develop one of its new "supercomputer" computer servers. The white rectangles indicate traditional planning processes. Here, SGI created the block diagram (the general plan) and the system specifications (the details behind the plan) that it wanted in its new computer. Notice, however, that product testing, indicated by the gray (computer software simulations) and black rectangles (prototype hardware testing), began long before SGI had completed its plans and detailed product specifications. The primary advantage of overlapping development is that it speeds up product development and makes the entire process much more flexible. In fact, SGI began software simulation testing just four months after product development began. And by having customers participate in product testing at an early stage, SGA had the flexibility to incorporate their feedback (and any last-minute changes in computer technology—which always occur at a rapid pace).[63]

product prototype
a full-scale, working model of a final product that is being tested for design, function, and reliability

The last critical component in the product-development process is *frequent testing of product prototypes*. A **product prototype** is a full-scale, working model that is being tested for design, function, and reliability. A good product plan or blueprint is essential. Very few new products succeed without them. But planning is no substitute for the hands-on learning that comes from frequent testing of product prototypes. For example, hoping to produce the ultimate multimedia home computer, a large technology company designed a state-of-the-art sound system for its personal computers. However, tens of thousands of dollars had been spent on development before anyone bothered testing the sound system with one of the company's computers. Only then did they find out that the sound system was so strong that it blurred the computer monitor's video screen.[64]

Prototype testing works best as a "hands-on" process. It begins by testing a prototype, making changes in the product based on what you learned, testing the new version of the prototype, and then making changes again, and so on. Netscape Corporation, maker of Netscape Navigator World Wide Web browser software, employs one of the best-known and most-public prototype product tests. When computer software is still in development, it's often called "beta" software. Netscape conducts prototype testing by releasing beta versions of its software to the public through its Web site. Thousands of people download beta versions of the software and then tell Netscape what they like or don't like about it. Then Netscape releases a "beta 2" version, which improves on "beta 1," and then "beta 3," and so on, before finally releasing the final version of the software.

Review 4
Special-Purpose Plans

Companies use special-purpose plans to deal with change, contingencies, and product development. Stretch goals are used to encourage workers to discover novel, creative ways of doing their work. Benchmarking can be used to set challenging, achievable stretch goals. Managers and workers should not be punished for failing to achieve stretch goals. Scenario planning helps managers anticipate and prepare for future contingency factors that could influence their businesses. The seven steps of scenario planning are (1) define the scenario scope, (2) identify the major stakeholders, (3) identify trends, (4) identify key uncertainties, (5) create initial scenarios, (6) check for consistency and plausibility, and (7) develop contingency plans for each scenario. Aggregate product plans help companies manage all products in development at any one time and avoid developing too many low-priority products. Product-development processes can be accelerated by planning to use cross-functional teams, promoting internal and external communication, using overlapping development phases, and frequently testing product prototypes.

What**Really**Happened?

Radio Shack is one of the best-recognized names in corporate America. However, when customers' needs change, and when new competitors arise to meet those needs, name recognition is no guarantee of success. Fortunately, Radio Shack's performance is on the rebound. Sales and profits are up, and, for the first time in a decade, Radio Shack plans to expand by building 500 new stores by the year 2000. Read the answers to the opening case to find out how Radio Shack is using planning to achieve its turnaround.

After your word processor finishes loading, you type "Radio Shack Master Plan" across the top of the page. But how to make a plan that works?

There are five steps to making a plan work: set specific goals, develop commitment to goals, develop action plans, track progress, and maintain flexibility. If there was a problem with Radio Shack's old business plan, it was that very few people inside or outside the company understood the company's goal of being "America's Technology Store." So when Tandy Corporation hired Len Roberts to be Radio Shack's new president, he began by redefining Radio Shack's vision, in other words, its basic purpose as a company. He said, "Analysts ask me, 'Don't you think that Radio Shack is behind the times? Don't you think that you need to radically change your merchandise strategy, your store formats, and even your name?' Yes, we would have to change all that if we were competing against places like Circuit City. Incredible Universe (another Tandy Corporation store) competes against Circuit City. We don't. *We are a consumer service company.* That's a different market niche." In other words, Radio Shack would compete based on service, not price.

Consistent with that vision, Roberts also emphasized that Radio Shack's new mission was to "demystify technology." With millions of customers unable to set the clock on their VCRs (is your VCR clock blinking 12:00 right now?), program their expensive security systems, or make basic changes to their computer software or hardware, Radio Shack's new mission is to make technology usable for the average person. Radio Shack wants to help frustrated consumers who don't want to have to get a Ph.D. in engineering to successfully use their VCRs to tape their favorite program each week. In fact, consistent with Radio Shack's new mission, company research indicated that customers didn't shop at Radio Shack because it had the lowest prices (It doesn't). Customers shopped at Radio Shack because its employees were patient, knowledgeable, and honest.

Technological products change so quickly that you can't afford to lock yourself into an inflexible plan that will be obsolete within a few years.

No industry changes faster than the electronics industry. For example, eight years ago, Radio Shack got 40 percent of its revenues by selling computers. Today, Radio Shack gets just 10 percent of its revenues from computer sales. Because it sells technology-based products, Radio Shack must have a plan that allows it to quickly adapt to these changes.

Options-based planning, in which the goal is to "keep your options open," is one way that companies are building flexibility into their planning processes. The options-based approach is to make small investments in many options or plans. When it becomes clear which option or plan is likely to work, you "strike" that option by making a much larger investment in it.

Radio Shack is keeping its options open by simultaneously pursuing several new tactical plans to achieve its mission of "demystifying technology." One new option is the Repair Shop at Radio Shack. If you need your VCR, camcorder, radio, TV, telephone, or computer fixed, Radio Shack will quote you a price, ship it to one of its 126 repair centers nationwide, and then return it with a 90-day guarantee. Another new option, designed to appeal to female customers who make 70 percent of all gift purchases, is Radio Shack's Gift Express. For just $4 plus shipping and handling, Radio Shack will wrap, pack, and send your gift anywhere in the U.S. A third option is Radio Shack Unlimited. The average Radio Shack sells approximately 3,000 products. However, by using Radio Shack Unlimited, which is Radio Shack's new-product catalog, customers can order as many as 250,000 different electronics products. By simultaneously pursuing these plans, Radio Shack is "keeping its options open" and building flexibility into its planning process.

Plus, if the plan is going to work, it has to be something that all managers in the company, from top to bottom, can believe in and make happen. So what will the plan have to look like to accomplish that?

To start, top management, like Radio Shack's President Len Roberts, has to develop strategic plans that make clear how the company will serve customers and position itself against competitors over the next two- to five-year period. Radio Shack has accomplished this with its clear focus on "demystifying technology." However, planning works best when the goals and action plans at the bottom and middle of the organization support the goals and action plans at the top of the organization. In fact, Roberts credits his store managers and customers for coming up with most of the ideas that the company is putting into action. Roberts also tries to spend as much time as he can in stores, finding out what concerns customers and managers. He holds regularly scheduled meetings with store managers. What payoff does Radio Shack get from having its president spend this much time with middle and lower-level managers? First, when you're trying to achieve complex goals, like turning around the performance of a company, action plans are much more effective when managers and subordinates develop them together (i.e., participatively). Second, planning works best when the people who create the plan are the same people who execute the plan.

Finally, you wonder, how did Radio Shack get in this mess in the first place? Even more important, if we get ourselves out of this mess, how can we make sure that we don't find ourselves in it again?

Surprisingly, it's common for companies to be caught unaware of major changes in their industry. For example, Wal-Mart is now the largest retail store chain in the U.S. But for 25 years before Wal-Mart, Sears was the largest retail store chain. Before Sears, the largest retail store chain was run by the W.T. Grant Company, which eventually went bankrupt. In each case, the management at W.T. Grant, Sears, and, to some extent, Radio Shack ignored the impending changes and trends in their businesses. When those changes occurred, they were not prepared to respond.

Fortunately for Radio Shack, management became aware of those changes in time. One way in which companies can plan for significant changes in their businesses and industry is to conduct scenario planning. The seven steps of scenario planning are to define the scenario scope, identify the major stakeholders, identify trends, identify key uncertainties, create initial scenarios, check for consistency and plausibility, and then develop contingency plans for each scenario. In fact, managers at Tandy, Radio Shack's parent company (Radio Shack accounts for 75 percent of Tandy's overall sales), began to conduct scenario planning in 1990. Tandy Chair John Roach said, "The genesis of the change came back in 1990, when I challenged our management team to think about how people will shop in the year 2000. I asked them, 'What would be the next wave in electronics retailing? And could we come up with an economic model that would be more favorable to the retailer?'"

Tandy came up with a three-part solution to the "Year 2000" scenario. First, create Computer City, Tandy's chain of computer hardware/software superstores. The computer industry had become so large that it was no longer enough to devote a small section of each Radio Shack store to computer sales. Second, create Incredible Universe, the football-field-sized electronics mall that sells everything from CDs to dishwashers to home entertainment systems. Incredible Universe combined one-stop technology shopping with low, shopping-club warehouse prices. (Tandy has since closed or sold its Incredible Universe and Computer City stores because they were not profitable.) Third, reposition Radio Shack so it did not compete with either of those stores. Radio Shack's new advertising slogan, "You've got questions. We've got answers," its vision as a consumer service company, and its mission of "demystifying technology" all indicate that the repositioning is off to a good start.

Sources: J. Fallows, "The Cutting Edge; Alas, Poor Kaypro . . . A Requiem for PCs Past," *Los Angeles Times*, 11 April 1994, 31. S. Hightower, "Radio Shack Marketing Blitz Aids 'Traumatized,'" *Marketing News*, 4 July 1994, 5. C. Miller, "Radio Shack Expands," *Marketing News*, 24 April 1995, 1. N. O'Leary, "Roberts' New Rule of Order: Demystify the Technology," *Brandweek*, 21 March 1994, 22. D. Olenick, "Back to the Future: Radio Shack Returns to Customer-Service Roots," *Home Furnishing News*, 18 September 1995, 1. B. Woods, "Radio Shack's Nationwide Computer, Electronics Repair," *Newsbytes News Network*, 17 February 1995.

Key Terms

action plan, p. 129
aggregate product plans, p. 150
benchmarking, p. 144
budgeting, p. 142
common-enemy mission, p. 138
distal goals, p. 129
goal commitment, p. 128
internal-transformation mission, p. 138
learning-based planning, p. 132
management by objectives, p. 138
mission, p. 135
operational plans, p. 141
options-based planning, p. 131
planning, p. 122
policy, p. 141
procedure, p. 141

What Would You Do-II?

Sportstown, U.S.A.

The end of another season. Wow. You've never been so physically and mentally exhausted in your life. Most fans think that being the coach of an NBA team is the stuff of dreams, but if they knew firsthand the abuse you took from overly aggressive, ego-driven sports writers, the lack of respect shown to you by your players, and the sheer impossibility of public life (like not being able to fill up your car without being bothered for an autograph), they wouldn't be so envious. Well, a couple of weeks of vacation on a secluded beach will fix the physical exhaustion, but, other than quitting coaching to become a TV analyst, there's no long-term cure for the mental fatigue.

Every year it's the same, one month off and then right back on the treadmill to get ready for the draft, studying hours of tape to decide what positions need to be filled on the team, and then studying hundreds of hours of tape to decide which college players you should draft to fill those positions. This year, you clearly need a point guard to run your offense (5th worst in the league). Unfortunately, the talent pool is very thin at the guard position this year. Besides, you don't have a first-round draft pick this year (you traded this year's first round pick to Seattle two years ago to move up from the 19th position to the 5th position in that draft). Your first draft pick is in the second round, the 32nd pick overall. With all those teams ahead of you, they'll certainly snap up any talented point guards before you get a chance at one. Well, there goes your chance of getting a point guard as good as Jason Kidd or John Stockton this year.

On the other hand, the draft pool is stocked with talented forwards, lots of them! However, two years ago (when you swapped draft positions with Seattle), your first pick in the draft was Eric Jones, a small (6'7") shooting forward, who averaged 23.2 points per game his junior year at Georgetown University. What a promising talent! Yet, what a disappointment so far! His first season, Eric averaged 18 minutes (NBA games are 40 minutes long), 3.2 rebounds, and just 6.8 points per game. But if not for that stress fracture, which wasn't discovered until the last month of the season, who knows how he might have played if he'd been healthy? Furthermore, he was young, having made the jump from college to the pros after his junior year.

This season, he was expected to improve a lot, especially since he was healthy all year. Again, though, he disappointed you, himself, and the fans, averaging just 22 minutes, 5.2 rebounds, and 9.7 points per game. He's a likeable kid. He does everything you ask him to in terms of practice during the season and physical training during the off-season. Unlike many pro athletes these days, he's not an attitude problem: no drugs, no arrests, no driving under the influence, at least not that you know of. But you can't afford to keep him in the small forward position if he continues to play this poorly. First-round draft picks, making $2.2 million a year, are supposed to pump in at least 20 points per game from the small forward position. At this rate, he's not even pulling 50 percent of his weight.

The question is, will he play better next year? The NBA is a tough place, requiring a combination of physical skill, strong will, and smarts. Many established players blossom in their third year in the league. By contrast, many wash up in their third year, too. What to do? It's well known that Eric was YOUR pick. Your general manager was willing to pick 19th that year, but you encouraged him to trade away this year's first-round pick to move up to the 5th position to get Eric. With two years left on your contract, it would be a big plus to have Eric "mature" this year. If he plays up to expectations, the team should win at least five or six more games, just on his efforts alone (and reporters would quit hounding you about the mistake you made when you drafted him). Furthermore, you've talked to Tom Love (a former star forward on the team, now in the NBA Hall of Fame) about providing one-on-one coaching for Eric next year. He's a good kid. But do you keep him and draft the best available athlete (maybe a leftover point guard) with the 32nd pick? Or do you try to trade Eric for a veteran point guard with a few good years left in his career and then draft a small forward in the second round to replace him? **If you were the coach, what would you do?**

Critical-Thinking Video Case

Planning & Implementing: Hudson's

The Dayton Hudson Corporation, with headquarters in Minneapolis, is the fourth-largest general merchandise retailer in the U.S. The corporation consists of Target, an upscale discount chain, Mervyns, a middle-market promotional department store, and the department store division, consisting of Dayton's, Hudson's, and Marshall Field's, all upscale department stores. Hudson's is opening a new store at a premier shopping mall in suburban Detroit. The new Hudson's, at 315,000 square feet, is the largest anchor store in the mall and will feature a gourmet food store, a beauty spa, a concierge desk, and marble floors. It will showcase Hudson's finest merchandise and reflect Hudson's latest thinking in store design and customer service. Hudson's will be the first anchor store in the mall. It is essential that the store open on time and in perfect condition. Planning for a new store is an immense task. Building and stocking the store with merchandise takes at least two years and costs millions of dollars.

Critical-Thinking Questions

1. How might Hudson's plan to build and open a new store?
2. How might Hudson's adapt its plan to meet its opening-day deadline?
3. How might Hudson's evaluate and provide feedback on the results of its planning process?

Management Decisions

What's Your Policy?

Ah, what's this, a Post-it note from the boss attached to a couple of newspaper articles? The first story is about a McDonald's manager who used the company voice-mail system to record "intimate exchanges" with a company co-worker. For reasons that were not made clear in the article, McDonald's later played the tape for his wife. The manager sued, claiming that his voice-mail messages were private and protected, because they could only be accessed by someone who possessed his voice-mail security password. McDonald's countered by claiming that since the voice-mail system was owned, run, and maintained by the company, nothing contained on the voice-mail system could be construed as personal or private.

The second news story is about Irene Wechselberg, a librarian at the University of California, Irvine. Irene works in the rare books department in the UC Library. Like most people, a large percentage of the e-mails that she sends and receives on her university e-mail account are business-related. However, some are personal. When Irene went on medical leave, her supervisor asked for her e-mail password, so that the library staff could keep up with her responsibilities. (No doubt, Irene subscribed to several professional LISTSERV groups that kept up on issues related to rare books.) When she refused, calling the request an "invasion of privacy," the university redirected all of her e-mail to her supervisor's computer. The campus is now in an uproar over this issue. The article quoted Daniel Tsang, a biographer and host of a campus radio show, as saying, "Just because the university owns the public buildings, does that mean the state has the right to install cameras in the bathroom?"

Oh, here's a second Post-it note from the boss. "ASAP, write a policy that makes clear to all employees the appropriate and inappropriate uses of e-mail. Without a clear policy, we're leaving ourselves exposed to problems, controversies, and potential lawsuits. Have a draft in my e-mail account by 9:00 A.M. Monday."

Questions

1. Before writing a rough draft of the e-mail policy, specify, in writing, the purpose of the policy and the outcomes it is to produce.
2. Write a rough draft of the new e-mail policy for your company. Be as specific as possible about appropriate and inappropriate uses of e-mail. Keep the policy short, no more than a page. Since it will be used to guide the actions of everyone in the company, make it easy to read and understand (no techno-speak).

Sources: M. Miller, "Should Email Be Private? UC, Employees Tangle Over Rights of University to Access Computers of Staff on Leave," *Los Angeles Times*, 12 November 1995. D.H. Seifman & C.W. Trepanier, "Email and Voicemail Systems," *Employee Relations Law Journal*, 1 December 1995. D. Young, "Office Email: There's No Right of Privacy," *Chicago Tribune*, 8 April 1996.

vi Ibid.

vii Ibid.

Management Decisions

Crisis Management Planning: Planning for Emergency Scenarios

Scenario planning helps managers anticipate and prepare for changes that might affect their businesses. It helps managers answer "what if" questions and prepare responses should those "what if" scenarios actually occur. Crisis management planning is a special kind of scenario planning that helps managers prepare for emergency scenarios. Barton (1993) defines a "crisis" as a major unpredictable event that may significantly damage an organization and its employees, products, services, financial condition, and reputation. Do you remember when Jack-in-the-Box undercooked hamburgers that were infected with the E.Coli bacterium? Several children in Seattle died as a result. That was a crisis. Do you remember when ABC accused Food Lion, a large grocery store chain, of repackaging old meat (meat that had not been sold before its stamped freshness date) and reselling it as new meat? After the story broke, thousands of customers quit shopping at Food Lion stores. Less than six months after the story aired, Food Lion profits had turned to multi-million-dollar losses. Furthermore, the value of Food Lion's stock was more than halved, from $7 billion to barely $3 billion. That was a crisis, too.

You first learned something about crisis management in the "Developing Your Management Potential" activity at the end of Chapter 2. (If you missed it, turn back to Chapter 2 for a look.) In that assignment, you learned how to deal with the press by responding to two crisis scenarios: the Szechuan Chinese Restaurant and the hotel night manager who finds a hotel guest who has accidentally been electrocuted. Although dealing with the press is a critically important skill, it's a skill needed *after* a crisis breaks. In fact, the best time to deal with a crisis is *before* it happens. Ironically, though, just half of all *Fortune* 500 companies have crisis-management plans in place. Yet, like the unprepared managers at Food Lion and Jack-in-the-Box, 97 percent of *Fortune* 500 CEOs were confident that they could deal with a crisis should one arise.

For this crisis-management planning scenario, let's return to the hotel where the customer is accidentally electrocuted. But this time, rather than focus on handling the crisis *after* it occurred (dealing with the press), we will focus on plans that the hotel chain should have had in place *before* the crisis occurred. Reread the scenario "Hotel Customer Dies in Strange Accident" on page 78 of Chapter 2 and use the questions below to put together the basics of a crisis-management plan.

Questions

1. One of the first steps in preparing a crisis-management plan is designating who is responsible for dealing with the press. In this scenario, was the night the manager the right person to speak to the press? Why or why not? If not the night manager, then who? Again, explain why.
2. The second step in crisis planning is developing an action plan that clearly indicates what steps need to be taken to deal with the crisis. Some common action steps in crisis-management plans are shown below in the form of questions. Complete the crisis-management plan by answering each of these questions.
   a. Who in the company needs to be contacted about this incident?
   b. Do we need to hire a photographer to document damage or evidence? Why or why not?

c. Will a press conference be necessary? Why or why not?
d. Whose responsibility is it to contact the accident victim's family?
e. What steps need to be taken to reassure the public?

Source: L. Barton, *Crisis in Organizations: Managing and Communicating in the Heat of Chaos* (Cincinnati, OH: South-Western College Publishing, 1993).

Develop Your Management Potential

What Do You Want To Be When You Grow Up?

What do you want to be when you grow up? Still not sure? Ask around. You're not alone. Chances are, your friends and relatives aren't certain either. Sure, they may have jobs and careers, but what you're likely to find out is that, professionally, many of them don't want to be where they are today. One reason this occurs is that people's interests change. Burnout is another reason that people change their minds about what they want to be when they grow up. For example, a former lawyer, Michael Stone, said, "I hated it." So he and a partner created a licensing agency that helps companies obtain licenses to sell products bearing the names and logos of corporations like Coca-Cola and Harley Davidson. Another reason some people are unhappy with their current jobs or careers is that they were never in the right one to begin with. For example, lawyer Marsha Cohen said that it took the results of a personality test for her to realize why she disliked her jobs in large organizations. The reason? She was an introvert. Today, she runs her own small practice in international business and is much happier.

Getting the job and career you want is not easy. It takes time, effort, and persistence. Moreover, in today's ever-more-mobile society, it's common for people to have three to five fairly different career paths over the course of their working lives. No matter what you decide to be "when you grow up," your career-planning process will be easier (and more effective!) if you take the time to develop a personal career plan.

Write a personal career plan by answering the following questions. (Hint: Type it up. Treat this seriously. If you do it effectively, this plan could guide your career decisions for the next five to seven years.)

1. Describe your strengths and weaknesses. Don't just rely on your opinions of your abilities. Ask your parents, relatives, friends, and employers what they think, too. Encourage them to be honest and then be prepared to hear some things that you may not want to hear. Remember, though, this information can help you pick the right job or career.
2. Write an advertisement for the job you want to have five years from now. Be specific. Describe the company, title, responsibilities, required education, required experience, salary, and benefits that you desire. If you're not sure where to begin, model the advertisement for your ideal job after the employment ads appearing in the Sunday job listings.
3. Create a detailed plan to obtain this job. In the short term, what classes do you need to take? Do you need to change your major? Do you need to get a business major or minor, or maybe a minor in a foreign language? What kind of summer work experience will move you closer to getting the job you want five years from now? What job do you need to get right out of college in order to get the work experience you need? At the very least, you should have a specific plan for each of the five years in your career plan. Don't worry too much about locking in your fourth- and fifth-year plans. Those are likely to change anyway. The value in planning is that it forces you to think about what you want and what steps you can take now to help achieve those goals.
4. Decide when you will monitor and evaluate the progress you're making with your plan. Career experts suggest that every six months is about right. How about your birthday and six months after your birthday? Others prefer January 1 and July 4, the beginning and middle of the calendar year. Whatever dates you choose, write them in your schedule. Furthermore, right now, before you forget, set five specific, challenging goals that you need to accomplish in the next six months in order to accomplish your career plans.

Sources: "20 Hot Job Tracks," *U.S. News & World Report*, 30 October 1995, 98-104. C. Boivie, "Planning for the Future . . . Your Future," *Journal of Systems Management* 44 (1993): 25-27. J. Connelly, "How to Choose Your Next Career," *Fortune*, 6 February 1995, 145-146. P. Sherrid, "A 12-Hour Test of My Personality," *U.S. News & World Report*, 31 October 1994, 109.

Chapter Five

Chapter 5 Outline

Decision Making

What Would **You** Do?

Mercedes-Benz Credit Corporation, Norwalk, CT. All auto manufacturers finance their own cars. GM has GMAC, General Motors Acceptance Corporation. Ford has FMC, Ford Motor Credit. In the U.S., Mercedes-Benz has MBCC, Mercedes-Benz Credit Corporation. At MBCC, your business is to make sure that when people buy or lease a Mercedes-Benz, they don't leave the Mercedes-Benz dealership to finance their new car. Instead of going to a bank or credit union, you want customers to get their loan or lease financing from MBCC, all without having to leave the car sales representative's office. Today, in an international teleconference with Stuttgart, Germany, home of Mercedes' world headquarters, your manager talked with you about downsizing and reengineering your division. Because of the widely publicized job cuts at large corporations like IBM, AT&T, and General Motors, you knew that top management really meant cost cutting and employee layoffs. The last few years, Mercedes has been through some tough times, losing market share, revenues, and profits to Toyota's Lexus division and to BMW, its German rival. With Germany having some of the highest labor costs in the world, nearly $40 an hour, Mercedes management looked for ways to cut costs. What was its initial answer? Move production out of high-cost Germany. Consequently, Mercedes "mini-Swatch" car will now be made in France (50 percent savings). Minivans will be made in Spain (50 percent savings). Also, a Mercedes four-wheel-drive sport-utility vehicle will be produced in Alabama (40 percent savings). Since you are located in the U.S., you couldn't figure out why your boss was suddenly talking to you about layoffs and reengineering. Sure, compared to other locations in the U.S. (Atlanta, Dallas-Fort Worth, Kansas City), Connecticut is an expensive place in which to do business. But it is still much cheaper than Germany. Nonetheless, your boss's exact words were, "Revenues are beginning to rebound, but your costs are still too high. You're going to have to reengineer the way you do things in order to cut costs and downsize." It wasn't until later in the day, when you checked your e-mail, that you understood why your boss was so adamant about cutting costs. There it was, message #5, subject "Continued Cost Cutting." The message, from the company CEO, said, "Due to competitive pressures, we aim to reduce costs by a total of 25 percent. In the last year, Mercedes-Benz has already completed half of its planned cost reductions. But we all know that the second part of this process will be the hardest." Well, that explains it. Amazingly, through all of the tough times, you managed to avoid layoffs by not filling jobs that came open when employees left the company. Now with business beginning to pick up, it seems you don't have a choice. Changes will have to be made. But there's got to be another way! You don't want to lay employees off. Besides, they're not just employees. They're your friends. They have families. You wonder, are too many jobs really the problem, or is it just the symptom of the real problem—whatever that is? Is cutting jobs the only alternative? Are there other ways to give top management what it wants? How do you decide who stays and who goes? In other words, how do you go about making this decision, and do you have to make the decision by yourself? There's got to be some creative way to handle this—something that doesn't involve layoffs—but what? **If you were the president of Mercedes-Benz Credit Corporation, what would you do?**

Sources: E. Brenner, "Effects of Downsizing Just Keep On Going," *New York Times*, 28 April 1996. "Mercedes-Benz Dealers Hitch a Ride on the Information Highway: New On-Line Service Gives Dealers a Marketing Advantage," *Business Wire*, 2 May 1996. T. Petzinger, Jr., "Georg Bauer Handed Burden of Downsizing to Employees," *The Wall Street Journal Interactive Edition,* 10 May 1996. "Two Cheers for Loyalty: Management Thinkers Are Rediscovering the Virtues of Loyalty," *The Economist*, 1 January 1996.

Even inexperienced managers know that decision making and problem solving are central parts of their jobs. Figure out what the problem is. Generate potential solutions. Pick the best solution. Make it work. However, experienced managers know how hard it really is to make good decisions and solve problems. One seasoned manager said: "I think the biggest surprises are the problems. Maybe I had never seen it before. Maybe I was protected by my management when I was in sales. Maybe I had delusions of grandeur, I don't know. I just know how disillusioning and frustrating it is to be hit with problems and conflicts all day and not be able to solve them very cleanly."[1] Undoubtedly, the president of Mercedes-Benz's Credit Corporation feels the same frustration and uncertainty about how to cut costs. Should cost reductions come from layoffs, as the boss suggested, or is there some other way to solve the problem? Any way you look at it, it's a tough decision.

decision making
the process of choosing a solution from available alternatives

rational decision making
a systematic process of defining problems, evaluating alternatives, and choosing optimal solutions

Decision making is the process of choosing a solution from available alternatives.[2] We begin the chapter by reviewing **rational decision making**, a systematic process in which managers define problems, evaluate alternatives, and choose optimal solutions that provide maximum benefits to their organizations. We discuss the steps of rational decision making as well as its limitations. In the second part of the chapter, we look at how managers can improve their decisions. Here we discuss methods for improving rational decision making and how managers can use groups and group decision techniques to improve decisions.

What Is Rational Decision Making?

Imagine that you've been away on business. Your first day back at the office, as you're sorting through your phone messages, you find this voice mail from the boss:

> *You're a computer nut, aren't you? Whaddya call yourself, an Internet geek? Well, you know more about this stuff than anyone else in the office. Here's what I need from you. You've got three weeks to get it done. I want you to prepare a presentation and write a report that details the problems we've been having with our computers. It should also summarize our current and future computer needs. Talk to everyone. Find out what they need and want. Be sure to consider upgrade options. I don't want to spend a ton of money to improve our systems, only to have them be obsolete in two years. Finally, come up with at least five plans or options for getting us where we need to be. Hey, almost forgot, you're probably going to have to do some educating here. Most of us in management don't speak "computer geek." Heck, half of the dinosaurs we've got in upper management think computers are $3,000 paper weights—Don't repeat that, O.K.? So be sure to explain in everyday language how we can decide which plans or options are best. Have a rough draft on my desk in three weeks.*

When your boss delegated this "computer problem," what he really wanted from you is a rational decision. In other words, the problem needs to be defined, analysis needs to be done, and alternatives need to be explored. Furthermore, the solution has to be "optimal," since the department is going to live with the computer equipment you recommend for the next 3 to 5 years.

BLASTFROMTHEPAST

Benjamin Franklin and Frederick W. Taylor

One of the earliest recorded instances of a rational approach to decision making in U.S. history can be found in Benjamin Franklin's "moral algebra," which he described as follows:

> *. . . my way is to divide half a sheet of paper by a line into two columns; writing over the one Pro and the other Con. Then, during three or four days' consideration, I put down under the different heads short hints of the different motives, that at different times occur to me, for or against the measure. When I have thus got them all together in one view, I endeavor to estimate their respective weights; and where I find two, one on each side, that seem equal, I strike them both out. If I find a reason pro equal to some two reasons con, I strike out the three. If I judge some two reasons con, equal to some three reasons pro, I strike out the five; and thus proceeding I find at length where the balance lies; and if, after a day or two of further consideration, nothing new that is of importance occurs on either side, I come to a determination accordingly.*[3]

However, the individual who had the greatest effect on how decisions are made in organizations is Frederick W. Taylor (1856-1915), the "Father of Scientific Management." Taylor once described Scientific Management as "seventy-five percent science and twenty-five percent common sense." Yet before Taylor, decision making in organizations could best be described as "seat-of-the-pants." Decisions were made haphazardly without any systematic study, thought, or collection of information. Prior to Taylor's time, most companies were very small, so few managers were needed. Most small companies were run by their owners or founders. For example, in 1849, Cyrus McCormick, founder of Chicago Harvester (predecessor of International Harvester), ran the largest factory in the U.S. Amazingly, it employed just 123 workers. In 1870, the Pullman company, a manufacturer of railroad sleeping cars, was the largest, with only 200 employees. However, the Industrial Revolution greatly increased the number of employees who worked in factories and companies. For example, while only 1.3 million people worked in manufacturing in 1860, that number had quadrupled to 5.3 million by 1890. With factories employing thousands of workers per location, companies then had a need for managers who knew how to organize and make good decisions.

Taylor filled this need for organized decision making by advocating the practice of Scientific Management. The goal of Scientific Management was to use systematic study to find the "one best way" of doing each task. In Scientific Management, managers have four duties or responsibilities. First, "develop a science" for each element of work. Study it. Analyze it. Determine the "one best way" to do the work. For example, one of Taylor's controversial proposals at the time was to give rest breaks to factory workers doing physical labor. Whereas we take morning, lunch, and afternoon breaks for granted, in Taylor's day, factory workers were expected to work without stopping. So when Taylor suggested the idea, and said that it would increase worker productivity, no one believed him. However, he showed that workers receiving frequent rest breaks were able to quadruple their daily work.

Second, scientifically select, train, teach, and develop workers to help them reach their full potential. Before Taylor, supervisors often hired on the basis of favoritism and nepotism. Who you knew was often more important than what you could do. Similarly, training and development of workers were extremely rare.

Third, cooperate with employees to ensure implementation of the scientific principles. Labor unrest was widespread at the time, with the number of labor strikes against companies doubling between 1893 and 1904. More often than not, workers and management viewed each other as the enemy. Taylor's advice ran contrary to common wisdom of the day. He said:

> *The majority of these men [workers and managers] believe that the fundamental interests of employees and employers are necessarily antagonistic. Scientific management, on the contrary, has for its very foundation the firm conviction that the true interests of the two are one and the same; that prosperity for the employer cannot exist through a long term of years unless it is accompanied by prosperity for the employee and vice versa; and that it is possible to give the workman what he most wants—high wages—and the employer what he wants—a low labor cost—for his manufactures.*[4]

The fourth responsibility of management, according to Scientific Management, was to divide the work and the responsibility equally between management and workers. Prior to Taylor, workers alone were held responsible for productivity and performance. But, according to Taylor:

The tremendous increase in factory workers during the Industrial Revolution created a need for managers who could organize and make good decisions.
© Hulton Getty

...almost every act of the workman should be preceded by one or more preparatory acts of the management which enable him to do his work better and quicker than he otherwise could. And each man should daily be taught by and receive the most friendly help from those who are over him, instead of being, at the one extreme, driven or coerced by his bosses, and at the other left to his own unaided devices.

Sources: G.R. Butler, "Frederick Winslow Taylor: The Father of Scientific Management and His Philosophy Revisited," *Industrial Management* 33 (1991): 23-26. B. Franklin, "A Letter to Joseph Priestly, 1772," reprinted in *B. Franklin, The Benjamin Franklin Sampler* (New York: Fawcett Publications, 1956). R. Reich, *The Next American Frontier* (New York: Times Books, 1983). T.L. Robinson, "Revisiting the Original Management Primer: Defending a Great Productivity Innovator," *Industrial Management* 34 (1992): 19-21.

After reading these next two sections, you should be able to:

1 explain the **steps to rational decision making**.

2 discuss the **limits to rational decision making**.

1 Steps to Rational Decision Making

Figure 5.1 shows the six steps of the rational decision-making process.

Let's learn more about each of these steps: **1.1** *define the problem,* **1.2** *identify decision criteria,* **1.3** *weight the criteria,* **1.4** *generate alternative courses of action,* **1.5** *evaluate each alternative, and* **1.6** *compute the optimal decision.*

1.1 *Define the Problem*

problem
a gap between a desired state and an existing state

The first step in decision making is identifying and defining the problem. A **problem** exists when there is a gap between a desired state—what managers want—and an existing state—the situation that the managers are facing. For example, the president of Kemp Mill Music, which sells tapes and CDs, knew his business was in trouble when Wal-Mart and Circuit City began selling popular CDs for $10 or less. Since his cost was $10.72 per CD,

Figure 5.1 **Steps of the Rational Decision-Making Process**

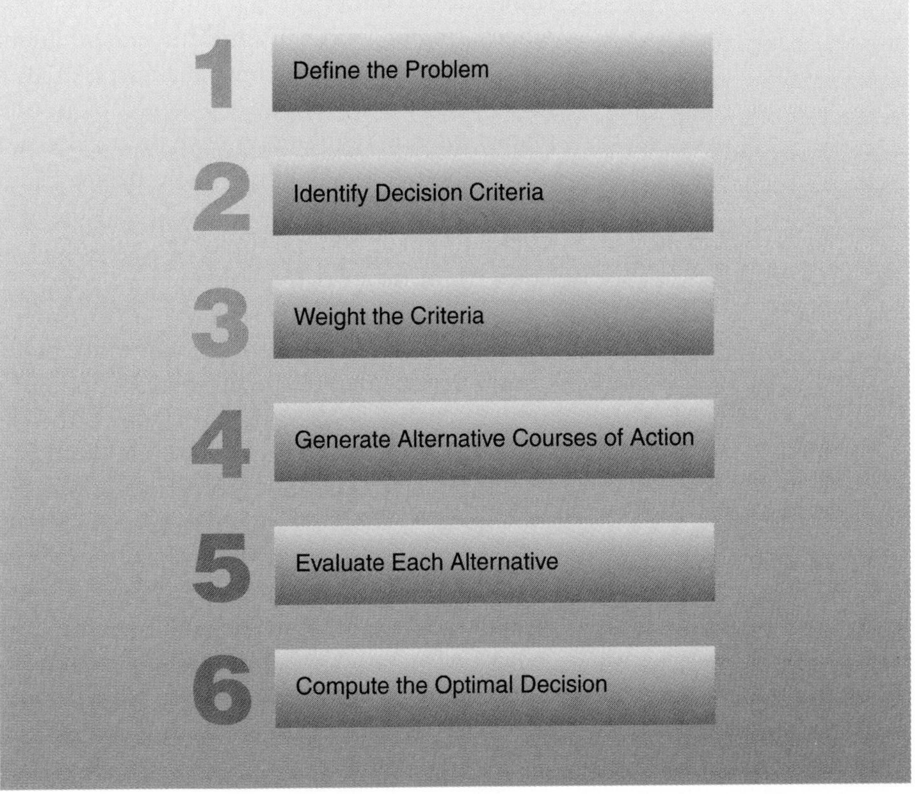

there was no way he could compete. Within nine months, Kemp Mill Music had to close 30 of its 36 music stores.[5]

The existence of a gap between an existing state and a desired state is no guarantee that managers will make decisions to solve problems. Three things must occur for this to happen.[6] First, managers have to be aware of the gap. They have to know there is a problem before they can begin solving it. For example, after noticing that people were spending more money on their pets, a new dog food company created an expensive, high-quality dog food. To emphasize the quality of the product, the dog food was sold in cans and bags with gold labels, red letters, and detailed information about product benefits and nutrients. However, the product didn't sell very well, and the company was out of business in less than a year. Company founders didn't understand why. When they asked a manager at a competing dog food company what their biggest mistake had been, the answer was, "Simple. You didn't have a picture of a dog on the package."[7] This problem would have been easy to solve, if management had only been aware of it.

Second, being aware of the gap between a desired state and an existing state isn't enough to begin the decision-making process. You also have to be motivated to reduce the gap. For example, business people have complained for years about unreasonable workplace regulation. However, Congress was not interested in solving this "problem," that is, until the 1995 Congressional Accountability Act subjected Congress to the same laws as private businesses. Now, like any business, Congress must give overtime pay to anyone who works more than 40 hours a week. Ironically, since it doesn't have the funds for overtime pay, legislative and office assistants, all of whom used to work 60 hours a week, are now limited by law to just 40. So, to limit hours, no one is allowed to work during lunch (even if they want to). Computers are turned off. Phones go unanswered. You can't even watch C-Span while eating your sandwich. At 6:00 p.m., office managers walk through the offices, ringing loud bells and turning off lights to force employees, who want to keep working, to go home. Not surprisingly, these changes have motivated many in Congress to take a second look at the unintended effects that workplace laws and regulations have on businesses.[8]

Finally, it's not enough to be aware of a problem and be motivated to solve it. You must also have the knowledge, skills, abilities, and resources to fix the problem. For example, the president of Kemp Mill Music most likely knew from the start that his company was in serious trouble. It's common practice for retail companies to closely track the prices and products being sold by competitors. So when Wal-Mart and Computer City started selling CDs for less than $10, he probably found out within days. Also, there's little doubt that he was motivated to solve the problem. No one wants to lose money and be forced to close stores. What prevented Kemp Mill Music from solving its problems (i.e., lowering prices) was that it didn't have the resources to fix them. First, with only 36 stores, Kemp Mill was never going to receive the volume price discounts that the recording companies give large retail chains like Wal-Mart and Computer City (a combined 2,500 stores). Second, because they make profits on the hundreds of other items that they sell, Wal-Mart and Computer City can afford to sell tapes and CDs at cost, just to lure people to their stores. However, since Kemp Mill only sells tapes and CDs, this strategy would put it out of business.

1.2 *Identify Decision Criteria*

decision criteria the standards used to guide judgments and decisions

Decision criteria are the standards used to guide judgments and decisions. Typically, the more criteria that a potential solution meets, the better that solution should be.

Let's return to the employee who was given the responsibility for making a rational decision about the office computer setup. What general kinds of factors would be important when purchasing computers for the office? Reliability, price, warranty, on-site service, and compatibility with existing software, printers, and computers would all be important, wouldn't they? However, you can't buy computer equipment without considering the technical details. So what kinds of specific factors would you want the office computer to have? According to *PC Magazine*, in the year 2001, state-of-the-art office computers will have a 64-bit computer chip that runs twice as fast as today's hottest computers, several gigabytes (not megabytes) of memory, an 15 to 20 gigabyte hard drive, a CD-ROM drive that plays DVD disks holding 8 gigabytes of data (including video and sound), a five-channel Dolby Digital sound subscriber link to the Internet that is 5 to 10 times faster than today—all for a price of $2,000 or less![9] These general and specific factors represent the criteria that could guide the purchase of computer equipment.

1.3 *Weight the Criteria*

After identifying decision criteria, the next step is deciding which criteria are more or less important. For example, despite *PC Magazine*'s advice, a 17-inch monitor and a CD-ROM drive aren't that important for business computers. In most cases, a lower-cost 15-inch monitor would suffice for office work (word processing, e-mail, and spreadsheets). And, as long as someone on the office network has a CD-ROM drive that can be accessed from any other computer on the network, then most office computers don't have to have a CD-ROM drive. On the other hand, a Pentium 400 computer chip, 128 megabytes of memory, network/Internet connections, and at least a 10 gigabyte hard drive are "must-haves" for today's desktop corporate computers. (Again, these specifications may be outdated by the time you read this.)

absolute comparisons
a process in which each decision criterion is compared to a standard or ranked on its own merits

While there are numerous mathematical models for weighting decision criteria, all require the decision maker to provide an initial ranking of the decision criteria. Some use **absolute comparisons**, in which each criterion is compared to a standard or ranked on its own merits. For example, *Consumer's Digest* uses a 12-point checklist when it rates and recommends new cars. Six points address the car's performance (starting and acceleration, fuel economy, handling and steering, shifting/transmission, ride quality, and braking), and six address the car's design (overall design, interior ergonomics, seating, accessories and amenities, cargo space, and fit and finish).[10]

Table 5.1 shows the absolute weights that someone buying a car might use. Because these weights are absolute, each criterion is judged on its own importance, using a 5-point scale, with "5" representing "critically important" and "1" representing "completely unimportant." In this instance, fuel economy, seating, and cargo space were rated most important, while shifting/transmission and accessories and amenities were rated least important.

relative comparisons
a process in which each decision criterion is compared directly to every other criterion

Another method is **relative comparisons**, in which each criterion is compared directly to every other criterion.[11] For example, moving down the first column of Table 5.2, we see that starting/acceleration has been rated less important (−1) than fuel economy; more important (+1) than handling and steering, shifting/transmission, and ride quality; but just as important as braking (0). Total weights, which are obtained by summing the scores in each column, indicate that fuel economy and starting/acceleration are the most important factors to this car buyer, while handling and steering, shifting/transmission, and ride quality are the least important.

Table 5.1

Absolute Weighting of Decision Criteria for a Car Purchase

5 critically important
4 important
3 somewhat important
2 not very important
1 completely unimportant

Performance Characteristics					
1. starting and acceleration	1	2	3	**4**	5
2. fuel economy	1	2	3	4	**5**
3. handling and steering	1	2	**3**	4	5
4. shifting/transmission	1	**2**	3	4	5
5. ride quality	1	2	**3**	4	5
6. braking	1	2	3	**4**	5
Design Characteristics					
1. overall design	1	2	3	**4**	5
2. interior ergonomics	1	2	**3**	4	5
3. seating	1	2	3	4	**5**
4. accessories and amenities	**1**	2	3	4	5
5. cargo space	1	2	3	4	**5**
6. fit and finish	1	2	**3**	4	5

Table 5.2 **Relative Comparison for Car Performance Characteristics**

Car Performance Characteristics	starting/ acceleration	fuel economy	handling and steering	shifting/ transmission	ride quality	braking
starting/ acceleration		+1	–1	–1	–1	0
fuel economy	–1		–1	–1	–1	–1
handling and steering	+1	+1		0	0	+1
shifting/ transmission	+1	+1	0		0	0
ride quality	+1	+1	0	0		0
braking	0	+1	–1	0	0	
Total Weight	**+2**	**+5**	**–3**	**–2**	**–2**	**0**

1.4

Generate Alternative Courses of Action

After identifying and weighting the criteria that will guide the decision-making process, the next step is to identify possible courses of action that could solve the problem. In general, at this step, the idea is to generate as many alternatives as possible. For instance, let's assume that you're in the insurance industry, and that your company wants to reduce costs by moving its headquarters out of Los Angeles. Why? Because real estate costs are astronomical, congested roadways lead to average commuting times of 2 to 3 hours per day, and, from your perspective, the regulatory environment is largely anti-business. Not surprisingly, the location of your new headquarters would have to meet the following criteria: a qualified labor force, high quality of life (easy commutes), low operating costs, low cost of living (low real estate costs), and a business-friendly state regulatory environment. After meeting with your staff, you generate a list of alternative locations: Atlanta, Baltimore, Chicago, Des Moines, Kansas City, Milwaukee, Minneapolis, Seattle, St. Louis, and Tampa.

Been There,

How Disney Keeps Ideas Coming

One of the key parts of decision making is generating alternative solutions, that is, keeping the ideas coming. This Fortune *magazine interview with Peter Schneider, Disney's feature animation president, explains how employees pitch film ideas three times a year to a panel consisting of CEO Michael Eisner, Roy Disney, brother of founder Walt Disney, and executives from Disney's animation group. People at each of these sessions refer to them as "gong shows."*

Q: How does a Gong Show get you the best ideas?

A: We have people thinking about what we should do next all the time. But lots of other people in the building, including secretaries, want to present their ideas too. So three times a year they get to do just that, pitching what they think would make a good animated film to me, Michael Eisner, Roy Disney, and my executive VP, Tom Schumacher.

Q: Isn't that a pretty scary audience?

A: Well, people with ideas get some help from their co-workers. Development helps them shape their pitch, for instance, so that it can be presented in three to five minutes, and coaches them on things such as the sort of visuals they could use. And if you're scared to death, someone else will hold your hand when you're up there. On the day of the Gong Show, it's very formal. The four of us all sit at a table and the room is full of people with ideas they want to submit. That way everybody gets to hear all of the ideas. It's not as though you're pitching alone. There's a group supporting you. We usually have about 40 presenters. That morning we pick names at random, so there's no advance order, but each person knows when it's his or her turn.

"You have to create an environment where people feel safe about their ideas."

Q: Still, it must be tough for people to get up and say what they think to Michael Eisner.

A: That's key, though. You have to create an environment where people feel safe about their ideas. And you do that by setting the example. Senior management has to take on the responsibility of saying, "Michael, you're wrong." When people see us saying that, it gives them permission to say it too.

Once all the ideas are presented, the four of us talk about which ones we liked and what aspects we liked about some of the others. Somebody may have a great concept, but the story may not be very good. Or somebody may have a great title. What we can't do is say, "Oh, that's fabulous. Great pitch, guys!" and when they leave, mumble, "What an idea! That was awful!" You must have immediate communication and not worry about people's egos and feelings and how to do it gently enough. You have to tell people why an idea didn't work. We don't pull our punches. If you do that enough, and people don't get fired or demoted, they begin to understand that no matter how good, bad, or indifferent the idea, it can be expressed, accepted, and thought about.

Q: What films came out of the Gong Show?

A: Most of Disney's animated features, in fact. In the case of Hercules, which is now in production, an animator came up with the central idea that a man is judged by his inner strength and not his outer strength. The title was also his idea, but we didn't go for his story line. In the end that came from the two guys who became the directors of the film.

Q: How much autonomy do you give those who lead a Disney project?

A: It's about putting the pieces together to allow people to do their job. It's about people clicking. So you want leadership to pick leadership. You want directors to pick their own art directors, the art directors to pick their head of background, heads of background to pick their own crew. You want people to have a sense of being chosen and wanted on a picture, not assigned, transferred, or exiled to it. You want people to say, "God, they want me."

Q: How often can you do that?

A: Seventy-five percent of the time. The other times we arrogantly say, even to directors, "Just do it." On one of our most successful projects, we told the director to shut up and do it. He was a very talented man but a bit indecisive in terms of where he wanted to go with his career. He didn't know if it was the right project. I said to him, "You've been offered to direct a major animated movie. Do it." He said, "But I don't think I like this and that." "Then change it," I said. "Get in there and start working." He did, and he became ecstatic about the work. But it was the process of it, not that he came in saying, "I know what to do with this movie." It was the process: Going to work, drawing the drawing, talking about it, arguing about it, fighting about it, redoing it, being there.

Q: But aren't you always going to have tension between the production side of the business and the creative side?

A: Always is right. But it's very healthy. Production's job is to ask whether every decision is worth it. We recently discussed making a small change at the end of Hunchback. We were in our last weeks, and the final four shots didn't quite fire off. We were talking about 30 feet of film, which is a significant change. Production said, "Guys, it's 30 feet." And we said, "Yeah, but it doesn't work." They finally agreed, but we didn't go with our first choice, which was time-consuming and expensive, and figured out a way to make the change faster and for less money.

People are getting more comfortable with the idea that this [gong show] is not about us and them. One of our managers organized a Ping-Pong tournament during lunch hours last year, and the winners played a final game with Michael Eisner and [president] Mike Ovitz. They said, "Oh, my God, Michael Eisner's playing Ping-Pong in our building. Wow, I'm important." I'm not sure they say that directly. But where else would the CEO be playing Ping-Pong with an hourly artist? The big guys lost the game, which goes to show people didn't feel they had to let Eisner win. The lines of hierarchy are so blurred that it makes no difference who you are to get access.

Source: J. McGowan, "How Disney Keeps Ideas Coming," *Fortune*, 1 April 1996, 131. This interview was edited for inclusion in this textbook.

1.5
Evaluate Each Alternative

The next step is to systematically evaluate each alternative against each criterion. Because of the amount of information that must be collected, this step can take much longer and be much more expensive than other steps in the decision-making process. For example, in order to evaluate the quality of locations for insurance companies, *Best's Review* (the "bible" for insurance companies) employed a research firm to conduct three in-depth surveys that asked top insurance executives how their locations affected their businesses. The research firm also mailed questionnaires to economic development offices in 25 cities. Those questionnaires contained questions about 50 items (i.e., state regulations governing insurance, number of insurance companies, number of insurance workers, etc.) specific to the insurance industry.[12]

Once the necessary information has been gathered, it is used to evaluate each alternative against each criterion. Table 5.3 shows how each of the ten cities fared on each criterion (higher scores are better). For example, Chicago and Des Moines have the best regulatory climates. But, because Chicago is a major city, it received the lowest score for operating costs, while Des Moines, which does not have a major airport, received the lowest score for accessibility.

1.6
Compute the Optimal Decision

The final step in the decision-making process is to compute the optimal decision by determining each alternative's optimal value. This is done by multiplying the rating for each criterion (step 5) by the weight for that criterion (step 3), and then summing those scores for each alternative course of action that you generated (step 4). For example, *Best's Review* rated the five decision

Table 5.3 **Criteria Ratings Used to Evaluate the Best Locations for Insurance Companies**

City	Regulatory Climate	Accessibility	Labor	Living Environment	Operating Costs	Weighted Average
Atlanta	3	5	4	6	4	4.35
Baltimore	5	4	2	4	5	4
Chicago	7	6	6	5	4	5.75
Des Moines	7	1	4	2	7	4.2
Kansas City	5	3	2	4	6	3.95
Milwaukee	6	2	4	3	5	4.05
Minneapolis	5	5	4	5	5	4.8
Seattle	4	4	3	6	4	4.2
St. Louis	3	5	1	4	5	3.5
Tampa	2	3	4	3	7	3.55

Source: K. Galloway, "America's Best Insurance Cities," *Best's Review/Property-Casualty Insurance Edition*, 1 November 1994, 38.

criteria in terms of importance to the final decision: regulatory climate (25 percent), accessibility (20 percent), labor (20 percent), living environment (20 percent), and operating costs (15 percent). Those weights are then multiplied by the ratings in each category. For example, St. Louis's optimal value of 3.5 (i.e., weighted average) is determined using the following calculation:

$$(.25*3) + (.20*5) + (.20*1) + (.20*4) + (.15*5) = 3.5$$

Table 5.4 shows that Chicago is clearly the best location for insurance companies, no doubt because of its extremely good accessibility, labor, and regulatory climate. By contrast, St. Louis is the worst location by virtue of its poor regulatory climate and weak labor force.

Review 1
Steps to Rational Decision Making

Rational decision making is a six-step process in which managers define problems, evaluate alternatives, and compute optimal solutions. The first step is identifying and defining the problem. Problems exist where there is a gap between desired and existing states. Managers won't begin the decision-making process unless they are aware of the gap, motivated to reduce it, and possess the necessary resources to fix it. The second step is defining the decision criteria that are used when judging alternatives. In step three, an absolute or relative comparison process is used to rate the importance of decision criteria. Step four involves generating as many possible courses of action (i.e., solutions) as possible. Potential solutions are assessed in step five by systematically gathering information and evaluating each alternative against each criterion. In step six, criterion ratings and weights are used to compute the optimal value for each alternative course of action. Rational managers then choose the alternative with the highest optimal value.

2 Limits to Rational Decision Making

In general, managers who diligently complete all six steps of the rational decision-making model will make better decisions than those who

Table 5.4 **Cities Ranked by Optimal Value**

Optimal Values	
1. Chicago	5.75
2. Minneapolis	4.80
3. Atlanta	4.35
4. Des Moines	4.20
Seattle	4.20
6. Milwaukee	4.05
7. Baltimore	4.00
8. Kansas City	3.95
9. Tampa	3.55
10. St. Louis	3.50

Source: K. Galloway, "America's Best Insurance Cities," *Best's Review/Property-Casualty Insurance Edition,* 1 November 1994, 38.

don't. So, when they can, managers should try to follow the steps in the rational decision-making model, especially for big decisions with long-range consequences.

However, it's highly doubtful that rational decision making can help managers "choose *optimal* solutions that provide *maximum* benefits to their organizations." The terms "optimal" and "maximum" suggest that rational decision making leads to perfect or near-perfect decisions. Of course, for managers to make perfect decisions, they have to operate in perfect worlds with no real-world constraints. For example, in an optimal world, the manager who was given three weeks to define, analyze, and fix computer problems in the office would have followed *PC Magazine*'s advice to buy all employees the "perfect personal computer" (i.e., Pentium 400, 128 megabytes of memory, etc.). And in arriving at that decision, our manager would not have been constrained by price ("$10,000 per computer? Sure, no problem.") or time ("Need six more months to decide? Sure, take as long as you need."). Furthermore, without any constraints, our manager could identify and weight an extensive list of decision criteria, generate a complete list of possible solutions, and then test and evaluate each computer against each decision criterion. Finally, our manager would have the necessary experience and knowledge with computers to easily make sense of all these sophisticated tests and information.

Of course, it never works like that in the real world. Managers face time and money constraints. They often don't have time to make extensive lists of decision criteria. And, they often don't have the resources to test all possible solutions against all possible criteria.

Let's see how **2.1** *bounded rationality,* **2.2** *common decision-making mistakes, and* **2.3** *risk and risky conditions make it difficult for managers to make completely rational, optimal decisions.*

2.1
Bounded Rationality

The rational decision-making model describes the way decisions *should* be made. In other words, decision makers wanting to make optimal decisions *should not* have to face time and costs constraints. They *should* have unlimited resources and time to generate and test all alternative solutions against all decision criteria. And, they *should* be willing to recommend any decision that produces optimal benefits for the company, even if that decision would harm their own jobs or departments. Of course, very few managers actually make rational decisions like they *should*. The way in which managers actually make decisions is more accurately described as "bounded (or limited) rationality."

bounded rationality
decision-making process restricted in the real world by limited resources, incomplete and imperfect information, and managers' limited decision-making capabilities

Bounded rationality means that managers try to take a rational approach to decision making, but are restricted by real-world constraints, incomplete and imperfect information, and their own limited decision-making capabilities. More specifically, at least four problems prevent managers from making rational decisions.[13] First, as described above, limited resources often prevent managers from making rational decisions. Managers only have so much time, so much money, and so many people or machines or offices to devote to a specific problem. When resources increase or decrease, managers change their decisions. For instance, when the South

Korean economy fell into a severe crisis in 1997 and 1998, many South Korean companies saw their sales drop dramatically. And, with fewer funds coming in, they were forced to cut a number of previously planned projects. For example, because of declining revenues, Daewoo Corporation suspended its plan to build two factories in northern France.[14] Because of limited resources, there is almost always a difference between what managers would like to do (i.e., rational decision making) and what they can do (i.e., bounded rationality).

information overload
situation in which decision makers have too much information to attend to

Second, attention problems limit the information that a decision maker can pay attention to at any one time. Often, attention problems stem from **information overload**, or too much information. For example, since *PC Magazine* uses 24 specific decision criteria to describe the "perfect PC," and since it typically tests approximately 50 computers every time it conducts a review, our rational decision maker would have to process 1,200 different pieces of information. This is simply too much information for one person to make sense of. Even 10 decision criteria and 10 computers would be too much.

PersonalProductivityTip

Bozo Saves Manager from Drowning!

Drowning in e-mail and information overload? If so, you're not alone. With group mailing lists, anyone can send e-mail to hundreds with just one click. The result? The number of e-mails sent and received has skyrocketed. Consequently, although much of it is irrelevant or worthless, it's increasingly common to spend 2 to 3 hours a day reading and responding to e-mail. One way to stay afloat is to use the Bozo filter in your e-mail software. Type in the names and topics (keywords) that you don't want to read about. The Bozo filter keeps them from popping up on your screen. Be careful, though. Don't "Bozo" the boss.

Sources: M. Rothschild, "When You're Gagging on E-mail," *Forbes ASAP*, 6 June 1994, 25-26.

Third, memory problems make it difficult to recall or retrieve stored information. Managers forget important facts and details. Companies don't always keep the best records. Since the new computer equipment has to be compatible with the old computer equipment, our manager's first task would be to find out what equipment the company already owns. However, if detailed records have not been kept, and if employees don't know the configuration of their computers ("Does it have a 486 or Pentium chip? What speed is the chip, 166, 200, or 233 megahertz?"), then each computer will have to be manually inspected to gather this information. Furthermore, information retrieval is not free. It costs time and money.

Fourth, expertise problems make it difficult for decision makers to organize, summarize, and fully comprehend all of the information that is available for making the decision. Realistically, even though our manager is a self-professed computer "geek," he or she probably doesn't have the required experience or knowledge to make sense of all of the test results and determine which computer is the "perfect PC." The difficulty of this task is illustrated by the fact that *PC Magazine* employs 30 full-time staffers in two research labs stuffed with hundreds of thousands of dollars of equipment to make such decisions. No one, not even managers, can possess expert knowledge about everything.

maximizing
choosing the best alternative

satisficing
choosing a "good enough" alternative

In theory, fully rational decision makers **maximize** decisions by choosing the optimal solution. However, limited resources, along with attention, memory, and expertise problems, make it nearly impossible for managers to maximize decisions. Consequently, most managers don't maximize—they "satisfice." Whereas maximizing is choosing the best alternative, **satisficing** is choosing a "good enough" alternative. With 24 decision criteria, 50 alternative computers to choose from, two computer labs with hundreds of thousands of dollars of equipment, and unlimited time and money, our manager could test all alternatives against all decision criteria and choose the "perfect PC." However, our manager's limited time, money, and expertise mean that only a few alternatives will be assessed against a few decision criteria. In practice, our manager will visit two or three computer or electronics stores, read a couple of recent computer reviews, and then get three or four bids from local computer stores that sell complete computer systems at competitive prices. The decision will be complete when our manager finds a "good enough" computer that meets a few decision criteria, most likely low price, a 10 gigabyte hard drive, and 128 megabytes of memory.

2.2 *Common Decision-Making Mistakes*

Another reason that managers have difficulty making rational decisions is that, like all decision makers, they are susceptible to these common mistakes: over-reliance on intuition, availability bias, representative bias, and the anchoring and adjustment bias.[15]

Have you ever had an "Aha!" experience, in which the solution to a problem you've been working on jumped into your head when you weren't thinking about it? If so, you've experienced intuition. While it's widely believed that scientists and business people only use logical, analytical, research-based methods, it's actually quite common for intuition to play a large role

Back to the Future

Decision Software Slays Satisficing?

Most decision makers "satisfice," accepting the first "good enough" solution that comes to mind. Furthermore, because of time pressures and situational limitations, intuitive, unstructured decision making is the norm rather than the exception. Together, these factors make it nearly impossible for managers and business people to maximize decisions.

However, computer software may do for decision making what it did for the nasty tasks of balancing your checkbook and doing your taxes—make it simpler, faster, and easier. If you've got a computer, you probably use Quicken (or a similar program) to balance your checkbook and stick to a budget. Likewise, if you do your own taxes, you probably use TurboTax (or a similar program) to figure out how much money you owe Uncle Sam (or, if you're lucky, how much he owes you). Millions of people swear by these programs. Avantos Software would like those same people to add decision-making software, called DecideRight, to their collection of computer tools. According to Walter Mossberg, who writes the Personal Technology column for *The Wall Street Journal*, DecideRight "does a far better job of organizing your options in a decision, and then ranking them by criteria you choose, than the traditional yellow legal pad with columns labeled 'pro' and 'con'—the method used by millions."

Here's how it works. DecideRight starts with its QuickBuild tool, which, in an interview-like style, walks decision makers through the decision-making process. Step one, label the decision. "What bank should we choose for the business?" Step two, enter the decision criteria. "Location, hours, fees, etc." Step three, enter the options you're considering. "Bank One, Central Bank & Trust, . . ." Step three, weight the decision criteria. For example, click on "location" and then drag and drop it on the high, medium, or low "importance" button on your screen. Step four, rate each option against each decision criterion. Again, all you do is drag and drop. If Central Bank & Trust is just right around the corner from your business, click on "Central Bank & Trust" and then drag and drop it onto the "excellent" button on your screen for location. Step five, the ranking of alternatives, is performed automatically. There's no math involved (unless you choose this option).

Not only does DecideRight automatically rank alternatives, but it also generates a report with charts and tables that explains why and how the decision was made. The report even explains why one alternative was chosen over another. Plus, it can create presentation slides in Microsoft PowerPoint and Lotus Freelance formats (the two most popular presentation software tools).

Decision-making software like DecideRight is no guarantee of good decisions. After all, Quicken can't guarantee that you'll always have money in the bank, and TurboTax can't guarantee a tax refund. But to the extent that tools like DecideRight encourage managers to work through the steps of the rational decision-making model, it should help them make *better* decisions.

Sources: K. Alesandrini, "Better Answers to Vital Questions," *Computer Shopper*, 26 January 1996. T. Carey, "It's Tax Time: Computer Life's Second Annual Guide to Tax Software Will Help Take the Edge off Doing Your Tax Returns," *Computer Life*, 13 May 1996. W. Kawamoto, "Software You Can Bank On: Personal-Finance Packages Make the Most of Your Money," *Computer Shopper*, 16 February 1996. W. Mossberg, "In Time for Elections: Software to Help You Make Up Your Mind," *The Wall Street Journal*, 8 February 1996. K. Yakai, To Do or Not To Do: Two Business-Oriented Decision Makers," *PC Magazine*, 23 January 1996.

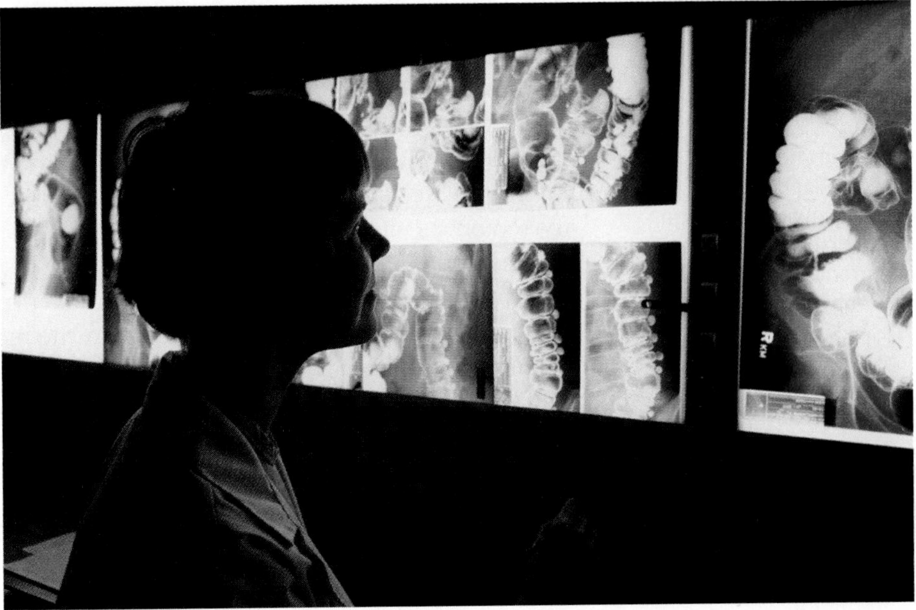

Like other decision makers, experienced radiologists may use some intuition in analyzing patterns of problems they have seen before.
© PhotoDisc, Inc.

in the decisions and discoveries of both professions. For example, physicist Albert Einstein, discoverer of the law of relativity, claimed, "I did not arrive at my understanding of the fundamental laws of the universe through my rational mind." Robert Pittman, CEO of Time Warner Enterprises, who helped create MTV and Nickelodeon's "Nick at Nite," says, "Research is not policy making. People make policy. Research just answers some questions. At the end of the day, it's a gut decision."[16]

Intuition works best for experienced decision makers who can quickly analyze patterns of problems that they've seen before. Unfortunately, over-reliance on intuition can lead even experienced decision makers to become overconfident, careless, and inconsistent. For example, nine radiologists participated in a study in which they examined 96 cases of possible stomach ulcers. Their task was to determine the likelihood that the ulcers were malignant. One week after initially reviewing these cases, the radiologists were shown the same cases again, but in a different order. Amazingly, these highly trained professionals, who knew that the purpose of the research was to study their diagnostic skills, arrived at different conclusions (malignant versus benign) for nearly one out of four patients (23 percent) in the second week of the study.[17] Put another way, if all 96 patients actually had cancer, 22 of the 96 would have been wrongly diagnosed as disease-free in the second week of the study.

Personal Productivity Tip

Don't Worry About Being Perfect

Is it always best to strive for optimal decisions? Probably not. Shooting for perfect solutions can freeze decision makers into inaction. They become so afraid of not making the perfect decision that they create "paralysis by analysis," where gathering data and information becomes more important than making decisions and taking action. Sometimes, it's better to make decisions, risk mistakes, and then learn from the mistakes when you make them. As one Hewlett-Packard group member said, "Why do we have to be perfect right away?" After all, the saying isn't "decisions make perfect," it's "practice makes perfect."

Sources: S. Sherman, "Secrets of HP's 'Muddled' Team," *Fortune*, 18 March 1996, 116-120.

The second common mistake occurs because decision makers have an availability bias when judging the frequency, probability, or causes of an event. The **availability bias** is the tendency of decision makers to give preference to recent information, vivid images that evoke emotions, and specific acts and behaviors that they personally observed. For example, since 1991, there has been a steady significant decline in the total number of crimes committed in the U.S. In particular, murders are down by 20 percent nationwide. However, during this same period, Americans actually *increased* their spending on security-related items from $39 to $55 billion a year. What accounts for this discrepancy? Television and the availability bias. Jason Knott, editor of *Security Sales* magazine, said, "The best advertising a security company has is the local television news." And, according to the Center

availability bias
unrecognized tendency of decision makers to give preference to recent information, vivid images that evoke emotions, and specific acts and behaviors that they personally observed

for Media & Public Affairs, network news has increased its coverage of murders by 336 percent between 1990 and 1995.[18] So, despite the fact that most people are actually much safer today than they were in 1990, they continue to purchase car alarms and home security systems because their minds are filled with the vivid images of murders that are televised to their homes via the local news.

representative bias unrecognized tendency of decision makers to judge the likelihood of an event's occurrence based on its similarity to previous events

The third common decision-making mistake is the **representative bias**, in which decision makers judge the likelihood of an event's occurrence based on its similarity to previous events and their likelihood of occurrence. For example, if a manager hired a graduate of ABC University, and that person just didn't work out, then that manager might tend to avoid hiring any other ABC graduates. In other words, in the manager's mind, one ABC graduate represents all ABC graduates. If one didn't succeed in the job, then the manager's unconscious expectation may be that others likely wouldn't succeed in the job either.

As another example, consider this riddle:

> *A father and son are en route to a baseball game when their car stalls on the railroad tracks. The father can't restart the car. An oncoming train hits the car. The father dies. An ambulance rushes the boy to a nearby hospital. In the emergency room, the surgeon takes one look and says: "I can't operate on this child; he's my son."*[19]

Researchers have found that it's common for people to invent strange scenarios — some involving extraterrestrials—to explain how this scenario could happen. However, since most surgeons are male, the representative bias prevents most people from considering the simple explanation that the surgeon is the boy's mother.

anchoring and adjustment bias unrecognized tendency of decision makers to use an initial value or experience as a basis of comparison throughout the decision process

The fourth common decision-making mistake is the **anchoring and adjustment bias**, in which judgment (good-bad, large-small, yes-no, etc.) is "anchored" by an initial value. Once the anchor is "dropped," two things happen: (1) all subsequent experiences are judged by their similarity to the anchor, and (2) all possible decision alternatives tend to cluster around the anchor. For example, if you were accidentally bumped up from coach to first-class seating the first time you flew to Europe on business, the fine food, free drinks, attentive service, and fully reclining seats would make every subsequent trans-Atlantic trip in coach seating seem miserable. Likewise, when negotiating salaries or selling prices, the first number discussed tends to serve as the anchor for the entire negotiation. For example, in house shopping, the "listing price" stated by the house seller is typically the anchor value for negotiations. Consequently, buyers and sellers tend to judge whether they got a "good deal" by how close the selling price was to the listing price.

2.3
Risk and Decision Making under Risky Conditions

conditions of certainty conditions in which decision makers have complete information and knowledge of all possible outcomes

Step five of the rational decision-making model assumes that managers can gaze into their crystal balls and accurately predict how well a potential solution will fix a problem. Furthermore, it is assumed that managers make decisions under **conditions of certainty**, with complete information and knowledge of all possible outcomes. It's like knowing who won the last ten Super Bowls and then traveling ten years back in time with $1,000 in your

Managers make decisions under conditions of risk. These risks in the auto industry could include plant closings and loss of thousands of jobs.
© PhotoDisc, Inc.

pocket. Because you already know who won, deciding which team to bet on is easy. Plus, you're a guaranteed winner.

conditions of risk
conditions in which decision makers face a very real possibility of making the wrong decision

Of course, if decision making were this easy, companies wouldn't need very many managers. In most situations, managers make decisions under **conditions of risk**, where there is a very real possibility of losing (making the wrong decision). Thus, risk and risky conditions make it difficult for managers to make completely rational, optimal decisions.

Furthermore, risk has a significant effect on how decision makers define and solve problems. Consider this problem from Max Bazerman's book, *Judgment in Managerial Decision Making*:

> *A large car manufacturer has recently been hit with a number of economic difficulties, and it appears as if three plants need to be closed and 6,000 employees laid off. The vice-president of production has been exploring alternative ways to avoid this crisis. She has developed two plans:*
>
> *Plan A: This plan will save one of three plants and 2,000 jobs.*
>
> *Plan B: This plan has a ⅓ probability of saving all three plants and 6,000 jobs, but has a ⅔ probability of saving no plants and no jobs.*

Did you choose Plan A? According to Bazerman, 80 percent of people given these choices choose Plan A rather than Plan B. However, what would you have done if you were faced with the following choices to the same problem?

Plan C: This plan will result in the loss of two of the three plants and 4,000 jobs.

Plan D: This plan has a ⅔ probability of resulting in the loss of all three plants and all 6,000 jobs, but has a ⅓ probability of losing no plants and no jobs.

This time, did you choose Plan D? Again, according to Bazerman, 80 percent choose Plan D. However, if you look closely at both sets of choices, you can see that Plans A and C both save 2,000 jobs, and Plans B and D both provide a ⅔ chance of losing all 6,000 jobs. So why would 80 percent of decision makers choose Plan A in the first context, while only 20 percent chose its equivalent, Plan C, in the second? Likewise, why would 20 percent of decision makers choose Plan B in the first context, while 80 percent chose its equivalent, Plan D, in the second?

positive frame
couching a problem in terms of a gain, thus influencing decision makers toward becoming risk-averse

The critical difference is how the problem is framed. A **positive frame** is the presentation of a problem in terms of a gain. When you begin with the belief that 6,000 people will lose their jobs, Plan A's ability to keep 2,000 jobs is clearly a gain. When faced with the prospect of a gain, decision makers tend to become risk-averse. In gambling terms, it's like quitting while you're ahead. You don't want to risk losing what you've already won. And in this situation, you start with 6,000 lost jobs, but Plan A helps you win 2,000 back. So most decision makers don't want to put that gain at risk.

negative frame
couching a problem in terms of a loss, thus influencing decision makers toward becoming risk-seeking

By contrast, a **negative frame**, such as that shown in Plan D, is the presentation of a problem in terms of a loss. With nothing left to lose (i.e., there's already a ⅔ chance of losing all 6,000 jobs), most decision makers become risk-seeking. In other words, if it's your last night in Las Vegas, and you've lost $900 of the $1,000 you brought to town, why not put your last $100 in a $100 slot machine? You only get one chance, but if it pays off, you'll get all of your money back and more. And if you lose, it doesn't really matter, you were going to lose that money anyway. In sum, risk not only affects how decision makers define problems, but it also affects the solutions they choose to fix those problems.

conditions of uncertainty
conditions in which decision makers don't know the odds of winning or losing

Managers also make decisions under **conditions of uncertainty**. How is uncertainty different from risk? With risk, a gambler knows there is a 1 in 52 chance of drawing a particular card, say, the ace of spades. But with uncertainty, you don't know how many cards there are, and you don't know how many aces of spades are in the deck or whether the deck even has an ace of spades. So under conditions of uncertainty, you can lose, but you don't even know the odds of winning or losing.[20]

risk propensity
a person's tendency to take or avoid risks

Very few people are willing to bet years of their lives and their own money under conditions of uncertainty. After all, why make the bet if you have no idea what your odds of success are? However, people differ in their willingness to embrace risks. For example, would you be willing to bungee jump off a bridge? Some, including me, wouldn't do it for all the money in the world. However, others would do it in a heartbeat. **Risk propensity** is a person's tendency to take or avoid risks. And it usually takes an individual with a high risk propensity to be willing to take risks under conditions of uncertainty.

One such person is Craig McCaw. McCaw founded and grew McCaw Cellular into the largest paging and cellular phone service provider in the world. Then, in 1994, he sold the company to AT&T for $11.5 billion. McCaw's new company, Teledesic, is attempting to become the first global digital Internet- and phone-service provider under conditions of extremely high uncertainty. Teledesic's incredibly ambitious plan is to put 840 satellites in orbit 435 miles above the earth's surface. However, with just four years before its first satellite launch, Teledesic faces huge uncertainties. What satellite design would work best? How should signals be transmitted from one satellite to another (radio waves or laser beams)? From what locations will the satellites be launched? And, perhaps the largest uncertainty of all, who will be willing to buy global Internet/phone service and at what price? Only someone like McCaw, who started a cellular phone company from scratch, could be comfortable in the face of these uncertainties.[21]

Review 2
Limits to Rational Decision Making

The rational decision-making model describes how decisions should be made in an ideal world without limits. However, bounded rationality recognizes that in the real world, managers' decision-making processes are restricted by limited resources, incomplete and imperfect information, and managers' limited decision-making capabilities. These limitations often prevent managers from being rational decision makers. So do common decision-making mistakes, such as over-reliance on intuition and the availability, representative, and anchoring and adjustment biases. The rational decision-making model assumes that decisions are made under conditions of certainty. However, most managerial decisions are made under conditions of risk, where there is limited information and knowledge and a very real chance of making a bad decision. Risk also affects how decision makers define and solve problems. Positive frames encourage decision makers to be risk averse, whereas negative frames encourage them to be risk seeking. Finally, managers also make decisions under conditions of uncertainty, in which the odds of winning or losing are unknown. It takes a high risk propensity to be willing to take risks under conditions of uncertainty.

Improving Decision Making

What's the biggest decision you've ever made? Was it choosing where to go to college? Was it choosing a major? Or was it a personal decision, such as deciding whether to get married, where to live, or which car or house to buy? Considering the lasting effect that decisions like these have on our lives, wouldn't it be great if we could learn how to make them better? Managers struggle with decisions, too. They wring their hands over who to hire or promote, or when and how somebody should be fired. They fret about which suppliers the company should do business with. They lose sleep over who should get how much for pay raises or how to change the company strategy to respond to aggressive competitors. And, considering the lasting effect that these decisions have on themselves and their companies, managers also want to learn how to make better decisions.

After reading these next two sections, you should be able to:

3 describe how **rules and testing can improve decision making.**

4 explain how **group decisions and group decision-making techniques can improve decision making.**

3 Using Rules and Testing to Improve Decision Making

In theory, rational decision making leads to optimal decisions. However, in practice, we know that real-world constraints, common decision-making mistakes, and risky situations make fully rational decisions difficult to achieve. Consequently, in the business world, managers are much more likely to "satisfice" and make "good enough" decisions than they are to "maximize" and make "optimal" decisions.

Let's see how managers can use **3.1** *decision rules and* **3.2** *multivariable testing to make better than "good enough" decisions.*

3.1 *Decision Rules*

decision rule
set of criteria that alternative solutions must meet to be acceptable to the decision maker

A **decision rule** is a set of criteria that alternative solutions must meet to be acceptable to the decision maker.[22] If an alternative doesn't meet the criteria in the decision rule, it is rejected. Nearly every kind of business uses basic decision rules. In restaurants, the general pricing decision rule is to price food at three times its cost, beer at four times cost, and hard liquor at six times cost. In clothing stores the rule is to sell clothing for 60 percent over wholesale, and then reduce that price by 20 percent every two weeks until the clothing has been sold. Decision rules improve decision making because they are easy to understand and simple to follow. Managers who don't have the time or resources to use the complete rational decision-making model can use simpler decision rules instead.

dictionary rule
decision rule that requires decision makers to rank criteria in order of importance and then test alternative solutions against those criteria in rank order, so that alternatives that meet the most important criterion must then meet the second most important criterion, and so on

There are two general kinds of decision rules: the dictionary rule and the threshold rule. In much the same way that a dictionary sorts words by their first letter and then their second letter, etc., the **dictionary rule** encourages decision makers to rank their criteria in order of importance and then assess alternative solutions against these criteria in rank order. Specifically, alternatives that meet the most important criterion then must meet the second most important criterion, and so on. For example, the first house that my wife and I owned had a living room and a family room. We found that the living room went basically unused, except when we had guests. So as our family grew and we started shopping for a larger house, the first thing we told the realtor was, "Don't show us any houses with two living areas. We want a house with one large living room." Second, because we've got three kids, "It would be great to have four bedrooms." We were willing to look at any houses that met those criteria.

minimum threshold rule
decision rule that requires alternative solutions to meet all the established minimum decision criteria

Sometimes decision makers need to make yes/no or accept/reject decisions. Should a bank accept or reject a mortgage application? Should MasterCard approve or deny a jeweler's request to charge your card $3,500 for a jewelry purchase? When these kinds of decisions must be made, companies often use the **minimum threshold rule**, which requires an alternative to pass all the established minimum decision criteria. For example, one of the most common problems seen in emergency rooms is injured ankles. However, only 15 percent of the five million ankle x-rays taken each year indicate fractures. In other words, doctors are ordering expensive x-rays much more than they need to. Recently, clinical research has resulted in the development of the "Ottawa rule," which states that physicians should send patients with ankle injuries for confirmatory x-rays only if there is (1) pain near the ankle joint, *and* (2) bone tenderness, *and* (3) an inability to bear weight on the ankle. All three criteria must be met before sending patients to have their ankles x-rayed. Studies showed that physicians using the Ottawa rule correctly ordered x-rays for 100 percent of the patients who fractured their ankles. Also, the Ottawa rule helped reduce the overall number of ankle x-rays by 34 percent.[23]

3.2
Multivariable Testing

In practice, analyzing alternatives is one of the weakest steps in the decision-making process. Much of the "analysis" that gets done is based on guesswork ("We think that Plan E has a 90 percent chance of working.") rather than on actual tests of possible solutions. Because it is based on data from small experiments rather than guesswork, **multivariable testing** (MVT) helps managers take a much more systematic approach to analyzing and evaluating potential solutions. At Southwestern Bell, where MVT is widely used, the vice president of information services said, "It takes the 'I believe' out of [decision making]. It broadens your problem-solving ability; puts some rigor in your thinking."[24]

multivariable testing
a systematic approach of experimentation used to analyze and evaluate potential solutions

Multivariable testing improves decision making in two important ways. First, instead of letting arguments determine what the best solution is (I really like that plan that Manufacturing came up with because . . .), MVT encourages managers to conduct small-scale experiments and let the data decide. Says MVT consultant and trainer Charles Holland, "The power of experimental design is not only its efficiency with data, but that it forces a team to make decisions based on facts. Hierarchy, politics, or emotions are refuted with data."[25] Second, rather then testing one solution at a time, multivariable testing encourages managers to examine the effects of several potential solutions at the same time. For example, SKF is the world's largest manufacturer of ball bearings. SKF wanted to cut costs by using a cheaper metal cage to hold the bearings in place, but worried that this might make the bearing less durable. Besides using cheaper metal, factory workers suggested two other changes. Make the inner ring of the bearing harder by changing the heat treatment and then reduce the clearance between the bearing and the outer ring of the cage. While none of these changes alone improved performance, MVT indicated that combining these three changes produced a ball bearing that was five times more durable than before.[26]

Table 5.5 shows a simple multivariable testing experiment that a small amusement park might use to increase park attendance on Tuesdays, typically the slowest day in the park. On the first Tuesday, Test 1, no changes are made. The park earns a profit of $4,000. On the next Tuesday, Test 2, the park runs a 2-for-1 admission special and gives everyone who enters the park a coupon for a free hotdog and a Coke between 11:00 a.m. and 1:00 p.m. The park earns just $2,000, losing money on all the free lunches it gave away to all those people who were admitted for free. On the next Tuesday, Test 3, parking is free and everyone who enters the park gets a free lunch

Table 5.5 **Multivariable Testing to Increase Amusement Park Attendance on Tuesdays**

Test	2-for-1	Free Lunch	Free Parking	Profits
Test 1				$4,000
Test 2	X	X		$2,000
Test 3		X	X	$9,000
Test 4	X		X	$5,000

coupon. The park makes $9,000. Finally, on the fourth Tuesday, the park again offers 2-for-1 admission, but this time with free parking. Profits this time are $5,000. What's the answer? It's obvious: Offer free parking and free lunch on Tuesdays.

MVT can be used in all kinds of businesses for many kinds of decisions. However, managers and employees will need to be trained on how to design simple experiments and how to gather and analyze basic statistical data. Nonetheless, despite its cost, MVT allows managers to test and evaluate potential solutions before committing large amounts of money to their use. So instead of arguing about what you "think" the best solution might be, use MVT to test alternative solutions.

Review 3
Using Rules and Testing to Improve Decision Making

Decision rules are a relatively simple method of improving decision making. The dictionary rule helps decision makers choose among multiple alternative solutions, whereas the threshold rule helps decision makers make yes/no or accept/reject decisions. Managers use multivariable testing to do a better job of analyzing and evaluating potential solutions. The basic idea is to experimentally test several potential solutions at the same time and let data, rather than beliefs, guide decision making.

4 Using Groups to Improve Decision Making

According to a study reported in *Fortune* magazine, 91 percent of U.S. companies use teams and groups to solve specific problems (i.e., make decisions).[27] For example, Wabash National, a little-known business that builds truck trailers for companies like Federal Express and Schneider Trucking, uses problem solving groups to increase productivity. In a class where workers learn how to work well together, they are told that when it comes to problem-solving, "None of us is as smart as all of us." Problem-solving groups have already saved the company money by figuring out how to eliminate time-consuming welding processes and by finding a simple way to line up rivet holes when connecting two pieces of metal.[28]

When done properly, like at Wabash National, group decision making can lead to much better decisions than individual decision making. In fact, numerous studies show that groups consistently outperform individuals on complex tasks.

Let's explore the **4.1** *advantages and pitfalls of group decision making, and see how the following group decision making methods—***4.2** *structured conflict,* **4.3** *the nominal group technique,* **4.4** *the Delphi technique, and* **4.5** *electronic brainstorming—can be used to improve decision making.*

4.1
Advantages and Pitfalls of Group Decision Making

Groups can do a much better job than individuals in two important steps of the decision-making process: defining the problem and generating alternative solutions. Four reasons explain why.

First, because group members usually possess different knowledge, skills, abilities, and experiences, groups will be able to view problems from multiple perspectives. This greatly increases the odds that decisions will solve the underlying causes of problems rather than problem symptoms. For example, Coca-Cola outsells Pepsi by nearly 3 to 1 in international sales. To improve its global sales, Pepsi has decided to change its trademark red, white, and blue can to a blue can (Coke is red). Furthermore, while Pepsi used to adapt the flavor of its soft drink for different tastes in different countries, now it has decided to change to a standard formula and taste throughout the world. Time will tell, but critics contend that by changing its flavor and trademark colors, Pepsi is focusing on the symptoms of the problem rather than the real cause of poor marketing and distribution (at least compared to Coke).[29]

Second, groups can find and access much more information than can individuals. For example, Cough, Harbour & Associates, an engineering consulting firm, uses a hiring team for interviewing potential employees. The company's director of human resources said, "We think we make better hiring decisions when we get a number of people involved. It's like working a crossword puzzle. If you get four people together, their chances of solving the puzzle are greater than if the four work separately."[30]

Third, the increased knowledge and information available to groups make it easier for them to generate more alternative solutions. Studies show that generating lots of alternative solutions is a critical part of improving the quality of decisions. Fourth, if groups are involved in the decision-making process, group members will be more committed to making chosen solutions work.

groupthink
a barrier to good decision making caused by pressure within the group for members to not disagree with each other

Although groups can do a better job of defining problems and generating alternative solutions, group decision making is subject to some pitfalls that can quickly erase these gains. One possible pitfall is groupthink. **Groupthink** occurs in highly cohesive groups when group members feel intense pressure not to disagree with each other, so that the group can approve a proposed solution.[31] Because groupthink leads to consideration of a limited number of solutions, and because it restricts discussion of any considered solutions, it usually results in poor decisions. Groupthink is most likely to occur under the following conditions:

- The group is insulated from others with different perspectives.
- The group leader begins by expressing strong preference for a particular decision.
- There is no established procedure for systematically defining problems and exploring alternatives.
- Group members have similar backgrounds and experiences.[32]

Personal Productivity Tip

Want to Help? Shhhhhh, Chew Your Nails

Managers sometimes impede group decision making by beginning the process by saying what they think should be done. Group members tend to place more importance on what their leaders say than on what other members say. This can impair group decision making by leading to premature acceptance of alternatives and decision criteria. So the best thing to do as a manager is to keep quiet. Do what this manager did when group members said, "Why don't you just tell us what to do so we can move on?" Her response? "I sat on my hands. Chewed on my fingernails."

Sources: S. Sherman, "Secrets of HP's 'Muddled' Team," *Fortune*, 18 March 1996, 116-120.

NASA's decision to launch the ill-fated space shuttle Challenger in 1986 is an example of groupthink. Despite cold weather conditions that would normally have postponed a launch, NASA placed heavy pressure on Morton Thiokol (maker of the o-rings) and other engineering firms involved in the launch decision to give their approval to launch. After being told twice that a launch was not recommended, NASA administrators pressured Morton Thiokol one last time for an OK. Because of the pressure and time constraints, Thiokol reversed its decision. Tragically, as Thiokol had originally feared, the o-rings failed, and the shuttle exploded, killing all aboard.[33]

A second potential problem with group decision making is that it takes considerable time. It takes time to reconcile schedules (so that group members can meet). Furthermore, it's the rare group that consistently holds productive task-oriented meetings to effectively work through the decision process. Some of the most common complaints about meetings (and thus decision making) are that the meeting's purpose is unclear, meeting participants are unprepared, critical people are absent or late, conversation doesn't stay focused on the problem, and no one follows up on the decisions that were made. Not surprisingly, given these difficulties, the *Valley News Dispatch*, a small paper in Tarentum, Pennsylvania, has this sign in the company conference room: "Are you lonely? Working on your own? Hate making decisions? HOLD A MEETING!"[34]

A third possible pitfall is that sometimes just one or two people dominate group discussion, restricting consideration of different problem definitions and alternative solutions. Another possible problem is that, unlike their own decisions and actions, group members often don't feel accountable for the decisions made and actions taken by the group.

While these pitfalls can lead to poor decision making, this doesn't mean that managers should avoid using groups to make decisions. When done properly, group decision making can lead to much better decisions. The pitfalls of group decision making are not inevitable. Most of them can be overcome through good management. Let's see how structured conflict, the nominal group technique, the Delphi technique, and electronic brainstorming help managers improve group decision making.

4.2 *Structured Conflict*

c-type conflict
disagreement that focuses on problem- and issue-related differences of opinion

Most people view conflict negatively. However, the right kind of conflict can lead to much better group decision making. **C-type conflict**, or cognitive conflict, focuses on problem- and issue-related differences of opinion.[35] In c-type conflict, group members disagree because their different experiences and expertise lead them to different views of the problem and its potential solutions. However, c-type conflict is also characterized by a willingness to examine, compare, and reconcile those differences to produce the best possible solution.

a-type conflict
disagreement that focuses on individual- or personally oriented issues

By contrast, **a-type conflict**, meaning "affective conflict," refers to the emotional reactions that can occur when disagreements become personal rather than professional. A-type conflict often results in hostility, anger, resentment, distrust, cynicism, and apathy. So, unlike c-type conflict, a-type conflict undermines team effectiveness by preventing teams from engaging in the kinds of activities, such as c-type conflict, that are critical to team effectiveness. Examples of a-type conflict statements would be, "your idea," "our idea," "my department," "you don't know what you are talking about," or "you don't understand our situation." Rather than focusing on issues and ideas, these statements focus on individuals.[36]

devil's advocacy
a decision-making method in which an individual or a subgroup is assigned the role of a critic

Devil's advocacy and dialectical inquiry are two methods that introduce structured c-type conflict into the group decision-making process. **Devil's advocacy** creates c-type conflict by assigning an individual or a subgroup the role of critic. The five steps of a devil's advocacy program are:

1. Generate a potential solution.
2. Assign a devil's advocate to criticize and question the solution.
3. Present the critique of the potential solution to key decision makers.
4. Gather additional relevant information.
5. Decide whether to use, change, or not use the originally proposed solution.[37]

dialectical inquiry
a decision-making method in which decision makers state the assumptions of a proposed solution (a thesis) and generate a solution that is the opposite (antithesis) of that solution

Dialectical inquiry creates c-type conflict by forcing decision makers to state the assumptions of a proposed solution (a thesis) and to then generate a solution that is the opposite (antithesis) of the proposed solution. The five steps of the dialectical inquiry process are:

1. Generate a potential solution.
2. Identify the assumptions underlying the potential solution.
3. Generate a conflicting counterproposal based on the opposite assumptions.
4. Have advocates of each position present their arguments and engage in a debate in front of key decision makers.
5. Decide whether to use, change, or not use the originally proposed solution.[38]

When properly used, both the devil's-advocacy and dialectical-inquiry approaches introduce c-type conflict into the decision-making process. Further, contrary to the common belief that conflict is bad, studies show that these methods lead to less a-type conflict, improved decision quality, and greater acceptance of decisions once they have been made.[39] See the "What Really Works" feature for more information on both techniques.

What Really Works

Devil's Advocacy and Dialectical Inquiry

Ninety percent of the decisions managers face are well-structured problems that recur frequently under conditions of certainty. For example, showing up at an airline ticket counter without your ticket is a well-structured problem. It happens every day (recurs frequently) and it's easy to determine if you have your ticket or not (conditions of certainty). Well-structured problems are solved with programmed decisions, in which a policy, procedure, or rule clearly specifies how to solve the problem. Thus, there's no mystery about what to do when someone shows up without a ticket. After you present identification to prove who you are, and after you pay a transaction fee (around $75), the airline gives you another ticket.

In some sense, programmed decisions really aren't decisions, because anyone with any experience knows what to do. There's no thought involved. What keeps managers up at night is that other 10 percent of problems. Ill-structured problems that are novel (no one's seen them before) and exist under conditions of uncertainty are solved with nonprogrammed decisions. Nonprogrammed decisions do not involve standard methods of resolution. Every time managers make a nonprogrammed decision, they have to figure out a brand new way of handling a brand new problem. That's what makes them so tough to handle.

Both the devil's advocacy and dialectical inquiry approaches to decision making can be used to improve nonprogrammed decision making. Both approaches work because they force decision makers to identify and criticize the assumptions underlying the non-programmed decisions they hope will solve ill-structured problems.

Devil's Advocacy

There is a 58 percent chance that decision makers who use the devil's-advocacy approach to criticize and question their solutions will produce better-quality decisions than decisions based on the advice of experts.

Devil's Advocacy

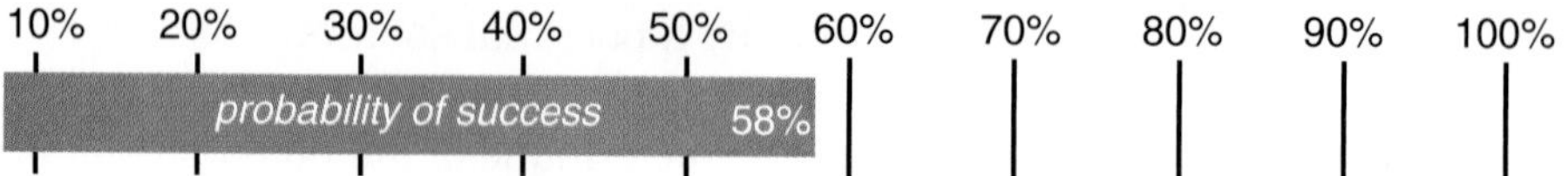

Dialectical Inquiry

There is a 55 percent chance that decision makers who use the dialectical-inquiry approach to criticize and question their solutions will produce better-quality decisions than decisions based on the advice of experts.

Dialectical Inquiry

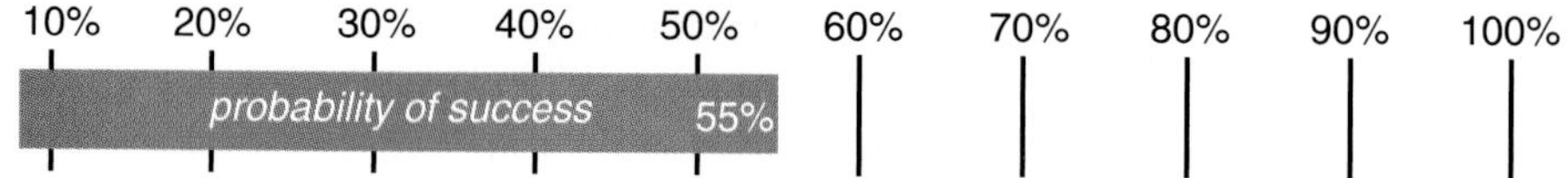

Note that in both cases, devil's advocacy and dialectical inquiry, each technique has been compared to decisions obtained by following experts' advice. So, while these probabilities of success, 55 percent and 58 percent, seem small, they very likely *understate* the effects of both techniques. In other words, the probabilities of success would have been much larger if both techniques had been compared to unstructured decision making processes.

Source: C.R. Schwenk, "Effects of Devil's Advocacy and Dialectical Inquiry on Decision Making: A Meta-Analysis," *Organizational Behavior and Human Decision Performance* 47 (1990): 161-176.

4.3 *Nominal Group Technique*

nominal group technique a decision-making method that begins and ends by having group members quietly write down and evaluate ideas to be shared with the group

"Nominal" means "in name only." Accordingly, the **nominal group technique** received its name because it begins with "quiet time," in which group members independently write down as many problem definitions and alternative solutions as possible. In other words, the nominal group technique begins by having group members act as individuals. After the "quiet time," the group leader asks each group member to share one idea at a time with the group. As they are read aloud, ideas are posted on flip charts or wall boards for all to see. This step continues until all ideas have been shared. The next step involves a discussion of the advantages and disadvantages of these ideas. The nominal group technique closes with a second "quiet time," in which group members independently rank the ideas presented. Group members then read their rankings aloud, and the idea with the highest average rank is selected.[40]

The nominal group technique improves group decision making by decreasing a-type conflict. However, in doing so, it also restricts c-type conflict. Consequently, the nominal group technique typically produces poorer-quality decisions than do the devil's-advocacy or dialectical-inquiry approaches. Nonetheless, more than 80 studies have found that nominal groups produce better-quality ideas than traditional group decisions.[41]

4.4 Delphi Technique

Delphi technique
a decision-making method in which a panel of experts respond to questions and to each other until reaching agreement on an issue

The **Delphi technique** is a decision-making method in which a panel of experts respond to questions and to each other until reaching agreement on an issue. The first step is to assemble a panel of experts. However, unlike other approaches to group decision making, it isn't necessary to bring the panel together in one place. Since the Delphi technique does not require the experts to leave their offices or disrupt their schedules, they are more likely to participate in the process. For example, a colleague and I were asked to conduct a Delphi technique assessment of the "ten most important steps for small businesses." With the help of the dean of my business school and a former mayor of the city, we assembled a panel of local top-level managers and CEOs.

The second step is to create a questionnaire consisting of a series of open-ended questions for the experts. For example, we asked our panel to answer these questions: "What is the most common mistake made by small-business persons?" "Right now, what do you think is the biggest threat to the survival of most small businesses?" "If you had one piece of advice to give to the owner of a small business, what would it be?"

In step 3, panel members' written responses are analyzed, summarized, and fed back to the panel for reactions until panel members reach agreement. In our Delphi study, it took about a month to get the panel members' written responses to the first three questions. Then, their written responses were summarized and typed into a brief report (no more than two pages). We sent the summary to the panel members and asked them to explain why they agreed or disagreed with these conclusions from the first round of questions. Asking why they agreed or disagreed is important, because it helps uncover panel members' unstated assumptions and beliefs. Again, this process of summarizing panel feedback and obtaining reactions to that feedback continues until panel members reach agreement. For our study, it took just one more round for panel members' views to reach a consensus. In all, it took approximately 3½ months to complete our Delphi study.

The Delphi technique is not an approach that managers should use for common decisions. Because it is a time-consuming, labor-intensive, and expensive process, the Delphi technique is best reserved for important long-term issues and problems. Nonetheless, the judgments and conclusions obtained from it are typically better than those you would get from one expert.

4.5 Electronic Brainstorming

brainstorming
a decision-making method in which group members build on each others' ideas to generate as many alternative solutions as possible

electronic brainstorming
a decision-making method in which group members use computers to build on each others' ideas and generate many alternative solutions

Brainstorming, in which group members build on others' ideas, is a technique for generating a large number of alternative solutions. Brainstorming has four rules:

1. The more ideas, the better.
2. All ideas are acceptable, no matter how wild or crazy they might be.
3. Use other group members' ideas to come up with even more ideas.
4. Criticism or evaluation of ideas is not allowed.

While brainstorming is great fun and can help managers generate a large number of alternative solutions, it does have a number of disadvantages. Fortunately, **electronic brainstorming**, in which group members use computers to communicate and generate alternative solutions, overcomes the disadvantages associated with face-to-face brainstorming.[42]

production blocking
a disadvantage of face-to-face brainstorming in which a group member must wait to share an idea because another member is presenting an idea

The first disadvantage that electronic brainstorming overcomes is **production blocking**, which occurs when you have an idea, but you have to wait to share it because someone else is already describing an idea to the group. This short delay may make you forget your idea or decide that it really wasn't worth sharing. But with electronic brainstorming, production blocking doesn't happen. With all group members seated at computers, everyone can type in their ideas whenever they occur. There's no "waiting your turn" to be heard by the group.

evaluation apprehension
fear of what others will think of your ideas

The second disadvantage that electronic brainstorming overcomes is **evaluation apprehension**, that is, being afraid of what others will think of your ideas. However, with electronic brainstorming, all ideas are anonymous. When you type in an idea and hit the "Enter" key to share it with the group, group members see only the idea. Furthermore, many brainstorming software programs also protect anonymity by displaying ideas in random order. So, if you laugh maniacally when you type "Cut top management's pay by 50 percent!" and then hit the "Enter" key, it won't show up immediately on everyone's screen. This makes it doubly difficult to determine whose comments belong to whom.

Figure 5.2 shows the typical layout for electronic brainstorming. All participants sit in front of computers around a U-shaped table. This configuration allows them to see their computer screens, each other, and a large main screen. Figure 5.3 shows what the typical electronic brainstorming group member will see on his or her computer screen. The first step in electronic brainstorming is to anonymously generate as many ideas as possible. It's common for groups to generate 100 ideas in a half-hour period. Step 2 is to edit the generated ideas, categorize them, and eliminate redundancies. Step 3 is to rank-order the categorized ideas in terms of quality. Step four, the last step, has three parts: generate a series of action steps, decide the best order for accomplishing these steps, and identify who is responsible for each step. All four steps are accomplished with computers and electronic brainstorming software.[43]

Figure 5.2 **Typical Layout for an Electronic Brainstorming Room**

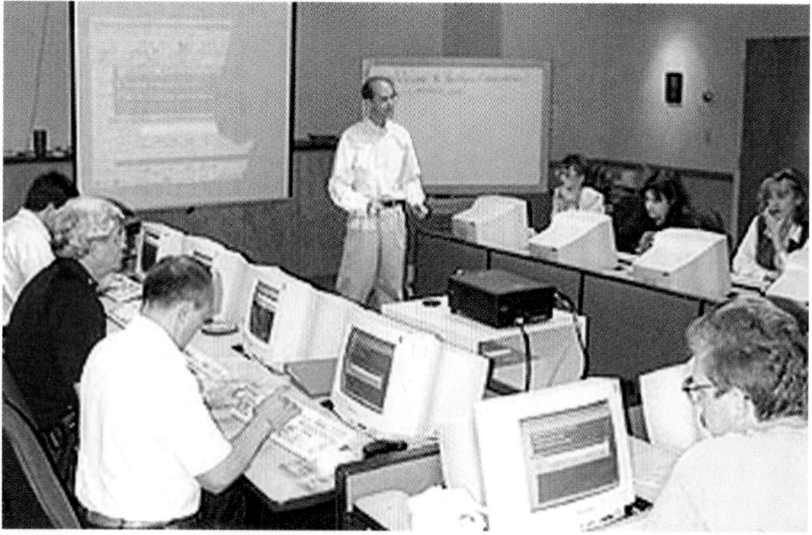

Source: "GroupSystems Tour Stop 4: Developing Consensus," Ventana Web Site. [Online] Available **www.ventana.com/html/vc_tour_stop_4__group_consensu.html,** 12 January 1999.

Figure 5.3

What You See on the Computer during Electronic Brainstorming

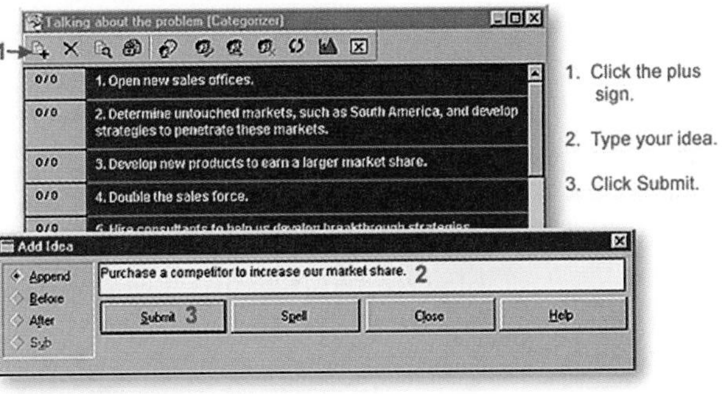

Source: "GroupSystems Tour Stop 2: Generating a List of Ideas," Ventana Web Site. [Online] Available **www.ventana.com/html/vc_tour_stop_2__categorizer.html,** 12 January 1999.

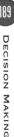

Studies show that electronic brainstorming is much more productive than face-to-face brainstorming. Compared to regular 4-person brainstorming groups, the same-sized electronic brainstorming groups produce 25 percent to 50 percent more ideas. Compared to regular 12-person brainstorming groups, the same-sized electronic brainstorming groups produce 200 percent more ideas! In fact, because production blocking (i.e., waiting your turn) is not a problem for electronic brainstorming, the number and quality of ideas generally increases with group size.[44]

Even though it works much better than traditional brainstorming, electronic brainstorming has disadvantages, too. An obvious problem is the expense of computers, networks, software, etc. However, as these costs continue to drop, electronic brainstorming will become cheaper.

Another problem is that the anonymity of ideas may bother people who are used to having their ideas accepted by virtue of their position (i.e., the boss). On the other hand, one CEO said, "Because the process is anonymous, the sky's the limit in terms of what you can say, and as a result it is more thought provoking. As a CEO, you'll probably discover things you might not want to hear but need to be aware of."[45]

A third disadvantage is that outgoing individuals who are more comfortable expressing themselves orally may find it difficult to express themselves in writing. Finally, the most obvious problem is that participants have to be able to type. Those who can't type, or who type slowly, may be easily frustrated and find themselves at a disadvantage to experienced typists. For example, one meeting facilitator was tipped off that an especially fast typist was pretending to be more than one person. Said the facilitator, "He'd type 'Oh, I agree' and then 'Ditto, ditto' or 'What a great idea,' all in quick succession, using different variations of uppercase and lowercase letters and punctuation. He tried to make it seem like a lot of people were concurring, but it was just him." Eventually, the person sitting next to him got suspicious and began watching his screen.[46]

Review 4
Using Groups to Improve Decision Making

When groups view problems from multiple perspectives, use more information, have a diversity of knowledge and experience, and become committed to solutions they help choose, they can produce better solutions than individual decision makers. However, group decisions suffer from these disadvantages: groupthink, slowness, discussions dominated by just a few individuals, and unfelt responsibility for decisions. Group decisions work best when group members encourage c-type conflict, and don't work as well when groups become mired in a-type conflict. The devil's-advocacy and dialectical-inquiry approaches improve group decisions because they bring structured c-type conflict into the decision-making process. By contrast, the nominal group technique and the Delphi technique both improve decision making by reducing a-type conflict through limited interactions between group members. Finally, because it overcomes the problems of production blocking and evaluation apprehension, electronic brainstorming is a more effective method of generating alternatives than face-to-face brainstorming.

What**Really**Happened?

When companies get into financial trouble, it seems that top management's automatic response is to lay off workers. In fact, according to the U.S. Department of Labor, 36 million jobs were eliminated through organizational downsizing from the late 1970s to the early 1990s. Furthermore, Wall Street usually cheers when it sees layoffs, believing them to be a sign that companies are serious about getting their costs under control. For example, when AT&T announced that it was laying off 40,000 workers, its stock price *increased* by $2.50. Said one stock analyst, "It's a good, aggressive move."

There is a danger for decision makers, however, when it becomes widely believed that there is only one way to solve a problem. When top management sits around a table and quickly decides that layoffs are the answer without considering any other options, this danger is called "groupthink" or "satisficing." Yet, regardless of the label you attach to it, premature definition of the problem ("We've got too many employees.") and limited consideration of alternative solutions ("We've got no choice. We have to start layoffs.") will almost always produce poor decisions and poor results. Read the answers to the opening case to find out how Mercedes-Benz Credit Corporation avoided these classic decision-making mistakes.

You wonder, are too many jobs really the problem, or is it just the symptom of the real problem—whatever that is?

The first step in decision making is defining the problem, that is, figuring out what's going wrong. The traditional way to do that is to look for gaps between desired states and existing states. The gap on which everyone was focused at Mercedes-Benz was profits. Instead of making money, Mercedes was losing several billion Deutschmarks a year. One way to define that gap is to conclude that costs are too high. The most popular way to cut costs these days is laying off employees.

However, at MBCC, the gap between revenues and costs wasn't defined as high costs; it was defined as low revenues. And the reason for the low revenues was poor customer service. MBCC has two sets of customers: those who buy and lease Mercedes-Benz cars and the Mercedes-Benz dealers who sell them. Neither group was satisfied with the service that MBCC provided, and that was the real reason why revenues weren't keeping up with costs.

Is cutting jobs the only alternative? Are there other ways to give top management what it wants?

The way in which you define the problem almost always restricts the solution you look for. If MBCC had defined the problem as high costs and started laying off employees, the already-poor customer service was sure to deteriorate even more. (Employees who are about to lose their jobs don't give great service. Neither do remaining employees who now have to do twice as much work.) So rather than cut jobs, the president of MBCC improved customer service by spending more money to hire and train more workers! The results speak for themselves. All customers' calls are answered by the third ring. But more important, 90 percent of the time, service representatives can solve customer problems in just one phone call.

How do you decide who stays and who goes? In other words, how do you go about making this decision, and do you have to make the decision by yourself?

When most companies announce layoffs, the decision comes straight from top management. However, usually groups can make better decisions than individuals. The advantages of group decisions are that groups view problems from multiple perspectives, they use more information, they have a diversity of knowledge and experience, and they become committed to solutions they help choose.

Amazingly, MBCC's president did the unthinkable: He gave his workers the task of reengineering the workplace. They were to decide if any jobs were to be cut, and if so, who was to be laid off. Two reasons prompted the president to make this innovative decision. First, he wanted "buy in." In other words, whatever the groups decided to do, he wanted their commitment to make it work. Second, he thought that the work groups themselves could produce the best decisions. After all, because they were closest to the problems, they should have the best ideas for solutions.

There's got to be some creative way to handle this—something that doesn't involve layoffs—but what?

When MBCC's president made the workers and work groups responsible for reengineering their workplace, he gave them this guarantee: Anyone who proposed changes that resulted in the elimination of their own jobs would be guaranteed a new job. MBCC's president said, "It was absolutely essential to establish a no-fear element in this whole change process."

This simple, but brilliant move unleashed worker creativity, allowing them to focus on the two most important steps of decision making: how to define the problem and how many different alternative solutions to consider.

With their creativity unleashed, here's what they decided to do. They wiped out most of their own jobs and departments. Previously, there had been eight levels of management. Now, there are four. Instead of having to wait for management approval, the employees redesigned the workplace so that cross-functional teams had immediate authority to do what they felt was necessary to satisfy customers. Private offices and closed doors were replaced with glass walls, open cubicles, and more conference rooms to encourage group decisions. Discussion databases, where employees posted problems for all to see, became a new source of ideas and solutions as everyone in the company posted suggestions and solutions.

In the end, these innovative approaches to decision making and problem solving gave top management what it wanted: a 31 percent increase in performance. But MBCC's president and employees got what they wanted, too. No one was laid off. In fact, business is so good that the number of new employees has increased by 19 percent. By the way, customers and car dealers got what they wanted too, thanks to the new services that MBCC created. When customers walk into a Mercedes-Benz dealership these days, they don't head out to the car lot to see what's available. Instead, the customer and salesperson sit at a computer to find a car that suits the customer's needs. Once a customer decides to buy, the computer spits out a payment plan and processes the credit application within minutes.

Sources: E. Brenner, "Effects of Downsizing Just Keep On Going," *New York Times*, 28 April 1996. "Mercedes-Benz Dealers Hitch a Ride on the Information Highway: New On-Line Service Gives Dealers a Marketing Advantage," *Business Wire*, 2 May 1996. T. Petzinger, Jr., "Georg Bauer Handed Burden of Downsizing to Employees," *The Wall Street Journal Interactive Edition,* 10 May 1996. "Two Cheers for Loyalty: Management Thinkers Are Rediscovering the Virtues of Loyalty," *The Economist*, 1 January 1996.

Key Terms

absolute comparisons p. 167
anchoring and adjustment bias p. 176
a-type conflict p. 184
availability bias p. 175
bounded rationality p. 173
brainstorming p. 187
conditions of certainty p. 176
conditions of risk p. 177
conditions of uncertainty p. 178
c-type conflict p. 184
decision criteria p. 166
decision making p. 162
decision rule p. 180
Delphi technique p. 187
devil's advocacy p. 185
dialectical inquiry p. 185
dictionary rule p. 180
electronic brainstorming p. 187
evaluation apprehension p. 188
groupthink p. 183
information overload p. 173
maximizing p. 173
minimum threshold rule p. 180
multivariable testing p. 181
negative frame p. 178
nominal group technique p. 186
positive frame p. 178
problem p. 164
production blocking p. 188
rational decision making p. 162
relative comparisons p. 167
representative bias p. 176
risk propensity p. 178
satisficing p. 173

What Would You Do-II?

Permission to Begin Napping?

"Control. This is American Airlines, Flight 74, nonstop from Dallas-Fort Worth to London."

"Roger, American 74."

"Control, pilot requests permission to begin napping."

Napping? Surprisingly, based on the results of an intriguing NASA study, a number of airlines have begun allowing their pilots to take short naps on long flights.

NASA studied the fatigue of airline pilots who were in the middle of an eight-flight travel period. Each of the eight flights lasted about nine hours and was followed by a 24-hour layover. Fatigue and attentiveness were measured by attaching electrodes to pilots' scalps and faces to monitor brain waves and eye movements. Pilots were then randomly assigned to two groups, a rest group and a no-rest group. Pilots in the rest group were allowed to take a 40-minute in-flight nap in their cockpit seats. For safety reasons, naps were only permitted when the planes had reached cruising altitude and had to end at least an hour before descent and landing, which are the most demanding and difficult parts of any flight. On average, while at cruising altitude, the no-rest pilots averaged 120 microsleep episodes in which they lost consciousness for more than two seconds. By contrast, the rest group only had 22 microsleep episodes. During descent and landing, the no-rest group had 22 microsleep episodes lasting more than five seconds. By contrast, the no-rest group had none. The study's authors also indicated that the need to sleep was so strong among the no-rest pilots that four experienced pilots fell asleep even after being told several times to keep working.

So, based on this and other research, British Airways, Australia's Quantas, Air New Zealand, Air Canada, Swissair, Finnair, and Lufthansa now permit their pilots to take short naps on long international flights. For these airlines, the goal of this policy is clear: to increase safety by keeping pilots fresh and alert.

However, not everyone thinks that allowing pilots to nap is a good idea. Gary Davis, deputy manager of the Federal Aviation Administration's Transportation Division, said that such an official napping policy could "strike fear" in passengers. Likewise, Karmjit Singh, assistant director of corporate affairs for Singapore Airlines, said the company "has investigated napping, but we're not pursuing it at this time." Cathay Pacific, a Hong Kong-based airline, Scandinavian Airlines, and the French pilots union also oppose napping. Regis Froger of the Syndicat National des Pilotes de Ligne union in France said, "It would be better to treat the causes of fatigue rather than its effect." He believes that scheduling that allows pilots sufficient rest and time between flights to adapt to the cumulative effects of jet lag would be better than napping.

Pilot fatigue is not something to take lightly. With fatigue estimated to be a factor in 21 percent of all crashes, something needs to be done. The question is, what? **If you were making this decision for an airline, would you allow pilots to nap on long international flights? What would you do?**

Source: C. Goldsmith, "Airlines Split on Question of Pilots' In-Flight Dozing," *The Wall Street Journal*, 20 January 1998. R. Parke, "Fatigue and Safety: New Research Reveals Weaknesses in Some Flight Operations," *Business & Commercial Aviation*, 1 September 1996. P. Sparaco, "Toward Safer Skies: Combating Fatigue to Enhance Safety," *Aviation Week & Space Technology*, 4, November 1996.

Critical-Thinking Video Case

Decision Making: Next Door Food Store

Next Door Food Store is a chain of 30 convenience stores and gas stations that meet the needs of people in a hurry. Convenience stores carry a limited range of products. The stores are kept small to move people in and out quickly. Convenience store customers demand that products be on the shelf 24 hours a day. To meet its customers' needs, Next Door Food Store had to make two fundamental decisions. First, what channels of distribution should it use to get items into the stores? Second, what items should it stock in its stores?

In making these decisions, Next Door Food Stores had the following goals: (1) manage the cost of distribution, (2) keep inventory levels low, (3) use just-in-time inventory, and (4) maintain a variety of products. However, in trying to achieve these goals, it faced the following constraints: (1) low volume compared with supermarkets, (2) small stores in terms of shelf space, (3) limited number of stores, (4) stores geographically dispersed, and (5) no trucking systems for shipping goods.

Critical-Thinking Questions

1. Should Next Door Food Stores build and operate a warehouse, or should they use wholesale distributors and vendors?
2. Coca-Cola offered Next Door Food Store $50,000 to be an exclusive distributor, meaning that they would remove all Pepsi products from their stores. What are the risks and rewards for Next Door Food Store if it accepts Coca-Cola's offer, and should they do it?
3. How does Next Door Food Store identify and respond to a merchandising trend?

Management Decisions

Sugar-Free Kool-Aid: Let's Brainstorm!

What comes to mind when you think of Kool-Aid? Summer? Pool parties and picnics? Third grade? Kool-pops that you made, poured into molds, and froze in the freezer? Was one of these flavors your favorite: Black Cherry, Cherry, Grape, Incrediberry, Kickin-Kiwi-Lime, Lemonade, Lemon-Lime, Man-o-Mangoberry, Oh-Yeah Orange-Pineapple, Orange, Pina-Pineapple, Pink Lemonade, Pink Swimmingo, Purplesaurus Rex, Raspberry, Rock-a-dile Red, Slammin' Strawberry-Kiwi, Strawberry, Strawberry-Raspberry, Tropical Punch, or Watermelon-Cherry?

When most people think of Kool-Aid, they think of kids. Just over a decade ago, Kool-Aid sales started to decline. In part, this was due to long-term demographic changes. Families were simply having fewer children. Since the makers of Kool-Aid obviously couldn't do anything to change demographic trends, the next best thing was to encourage groups other than kids, such as teens and adults, to drink more Kool-Aid. With the explosion in popularity of diet drinks, the answer seemed simple: Sugar-Free Kool-Aid. However, Kool-Aid's management knew that it would still have a tough time convincing teens and adults to make Sugar-Free Kool-Aid their drink of choice. So, to figure how they might do this, Kool-Aid sponsored a contest for MBA students at the top business schools in the nation. MBA student teams submitted their ideas, and the teams with the most promising proposals were flown to New York to make formal presentations. Unfortunately, their suggestions were not very creative. Kool-Aid management was extremely disappointed with the results.

The purpose of this in-class management-decision activity is to correct that problem by using brainstorming to generate as many ideas as possible for selling Sugar-Free Kool-Aid to teens and adults. The rules of brainstorming are:

- The more ideas, the better.
- All ideas are acceptable, no matter how wild or crazy they might be.
- Build on other group members' ideas to come up with even more ideas.
- Criticism or evaluation of ideas is not allowed.

Remember, creativity requires playfulness. Make this fun! Be wild and crazy! And, most important, don't criticize others' ideas. No moaning, groaning, or commenting allowed (or aloud). The first step in brainstorming is to generate as many different ideas as possible. Evaluation comes later.

Question

1. Think of as many ways as possible to get teens and adults to buy and use Sugar-Free Kool-Aid.

Management Decisions

Bad Shoppers! No More Sales for You!

When was the last time you paid full price for something? Hard to remember, isn't it? Most shoppers are addicted to buying clothing, cars, airline tickets, and computers/electronics "on sale." Barbara Meyer, a Chicago resident who shops at Marshall Field's (an upscale retailer), said, "An OK sale is 25 percent. A good sale is

40 percent. But if you can wait, you can do even better than that. I know everyone has to make their money, but I just feel taken somehow when I pay full price."

Of course, shoppers' savings come at the expense of profits. With several years of weak profits behind them, retailers are trying to cure shoppers' addiction to sales by using a "one-half" strategy (and they don't mean one-half off). For example, Dayton Hudson Corp. has cut the number of its yearly sales events in half, from 140 to 70. Another one-half strategy, used by Ann Taylor Stores, is to cut the number of displayed items by one half. "If there's a jacket you love and you see only six on a rack, you're more likely to pay full price for it," says Ann Taylor's chief executive.

Besides halving sales and reducing inventory, some retailers plan to replace frequent sales with "value shopping," otherwise known as "everyday low prices." However, to earn respectable profits, the everyday low prices won't be quite as low as the sale prices that consumers have become accustomed to.

Questions

1. Similar to the devil's-advocacy and dialectical-inquiry approaches discussed in the chapter, begin by describing the basic assumptions of retailers' "one-half" and "value-pricing" plans. In other words, explain in your own words why retailers think these plans will work. List and explain at least three assumptions.

2. The second step in devil's advocacy and dialectical inquiry is to develop a critique of the original plan. So using the assumptions that you wrote for question 1 (i.e., the basics of retailers' plans), explain why each assumption is wrong.

Develop Your Management Potential

Best Practices

Ninety percent of all problems are routine problems. This means that they recur frequently and that a standard method of resolution already exists for solving them. Experienced managers view routine problems as "no-brainers." The difficulty for new managers is that the first time they encounter a routine problem, it's not routine—it's new, and they don't know how to solve it. For example, you've got an employee who comes in late. You've already talked to this person about it, but it didn't do any good. What do you do? Or, the first time you prepare your department's budget, how do you do it? What are the steps? How do you figure out how much to spend on each category? As a manager, where can you get solutions the first time you encounter routine problems?

Often the best answers come from what business consultants call "best practices." "Best practices" is a three-step method of decision making. First, ask for help. "Does anybody know how to . . . ? Does anybody know anybody who knows how to . . . ?" Second, talk to the "experts" who have faced the problem before. Find out what they do and why. Third, do what they do, or adapt what they do to your problem and circumstances.

Questions

1. Choose a problem on which you need help. Make sure it's a routine problem that is new to you, but that it's also a problem that others will know how to solve. (It doesn't have to be a management problem. It could be figuring out what car to buy.) Write a clear statement of the problem.

2. Find three people to talk to about the problem. Ask around the dorm, the apartment complex, or at work. Another option, if you've got an Internet connection, is to post your question to the appropriate Usenet group—there are thousands. Share your problem with each of three "experts." Ask them what they'd do and why they recommended the solutions that they did. The "why" is just as important as the "what." Then describe their advice, the "what" and the "why," in writing.

3. Now that you've considered what the "experts" have to say, choose the "expert" advice that is appropriate for your problem and circumstances. Integrate that into a final plan that explains your choice and what steps you will take to solve your problem.

Chapter Six

196

Chapter 6 Outline

Managing Information

What Would **You** Do?

MTC Headquarters, Petaluma, California. There it is, the company phone bill, sitting on top of the pile of mail that your assistant put on your desk this morning. You've tried to ignore it all day, but there's no point putting it off anymore. Ok, what's the damage? Ouch! That's 30 percent more than last month. This is killing us! Ironically, the company you work for, MTC Telecommunications, is in the business of helping others reduce their phone costs. MTC sells cellular phones that work in countries all over the world (most cellular accounts are limited to a particular geographical region). It also sells switching services that automatically find the cheapest way to route international phone connections. However, with 15,000 sales representatives selling in 160 different countries, more than 90 percent of the company's long-distance phone calls, faxes, and voice mails are expensive international calls. Most of the cost is attributable to the dial-up ordering system that was put in place several years ago. For example, by using a laptop computer, modem, and company phone account, a sales representative anywhere in the world can tap into the company computer system in California to activate a new account. After entering the appropriate information, the sales rep presses the "Enter" key on the laptop to instantaneously activate the account, all while sitting in the customer's office. Not surprisingly, with no six-week waiting period and no equipment installation, customers love MTC's ability to immediately reduce their phone costs. But despite using its own low-cost services, MTC's phone expenses are growing just as quickly as its business. With only $100 million in revenues, you've got to get your phone expenses down to keep your prices competitive. But how? The phone, fax, voice mail, and dial-up order systems are the cardiovascular system of the company. Without information and orders flowing back and forth through them, the company would cease to exist. Furthermore, quick activation and troubleshooting of accounts are your primary advantages over competitors. So telling sales reps to cut costs by reducing phone use is like a newspaper deciding to reduce costs by not printing so many newspapers each day. Simply put, if you cut costs in this way, you cut revenues, too. So how do you find a way to cut costs and still maintain your competitive advantage and the critical flow of information from sales reps to headquarters and back? Furthermore, customers are now expressing a desire to tap directly into their accounts, so they can more closely monitor expenses without waiting for the monthly bill. How can you do that without incurring greater costs? **If you were the chief information officer at MTC, what would you do?**

Sources: T. Duffy, "Intranet Radically Reduces Costs," *PC Week Web Site.* [Online] Available **http://www.pcweek.com/@netweek/0527/27mtc.html,** 30 May 1996. M. Halper, "So Does Your Web Site Pay?" *Forbes,* 25 August 1997, 117. L. Patterson, "Get Smart: Tools to Raise Your Company's IQ," *Forbes ASAP*, 7 April 1997, 62. B. Ziegler, "Technology (A Special Report): Working Together," *The Wall Street Journal*, 18 November 1996, R21.

Personal Productivity Tip

Bits and Bytes

A "bit," b, is the smallest piece of computer data. It is a binary digit with a value of zero or one. A "byte," B, is 8 bits. Since "kilo" is 2 to the 10th power, a "kilobyte," KB, is 1,024 bytes. A "megabyte," MB, is 1,048,576 bytes (1,024 X 1,024). A "gigabyte," GB, which is the unit used to measure hard drive size in personal computers, is 1,073,741,824 bytes (1,024 to the third power). A "terabyte," TB, the unit used to measure hard drive size in mainframe computers, is 1,099,511,627,776 bytes (1,024 to the fourth power).

Source: "Cnet Glossary of Computer and Internet Terms," Cnet Web site. [Online] Available **http://www.cnet.com/Resources/Info/Glossary/index.html,** 15 June 1998.

Moore's law
Prediction that every 18 months, the cost of computing will drop by 50 percent as computer-processing power doubles

A generation ago, computer hardware and software had little to do with managing business information. Rather than storing information on hard drives, managers stored it in filing cabinets. Instead of uploading daily sales and inventory levels by satellite to corporate headquarters, they mailed hard-copy summaries to headquarters at the end of each month. Instead of word processing, there was the electric typewriter. Instead of spreadsheets, there were adding machines. Managers didn't communicate by e-mail; they communicated by sticky notes. Phone messages weren't left on voice mail. Assistants and co-workers wrote them down. Workers didn't use desktop or laptop computers as a daily tool to get work done; they scheduled limited access time to run batch jobs on the mainframe computer (and prayed that the batch job computer code they wrote would work—it often didn't).

Yet today, a generation later, computer hardware and software are an integral part of managing business information. In large part, this is due to something called **Moore's law**. Gordon Moore is one of the founders of Intel Corporation, which makes 80 percent of the integrated processors used in personal computers. In 1966, Moore predicted that every 18 months, the cost of computing would drop by 50 percent as computer-processing power doubled.[1] As shown in Figure 6.1, Moore was right. Every few years, computer power, as measured by the number of transistors per computer chip, *has* more than doubled. Consequently, the computer sitting in your lap or on your desk is not only smaller, but also much cheaper and more powerful than the large mainframe computers used by Fortune 500 companies in the early 1990s. In fact, if car manufacturers had achieved the same power increases and cost decreases attained by computer manufacturers, a fully outfitted Lexus or Mercedes sedan would cost less than $1,000!

We begin this chapter by explaining why information matters. In particular, you will learn the value, cost, and strategic importance of information to companies. Next, you will investigate the much more powerful (and cheaper!) information technologies that are changing the way companies use information. Finally, you will learn how companies capture, store, and process information, how information is accessed and shared with those within and outside the company, and how knowledge and expertise (not just information or data) are shared, too.

Figure 6.1 **Moore's Law**

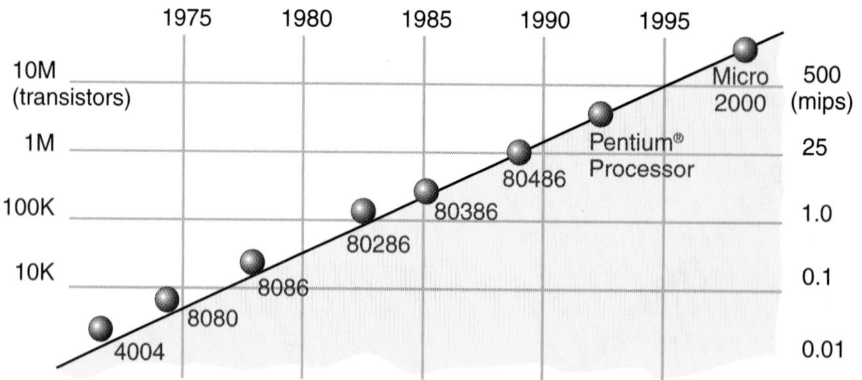

Source: "Processor Hall of Fame: What Is Moore's Law?" Intel Corporation. [Online] Available **www.intel.com/intel/museum/25anniv/Hof/moore.htm,** 8 January 1999.

Why Information Matters

raw data
facts and figures

information
useful data that can influence peoples' choices and behavior

Raw data are facts and figures. For example, 5, $18.40, 64, and 870 are some data that I used the day I wrote this section of the chapter. However, facts and figures aren't particularly useful unless they have meaning. For example, you probably can't guess what these four pieces of raw data represent, can you? And if you can't, those data are useless. That's why researchers make the distinction between raw data and information. While raw data consists of facts and figures, **information** is useful data that can influence someone's choices and behavior. So what did those four pieces of data mean to me? Well, 5 stands for channel 5, the local NBC affiliate on which I watched part of the men's French Open Tennis finals. $18.40 is how much it cost me to buy plumbing parts at Wal-Mart so I could fix two leaky faucets. 64 is for the 64 megabytes of memory that I want to add to my laptop computer. (Prices are low right now; I'll probably buy it.) And 870 means that I should have had the oil changed on my car 870 miles ago.

After reading the next two sections, you should be able to:

1 describe the **characteristics of useful information** (i.e., its value and costs).

2 explain the **strategic importance of information**.

1 Characteristics and Costs of Useful Information

Information is useful when it is **1.1** *accurate,* **1.2** *complete,* **1.3** *relevant, and* **1.4** *timely. However, there can be significant* **1.5** *acquisition,* **1.6** *processing,* **1.7** *storage,* **1.8** *retrieval, and* **1.9** *communication costs associated with useful information.*

1.1 *Accurate Information*

Information is useful when it is accurate. To be accurate, information must be reliable and valid. For instance, airline maintenance crews can't service and fix passenger jets unless they receive accurate information from plane crews or from the plane's own information system. In fact, at one time, the information systems on Boeing's 747 passenger jets indicated a large number of false problems—problems that didn't really exist.[2] If, for example, a member of the crew accidentally flipped a circuit breaker off, the 747's information system would indicate that the plane needed to be taken out of service to be fixed. However, simply resetting the circuit breaker switch would fix the problem. Since maintenance costs represent 20 percent of the cost of running an airline, inaccurate information can lead to expensive mistakes.

1.2 *Complete Information*

Information is useful when it is complete. To be complete, the amount of information must be sufficient to identify the problem and begin to identify potential solutions. Aircraft manufacturers recognized the importance of providing flight crews and maintenance personnel with more information about how their jets were running. Consequently, new-generation planes, like Boeing's 777, contain 600 computer sensors that airlines can use to fix problems and schedule maintenance. United Airlines feeds this information

The Boeing 747's onboard information system supplies useful information about the plane's condition to flight and maintenance crews.
© Paul Chesley/Tony Stone Images

into a system called AMIS, Aircraft Maintenance Information System. In turn, ground crews use laptop computers to run diagnostic tests on information gleaned from AMIS, while flight crews use computer monitors to access hundreds of color graphs that continuously monitor and display the plane's performance.[3]

1.3
Relevant Information

Information is useful when it is relevant. Information is relevant when it pertains to the problem, so that decision makers can use it to define the problem and begin to identify potential solutions. The Federal Aviation Administration (FAA) classifies maintenance problems on planes into three categories.[4] Once a priority-one problem has been identified, it must be fixed after the plane lands, or before it is allowed to take off. Anything that could lead to engine failure would be a priority-one problem. A priority-two problem does not require immediate action. The FAA allows planes with priority-two problems to take off, fly, and land for a specified time period. But the plane must be fixed within this timeframe, or the FAA will ground the plane. Priority-three problems are minor maintenance problems, like broken refrigerators or video monitors, that airlines can fix at their own discretion. Since the new information systems, like United's AMIS system, provide information on all three kinds of problems, flight crews and maintenance crews are much more likely to have the relevant information they need to make good decisions.

1.4

Timely Information

Finally, information is useful when it is timely. To be timely, the information must be available when needed to define a problem or begin to identify possible solutions. If you've ever thought, "I wish I'd known that ahead of time," then you understand the importance of timely information. For the airlines, the information that can now be obtained on plane performance is not only more accurate, more complete, and more relevant, but also more timely. In fact, United Airline's maintenance crews track the performance and problems of their planes while they're en route to their destinations. For example, if you're 35,000 feet over the Pacific on the way back to San Francisco from your business trip to South Korea, United's west coast ground crews are tracking the performance of your plane on their computer workstations. And because problems can be identified while planes are in the air, ground crews now have several hours to gather the tools, parts, and mechanical expertise needed to begin repairs as soon as the plane stops at the passenger gate. The timeliness of this information greatly increases the chances of keeping planes in service and on time.[5]

1.5

Acquisition Costs

acquisition cost
the expense of obtaining data that you don't have

Acquisition cost is the cost of obtaining data that you don't have. For example, Acxiom Inc. gathers and processes data for direct-mail marketing companies. If you've received an unsolicited, "preapproved" credit card application recently (and who hasn't?), chances are Acxiom helped the credit card company gather information about you. Where does Acxiom get that information? The first place it turns is to companies that sell consumer credit reports at a wholesale cost of $1 each. Acxiom also obtains information from retailers. Each time you use your credit card, retailers' checkout scanners gather information about your spending habits and product preferences. Many retailers sell this information to companies like Acxiom that use it for market research. So why pay for this information? Because acquiring it can help credit card companies do a better job of identifying who will mail back a signed credit card application and who will rip the credit card application in half and toss it in the trash.[6]

1.6

Processing Costs

processing cost
the expense of turning raw data into usable information

Processing cost is the cost of turning raw data into usable information. Indeed, Max Gould, Aetna Life & Casualty's chief technology officer, says, "We have massive amounts of data. But whether we have massive amounts of information is another question."[7] Often, companies already have the data they want, but it's not in the form or combination that they need it to be in. When Prudential Insurance wanted to build a better customer database, it realized that it had good information on more than 10 million households, information that could help it do a better job of targeting its insurance, money market, and real estate services to those customers. However, the processing costs were enormous, because the raw data had to be processed from 15 different computer systems that stored the data in incompatible formats.

1.7
Storage Costs

storage cost
the expense of physically or electronically archiving information for later use and retrieval

Storage cost is the cost of physically or electronically archiving information for later use and retrieval. One of the reasons that credit card companies hire Acxiom to help them identify good customer prospects is that Acxiom maintains a database of the following information about 195 million Americans: age, estimated income, home ownership, cars owned, occupation, children, number of credit cards, and so on. All of that information is stored in Acxiom's "data warehouse" outside of Little Rock, Arkansas. Acxiom uses 16 mainframes and 600,000 computer tapes to process and store all of that information. In all, Acxiom has 350 terabytes (a terabyte is the equivalent of 500 million pages of single-spaced text) of information in storage in its data warehouse. And, it intends to store even more. Axciom's CEO says, "Our customers today are saying, 'Save everything, because we might find a use for this information a year from now.' "[8]

1.8
Retrieval Costs

PersonalProductivityTip

Using Spiders and Agents on the Web

The fastest way to find information on the Internet is to visit a search site like Excite (**http://www.excite.com**) or Yahoo (**http://www.yahoo.com**). Enter the information you want, say, "travel reservations," and receive a list of sites that contain the information you want. Search sites catalog the Internet by sending software "spiders" to jump from site to site until they're finished gathering information. Software "agents" can also help find information. Tell an agent to find the cheapest flights from Dallas to Chicago. Go get some coffee. When you come back, your agent will have automatically found and organized the information you requested.

Source: P.E. Ross & N. Hutheesing, "Along Came the Spiders," *Forbes*, 23 October 1995, 210-216.

Retrieval cost is the cost of accessing already-stored and processed information. One of the most common misunderstandings about information is that it is easy and cheap to retrieve once the company has it. Not so. First, you have to find the information. Then, you've got to convince whoever has it to share it with you. Then the information has to be processed into a form that is useful for you. By the time you get the information you need, it may not be timely anymore.

For example, R.R. Donnelly & Sons is the largest printer of phone books in the world. Donnelly designed software that would make it easier to convert electronic information into the metal printing plates that are used to print each page of the phone book. When the software didn't work like it was supposed to, the printers who used the software to make the metal printing plates would call the software designers to get the information they needed to fix the problem. An assistant would then forward the request for information. However, it would often take several weeks (sometimes months!) for the software designers to provide the information that would fix the problem.[9] Because phone book information is "perishable" (people move, numbers change, new numbers are added), the printers not only lost production time, but they also frequently had to start over in order to print the most up-to-date information in the phone book. In theory, retrieval should be quick and easy. In practice, it often isn't.

1.9
Communication Costs

retrieval cost
the expense of accessing already-stored and processed information

communication cost
the expense of transmitting information from one place to another

Communication cost is the cost of transmitting information from one place to another. For example, the most important information that an electric utility company collects each month is the information from the electric meter attached to the side of your house. Traditionally, electric companies have employed meter readers to walk from house to house to gather information that would then be entered into company computers. However, meter readers are losing their jobs to radio networks that work by placing a small transceiver in your electric meter. Every five minutes, the transceiver uses radio waves to transmit data indicating how much electricity was used at your house. The data is transmitted to a nearby electric pole that holds a small computer. The small computer forwards the information to a somewhat larger computer within a quarter-mile range, which then sends the information to a base-station computer that is no more than nine miles away. The base-station computer completes the communication process by forwarding the information via phone lines or microwave towers to company headquarters. The cost: less than $1 per month for each household.[10]

Review 1: *Characteristics and Costs of Useful Information*

Raw data are facts and figures. Raw data don't become information until they are in a form that can affect decisions and behavior. For information to be useful, it has to be reliable and valid (accurate), of sufficient quantity (complete), pertinent to the problems you're facing (relevant), and available when you need it (timely). Useful Information does not come cheaply. The five costs of obtaining good information are the costs of acquiring, processing, storing, retrieving, and communicating information.

2 Strategic Importance of Information

Information has strategic importance for organizations, because it can be used **2.1** *to obtain first-mover advantage and* **2.2** *to sustain a competitive advantage once it has been created.*

2.1 *First-Mover Advantage*

first-mover advantage the strategic advantage that companies earn by being the first to use new information technology to substantially lower costs or to make a product or service different from competitors

First-mover advantage is the strategic advantage that companies earn by being the first in an industry to use new information technology to substantially lower costs or to differentiate a product or service from competitors. For example, Amazon.com (**http://www.amazon.com**) is the first store to sell books solely over the Internet. The first-mover advantages it has over traditional bookstores are numerous and substantial. First, unlike retail bookstores that are constrained by the limits of shelf space and square footage, there is no limit to the number of books that Amazon.com can sell from its Web site. With 2.5 million books for sale on its site, Amazon.com has ten times as many books as Borders' or Barnes & Noble's super-sized bookstores. Second, it is open for business worldwide 24 hours a day. Anyone with access to the Internet can "stroll" its electronic aisles at any time from anywhere. Third, unlike traditional stores, Amazon.com doesn't order most books until it sells them. So it has much less cash tied up in unsold inventory. Fourth, except for the warehouse, there are no real estate costs, and no stores to build and maintain. Finally, the Internet encourages interaction with customers, who are encouraged to write reviews of books they have purchased. College professor Don Pierstorff says, "It's not in my nature to be hip, but Amazon is the finest bookstore I've ever been to."[11]

In all, first-mover advantages can be sizable. On average, first movers earn 30 percent market share compared to 19 percent for companies that follow.[12] For example, banks that were early adopters of ATM technology were able to increase both market share and profits by 26 percent over nonadopters

Banks that were quick to adopt ATM technology gained first-mover advantage in market share over their competitors. © PhotoDisc, Inc.

of ATM technology.[13] Likewise, over 70 percent of today's market leaders started as first movers.[14]

2.2
Sustaining a Competitive Advantage

However, sustaining a competitive advantage through information technology is not easy to do. For example, smaller banks with fewer ATMs eventually caught up with larger banks by forming ATM networks like Plus and Cirrus. Because these networks allow ATM machines to process transactions on most bank cards (as long as you're willing to pay a small fee, typically $1 or less), it didn't matter whether a bank had 2 or 200 ATM machines. Furthermore, because new information technology always costs more when it is new, first-mover strategies are typically much more expensive than adopting technology after it has been established (and prices have fallen). This means that companies that establish first-mover advantage and then lose it can lose substantial amounts of money and market share. In many instances, this can put the company that had first-mover advantage out of business.

According to the resource-based view of information technology shown in Figure 6.2, companies need to address three critical issues in order to sustain a competitive advantage through information technology. First, does the information technology create value for the firm by lowering costs or providing a better product or service? If an information technology doesn't add value, then investing in it would put a firm at a competitive disadvantage to companies that choose information technologies that do add value. Second, is the information technology the same or different across competing firms? If all the firms have access to the same information technology and use it in the same way, then no firm has an advantage over another (i.e., competitive parity). Third, is the firm's use of information technology difficult for another company to create or buy? If so, then a firm has established a sustainable competitive advantage over competitors through information technology. If not, then the competitive advantage is just temporary, and competitors should eventually be able to duplicate the advantages the leading firm has gained from information technology.

In short, the key to sustaining a competitive advantage is not faster computers, more memory, and larger hard drives. The key is using information technology to continuously improve and support the core functions of a business. Companies that achieve first-mover advantage with information

Figure 6.2 **Using Information Technology to Sustain a Competitive Advantage**

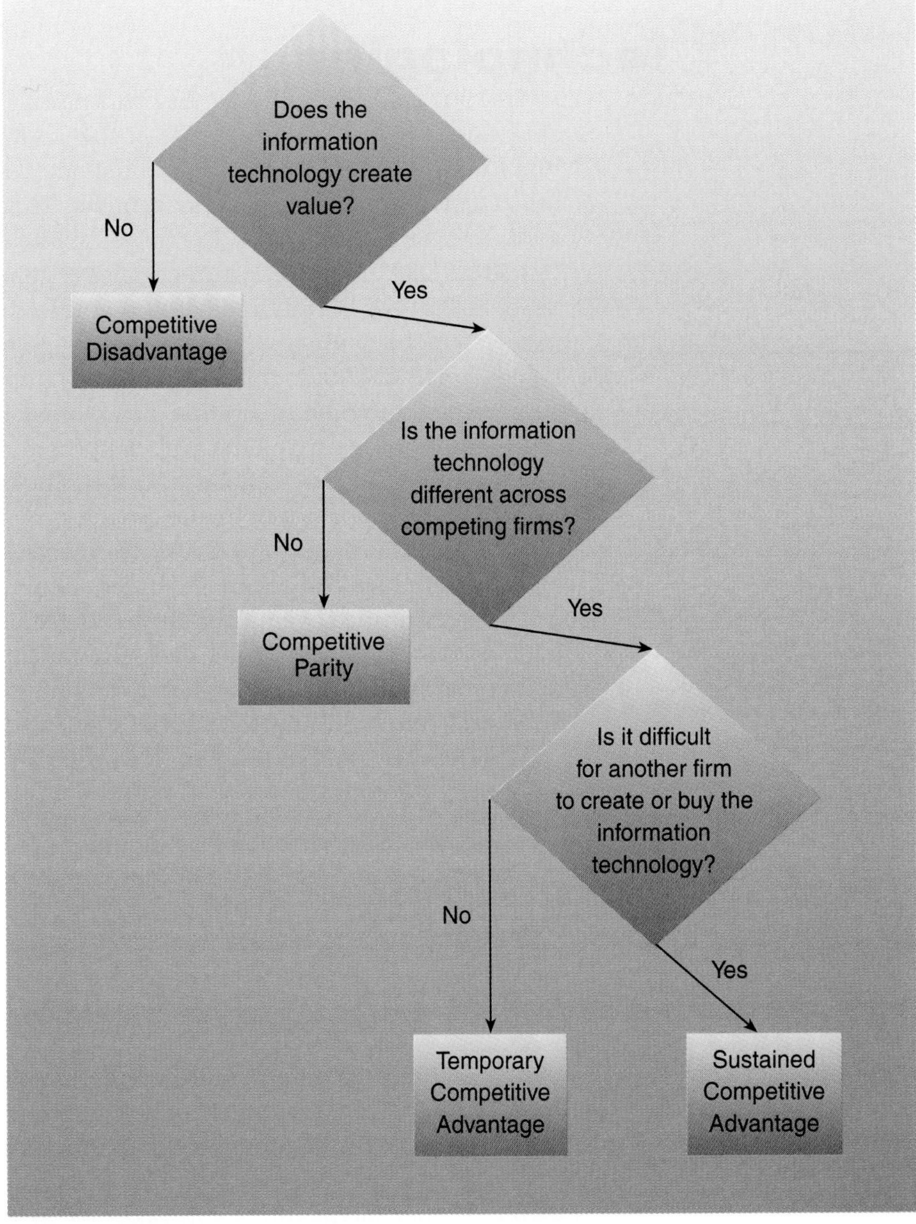

Source: Adapted from F.J. Mata, W.L. Fuerst, & J.B. Barney, "Information Technology and Sustained Competitive Advantage: A Resource-Based Analysis," *MIS Quarterly,* December 1995, 487-505.

technology and then sustain it with continued investment in the technology create a moving target that competitors will have difficulty hitting.

Review 2: *Strategic Importance of Information*

The first company to use new information technology to substantially lower costs or differentiate products or services often gains first-mover advantage, higher profits, and larger market share. However, creating a first-mover advantage can be difficult, expensive, and risky. According to the resource-based view of information technology, sustainable competitive advantage occurs when information technology adds value, is different across firms, and is difficult to create or acquire.

Information Technologies

In 1907, Metropolitan Life Insurance built a huge office building in New York City for its brand new, state-of-the art information technology system. What was the system that represented such a breakthrough in information management? The advanced system was card files. That's right, the same card file systems that every library in America used before computers. Metropolitan Life's information "technology" consisted of 20,000 separate file drawers that sat in hundreds of file cabinets more than 15 feet tall. This filing system held 20 million insurance applications, 700,000 accounting books, and 500,000 death certificates. Metropolitan Life employed 61 workers who did nothing but sort, file, and climb ladders to pull files as needed.[15]

Less than a century later, the cost, inefficiency, and ineffectiveness of this system that was previously state-of-the art would put a contemporary insurance company out of business within months. Today, if storms, fire, or accidents damage policyholders' property, insurance companies write checks on the spot to cover the losses. When policyholders buy a car, they call their insurance agent from the car dealership to activate their insurance before driving off in their new car. And now, insurance companies are marketing their products and services to customers directly from the Internet.

Wow! From card files to Internet files in 90 years. The rate of change in information technology is spectacular. After reading the next two sections, you should be able to:

3 explain the basics of **capturing, storing, and processing information**.

4 describe how companies can **share and access information and knowledge**.

3 Capturing, Storing, and Processing Information

When you go to your local Rite Aid pharmacy to pick up a prescription, the pharmacist reviews an electronic file that shows all of the medications you're now taking. That same system automatically checks to make sure that your new prescription won't create adverse side effects by interacting with the other medications you take. When you pay for your prescription, Rite Aid's point-of-sale information system determines whether you've written any bad checks lately (to Rite Aid or other stores), records your payment, and then checks with the computer of the pharmaceutical company that makes your prescription drugs to see if it's time to reorder.

In this section, you will learn about the information technologies that companies like Rite Aid use to **3.1** *capture,* **3.2** *store, and* **3.3** *process information.*

3.1 *Capturing Information*

There are two basic methods of capturing information, manual and electronic. Manual capture of information is a labor-intensive process by which data are recorded and entered by hand into a data storage device. For example, when you applied for a driver's license, you recorded personal information about yourself by filling out a form. Then, after passing your driver's test, someone typed your handwritten information into the department of motor vehicles' computer database, so that local and state police could access it from their patrol cars when they pulled you over for speeding (Isn't information great?). The problem with manual capture of information is that it is slow, expensive, and often inaccurate.

Consequently, companies are relying more on electronic capture, in which data are electronically recorded and entered into electronic storage devices. For example, scientists are now using a software program called WinWedge 32 to electronically capture research data. By connecting their scientific instruments (scales, thermometers, etc.) directly to the computer, WinWedge 32 can automatically record the data from these instruments into a computer spreadsheet (like Lotus 1-2-3 or Microsoft Excel). Bill Moir, who does research for the U.S. Forest Service, says that the software allows him and other researchers to " . . . dump data directly into the computer with no hand-entry errors and less time spent doing it."[16]

bar code
a visual pattern that represents numerical data by varying the thickness and pattern of vertical bars

Bar codes and document scanners are the most common methods of electronically capturing data. **Bar codes** represent numerical data by varying the thickness and pattern of vertical bars. The primary advantage that bar codes offer is that the data they represent can be read and recorded in an instant with a hand-held or pen-type scanner. One pass of the scanner (ok, sometimes several) and "Beep!" the information has been captured.

Bar codes were invented in 1952 and were first used to track parts inventory in factories in 1961. In 1967, railroad companies began using bar codes for tracking railroad cars. In 1973, the grocery business adopted the Universal Product Code, which required product manufacturers to place bar codes on their products or product labels. However, it took nearly two decades for bar code scanners to become standard equipment in most retail and grocery stores. Yet, once adopted, bar codes cut checkout times in half, reduced data entry errors by 75 percent, and saved stores money because stockers didn't have to go through the labor-intensive process of placing a price tag on each item in the store.[17]

electronic scanner
an electronic device that converts printed text and pictures into digital images

optical character recognition
software to convert digitized documents into ASCII text (American Standard Code for Information Interchange) that can be searched, read, and edited by word processing and other kinds of software

Because they are inexpensive and easy to use, **electronic scanners**, which convert printed text and pictures into digital images, have become an increasingly popular method of electronically capturing data. However, text that has been digitized cannot be searched or edited like the regular text in your word processing software. Therefore, companies can use **optical character recognition** software to scan and convert original or digitized documents into ASCII text (American Standard Code for Information Interchange). ASCII text can be searched, read, and edited in standard word processing, e-mail, desktop publishing, database management, and spreadsheet software.

3.2
Storing Information

Some common options for storing information are paper, microfiche, CD-ROM, DVD disks, tape, and hard drives. Paper is the most common form of data storage. However, paper storage is expensive, takes tremendous amounts of space, and requires manual search processes, which are slow and error-laden. Furthermore, only one person at a time can access paper-stored data.

Microfilm, sometimes called microfiche, is one of the oldest nonpaper methods of data storage. Information is stored on **microfilm** by literally taking a picture of the data. Because each page of data is stored on a small photographic slide, a reel of microfilm can store hundreds of pages of data. This is why libraries have used microfilm to store back issues of newspapers and magazines. Microfilm is inexpensive, permits faster retrieval than paper, requires little storage space, and is a particularly good method for long-term archives of infrequently accessed data. However, microfilm can only be viewed by one person at a time. Access to information is available only where the microfilm is stored. Searching for information is faster than paper, but still relatively slow.

microfilm
small photographic slides used to store data. A reel of microfilm can store hundreds of pages of data.

Recent advances now make it practical and affordable for even small businesses to record data on **CD-ROMs (compact disk read only memory)**, 5¼" disks that hold 650 megabytes of text, sound, or graphic data. With easy-to-use software, it takes about 30 minutes for a compact disk recorder (CD-R), which costs less than $500, to finish writing data to a CD-ROM disk, which costs less than $5.[18] This makes storing data on recordable CD-ROMs one of the cheapest forms of data storage.

CD-ROM (compact disk read only memory)
a 5¼" compact disk that holds up to 650 megabytes of text, sound, or graphic data

However, this great storage bargain will get even better as CD-ROMs are replaced by larger-capacity **DVDs, digital video disks**, that hold 4.7 gigabytes of information per side, or 9.4 gigabytes per disk. (The next generation of DVD technology will nearly double that capacity to 17 gigabytes per disk!) And since DVD technology is fully backward compatible, companies can use DVD drives to read data they previously stored on CD-ROMs. Although the technological standards are still being worked out, by the time you read this, digital video disk recorders (DVD-Rs) should be widely available, making them a cheap and worthwhile storage option for most companies.[19]

DVD (digital video disk)
a 5¼" compact disk that holds up to 17 gigabytes of text, sound, or graphic data

In the past, **data storage tapes**, which are magnetic tapes used to record data, were used to archive data for long-term storage in separate off-site locations. **Archived data** were kept just in case they were needed, but were otherwise not used by workers or managers. However, because of advances in technology, data storage tapes are now often used for **secondary storage** of data that are regularly, but infrequently used on-site by workers to do their jobs.[20] An example of data tape storage would be the Ditto Max tape drive, made by Iomega Corporation, which connects to your personal computer. Pop in a tape, which can hold up to 10 gigabytes of information (probably much more by the time you read this), and you can access or archive gigabytes of data with the click of a mouse.[21] Furthermore, despite the fact that they store so much data, most tape cartridges are small. Many are the same size as standard floppy disks (which fit in your shirt pocket), only thicker. This small size makes data storage tapes portable. Consequently, data storage tapes are increasingly used to share or transport large amounts of data to others.

data storage tape
a magnetic tape used to record and store data

archived data
data kept in long-term storage in separate off-site locations

secondary storage
stored data that are regularly, but infrequently used on-site by workers to do their jobs

Primary storage is for the data that workers and managers use most often in performing their jobs. The most common form of primary storage is hard drive storage. **Hard drives**, which are usually mounted inside computers, are magnetic disks that allow users to read *and* write (store) data. If you've got a personal computer, the hard drive is where all of your data and software are stored. Compared to CD-ROMs, DVDs, and tape storage, hard drives permit the fastest data retrieval. And, because of competition and advances in technology, the hard drives sold today easily hold ten to twenty times as much information as those sold just a few years ago. But, even better, hard drive prices

primary storage
stored data that workers and managers use most often in performing their jobs

hard drive
a magnetic disk, usually mounted inside a computer, that allows users to read its stored data and write data to it

Your computer's hard drive is a magnetic disk that serves as the primary storage area for your data and software.
© PhotoDisc, Inc.

Personal Productivity Tip

Your Hard Drive *Will* Crash, So Buckle Up with a Backup

In theory, a hard drive will work eight hours a day for 102 years before crashing. Of course, the theory ignores power failures, computer viruses, spilled drinks, or dropped laptop computers. To protect yourself and your data, buy a tape backup drive ($200 or less). Once a day, make a backup copy of all new files. Once a month, back up your entire hard drive. Backing up data is faster and cheaper than the $500 to $2,000 it will cost for a specialist to try (no guarantees) to retrieve your data from your dead hard drive.

Source: S. Kichen, "Avoiding Disaster," *Forbes,* 26 February 1996, 104-108.

RAID (redundant array inexpensive disk)
a collection of hard drives connected together so that they perform as if they were one large hard drive, to protect data from hard drive failure

dropped by 50 percent to 75 percent during the same period. (At the time this was written, you could purchase a 12 gigabyte hard drive for approximately $400.[22]) Consequently, most companies should be able to buy all of the hard drive storage that they need.

Despite these significant advantages, hard drives have one very serious disadvantage: they crash—they just lock up. Hard-drive crashes can destroy data and produce immediate work stoppages. For example, like millions of workers, the engineering group at ITT Aerospace relies on hard drives to store the data and engineering design software that it uses every day. Unfortunately, ITT Aerospace's primary network hard drive kept crashing. With the hard drive down, none of the engineers could work. Hank Hoffman, one of the engineers in the group, said, "Our systems are mission-critical, so we can't afford that kind of downtime."[23] Hoffman's solution to this problem was to install a RAID hard drive system.

RAID is short for **redundant array inexpensive disk** system. The idea behind RAID was hatched when scientists at the University of California, Berkeley determined that clustering a series of small disk drives together would be cheaper and more reliable (i.e., less prone to disk crashes) than a single large disk.[24] For example, a RAID hard drive system might consist of ten 2-gigabyte hard drives connected together to act as one large 20-gigabyte hard drive. RAID works by mirroring or duplicating data on at least three different drives. So if you wrote a 20-page report, that report would be stored on at least three of the ten hard drives in the RAID system. If the small drive that holds the original copy of your report crashes, then the RAID system automatically begins using one of the other copies.

RAID systems are so reliable that most users will never even know there was a problem. Quaker Oats Co. has now switched all of its payroll, sales, and financial applications to RAID systems. David Blanchard, a systems analyst for Quaker Oats, explained that "We can't afford downtime here." Likewise, ITT Aerospace hasn't had any downtime from hard drive crashes since it installed a RAID system.[25] RAID systems are more expensive, but having reliable access to critical software and data is much less expensive than the loss of data, work, and customers that could result from the crash of a critical hard drive.

3.3 *Processing Information*

processing information transforming raw data into meaningful information

Processing information means transforming raw data into meaningful information that can be applied to business decision making. Evaluating sales data to determine the best- and worst-selling products, examining

Back to the Future

Can you Strike Gold with Data Mining?

With automated, electronic capture of data, increased processing power, and cheaper and more plentiful ways to store data, managers no longer worry about getting data. Instead, they scratch their heads about how to use the overwhelming amount of data that pours into their businesses every day. Furthermore, most managers know little about statistics and have neither the time nor the inclination to learn how to use them to analyze data.

One promising tool to help managers dig out from under the avalanche of data is data mining. **Data mining** is the process of discovering unknown patterns and relationships in large amounts of data. For example, IBM has provided several National Basketball Association teams with data mining software called Advanced Scout. Advanced Scout allows basketball coaches to ask "What if?" questions like "What if I start a certain lineup or run certain plays?" "When should we go for more three-pointers?" and "Does this strategy lead to victory?" Dr. Inderpal Bhandari, a computer scientist at IBM, said, "The beauty of Advanced Scout is that it requires little computer training or data analysis background. It was written with the coach in mind."

Bob Salmi, assistant coach for the New York Knicks, said, "Using Advanced Scout is like having another coach on your team. There are patterns in all data. As coaches, we have ideas about why we win or lose, based on player performance and statistics. This technology allows us to get quick answers to questions and automatically identify patterns that may mean the difference between winning and losing. The ability to analyze data quickly and see previously unsuspected patterns in data can only help us make more intelligent decisions." Plus, Advanced Scout is easy to use. It asks users simple questions and makes suggestions that may help them find what they're looking for.

At this point in its early development, there are two kinds of data mining. Supervised data mining usually begins with the user telling the data mining software to look and test for specific patterns and relationships in a data set. For instance, a grocery store manager might instruct the data mining software to determine if coupons placed in the Sunday paper increased or decreased profits. Unsupervised data mining is when the user simply tells the data mining software to uncover whatever patterns and relationships it can find in a data set.

For example, Dr. John Nearhos is the general manager of the professional review division at Australia's Health Insurance Commission, which processes 300 million health insurance claims and makes eight billion dollars of payments each year. Dr. Nearhos gave IBM 10 data tapes with a total of three gigabytes of information, and asked the company to use its data mining software to find anything that might help the commission cut costs. Three days later, the software had uncovered an illegal billing practice that was costing the commission millions of dollars that it shouldn't have to pay. Dr. Nearhos said, "I don't know if we would have ever made the connection on our own. I was able to make a call and put a stop to it that day. Data mining targets the problem areas for us, and we can do the rest."

At this point, data mining is much more of a promise than realized potential. It remains unproven and expensive. (It took IBM three days of raw mainframe power to find the illegal billing practice.) But if it follows the path of most technology, it will become even easier and cheaper to use in the future.

Sources: A. Crowley, "Pattern Matching: Industries from Sports to Health Care Are Examining Data Mining Methods," *PC Week Online,* 4 June 1996. "Data Mining: Advanced Scout," IBM Research Web Site. [Online] Available **http://www.research.ibm.com/xw-scout**, 31 December 1995. M.G. Stillwell, "Data Mining and Discovery." [Online] Available **http://alf.usask.ca/grads/mgs310/Cmpt826S3/cmpt826sum3.html**, 15 November 1995.

repair records to determine product reliability, or monitoring the cost of long-distance phone calls are all examples of processing raw data into meaningful information. There are three kinds of computer processing: centralized, distributed, and shared processing.

data mining
the process of discovering unknown patterns and relationships in large amounts of data

centralized processing
processing and storing data from individual computer terminals on mainframe computers, which have gigabytes of memory and terabytes of hard drive storage space

Centralized processing means that data entered into individual computer terminals are stored and processed on mainframe computers that have hundreds of megabytes of memory and hundreds of gigabytes of hard drive storage space.[26] Not surprisingly, companies use mainframes when they need to store and process vast amounts of information. For example, with 30 million customers who speak and read 19 different languages, nothing but a mainframe computer would allow *Reader's Digest* magazine to keep track of its customer base.

Because of their enormous processing and storage capabilities, mainframe computers are often used in transaction and automated processing systems. **Transaction processing systems** are centralized mainframe systems that record the thousands of routine, daily transactions involved in running a business, such as reservations, orders, sales, purchasing, payroll and expenses.[27] For example, West Coast department store chain Carter Hawley Hale uses a transaction processing system to run its shipping and distribution centers and handle thousands of shipping transactions every day.[28]

transaction processing systems
centralized mainframe systems that record the thousands of routine, daily transactions involved in running a business

automated processing
using mainframe systems to automatically collect and process data into useful information

Mainframes are also frequently used to do **automated processing**, which is using information technology (rather than people) to automatically collect and process data into useful information. For example, some companies are experimenting with automated check-ins using stand-alone kiosks that resemble ATMs.[29] Slide in your credit card, punch in the information, and presto: The kiosk, which is typically connected to a mainframe computer hundreds of miles away, handles your transaction, and provides a receipt. Alamo Rental Car uses its Alamo Express Plus kiosks to check in its customers in less than 60 seconds.[30] And, at a cost of only $15,000 to $20,000 per kiosk, the savings in wages alone can pay for a check-in kiosk in just six months.

distributed processing
processing and storing data in desktop computers

Unlike mainframe computers in which data are centrally processed and stored in one large computer, **distributed processing** is processing and storing data in desktop computers. The basic idea behind distributed processing is to give the managers and workers closest to the data the tools they need to quickly and easily transform data into information. Rather than waiting for corporate data centers to generate reports based on information retrieved from company mainframes, managers and workers empowered with desktop computers can quickly capture and process the data themselves. For example, the president and CEO of People's Bank of Connecticut said that "The PC [personal computer] is a critical element in our long-term strategy." In fact, the PC is so important that People's is replacing mainframe terminals (computer terminals that can only be used to access mainframe computers) with desktop computers. The goal is to use desktop computers to give employees quicker access to more information about customers' needs and bank products.[31] When a new customer comes in for a car loan, it's much faster and easier for a People's Bank loan officer to run the numbers on a desktop PC than a mainframe computer.

shared processing
information processing that is shared by two kinds of computers, clients and servers, across a client/server network

client/server network
individual computers connected together through a server computer, so that they can share data and software stored on the server

Shared processing, which is based on client/server networks, represents a middle ground between centralized (mainframes) and distributed processing (desktop computers). **Shared processing** literally means that the processing of information is shared between two kinds of computers, clients and servers. In a **client/server network**, individual computers are connected together

client
a desktop computer connected to a network through a server

server
a larger, more powerful computer than client computers that stores data and software requested by clients on a network; also called a file server

network
a system of cable wires or optic fibers that connect computers and allow them to send data to and receive data from each other

PersonalProductivityTip

Five Ways To Get More from Your Computer

1. Buy twice the chip speed, three times the hard drive, and four times the memory you think you'll need.
2. Keep it simple. Buy basic software (or last year's version).
3. Create a built-in help group by buying the same computer stuff that your friends and co-workers use.
4. Read Internet news groups that discuss your software or hardware. Ninety percent of the time, others will be experiencing the same problems you are and someone will discuss how to fix it.
5. Read your computer/software manual or help file. Teach yourself how to use the $2,000 computer on your desk. It's not that hard.

Source: G. Kawasaki, "Get More Out of Your Computer," *Forbes*, 26 February 1996), 112.

through a network, so that they can share data and software stored on the server. The **client** is usually a desktop computer, while the **server** is a larger computer (though not as large as a mainframe) with ten to one hundred times the capacity of the desktop computer. Servers store data and software that can be used by clients on the network. When a client computer requests data from a server (also called a "file server" because it holds data files), that request is processed over a computer network. Like phone lines, a **network** is a system of cable wires or optic fibers that connect computers and allow them to send and receive data.

So which kind of processing—centralized (mainframes), distributed (desktops), or shared (client/server)—should you use to manage information in your company? In the past, because of prohibitive costs, companies tended to rely on one kind of processing. Today, however, most companies use a combination of processing approaches. Larger companies are likely to use mainframes, desktops, and client/ server networks. For example, when American Airline's Sabre Division handles more than 3,000 ticket reservations a second, or when Allstate handles 7,000 claims per day (after a major hurricane struck Florida), there is no substitute for the power and capacity of a mainframe computer.[32] Yet even smaller companies with no more than three or four employees will benefit by combining desktop computers with a client/server network.

So, with the information technology tools available today and even better ones on the horizon, the question managers should be asking is which combination of processing and storage best meets their information management needs. Table 6.1, which summarizes the standard memory, storage, processing speed, and cost of desktop, server, and mainframe computers, is a good place to begin answering that question.

Review 3: *Capturing, Storing, and Processing Information*

Electronic data capture (bar codes and scanners) is much faster, easier, and cheaper than manual data capture. The most common form of data storage, paper, is slow, expensive, and takes space. Microfilm saves space, but is a time-consuming method of retrieving information. Recordable CD-ROMs and DVDs allow fast information retrieval and are now one of the cheapest methods of data storage. Data storage tapes are primarily used to archive data for long-term and secondary storage. Hard drives are the most common method of primary storage, but drive failures can destroy data and

Table 6.1 **Cost and Configuration for Desktop, Server, and Mainframe Computers**

Computer	*Price*	*Processor*	*Memory*	*Storage*
Desktop	$1,000 to $3,000	200–400 MHz Pentium II processor	32–64 megabytes	4–8 gigabytes
Servers	$5,000 to $20,000	Up to 4 400 MHz Pentium II processors	Up to 4 gigabytes	Up to 350 gigabytes of total storage
Mainframes	$500,000 to $5,000,000	Up to 20 500 MHz processors	8–32 gigabytes	4–8 terabytes

lead to work stoppages. However, RAID hard drives can be used to protect data from hard drive crashes. Centralized processing relies on mainframe computers, which are used for transaction processing and automated processing. Distributed processing relies on desktop computers. Shared processing relies on client/server networks.

4 Accessing and Sharing Information and Knowledge

Imagine a situation where the only way customers could contact your company would be to fax a company in Switzerland, which would then fax the customer faxes to you. A company would have to be crazy to do that, right? Well, that's exactly the situation that Ingersoll-Rand, a $5 billion manufacturing company, put itself in with its international customers. For example, Sermatec, which sells Ingersoll-Rand air compressors in Santiago, Chile, would fax its order for more air compressors to Ingersoll-Rand's international trading company in Switzerland, which would then fax the order to factories in North Carolina, Pennsylvania, and Tennessee. Sermatec's General Manager said, "It would take up to two weeks just to get confirmation that I'd placed an order." With no direct contact and no way to find out the status of orders, distributors might as well have put a message in a bottle and dropped it in the ocean with the hope that Ingersoll-Rand would someday get the message and respond.

It didn't take long for Ingersoll-Rand's manager of global business systems to realize that "We had to make a change, and we had to make it quickly." So the company installed a $1.5 million system that lets customers make orders and check on pricing, inventory, and the status of previous orders from their own office computers. With instant access to this information, Sermatec increased it sales. Now when a customer calls about the price and availability of an Ingersoll-Rand part or product, Sermatec logs onto the system to provide an immediate answer. Moreover, Ingersoll-Rand has reduced product delivery times to distributors like Sermatec from well over a month to three days.[33]

Today, information technologies are letting companies communicate, share, and provide data access to workers, managers, and customers in ways that were unthinkable just a few years ago.

After reading this section, you should be able to explain how companies use information technology to improve **4.1** *communication,* **4.2** *internal access and sharing of information,* **4.3** *external access and sharing of information, and* **4.4** *the sharing of knowledge and expertise.*

4.1 *Communication*

e-mail
the transmission of messages via computers

E-mail, voice-messaging, and conferencing systems are changing how managers, workers, and customers communicate and work with each other. **E-mail**, the transmission of messages via computers, is the fastest growing form of communication in organizations. By the year 2000, more than 100 million people worldwide will be using e-mail to send messages, up from 80 million in 1998.[34] Why is e-mail so popular? First, it's the cheapest way to send a message. For example, a two-page document sent from Baltimore to Portland would cost $15.50 by Federal Express, $10.75 by the U.S. Postal

Service's overnight delivery, 32 cents by regular U.S. mail, 50 cents to $1.50 by fax, and just 7 cents by e-mail.[35] Second, e-mail is substantially faster, usually appearing in the receiver's electronic mailbox within half an hour (sometimes within minutes). Third, e-mail, because of its similarity to regular mail (which devoted e-mail users call "snail mail"), is easy to learn and use.

Of course, the ease and simplicity of e-mail create its own disadvantage: too much e-mail! Patricia Baldwin, director of business simplification for Sun Microsystems, makers of Unix-based computers and the Java software language, gets more than 250 e-mails a day. Of those 250 messages, no more than 20 have any significant impact on her job.[36] Unfortunately, the volume of e-mail that Patricia receives is not unique.

voice messaging telephone answering system that records audio messages

Voice messaging, or "voice mail," is a telephone answering system that records audio messages. Surveys indicate that 89 percent of respondents believe that voice messaging is critical to business communication, 78 percent believe that it improves productivity, and 58 percent would rather leave a message on a voice messaging system than with a receptionist.[37] Fred DeLuca, who runs Subway Sandwiches, said, "We started using voice mail about nine years ago. I like it because you don't have to have any special equipment—you see a phone, you make a call." Fred also likes voice mail because "voice messages have more texture—expression and emotion—than e-mail or a memo does. Some people aren't readers; they're talkers, and you just can't capture them in writing the way you can in speech."[38]

Voice messaging systems are easy to use and cut costs because workers don't have to spend their time recording and forwarding messages. However, handling voice messages can take a considerable amount of time. Fred DeLuca said, "I get about 60 messages a day from employees and franchisees, and I listen to all of them. For my sanity, I set a time limit of 75 seconds, because people can be long-winded when they're excited. When I hear, 'You have 30 messages,' I know right away that I'll spend 60 minutes on voice mail. I take 2 minutes per message, listening and returning or forwarding."[39] By contrast, because people read six times faster than they can listen, 30 e-mail messages can usually be handled in 10 to 15 minutes.[40] Plus, some companies have found that customers prefer to talk to "real" people, even if only to leave a message. Winguth, Dohahue & Co., an executive search firm in Los Altos, California, scrapped its $20,000 voice messaging system. Owner Ed Winguth said, "At first clients said it was terrific that we were in the 21st century. But soon customers started saying it was too cold and annoying. These were CEOs and VPs calling in. Our repeat customers really got annoyed."[41]

conferencing system communications system that lets two or more users in different locations see and talk to each other as if they were in the same room

document conferencing communications system that allows two or more people in different locations to simultaneously view and make comments about a document

application sharing communications system that allows two or more people in different locations to make changes in a document by sharing control of the software application running on one computer

Unlike e-mail and voice mail, which only permit users to leave messages, **conferencing systems** allow two or more users in different locations to see and talk to each other as if they were working side by side in the same room. There are three kinds of conferencing systems: document conferencing, application sharing, and video conferencing.[42] The key similarity across all three is that time and space don't matter when it comes to getting work done. No matter where people are, conferencing systems allow them to work together.

Document conferencing, also called "white boarding," allows two or more people to use computers to simultaneously view and make comments about a document. **Application sharing** takes document conferencing several steps further by allowing two or more people in different locations to actually make changes in a document by sharing control of the software

Personal Productivity Tip

Privacy Through Public Key Encryption

One of the biggest fears about computers is privacy. However, you can use a system called "public key encryption" to protect your files. First, give copies of your "public key" to anyone who sends you files or e-mail. Have them use the public key, which is actually a piece of software, to encrypt files before sending them to you. The only way to decrypt the files is with a companion "private key," that you keep to yourself. If you want to learn more, or want to begin encrypting your own files, download a free program called Pretty Good Privacy from **http://web.mit.edu/pgp**.

Source: G. Kawasaki, "Get More Out of Your Computer," *Forbes,* 26 February 1996, 112.

application running on one computer. Here's how it works. A lawyer in Chicago and her client, a business person in San Francisco, are making the final changes on a contract for the business person's company. Step one: The lawyer and the business person talk on the phone while they work. Step two: Both use a second phone line or a company network to connect their computers as they talk. Step three: The lawyer opens the contract in word processing software and then starts the application sharing software. (Several companies make this software: Netscape's Conference, **http://www.netscape.com/**, Microsoft's NetMeeting, **http://www.microsoft.com/netmeeting/**, and Intel's TeamStation System, **http://www.intel.com/proshare/conferencing/demo/.**) Seconds later, the first page of the contract appears on the lawyer's computer in Chicago, and a few seconds after that, it appears on the business person's computer in San Francisco. Now, both can make changes to the document. For example, the lawyer could change $5,000 to $50,000 on the first page while the business person is correcting a misspelling on page 20.[43] As the changes are being made, the computers communicate the changes over the phone line or network, so that both parties can work on identical versions of the file at all times.

There are numerous advantages to application sharing. Companies save an enormous amount of money and time by eliminating or reducing travel. Rather than holding a meeting to talk about proposed changes and then making them, the changes are made instantly. Therefore, there are no follow-up notes, e-mails, or faxes to make sure that agreed-on changes actually get made. Beyond the initial cost of the software, the only expense is for long-distance phone calls. Even that can be eliminated if both parties have fast enough systems to use the Internet to transmit their phone calls. Unlike videoconferencing, which is discussed next, document sharing runs well over standard phone lines. Thus, most companies and business people can use it now without having to invest funds for additional equipment.

desktop videoconferencing communications system that allows two or more people in different locations to use video cameras and computer monitors to see and hear each other and share documents

Desktop videoconferencing allows two or more people in different locations to use video cameras and computer monitors to see and hear each other and to share documents. Unlike application sharing, desktop videoconferencing does not work well over regular phone lines. For adequate transmission of audio and video, participants need access to a high-speed network or high-speed connection to the Internet. All participants also need to place an audio microphone and a small inexpensive video camera on top of their personal computer. As shown in Figure 6.3, a participant in a desktop video

Using video cameras, microphones, and computer monitors, people in different locations can work together and share documents through videoconferencing.
© Corbis/R. W. Jones

Figure 6.3 **Desktop Videoconferencing**

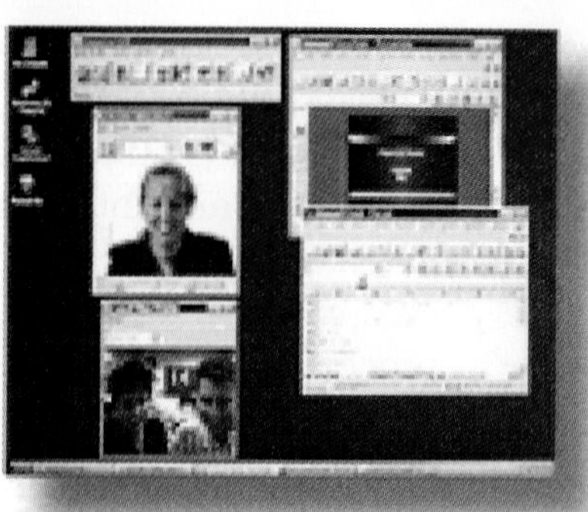

conference sees (and hears) live pictures of other participants. Also, like document sharing, participants can see the files they are sharing. (See "Back to the Future: A Global 'Walk Down the Hallway'" in Chapter 8 for a full discussion of the uses of videoconferencing.) While desktop videoconferencing is more expensive and harder to make work than application sharing, companies with high-speed networks should have few problems taking advantage of this technology.

4.2
Internal Access and Sharing

executive information system (EIS) data processing system that uses internal and external data sources to provide the information needed to monitor and analyze organizational performance

Two kinds of information technology are used by executives, managers, and workers inside the company to access and share information: executive information systems and intranets. An **executive information system (EIS)** uses internal and external sources of data to provide managers and executives the information they need to monitor and analyze organizational performance.[44] The goal of an EIS is to provide accurate, complete, relevant, and timely information to managers.

For example, with the click of a mouse, senior and middle managers at United Cigar Stores can pull up graphs and charts of weekly and monthly sales on their computers to see if they're on target. If they're not, they can "drill down" for more information to help them figure out whether the problem is at the divisional, regional, or district level. The managers can look at charts and graphs of data for each of the company's 476 stores. Data can even be cross-referenced, looking at how, for example, various products (cigars, pipe tobacco, or cigarettes) sell in particular stores (hotel shops versus malls) or areas (Vancouver, Toronto, etc.).[45]

Since most managers are not computer experts, EISs must be easy to use and must provide information that managers want and need. Consequently, most EIS programs use touch screens, "point and click" commands, and easy-to-understand displays, such as color graphs, charts, and written summaries so that little learning or computer experience is required. In addition, basic commands such as *find, compare,* and *show* allow managers to easily and quickly get the information they need to make good decisions. For example, at Du Pont Chemical, the EIS is directly linked to the company e-mail system. When managers find interesting information, a couple of mouse clicks sends color charts and graphs on their way to the appropriate people. At Frito-Lay, the EIS gives managers touch-screen access

BLASTFROMTHEPAST

The History of Managing Information

The earliest recorded use of written information occurred nearly 60,000 years ago when Cro-Magnons, from whom modern humans descended, created and recorded a lunar calendar. The calendar, consisting of 28 symbols carved into a reindeer antler, was used to track and kill deer, bison, and elk that would gather at river crossings when, as the Cro-Magnons' lunar calendar indicated, the waters would be high.

For most of recorded history, information has been costly, difficult to obtain, and slow to spread. Because of the immense labor and time it took to hand-copy information, books, manuscripts, and written documents of any kind were rare and extremely expensive. Word of Joan of Arc's death in 1431 took 18 months to travel from France across Europe to Constantinople (now Istanbul, Turkey). Most people literally heard news and information from the town crier (Hear ye, Hear ye!) or from minstrel and acting groups who relayed information as they traveled from town to town. There were no newspapers. The average person could not read or write.

However, accurate, timely, relevant, and complete information has been important to businesses throughout history. Indeed, 99 percent of the stone tablets and animal-skin documents unearthed in our earliest cities were business and economic texts. Why? Because traders, crafts people, and local business people have always needed some way to keep track of trades, orders, and how much money (or gold, or pigs, or chickens) was owed to whom. Consequently, businesses have pushed for and been quick to adopt new information technologies that reduced the cost or increased the speed with which they could acquire, store, retrieve, or communicate information.

The first "technologies" to revolutionize the business use of information were paper and the printing press. In the 14th century, water-powered machines were created to pulverize rags into pulp to make paper. Paper prices, which were already cheaper than animal-skin parchments, quickly dropped by 400 percent. Less than a half-century later, Johannes Gutenberg invented the printing press, which greatly reduced the price and time needed to copy written information. For instance, in 1483 in Florence, Italy, a scribe would charge one florin (then, an Italian unit of money) to hand-copy one document page. By contrast, it would cost just three florins to have a printer set up and print 1,025 copies of the same document. Within 50 years of its invention, Gutenberg's printing press cut the cost of information by 1,000 percent!

And what Gutenberg's printing press did for publishing, the manual typewriter did for daily communication. Before 1850, most business correspondence was written by hand and copied using the "letter press." With the ink still wet, the letter would be placed into a tissue paper "book." A hand press would then be used to squeeze the "book" and copy the still wet ink onto tissue paper. By the 1870s, manual typewriters made it cheaper, easier, and faster to produce and copy business correspondence. Of course, in the 1980s, slightly more than a century later, typewriters were replaced by personal computers and word processing software for identical reasons.

The decreased cost and widespread use of printed information produced a growing need to organize and make sense of the explosion of information that overwhelmed the typical business. The cash register, invented in 1879, kept sales clerks honest by recording all sales transactions on a roll of paper securely locked inside the machine. But managers soon realized that its most important contribution was better management and control of their business. For example, department stores could track performance and sales by installing separate cash registers in the food, clothing, and hardware departments.

Time clocks, introduced in the 1890s, helped businesses keep track of worker hours and costs. Vertical file cabinets and the Woodruff file, invented in 1868, represented major advances in information storage and retrieval. Once sales orders or business correspondence were put in the proper file drawer, they could easily and quickly be found by anyone familiar with the system.

Finally, businesses have always looked for information technologies that would speed access to timely information. For instance, the Medici family, which opened banks throughout Europe in the early 1400s, used posting messengers to keep in contact with their more than 40 "branch" managers. The post messengers, which predate the U.S. Postal Service Pony Express by 400 years, could travel 90 miles per day, twice what average riders could cover, because the Medicis were willing to pay for the expense of providing them with fresh horses.

Sources: J. Burke, *The Day the Universe Changed* (Boston: Little, Brown & Company, 1985). S. Lubar, *Infoculture: The Smithsonian Book of Information Age Inventions* (Boston: Houghton, Mifflin, 1993). M. Rothschild, "Cro-Magnon's Secret Weapon," *Forbes ASAP: A Technology Supplement* 2 (13 September 1993): 19.

to monthly sales reports, distribution patterns, and outside data on competitors and suppliers that can be obtained from the Dow Jones News Retrieval Service. Table 6.2 describes the capabilities of two of the best-selling products that companies use for EIS programs.

intranets
private company networks that allow employees to easily access, share, and publish information using Internet software

Intranets are private company networks that allow employees to easily access, share, and publish information using Internet software. At Geffen Records, employees can pull up phone lists, schedules, news, and the release dates for new CDs. At Boeing, employees can access messages from top company leadership, information bulletins, and the doctor and hospital directory wherever they live. The intranet also helps its engineers work together to design planes wherever they're located. At Turner Entertainment Group, employees can access information about CNN, the Cartoon Network, and the company newsletter; do company research; file expense reports; order supplies; and change their health insurance provider.[46]

Intranets are exploding in popularity. In 1995, the Business Research Group estimated that only 11 percent of midsize to large companies were us-

Table 6.2

Characteristics of Best-Selling Executive Information Systems

Ease of Use

- **Few commands to learn**. Simply drag-and-drop or point-and-click to create charts and tables or get the information you need.
- **Save important views**. Need to see weekly sales by store every Monday? Save that "view" of the data, and it will automatically be updated with new data every week.
- **3-D charts to display data.** Column, square, pie, ring, line, area, scatter, bar, cube, etc.
- **Geographic dimensions**. Different geographic areas are automatically color-coded for easy understanding.

Analysis of Information

- **Track sales**. Track sales performance by product, region, account, and channel.
- **Easy-to-understand displays**. Information is displayed in tabular and graphical charts.
- **Time periods**. Data can be by current year, prior year, year to date, quarter to date, and month to date.

Identifying Problems and Exceptions

- **Compare to standards.** Compares actual company performance (actual expenses versus planned expenses, or actual sales by sales quotas).
- **Trigger exceptions**. Allows users to set triggers (5 percent over budget, 3 percent under sales quota), which then highlight negative exceptions in red and positive exceptions in green.
- **Drill down.** Once exceptions have been identified, users can drill down for more information to determine why the exception is occurring.
- **Detect & alert newspaper**. When things go wrong, the EIS delivers a "newspaper" via e-mail to alert managers to problems. The newspaper offers an intuitive interface for easily navigating and further analyzing the alert content.
- **Detect & alert robots**. Detect & alert robots keep an extra "eye" out for events and problems. Want to keep an eye out for news about one of your competitors? Use a news robot to track stories on Dow Jones News Retrieval. Robots can also be used to track stock quotes, internal databases, and e-mail messages.

Sources: Pilot Software home page, "Decision Support Suite Benefits." [Online] Available **http://www.pilotsw.com/products/benefits.htm**, 15 June 1998. Comshare home page. [Online] Available **http://www.comshare.com/**, 15 June 1998.

ing intranets. Today, more than 70 percent have their own intranets.[47] The reasons for this phenomenal growth are many. First, executive information systems can cost as much as several hundred thousand dollars to install for a small group of managers. In comparison, intranets, which can be used by everyone in the company, are inexpensive. Much of the software required to set up an intranet is either **freeware** (no cost) or **shareware** (try before you buy, and usually less expensive than commercial software).

freeware
computer software that is free to whoever wants it

shareware
computer software that you can try before you buy, but, if you keep it beyond the trial period, usually 30 days, you must buy it

Second, using intranets is intuitive and easy. Point your cursor over a word or symbol that you're interested in. If the cursor turns from an arrow into a hand, indicating that the word or symbol is a link to further information, then click it. Presto! The information you want appears on the screen. That's all there is to it. As a result, companies are rushing to put as much information as they can on their intranets. Indeed, a study of 323 companies in 10 different industries found that 23 percent of company intranets contained information on company benefits; 18 percent had information about savings plans, profit sharing, or company stock plans; 70 percent had information about jobs; 6 percent allowed managers to conduct performance appraisals online; 24 percent were used for training; and 57 percent were used for corporate communications.[48]

Third, it doesn't matter if the people in marketing use the Macintosh operating system, the finance folks use Windows, and the information systems people use Unix systems—everyone can easily access information if it's available on the company intranet.[49] Intranets work across all kinds of computers and computer operating systems.

Fourth, if you already have a computer network in place, chances are your company already has the computer equipment and expertise to quickly and easily roll out an intranet.

Fifth, while it's not seamless, many software programs easily convert electronic documents from proprietary word processing (Word Perfect, Microsoft Word, etc.), spreadsheet (Lotus 1-2-3, Microsoft Excel), or graphics (Lotus Freelance or Microsoft PowerPoint) formats to the hypertext markup language (HTML) used to display text and graphics on the Internet and intranets. Indeed, many HTML software editors are now as easy to use as word processors. So when employees have information that others in the company want access to, HTML editors make it easy to publish information on the company intranet for all to see. Boeing's intranet contains everything from corporate-policy material to maintenance manuals, and Boeing encourages its employees to publish any information that others might find useful.[50]

4.3 *External Access and Sharing*

Historically, companies have been unable or reluctant to let outside groups have access to corporate information. However, two information technologies—electronic data interchange and the Internet—are not only making it easier to share company data with external groups like suppliers and customers, but also the reduced costs, higher productivity, better customer service, and faster communications they produce have managers scrambling to find ways to use them in their own companies.

electronic data interchange (EDI)
the direct electronic transmission of purchase and ordering information from one company's computer system to another company's computer system

Electronic data interchange, or **EDI**, is the direct electronic transmission of purchase and ordering information from one company's computer system to another company's computer system. For example, when a Wal-Mart checkout clerk drags a CD across the checkout scanner, Wal-Mart's computerized inventory system automatically reorders another copy of that CD through the direct EDI connection that its computer has with the manufacturing and shipping computer at the company that published the CD, say Atlantic Records. No one at Wal-Mart or Atlantic Records fills out paperwork. No phone calls are made. There are no delays to wait to find out whether Atlantic has the CD in stock. The transaction takes place instantly and automatically.

EDI saves companies money by eliminating step after step of manual information processing. One study found that EDI could save manufacturing companies $18 per transaction, retail companies $23 per transaction, and wholesalers $11 per transaction.[51] Of course, those are just averages. Some companies save more. R.J. Reynolds Tobacco Company, which deals with more than 1,400 suppliers and tens of thousands of orders per year, said that EDI reduced the cost of orders from between $75 and $125 to just 93 cents![52] And when you consider that 70 percent of the data output from one company, like a purchase order, ends up as data input at another company, such as a sales invoice or shipping order, EDI also reduces data entry errors. Finally, EDI reduces order and delivery times. Hotel and motel chains like Marriott and Hilton have found that EDI has reduced the average time for food and beverage orders to their kitchens by half, from six days to three days.[53]

Internet
a global network of networks that allows users to send and retrieve data from anywhere in the world

Similar to the way in which EDI is used to handle transactions with suppliers, companies are reducing paperwork and manual information processing by using the Internet to electronically automate transactions with customers. The **Internet** is a global network of networks that allows users to send and retrieve data from anywhere in the world. Companies like Southwest Airlines (**http://www.iflyswa.com/**), United Airlines (**http://www.ual.com/**), and American Airlines (**http://www.americanair.com/**), as well as independent travel sites like Microsoft Expedia (**http://expedia.msn.com/**), have Internet sites where customers can purchase tickets without calling a ticket agent or the airline's toll-free number.

Been There,

John Edwardson and Andrew Studdert of United Airlines

John Edwardson, President, and Andrew Studdert, Chief Information Officer, are two key managers who helped United Airlines use information technology to return to profitability after $1.3 billion in losses in the early 1990s.

Q: John, what do you want IS [Information Services] to do for you at United?

A: I'm looking at IS as a critical change agent. When I worked at Northwest, I considered United a real leader in terms of information services and automation. When I got here, I found that they had lost their focus. What happened here I've seen at hundreds of companies, and it usually isn't the fault of IS. It's the user departments who say, "You know what I want, and I don't have much time, so just go build this for me." I met people in IS who had talked with their customers on the telephone but had never met them. It was stunning to me that they had never met face to face, and they worked in the same buildings! I also see IS as a revenue-generating unit.

"When you boil it down, IS is a people business."

Q: By what measures?

A: Historically we had taken the attitude that we wouldn't sell the software we developed. We thought we had a competitive advantage that way.

to automate the creation of company contracts. Step 1: Choose from a menu of 20 types of contracts. Step 2: Answer 25-35 questions designed to fill out the contract details and to choose the right legal language and protection for the company. With the expert system, it takes an average of half an hour to complete and print a standard multimillion dollar contract. Without the expert system, the same contract took four hours of a purchasing manager's time, four hours of word processing, and two hours of an attorney's time. One of the managers who uses the expert system said, "I can just go bing, bam, boom, and it's done. My manager can feel confident that we've got all of the bases covered with each of the [legal] clauses."[57]

Most expert systems work by using a collection of "if-then" rules to sort through information and recommend a course of action. For example, let's say that you're using your American Express card to help your spouse celebrate a promotion. You buy dinner, and then some movie tickets. After the movie, you and your spouse stroll by a travel office that displays a Las Vegas poster in its window. Thirty minutes later, caught up in the moment, you find yourselves at the airport ticket counter trying to purchase last-minute tickets to Vegas. But there's just one problem. American Express didn't approve your purchase. In fact, the ticket counter agent is on the phone with an American Express customer service agent.

So what put a temporary halt to your weekend escape to Vegas? An expert system that American Express calls "Authorizer's Assistant." The first "if-then" rule that prevented your purchase was the rule, "*if* a purchase is much larger than the cardholder's regular spending habits, *then* deny approval of the purchase." This rule is built into American Express's transaction-processing system that handles thousands of purchase requests per second. Now that the American Express customer service agent is on the line, he or she is prompted by the Authorizer's Assistant to ask the ticket counter agent to examine your identification. You hand over your driver's license and another credit card to prove you're you. Then, the ticket agent asks for your address, phone number, social security number, and your mother's maiden name, and relays the information to American Express. Finally, your ticket purchase is approved. Why? Because you met the last series of "if-then" rules. *If* the purchaser can provide proof of identity, and *if* the purchaser can provide personal information that isn't common knowledge, *then* approve the purchase.

Review 4:
Accessing and Sharing Information and Knowledge

E-mail, voice-messaging, and conferencing systems are changing how we communicate and work with each other. E-mail is cheap, fast, and easy to use. Though also easy to use, voice messages take more time to process than e-mail. Application sharing and document and video conferencing let people in different locations work as if they were together in the same room. Executive information systems and intranets facilitate internal sharing and access to company information. Electronic data interchange and the Internet allow external groups, like suppliers and customers, to easily access company information. Both decrease costs by reducing or eliminating data entry, data errors, and paperwork, and by speeding up communication. Organizations use decision support systems and expert systems to capture and share specialized knowledge with nonexpert employees.

What**Really**Happened?

At the beginning of this chapter, you learned about MTC Telecommunications, which is in the business of providing low-cost domestic and international phone service. Ironically, with 15,000 sales representatives in 160 different countries making thousands of international phone calls to place orders and service customer accounts, MTC's own phone expenses were astronomical. However, with the help of new information technologies, MTC found a way to lower its costs and better manage its business. Let's find out how MTC did it.

So how do you find a way to cut costs and still maintain your competitive advantage and the critical flow of information from sales reps to headquarters and back?

There are five costs associated with information: acquisition, processing, storage, retrieval, and communication. MTC's worldwide sales force would communicate with corporate headquarters in California by using long-distance phone service to make calls, send faxes, and leave messages (i.e., to acquire, process, store, retrieve, and communicate information). But with the cost of international phone calls at $300,000 a month and growing, MTC had to do something.

To cut costs without cutting service, MTC replaced its phone-based system with a secure company intranet. So instead of making long-distance calls, sales representatives now dial up their local Internet service providers. Once on the Internet, sales reps can connect directly to the company intranet (basically, an Internet connection, but only for those who work for MTC) at no extra cost. Using Internet software like Netscape Navigator or Microsoft's Internet Explorer, sales reps can examine accounts or change their customers' credit limits. And, rather than leaving voice-mail messages, sales reps and company staffers can communicate via e-mail at much less cost to the company. Furthermore, MTC maintains the privacy and security of its communications by giving sales reps confidential user IDs and passwords, and by using something called "secure sockets layer technology" to encrypt all communications, so that they're unreadable to anybody not on the company intranet.

Besides greatly reducing the number of international phone calls, the company intranet is saving money in other ways. Because the intranet connects sales reps directly to the information they need to service current accounts or activate new ones, MTC believes that it could grow its sales staff worldwide from its present level of 15,000 to 100,000 without adding any additional support staff at company headquarters. For instance, if a client in India is having trouble with its MTC phone connections, the MTC sales rep in that part of India logs onto the company intranet and fills out a computer form describing the problem, and then MTC's computers take care of the rest. In most instances, no one at headquarters needs to do anything to solve the problem.

MTC is also saving travel and training expenses by publishing training materials on the company intranet. Now, any sales rep anywhere in the world can access training materials whenever needed for the cost of a local telephone call. It used to cost MTC between $50,000 and $100,000 per training class, primarily due to the travel expense of bringing international sales reps to company headquarters in the U.S.

Furthermore, customers are now expressing a desire to tap directly into their accounts, so they can more closely monitor expenses without waiting for the monthly bill. How can you do that without incurring greater costs?

Similar to the way that MTC is using its company intranet to reduce costs and increase response times for its sales reps, it is now using the Internet to bill customers and let customers access detailed information about their accounts. Since many of its corporate accounts have phone bills that are hundreds of pages long, MTC may save as much as $5 to $10 in mailing costs per customer by sending bills to customers via the Internet. Plus, customers can access MTC's Web site to download charts and statistical information to help them monitor and control the expense of long-distance phone calls.

So why is MTC so aggressive about using information technology to connect its sale reps, headquarter staffers, and customers to each other and to the company database? Because, often, the first company to use new information technology to substantially lower costs or differentiate its products or services gains first-mover advantage that can lead to higher profits and larger market share. Creating a first-mover advantage can be difficult and expensive. MTC said that it cost several hundred thousand dollars to put these systems in place. However, it took only about six months for the system to pay for itself in cost savings.

Sources: T. Duffy, "Intranet Radically Reduces Costs," PC Week Web site. [Online] Available **www.pcweek.com/@netweek/0527/27mtc.html**, 30 May 1996. M. Halper, "So Does Your Web Site Pay?" *Forbes,* 25 August 1997, 117. L. Patterson, "Get Smart: Tools to Raise Your Company's IQ," *Forbes ASAP,* 7 April 1997, 62. B. Ziegler, "Technology (A Special Report): Working Together," *The Wall Street Journal,* 18 November 1996, R21.

Key Terms

acquisition cost p. 201

application sharing p. 214

archived data p. 208

automated processing p. 211

bar code p. 207

CD-ROM, (compact disk read only memory) p. 208

centralized processing p. 211

client p. 212

client/server network p. 211

communication cost p. 202

conferencing system p. 214

data mining p. 210

data storage tape p. 208

decision support system (DSS) p. 222

desktop videoconferencing p. 215

distributed processing p. 211

document conferencing p. 214

DVD (digital video disk) p. 208

electronic data interchange (EDI) p. 219

electronic scanner p. 207

e-mail p. 213

executive information system (EIS) p. 216

expert system p. 222

first-mover advantage p. 203

freeware p. 219

hard drive p. 208

information p. 199

Internet p. 220

intranets p. 218

knowledge p. 221

microfilm p. 208

Moore's law p. 198

network p. 212

optical character recognition p. 207

primary storage p. 208

processing cost p. 201

processing information p. 210

RAID (redundant array inexpensive disk) p. 209

raw data p. 199

retrieval cost p. 202

secondary storage p. 208

server p. 212

shared processing p. 211

shareware p. 219

storage cost p. 202

transaction processing systems p. 211

voice messaging p. 214

What Would You Do-II?

Hackersville, U.S.A.

According to the Computer Security Institute, half of the 428 organizations that participated in a survey on computer crime and security admit to being victims of unauthorized access to their computer systems. In all these, unauthorized computerized break-ins are estimated to cost businesses more than $10 billion per year.

Unfortunately, hackers don't restrict themselves to computer systems. John Haugh, author of *Toll Fraud and Telabuse*, said that "business losses from telephone fraud or 'hacking' are estimated at $4 billion per year. Companies with a typical PBX phone system risk a 1-in-18 chance of being hacked, and the average loss per hack is over $60,000." How do they do it? One method is "social engineering." Pretend that you're an employee, call whoever is in charge of phone access codes, and say that you lost or forgot your password/code. If the person is willing to give it to you, you've got instant access.

The raw, brute power of a "war dialer" is another technique. "War dialing" is a computer program that can find and crack a four-digit code or password in 20 minutes, and an eight-digit code or password in six hours. A hacker who gets control of your company's phone system on Saturday morning, and then opens up your phone lines to other hackers and associates, could run up $1,500 in charges per phone line by Monday morning. For example, a regional office with 250 phone lines could get hit for $375,000 in charges over the weekend!

By many estimates, though, computer and phone system hackers aren't the most serious threats to company security. The greatest threats come from competitors and employees. Richard Power of the Computer Security Institute (CSI) in San Francisco said that "competitors are the single greatest threat in computer crime." A study by CSI and the FBI found that more than half of 453 companies reported being very concerned about electronic snooping by competitors. However, the same study also indicated that close to half of reported electronic espionage cases involve company insiders, who more often than not, find it incredibly easy to steal company data or secrets.

Should your company be worried? You bet. In less than a decade, the number of computers in companies has soared from 10 million to more than 100 million. Furthermore, while only 15 percent of workplace computers were networked in 1990, today more than half are, and the percentage of networked computers continues to grow. The surging popularity of the Internet also represents a threat, especially to companies that put the pages for their Web site on the same computer systems as their proprietary data. According to the Society for Industrial Security, the combination of easy internal and external access to company data created by company networks and the Internet has increased the number of electronic security break-ins from one every three months in 1980 to more than 30 per month today. In short, competitors, hackers, managers, and employees can steal, change, destroy, or give others your company's most sensitive and critical data. **If you were in charge of electronic security for your company, what basic steps could you take to reduce these threats to your communications and computer systems?** (Hint: You don't have to be a computer expert. Simply think about the ways in which employees access computers and the phone system in the places you've worked. Then come up with simple methods to make that access more secure.)

Sources: W. Dutcher, "Locking the Corporate Vault: Achieving a Balance Between Security and Accessibility Can Be Tricky," *PC Week* 3 (11 March 1996): N1. K.J. Higgins, "Swarming Your Sites," *Communications Week* 4 (8 April 1996): 37. D.S. Linthicum, "Secure Your Web Server to Protect Your Data," *Computer Shopper*, March 1996, 138. "Security Shopping List," *VarBusiness*, 1 March 1996. C. Steffens, "What You Should Know about PBX Security," *Telecommunications* 27, no. 2 (October 1993): 53. B. Violino, "Crime Fighters—Corporate SWAT Teams Battle Mounting Security Threats," *Information Week*, 13 May 1996. J. Young, "Spies Like Us," *Forbes* 14 (3 June 1996): 70.

Critical-Thinking Video Case

Management Information Systems: Archway Cookies

Archway Cookies is the third-largest cookie manufacturer in the United States and is well known for its high-quality home-style cookies. Archway's bake-to-order system, where cookies are ordered, baked, and sent to distributors within 48 hours, has been a key part of its success. As Archway has grown, so has its need for an advanced management information system.

Critical-Thinking Questions

1. Why would Archway change to a new management information system?
2. What benefits are expected from adopting the new integrated management information system?
3. What challenges does Archway face in implementing the new management information system?

Management Decisions

Red Truck Tours

Since 1988, vacationers have flocked to Red Truck Tours, so they can visit 700-year-old Sinaguan Indian cliff dwellings, study ancient pictographs painted on rock walls, hike to the top of canyons for breath-taking views 2,000 feet above the desert floor, and visit the sacred prehistoric sites of Native American culture. Growing every year in popularity, Red Truck Tours delights nearly 250 passengers a day with its unique day-trips in the southwestern United States.

While the company's owners have welcomed growth, they've also found that it's become more difficult to manage the business. For example, the company once had an office in one location. Now it has offices in four locations. Where it once had two basic tours, it now offers four. Furthermore, it's willing, if customers request, to offer unique combinations of the basic tours.

Since its inception, the company has used handwritten wall charts to schedule tours, tour leaders, and drivers. This worked well when it had just one office and two tours. But now one of the key difficulties is simply communicating the reservation and scheduling information between the four offices. At any one time, the odds are very high that reservation agents are unintentionally working from different wall charts in each office. Unfortunately, this has produced confusion, overbooking, and other booking errors. Moreover, the wall charts, which only show one week at a time, have made it difficult to do accurate long-term scheduling.

The owners of Red Truck Tours realize that if they want to continue to grow, they're going to have to do a better job of managing tour and scheduling information. This means investing in information technology. Considering the company's four offices and its need to manage office workers, drivers, tour guides, and mechanics (for truck maintenance and repair), recommend an information technology plan for Red Truck Tours.

Questions

1. What kind of computer setup would you recommend for Red Truck? Why? Be specific.
2. Given the difficulties of communicating information between four offices, what would you recommend that Red Truck do to make it easier to share information internally and externally. Why? Again, be specific.

Source: "Network Solution Drives Success for Pink Jeep Tours," SmallBiz: The Microsoft Small Business Resource Web site. [Online] Available **www.microsoft.com/smallbiz**, 8 July 1996.

Management Decisions

In-House or Outsource?

As founder of Adoge's, the largest department store chain west of the Rockies (117 stores), you've watched your business grow over four decades. In the 1960s, your primary competition was Sears, the Sears catalog, and what remained of soon-to-be-obsolete five-and-dime stores. In the 1970s, you competed against Sears, J.C. Penney, the Sears and Penney's catalogs, and a growing threat called Kmart. In the 1980s, as Sears struggled, your early competition was J.C. Penney and Kmart. But by the end of the decade and well into the 90s, large national chains like Wal-Mart, Office Depot, and Home Depot were your primary competition.

Each time a new competitor rolled in, you regrouped and met the challenge. The last few years have been disappointing, though. Wal-Mart, Office Depot, and Home Depot have been at the forefront of innovative uses of information technology in the retail industry and have made significant dents in your business. From the scanners that ring up sales and keep track of inventory to the use of electronic data interchange that provides a direct connection to suppliers, every item delivered, displayed, and bought in your competitors' stores is tracked, scanned, and analyzed by ever-improving information technology. So if Adoge's wants to make it into the 21st century, it will have to regroup and meet the challenge of modernizing the way it manages information. A new mainframe, more client/server networks, state-of-the-art desktop computers, teleconferencing for training employees and for purchasers to use when selecting merchandise, e-mail for every employee—basically, if there's information or communication to be found, you're going to throw technology and computers at it.

But there's one thing you're not sure of. Should you manage all of this technology in-house, or should you outsource it to a company like Electronic Data Systems or Andersen Consulting, which specializes in running complete information technology systems for companies? Outsourcing has certainly become more popular, growing from a $7-to-$12 billion industry in 1992, to a $38-to-$50 billion industry today.

These numbers indicate that lots of companies think outsourcing is a good idea. But could you have your Information Services Department manage it? Of course, IS would need a bigger budget, more employees, and probably some training, but you're going to be giving them much more to manage, so that seems reasonable. On the other hand, most IS outsourcing firms would want you to sign a contract guaranteeing your commitment to them for five years. That seems like a long time. However, it might really be like buying an extended service plan on a new car; whatever goes wrong, you're covered for five years (or 100,000 miles?) by a team of information technology professionals. Well, let's try to think this through . . .

Additional Internet Resources

- **Ask the Outsourcing Experts (*www.outsourcing-experts.com/index.html*).** This site contains information about outsourcing. Be sure to search the questions and answers to get a feel for the issues related to outsourcing information technology.
- **Outsourcing Interactive (*www.outsourcing.com/OSM1How.htm*).** This site contains a section on how and why to outsource.

Questions

1. Which is more likely to be cheaper, an outsourcing firm or an in-house information services department? Why?
2. Which is more likely to do a better job of managing information technology for your company, an outsourcing firm or an in-house information services department? Why?
3. Which is more likely to help Adoge create and sustain a competitive advantage in its western retail markets, an outsourcing firm or an in-house information services department? Why?

Sources: M.J. Earl, "The Risks of Outsourcing IT," *Sloan Management Review,* Spring 1996, 26-32. M.C. Lacity & R. Hirschheim, "The Information Systems Outsourcing Bandwagon," *Sloan Management Review,* Fall 1993, 73-86. M.C. Lacity, L.P. Willcocks, & D.F. Feeney, "The Value of Selective IT Sourcing," *Sloan Management Review,* Spring 1996, 13-25. F.W. McFarlan & R.L. Nolan, "How to Manage an IT Outsourcing Alliance," *Sloan Management Review,* Winter 1995, 9-23.

Develop Your Management Potential

Becoming Comfortable with Computers

Some top executives become comfortable with computers by taking crash courses. Computer Associates International Inc., one of the world's largest software companies, runs a four-day, $7,000 technology boot camp for CEOs who know absolutely nothing about computers. For example, at one camp, a CEO raised his hand to ask if the computer mouse belonged on the floor. Charles Wang, the chairman of Computer Associates, had to tell him "No, no, no! It's not an accelerator pedal!" Most CEOs find technology boot camps give them the basic skills to get past their fear of technology. Marvin Levy, the CEO of Miller International Inc., a clothing maker and retailer in Denver, knew nothing about computers before his boot camp. Now he uses a laptop computer at least two hours a day to check and send e-mail, run financial analyses, and keep up with what his competitors are doing via the Internet. Regarding the importance of computer skills to today's executives,

Mr. Levy said, "I am the last person who will ever be CEO of this firm [and] come into the job without a substantial amount of computer literacy."

Since it's doubtful that you can convince anybody at your company to spend seven grand to send you to computer boot camp, you're probably going to have to teach yourself if you want to become comfortable with computers. In fact, that's how most people do it. Learning about computers takes time. But it pays off. Managers and employees who know how to use computers make 20 to 30 percent more over the course of their lifetimes. That's right, 20 to 30 percent more! That should grab your attention.

Reading about computers is one of the best ways to get started. Lots of people like the "Dummies" series, such as *Windows for Dummies* or *Word Perfect for Dummies*. Another way to learn is to read and subscribe to computer magazines like *PC World* or *Mac World*. To start becoming more comfortable with computers, do the following:

1. Pick a computer topic that you'd like to learn more about. It could be deciding which desktop or laptop computer to buy, how to put together a Web page, or how to choose the right modem or graphics card when you upgrade your computer.
2. Then read and make copies of three articles published in the last 12 months on that topic. Visit your library. Or, better yet, use the computer to find these articles.
   a. One way is to use electronic sources like InfoTrac, FirstSearch, or whatever is available in your library. Type in the keywords you're interested in and print the articles that seem relevant.
   b. A better way to do this search, though, is to use the Internet, where there are two particularly good sites to find current information. CMP MEDIA Inc., one of the largest publishers of computer magazines, runs the first site. Go to CMP's home page at **www.cmpnet.com**. Enter your search terms into the *Search CMPnet* box and then click the *Enter* button. The second site, ZDNet, is run by Ziff-Davis Publishing, which publishes over a dozen leading computer magazines. Go to **http://xlink.zdnet.com/cgi-bin/texis/xlink/** xlink/welcome.html. Enter your search terms into the *Search ZDNet* box and then click *Find It!*
3. After selecting/finding three articles, write a two-page summary about the topic. Note the advantages, disadvantages, and key features/information that you learned.

Chapter Seven

Chapter 7 Outline

Control

What Would **You** Do?

O'Hare Airport, Chicago, Illinois. The World Trade Center explosion in New York City was first. Then, there was the federal building in Oklahoma City. A year after that, the living quarters of U.S. armed forces in Riyadh, Saudi Arabia were bombed. Then, less than a month later, an explosion blew TWA flight 800 out of the sky just off the shore of Long Island, New York. And, twelve days after that, an explosion ripped through Atlanta's Olympic Centennial Park during the Olympic games. While it was later determined that the TWA 800 explosion resulted from an electrical glitch, the other four incidents, three of which occurred on U.S. soil, were clearly categorized as terrorist acts. And who knows how many more will occur? As head of security for O'Hare Airport, you've seen security crises like this before. There was a rash of plane hijackings in the 1970s, and more hijackings, bombs, and terrorist activities, especially in Europe and the Middle East, in the 1980s. The response before was always the same—temporarily tighten up security. For example, during the Gulf War, passengers couldn't get into a major U.S. airport without a ticket showing that they had a flight in the next few hours. Of course, when the threats subsided, and they always did, security returned to normal levels. This time, however, your gut tells you that increased security is here to stay. Federal authorities had warned of increased terrorist activity as long as a year before the bombings in Riyadh and Atlanta. Not surprisingly, these activities led the press and the government to pay more attention to security issues (translation: to demonstrate the holes in current levels of security). Days after TWA flight 800 went down, two French reporters tested the security at JFK International, the airport from which flight 800 originated. They did it by simply walking into the flow of passengers leaving the terminal. And when a locked door blocked their progress, they didn't have to wait long for passengers leaving the terminal to open it. The reporters said, "We were not checked. If we had been carrying a bomb, we could have given it to an accomplice boarding the plane." Likewise, in a security test, federal investigators were able to gain access to supposedly secure areas in 15 out of 20 airports. Mary Schiavo, former inspector general of the Federal Aviation Administration, concluded, "My staff was able to literally get out on the tarmac, get on the runway, get on planes, get in cockpits and witness a number of test devices go through security." In one instance, investigators proved their point by leaving a note in the cockpit for the flight crew to find. So the question for you isn't whether security will increase. It already did when the president ordered Level 3 security at all airports immediately following the explosion of TWA flight 800. (As a result, cars could not park in front of airport terminals, and passengers had to show photo I.D.s and answer specific questions about their luggage.) The question is how and where to increase security to a reasonable level at a reasonable cost with minimal delays to passengers. The best place to start is to determine how well airports and airlines are performing when it comes to airline safety and security. After determining where the problems are, the next step is to figure out how to solve them. For example, nearly all passengers and carry-on luggage are x-rayed and inspected. However, security experts maintain that the biggest risk is from baggage stowed in a plane's storage compartment. So, given this risk, should airports buy expensive machines to x-ray the thousands of pieces of stowed luggage they handle every day? In some European and Middle Eastern countries, highly paid, highly trained security professionals and paramilitary forces are in charge of airline security. Should U.S. airports invest in a better-trained, better-paid security force? Would passengers be willing to pay extra for this level of security? It worked with cars. Customers were willing to pay extra for airbags and anti-lock brakes—in fact, they're now standard equipment on most cars. And how much earlier would passengers be willing to arrive at airports to accommodate security procedures? **If you were the head of security for O'Hare Airport, what would you do?**

Sources: S. Bell, "Reporters Expose Gap at JFK," *London Times*, 22 July 1996. J. Cole, "No Evidence of TWA 800 Missile, Experts Say," *The Wall Street Journal*, 9 December 1997, B5. J. Dahl & L. Miller, "Which Is the Safest Airline? It All Depends on Criteria," *The Wall Street Journal Interactive Edition*, 24 July 1996. J. Kifner, "Few Checks on Workers with Access to Planes," *New York Times*, 29 July 1996. D. Lenckus & G. Souter, "Risk Managers Review Security: TWA Crash, Olympics Bombing Raise Profile of Terrorism Risk," *Business Insurance*, 5 August 1996. G. Stoller, "Scanning Luggage for Bombs: More Detectors Prowl Baggage, But Not Enough," *USA Today*, 18 February 1998, 1B.

Did you or someone you know fly soon after the bombings of the World Trade Center, the federal building in Oklahoma City, the U.S. armed forces living quarters in Saudi Arabia, or Atlanta's Olympic Centennial Park? If you became concerned about safety and security after these or other similar events, then whether you knew it or not, you were also concerned with control. **Control** is a regulatory process of establishing standards that will achieve organizational goals, comparing actual performance to those standards, and then, if necessary, taking corrective action to restore performance to those standards.

control
a regulatory process of establishing standards to achieve organizational goals, comparing actual performance against the standards, and taking corrective action, when necessary

Control is achieved when behavior and work procedures conform to standards, and company goals are accomplished.[1] After the bombings, control became even tighter as authorities tried to guarantee the goal of personal safety by making sure security procedures were followed. However, control is not just an after-the-fact process. Preventive measures, such as having passengers or Olympic stadium ticket holders pass through metal detectors, are also a form of control. In fact, we should remember that control is the last step in the first function of management, making things happen. To review, making things happen is a function of planning what you want to accomplish (Chapter 4), deciding how to achieve those plans (Chapter 5), gathering and managing the information needed to make good decisions (Chapter 6), and controlling behavior and processes through preventive or corrective action (Chapter 7).

We begin this chapter by examining the basic control process used in organizations. Then we examine whether control is always necessary or possible (it isn't). In the third part of the chapter, we go beyond the basics to an in-depth examination of the different methods that companies use to achieve control. We finish the chapter by taking a look at the things that companies choose to control (i.e., finances, product quality, customer retention, etc.).

Basics of Control

If you wanted to control traffic speeds in your town, how would you do it? Well, most municipalities put in speed bumps, lower speed limits, put up traffic lights, or write more speeding tickets. However, the city of Culemborg in the Netherlands is planning to use sheep to slow down speeding cars on its neighborhood streets. Why sheep? One of the city council members, who had observed the driving patterns on country roads in rural England, said, "After all, it's impossible to speed past the sheep [in the middle of the road] if you drive in the Yorkshire Dales." When animal rights groups complained that this was a bad idea, the city responded by erecting a special kind of fence to prevent the sheep from wandering onto busier, high-speed roads where they would clearly be endangered. However, Culemborg's city leaders were apparently not familiar with the tradition of some Yorkshire locals who "accidentally" hit sheep, hoping to make off with a free supply of lamb chops.[2] The city plans to release five or six sheep at first. If motorists actually do slow down, as many as 100 sheep may eventually be released onto city streets.

After reading the next two sections, you should be able to:

1. describe the basic **control process**.
2. answer the question: **Is control necessary or possible?**

The city of Culemborg in the Netherlands devised a rather creative form of traffic control: the international use of sheep in the road.
© Corbis/Patrick Ward

1 The Control Process

The basic control process **1.1** *begins with the establishment of clear standards of performance,* **1.2** *involves a comparison of actual performance to desired performance,* **1.3** *takes corrective action, if needed, to repair performance deficiencies,* **1.4** *is a dynamic process, and* **1.5** *consists of three basic methods: feedback control, concurrent control, and feedforward control.*

1.1 *Standards*

standards
a basis of comparison when measuring the extent to which various kinds of organizational performance are satisfactory or unsatisfactory

The control process begins when managers set goals, like satisfying 90 percent of customers, or increasing sales by 5 percent. Companies then specify the performance standards that must be met to accomplish those goals. **Standards** are a basis of comparison for measuring the extent to which organizational performance is satisfactory or unsatisfactory. For example, many pizzerias use 30 minutes as the standard for delivery times. Since anything longer than that is viewed as unsatisfactory, they'll typically reduce their prices if they can't deliver a hot pizza to you in 30 minutes or less.

So how do managers set standards? How do they decide which levels of performance are satisfactory and which are unsatisfactory? The first criterion for a good standard is that it must enable goal achievement. If you're meeting the standard, but still not achieving company goals, then the standard may have to be changed. For example, Best Buy, which sells electronics and appliances, used to allow customers to return or exchange goods without receipts. However, the company lost a substantial amount of money when, without making a purchase, people would take goods directly from store shelves to the service counter to exchange or get a cash refund. Today, Best Buy's new standard is "No refunds or exchanges without a receipt. Period."[3]

Companies also determine standards by listening to customers or observing competitors. When study after study indicated that customers preferred Burger King's menu to its own, McDonald's finally decided to introduce the

Big Xtra, a burger with lettuce, tomato, mayonnaise, and ketchup that is clearly a knockoff of Burger King's Whopper (though McDonald's management denies that this is so).[4]

Also, as you learned in Chapter 4, standards can be determined by benchmarking other companies. *Benchmarking* is the process of determining how well other companies (though typically not competitors) perform business functions or tasks. In other words, benchmarking is the process of determining other companies' standards.

The first step in setting standards is to determine what to benchmark. Companies can benchmark anything, from cycle time (how fast) to quality (how well). The next step is to identify the companies against which to benchmark your standards. Since this can require a significant commitment on the part of the benchmarked company, it can take time to identify and get agreement from them to be benchmarked. The last step is to collect data to determine other companies' performance standards. For example, countless companies have visited MBNA, the credit card company, to learn how to respond quickly, if not immediately, to customer requests. Indeed, visitors learn that MBNA answers its phones by the second ring 98.5 percent of the time, and that it takes no more than 30 minutes to approve (or deny) customer requests for higher credit limits.[5]

1.2 Comparison to Standards

The next step in the control process is to compare actual performance to performance standards. While this sounds straightforward, the quality of the comparison largely depends on the measurement and information systems a company uses to keep track of performance. The better the system, the easier it is for companies to track their progress and identify problems that need to be fixed.

For example, Regal Cinemas, a Knoxville, Tennessee-based movie theater company with more than 650 screens, makes twice the profits of its larger and better-known competitors because it keeps such tight controls on its costs. To keep costs down, Regal uses its information system to keep close track of concessions, which are typically where theaters make most of their profits. If a Regal theater misplaces or damages a box of paper drink cups, Regal uses its computer system to charge the theater manager the full retail price of the drink, not just the replacement cost of the cups. With an information system this accurate, Regal's theater managers and employees don't waste cups, popcorn, popcorn oil, or anything else. However, it's important to point out that Regal's information system isn't used just to track negative performance discrepancies. Indeed, Regal managers who exceed company standards can earn bonuses as large as half the amount of their base salaries.[6]

1.3 Corrective Action

The next step in the control process is to identify performance deviations, analyze those deviations, and then develop and implement programs to correct them. This is similar to the planning process discussed in Chapter 4: Regular, frequent performance feedback allows workers and managers to track their performance and make adjustments in effort, direction, and strategies.

Back to the Future

Computers and Control: The Promise and the Perils

In the "old" days, there was no better way for college students to feed themselves and their friends cheaply than the dormitory food card. Flash the card, fill a tray, eat the slop, and then pass the food card to a friend, who reuses it to gain entrance to the cafeteria. Where else could six people eat for the price of one? But that was before university cafeterias clamped down on food card fraud by using computers. For example, the University of Georgia now uses a $2,000 hand scanner to admit students to the cafeteria. Students put their right hand on the scanner and use their left hand to "swipe" their dorm food card through an attached electronic card reader, just like a credit card. If the palm print on the hand scanner matches the hand image stored on the magnetic strip on the back of the dorm food card, the turnstile unlocks, admitting the student to the cafeteria. If not, well, it's time to make that trip to Taco Bell after all.

Hand scanners represent the promise of computers and control: cheap, automatic, and nearly foolproof. This is what managers hope for when using computers to control key corporate resources and expenditures. Unfortunately, relying on computers for control holds nearly as much peril as promise. For example, most companies designate an accounts payable department or person to pay company bills in a timely, accurate manner. However, in recent years, thanks to the use of computers, companies have begun slashing the size of their accounts payable departments to reduce costs. Niagra Mohawk Power in Syracuse, New York, cut its accounts payable department in half. Occidental Chemical and General Electric cut their accounts payable departments by one third.

Initially, these moves saved money by cutting payroll expenses. But they have also resulted in a rash of accounts payable errors, now that computers make most of the payments instead of accounts payable staffers. At Niagra Mohawk Power, the computer made a $10,680 error by paying a maintenance company twice for the same purchase. An experienced accounts payable clerk would have easily caught this mistake, but different purchase order numbers tripped up the computer on the otherwise identical purchase orders. At Occidental Chemical, duplicate payments have doubled to nearly half a million dollars a year and are likely to increase. According to Ronald Loder, president of a payables consulting firm, computer-related accounts payable problems are likely to get worse before they get better. Mr. Loder said, "Payable clerks are blessed with intuition, memory, recognition and the ability to make educated guesses. Computers are dumb and dumber in these areas."

Another area in which computers may actually hurt rather than help managerial control is employee Internet use. A survey of 1,000 companies in the United Kingdom revealed that 55 percent were very worried about how much time employees would waste surfing the Internet on company time. For example, one manager said, "I have one employee who will read the Italian newspapers for an hour or two. And there's another who spends a lot of time looking at, uh, photos. I'm not going to say any more on that." And, since employees are sitting at their computers as they surf, it often looks as if they're working. Unfortunately, it doesn't take much unauthorized surfing before the costs to company productivity become staggering. Mark Ryan, a systems manager for Blick Rothenberg chartered accountants in London, said, "Even if an employee spends just 30 minutes a day on the Net for personal use, that costs British businesses half a billion pounds [roughly a billion dollars] annually."

Ironically, one solution to unsanctioned Net surfing on company time may be tighter computer control. Software that was originally created to prevent children from visiting adult-oriented Web sites is now being used by a number of companies to partially restrict Internet access. Other software also makes it possible to monitor the keystrokes, mouse clicks, and Internet moves made on every computer on the company network. Compaq Computers used that approach to identify and then fire 20 employees who had made more than 1,000 visits to sexually explicit Web sites on company time with company computers.

In the end, computers are two-edged swords when it comes to managerial control. They hold enormous potential for gaining better control of key resources, processes, and expenses. However, the same computer power that makes it possible for companies to obtain better control also makes it easier for employees to evade that control. In the long run, the same people who put the "boss button" on computer games—push it, and a spreadsheet appears on your screen to make it look as if you were working instead of playing Duke Nuke'm—will continue to find ways to ensure that workers can waste time on company computers.

Sources: L. Berton, "Firms Find Computers Can't Spot Many Errors on Fraud," *The Wall Street Journal Interactive Edition*, 5 September 1996. E. Carlson, "Some Forms of Identification Can't Be Handily Faked," *The Wall Street Journal*, 14 September 1993, B2. C. Durcanin, "Employee Surfing Creates a New Business Headache," *The Wall Street Journal Interactive Edition*, 2 September 1996.

One example of identifying and correcting performance deviations is the service-quality audit conducted by a prestigious New York City hotel known for its first-class service. The purpose of the quality audit was to identify the frequency and cost of service errors and what it would cost to prevent them. The most common error, occurring nearly 70 times per day at an annual cost of nearly a quarter million dollars, was not posting minibar and phone charges to guests' bills. Following discussions with managers and employees, the hotel took the following steps to correct the problem: (1) During check-in, verify whether guests in the same room have separate bills and charges. (2) Have the night clerk double-check all the phone and minibar charges for guests checking out the next morning. (3) Include a list of phone, minibar, and other charges (and when they were incurred) with the bill provided to guests in their rooms on the morning they check out. (4) Reduce checkout times and errors by providing the front desk a master list of all of the minibar, phone, and extra charges for guests checking out that day. Importantly, it only cost the hotel $25,000 to implement these corrective actions and begin reducing the $250,000 annual cost of these mistakes.[7]

1.4 *Dynamic Process*

PersonalProductivityTip

Identify Your Time Wasters
With organizational downsizing and dual careers, everyone has less of their most important resource, time. However, we can get back 2–4 hours a day by identifying and eliminating habitual time-wasting activities, such as telephone interruptions, the inability to say no, drop-in visitors, poorly run meetings, junk mail, and junk e-mail. When squeezed for time, tell callers how much time you have to talk. When visitors drop in unexpectedly, schedule an appointment. Check your e-mail at regular intervals, first thing in morning or after lunch, or on the hour, and then don't touch it until the appointed time. List your top five time-wasters. Start eliminating them today!
Source: C.S. Frings, "Develop Powerful Leadership Skills," *Medical Laboratory Observer,* 1 July 1996, 64.

As shown in Figure 7.1, control is a continuous, dynamic process. It begins with actual performance and measures of that performance. Managers then compare performance to the pre-established standards. If they identify deviations from standard performance, they analyze the deviations and develop corrective programs. Then implementing the programs (hopefully) achieves the desired performance. To maintain performance levels at standard, managers must repeat the entire process again and again in an endless feedback loop. So control is not a one-time achievement or result. It continues over time (a dynamic process) and requires daily, weekly, and monthly attention from managers.

For example, at Pepsi, when the weekly Nielsen numbers come in, indicating the popularity of the television shows on which Pepsi bought commercial time, 70 people immediately begin analyzing and questioning the numbers to see if Pepsi got the audiences it wanted for its advertising dollar. If it didn't, the company may cancel its advertising on shows that didn't measure up and purchase advertising time on shows that appear to hold more promise. Likewise, each Friday, senior managers at *USA Today* receive a packet of reports showing how the paper performed in terms of sales and advertising revenue that week, and how that week compares to the previous week and the same week a year ago.[8]

Sure, it's a cliche, but it's just as true in business as it is in sports: If you take your eye off the ball, you're going to strike out. Control is an ongoing, dynamic process.

1.5 *Feedback, Concurrent, and Feedforward Control*

feedback control
a mechanism for gathering information about performance deficiencies after they occur

There are three basic control methods: feedback control, concurrent control, and feedforward control.[9] **Feedback control** is a mechanism for gathering information about performance deficiencies after they occur. This information is then used to correct or prevent performance deficiencies. Study after study has clearly shown that feedback improves both individual and organizational performance. In most instances, any feedback is better than

Figure 7.1 **Cybernetic Control Process**

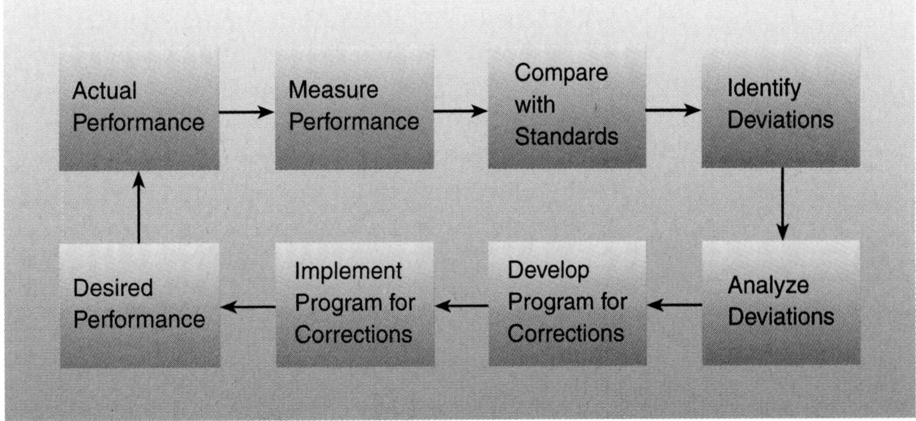

Source: H. Koontz & R.W. Bradspies, "Managing Through Feedforward Control: A Future Directed View," *Business Horizons,* June 1972, 25-36.

no feedback. However, if there is a downside to feedback, it is that it sometimes occurs too late. Sometimes it comes after big mistakes have been made.

For example, while everyone knows about Microsoft's current success with its Windows operating system, relatively few know that Microsoft's first try at writing operating software for networked computers and file servers was a bust. This program—the early version of Windows NT ("NT" stands for "new technology")—was huge and painfully slow. Unfortunately, the Windows NT development team did not become aware of these problems until the product shipped and customers began complaining. Why hadn't the team gotten any early indication (i.e., feedback) of these problems? Because, unlike most of their customers who were running slower computers with little computer memory, the NT development team used fast, state-of-the-art computers with nearly four times more memory.[10] So Windows NT ran great for them, but terribly for regular users.

Concurrent control
a mechanism for gathering information about performance deficiencies as they occur, eliminating or shortening the delay between performance and feedback

Concurrent control is a mechanism for gathering information about performance deficiencies as they occur. Thus, it is an improvement over feedback, because it attempts to eliminate or shorten the delay between performance and feedback about the performance. Because it had not been aware of the slow speed (and other problems) in the initial version of Windows NT, the NT development team abandoned its reliance on late-coming customer feedback and quickly adopted a development model based on concurrent control and feedforward control (discussed below).

For example, rather than waiting for customer complaints to come to them, the NT development team developed concurrent controls by establishing systematic, ongoing relationships between the team engineers and NT customers. When there was a problem, they heard about it immediately. Furthermore, NT programmers took turns answering the help line that NT customers called for technical support. They traveled to companies using NT, so that they could talk to customers directly and find out how they were using NT and where its performance fell short. Microsoft sent thousands of test copies of redesigned NT software to officially approved beta-testers who, through regular phone calls and e-mails, told the development team what they liked and didn't like.

feedforward control
a mechanism for monitoring performance inputs rather than outputs to prevent or minimize performance deficiencies before they occur

Feedforward control is a mechanism for gathering information about performance deficiencies before they occur. In contrast to feedback and concurrent control, which provide feedback on the basis of outcomes and results, feedforward control provides information about performance deficiencies by monitoring inputs, not outputs. Thus, feedforward seeks to prevent or minimize performance deficiencies before they occur. So rather than waiting for customer feedback, the Windows NT team used feedforward controls by establishing a special 16-member team of programmers whose sole job was to inspect the underlying computer code (the input). Then, literally step by step, they rewrote, redesigned, or created new computer code to make Windows NT run faster. It worked. While newer versions of the Windows NT software have grown from 6.1 to 16.5 million lines of code, it now runs eight times faster than the original and uses one-third less memory. Table 7.1 lists guidelines that companies can follow to get the most out of feedforward control.

Review 1: *The Control Process*

The first step in the control process is to set goals and performance standards. The second is to compare actual performance to performance standards. The better a company's information and measurement systems, the easier it is to make these comparisons. The last step is to identify and correct performance deviations. However, control is a continuous, dynamic process, not a one-time achievement or result. Control requires frequent managerial attention. The three basic control methods are feedback control (after the fact performance information), concurrent control (simultaneous performance information), and feedforward control (preventive performance information).

2 Is Control Necessary or Possible?

control loss
situation in which behavior and work procedures do not conform to standards

Control is achieved when behavior and work procedures conform to standards, and goals are accomplished. By contrast, **control loss** occurs when behavior and work procedures do not conform to standards.[11] Control loss usually prevents goal achievement. For example, several years ago, the Fidelity Investment Magellan Fund, which is the largest and, historically, one of the best-performing stock mutual funds, made a $2.4 billion dollar mis-

Table 7.1

Guidelines for Using Feedforward Control

1. Thorough planning and analysis are required.
2. Careful discrimination must be applied in selecting input variables.
3. The feedforward system must be kept dynamic.
4. A model of the control system should be developed.
5. Data on input variables must be regularly collected.
6. Data on input variables must be regularly assessed.
7. Feedforward control requires action.

Source: H. Koontz & R.W. Bradspies, "Managing Through Feedforward Control: A Future Directed View," *Business Horizons,* June 1972, 25-36.

take. When the accountants were closing the books in December, they accidentally recorded a $1.2 billion loss as a gain, thus overstating end-of-year returns by $2.4 billion. Fortunately, because it was a simple error and because it was quickly corrected, no one lost any money. However, this highly publicized mistake, which came just six months after a similar well-publicized error, did damage Fidelity's reputation with investors and in the financial community.[12]

When control losses occur, managers need to find out what they could have done, if anything, to prevent these mistakes from occurring. In Fidelity's case, there was a simple solution: Be sure to show the end-of-year summary statement to the fund manager before releasing it to mutual fund shareholders and the public. Any fund manager would easily catch a mistake of that size.

In general, when control loss occurs, managers need to ask three questions: **2.1** *Is more control necessary?* **2.2** *Is more control possible? and* **2.3** *If more control is necessary but not possible, what should we do instead?*

2.1 *Is More Control Necessary?*

degree of dependence
the extent to which a company needs a particular resource to accomplish its goals

resource
anything that can be used to fulfill a need or solve a problem

resource flow
the extent to which companies have access to critical resources

Two factors can help managers determine whether more (or different) control is necessary: the degree of dependence and resource flows.[13] **Degree of dependence** is the extent to which a company needs a particular resource to accomplish its goals. The more important a resource is for meeting organizational standards and goals, the more necessary it is to control that resource.

Note, however, that resources are more than just raw materials. A **resource** is anything that can be used to fulfill a need or solve a problem. Thus, resources can include employee skills, space, intellectual capability, capital ($), specialized know-how, a cohesive corporate culture, etc. Basically, critical resources, whatever form they take, make it easier for managers and employees to carry out the work processes that conform to standards and lead to goal accomplishment.

For example, a key to profitability in the airline industry is the proportion of filled seats on each flight. With enormous fixed expenses, it costs an airline almost as much money to fly a plane empty as it does to fly it full. So one of the keys to success is to put more people on each plane.[14] Today, computerized yield systems are the key resource that airlines use to make sure their flights are as full as possible. Without them (i.e., a high degree of dependence), most airlines could not compete or earn a profit. Sophisticated computerized yield systems fill seats by constantly raising and lowering prices in response to customer demand and competitor pricing. If done right, most planes will only be partially full several weeks before departure. Then, at the last minute, the airline can fill the remaining seats with business travelers who, unlike leisure travelers, are willing to pay much higher prices for immediate travel.

The second factor that determines whether more control is necessary is resource flow. **Resource flow** is the extent to which companies have easy access to critical resources. For example, after a year-long drought, the city council of San Antonio, Texas, did what city councils normally do when facing a drought: They placed restrictions on lawn and landscape watering. However, the drought had become so bad that the council discussed restricting the

Computerized yield systems help airlines constantly adjust seat prices in response to changes in customer demand and competitor pricing.

amount of water that homeowners could use in existing pools and even considered forbidding the construction of new pools. Leif Zars, owner of Gary's Pools in San Antonio, immediately recognized that this could put his company out of business. In other words, the city council was just about to cut off the flow of his key resource, water.[15] After all, who would want a pool without water?

When companies have a difficult time getting the critical resources they need, they usually try to increase resource flows by creating or obtaining some form of control over them. For Leif Zars, the question was, how could he control the amount of water that the city made available to homeowners? Well, the straight answer is that he couldn't. Nor could he exert much control or influence over the city council, at least probably not more than any other San Antonio resident. But what Leif Zars could do was help pool owners control the amount of water evaporation in their pools. And if he could do that, perhaps the city council could be convinced not to stop the construction of new pools.

Since most pool owners were unwilling to use expensive, unwieldy tarps to cover their pools, Zars invented cheap, easy-to-use evaporation shields. It only took about 12 lightweight plastic shields, which cost just $3 apiece, to cover most pools. And when used, they reduced water loss to nearly nothing. So rather than restricting new pool construction, Zars wanted the city council to mandate that all pool owners reduce water use by covering their pools to reduce water evaporation.

2.2 *Is More Control Possible?*

Degree of dependence and resource flows can help determine whether control is needed. However, the cost of control and cybernetic feasibility help determine whether control is possible. First, to determine whether more control is possible (or worthwhile), managers need to carefully assess the costs, benefits, and unintended consequences of control, because sometimes the costs of control exceed its benefits. For example, one of the reasons that the number of U.S. pharmaceutical companies producing major vaccines has

Personal Productivity Tip

Gain Control—Lower Your Expectations

Control loss occurs when performance falls short of standards. When this happens, the automatic response is to put in more hours and do everything possible to meet the standard. But remember: One way to maintain control is to change goals. This may seem like an admission of failure. But in many cases, it's just being realistic. You can't excel at everything. Disappointed because you're ten pounds over your high school weight? Celebrate that it's *only* ten pounds and not twenty. Bummed because you didn't get that raise? Be glad you've still got your job. Selectively lower your expectations and regain control.

dropped significantly is that the cost of controlling legal risk (through liability insurance and in-house legal staffs) is just too high.[16] Indeed, the threat of lawsuits has led 47 percent of companies to drop one or more products, has encouraged 25 percent of companies to drop research and development programs, and has stopped 39 percent of companies from bringing new products to market.[17] Before choosing to implement control, managers should be confident that the benefits exceed the costs.

An often-overlooked factor in determining the cost of control is the set of unintended consequences that sometimes accompany increased control. Control systems help companies, managers, and workers accomplish their goals, but at the same time that they help solve some problems, they can create others. For example, in Chapter 4, you learned that Delta Airlines wanted to reduce its costs from 9.76 cents per seat-mile to 7.5 cents per seat-mile. In many respects, Delta succeeded, lowering its costs and returning to solid profitability. However, in some places, the cost-cutting was so deep that Delta's performance suffered in other key areas. For example, Delta used to keep one mechanic at each gate to fix minor problems between flights. Yet, after cost-cutting, it only assigned one mechanic to every three or four gates. Because the mechanic could only repair one plane at a time, the unintended consequence was that many flights were delayed. At the time, this caused Delta to fall to last among domestic airlines in on-time arrivals.[18]

cybernetic feasibility
the extent to which it is possible to implement each step in the control process

The second factor that helps managers determine whether control is possible is cybernetic feasibility. **Cybernetic feasibility** is the extent to which it is possible to implement each step in the control process: clear standards of performance, comparison of performance to standards, and corrective action. If one or more steps cannot be implemented, then maintaining effective control may be difficult or impossible.

For example, companies traditionally have a very tough time making employees follow corporate travel procedures (i.e., clear standards, but poor corrective action). Instead of calling the officially approved company travel agency, employees typically make their own reservations, or call their own travel agents. American Express, which in addition to its charge-card business is one of the world's largest travel companies, estimates that American companies lose $15 billion a year because managers and employees don't follow travel policies. Companies should certainly try to control travel expenses. But with so many ways to arrange travel outside of the officially sanctioned corporate methods, controlling travel will always be difficult—especially now, with online travel agencies making it even easier for employees to book their own travel.[19]

2.3 *Quasi-Control: When Control Isn't Possible*

quasi-control
reducing dependence or restructuring dependence when control is necessary but not possible

reducing dependence
abandoning or changing organizational goals to reduce dependence on critical resources

If control is necessary, but not possible because of costs or cybernetic infeasibility, then managers can use two **quasi-control** options: reducing dependence or restructuring dependence. **Reducing dependence** involves an explicit choice to abandon or change organizational goals by reducing dependence on critical resources. Companies are likely to choose to reduce dependence under the same conditions that they would choose control. The difference, however, is that companies choose to reduce dependence when control is not possible, that is, when the cost is too high or cybernetic feasibility is near zero.

For example, over the last 20 years, PepsiCo operated three distinct businesses: soft drinks (Pepsi, Mountain Dew, etc.), fast-food restaurants (Pizza Hut, Taco Bell, and Kentucky Fried Chicken), and snack foods (Frito-Lay). Each business was a resource that Pepsi used to earn profits. However, in the last decade, no matter what it tried, Pepsi found that it couldn't be successful in all three businesses at the same time. Increasingly, money invested in the restaurants was needed to fight Coca-Cola in the soft drink business. So, rather than continue to depend on three different resources, Pepsi reduced its dependence by deciding to focus on just two. Consequently, it sold its restaurants for more than $11 billion and reinvested the proceeds in its soft drink and snack food businesses.[20]

restructuring dependence exchanging dependence on one critical resource for dependence on another

Instead of reducing dependence when control is not possible, companies can choose to **restructure dependence**—exchange dependence on one critical resource for dependence on another. One area in which companies are exchanging resources is to substitute private planes for commercial air travel. Surprisingly, traveling by private plane has a number of advantages over traveling via commercial airlines. To start, compared to last-minute business class tickets, which are much more expensive now than just a few years ago and approximately three to five times the cost of coach class tickets, corporate planes can be cheaper to fly. Tim Quinn, who owns a construction company, saw his monthly air-travel expenses drop almost in half, from $11,000 to $6000, even after making the monthly payments for his company plane.

Another advantage of exchanging private plane travel for commercial air travel is that private planes can get to many more destinations. While commercial airlines fly into 550 airports nationwide, smaller, private planes can fly into more than 5,500 different airports. Also, private planes are useful tools, not the fancy perks that most people believe them to be. Maytag spokesperson Tom Schwartz said that Maytag's two jets "don't have legroom, you can't stand up, and there's no lavatory." He said, "It would be a mistake to think of this as an executive perk."[21]

There are three advantages to restructuring dependence. First, like private planes, the new critical resource may be more controllable. Second, even better, the new critical resource may not require any control at all. Third, the company does not have to change its goals.

Review 2:
Is Control Necessary or Possible?

Figure 7.2 summarizes the questions that managers should answer to determine if control is necessary or possible. First, if the degree of dependence on a critical resource is high, or if resource flows are poor, managers will want to initiate greater control over critical resources. However, if resource flows and the degree of dependence are low, managers do not need to do anything to increase control. Next, if cybernetics (i.e., the basic control process) is feasible, managers should determine if the cost of control is acceptable. If it is, then managers should choose to regulate or control the degree of dependence on critical resources. However, if cybernetics is not feasible, the next step is deciding whether goals can be changed. If goals are fixed and unchangeable, then managers should restructure their dependence on critical resources by exchanging dependence on one critical resource for dependence

Figure 7.2 **Is Control Necessary or Possible?**

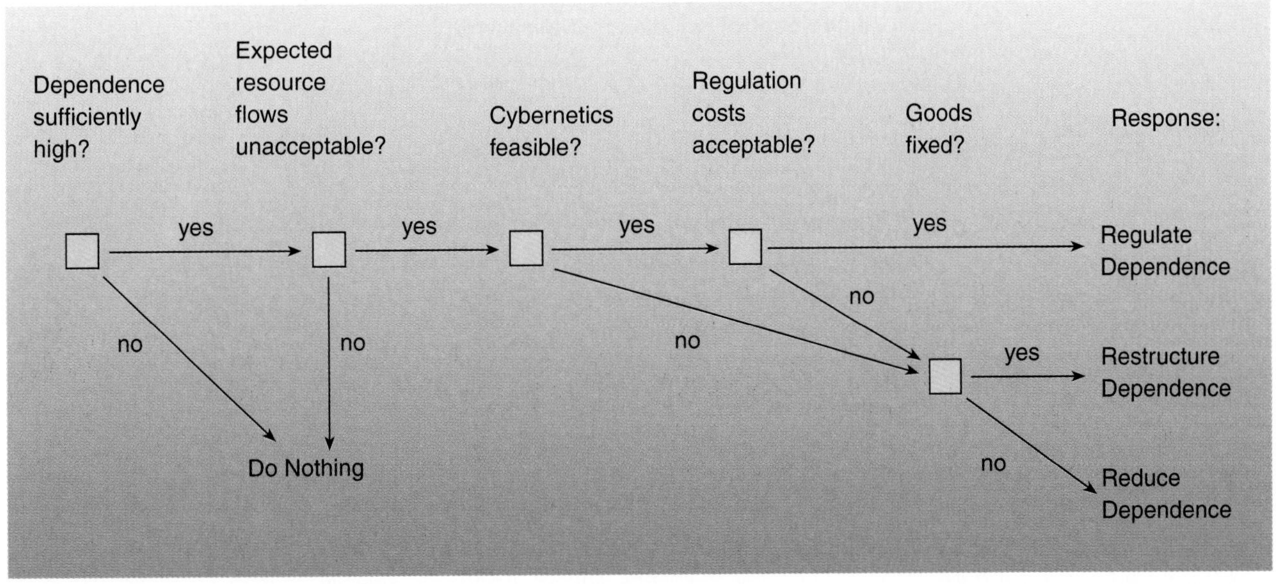

Source: S.G. Green & M.A. Welsh, "Cybernetics and Dependence: Reframing the Control Concept," *Academy of Management Review*, 13 (1988): 287-301.

on another. On the other hand, if goals can be changed, then managers should reduce dependence on critical resources by abandoning or changing key goals.

How and What to Control

Have you developed a taste for gourmet coffee? With gourmet coffee seemingly everywhere, chances are you have or someone in your office has. However, the popularity of specialty coffees and coffee shops has created a problem in many offices: the long coffee break. Instead of wandering down the hall to brew a fresh pot of regular coffee and chat with co-workers during a 15-minute coffee break, workers are now running out of their offices to find the nearest gourmet coffee shop. In the marketing department for the Pittsburgh Symphony, the department manager declared coffee shops off limits after finding five department staffers missing well beyond their regular coffee breaks.[22]

The question for aspiring managers is, how would you handle this situation? Should you declare coffee shops off-limits? Should you simply discuss it with employees and rely on them to exercise their own judgment? Should you closely watch for potential violators and then punish them? And then there is the question of whether long coffee breaks are something that managers should even try to control. Paul Ivers, who works for Lotus Development Corporation, believes that there's nothing wrong with trips to the coffee shop. He said, "It's not good to be doing something straight for nine to ten hours." Likewise, Carol Raymer, who is a manager at Federal Express (and gets six to eight cups a day from the coffee shop in her office building!), said, "You talk to customers and issues come up. It's a good networking place."

After reading the next two sections, you should be able to:

3 discuss the various **methods** that managers can use to maintain **control.**

4 describe the **behaviors, processes, and outcomes** that managers are choosing **to control** in today's organizations.

3 Control Methods

There are five different methods that managers can use to achieve control in their organizations: **3.1** *bureaucratic,* **3.2** *objective,* **3.3** *normative,* **3.4** *concertive, and* **3.5** *self-control.*

BLASTFROMTHEPAST

From 1870 to the Present—Five Eras of Management Control

According to researchers Stephen Barley and Gideon Kunda, there have been five eras of management control since 1870: industrial betterment, scientific management, human relations, systems rationalization, and organizational culture and quality.

Industrial Betterment, 1870–1900

Industrial betterment, which was preceded by an era in which employers did not care about the general welfare or working conditions of employees, is best characterized as paternalistic. Just as parents provide for their children, many large companies sought to provide and care for their employees during this time. Some companies practiced industrial betterment by building libraries, parks, gymnasiums, and subsidized housing for employees. Others improved horrid working conditions by making unsanitary and unsafe factory jobs clean and safe. Still others paid for social clubs, and established profit-sharing and benefit plans not found in companies before that time. YMCAs, the Young Men's Christian Associations, were established by railroad companies to attend to the physical and spiritual needs of the employees who rode the rails from coast to coast. Although "industrial betterment" sounds virtuous, it had the larger goal of attracting and producing a reliable workforce. For example, the railroads were hopeful that in ministering to their workers, YMCAs would also reduce the widespread drunkenness that created an unstable, unreliable, unsafe workforce.

Scientific Management, 1900–1922

By contrast to the paternalistic view of industrial betterment, scientific management, founded by Frederick W. Taylor (see "Blast from the Past" in Chapter 5), was concerned with efficiency, finding the most efficient combination of procedures to produce a product. Scientific management was built on three ideas. First, controlled, scientific study of work would lead to greater efficiency. Second, all employees are rational. If shown a superior way to do the work, they will embrace it. Third, employees are primarily motivated by money.

Building on these beliefs, Taylor introduced the then-novel idea of piece-rate payment plans, in which workers were paid according to their output. Not surprisingly, Taylor held little respect for industrial betterment. He said, "No self-respecting workman wants to be given things; every man wants to earn things."

Human Relations, 1925–1955

Unlike the efficiency focus of scientific management, the human relations approach to control assumed that social interaction and the need to belong to work groups were more important to employees than money. The human relations approach advocated the importance of supervisor training, communication, and group dynamics and processes. So rather than just paying workers to work harder, this approach assumed that workers would be more motivated if supervisors treated employees better, if work groups participated in decision making, and if jobs were redesigned to allow rather than restrict social interaction between employees. Although this approach bears similarities to industrial betterment, there is one key difference: Industrial betterment sought to improve the company workforce, whereas human relations took as its goal the improvement of the company itself.

Systems Rationalism, 1955–1980

In contrast to human relations, which placed employee considerations at the heart of its control philosophy, the systems rationalization or systems approach chose to ignore employees to focus exclusively on seeking universal principles or functions that would help an entire organization run like a smooth machine. Using ideas from electrical engineering and computer science, the systems approach sought ways to plan, forecast, and control the performance of the entire organization. Managers focused on organizational inputs and outputs. Supervisor training was unimportant, because it was the larger management system in the company, not its supervisors, which determined success or failure.

Organizational Culture and Quality, 1980–Present

Finally, in contrast to the sterile approach of systems management, the pendulum of organization control swung the other way to embrace organizational culture and quality. Here, rather than focusing on efficiency or on units of the company as parts of a larger system, leaders and companies maintained control through the shared beliefs, values, and actions of their managers and workers. Concerns shifted from inputs and outputs to employee commitment and motivation, teamwork, values, vision, and morale. The goal was to have employees perceive that the organization was committed to producing a quality product or service. Inspired by this vision or goal, employees and managers would work harder and with greater commitment for the company and its customers.

With downsizing and the loss of millions of corporate jobs throughout the 1990s, some would argue that companies have already left the era of culture and quality. Indeed, Barley and Kunda argue that historically, control philosophies have cycled between rational efficiency-based approaches (scientific management and systems rationalism) and employee-based approaches (industrial betterment, human relations, and corporate culture and quality).

Source: S.R. Barley & G. Kunda, "Design and Devotion: Surges of Rational and Normative Ideologies of Control in Management Discourse," *Administrative Science Quarterly* 37 (1992): 363-399.

3.1 *Bureaucratic Control*

bureaucratic control
use of hierarchical authority to influence employee behavior by rewarding or punishing employees for compliance or noncompliance with organizational policies, rules, and procedures

When most people think of managerial control, what they have in mind is bureaucratic control. **Bureaucratic control** is top-down control, in which managers try to influence employee behavior by rewarding or punishing employees for compliance or noncompliance with organizational policies, rules, and procedures. However, most employees would argue that bureaucratic managers emphasize punishment for noncompliance much more than rewards for compliance. For example, in the Sejen Electronics TV manufacturing plant in Zhuhai, China, Kim Jin Sun, the manager who runs the plant, found several workers napping during their breaks. Consequently, she punished all 100 of her workers by making them kneel before her. When asked why she intimidated the workers this way, she responded, "It was the best way to make them understand that they had done wrong. Kneeling down in Korea isn't considered as shameful as in China. I didn't mean to demean them as human beings. It was just a management strategy I had to resort to."[23]

Ironically, bureaucratic management and control were created to prevent just this type of managerial behavior. By encouraging managers to apply well-thought-out rules, policies, and procedures in an impartial, consistent manner to everyone in the organization, bureaucratic control is supposed to make companies more efficient, effective, and fair. Perversely, it frequently has just the opposite effect. Managers who use bureaucratic control often put following the rules above all else. For example, this story comes from an Internet site called "When Winners Work for Losers" (**http://www.myboss.com/**):

> *After working in the defense industry for 20 years, I was suddenly faced with two layoffs in two years. After my second "mandatory vacation," all financial resources were exhausted. My mother, who lived with me, was diagnosed with ovarian cancer and required very expensive painkilling medications not covered under her insurance. Through a temporary agency, I got a job at a major credit-reporting firm. This company had a policy of docking any worker 50 cents per hour for any*

time missed, regardless of the reason. I went to the on-site supervisor in hopes of getting an exception to the policy, because I was the only person who could get my mother to her doctor's appointments.

She refused to intervene with the agency, even though her own mother was ill and it was well known that she took time to ensure her mother's medical care. She refused to discuss the issue with me saying (her exact words) that it was a dead issue. It certainly was, because my mother died one month later without being able to get to the doctor.

To add insult to injury, I left the job one hour after the Hospice nurses called to say my mother had died. The agency, true to policy, docked me 50 cents per hour.[24]

Another characteristic of bureaucratically controlled companies is that due to their rule- and policy-driven decision making, they are highly resistant to change and slow to respond to customers and competitors. Even Max Weber, the German philosopher who is largely credited with popularizing bureaucratic ideals in the late 19th century, referred to bureaucracy as the "iron cage." He said, "Once fully established, bureaucracy is among those social structures which are the hardest to destroy."[25] Of course, the federal government, with hundreds of bureaus, agencies, and departments, is typically the largest bureaucracy in most countries. And, because of the thousands of career bureaucrats who staff those offices, even presidents and Congress have difficulty creating change. When General Dwight Eisenhower defeated incumbent Harry Truman to become president, Truman, who as president had dealt with government bureaucracies, quipped, "Poor Ike. It won't be a bit like the army. He'll sit here and he'll say, 'Do this, do that,' and nothing will happen."[26]

3.2 *Objective Control*

objective control
use of observable measures of worker behavior or outputs to assess performance and influence behavior

behavior control
regulation of the behaviors and actions that workers perform on the job

In many companies, bureaucratic control has evolved into **objective control**, which is the use of observable measures of employee behavior or outputs to assess performance and influence behavior. Objective control differs from bureaucratic control in that managers focus on the observation or measurement of worker behavior or outputs rather than policies and rules.

Behavior control is the regulation of the behaviors and actions that workers perform on the job. The basic assumption of behavior control is that if you do the right things (i.e., the right behaviors) every day, then those things should lead to goal achievement. However, behavior control is still management-based, which means that managers are responsible for monitoring, rewarding, and punishing workers for exhibiting desired or undesired behaviors. When Alan Greenberg, the CEO of Bear Stearns, a Wall Street investment company, wrote the following memo to his firm's managing partners, he was enacting behavioral control about the importance of always being available.

Bear Stearns is moving forward at an accelerated rate and everyone is contributing. It is absolutely essential for us to be able to talk to our [the firm's] partners at all times. All of us are entitled to eat lunch, play golf and go on vacation. But you must leave word with your secretary or associates where you can be reached at all times. Decisions have to be made and your input can be important!

I conducted a study of the 200 firms that have disappeared from Wall Street over the last few years, and I discovered that 62.349 per-

cent went out of business because the important people did not leave word where they went when they left their desk if even for 10 minutes. That idiocy will not occur here![27]

Greenberg has also written pointed memos to his "troops" about not returning phone calls ("Do you realize what a negative effect not returning a call has on an associate or client?"), the expense of overusing Federal Express to mail documents ("I can assure you that future use of Federal Express is going to be very closely monitored. The fact that it wasn't up to now is my fault, and I take full blame."), and the importance of reporting any suspicious behavior that might violate Bear Stearns' standards of honesty and integrity ("If you think somebody is doing something off the wall or his/her decision making stinks, go around the person, and that includes me."). All are examples of attempts to initiate behavioral control.

output control
regulation of worker results or outputs through rewards and incentives

Instead of measuring what managers and workers do, **output control** measures the results of their efforts. Whereas behavior control regulates, guides, and measures how workers behave on the job, output control gives managers and workers the freedom to behave as they see fit as long as it leads to the accomplishment of pre-specified, measurable results. Output control is often coupled with rewards and incentives. However, three things must occur for output control and rewards to lead to improved business results.

First, output control measures must be reliable, fair, and accurate. Second, employees and managers must believe that they can produce the desired results. For example, Monsanto made the mistake of linking worker pay in one of its manufacturing plants to overall plant performance. Employees didn't like this output measure because they didn't feel they could have an impact on what was going on in the entire plant. So Monsanto now ties the bonuses to outcome controls that track the performance of much smaller groups of 50 to 60 employees. Said one employee, "Once you feel some sort of ownership, it works well."[28]

Third, the rewards or incentives tied to outcome control measures must truly be dependent on achieving established standards of performance. For example, it seems that each year *The Wall Street Journal* or *Business Week* runs a story about how Disney CEO Michael Eisner earned another multimillion dollar bonus that year. However, few people realize that several years ago, Eisner did not receive a bonus. The Walt Disney Company fell short of its goals for growth in net income and shareholder's equity (the price of its stock), so Eisner only received his annual salary of $750,000 that year. Ok, so you're not shedding any tears for Mr. Eisner because the poor guy "only" received three-quarters of a million that year. However, in the three years preceding this no-bonus year, Eisner received bonuses of $10.5, $4.7, and $6.7 million.[29] So for output control to work with rewards, the rewards must truly be at risk if performance doesn't measure up.

3.3
Normative Control

Rather than monitoring rules, behavior, or outputs, another way to control what goes on in organizations is to shape the beliefs and values of the people who work there through normative control. With **normative controls**, a company's widely shared values and beliefs guide workers' behavior and decisions. For example, at Nordstrom, a Seattle-based department store chain, one value permeates the entire workforce from top to bottom: extraordinary

normative control
regulation of workers' behavior and decisions through widely shared organizational values and beliefs

customer service. The first day of work at Nordstrom, trainees begin their transformation to the "Nordstrom way" by reading the employee handbook. Sounds boring, doesn't it? But Nordstrom's handbook is printed on one side of a 3" x 5" note card. In its entirety, it reads:

> *Welcome to Nordstrom's. We're glad to have you with our company. Our Number One goal is to provide outstanding customer service. Set both your personal and professional goals high. We have great confidence in your ability to achieve them. Nordstrom Rules: Rule #1: Use your good judgment in all situations. There will be no additional rules. Please feel free to ask your department manager, store manager or division general manager any question at any time.*[30]

That's it. No lengthy rules. No specifics about what behavior is or is not appropriate. Use your judgment.

Normative controls are created in two ways. First, companies that use normative controls are very careful about whom they hire. While many companies screen potential applicants on the basis of their abilities, normatively controlled companies are just as likely to screen potential applicants based on their attitudes and values. For example, before building stores in a new city, Nordstrom will send its human resource team into town to interview prospective applicants. In those few instances in which it could not find enough qualified applicants, applicants who would embody the service attitudes and values that Nordstrom is known for, the company has canceled its expansion plans in those cities. Nordstrom would rather give up potential sales in lucrative markets than do business using people who could not provide Nordstrom's level of service.[31]

Second, with normative controls, managers and employees learn what they should and should not do by observing experienced employees and by listening to the stories they tell about the company. At Nordstrom, they even have a name for these stories, "heroics," many of which are inspired by the company motto, "Respond to Unreasonable Customer Requests!"[32]

"Nordies," as Nordstrom employees call themselves, like to tell the story about a customer who just had to have a pair of burgundy Donna Karan slacks that had gone on sale. However, she could not find her size. The sales associate, who was helping her, contacted five nearby Nordstrom stores. She could not find the customer's size. So rather than leave the customer dissatisfied with her shopping experience, the sales associate went to her manager for petty cash and then went across the street and paid full price for the slacks at a competitor's store. She then resold them to the customer at Nordstrom's lower sale price.[33] Obviously, Nordstrom would quickly go out of business if this were the norm. However, this story makes clear the attitude that drives employee performance at Nordstrom in ways that rules, behavioral guidelines, or output controls could not.

3.4 *Concertive Control*

concertive control
regulation of workers' behavior and decisions through work group values and beliefs

Whereas normative controls are based on the strongly held, widely shared beliefs throughout a company, **concertive controls** are based on beliefs that are shaped and negotiated by work groups.[34] So while normative controls are driven by strong organizational cultures, concertive controls usually arise when companies give autonomous work groups complete re-

Members of an autonomous work group, such as these computer game programmers, control their own group's processes, outputs, and behavior.
© Dennis O'Clair/Tony Stone Images

autonomous work groups
groups that operate without managers and are completely responsible for controlling work group processes, outputs, and behavior

sponsibility for task completion. **Autonomous work groups** are groups that operate without managers and are completely responsible for controlling work group processes, outputs, and behavior. These groups do their own hiring, firing, worker discipline, work schedules, materials ordering, budget making and meeting, and decision making.

Concertive control is not established overnight. Autonomous work groups evolve through two phases as they develop concertive control. In phase one, autonomous work group members learn to work with each other, supervise each other's work, and develop the values and beliefs that will guide and control their behavior. And because they develop these values and beliefs themselves, work group members feel strongly about following them.

For example, a member of an autonomous team at ISE Electronics, a small manufacturer of electronic boards, said, "I feel bad, believe it or not. Last Friday, we missed a shipment. I feel like *I* missed the shipment since I'm the last person that sees what goes to ship. But Friday we missed the shipment by two boards and it shouldn't have been missed. But it was and I felt bad because it's me, it's a reflection on me, too, for not getting the boards out the door."[35] Another member of the same team said, "Under the old system [management-led bureaucratic control], who gave a hoot if the boards shipped today or not? We just did our jobs. Now, we have more buy-in by the team members. We feel more personal responsibility for the product."[36]

The second phase in the development of concertive control is the emergence and formalization of objective rules to guide and control behavior. The beliefs and values developed in phase one usually develop into more objective rules as new members join teams. The clearer those rules, the easier it becomes for new members to figure out how and how not to behave.

For example, a team member at ISE electronics described how the team dealt with members showing up late to work: "Well, we had some disciplinary thing, you know. We had a few certain people who didn't show up on time and made a habit of coming in late. So the team got together and kinda set some guidelines and we told them, you know, 'If you come in late the third time and you don't wanna do anything to correct it, you're gone.' That was a team decision that this was a guideline that we were gonna follow."[37] Again, the key difference in concertive control is that the teams and not management enforced these rules.

Ironically, concertive control may lead to even more stress for workers to conform to expectations than bureaucratic control. Under bureaucratic control, most workers only have to worry about pleasing "the boss." But with concertive control, they have to keep the rest of their team members satisfied with their behavior. For example, one team member said, "I don't have to sit there and look for the boss to be around; and if the boss is not around, I can sit there and talk to my neighbor or do what I want. Now the whole team is around me and the whole team is observing what I'm doing."[38] Plus, with concertive control, team members have a second, much more stressful role to perform—that of making sure that their team members adhere to team values and rules.

3.5 *Self-Control*

self-control (self-management) control system in which managers and workers control their own behavior by setting their own goals, monitoring their own progress, and rewarding themselves for goal achievement

Self-control, also known as **self-management**, is a control system in which managers and workers control their own behavior.[39] However, self-control is not anarchy in which everyone gets to do whatever they want. In self-control or self-management, leaders and managers provide workers with clear boundaries within which they may guide and control their own goals and behaviors.[40] Leaders and managers also contribute to self-control by teaching others the skills they need to maximize and monitor their own work effectiveness. In turn, individuals who manage and lead themselves establish self-control by setting their own goals, monitoring their own progress, rewarding or punishing themselves for achieving or for not achieving their self-set goals, and constructing positive thought patterns that remind them of the importance of their goals and their ability to accomplish them.[41]

One technique for reminding yourself of your goals is daily affirmation, in which you write down or speak your goals aloud to yourself several times a day. Skeptics contend that daily affirmations are nothing more than positive thinking. However, an affirmation is just a simple way to help control what you think about and how you spend your time. Basically, it's a technique to prevent (i.e., control) yourself from getting sidetracked on unimportant thoughts and activities.

Scott Adams, who illustrates the cartoon strip "Dilbert," was skeptical that affirmations would work, but he gave them a try. His first affirmations were to see the price of a company's stock rise and to impress a particular woman. Both happened. Then when he was getting ready to take the GMAT test to get into an MBA program, every day he wrote that he wanted a score of a 94. His score was a 94. When he began affirming, "I will be the best cartoonist on the planet," "Dilbert" ballooned in popularity. Where it once appeared in only 100 newspapers, it now appears in more than 1,100. What's he affirming now? "I will win a Pulitzer Prize."[42] Ok, start writing, "I will get an 'A' in Management. I will get an 'A' in Management. . . . "

Personal Productivity Tip

Learn to Say No!

Control is not just setting standards and identifying performance discrepancies. A key issue in control is deciding what to control and what to ignore. We can't do everything, and that means that sometimes we have to say no when we're asked to participate. Here are four tips for saying no. First, listen to show interest and understanding. Second, say no immediately to avoid raising false expectations concerning your involvement. Three, explain why you can't, so that the reasons for your refusal are understood. Fourth, offer alternatives to your participation. "I can't, but you should contact Mary Smith. Mary knows how to do this."

Sources: V.M. Parachin, "Overcoming Work Addiction: Twelve Ways to Slow Down and Take Care of Yourself," *Vibrant Life,* 13 March 1996, 10.

Review 3: *Control Methods*

There are five methods of control: bureaucratic, objective, normative, concertive, and self-control (self-management). Bureaucratic and objective controls are top-down, management- and measurement-based. Normative and concertive controls represent shared forms of control, because they evolve from companywide or team-based beliefs and values. Self-control, or self-management, is a control system in which managers largely, but not completely, turn control over to the individuals themselves.

Bureaucratic control is based on organizational policies, rules, and procedures. Objective controls are based on reliable measures of behavior or outputs. Normative control is based on strong corporate beliefs and careful hiring practices. Concertive control is based on the development of values, beliefs, and rules in autonomous work groups. Self-control is based on individuals' setting their own goals, monitoring themselves, and rewarding or punishing themselves with respect to goal achievement.

We end this section by noting that there are more or less appropriate circumstances for using each of these control methods. Examine Table 7.2 to find out when each of these five control methods should be used.

Table 7.2

When to Use Different Methods of Control

Bureaucratic Control

- when it is necessary to standardize operating procedures
- when it is necessary to establish limits

Behavior Control

- when it is easier to measure what workers do on the job than what they accomplish on the job
- when "cause-effect" relationships are clear, that is, when companies know which behaviors will lead to success and which won't
- when good measures of worker behavior can be created

Output Control

- when it is easier to measure what workers accomplish on the job than what they do on the job
- when good measures of worker output can be created
- when it is possible to set clear goals and standards for worker output
- when "cause-effect" relationships are unclear

Normative Control

- when organizational culture, values, and beliefs are strong
- when it is difficult to create good measures of worker behavior
- when it is difficult to create good measures of worker output

Concertive Control

- when responsibility for task accomplishment is given to autonomous work groups
- when management wants workers to take "ownership" of their behavior and outputs
- when management desires a strong form of worker-based control

Self-Control

- when workers are intrinsically motivated to do their jobs well
- when it is difficult to create good measures of worker behavior
- when it is difficult to create good measures of worker output
- when workers have or are taught self-control and self-leadership skills

Sources: L.J. Kirsch, "The Management of Complex Tasks in Organizations: Controlling the Systems Development Process," *Organization Science* 7 (1996): 1-21. S.A. Snell, Control Theory in Strategic Human Resource Management: The Mediating Effect of Administrative Information," *Academy of Management Journal* 35 (1992): 292-327.

4 What to Control?

In the second part of this chapter we asked, "Is control necessary or possible?" In part three we asked, "How should control be obtained?" In this fourth and final section, we ask the equally important question "What should managers control?" The way their managers answer this question has critical implications for most businesses.

Take the example of Piccadilly's Cafeterias, which is based in Baton Rouge, Louisiana. Piccadilly's hired a new CEO, who decided that the company needed to control costs to be more competitive. At a meeting with other top managers, he announced his plans. The recipe for chocolate pie, the most popular item on the menu, would be changed to save a few pennies a slice. Lemon pie, once made from scratch, would be made from cheaper premade lemon filling scooped out of 48-pound buckets. Eight-ounce steaks would now be seven-ounce steaks. At first, this worked, with profits rising 24 percent the first three years. Eventually, though, customers wised up to the fact that the food just wasn't as good anymore. Said one customer who had been coming to Picadilly's every Sunday for 12 years, "Them mashed potatoes got lumpy and didn't taste fresh and those pie crusts weren't flaky but got mushy."[43] Not long afterwards, Picadilly's posted its first loss in nearly 50 years.

Picadilly's lost its customers and its profitability because it cared (i.e., controlled) about just one thing—reducing costs. Companies need to have a clear vision. They can't be everything to everybody. However, most companies successfully carry out their visions and missions by doing a multitude of small things right. As for Picadilly's, customers and profits didn't come back until management replaced its cheap "heat and eat" food with food created according to the company founder's recipes. In other words, Picadilly's business didn't thrive until management balanced its need to make a profit with its customers' need to get good food at a good price.

After reading this section, you should be able to explain **4.1** *the balanced scorecard approach to control, and how companies can achieve balanced control of company performance by choosing to control* **4.2** *economic value added,* **4.3** *customer defections,* **4.4** *quality, and* **4.5** *waste and pollution.*

4.1 *The Balanced Scorecard*

In most companies, performance is measured using standard financial and accounting measures, such as return on capital, return on assets, return on investments, cash flow, net income, net margins, etc. That's why employees at Americas Marketing and Refining (AM&R), the largest division of Mobil Oil Corporation, were not looking forward to their quarterly meeting with their tough division vice-president. On most of these traditional measures, division performance had been poor, and lower-level employees and managers expected to be blasted for their poor performance. In the past, poor financial performance usually led to firings and layoffs. So no one wanted to go to the meeting.

However, this time it was different. After opening the meeting with a discussion of the poor financial results, the meeting turned positive. Market share had improved. Operating expenses were down. And employees, as measured by a recent attitudinal survey, were satisfied with their jobs and their bosses. The VP declared, "In all the areas we could control, we moved the needle in the right direction." The employees, who expected to be handed their heads, were shocked by the praise. Greg Berry, the division's manager of business and performance analysis, said, "It was a total departure from the past. Here was a Mobil executive saying, 'Hey, we didn't make any money, but I feel good about where the business is going.'"[44]

balanced scorecard measurement of organizational performance in four equally important areas: finances, customers, internal operations, and innovation and learning

The **balanced scorecard** encourages managers to look beyond traditional financial measures to four different perspectives on company performance. How do customers see us (the customer perspective)? What must we excel at (the internal perspective)? Can we continue to improve and create value (the innovation and learning perspective)? How do we look to shareholders (the financial perspective)?[45]

The balanced scorecard has several advantages over traditional control processes that rely solely on financial measures. First, it forces managers at each level of the company to set specific goals and measure performance in each of the four areas. For example, Mobil Oil's AM&R division uses 23 different measures in its balanced scorecard. Of those 23, only five are standard financial measures of performance.

Figure 7.3 shows the balanced scorecard used by a large semiconductor company. This company does measure its performance in traditional financial terms—cash flows, quarterly sales growth, and increased market share

Figure 7.3 **Example of a Balanced Scorecard**

Financial Perspective		Customer Perspective	
Goals	***Measures***	***Goals***	***Measures***
Survive	Cash flow	New products	Percent of sales from new products
Succeed	Quarterly sales growth and operating income by division		Percent of sales from proprietary products
Prosper	Increased market share and ROE	Responsive supply	On-time delivery
		Preferred customer	Share of key accounts' purchases
		Customer partnership	Number of cooperative engineering efforts

Internal Business Perspective		Innovation and Learning Perspective	
Goals	***Measures***	***Goals***	***Measures***
Technology capability	Manufacturing geometry vs. competition	Technology leadership	Time to develop next generation product
Manufacturing excellence	Cycle time, Unit cost	Product focus	Percent of products equaling 80% sales
Design productivity	Silicon efficiency, Engineering efficiency	Time to market	New product introduction vs. competition
New product introduction	Actual introduction schedule vs. plan		

Source: R.S. Kaplan & D.P. Norton, "The Balanced Scorecard: Measures that Drive Performance," *Harvard Business Review,* January-February 1992, 71-79.

and return on equity. But it also measures the percentage of sales from new products and on-time deliveries (customer perspective), unit costs and whether the company met the projected schedule for new product introductions (internal business perspective), and how long it takes to develop the next generation of new products and how well it rolls out new products compared to its competition (innovation and learning perspective).

suboptimization
performance improvement in one part of an organization but only at the expense of decreased performance in another part

The second major advantage of the balanced scorecard approach to control is that it minimizes the chances of **suboptimization**, where, like at Picadilly Cafeterias, performance improves in one area, but only at the expense of decreased performance in others. For example, at Mobil Oil's AM&R division, everyone in the plant now measures performance based on the balanced scorecard. When the division's executive team meets, all managers must bring their copy of the balanced scorecard to explain how their actions will affect finances, customers, internal business, and innovation and learning. AM&R's vice-president said, "It's the basis of every conversation. When I go out in the field and talk with a guy running a coker on the midnight shift at one of our refineries, he can tell me what he's doing to impact the scorecard."[46]

Let's examine some of the ways in which companies are controlling the four basic parts of the balanced scorecard: the financial perspective (economic value added), the customer perspective (customer defections), the internal perspective (total quality management), and the innovation and learning perspective (waste and pollution).

4.2
The Financial Perspective: Controlling Economic Value Added

The traditional approach to controlling financial performance focuses on measures such as analysis of financial ratios, cash flow, capital budgets, balance sheets, and income statements. For years, management textbooks have recommended that managers use these measures to monitor and control the financial performance of their companies. In reality, though, most managers don't (but should) have a good understanding of accounting measures.[47] (If you struggle with these, you might find help in the following books: *Accounting the Easy Way* by Peter J. Eisen, *Accounting for Dummies* and *How to Read a Financial Report: Wringing Vital Signs Out of the Numbers*, both by John A. Tracy.) Furthermore, the complexity and sheer amount of information contained in these measures can shut down the brains and glaze over the eyes of even the most experienced managers.[48]

On the other hand, the balanced scorecard focuses on one simple question when it comes to finances: How do we look to shareholders? One of the best ways to answer that question is through something called economic value added.

economic value added (EVA)
the amount by which company profits (revenues minus expenses minus taxes) exceed the cost of capital

Conceptually, **economic value added (EVA)** is fairly easy for managers and workers to understand. It is the amount by which profits (after expenses) exceed the cost of capital in a given year. It is based on the simple idea that it takes capital to run a business, and capital comes at a cost. While most people think of capital as cash, capital is more likely to be found in a business in the form of computers, manufacturing plants, employees, raw materials, etc. And just like the interest that a homeowner pays on a mortgage or that a college student pays on a student loan, there is a cost to that capital.

The most common costs of capital are the interest paid on long-term bank loans used to buy all those resources, the interest paid to bondholders (who lend organizations their money), and the dividends (cash payments) and growth in stock value that accrue to shareholders. EVA is positive when company profits (revenues minus expenses minus taxes) exceed the cost of capital in a given year. In other words, if a business is to truly grow, its revenues must be large enough to cover both short-term costs (annual expenses and taxes) and long-term costs (the cost of borrowing capital from bondholders and shareholders). If you're a bit confused, Robert Goizueta, the former CEO of Coca-Cola, explained it this way: "You borrow money at a certain rate and invest it at a higher rate and pocket the difference. It is simple. It is the essence of banking."[49]

Been There,

Economic Value Added at Armstrong World Industries

Armstrong World Industries is a manufacturer of floor coverings, building products, and furniture. In this interview, CEO George Lorch explains how the company uses economic value added (EVA) to guide company decisions and align corporate and shareholder interests.

Q. How does economic value added (EVA) give Armstrong better analysis than conventional measurements?
A. It more closely aligns us to the shareholders' interests, number one. It takes into account our cost of debt and equity capital and really reflects what we need to provide to the shareholder as an adequate return. All the elements that go into that calculation force us to focus on important things: growth, which is profitable sales revenue; our margins, which we arrive at after we take into account our cost; the operating assets it takes to drive that profitability; and taxes.

Q. Will EVA ever replace more traditional ways of measuring financial performance?
A. No. There is no one measurement system that is absolutely the best. A company has to look at what it is trying to do and pick the best system. EVA holds a company accountable for the cost of capital it uses to expand and operate its business and attempts to show whether a company is creating real value for its shareholders.

Q. Your salaried people are on incentive-based compensation.
A. Every salaried person is on EVA as a measurement. One hundred percent of my incentive compensation is based on how well we do against our EVA target. Take my assistant. Her incentive compensation is also based 100 percent on our ability to generate the targeted EVA. A president of one of our worldwide businesses—30 percent of his or her incentive would be based on the corporate EVA. Fifty percent would be based on the operation's EVA for that business. The balance would be on personal objectives, all of which are tied specifically to things they must do to drive the financial performance of the business.

"They will work a lot harder and a lot smarter, because the reward will be there if they're able to perform."

Q. Did it take you a long time to set this up?
A. It took us a few months.

Q. Did you have any people who were less than enthusiastic about this?
A. No. The greatest apprehension on the part of the senior management group was where the EVA target would be set for [each manager's] business. Would we be fair, or would we put them in Never Never Land, where they wouldn't have a chance to make any decent bonus money? Once they understood what the numbers were and compared them to the ROA target, they said, "Yeah. That looks fair."

The farther into the organization you go, the greater the percentage payout is tied directly to that business and the personal objectives. You put the incentive money as close to the target as you can. Somebody who is, let's say, a product manager in our flooring business in North America will be driven by actions that they can control within their business. So, that's what we want to have the incentive follow.

Q. Can you cite an example?
A. The leader of our worldwide flooring business or building products business is an executive officer of this

company and one of the five top-paid guys. You want those guys to be rewarded based on how well the total company does. In our executive compensation plan that follows this measurement, we have benchmarked ourselves against peer companies in our group and [against] a cross section of American business. We tried to put more opportunity into the incentive side of compensation, so that we really drive performance to align us more closely with what the shareholder wants. If we really do well, as we did last year, our people at all levels of this incentive thing make a lot of money. When we don't do very well, they won't make much money. Under the old plan, the threshold to begin to earn incentive compensation was 4 percent ROA. The threshold under the new plan is 7.1 percent. So, you see, we gave up mediocre performance for extraordinary performance, because under the old plan, there was a cap on how much incentive money you could earn. We've taken the cap off the incentive.

Q. But, they've got to work a lot harder.
A. They will work a lot harder and a lot smarter, because the reward will be there if they're able to perform. Last year—I'm going to go from memory, now—our performance, ROA-wise, was 10.4 percent against a target of 8 percent. If we do as well this year as we did last year, there's going to be some very handsome rewards out there.

Q. Your incentive compensation is 100 percent based on the total performance of the company. What happens if you've got great performance across various sectors, and one falls off the face of the earth?
A. My incentive compensation is based on the total company. So, if we've got six business units that do great and one that doesn't, and if it pulls us below the target level, I don't get anything. I like to think that better than 60 percent of my compensation is at risk all the time.

Q. Is there too much concentration, then, on the short-term bottom line to the detriment of longer-term factors?
A. No. They have long-term incentive compensation in stock options and performance-restricted shares. The longer, term-restricted shares reflect a three-year performance relative to total appreciation of our stock plus the reinvested dividends, measured against the Standard & Poor's 500 performance. Accountability is the important issue, but even more important is that these incentive plans change behavior. They give people a sense of urgency, and they force people to focus on the things that really matter.

Q. What kind of feedback on EVA have you had from your CEO counterparts?
A. I've gotten more questions about "Why did you do this? . . . How difficult is it to communicate?" and "What are the benefits?" There are some very, very fine companies that have already adopted EVA—Coca-Cola, AT&T, Quaker Oats. Before we implemented this thing, I talked to those CEOs about their use of EVA and how they structured their incentive programs. It gave me a lot of confidence that what we were doing was the right thing. This is not something that you whip up in 30 days.

Source: B. Ettore, "George Lorch Explains Economic Value Added," *Management Review* 3 (September 1995): 50. This interview was edited for inclusion in this textbook.

Done That

So why is EVA so important? First and most important, since it includes the cost of capital, it shows whether a business, division, department, or profit center is really paying for itself. For example, soon after Goizueta became Coke's CEO, Coke management used EVA to take a hard look at its fountain business (selling coke concentrate to restaurants). Goizueta said, "And we found out that we're making much less than our cost of capital, which at that time, with no debt, was about 16 percent. So what we thought was a great business [using the traditional accounting and financial measures] was, in fact, a lousy business."[50]

Second, because EVA can easily be determined for subsets of a company, such as divisions, regional offices, manufacturing plants, and sometimes even departments, it makes managers at all levels pay much closer attention to how they run their segment of the business. For example, at Coke, when the managers of the fountain business realized that they weren't even covering the cost of capital (i.e., a negative EVA), they looked for ways to do more with less capital. They determined that instead of delivering Coke concentrate in thousands of small 20-gallon steel containers, they could save money by delivering it to restaurants in huge tanker trucks.[51] In other words, EVA motivates all managers to think like small business owners who must scramble to contain costs and generate enough business to meet their bills each month.

Finally, unlike many kinds of financial controls, EVA doesn't specify what should or should not be done to improve performance. Thus, it encourages managers and workers to be creative as they try to find ways to improve EVA performance.

For example, CSX Intermodal uses trains to transport cargo containers across the country to waiting trucks or ships. When CSX managers found out that the company had an EVA of negative $70 million, they started making changes. CSX used to use four engine cars to pull a regularly scheduled train from New Orleans to Jacksonville at an average speed of 28 mph. However, the train usually arrived six to eight hours before it was to be unloaded. So managers made better use of their capital by using only three engine cars, which pulled the train at an average speed of 25 mph. The train still arrived three hours before it was scheduled to be unloaded, but with three rather than four engines, it used 25 percent less fuel.[52]

Table 7.3 shows the capital, return on capital, and cost of capital, for some major companies. Remember that EVA is the amount by which profits (after expenses) exceed the cost of capital in a given year. So the more that return on capital exceeds the cost of capital, the better a company is using investors' money.

4.3 The Customer Perspective: Controlling Customer Defections

The second aspect of organizational performance that the balanced scorecard helps managers monitor is customers. It does so by forcing managers to address the question "How do customers see us?" Unfortunately, most companies try to answer this question through customer satisfaction surveys that are often misleadingly positive. Most customers are reluctant to talk about their problems, because they don't know who to complain to, or they don't think that complaining will do any good. Indeed, a study by the federal Office of Consumer Affairs indicated that 96 percent of unhappy customers never complain to anyone in the company.[53]

Table 7.3 **Leading Companies, as Measured by Economic Value Added**

Companies	***Economic Value Added $millions***	***Capital $millions***	***Return on Capital***	***Cost of Capital***
Coca-Cola	$2,442	$10,814	36.0%	9.7%
General Electric	$2,515	$53,567	17.7%	12.7%
Microsoft	$1,727	$ 5,680	47.1%	11.8%
Intel	$3,605	$17,483	36.4%	13.6%
Merck	$1,688	$22,219	23.0%	14.5%
Philip Morris	$3,119	$42,885	20.1%	12.5%
Exxon	$1,334	$88,396	12.0%	10.4%
Procter & Gamble	$ 576	$25,032	14.3%	11.9%
Johnson & Johnson	$1,327	$18,138	21.8%	13.3%
Bristol-Myers Squibb	$1,515	$14,107	24.1%	12.8%

Source: R. Teitelbaum, "America's Greatest Wealth Creators," *Fortune*. [Online] Available **http://www.pathfinder.com/fortune/1997/971110/fea.pdf,** 10 November 1997.

Another reason that customer satisfaction surveys can be misleading is that sometimes even very satisfied customers will leave to do business with competitors. Dave Nichol, founder of the President's Choice brand, explained why: "Customer loyalty is the absence of something better."[54] So even if customers are pleased, they may go elsewhere if they believe they can get a better product or service.

Finally, customer satisfaction surveys can be misleading because they greatly overestimate the degree to which customers will buy from a company again. For example, it's common for automakers to advertise that "90 percent of customers are satisfied with their cars." But what they don't say in their advertising is that only 30 percent to 40 percent of car buyers purchase their next car from the same company.[55]

Rather than poring over customer satisfaction surveys from current customers, studies indicate that companies may do a better job of answering the question "How do customers see us?" by closely monitoring **customer defections**, that is, by identifying which customers are leaving the company and measuring the rate at which they are leaving. In contrast to customer satisfaction surveys, customer defections and retention have a much greater effect on profits.

customer defections performance assessment in which companies identify which customers are leaving and measure the rate at which they are leaving

For example, very few managers realize that it costs five times as much to obtain a new customer as it does to keep a current one. In fact, the cost of replacing old customers with new ones is so great that most companies could double their profits by increasing the rate of customer retention by just 5–10 percent per year.[56] And, if a company can keep a customer for life, the benefits are even larger. For Taco Bell, keeping a customer is worth $11,000 in lifetime sales. For a Cadillac dealer, the value is $332,000. For a grocery store, it can approach $200,000.[57]

Beyond the clear benefits to the bottom line, the second reason to study customer defections is that customers who have defected to other companies are much more likely than current customers to tell you what you are doing wrong. Perhaps the best way to tap into this source of good feedback is to have top-level managers from various departments talk directly to customers who have left. Some might argue that it's a waste of valuable executive time to have upper-level managers make these calls, but there's no faster way to get the people in charge to realize what needs to be done than to hear it directly from customers who decided that their company's performance was lacking.

For example, when the top managers at Microscan Technologies, which makes microbiological testing equipment, talked to customers who defected, they found out their products were too expensive and unreliable, and that the company was doing a poor job of responding to customer needs and complaints. And, the harder and longer that upper-level management listened, the clearer it became that these weren't arbitrary perceptions but real problems.[58] Two years after beginning to solve the problems identified by customer defectors, Microscan became the market leader in its industry.

Finally, companies that understand why customers leave can not only take steps to fix ongoing problems, but can also identify which customers are likely to leave and make changes to prevent them from leaving. For example, a large bank discovered that departing customers would send signals that they were getting ready to leave. A small business that made regular overnight deposits would make them less frequently. Or a customer with a

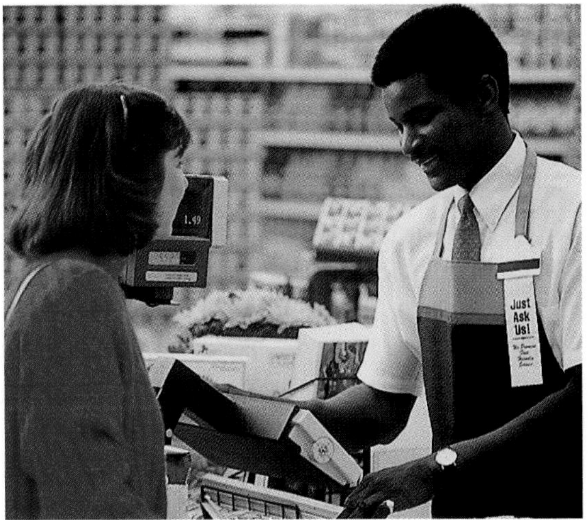

Since it costs five times as much to obtain a new customer as it does to keep a current one, it pays to keep customers happy.
© Jeff Zaruba/Tony Stone Images

personal bank account who withdrew money each Friday might only withdraw money once or twice a month. Since these changes usually occurred before customers left, the bank used its computers to create a daily "retention alert" that would identify customers whose regular interaction patterns had changed. Then, each of those customers would receive a personal phone call from bank account managers to determine what could be done to solve their problems and keep their business.[59]

Likewise, Citibank mails postcards to credit card holders when their credit card usage suddenly drops. The post cards say, "Call 1-800 . . . now and tell us why, and we'll make you an offer that will make your card even more valuable to you." When a customer called to explain that his Discover Card paid a cashback bonus, Citibank kept the customer's business by offering him an identical cashback deal.[60]

4.4 *The Internal Perspective: Controlling Quality*

The third part of the balanced scorecard, the internal perspective, consists of the processes, decisions, and actions that managers and workers make within the organization. So, in contrast to the financial perspective of EVA and the outward-looking customer perspective, the internal perspective asks the question "What must we excel at?" For McDonald's, the answer would be quick, low-cost food. For America Online, the answer would be reliability—when your modem dials, the network should be up and running and you should be able to connect without getting a busy signal. Yet no matter what area a company chooses, the key is to excel in that area. Consequently, the internal perspective of the balanced scorecard usually leads managers to a focus on quality.

Quality is typically defined and measured in three ways: excellence, value, and conformance to expectations.[61] When the company defines its quality goal as *excellence*, then managers must try to produce a product or service of unsurpassed performance and features. For example, by almost any count, Singapore International Airlines (SIA) is "the best" airline in the world. It has been named so eight of the last nine years by readers of *Conde Nast Traveler* magazine.[62] Even SIA's competitors recognize its excellence. *Air Transport World*, the magazine read by those who work in the airline industry, stated, "SIA aimed to be the best and most successful airline in the world."[63] SIA was the first airline to introduce a choice of meals, and complementary drinks and earphones in coach class in the 1970s. Today, it continues to innovate, introducing the first worldwide video, news, telephone, and fax service on any airline. This system offers 22 video channels with movies, news, and documentaries, 12 audio channels, and 10 different Nintendo games.

value
customer perception that the product quality is excellent for the price offered

Value is the customer perception that the product quality is excellent for the price offered. At a higher price, for example, customers may perceive the product to be less of a value. When a company emphasizes value as its quality goal, managers must simultaneously control excellence, price, durability, or other features of a product or service that customers strongly associate with value. One company that has put value at the core of everything it does is Lands' End, the catalog company that sells quality clothing and accessories at reasonable prices. In its advertising, Lands' End said, "Value is more than price. Value is the combination of product quality, world class customer service and a fair price." Lands' End puts its commitment to value into practice through its eight principles of doing business, which are shown in Table 7.4.

When a company defines its quality goal as conformance to specifications, employees must base decisions and actions on whether services and

Table 7.4

The Lands' End Principles of Doing Business

Principle 1.	We do everything we can to make our products better. We improve material, and add back features and construction details that others have taken out over the years. We never reduce the quality of a product to make it cheaper.
Principle 2.	We price our products fairly and honestly. We do not, have not, and will not participate in the common retailing practice of inflating mark-ups to set up a future phony "sale."
Principle 3.	We accept any return for any reason, at any time. Our products are guaranteed. No fine print. No arguments. We mean exactly what we say: GUARANTEED. PERIOD.
Principle 4.	We ship faster than anyone we know of. We ship items in stock the day after we receive the order. At the height of the last Christmas season the longest time an order was in the house was 36 hours, excepting monograms which took another 12 hours.
Principle 5.	We believe that what is best for our customer is best for all of us. Everyone here understands that concept. Our sales and service people are trained to know our products, and to be friendly and helpful. They are urged to take all the time necessary to take care of you. We even pay for your call, for whatever reason you call.
Principle 6.	We are able to sell at lower prices because we have eliminated middlemen; because we don't buy branded merchandise with high protected mark-ups; and because we have placed our contracts with manufacturers who have proven that they are cost conscious and efficient.
Principle 7.	We are able to sell at lower prices because we operate efficiently. Our people are hard-working, intelligent, and share in the success of the company.
Principle 8.	We are able to sell at lower prices because we support no fancy emporiums with their high overhead. Our main location is in the middle of a 40-acre cornfield in rural Wisconsin.

Source: "The Lands' End Principles of Doing Business," Lands' End Web Site. [Online] Available http://www.landsend.com/spawn.cgi?target=EDITPRIN1992&mode=GRAPHIC&refer=NODECOMP0795&sid=0933282560042, 26 June 1998.

products measure up to standard specifications. In contrast to excellence and value-based definitions of quality that can be somewhat ambiguous, measuring whether products and services are "in spec" is relatively easy. Furthermore, while conformance to specifications is usually associated with manufacturing, it can be used equally well to control quality in nonmanufacturing jobs. Table 7.5 shows a quality checklist that a cook or restaurant owner would use to ensure quality when buying fresh fish.

The way in which a company defines quality affects the methods and measures that workers use to control quality. Accordingly, Table 7.6 shows the advantages and disadvantages associated with the excellence, value, and conformance to specification definitions of quality.

4.5 The Innovation and Learning Perspective: Controlling Waste and Pollution

The last part of the balance scorecard, the innovation and learning perspective, addresses the question "Can we continue to improve and create value?" Thus, the innovation and learning perspective is concerned with new product development (discussed in Chapter 4), continuous improvement in ongoing products and services (discussed in Chapter 15), and relearning and redesigning the processes by which products and services are created (discussed in Chapter 10). Since all three categories are discussed in more detail elsewhere in the text, this section reviews an increasingly important topic, waste and pollution minimization, that is affected by all three of these issues.

As shown in Figure 7.4, there are four levels of waste minimization, with waste prevention and reduction producing the greatest minimization of waste and waste disposal producing the smallest minimization of waste.[64] The top level is *waste prevention and reduction*, in which the goals are to prevent waste and pollution before they occur, or to reduce them when they do occur. There are three strategies for waste prevention and reduction.

1. *Good housekeeping*—regularly scheduled preventive maintenance for offices, plants, and equipment. Making sure to quickly fix leaky valves, or making sure machines are running properly so they don't use more fuel than necessary are examples of good housekeeping.

Table 7.5 **Conformance to Specifications Checklist for Buying Fresh Fish**

Quality Checklist for Buying Fresh Fish		
Fresh Whole Fish	***Acceptable***	***Not Acceptable***
Eyes	clear, bright, bulging, black pupils	dull, sunken, cloudy, gray pupils
Gills	bright red, free of slime, clear mucus	brown to grayish, thick, yellow mucus
Flesh	firm and elastic to touch, tight to the bone	soft and flabby, separating from the bone
Smell	inoffensive, slight ocean smell	ammonia, putrid smell
Skin	opalescent sheen, scales adhere tightly to skin	dull or faded color, scales missing, or easily removed
Belly Cavity	no viscera or blood visible, lining intact, no bone protruding	incomplete evisceration, cuts or protruding bones, off-odor

Source: "Setting Specs (Specifications for Better Seafood Products)" in "Seafood Service: 7 Steps to Selling Seafood," *Restaurant Business* 2 (1 Sept 1993): S12.

Table 7.6

Advantages and Disadvantages of Different Measures of Quality

Advantages	Disadvantages
Quality as Excellence	
Advantages	*Disadvantages*
Promotes clear organizational vision.	Provides little practical guidance for managers.
Being/providing the "best" motivates and inspires managers and employees.	Excellence is ambiguous. What is it? Who defines it?
Appeals to customers, who "know excellence when they see it."	Difficult to measure and control.
Quality as Value	
Advantages	*Disadvantages*
Customers recognize differences in value.	Can be difficult to determine what factors influence whether a product/service is seen as having value.
Easier to measure and compare whether products/services differ in value.	Controlling the balance between excellence and cost (i.e., affordable excellence) can be difficult.
Quality as Conformance to Specifications	
Advantages	*Disadvantages*
If specifications can be written, conformance to specifications is usually measurable.	Many products/services cannot be easily evaluated in terms of conformance to specifications.
Should lead to increased efficiency.	Promotes standardization, so may hurt performance when adapting to changes is more important.
Promotes consistency in quality.	May be less appropriate for services, which are dependent on a high degree of human contact.

Source: C.A. Reeves & D.A. Bednar, "Defining Quality: Alternatives and Implications," *Academy of Management Review* 19 (1994): 419-445.

2. *Material/product substitution*—replacing toxic or hazardous materials with less harmful materials. For example, Maytag redesigned its dishwashers, substituting a molded polypropylene tub and door liner for the porcelain enamel steel tub it had used for years. Not only was the new material cheaper and lighter, but it also eliminated the paint residue and metal sludge that were by-products of the old porcelain enamel steel tub.[65]
3. *Process modification*—changing steps or procedures to eliminate or reduce waste. For example, Coors found ways to make its beer bottles thinner. The results were annual savings of $2 million and a 38-million-pound reduction in the amount of glass used each year to bottle Coors beer.[66]

The second level of waste minimization is *recycle and reuse*. At this level, wastes are reduced by reusing materials as long as possible, or by collecting materials for on- or off-site recycling. For example, Red Spot Paint and Varnish Company, which makes specialized protective coatings for the plastics used in automobiles, was using nearly 1,000 gallons of cleaning solvents in its factory every day. However, through simple trial and error, the company found out that it could reuse the solvents until they contained 15 percent solids (sort of like reusing soapy water until it gets too dirty to clean anymore). This simple change reduced solvent use by 90 percent to just 100 gallons a day.[67]

Figure 7.4 **Four Levels of Waste Minimization**

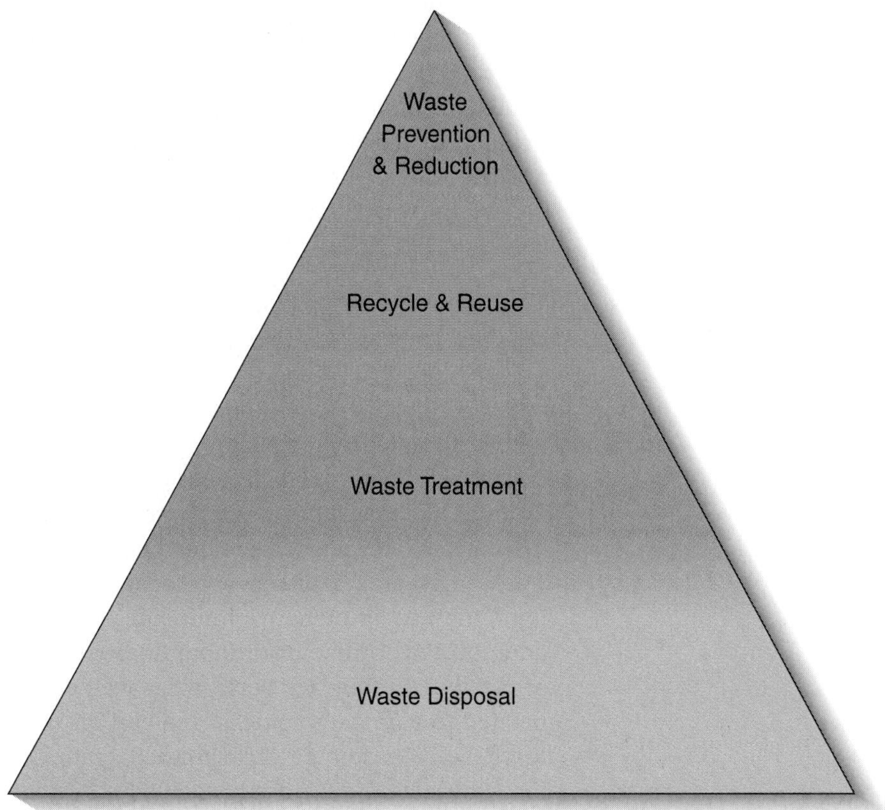

Source: D.R. May & B.L. Flannery, "Cutting Waste with Employee Involvement Teams," *Business Horizons,* September-October 1995, 28-38.

A growing trend in recycling is a process called "design for disassembly," where products are redesigned from the start for easy disassembly, recycling, and reuse once they are no longer usable. For example, by 2003, the European Union will not allow companies to sell products unless the entire product and its packaging can be recovered for recycling. Companies, not consumers, will be held responsible for recycling the products they manufacture. Consequently, cereal makers, car companies, appliance makers, etc., must design their products from the start with recycling in mind.[68]

The third level of waste minimization is *waste treatment*, where companies use biological, chemical, or other processes to turn potentially harmful waste into harmless compounds or useful by-products. For example, one of the processes in the manufacture of steel sheets is called "pickling." Pickling is simply bathing the steel in an acid solution to clean impurities and oxides (that would rust) from the surface of the steel sheet. Getting rid of the "pickle juice" has always been a problem. Not only is the juice an acid, but it also contains ferric chloride and other metals that prevent steel makers from dumping it into local water supplies. Fortunately, Magnetics International has found a safe, profitable way to treat the pickle juice. It sprays the juice into a 100-foot high chamber at 1,200 degrees Fahrenheit. The iron chloride in the juice reacts with oxygen at that temperature to form pure iron oxide, which can be transformed into a useful magnetic powder. Inland Steel is now using this process to transform pickle juice into 25,000 tons of magnetic powder that can be reused in electric motors, stereo speakers, and refrigerator gaskets.[69]

The fourth and last level of waste minimization is *waste disposal.* Wastes that cannot be prevented, reduced, recycled, reused, or treated should be safely disposed of in environmentally secure landfills that prevent leakage and damage to soil and underground water supplies. Contrary to common belief, all businesses, not just manufacturing firms, have waste-disposal problems. For example, although the fluorescent lights used in most businesses are environmentally friendly because they last longer and use less electricity, burned out fluorescent bulbs contain Mercury, a hazardous waste.[70]

Review 4:
What to Control?

Deciding what to control is just as important as deciding whether to control or how to control. In most companies, performance is measured using financial measures alone. However, the balanced scorecard encourages managers to measure and control company performance from four perspectives: financial, customers, internal operations, and innovation and learning. One way to measure financial performance is through economic value added (EVA). Unlike traditional financial measures, EVA helps managers assess whether they are performing well enough to pay the cost of the capital needed to run the business. Instead of using customer satisfaction surveys to measure customer performance, companies should pay attention to customer defectors, who are more likely to speak up about what the company is doing wrong. Performance of internal operations is often measured in terms of quality, which is defined in three ways: excellence, value, and conformance to expectations.[71] Minimization of waste has become an important part of innovation and learning in companies. The four levels of waste minimization are waste prevention and reduction, recycle and reuse, waste treatment, and waste disposal.

What**Really**Happened?

Airline security is a classic control problem, because it involves setting goals and performance standards, comparing actual performance to those goals and standards, and then identifying and correcting performance deviations. With most terrorist acts occurring overseas, neither the Federal Aviation Administration (FAA) nor U.S. airlines have had to pay more than minimal attention to airline security. But with the bombing of the World Trade Center, the federal building in Oklahoma City, and Atlanta's Olympic Centennial Park, no one is taking airline safety for granted anymore. Let's see how the issues surrounding control in organizations affect the way in which airports, airlines, and the FAA try to maintain control of airline safety.

The best place to start is to determine how well airports and airlines are performing when it comes to airline safety and security.

A basic assumption in the control process is that it's possible to measure performance. Indeed, many argue that if the FAA can measure airline performance in terms of on-time arrivals, it should be able to do the same thing with respect to safety and security. In theory, it should. But what's the best way to do it?

For example, would it be best to rank airlines based on safety and security results or by the safety and security procedures that they have in place? Most people would say results. However, results measures can be highly misleading. There just aren't that many safety incidents each year (the average is around 40). Consequently, small changes in year-to-year performance can lead to big changes in safety rankings. For example, TWA, which was the safest airline in 1993, was the least safe in 1994. Was there a huge change in TWA's security and safety practices? Probably not. What bumped TWA from the top of the safety list to the bottom in just one year was that it had two fatal crashes in 1994. In other words, TWA's standings in the rankings probably had more to do with poor circumstances and bad luck than with its actual safety and security practices.

The second problem is how the FAA defines accidents. Right now, an accident is defined as any incident involving a death, serious injury, or substantial damage to an aircraft. Consequently, terrorist attacks, crashes, luggage trucks bumping into planes, and serious burns resulting from spilled coffee are all classified as accidents. At its core, control relies on measures that allow managers to compare actual performance to desired performance. So if the FAA wants to obtain better control over airline safety and security, it will have to do a better job of measuring both.

After determining where the problems are, the next step is to figure out how to solve them. For example, nearly all passengers and carry-on luggage are x-rayed and inspected. However security experts maintain that the biggest risk is from baggage stowed in a plane's storage compartment. So, given this risk, should airports buy expensive machines to x-ray the thousands of pieces of stowed luggage they handle every day?

These questions address a basic issue in the control process: Is control necessary or possible? While there's little argument concerning the increased need to control airline safety and security, there's plenty of disagreement over whether these machines will improve security. For example, InVision Technologies sells a $1 million machine that checks baggage for explosive devices and material. InVision has sold 20 machines to airports in Brussels, London, Manchester, and Manila, and has many more on order for other airports in Asia and Europe. Thus far, however, it has sold only three machines in the U.S. Critics contend that scanning machines can only process a limited number of bags per hour and are just as likely to flag a plastic hair dryer as they are plastique explosive.

Instead of using scanning devices, El Al, Israel's airline, has achieved the best airline security in the world by largely relying on people to do the screening. Luggage is hand-searched. Toothpaste tubes are squeezed. Socks are turned inside out. Baggage is checked for hidden compartments where a bomb might be stored. Suspicious passengers and their luggage are led away and searched in special rooms. All passengers must answer a series of questions designed to identify potential security risks, such as potential terrorists or, more likely, unsuspecting passengers who were tricked into carrying explosive devices onto the plane. In one instance, the questions helped El Al's security agents identify a bomb-carrying German who thought he was smuggling drugs. The bomb would have killed him and everyone else on board.

In some European and Middle Eastern countries, highly paid, highly trained security professionals and

paramilitary forces are in charge of airline security. Should U.S. airports invest in a better-trained, better-paid security force?

There are five different methods of control: bureaucratic, objective, normative, concertive, and self-management. By using highly paid, highly trained security professionals, European and Middle Eastern countries are using normative control, which is based on strong beliefs and careful hiring practices, to strengthen security.

However, in the U.S., the emphasis has been on objective control, where the key measure of performance has been cost, not security. For example, most of the security agents in U.S. airports are paid approximately $7 an hour and receive no more than a half-day of training before beginning their jobs. Many of the workers who perform basic service on the planes or who load and unload cargo are hired at minimum wage. And, to keep hiring costs down, most are hired without having had their backgrounds or work experience checked. Henry DeGeneste, who was the superintendent of the New York-New Jersey Port Authority Police in charge of New York City's three major airports, said, "This is the major hole in the system. I would be less concerned with the luggage screening; what I would be concerned with is what [who] goes on the tarmac. For a terrorist, the best would probably be a job in the catering company, secondly the baggage handlers, the cleaners, too. Anybody that's carrying things on the plane."

Would passengers be willing to pay extra for this level of security? It worked with cars. Customers were willing to pay extra for airbags and anti-lock brakes—in fact, they're now standard equipment on most cars. And how much earlier would passengers be willing to arrive at airports to accommodate security procedures?

Control systems in organizations are traditionally focused on measuring or achieving one major goal. For businesses, that goal is profit. In this case, the goal is safety and security.

The balanced scorecard approach to control argues that all organizations need to measure and control performance in four areas: financial, customers, internal operations, and innovation and learning, instead of just one area. So, when it comes to security, airports and airlines cannot overlook the reactions that travelers have to tighter security procedures. On this topic, Carol Hallett, president of the Air Transport Association, said, "The public is very accepting of longer lines and longer processing times [at airport check-in areas] if they feel it will protect them and improve safety."

Thus far, increased security procedures have produced only longer check-in times, averaging 1–1½ hours. But would American travelers be willing to check in three hours early, as passengers on El Al airline must do? Thus far, there's no clear answer. One traveler, Alan Binder, said, "I would tolerate a 5 percent increase in time and/or money spent on airline travel in order to beef up airport security. This may seem rather cheap (or it may not), but I can't help but feel that this is the maximum amount of increase necessary to truly make airline travel as safe as possible." However, another traveler, John Bresemann, said, "I'm willing to pay a little extra to bring security (especially on international flights) up to par with other countries. But if the purpose is to save lives, the money would be better spent on finding a cure for deadly diseases, or increasing safety in automobiles. The TWA tragedy is terrible, but these tragedies are few and far between. Just because they get more publicity, doesn't make them more important."

Sources: J. Dahl & L. Miller, "Which Is the Safest Airline? It All Depends on Criteria," *The Wall Street Journal Interactive Edition,* 24 July 1996. G. Stoller, "Scanning Luggage for Bombs: More Detectors Prowl Baggage, But Not Enough," *USA Today*, 18 February 1998, 1B. J. Kifner, "Few Checks on Workers with Access to Planes," *New York Times,* 29 July 1996. D. Lenckus & G. Souter, "Risk Managers Review Security: TWA Crash, Olympics Bombing Raise Profile of Terrorism Risk," *Business Insurance,* 5 August 1996. S. McCartney, M. Brannigan, & S. Carey, "Fliers Likely to See Delays, But Not Soaring Fares," *The Wall Street Journal Interactive Edition,* 26 July 1996. "MSNBC Question of the Day: How much more are you prepared to pay in terms of increased air fares, increased time, increased parking fees and the like for more security at airports and on airlines?" MSNBC Web Site. [Online] Available **www.msnbc.com/news/21031.asp**, 1 August 1996.

Key Terms

autonomous work groups p. 249

balanced scorecard p. 253

behavior control p. 246

bureaucratic control p. 245

concertive control p. 248

concurrent control p. 237

control p. 232

control loss p. 238

customer defections p. 258

cybernetic feasibility p. 241

degree of dependence p. 239
economic value added (EVA) p. 254
feedback control p. 236
feedforward control p. 238
normative control p. 247
objective control p. 246
output control p. 247
quasi-control p. 241
reducing dependence p. 241
resource p. 239
resource flow p. 239
restructuring dependence p. 242
self-control (self-management) p. 250
standards p. 233
suboptimization p. 254
value p. 260

What Would You Do-II?

Amherst, Massachusetts.

It's only 9:30, and you've already bugged your assistant for some aspirin to relieve your throbbing headache. This is the third month in a row that your department has failed to meet its performance objectives, and your boss has been on your case again about substandard performance. Another quarter like this, and you know she's going to fire you. As the head of the northeast division for Tom's Terrific Travel, you supervise more than 100 travel agents, who book everything from standard airline reservations to cruises, ski vacations, hotel reservations, and Eurail passes for riding the trains in Europe. Most people think being a travel agent is simple, but it's not. It can take years for travel agents to become familiar with all of the different computer systems used by different industries and companies. Plus, there are hundreds of locations and ever-changing trip packages and promotions to learn. Then there's dealing with the public. Put it all together, and you have a challenging job.

After gulping down the aspirin, you tell your assistant to buzz you when the sales representative from Intec Industries arrives. You're hoping that what Intec has to offer will be the beginning of the end of your problems. The brochures sounded promising; they always do, but you have some serious doubts, too. Intec sells technology that will allow you to electronically monitor the work of your travel agents. Punch a button, and you can immediately listen to your agents as they talk to customers. Click your computer mouse, and real-time graphs appear showing the average number of phone calls, the length of those calls, the number of ticket bookings, and the number and length of work breaks taken by each agent. Activate a program called TTY Watcher, and you can watch what agents are doing on their computers. You can view what's on their screens, and even see what they're typing on their keyboards. Together, the phone and computer technology makes it easy to closely monitor the performance of everyone in the division. You couldn't get better, more up-to-date information if you were looking over their shoulders as they did their jobs.

On the positive side, Intec's technology should help new travel agents get up to speed faster. By monitoring how they deal with customers and how they use the different computer systems, you can quickly identify problems and coach the employees yourself or recommend additional training. In one of its brochures, Intec quotes an employee whose work has been monitored in this manner: "If they see you doing something on the screen that they think you can do a quicker way, they can tell you—they can advise you of it. They can even tell you ways to talk to people, or they can tell you ways to do things quicker to end your call quicker, so it's pretty helpful."

On the negative side, which Intec somehow forgot to mention in its brochure, there's bound to be strong employee resistance. You expect to hear comments about "Big Brother" or the "dark side of the force." You've even read newspaper stories about the stress that these systems cause workers. In some companies, employees have to be taking calls 88 percent of their workday. As soon as one call ends, the automatic forwarding system starts another. And if the calls take too long, or if employees take too long to go the bathroom (indicated by the lack of activity on the phone and computer), Intec's technology records it all.

You desperately need to find a way to improve and control performance in your division. But on the other hand, you rose from the ranks, having been a travel agent for 4 1/2 years before going into management. You know how tough a travel agent's job is. And, frankly, you're not so sure that you'd like your boss to have the capability to monitor your every move in the office. **If you were in charge of the Northeast Division of Tom's Terrific Travel, what would you do?**

Sources: J.R. Aiello & K.J. Kolb, "Electronic Performance Monitoring and Social Context: Impact on Productivity and Stress," *Journal of Applied Psychology* 80 (1995): 339-353. D. Charles, "High-Tech Spy Equipment in the Workplace," *All Things Considered* (National Public Radio), 1 April 1996. T.L. Griffith, "Teaching Big Brother to Be a Team Player: Computer Monitoring and Quality," *Academy of Management Executive* 7 (1993): 73-80. J.R. Hayes, "Memo Busters," *Forbes,* 24 April 1995, 174-175. J.R. Larson, Jr. & C. Callahan, "Performance Monitoring: How It Affects Work Productivity," *Journal of Applied Psychology* 75 (1990): 530-538. J. McKay, "Electronic Slavery," *Pittsburgh Post-Gazette,* 2 July 1995, C1.

Critical-Thinking Video Case

Control: Sunshine Cleaning Systems

In 1976, former professional baseball player, Larry Calufetti, founded Sunshine Cleaning Systems, a privately held company in Fort Lauderdale. Today, Sunshine also has offices in Tampa, Orlando, and West Palm Beach. Sunshine is one of the largest contract cleaning companies in the state of Florida. It cleans entire facilities inside and out. It also specializes in cleaning windows, carpets, ceilings, and even construction sites. Customers include sports facilities, office buildings, stores, malls, the Orlando Convention Center, and the Fort Lauderdale Airport.

In this video, you will learn how Sunshine Cleaning Systems maintains extremely high standards for its key customers while controlling costs. As you watch the video, consider the following critical-thinking questions.

Critical-Thinking Questions

1. What types of effective control systems could Sunshine develop to enable it to provide cost-effective quality service?
2. How could Sunshine control quality through an inspection process?

Management Decisions

Controlling Employee Health Costs

Since 1960, the inflation rate for health care costs has outstripped the overall rate of inflation by 50 to 100 percent year after year. For example, in 1985, the average cost per employee for health benefits was $1,724 per year. Ten years later, the average had more than doubled, to $3,741. Not surprisingly, companies are doing everything they can, from managed care to health maintenance organizations, to cut medical costs.

In the last decade, more companies have turned to wellness programs, which have roots in preventive medicine. Instead of reducing the costs of current medical treatments, or encouraging doctors and hospitals to use lower cost treatments, wellness programs try to reduce costs by preventing employees from getting sick in the first place. Since nearly 70 percent of all illnesses are preventable, wellness programs encourage employees to exercise more, quit smoking, eat a low-fat diet, and manage stress in hopes that these lifestyle changes will help them lose weight, lower cholesterol, lower blood pressure, and reduce the incidence of strokes, heart attacks, cancer, diabetes, and other illnesses. Furthermore, studies show that wellness programs work. Low-risk employees who exercise regularly, quit smoking, eat right, and manage their stress average $200 a year in health claims compared to over $1,600 a year on average for high-risk employees who don't practice these preventive guidelines. Indeed, of the 48 studies on work site wellness programs in the last decade, only one failed to show a cost savings for the company.

Ironically, while studies show that wellness programs do exactly what they're supposed to when employees join them, they also show that it's very difficult to get most employees to actually join and continue to participate in wellness programs. David Anderson, vice president of operations at StayWell Health Management Systems, said, "One of the real problems [confronting] wellness programs is that the healthier employees are the ones more interested in getting involved." Of course, this does little to reduce costs, since these employees are already healthier than most.

Questions

1. Explain how you could use bureaucratic control ideas to encourage more employees, especially those who really need it, to participate in wellness programs.
2. Explain how you could use self-control ideas to encourage more employees, especially those who really need it, to participate in wellness programs.
3. Explain how you could use objective control ideas to encourage more employees, especially those who really need it, to participate in wellness programs.

Sources: L. Litvan, "Preventive Medicine," *Nation's Business*, 1 September 1995, 32. M. Parent, "How to Launch a Corporate Fitness Program," *Boston Business Journal,* 28 June 1996, 39. L. Postman, "Employers Banking on Worker Wellness," *Indianapolis Business Journal,* 10 June 1996, 25. M.A. Robbins, "Giving Workers Healthy Incentives," *Trustee,* 1 February 1996, 30. D. Stokols, K.R. Pelletier, & J.E. Fielding, "Integration of Medical Care and Worksite Health Promotion," *The Journal of the American Medical Association,* 12 April 1995. "Wellness Programs Pay Dividends," *Business & Health,* 1 March 1995, 23.

Management Decisions

Ditch the Life Rafts?

Do you ride your bike without wearing a helmet? Do you drive your car without wearing your seat belt? If you do, it's your choice. But would you choose to fly on an offshore plane if you knew that it didn't have life rafts on board? Several airlines, Delta, Continental, USAir, American, and Alaskan Airlines, have petitioned the FAA for the right to not put life rafts on flights that are never more than 162 miles offshore. Flights from New York to Miami or from Houston to New Orleans, or along the U.S. East Coast and Gulf Coast are examples of such flights. Since the minimum altitude on these flights is 25,000 feet, the airlines argue that jets that lose power to all of their engines (an incredibly rare occurrence) would still be high enough and close enough to the shore to easily glide inland for a safe landing.

The airlines want to remove the rafts to save expenses and fuel. Usually planes are required to have 3–4 rafts on board. With each raft costing about $5,500 and weighing about 100 pounds, the airlines can save approximately $15,000–$20,000 per plane on the cost of rafts plus another $20,000 annually in fuel costs (by eliminating the extra weight). For Delta alone, the savings would be more than $3 million per year. However, critics contend that cost savings should not come before safety. They argue that while passengers' life jackets may keep them afloat if a plane ditches at sea, the passengers could still die of hypothermia in cold waters or from shark attacks in warmer waters. Furthermore, rafts keep passengers together in one place, making search and rescue operations easier.

Additional Internet Resources

- Revere Survival Products (**www.reveresupply.com/**). Follow the link on aviation survival.
- Equipped to Survive: Aviation Life Raft Reviews (**www.equipped.com/avraft.htm**).
- FAA Advisory Circular 120-47: Survival Equipment for Use in Overwater Operations (**http://www.equipped.com/ac120_47.htm**).

Questions

1. If this were your choice to make, would you choose to keep or ditch the life rafts? Use the terms and ideas from the section "Is Control Really Necessary?" to justify your choice.
2. Explain your decision using the balanced scorecard approach to control.

Sources: J.S. Hirsch, "Airlines Ditch Life Rafts on Some Flights to Cut Costs," *The Wall Street Journal Europe,* 6 January 1995, 4. Reuters News Service, "Delta Cuts Life Rafts from Offshore Flights," *Houston Post,* 6 January 1995, C1. Reuters News Service, "Flights to Skip Life Rafts," *Calgary Herald,* 6 January 1995, D3. "US Airlines Remove Life Rafts on Some Over-Water Flights to Save Money," *Agence France-Presse*, 5 January 1995.

Develop Your Management Potential

Learning from Failure

"There is the greatest practical benefit of making a few failures early in life." —T.H. Huxley

No one wants to fail. Everyone wants to succeed. However, some business people believe that failure can have enormous value. At Microsoft, founder and CEO Bill Gates encourages his managers to hire people who have made mistakes in their jobs or careers. A Microsoft vice president said, "We look for somebody who learns, adapts, and is active in the process of learning from mistakes. We always ask, what was a major failure you had? What did you learn from it?" Another reason that failure is viewed positively is that it is often a sign of risk taking and experimentation, both of which are in short supply in many companies. John Kotter, a Harvard Business School professor says, "I can imagine a group of executives 20 years ago discussing a candidate for a top job and saying, 'This guy had a big failure when he was 32.' Everyone else would say, 'Yep, yep, that's a bad sign.' I can imagine that same group considering a candidate today and saying, 'What worries me about this guy is that he's never failed.' " Jack Matson, who teaches a class at the University of Michigan called Failure 101, says, "If you are doing something innovative, you are going to trip and fumble. So the more failing you do faster, the quicker you can get to success."

One of the most common mistakes that occurs after failure is the *attribution error*. An *attribution* is to assign blame or credit. When we succeed, we take credit for the success by owning up to our strategies, how we behaved, and how hard we worked. However, when we fail, we ignore our strategies, or how we behaved, or how hard we worked (or didn't). Instead, when we fail, we assign the blame to other people, or to the circumstances, or to bad luck. In other words, the basic attribution error is that success is our fault but failure isn't. The disappointment we feel when we fail often prevents us from learning from our failures.

What this means is that attribution errors disrupt the control process. The three basic steps of control are to set goals and performance standards, to compare actual performance to performance standards, and to identify and correct performance deviations. When we put all of the blame on external forces rather than our own actions, we stop ourselves from identifying and correcting performance deviations. Furthermore, by not learning from our mistakes, we make it even more likely that we will fail again.

Your task in this Developing Your Management Potential is to begin the process of learning from failure. This is not an easy thing to do. When *Fortune* magazine writer Patricia Sellers wrote an article called "So You Fail," she found most of the people she contacted reluctant to talk about their failures. She wrote,

> *Compiling this story required months of pleading and letter writing to dozens of people who failed and came back. 'If it weren't for the 'F' word, I'd talk,' lamented one senior executive who got fired twice, reformed his know-it-all management style, and considered bragging about his current hot streak. Others cringed at hearing the word "failure" in the same breath as "your career."*

Questions

1. Identify and describe a point in your life when you failed. Don't write about simple or silly mistakes. The difference between a failure and a mistake is how badly you felt afterwards. Years afterwards, a real failure still makes you cringe when you think about it. What was the situation? What were your goals? And how did it turn out?

2. Describe your initial reaction to the failure. Were you shocked, surprised, angry, or depressed? Initially, who or what did you blame for the failure? Explain.

3. One purpose of control is to identify and correct performance deviations. With that in mind, describe three mistakes that you made that contributed to your failure. Now that you've had time to think about it, what would you have done differently to prevent these mistakes? Finally, summarize what you learned from your mistakes that will increase your chances of success the next time around.

Sources: S. Caulkin, "If You Want to Stay a Winner, Learn from Your Mistakes," *The Observer,* 3 March 1996, 7. J. Hyatt, "Failure 101," *Inc.,* January 1989, 18. B. McMenamin, "The Virtue of Making Mistakes," *Forbes,* 9 May 1994, 192-194. P. Sellers, "So You Fail," *Fortune,* 1 May 1995, 48-66. P. Sellers, "Where Failures Get Fixed," *Fortune,* 1 May 1995, 64. B. Weiner, I. Freize, A. Kukla, L. Reed, S. Rest, & R.M. Rosenbaum, "Perceiving the Causes of Success and Failure," in *Attribution: Perceiving the Causes of Behavior,* eds. E. Jones, D. Kanouse, H. Kelley, R. Nesbitt, S. Valins, and B. Weiner (Morristown, NJ: General Learning Press, 1971): 45-61.

Part Three

Meeting the Competition

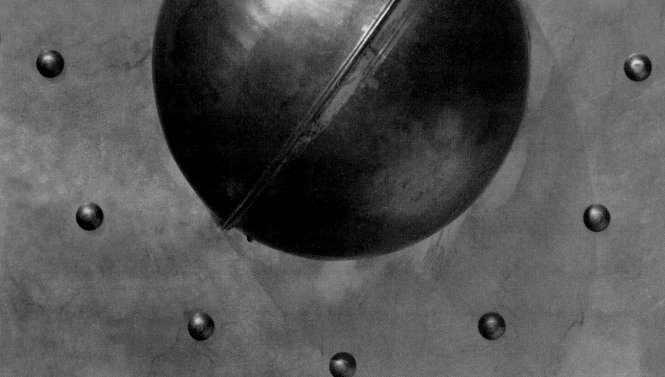

Chapter Eight

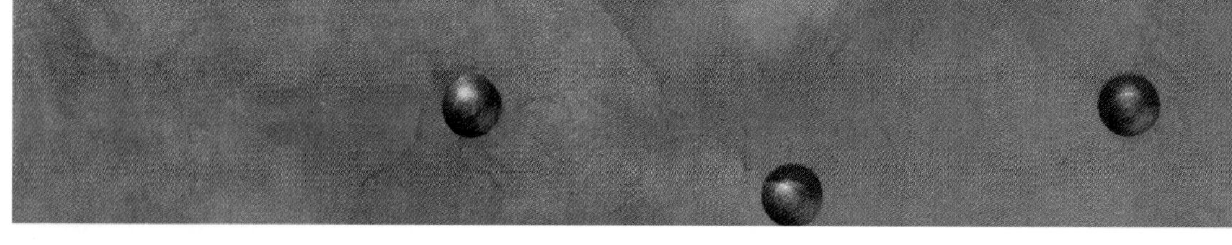

Chapter 8 Outline

Global Management

What Would **You** Do?

McDonald's Plaza, Oak Brook, IL. McDonald's opens more than 2,000 new restaurants each year, roughly one every four hours. Furthermore, 85 percent of those new stores open *outside* the U.S. As head of McDonald's International, you have been charged with continuing that growth by setting up new McDonald's in Hungary, Poland, the Czech Republic, Slovakia, Romania, Bulgaria, and East Germany. The plan is to add 700 restaurants in Eastern Europe over the next three years. Of course, you have done this before. After all, McDonald's already has more than 12,000 foreign stores. But this is different. Most of McDonald's foreign stores are in Japan, Canada, Great Britain, West Germany, Australia, and France, all thriving industrial economies. In contrast, even a decade after the fall of communism, transportation systems in Eastern Europe are poor, and basic farm produce, such as potatoes, tomatoes, lettuce, and onions, is scarce. Furthermore, the produce you can buy doesn't come close to meeting the high standards that McDonald's maintains in every store worldwide. Even worse, since the communist system guaranteed everyone a job (firing workers was nearly impossible), and since it paid workers the same no matter how much they produced or the quality of what they produced, you wonder if three decades of communist rule has ruined the work ethic. Will you be able to get workers who will smile, work hard, or even know what quick, efficient, courteous customer service is? You turn the TV off and sit at your desk to plan McDonald's "invasion" of Eastern Europe. At the top of your notepad you have written "Key Decisions." Should you import your supplies from the U.S. or from Western Europe, or try to obtain them locally? Should you hire local workers and managers? If you do, how will you train them? Which countries should you enter first, and why? Should you set up company-owned stores, or look for local investors who pay for the rights to a McDonald's franchise? Or, should you set up joint ventures? Finally, will you have to make changes in your menu to adapt to local tastes and traditions? **If you were the head of McDonald's International, what would you do?**

Sources: S. Chandler, "Foreign Woes Shadow McDonald's 2nd Quarter," *Chicago Tribune*, 21 July 1998. "Bloomberg News. McDonald's to Continue to Expand in Asia Restaurants," *Los Angeles Times*, 10 April 10 1998, D3. R. Gibson, "McDonald's Profit Rises 19% on Boom in Business Abroad," *The Wall Street Journal,* 26 January 1996, A4. R. Gibson, "For McDonald's, 11 Nations Have 85% of Outlets," *The Wall Street Journal Europe,* 3 April 1998, 6. R. Gibson & M. Moffett, "Why You Won't Find Any Egg McMuffins for Breakfast in Brazil," *The Wall Street Journal,* 23 October 1997, A1. A.E. Serwer, "McDonald's Conquers the World," *Fortune,* 17 October 1994, 103–116. J. Whalen, "McDonald's Salivates at Overseas Potential," *Crain's Chicago Business,* 31 July 1995.

McDonald's expansion into Eastern Europe is an example of the key issue in global business: How can you be sure that the way you run your business in one country is the right way to run that business in another? This chapter discusses how organizations make those decisions. We will start by examining global business in two ways: first, by exploring its impact on U.S. businesses; and second, by reviewing the basic rules and agreements that govern global trade. Next, we will examine how and when companies go global by examining the tradeoff between consistency and adaptation, and by discussing how to organize a global company. Finally, we will look at how companies decide where to expand globally. Here, we will examine how to find the best business climate, the importance of adapting to cultural differences, and how to better prepare employees for international assignments.

What Is Global Business?

global business
the buying and selling of goods and services by people from different countries

Business is the buying and selling of goods or services. Buying this textbook was a business transaction. So was selling your first car. So was getting paid for babysitting or for mowing lawns. **Global business** is the buying and selling of goods and services by people from different countries. The Timex watch on my wrist as I write this chapter was purchased at a Wal-Mart in Texas. But since it was made in the Philippines, I participated in global business when I wrote Wal-Mart a check. Wal-Mart, in turn, paid Timex, which then paid the company that employs the Filipino managers and workers who made my watch.

Of course, there is more to global business than buying imported products at Wal-Mart. After reading these next two sections, you should be able to:

1. describe the **impact of global business** on the U.S.
2. discuss the **trade rules and agreements** that govern global trade.

1 Impact of Global Business

You are shopping at the local mall. Someone with a clipboard asks you to respond to this short questionnaire about global business. Mark your answers true or false.

1.1. _____ *"Foreigners," especially the Japanese, are buying up American companies at an astounding rate, and now control a large part of our economy.*

1.2. _____ *American companies are no longer competitive in the world market, especially in high-tech industries.*

1.3. _____ *If given a choice, Americans will buy American-made goods rather than foreign-made goods.*

National polls show that nearly half of all Americans want to prevent foreign companies from buying U.S. companies that have developed new technologies. The polls also show that 62 percent of Americans want to protect U.S. companies from foreign competition and that more than 87 percent believe that Japan is far ahead of the U.S. in exporting high-technology products. Of the Americans polled, 85 percent say they will try to buy American-made products when they have a choice.[1] Overall, 58 percent believe that foreign trade has been bad for the U.S. economy.[2] So if you responded like most Americans, you probably answered "true" to each question. However, none of the statements in our short questionnaire accurately describes the influence of global business in the U.S. Let's see why.

1.1

"Foreigners," especially the Japanese, are buying up American companies at an astounding rate, and now control a large part of our economy.

direct foreign investment a method of investment in which a company builds a new business or buys an existing business in a foreign county

Direct foreign investment is a method of investment in which a company builds a new business or buys an existing business in a foreign country. Kao corporation, maker of Japanese laundry detergent and body soaps and shampoos, made a direct foreign investment when it purchased Andrew Jergens Company, which makes hair- and skin-care products.

With polls showing that, by 64 percent to 16 percent, Americans believe that Asian countries engage in unfair trade practices, it's not surprising that newspapers periodically run stories proclaiming that the "Japanese are Buying America."[3] In reality, though, the headlines should read, "Foreign Invasion: The World Buys America," because companies from Germany, Belgium, England, Canada, Mexico, and many other countries own businesses in the U.S. Figure 8.1 shows which countries have the largest direct foreign investment in the U.S. Contrary to common opinion, companies from the United Kingdom, not Japan, have the largest investments in the U.S. In fact, Japanese investment represents only 19 percent of all direct foreign investment in the U.S.

Figure 8.1 **Direct Foreign Investment in the U.S., Five-Year Average, 1993–1997**

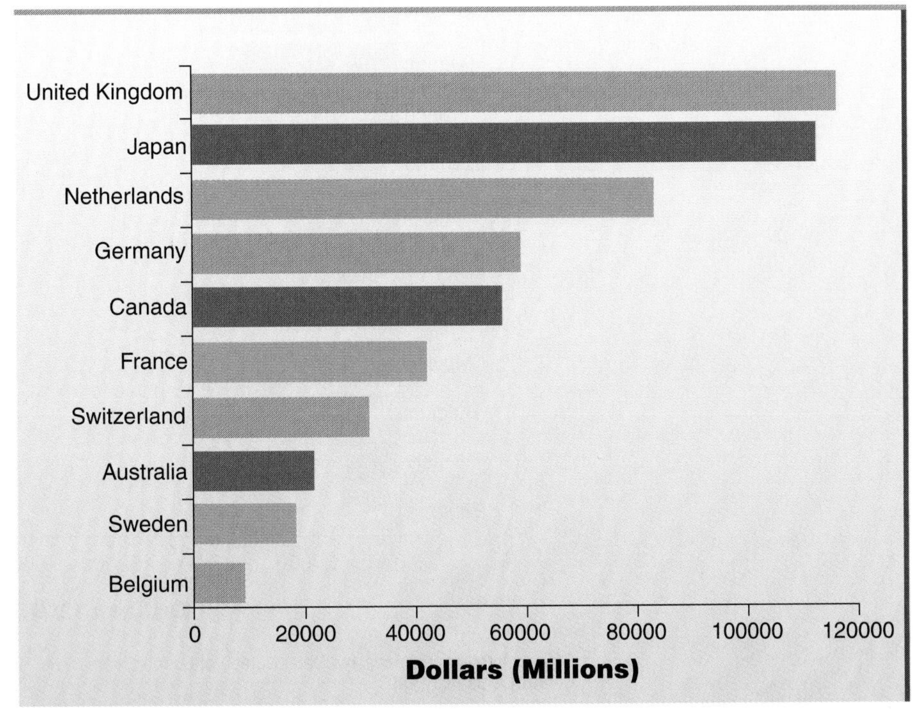

Source: International Accounts Data, Bureau of Economic Analysis. [Online] Available **www.bea.doc.gov/bea/di1.htm**, 9 January 1998.

However, direct foreign investment in the U.S. is just half the picture. U.S. companies also have made large direct foreign investments in businesses throughout the world. Figure 8.2 shows that U.S. companies have made their largest direct foreign investments in the United Kingdom, the Netherlands, Germany, Japan, France, and Switzerland. In fact, U.S. companies have invested *more* abroad than *all* the foreign companies combined that have invested in the U.S. Furthermore, a United Nations study found that direct foreign investment of U.S. companies was four times greater than Japanese companies and double that of British companies.[4] These figures make it clear that Americans have misplaced fears about direct foreign investment. Perhaps the newspaper headlines should read, "Yankee Invasion, U.S.A. Buys the World."

Overall, direct foreign investment throughout the world has *more than doubled* in the last decade. So whether foreign companies invest in the U.S. or U.S. companies invest abroad, direct foreign investment is an increasingly important and common method of conducting global business.

1.2

American companies are no longer competitive in the world market, especially in high-tech industries.

Nearly 90 percent of Americans consider this a serious problem. However, data from the National Science Board, shown in Figure 8.3, show that U.S. companies lead Japan, Germany, France, the United Kingdom, China, and

Figure 8.2 **U.S. Direct Foreign Investment Abroad, 1997**

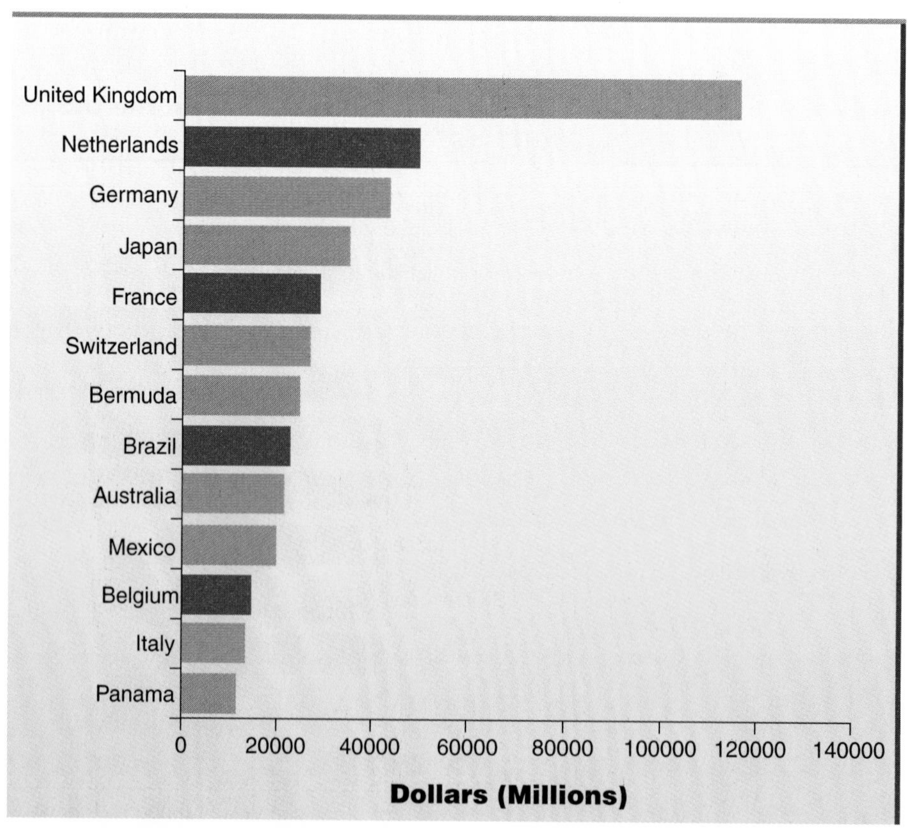

Source: International Accounts Data, Bureau of Economic Analysis. [Online] Available **www.bea.doc.gov/bea/di1.htm**, 9 January 1999.

Figure 8.3 **Global High-Technology Market Share**

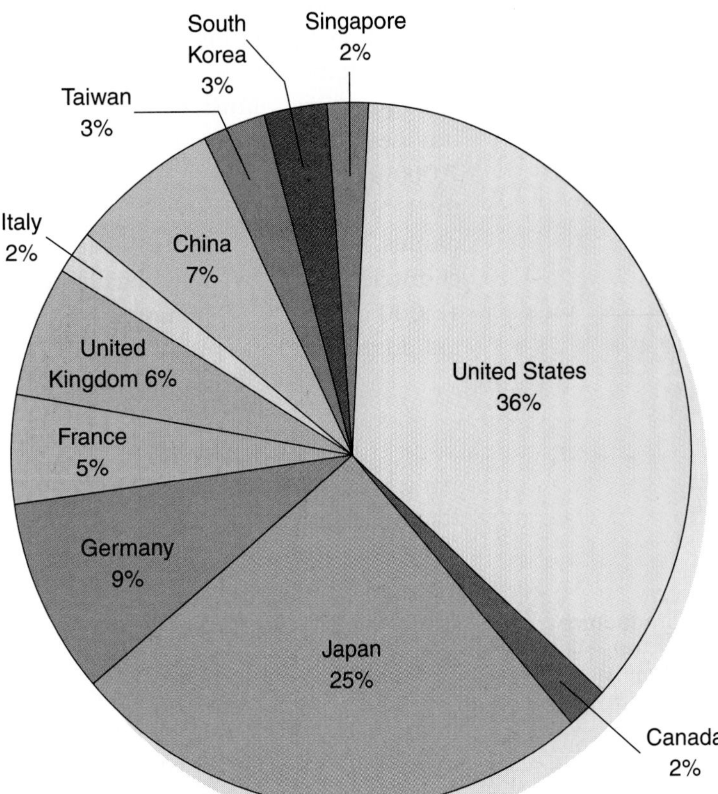

Source: Science & Engineering Indicators, 1998. National Science Board. [Online] Available **www.nsf.gov/sbe/srs/seind98/frames.htm**, 9 January 1998.

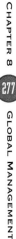

South Korea in global high-technology market share. Furthermore, the U.S. share of the global high-technology markets has increased, not decreased, since 1980. By 1995, U.S. high-tech companies were market leaders in four out of the seven global high-technology industries: aircraft, scientific instruments, computers and office equipment, and pharmaceuticals.[5]

So why do most Americans believe that the U.S. is falling behind the rest of the world? It may be because U.S. companies once dominated global markets. Immediately following World War II, U.S. companies accounted for 75 percent of the **world gross national product**. World GNP is the value of all the goods and services produced annually worldwide. While U.S. companies continued to dominate world trade through the early 1960s, by the early 1990s, U.S. companies produced only 19.4 percent of the world's gross national product.[6]

world gross national product
the value of all the goods and services produced annually worldwide

To many Americans, the drop from 75 percent to 19.4 percent of world GNP is proof of U.S. industrial decline. However, these figures suggest much more about the rest of the world's economy than they do about the U.S. economy. After the war, U.S. companies faced little competition. Bombing had destroyed factories throughout Japan, Europe, and Russia. By contrast, not one manufacturing plant was destroyed in the continental U.S. With foreign competitors having to rebuild, literally from the ground up, is it any wonder that U.S. companies dominated the world market then?

Today, in contrast to the postwar global economy, U.S. companies face stiff competition throughout the world. The economies of France, Germany, Italy,

Japan, and the United Kingdom, which the war decimated, are now part of a group of seven countries that account for more than 70 percent of the world's GNP (Canada and the U.S. are the other two members). This is roughly the same portion of world GNP controlled by the U.S. alone following the war.

Another sign of increased competition in world markets is the *number* of multinational corporations and *where* those multinational corporations are headquartered. **Multinational corporations** are corporations that own businesses in two or more countries. In 1970, more than half the world's 7,000 multinational corporations were headquartered in just two countries, the U.S. and Britain. Today, there are more than 35,000 multinational companies.[7] Roughly 17,000 of the multinationals are headquartered in four countries: Switzerland, Germany, Japan, and the U.S. The remaining 18,000 multinationals, more than two and a half times the number of multinationals in 1970, are headquartered throughout the rest of the world!

multinational corporation
corporation that owns businesses in two or more countries

1.3

If given a choice, Americans will buy American-made goods rather than foreign-made goods.

Americans say they prefer to "buy American," but if they do, why does the demand for imported products increase year after year? There are a number of potential explanations. The first is that consumers often don't know or pay attention to **country of manufacture** when making purchases. Stop reading for a minute. Take your shoes off. Where were they made? What about the VCR in your house, or your computer, or your backpack? Did you learn where these products were manufactured before you purchased them? Chances are, you didn't. Many consumers don't know or care about country of manufacture.

country of manufacture
country where product is made and assembled

A second explanation for rising imports is that consumers want to buy American and think they are buying American but, in fact, are unknowingly buying imported products. For example, take your Uncle Fred, who bleeds red, white, and blue. That Chrysler minivan in his driveway—he bought it because it was a good "American" car. However, Chrysler assembles most of its minivans in Canada. That Honda Accord Uncle Fred's been giving you a hard time about—it was made in Marysville, Ohio. Uncle Fred has confused the country of manufacture, where the product is made, with the **country of origin**, which is the company's home country. However, this is an easy mistake to make in today's global marketplace.

country of origin
the home country for a company, where its headquarters is located

The third explanation for the continued increases in sales of imported products is that consumers know that many products they purchase are imported, but they just don't care. For example, until recently, Japan had closed its markets to foreign-grown apples, claiming that imported apples contained insects that would infest Japanese orchards. With no foreign competition, Japanese apples were expensive, about $5 for a bag of six "bargain" apples, and about $6 for a flawless, gourmet apple. The president of the Aomori Apple Association said, "This is Japanese culture. Japanese don't want apples with scratches or uneven color, even if they taste fine." However, Japan is now allowing apples to be imported from "approved" apple orchards in Washington state. If the president of the Aomori Apple Association is wrong, Japanese consumers will buy American apples because they cost about a third less. Early indications are that value will win out. Sadako Watanabe, a Japanese grandmother, said, "If they taste good, I'll keep buying them."[8]

Review 1: *Impact of Global Business*

Contrary to common opinion, the Japanese don't "own" a disproportionate share of U.S. assets, American companies are competitive in world markets, and consumers are less concerned with patriotism than value. In the last decade, direct foreign investment has doubled, making world markets much more competitive than they used to be. Yet despite this competition, American companies (and German companies, and Japanese companies, and . . .) continue to expand to meet the demands of consumer-driven world markets.

2 Trade Rules and Agreements

The rules governing global trade are many and complex, and have changed tremendously in the last few years.

Let's learn about **2.1** *the various kinds of tariff and nontariff trade barriers,* **2.2** *the global and regional trade agreements that are reducing trade barriers worldwide, and* **2.3** *how consumers are responding to these unprecedented changes in trade rules and agreements.*

2.1 *Trade Barriers*

trade barriers
government-imposed regulations that increase the cost and restrict the number of imported goods

protectionism
a government's use of trade barriers to shield domestic companies and their workers from foreign competition

tariff
a direct tax on imported goods

Although most consumers don't especially care where the products they buy come from, national governments have preferred that consumers buy domestically made products in hopes that such purchases would increase the number of domestic businesses and workers. However, governments have done much more than hope that you buy from domestic companies. For most of this century, governments have actively used **trade barriers** to make it much more difficult or expensive (or sometimes impossible) for you to buy imported goods. For example, the Canadian government placed an 80 percent excise tax on the Canadian editions of U.S. magazines. Many "Canadian" magazines, such as *Time* or *Newsweek*, are simply U.S. editions that have been repackaged for the Canadian market by replacing a few U.S. stories with a few Canadian stories. Canadian magazine publishers encouraged their government to enact the excise tax. They knew that given a choice between a Canadian sports magazine and *Sports Illustrated Canada*, which now costs nearly twice as much, thanks to the excise tax, most Canadian sports fans would buy the Canadian magazine. In fact, because of this excise tax, the Canadian edition of *Sports Illustrated Canada* is no longer published. By establishing this tax, the Canadian government engaged in **protectionism**, which is the use of trade barriers to protect local companies and their workers from foreign competition.[9]

Governments have used two general kinds of trade barriers: tariff and nontariff barriers. A **tariff** is a direct tax on imported goods. Like the Canadian excise tax on U.S. magazines, tariffs increase the cost of imported goods relative to domestic goods. For example, the U.S. import tax on trucks is 25 percent. This means that U.S. buyers will pay $25,000 for a $20,000

nontariff barriers nontax methods of increasing the cost or reducing the volume of imported goods

quota limit on the number or volume of imported products

voluntary export restraints voluntarily imposed limits on the number or volume of products exported to a particular country

Toyota T-1 truck, with the $5,000 tariff going to the U.S. government. **Nontariff barriers** are nontax methods of increasing the cost or reducing the volume of imported goods. There are five types of nontariff barriers: quotas, voluntary export restraints, government standards, government subsidies, and customs valuation/classification. Because there are so many different kinds of nontariff barriers, they can be an even more potent method of shielding domestic industries from foreign competition.

Quotas are specific limits on the number or volume of imported products. For example, the U.S. places quotas on the number of Chinese area rugs that can be imported each year. Yet demand for these rugs is so strong that they often reach the quota limit in August or September. Once they reach this quota, importation of Chinese rugs is forbidden until January 1 of the next year.

Voluntary export restraints are similar to quotas in that there is a limit on how much of a product can be imported annually. The difference is that the exporting country rather than the importing country imposes the limit. However, the "voluntary" offer to limit imports usually occurs because of the implicit threat of forced trade quotas by the importing country. For example, the European Union holds yearly "monitoring talks" with Japanese auto manufacturers to discuss limits on the number of imported Japanese cars. When the sales of European-made cars fell significantly, the Japanese "voluntarily" agreed to cut their imports by 100,000 cars.[10] However, according to the World Trade Organization (see the discussion on the General Agreement on Trade and Tariffs below), countries should have phased out voluntary export restraints after 1999.[11]

In theory, government standards are specified for imports to protect the health and safety of citizens. In reality, government standards are often used to restrict or ban imported goods. For example, China is the only nation in the world that requires U.S.-grown grain to be 100 percent fungus free. Although preventing the importation of a fungus-infected agricultural product sounds reasonable enough, having a very small percentage of fungus is normal for harvested wheat. Since there is no chance that the fungus

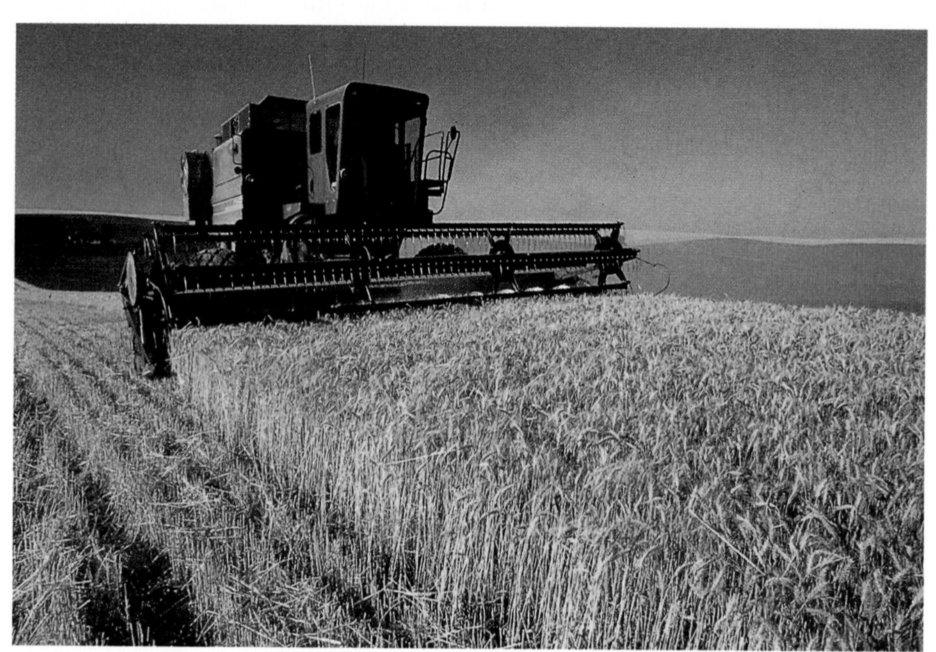

Government standards can protect citizens from unhealthy foreign imports, but sometimes governments apply unreasonable standards, such as 100 percent fungus-free wheat, to protect domestic growers. © 1995 Bill Stormont/The Stock Market

Personal Productivity Tip

Customs and Carnet

When you travel, you can take home $400 worth of souvenirs duty-free (i.e., tax-free). After $400, the duty is 10 percent. Over $1,400, the duty depends on the item. However, you don't want to be charged a duty on items used in your business, like samples or professional equipment. To avoid duties on these items, apply for a *carnet* (car-nay) that allows duty-free admission of business goods into a country and duty-free re-admission when you return home. In Europe, a carnet saves the expense of import tariffs and value-added taxes (roughly 20 percent). To find out more, call the U.S. Council for International Business, 1-800-227-6387.

Sources: U.S. Customs Service, "Know Before You Go." [Online] Available **www.customs.ustreas.gov/text/travel/kbygo.htm**, 24 January 1999. U.S. Council for International Business, "Welcome to the World of Dutyfree Exports: ATA Carnet —The Merchandise Passport." [Online] Available **www.imex.com/uscib/carnet/carnet.htm**, 24 January 1999.

will spread once wheat has been harvested, and since China is the only nation to insist on this standard, the Chinese government is actually using this government standard to protect the economic health of its wheat farmers, rather than the physical health of its consumers.[12]

Many nations also use **subsidies**, such as long-term, low-interest loans, cash grants, and tax deferments, to develop and protect companies in special industries. European and Japanese governments have invested billions of dollars to develop airplane manufacturers and steel companies, while the U.S. government has provided subsidies for manufacturers of computer chips. Not surprisingly, businesses complain about unfair trade practices when other companies receive government subsidies. For example, Boeing Corporation, the world's largest manufacturer of commercial airplanes, frequently complains to U.S. government officials about the millions of dollars in direct government subsidies that Airbus, a European manufacturer of commercial airplanes, receives each year from European governments.[13]

The last nontariff barrier is customs classification. As products are imported into a country, they are examined by customs agents, who must decide into which of nearly 9,000 categories they should classify a product. Classification is important, because the category assigned by customs agents can affect the size of the tariff and consideration of import quotas. For example, the U.S. Customs Service changed the tariff on 33,000 girls' ski jackets because corduroy trim had been sewn on the jackets' sleeves. Without the trim, they would have classified the jackets as "garments designed for rain wear, hunting, fishing, or similar uses," which have a tariff of only 10.6 percent. Yet with the trim, they categorized the jackets as "other girls' wearing apparel" and earned a higher tariff of 27.5 percent.[14]

2.2 *Trade Agreements*

Thanks to the trade barriers described above, buying imported goods has often been much more expensive and difficult than buying domestic goods. However, the regulations governing global trade were transformed in the 1990s. The most significant change was that 124 countries agreed to adopt the **General Agreement on Tariffs and Trade (GATT)**.

subsidies
government loans, grants, and tax deferments given to domestic companies to protect them from foreign competition

Through tremendous decreases in tariff and nontariff barriers, GATT will make it much easier and cheaper for consumers in all countries to buy foreign products. First, by the year 2005, GATT will cut average tariffs worldwide by 40 percent. Second, GATT will eliminate tariffs in ten specific industries: beer, alcohol, construction equipment, farm machinery, furniture, medical equipment, paper, pharmaceuticals, steel, and toys. Third, GATT puts stricter limits on government subsidies. For example, GATT places limits on how much national governments can subsidize company research in electronic and high-technology industries. Fourth, GATT protects intellectual property such as trademarks, patents, and copyright. Protection of intellectual property has been an increasingly important issue in global trade because of widespread product piracy. For example, Chinese bootleggers were selling illegal copies of Disney's *The Lion King* and *Mulan* videos even *before* Disney could get its official copies to stores in the United States.[15] Product piracy like this costs companies billions in lost revenue each year. Finally, trade disputes between countries will be fully settled by arbitration panels from the World Trade Organization. In the past, countries could ignore arbitration panel rulings by using their veto power to cancel arbitration

GATT (General Agreement on Tariffs and Trade)
worldwide trade agreement that will reduce and eliminate tariffs, limit government subsidies, and protect intellectual property

decisions. For instance, the French government has routinely vetoed rulings that it unfairly subsidized French farmers with extraordinarily large cash grants. However, countries that are members of the World Trade Organization (every country that agrees to GATT is a member) will no longer have veto power. Thus, World Trade Organization rulings will be complete and final. For more information about GATT and the World Trade Association (WTO), go to the WTO web site at **www.wto.org**.

regional trading zones areas in which tariff and nontariff barriers on trade between countries are reduced or eliminated

The second major development in the historic move toward reduction of trade barriers has been the creation of **regional trading zones**, in which tariff and nontariff barriers are reduced or eliminated for countries within the trading zone. The largest and most important trading zones are in Europe (the Maastricht Treaty), North America (the North American Free Trade Agreement, NAFTA), South America (the Free Trade Area of the Americas, FTAA), and Asia (ASEAN, Association of South East Nations, and APEC, Asia-Pacific Economic Cooperation). The map in Figure 8.4 shows the extent to which free trade agreements govern global trade.

Maastricht Treaty of Europe regional trade agreement between most European countries

In 1992, the countries of Belgium, France, Germany, Italy, Luxembourg, the Netherlands, Denmark, Ireland, United Kingdom, Greece, Portugal, and Spain implemented the **Maastricht Treaty of Europe**. The purpose of this treaty was to transform their 12 different economies and 12 currencies into

Figure 8.4 **Global Map of Regional Trade Agreements**

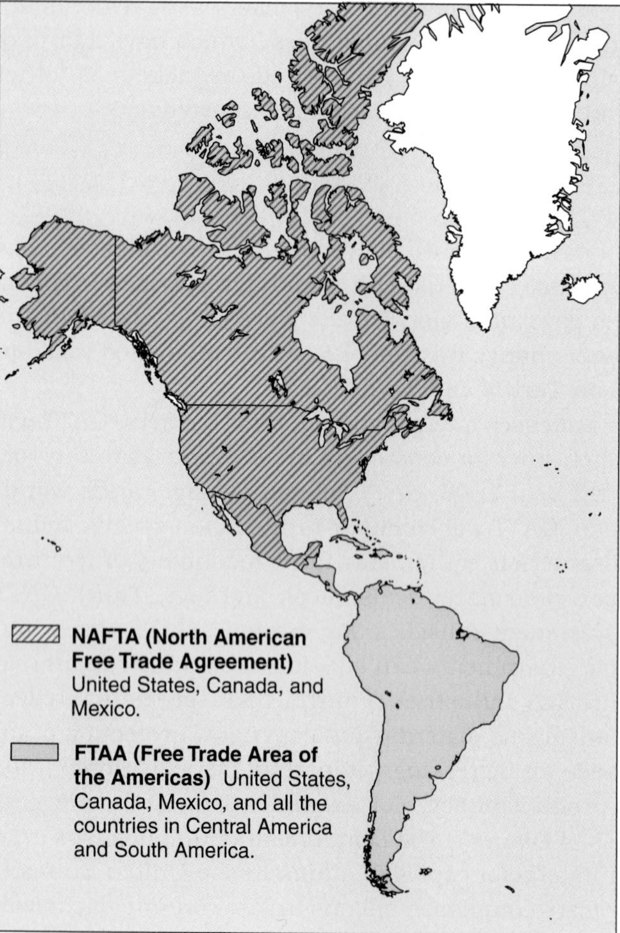

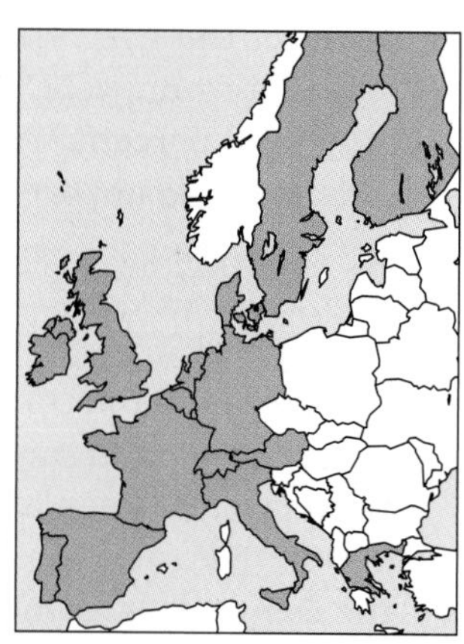

Maastricht Treaty of Europe Belgium, France, Germany, Italy, Luxembourg, Netherlands, Denmark, Ireland, United Kingdom, Greece, Portugal, Spain, Austria, Finland, and Sweden.

ASEAN Indonesia, Thailand, Philippines, Malaysia, Singapore, and Brunei.

APEC Indonesia, Thailand, Philippines, Malaysia, Singapore, Brunei, United States, Canada, Japan, South Korea, Australia, New Zealand, China, Taiwan, and Hong Kong.

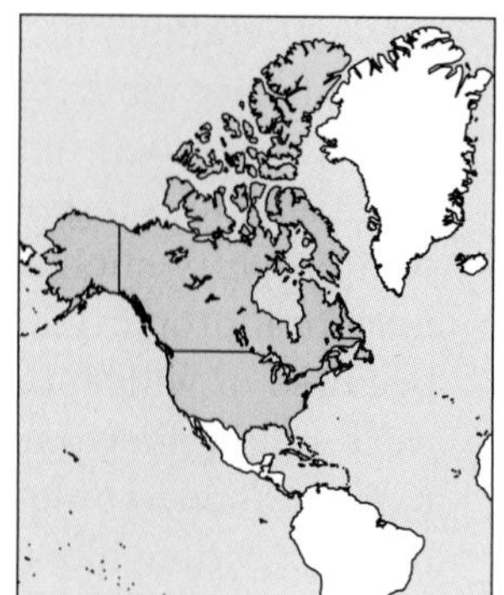

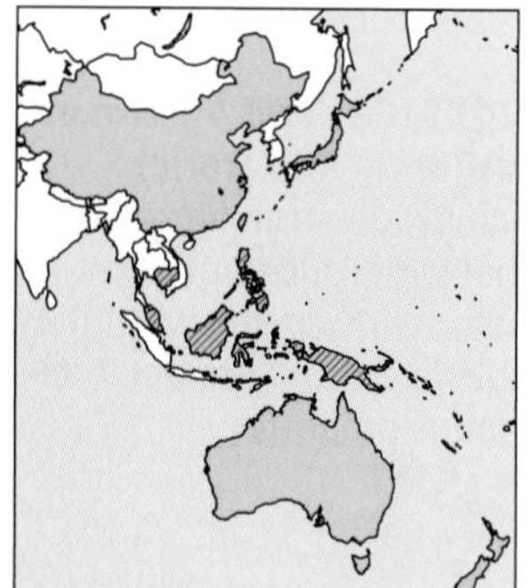

one common economic market, called the European Union, and one common currency, the euro. Austria, Finland, and Sweden are now members, too.[16]

Prior to the treaty, trucks carrying products were stopped and inspected by customs agents at each border. Furthermore, since the required paperwork, tariffs, and government product specifications could be radically different in each country, companies often had to file 12 different sets of paperwork, pay 12 different tariffs, and produce 12 different versions of their basic product to meet various government specifications.

Likewise, open business travel, which we take for granted in the U.S. as we travel from state to state, was complicated by inspections at each border crossing. For example, if you lived in Germany, but worked across the border in Luxembourg, your car was stopped and your passport was inspected twice a day, every day, as you traveled to and from work. Also, every business transaction required a currency exchange, for example, from German deutsche marks to Italian lira, or from French francs to British pounds. Imagine all of this happening to millions of trucks, cars, and business people, and you can begin to appreciate the difficulty and cost of conducting business across Europe before the Maastricht Treaty.

For more information about the Maastricht treaty and the European Union, go to *http://europa.eu.int/index-en.htm.* For more about Europe's new currency, the euro, which, by July 1, 2002, will replace the currencies of 11 countries (Austria, Belgium, Finland, France, Germany, Ireland, Italy, Luxembourg, Netherlands, Portugal, and Spain), see **http://europa.eu.int/euro/html/home5.html?lang=5**.

NAFTA (North American Free Trade Agreement) regional trade agreement between the United States, Canada, and Mexico

NAFTA, the **North American Free Trade Agreement** between the United States, Canada, and Mexico, went into effect January 1, 1994. More than any other regional trade agreement, NAFTA liberalizes trade between countries so that businesses can plan for one market, North America, rather than for three separate markets, the U.S., Canada, and Mexico. One of NAFTA's most important achievements was to eliminate most product tariffs. On January 1, 1994, product tariffs were eliminated on the first and

NAFTA has paved the way for goods to flow freely between Mexico, Canada, and the United States.

largest group of products traded among the three countries. The result? Just six months after NAFTA went into effect, U.S. exports were up by 10 percent to Canada and 17 percent to Mexico. Overall, both Mexican and Canadian exports to the U.S. have doubled since NAFTA went into effect.[17] In fact, trade between Mexico and the U.S. is so strong that more than 2,500 eighteen-wheeler trucks full of U.S. and Mexican products cross the border at Laredo, Texas, each day.[18] Cross-border traffic is heavy between the U.S. and Canada, too. Canadian Pacific, one of Canada's largest railroad companies, saw an immediate 10 percent increase in its north-south shipments after NAFTA went into effect.

The second set of NAFTA product tariffs was eliminated in 1998, with the third and final set to be eliminated in 2003. Importantly, NAFTA also prevents Canada, the U.S., and Mexico from increasing existing tariffs or introducing new tariffs. For more information about NAFTA, see **www.sice.oas.org/trade/nafta/naftatce.stm.**

FTAA (Free Trade Area of the Americas) regional trade agreement that, when signed, will create a regional trading zone encompassing 36 countries in North and South America

The goal of **FTAA**, **Free Trade Area of the Americas**, is to establish a free trade zone similar to NAFTA throughout the Western Hemisphere. If created, FTAA would be the largest trading zone in the world, consisting of 850 million people in 36 countries in both North and South America. Similar to NAFTA, FTAA pledges to support trade "without barriers, without subsidies, without unfair practices, and with an increasing stream of productive investments."[19] Negotiations may take a decade. However, leaders from each of the 36 countries have agreed to finish FTAA negotiations by 2005. For more information about FTAA, see **www.ftaa-alca.org.**

ASEAN (Association of South East Nations) regional trade agreement between Indonesia, Thailand, Philippines, Malaysia, Singapore, and Brunei

APEC (Asia-Pacific Economic Cooperation) regional trade agreement between the US, Canada, Japan, South Korea, Australia, New Zealand, China, Taiwan, Hong Kong, and members of ASEAN

ASEAN, the **Association of South East Nations**, and **APEC**, **Asia-Pacific Economic Cooperation**, are the two largest and most important regional trading groups in Asia. ASEAN is a trade agreement between Indonesia, Thailand, Philippines, Malaysia, Singapore, and Brunei that, together, form a market of more than 330 million people. APEC is a broader agreement between the U.S., Canada, Japan, South Korea, Australia, New Zealand, China, Taiwan, Hong Kong, and members of ASEAN. U.S. trade with ASEAN countries is sizable, exceeding $75 billion a year. In fact, the United States is ASEAN's largest trading partner, while the six member nations of ASEAN are the U.S.'s fifth-largest trade group. ASEAN member countries have agreed to create an ASEAN free trade area beginning in 2003 that will limit tariffs to no more than 5 percent of the cost of a product.[20] Likewise, APEC countries, which include members of ASEAN, have agreed to begin reducing trade barriers in the year 2000, though it will take until 2020 for all trade barrier reductions to be completely phased in. For more information about ASEAN, see **www.asean.or.id.** For more information about APEC, see **www.apecsec.org.sg.**

2.3
Consumers, Trade Barriers, and Trade Agreements

In Tokyo, a Coke costs $1.10. In Geneva, a small cup of regular coffee costs $1.20. In Germany, a newspaper costs $1.50. In the U.S., each of these items costs about 50 cents. While not all products are two to three times as expensive in these countries, a World Bank study did find that American consumers get much more for their money than any other consumers in the world. For example, the average Swiss consumer earns nearly $35,410 a year, compared to the average American who earns $24,750.[21] Yet after both incomes are compared for how much they can buy (for example, a

Big Mac that costs an average of $2.56 cents in the U.S. costs $3.87 in Switzerland), the Swiss income is equivalent to just $23,620! So while U.S. incomes are lower, they still buy more for the average American.[22] Other studies find similar results. Despite having larger average annual incomes than American workers, German and Japanese consumers are only able to buy approximately 83 percent of what the average American consumer can buy.[23]

Although the connection is not obvious, one reason that Americans get more for their money is that the U.S. marketplace has been one of the easiest for foreign companies to do business in. Some U.S. industries, such as textiles, have been heavily protected from foreign competition through many trade barriers. But, for the most part, American consumers (and businesses) have had plentiful choices among American-made and foreign-made products. More important, the high level of competition between foreign and domestic companies that creates these choices helps to keep prices low in the U.S. Furthermore, it is precisely this lack of choice, and the low level of competition, that keeps prices higher in countries that have not been as open to foreign companies and products. For example, Japanese trade barriers are estimated to cost Japanese consumers more than $100 billion a year! This figure is equivalent to a 178 percent increase in cost across the 47 product categories studied by Japanese economists.[24] To illustrate how large a difference this can be, consider that a set of golf balls that retails for $19.99 in the U.S. typically costs a Japanese golfer $72.00! Not surprisingly, polls show that price, not quality, is the most important consideration for Japanese consumers.[25]

Review 2: *Trade Rules and Agreements*

Tariffs and nontariff trade barriers, such as quotas, voluntary export restraints, government standards, government subsidies, and customs classifications, have made buying foreign goods much harder or expensive than buying domestically produced products. However, worldwide trade agreements, such as GATT, along with regional trading agreements, like the Maastricht Treaty of Europe, NAFTA, FTAA, ASEAN, and APEC, substantially reduced tariff and nontariff barriers to international trade. Companies have responded by investing in growing markets in Asia, Eastern Europe, and Latin America. Consumers have responded by purchasing products based on value, rather than geography.

How to Go Global?

Once a company has decided that it *will* go global, it must decide *how* to go global. For example, if you decide to sell in Singapore, should you try to find a local business partner who speaks the language, knows the laws, and understands the customs and norms of Singapore's culture, or should you simply export your products from your home country? What do you do if you are also entering Eastern Europe, perhaps starting in Hungary? Should you use the same approach in Hungary that you used in Singapore?

While there is no magical formula to answer these questions, after reading these next two sections, you should be able to:

3 explain why companies choose to **standardize or adapt** their business procedures.

4 explain the different ways that companies can **organize to do business globally**.

3 Consistency or Adaptation?

In this section, we return to a key issue in the chapter: How can you be sure that the way you run your business in one country is the right way to run that business in another? In other words, how can you strike the right balance between global consistency and local adaptation?

Global consistency means that when a multinational company has offices, manufacturing plants, and distribution facilities in different countries, it will run those offices, plants, and facilities based on the same rules, guidelines, policies, and procedures. Managers at company headquarters value global consistency, because it simplifies decisions. For example, IBM's international sales used to be organized by country. Under this system, if a multinational company with offices in ten different countries wanted to purchase IBM personal computers, it would deal with ten different IBM offices, and would likely get different prices and levels of service from each one. Today, multinational customers only have to deal with IBM's central sales of-

Back to the Future

A Global "Walk Down the Hallway"

Typically, when managers consider how to use technology to conduct global business, they think about teleconferencing. The advantage that teleconferencing has over international phone calls is that teleconferencing equipment transmits voice and live video. Both "callers" can see each other as they talk. Teleconferencing also permits simultaneous viewing of charts, graphs, data, and videotape. In many respects, because of these features, a well-managed teleconference can be nearly as useful for doing business as actually being there for the meeting. However, with teleconferencing, you don't lose a full business day by flying 12 hours there and 12 hours back. Furthermore, you were rested and mentally sharp during the meeting, because you got eight full hours of sleep in your own bed. In contrast, you would have been lucky to eke out a fitful four hours of sleep on the airplane. Also, because you didn't change 11 time zones, you weren't plagued by seven days of jet lag after the meeting was over.

Fortunately, technological advances will make teleconferencing cheaper, more accessible, and a better communication tool. A few years ago, international teleconferencing cost about $300 an hour for satellite transmission, not counting the minimum $10,000 setup cost to purchase teleconferencing equipment. Today, a $200 investment allows workers to teleconference from their personal computers (a camera, the size of a wallet, sits on top of each person's computer). Instead of using a satellite link-up and a TV screen, participants view their partners through a small application window on their computer screen. Voices, which are transmitted via standard microphones, are received through the computer's audio board and heard through the computer speakers. Since the teleconference can be transmitted over POTS (plain old telephone service), hourly charges will be less than half the cost of satellite link-ups. However, if the personal computers are linked up to the companies' local area networks that, in turn, may be connected to the Internet, there could be no hourly cost for a teleconference!

The greatest advantage of personal computer-based teleconferencing may be that it permits application sharing. This means that teleconference participants can share word processing, spreadsheet, and graphics software as they teleconference. When your colleague in Frankfurt changes the spreadsheet cell for March sales revenue, that change shows up instantaneously in the same spreadsheet on your computer in Los Angeles. Advances in teleconferencing equipment and software like these will eventually allow global colleagues to work together as if they had walked down the hallway to work side by side in the same office.

Sources: R. Collis, "If You Have Ever Felt That Stepping Off a Long-Haul Flight into a Business Meeting Is a Form of Virtual Reality (Couldn't We Have Done This on the Phone?), Here Comes Rosenbluth International," *International Herald Tribune*, 25 September 1998, 12. J.S. Cohen, "As Technology Blossoms, So Does the Popularity of Corporate Cybergatherings," *Chicago Tribune*, 10 August 1998. K. Jurek, "Business Travel Could Be Stunted," *Crain's Cleveland Business*, 2 November 1998, 35.

fice. Once a deal has been cut, they can expect similar prices and service in each location.[26]

Local adaptation is a company policy to modify its standard operating procedures to adapt to differences in foreign customers, governments, and regulatory agencies. Local adaptation is typically more important to local managers who are charged with making the international business successful in their countries. In his book, *Blunders in International Business*, David Ricks describes an ill-fated advertising theme used by Sumitomo Corporation of Japan to introduce a new kind of steel pipe to the U.S. market. Following the advice of a Japanese advertising agency, the steel was named "**S**umitomo ***H***igh ***T***oughness," and was advertised in full-page advertisements with nearly full-page letters as ***SHT***, the steel "made to match its name." Sumitomo could probably have prevented this mistake if they had given some control of their advertising to local managers who understood the culture and language.

Multinational companies struggle to find the correct balance between global consistency and local adaptation. If they lean too much toward global consistency, they run the risk of using management procedures poorly suited to particular countries' markets, cultures, and employees. However, if companies focus too much on local adaptation, they run the risk of losing the cost efficiencies and productivity that result from using standardized rules and procedures throughout the world. Indeed, Texas Instruments, Digital Equipment, and Ford redesigned their international offices precisely because they became "slow-moving—and at times redundant—clones of corporate headquarters."[27] These companies found that their foreign offices operated independently, not communicating, not coordinating, and sometimes even competing with each other.

Review 3:
Consistency or Adaptation?

Global business requires a balance between global consistency and local adaptation. Global consistency means using the same rules, guidelines, policies, and procedures in each foreign location. Managers at company headquarters like global consistency, because it simplifies decisions. Local adaptation means adapting standard procedures to differences in foreign markets. Local managers prefer a policy of local adaptation, because it gives them more control. Not all businesses need the same combinations of global consistency and local adaptation. Some thrive by emphasizing global consistency and ignoring local adaptation. Others succeed by ignoring global consistency and emphasizing local adaptation.

4 Forms for Global Business

Besides determining whether to adapt organizational policies and procedures, a company must also determine how to organize itself for successful entry into foreign markets. Historically, companies have generally followed the *phase model of globalization*.

This means that companies made the transition from a domestic company to a global company in sequential phases, beginning with **4.1** *exporting, followed by* **4.2** *cooperative contracts, moving next to* **4.3** *strategic alliances, and finishing with* **4.4** *wholly owned affiliates. At each step, the company would grow much larger, would use those resources to enter more global markets, would be less dependent on home country sales, and would be more committed in its orientation to global business. However, evidence suggests that some companies do not follow the phase model of globalization.*[28] *Some skip phases on their way to becoming more global and less domestic. Others, known as* **4.5** *global new ventures, don't follow the phase model at all. This section reviews these forms of global business.*[29]

4.1 Exporting

exporting
selling domestically produced products to customers in foreign countries

When companies produce products in their home countries and sell those products to customers in foreign countries, they are **exporting**. For example, few realize that India is the second-largest exporter of computer software in the world (U.S. software companies are first). In fact, when Digital Equipment Corporation's Japanese subsidiary needed software that automatically translated English words into Japanese characters, they hired Indian rather than Japanese software engineers, because they were cheaper and, according to DEC, more talented.[30]

Exporting has many advantages as a form of global business. It makes the company less dependent on sales in its home market and provides a greater degree of control over research, design, and production decisions. Namaste Exports is an Indian manufacturer and exporter of leather clothing. The company was founded when Narayan Bhat began selling the purses that his wife made in their home. In contrast to its humble beginnings when all of what it made was sold in India, the company now gets more than 80 percent of its sales from Europe.[31]

While advantageous in a number of ways, exporting also has its disadvantages. The primary disadvantage is that many exported goods are subject to tariff and nontariff barriers that can substantially increase their final cost to consumers. A second disadvantage of exporting is that transportation costs can significantly increase the price of an exported product. For example, a 50-pound box of Nicaraguan sweet-onions costs about $17, but shipping those onions to the U.S. costs $5, adding more than 29 percent to the price.[32] Another disadvantage of exporting is that companies that export are dependent on foreign importers for distribution of their products. For example, if the foreign importer makes a mistake on the paperwork that accompanies a shipment of imported goods, those goods can be returned to the foreign manufacturer at the manufacturer's expense.

cooperative contract
an agreement in which a foreign business owner pays a company a fee for the right to conduct that business in his or her country

4.2 Cooperative Contracts

When an organization decides to expand its business globally, but does not want to make large financial commitments to do so, it will sign a **cooperative contract** with a foreign business owner, who pays the company a fee for the right to conduct that business in his or her country. There are two kinds of cooperative contracts: licensing and franchising.

licensing
agreement in which a domestic company, the *licensor,* receives royalty payments for allowing another company, the *licensee,* to produce its product, sell its service, or use its brand name in a specified foreign market

Under a **licensing** agreement, a domestic company, the *licensor*, receives royalty payments for allowing another company, the *licensee,* to produce its product, sell its service, or use its brand name in a particular foreign market. For example, brands such as Peter Paul Mounds, Almond Joy, and

Lowenbrau, which consumers associate with American companies, are not really American products. British company Cadbury Schweppes licenses Peter Paul Mounds and Almond Joy candy bars for U.S. production to Hershey foods.

One of the most important advantages of licensing is that it allows companies to earn additional profits without investing more money. As foreign sales increase, the royalties paid to the licensor by the foreign licensee increase. Moreover, the licensee, not the licensor, invests in production equipment and facilities to produce the licensed product. Licensing also helps companies avoid tariff and nontariff barriers. Since the licensee manufactures the product within the foreign country, tariff and nontariff barriers don't apply. For example, Britvic Corona is licensed to bottle and distribute Pepsi-Cola within Great Britain. Because it bottles Pepsi in England, tariff and nontariff barriers do not affect the price or supply of these products.

The biggest disadvantage associated with licensing is that the licensor gives up control over the quality of the product or service sold by the foreign licensee. Other than specific restrictions in the licensing agreement, the licensee controls the entire business, from production, to marketing, to final sales. Many licensors include inspection clauses in their license contracts, but closely monitoring product or service quality from thousands of miles away can be difficult. An additional disadvantage is that licensees can eventually become competitors, especially when a licensing agreement includes access to important technology or proprietary business knowledge.

franchise
a collection of networked firms in which the manufacturer or marketer of a product or service, the *franchisor,* licenses the entire business to another person or organization, the *franchisee*

A **franchise** is a collection of networked firms in which the manufacturer or marketer of a product or service, the *franchisor,* licenses the entire business to another person or organization, the *franchisee.* For the price of an initial franchise fee plus royalties, franchisors provide franchisees training, help with marketing and advertising, and an exclusive right to conduct business in a particular location. Most franchise fees run between $5,000 and $35,000. However, McDonald's, one of the largest franchisors, charges $200,000 to $900,000 up front for a franchise outside the United States[33] Since typical royalties range from 2 percent to 8 percent of gross sales, franchisors are well rewarded for the help they provide to franchisees.[34] Well over 400 U.S. companies franchise their businesses to foreign franchise partners.

Overall, franchising is a fast way to enter foreign markets. During the 1980s, U.S. franchisors increased their global franchises by an astronomical 79 percent, for a total of almost 40,000 global franchise units! Because it gives the franchisor additional cash flows from franchisee fees and royalties, franchising can be a good strategy when a company's domestic sales have slowed. For example, Pizza Hut, Taco Bell, and Kentucky Fried Chicken, are accepting almost no new U.S. franchises, because the U.S. market is saturated with fast-food outlets. McDonald's is only adding about 5 percent more U.S. stores per year through franchising. By contrast, these restaurants are experiencing or predicting phenomenal growth in global franchises. In the last decade, McDonald's has nearly doubled its number of overseas stores. Pizza Hut plans to open 300 new stores in Asia by the year 2,000, while KFC plans to build more than 1,100 new stores in Asia during the same period.[35]

Despite its many advantages, franchisors face a loss of control when they sell businesses to franchisees who are thousands of miles away. Although there are successful exceptions, franchising success may be somewhat culture-bound. In other words, because most global franchisors begin by

By franchising globally, KFC has gained new sources of cash flows,despite the already-saturated U.S. fast-food market. © Corbis/Kevin R. Morris

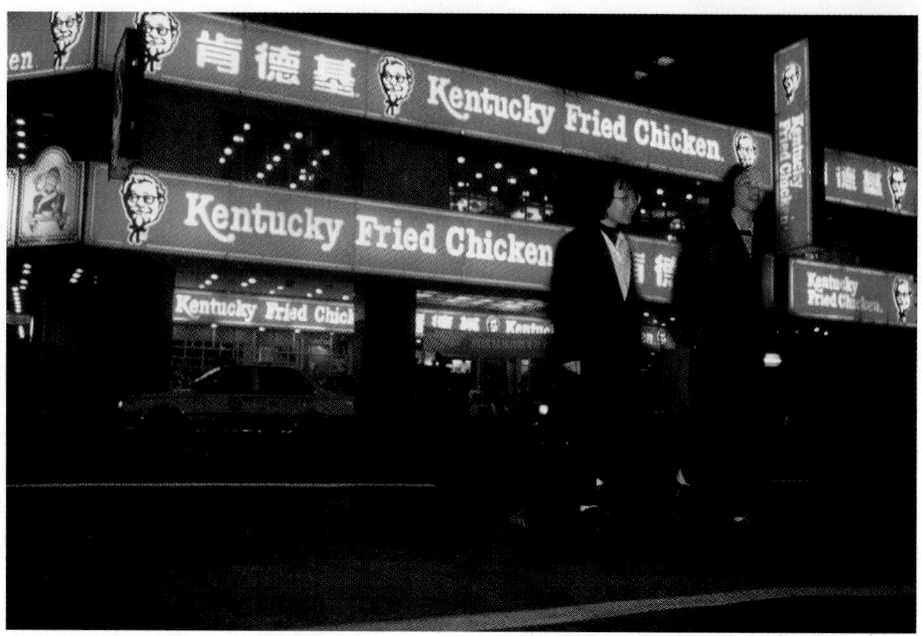

franchising their businesses in similar countries or regions (Canada is by far the first choice for American companies taking their first step into global franchising), and because 65 percent of franchisors make absolutely no change in their business for overseas franchisees, that success may not generalize to cultures with different lifestyles, values, preferences, and technological infrastructures. Because of this, simple things taken for granted in one's own country can trip up the most successful businesses when they franchise overseas. For example, in Eastern Europe, less than half the households have working phones. Domino's Pizza might find it difficult to franchise its pizza delivery business under those circumstances.

4.3 *Strategic Alliances*

strategic alliance
agreement in which companies combine key resources, costs, risk, technology, and people

joint venture
a strategic alliance in which two existing companies collaborate to form a third, independent company

Companies forming **strategic alliances** combine key resources, costs, risks, technology, and people. The most common strategic alliance is a **joint venture,** which occurs when two existing companies collaborate to form a third company. The two founding companies remain intact and unchanged, except that, together, they now own the newly created joint venture.

One of the oldest, most successful global joint ventures is Fuji-Xerox, which is a joint venture between Fuji Photo Film of Japan and Xerox Corporation, based in the U.S., which makes copiers and automated office systems. More than 35 years after its creation, Fuji-Xerox employs nearly 30,000 employees and has close to $7 billion in revenues. Fuji-Xerox is largely responsible for copier sales in Asia, whereas Xerox is responsible for North American sales. Rank Xerox, which is a Xerox subsidiary, is responsible for sales in Europe.[36]

One of the advantages of global joint ventures is that, like licensing and franchising, they help companies avoid tariff and nontariff barriers to entry. Another advantage is that companies participating in a joint venture bear only part of the costs and the risks of that business. Many companies find this attractive, because of how expensive it is to enter foreign markets or develop new products. Toshiba Corporation of Japan uses joint ventures to lower the cost of development in its high-technology businesses, such as computer chips, flat panel computer screens, and giant turbines for electrical plants. Toshiba estimates that it will cost more than a billion dollars to develop the next generation of computer memory chips. Consequently, Toshiba has formed a joint venture with IBM and Siemens.[37]

Global joint ventures can be especially advantageous to smaller, local partners that link up with larger, more-experienced foreign firms that can bring advanced technology, management, and business skills to the joint venture. After the Berlin Wall fell, General Motors, the world's largest auto manufacturer, committed to a joint venture with German Automobil Werke Eisenach, an automobile manufacturer in Eisenach, Germany (formerly East Germany). Together, General Motors and GEW-Eisenach built a brand new factory that allowed General Motors to introduce the most up-to-date manufacturing machines, teamwork-based assembly, and just-in-time inventory systems, none of which had been used in the antiquated factory that GEW-Eisenach used to manufacture East German cars.[38]

Global joint ventures are not without problems, though. Because companies share costs and risk with their joint venture partners, they must also share their profits. At one time, sharing of profits created some tension between Fuji Color Film, Xerox, and their joint venture Fuji-Xerox. In fact, Xerox struggled so long before turning itself around that business experts used to joke that Fuji-Xerox, which had been highly profitable, should purchase Xerox.[39] Setting up global joint ventures is also complex, often requiring detailed contracts that specify the obligations of each party. Toshiba, which participated in its first global joint ventures in the early 1900s by making light bulb filaments with General Electric, treats joint ventures like a marriage of two companies and views the contract as a prenuptial agreement.[40] In other words, the joint venture contract specifies how much each company will invest, what its rights and responsibilities are, and what it is entitled to if the joint venture does not work out. These steps are important, because it is estimated that the rate of failure for global joint ventures is as high as 33 percent to 50 percent.[41] Global joint ventures can also be difficult to manage, because they represent a merging of four cultures: the country and the organizational cultures of the first partner, and the country and the organizational cultures of the second partner.

4.4
Wholly Owned Affiliates (Build or Buy)

Approximately one-third of multinational companies enter foreign markets through wholly owned affiliates. Unlike licensing, franchising, or joint ventures, **wholly owned affiliates** are 100 percent owned by the parent company. For example, Honda Motors of America, in Marysville, Ohio, is 100 percent owned by Honda Motors of Japan. Ford Motor of Germany, in Cologne, is 100 percent owned by the Ford Motor Company in Detroit, Michigan.

wholly owned affiliates foreign offices, facilities, and manufacturing plants that are 100 percent owned by the parent company

The primary advantage of wholly owned businesses is that they give parent companies all of the profits and complete control over foreign facilities. The biggest disadvantage is the expense of building new operations or buying existing businesses. While the payoff can be enormous if wholly owned affiliates succeed, the losses can be immense if they fail. For example, when

Volkswagen spent over a quarter of a billion dollars to purchase and modernize an auto manufacturing plant from Chrysler, everyone, including the state of Pennsylvania that lured Volkswagen to Pennsylvania with a $63 million tax break, thought Volkswagen would be wildly successful. However, nearly a decade later, Volkswagen sales had dropped and the plant, which was running at only 40 percent of capacity, was losing $120 million a year. Twenty-five hundred workers lost their jobs when Volkswagen closed the plant for good.[42]

Acquiring foreign businesses is sometimes resented by local businesses, customers, or workers. In fact, worker resentment may have contributed to Volkswagen's plant shutdown. Volkswagen's U.S. auto workers walked off their jobs and shut down the plant to protest being paid $1 to a $1.50 less an hour than other U.S. auto workers.[43]

4.5
Global New Ventures

It used to be that companies slowly evolved from being small and selling in their home markets to being large and selling to foreign markets. Furthermore, as companies went global, they usually followed the phase model of globalization. However, three trends have combined to allow companies to skip the phase model when going global. First, quick, reliable air travel can transport people to nearly any point in the world within one day. Second, low-cost communication technologies, such as international e-mail, teleconferencing, and phone conferencing, make it easier to communicate with global customers, suppliers, managers, and employees. Third, there is now a critical mass of business people with extensive personal experience in all aspects of global business.[44] This combination of events has made it possible to start companies that are global from inception. With sales, employees, and financing in different countries, **global new ventures** are new companies founded with an active global strategy.[45]

global new ventures
new companies with sales, employees, and financing in different countries that are founded with an active global strategy

While there are several different kinds of global new ventures, they share two common factors. First, the company founders successfully develop and communicate the company's global vision. For example, unlike many large investment firms that began and specialized in transactions within a particular country, the International Investment Group was founded to help global clients and businesses. IIG helps with global trading and offers global investment advice to clients in the U.S., India, France, Switzerland, and Great Britain.[46]

Second, rather than going global one country at a time, new global ventures bring a product or service to market in several foreign markets at the same time. National GYP-Chipper, based in Pflugerville, Texas, manufactures and sells a $10,000 machine that crushes scrap gypsum (drywall) into a recyclable powder.[47] It is cheaper and faster for building contractors to grind up used or leftover drywall board into a recyclable powder than it is to pay to have it hauled to the dump. Because National Gyp-Chipper feared that potential overseas competitors would copy its machine, it established licensing contracts with companies in Britain, Japan, and Canada, and was seeking other relationships in Europe and the Middle East. By entering so many markets so quickly, National Gyp-Chipper hoped to get ahead of and deter any copycat competitors.

Review 4: *Forms for Global Business*

The phase model of globalization says that as companies move from a domestic to a global orientation, they use these organizational forms in sequence: exporting, cooperative contracts (licensing and franchising), strategic alliances, and wholly owned affiliates. Yet, not all companies follow the phase model. For example, global new ventures are global from their inception.

Where to Go Global?

Deciding where to go global is just as important as deciding how your company will go global. After reading these next three sections, you should be able to:

5 explain how to **find a favorable business climate**.

6 discuss the importance of **identifying and adapting to cultural differences**.

7 explain how to successfully **prepare workers for international assignments**.

5 Finding the Best Business Climate

When deciding where to go global, companies try to find countries or regions with promising business climates.

An attractive global business climate **5.1** *positions the company for easy access to growing markets,* **5.2** *is an effective but cost-efficient place to build an office or manufacturing site, and* **5.3** *minimizes the political risk to the company.*

5.1 *Growing Markets*

The most important factor in an attractive business climate is access to a growing market. For example, no product is known and purchased by as many people throughout the world as Coca-Cola. Yet, even Coke, which is available in 195 countries, still has tremendous potential for further global growth. Presently, the Coca-Cola Company gets about 80 percent of its sales from its 16 largest markets. The remaining 20 percent is spread across the other 179 countries in which Coke does business. Coke's former CEO said, "We have really just begun reaching out to 95 percent of the world's population that lives outside the U.S."[48]

purchasing power
a comparison of the relative cost of a standard set of goods and services in different countries

Two factors help companies determine the growth potential of foreign markets: purchasing power and foreign competitors. **Purchasing power** is measured by comparing the relative cost of a standard set of goods and services in different countries. Earlier in the chapter we noted that a Coke costs $1.10 in Tokyo. But because a Coke only costs about 50 cents in the U.S., the average American would have more purchasing power. Purchasing power is surprisingly strong in countries like Mexico, India, and China, which have low average levels of income. This is because consumers still have money to spend after paying for basic living expenses, such as food, shelter, and transportation, which are very inexpensive in those countries. To illustrate, the average Chinese household spends only 5 percent of household income on basic living expenses, while the average American household spends 45 percent to 50 percent.[49] Because basic living expenses are so small, purchasing power is strong, and millions of Chinese, Mexican, and Indian consumers increasingly have extra money to spend on what they want, in addition to what they need.

Consequently, countries with high levels of purchasing power are good choices for companies looking for attractive global markets. Coke has found that the per capita consumption of Coca-Cola, how many Cokes a person drinks per year, rises directly with purchasing power. In Eastern Europe, as countries began to embrace capitalism after the fall of communism, per capita consumption of Coke increased from 20 to 31 cokes in just two years. It is predicted to more than triple to 71 by the year 2,000.[50] Figure 8.5 shows the millions of new middle-class consumers throughout the world who, thanks to purchasing power, have growing disposable incomes.

The second part of assessing growing global markets is to analyze the degree of global competition, which is determined by the number and quality of companies that already compete in foreign markets. Before J.C. Penney began developing stores in foreign markets, it sent a small team of experienced retailers to scout its global competition. In East Berlin, the team found display windows with nothing more than one dusty shirt on display. In Istanbul,

Figure 8.5

Number of New Middle-Class Workers Who Now Have Disposable Incomes

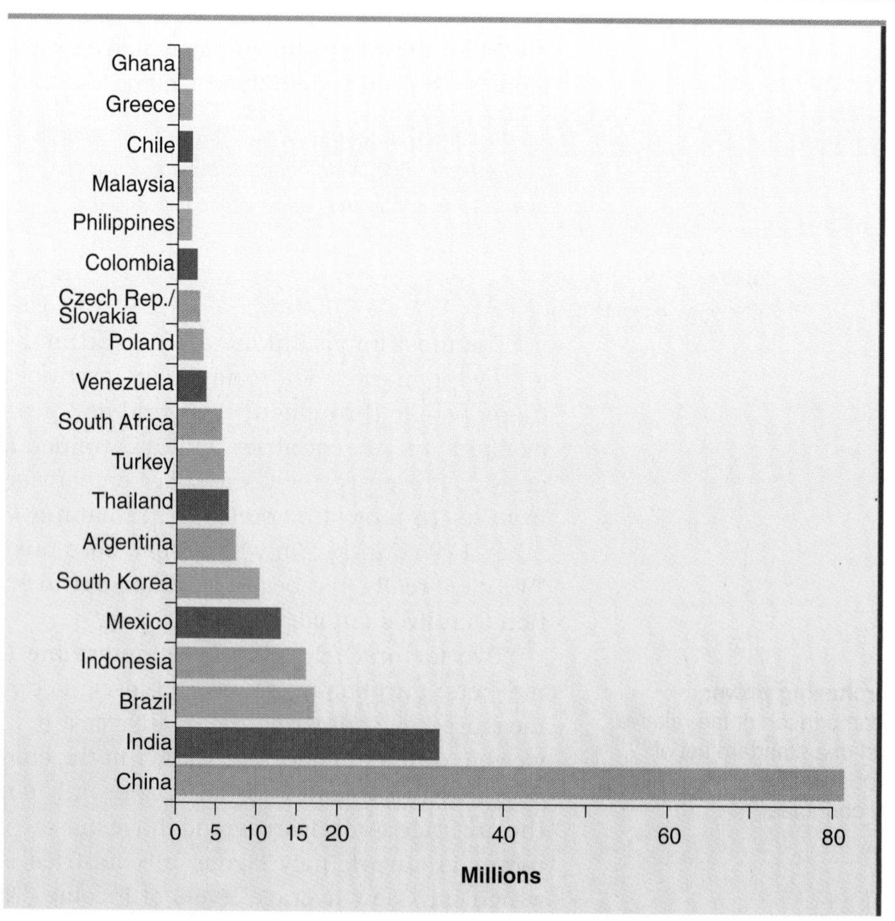

Source: "The Big Rise: Middle Classes Explode Around the Globe, Bringing New Markets and New Prosperity," *Fortune*, 30 May 1994, 74–90.

they found retail stores with plumbing supplies next to the women's lingerie and clothing. Because its top-selling stores were right on the U.S.-Mexican border, Penney's managers didn't even have to leave the U.S. to assess its competition in Mexico. Studies confirmed that 60 percent of the sales in these U.S. stores came from Mexicans who crossed the border to shop.[51] Because its foreign competitors were weak in marketing, customer service, and product distribution, J.C. Penney followed through on its plan to expand into global markets.

5.2
Choosing an Office/Manufacturing Location

Companies do not have to establish an office or manufacturing location in each country they enter. They can license, franchise, or export to foreign markets, or they can serve a larger region from one country. Thus, the criteria for choosing an office/manufacturing location are different from the criteria for entering a foreign market.

Rather than focusing on costs alone, companies should consider both qualitative and quantitative factors. Two key qualitative factors are work force quality and company strategy. Work force quality is important because it is often difficult to find workers with the specific skills, abilities, and experience that a company needs to run its business. Work force quality was the most important consideration when Lands' End, a mail-order catalog company, built a communications center in Oakham, England. Lands' End's project manager for the Oakham location said, "We operate a service business over the phone. We need polite operators with neutral accents, so quality of labor was one through five on our list of priorities."[52] A company's strategy is also important when choosing a location. For example, a company pursuing a low-cost strategy may need plentiful raw materials, low-cost transportation, and low-cost labor. A company pursuing a differentiation strategy (typically a higher-priced, better product or service) may need access to fine-quality materials and a highly skilled and educated work force.

Quantitative factors, such as the kind of facility being built, tariff and nontariff barriers, exchange rates, and transportation and labor costs, should also be considered when choosing an office/manufacturing location. Regarding the kind of facility being built, a real estate specialist in company location decisions said, "If it's an assembly plant, a company might be inclined to look for incentives that would subsidize its hiring. With a distribution facility, an adequate transportation network will likely be critical. A corporate headquarters will need a good communications network, a multilingual labor force, and easy access by air. On the other hand, a research and development operation will require proximity to a high-tech infrastructure and access to good universities."[53]

Figure 8.6 shows consulting company Arthur Andersen's rankings for the world's top cities for global business. This information is a good starting point if your company is trying to decide where to put an international office or manufacturing plant.

5.3
Minimizing Political Risk

When managers think about political risk in global business, they envision burning factories and riots in the streets. Although political events

Figure 8.6 **World's Best Cities for Business**

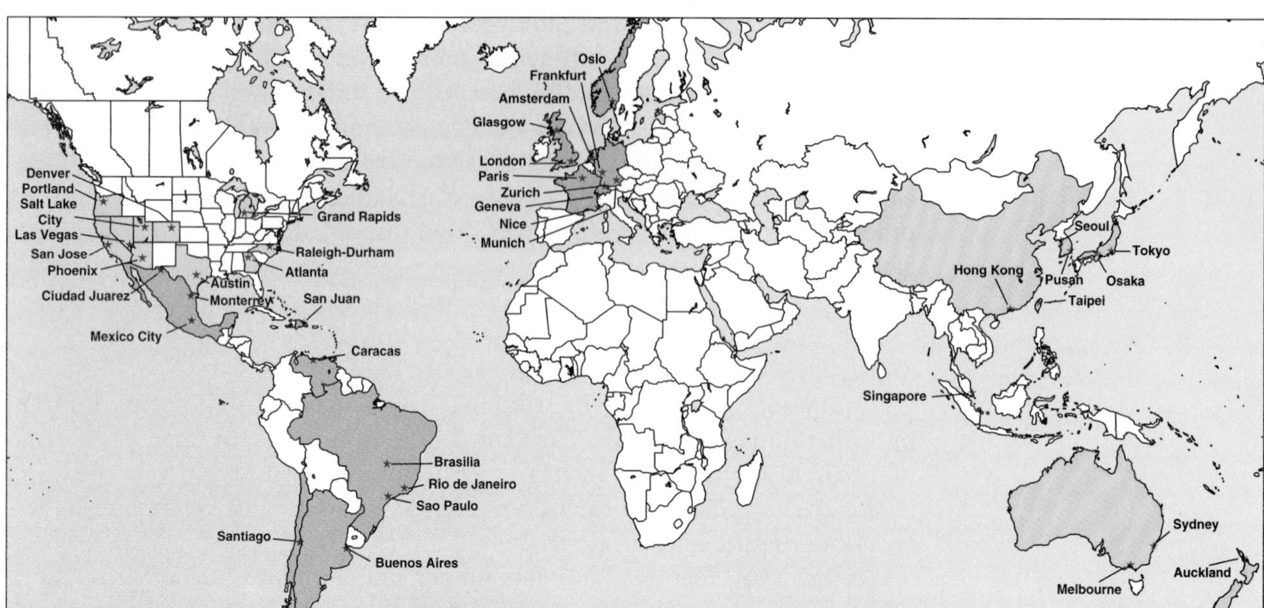

North America	Latin America	Europe	Asia Pacific
1. Austin, TX	1. Santiago	1. London	1. Singapore
2. Las Vegas, NV	2. Monterrey	2. Paris	2. Tokyo
3. Salt Lake City, UT	3. Buenos Aires	3. Glasgow	3. Osaka
4. Phoenix, AZ	4. Rio de Janeiro	4. Zurich	4. Hong Kong
5. San Jose, CA	5. Mexico City	5. Geneva	5. Auckland
6. Raleigh-Durham, NC	6. Sao Paulo	6. Amsterdam	6. Sydney
7. Portland, OR	7. Cuidad Juarez	7. Oslo	7. Melbourne
8. Atlanta, GA	8. Brasilia	8. Nice	8. Seoul
9. Denver, CO	9. San Juan	9. Frankfurt	9. Taipei
10. Grand Rapids, MI	10. Caracas	10. Munich	10. Pusan

Source: "Fortune Best Cities 1998," Arthur Andersen Real Estate and Hospitalities Group. [Online] Available at **www.arthurandersen.com/rehsg/bestcities/winners.asp**, 9 January 1999.

such as these receive dramatic and extended coverage from the press, the political risks that most companies face usually will not be covered as breaking stories on CNN. However, the negative consequences of ordinary political risk can be just as devastating to companies that fail to identify and minimize those risks.

When conducting global business, companies should attempt to identify two types of political risk: political uncertainty and policy uncertainty.[54] **Political uncertainty** is associated with the risk of major changes in political regimes that can result from war, revolution, death of political leaders, social unrest, or other influential events. **Policy uncertainty** refers to the risk associated with changes in laws and government policies that directly affect the way foreign companies conduct business. This is the most common form of political risk in global business and perhaps the most frustrating. For example, the busiest McDonald's in the world used to be in a prime location in Wangfujing, China—that is, until the Chinese government broke McDonald's 20-year lease after only two years, telling McDonald's that it would have to build a brand new store just blocks away from the original location. The Chinese government broke McDonald's lease so that a Hong Kong billionaire could develop the location. Ironically, after agreeing to let

political uncertainty
the risk of major changes in political regimes that can result from war, revolution, death of political leaders, social unrest, or other influential events

policy uncertainty
the risk associated with changes in laws and government policies that directly affect the way foreign companies conduct business

him build on the site, the Chinese government retracted that permission, too.[55]

Several strategies can be used to minimize or adapt to the political risk inherent to global business. An *avoidance strategy* is used when the political risks associated with a foreign country or region are viewed as too great. If firms are already invested in high-risk areas, they may divest or sell their businesses. If they have not yet invested, they will likely postpone their investment until the risk shrinks. For example, many international companies left Hong Kong when it reverted from British rule, under which it had been a free democracy, to socialist rule under the Chinese government.

Control is an active strategy to prevent or reduce political risks. Firms using a control strategy will lobby foreign governments or international trade agencies to change laws, regulations, or trade barriers that hurt their business in that country.

Another method for dealing with political risk is *cooperation*, which makes use of joint ventures and collaborative contracts, such as franchising and licensing. Although cooperation does not eliminate the political risk of doing business in a country, it does limit the risk associated with foreign ownership of a business. For example, a German company forming a joint venture with a Chinese company to do business in China may structure the joint venture contract so that the Chinese company owns 51 percent or more of the joint venture. Doing so qualifies the newly formed joint venture as a Chinese company and exempts it from Chinese laws that apply to foreign-owned businesses.[56]

Review 5: *Finding the Best Business Climate*

The first step in deciding where to take your company global is finding an attractive business climate. Be sure to look for a growing market where consumers have strong purchasing power and foreign competitors are weak. When locating an office or manufacturing facility, consider both qualitative and quantitative factors. In assessing political risk, be sure to examine political uncertainty and policy uncertainty. If the location you choose has considerable political risk, you can avoid it, try to control the risk, or use a cooperation strategy.

6 Becoming Aware of Cultural Differences

Some of the more interesting and amusing aspects of global business are the unexpected confrontations that people have with cultural differences, "the way they do things over there." For example, as part of a class assignment in global business, a high school class in Dearborn, Michigan, and a high school class in Valle, Spain agreed to form a global "joint venture." The two classes agreed that the U.S. students would buy Spanish products from the Spanish high school students and resell them at a profit to other American students. Likewise, the Spanish students would purchase American products from the American students and then resell them at a profit to their Spanish friends. Now, what to buy from each other? The American students decided to buy giant beach towels showing teenaged Spanish lovers.

Through forming a virtual joint venture, students in the United States and Spain learned a lesson in cultural differences. © Alan Levenson/Tony Stone Images

One of the towels showed a boy helping his girlfriend remove her shirt. Another showed him unzipping her jeans. In Spain's culture, which is much more relaxed about sexuality than American culture, no one gives these towels a second thought. Of course, despite protestations of censorship, the U.S. high school teacher vetoed the towels as too suggestive.[57]

However, U.S. sensitivities about sexual issues are nothing compared to those in Iran's Islamic culture. All Iranian advertising must be approved by the conservative (at least from an American perspective) Ministry of Islamic Guidance, whose job is to prevent anything of a sexual or Western nature from being displayed. For example, a billboard ad for women's underwear consisted of a picture of a green box with nothing more than the words "soft and delicate" written on it. Not surprisingly, no one knew what the ad was about. Despite approval by the Ministry of Islamic Guidance, billboards displaying giant red lips, which were used to advertise Goldstar televisions from South Korea, were burned down twice by Iranians who felt the ad was too sexual.[58]

national culture
the set of shared values and beliefs that affects the perceptions, decisions, and behavior of the people from a particular country

National culture is the set of shared values and beliefs that affects the perceptions, decisions, and behavior of the people from a particular country. The first step in dealing with culture is to recognize that there are meaningful differences in national cultures. Geert Hofstede has spent the last 20 years studying cultural differences in 53 different countries. His research shows that there are five consistent differences across national cultures: power distance, individualism, short-term versus long-term orientation, masculinity, and uncertainty avoidance.[59]

Power distance is the extent to which people in a country accept that power is distributed unequally in society and organizations. In countries where power distance is weak, such as Denmark and Sweden, employees don't like for their organizations or their bosses to have power over them or to tell them what to do. They want to have a say in decisions that affect them. *Individualism* is the degree to which societies believe that individuals should be self-sufficient. In individualistic societies, employees put loyalties to themselves first, and loyalties to their company and work group second.

Short-term/Long-term orientation addresses whether cultures are oriented to the present and seek immediate gratification, or to the future and defer gratification. Not surprisingly, countries with short-term orientations are consumer driven, whereas countries with long-term orientations are savings driven.

Masculinity, and its opposite, *femininity*, capture the difference between highly assertive and highly nurturing cultures. Masculine cultures emphasize assertiveness, competition, material success, and achievement, whereas feminine cultures emphasize the importance of relationships, modesty, caring for the weak, and quality of life.

The cultural difference of *uncertainty avoidance* is the degree to which people in a country are uncomfortable with unstructured, ambiguous, unpredictable situations. In countries with strong uncertainty avoidance like Greece and Portugal, people are aggressive and emotional and seek security (rather than uncertainty).

Cultural differences affect perceptions, understanding, and behavior. Recognizing cultural differences is critical to succeeding in global business. However, Hofstede said we should recognize that these cultural differences are based on averages—the average level of uncertainty avoidance in Portugal, or the average level of power distance in Argentina, etc. Hofstede said, "If you are going to spend time with a Japanese colleague, you shouldn't assume that overall cultural statements about Japanese society automatically apply to this person."[60]

After becoming aware of cultural differences, the second step is deciding how to adapt your company to those cultural differences. Unfortunately, studies investigating the effects of cultural differences on management practice point more to difficulties than to easy solutions. One problem is that different cultures will probably perceive management policies and practices differently. For example, blue-collar workers in France and Argentina, all of whom performed the same factory jobs for the same multinational company, perceived the company's corporate-wide safety policy differently.[61] French workers perceived that safety wasn't very important to the company, but Argentine workers thought that it was. The fact that something as simple as a safety policy can be perceived differently across cultures shows just how difficult it can be to standardize management practices across different countries and cultures.

Another difficulty is that cultural values are changing, albeit slowly, in many parts of the world. The fall of communism in Eastern Europe and the former Soviet Republic and the broad economic reforms in China have combined to produce sweeping changes on two continents. Thanks to increased global trade resulting from GATT and other regional free trade agreements, major economic transformations are also under way in India, Mexico, Central America, and South America. The difficulty that companies face when trying to adapt management practices to cultural differences is that they may be adapting the way they run their businesses based on outdated and incorrect assumptions about a country's culture.

Review 6:
Becoming Aware of Cultural Differences

National culture is the set of shared values and beliefs that affects the perceptions, decisions, and behavior of the people from a particular country. The first step in dealing with culture is to recognize meaningful differences, such as power distance, individualism, short-term/long-term orientation, masculinity, and uncertainty avoidance. Cultural differences should be carefully interpreted, because they are based on averages, not individuals. Adapting managerial practices to cultural differences is difficult, because policies and practices can be perceived differently in different cultures. Another difficulty is that cultural values may be changing in many parts of the world. Consequently, when companies try to adapt management practices to cultural differences, they need to be sure that those changes are not based on outdated assumptions about a country's culture.

7 Preparing for an International Assignment

Personal Productivity Tip

Passports

To find out where to apply for a passport, call the post office. Allow two months for processing. Bring proof of U.S. citizenship (birth certificate or certificate of naturalization), proof of identity (picture ID), and two photos (2 inches by 2 inches). To renew by mail, send your application, old passport, two photos, and renewal fee to the National Passport Center, P.O. Box 371971, Pittsburgh, PA 15250-7971. In an emergency, a private passport service can obtain a passport in several days. If you lose your passport, contact the local police and the U.S. embassy or consulate. A photocopy of your passport will make it easier to obtain a replacement.

Sources: U.S. State Department, Passport Services and Information. [Online] Available **http://travel.state.gov/passport_services.html**, 26 January 1999.

expatriate
someone who lives outside his or her native country

Around a conference table in a large U.S. office tower, three American executives sat with their new boss, Mr. Akiro Kusumoto, the newly appointed head of a Japanese firm's American subsidiary, and two of his Japanese lieutenants. The meeting was called to discuss ideas for reducing operating costs. Mr. Kusumoto began by outlining his company's aspiration for its long-term U.S. presence. He then turned to the budgetary matter. One Japanese manager politely offered one suggestion, and an American then proposed another. After gingerly discussing the alternatives for quite some time, the then exasperated American blurted out: 'Look, that idea is just not going to have much impact. Look at the numbers!' In the face of such bluntness, uncommon and unacceptable in Japan, Mr. Kusumoto fell silent. He leaned back, drew air between his teeth, and felt a deep longing to return East. He realized his life in this country would be filled with many such jarring encounters, and lamented his posting to a land of such rudeness.[62]

Mr. Kusumoto is a Japanese **expatriate**, someone who lives outside his or her native country. The cultural shock that he was experiencing is common. The difficulty of adjusting to language, cultural, and social differences is the primary reason that so many expatriates fail in overseas assignments. For example, it is estimated that 10 percent to 45 percent of American expatriates sent abroad by their companies will return to the U.S. before they have successfully completed their international assignments.[63] Of those who do complete their international assignments, as many as 30 percent to 50 percent are judged by their companies to be no better than marginally effective.[64]

Since the average cost of sending an employee on an international assignment can run between $200,000 and $1.2 million, failure in those assignments can be extraordinarily expensive.[65]

However, the chances for a successful international assignment can be increased through **7.1** *language and cross-cultural training, and* **7.2** *consideration of spouse, family, and dual-career issues.*

7.1 *Language and Cross-Cultural Training*

The purpose of pre-departure language and cross-cultural training is to reduce the uncertainty that expatriates feel, the misunderstandings that take place between expatriates and natives, and the inappropriate behaviors

Personal Productivity Tip

Money and International Travel

Credit cards, such as Visa, MasterCard, and American Express, are accepted worldwide and offer the best exchange rates. Traveler's checks are replaceable if lost or stolen. Carry enough local currency to pay for food, transportation, and lodging your first day in a country. If you need more, you can exchange local currency at hotels, post offices, or for-profit currency exchange stores. However, because of the 2 percent to 10 percent exchange fees, many travelers now use ATM machines to withdraw cash directly from their personal bank ccounts. ATMs are widely available (see **www.mastercard.com/atm** for the Cirrus network), and they offer exchange rates as good as credit cards.

that expatriates unknowingly commit when they travel to a foreign country. Indeed, simple things like using a phone, finding a public toilet, asking for directions, knowing how much things cost, exchanging greetings, or ordering in a restaurant can become tremendously complex when expatriates don't know a foreign language or a country's customs and cultures. In his book *Blunders in International Business*, David Ricks tells the story of an American couple in Asia. After a walk with their dog, the Americans had dinner at a local restaurant. Since the waiters and waitresses did not speak English, they ordered by pointing to items on the menu. Because their dog was hungry, they pointed to the dog and to the kitchen. The waiter had trouble understanding, but finally took the dog to the kitchen. The American couple assumed that this meant the dog could not be fed in the dining room, but was going to be fed in the kitchen. Unfortunately, to the couple's dismay, the waiter and the chef returned later to proudly show them how well they had cooked the poodle.

Expatriates who receive pre-departure language and cross-cultural training make faster adjustments to foreign cultures and perform better on their international assignments (and are better at ordering in foreign restaurants).[66] Unfortunately, only a third of the managers who go on international assignments receive any kind of pre-departure training. This is somewhat surprising given the failure rates for expatriates and the high cost of those failures. It is also surprising because, with the exception of some language courses, pre-departure training is not particularly expensive or difficult to provide.

What Really Works

Cross-Cultural Training

Most expatriates will tell you that cross-cultural training helped them adjust to foreign cultures. However, anecdotal data is not as convincing as systematic studies. Twenty-one studies, with a combined total of 1,611 participants, have examined whether cross-cultural training affects the self-development, perceptions, relationships, adjustment, and job performance of expatriates. Overall, they show that cross-cultural training works extremely well in most instances.

Self-Development

When you first live in another country, you must learn how to make decisions that you took for granted in your home country: how to get to work, how to get to the grocery, how to pay your bills, and so on. If you've generally been confident about yourself and your abilities, an overseas assignment can challenge that sense of self. However, cross-cultural training helps expatriates deal with these and other challenges. Expatriates who receive cross-cultural training are 79 percent more likely to report healthy psychological well-being and self-development than those who don't receive training.

Psychological Well-Being & Self Development

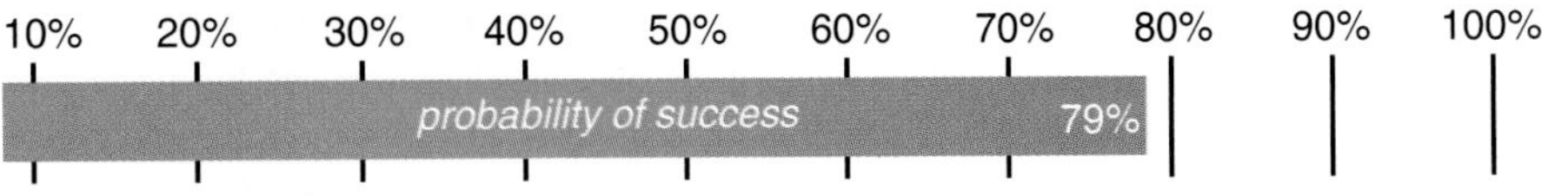

Fostering Relationships

One of the most important parts of an overseas assignment is establishing and maintaining relationships with host nationals. If you're in Brazil, you need to make friends with Brazilians. However, many expatriates make the mistake of making friends only with expatriates from their home country. In effect, they become social isolates in a foreign country. They work and live there, but as much as they can, they speak their native language, eat their native foods, and socialize with other expatriates from their home country. Cross-cultural training makes a big difference in whether expatriates establish relationships with host nationals. Expatriates who receive cross-cultural training are 74 percent more likely to have established such relationships.

Fostering Relationships with Native Citizens

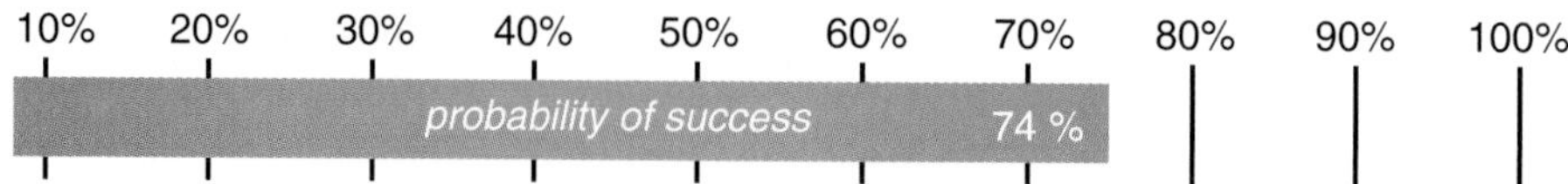

Accurate Perceptions of Culture

Another thing that distinguishes successful from unsuccessful expatriates is that they understand the cultural norms and practices of the host country. For example, many Americans do not understand the famous pictures they have seen of Japanese troops turning their backs to American military commanders on V-J day, the day that Japan surrendered to the United States in World War II. Americans viewed this as a lack of respect, when in fact in Japan, turning one's back in this way is a sign of respect. Cross-cultural training makes a big difference in the accuracy of perceptions concerning host country norms and practices. Expatriates who receive cross-cultural training are 74 percent more likely to have accurate perceptions.

Accurate Cultural Perceptions

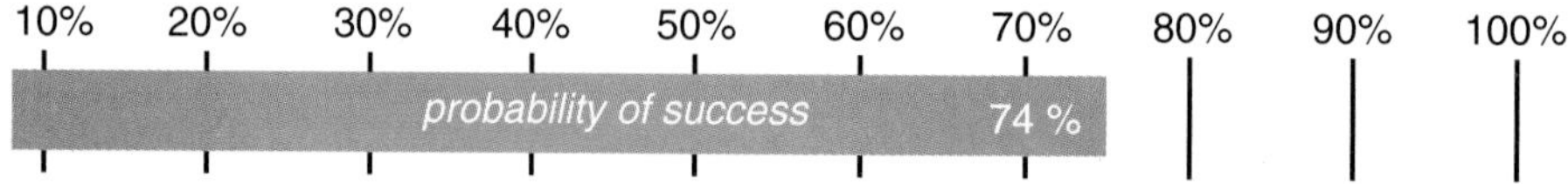

Rapid Adjustment

New employees are most likely to quit in the first six months, because this initial period requires the most adjustment: learning new names, new faces, new procedures, and new information. It's tough. Of course, expatriates have a much tougher time making a successful adjustment, because besides learning new names, faces, procedures, and information, expatriates are learning new languages, new foods, new customs, and often new lifestyles. Expatriates who receive cross-cultural training are 74 percent more likely to make a rapid adjustment to a foreign country.

Rapid Adjustment to Foreign Cultures and Countries

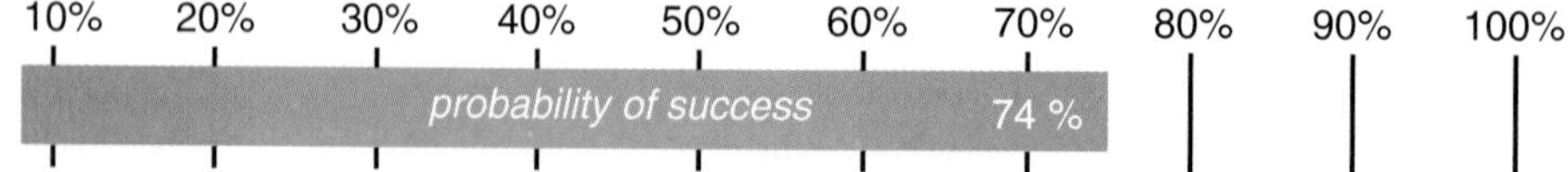

Job Performance

It's good that cross-cultural training improves self-development, fosters relationships, improves the accuracy of perceptions, and helps expatriates make rapid adjustments to foreign cultures. However, from an organizational standpoint, the ultimate test of cross-cultural training is whether it improves expatriates' job performance. The evidence shows that cross-cultural training makes a significant difference in expatriates' job performance. This is not quite as big a difference as for the other factors. However, it is estimated that cross-cultural training for 100 managers could bring about $390,000 worth of benefits to a company, nearly $4,000 per manager. This is an outstanding return on investment, especially when you consider the high rate of failure for expatriates. Expatriates who have received cross-cultural training are 71 percent more likely to have better on-the-job performance than those who did not receive cross-cultural training.

On-the-Job Performance

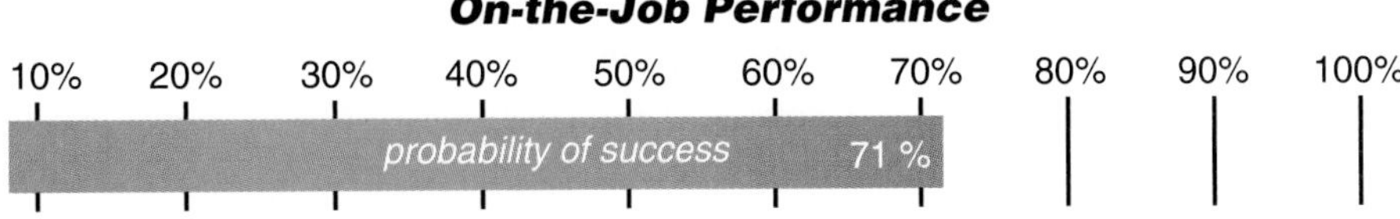

Source: S.P. Deshpande & C. Viswesvaran, "Is Cross-Cultural Training of Expatriate Managers Effective: A Meta-Analysis," *International Journal of Intercultural Relations* 16, no. 3 (1992): 295–310.

For example, a U.S. electronics manufacturer prepared workers for assignments in South Korea by using a combination of documentary training, cultural simulations, and field experiences. *Documentary training* focuses on identifying the critical specific differences between various cultures. Trainees learned that U.S. subordinates will normally look their boss in the eye, whereas Korean subordinates avoid eye contact unless their boss asks them a question. Trainees also learned about other U.S.-South Korean differences, such as how to greet business people, how to behave toward South Korean women or elders, and how to respect privacy.

After learning critical specific differences in documentary training, trainees participated in a *cultural simulation*, in which they had the opportunity to practice adapting to cultural differences. For example, the trainees participated in a simulated cocktail party in which company managers who had spent time in South Korea posed as South Korean business people and their spouses. Trainees practiced South Korean greetings, introductions, and communication styles, and then received feedback on their performance.

Field simulation training, a technique made popular by the U.S. Peace Corps, places trainees in an ethnic neighborhood for three to four hours to talk to residents about cultural differences. In this instance, trainees explored a nearby South Korean neighborhood, talking to shopkeepers and people on the street about South Korean politics, family orientation, and day-to-day living practices.

7.2
Spouse, Family, and Dual-Career Issues

At the request of his company, "Sam" and his wife "Janet" moved to London for Sam's international assignment. Their plush apartment was across the street from world-famous Harrods department store and was also close to London's best parks, museums, and gardens. The company also paid them enough to afford full-time childcare. By most accounts, Sam and Janet should have had a wonderful experience in London. However, Janet was miserable. Consequently, so was Sam. Their social life was active, but revolved around Sam's business clients. Janet was lonely. She missed her job, which she gave up to come to London. She also missed her friends in Atlanta. Sam and Janet were divorced after returning to the U.S.[67]

Not all international assignments turn out so badly for expatriates and their families, but the evidence clearly shows that how well an expatriate's spouse and family adjust to the foreign culture is the most important factor in determining the success or failure of an international assignment.[68] Unfortunately, despite its importance, there has been little systematic research on what does and does not help expatriates' families successfully adapt. However, a number of companies have found that adaptability screening and intercultural training for families can lead to more successful overseas adjustment.

Adaptability screening is used to assess how well managers and their families are likely to adjust to foreign cultures. For example, Prudential Relocation Management's international division has developed an "Overseas Assignment Inventory" to assess spouse and family's open-mindedness, respect for others' beliefs, sense of humor, and marital communication. Likewise, AMP Inc., based in Pennsylvania, conducts extensive psychological screening on expatriates and their spouses when making international assignments. But adaptability screening is not just companies assessing employees; it can also mean that employees screen international assignments for desirability. Since more employees are becoming aware of the costs of international assignments (spouses having to give up or change jobs, children having to change schools, having to learn a new language, etc.), some companies are willing to pay for a pre-assignment trip for the employee and his or her spouse to investigate the country *before* accepting the international assignment.[69]

Language and cross-cultural training for families is just as important as language and cross-cultural training for expatriates. In fact, it may be more important, because unlike expatriates, whose professional jobs often shield them from the full force of a country's culture, spouses and children are often fully immersed in foreign neighborhoods and schools. Households must be run, shopping must be done, and bills must be paid. Likewise, children and their parents must deal with different cultural beliefs and practices about discipline, alcohol, dating, and other issues.

For example, one of the ways in which Japanese parents discipline their children is to lock them out of the house. It's the American equivalent of timeout. But instead of sending their children to their rooms, Japanese parents lock their children out of the house for selfish behavior. The child usually cries loudly outside the house, begging his or her parents' forgiveness, and begging to be let in. Occasionally, American neighbors will misinterpret this method of discipline as child abuse and call the police, causing great embarrassment to themselves, the police, and the Japanese expatriate's family.[70] Language and cross-cultural training can help reduce uncertainty about how to act and decrease misunderstandings between expatriates, their families, and locals.

Review 7:
Preparing for an International Assignment

Many expatriates return prematurely from international assignments because of poor performance. However, this is much less likely to happen if employees receive language and cross-cultural training, such as documentary training, cultural simulations, or field experiences, before going on assignment. Adjustment of expatriates' spouses and families, which is the most important determinant of success in international assignments, can be improved through adaptability screening and intercultural training.

What**Really**Happened?

Anyone who has traveled to Eastern Europe in the last few years knows that McDonald's "invasion" was successful. "It's hard for Americans to understand, but McDonald's is almost heaven sent to these people," says Tim Fenton, who heads McDonald's Poland. "It's some of the best food around. The service is quick, and people smile. You don't have to pay to use the bathroom. There's air conditioning. The place isn't filled with smoke. We tell you what's in the food. And we want you to bring the kids." Learn how McDonald's does business all over the world by reading the answers from the opening case, *What Would You Do?*

Should you import your supplies from the U.S. or from Western Europe, or try to obtain them locally?

At first, McDonald's will usually import supplies to meet its high standards. For example, french fries for its Polish stores are produced in a plant in Aldrup, Germany. McDonald's also imports onions from California. However, if local suppliers can be found, McDonald's will develop a relationship with them. For example, a German supplier, that now sells McDonald's $40 million of condiments a year, started 20 years ago with a $100 order for mustard and mayonnaise. Most often, however, McDonald's relies on its U.S. suppliers to follow it overseas. OSI industries, which supplies beef patties to McDonald's in the U.S., has joined with local companies to form joint ventures in 17 different countries.

Should you hire local workers and managers? If you do, how will you train them?

A startup team composed of 50 workers from Britain, Germany, Russia, and the U.S. did the initial setup work in Poland: finding locations, overseeing construction, working with government officials, and hiring and training workers. Two years after the startup, all the workers were Polish, except the manager, who is American. Eventually, a Pole will replace him, too. Foreign managers with two to five years of experience are eligible for training at Hamburger University, near Chicago. Courses in team building, staffing and retention, and total quality management are simultaneously translated into 22 different languages for managers from 72 different countries. Besides its main campus near Chicago, McDonald's also runs Hamburger Universities in England, Japan, Germany, and Australia, as well as ten international training centers.

Which countries should you enter first, and why?

Like many other companies, McDonald's chose to put many of its new stores in East Germany, Hungary, Poland, and the Czech Republic. Collectively, these countries were closer to existing markets, made clear breaks from communism to capitalism (i.e., political stability), encouraged direct foreign investment, and had well-trained, low-cost workers.

Should you set up company-owned stores, or look for local investors who pay for the rights to a McDonald's franchise? Or, should you set up joint ventures?

In Europe, which resembles the U.S. market in many ways, McDonald's usually runs wholly owned subsidiaries, for example, McDonald's Poland. In turn, subsidiaries operate company-owned stores and license franchises. Potential franchisees who survive a two-year screening process pay $240,000 for a 20-year franchising contract. In Asia, McDonald's prefers joint ventures, because entering those markets is much more difficult. The 50-50 split in ownership encourages local partners to handle difficult negotiations with government officials. Finally, in markets with the greatest political risk, McDonald's limits its risk by not putting up any of its own money. It just licenses its name and enforces its worldwide standards for quality. However, McDonald's can buy in later if it chooses.

Finally, will you have to make changes in your menu to accommodate local tastes and traditions?

Although it maintains a standard menu worldwide, McDonald's does try to accommodate local tastes. It sells McSpaghetti, made of noodles, in the Philippines, and MacLak, which is a salmon sandwich, in Norway.

Sources: S. Chandler, "Foreign Woes Shadow McDonald's 2nd Quarter," *Chicago Tribune*, 21 July 1998. "Bloomberg News. McDonald's to Continue to Expand in Asia Restaurants," *Los Angeles Times*, 10 April 10 1998, D3. R. Gibson, "McDonald's Profit Rises 19% on Boom in Business Abroad," *The Wall Street Journal*, 26 January 1996, A4. R. Gibson, "For McDonald's, 11 Nations Have 85% of Outlets," *The Wall Street Journal Europe*, 3 April 1998, 6. R. Gibson & M. Moffett, "Why You Won't Find Any Egg McMuffins for Breakfast in Brazil," *The Wall Street Journal*, 23 October 1997, A1. A.E. Serwer, "McDonald's Conquers the World," *Fortune*, 17 October 1994, 103–116.

Key Terms

APEC (Asia-Pacific Economic Cooperation) p. 284

ASEAN (Association of South East Nations) p. 284

cooperative contract p. 288

country of manufacture p. 278

country of origin p. 278

direct foreign investment p. 275

expatriate p. 300

exporting p. 288

franchise p. 289

FTAA (Free Trade Area of the Americas) p. 284

GATT (General Agreement on Tariffs and Trade) p. 281

global business p. 274

global new ventures p. 292

joint venture p. 290

licensing p. 288

Maastricht Treaty of Europe p. 282

multinational corporation p. 278

NAFTA (North American Free Trade Agreement) p. 283

national culture p. 298

nontariff barriers p. 280

policy uncertainty p. 296

political uncertainty p. 299

protectionism p. 279

purchasing power p. 293

quota p. 280

regional trading zones p. 282

strategic alliance p. 290

subsidies p. 281

tariff p. 279

trade barriers p. 279

voluntary export restraints p. 280

wholly owned affiliates p. 291

world gross national product p. 277

What Would You Do-II?

Mazda Motors Headquarters, Tokyo, Japan

It's 8:30 Friday night, and you're still at the office. After a late dinner with some Japanese co-workers, you'll return to the office early Saturday morning to ponder the biggest management decision you've ever made.

Three years ago, at the request of your employer, Ford Motor Company, you packed up everything from your Detroit home and came to Japan to work for Mazda Motor Corporation. In a historical decision, Japanese bankers had asked the American managers who run Ford Motor Company to take over management of Mazda. Ford, which owns 33.4 percent of Mazda, was asked to assume day-to-day control of Mazda, because Mazda's management had lost more than a billion and a half dollars in five years and was having difficulty repaying $8 billion in bank loans. When the Japanese bankers called Ford, Ford called you.

To return Mazda to profitability, you and Mazda's top management have cut long-term costs by 25 percent, cut production of vehicles for the Japanese market by 22 percent, and cut production of vehicles for export (to the U.S. and other countries) by more than 50 percent! However, the most painful cut would be elimination of Mazda's guarantee of lifetime employment, which large Japanese firms have traditionally offered to their workers. No matter how bad things get, no matter how much money the company loses, large Japanese companies have promised their workers they will not lose their jobs.

One thing you learned when Ford lost billions of dollars and had to lay off thousands of workers was that the best job security in the world is to be competitive. However, Mazda managers are strongly resisting elimination of lifetime employment. A Mazda manager said, "They (Ford managers) think lifetime employment is a Japanese business practice that is going to change in the future. It's difficult for them to understand our idea that employees come first."

The question is: Who is right? What should take precedence, the cultural factors in Japan that guarantee lifetime employment or the business factors that require Mazda to reduce its costs, focus its product line, and ultimately return to profitability? It's a tough call. You've heard horror stories from your American friends in Japan who work for other companies. When their companies tried to use American ideas in their Japan offices, they didn't work very well. On the other hand, Japanese auto companies have too much capacity. Japanese auto factories have the capacity to build 14 million cars a year, but Japanese consumers only buy 11 million a year, so something's got to give. And with Mazda sales down nearly 50 percent in the last five years, Mazda can't pay its loans and keep factories open unless it is profitable. With so much excess capacity, layoffs would clearly help get costs in line. But would layoffs, which would destroy the promise of lifetime employment, damage employee morale and threaten Mazda's reputation in Japan? What's the right answer? **If you were Ford's manager at Mazda headquarters, what would you do?**

Sources: E. Fingleton, "Jobs for Life: Why Japan Won't Give Them Up," *Fortune* 20, no. 5 (March 1995): 119. M.A. Lev, "Ford Executive Retools Mazda—Undramatically," *Chicago Tribune*, 31 March 1997. V. Reitman & O. Suris, "Ford Asked To Take the Wheel at Mazda," *Asian Wall Street Journal*, 21 November 1994, 1. V. Reitman & A. B. Henderson, "International: Mazda Cuts Output as Troubles Mount," *The Wall Street Journal*, 26 April 1995, A12. L. Shuchman, "Mazda Narrows Loss and Projects Profit in Spite of Weak Automarkets in Asia," *The Wall Street Journal*, 27 May 1998, A17. S. Sugawara, "Ford's Effort to Save Mazda Offers Guide to Crossing Cultural Gaps," *The Washington Post*, 14 June 1998, H1. K. Yung, "Mazda Hopes to Turn Corner in U.S. This Year," *The Detroit News*, 14 April 1998, B4.

Critical-Thinking Video Case

Global Strategy: Enforcement Technology, Inc.

Enforcement Technology, Inc., or ETEC, is the world's leading producer of hand-held enforcement systems used for parking and traffic administration. Headquartered in Southern California, the company has sales and service locations throughout the United States, with international offices in Australia and Argentina. ETEC manufactures and services its own hardware and software under the AutoCITE brand name. Law enforcement agencies in San Diego, Seattle, and Chicago, as well as numerous college campuses, use ETEC's AutoCITE system. ETEC's products are also used in Australia, Mexico, Canada, and Argentina.

Critical-Thinking Questions

1. What differences between doing business in the United States and other countries affect ETEC's global strategy?
2. In development of their global strategy, what adaptations will enable ETEC to successfully serve the international marketplace?

Management Decisions

Hearts at Home and Going Native

In the last five years, your company has considerably improved the way in which it prepares employees for international assignments. Except emergencies, employees are typically given four to five months' notice before being sent abroad. Employees, their spouses, and their families are carefully screened and selected. Moreover, all employees and their families receive two months of extensive language and cultural training before beginning an international assignment. Although these steps have greatly improved the success and performance of your company's expatriates, you're still running into two serious problems.

Problem number one is the expatriate who "goes native." Expatriates who go native are strongly committed to doing what is right for the foreign office, even at the expense of ignoring parent company policy. For example, "Gary," a manager who had spent half his 15 years with a company on three different overseas assignments, stated, "My first commitment is to the unit here (in France). In fact, half the time I feel as if corporate is a competitor I must fight rather than a benevolent parent I can look to for support." While he had only six months remaining on his French assignment, Gary had already asked the home office for an extended stay.

Problem number two is the expatriate whose "heart is still at home." Consider "Earl" who, after two decades with the parent company, was promoted to managing director of European headquarters. However, unlike managers who "go native," this was Earl's first international assignment. Consequently, his allegiance was "first and foremost" to the parent company rather than the European office. In fact, when his two years as managing director are up, he is going straight back to the states.

Expatriates who go native make it very difficult for companies to achieve global consistency in their operations. Expatriates whose hearts are at home ignore the importance of local adaptation. As one senior manager put it, "How can we get expatriate managers who are committed to the local overseas operation during their international assignments, but who remain loyal to the parent firm?"

Questions

1. What steps would you take to reduce the chances that an expatriate would go native?
2. What steps would you take to reduce the chances that an expatriate would leave his or her heart at home?
3. What steps could be taken to encourage expatriates to develop a dual allegiance to the parent company *and* the overseas operation?

Sources: J.S. Black, "Serving Two Masters: Managing the Dual Allegiance of Expatriate Employees," *Sloan Management Review,* Summer 1992, 61–71. H.B. Gregersen, "Commitments to a Parent Company and a Local Work Unit during Repatriation," *Personnel Psychology* 45 (1992): 29–54. J. Kaufman, "In China, John Aliberti Gets VIP Treatment; At Home, Grass Grows in the Patio," *The Wall Street Journal*, 19 November 1996, A1.

Management Decisions

When in China, Negotiate Like the Chinese Do?

You are the Chief Executive Officer of a medium-sized machine manufacturing company in Baton Rouge, Louisiana. Twelve months ago, one of your best customers referred a Chinese manufacturer to you for business. Since then, a delegation of Chinese managers has twice visited your Louisiana factory. You, your sales manager, and your plant manager took a ten-day trip to China to visit the Chinese company and to investigate shipping, banking, and customs procedures. After months of preparation, you are ready to begin formal negotiations. In ten days, representatives from your company will meet in Hong Kong with representatives from the Chinese company to negotiate a contract specifying the size, price, and delivery date of what you believe will be the largest overseas shipment your company has ever made.

You're concerned, however, because no one on your team has any experience negotiating with the Chinese, who are patient and skilled negotiators. As you were considering your options, these questions occurred to you:

Questions

1. Should you, the CEO, attend and be part of the negotiations?
2. Americans and Chinese typically have very different negotiating styles. Since the Chinese are unlikely to adopt an American style of negotiating, would negotiations go better if your team was prepared to negotiate "Chinese-style"?
3. Your sales manager feels that you should hire a Hong Kong consultant with extensive experience dealing with the Chinese to negotiate for your company. You can see the merit in this, but you also know that "guanxi," or personal relationships, is one of the most important parts of doing business in China. If you hired a Hong Kong consultant to do the negotiations, would you damage the "guanxi" that it has taken you six months to establish?

Sources: S. Lubman, Round and Round: To Survive Your Business Negotiations, You'll Need Patience, Skill—and Perhaps an Extra Coat," *The Wall Street Journal,* 10 December 1993, R3. I. Matthee, "Accountant Opens Trade Doors: Firm Helps Businesses Gain Access to China," *Seattle Post-Intelligencer*, 3 October 1997, E1. M.A. Sabo & S. Leith, "What West Michigan Wants: A Payoff on the Business Gamble and the Costly Foothold," *The Grand Rapids Press*, 21 June 1998, D1. S.E. Weiss, "Negotiating with 'Romans'— Part 1," *Sloan Management Review,* Winter 1994, 51–61. T. Yeung & L.L. Yeung, "Negotiations in the People's Republic of China: Results of a Survey of Small Businesses in Hong Kong," *Journal of Small Business Management,* 1 January 1995, 70.

Develop Your Management Potential

Are you Nationminded or Worldminded?

There are three parts to this assignment. Step 1: Complete the questionnaire shown below. Step 2: Determine your score. Step 3: Develop a plan to increase your global managerial potential.

Step 1: Use the six-point rating scale to complete the questionnaire shown below.

Rating Scale

6 Strongly Agree	3 Mildly Disagree
5 Agree	2 Disagree
4 Mildly Agree	1 Strongly Disagree

_____ 1. Our country should have the right to prohibit certain racial and religious groups from entering it to live.

_____ 2. Immigrants should not be permitted to come into our country if they compete with our own workers.

_____ 3. It would be a dangerous procedure if every person in the world had equal rights which were guaranteed by an international charter.

_____ 4. All prices for exported food and manufactured goods should be set by an international trade committee.

_____ 5. Our country is probably no better than many others.

_____ 6. Race prejudice may be a good thing for us because it keeps many undesirable foreigners from coming into this country.

_____ 7. It would be a mistake for us to encourage certain racial groups to become well educated because they might use their knowledge against us.

_____ 8. We should be willing to fight for our country without questioning whether it is right or wrong.

_____ 9. Foreigners are particularly obnoxious because of their religious beliefs.

_____ 10. Immigration should be controlled by a global organization rather than by each country on its own.

_____ 11. We ought to have a world government to guarantee the welfare of all nations irrespective of the rights of any one.

_____ 12. Our country should not cooperate in any global trade agreements which attempt to better world economic conditions at our expense.

_____ 13. It would be better to be a citizen of the world than of any particular country.

_____ 14. Our responsibility to people of other races ought to be as great as our responsibility to people of our own race.

_____ 15. A global committee on education should have full control over what is taught in all countries about history and politics.

_____ 16. Our country should refuse to cooperate in a total disarmament program even if some other nations agreed to it.

_____ 17. It would be dangerous for our country to make international agreements with nations whose religious beliefs are antagonistic to ours.

_____ 18. Any healthy individual, regardless of race or religion, should be allowed to live wherever he or she wants to in the world.

_____ 19. Our country should not participate in any global organization which requires that we give up any of our national rights or freedom of action.

_____ 20. If necessary, we ought to be willing to lower our standard of living to cooperate with other countries in getting an equal standard for every person in the world.

_____ 21. We should strive for loyalty to our country before we can afford to consider world brotherhood.

_____ 22. Some races ought to be considered naturally less intelligent than ours.

_____ 23. Our schools should teach the history of the whole world rather than of our own country.

_____ 24. A global police force ought to be the only group in the world allowed to have armaments.

_____ 25. It would be dangerous for us to guarantee by international agreement that every person in the world should have complete religious freedom.

_____ 26. Our country should permit the immigration of foreign peoples even if it lowers our standard of living.

_____ 27. All national governments ought to be abolished and replaced by one central world government.

_____28. It would not be wise for us to agree that working conditions in all countries should be subject to international control.

_____29. Patriotism should be a primary aim of education so our children will believe our country is the best in the world.

_____30. It would be a good idea if all the races were to intermarry until there was only one race in the world.

_____31. We should teach our children to uphold the welfare of all people everywhere even though it may be against the best interests of our own country.

_____32. War should never be justifiable even if it is the only way to protect our national rights and honor.

Step 2: Determine your score by entering your response to each survey item below, as follows. In blanks that say *regular scoring*, simply enter your response for that item. If your response was a 4, place a 4 in the *regular scoring* blank. In blanks that say *reverse scoring*, subtract your response from 6 and enter the result. So if your response was a 4, place a 2 (6 – 4 = 2) in the *reverse scoring* blank.

1. reverse score _____	17. reverse score _____
2. reverse score _____	18. regular score _____
3. reverse score _____	19. reverse score _____
4. regular score _____	20. regular score _____
5. regular score _____	21. reverse score _____
6. reverse score _____	22. reverse score _____
7. reverse score _____	23. regular score _____
8. reverse score _____	24. regular score _____
9. reverse score _____	25. reverse score _____
10. regular score _____	26. regular score _____
11. regular score _____	27. regular score _____
12. reverse score _____	28. reverse score _____
13. regular score _____	29. reverse score _____
14. regular score _____	30. regular score _____
15. regular score _____	31. regular score _____
16. reverse score _____	32. regular score _____

Total your scores from items 1–16 _____
Total your scores from items 17–32 _____
Add together to compute *total score* _____

Higher scores show greater worldmindedness.

Step 3: Develop a plan to increase your global managerial potential.

People don't change from being nation-minded to worldminded overnight. Below you'll find the outlines of a plan to increase your worldmindedness. You need to fill in the details to make it work. This plan is based on foreign languages, living overseas, global news and television, and your openness to the different cultural experiences available right where you live!

3A. **Language.** How many languages do you speak fluently? If you're an average American student, you speak one language, American English. Develop a plan to become fluent in another language. Specify the courses you would need to take to become conversationally fluent. A minimum of two years is recommended. Even better is minoring in a language! What courses would you have to take to complete a minor?

3B. **Living overseas.** Develop a plan to study overseas. List the facts for two different overseas study programs available at your university or another university. Be sure to specify how long the program lasts, whether you would receive language training, where you would live, the activities in which you would participate, and any other important details.

3C. **Global news and television.** Another way to increase your worldmindedness is to increase the diversity of your news sources. Most Americans get their news from local TV and radio, or from the major networks, ABC, NBC, and CBS. Luckily, you don't have to leave the country to gain access to foreign news sources. Furthermore, you don't have to speak a foreign language. Many foreign newspapers and television and radio shows are presented in English. List the foreign newspapers and television and radio shows available to you where you live. Hint: Check your university library, CNN, PBS, and the Internet. Be sure to indicate where you can find the newspapers, the day and time the shows are on, and whether the newspapers or TV shows are in English or a foreign language.

3D. **Local cultural experiences.** Many American students wrongly assume that they have to travel overseas to gain exposure to foreign cultures. Fortunately, many American cities and universities are rich in such experiences. Ethnic neighborhoods, restaurants, festivals, foreign films, and art displays, along with ethnic Americans who continue to live and celebrate their heritage, present ample opportunities to sample and learn about foreign cultures right here in our own backyards.

Specify a plan of foreign restaurants, ethnic neighborhoods, and cultural events that you could attend this year.

Sources: R. W. Boatler, "Study Abroad: Impact on Student Worldmindedness," *Journal of Teaching in International Business* 2, no. 2 (1990):17–13. R.W. Boatler, "Worldminded Attitude Change in a Study Abroad Program: Contact and Content Issues," *Journal of Teaching in International Business* 3, no. 4 (1992): 59–68. H. Lancaster, "Learning to Manage in a Global Workplace (You're on Your Own)," *The Wall Street Journal*, 2 June 1998, B1. D.L. Sampson & H.P. Smith, "A Scale to Measure Worldminded Attitudes," *Journal of Social Psychology* 45, 1957, 99–106.

Chapter 9 Outline

Organizational Strategy

What Would **You** Do?

Kodak Headquarters, Rochester, NY. For years, Eastman Kodak has marketed its products with memorable commercials depicting "Kodak moments," those special times in our lives, such as birthdays, holidays, weddings, and graduations, that deserve to be captured forever (on Kodak film with a Kodak camera and printed on Kodak photographic paper). So when people think of Eastman Kodak, they think "pictures." However, over the last decade, Kodak moved away from its roots, spending ten billion dollars to buy medical companies that develop pharmaceuticals and medical diagnostic tests and equipment. With medical sales accounting for nearly one-fourth of Kodak's annual sales, a Kodak moment no longer meant just "pictures"—it also meant "Take 3 pills per day" or "Squeeze a drop of blood from your finger onto the blue strip to test your glucose level." Unfortunately, Kodak's diversification strategy hasn't worked very well. Because it paid less attention to its core business, Kodak saw its world market share in film drop from 67 percent in the 1970s to approximately 45 percent today. Likewise, Fuji Film, a Japanese film company, Agfa, a German film producer, and 3M, the innovative U.S. conglomerate, managed to reduce Kodak's U.S. market share from 80 percent to 70 percent in less than a decade. Their strategy was simple. Sell low-cost film to retailers, who could then repackage it as their own private label film (i.e., Sam's Pharmacy Film). This low-cost attack strategy forced Kodak to cut its own prices, producing a one-year loss of $1.5 billion, the worst in company history. With huge losses and billions in debt to pay off after its spending spree to acquire medical companies, Kodak management took out its ax and started swinging. The company went through five painful restructurings, eventually eliminating 40,000 jobs in an effort to cut costs and stop the huge losses. The prognosis for the company was so bad that one stock analyst speculated that turning around Kodak would "be one of the greatest feats in business annals." Another said, "Making Kodak grow is not like teaching an elephant to dance. It's like cloning an elephant into a mouse." Although its recent performance has been terrible, many believe that digital photography will darken Kodak's future even more. With film-based photography, Kodak makes money selling film and cameras, film and developing equipment, film development chemicals, and photographic paper. But digital camera users can snap pictures and transfer them to a personal computer for viewing in just minutes. The good news for Kodak is that its reputation and long history in the photography business should give it instant credibility as its sells the new digital cameras. Unfortunately, competition in digital photography will be fierce. Kodak estimates that at least 600 other companies worldwide have entered the digital photography business in one form or another (i.e., digital cameras, software for manipulating digital images, or CDs for storing images). Even worse, however, is that with digital photography, consumers don't need Kodak film, Kodak photographic paper, Kodak chemicals (for film labs), or Kodak film and print developing equipment (for film labs) to view digital pictures. If Kodak is to compete in the long term, it must develop a strategy that addresses these key questions. First, how can Kodak create a sustainable advantage over its competitors? Second, are there potential business opportunities among the obvious and numerous threats to Kodak's business? Third, what business is Kodak really in, medicine or photography, and do these businesses make sense together? Finally, what should Kodak's new strategy be? Should it be growth, stability, or retrenchment/recovery? **If you were in charge of Kodak's strategy, what would you do?**

Sources: M. Bulkeley, "Kodak Profit, Helped by Cost Cutting, Hits Forecasts Despite 7% Sales Decline," *The Wall Street Journal*, 15 April 1998, A4. S.N. Chakravarty, "How an Outsider's Vision Saved Kodak," *Forbes*, 13 January 1997, 45-47. J.P. Donlon, "The Big Picture (Interview with Eastman Kodak CEO George Fisher)," *Chief Executive*, November 1995, 34-37. L. Grant, "The Bears Back Off Kodak," *Fortune*, 24 June 1996, 24-26. D. Grotta & S.W. Grotta, "Heave-Ho Silver!" *PC Magazine*, 7 January 1997, 145-178. L. Johannes, "Kodak Reports Loss of $744 Million Including Big Restructuring Charge," *The Wall Street Journal*, 16 January 1998, A4. M. Maremont, "Kodak's New Focus," *Business Week*, 30 January 1995. J.F. Peltz, "Kodak Takes Another Shot at Restructuring the Company Hopes to Recapture Its BlueChip Status with Film, but Even That Business Is Troubled," *Los Angeles Times*, 30 October 1994.

In Chapter 4, you learned that *strategic plans* are overall company plans that clarify how a company intends to serve customers and position itself against competitors over the next two to five years. Kodak's problems show that picking the wrong strategic plan can have devastating consequences. This chapter begins with an in-depth look at how managers create and use strategies to obtain a sustainable competitive advantage. Then you will learn the three steps of the strategy-making process. Next, you will learn about corporate-level strategies that help managers answer the question: What business or businesses should we be in? You will then examine the industry-level competitive strategies that help managers determine how to compete successfully within a particular line of business. The chapter finishes with a review of the firm-level strategies of direct competition and entrepreneurship.

Basics of Organizational Strategy

It should have been a time of celebration for Steve Case, founder and CEO of America Online (AOL), the leading online computer company, which provides services such as e-mail, Internet access, chat rooms, etc. Under Case's guidance, AOL had grown from being one of the smallest online service providers to the largest in less than a decade. The last few years, in particular, had been especially good, because AOL doubled its customer base and finally achieved consistent profits. Even better, at the same time that AOL was thriving, its major competitors, CompuServe and Prodigy, were shrinking and losing money. It should have been a time to celebrate.

However, celebration turned to crisis when AOL changed its variable-rate pricing plan ($9.95 a month for five online hours and $2.95 for every additional hour) to a flat-rate $19.95 a month, unlimited-connect-time pricing plan. AOL had good reasons for the change. Its once fast growth had slowed to a crawl, because it was losing customers to Internet service providers, most of whom provided unlimited access to the Internet, typically for $19.95 or less per month. However, with the hourly price charges gone, the number of daily online sessions immediately jumped by one-third, from six to nine million per day. Furthermore, the length of those nine million online sessions more than doubled, increasing from an average of 14 minutes per session to 32 minutes per session.[1] With so many more customers accessing their accounts for longer periods, AOL's phone lines were nearly inaccessible. For a large percentage of its subscribers, busy signals replaced instant online access. To make things worse, the strain on AOL's computers led to three highly publicized network breakdowns.

Less than six weeks after changing its pricing plan, thousands of customers per day canceled their accounts to sign with CompuServe or with local Internet service providers. Daily news stories chronicled the frustration of subscribers who could not use their accounts. Sensing opportunity, AOL's competitors, such as Internet America, which provides Internet access in Dallas, began touting its flat-rate pricing *and* accessible service. For example, Internet America's radio ads said, "The Internet's a great way to send e-mail around town or around the world, . . . , or do any of the other things that make the Internet fun and rewarding, if you can just get past these (bleeped-out expletive) busy signals."[2]

How can a company like AOL, which dominates an industry, keep its competitive advantage? What steps can AOL and other companies take to better manage the strategy-making process?

After reading the next two sections, you should be able to:

1 explain the components of **sustainable competitive advantage** and why it is important.

2 describe the steps involved in the **strategy-making process**.

1 Sustainable Competitive Advantage

resources
the assets, capabilities, processes, information, and knowledge that an organization uses to improve its effectiveness and efficiency and to create and sustain an advantage over competitors

competitive advantage
providing greater value for customers than competitors can

An organization's **resources** are the assets, capabilities, processes, information, and knowledge that the organization controls. Firms use their resources to improve organizational effectiveness and efficiency. Resources are critical to organizational strategy, because they can help companies create and sustain an advantage over competitors.[3]

Organizations can achieve a **competitive advantage** by using their resources to provide greater value for customers than competitors can. For example, prior to its recent troubles, AOL created competitive advantage for itself and value for its customers through its simplicity. To get online with AOL, you put its software disk in your computer, typed "Install," and followed the directions (enter your name, credit card number, etc.) as the software automatically dialed AOL's free sign-up number. In less than five minutes, you were an AOL subscriber with 10 to 100 free hours of full access. Furthermore, the software's simple-to-understand menus, icons, and instructions made AOL's service easy and intuitive, even for those who knew little about computers. Other online services were more difficult to use.

sustainable competitive advantage
a competitive advantage that other companies have tried unsuccessfully to duplicate and have, for the moment, stopped trying to duplicate

A competitive advantage becomes a **sustainable competitive advantage** when other companies cannot duplicate the value a firm is providing to customers. Importantly, sustainable competitive advantage is not the same as a long-lasting competitive advantage, though companies obviously want a competitive advantage to last a long time. Instead, a competitive advantage is *sustained* if that advantage still exists after competitors have tried unsuccessfully to duplicate the advantage and have, for the moment, stopped trying to duplicate it. For example, CompuServe lost $100 million dollars trying to establish WOW!, an easy-to-use online service that was similar in ways to AOL. However, Wow!, which was supposed to give parents much more control over what their children could view online, only attracted 100,000 subscribers. Unable to duplicate America Online's success, CompuServe shut down Wow! less than a year after it began.[4] Once that happened, the competitive advantage that AOL created with its easy-to-use software became, for the time being, a sustainable competitive advantage.

Four conditions must be met if a firm's resources are to be used to achieve a sustainable competitive advantage. The resources must be valuable, rare, imperfectly imitable, *and* nonsubstitutable.

valuable resource
a resource that allows companies to improve efficiency and effectiveness

Valuable resources allow companies to improve their efficiency and effectiveness. Unfortunately, changes in customer demand and preferences, competitors' actions, and technology can make once-valuable resources much less valuable. For example, when America Online charged $9.95 a month for five online hours and $2.95 for every additional hour, it had sufficient resources, meaning phone lines, network computers, and available support staff, to successfully handle the business growth it was experiencing. However, when it switched to the $19.95 flat rate plan with unlimited connection hours, those once-valuable resources became an obstacle to efficiency and effectiveness, because they could not keep up with surging customer demand for online access.

For sustained competitive advantage, valuable resources must also be rare resources. Think about it. How can a company sustain a competitive advantage if all of its competitors have similar resources and capabilities? Consequently, **rare resources**, resources that are not controlled or possessed by many competing firms, are necessary to sustain a competitive advantage. When America Online first created the ability to automatically charge monthly bills to customers' credit cards, none of its competitors were offering this service. However, any competitive advantage gained from this was short-lived, because within months, CompuServe, Prodigy, and other online services and Internet providers soon had the same capability. What was initially a rare resource, the capability to bill to credit cards, had become commonplace.

rare resource
a resource that is not controlled or possessed by many competing firms

As the previous example shows, valuable, rare resources can create temporary competitive advantage. However, for sustained competitive advantage, other firms must be unable to imitate or find substitutes for those valuable, rare resources. **Imperfectly imitable resources** are impossible or extremely costly or difficult to duplicate. For example, despite numerous attempts by competitors, such as CompuServe, AOL's ease-of-use and simplicity have, thus far, been an imperfectly imitable resource. *PC Magazine* said, "AOL's graphical interface, with menus made up of single-click art icons, folders, and other documents, is a best-of-breed design. The total effect is coherent and easy to navigate. Some interface elements are even animated, adding still more visual appeal."[5] By contrast, *PC Magazine* said, "Honorable mention goes to CompuServe. Its aging, inconsistent interface makes it unduly hard to navigate, but its breadth and depth of content are still unrivaled in the online world." In other words, despite significant efforts, CompuServe has not been able to imitate AOL's simplicity and ease-of-use. Indeed, over the first decade in the online service business, it was AOL's intuitive design and ease-of-use that helped it displace CompuServe as the industry leader.

imperfectly imitable resource
a resource that is impossible or extremely costly or difficult for other firms to duplicate

Valuable, rare, imperfectly imitable resources can produce sustainable competitive advantage only if they are also **nonsubstitutable resources**, meaning that no other resources can replace them and produce similar value or competitive advantage. For example, as described above, the resource that has brought AOL its strongest competitive advantage is its simplicity and ease-of-use. In the online/Internet service business, this resource has proved valuable, rare, and imperfectly imitable. However, AOL's service and connectivity problems (i.e., constant busy signals) have made customers aware that local Internet Service Providers (ISPs) are potential substitutes for online access. ISPs do one thing—provide access to the Internet. That's it. Unlike AOL, there's no automated sign-up. There's no award-winning, easy-to-use software. (Typically, you have to download the software on your own.) And, ISPs generally don't offer extensive, proprietary content

nonsubstitutable resource
a resource, without equivalent substitutes or replacements, that produces value or competitive advantage

for members. (See **www.aol.com/webcenters/home.adp** for a long list of exclusive content on AOL.)

So what do local ISPs have in the way of resources than can substitute for everything AOL has to offer? First, most ISPs have direct links to Internet sites that allow their customers to download free, simple-to-use software for e-mail and browsing the Web, the most popular tasks on the Internet. While not as easy to use as AOL, most people can be up and running within days of activating their Internet accounts. The second substitute for AOL's resources is the level of customer support that some local ISPs provide. For example, Q Networks, an ISP in Kansas City, provides extensive service and online support (see **http://www.qni.com**) to its 20,000 individual and commercial customers. Q Networks' founder and president said, "Customers are not just numbers to us. It's a very tight-knit community. When we do well, it's posted on the Internet." Current customers refer 93 percent of Q Networks' new customers. Moreover, unlike AOL, which was hemorrhaging thousands of customers per day at the peak of its problems, Q Networks only has a .3 percent rate of annual customer turnover.[6] In summary, AOL's resources that provide customers with simplicity and ease-of-use have been valuable, rare, and imperfectly imitable. However, if customers decide that the Internet access provided by ISPs is an acceptable substitute, then AOL will not have a sustainable competitive advantage.

Review 1: *Sustainable Competitive Advantage*

Firms can use their resources to create and sustain a competitive advantage, that is, to provide greater value for customers than competitors can. A competitive advantage becomes sustainable when other companies cannot duplicate the benefits it provides and have, for now, stopped trying. To provide a sustainable competitive advantage, the firm's resources must be valuable (capable of improving efficiency and effectiveness), rare (not possessed by many competing firms), imperfectly imitable (extremely costly or difficult to duplicate), and nonsubstitutable (competitors cannot substitute other resources to produce similar value).

2 Strategy-Making Process

Companies use a *strategy-making process* to create strategies that produce sustainable competitive advantage.[7] Figure 9.1 displays the three steps of the strategy-making process.

Step one is to **2.1** *assess the need for strategic change. Step two is to* **2.2** *conduct a situational analysis. Step three is to* **2.3** *choose strategic alternatives. Let's examine each of these steps in more detail.*

Figure 9.1 **Three Steps of the Strategy-Making Process**

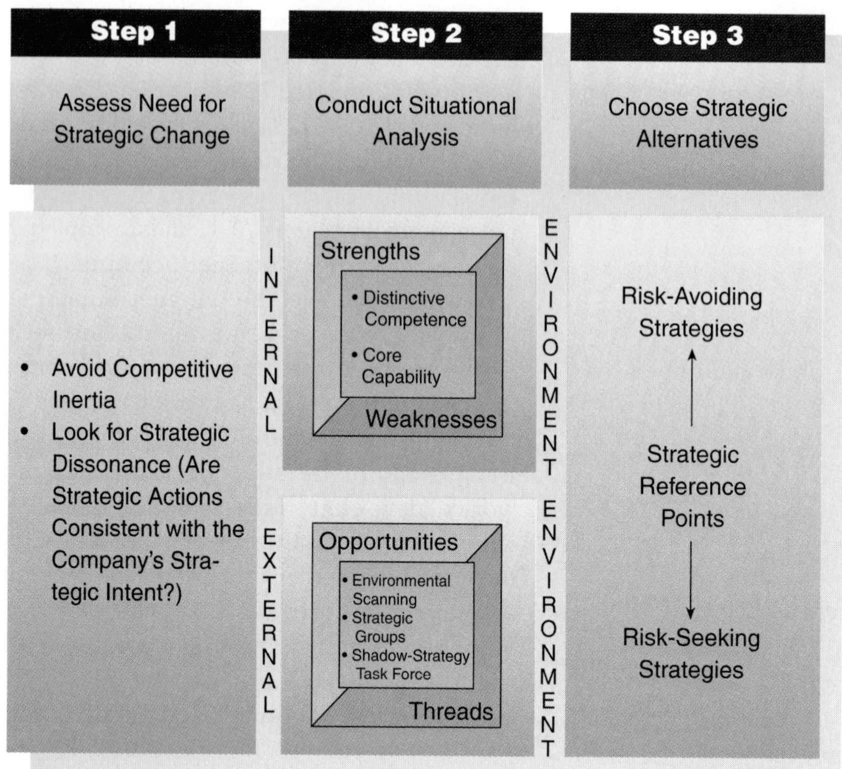

What Really Works

Strategy-Making for Firms, Big and Small

The strategy-making process (assessing the need for strategic change, conducting a situational analysis, and choosing strategic alternatives) is the method by which companies create strategies that produce sustainable competitive advantage. For years, it had been thought that strategy-making was something that only large firms could do well. It was believed that small firms did not have the time, knowledge, or staff to do a good job of strategy-making. However, two meta-analyses indicate that strategy-making can improve the profits, sales growth, and return on investment of both big *and* small firms.

Strategy-Making for Big Firms

There is a 72 percent chance that big companies that engage in the strategy-making process will be more profitable than big companies that don't. However, strategy-making not only improves profits, but also helps companies grow. Specifically, there is a 75 percent chance that big companies that engage in the strategy-making process will have greater sales and earnings growth than big companies that don't. Thus, in practical terms, the strategy-making process can make a significant difference in a big company's profits and growth.

Strategic Planning & Profits for Big Companies

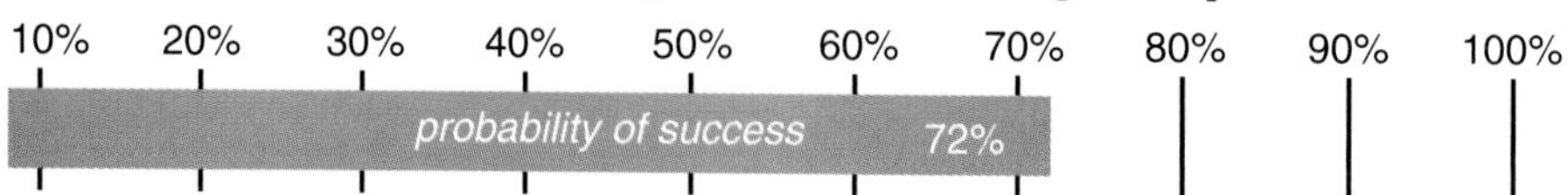

Strategic Planning & Growth for Big Companies

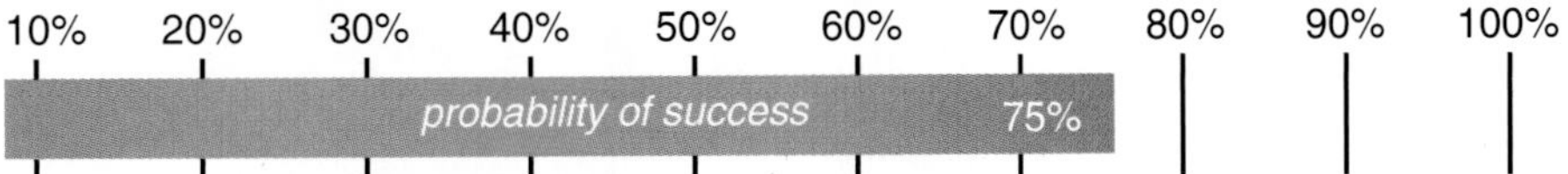

Strategy-Making for Small Firms

However, strategy-making can also improve the performance of small firms. There is a 61 percent chance that small firms that engage in the strategy-making process will have more sales growth than small firms that don't. Likewise, there is a 62 percent chance that small firms that engage in the strategy-making process will have a larger return on investment than small companies that don't. Thus, in practical terms, the strategy-making process can make a significant difference in a small company's profits and growth, too.

Strategic Planning & Sales Growth for Small Companies

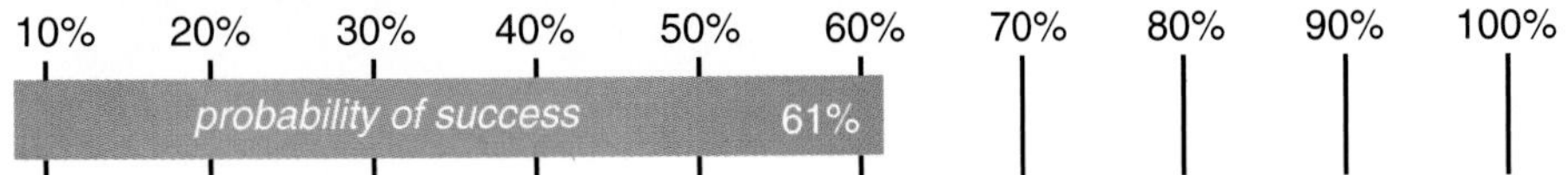

Strategic Planning & Return on Investment for Small Companies

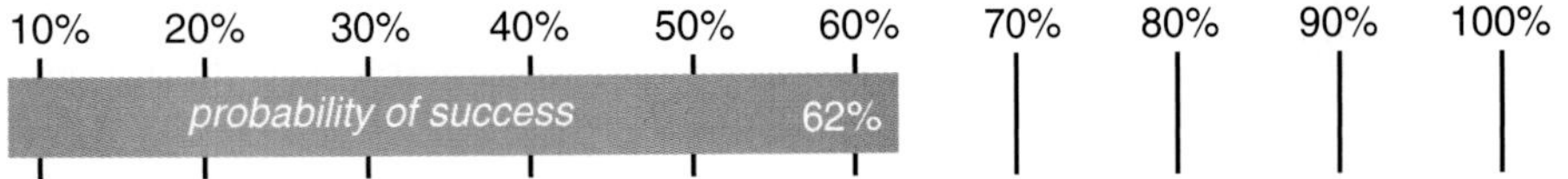

Sources: S. Hart & C. Banbury, "How Strategy-Making Processes Can Make a Difference," *Strategic Management Journal* 15 (1994): 251-269. C.C. Miller & L.B. Cardinal, "Strategic Planning and Firm Performance: A Synthesis of More Than Two Decades of Research," *Academy of Management Journal* 37 (1994): 1649-1665. C.R. Schwenk, "Effects of Formal Strategic Planning on Financial Performance in Small Firms: A Meta-Analysis," *Entrepreneurship Theory and Practice*, Spring 1993, 53-64.

2.1 *Assessing the Need for Strategic Change*

The external business environment is much more turbulent than it used to be. With customers' needs constantly growing and changing, and with competitors working harder, faster, and smarter to meet those needs, the first step in strategy-making is determining the need for strategic change. In other words, the company needs to determine whether or not it needs to change its strategy to sustain a competitive advantage. [8]

It might seem that determining the need for strategic change would be easy to do, but in reality, it's not. There's a great deal of uncertainty in strategic business environments. Furthermore, top-level managers are often slow to recognize the need for strategic change, especially at successful companies that have created and sustained competitive advantages. Because they are acutely aware of the strategies that made their companies successful, they continue to rely on them, even as the competition changes. In other words, success often leads to **competitive inertia**—a reluctance to change strategies or competitive practices that have been successful in the past.

competitive inertia
a reluctance to change strategies or competitive practices that have been successful in the past

For example, just a few years ago, no one in the cable TV industry believed that direct broadcast satellite dishes would threaten their business. With huge satellite dishes costing over $1,000, why would the 65 million Americans who already had cable TV in their homes pay more than $1,500

The threat from developing satellite dish technology woke up cable TV companies to sustain competitive advantage.
© Andy Sacks/Tony Stone Images

Personal ProductivityTip

Thinking Strategically? Be Foolish!

You've all heard "Don't be foolish! This is serious!" However, being foolish occasionally may actually be a good thing, because it encourages you to challenge conventional thinking and see things you might normally miss. For example, as a researcher at AT&T's Bell Labs, David Isenberg dressed as a court jester while holding a conference called "What If Minutes Were Free?" At the time, many in AT&T thought the conference foolish. But with the advent of free Internet phone calls, Isenberg no longer looks the fool. So next time you're thinking strategically, be foolish! It may help you and your company see the need for strategic change.

Sources: T. Petzinger, Jr., A Smart Business Model Is Seen in a 'Stupid Network', Somebody Had to Play the Fool, and David Isenberg Figured It Might as Well Be Him," *The Wall Street Journal Interactive Edition*, 20 February 1998.

strategic dissonance
a discrepancy between upper management's intended strategy and the strategy actually implemented by lower levels of management

to install an unsightly ten-foot-diameter satellite dish in their yard to get the same number of channels that they could get from their local cable company for only a $50 installation fee and $25 a month? Managers of cable TV companies would laugh that "DBS" (direct broadcast satellite) really stood for "Don't Be Stupid." However, now that satellite dishes are smaller (two feet in diameter), cost less than $200, and offer 200 channels compared to the 40 or fewer channels available on most cable systems, no one who manages a cable company is laughing anymore. Indeed, the number of DBS subscribers is predicted to quadruple from four million to sixteen million in the next few years.[9]

So, besides being aware of the dangers of competitive inertia, what can managers do to improve the speed and accuracy with which they determine the need for strategic change? One method is to actively look for signs of strategic dissonance. **Strategic dissonance** is a discrepancy between upper management's intended strategy and the strategy actually implemented by the lower levels of management. Upper management sets overall company strategy, but middle and lower-level managers must carry out the strategy. Middle and lower-level managers are held directly responsible for meeting customers' needs and responding to competitors' actions. While strategic dissonance can indicate that these managers are not doing what they should to carry out company strategy, it can also mean that the intended strategy is out of date and needs to be changed.

For example, few people know that Intel, the leading manufacturer of microprocessors for personal computers (i.e., Pentium microprocessors), began as a manufacturer of DRAM memory chips for computers (a related, but very different business). However, it took Intel's upper management several years to realize that its intended strategy to be a "memory company" was not consistent with its actions toward being a "microprocessor company." Andy Grove, then Intel's CEO, said that top management finally recognized the need for strategic change when it began to look at its managers' actions. Grove said,

Don't ask managers, What is your strategy? Look at what they do! Because people will pretend... The fact is that we [Intel] had become a non-factor in DRAMs [memory chips], with 2–3% market share. The DRAM business just passed us by! Yet, many people were still holding to the "self-evident truth" that Intel was a memory company. One of the toughest challenges is to make people see that these self-evident truths are no longer true...I recall going to see Gordon Moore [Intel's founder] and asking him what a new management would do if we were replaced. The answer was clear: Get out of DRAMs [and focus on microprocessors]. So, I suggested to Gordon that we go through the revolving door, come back in, and just do it ourselves.[10]

Determining the need for strategic change is a difficult process, but can be improved by actively looking for signs of strategic dissonance, a difference between the intended strategy and what managers are actually doing.

2.2 Situational Analysis

situational (SWOT) analysis
an assessment of the strengths and weaknesses in an organization's internal environment and the opportunities and threats in its external environment

A situational analysis can also help managers determine the need for strategic change. A **situational analysis**, also called a **SWOT analysis** for *strengths, weaknesses, opportunities*, and *threats*, is an assessment of the strengths and weaknesses in an organization's internal environment and the opportunities and threats in its external environment.[11] Ideally a SWOT analysis helps a company determine how to increase internal strengths and minimize internal weaknesses while simultaneously maximizing external opportunities and minimizing external threats. However, a basic situational analysis of Apple Computer shows this is not always easy to do. One of Apple's strengths used to be that its computers were much easier to learn and use than others on the market. Indeed, millions of customers were willing to pay much more for an Apple because this was so. However, there have been key changes in Apple's external environment. One of the most important was the introduction of Microsoft's Windows 95 (followed by Windows 98) software, which made IBM-compatible computers much easier to use. Consequently, Apple's strength, coupled with the much higher prices that Apple charged for its computers, eventually became a tremendous weakness. The result: Apple's share of the personal computer market plummeted from 16 percent to 4 percent in less than three years.[12]

As Apple's experience shows, competitive advantages can erode over time if internal strengths eventually become weaknesses. Consequently, an analysis of an organization's internal environment, that is, a company's strengths and weaknesses, begins with an assessment of distinctive competencies and core capabilities. A **distinctive competence** is something that a company can make, do, or perform better than its competitors. For example, *Consumer Reports* magazine consistently ranks Toyota cars number one in quality and reliability. Likewise, by finishing first in passenger satisfaction, on-time performance, and baggage handling (fewest mishandled bags per 1,000 customers), Southwest Airlines regularly wins the U.S. Department of Transportation's "triple-crown" for superior airline performance.[13]

distinctive competence
what a company can make, do, or perform better than its competitors

While distinctive competencies are tangible—for example, a product or service is faster, cheaper, or better—the core capabilities that produce distinctive competencies are not. **Core capabilities** are the less visible,

Apple Computer lost much of its market share when Windows made IBM-compatible machines as easy to use as Apples. CEO Steve Jobs is leading Apple's drive to reclaim its strength in ease of use, with the introduction of the iMac computer.
© Corbis/AFP

core capabilities
the internal decision-making routines, problem-solving processes, and organizational cultures that determine how efficiently inputs can be turned into outputs

internal decision-making routines, problem-solving processes, and organizational cultures that determine how efficiently inputs can be turned into outputs.[14] Distinctive competencies cannot be sustained for long without superior core capabilities. Southwest Airlines' unique corporate culture is a core capability that helps it achieve its distinctive competencies in airline performance. At Southwest, employees know that company management truly values them. One example of that value occurs each year on the busiest flying day of the year, the Wednesday before Thanksgiving. On that day, CEO Herb Kelleher and other top managers show their support for Southwest's employees by helping exhausted ground crews load baggage onto planes. Southwest's employees, in turn, work even smarter, harder, and longer than most employees. Consequently, at Southwest, the corporate culture is *the* core capability that enables Southwest to create distinctive competencies in on-time performance, baggage handling, and customer satisfaction.[15]

After examining internal strengths and weaknesses, the second part of a situational analysis is to look outside the company and assess the opportunities and threats in the external environment. In Chapter 2, you learned that *environmental scanning* is searching the environment for important events or issues that might affect the organization. With environmental scanning, managers usually scan the environment to stay up-to-date on important factors in their environment, such as pricing trends and changes in technology in the industry. However, in a situational analysis, managers use environmental scanning to identify specific opportunities and threats that can either improve or harm the company's ability to sustain its competitive advantage. Identification of strategic groups and formation of shadow-strategy task forces are two ways to do this.

strategic group
a group of companies within an industry that top managers choose to compare, evaluate, and benchmark strategic threats and opportunities

core firms
the central companies in a strategic group

secondary firms
the firms in a strategic group that follow related, but somewhat different strategies than do the core firms

transient firms
the firms in a strategic group whose strategies are changing from one strategic position to another

Strategic groups are not "actual" groups, but are selected for study by managers. A **strategic group** is a group of other companies within an industry that top managers choose for comparing, evaluating, and benchmarking their company's strategic threats and opportunities.[16] Typically, managers include companies as part of their strategic group if they compete directly with those companies for customers or if those companies use strategies similar to theirs. For example, it's likely that the managers at Gannett Company, the largest U.S. newspaper publisher (84 daily newspapers and USA Today), assess strategic threats and opportunities by comparing themselves to a strategic group consisting of the other major newspaper companies. This would probably include the Tribune Company (the *Chicago Tribune*, the *Ft. Lauderdale Sun-Sentinel*, *Orlando Sentinel*, and many other newspapers) and Knight-Ridder (the *Detroit Free Press*, the *Philadelphia Inquirer*, the *Miami Herald*, and many other newspapers). By contrast, given that Gannett owns 84 daily newspapers in 40 states with a total circulation approaching 7 million readers, it's unlikely that Gannett management worries much about *The Arkansas Democrat Gazette*. The *Gazette* is a fine paper, having won numerous awards for its writing and news coverage, but with a total circulation of 175,000, mostly within Arkansas, managers at Gannett would probably not include it in their strategic group.

In fact, when scanning the environment for strategic threats and opportunities, managers tend to categorize the different companies in their industries into several kinds of strategic groups: core, secondary, and transient firms.[17] The first kind of strategic group consists of **core firms**, that is, central companies in a strategic group. Gannett's core firms would be the Tribune Company and Knight-Ridder publishing. When most managers scan their environments for strategic threats and opportunities, they do so by primarily scanning the strategic actions of core firms.

Secondary firms are firms that use related but somewhat different strategies than core firms. For Gannett, this might be the New York Times Company, which publishes the *New York Times*, the *Boston Globe*, and 20 other small newspapers. However, the New York Times Company is somewhat different, in that it also publishes magazines, runs TV and radio stations, operates two paper mills, and sells wire and photo services to other newspapers publishers. Managers are aware of the potential threats and opportunities posed by secondary firms. However, they spend more time assessing the threats and opportunities associated with core firms.

Transient firms are companies whose strategies are changing from one strategic position to another. An example for Gannett would be the Times Mirror Company, which publishes the *Los Angeles Times* and is the third-largest newspaper publisher in the U.S. Times Mirror sold its cable TV and book publishing businesses to refocus on the newspaper business. Because their strategies are changing, managers may not know what to think about transient firms. Consequently, managers may often overlook or be wrong about the potential threats and opportunities posed by transient firms.

So, what external threats and opportunities did Gannett see after assessing its strategic groups? In terms of threats, Gannett saw little chance for growth in several areas, selling all five of its remaining radio stations and its outdoor advertising company (i.e., billboards). In terms of opportunities, Gannett has focused on technology and television, establishing InfiNet, an

Internet access and service company designed to help newspapers go online, and purchasing five television stations in the last few years.[18]

Because top managers tend to limit their attention to the core firms in their strategic group, some companies have started using shadow-strategy task forces to more aggressively scan their environments for strategic threats and opportunities. The goal of a **shadow-strategy task force** is to actively seek out its own company's weaknesses and then, thinking like a competitor, determine how other companies could exploit them for competitive advantage.[19] Furthermore, to make sure that the task force challenges conventional thinking, its members should be independent-minded, come from a variety of company functions and levels, and have the access and authority to question the company's current strategic actions and intent. For example, Ciba-Geigy's Industrial Dye division makes color dyes used in carpet manufacturing. One of the difficulties in this business is ensuring color consistency, that is, making sure that the dark gray carpet manufactured today looks the same color as the dark gray carpet manufactured next week. Ciba-Geigy's shadow-strategy task force determined that if its competitors could find ways to consistently, precisely, and cheaply match color carpet dyes (so that carpet colors looked the same regardless of when and where they were manufactured), Ciba-Geigy would be at a considerable competitive disadvantage. After the shadow-strategy task force challenged top management with its conclusions, the company went about developing distinctive competencies in dye research and manufacturing, which allowed it to make dyes with scientific preciseness.[20]

shadow-strategy task force
a committee within the company that analyzes the company's own weaknesses to determine how competitors could exploit them for competitive advantage

In short, there are two basic parts to a situational analysis. The first is to examine internal strengths and weaknesses by focusing on distinctive competencies and core capabilities. The second is to examine external opportunities and threats by focusing on environmental scanning, strategic groups, and shadow-strategy task forces.

2.3 *Choosing Strategic Alternatives*

After determining the need for strategic change and conducting a situational analysis, the last step in the strategy-making process is to choose strategic alternatives that will help the company create or maintain a sustainable competitive advantage. According to Strategic Reference Point Theory, managers choose between two basic alternative strategies. They can choose a conservative, *risk-avoiding strategy* that aims to protect an existing competitive advantage. Or, they can choose an aggressive, *risk-seeking strategy* that aims to extend or create a sustainable competitive advantage. For example, Menards is a hardware store chain with 128 locations throughout the Midwest. When hardware giant Home Depot entered the Midwest several years ago, Menards faced a basic choice: avoid risk by continuing with the strategy it had in place before Home Depot's arrival, or seek risk by trying to further its competitive advantage against Home Depot, which is six times its size. Some of its competitors decided to fold. Kmart closed all of its Builder's Square hardware stores when Home Depot came to Minneapolis. Handy Andy liquidated its 74 stores when Home Depot came to the Midwest. But Menards decided to fight, spending millions to open 35 new stores at the same time that Home Depot was opening 44 of its new stores.[21]

The choice to be risk-seeking or risk-avoiding typically depends on whether top management views the company as falling above or below

strategic reference points the strategic targets managers use to measure whether a firm has developed the core competencies it needs to achieve a sustainable competitive advantage

strategic reference points. **Strategic reference points** are the targets that managers use to measure whether their firm has developed the core competencies that it needs to achieve a sustainable competitive advantage. For example, if a hotel chain decided to compete by providing superior quality and service, then top management would track the success of this strategy through customer surveys or published hotel ratings, such as those provided by the prestigious *Mobil Travel Guide*. By contrast, if a hotel chain decided to compete on price, it would regularly conduct market surveys that checked the prices of other hotels. The competitors' prices are the hotel managers' strategic reference points against which to compare their own pricing strategy. If competitors can consistently underprice them, then the managers need to determine whether their staff and resources have the core competencies to compete on price.

As shown in Table 9.1, when companies are performing above or better than their strategic reference points, top management will typically be satisfied with company strategy. Ironically, this satisfaction tends to make top management conservative and risk-averse. After all, since the company already has a sustainable competitive advantage, the worst thing that could happen would be to lose it. Consequently, new issues or changes in the company's external environments are viewed as threats. But when companies are performing below or worse than their strategic reference points, top management will typically be dissatisfied with company strategy. However, in this instance, managers are much more likely to choose a daring, risk-taking strategy. After all, if the current strategy is producing substandard results, what has the company got to lose by switching to risky new strategies in the hopes that it can create a sustainable competitive advantage? Consequently, for companies in this situation, new issues or changes in external environments are viewed as opportunities for potential gain.

However, Strategic Reference Point Theory is not deterministic. Managers are not predestined to choose risk-averse or risk-seeking strategies for their companies. Indeed, one of the most important points in Strategic Reference Point Theory is that managers *can* influence the strategies chosen at their companies by *actively changing and adjusting* the strategic reference points they use to judge strategic performance. To illustrate, if a company

Table 9.1 **Strategic Reference Points**

	Current Situation	Perception of New Issues	Response or Behavior
Above ↑	• Satisfied • Sitting on Top of the World	• Threat • Potential Loss • Negative	• Risk-averse • Conservative • Defensive
Strategic Reference Points			
↓ **Below**	• Dissatisfied • At the Bottom Looking Up	• Opportunity • Potential Gain • Positive	• Risk-taking • Daring • Offensive
	Current Situation	**Perception of New Issues**	**Response or Behavior**

Source: A. Fiegenbaum, S. Hart, & D. Schendel, Strategic Reference Point Theory, *Strategic Management Journal* 17 (1996): 219-235.

has become complacent after consistently surpassing its strategic reference points, then top management can change the company's strategic risk orientation from risk-averse to risk-taking by raising the standards of performance (i.e., strategic reference points). Indeed, this is what happened at Menards.

Instead of being satisfied with just protecting its existing stores (a risk-averse strategy), founder John Menard changed the strategic referent points the company had been using to assess strategic performance. To encourage a daring, offensive-minded strategy that would allow the company to open nearly as many new stores as Home Depot, he determined that Menards would have to beat Home Depot on not one or two, but four strategic reference points: price, products, sales per square foot, and "friendly accessibility." Preliminary data indicate that the Menard's strategy is well on its way to succeeding. In terms of price, market research indicates that a 100-item shopping cart of goods is consistently cheaper at Menards. In terms of products, Menards sells 50,000 products per store, the same as Home Depot. In terms of sales per square foot, Menards ($360 per square foot) strongly outsells Home Depot ($290 per square foot). Finally, unlike Home Depot's warehouse-like stores, Menards' stores are built to resemble grocery stores. Shiny tiled floors, wide aisles, and easy-to-reach products all make Menards a "friendlier" place for shoppers.[22]

So even when (perhaps *especially* when) companies have achieved a sustainable competitive advantage, top managers must adjust or change strategic reference points to challenge themselves and their employees to develop new core competencies for the future. In the long run, effective organizations will frequently revise their strategic reference points to better focus managers' attention on the new challenges and opportunities that occur in their ever-changing business environments.

Personal Productivity Tip

To Which Party Do You Belong?

One of the most difficult steps in strategy-making is getting top managers to recognize the need for strategic change. Professor Gary Hamel advises senior executives to answer two questions. First, over time, have they become more or less willing to challenge conventional thinking about their business? Second, have they become more or less curious about the changes taking place outside their industry? Ralph Waldo Emerson wrote, "There are always two parties, the party of the past and the party of the future; the establishment and the movement." Hamel, paraphrasing Emerson, asks top managers "To which party do you belong? the past or the future?"

Source: G. Hamel, "Strategy as Revolution," *Harvard Business Review*, July-August 1996, 69-82.

Review 2
Strategy-Making Process

The first step in strategy-making is determining whether a strategy needs to be changed in order to sustain a competitive advantage. Because uncertainty and competitive inertia make this difficult to determine, managers can improve the speed and accuracy of this step by looking for differences between top management's intended strategy and the strategy actually implemented by lower-level managers (i.e., strategic dissonance). The second step is to conduct a situational analysis that examines internal strengths and weaknesses (distinctive competencies and core capabilities), as well as external threats and opportunities (environmental scanning, strategic groups, and shadow-strategy task forces). In the third step of strategy-making, Strategic Reference Point Theory suggests that when companies are performing better than their strategic reference points, top management will typically choose a risk-averse strategy. When performance is below strategic reference points, risk-seeking strategies are more likely to be chosen. Importantly, however, managers *can* influence the choice of strategic alternatives by actively changing and adjusting the strategic reference points they use to judge strategic performance.

Corporate-, Industry-, and Firm-Level Strategies

Several years ago, Walter Young received a call from an investment banker who wanted to know if he was interested in running Champion Enterprises, maker of recreational vehicles, recreational buses, and manufactured homes, and seller of home insurance, home financing, and numerous other products and services. Despite the fact that Champion had lost $30 million over the last five years, Young decided to take the job. The first question he asked himself and Champion's managers was "What business are we in?" Were they in the money-lending business? No. Were they in the property-selling business? No. What about housing parts or insurance? No, not those either. After serious consideration, Walter Young and his managers decided that Champion Enterprises should only be in one business, "supplying affordable housing." So Champion stopped selling property. Plus, it got out of the housing component, insurance, and RV businesses, selling them to others. As a result, Champion now has one focus: selling low-cost, pre-manufactured housing.

With its business, supplying affordable housing, now clear, Young and his managers asked themselves a second important question: "How should we compete in this industry?" At first, the answer was "cut costs." Accordingly, Young lowered Champion's expenses, cutting the number of staffers at corporate headquarters from 260 to 12. Then, he further cut costs by reducing the number of different models of manufactured houses that the company would build. After bringing costs in line, the answer was growth. In the last four years, Champion has strengthened its core business by purchasing seven other pre-manufactured housing companies. Together, these moves have doubled Champion's revenues and increased its market share, making it second only to industry leader Redman Industries. [23]

What business are we in? How should we compete in this industry? Who are our competitors and how should we respond to them? These simple, but powerful questions are at the heart of corporate-, industry-, and firm-level strategies.

After reading the next three sections, you should be able to:

3 explain the different kinds of **corporate-level strategies**.

4 describe the different kinds of **industry-level strategies**.

5 explain the components and strategies of **firm-level strategies**.

Table 9.2 provides an overview of the various corporate-, industry-, and firm-level strategies that you'll learn about in these sections.

3 Corporate-Level Strategies

corporate-level strategy the overall organizational strategy that addresses the question "What business or businesses are we in or should we be in?"

Corporate-level strategy is the overall organizational strategy that addresses the question "What business or businesses are we in or should we be in?" For example, in recent years, Ford Motor Company has decided to focus more on its core business of manufacturing cars. Consequently, Ford decided to sell three companies that it owned: Budget Rent-a-Car (the fifth-largest rental car company), its heavy truck operations, and a financial unit called USL Capital.[24]

Table 9.2: **Corporate-, Business-, and Firm-Level Strategies.**

Corporate-Level Strategies	Positioning Strategies
Corporate-Level Strategies	**Positioning Strategies**
Portfolio Strategy	• Cost leadership
• Acquisitions, unrelated diversification, related diversification, single businesses	• Differentiation
• Boston Consulting Group Matrix	• Focus
■ Stars	**Adaptive Strategies**
■ Question marks	• Defenders
■ Cash cows	• Analyzers
■ Dogs	• Prospectors
Grand Strategies	• Reactors
• Growth	***Firm-Level Strategies (Direct Competition)***
• Stability	**Direct Competition**
• Retrenchment/recovery	• Market commonality
Industry-Level Strategies	• Resource similarity
Five Industry Forces	**Strategic Moves of Direct Competition**
• Character of rivalry	• Attack
• Threat of new entrants	• Response
• Threat of substitute products or services	**Entrepreneurial Orientation**
• Bargaining power of suppliers	• Autonomy
• Bargaining power of buyers	• Innovativeness
	• Risk taking
	• Proactiveness
	• Competitive aggressiveness

Let's learn more about how companies decide which businesses they should be in by examining the two major approaches to corporate-level strategy, **3.1** *portfolio strategy and* **3.2** *grand strategies.*

3.1 Portfolio Strategy[25]

diversification
a strategy for reducing risk by buying a variety of items (stocks or, in the case of a corporation, types of businesses), so that the failure of one stock or one business does not doom the entire portfolio

portfolio strategy
corporate-level strategy that minimizes risk by diversifying investment among various businesses or product lines

One of the standard strategies for stock market investors is **diversification**: buy stocks in a variety of companies in different industries. The purpose of this strategy is to reduce risk in the overall stock portfolio (i.e., the entire collection of stocks). The basic idea is simple: If you invest in ten companies in ten different industries, you won't lose your entire investment if one company performs poorly. Furthermore, because they're in different industries, one company's losses are likely to be offset by another company's gains. Portfolio strategy is based on these same ideas.

Portfolio strategy is a corporate-level strategy that minimizes risk by diversifying investment among various businesses or product lines. Like an investor who invests in a variety of stocks, portfolio strategy guides the strategic decisions of corporations that compete in a variety of businesses. For example, it could be used to guide the strategy of a company like 3M, which makes 50,000 products for 16 different industries. Similarly, it could be used by Johnson & Johnson, which has 170 divisions making health care products for the pharmaceuticals, diagnostics, consumers, and health care professionals markets. And, just as investors consider the mix of stocks in their stock portfolio when deciding which stocks to buy or sell, portfolio strategy provides the following guidelines to help managers acquire companies that fit well with the rest of their corporate portfolio and sell those that don't.

First, the more businesses in which a corporation competes, the smaller its overall chances of failing. Think of a corporation as a stool and its businesses as the legs of the stool. The more legs or businesses added to the stool, the less likely it is to tip over. Using this analogy, portfolio strategy reduces 3M's risk of failing, because the corporation's survival depends on essentially 16 different businesses. Because the emphasis is on adding "legs to the stool," managers who use portfolio strategy are often on the lookout for **acquisitions**, that is, other companies to buy.

acquisition
purchase of a company by another company

unrelated diversification
creating or acquiring companies in completely unrelated businesses

Second, beyond adding new businesses to the corporate portfolio, portfolio strategy can reduce risk even more through **unrelated diversification—** creating or acquiring companies in completely unrelated businesses. If the businesses are unrelated, then losses in one business or industry will have minimal effect on the performance of other companies in the corporate portfolio. One of the best examples of unrelated diversification is Samsung Corporation of Korea. Samsung has eight businesses in electronics (video and audio products, appliances, information systems, computers, and semiconductors), four companies in its machinery business group (power plants, waste-treatment facilities, infrastructure, and material-handling systems), five companies in chemicals (high-polymer composites, engineering plastics, and specialty chemicals), five companies in finance and insurance (life, property, and casualty insurance, as well as credit cards and securities), and sixteen other companies in businesses ranging from automobiles to hotels to entertainment. Because most internally grown businesses tend to be related to existing products or services, acquiring new businesses is the preferred method of unrelated diversification.

BCG matrix
a portfolio strategy, developed by the Boston Consulting Group, that managers use to categorize the corporation's businesses by growth rate and relative market share, helping them decide how to invest corporate funds

star
a company with a large share of a fast-growing market

question mark
a company with a small share of a fast-growing market

cash cow
a company with a large share of a slow-growing market

dog
a company with a small share of a slow-growing market

Third, investing the profits and cash flows from mature, slow-growth businesses into newer, faster-growing businesses can reduce long-term risk. The best-known portfolio strategy for guiding investment in a corporation's businesses is the Boston Consulting Group (BCG) matrix. The **BCG matrix** is a portfolio strategy that managers use to categorize their corporation's businesses by growth rate and relative market share, helping them decide how to invest corporate funds. The matrix, shown in Figure 9.2, separates businesses into four categories, based on how fast the market is growing (high-growth or low-growth) and the size of the business's share of that market (small or large). **Stars** are companies that have a large share of a fast-growing market. To take advantage of a star's fast-growing market and its strength in that market (large share), the corporation must invest substantially in it. However, the investment is usually worthwhile, because many stars produce sizable future profits. **Question marks** are companies that have a small share of a fast-growing market. If the corporation invests in these companies, they may eventually become stars, but their relative weakness in the market (small share) makes investing in question marks more risky than investing in stars. **Cash cows** are companies that have a large share of a slow-growing market. Companies in this situation are often highly profitable, hence the name "cash cow." Finally, **dogs** are companies that have a small share of a slow-growing market. As the name "dogs" suggests, having a small share of a slow-growth market is often not profitable.

Since the idea is to redirect investment from slow-growing to fast-growing companies, the Boston Consulting Group matrix starts by recommending that, while they last, the substantial cash flows from cash cows should be reinvested in stars to help them grow even faster and obtain even more market share. Using this strategy, current profits help produce future profits.

Figure 9.2 **Boston Consulting Group Matrix**

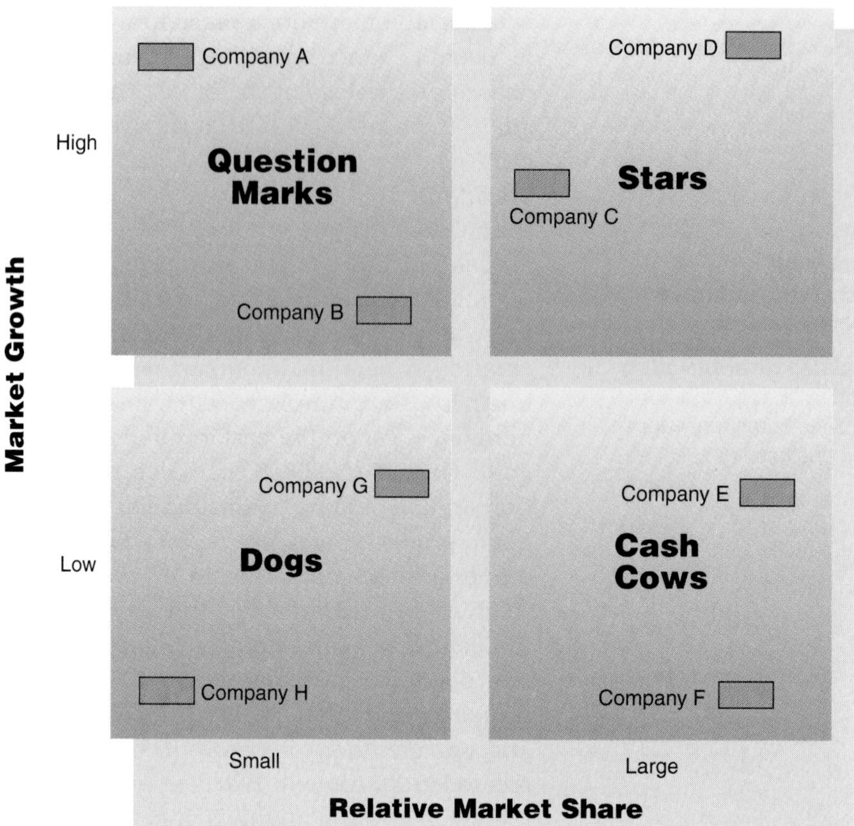

Cash flows should also be directed to some question marks. Though riskier than stars, question marks have great potential because of their fast-growing market. However, managers must decide which question marks are most likely to turn into stars and therefore warrant further investment, and which ones are too risky and should be sold. Finally, because dogs lose money, the corporation should "find them new owners" or "take them to the pound." In other words, dogs should be sold to other companies, or should be closed down and liquidated for their assets.

While the BCG matrix and other forms of portfolio strategy are relatively popular among managers, portfolio strategy has some drawbacks. The most significant is that the evidence does not support the usefulness of acquiring unrelated businesses. As shown in Figure 9.3, there is a U-shaped relationship between diversification and risk. The left side of the curve shows that single businesses with no diversification are extremely risky (if the single business fails, the entire business fails). So, in part, the portfolio strategy of diversifying is correct—competing in a variety of different businesses can lower risk. However, portfolio strategy is partly wrong, too—the right side of the curve shows that conglomerates composed of completely unrelated businesses are even riskier than single, undiversified businesses.

The second set of problems with portfolio strategy has to do with the dysfunctional consequences that occur when companies are categorized as stars, cash cows, question marks, or dogs. Contrary to expectations, the BCG matrix often yields incorrect judgments about a company's future potential. This is because it relies on past performance (i.e., previous market share and previous market growth), which is a notoriously poor predic-

Figure 9.3 **U-shaped Relationship Between Diversification and Risk**

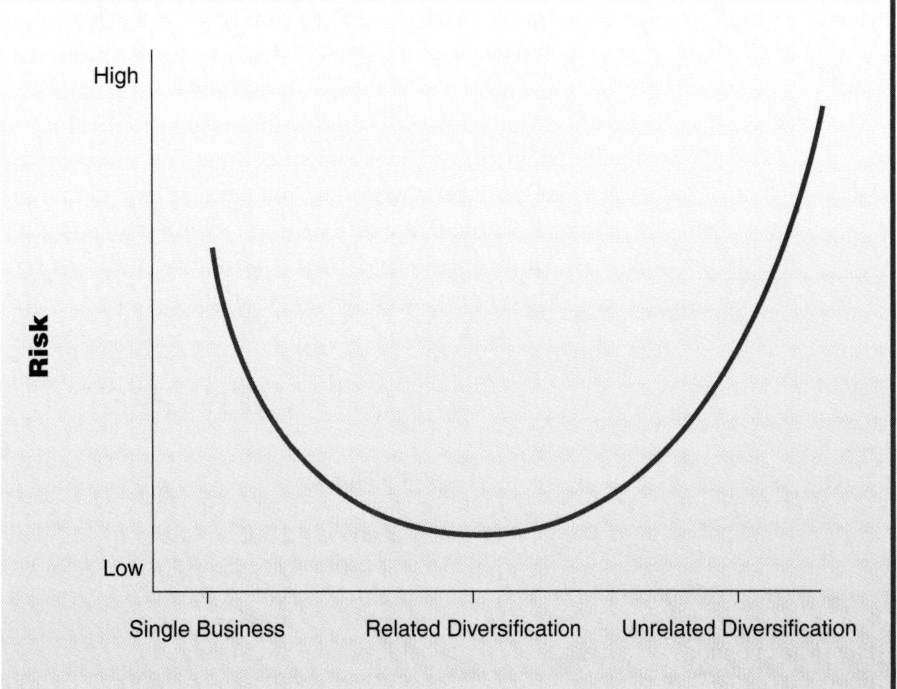

Source: M. Lubatkin & P.J. Lane, "Psst...The Merger Mavens Still Have It Wrong!" *Academy of Management Executive* 10 (1996): 21-39.

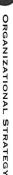

tor of future company performance. For example, in the early 1980s, Coca-Cola would clearly have been categorized as a dog. Growth in soft-drink sales had slowed dramatically. *Business Week* magazine even ran a cover story called "The Graying of the Soft Drink Industry," which suggested that the business was destined to shrink as young cola drinkers aged. Pepsi was gaining market share at Coke's expense. Plus, the company embarrassed itself worldwide with its failed introduction of new Coke. If any company could be characterized as a "dog" at that time, it was Coca-Cola. However, since that time, Coke has outperformed all other companies, including such stalwarts as General Electric, Intel, Wal-Mart, and Microsoft, returning over $60 billion in dividends and stock price appreciation to its shareholders.[26]

Furthermore, using the BCG matrix can also weaken the strongest performer in the corporate portfolio, the cash cow. As funds are redirected from cash cows to stars, corporate managers essentially take away the resources needed to take advantage of the cash cow's new business opportunities. The result is that the cash cow becomes less aggressive in seeking new business or in defending its present business. Finally, labeling a top performer as a cash cow can harm employee morale. Instead of working for themselves, cash cow employees realize that they have inferior status because their successes are now being used to fund the growth of stars and question marks.

related diversification
creating or acquiring companies that share similar products, manufacturing, marketing, technology, or cultures

So, what kind of portfolio strategy does the best job of helping managers decide which companies to buy or sell? The U-shaped curve in Figure 9.3 indicates that the best approach is probably **related diversification**, in which the different business units share similar products, manufacturing, marketing, technology, or cultures. The key to related diversification is to acquire or create new companies with core capabilities that complement the core capabilities of businesses already in the corporate portfolio. We began this section with the example of 3M and how its 50,000 products are sold in over 16 different industries. While seemingly different, most of 3M's product divisions are based in some fashion on its distinctive competencies in adhesives and tape (i.e., wet or dry sandpaper, Post-it notes, Scotchgard fabric protector, transdermal skin patches, reflective material used in traffic signs, etc.). Furthermore, all of 3M's divisions share its strong corporate culture that promotes and encourages risk-taking and innovation. In sum, in contrast to single, undiversified businesses or unrelated diversification, related diversification reduces risk, because the different businesses can work as a team, relying on each other for needed experience, expertise, and support.

Table 9.3 details the problems associated with portfolio strategy and recommends ways that managers can increase their chances of success through related diversification.

BLASTFROMTHEPAST

Five Decades of Diversification Strategies

According to Michael Gold and Kathleen Luchs, there have been four distinct periods of thought about corporate diversification strategies: conglomerates and general management skills in the 1950s and 1960s, corporate strategy and portfolio planning in the 1970s, restructuring and value-based planning in the 1980s, and synergy and "core" portfolios in the 1990s.

1950s & 1960s: Conglomerates and General Management Skills

The 1950s and 1960s saw the rise of "professional managers," who were assumed capable of managing any organization in any industry. It was argued that general management skills made managers interchangeable. If a manager was successful at an insurance company, then that success should be transferable to a steel company or a hospital. Human and conceptual skills, not specific work experience or knowledge, were thought to be the keys to good management.

Of course, if the same management skills and principles could be used to ensure success in any industry, then it didn't really matter what business you were in. Consequently, unquestioned faith in general management skills led to the rise of conglomerates, large collections of unrelated businesses under one company name. One of the largest conglomerates was ITT Corporation. As its name, International Telephone and Telegraph, suggests, ITT began as an international phone company and manufacturer. However, when Harold Geneen became ITT's president in 1959, he began a decade-long acquisition binge that ended with ITT owning 300 different companies. In one board meeting alone, Mr. Geneen suggested buying a baking company, a glassmaker, a company that taught speedwriting, and a company that manufactured hydraulic equipment for ships. During this time, ITT also bought Avis, Sheraton Hotels, Harftford Insurance, Levitt & Sons home builders, a TV company in England, and a cosmetics company in France.

1970s: Corporate Strategy and Portfolio Planning

By the end of the 1960s, enthusiasm for conglomerates and general management skills dimmed considerably. Studies indicated that conglomerates following a strategy of unrelated diversification were able to grow revenues and build market share, but were significantly less profitable and efficient than most other companies.

In the 1970s, three key ideas about diversification emerged in response to the failings of conglomerates. First, strategy was more than long-term planning. It was a way of determining a company's basic direction and taking advantage of future opportunities. Second, the purpose of strategy was to help top managers decide what business they should be in (i.e., corporate-level strategy). Third, unlike the haphazard, almost random diversification in the 1960s, portfolio planning tools, such as the GE Business Screen or the Boston Consulting Group matrix, helped managers put together a "balanced portfolio" of businesses. By selling weak companies and shifting resources from mature to promising companies, managers hoped to ensure future growth and to maximize overall corporate performance rather than the performance of any single business unit. One CEO said, "I was finding it very difficult to manage and understand so many different products and markets. I just grabbed at portfolio planning, because it provided me with a way to organize my thinking about our businesses and the resource allocation issues facing the total company. I became and still am very enthusiastic." Indeed, it's estimated that nearly half of Fortune 500 companies used portfolio planning during this time.

1980s: Restructuring and Value-Based Planning

By the end of the 1970s, top managers realized that managing a "balanced" portfolio of different companies was much more difficult than they had thought. The most serious mistake was applying the same management systems (i.e., financial planning, capital investment, incentive systems, and strategy-making processes) to very different business subunits. The lesson learned was that different types of businesses had to be managed differently, not the same.

In large part, diversification strategies in the 1980s were used to "correct" the excesses of the conglomerate-based, unrelated diversification of the 1960s and 1970s. The first correction was to cut headquarters costs, mostly by cutting the large number of headquarters staffers who had been needed to help manage large portfolios of companies. The second correction was to evaluate company value using stock market and economic measures, such as discounted cash flows and return on equity, rather than revenue growth and market share. Using these tools, managers discovered a huge "value gap" between what accounting book values indicated their corporate assets (i.e., business units) were worth and what the stock market indicated they were worth. In other words, in direct contrast to the 1960s and 1970s, managers now believed that different business units would be more valuable apart than together. These views produced the third correction, corporate restructuring, which let managers "fully value" these assets by selling the business units acquired during the acquisition binges of the 1960s and 1970s. The last correction was that managers came to believe that the most successful companies "stuck to their knitting," focusing on achieving quality, low costs, and excellence in just one business or in several related businesses.

1990s: Synergy and "Core" Portfolios

Just as the diversification strategies of the 1970s can be seen as an attempt to refine and improve the strategies of the 1960s, the diversification strategies in the 1990s can be seen as an attempt to refine and improve the strategies of the 1980s. With the dismantling of corporate conglomerates largely complete, diversification strategies in the 1990s have revolved around three ideas: synergy, core competencies, and dominant logic.

First, the basic idea of synergy is that related diversification works best. Consequently, acquisitions should be limited to companies that have complementary parts that make the companies stronger together than they were apart. In other words, synergy occurs when 1 + 1 = 3. Second, corporate portfolios are not collections of businesses, but collections of core competencies, meaning unique skills and capabilities. Walter Kiechel of *Fortune* magazine wrote, "To the extent that such skills can be exploited by each of the company's businesses, they represent a reason for having all of those businesses under one corporate umbrella . . . ." Third, dominant logic is the general way in which managers perceive and think about the business and its problems. Dominant logic influences the opportunities and threats that managers see and the strategic alternatives they consider. So, to improve the chances that diversification will work, managers should strive for good "fit," and they should acquire companies in industries that have similar dominant logic. For example, a poor "fit" would probably occur if the dominant logic of corporate management was growth and the dominant logic of the acquired firm was retrenchment.

For now, synergy, core competencies, and dominant logic are the leading beliefs about corporate diversification. However, in time, just as with conglomerates, portfolio planning, and restructuring and value-based planning, these ideas are likely to be challenged as well.

Sources: D. Dowling, "On the March, ITT Sets Breakaway Pace: Firm Loosens the Conglomerate Grip," *The StarLedger Newark*, 26 November 1995. M. Goold & K. Luchs, "Why Diversify? Four Decades of Management Thinking," *Academy of Management Executive* 7 (1993): 7-25. R.G. Hamermesh, *Making Strategy Work* (New York: John Wiley & Sons, 1986). B. Orwall, R.L. Rundle, & F. Rose, "Hilton and ITT Took Two Different Paths to this Confrontation, But Both Companies Wrestled with a Similar Demon: A Serious Lack of Focus," *The Wall Street Journal Europe*, 30 January 1997.

3.2 *Grand Strategies*

grand strategy
a broad corporate-level strategic plan used to achieve strategic goals and guide the strategic alternatives that managers of individual businesses or subunits may use

A **grand strategy** is a broad strategic plan used to help an organization achieve its strategic goals.[27] Grand strategies guide the strategic alternatives that managers of individual businesses or subunits may use. There are three kinds of grand strategies: growth, stability, and retrenchment/recovery.

The purpose of a **growth strategy** is to increase profits, revenues, market share, or the number of places (stores, offices, locations) in which the company does business. Companies can grow in several ways. They can grow externally by merging with or acquiring other companies. In recent years, some of the largest mergers and acquisitions have occurred in the

Table 9.3 **Portfolio Strategy: Problems and Recommendations**

Problems with Portfolio Strategy

- Unrelated diversification does not reduce risk.
- Uses present performance to predict future performance.
- Assessments of a business's growth potential are often inaccurate.
- Cash cows fail to aggressively pursue opportunities and defend themselves from threats.
- Being labeled a "cash cow" can hurt employee morale.
- Companies often overpay to acquire stars.
- Acquiring firms often treat acquired stars as "conquered foes." Key stars' managers, who once controlled their own destiny, often leave because they are now treated as relatively unimportant middle managers.

Recommendations for Making Portfolio Strategy Work

- Don't be so quick to sell dogs or question marks. Instead, management should commit to the markets in which it competes by strengthening core capabilities.
- Put your "eggs in similar (not different) baskets," by acquiring companies in related businesses.
- Acquire companies with complementary core capabilities.
- Encourage collaboration and cooperation between related firms and businesses within the company.
- "Date before you marry." Work with a business before deciding to acquire it.
- When in doubt, don't acquire new businesses. Mergers and acquisitions are inherently risky and difficult to make work. Only acquire firms that can help create or extend a sustainable competitive advantage.

Sources: M. Lubatkin, "Value-Creating Mergers: Fact or Folklore?" *Academy of Management Executive* 2 (1988): 295-302. M. Lubatkin & S. Chatterjee, "Extending Modern Portfolio Theory into the Domain of Corporate Diversification: Does It Apply?" *Academy of Management Journal* 37 (1994): 109-136. M.H. Lubatkin & P.J. Lane, "Psst . . . The Merger Mavens Still Have It Wrong!" *Academy of Management Executive* 10 (1996): 21-39.

growth strategy
strategy that focuses on increasing profits, revenues, market share, or the number of places in which the company does business

telecommunications industry, with WorldCom acquiring MCI Communications, Bell Atlantic acquiring Nynex, and Southwestern Bell Communications acquiring Pacific Telesis Group.[28]

Another way to grow is internally, directly expanding the company's existing business or creating and growing new businesses. Reuters, a British news agency, has grown over the last decade by creating new businesses. Reuters' CEO said, "Acquisitions are about buying market share. Our challenge is to create markets. There is a difference. Creating markets is something two out of three times you fail to do. But the third time, if you create it and you're the first, it can grow rapidly." Proof of that rapid growth can be found in Reuters' rising sales that have increased by a factor of 9 in the last 12 years. In the next 12 years, Reuters expects to achieve similar growth by growing many of its new businesses on the Internet. For now, Reuters is the leading news provider on the Internet, with its news reports available at 35 different Web sites. However, Reuters' Reality Online division also designs transaction-based Web sites for stock brokerage companies like Charles Schwab and Quick & Reilly that allow customers to research, buy, and sell investments via the World Wide Web.[29]

stability strategy
strategy that focuses on improving the way in which the company sells the same products or services to the same customers

The purpose of a **stability strategy** is to continue doing what the company has been doing, but just do it better. Consequently, companies following a stability strategy try to improve the way in which they sell the same products or services to the same customers. For example, Danzas Corporation, an international air and sea freight company, is pursuing a stability strategy. Danzas, using what it calls its "core carriers strategy," has decided to limit the number of customers it serves and the number of air hubs and seaports where it will handle freight. The reason? To improve the quality of service it provides to its four core customers, Hapag-Lloyd, DSR-Senator Lines, Cho Yang, and Mediterranean Shipping Company, each of which has a long-term contract with the company.[30] Companies often choose a stability strategy when their external environment doesn't change much, or after they have struggled with periods of explosive growth.

Been There,

Nestlé CEO, Helmut Maucher, Discusses Strategy

A decade ago, half of Nestlé's profits came from one product, Nescafé instant coffee. Likewise, most of its revenues came from one market, Europe. However, today, after a decade of worldwide acquisitions, Nestlé is the most global food company in the world. In fact, Nestlé sells more than 8,500 food products in over 100 countries. Some of its best-known products are Nescafé and Taster's Choice instant coffees, Perrier mineral water, Nestea iced tea, Coffee-Mate coffee creamer, Stouffer's frozen foods, the Nestlé Crunch candy bar, and Friskies cat food. CEO Helmut Maucher, who oversaw this expansion, talks about Nestlé's past and future strategies.

Q: How can Nestlé hope to maintain the momentum and the earnings growth that the company has enjoyed over the past decade?

A: In the past 15 years, we put Nestlé on a new footing to prepare for competition and the global markets of the future. We believe we have more or less done our homework: We are now in all the big markets, and we're in all those product areas that we want to be in. We've streamlined our organization and focused it in terms of strategic direction. Acquisitions will still be part of our future strategy, but to a lesser extent. Internal growth from the assets we now have in our hands will play a much more important role.

"Our policy has been to spread risks over different countries and different product areas . . . ."

Q: What can be done to reduce the risks of currency fluctuation against the Swiss franc and the ups and downs of commodities from which your products are made?

A: When I started here we relied heavily on Europe, and half of our profit came from Nescafé instant coffee. If anything were to have happened to coffee, we would really have been in trouble. Now we've expanded into pet food, ice cream, water, and other areas. Our policy has been to spread risks over different countries and product areas, without embarking on serious diversification: We're still 95 percent concentrated on food products. Commodities do certainly fluctuate, but coffee and cocoa prices have much less of an effect on us than in the past, because of a widening of our activities. This will never endanger our profit-and-loss account.

Q: In the past decade two-thirds of Nestlé's growth came from acquisitions. But now the emphasis seems to be on organic, internal growth. Are you turning away from acquisitions because prices are too high or because there's nothing left to buy?

A: Two big strategic items are now behind us: getting into certain countries, and [getting a presence in] product areas where we were weak. That's why there's no longer the same need to be acquisitive. We made a few big decisions about major acquisitions that will take us into the next century, but now we don't need to do any more of these. But now we have all the elements in our hands to provide us with the organic growth we need.

Q: Financial markets are schizophrenic: They like to see signs of long-term strategic thinking, but they also demand very short-term performance. What do you say to investors who demand near-term results at the expense of long-term vision?

A: Back in the days when everyone was praising the so-called stakeholder approach, I always said, "Please don't forget the shareholder, because he is our main priority." We are there to get long-term results for our shareholders. But if an investor from New York presses me to produce returns over the next two months, I'll reply: "No. I can't satisfy somebody whose interest is simply to see an increase in the value of Nestlé shares because he needs to sell again." I have a responsibility to those long-term shareholders in Nestlé who feel a sense of ownership. I just can't afford to get nervous about some of these short-term games.

Q: How do you ensure a smooth second stage of sales growth in emerging markets?

A: The greatest growth potential for us comes in countries with per capita incomes between $2,000 and $20,000. In China, for example, the level is $350 per capita, which means we have a huge population moving into that growth zone. They'll eat more chocolate, drink more Nescafé and buy better-tasting, quality food, including convenience food. Once countries like China and India find themselves at the upper end of that growth zone, we might have annual sales of 200 billion Swiss Francs.

Source: R. House, "Helmut Maucher of Nestlé: Sweet Success," *Institutional Investor* 25, no. 2 (January 1997). This interview was edited for inclusion in this textbook.

Done That

retrenchment strategy
strategy that focuses on turning around very poor company performance by shrinking the size or scope of the business

The purpose of a **retrenchment strategy** is to turn around very poor company performance by shrinking the size or scope of the business. The first step of a typical retrenchment strategy might include significant cost reductions, layoffs of employees, closing of poorly performing stores, offices, or manufacturing plants, or closing or selling entire lines of products or services.[31] For example, after its share of the U.S. car market dropped from 50 percent in the 1970s to its present level near 30 percent, General Motors had too many automobile assembly plants. So, since 1992, GM has pursued a retrenchment strategy, in which it has laid off nearly one-third of its workforce and closed or sold 12 U.S. car plants. However, to get its production capacity in line with demand for its products, some analysts believe that GM may have to close another seven plants and cut 50,000 of its remaining 240,000 assembly line jobs.[32]

recovery
the strategic actions taken after retrenchment to return to a growth strategy

After cutting costs and reducing a business's size or scope, the second step in a retrenchment strategy is recovery. **Recovery** consists of the strategic actions that a company takes to return to a growth strategy. This two-step process of cutting and recovery is analogous to pruning roses. Prior to each growing season, roses should be cut back to two-thirds of their normal size. However, pruning doesn't damage the roses; it makes them stronger and more likely to produce beautiful, fragrant flowers. The retrenchment-and-recover process is similar. Cost reductions, layoffs, and plant closings are sometimes necessary to restoring companies to "good health." But like pruning, those cuts are intended to allow companies to eventually return to growth strategies (i.e., recovery). For example, to restore its sagging profits to normal levels, AT&T announced that it would cut 40,000 jobs and reduce annual expenses by $2.6 billion. Furthermore, AT&T told investors to expect below-average profits over the next few years, as the company invests $9 billion a year to install the new telecommunications equipment needed to begin its brand new local phone service (in addition to its core long-distance phone service). AT&T's chairman said that this spending "will put increasing strain on our financial performance," but should "put AT&T on a path for powerful growth."[33] So when company performance drops significantly, a strategy of retrenchment and recovery may help companies return to a successful growth strategy.

Review 3: *Corporate-Level Strategies*

Corporate-level strategies, such as portfolio strategy and grand strategies, help managers determine what businesses they should be in. Portfolio strategy focuses on lowering business risk by being in multiple, unrelated businesses and by investing the cash flows from slow-growth businesses into faster growing businesses. One portfolio strategy, the BCG matrix, suggests that cash flows from cash cows should be reinvested in stars and in carefully chosen question marks. Dogs should be sold or liquidated. However, portfolio strategy has several problems. Acquiring unrelated businesses actually increases risk rather than lowering it. The BCG matrix is often wrong when predicting companies' (i.e., dogs, cash cows, etc.) future potential. And redirecting cash flows can seriously weaken cash cows. The most successful way to use the portfolio approach to corporate strategy is to reduce risk through related diversification.

The three kinds of grand strategies are growth, stability, and retrenchment/recovery. Companies can grow externally by merging with or acquiring other companies, or they can grow internally through direct expansion or creating new businesses. Companies choose a stability strategy—selling the same products or services to the same customers—when their external environment changes very little or after they have dealt with periods of explosive growth. Retrenchment strategy, shrinking the size or scope of a business, is used to turn around poor performance. If retrenchment works, it is often followed by a recovery strategy that focuses on growing the business again.

4 Industry-Level Strategies

industry-level strategy corporate strategy that addresses the question "How should we compete in this industry?"

Industry-level strategy is a corporate strategy that addresses the question "How should we compete in this industry?" For example, the strategy of most nursing homes has been to provide medical care for elderly people who were no longer able to physically take care of themselves. However, in recent years, nursing homes have had to compete with assisted-living facilities. Assisted-living facilities don't offer the serious medical support available at most nursing homes. Although they provide assistance with things such as bathing and dressing, they have a different goal: to help residents be independent and active for as long as possible. Consequently, assisted-living facilities are much more livable than traditional nursing homes. For example, all of Sunrise Assisted Living's facilities resemble Victorian mansions. Open porches, lots of big windows, curved staircases, carpeted floors, and comfortable couches and living areas replace the dark lighting, tile floors, and narrow hallways found in most nursing homes.[34]

Let's find out more about industry-level strategies by discussing **4.1** *the five industry forces that determine overall levels of competition in an industry, and* **4.2** *the positioning strategies and* **4.3** *adaptive strategies that companies can use to achieve sustained competitive advantage and above-average profits.*

4.1
Five Industry Forces

According to Harvard professor Michael Porter, five industry forces—character of rivalry, threat of new entrants, threat of substitute products or services, bargaining power of suppliers, and the bargaining power of buyers—determine an industry's overall attractiveness and potential for long-term profitability. The stronger these forces, the less attractive the industry becomes to corporate investors, because it is more difficult for companies to be profitable. Porter's industry forces are illustrated in Figure 9.4. Let's examine how these industry forces are bringing changes to several kinds of industries.

character of the rivalry a measure of the intensity of competitive behavior between companies in an industry

Character of the rivalry is a measure of the intensity of competitive behavior between companies in an industry. Is the competition among firms aggressive and cutthroat, or do competitors focus more on serving customers than attacking each other? Both industry attractiveness and profitability decrease when rivalry is cutthroat. For example, selling cars is a highly competitive business. Pick up a local newspaper on Friday, Saturday, or Sunday morning, and you'll find dozens of pages of car advertising ("Anniversary Sale-A-Bration," "Ford March Savings!" and "$99 Down, You Choose!"). In fact, competition is so intense that if it weren't for used car sales, repair work, and replacement parts, many auto dealers would actually lose money.

threat of new entrants a measure of the degree to which barriers to entry make it easy or difficult for new companies to get started in an industry

The **threat of new entrants** is a measure of the degree to which barriers to entry make it easy or difficult for new companies to get started in an industry. If it is easy for new companies to get started in the industry, then competition will increase and prices and profits will fall. However, if there are sufficient barriers to entry, such as large capital requirements to buy expensive equipment or plant facilities or the need for specialized knowledge, then competition will be weaker and prices and profits will generally be higher. For example, anyone wanting to start a new car dealership would

Figure 9.4 **Porter's Five Industry Forces**

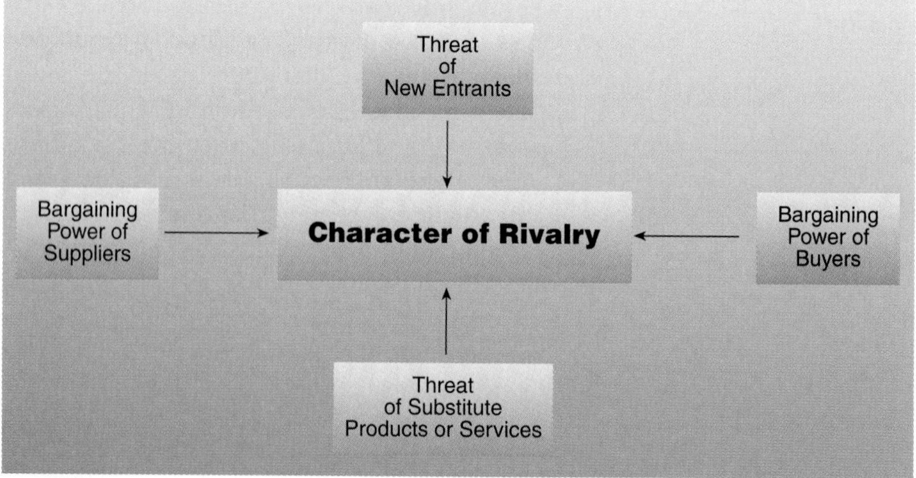

Source: M.E. Porter, *Competitive Strategy: Techniques for Analyzing Industries and Competitors* (New York: Free Press, 1980).

have to give a large sum of money to one of the major auto manufacturers (i.e., GM, Ford, etc.) to become an official dealer. Then, on top of that, they would have to spend millions more to purchase sufficient land and construct buildings to showcase cars, hold dealership offices, and house repair bays and parts inventory. Not surprisingly, the number of new auto dealerships has steadily declined over the last two decades. However, the Internet has now made it possible for Internet sites like Autobytel (**www.autobytel.com**), AutoWeb (*www.autoweb.com*), and CarPoint (**carpoint.msn.com**) to bypass these barriers to entry, increase competition, and drive down auto prices.

So how does Internet-based auto-buying work? Well, on Autobytel's *free* Web site, customers indicate when and what they plan to buy. Autobytel then contacts a participating local car dealer (3 percent of dealers nationwide), who phones the customer (within 48 hours) with a low, no-haggle price for the car model the customer wants. One Autobytel customer said, "When he [car salesman] quoted me a price, I nearly fell over–[it was] nearly $7,000 less than what we were quoted earlier in the week at the dealership down the road." Another said, "I filled out your query and was contacted by the same dealership I had haggled with before. They found a vehicle, quoted a price (which was $1,500 dollars less than the one we had agreed to two weeks prior), and we reached a financing plan in 20 minutes."[35] Autobytel earns money by charging dealers an annual fee of $2,500, and $500 to $1,500 a month per car brand (i.e., Ford, Chevy, etc.). In return, dealers receive exclusive territories, low costs (by not having to advertise in local papers or on local radio and TV stations), and customers who are much more likely to buy.[36] As for the threat to car dealers who are not aligned with these Internet car-selling sites, it's likely to grow. Today, 16 percent of car buyers buy online, but within several years, it's estimated that more than half of all car buyers will purchase their cars this way.[37]

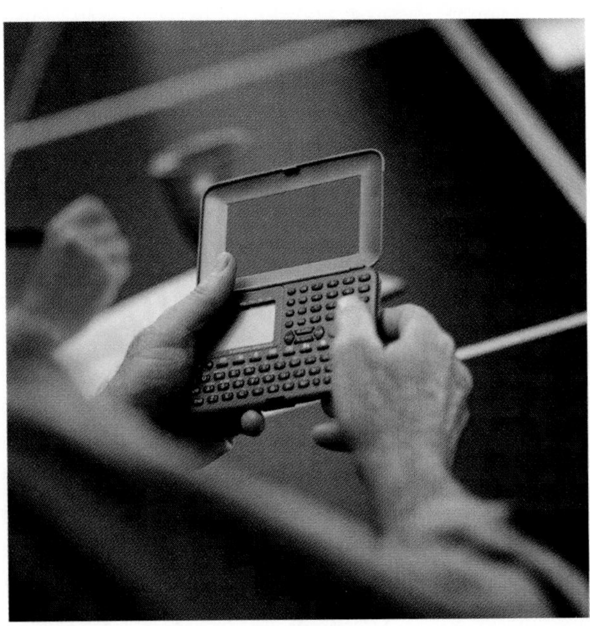

Intel is one of many suppliers of chips to the consumer electronics industry, so it has less bargaining power in that industry than in personal computers, where it is the dominant supplier. © PhotoDisc, Inc.

threat of substitute products or services
a measure of the ease with which customers can find substitutes for an industry's products or services

The **threat of substitute products or services** is a measure of the ease with which customers can find substitutes for an industry's products or services. If customers can easily find substitute products or services, the competition will be greater and profits will be lower. If there are few or no substitutes, competition will be weaker and profits will be higher. Generic medicines are some of the best-known examples of substitute products. Under U.S. patent law, a company that develops a drug has exclusive rights to produce and market that drug for 20 years. During this time, if the drug sells well, prices and profits are generally high. However, at the end of 20 years, after the patent has expired, any pharmaceutical company can manufacture and sell the same drug. When this happens, drug prices drop substantially, and the company that developed the drug typically sees its revenues drop sharply. For example, Capoten, a heart drug sold by Bristol-Myers Squibb, sold for 57 cents a pill while under patent, and just 3 cents a pill as a generic brand when produced by Bristol-Myers Squibb's competitors. Not surprisingly, Bristol-Myers Squibb's sales of Capoten fell 83 percent from $146 million to $25 million the year the drug went off patent protection.[38]

bargaining power of suppliers
a measure of the influence that suppliers of parts, materials, and services to firms in an industry have on the prices of these inputs

Bargaining power of suppliers is a measure of the influence that suppliers of parts, materials, and services to firms in an industry have on the prices of these inputs. If an industry has numerous suppliers from whom to buy parts, materials, and services, companies will be able to bargain with suppliers to keep prices low. On the other hand, if there are few suppliers, or if a company is dependent on a supplier with specialized skills and knowledge, then suppliers will have the bargaining power to dictate price levels. Intel, which supplies more than an 80 percent of the microprocessors used in personal computers, has clearly had much more bargaining power than manufacturers of personal computers, who have had little choice but to buy their computer chips from Intel. As a result of this dominance, Intel clearly controlled the pricing of microprocessors and became one of the most profitable companies this decade. By contrast, Intel has little bargaining power in the exploding market for consumer electronics, such as hand-held and palm-sized computers, digital cameras, video game players, televisions, etc. In this market, which is much larger than the market for personal computers, almost no manufacturer buys chips from Intel. Instead, they buy much cheaper and much faster chips from several companies like NEC, Hitachi, and LSI Logic. David Robinson of General Instrument, which manufactures digital set-top cable TV boxes, said that, for these kinds of chips, "Intel is running dead last." [39]

bargaining power of buyers
a measure of the influence that customers have on a firm's prices

Bargaining power of buyers is a measure of the influence that customers have on the firm's prices. If a company is dependent on just a few high-volume buyers, those buyers will typically have enough bargaining power to dictate prices. By contrast, if a company sells a popular product or service to multiple buyers, then the company has more power to set prices. When it comes to purchasing cars, one of the ways in which consumers are increasing their bargaining power is to concentrate it in the hands of vehicle buying services now available at credit unions, Sam's Discount Warehouses, or AAA. For example, AAA Auto Club operates a free, no-haggle buyer's service in which it pre-negotiates car prices for its members. A toll-free phone call to AAA starts the process. AAA then contacts local dealers to see if they have the car that the customer wants. If they do, and the AAA member wants to buy, they simply sign a pre-negotiated purchase agreement that guarantees a low price, which typically averages $100 over dealer cost for U.S. models and $400 over dealer cost for foreign models.[40] No haggling. No tricky negotiating ploys by salespeople.

4.2 *Positioning Strategies*

After analyzing industry forces, the next step in industry-level strategy is to effectively protect your company from the negative effects of industry-wide competition and to create a sustainable competitive advantage. According to Michael Porter, there are three positioning strategies: cost leadership, differentiation, and focus.

cost leadership
the positioning strategy of producing a product or service of acceptable quality at consistently lower production costs than competitors can, so that the firm can offer the product or service at the lowest price in the industry

Cost leadership means producing a product or service of acceptable quality at consistently lower production costs than competitors, so that the firm can offer the product or service at the lowest price in the industry. Cost leadership protects companies from industry forces by deterring new entrants, who will have to match low costs and prices. Cost leadership also forces down the prices of substitute products and services, attracts bargain-seeking buyers, and increases bargaining power with suppliers, who have to keep their prices low if they want to do business with the cost leader. AirTran airlines is an example of a cost leadership strategy. Its founders started the company based on one simple fact and two simple questions. The fact: Twenty million people drive to Florida each year for vacation. The questions: If prices were low enough, wouldn't they rather fly? And where else would they like to fly if prices were low enough? How low are AirTran's prices? President Lewis Jordan said, "It wouldn't take a lot to study our costs and figure out that if we wanted to cut our fares in half, we could run for a long time on the cash we have built up and be very competitive. If a big carrier was going to match us across the board, they would have to bleed hundreds of millions of dollars" to put AirTran out of business.[41]

differentiation
the positioning strategy of providing a product or service that is sufficiently different from competitors' offerings such customers are willing to pay a premium price for it

Differentiation means making your product or service sufficiently different from competitors' offerings that customers are willing to pay a premium price for the extra value or performance that it provides. Differentiation protects companies from industry forces by reducing the threat of substitute products. It also protects companies by making it easier to retain customers and more difficult for new entrants trying to attract new customers. Anyone who has been to the movies lately should recognize that the major theater companies are using differentiation to steal customers from each other. For example, Edwards Theatres Circuit has 500 movie screens in southern California. Over the next few years, the company plans to add 500 more. However, these new screens will all be part of huge multi-screen complexes. For instance, Edwards is building a 22-screen movie complex in Ontario, California. Unlike traditional 2-to-6 screen complexes, these behemoths will have wider, softer, sloped stadium-style seating, larger screens, higher-priced flavored coffee and specialty foods, and extremely powerful digital sound systems guaranteed to knock viewers back into their seats. Why spend millions on these new multi-screen complexes? Because many regular movie customers will choose these high-tech, high-comfort theaters over traditional theaters. And because people who would normally pay $3 to rent a movie at BlockBuster are more likely to go to the movies when their $7 or $8 buys them a theater experience that they can't get at home.[42]

focus strategy
the positioning strategy of using cost leadership or differentiation to produce a specialized product or service for a limited, specially targeted group of customers in a particular geographic region or market segment

A **focus strategy** means that a company uses either cost leadership or differentiation to produce a specialized product or service for a limited, specially targeted group of customers in a particular geographic region or market segment. Focus strategies typically work in market niches that competitors have overlooked or have difficulty serving. Alpine Log Homes is a company that follows a focus strategy. First, as its name indicates, Alpine Log Homes serves a specialized niche in the home construction industry: manufacturing log houses. However, Alpine is even more focused than that. With the average Alpine log home running 6,500 square feet and costing $1.2 million, Alpine serves just the high end of the log home market. Other than price, what differentiates Alpine's log homes is the number of options available (indoor swimming pools, movie theaters, heated indoor parking) and the fact that its logs are hand-hewn (most logs in log homes are cut and shaped in factories). Finally, Alpine maintains its differentiation focus strategy by building only 75 log homes per year.[43]

4.3
Adaptive Strategies

Adaptive strategies are another set of industry-level strategies. While the aim of positioning strategies is to minimize the effects of industry competition and build a sustainable competitive advantage, the purpose of adaptive strategies is to choose an industry-level strategy that is best suited to changes in the organization's external environment. There are four kinds of adaptive strategies: defenders, analyzers, prospectors, and reactors.[44]

defenders
an adaptive strategy aimed at defending strategic positions by seeking moderate, steady growth and by offering a limited range of high-quality products and services to a well-defined set of customers

Defenders seek moderate, steady growth by offering a limited range of products and services to a well-defined set of customers. In other words, defenders aggressively "defend" their current strategic position by doing the best job they can to hold on to customers in a particular market segment. For, example Pitney Bowes sells 85 percent of the postage meters used to automatically weigh and "stamp" mail with an official U.S. Postal Service metered mark. (Take a look at the envelope containing one of your monthly bills. Notice the pinkish/red meter mark where you'd normally find a stamp.) However, Pitney Bowes' domination of that market is coming under attack. A new entrant, PC Postage, has invented a computer chip/software combination that will allow businesses and individuals to use a desktop computer and printer to stamp mail with a postal service meter mark. Buying refills is easier, too. Just log on to the PC Postage secure Web site, enter your business credit card, and download your refill, all without going to the post office. However, Pitney Bowes intends to defend its business and is not giving up without a fight. It has developed a digital postmark, with all of the convenience of PC Postage, which also helps the U.S. Postal Service reduce postal fraud (fake meter stamps).[45]

prospectors
an adaptive strategy that seeks fast growth by searching for new market opportunities, encouraging risk taking, and being the first to bring innovative new products to market

Prospectors seek fast growth by searching for new market opportunities, encouraging risk taking, and being the first to bring innovative new products to market. Prospectors are analogous to gold miners who "prospect" for gold nuggets (i.e., new products) in hopes that it will lead them to a mine that has a rich deposit of gold (i.e., fast growth). Regnery Publishing, a small book publisher, is using a prospector strategy to achieve fast growth. Regnery grows by publishing controversial books, such as *Unlimited Access*, in which former FBI agent Gary Aldrich accused President Clinton of sneaking out of the White House for midnight trysts at a Washington hotel. It also published Detective Mark Fuhrman's best-seller, *Murder in Brentwood*.

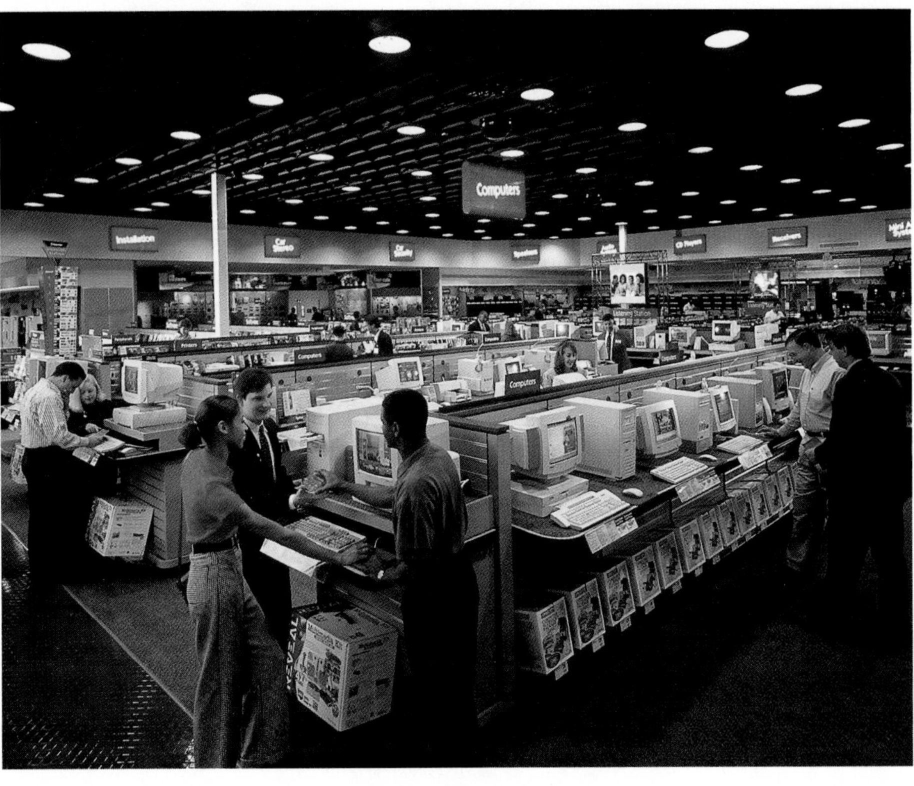

Many small computer manufacturers compete by using an analyzer strategy, following the lead of major PC makers. © Jeff Zaruba/The Stock Market

Fuhrman is the controversial LAPD detective who, in O.J. Simpson's murder trial, allegedly lied about his use of racial slurs. Concerning the risks that Regnery takes with its prospector strategy, Phyllis Gran, president of Penguin Putnam, a large publisher, said, "We wouldn't do the Fuhrman book because I don't think any of our editors would want to sponsor it."[46]

analyzers
an adaptive strategy that seeks to minimize risk and maximize profits by following or imitating the proven successes of prospectors

Analyzers are a blend of the defender and prospector strategies. Analyzers seek moderate, steady growth *and* limited opportunities for fast growth. Analyzers are rarely first to market with new products or services. Instead, they try to simultaneously minimize risk and maximize profits by following or imitating the proven successes of prospectors. For example, while 75 percent of personal computers are made by the 20 largest PC manufacturers (Compaq, Dell, IBM, Gateway, etc.), the remaining 25 percent are made by 100,000 small manufacturers, most of whom use an analyzer strategy. One such company is Adam Computers, which manufactures and sells 7,000 computers a year in Dallas. Rather than trying to design new computer products (a prospector strategy), Adams typically makes computers with the same options and configurations as the large PC manufacturers offer. However, Adam Computers distinguishes itself by offering personal service. Instead of impersonal Web sites and 24-hour phone support, small manufacturers like Adam Computers frequently send service technicians to customers' homes to make repairs. Likewise, when customers call with a question, they can often talk directly to the technician who manufactured their computer.[47]

reactors
an adaptive strategy of not following a consistent strategy, but instead reacting to changes in the external environment after they occur

Finally, unlike defenders, prospectors, or analyzers, **reactors** do not follow a consistent strategy. Furthermore, rather than anticipating and preparing for external opportunities and threats, reactors tend to "react" to changes in their external environment after they occur. Not surprisingly, reactors tend to be poorer performers than defenders, prospectors, or analyzers. One likely example of a reactor is your local bowling alley. Bowling peaked in popularity in the early 1970s. At that time, ten million Americans eagerly signed up to participate in regular bowling leagues lasting 35 weeks a year. However, 20 years later, only five million Americans count themselves as regular bowlers. As would be expected, many bowling alleys have gone out of business. Consistent with a reactor strategy, the surviving bowling alleys have only recently begun to take actions to reverse these declines. Bowling alley owners can only hope that innovations such as "no gutter" bowling for small children (on weekends), traditional leagues for retirees (on week days), and "cosmic bowling" with pounding music, glow-in-the-dark pins, laser lights, and fog machines (for teenagers on weekend nights) will bring customers back.[48]

Review 4: *Industry-Level Strategies*

Industry-level strategies focus on how companies choose to compete in their industry. Five industry forces determine an industry's overall attractiveness to corporate investors and potential for long-term profitability. Together, a high level of new entrants, substitute products or services, bargaining power of suppliers, bargaining power of buyers, and rivalry between competitors combine to increase competition and decrease profits. Three positioning strategies can help companies protect themselves from the negative effects of industry-wide competition. Under a cost leadership strategy, firms try to keep production costs low, so that they can sell products at prices lower than competitors'. Differentiation is a strategy aimed at making a product or service sufficiently different from competitors that it can command a premium price. Using a focus strategy, firms seek to produce a specialized product or service for a limited, specially targeted group of customers. The four adaptive strategies help companies adapt to changes in the external environment. Defenders want to "defend" their current strategic positions. Prospectors look for new market opportunities by bringing innovative new products to market. Analyzers minimize risk by following the proven successes of prospectors. Reactors do not follow a consistent strategy, but instead react to changes in their external environment after they occur.

5 Firm-Level Strategies

firm-level strategy corporate strategy that addresses the question "How should we compete against a particular firm?"

Firm-level strategy addresses the question "How should we compete against a particular firm?" For example, over the last two decades, McDonald's has dominated its nearest rival, Burger King, in terms of sales, profits, market share, and growth. Consequently, McDonald's is twice Burger King's size. However, over the last few years, Burger King has become the attacker and McDonald's the nervous follower. Burger King started its attack by heavily advertising that its Whopper sandwich was bigger than McDonald's Big Mac. McDonald's responded by creating larger, more expensive Deluxe sandwiches like the Arch Deluxe hamburger. When it did, Burger King's sales (not McDonald's) increased by 11 percent. To keep weight and health-conscious customers coming in, Burger King created a grilled chicken sandwich. Several years later, McDonald's did the same. Then, Burger King attacked McDonald's stranglehold on the fast-food breakfast business, introducing its own croissant and biscuit breakfast sandwiches and selling them for 20 to 25 cents less than McDonald's better-known Egg McMuffin and Sausage McMuffin sandwiches. Moreover, Burger King was able to lower prices on items across its entire menu at the same time that McDonald's food prices increased by 4 percent to 8 percent.[49]

All told, Burger King's aggressive attacks have worked. Burger King's sales are increasing while McDonald's are decreasing. Indeed, an internal McDonald's memo indicated that price cuts might be needed because of an "overt competitive attack by BK."[50]

Let's find out more about firm-level competition between companies by reading about **5.1** *the basics of direct competition,* **5.2** *the strategic moves involved in direct competition between companies, and* **5.3** *the firm-level strategy of entrepreneurship.*

5.1 Direct Competition

While Porter's five industry forces indicate the overall level of competition in an industry, most companies do not compete directly with all the firms in their industry. For example, McDonald's and Red Lobster are both in the restaurant business, but no one would characterize them as competitors. McDonald's offers low-cost, convenient fast food in a "seat yourself" restaurant, while Red Lobster offers mid-priced, sit-down seafood dinners complete with servers and a bar.

direct competition
the rivalry between two companies that offer similar products and services, acknowledge each other as rivals, and act and react to each other's strategic actions

market commonality
the degree to which two companies have overlapping products, services, or customers in multiple markets

resource similarity
the extent to which a competitor has similar amounts and kinds of resources

Instead of "competing" with the industry, most firms compete directly with just a few companies. **Direct competition** is the rivalry between two companies offering similar products and services that acknowledge each other as rivals and take offensive and defensive positions as they act and react to each other's strategic actions.[51] Two factors determine the extent to which firms will be in direct competition with each other: market commonality and resource similarity. **Market commonality** is the degree to which two companies have overlapping products, services, or customers in multiple markets. The more markets in which there is product, service, or customer overlap, the more intense the direct competition between the two companies. **Resource similarity** is the extent to which a competitor has similar amounts and kinds of resources, that is, similar assets, capabilities, processes, information, and knowledge used to create and sustain an advantage over competitors. From a competitive standpoint, resource similarity means that the strategic actions that your company takes can probably be matched by your direct competitors.

Figure 9.5 shows how market commonality and resource similarity interact to determine when and where companies are in direct competition.[52] The overlapping area (between the triangle and the rectangle or between the differently colored rectangles) in each quadrant depicts market commonality. The larger the overlap, the greater the market commonality. Shapes depict resource similarity, with rectangles representing one set of competitive resources and triangles representing another. Quadrant I shows two companies in direct competition, because they have similar resources at their disposal and a high degree of market commonality, as they try to sell similar products and services to similar customers. McDonald's and Burger King would clearly fit here as direct competitors.

Figure 9.5 **A Framework of Direct Competition**

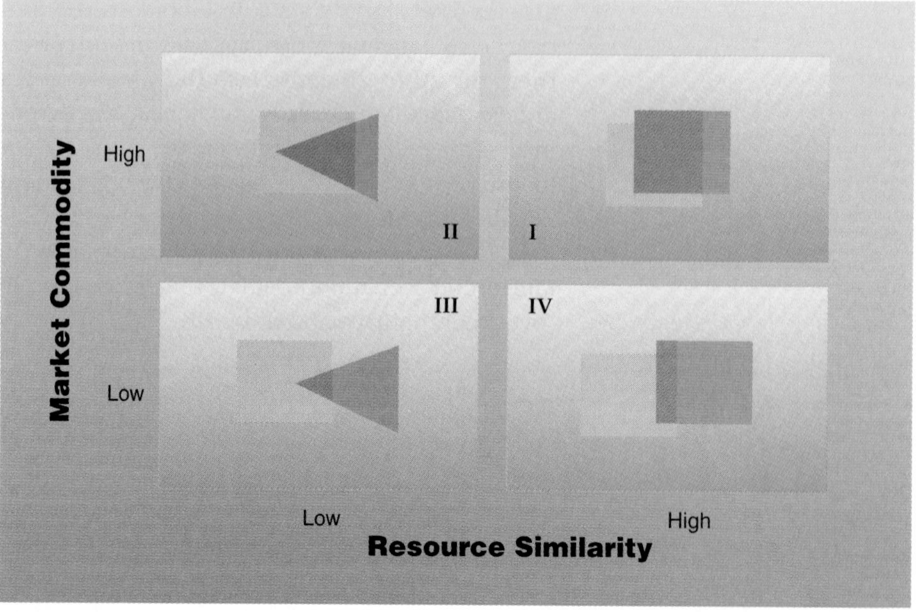

Source: M. Chen, "Competitor Analysis and Interfirm Rivalry: Toward a Theoretical Integration," *Academy of Management Review* 21 (1996): 100-134.

In Quadrant II, the overlapping parts of the triangle and rectangle show two companies going after similar customers with some similar products or services, but doing so with different competitive resources. McDonald's and Wendy's restaurants would fit here. Wendy's is after the same lunchtime and dinner crowds that McDonald's is. However, it is less of a direct competitor to McDonald's than Burger King is, because Wendy's hamburgers, fries, and shakes are more expensive. A representative from Wendy's said, "We believe you win customers by consistently offering a better product at a strong, everyday value." Plus, Wendy's is now competing less with McDonald's as it expands its Tim Horton's chain. Tim Horton's is a baked-goods store that also serves bagels, soups, deli sandwiches, cookies, and soft drinks.[53]

In Quadrant III, the very small overlap shows two companies with different competitive resources and little market commonality. McDonald's and Boston Market restaurants fit here. Although both are in the fast-food business, there's almost no overlap in terms of products and customers. For example, Boston Market sells rotisserie chicken, turkey sandwiches, meat loaf, and vegetables, none of which are available at McDonald's. Furthermore, Boston Market customers aren't likely to eat at McDonald's. In fact, Boston Market is not really competing with other fast-food restaurants, but with eating at home. Company surveys show that close to half of its customers would have eaten at home, not at another restaurant, if they hadn't come to Boston Market.[54]

Finally, in Quadrant IV, the small shaded overlap between the two rectangles shows two companies competing with similar resources but with little market commonality. Surprisingly, McDonald's and Burger King fit here too. However, the major difference from Quadrant I is that Quadrant IV represents direct competition between McDonald's and Burger King in Japan, not the U.S. Both sell burgers and fries in Japan (i.e., similar products). However, unlike the U.S. market, market commonality is low, because of Burger King's small size and because few Japanese fast-food customers have ever heard of it. Jun Fujita, an assistant manager at a Tokyo McDonald's, said, "We don't see them as a threat at all. Who has ever heard of Burger King?"[55] This example also illustrates the point that even between direct competitors, competition in each market (i.e., geographic regions, particular products or services, etc.) is unique. Furthermore, direct competitors have different strengths and weaknesses in different markets. For example, although Burger King has been gaining on McDonald's in the U.S., McDonald's is clearly dominant in Japan. McDonald's has been in Japan for 25 years and has over 2,000 restaurants. By contrast, Burger King hopes to open 200 restaurants in Japan over the next 5 years.

5.2 Strategic Moves of Direct Competition

attack
a competitive move designed to reduce a rival's market share or profits

response
a competitive countermove, prompted by a rival's attack, to defend or improve a company's market share or profit

While corporate-level strategies help managers decide what business to be in and business-level strategies help them determine how to compete within an industry, firm-level strategies help managers determine when, where, and what strategic actions should be taken against a direct competitor. There are two basic strategic moves in direct competition between firms: attacks and responses.

An **attack** is a competitive move designed to reduce a rival's market share or profits. For example, with its Pampers and Luv's brands, Procter & Gamble is the largest maker of disposable baby diapers. However, Procter & Gamble's market share is being attacked by Paragon Trade Brands. Paragon, which manufactures the cheaper, private label diapers that grocery and discount stores sell under their own store brand names, now has a 16 percent share of the disposable-diaper market.[56]

A **response** is a countermove, prompted by a rival's attack, designed to defend or improve a company's market share or profit. For example, in an extremely aggressive response, Procter & Gamble is suing Paragon for damages and lost profits, alleging that Paragon violated the patents it has for putting elastic in diapers to prevent leaking around a baby's legs. To those unfamiliar with the diaper business, "elastic around the legs" may not sound like an especially important thing. However, Andrew Urban, a diaper-technology consultant, called this design "one of the most important advances in diapers" since the invention of tight-fitting hourglass-shaped diapers.[57] Consequently, Procter & Gamble's intent is to force Paragon to stop making diapers with elastic in the legs or to make it pay a royalty for each diaper. Either would greatly reduce Paragon's profitability.

Personal Productivity Tip

Competitive Intelligence, Shopping the Competition

One of the best ways to keep abreast of the need for strategic change is to "shop the competition." Every time David Glass, Wal-Mart CEO, visits a local Wal-Mart store, he also visits the nearby Kmart or Target store. When FedEx wants to benchmark its delivery services against the competition, it has FedEx employees, posing as customers, mail identical packages with identical destinations at FedEx *and* UPS offices. Likewise, when Burger King wants to study the efficiency of its drive-through windows, it sends researchers through the drive-through windows at Burger King, McDonald's, and Wendy's. Curious about what your competitors are up to? Go shopping.

Sources: J. Kass, "Business Intelligence Operatives Organize Information: Group Helps Companies Stay Ahead, Advising Them on Knowing Their Customers, Competitors and Industry," *Los Angeles Times*, 11 April 1995.

Attacks and responses can include smaller, more tactical moves, like price cuts, specially advertised sales or promotions, or improvements in service. However, they can also include resource-intensive strategic moves, such as expanding service and production facilities, introducing new products or services within the firm's existing business, or entering a completely new line of business for the first time. Of these, market entries and exits are probably the most important kinds of attacks and responses. Entering a new market is a clear offensive signal to an attacking or responding firm that your company is committed to gaining or defending market share and profits at their expense. By contrast, exiting a market is an equally clear defensive signal that your company is retreating.[58] For example, because its core computer business is struggling, Apple Computers has decided that it can no longer afford to make and sell its Newton "palmtop" computers, which can be used to take handwritten notes and to store calendars, lists of contacts, phone numbers, etc. Apple's exit from the palmtop computer market is ironic for two reasons. First, the Apple Newton was one of the first palmtop computers introduced to the market. Second, Apple's exit comes at a time when demand for palmtop computers is projected to increase dramatically over the next few years.[59]

Figure 9.6 shows that market commonality and resource similarity determine the likelihood of an attack or response, that is, whether a company is likely to attack a direct competitor or to strike back with a strong response when attacked. When market commonality is strong and companies have overlapping products, services, or customers in multiple markets, there is less motivation to attack and more motivation to respond to an attack. The reason for this is straightforward: when firms are direct competitors in a large number of markets, there is much more at stake. If Kmart cuts prices in its lawn-and-garden department so that they're 10 percent lower than Wal-Mart's prices, it knows that Wal-Mart, which has a store within several miles of nearly every Kmart store, will strike back by immediately cutting its lawn-and-garden prices so that its prices are cheaper. The result is that both Kmart and Wal-Mart will sacrifice profits from the lawn-and-garden department in thousands of stores.

While market commonality affects the likelihood of an attack or a response to an attack, resource similarity largely affects response capability, that is, how quickly and forcefully a company can respond to an attack. When resource similarity is strong, the responding firm will generally be able to match the strategic moves of the attacking firm. Consequently, firms are less likely to attack firms with similar levels of resources, because they're unlikely to gain any sustained advantage when the responding firm strikes back. On the other hand, if one firm is substantially stronger than another (i.e., low resource similarity), then a competitive attack is more likely to produce sustained competitive advantage. For example, CVS drugstores, which has 4,000 stores, is one of the fastest-growing drugstore chains. CVS attacks competitors, mostly weaker, independently owned and

Figure 9.6 **Likelihood of Attacks and Responses in Direct Competition**

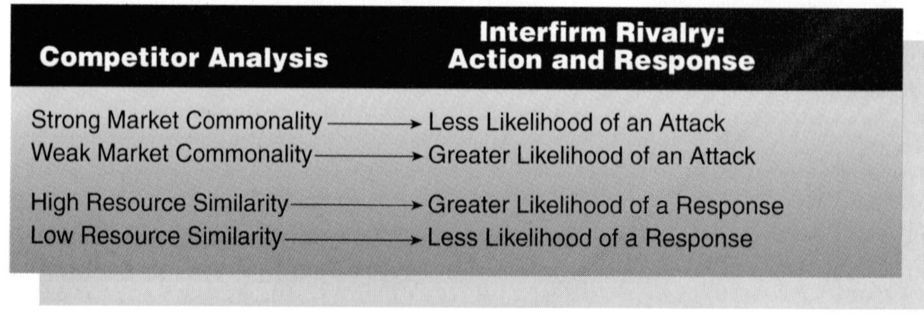

Competitor Analysis
Interfirm Rivalry: Action and Response
Strong Market Commonality → Less Likelihood of an Attack
Weak Market Commonality → Greater Likelihood of an Attack
High Resource Similarity → Greater Likelihood of a Response
Low Resource Similarity → Less Likelihood of a Response

Source: M. Chen, "Competitor Analysis and Interfirm Rivalry: Toward a Theoretical Integration, *Academy of Management Review* 21 (1996): 100-134.

operated pharmacies, by quickly opening up several nearby stores. Then, to lure shoppers to its stores and away from competitors, it negotiates sole-provider contracts with local health maintenance organizations. Consequently, HMO members who get their prescriptions filled at CVS pay less money out of their own pockets. Finally, CVS pressures its rivals with repeated buyout offers. One competitor, Jack Morgan, watched helplessly as his former customers began going to a nearby CVS store to fill their prescriptions. With his sales cut in half, he sold out to CVS. "I didn't have much choice," Mr. Morgan said. "You can't compete with CVS."[60]

In general, the greater the number of moves (i.e., attacks) a company initiates against direct competitors, and the greater a firm's tendency to respond when attacked, the better its performance. More specifically, attackers and early responders (companies that are quick to launch a retaliatory attack) tend to gain market share and profits at the expense of late responders. This is not to suggest that a "full-attack" strategy always works best. In fact, attacks can provoke harsh retaliatory responses. Consequently, when deciding when, where, and what strategic actions to take against a direct competitor, managers should always consider the possibility of retaliation.

5.3 *Entrepreneurship: A Firm-Level Strategy*

Firm-level strategy addresses how one company should compete against another. Furthermore, of the various kinds of attacks and responses used in direct competition, market entry is perhaps the most forceful attack or response, because it sends the clear signal that the company is committed to gaining or defending market share and profits at a direct competitor's expense.

entrepreneurship
the process of entering new or established markets with new goods or services

Since **entrepreneurship** is the process of entering new or established markets with new goods or services, entrepreneurship is also a firm-level strategy. In fact, the basic strategic act of entrepreneurship is new entry—creating a new business from a brand new startup firm or from an existing firm. For example, each year five million pounds of formulated insecticide are used to protect potato crops from pests and diseases. However, instead of applying agricultural chemicals, farmers can now simply plant Monsanto Corporation's NewLeaf Plus potatoes, which, thanks to biotechnology engineering, are pest and disease resistant. Because Monsanto has been in the agricultural chemical business for decades, its new biotech products, like the NewLeaf Plus potato, are strong evidence that the company is now using an entrepreneurial strategy to enter brand new markets with brand new products and services.[61]

entrepreneurial orientation
the set of processes, practices, and decision-making activities that lead to new entry, characterized by five dimensions: autonomy, innovativeness, risk-taking, proactiveness, and competitive aggressiveness

While the goal of an entrepreneurial strategy is new entry, the process of carrying out an entrepreneurial strategy depends on the ability of the company's founders or existing managers to foster an entrepreneurial orientation. An **entrepreneurial orientation** is the set of processes, practices, and decision-making activities that lead to new entry. Five key dimensions characterize an entrepreneurial orientation: autonomy, innovativeness, risk-taking, proactiveness, and competitive aggressiveness.[62] Without these, an entrepreneurial strategy is unlikely to succeed.

1. *Autonomy.* If a firm wants to successfully develop new products or services to enter new markets, it must foster creativity among employees. To be creative, employees need the freedom and control to develop a new

idea into a new product or service opportunity without interference from others. In other words, they need autonomy. For example, when IBM was developing its first personal computer in the early 1980s, it created a dozen design teams, gave them complete freedom to design what they wanted, and sent them to different locations away from IBM's regular offices. In fact, the winning team worked out of an old rundown manufacturing plant in Boca Raton, Florida. Furthermore, to prevent interference or influence from IBM's existing business, almost no one in the company knew these teams existed.

2. *Innovativeness.* Entrepreneurial firms also foster innovativeness by supporting new ideas, experimentation, and creative processes that might produce new products, services, or technological processes. One example is Great Plains Software, which makes accounting software for small companies. With 63 other firms also producing accounting software, the obvious question was how to make the company's accounting software stand out in a crowded market. The answer was to provide extensive phone support to customers who purchased the software. The innovation was to charge for that support, something that no software company had dared try. In fact, Great Plains found that customers were more than willing to pay a fixed amount for unlimited support, because Great Plains was not only helping them learn to use its software, but was also helping them set up their accounts and ledgers correctly. Today, customers who pay a fixed annual fee for support are guaranteed to be called back in 30 minutes by their own personal support representative.[63]
3. *Risk taking.* Entrepreneurial firms are also willing to take some risks, by making large resource commitments that may result in costly failure.[64] Another way to conceptualize risk-taking is to think of it as managers' preferences for bold rather than cautious acts. For example, after travelling to Italy and noticing that Italians cooked pasta for their dogs, Richard Thompson decided to start Pet Pasta Products. With Americans spending over $9 billion a year on pet food, and much of that for premium brands that look tasty and promise superior nutritional benefits, Thompson figured that products like Pasta Plus dog food would be fast sellers. However, in four years of business, the company has spent $30 million and not yet earned a profit. Thompson, however, is not deterred. He said, "I'm the only one with the guts to take on these guys [Purina, Heinz, and Mars pet foods]....I've gambled my fortune that this will work!"[65]
4. *Proactiveness.* Entrepreneurial firms have the ability to anticipate future problems, needs, or changes by developing new products or services that may not be related to their current business, by introducing new products or services before the competition does, and by dropping products or services that are declining (and likely to be replaced by new products or services).[66] Internet Security Systems (ISS) anticipated the security risks associated with corporate e-mail, Internet access, and company intranets by developing software that helps companies protect company data and computer systems. For example, ISS's software scans company password databases, looking for 25,000 easy-to-crack account passwords, like "Spot," "Steelers," and "Startrek." When it finds them, users must then submit a more-secure password. In all, ISS's software shuts down over 200 computer hacker tricks that compromise corporate computer security. Christopher Klaus, the 23-year-old company founder, said, "We make sure all the windows are closed and the doors are locked."[67]

5. *Competitive aggressiveness.* Because new entrants are more likely to fail than are existing firms, they must be aggressive if they want to succeed. A new firm often must be willing to use unconventional methods to directly challenge competitors for their customers and market share. A new company called Fresh Picks is using this approach to enter the highly competitive retail business of selling music CDs to consumers. In recent years, music stores like Wherehouse Entertainment and Camelot Music have ended up in bankruptcy, losing business to the likes of Wal-Mart, Kmart, and Circuit City. So instead of setting up music stores, Fresh Picks wants to sell CDs in grocery stores by setting up CD display cases holding up to 400 different selections. Why grocery stores? In France, supermarkets already sell half of all CDs. In the United Kingdom, it's roughly 12 percent. Fresh Picks' President Michael Rigby said, "Customers go into a supermarket with an open shopping list and a 100 percent intent to spend."[68]

Review 5: *Firm-Level Strategies*

Firm-level strategies are concerned with direct competition between firms. Market commonality and resource similarity determine whether firms are in direct competition and thus likely to attack each other or respond to each other's attacks. In general, the more markets in which there is product, service, or customer overlap, and the greater the resource similarity between two firms, the more intense the direct competition between them. When firms are direct competitors in a large number of markets, attacks are less likely, because responding firms are highly motivated to quickly and forcefully defend their profits and market share. By contrast, resource similarity affects response capability, meaning how quickly and forcefully a company responds to an attack. When resource similarity is strong, attacks are much less likely to produce a sustained advantage, because the responding firm is capable of striking back with equal force. Market entries and exits are the most important kinds of attacks and responses. Entering a new market is a clear offensive signal, while exiting a market is a clear signal that a company is retreating. In general, attackers and early responders gain market share and profits at the expense of late responders. However, attacks must be carefully planned and carried out, because they can provoke harsh retaliatory responses. Firm-level strategy addresses how one company should compete against another. Of the various kinds of attacks and responses used in direct competition, market entry is perhaps the most forceful attack or response, because it sends the clear signal that the company is committed to gaining or defending market share and profits at a direct competitor's expense. Finally, the basic strategic act of entrepreneurship is new entry. To carry out an entrepreneurial strategy, a company must create an entrepreneurial orientation by encouraging autonomy, innovativeness, risk taking, proactiveness, and competitive aggressiveness.

What**Really**Happened?

In the opening case, you learned that Kodak struggled after spending nearly $10 billion to diversify into pharmaceuticals and medical testing equipment. Read the answers to the opening case to find out how, with a new CEO (George Fisher) and a new strategy, Kodak is trying to turn around its performance.

First, how can Kodak create a sustainable advantage over its competitors?

To provide a sustainable competitive advantage, firm resources must improve efficiency and effectiveness (i.e., be valuable), must not be possessed by many competing firms (i.e., rare), must be extremely costly or difficult to duplicate (i.e., imperfectly imitable), and must be nonsubstitutable (i.e., competitors cannot substitute other resources to produce similar value). While Kodak has cut costs significantly and is now run more efficiently, it's not yet clear that Kodak's distinctive competencies and core capabilities are rare, imperfectly imitable, or nonsubstitutable. Kodak produces high-quality photographic film, paper, and cameras, but there are at least a dozen other companies that sell these products, too. Furthermore, there are even more companies competing to set the standard for digital cameras and pictures. At this point, it's obvious that Kodak has a lot of work to do to create a sustainable competitive advantage, especially in digital photography.

Second, are there potential business opportunities among the obvious and numerous threats to Kodak's business?

The biggest change in Kodak's strategy is that CEO George Fisher sees digital photography and imaging as a strategic opportunity for Kodak's business rather than a strategic threat. He says, "Not too many years ago, the company feared that digital was somehow going to wipe out film. We don't see that happening. Hence digital is now being embraced more as a way to grow not just the total enterprise but the film business as well." One example of this change in perspective is Kodak's Advantix camera, which combines the best technological components of traditional and digital photography. The Advantix uses regular Kodak film, because traditional photographic film easily produces much higher quality pictures than digital cameras (at least for now). However, each picture taken by the Advantix stores digital information about the camera speed, light exposure, etc., that can be used to produce even higher quality pictures. Another indication that Kodak now sees digital photography as an opportunity is that it sells the broadest range of digital cameras on the market, from basic digital cameras selling for less than $300 all the way to professional digital cameras costing as much as $15,000.

Third, what business is Kodak really in, medicine or photography, and do these businesses make sense together?

Corporate-level strategy helps managers answer the question "What business are we in?" CEO Fisher concluded that "The company was trying to do too many things at once and wasn't able to afford to do any of them well enough." So Fisher answered this question by declaring that Kodak's business was imaging, be it traditional photographic film and paper imaging or digital imaging. "And if that [digital imaging] eats up some of the film business, so be it." With this decided, it took Fisher less than six months to sell Kodak's pharmaceutical, medical testing, and chemical businesses for $8 billion. This money was then used to pay off the long-term debt the company had accumulated while buying these companies.

Finally, what should Kodak's new strategy be? Should it be growth, stability, or retrenchment/recovery?

With five restructurings and the layoff of 40,000 employees, Kodak has obviously been going through a period of retrenchment. Now that it has begun to recover, Kodak wants to return to a growth strategy, so it can increase profits, market share, and the number of places in which it does business. However, this time, instead of growing by acquiring unrelated companies (i.e., unrelated diversification), Kodak is pursuing internal growth by growing its current business and by growing new businesses. CEO Fisher believes that Kodak can grow its core photographic film and paper business 7 percent to 9 percent per year. He said, "Half the people in the world have yet to take their first picture. The opportunity is huge, and it's nothing fancy. We just have to sell yellow boxes of film." In all, Fisher expects Kodak to pursue five major areas of growth: product differentiation, geographic expansion (global), digital imaging, equipment manufacturing, and imaging services (electronic photo delivery).

Sources: M. Bulkeley, "Kodak Profit, Helped by Cost Cutting, Hits Forecasts Despite 7% Sales Decline," *The Wall Street Journal*, 15 April 1998, A4. S.N. Chakravarty, "How an Outsider's Vision Saved Kodak," *Forbes*, 13 January 1997, 45-47. J.P. Donlon, "The Big Picture (Interview with Eastman Kodak CEO George Fisher)," *Chief Executive*, November 1995, 34-37. L. Grant, "The Bears Back Off Kodak," *Fortune*, 24 June 1996, 24-26. D. Grotta & S.W. Grotta, "Heave-Ho Silver!" *PC Magazine*, 7 January 1997, 145-178. L. Johannes, "Kodak Reports Loss of $744 Million Including Big Restructuring Charge," *The Wall Street Journal*, 16 January 1998, A4. M. Maremont, "Kodak's New Focus," *Business Week*, 30 January 1995. J.F. Peltz, "Kodak Takes Another Shot at Restructuring the Company Hopes to Recapture Its BlueChip Status with Film, but Even That Business Is Troubled," *Los Angeles Times*, 30 October 1994.

Key Terms

acquisition p. 329
analyzers p. 343
attack p. 347
bargaining power of buyers p. 340
bargaining power of suppliers p. 340
BCG matrix p. 329
cash cow p. 329
character of the rivalry p. 338
competitive advantage p. 315
competitive inertia p. 319
core capabilities p. 322
core firms p. 323
corporate-level strategy p. 327
cost leadership p. 341
defenders p. 342
differentiation p. 341
direct competition p. 345
distinctive competence p. 321
diversification p. 328
dog p. 329
entrepreneurial orientation p. 349
entrepreneurship p. 349
firm-level strategy p. 344
focus strategy p. 342
grand strategy p. 333
growth strategy p. 333
imperfectly imitable resource p. 316
industry-level strategy p. 337
market commonality p. 345
nonsubstitutable resource p. 316
portfolio strategy p. 328
prospectors p. 342
question mark p. 329
rare resource p. 316
reactors p. 343
recovery p. 336
related diversification p. 331
resource similarity p. 345
resources p. 315
response p. 347
retrenchment strategy p. 336
secondary firms p. 323
shadow-strategy task force p. 324
situational (SWOT) analysis p. 321
stability strategy p. 334
star p. 329
strategic dissonance p. 320
strategic group p. 323
strategic reference points p. 325
sustainable competitive advantage p. 315
threat of new entrants p. 338
threat of substitute products or services p. 340
transient firms p. 323
unrelated diversification p. 329
valuable resource p. 315

What Would You Do-II?

Neenah, Wisconsin

It's 9:00 p.m. Sunday night, and your local grocery store is packed with parents filling shopping carts with the milk, bread, and cereal they need to get their kids going on Monday morning. Waiting in the checkout line (of course, only one checkout lane is open), you smile when you notice that half the carts are filled with Kimberly-Clark products, particularly disposable diapers and wipes. The diaper business is a good one. From birth to potty training, which typically lasts about three years, the average child uses 6,000 disposable diapers. At a cost of about $30 a week, the total cost comes to about $4,700 per child. Even better, the market has grown to the point where disposable diapers now cover 94 percent of U.S. babies' bottoms.

Yes, it's a good business to be in, but it's a cutthroat business. Your company, Kimberly-Clark, has been battling with market leader Procter & Gamble (P&G) for nearly three decades. It began when P&G introduced Pampers, the first disposable diaper, in 1961. Seven years later, Kimberly-Clark produced its first disposable, Kimbies. In the 1970s, P&G innovated by adding tape closures to Pampers to replace the safety pins that parents used to keep disposable diapers on babies. P&G also introduced sizes for toddlers and premature infants. These aggressive moves killed Kimbies' sales, forcing Kimberly-Clark to pull Kimbies from the market. However, in 1978, Kimberly-Clark introduced Huggies, diapers with elastic around the legs to prevent leakage. Then, in 1983, Kimberly-Clark added refastenable tape closures to Huggies. Now parents could unfasten the diaper to see if it was dirty and then refasten it for continued use if it wasn't. The result: P&G's profits and market share dropped significantly. However, three years later, P&G responded with Pampers Ultras, ultra-absorbent diapers that were half the thickness of regular disposable diapers. A year later, Kimberly-Clark followed with Huggies SuperTrim.

Attack, response, and attack: The battle continues today. But instead of a domestic battle, it has become a battle for global dominance of the diaper market. Right now, the fiercest scuffles are in Europe. When Kimberly-Clark introduced its diapers in Europe, P&G responded with a deep price cut. P&G's move forced Kimberly-Clark to match the lower prices, costing Kimberly-Clark over $80 million in lost profits. Another factor complicating Kimberly-Clark's move into Europe is that European grocery stores are small and have much more limited shelf space. Consequently, stores only carry a small selection of well-known brands, like P&G's Pampers, and are reluctant to add new brands that might not sell as well. Because of these difficulties, Kimberly-Clark doesn't expect its European diaper business to break even for several years.

Slam! The carry-out assistant finishes putting the groceries in your car and closes the trunk. As you pull out of the parking lot, you wonder what the company needs to do to create a sustained competitive advantage against P&G. Since the company has a variety of business units (trucking, beauty/barbershops, a regional airline, cigarette papers, pulp and paper mills that process a variety of raw materials used in Kimberly-Clark products) in addition to diapers, there's no shortage of strategic alternatives. What kind of corporate-level strategy should the company pursue? Should it be growth, stability, or retrenchment/recovery? Also, what kind of diversification strategy should Kimberly-Clark employ? Likewise, what kind of industry-level strategy should the company follow: cost-leadership, differentiation, or focus? Or might an adaptive strategy be better? But which one: defender, prospector, analyzer, or reactor? Finally, given the brutal competition with P&G, how aggressive should Kimberly-Clark be in its firm-level competition? How quick should it be to attack and respond to P&G? And, if Kimberly-Clark chooses to attack or respond to P&G, how should it do so? **If you were in charge of the strategy-making process at Kimberly-Clark, what would you do?**

Sources: D. Decwikiel-Kane, "Oh, How Diapers Have Changed/The Disposable Changed Diapers for Babies," *Greensboro News & Record*, 4 November 1996. B. Deener, "Continental Divide: Kimberly-Clark Faces Tough Competition in Europe from Rival P&G," *The Dallas Morning News*, 16 July 1995. B. Deener, "KimberlyClark Plans to Acquire Scott Paper," *The Dallas Morning News*, 18 July 1995. G. Lazarus, "Procter Wipes Up Towelette Brands," *Chicago Tribune*, 24 May 1996. R. Lenzner & C. Shook, "The Battle of the Bottoms," *Forbes*, 24 March 1997, 98-104. R. Narisetti, "P&G to Embark on an Overhaul of Diaper Lines," *The Wall Street Journal Europe*, 10 June 1996.

Critical-Thinking Video Case

Entrepreneurship: Second Chance Body Armor

Owner/inventor Richard Davis had a violent encounter that led him to develop a product to save lives. After being shot twice, he developed body armor that was comfortable enough for people to wear every day. Today, Second Chance is a major supplier of body armor to law enforcement agencies across the U.S. This body armor has saved at least 600 police officers' lives.

Critical-Thinking Video Case

In this video, you learn how Richard Davis started Second Chance Body Armor and the innovative steps he had to take to make law enforcement agencies aware of the life-protecting benefits of his new product. As you watch the video, consider the following critical-thinking questions.

Critical-Thinking Questions

1. What types of challenges do entrepreneurs face when they start a business?
2. How would Second Chance maintain an advantage over their competition?
3. What are the advantages and disadvantages of being an entrepreneur?

Management Decisions

Absolutely, Positively Overnight

It begins at 11:00 p.m. each night. Every 90 seconds an orange, blue, and white FedEx cargo plane lands at the Memphis airport. By 1:00 a.m., all the planes have arrived. As FedEx workers scurry between planes, loading and unloading packages and cargo containers, activity is everywhere. The scene is not unlike a busy colony of ants lucky enough to find itself underneath a park picnic table. Before the planes return to the runway several hours later, stuffed to the cockpit with packages guaranteed to be delivered to their final destinations "absolutely, positively overnight," FedEx's 9,000 Memphis workers will have sorted one million packages in less than four hours. However, the daily numbers for the entire company are even more impressive: 562 cargo planes and 372,000 vans delivering 2.5 million packages in 211 countries.

Thanks to the increasing pace of the business world (and the human tendency to want immediate gratification, despite determined procrastination), FedEx has had unparalleled growth over the last two decades. Revenues have grown from zero, when FedEx invented the overnight delivery business a quarter century ago, to more than $10 billion a year. But can FedEx achieve the same explosive growth in the next 25 years that it had in its first 25? Unlike 1973, when founder and CEO Fred Smith started the company, FedEx faces numerous competitors, as well as technology (e.g., faxes and the Internet) that no one had even imagined a quarter century ago.

Additional Internet Resources

- FedEx Home Page (**www.fedex.com**). This site contains information about FedEx's services, software, tracking, and delivery services.
- United Parcel Service Home Page (**www.ups.com**). This site contains information about UPS's services, software, tracking, and delivery services.
- U.S. Postal Service Home Page (**www.usps.gov**). This site contains information about the United States Postal Service. In particular, be sure to check out "Express Mail" and information about postal rates, especially for express mail.

Questions

1. Conduct a situational analysis for FedEx. What are its internal strengths (i.e., core competencies) and weaknesses? What strategic opportunities and threats does it face?
2. Assume that CEO Fred Smith has made you head of FedEx's shadow-strategy task force. Thinking like a competitor, actively determine FedEx's weaknesses and how a competitor could exploit them for competitive advantage.

Sources: D.A. Blackmon, "FedEx Plans to Establish a Marketplace in Cyber Space–Shipper Aims to Deliver the Goods as it Moves into Internet Commerce," *The Wall Street Journal*, 9 October 1996. D.A. Blackmon, "Federal Express Sees Strong 4Q, Backs Yr View above $3/Shr," *Dow Jones News Service*, 31 March 1997. D.A. Blackmon, "Federal Express Plans 3-Day Service to Challenge UPS," *The Wall Street Journal*, 2 April 1997. "Dietzgen's New Same-Day Satellite Document Delivery Service for Architectural and Engineering Blueprints Takes Direct Aim at Overnight Courier Business," *Business Wire*, 21 March 1997. T. Lappin, "FedEx: The Airline of the Internet," *Wired Magazine*, December 1996.

Management Decisions

How About a "Cuppa?"

In Great Britain, when someone asks, "How about a cuppa?" they're asking if you want a cup of tea. And with an average of 3.6 "cuppas" a day per person, Great Britain, which has a population just one-fourth the size of the U.S., consumes an amazing 10 percent of the world's tea each year—more than North America and Europe put together. In Great Britain, people of all ages and economic levels drink tea, bringing annual sales to more than $750 million per year. Indeed, the British drink so much tea that market researchers estimate that tea accounts for 42 percent of all liquid intake in Great Britain.

Yet even in tea-crazed Britain, tea is not as popular as it once was. Tea still outsells coffee and soft drinks combined, but tea sales are no longer growing. By contrast, coffee sales, especially among young professionals, are increasing approximately 4 percent per year. Mark Beales, a coffee marketing manager at Nestle Foods, said, "It's seen to be more sophisticated than tea now. Out-of-home consumption is being driven by the increasing number of quality café bars, which improves the perception of coffee and makes it more widely available." With sales of soft drinks increasing, too, especially among children and teens, the long-term prospects for tea don't look promising.

Questions

1. Using Michael Porters' Industry Forces model, explain how each of the five forces will affect the tea industry's overall attractiveness and potential for long-term profitability.

2. If you worked for one of the leading tea companies in Britain (tea bags account for 83 percent of all tea sold by these companies), what industry-level strategy would you recommend to the company? Would it be focus, cost-leadership, differentiation, defender, prospector, analyzer, reactor, or a combination of these strategies? Explain which you recommend, why you recommend it, and how the company should use that strategy to gain competitive advantage.

Sources: E. Beck, "New 3-D Tea Bag Rattles Some Tea Cups in the U.K," *The Wall Street Journal Interactive Edition*, 24 March 1997. L. Bray, "Boiling Points: Life Is Not an Easy Ride for Tea and Coffee Manufacturers These Days, with Innovation in Other Beverage Categories Increasing All the Time," *Grocer*, 16 November 1996, 45-46. N. Clayton, "Workforce Is Showing Bags of Innovation," *The Times of London*, 2 October 1994. R. Mulholland, "Storm Brewing in Britain's Teacups," *Agence France-Presse*, 24 February 1996. R. Turcsik, "A Bountry of Teas," *Supermarket News*, 13 November 1995, 42-43.

Develop Your Management Potential

Strategic Planning, Protean Careers, and Psychological Success

For most of the 20th century, planning for a career has been as simple as planning for your next job. This is because most 20th century careers have been linear—a progressive series of upward job promotions in the same field. For example, college graduates might begin a marketing career by starting as sales representatives. Then, over time, as they acquired knowledge and experience, they could expect to be promoted to marketing jobs with more authority and responsibility, perhaps sales manager or account manager. Eventually, they would retire, having spent their entire career in marketing-related jobs.

Today, however, careers are much more likely to be protean than linear. The term "protean" comes from the mythical Greek god Proteus, who would change shapes to keep others from finding him and obtaining his knowledge about all things past, present, and future. So, by contrast to linear careers in which the next job was simply a step up from one's previous job, protean career paths change frequently. If the ladder is the appropriate symbol for linear careers, then a parachute is the best symbol for protean careers, as people jump from one set of jobs to a completely different set of jobs. Instead of a job path that heads straight up the same career ladder, the job path in protean careers zigs and zags as "career jumpers" land their job parachutes far away from their original targets.

Of course, this creates a problem. How do you plan for a protean career when it's highly likely that what you do in your current job will be completely unrelated to what you do in your next job or the job after that? Fortunately, there is something you can do to plan for a protean career.

Since there's no way to know when a significant job change may present itself, career experts recommend that you focus on psychological success rather than that next job or promotion. A common reaction to this advice is that the "experts" have got it backwards. It's widely believed that you can't achieve career success, happiness, or wealth without keeping an eye on that next promotion. The "experts" have two responses. First, several decades of research clearly indicate that there's only a tiny positive relationship between money (which, for most of us, comes from getting promoted) and happiness. In fact, only 2 percent of the differences between happy and miserable people stem from money. Second, many business people don't achieve real success until they let go of their "careerist" goals (i.e., promotion after promotion) and focus on enjoying and excelling at their jobs. Ironically, after this occurs, promotions and other career opportunities tend to take care of themselves. In other words, over the long run, that is, from a strategic perspective, it makes more sense to worry about whether you enjoy what you're doing than when and where that next promotion will come from and how much more money you'll earn when you get it.

Begin your plan for a protean career by answering the following questions.

Questions

1. Of all the jobs you've had, which made you feel the best about yourself as a person? What did you enjoy most about this job? Be specific. Now, of all the jobs you've had, which made you feel the worst about yourself as a person? What was the worst part of this job? Finally, describe three significant differences between your best and worst jobs.

2. What do you do in your free time? Do you have any hobbies or interests in which you become readily absorbed? Describe your favorite outside interest or hobby. List three reasons why this activity or interest is so much fun for you.

Sources: K.R. Brousseau, M.J. Driver, K. Eneroth, & R. Larsson, "Career Pandemonium: Realigning Organizations and Individuals," *Academy of Management Executive*, November 1996, 52-66. D.T. Hall, "Protean Careers of the 21st Century," *Academy of Management Executive*, November 1996, 8-16. D. Seligman, "Does Money Buy Happiness?" *Forbes*, 21 April 1997, 394-396.

Chapter ten

Chapter 10 Outline

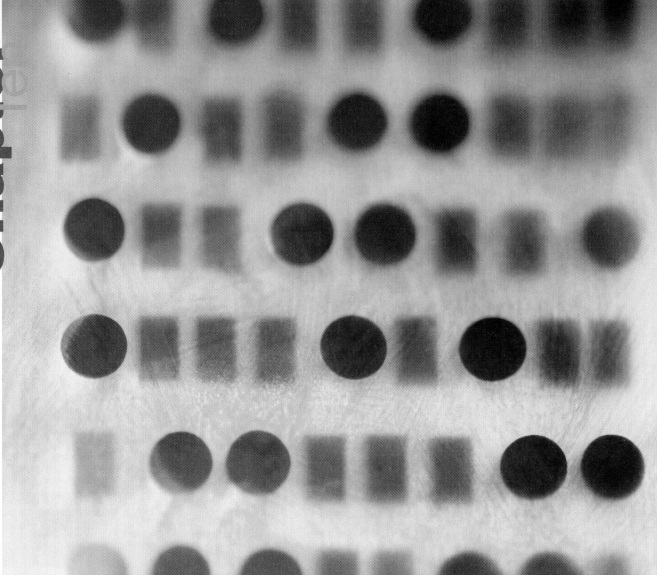

Innovation and Change

What Would **You** Do?

IBM Headquarters, Armonk, NY. Not in your briefcase. Not in the glove compartment. Not in your coat pocket. Darn! Where did you put those antacids? Ah, there they are on the floor. Better get them while the light is still red. Ugh, cherry, nasty. But the stress is killing your stomach. Every time you think about lunch and your management consultant's advice, your stomach turns. Her message was direct: If IBM doesn't change, it will join a long list of once-large corporate dinosaurs that have shrunk in size and profitability or, even worse, gone out of business. Her words painted a frightening picture. "Sears, General Motors, and U.S. Steel. For decades, these companies dominated their industries. You name it: clothing, furniture, tools, appliances, lawn mowers, car batteries, in the store or by catalog. Sears sold it all and dominated retailing. General Motors sold six out of every ten cars made in the U.S. Sixty percent! In fact, GM was so large and contributed so much to the U.S. economy that its domination of the auto industry was expressed in the well-known phrase: 'What's good for General Motors is good for the country.' U.S. Steel so dominated the steel industry that it was larger than its next three competitors combined." "Then," she warned, "their businesses changed but they didn't." She explained, "Wal-Mart, not Sears, now dominates retailing. JC Penney's catalog sales now dwarf Sears' catalog sales. In the auto industry, GM's market share dropped nearly in half, from just over 60 percent to barely over 30 percent. Who has that 30 percent now? Toyota, Honda, Ford, and Chrysler, that's who. And, in steel, mini-mills, like those run by Nucor Corporation, cut U.S. Steel's business in half as easily as a hot knife cuts through warm butter. Cut in half in less than a decade. The mini-mills were cheaper, faster, and easily out-innovated slow-moving U.S. Steel. And the same thing will happen to you. If you don't change, IBM will be the next giant to fall."

Unfortunately, you know she's right. IBM has to change. IBM (short for International Business Machines) once dominated sales of office equipment, first with typewriters, then mainframe computers, and then personal computers. Today, however, typewriters, replaced by computers, are a dead business. Mainframe sales, which accounted for half of IBM's revenues, are off by one-third. And in personal computers, where it once had more than 70 percent of the market, IBM now has a 7 percent market share behind Gateway, Compaq, and Dell Computers, none of which were even in business when IBM began selling personal computers. But how do you quickly and effectively change a company like IBM? Should the change be slow and gradual or quick and revolutionary? IBM has a long history and a strong culture. So, any changes that you try to make will probably be resisted. How can you identify and manage that resistance so IBM can make the changes that it needs to make? In the fast-paced environment of computers, it takes IBM much too long to develop and bring new products to market. How can you speed up that process?

If you were at IBM, what would you do?

Sources: A. Goldstein, "Big Blue Pulls Ahead of the Pack," *Dallas Morning News*, 14 February 1999, 1H. L. Hays, "Another Top IBM Executive Quits Amid Reorganization by Gerstner," *The Wall Street Journal Europe*, 10 January 1995. "IBM's Finances: Now Comes the Hard Part," *Infoperspectives* 18 (1 April 1997). D.Q. Mills, "The Decline and Rise of IBM," *Sloan Management Review* 37 (1 June 1996). R. Narisetti, "How IBM Turned Around Its Ailing PC Division," *The Wall Street Journal*, 12 March 1998, B1. S. Sherman, "Is He Too Cautious to Save IBM?" *Fortune*, 3 October 1994. B. Ziegler, "IBM's Research Cutbacks Now Seem to Be Brilliant," *The Wall Street Journal*, 6 October 1997.

organizational innovation
the successful implementation of creative ideas in organizations

creativity
the production of novel and useful ideas

We begin this chapter by reviewing the issues associated with organizational innovation. **Organizational innovation** is the successful implementation of creative ideas in an organization.[1] **Creativity**, which is a form of organizational innovation, is the production of novel and useful ideas.[2] For example, the reason that IBM lost so much money and market share wasn't poor creativity, it was poor innovation. IBM was consistently slow to implement the ideas it developed in its award-winning research and development labs. A prime example of IBM's failed innovation efforts was the RISC chip. RISC, which is short for reduced instruction-set computing, makes computer chips execute their tasks much faster. IBM developed RISC, but Sun Microsystems, and later Intel Corporation, brought RISC technology into their products long before IBM did.[3] So, in the first part of this chapter, you will learn why innovation matters and how to manage innovation to create and sustain a competitive advantage.

organizational change
a difference in the form, quality, or condition of an organization over time

In the second half of this chapter, you will learn about organizational change. **Organizational change** is a difference in the form, quality, or condition of an organization over time.[4] For example, after being one of the most profitable companies in the world between 1950 and 1990, IBM lost more than $10 billion between 1991 and 1993. Those incredible losses prompted numerous changes at IBM, beginning with the replacement of its CEO. Also, out of financial necessity, IBM had to renege on its guarantee of lifetime employment for its workers. As the company struggled to stem its billion-dollar losses, more than 170,000 managers and workers lost their jobs. In the second half of this chapter, you will learn why changes like these occur. You will also learn about the risk of not changing, the different kinds of change, and the ways in which companies can manage change.

Organizational Innovation

Do you remember the first time, probably as a child, that you saw a blimp floating overhead? It moved slowly, was clearly visible for miles, and held your attention as it got closer, passed overhead, and then floated away. Interestingly, the things that make blimps fascinating to kids also make them great for advertising (i.e., slow, visible, holds attention). For example, Goodyear Tires, Anheuser-Busch (Budweiser Beer), and Blockbuster Video use blimps to advertise their products. Company names are clearly displayed on the side of their blimps at sporting events that are attended by thousands and seen by millions on TV. Blimps are so commonplace that major sporting events such as Monday Night Football, the Superbowl, the U.S. Open Golf Tournament, and the World Series would seem incomplete without traditional overhead camera shots from the blimp. Even when games occur inside domed stadiums, blimp-mounted cameras are still used to transmit pictures of city skylines or nearby mountains, oceans, or deserts.

Today, however, the "Lightship," an innovative new blimp made by the American Blimp Company, is revolutionizing the blimp business and the advertising revenues that go with it. Lightships have several advantages over traditional blimps. To start, they're much smaller and cheaper. A typical, full-size blimp costs about $300,000 a month to operate. Most of that cost is for the 24 people who work in the blimp's ground and flight crews. Because American Blimp's Lightships are smaller, it takes only 14 people to staff the ground and flight crews. Consequently, monthly costs run around $200,000, one-third less than full-size blimps. Another advantage is that Lightships are lighted from the inside. So, when it gets dark, the company name and logo on the side of the blimp are still visible! This is critical since most sporting events take place at night to maximize the size of their TV audience.[5]

Organizational innovation, like American Blimp's new Lightships, is the successful implementation of creative ideas in an organization.[6] After reading the next two sections on organizational innovation, you should be able to:

1 explain why **innovation matters** to companies.

2 discuss the different methods that managers can use to effectively **manage innovation** in their organizations.

1 Why Innovation Matters

When was the last time you used a record player to listen to music, tuned up your car, baked cookies from scratch, or manually changed the channel on your TV? Because of product innovations and advances in technology, it's hard to remember, isn't it? In fact, since compact discs began replacing vinyl record albums nearly a decade ago, many of you may *never* have played a record album. Lots of people used to tune up their own cars because it was easy, quick, and cheap. Change the points, spark plugs, and distributor cap, and your car was good for another six months or 12,000 miles. Today, with advanced technology and computerized components, almost no one tunes up their cars anymore. It's far too complex for weekend mechanics. Nobody makes cookies from scratch anymore, either. Millions of kids think that baking cookies means adding water to a powered mix or getting pre-made cookie dough out of the refrigerator. As for manually changing the channels on your TV, ok, you may have done that recently, but only because you couldn't find the remote.

We can only guess what changes technological innovations will bring in the next 20 years. Maybe we'll be listening to compact chips rather than compact discs. Maybe cars won't need tune-ups. Maybe we'll use the Internet to have cookies delivered hot to our homes like pizza. And maybe TVs will be voice-activated, so it doesn't matter if you lose the remote (just don't lose your voice). Who knows? The only thing we do know about the next 20 years is that innovation will continue to change our lives. For a fuller appreciation of how technological innovation has changed our lives, see the "Blast from the Past" on technological innovation in the 20th century

Let's begin our discussion of innovation by learning about **1.1** *technology cycles and* **1.2** *innovation streams.*

BLASTFROMTHEPAST

Technological Innovation in the 20th Century

There's no better way to understand how technology has repeatedly and deeply changed modern life than to read a year-by-year list of innovations in the 20th century. The first time through the list, simply appreciate the amount of change that has occurred in this century. It's astonishing. However, the second time through, look at each invention and ask yourself two questions: What brand new business or industry was created by this innovation? And, what old business or industry was made obsolete by this innovation?

1900–1910
- electric typewriter
- air conditioner
- airplane
- reinforced concrete
- skyscraper
- vacuum tube
- plastic
- chemotherapy
- electric washing machine

1911–1920
- artificial kidney
- mammography
- 35mm camera
- zipper
- sonar
- tank
- Band-Aid
- submachine gun

1921–1930
- self-winding watch
- TB vaccine
- frozen food
- commercial fax service
- talking movies
- black and white television
- penicillin
- jet engine
- supermarket

1931–1940
- defibrillator
- radar
- Kodachrome film
- helicopter
- nylon
- ballpoint pen
- first working computer
- fluorescent lighting
- color television

1941–1950
- aerosol can
- nuclear reactor
- atomic bomb
- first modern herbicide
- microwave oven
- bikini
- disposable diaper
- ENIAC computer
- mobile phone
- transistor
- credit card

1951–1960
- Salk's polio vaccine
- DNA
- oral contraceptive
- solar power
- Tylenol
- Sputnik
- integrated circuit
- breast implant

1961–1970
- measles vaccine
- navigation satellite
- miniskirt
- video recorder
- soft contact lenses
- coronary bypass
- handheld calculator
- computer mouse
- Arpanet (prototype Internet)
- bar-code scanner
- lunar landing

1971–1980
- compact disc
- Pong (first computer game)
- word processor
- gene splicing
- Post-it note
- Ethernet (computer network)
- laser printer
- personal computer
- VHS video recording
- fiber-optics
- linked ATMs
- magnetic resonance imaging

1981–1990
- MS-DOS
- space shuttle
- clone of IBM personal computer
- cellular-phone network
- computer virus
- human embryo transfer
- CD-ROM
- Windows software
- 3-D video game
- disposable contact lenses
- Doppler radar
- RU-486 (abortion pill)
- global positioning system by satellite
- stealth bomber
- World Wide Web

1991–Today
- baboon-human liver transplant
- taxol (cancer drug)
- mapping of the male chromosome
- Pentium processor
- channel tunnel opens
- HIV protease inhibitor
- gene for obesity discovered
- Java (computer language)
- cloning of an adult mammal

Source: T. Gideonse, "Decade by Decade: A Rich Century of Better Mousetraps," *Newsweek Special Issue: The Power of Invention,* Winter 1997-1998, 12-15.

1.1 *Technology Cycles*

technology cycle
cycle that begins with the "birth" of a new technology and ends when that technology reaches its limits and is replaced by a newer, substantially better technology

In Chapter 2, you learned that *technology* is the knowledge, tools, and techniques used to transform inputs (raw materials, information, etc.) into outputs (products and services). A **technology cycle** begins with the "birth" of a new technology and ends when that technology reaches its limits and "dies" as it is replaced by a newer, substantially better technology.[7] For example, technology cycles occurred when air conditioning supplanted fans, when Henry Ford's Model T replaced horse-drawn carriages, when planes replaced trains as a means of cross-country travel, when vaccines that prevented diseases replaced medicines designed to treat them, and when battery-powered wristwatches replaced mechanically powered, stem-wound wristwatches.

S-curve pattern of innovation
a pattern of technological innovation characterized by slow initial progress, then rapid progress, and then again by slow progress as a technology matures and reaches its limits

From Gutenberg's invention of the printing press in the 1400s to the rapid advance of the Internet in the last few years, studies of hundreds of technological innovations have shown that nearly all technology cycles follow the typical **S-curve pattern of innovation** shown in Figure 10.1.[8] Early in a technology cycle, there is still much to learn and progress is slow, as depicted by point A on the S-curve. The flat slope indicates that increased effort (i.e., money, research and development) brings only small improvements in technological performance. Intel's technology cycles have followed this pattern. Intel spends billions to develop new computer chips and to build new production facilities to produce them. Intel has found that the technology cycle for its integrated circuits (that power personal computers) is about three years. In each three-year cycle, Intel introduces a new chip, improves the chip by making it a little bit faster each year, and then replaces that chip at the end of the cycle with a brand new chip that is substantially faster than the old chip. But, at first, those billions typically produce only small improvements in performance. For instance, as shown in Figure 10.2, Intel's first 60 megahertz (MHz) Pentium processors ran at a speed of 60 based on the iComp Index.[9] (The iComp Index is a benchmark test for measuring relative computer speed. For example, a computer with an iComp score of 200 is twice as fast as a computer with an iComp score of 100). Yet, six months later, Intel's new 75 MHz Pentium was only slightly faster, with an iComp speed of 67.

Figure 10.1 **S-Curves and Technological Innovation**

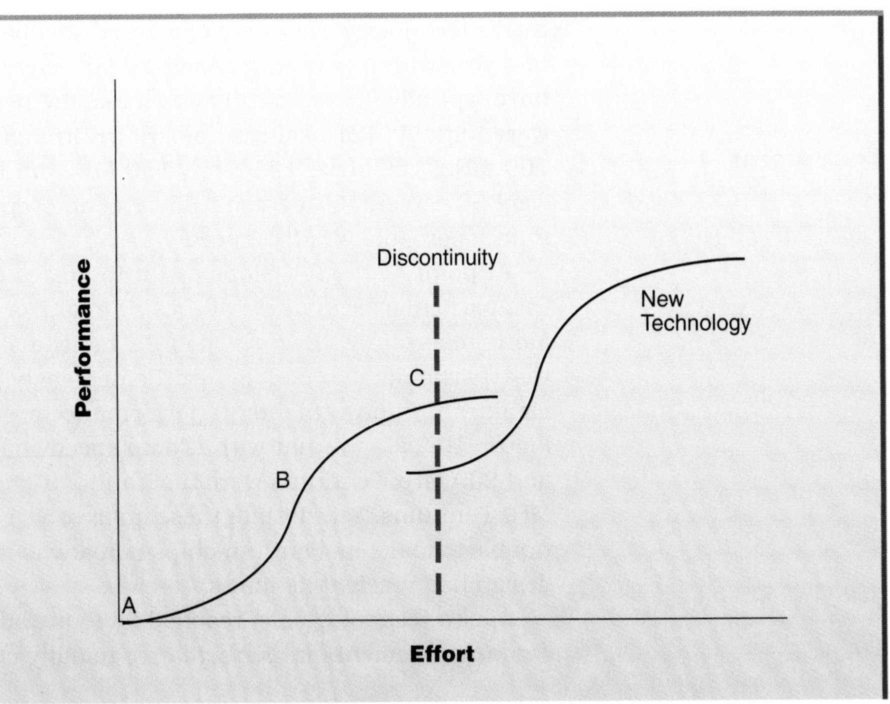

Source: R.N. Foster, *Innovation: The Attacker's Advantage* (New York: Summitt, 1986).

Figure 10.2 **iComp Index 2.0 Comparing the Relative Performance of Different Intel Microprocessors**

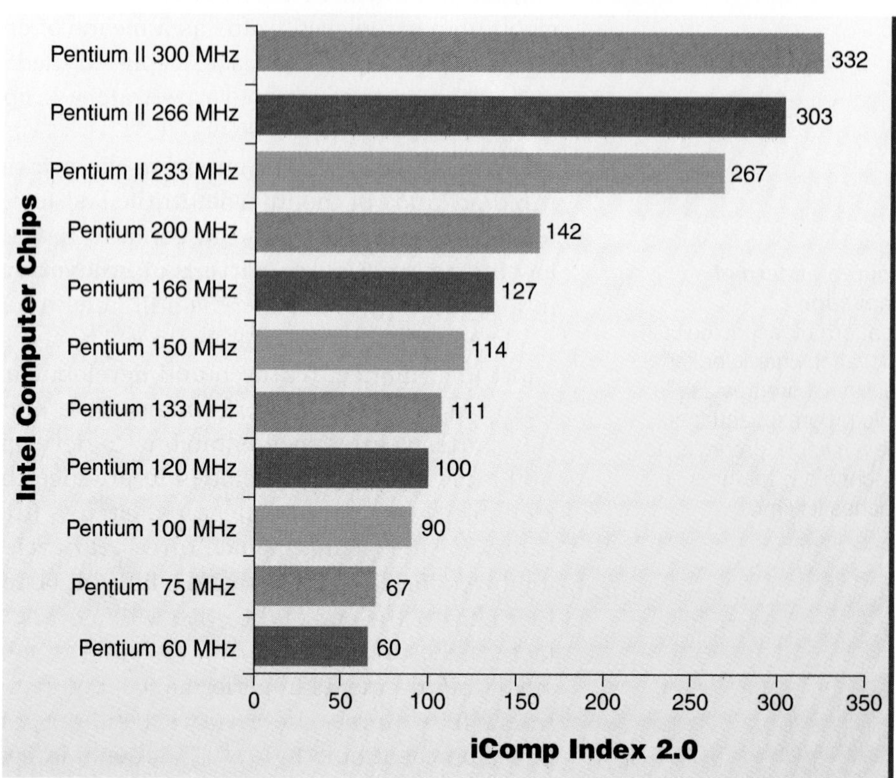

Source: "iComp Index 2.0," Intel Corporation Web Site. [Online] Available **www.intel.com/procs/performance/icomp/index.htm**, 3 March 1999.

Fortunately, as the technology matures, researchers figure out how to get better performance from the new technology. This is represented by point B of the S-curve in Figure 10.1. The steeper slope indicates that small amounts of effort will result in significant increases in performance. Again, Intel's technology cycles have followed this pattern. In fact, after six months to a year with a new chip design, Intel's engineering and production people have typically figured out how to make the new chips much faster than they were initially. For example, as shown in Figure 10.2, Intel soon rolled out 100 MHz, 120 MHz, 133 MHz, 150 MHz, and 166 MHz Pentium chips that were 50 percent, 67 percent, 85 percent, 90 percent, and 111 percent faster than its original 60 MHz speed.

At point C, the flat slope again indicates that further efforts to develop this particular technology will result in only small increases in performance. More importantly, however, point C indicates that the performance limits of that particular technology are being reached. In other words, additional significant improvements in performance are highly unlikely. For example, Figure 10.2 shows that with iComp speeds of 127 and 142, Intel's 166 MHz and 200 MHz Pentiums were 2.12 and 2.37 times faster than its original 60 MHz Pentiums. Yet, despite these impressive gains in performance, Intel was unable to make its Pentium chips run any faster, because the basic Pentium design had reached its limits.

After a technology has reached its limits at the top of the S-curve, significant improvements in performance usually come from radical new designs or new performance-enhancing materials. In Figure 10.1, that new technology is represented by the second S-curve. The changeover or discontinuity between the new and old technologies is represented by the dotted line. At first, the new and old technologies will likely coexist. Eventually, however, the new technology will replace the old technology. When that happens, the old technology cycle will be complete and a new one will have started. The changeover between Intel's Pentium processors, the old technology, and its Pentium II processors, the new technology (these chips are significantly different technologies despite their similar names), took approximately a year. Figure 10.2 shows this changeover or discontinuity between the two technologies. With an iComp speed of 267, the first Pentium II (233 MHz) was 88 percent faster than the last and fastest 200 MHz Pentium processor. And because their design and performance are significantly different (and faster) than Pentium II chips, Intel's new Pentium III chips represent the beginning of yet another S-curve technology cycle in integrated circuits.

While the evolution of Intel's Pentium chips has been used to illustrate the idea of S-curves and technology cycles, it's important to note that technology cycles and technological innovation don't necessarily mean "high technology." Remember, *technology* is simply the knowledge, tools, and techniques used to transform inputs (raw materials, information, etc.) into outputs (products and services). So a technology cycle occurs whenever there are major advances or changes in the *knowledge*, *tools*, and *techniques* of a field or discipline. For example, one of the most important technology cycles in the history of civilization occurred in 1859, when 1,300 miles of central sewer line were constructed throughout London to carry human waste to the sea more than 11 miles away. This extensive sewer system replaced the widespread practice of directly dumping raw sewage into streets, where people walked through it and where it drained into public wells that supplied drinking water. Though the relationship wasn't known at the time, preventing waste runoff from contaminating water supplies stopped the spread of cholera that had killed millions of people for centuries in cities throughout the world.[10] Safe water supplies immediately translated into better health and longer life expectancies. Indeed, the water you drink today is safe thanks to this "technology" breakthrough. So when you think about technology cycles, don't automatically think "high technology." Instead, broaden your perspective by considering advances or changes in knowledge, tools, and techniques.

1.2 *Innovation Streams*

In Chapter 9, you learned that organizations can create *competitive advantage* for themselves if they have a *distinctive competence* that allows them to make, do, or perform something better than their competitors. Furthermore, a competitive advantage becomes sustainable if other companies cannot duplicate the benefits obtained from that distinctive competence. Technological innovation, however, makes it possible not only to duplicate the benefits obtained from a company's distinctive advantage, but also to quickly turn a company's competitive advantage into a competitive disadvantage. For example, through the 1970s, National Cash Register (NCR) was the leading U.S. producer of, well, cash registers. But in 1971, NCR announced that it was taking a $140 million write-off for millions of brand new cash registers. If the cash registers were brand new, why couldn't NCR sell them? NCR's cash registers were electromechanical and had been made obsolete by newer, more powerful, and cheaper electrical cash registers.[11] Technological innovation had turned NCR's competitive advantage into a competitive disadvantage. And, in the last decade, the same electrical cash registers that began NCR's downfall were themselves made obsolete by scanners that automatically scanned prices and product information from bar codes into computerized cash registers.

As NCR's example shows, companies that want to sustain a competitive advantage must understand and protect themselves from the strategic threats of innovation. Over the long run, the best way to do that is for a company to create a stream of its own innovative ideas and products year after year. Consequently, we define **innovation streams** as patterns of innovation over time that can create sustainable competitive advantage.[12] Figure 10.3 shows a typical innovation stream consisting of a series of technology cycles. Recall that technological cycles begin with a new technology and end when

innovation streams patterns of innovation over time that can create sustainable competitive advantage

Figure 10.3 **Innovation Streams: Technology Cycles over Time**

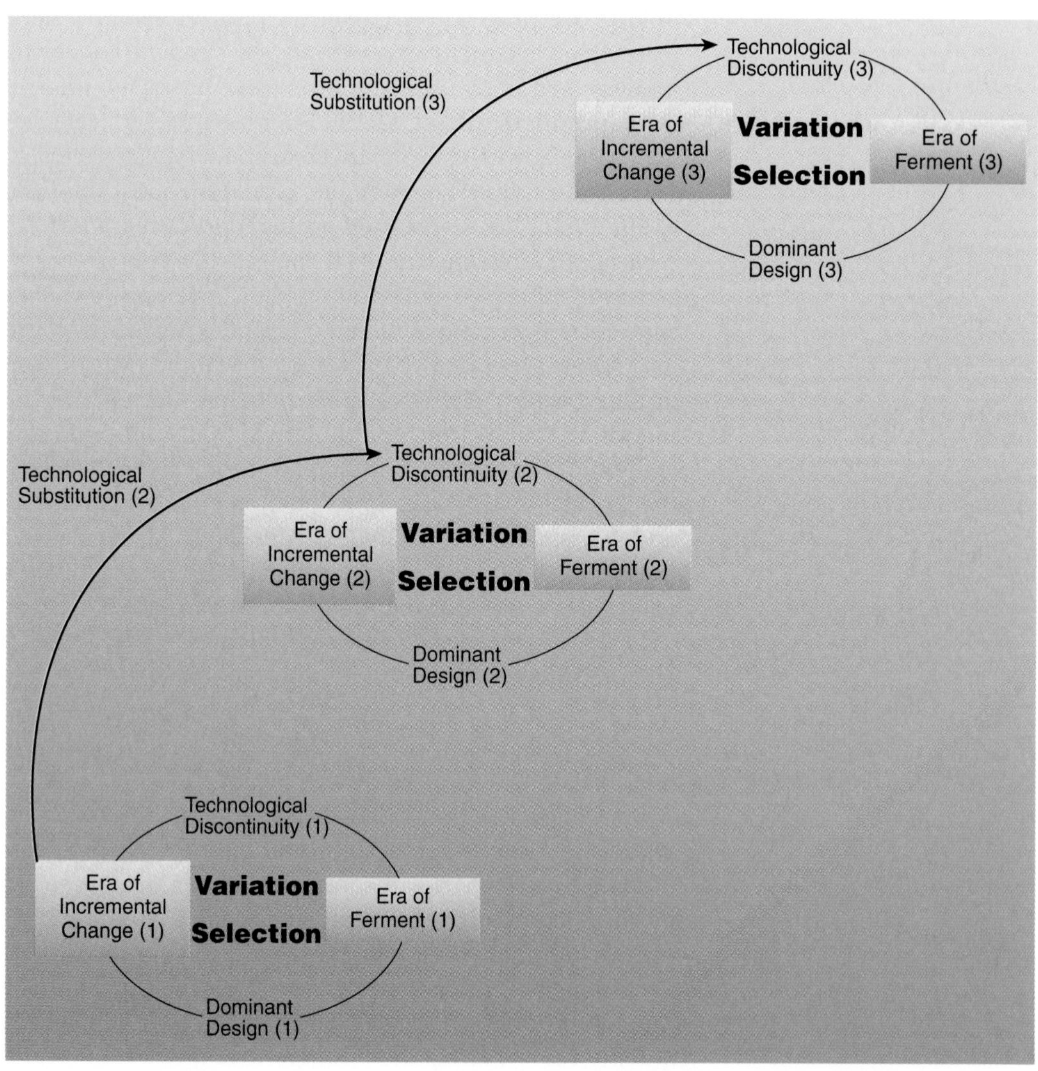

Source: M.L. Tushman, P.C. Anderson, & C. O'Reilly, "Technology Cycles, Innovation Streams, and Ambidextrous Organizations: Organization Renewal Through Innovation Streams and Strategic Change," in *Managing Strategic Innovation and Change,* eds. M.L. Tushman & P. Anderson (1997), 3-23.

that technology is replaced by a newer, substantially better technology. The innovation stream in Figure 10.3 shows three such technology cycles.

technological discontinuity
scientific advance or unique combination of existing technologies that creates a significant breakthrough in performance or function

An innovation stream begins with a **technological discontinuity**, in which a scientific advance or a unique combination of existing technologies creates a significant breakthrough in performance or function. For example, coronary bypass surgery, which is a common treatment for heart attacks, has saved millions of lives. Because of the intrusive nature of the surgery—an incision is made from the belly button to the middle of the chest, the breast bone is sawed through, and then a metal ratchet is used to spread the rib cage open—it takes anywhere from 3 to 6 months to recover from the operation. However, thanks to miniature lights, cameras, and surgical tools, surgeons can now do bypass operations by making several small, key-sized holes in the chest. The trauma associated with this new technique is so small that people can be back at work or on the golf course 3 to 4 days after the surgery.[13]

era of ferment
phase of a technology cycle characterized by technological substitution and design competition

technological substitution
purchase of new technologies to replace older ones

Technological discontinuities are followed by an **era of ferment** characterized by technological substitution and design competition. **Technological substitution** occurs when customers purchase new technologies to replace older technologies. For example, in the first half of the 1800s, letters, messages, and news traveled slowly by boat, train, or horseback, such as the famous Pony Express that, using a large number of fresh riders and fresh horses, could deliver mail from St. Joseph, Missouri, to Sacramento, California, in 10 days.[14] However, between 1840 and 1860, many businesses began using the telegraph, because it allowed messages and news to be sent cross-country (or even around the world) in minutes rather than days, weeks, or months.[15] Indeed, telegraph companies were so successful that the Pony Express went out of business almost immediately after the completion of the transcontinental telegraph, which linked telegraph systems from coast to coast.

design competition
competition between old and new technologies to establish a new technological standard or dominant design

An era of ferment is also characterized by **design competition** in which the old technology and several different new technologies compete to establish a new technological standard or dominant design. Because of large investments in old technology, and because the new and old technologies are often incompatible with each other, companies and consumers are reluctant to switch to a different technology during design competition. Indeed, the telegraph was so widely used as a means of communication in the late 1800s that, at first, almost no one understood why telephones would be a better way to communicate. In his book *Interactive Excellence: Defining and Developing New Standards for the Twenty-first Century*, Edwin Schlossberg wrote, "People could not imagine why they would want or need to talk immediately to someone who was across town or, even more absurdly, in another town. Although people could write letters to one another, and some could send telegraph messages, the idea of sending one's voice to another place and then instantly hearing another voice in return was simply not a model that existed in people's experience. They also did not think it was worth the money to accelerate sending or hearing a message."[16] Also, during design competition, the changeover from older to newer technologies is often slowed by the fact that older technology usually improves significantly in response to the competitive threat from the new technologies.

dominant design
a new technological design or process that becomes the accepted market standard

An era of ferment is followed by the emergence of a **dominant design**, which becomes the accepted market standard for technology.[17] Dominant designs emerge in several ways. One is critical mass, meaning that a particular technology can become the dominant design simply because most people use it. Since millions more people bought VCRs that used VHS tapes, VHS tapes beat out Sony's Beta format to become the dominant design for VCRs. Likewise, a design can become dominant if it solves a practical problem. For example, the QWERTY keyboard (look at the top left line of letters on a keyboard) became the dominant design for typewriters, because it slowed typists who, by typing too fast, caused mechanical typewriter keys to jam. Ironically, despite the fact that computers can easily be switched to the Dvorak keyboard layout, which doubles typing speed and cuts typing errors by half, QWERTY lives on as the standard keyboard. Thus, the best technology doesn't always become the dominant design.

Another way in which dominant designs emerge is through independent standards bodies. The International Telecommunication Union (**www.itu/ch/**) is an independent organization that establishes standards for the communications industry. The ITU was founded in Paris in 1865, because all the countries in Europe had different telegraph systems that could not communicate with each other. Messages crossing borders had to be transcribed from one country's system before they could be coded and delivered on another. After three months of negotiations, 20 countries signed the International Telegraph Convention that standardized equipment and instructions, so that telegraph messages could flow seamlessly from country to country. Today, as in 1865, various standards are proposed, discussed, negotiated, and changed until agreement is reached on a final set of standards that communication industries (i.e., Internet, telephony, satellites, radio, etc.) will follow worldwide.

Yet, no matter how they occur, the emergence of a dominant design is a key event in an innovation stream. First, emergence of a dominant design indicates that there are winners and losers. Technological innovation is both competence enhancing and competence destroying. Companies that bet on the wrong design or on the old technology often struggle, while companies that bet on the now-dominant design usually prosper. In fact, more companies are likely to go out of business in an era of ferment than in an economic recession or slowdown. Second, the emergence of a dominant design signals a change away from design experimentation and competition to **incremental change**, a phase in which companies innovate by lowering the cost and improving the functioning and performance of the dominant design. For example, during a technology cycle, manufacturing efficiencies let Intel cut the cost of its chips by half to two-thirds, all while doubling or tripling the chips' speed. This focus on improving the dominant design continues until the next technological discontinuity occurs.

incremental change
the phase of a technology cycle in which companies innovate by lowering costs and improving the functioning and performance of the dominant technological design

Review 1:
Why Innovation Matters

Technology cycles typically follow an S-curve pattern of innovation. Early in the cycle, technological progress is slow and improvements in technological performance are small. However, as a technology matures, performance improves quickly. Finally, small improvements occur as the limits of a technology are reached. At this point, significant improvements in performance must come from new technologies.

The best way to protect a competitive advantage is to create a stream of innovative ideas and products. Innovation streams begin with technological discontinuities that create significant breakthroughs in performance or function. Technological discontinuities are followed by an era of ferment, in which customers purchase new technologies (technological substitution) and companies compete to establish the new dominant design (design competition). Dominant designs emerge because of critical mass, because they solve a practical problem, or because of the negotiations of independent standards bodies. Because technological innovation is both competence enhancing and competence destroying, companies that bet on the wrong design often struggle, while companies that bet on the eventual dominant design usually prosper. Emergence of a dominant design leads to a focus on incremental change, lowering costs, and small, but steady improvements in the dominant design. This focus continues until the next technological discontinuity occurs.

2 Managing Innovation

The previous discussion of technology cycles and innovation streams showed that managers must be equally good at managing innovation in two very different circumstances. First, during eras of ferment, companies must find a way to anticipate and survive the technological discontinuities that can suddenly transform industry leaders into losers and industry unknowns into industry powerhouses. Companies that can't manage innovation following technological discontinuities risk quick organizational decline and dissolution. Second, after a new dominant design emerges following an era of ferment, companies must manage the very different process of incremental improvement and innovation. Companies that can't manage incremental innovation slowly deteriorate as they fall farther behind industry leaders.

Unfortunately, what works well when managing innovation after technological discontinuities doesn't work well when managing innovation during periods of incremental change (and vice versa). Consequently, to successfully manage innovation streams, companies need to be good at three things: **2.1** *managing the sources of innovation,* **2.2** *managing innovation during discontinuous change, and* **2.3** *managing innovation during incremental change.*

2.1 *Managing Sources of Innovation*

Innovation comes from great ideas. So a starting point for managing innovation is to manage the sources of innovation, that is, where new ideas come from. One place that new ideas originate is with brilliant inventors. For example, do you know who invented the telephone, the light bulb, electricity, air conditioning, radio, television, automobiles, the jet engine, computers, and the Internet? Respectively, these innovations were created by Alexander Graham Bell, Thomas Edison, Pieter van Musschenbroek, Willis Carrier, Guglielmo Marconi, John Baird and Philo T. Farnsworth, Gottlieb Daimler and Wilhelm Maybach, Sir Frank Whittle, Charles Babbage, and Vint Cerf and Robert Kahn. These innovators and their innovations forever

Innovation begins with creativity.

changed the course of modern life. However, only a few companies have the likes of an Edison, Marconi, or Graham Bell working for them. Given that great thinkers and inventors are in short supply, what might companies do instead to ensure a steady flow of good ideas?

Well, when we say that innovation begins with great ideas, we're really saying that innovation begins with creativity. *Creativity* is the production of novel and useful ideas.[18] While companies can't command creativity from employees ("You *will* be more creative!"), they can jump-start innovation by building **creative work environments,** in which workers perceive that creative thoughts and ideas are welcomed and valued. As shown in Figure 10.4, creative work environments have five components that encourage creativity: challenging work, organizational encouragement, supervisory encourage-

creative work environments
workplace cultures in which workers perceive that new ideas are welcomed, valued, and encouraged

Figure 10.4 **Components of Creative Work Environments**

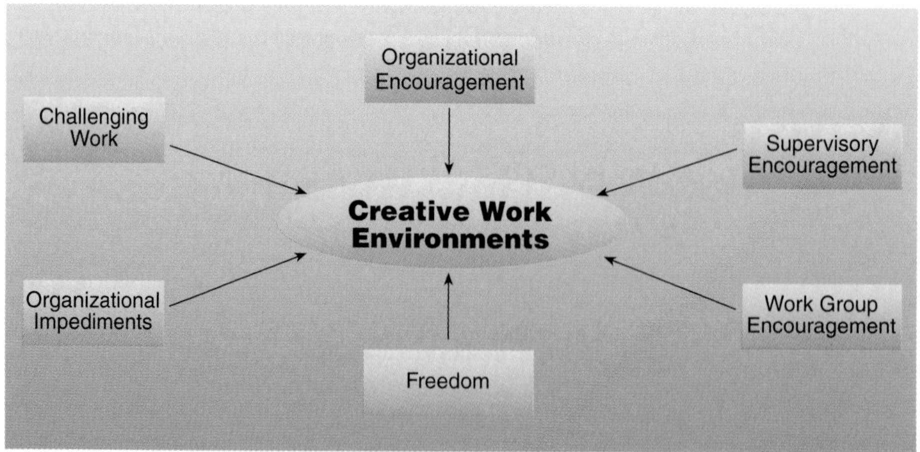

Source: T.M. Amabile, R. Conti, H. Coon, J. Lazenby, & M. Herron, "Assessing the Work Environment for Creativity," *Academy of Management Journal* 39 (1996): 1154-1184.

ment, work group encouragement, and freedom. A sixth component, organizational impediments, must be managed so as not to discourage creativity.[19]

Work is *challenging* when it requires hard work, demands attention and focus, and is seen as important to others in the organization. Researcher Mihaly Csikszentmihalyi (pronounced ME-high-ee CHICK-sent-me-high-ee) said that challenging work promotes creativity because it creates a rewarding psychological experience known as "flow." **Flow** is a psychological state of effortlessness, in which you become completely absorbed in what you're doing and time seems to fly. (You begin work, become absorbed in it, and then suddenly realize that several hours have passed.) When flow occurs, who you are and what you're doing become one. Csikszentmihalyi first encountered flow when studying artists. He said, "What struck me by looking at artists at work was their tremendous focus on the work, this enormous involvement, this forgetting of time and body. It wasn't justified by expectation of rewards, like, 'Aha, I'm going to sell this painting.'"[20] Csikszentmihalyi has found that chess players, rock climbers, dancers, surgeons, and athletes regularly experience flow, too. A key part of creating flow experiences, and thus creative work environments, is to achieve a balance between skills and task challenge. When workers can do more than what is required of them, they become bored. Anxiety occurs when workers' skills aren't sufficient to accomplish a task. However, when skills and task challenge are balanced, flow and creativity can occur.

A creative work environment requires three kinds of encouragement: organizational, supervisory, and work group encouragement. *Organizational encouragement* of creativity occurs when management encourages risk taking and new ideas, supports and fairly evaluates new ideas, rewards and recognizes creativity, and encourages the sharing of new ideas throughout different parts of the company. *Supervisory encouragement* of creativity occurs when supervisors provide clear goals, encourage open interaction with subordinates, and actively support development teams' work and ideas. *Work group encouragement* occurs when work group members have diverse experience, education, and backgrounds; when there is a mutual openness to ideas; when there is positive, constructive challenge to ideas; and when there is shared commitment to ideas.

An example of organizational and supervisory encouragement can be found at Toro Corporation, which makes lawn mowers and equipment. Toro tried to encourage innovation by announcing that innovative ideas that failed would not be punished. Encouraged by this announcement, a team of engineers used an experimental molding technique to cut the cost and time it took to make the metal hoods for Toro riding lawn mowers. The experimental molding technique worked great in the lab, but failed miserably at the fast speeds required in Toro's production facilities. Despite the company's pronouncements that innovation would not be punished, all the team members expected to be fired when Toro's CEO asked for a meeting with them. On arriving at the CEO's office, instead of finding pink slips, they found balloons, cake, and a pleased CEO who wanted to celebrate their efforts.[21] For more on creativity and failure, see the "Been There, Done That" feature about British comedian John Cleese's thoughts on creativity and the importance of making mistakes.

Personal Productivity Tip

Cultivate Your Most Demanding Customer or Boss

Once you're successful, it can be difficult to change. One way to battle complacency is to cultivate your most demanding customer or boss, the one who always wants more. Silicon Graphics designed its next generation of computers by helping Disney's Imagineering group design a new "Aladdin" theme park ride. Since Disney wanted the ride to look exactly like the movie, SG designed new virtual reality headgear that makes it look like you're actually riding a magic carpet. After meeting Disney's demanding standards, SG can sell its greatly improved computers to others. To force yourself to keep changing, cultivate a demanding customer or boss!

Source: A. Deitschman, "The Managing Wisdom of High-Tech Superstars," *Fortune,* 17 October 1994.

flow
a psychological state of effortlessness, in which you become completely absorbed in what you're doing and time seems to pass quickly

Personal Productivity Tip

Listen to All Ideas, Big and Small

Companies can encourage innovation by listening to all ideas, big and small. For example, with a wall of nearly 50 TVs in each store, and over 30 million visitors a week to its electronics departments, Wal-Mart has begun airing in-store commercials via the new Wal-Mart TV Network. The idea for this innovative method of advertising came from an electronics department employee. Likewise, American Airlines has saved millions from the thousands of ideas generated by employees through its "IdeAAs in Action" suggestion program. Big or small, the next breakthrough idea could come from anyone or anywhere in your company. Listen hard or you may miss it.

Sources: Y. Ono, "Wal-Mart Uses TV-Set Displays for In-Store Ad Network," *The Wall Street Journal Interactive Edition,* 7 October 1997.

Been There,

"The Importance of Mistakes"

John Cleese on Innovation and Creativity in Organizations

For years, John Cleese, of Monty Python fame and star/writer of movies such as "A Fish Called Wanda," has also created management and marketing training videos for the corporate world (see **www.video-arts.com***). Cleese, widely regarded as a creative and comic genius, shared his thoughts about organizational innovation and creativity in a speech entitled "The Importance of Mistakes."*

Cleese: I want to suggest to you that unless we have a tolerant attitude toward mistakes—I might almost say a positive attitude toward them—we shall be behaving irrationally, unscientifically and unsuccessfully.

Of course, if you now say to me, "Look here, you weird limey, are you seriously advocating relaunching the Edsel?" I will reply, "No, Mac. There are mistakes and mistakes." There are true copper-bottomed mistakes like wearing a black bra under a white blouse, or, to take a more masculine example, starting a land war in Asia. I'm talking about mistakes that at the time they were committed did have a chance.

". . . if we can't take the risk of saying or doing something wrong, our creativity goes right out the window."

Let's first concentrate on taking the risk of making a mistake. Has it occurred to you that if you don't take this risk, you can't do or say anything useful?

For example, if you ask me now "What is the time?" I could give you the following guaranteed-true answer. "It is between five o'clock in the morning and midnight." Right? You can't argue with that. No chance of error there. Or I could tell you that it is 23 minutes of 2, when it is in fact 24 minutes of 2. Which of those is more useful to you? The true one or the mistake?

It's self-evident that if we can't take the risk of saying or doing something wrong, our creativity goes right out the window. Because the essence of creativity is not the possession of some special talent, it is much more the ability to "play." MacKinnon's research at Berkeley in the 1960s and 1970s on professionals rated by their colleagues as "highly creative" showed they were no different in intelligence from their less creative colleagues—but that they took longer to study problems and "played with them" more. Highly creative people know better how to get themselves into a mode where they are able to respond more spontaneously to their intuitions, to explore out of pure curiosity, to follow little impulses with interest without immediately imposing critical thought.

For a group to function more creatively, people must lose their inhibitions. They must gain the confidence to contribute spontaneously to what's happening, and the inhibition arises because of the fear of looking foolish. Yes! It's nothing more than the fear of making mistakes. While people are held back by this fear, while they go over each thought they had six times before expressing it in case someone will think it's "wrong," nothing useful can happen creatively.

Now, to come to the second half of my argument, a positive attitude toward mistakes will allow them to be corrected rapidly when they occur.

In organizations where mistakes are not allowed, you get two types of counterproductive behavior. First, since mistakes are "bad," if they're committed by people at the top, the feedback arising from those mistakes has to be ignored or selectively reinterpreted, in order that those top people can pretend that no mistake has been made. So it doesn't get fixed. Second, if they're committed by people lower down in the organization, mistakes get concealed.

Taking concealment first, Peter Parker, the very successful former head of British Rail, said recently, "The hardest thing in management is the mistake concealer. If someone walks into my office saying, 'I screwed up,' I say, 'Come on in.'"

In the healthiest organizations, the taboo is not on making mistakes, it's on concealing them. But in a mistake-denying culture, they are concealed and therefore not corrected. Worse, lies have to be told.

This is the essence of a particular form of comedy that has traditionally been popular in Europe—the farce. In America, you have a similar form of entertainment, usually called Something-Gate, where entire departments of government officials pass their working days trying unsuccessfully to conceal one key mistake. This type of comedy is less successful in Britain, simply because the government there has much greater power to suppress the best jokes in the name of national security.

Next, let's see what happens if the people at the top of organizations are determined to show they are infallible. Peter Drucker has a nice example of ignored feedback when he refers to a product he calls the "investment in managerial ego." This is a product that the manager believed in, nay, fought for and which has been repackaged, its salesmen retrained, its advertising changed and then the agency subsequently sacked, which was then relaunched as a seasonal product—but which has never actually sold. The manager has always reinterpreted the feedback from the marketplace so as to avoid acknowledging that the product has been a mistake.

If the corporate ego is so huge and unrealistic that failures have to be repackaged as successes, then disaster cannot be very far down the road. If the heads of organizations cannot bear to receive feedback that may suggest that mistakes have been made and need correction, then they will increasingly be surrounded by yes-men and will be increasingly cut off from the feedback they need to stay on course. (I still treasure, incidentally, Sam Goldwyn's memo: "I don't want any yes-men in this organization. I want people to speak their minds—even if it does cost them their jobs.")

So once the corporate ethos is that the corporation cannot have made a mistake, then it's going to go further and further off course. The CEO becomes a bit like a pilot in an aircraft who says to the altimeter, "What's the height?" And hears the altimeter reply, "What would you like it to be?"

The leading philosopher of science of this century, Karl Popper, says that scientists do not sit around dispassionately observing clusters of phenomena and then come up with rational explanations of them. He suggests that scientists really get "hunches" and then look around for examples to fit in with their ideas. And that, therefore, in the pursuit of scientific truth, when they have worked out their hypothesis, they should test it, not with tests to prove it right, but with tests specifically designed to prove it wrong. In Popper's words, falsifiable. All of which shows that current philosophical and scientific thought has arrived at the startling realization that we learn only from our mistakes.

Now we reach the real problem. If all the evidence from business, science and psychology suggests that the best results are obtained by risking mistakes, and by having a positive attitude toward them when they occur, why are we all so nervous about making them?

I'm sure that the answer is quite simply that we all have these ridiculous things called egos. Once you've got an ego, you want to be right. I've noticed this even in my 3-year-old daughter. If I ask her a question and she doesn't know the answer, she doesn't want to guess in case she makes a mistake. She changes the subject, even though I tell her it doesn't matter.

How can we solve this problem? You may be able to persuade yourself and others that admitting small mistakes right away protects your ego more efficiently than running the risk of making a far greater and more painful mistake later.

For example, I chose to show my latest film here in New York in a rough form, and actually encouraged people to damage my ego by criticizing it, so that I can eliminate some of the mistakes and improve it. I feel safer doing this than sheltering myself from adverse criticism now only to run the risk of discovering in a few months' time that it's Britain's answer to Heaven's Gate. People say nobody likes criticism. True, but I feel safer getting the pain up front.

Finally, the most effective way that we can create an atmosphere of tolerance and positiveness toward mistakes is, of course, to model it. In the early stages of a discussion, say that you don't know the solution, throw up a couple of ideas that, after examination, you casually discard saying, "Okay, I don't think that was very useful." Better still, discuss a couple of recent mistakes that you've made and learned from.

Any ego-loss suffered is more than compensated for in my experience by the ego-gain in showing you're the kind of guy who's big enough to admit when he's wrong.

Taken from the Video Arts programme, "The Importance of Mistakes" and reproduced with the permission of Video Arts Limited.

Done That

Freedom means having autonomy over one's day-to-day work, and a sense of ownership and control over one's ideas. Numerous studies have indicated that creative ideas thrive under conditions of freedom. At 3M, engineers and scientists can spend 5 percent of their time, roughly a half day per week, doing whatever they want, as long as it's related to innovation and new product development. At Du Pont, engineers and scientists are given a full day per week to do the same: Read, stay home, surf the Internet, visit competitors, or take a class—as long as it has something to do with innovative ideas. Phone company Bell Atlantic takes the idea of freedom even farther with its Champion program. Employees who qualify as "idea champions" take a fully paid leave from their regular jobs to be trained on how to write a business plan, organize a development schedule, and spend the money the company gives them to develop their idea into a product or business. Champions are also allowed to invest 10 percent of their salary in their projects and can choose to give up their annual bonus in exchange for 5 percent of the revenues from their ideas, should they ever become profitable. In its first three years, the Champion program has led to two government patents, with eleven more patents pending. [22]

Work environments that generally foster creativity may also have some impediments to creativity. Internal conflict and power struggles, rigid management structures, and a conservative bias toward the status quo can all discourage creativity. They create the perception that others in the organization will decide which ideas are acceptable and deserve support. One of the ways in which 3M avoids a conservative, anti-innovation bias is through a reward structure based on the "4/30" rule. The 4/30 rule states that 30 percent of a 3M division's sales must come from products that are no more than four years old. The logic behind this rule is simple, but powerful: Each year, four-year-old products become five years old and can't be counted toward the 30 percent of sales. Thus, the 4/30 rule encourages everyone at 3M to be on the lookout for and open to new ideas.[23]

2.2 *Managing Innovation during Discontinuous Change*

experiential approach to innovation
an approach to innovation that assumes a highly uncertain environment, and uses intuition, flexible options, and hands-on experience to reduce uncertainty and accelerate learning and understanding

design iteration
a cycle of repetition in which a company tests a prototype of a new product or service, improves on that design, and then builds and tests the improved prototype

testing
systematic comparison of different product designs or design iterations

A study of 72 product development projects (i.e., innovation) in 36 computer companies across the U.S., Europe, and Asia found that companies that succeeded in periods of discontinuous change (in which a technological discontinuity created a significant breakthrough in performance or function) typically followed an experiential approach to innovation.[24] The **experiential approach to innovation** assumes that innovation is occurring within a highly uncertain environment, and that the key to fast product innovation is to use intuition, flexible options, and hands-on experience to reduce uncertainty and accelerate learning and understanding. There are five parts to the experiential approach to innovation: design iterations, testing, milestones, multifunctional teams, and powerful leaders.[25]

An "iteration" is a repetition. So, a **design iteration** is a cycle of repetition in which a company tests a prototype of a new product or service, improves on the design, and then builds and tests the improved product or service prototype. As you learned in Chapter 4, a product prototype is a full-scale working model that is being tested for design, function, and reliability. **Testing** is a systematic comparison of different product designs or design iterations. Companies that want to create a new dominant design following a technological discontinuity quickly build, test, improve, and retest a series of different product prototypes.

For example, it took a number of design iterations for Starbucks and its suppliers to successfully create a paper coffee cup that would keep coffee hot but not burn customers' hands. To prevent customers from burning themselves, Starbucks had either stacked two paper cups together or used cardboard sleeves that slid over the outside of the cup. However, customers complained that sleeves fell off or prevented cups from fitting into cup holders and that using two cups was wasteful. As a result, Starbucks and its suppliers worked for three years to come up with a paper cup that was light, cheap, environment friendly, and heat insulating. Prototypes ranged from a layered cup that folded and wrapped one long piece of paper into three layers of paper, to a Japanese-designed cup coated with a special plastic. Testing was both practical, using human hands to pick up different cups filled with steaming coffee, and scientific, using an infrared temperature gauge to test cups' external temperatures. The breakthrough cup design, now being tested in Starbucks stores, sandwiches a thin air layer between an inner polyethylene liner and outer layer of brown recycled paper.[26]

By trying a number of very different designs, or by making successive improvements and changes in the same design, frequent design iterations reduce uncertainty and improve understanding. Simply put, the more prototypes you build, the more likely you are to learn what works and what doesn't. Plus, building a number of prototypes also means that designers and engineers are less likely to "fall in love" with a particular prototype. Instead, they'll be more concerned with improving the product or technology as much as they can. Testing speeds up and improves the innovation process, too. Testing two very different design prototypes against each other, or testing the new design iteration against the previous iteration, quickly makes product design strengths and weaknesses apparent. Likewise, testing uncovers errors early in the design process when they are easiest to correct. Finally, testing accelerates learning and understanding by forcing engineers and product designers to examine hard data about product performance. When there's hard evidence that prototypes are testing well, the confidence of the design team grows. Also, personal conflict between design team members is less likely when testing focuses on hard measurements and facts rather than personal hunches and preferences.

PersonalProductivityTip

Testing 1-2-3, Testing 1-2-3

Ideas are no substitute for real-world testing. Team New Zealand used daily testing, two identical racing boats, and sophisticated design software to prepare for the America's Cup yacht races. Each day, one boat would use the new design generated by the computer. Then, the two boats would race to determine which was better. Afterwards, the simulation was reprogrammed using data gathered during that race. In the morning, another configuration would be race-tested the same way. The result? Team New Zealand defeated Team USA by the largest margin in history. Not sure which idea is best? Give them a try and put them to the test.

Sources: M. Iansiti & A. MacCormack, "Developing Products," *Harvard Business Review*, September-October 1997, 108-117.

Milestones are formal project review points used to assess progress and performance. For example, a company that has put itself on a 12-month schedule to complete a project might schedule milestones at the 3-month, 6-month, and 9-month points on the schedule. By making people regularly assess what they're doing, how well they're performing, and whether they need to take corrective action, milestones provide structure to the general chaos that follows technological discontinuities. Milestones also shorten the innovation process by creating a sense of urgency that keeps everyone on task. For example, when Florida Power & Light was building its first nuclear power facility, the company's construction manager passed out 2,000 desk calendars to company employees, construction contractors, vendors, and suppliers, so that everyone involved in the project was aware of the construction timeline. Contractors that regularly missed deadlines were replaced.[27] Finally, milestones are beneficial for innovation, because meeting regular milestones builds momentum by giving people a sense of accomplishment.

milestones
formal project review points used to assess progress and performance

Multifunctional teams are work teams composed of people from different departments. Multifunctional teams accelerate learning and understanding by mixing and integrating technical, marketing, and manufacturing activities. By involving all key departments in development from the start, multifunctional teams speed innovation through early identification of problems that would typically not have been identified until much later. DaimlerChrysler Corporation felt so strongly about the importance of multifunctional teams that it built a brand new 950,000-square-foot, 15-story headquarters to bring its engineers, car designers, marketers, accountants, and manufacturing specialists together under one roof. Previously, each group was in a separate part of the company's old headquarters complex. Plus, it was impossible to bring them together at the same time, because

multifunctional teams
work teams composed of people from different departments

there wasn't a large enough meeting facility. However, in DaimlerChrysler's new building, all these different groups have offices together. Furthermore, the building's openness, which comes from using glass for walls in offices and corridors, encourages even more interaction between the members of the multifunctional teams responsible for designing new cars. Today, thanks to multifunctional teams and its new offices, DaimlerChrysler can design and build a new car 40 percent faster than it used to.[28]

Powerful leaders provide the vision, discipline, and motivation to keep the innovation process focused, on time, and on target. Powerful leaders are able to get resources when they are needed, are typically more experienced, have high status in the company, and are held directly responsible for product success or failure. On average, powerful leaders can get innovation-related projects done nine months faster than leaders with little power or influence. One such powerful leader is Sherm Mullin, who headed Lockheed Corporation's Advanced Development company, which developed the F-117 Stealth fighter and is now developing the new Advanced Tactical Fighter jet for the U.S. Air Force. When Mullin brought the ATF design team together, the first slide in his presentation to the group was "Lead, follow, or get the hell out of the way." This was his way of telling them that the project would come in on time and under budget. Furthermore, Mullin runs a tight operation. When developing new planes, he creates small teams of highly motivated workers, gives them demanding schedules and small budgets, and then isolates them from the rest of Lockheed to keep management "off their backs." He said, "You don't let anyone in, and you give them the freedom to do their thing." The key challenge, he said, is "to do it faster and cheaper."[29]

2.3
Managing Innovation during Incremental Change

While the experiential approach is used to manage innovation during periods of discontinuous change, a compression approach can be used during periods of incremental change, in which the focus is on systematically improving the performance and lowering the cost of the dominant technological design. A **compression approach to innovation** assumes that innovation is a predictable process, that incremental innovation can be planned using a series of steps, and that compressing the time it takes to complete those steps can speed up innovation. There are five parts to the compression approach to innovation: planning, supplier involvement, shortening the time of individual steps, overlapping steps, and multifunctional teams.[30]

compression approach to innovation
an approach to innovation that assumes that incremental innovation can be planned using a series of steps, and that compressing those steps can speed innovation

In Chapter 4, *planning* was defined as choosing a goal and a method or strategy to achieve that goal. When *planning for incremental innovation*, the goal is to squeeze or compress development time as much as possible, and the general strategy is to create a series of planned steps to accomplish that goal. Planning for incremental innovation helps avoid unnecessary steps. Plus, planning allows developers to sequence steps in the right order to avoid wasted time and shorten the delays between steps. Planning also reduces misunderstandings and decreases coordination problems regarding when and how things are to be done.

generational change
change based on incremental improvements to a dominant technological design such that the improved technology is fully backward compatible with the older technology

Most planning for incremental innovation is based on the idea of generational change. **Generational change** occurs when incremental improvements are made to a dominant technological design such that the improved version of the technology is fully backward compatible with the older version.[31] So unlike technological discontinuities that result in the replacement of older technologies, generational change allows the old and newer versions of the same technological design to coexist in the marketplace. For example, Sony used the idea of generational change to extend the life of its Sony Walkman products. After inventing the Walkman tape player in 1978, Sony introduced 250 different kinds of Walkmans over the next decade. However, there were few significant changes in the basic Walkman over that time. In fact, 85 percent of the new models simply represented small improvements (i.e., generational change) based on a four-point plan that Sony developed. First, make the Walkmans smaller. Second, make them cheaper. Third, when possible, add small improvements. For example, while the first Walkman only played audio tapes, subsequent Walkmans added AM/FM stereo radio, auto reverse, Dolby sound, water resistance, TV audio band, digital tuning, and enhanced bass. Finally, make minor cosmetic changes in the Walkman's color and appearance. Together, these generational changes have helped Sony maintain above-average profits and a 50 percent share of this market.[32]

Because the compression approach assumes that innovation can follow a series of preplanned steps, one of the ways to shorten development time is *supplier involvement*. Delegating some of the preplanned steps in the innovation process to outside suppliers reduces the amount of work that internal development teams must do. Plus, suppliers provide an alternative source of ideas and expertise that can lead to better designs. For example, when Whirlpool, a leading manufacturer of appliances, decided to completely redesign its products, it involved one of its key partners, Inland Steel, from the start. Inland used its expertise in metals to help Whirlpool tear down and analyze each component of its competitors' washers, dryers, and refrigerators.

Supplier involvement also takes advantage of distinctive competencies by allowing both the development team and the suppliers to do what they do best. Said Whirlpool manager Jack Crank, "We know how to make the world's best appliances, but that doesn't mean we are also experts in metallurgy or all of the processes necessary to get maximum benefit from a particular metal. They [Inland] test materials, help us set specifications for metals, make steel that exactly fits our needs and get it to us on time—all of which saves us money and raises the quality of our products."[33] In general, the earlier suppliers are involved, the quicker they are to catch and prevent future problems, such as unrealistic designs or mismatched product specifications.

Another way to shorten development time is to simply *shorten the time of individual steps* in the innovation process. One of the most common ways to do that is through computer-aided design (CAD). CAD speeds up the design process by allowing designers and engineers to make and test design changes using computer models. In many steps of the design process, Ford found that CAD models and computer simulations can replace physical testing of expensive automobile prototypes. And since computer-based CAD systems store design specifications and characteristics in computer files (the same way that a personal computer stores word processing files), CAD speeds innovation by making it easy to access and reuse previous designs. At Ford, product designers and engineers use desktop and laptop computers to access a design knowledge base containing standard parts, standard design guides (that walk designers through the process of creating new parts), and detailed performance and testing information. The design knowledge base is accessible to any computer connected to Ford's company network. Finally,

When Whirlpool wanted to redesign its products, it enlisted the help of its key supplier, Inland Steel, for its expertise in metals.
© Brownie Harris/
The Stock Market

CAD systems improve communication and organization by making sure that all design team members work with the latest design iteration. If the engineers in charge of engine design change the size of an engine from four to six cylinders, those changes are automatically registered in what Ford calls the "common total vehicle data model." So when the designers in charge of the car's suspension system log on, they'll find that the engine has been changed and can make the necessary changes to the car's suspension system.[34]

In a sequential design process, each step must be completed before the next step begins. But sometimes multiple development steps can be performed at the same time. *Overlapping steps* shortens the development process by reducing the delays or waiting time between steps. By using overlapping rather than sequential steps, most car companies have reduced the time it takes to develop a brand new car from five years to three years. However, they still develop new models sequentially. First they design and build, say, a four-door sedan. Then, after perfecting the design and manufacture of the sedan, two or three years later they introduce the two-door coupe. A couple of years after that, they introduce the station wagon version of the same model. Toyota, however, has taken the notion of overlapping steps even further by developing all three versions (four-door sedan, two-door coupe, and station wagon) simultaneously. By overlapping model development, Toyota has cut its total development time for all three models in half! This has helped Toyota bring 18 new or redesigned cars to market in the last two years. And, its new Picnic and Corolla Spacio models went into production a record 14½ months after designs were approved, well under the three years it normally takes to develop a brand new car.[35]

Review 2
Managing Innovation

To successfully manage innovation streams, companies must manage the sources of innovation and learn to manage innovation during both discontinuous and incremental change. Since innovation begins with creativity, companies can manage the sources of innovation by supporting a creative work environment, in which creative thoughts and ideas are welcomed, valued, and encouraged. Creative work environments provide challenging work; offer organizational, supervisory, and work group encouragement; allow significant freedom; and remove organizational impediments to creativity.

Companies that succeed in periods of discontinuous change typically follow an experiential approach to innovation. The experiential approach assumes that intuition, flexible options, and hands-on experience can reduce uncertainty and accelerate learning and understanding. This approach involves frequent design iterations, frequent testing, regular milestones, creation of multifunctional teams, and use of powerful leaders to guide the innovation process.

A compression approach to innovation works best during periods of incremental change. This approach assumes that innovation can be planned using a series of steps, and that compressing the time it takes to complete those steps can speed up innovation. The five parts to the compression approach are planning (generational change), supplier involvement, shortening the time of individual steps (computer-aided design), overlapping steps, and multifunctional teams.

Organizational Change

"Ding-dong. Avon calling." When people think of Avon, they think of their local "Avon Lady." In the U.S. alone, Avon has nearly 450,000 Avon Ladies who, using the company's distinctive one-on-one marketing approach, have been selling Avon products directly to customers for decades. Now, however, Avon management is testing the idea of selling Avon products through Avon retail stores. This strategy has been successful overseas, particularly in Malaysia, where 145 Avon stores now account for half of Avon's Malaysian sales. The company is also testing a direct-mail catalog. Early results indicate that catalog customers spend twice as much per order as customers who place orders through Avon Ladies. While these changes look promising, they are also risky, because they're likely to cut into the sales and earnings of Avon's U.S. sales force, which accounts for 98 percent of U.S. sales! Avon hopes to keep its Avon Ladies happy by giving them franchising opportunities with its new Avon stores. Or, it may try to refer store customers to them for additional sales. However, when Avon has tried to make changes before, its Avon Ladies have responded angrily. For example, when management tried to cut costs by eliminating sales representative discounts on a limited number of Avon products, 25,000 Avon Ladies quit their jobs in protest.[36]

Why would a company like Avon consider such drastic changes in the way it does business? And, with the strong resistance it expects from its sales force, how can it implement these changes successfully? After reading these next two sections on organizational change, you should be able to:

3 discuss **why change occurs and why it matters**.

4 discuss the different methods that managers can use to better **manage change** as it occurs.

3 Why Change Occurs and Why It Matters

Businesses operate in a constantly changing environment. Recognizing and adapting to internal and external changes can mean the difference between continued success and going out of business.

Let's learn **3.1** *how change forces and resistance forces bring about change and* **3.2** *how companies that fail to change run the risk of organizational decline.*[37]

3.1
Change Forces and Resistance Forces

change forces
forces that produce differences in the form, quality, or condition of an organization over time

resistance forces
forces that support the existing state of conditions in organizations

According to social psychologist Kurt Lewin, change is a function of the forces that promote change and the opposing forces that slow or resist change.[38] **Change forces** lead to differences in the form, quality, or condition of an organization over time. By contrast, **resistance forces** support the status quo, that is, the existing state of conditions in organizations.

Figure 10.5 illustrates how the relative strengths of resistance and change forces interact to bring about different levels of change. Change can be nonexistent, sporadic, continuous, or discontinuous, depending on whether change forces are stronger or weaker than resistance forces. At one extreme, when resistance forces are strong and change forces are weak, there is *no change*. For example, prior to 1983, AT&T essentially controlled both the local and the long-distance phone service markets, as well as the production of telephone equipment. If you needed phone service or equipment, you called AT&T. While AT&T offered reliable service, the lack of competition in the local phone service (almost no competition), long-distance phone service (only MCI), and phone equipment markets (no competition) meant that there was little reason for AT&T to change or innovate. Consequently, the service that AT&T offered to consumers was nearly the same in 1983 as it was in 1963.[39]

When resistance and change forces are both weak, chance events can lead to *sporadic change* that occurs in random patterns or for accidental reasons. For example, Ontrack Data International became a successful small company by writing software that allowed computer manufacturers (or anyone installing a new hard drive) to shorten the time it takes to install and format computer hard drives from twenty four hours to less than one hour. Today, however, Ontrack accidentally finds itself in the "disk doctor" business. Why? Because Ontrack was so good at fixing hard drives and retrieving data from crashed drives, the disk drive manufacturers themselves began referring customers with hard drive problems to Ontrack. Now, Ontrack gets more than 60 percent of its revenues from "disk doctoring" and only 20 percent of its revenues from its original software products.[40]

Figure 10.5 **How Change and Resistance Forces Create Change**

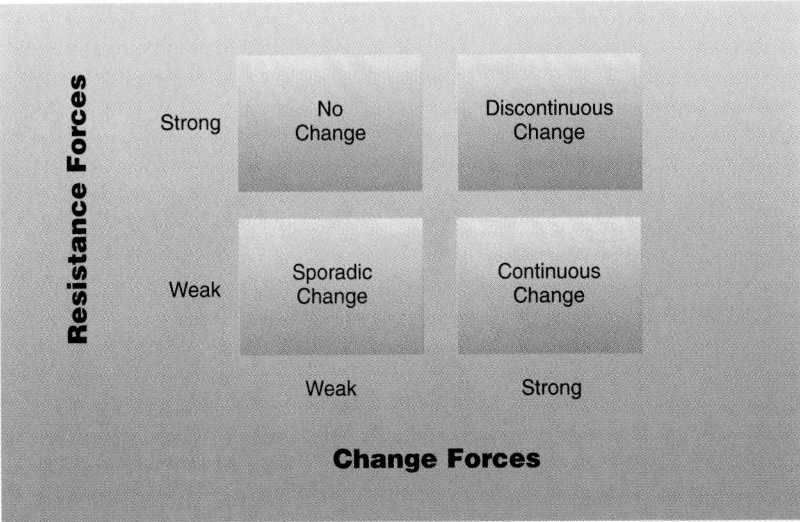

Source: P. Strebel, "Choosing the Right Change Path," *California Management Review,* Winter 1994, 29-51.

When change forces are strong and resistance forces are weak, *continuous change* occurs, as organizations are forced to adapt to ongoing change forces. Over the last three decades, companies have clearly struggled to keep up with the continuous changes in computer technology. For example, Intel's first microprocessor computed 60,000 instructions per second. However, by the year 2010, it's estimated that Intel's microprocessors will be capable of computing more than 100 billion instructions per second.[41] Not surprisingly, companies have had to increase the amount of money they spend on technology. It's now estimated that 41 percent of capital investments (i.e., money spent for long-term improvement of the firm) is spent on information technology compared to just 31 percent five years ago."[42]

If both change and resistance forces are strong, and the resistance forces can no longer hold back the change forces, sudden *discontinuous change* can occur. Discontinuous change is similar to an arm-wrestling match between two 250-pound men. Both men are strong, but after awhile, one is likely to lose his grip or tire. When that happens, the match will end seconds later, as the winner suddenly overpowers the loser. Although few change forces affected AT&T in the 1960s and 1970s, the company experienced discontinuous change in 1983. Then, after a decade-long antitrust lawsuit, a Justice Department decree broke up "Ma Bell," which had been one huge company, into eight separate companies. After the breakup, there was one long-distance company (AT&T) and seven separate, newly independent local phone service companies (which came to be known as the "Baby Bells").[43]

organization decline
a large decrease in organizational performance that occurs when companies don't anticipate, recognize, neutralize, or adapt to the internal or external pressures that threaten their survival

3.2 *Organizational Decline: The Risk of Not Changing*

Organization decline occurs when companies don't anticipate, recognize, neutralize, or adapt to the internal or external pressures that threaten their survival.[44] In other words, decline occurs when organizations don't recognize the need for change. GM's loss of market share in the automobile

Overconfidence blinded Barney's management to the need for change, resulting in the company's demise.
© Corbis/Lynn Goldsmith

industry (from 60 percent to 30 percent) is an example of organizational decline. There are five stages of organizational decline: blinded, inaction, faulty action, crisis, and dissolution.[45]

In the *blinded stage*, decline begins because key managers don't recognize the internal or external changes that will harm their organizations. This "blindness" may be due to a simple lack of awareness about changes. It may stem from an inability to understand the significance of changes. Or, it may simply come from the overconfidence that can develop when companies have been successful. In the case of Barney's, a tiny men's discount clothing store on 17th Street and Seventh Avenue in New York City that grew into a collection of stores in Beverly Hills, Chicago, London, and Tokyo (and a dozen other international cities), selling some of the most expensive and fashionable designer clothes in the world, the overconfidence of the founder's grandsons, Gene and Bob Pressman, eventually led to the company's demise.[46] In his book *The Rise and Fall of The House of Barneys: A Family Tale of Chutzpah*, Joshua Levine of *Forbes* magazine described how overconfidence led the Pressmans to spend more time working out at the gym than running the company.[47] Confident of their success, the Pressmans blindly overspent and overbuilt the company. Indeed, just three years after opening a luxurious $270 million store on Madison Avenue in New York City, complete with marble floors, silver-plated windows, and an extravagantly priced restaurant, expresso bar, beauty salon, and health club, Barney's filed for bankruptcy.

In the *inaction stage*, as organizational performance problems become more visible, management may recognize the need to change but still take no action. The managers may be waiting to see if the problems will correct themselves. Or, they may find it difficult to change previous practices and policies that once led to success. Another possible reason is that they wrongly assume that they can make changes to correct problems, so they don't feel the problems are urgent. For example, when Barney's expanded from men's into women's clothing, management budgeted $12 million to buy and convert a building into a 70,000 square foot store for women's clothing. However, management ended up spending $25 million, more than double the estimated cost. While most managers would have been worried sick about spending twice their budget for a project like this, one of Barney's top managers exclaimed, "What's money?"[48]

In the *faulty action stage*, due to rising costs and decreasing profits and market share, management will announce "belt-tightening" plans designed to cut costs, increase efficiency, and restore profits. In other words, rather than recognizing the need for fundamental changes, managers assume that if they just run a "tighter ship," company performance will return to previous levels. Barney's fit this pattern, too. Rather than reexamine the basic need for change, Barney's management focused on cost cutting. Company managers and staff were no longer allowed to spend hundreds of thousands of dollars a year on perks such as cellular phones, cars, and entertainment. In fact, clothing allowances for some senior managers had been as much as $20,000 a year.[49] Unfortunately for Barney's, even this belt-tightening was too little too late.

In the *crisis stage*, bankruptcy or dissolution (i.e., breaking up and selling the different parts of the company) is likely to occur unless the company completely reorganizes the way it does business. At this point, however, companies typically lack the resources needed to fully change how they run their businesses. Cutbacks and layoffs will have reduced the level of talent among employees. Furthermore, talented managers who were savvy enough to see the crisis coming will have begun taking jobs with other companies (often with competitors). Because of rising costs and lower sales, cash is tight. And, lenders and suppliers are unlikely to extend further loans or credit to ease the cash crunch. For example, after giving Barney's more than $180 million in loans, Barney's bankers refused to loan the company any more money.

In the *dissolution stage*, after failing to make the changes needed to sustain the organization, the company is dissolved through bankruptcy proceedings or by selling assets in order to pay suppliers, banks, and creditors. At this point, a new CEO may be brought in to oversee the closing of stores, offices, and manufacturing facilities, the final layoff of managers and employees, and the sale of assets to pay bills and loans. In fact, after filing for bankruptcy, Barney's closed four stores, including the original Barney's at Seventh Avenue and 17th Street.[50] Then, three years later, Barney's was sold to two investment companies that brought in new management to rebuild the company.[51]

Finally, because decline is reversible at each of the first four stages, not all companies in decline reach final dissolution like Barney's did. For example, after nearly a decade in decline, GM has cut costs, stabilized its market share, and had several consecutive years of small profits.

Review 3: *Why Change Occurs and Why It Matters*

Change is a function of the relative strength of the change forces and resistance forces that occur inside and outside of organizations. Change can be nonexistent, sporadic, continuous, or discontinuous, depending on whether change forces are stronger or weaker than resistance forces. The five-stage process of organizational decline begins when organizations don't recognize the need for change. In the blinded stage, managers don't recognize the changes that threaten their organization's survival. In the inaction stage, management recognizes the need to change, but doesn't act, hoping that the problems will correct themselves. In the faulty action stage, management focuses on cost cutting and efficiency rather than facing up to fundamental changes needed to insure survival. In the crisis stage, failure is likely unless fundamental reorganization occurs. Finally, in the dissolution stage, the company is dissolved through bankruptcy proceedings, by selling assets to pay creditors, or through the closing of stores, offices, and facilities. However, if companies recognize the need to change early enough, dissolution may be avoided.

4 Managing Change

According to the Air Travelers Association, the worst safety record in the skies belongs to China Airlines, a Taiwan-based air carrier. Over the last decade, China Airlines has had six plane crashes in which more than 700 people were killed. As a result, company management hired Lufthansa Technik, a division of German-based Lufthansa Airlines, to revamp its training programs and improve its safety record. However, Lufthansa Technik has had difficulty making changes. Said Alfred Kupferschmied, "We had a lot of resistance to changes from the pilots. We had to convince them that this is a better way to operate an airline." However, because of their military backgrounds, China Airline's pilots were used to in-flight decisions being made according to one's rank. So, when Lufthansa Technik trained copilots to actively question and overrule their captains in crisis situations (where passenger safety becomes more important than rank), they resisted.[52]

resistance to change opposition to change resulting from self-interest, misunderstanding and distrust, or a general intolerance for change

Resistance to change, like that shown by China Airline's pilots, is caused by self-interest, misunderstanding and distrust, and a general intolerance for change.[53] People resist change out of *self-interest*, because they fear that change will cost or deprive them of something they value. For example, resistance might stem from a fear that the changes will result in a loss of pay, power, responsibility, or even perhaps one's job. People also resist change because of *misunderstanding and distrust*, that is, they don't understand the change or the reasons for it, or they distrust the people, typically management, behind the change. Ironically, when this occurs, some of the strongest resisters may support the changes in public, nodding and smiling their agreement, but then ignore the changes in private and just do their jobs as they always have. Management consultant Michael Hammer calls this deadly form of resistance the "Kiss of Yes."[54]

Resistance may also come from a generally low tolerance for change. Some people are simply less capable of handling change than others. People with a *low tolerance for change* are threatened by the uncertainty associated with change and worry that they won't be able to learn the new skills and behaviors needed to successfully negotiate change in their companies.

Because resistance to change is inevitable, successful change efforts require careful management. So, in this section you will learn about **4.1** *managing resistance to change,* **4.2** *different change tools and techniques,* **4.3** *managing conversations to promote change, and, finally,* **4.4** *what* not *to do when leading organizational change.*

4.1 *Managing Resistance to Change*

unfreezing getting the people affected by change to believe that change is needed

change intervention the process used to get workers and managers to change their behavior and work practices

refreezing supporting and reinforcing the new changes so they "stick"

According to Kurt Lewin, managing organizational change is a basic process of unfreezing, change intervention, and refreezing. **Unfreezing** is getting the people affected by change to believe that change is needed. During the **change intervention** itself, workers and managers change their behavior and work practices. **Refreezing** is supporting and reinforcing the new changes so they "stick."

Resistance to change, like that of China Airline's pilots, is an example of frozen behavior. Given the choice between changing and not changing, most people, including pilots, would rather not change. Because resistance to change is natural and inevitable, managers need to unfreeze resistance to change to create successful change programs. The following methods can be used to manage resistance to change: education and communication, participation, negotiation, top management support, and coercion.[55]

When resistance to change is based on insufficient, incorrect, or misleading information, managers should *educate* employees about the need for change and *communicate* change-related information to them. Managers must also supply the information and funding or other support employees need to make changes. For example, when GTE Mobilnet, the cellular phone division of GTE, began a customer connection initiative to better serve its customers, one of the small changes it wanted was to make sure that GTE's cell phones had batteries in them when customers purchased them. Unfortunately, GTE had difficulty getting service workers to take the time (eight hours) to pre-charge and install the batteries in new cell phones. Surprisingly, the workers just didn't understand why this mattered. So GTE began educating them about why this was important to customers and the company. Repeatedly, GTE managers communicated this basic message:

> *You can't see why you need to bother with this? Here are sales figures showing how much revenue we lose by making customers wait to use the phone. The average customer, like a kid with a new toy, calls everybody he knows from Boston to Baton Rouge when he first gets the thing, but only if it has a charged battery in it. Don't have room to stock all those extra batteries? We'll help you redesign your workspace to accommodate them. Can't predict how many of which battery you'll need on hand at any given time? We'll provide data to help you with those projections, and teach you how to use them. Can't afford for any of this to come out of your operating budget? We'll fund it for you.*[56]

Another way to reduce resistance to change is to have those affected by the change *participate in planning and implementing the change process*. Employees who participate have a better understanding of change and the need for it. Furthermore, employee concerns about change can be addressed as they occur if employees participate in the planning and implementation process. For example, when Avis, the car rental company, became employee-owned, it made hundreds of significant changes in the way the company was run. This degree of change would be difficult for any company. But Avis handled it by creating more than 150 employee-participation groups. On the first Thursday of every month, these groups meet to discuss specific problems and find ways to increase company productivity. Because other Avis employees elect the people who attend as representatives, there is typically

Building contractor McDevitt Street Bovis avoids many of the problems common to the building trade by negotiating agreements on the obligations of each participant before the project begins.

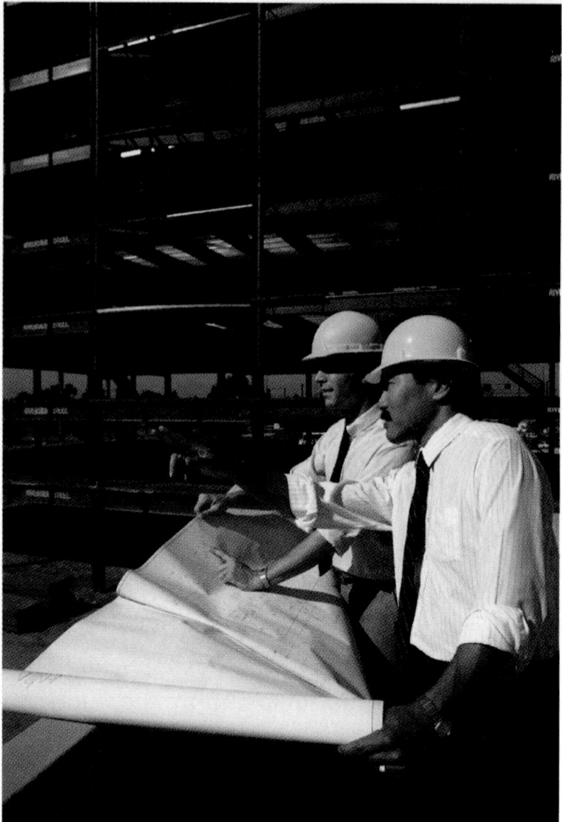

little resistance to the changes and recommendations made by Avis's employee-participation groups.[57]

Employees are less likely to resist change if they are allowed *to discuss and agree on who will do what* after change occurs. For example, construction projects are notoriously hard to manage. It's difficult to get clients, architects, contractors, and subcontractors to agree on things like prices, materials, schedules, or who should be held responsible for unexpected changes and expenses. Often, lawsuits have to be filed to force reluctant parties to fulfill their responsibilities. However, McDevitt Street Bovis (MSB), a major building contractor, avoids these problems by meeting to negotiate an agreement in which MSB, its clients, and its subcontractors put each others' expectations and obligations into writing before construction begins. This way, when problems or changes occur, the parties involved are much more likely to fulfill their responsibilities. The power of this negotiating procedure is evident in a single fact: unlike most building contractors, MSB has never been sued by a client when it negotiates an agreement ahead of time.[58]

Resistance to change also decreases when change efforts receive *significant managerial support.* Top managers must do more than talk about the importance of change. They must provide the training, resources, and autonomy needed to make change happen. For example, at Monarch Marking Systems, Elfie Winter's team was responsible for redesigning how the company manufactured its price-marking tool (which is used to put price tags on items in stores). Her boss demonstrated managerial support by making Elfie's team fully responsible for designing a solution, for working out the necessary changes with other departments, and for making arrangements with company suppliers. He told Elfie and her once-resistant co-workers, "Go make it happen and then tell us about it." When Elfie and her co-workers were finished, they had reduced the amount of space it takes to assemble the product by 70 percent, cut inventory by $127,000, reduced late shipments by 90 percent, and doubled productivity.[59]

coercion
use of formal power and authority to force others to change

Finally, use of formal power and authority to force others to change is called **coercion**. Because of the intense negative reactions it can create (i.e., fear, stress, resentment, sabotage of company products), coercion should only be used when a crisis exists or when all other attempts to reduce resistance to change have failed.

Table 10.1 summarizes some additional suggestions for what managers can do when employees resist change.

4.2
Change Tools and Techniques

If your boss came to you and said, "Alright, genius, you wanted it. You're in charge of turning around the division." How would you start? Where would you begin? How would you encourage change-resistant managers to change? What would you do to include others in the change process? How would you get the change process off to a quick start? Finally, what long-term approach would you use to promote long-term effectiveness and performance? Results-driven change, the General Electric Workout, transition management teams, and organizational development are different change tools and techniques that can be used to address these issues.

One of the reasons that organizational change efforts fail is that they are activity oriented, meaning that they primarily focus on changing company procedures, management philosophy, or employee behavior. Typically, there

Table 10.1 **What to Do When Employees Resist Change**

UNFREEZING	CHANGE	FREEZING
• **Share Reasons**: Share the reason for change with employees. • **Empathize**: Be empathetic to the difficulties that change will create for managers and employees. • **Communicate**: Communicate the details simply, clearly, extensively, verbally, and in writing.	• **Benefits**: Explain the benefits, "What's in it for them." • **Champion**: Identify a highly respected manager to manage the change effort. • **Input**: Allow the people who will be affected by change to express their needs and offer their input. • **Timing**: Don't begin change at a bad time, for example, during the busiest part of the year or month. • **Security**: If possible, maintain employees' job security to minimize fear of change. • **Training**: Offer training to ensure that employees are both confident and competent to handle new requirements. • **Pace**: Change at a manageable pace. Don't rush	• **Top Management Support**: Send consistent messages and free resources. • **Publicize Success**: Let others know when and where change is working. • **Employee Services**: Offer counseling or other services to help employees deal with the stress of change.

Source: G.J. Iskat & J. Liebowitz, "What to Do When Employees Resist Change," *Supervision,* 1 August 1996.

is much buildup and preparation as consultants are brought in, presentations are made, books are read, and employees and managers are trained. There's a tremendous emphasis on "doing things the new way." But for all the focus on activities, on "doing," there's almost no focus on results, on seeing if all this activity has actually made a difference.

results-driven change change created quickly by focusing on the measurement and improvement of results

By contrast, **results-driven change** supplants the sole emphasis on activity with a laser-like focus on quickly measuring and improving results.[60] For example, at Monarch Marking Systems, quality-assurance engineer Steve Schneider guided the company's results-driven change process by first identifying everything in Monarch's factory that could be measured easily. He found 162 measures in all.[61] He further emphasized the importance of quick results by declaring that problem-solving teams had only 30 days to solve a particular problem. He encouraged workers to get to it, saying, "It's a project, not a process."

Another advantage of results-driven change is that managers introduce changes in procedures, philosophy, or behavior only if they are likely to improve measured performance. In other words, managers actually test to see if changes make a difference. Consistent with this approach, Schneider announced that Monarch's problem-solving teams could make any permanent changes they wanted, as long as those changes improved one of the 162 different measures of performance.

A third advantage of results-driven change is that quick, visible improvements motivate employees to continue to make additional changes to improve measured performance. For example, one team at Monarch used cross-training to reduce the number of job categories from 120 to 32. Another, encouraged by the success of 90 other problem-solving teams, trained machine operators how to enter production data directly into the computer on the factory floor, eliminating the 7,600 hours of staff work that it used to take to enter those data from paper records. Consequently, unlike most change efforts, the quick successes associated with results-driven change were particularly effective at reducing resistance to change. Table 10.2 describes the basic steps of results-driven change.

General Electric Workout a three-day meeting in which managers and employees from different levels and parts of an organization quickly generate and act on solutions to specific business problems

The **General Electric Workout** is a special kind of results-driven change. It is a three-day meeting that brings together managers and employees from different levels and parts of an organization to quickly generate and act on solutions to specific business problems.[62] On the first morning of a workout, the boss discusses the agenda and targets specific business problems that the group is to try to solve. Then, the boss leaves, and an outside facilitator breaks the group, typically 30 to 40 people, into five or six teams and helps them

Table 10.2 **Results-Driven Change Programs**

1. Create measurable, short-term goals to improve performance.
2. Use action steps only if they are likely to improve measured performance.
3. Management should stress the importance of immediate improvements.
4. Consultants and staffers should help managers and employees achieve quick improvements in performance.
5. Managers and employees should test action steps to see if they actually yield improvements. Action steps that don't should be discarded.
6. It takes few resources to get results-driven change started.

Source: R.H. Schaffer & H.A. Thomson, J.D, "Successful Change Programs Begin with Results," *Harvard Business Review on Change* (Boston: Harvard Business School Publishing, 1998), 189-213.

spend the next day and a half discussing and debating solutions. On day three, in what GE calls a "town meeting," the teams present specific solutions to their boss, who has been gone since day one. As each team spokesperson makes specific suggestions, the boss has only three options: agree on the spot, say no, or ask for more information so that a decision can be made by a specific agreed-on date. Amand Lauzon is a GE boss who sweated his way through a town meeting. To encourage him to say yes, his workers set up the meeting room so that he couldn't make eye contact with his boss. He said, "I was wringing wet within half an hour. They had 108 proposals, I had about a minute to say yes or no to each one, and I couldn't make eye contact with my boss without turning around, which would show everyone in the room that I was chicken."[63] In the end, Lauzon agreed to all but eight suggestions. Furthermore, once those decisions were made, no one at GE was allowed to overrule them.

transition management team (TMT)
a team of 8 to 12 people whose full-time job is to completely manage and coordinate a company's change process

While the GE Workout clearly speeds up change, it may fragment change, as different managers approve different suggestions in different town meetings across a company. By contrast, a transition management team provides a way to coordinate change throughout an organization. A **transition management team (TMT)** is a team of 8 to 12 people whose full-time job is to manage and coordinate a company's change process.[64] One member of the TMT is assigned the task of anticipating and managing the emotions and behaviors related to resistance to change. Despite their importance, many companies overlook the impact that negative emotions and resistant behaviors can have on the change process. Also, TMTs report to the CEO every day, decide which change projects are approved and funded, select and evaluate the people in charge of different change projects, and make sure that different change projects complement one another. For example, entertainment company Viacom used a TMT to handle the changes that occurred when it acquired two much larger companies, Paramount Communications (TV and films) and Blockbuster Entertainment. The TMT reported directly to the CEO and included managers from Viacom, Paramount, and Blockbuster. Furthermore, Viacom's TMT was charged with eliminating duplication in television production, distribution and sales, and overhead and administrative costs in order to cut $200 million in expenses.[65]

It is also important to say what a TMT is not. A TMT is not an extra layer of management further separating upper management from lower managers and employees. A TMT is not a steering committee that creates plans for others to carry out. Instead, the members of the TMT are fully involved with making change happen on a daily basis. Furthermore, it's not the TMT's job to determine how and why the company will change. That responsibility belongs to the CEO and upper management. But it is the TMT's responsibility to accomplish those changes and make them stick. Finally, a TMT is not permanent. Once the company has successfully changed, the TMT is disbanded. Table 10.3 lists the primary responsibilities of TMTs.

organizational development
a philosophy and collection of planned change interventions designed to improve an organization's long-term health and performance

Organizational development is a philosophy and collection of planned change interventions designed to improve an organization's long-term health and performance. Organizational development takes a long-range approach to change, assumes that top management support is necessary for change to succeed, creates change by educating workers and managers to change ideas, beliefs, and behaviors so problems can be solved in new ways, and emphasizes employee participation in diagnosing, solving, and evaluating problems.[66] As shown in Table 10.4, organizational development interventions begin with recognition of a problem. Then, the company designates a

Table 10.3 The Primary Responsibilities of Transition Management Teams

1. Establish context for change and provide guidance.
2. Stimulate conversation.
3. Provide appropriate resources.
4. Coordinate and align projects.
5. Ensure congruence of messages, activities, policies, and behaviors.
6. Provide opportunities for joint creation.
7. Anticipate, identify, and address people problems.
8. Prepare the critical mass.

Source: J.D. Duck, "Managing Change: The Art of Balancing," *Harvard Business Review on Change* (Boston: Harvard Business School Publishing, 1998) 55-81.

change agent
the person formally in charge of guiding a change effort

change agent to be formally in charge of guiding the change effort. This person can be someone from the company or a professional consultant. The change agent clarifies the problem, gathers information, works with decision makers to create and implement an action plan, helps to evaluate the plan's effectiveness, implements the plan throughout the company, and then leaves only after making sure the change intervention will continue to work.

Organizational development interventions are aimed at changing large systems, small groups, or people.[67] More specifically, the purpose of *large system interventions* is to change the character and performance of an organization, business unit, or department. The purpose of a *small group intervention* is to assess how a group functions and help it work more effectively toward the accomplishment of its goals. The purpose of a *person-focused intervention* is to help people become aware of their attitudes and behaviors and acquire new skills and knowledge to increase interpersonal effectiveness. Table 10.5 describes the most frequently used organizational development interventions for large systems, small groups, and people. For additional information about changing systems, groups, and people, see "What Really Works: Change the Work Setting or Change the People? Do Both!"

Table 10.4 General Steps for Organizational Development Interventions

1. Entry	A problem is discovered and the need for change becomes apparent. Search begins for someone to deal with the problem and facilitate change.
2. Start-up	A change agent enters the picture and works to clarify the problem and gain commitment to a change effort.
3. Assessment and Feedback	The change agent gathers information about the problem and provides feedback about it to decision makers and those affected by it.
4. Action Planning	The change agent works with decision makers to develop an action plan.
5. Intervention	The action plan, or organizational development intervention, is carried out.
6. Evaluation	The change agent helps decision makers assess the effectiveness of the intervention.
7. Adoption	Organizational members accept ownership and responsibility for the change, which is then carried out through the entire organization.
8. Separation	The change agent leaves the organization after first ensuring that the change intervention will continue to work.

Source: W.J. Rothwell, R. Sullivan, & G.M. McLean, *Practicing Organizational Development: A Guide For Consultants* (San Diego: Pfeiffer & Company, 1995).

Table 10.5 **Different Kinds of Organizational Development Interventions**

Large System Interventions	
Sociotechnical Systems	An intervention designed to improve how well employees use and adjust to the work technology used in an organization.
Survey Feedback	An intervention that uses surveys to collect information from organizational members, reports the results of that survey to organizational members, and then uses those results to develop action plans for improvement.
Small Group Interventions	
Team Building	An intervention designed to increase the cohesion and cooperation of work group members.
Unit Goal Setting	An intervention designed to help a work group establish short- and long-term goals.
Person-Focused Interventions	
Counseling/Coaching	An intervention designed so that a formal helper or coach listens to managers or employees and advises them how to deal with work or interpersonal problems.
Training	An intervention designed to provide individuals the knowledge, skills, or attitudes they need to become more effective at their jobs.

Source: W.J. Rothwell, R. Sullivan, & G.M. McLean, *Practicing Organizational Development: A Guide For Consultants* (San Diego: Pfeiffer & Company, 1995).

What Really Works

Change the Work Setting or Change the People? Do Both!

Let's assume that you believe that your company needs to change. Congratulations! Just recognizing the need for change puts you ahead of 80 percent of the companies in your industry. But now that you've recognized the need for change, how do you make change happen? Should you focus on changing the work setting or the behavior of the people who work in that setting? It's a classic chicken or egg type of question. Which would you do?

A recent meta-analysis based on 52 studies and a combined total of 29,611 study participants indicated that it's probably best to do both!

Changing the Work Setting

An organizational work setting has four parts: organizing arrangements (control and reward systems, organizational structure), social factors (people, culture, patterns of interaction), technology (how inputs are transformed into outputs), and the physical setting (the actual physical space in which people work).

Overall, there is a 55 percent chance that organizational change efforts will successfully bring changes to a company's work setting. While the odds are still 55-45 in your favor, this is undoubtedly a much lower probability of success than you've seen with the management techniques discussed in other chapters. This simply reflects how strong resistance to change is in most companies.

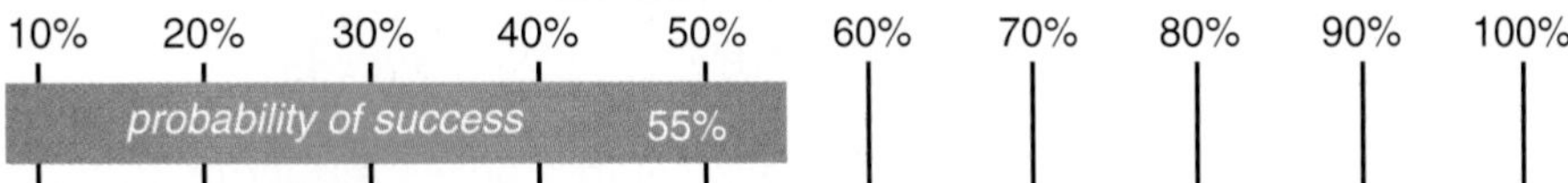

Changing the People

Changing people means changing individual work behavior. The idea is powerful. Change the decisions people make. Change the activities they perform. Change the information they share with others. And change the initiatives they take on their own. Change these individual behaviors and collectively you change the entire company. Overall, there is a 57 percent chance that organizational change efforts will successfully change people's individual work behavior. If you're wondering why the odds aren't higher, consider how difficult it is to simply change personal behavior. It's incredibly difficult to quit smoking, change diet, or maintain a daily exercise program. Not surprisingly, changing personal behavior at work is also difficult. Thus, viewed in this context, a 57 percent chance of success is a notable achievement.

Probability of Success

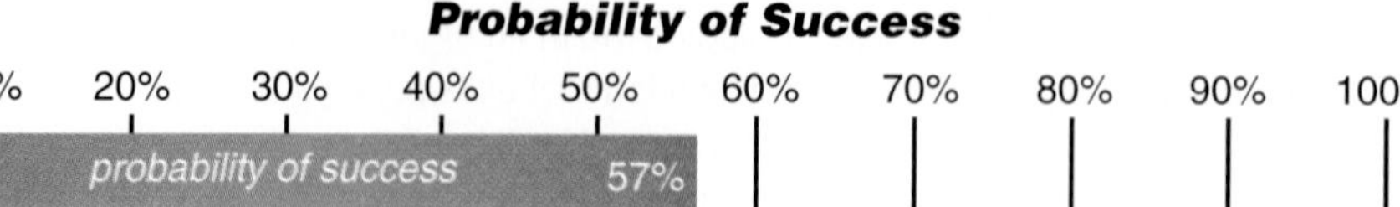

Changing Individual Behavior and Organizational Performance

The point of changing individual behavior is to improve organizational performance (i.e., higher profits, market share, and productivity, and lower costs). Overall, there is a 76 percent chance that changes in individual behavior will produce changes in organizational outcomes. So if you want to improve your company's profits, market share, or productivity, focus on changing the way that your people behave at work.

Probability of Success

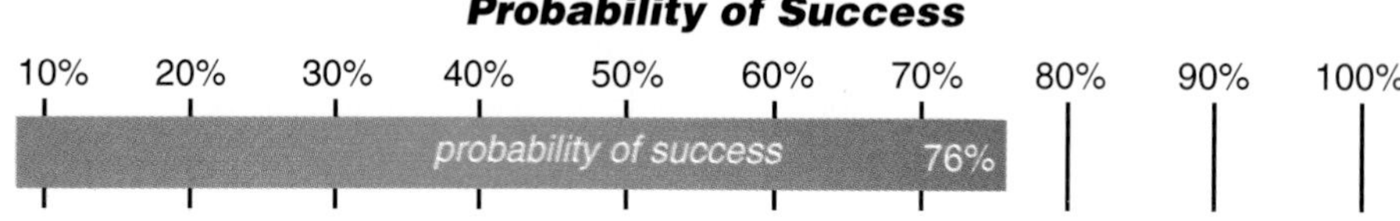

Source: P.J. Robertson, D.R. Roberts, & J.I. Porras, "Dynamics of Planned Organizational Change: Assessing Empirical Support for a Theoretical Model," *Academy of Management Journal* 36 (1993): 619-634.

4.3
Managing Conversations to Promote Change

Think about where you have worked. How well and often did managers, especially top management, talk to you and other employees? Was it one-way, top-down communication, or did management listen and respond to the ideas of lower-level managers and employees? How did people from different parts of the company talk to each other? Did they try to understand each other, or did they talk past each other by using terms and ideas particular to their jobs or departments?

organizational dialogue the process by which people in an organization learn to talk effectively and constructively with each other

Organizational dialogue is the process by which people in an organization learn to talk effectively and constructively with each other.[68] Unfortunately, in most companies, the quality of organizational dialogue isn't very good. But when change forces are strong and managers and workers are stressed, organizational dialogue can be nonexistent. Consequently, the way managers and workers talk (or don't talk) to each other can be a significant barrier to successful change efforts.

According to this line of thinking, talk is not cheap. Conversations shape attitudes, intentions, and actions. What is said or not said really matters. So when organizational dialogue breaks down, change efforts break down, too. From this perspective, managing change is akin to managing the conversations that make up organizational dialogue.

The dark-colored boxes in Figure 10.6 show the four kinds of conversations that managers can use to influence change in organizations.[69] When change efforts work, change begins with initiative conversations. These are followed by conversations about understanding, performance, and closure. However, the light-colored boxes in Figure 10.6 show that each of those con-

Figure 10.6 **Managing Conversations to Initiate Change**

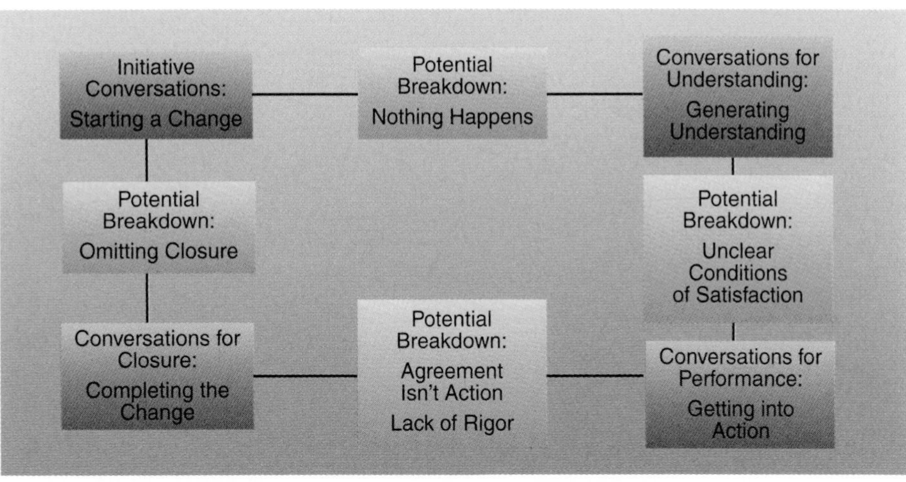

Source: J. Ford & L.W. Ford, "The Role of Conversations in Producing Intentional Change in Organizations," *Academy of Management Review* 20 (1995): 541-570.

versations is subject to potential breakdowns: nothing happens, unclear conditions of satisfaction, agreement isn't action, lack of rigor, and omitting closure. When breakdowns happen, change may fail. Let's examine each of these change conversations and breakdowns in more detail. As we do so, refer to Table 10.6, which shows a conversation among hospital managers who are discussing the need for a quality-improvement plan.

initiative conversations
conversations that start the change process by discussing what should or needs to be done to bring about change

Initiative conversations start the change process by discussing what should or needs to be done to bring about change. Initiative conversations begin with phrases like "I propose . . . ," "Tell me what we should do about . . . ," "We should stop . . . and start . . . ," "It is time we undertake . . . ," and "What do you think about. . . . " For example, in Table 10.6, the hospital CEO begins an initiative conversation by stating, "I want us to implement a quality-improvement program."

Naturally, talking about change only matters if it leads to action to promote change. Consequently, if *nothing happens* after talking about what needs to be done to bring about change, then the change process will stop. This kind of breakdown occurs for two reasons. First, the people who want to initiate change may be unable to actually make change happen. Second, if previous initiatives for change have been ignored or dismissed as unimportant, the people who have initiative conversations about what changes need to occur may not tell anyone with the power or authority to make change happen. In both instances, despite the fact that change clearly needs to occur, frustration sets in, because nothing happens.

conversations for understanding
conversations that generate a deeper understanding of why change is needed, what problems have been occurring, and what might be done to solve those problems

If a breakdown is avoided, initiative conversations should be followed by conversations for understanding. **Conversations for understanding** generate a deeper understanding of why change is needed, what problems have been occurring, and what might be done to solve those problems. For example, in the conversation of understanding shown in Table 10.6, the hospital managers discuss why change is needed ("First, we are getting far too many complaints from our patients."), and try to figure out why problems have been occurring ("The staff may be doing a better job as individual workers but not as a team. There must be some reason for the complaints.").

Table 10.6	A Hospital Staff's Change Conversations about a Quality-Improvement Plan
Conversation	***Statements***
Initiative	CEO: I want us to implement a quality-improvement program.
Understanding	Director of Administration: What's this all about?
	CEO: Several things. First, we are getting far too many complaints from our patients. Second, the current climate for reform makes quality essential, and, third, I am convinced we can deliver better care.
	Director of Nursing: I'm not sure we need to improve quality. We have a well-trained staff and they do a good job. The average performance ratings of the nurses are up, and any changes would just give them more work to do.
	CEO: The staff may be doing a better job as individual workers but not as a team. There must be some reason for the complaints.
	CEO: Okay, so we are all agreed that we should undertake a quality-improvement program. Now, how will we know if the program works?
	Director of Administration: What if we used the number of formal complaints received to tell? We received over 100 complaints last month, both written and verbal. That translates into about three complaints per thousand patients.
(Condition of satisfaction)	Director of Nursing: Okay, so if the number of complaints is less than 1 per thousand per month by the end of this calendar year, we will say the program worked.
Performance	CEO to Director of Administration: Will you contact each of the department heads and ask them to generate a list of things they think could contribute to us getting fewer complaints and then to bring that list with them to a meeting on the sixth of this month at 1 p.m.?
	Director of Administration: Yes. Do you want us to make a list also?
	CEO: No.
	Director of Nursing: I will meet with my supervisors and ask them to generate a similar list and ask them to bring the list to a meeting on the eighth of this month starting at 3 p.m.
	CEO: Great. Then, at the meetings, we will identify things that can be done and assign them to some project teams.
Closure	CEO: I want to thank each of you for the work you did here today. Your willingness to press in on the issue made it possible for us to see what is needed to get our quality program well-defined. Does anyone have anything to say about the meeting or what happened here?

Source: J. Ford & L.W. Ford, "The Role of Conversations in Producing Intentional Change in Organizations," *Academy of Management Review* 20 (1995): 541-570.

conditions of satisfaction a statement of the specific, measurable, and observable conditions that must be met in order for change to be successful

A conversation for understanding breaks down when *there is no clear understanding of the conditions of satisfaction.* **Conditions of satisfaction** are the specific, measurable, and observable conditions that must be met in order for change to be successful. For example, in Table 10.6, the Director of Nursing clearly describes the conditions of satisfaction by stating, "OK, so if the number of complaints is less than 1 per thousand per month by the end of the calendar year, we will say the program worked." Without clear conditions of satisfaction, people are not sure about what to do or what to change. Furthermore, they're unable to determine if what they're doing or changing is working.

conversations for performance conversations about action plans, in which managers and workers make specific requests and promise specific results

If the conditions of satisfaction can be clearly stated, the next step is a conversation for performance. **Conversations for performance** are conversations about action plans, in which managers and workers make specific requests and promise specific results. For example, in Table 10.6, the CEO made a specific performance-related request with this statement: "Will you contact each of the department heads and ask them to generate a list of things they think could contribute to us getting fewer complaints. . . ." The Director of Nursing promised a specific result when she said, "I will meet with my supervisors and ask them to generate a similar list and ask them to bring the list to a meeting on the eighth of this month starting at 3 p.m." If done properly, the specific requests and promises discussed in performance conversations will be closely linked to the specific, measurable, and observable conditions set forth in the conditions of satisfaction.

Conversations for performance break down in two ways. The first breakdown is that managers may not realize that *agreement isn't action*. In fact, many managers rely exclusively on conversations for understanding when managing change processes. Unfortunately, a general understanding about why change is needed is not enough to produce change-related actions. For example, just because the hospital managers (Table 10.6) agree that the number of complaints per 1,000 patients needs to be reduced doesn't mean they'll take any specific actions to reduce it. If managers want specific changes to occur, then the specific requests and promises that occur in conversations for performance must follow agreement and understanding.

The second kind of breakdown at this point is the *lack of rigor* used when managing conversations for performance. Specifically, managers may assume that people know what they should be doing and may not ask them to take specific actions or ask them to indicate what specific actions they intend to take. Consequently, people just "do their best." Furthermore, managers compound this breakdown by not specifying the deadline for that result. In the end, workers get around to the change "as soon as possible" or "when they have the time." So, from this perspective, breakdowns don't occur because of resistance to change, but from managers not being clear about what specific actions will be taken, who will do them, and when they will be done.

conversations for closure conversations that end the change process by indicating that the work is done and the change process is complete

If conversations for performance have focused on specific requests and promises and specific actions have been taken to create successful change, then the last step in this process is a conversation for closure. **Conversations for closure** end the change process by indicating that the work is done. Congratulations may be expressed if the change was successful. Regrets may be expressed if it was not. Yet, regardless of the results, the process is declared complete. In fact, closure is so important that *omitting closure* is the last possible breakdown in the change process. When it becomes obvious to everyone that the intended results have been achieved, or that they will not be achieved (or at least not on schedule), managers need to express thanks for what has been accomplished. When successes, losses, creativity, and hard work are not recognized, people feel unappreciated. Even worse, they may become resentful, cynical, and unlikely to fully participate in future change efforts.

One way to achieve closure is to celebrate the successes, losses, creativity, and hard work of the people and groups involved in the change process. For example, Southwest Airlines celebrates each time it begins flying to a new city (a change process that takes between three and six months to complete). When Southwest began flights at Chicago's Midway Airport, it threw a party at which Chicago's mayor and Southwest's CEO fastened a ten-foot seatbelt together to signify the importance of Southwest coming to Chicago. When Southwest opened service at Baltimore/Washington International Airport, it celebrated its $49 one-way ticket prices by flying 49 Baltimore fifth-graders to Cleveland to spend a day at the Cleveland Zoo. Celebrations publicize outstanding performance, renew and energize employees, and allow people throughout the company to build relationships in an informal setting.[70]

Celebrations bring closure to change processes, because they mark beginnings, ends, and milestones. See Table 10.7 for more reasons why Southwest Airlines celebrates change.

4.4
What Not to Do When Leading Change

So far, you've learned about the basic change process (unfreezing, change, refreezing), managing resistance to change, the four kinds of change tools and techniques (results-driven change, the GE Workout, transition management teams, and organizational development), and using conversations to promote change. However, John Kotter of the Harvard Business School argues that knowing what *not* to do is just as important as knowing what to do when it comes to achieving successful organizational change.[71]

Table 10.8 shows the most common errors that managers make when they lead change. The first two errors occur during the unfreezing phase, in which managers try to get the people affected by change to believe that change is really needed. The first and potentially most serious of these errors is *not establishing a great enough sense of urgency*. Indeed, Kotter estimates that more than half of all change efforts fail because the people affected by change are just not convinced that change is necessary. However, people will feel a greater sense of urgency about change if a leader in the company makes a public, candid assessment of the company's problems and weaknesses. For example, Continental Airlines CEO Gordon Bethune said, "We had a crappy product, and we were trying to discount ourselves into profitability. Nobody wants to eat a crummy pizza, no matter if it's 99 cents."[72] Plus, by sharing extensive (and depressing) financial information with Continental's workers, Bethune made it clear that the company was truly at risk of going bankrupt. And because employees knew that neither Pan Am nor Eastern Airlines ever recovered after declaring bankruptcy, resistance to change evaporated at Continental as employees concluded that accepting change was the only reasonable option.[73]

The second mistake that occurs in the unfreezing process is *not creating a powerful enough coalition*. Change often starts with one or two people, but in order to build enough momentum to change an entire department, division, or company, change has to be supported by a critical and growing group of people. Besides top management, Kotter recommends that key employees, managers, board members, customers, and even union leaders be members of a *core change coalition*, which guides and supports organizational change. Furthermore, it's important to strengthen this group's resolve by periodically

Table 10.7 **Why Southwest Airlines Celebrates Change**

1. Celebration provides an opportunity for building relationships.
2. Celebration gives us a sense of history.
3. Celebration helps us envision the future.
4. Celebration is a way of recognizing major milestones.
5. Celebration helps reduce stress.
6. Celebration inspires motivation and reenergizes people.
7. Celebration builds self-confidence and removes fear.
8. Celebration helps us mourn the losses associated with change.

Source: K. Freiberg & J. Freiberg, *Nuts! Southwest Airlines' Crazy Recipe for Business and Personal Success* (Austin, TX: Bard Press, 1996).

Table 10.8

Errors Managers Make When Leading Change

Unfreezing

1. Not establishing a great enough sense of urgency.
2. Not creating a powerful enough guiding coalition.

Change

3. Lacking a vision.
4. Undercommunicating the vision by a factor of ten.
5. Not removing obstacles to the new vision.
6. Not systematically planning for and creating short-term wins.

Refreezing

7. Declaring victory too soon.
8. Not anchoring changes in the corporation's culture.

Source: J.P. Kotter, "Leading Change: Why Transformation Efforts Fail," *Harvard Business Review* 73, no. 2 (March-April 1995): 59.

bringing its members together for off-site retreats. At Merck, a leading pharmaceutical firm, CEO Raymond Gilmartin uses off-site retreats to break down barriers and build confidence. He said, "What goes on during the breaks and during the dinners or lunches is often just as important" as what is discussed in the meetings. Likewise, to encourage an openness to change, IBM CEO Lou Gerstner takes his top 40 managers to an off-site retreat every six weeks. The purpose? To get IBM's managers to challenge their thinking and to learn to view IBM's business from different perspectives.[74]

The next four errors that managers make occur during the change phase, in which a change intervention is used to try to get workers and managers to change their behavior and work practices.

Lacking a vision for change is a significant error at this point. As you learned in Chapter 4, a *vision* is a statement of a company's purpose or reason for existing. A vision for change makes clear where a company or department is headed and why the change is occurring. Change efforts that lack vision tend to be confused, chaotic, and contradictory. By contrast, change efforts guided by visions are clear, easy to understand, and can be effectively explained in five minutes or less. At Continental Airlines, the initial change vision was simple: "getting passengers where they were supposed to be on time."[75] With this clear-cut vision focusing managers and workers, Continental now ranks third in on-time arrivals and second in baggage handling. Previously, it had ranked tenth on both.

Undercommunicating the vision by a factor of ten is another mistake in the change phase. According to Kotter, companies mistakenly hold just one meeting to announce the vision. Or, if the new vision receives heavy emphasis in executive speeches or company newsletters, senior management then undercuts the vision by behaving in ways contrary to it. Successful communication of the vision requires that top managers link everything the company does to the new vision and that they "walk the talk" by behaving in ways consistent with the vision. Furthermore, even companies that begin change with a clear vision sometimes make the mistake of *not removing obstacles to the new vision*. Insisting on change, but then failing to redesign jobs, pay plans, and technology to support the new way of doing things leaves formidable barriers to change in place. One way Continental removed obstacles to its new vision was by completely rewriting its employee policy manual. CEO Bethune said, "And we don't call it a manual anymore; we call it guidelines. The new guidelines are supposed to help employees solve problems—give them a sense of where the boundaries are when they run into trouble. But in the general pursuit of their jobs, we want them to use their heads and use their resources." In short, ". . . if you find yourself in the middle of something complicated, something unusual, something that just doesn't fit, then use your head and make the best decision you can."[76]

Similar to results-driven change, another error in the change phase is *not systematically planning for and creating short-term wins.* Most people don't have the discipline and patience to wait two years to see if the new change effort works. Change is threatening and uncomfortable, so for people to continue to support it, they need to see an immediate payoff. Kotter recommends that managers create short-term wins by actively picking people and projects that are likely to work extremely well early in the change process. The short-term wins at Continental came in the form of $65 checks. Bethune told managers and employees that every employee would get a check for $65 each month that Continental finished in the top five in on-time arrivals (as rated by the Department of Transportation). The first time that Continental made it into the top five, it sent out $2.5 million worth of $65 checks to its employees. Bethune said, ". . . we didn't just drop 65 extra dollars into their paychecks and have the whole impact of their bonus disappear. Nor did we let them start calculating how much of it they lost to taxes. We gave each employee $65 in a special check—we took the withholding out of their regular paychecks so they got 65 actual dollars."[77]

The last two errors that managers make occur during the refreezing phase, when attempts are made to support and reinforce changes so they "stick."

Declaring victory too soon is a tempting mistake in the refreezing phase. Managers typically declare victory right after the first large-scale success in the change process. For instance, it would have been easy for Continental to declare victory the first time that it made it into the top five in on-time arrivals. Ironically, declaring success too early has the same effect as draining the gasoline out of a car. It stops change efforts dead in their tracks. With success declared, supporters of the change process stop pushing to make change happen. After all, why "push" when success has been achieved? Rather than declaring victory, managers should use the momentum from short-term wins to push for even bigger or faster changes. This maintains urgency and prevents change supporters from slacking off before the changes are frozen into the company's culture. For example, after quickly moving into the top five in on-time arrivals, Continental maintained urgency by raising the requirements for monthly, on-time bonuses. Now, instead of the top five, Continental had to finish third or higher in on-time arrival. However, when it raised the bar, it also raised the reward, increasing the on-time bonus from $65 to $100.

The last mistake that managers make is *not anchoring changes in the corporation's culture.* An *organization's culture* is the set of key values, beliefs, and attitudes shared by organizational members that determines the "accepted way of doing things" in a company. As you learned in Chapter 2, cultures are extremely difficult and slow to change. Kotter said that two things help anchor changes in a corporation's culture. The first is directly showing people that the changes have actually improved performance. At Continental, this was easily demonstrated by the company's improved Department of

Transportation rankings for on-time arrival and baggage handling. The second is to make sure that the people who get promoted fit the new culture. If they don't, it's a clear sign that the changes were only temporary.

When did CEO Gordon Bethune know that the changes he was seeking were anchored in Continental's culture? He was getting on a Continental flight at the last minute, right as the gate agent was scrambling to get the plane out of the gate on time. Bethune, whose back was to the agent, heard him say, " Excuse me, sir, you'll have to sit down. The plane has to leave." The flight attendant became upset and said to the agent, "Do you know who that is? That's Mr. Bethune!" The agent responded, "That's very nice, but we gotta go. Tell him to sit down." Bethune said that this ". . . is how Continental Airlines stays on time—and how it has changed for the better."[78]

Review 4: *Managing Change*

The basic change process is unfreezing, change, and refreezing. Resistance to change, which stems from self-interest, misunderstanding and distrust, and a general intolerance for change, can be managed through education and communication, participation, negotiation, coercion, and top management support. When change efforts work, change begins with initiative conversations and is followed by conversations about understanding, performance, and closure. But when conversations break down, change efforts break down, too. Change conversations can break down in five ways: nothing happens, unclear conditions of satisfaction, agreement isn't action, lack of rigor, and omitting closure.

Managers can use a number of change techniques. Results-driven change and the GE Workout reduce resistance to change by getting change efforts off to a fast start. Transition management teams, which manage a company's change process, coordinate change efforts throughout an organization. Organizational development is a collection of planned change interventions (large system, small group, person-focused) guided by a change agent that are designed to improve an organization's long-term health and performance. Finally, knowing what *not* to do is as important as knowing what to do to achieve successful change. Managers should avoid these errors when leading change: not establishing urgency, not creating a guiding coalition, lacking a vision, undercommunicating the vision, not removing obstacles to the vision, not creating short-term wins, declaring victory too soon, and not anchoring changes in the corporation's culture.

What**Really**Happened?

In the opening case, you learned about the financial difficulties that IBM experienced as a result of its inability to change or to bring innovative products to market. Read the answers to the opening case to find out how IBM is addressing these problems.

But how do you quickly and effectively change a company like IBM? Should the change be slow and gradual or quick and revolutionary?

It's never easy to change a company, especially one as large as IBM (revenues over $80 billion and more than 200,000 employees). However, in less than five years, CEO Gerstner and his management team have managed to bring change to IBM and return it to solid profitability.

Organizational change is a function of the relative strength of the change forces and resistance forces that occur inside and outside of organizations. Change can be nonexistent, sporadic, continuous, or discontinuous, depending on whether change forces are stronger or weaker than resistance forces. Many analysts and experts have been frustrated by what they see as Gerstner's steady, continuous approach to changing IBM. They criticized Gerstner and IBM for being "incrementalists" and for not changing the basic way IBM does business. Essentially, they wanted Gerstner to greatly increase the change forces within IBM, for example, changing the management structure, changing the reward systems, and so forth. And Gerstner has done some of these things. Today, 75 percent of an IBM manager's bonus is tied to overall company profitability compared to just 25 percent before Gerstner arrived. With so much more money riding on the company's success, IBM managers have been quicker to change.

However, most of Gerstner's efforts so far have been aimed at weakening resistance forces that promote and protect the status quo in all organizations. And at IBM, the greatest deterrent to change was its guarantee of lifetime employment. As long as you were a good performer, you'd have a job of some kind at IBM, even if your division or job no longer existed. This guarantee was supposed to demonstrate IBM's commitment to its workforce and, in turn, gain workers' loyalty. In practice, however, IBM managers guaranteed jobs to all employees, regardless of job performance. Not surprisingly, in annual attitude surveys IBM's best performers complained that company management was too soft on poor performers who, in their view, should have been fired. So, in a move that many would describe as revolutionary for IBM, Gerstner began a program of layoffs that would eventually cut IBM's workforce in half, from just over 400,000 employees to approximately 200,000 today. And with layoffs occurring, IBMers who previously had every reason to resist change (i.e., lifetime job guarantee) began listening to what needed to be done to stem IBM's losses and restore profitability. Said Gerstner, "Transforming IBM is not something we can do in one or two years. The better we are at fixing some of the short-term things, the more time we have to deal with the long-term issues. You can't really start addressing the long-term issues unless you've got a stabilization."

IBM has a long history and a strong culture. So, any changes that you try to make will probably be resisted. How can you identify and manage that resistance so IBM can make the changes that it needs to make?

The basic change process is one of unfreezing, change, and then refreezing. Unfreezing is getting the people affected by change to believe that change is needed. During the change intervention itself, workers and managers change their behavior and work practices. Refreezing is supporting and reinforcing the new changes so they "stick." This basic change process of unfreezing, change, and refreezing works best by first reducing resistance to change.

Gerstner has managed resistance to change by focusing on participation and by selectively using coercion. Participation reduces resistance to change by having those affected by change participate in the planning and implementation of the change process. Whereas the "old IBM" was incredibly slow to make decisions, Gerstner has tried to force IBMers to quickly act on decisions. He does this by making snap, on-the-spot decisions and then granting full authority to particular individuals to make those decisions happen. For example, Gerstner began eight reengineering projects in areas such as hardware development and production processes, and then made sure that each project was "owned" by a manager who was fully responsible for it.

Coercion is the use of formal power and authority to force others to change. Because of the negative reactions it can create, coercion should only be used when a crisis exists or when other change techniques have failed. When IBM needed to downsize its workforce in France, it offered French workers this deal: You can save your jobs if you replace your guaranteed annual bonus with a compensation package that ties your earnings to company performance.

In the fast paced environment of computers, it takes IBM much too long to develop and bring new products to market. How can you speed up that process?

IBM has never had problems coming up with new ideas. For example, IBM invented computer hard drives and memory, two of the key components of modern computers. IBM's mistake, however, was that it has been slow to bring its new inventions and new product ideas to market. Until recently, IBM seems not to have understood that technology cycles follow an S-curve pattern of innovation. Early in the cycle, technological progress is slow and improvements in technological performance are small. However, as a technology matures, performance improves quickly. Finally, small improvements occur as the limits of a technology are reached. At this point, significant improvements in performance must come from new technologies. It's at this last point that IBM has been consistently outgunned by competitors such as Intel and Microsoft who have been much quicker to introduce new technologies.

Over the long run, the best way for a company to protect its competitive advantage is to create a stream of innovative ideas and products. To do this well, the company must learn how to manage the sources of innovation, how to manage innovation during discontinuous change, and how to manage innovation during incremental change. In the last few years, IBM has made significant strides in these areas by doing a much better job of bringing new technologies to market. A former IBM researcher said, "The difference that the Gerstner regime introduced was, it wasn't enough anymore to just move ideas into the product world. What was important for us in Research was to understand what the market wanted."

For example, IBM has a new program called "First of a Kind," in which new research projects are shared with IBM customers who use them to solve real-world problems. One of the more successful "First of a Kind" products was IBM's voice-dictation software. After developing the software, IBM shared it with radiologists in New York and Boston hospitals. When reading x-rays, these doctors usually dictated their findings onto audio tapes that were later transcribed and placed in patients' files. Now, however, the doctors simply dictate their notes directly to a computer that, using IBM's software, instantly converts them to written files. IBM now sells this software worldwide.

Sources: A. Goldstein, "Big Blue Pulls Ahead of the Pack," *Dallas Morning News*, 14 February 1999, 1H. L. Hays, "Another Top IBM Executive Quits Amid Reorganization by Gerstner," *The Wall Street Journal Europe*, 10 January 1995. "IBM's Finances: Now Comes the Hard Part," *Infoperspectives* 18 (1 April 1997). D.Q. Mills, "The Decline and Rise of IBM," *Sloan Management Review* 37 (1 June 1996). R. Narisetti, "How IBM Turned Around Its Ailing PC Division," *The Wall Street Journal*, 12 March 1998, B1. S. Sherman, "Is He Too Cautious to Save IBM?" *Fortune*, 3 October 1994. B. Ziegler, "IBM's Research Cutbacks Now Seem to Be Brilliant," *The Wall Street Journal*, 6 October 1997.

Key Terms

change agent p. 390

change forces p. 380

change intervention p. 385

coercion p. 387

compression approach to innovation p. 376

conditions of satisfaction p. 394

conversations for closure p. 395

conversations for performance p. 394

conversations for understanding p. 393

creative work environments p. 370

creativity p. 360

design competition p. 367

design iteration p. 374

dominant design p. 367

era of ferment p. 367

experiential approach to innovation p. 374

flow p. 371

General Electric Workout p. 388

generational change p. 376

incremental change p. 368

initiative conversations p. 393

innovation streams p. 366

milestones p. 375

multifunctional teams p. 375

organization decline p. 381

organizational change p. 360

organizational development p. 389

organizational dialogue p. 392

organizational innovation p. 360

refreezing p. 385

resistance forces p. 380

resistance to change p. 384

results-driven change p. 388

S-curve pattern of innovation p. 363

technological discontinuity p. 367

technological substitution p. 367

technology cycle p. 362

testing p. 374

transition management team (TMT) p. 389

unfreezing p. 385

What Would You Do-II?

Cyberspace

It's 2:00 a.m. Do you know how your investments are doing? Just a few years ago, if your investments were keeping you up at night, you'd have to wait until 9:00 the next morning to call your full-service broker. Today, however, sleepless investors can calm their nerves (hopefully) by logging onto the Internet at any time from anywhere to check on their investment portfolios.

One of the companies leading the charge to Internet investing is E*TRADE (**www.etrade.com**). Bill Porter founded E*TRADE in 1982, because he couldn't understand why he should pay a discount broker $100 per stock trade when the same thing could be accomplished for much less using computers. Porter's idea was brilliant, but years ahead of its time. The company grew, but very slowly, for a decade. In fact, electronic stock trading didn't catch on until online services like America Online and CompuServe became popular in the early 1990s. Then with the advent of public Internet access in the mid-1990s, E*TRADE's online business skyrocketed. In 1992, E*TRADE was conducting just a few hundred trades per day for its customers and annual revenues were only $848,000. Today, thanks to its Web site, the company adds more than 500 new customer accounts (worth $8 million to $10 million in assets) per day! Since moving to the Internet, E*TRADE has been growing at a rate of 50 percent per quarter!

The reasons for E*TRADE's explosive growth are straightforward: low prices and great investment information. Let's say you're buying 100 shares of Coca-Cola stock, which sells for about $65 per share (at the time this was written). E*TRADE charges a $14.95 commission for this trade. The same cost at a full-service broker like Merrill Lynch would be $101.45. The $86.50 difference is more than enough to buy another share of Coke's stock!

The second reason for E*TRADE's growth is its first-class information and research services, which rival those available to professional stockbrokers and investors. E*TRADE customers can personalize their own Web investment pages to automatically track and update their stock portfolios and any major market indices, such as the Dow Jones or NASDAQ markets. Customers also have free access to data on stock quotes, statistical charts, financial news, commentary by financial experts, and company earnings estimates. The major difference is that, unlike full-service brokerages, E*TRADE doesn't have stockbrokers to hold investors' hands and help them make decisions. But, then again, unlike full-service brokerages, E*TRADE's online investment research and information is available 24 hours a day, 7 days a week.

In all, E*TRADE has developed a model for Internet investing that today's independent-minded, technology-capable customers love. However, the company faces serious challenges. E*TRADE was once the most innovative Internet investment company around. But now more than 40 other Internet investment companies offer similar prices and services. (See **www.yahoo.com/Business_and_Economy/Companies/ Financial_Services/Investment_Services/ Brokerages/** for a list.) What E*TRADE offers its customers isn't so innovative anymore. For example, Ameritrade charges a flat fee of $8 for any size stock trade, nearly half what E*TRADE charges. Likewise, Charles Schwab has rolled out a $29.95 monthly flat fee plan that allows customers to trade up to 1,000 shares per month (3 cents per share above 1,000) and gives them full access to Schwab's telephone, office branch, and online services. Michael Gazala, an investment analyst with Forrester Research Inc., said, "When they [E*TRADE] started out, they definitely had a pretty unique value proposition." [But now], "I don't know if there's a unique value proposition to E*TRADE that's not being met equally well by Schwab or Fidelity."

If you were in charge of E*TRADE, what would you do?

(Hint: Figure out where E*TRADE is on the standard S-curve pattern of innovation. Also, figure out what phase of the innovation stream E*TRADE is in right now. Finally, take a look at E*TRADE's Web site and its current offerings and promotions. Then see, listed below, what its major competitors are doing.)

- Ameritrade (**www.ameritrade.com/**)
- Charles Schwab (**www.eschwab.com/**)
- Datek (**www.datek.com/**)
- Fidelity Investments (**personal451.fidelity.com/**)
- National Discount Brokers (**www.ndb.com/**)
- Quick & Reilly (**www.quick-reilly.com/**)

Sources: R. Buckman, "E*TRADE Faces More Rivals," *Dow Jones News Service,* 27 December 1997. R. Buckman, "Some Online Broker Fees Are Climbing," *The Wall Street Journal,* 16 March 1999, C1. R. Buckman & A. Lucchetti, "Cooling It: Wall Street Firms Try to Keep Internet Mania from Ending Badly—They Upgrade Their Systems, Stiffen Trading Limits to Curb the Speculation," *The Wall Street Journal,* 24 February 1999, A1. C. Byron, "Money Talks: Flame Your Broker!" *Esquire,* 5 May 1997. H.R. Gold & T.W. Carey, "Getting Wired," *Barron's,* 6 May 1996. T. Hoffman, "Schwab Bolsters Internet Effort under Flat-Fee Plan," *ComputerWorld,* 22 December 1997. S. Thurm, "For Frazzled Online Brokers, Technology Is the Problem," *The Wall Street Journal,* 4 March 1999, B6. M. Veverka, "E*TRADE, Compelling but Risky, Isn't Just Another Internet Stock," *The Wall Street Journal,* 3 March 1997. J. Wyatt & M. Atanasov, "E*TRADE: Is This Investing's Future?" *Fortune,* 3 March 1997.

Critical-Thinking Video Case

Managing Change: Central Michigan Community Hospital

Central Michigan Community Hospital is a nonprofit, regional healthcare system. It includes a full-service 151-bed hospital, a medical staff of over 120 doctors, a walk-in urgent care center, wellness centers, occupational medicine, home healthcare, and numerous other services. In 1994, it was designated one of the top 100 hospitals in the U.S.

The hospital is riding a tidal wave of change in the healthcare environment. It is striving to meet the changing demands of patients, employees, insurance companies, and the state and federal governments, so it can continue to provide quality care at a cost-effective price. As you watch the video, consider the following critical-thinking questions.

Critical-Thinking Questions

1. What types of changes should Central Michigan Community Hospital make to compete in the next century?
2. What can Central Michigan Community Hospital employees do to make these changes successful?

Management Decisions

Freedom Not to Worry about Products and Profits?

What a great opportunity! Head of company research and development for Microtel, a *Fortune* 100 high-tech company. This is the job you've been wanting for years. And what better time to get it? Thanks to the innovative products and technology produced by your R&D labs, profits are strong and market share is growing. There's only one downside. Microtel's success has attracted numerous competitors and dozens of new startup companies, all intent on taking a substantial chunk of your customers and profits. If the company doesn't maintain its stream of innovative products, it's sure to lose its competitive advantage to one of these hungry competitors. This morning, when you met with Microtel's CEO, you were given one directive: "Find a way to increase the level of innovation we get from our R&D labs. How you do it is up to you. Just make it happen." Your reply was quick and confident, "You can count on me." But as you were leaving the office, you really weren't sure just how to improve on Microtel's already fine record of innovation.

In general, there are two lines of thought about how to get the most out of R&D labs. The first is to focus on basic research and give researchers the freedom they need to pursue the ideas that intrigue them. This is the model that Bell Labs, formerly AT&T's research & development lab, followed for over 60 years. During that time, Bell Labs researchers came up with more than 25,000 patents, more than one per day, as they invented motion pictures with sound, long-distance transmission of TV signals, stereo recording, transistors, solar power cells, lasers, communications satellites, and cellular phones. Not surprisingly, seven Bell Labs scientists won Nobel Prizes for science during that time, more than any other lab in the world. Under the basic research model, leading scientists study what they want and never have to worry about profits. Furthermore, they have "signatory authority," meaning that they control their own research budgets and have the ability (within that budget) to purchase whatever equipment they need to conduct their research.

The second line of thought is that innovation can be improved by holding researchers accountable for developing marketable ideas that can be turned into practical products. For example, at ICL PLC, the British computer company owned by Fujitsu of Japan, researchers are expected to maintain close contact with customers. When ICL PLC developed a new computer system for Cathay Pacific Airlines, management told the researchers to "get out of their Jesus sandals and into business suits. . . . we're going to transfer you (to Asia) along with the technology." In general, moves like this are designed to make researchers aware of three questions: What can the company do with your idea/technology/product? How big is the market for it? And how much money can the company make from it?

Questions

1. Both approaches have tradeoffs. After reviewing the chapter discussion concerning innovation streams and technology cycles, describe two important advantages and two serious disadvantages for the "basic research" model described above.
2. Describe two important advantages and two serious disadvantages for the "profits and products" model described above.
3. If you were running Microtel's R & D lab, which would you choose, the "basic research" model or the "profits and products" model? Explain your choice and the reasons for it.

Sources: S. Ascarelli, "European Telecom R&D Labs Adjusting—Scientists Must Think in Terms of Profit and Loss, *The Wall Street Journal,* 15 March 1996. L. Hooper, "Technology (A Special Report): Genius—The Creative Edge: Nurturing High-Tech Talent Requires a Delicate Balancing Act; But the Payoff Can Be Huge," *The Wall Street Journal,* 24 May 1993. J. Keller, "Technology (A Special Report): Finding and Feeding—Ignoring the Bottom Line—NEC's U.S. Research Lab Has a Theory: The Freedom Not to Worry about Products May Lead to the Best Products of All," *The Wall Street Journal,* 24 May 1993. G. Naik, "Corporate Research: How Much Is It Worth? Top Labs Shift Research Goals to Fast Payoffs," *The Wall Street Journal,* 22 May 1995. B. Ziegler & G. Naik, "Bell Labs Faces Mundane Future under Breakup Plan," *The Wall Street Journal,* 22 September 1995.

Management Decisions

Hot Spots

Repeatedly throughout history, entire industries have become associated with particular regions, locations, or cities. For example, in the mid 15th century, because of nearby silver and soft metal mines, the German towns of Augsberg, Regensburg, Ulm, and Nuremburg became the center of Europe's metalworking industry. In the 17th century, the British Navigation Act of 1651 required that all trade with England or its numerous colonies throughout the New World be conducted using British ships. The result was that London became the busiest seaport in the world and thus the center of international trade in tobacco, spices, tea, and other goods. Today, we continue to associate particular industries with particular locations: Paris with the fashion industry, New York and Wall Street with finance, Detroit with the automobile, and Hollywood with the entertainment industry.

The development of a particular industry in a particular location is known as a "hot spot." *Hot spots* are regional clusters of companies in the same industry that require similar kinds of resources and that grow faster than the industry average. Hot spots are thought to be especially important to the development and growth of technology companies, whose success depends on the ability to create innovative products and technologies. Indeed, the standard advice for innovation- or technology-based companies is that they be located in or near high-tech hot spots. For example, Silicon Valley in Northern California, near Palo Alto, Santa Clara, and San Jose, is perhaps the best-known hot spot in the world for the computer hardware industry. There are more major computer companies (e.g., Intel, Cisco, Hewlett-Packard) and more new startups of hardware computer companies in Silicon Valley than anywhere else in the world.

However, the wisdom of locating innovation-based companies in geographical hot spots is now being questioned. Critics claim that the disadvantages of locating in hot spots can easily outweigh the advantages. Furthermore, as hot spots "burn out," the advantages that once made them great places to start and grow a business may actually become serious disadvantages.

To gain some experience with the idea of "hot spots," imagine that you started a computer-related business while in college. Now that you've graduated, you have to decide where to formally locate your business. After some initial consideration, you limit your final choices to three locations: Silicon Valley (San Jose, California), the hottest of the technology hot spots; Austin, Texas, an up-and-coming hot spot; and Seattle, Washington, another hot spot on the rise. As you decide where to locate your company, you'll want to consider the following factors: cost of living, cost of office space, availability and cost of employees, access to customers and important business partners or suppliers, etc. Use the Internet resources shown below to research each of these locations. Then answer the questions to explain your reasons for your choice.

Internet Resources

- ***Money*** **Magazine's Best Places to Live (http://pathfinder.com/money/bestplaces/index.html)**. This site's screening tool helps you sort through America's 300 largest metro areas to find the best spot to live, work, or play. Also, check for this year's best places to live. Be sure to enter "San Jose," "Seattle," and "Austin" into the *City Details* search engine to learn more about each of these cities.
- ***Money*** **Magazine's Cost of Living Comparator (http://pathfinder.com/money/besplaces/col/compare.html)**. Use the Cost of Living Comparator to compare San Jose, Seattle, and Austin.
- ***Fortune*** **Magazine's Best Cities for Business (http://cgi.pathfinder.com/fortune/)**. Look for the "Search Fortune" box. Enter "best cities for business," and the search will return several articles for you to read. Read what *Fortune* has to say about these top cities (including Austin and Seattle). The URL **http://www.pathfinder.com/fortune/bestcities/index.html** takes you directly to *Fortune's* top-ten U.S. cities for business.
- **"Rating the Regions: Our experts call it!" (http://www.forbes.com/asap/97/0825/064.htm)**. Also see this *Forbes ASAP* article, in which corporate location experts discuss their views on various high-tech hot spots.

Questions

1. What were the two most important criteria that you used when deciding where to locate your company? Why? What were the two least important criteria you used? Why?
2. Which location did you choose? Explain your choice by writing a brief paragraph about each location—Silicon Valley, Austin, and Seattle—that explains the advantages and disadvantages each offers your business.

Sources: K. Alesandrini, "In Search of Greener Valleys," *Computer Shopper,* 1 December 1997. C.M. Anders, "Santa Clara No Longer Hot—Its Insane Housing Prices Skyrocketing in Silicon Valley," *San Francisco Examiner,* 6 July 1997. J. Burke, *The Day the Universe Changed* (Boston: Little, Brown, and Company, 1985). M. Dickerson, "Phoenix Ascending: Southwest Boomtown Rides Diversified Industries; Arizona's Valley of the Sun Shines in Reinventing Itself as a Hotbed of Startup and Tech Companies," *Austin American-Statesman,* 21 December 1997. R. Pouder & C.H. St. John, "Hot Spots and Blind Spots: Geographical Clusters of Firms and Innovation," *Academy of Management Journal* 21 (1996): 1192-1225. C. Rosen, "The Best Locations: Hot Today, Cold Tomorrow? Industry Executives Weigh the Pros and Cons of Establishing Roots in Different Regions," *Electronic Buyers' News,* 17 February 1997.

Develop Your Management Potential

A Personal Force Field Analysis

In the "What Really Works" section of this chapter, you learned that when people change their behavior in the workplace, there is a 76 percent chance that organizational profits, market share, and productivity can be improved. However, you also learned that organization-wide change efforts have only a 57 percent chance of successfully changing people's work behavior. So changing people's behavior works great. The hard part is figuring out how to get them to change their behavior. This "Develop Your Management Potential" assignment reviews how you can use a personal force field analysis to change your behavior at work.

At the beginning of this chapter, you learned that organizational change is a function of change forces and resistance forces. Change forces lead to differences in the form, quality, or condition of an organization over time. Resistance forces support the status quo, that is, the existing state of conditions in organizations. One of the ways that managers prepare for specific organizational change is to carefully conduct an organizational force field analysis by listing the change and resistance forces that support and oppose that change. For example, Table 10-9 lists the resistance forces and change forces that oppose and support the possibility of changing a company's corporate headquarters from New York City to Dallas.

Listing resistance and change forces is also a useful way to conduct a personal force field analysis. The first step of a personal force field analysis is to clearly describe how or what behavior you intend to change. For example, if you're always late with your expense reports, you might write, "I will turn in my expense reports within three days of returning from a business trip." In Chapter 4, you learned that to be effective, goals need to be S.M.A.R.T.: specific, measurable, attainable, realistic, and timely. Descriptions of the behaviors you intend to change should follow the S.M.A.R.T. guidelines, too.

The second step of a personal force field analysis is to list and describe resistance forces, that is, the reasons that make it difficult for you to change your behavior. Since resistance to change is caused by self-interest, misunderstanding and distrust, and a general intolerance for change, be sure to assess whether these factors are making it difficult for you to change your behavior. For example, are you turning your expense reports in late because turning them in on time will cost or deprive you of something of value (i.e., self-interest)? Probably not, because if you turned the expense reports in on time, you'd get your money back sooner.

Are you turning in your expense reports late because you misunderstand or distrust the reasons for turning in your expense report on time

Table 10-9 **Resistance and Change Forces**

Possible Change: Moving Corporate Headquarters from New York City to Dallas

Resistance Forces	*Change Forces*
• Many employees may not want or be able to move. • Large expense of making the move, buying or building a new headquarters, and selling old headquarters. • Negative publicity from local press generated by just considering the move. • New York City officials may offer incentives to encourage firm to stay.	• Much lower cost of living and no state income tax will make it easier to attract and retain a talented work force. • Lower real estate and energy costs will significantly lower the cost of maintaining corporate headquarters. • Significant customer base has developed in the South, Southwest, and Western regions of the country. • Dallas city officials may offer incentives to encourage firm to move.

or distrust the people who review the expenses? Well, we might be on to something here. Misunderstanding probably isn't the problem. What's to misunderstand about an expense report? You fill it out, turn it in, and get reimbursed. In this case, it's more likely that your resistance stems from distrust of the people who review the reports. Perhaps, in the past, you felt that you weren't fairly reimbursed. If so, why turn in your expense report on time when you don't expect to get back all the money you're owed?

Finally, are you turning in your expense reports late because you have a low tolerance for change? In this case, however, a low tolerance for change probably has more to do with habitual behavior than with any uncertainty associated with the change process.

The final step of a personal force field analysis is to list the change forces, that is, the reasons prompting you to consider changing your behavior. At this step, it can be useful to separate your reasons by category, such as personal or organizational benefits, or personal or organizational consequences (i.e., the negative consequences associated with not changing your behavior). For example, turning in your expense report on time gets you your money faster, a personal benefit; helps the organization stay current with its expenses, an organizational benefit; and helps you avoid getting yelled at by your boss for being late with the expense report, which is a personal negative consequence.

Now use these steps to conduct a personal force field analysis.

Questions

1. Clearly describe how or what behavior you intend to change. Be sure your description is S.M.A.R.T.: specific, measurable, attainable, realistic, and timely.

2. List and describe the resistance forces that make it difficult for you to change this behavior. Do these reasons have anything to do with
   - *Self-interest?* Will the change cost or deprive you of something you value?
   - *Misunderstanding and distrust?* Do you not understand the change or the reasons for it? Do you distrust the people behind the change? In other words, is someone other than yourself pressuring you to make this change?
   - *A general intolerance for change?* Are you simply less capable of handling change than others? Are you worried that you won't be able to learn the new skills and behaviors needed to successfully negotiate this behavior change?

3. List and describe the change forces that are leading you to consider changing your behavior. Separate your reasons into personal or organizational benefits, or personal or organizational consequences (i.e., the negative consequences associated with not changing your behavior).

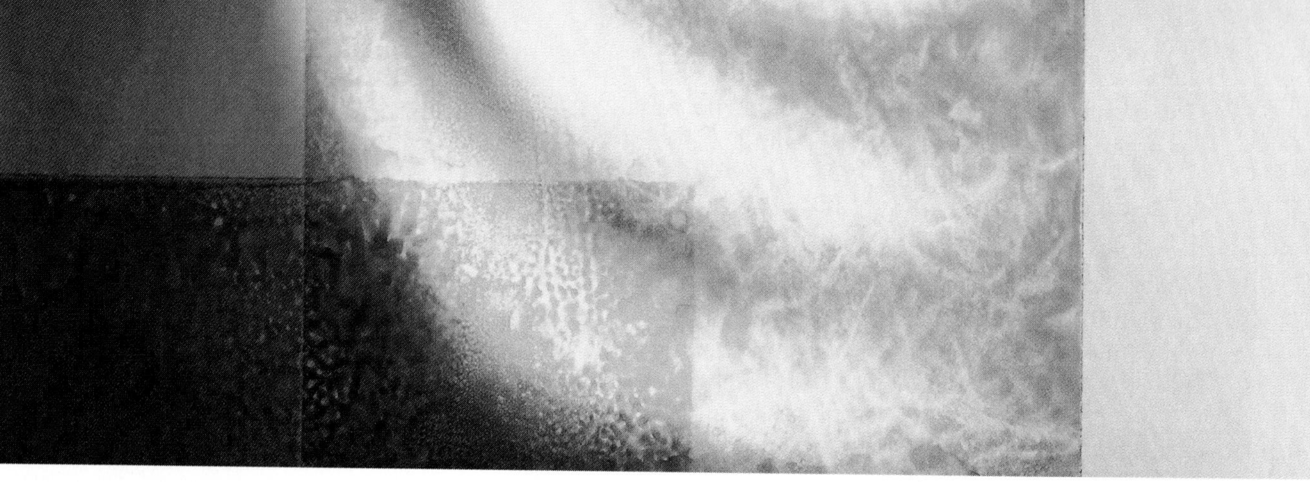

Chapter 11 Outline

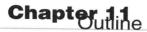

Designing Adaptive Organizations

What Would **You** Do?

American Express Corporation Headquarters, New York, NY. For decades, American Express used the well-known advertising slogan, "The American Express Card: Don't Leave Home Without It." Unfortunately, since the mid-1980s, consumers have been largely ignoring this advice. Instead of leaving home with their American Express cards, consumers have been much more likely to leave home with either a Visa or a MasterCard. American Express, which once had a 26 percent share of the credit and charge card markets, has fallen to a 16.2 percent share, well behind Visa's 48.7 percent market share and MasterCard's 27.3 percent.

Along the way, American Express has made a number of critical mistakes. The worst was not teaming up with American Airlines in 1985 for a joint credit card offering frequent flyer miles. When American Express promptly dismissed the idea, American Airlines issued a joint card with Citibank instead. Today, because every dollar charged to a Citibank/AAadvantage Visa card earns one free air mile on American Airlines (25,000 AAdvantage miles earn a free round-trip ticket to anywhere in the continental U.S.), there are now four million Citibank/AAdvantage cardholders. A large percentage of those customers have canceled or quit using their American Express cards precisely because they *weren't* earning air miles. Five years later, AT&T approached American Express with a similar offer. Again, American Express said no to issuing a joint card. Today, consumers earn discounts on their long-distance phone bills when they make charges on their no-annual-fee AT&T Universal MasterCards. With more than $13 billion a year in total charges, the AT&T Universal MasterCard is now the sixth most frequently used consumer credit card in the U.S. Today, more than a decade after it turned down American Airlines, American Express finally has an air miles program, called "Membership Rewards," that allows customers to earn air miles on more than a dozen different airlines.

In addition to these lost opportunities, American Express has seen its costs rise and has been slow to respond to competitors. Thomas Ryder, president of American Express's International Travel Related Services, said, "We have been slow to launch new products, we operate at a cost disadvantage, and market share is an issue almost everywhere." Cost pressures became so severe that the company recently laid off 3,300 employees, bringing the total number of layoffs to over 15,000 in the last decade. In a letter explaining the layoffs, CEO Harvey Golub stated, "We concluded that TRS' [Travel Related Services] product-oriented processes, as well as its marketing and operational structure, have three important deficiencies: They cost us significantly more than those of our most efficient competitors; we are too slow to change and adapt, particularly in introducing new products; and we are not flexible enough to meet the needs of specific, more targeted customer segments." Furthermore, Golub indicated that American Express's competitors are "not standing still" and that "some of them are introducing new products and services faster and at margins that are superior to ours."

After a decade of poor performance, American Express has decided that it needs to "reengineer" and "restructure" the way it does business if it ever wants to return to the success it once had. Of course, the difficult question is "how?" How should the company be organized? Should it be by function, product, customer, or geography? Second, what changes should be made in who makes what decisions? Should the approach be centralized or highly decentralized? Third, if American Express wants to truly "reengineer" the way it does business, should it focus on reengineering its internal processes, the way it does business internally, or should it reengineer its external processes, the way it does business with other companies?

If you were in charge of the "reengineering" and "restructuring" at American Express, what would you do?

Sources: "Amexco 'reengineers'," *Travel Weekly*, 10 February 1997. D. Brady & S.E. Frank, "American Express Recasts Overseas Part of the Travel Unit," *The Wall Street Journal*, 24 May 1996. L. Fickenscher, "Rivals Spurred American Express Revamping," *American Banker*, 12 October 1994. S.E. Frank, "Credit Cards: Amex Strategy on Cards Way to Growth," *The Wall Street Journal*, 28 April 1997. S.E. Frank, "American Express Posts 15% Net Rise on Card Strengths," *The Wall Street Journal Interactive Edition*, 25 April 1997. S.E. Frank, "American Express Stages Its First Gain in Credit-Card Market Share in Decade," *The Wall Street Journal Interactive Edition*, 24 March 1998. D. Jones, "Amexco Cuts Not Lost on the Industry," *Travel Weekly*, 17 February 1997. S. Oliver, "The Battle of the Credit Cards," *Forbes*, 1 July 1996.

No one builds a house without first looking at the design. Put a window there. Take out a wall here. Soon you've got the design you want. Only then do you start building. These days, the design of a company is just as important as the design of a house. As the American Express case shows, if you don't have the right design, the company's performance can quickly fall apart like a house of cards.

organizational structure the vertical and horizontal configuration of departments, authority, and jobs within a company

This chapter begins by reviewing the traditional organizational structure approach to organizational design. **Organizational structure** is the vertical and horizontal configuration of departments, authority, and jobs within a company. For example, Figure 11.1 shows Microsoft's organizational chart. From this chart, you can see the vertical dimensions of the company—who reports to whom, the number of management levels, who has authority over what, etc. Founder Bill Gates is the CEO. President Steve Ballmer reports directly to him. Four group vice-presidents (one of whom is also an executive vice-president) report directly to Ballmer. In turn, each vice-president oversees a number of divisions. For instance, Pete Higgins, the group vice-president of Interactive Media, is also in charge of the Desktop Finance and Consumer Input Devices (keyboards, mice, etc.) divisions.

The organizational chart also displays Microsoft's horizontal dimensions—who does what jobs, the number of different departments, etc. For instance, in addition to the Interactive Media group, Microsoft has groups in Platform & Applications (where software such as Windows 98, Windows NT, and Microsoft Office is written); Operations (manufacturing, delivery, and corporate functions); and Sales & Support (small and large organizations, schools and universities, and consumers). In the first half of the chapter, you will learn about the traditional vertical and horizontal approaches to organizational structure, including departmentalization, organizational authority, and job design.

organizational process the collection of activities that transforms inputs into outputs that customers value

In the second half of the chapter, you will learn how contemporary organizations are becoming more adaptive by redesigning their internal and external processes. An **organizational process** is the collection of activities that transforms inputs into outputs that customers value.[1] For example, Figure 11.2 shows the basic internal and external processes that Microsoft uses to write computer software. The process starts when Microsoft gets feedback from customers through Internet newsgroups (set your Internet News software to **msnews.microsoft.com**), e-mail, phone calls, or letters. This information helps Microsoft understand customers' needs and problems and identify important software issues and needed changes and functions. Microsoft then rewrites the software, testing it internally at the company and then externally through its beta-testing process. In beta testing, early versions of software are distributed to beta testers (i.e., customers who volunteer or are selected by Microsoft), who give the company extensive feedback, which is then used to make improvements. The beta-testing process may take as long as a year and involve thousands of customers. After "final" corrections are made to the software, the company distributes and sells it to customers, who start the process again by giving Microsoft more feedback.

This process view of Microsoft, which focuses on how things get done, is very different from the hierarchical view of Microsoft (go back to Microsoft's organizational chart in Figure 11.1), which focuses on accountability, responsibility, and position within the chain of command. In the second half of the chapter, you will learn how companies are using reengineering, empowerment, and behavior informality to redesign their internal organiza-

Figure 11.1 **Microsoft Corporation's Organizational Chart**

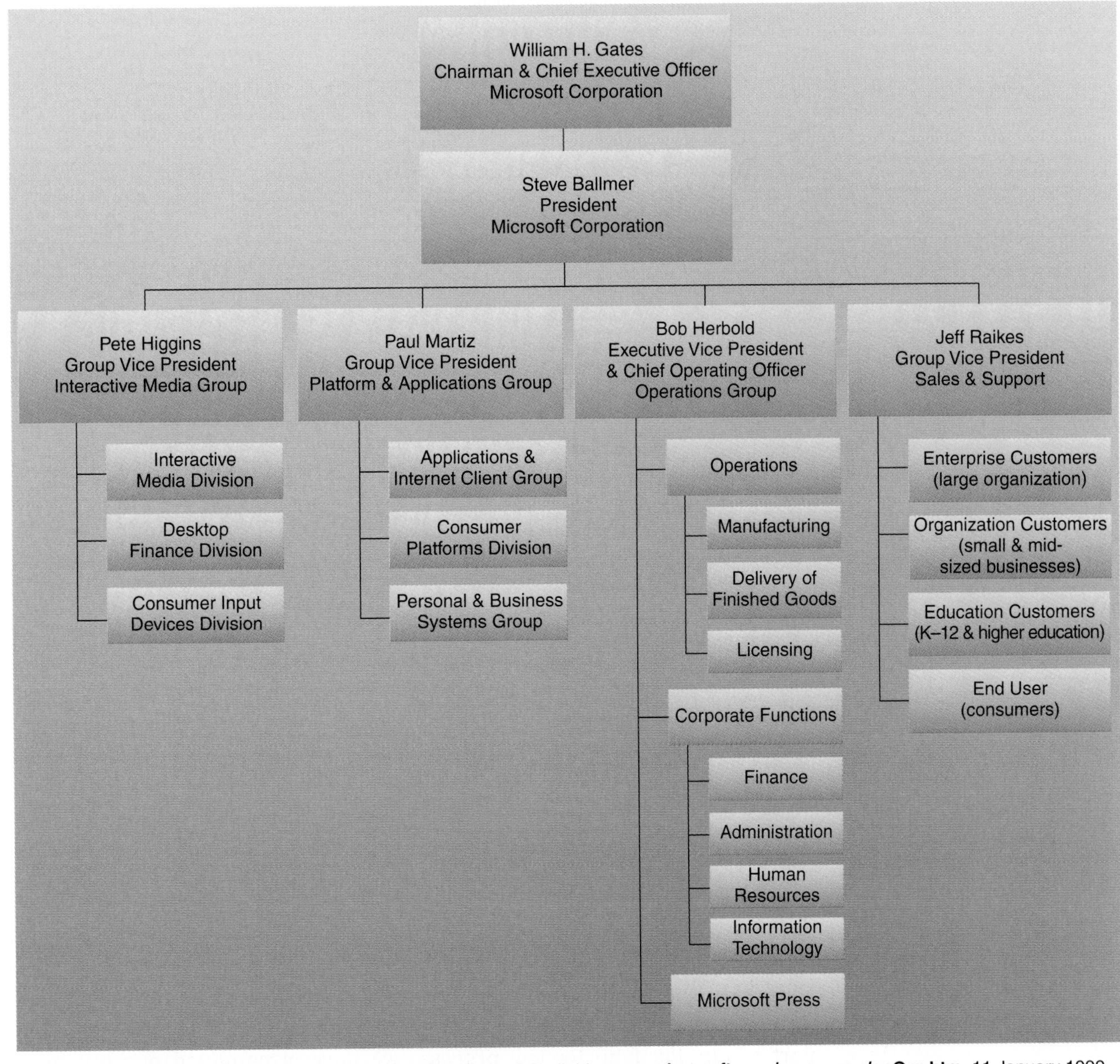

Source: "Organizational Overview," Microsoft Web site. [Online] Available **www.microsoft.com/presspass/cpOrg.htm**, 11 January 1999.

tional processes. The chapter ends with a discussion about the ways in which companies are redesigning their external processes, that is, how they are changing to improve their interactions with those outside the company. In that discussion, you will explore the basics of modular, virtual, and boundaryless organizations.

Designing Organizational Structures

Best known as the maker of Reynolds Wrap (the aluminum foil used to keep leftovers fresh in your fridge), Reynolds Metals is an integrated manufacturer, distributor, and marketer of processed and unprocessed aluminum products. Reynolds, which had been organized geographically, with separate

Figure 11.2 **Process View of Microsoft's Organization**

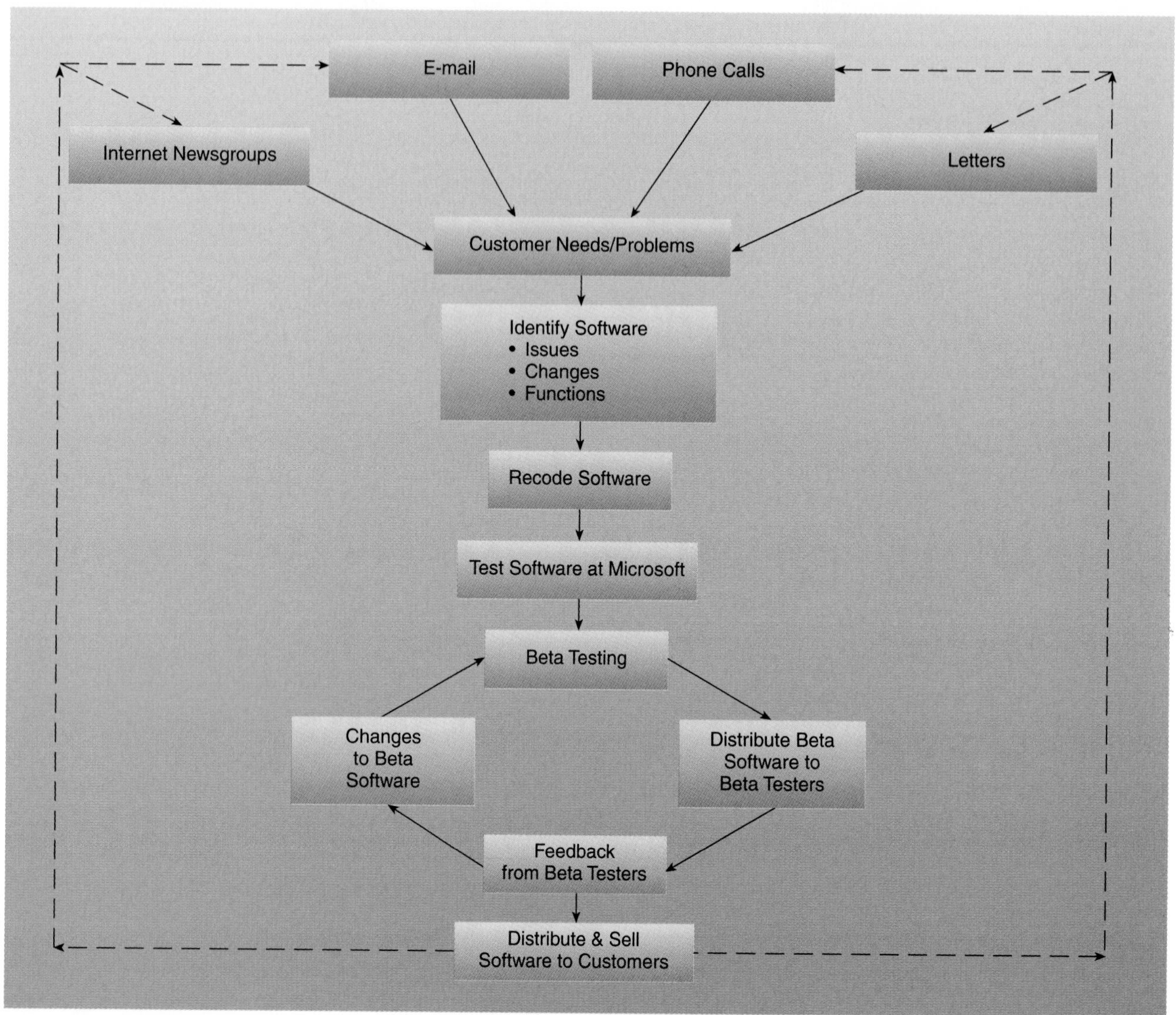

U.S. and regional operations around the world, announced that it was restructuring. Jeremiah Sheehan, Reynolds' chairman and CEO, said that "As part of our Portfolio Review process, we have streamlined our business focus and assessed new organization structures appropriate for managing our businesses in the future. As a result, we are reorganizing the structure of the company into six worldwide, market-focused businesses . . .".[2] So instead of having U.S., Latin American, European, and Far Eastern divisions, Reynolds will now use a product structure, with separate divisions focusing on aluminum cans, building and construction, consumer products, infrastructure, packaging, and transportation.

Why would a large company like Reynolds, with 29,000 employees and $7 billion in annual revenues, completely restructure its global organizational design? What does it expect to gain as a result of this massive change? After reading these next three sections, you'll have a better understanding of the importance of organizational structure, because you should be able to:

1 describe the **departmentalization** approach to organizational structure.

2 explain **organizational authority**.

3 discuss the different methods for **job design**.

1 Departmentalization

departmentalization subdividing work and workers into separate organizational units responsible for completing particular tasks

Traditionally, organizational structures have been based on some form of departmentalization. **Departmentalization** is a method of subdividing work and workers into separate organizational units that take responsibility for completing particular tasks.[3] For example, the Sony Corporation has separate departments or divisions for electronics, music, movies, television, games, and theaters. Likewise, Bayer, a German-based company, has separate departments or divisions for healthcare, agriculture, polymers, chemicals, and photography.

Traditionally, organizational structures have been created by departmentalizing work according to five methods: **1.1** *functional,* **1.2** *product,* **1.3** *customer,* **1.4** *geographic, and* **1.5** *matrix.*

1.1 *Functional Departmentalization*

functional departmentalization organizing work and workers into separate units responsible for particular business functions or areas of expertise

The most common organizational structure is functional departmentalization. Companies tend to use this structure when they are small or just starting out. **Functional departmentalization** organizes work and workers into separate units responsible for particular business functions or areas of expertise. For example, a common set of functions would consist of accounting, sales, marketing, production, and human resources departments.

However, not all functionally departmentalized companies have the same functions. For example, Figure 11.3 shows functional structures for an insurance company and an advertising agency. The light-colored boxes indicate that both companies have sales, accounting, human resources, and information systems departments. The darker boxes are different for each company. As would be expected, the insurance company has separate departments for life, auto, home, and health insurance. By contrast, the advertising agency has departments for artwork, creative work, print advertising, and radio advertising. So the kind of functional departments in a functional structure depends, in part, on the business or industry a company is in.

Functional departmentalization has some advantages. First, it allows work to be done by highly qualified specialists. While the accountants in the accounting department take responsibility for producing accurate revenue and expense figures, the engineers in research and development can focus their efforts on designing a product that is reliable and simple to manufacture. Second, it lowers costs by reducing duplication. When the engineers in research and development come up with that fantastic new product, they don't have to worry about creating an aggressive advertising campaign to sell it. That task belongs to the advertising experts and sales representatives in marketing. Third, with everyone in the same department having similar work experience or training, communication and coordination are less problematic for departmental managers.

Figure 11.3 **Functional Departmentalization**

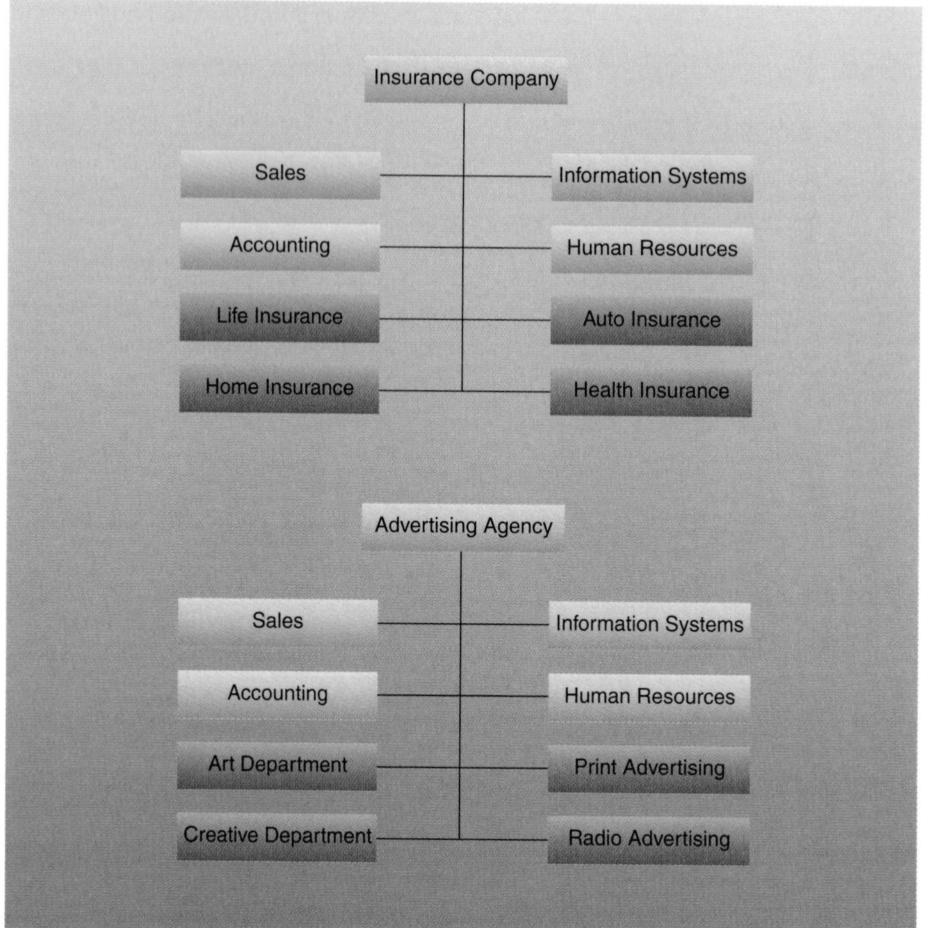

However, functional departmentalization has a number of disadvantages, too. To start, cross-department coordination can be difficult. Managers and employees are often more interested in doing what's right for their function than in doing what's right for the entire organization. A good example is the traditional conflict between marketing and manufacturing. Marketing typically pushes for spending more money to make more products with more accessories and capabilities to meet customer needs. By contrast, manufacturing pushes for fewer products with simpler designs, so that manufacturing facilities can ship finished products on time and keep costs within expense budgets. As companies grow, functional departmentalization may also lead to slower decision making and produce managers and workers with narrow experience and expertise.

product departmentalization organizing work and workers into separate units responsible for producing particular products or services

1.2 *Product Departmentalization*

Product departmentalization organizes work and workers into separate units responsible for producing particular products or services. Figure 11.4 shows the product departmentalization structure used by the General Electric Corporation. GE is organized along 12 different product lines: aircraft

Figure 11.4 **Product Departmentalization: General Electric Corporation**

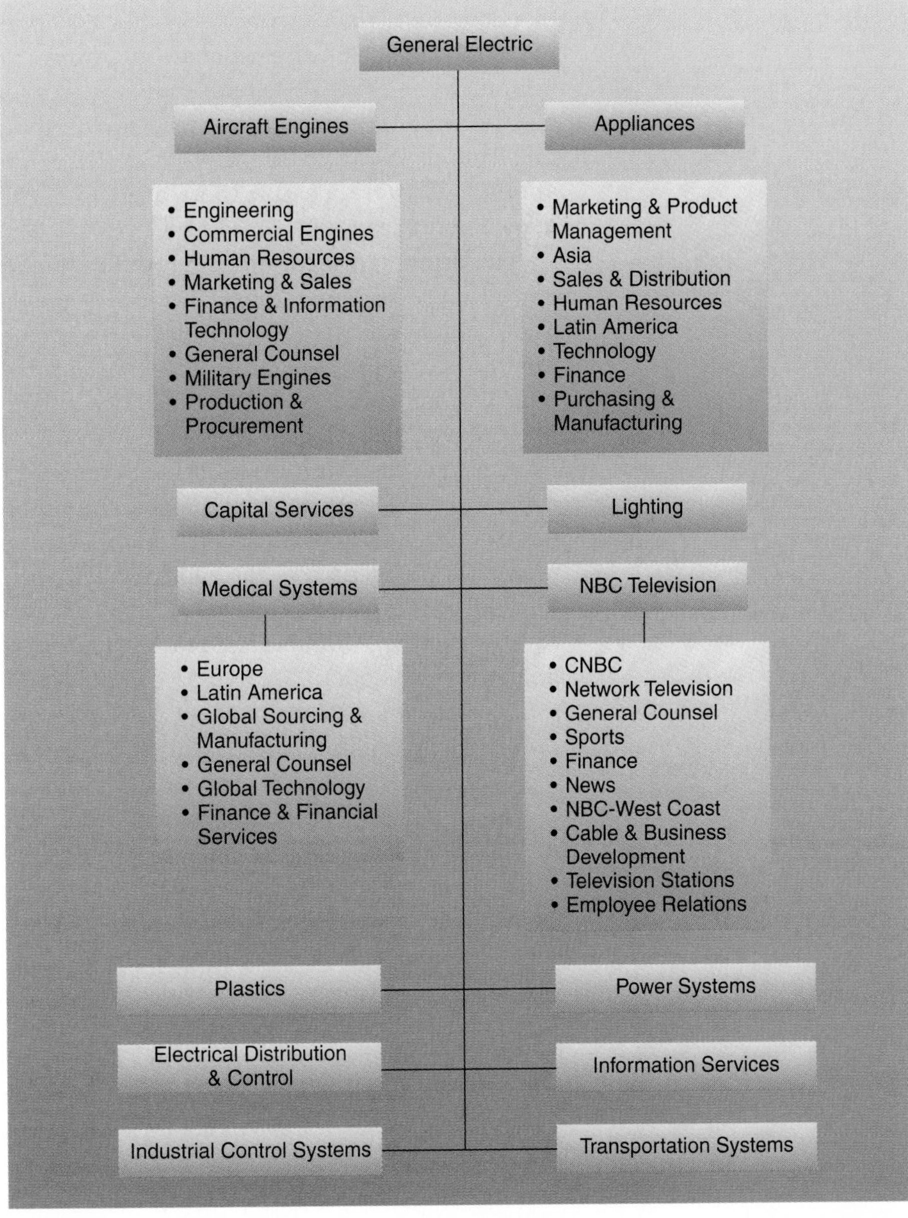

Source: "Operating Management," GE Web site. [Online] Available **www.ge.com/annual97/opmanage/index.htm**, 11 January 1999.

engines, appliances, capital services, lighting, medical systems, NBC television, plastics, power systems, electrical distribution & control, information services, industrial control systems, and transportation systems.

One of the advantages of product departmentalization is that, like functional departmentalization, it allows managers and workers to specialize in one area of expertise. However, unlike the narrow expertise and experiences in functional departmentalization, managers and workers develop a broader set of experiences and expertise related to an entire product line. Likewise, product departmentalization makes it easier for top managers to assess work-unit performance. For example, because of their clear separation, it is a relatively straightforward process for GE's top managers to evaluate the performance of their 12 different product divisions. For instance, GE's Aircraft Engines product division outperformed GE's Power Systems product division. Both had similar revenues, $7.8 billion for Aircraft Engines and $7.5 billion for Power Systems, but Aircraft Engines had a profit of $1.05 billion, while Power Systems had a profit of just $758 million.[4] Finally, because managers and workers are responsible for the entire product line rather than for separate functional departments, decision making should be faster, because there are fewer conflicts (compared to functional departmentalization).

The primary disadvantage of product departmentalization is duplication. For example, you can see in Figure 11.4 that the Aircraft Engines and Appliances divisions both have Human Resources, Finance, and Sales departments. Likewise, the Medical Systems and NBC Television divisions both have Finance and General Counsel departments. Duplication like this often results in higher costs.

A second disadvantage is that it can be difficult to achieve coordination across the different product departments. For example, GE would probably have difficulty standardizing its policies and procedures in product departments as different as the Lighting (light bulbs and lighting products for homes, offices, and factories) and Capital Services (corporate debt and equity financing, commercial real estate, insurance, and personal credit and financing) divisions.

1.3 *Customer Departmentalization*

customer departmentalization organizing work and workers into separate units responsible for particular kinds of customers

Customer departmentalization organizes work and workers into separate units responsible for particular kinds of customers. For example, Figure 11.5 shows that American Express is organized into departments that cater to consumers (Cards: credit and charge cards), travelers (Travel: travelers' checks, airline tickets, vacations, and worldwide travel offices), investors (Financial Services: advisors, mutual and money market funds, etc.), shoppers (Shopping: catalog, gift, and online shopping), and businesspeople (Business Services: business travel, corporate cards, and financing, accounting, planning, and lending for small businesses).

The primary advantage to customer departmentalization is that it focuses the organization on customer needs rather than on products or business functions. Furthermore, creating separate departments to serve specific kinds of customers allows companies to specialize and adapt their products and services to customer needs and problems.

The primary disadvantage of customer departmentalization is that, like product departmentalization, it leads to duplication of resources. Furthermore, like product departmentalization, it can be difficult to achieve coordination across different customer departments. Finally, the emphasis on meeting customers' needs may lead workers to make decisions that please customers but hurt the business.

Figure 11.5 **Customer Departmentalization: American Express Corporation**

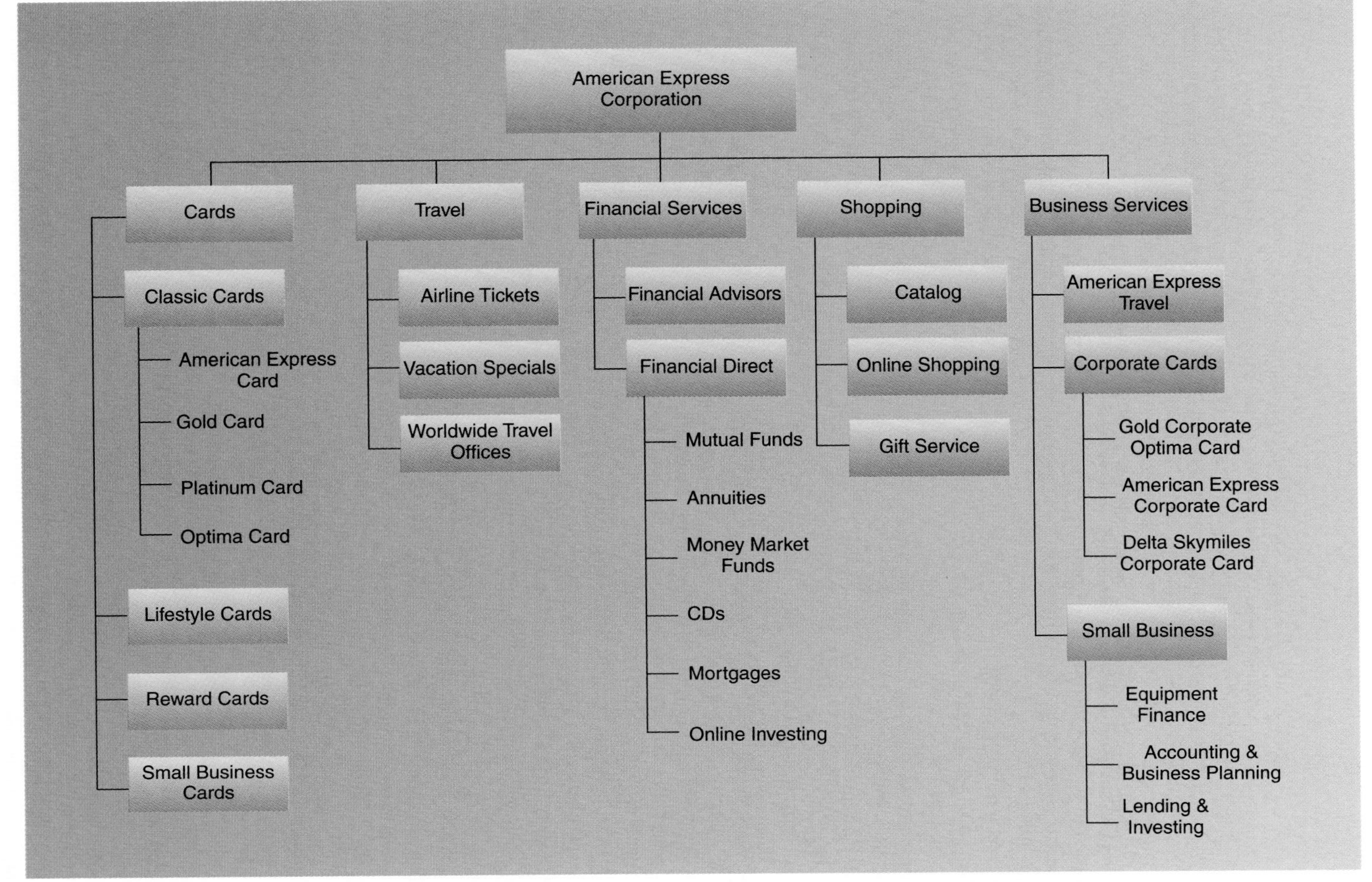

Source: "About American Express," American Express Web site. [Online] Available **www.americanexpress.com/corp/?aexp_nav=hp_corp**, 11 January 1999.

Been There,

igus and the Solar System

*Frank Blasé is CEO of the igus corporation (**www.igus.de/index.html** and **www.igus.com**) in Cologne, Germany. igus designs, manufactures, and sells products (bearings, chainflex cables, and energy chain systems) that carry and protect cables and hoses on machines. igus products are used on items ranging from factory machines to robots to 10-story cranes to medical lab equipment to network television cameras at sporting events. Frank discussed the unique organizational design used at igus.*

Q: After getting your MBA, you worked for a large, Fortune 500 firm. Then, out of frustration with the company, you quit to return to Germany to help your father run igus. How did it go at first?

A: (He laughs.) The first three years were totally unexpected. Nothing I did worked. Nobody bought products. We tried to establish a presence abroad with a U.S. business partner. Unfortunately, after spending lots of money on advertising, the partnership only lasted three weeks. In all, the first three years were humbling and frustrating.

"... with this solar system structure, we get our orders and direction from customers."

Q: What did you do? How did you fix things?

A: The key was customers. We knew we needed to get our customers more involved with igus. And, in turn, we needed to find a way to get our employees to pay more attention to customers, to be glad to take a $5 order, or to hear customer complaints. In short, when we did things right, there was an energy, almost a light, you might say, that came directly from customers.

Q: O.K. So how did you create a focus on customers?

A: By creating an organization structure based on the solar system. The planets in a solar system rotate around the sun. Well, in igus' solar system, the sun was the customer and the planets were teams of igus workers (from tooling, injection molding, product assembly, and accounting). Since the sun gives off energy and all things need energy to survive, the basic idea of this solar system structure was to make sure that everyone in igus had regular, consistent exposure to customers. It's just like a planet's orbit. Of course, some employee teams such as in-house services, maintenance and repairs, and factory planning may have less interaction (i.e., longer orbits), while others like sales people may have more frequent interaction (i.e., shorter orbits). And, unlike hierarchical organizations in which everyone gets their orders from top management, here at igus with this solar system structure, we get our orders and direction from customers.

Q: I noticed that you even have a large solar system chiseled into the building near the front entrance.

A: That's by design. British architect Nicholas Grimshaw, who is known for his high-tech designs, used the ideas behind this solar system structure when planning the building. For example, there is total transparency through the entire building. The offices are not separated from the factory. Likewise, thanks to glass walls, you can see from the factory into the offices (and vice versa), as well as from one end of the factory to another.

Q: That's really different. In most companies, it's rare for office workers and factory workers to see each other, or much less interact with each other.

A: Well, we wanted to make sure that everyone was treated the same. Every office, including mine, has the same industrial furniture kit. The same wooden table that I use as my desk is the same kind of wooden table that is used to pack boxes for shipping products. The chairs, whether they're in the offices or out in the factory, are all alike. Furthermore, we all have the same social areas. The cafeteria, which provides free food for all, opens as early as 5:30 a.m. to encourage everyone to interact from the beginning of the day to the end of the day. Finally, there's just one bathroom area that is used by both office and factory workers. Surprisingly, it's a place you run into people that you might not otherwise see. Having one bathroom area (though it's not unisex) actually leads to better communication.

Q: Is there anything else you do at igus to reinforce this egalitarian culture and the importance of customers?

A: First, we send out a weekly newsletter. I write this every Saturday and then e-mail it to everyone in the company. This newsletter covers what's new, the trade shows igus will be going to, the percentage increases and decreases in sales and market share, etc. Though both good and bad news can be found in the newsletter, we do try to stress the positive. Even when we make a mistake, it can still be presented as "see what we learned." Second, all serious job applicants must spend an unpaid day with the company before they are hired. Because we're different, we want them to know us and us to know them before making a job offer. This alone tends to screen out most applicants. Only 10–15 percent agree to do this. We make sure that applicants talk to the employees, that they learn about our culture, and that they learn about vacations, overtime, and other official things like that. We're bluntly honest because we don't want people to have false hopes. We want them to know what they're getting into. Finally, at the end of the day, there's a team appraisal. If the team with which an applicant will be working doesn't like the job candidate, they don't get hired. So not only are our teams highly involved with customers, we also make sure that they play a critical role in deciding who gets hired.

Done That

1.4
Geographic Departmentalization

geographic departmentalization organizing work and workers into separate units responsible for doing business in particular geographical areas

Geographic departmentalization organizes work and workers into separate units responsible for doing business in particular geographical areas. For example, Figure 11.6 shows the geographic departmentalization used by Coca-Cola Enterprises (CCE), the largest bottler and distributor of Coca-Cola products in the world. (The Coca-Cola Company develops and advertises soft drinks. CCE, which is a separate company with its own stock, buys the soft drink concentrate from the Coca-Cola Company, combines it with other ingredients, and then distributes the final product in cans, bottles, or fountain containers.) As shown in Figure 11.6, CCE has four regional groups: Central North America, Eastern North America, Western North America, and Europe. The table below Figure 11.6 shows that each of these four regions would be a sizable company by itself. For example, the European group serves a population of 137 million people in Belgium, France, Great Britain, and the Netherlands, sells more than 825 million cases of soft drinks a year, employs more than 7,907 people, and runs 28 bottling facilities.

The primary advantage of geographic departmentalization is that it helps companies respond to the demands of different markets. This can be especially important when selling in different countries. For example, CCE's geographic divisions sell products suited to the taste preferences in different countries. CCE bottles and distributes the following products in Europe but not in the U.S.: Aquarius, Bonaqua, Buxton Mineral Water, Coca-Cola light, Cresta flavors, Finley, Kia-Ora, Kinley, Lilt, Oasis, and Roses. Another advantage is that geographic departmentalization can reduce costs by locating unique organizational resources closer to customers. For instance, it is much cheaper for CCE to build bottling plants in Belgium than to bottle Coke in England and then transport it across the English Channel.

matrix departmentalization a hybrid organizational structure in which two or more forms of departmentalization, most often product and functional, are used together

The primary disadvantage of geographic departmentalization is that it can lead to duplication of resources. For example, while it may be necessary to adapt products and marketing to different geographic locations, it's doubtful that CCE needs significantly different inventory tracking systems from location to location. Also, even more so than with the other forms of departmentalization, it can be especially difficult to coordinate departments that are literally thousands of miles from each other and whose managers have very limited contact with each other.

1.5
Matrix Departmentalization

Matrix departmentalization is a hybrid structure in which two or more forms of departmentalization are used together. The most common matrix combines product and functional forms of departmentalization. Figure 11.7

 Geographic Departmentalization: Coca-Cola Enterprises

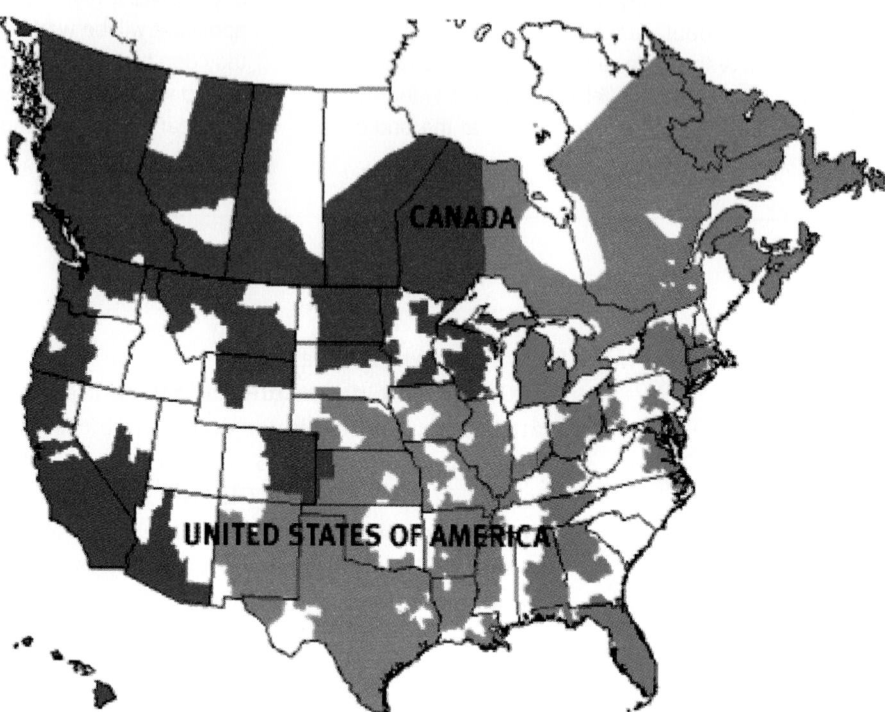

	Central North America Group	Eastern North America Group	European Group	Western North America Group	Total
Population	57 Million	83 Million	137 Million	61 Million	338 Million
Unit Cases	810 Million	1,025 Million	825 Million	710 Million	3.4 Billion
Employees	14,349	21,477	7,907	12,100	55,833
Facilities	121	128	28	118	395

Source: "Territories," Coca-Cola Enterprises Web site. [Online] Available **www.cokecce.com/territories.html,** 14 April 1999.

shows the matrix structure used by Pharmacia & Upjohn, a pharmaceutical company. Across the top of Figure 11.7, you can see that the company uses a functional structure (research, development, manufacturing, and marketing) within each of its three largest geographic markets, the U.S., Europe, and Japan. However, down the left side of the figure, notice that the company is using a product structure to research and develop drugs for the central nervous system, infectious diseases, metabolic and inflammatory diseases, as well as thrombosis, women's health, ophthalmology, critical care, urology, and oncology.

The boxes in the figure represent the matrix structure, created by the combination of the functional/geographic and product structures. For example, in Europe, the Metabolic Diseases group has four functional departments: Research, Development, Manufacturing, and Marketing. In the U.S., the Oncology group has the same set of functional departments.

Several things distinguish matrix departmentalization from the other traditional forms of departmentalization.[5] First, most employees report to two bosses, a functional boss and a project or product boss. For example, in Figure 11.7, a research employee in the European Metabolic Diseases group would have a boss from the European Research department and a boss from the European Metabolic Diseases product group. Second, by virtue of the function-by-project design, matrix structures lead to much more cross-functional interaction than other forms of departmentalization. In fact, while

Figure 11.7 **Matrix Departmentalization: Pharmacia & Upjohn**

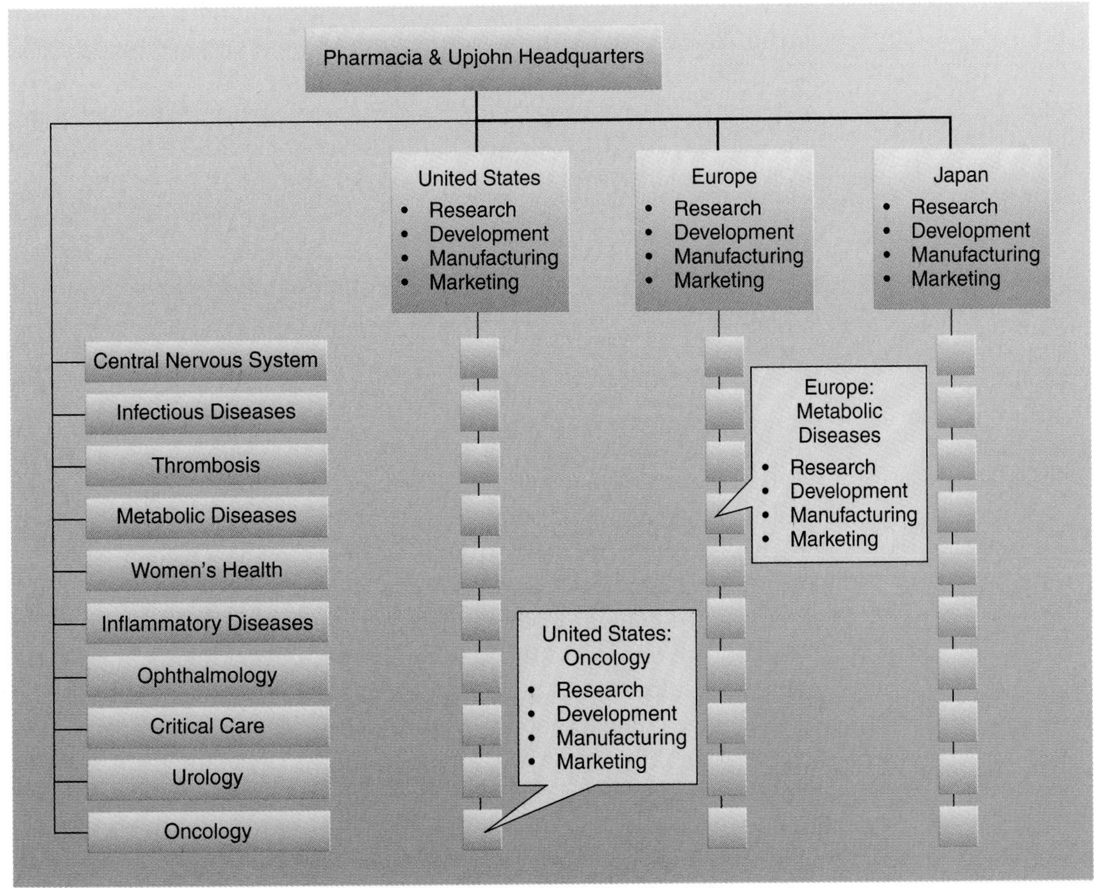

Source: "Financial Reports," *Pharmacia & Upjohn Annual Report.* [Online] Available **www.upjohn.com/business/financial.asp**, 11 January 1999.

matrix workers are members of only one functional department (based on their work experience and expertise), it is common for them to be members of several ongoing project groups. Third, because of the high level of cross-functional interaction, matrix departmentalization requires significant coordination between functional and project managers. In particular, these managers have the complex job of tracking and managing the multiple project and functional demands on employees' time.

The primary advantage of matrix departmentalization is that it allows companies to efficiently manage large, complex tasks like researching, developing, and marketing pharmaceuticals. Efficiency comes from avoiding duplication. For example, rather than having an entire marketing function for each project, the company simply assigns and reassigns workers from the marketing department as they are needed at various stages of product completion. More specifically, an employee from a department may simultaneously be part of five different ongoing projects, but may only be actively completing work on a few projects at a time.

Another advantage is the ability to carry out large, complex tasks. Because of the ability to quickly pull in expert help from all the functional areas of the company, matrix project managers have a much more diverse set of expertise and experience at their disposal than do managers in the other forms of departmentalization.

The primary disadvantage of matrix departmentalization is the high level of coordination required to manage the complexity involved with running large, ongoing projects at various levels of completion. Matrix structures are notorious for confusion and conflict between project bosses, or between project and functional bosses. Disagreements or misunderstandings about project schedules, budgets, available resources, and the availability of employees with particular functional expertise are common. Another disadvantage is that matrix structures require much more management skill than the other forms of departmentalization.

simple matrix
a form of matrix departmentalization in which project and functional managers negotiate conflicts and resources

complex matrix
a form of matrix departmentalization in which project and functional managers report to matrix managers, who help them sort out conflicts and problems

Because of these problems, many matrix structures evolve from the **simple matrix**, in which project and functional managers negotiate conflicts and resources, to the **complex matrix**, in which specialized matrix managers and departments are added to the organizational structure. In the complex matrix, project and functional managers report to the same matrix manager, who helps them sort out conflicts and problems.

Review 1: *Departmentalization*

There are five traditional departmental structures: functional, product, customer, geographic, and matrix. Functional departmentalization is based on the different business functions or expertise used to run a business. Product departmentalization is organized according to the different products or services a company sells. Customer departmentalization focuses its divisions on the different kinds of customers that companies have. Geographic departmentalization is based on the different geographical areas or markets in which the company does business. Matrix departmentalization is a hybrid form that combines two or more forms of departmentalization, the most common being the product and functional forms. There is no "best" departmental structure. Each structure has advantages and disadvantages.

2 Organizational Authority

authority
the right to give commands, take action, and make decisions to achieve organizational objectives

The second part of traditional organizational structures is authority. **Authority** is the right to give commands, take action, and make decisions to achieve organizational objectives.[6]

Traditionally, organizational authority has been characterized by the following dimensions: **2.1** *chain of command,* **2.2** *line versus staff authority,* **2.3** *delegation of authority, and* **2.4** *degree of centralization.*

2.1 *Chain of Command*

chain of command
the vertical line of authority that clarifies who reports to whom throughout the organization

unity of command
a management principle that workers should report to just one boss

Turn back a few pages to Microsoft's organizational chart in Figure 11.1. If you place your finger on any position in the chart, say, the Director of Human Resources (under Corporate Functions in the Operations Group), you can trace a line upward to the company CEO, Bill Gates. This line, which vertically connects every job in the company to higher levels of management, represents the chain of command. The **chain of command** is the vertical line of authority that clarifies who reports to whom throughout the organization. People higher in the chain of command have the right, *if they so choose,* to give commands, take action, and make decisions concerning activities occurring anywhere below them in the chain. In the following discussion about delegation and decentralization, you will learn that managers don't always choose to exercise their authority directly.[7]

One of the key assumptions underlying the chain of command is **unity of command**, which means that workers should report to just one boss.[8] In practical terms, this means that only one person can be in charge at a time. Matrix organizations, in which employees have two bosses, automatically violate this principle. This is one of the primary reasons that matrix organizations are difficult to manage. The purpose of unity of command is to prevent the confusion that might arise when an employee receives conflicting commands from two different bosses. For example, someone walks into an emergency room, describing symptoms similar to a heart attack. The first person in charge, most likely a nurse, makes the initial assessment, assigns the patient to a treatment room, and gets the necessary doctors, nurses, and equipment to begin evaluation and treatment. Then the emergency room physician, who is higher than the nurse in the chain of command, takes charge and begins the process of determining whether the patient is really having a heart attack by conducting an examination, ordering tests, and taking the patient's medical history. If the physician calls in a cardiologist for consultation, the cardiologist becomes the person in charge, and makes the final treatment decision. Despite the number of people involved in the process, it's clear who is in charge at each point, because the emergency room follows the principle of unity of command.

2.2 *Line Versus Staff Authority*

line authority
the right to command immediate subordinates in the chain of command

A second dimension of authority is the distinction between line and staff authority. **Line authority** is the right to command immediate subordinates in the chain of command. For example, in the Microsoft organizational chart in Figure 11.1, Pete Higgins has line authority over the manager of the Interactive Media Division. Higgins can issue orders to that division manager and expect them to be carried out.

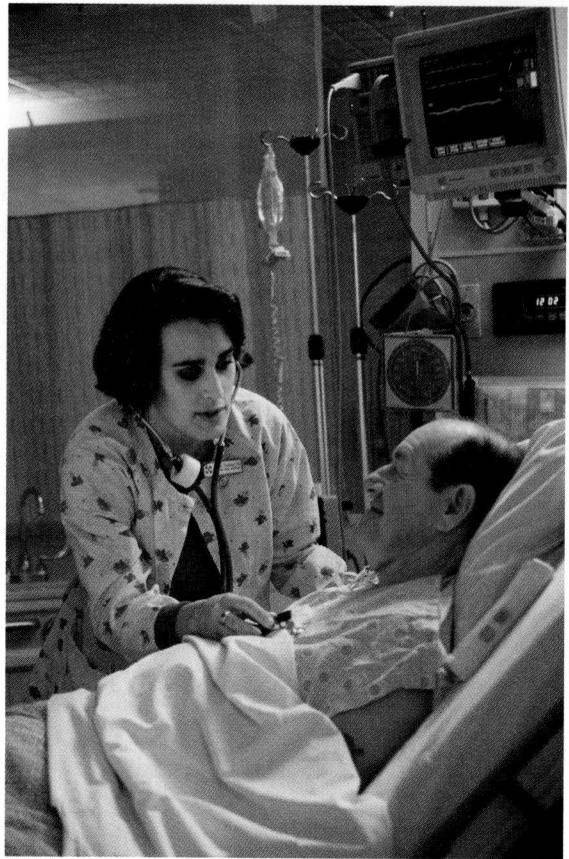

The emergency room follows unity of command, so everyone knows who is in charge at any given time.
© Corbis/Warren Morgan

staff authority
the right to advise but not command others who are not subordinates in the chain of command

Staff authority is the right to advise but not command others who are not subordinates in the chain of command. For example, at Microsoft, a manager in Human Resources might advise Higgins in making a hiring decision but cannot order him to hire a certain applicant.

line function
an activity that contributes directly to creating or selling the company's products

staff function
an activity that does not contribute directly to creating or selling the company's products, but instead supports line activities

The terms "line" and "staff" are also used to describe different functions within the organization. A **line function** is an activity that contributes directly to creating or selling the company's products. So, for example, activities that take place within the manufacturing and marketing departments would be considered line functions. A **staff function** is one that does not contribute directly to creating or selling the company's products, but instead supports line activities. Typical staff functions within an organization are accounting, human resources, and legal services. For example, marketing managers might consult with the legal staff to make sure the wording of a particular advertisement is legal.

2.3
Delegation of Authority

delegation of authority
the assignment of direct authority and responsibility to a subordinate to complete tasks for which the manager is normally responsible

Managers can exercise their authority directly by completing the tasks themselves, or they can choose to pass on some of their authority to subordinates. **Delegation of authority** is the assignment of direct authority and responsibility to a subordinate to complete tasks for which the manager is normally responsible.

When a manager delegates work, three transfers occur, as illustrated in Figure 11.8. First, the manager transfers full responsibility for the assign-

Figure 11.8 Delegation: Responsibility, Authority, and Accountability

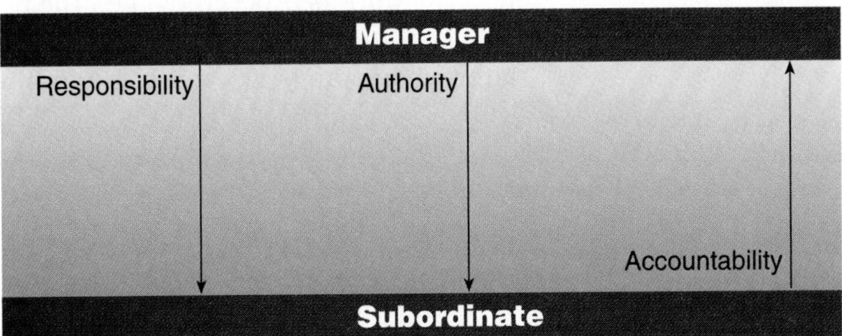

Source: C.D. Pringle, D.F. Jennings, and J.G. Longenecker, *Managing Organizations: Functions and Behaviors* (Columbus, OH: Merrill Publishing, 1988), 210.

ment to the subordinate. Many managers find giving up full responsibility somewhat difficult. For example, Joseph Liemandt, CEO of Trilogy Development Group, said, "You always hate to delegate something that you like to do, but you have no choice if the company is going to grow."[9] Indeed, most managers have way too much to do. So, from a practical perspective, they can't assume new responsibilities that come with change and growth until they fully delegate old ones.

Another problem is that managers often fear that the task won't be done as well if they don't do it themselves. However, CEO Liemandt said, "If you can delegate a task to somebody who can do it 75 percent to 80 percent as well as you can today, you delegate it immediately." Why? Because many tasks needn't be done perfectly; they just need to be done. And delegating tasks that someone can already do frees managers to assume other important responsibilities.

Sometimes managers delegate "full responsibility" only to later interfere with how the employee is performing the task. "Why are you doing it that way? That's not the way I do it." In short, delegating full responsibility means that the employee—not the manager—is now completely responsible for task completion.

Second, delegation transfers to the subordinate full authority over the budget, resources, and personnel needed to do the job. To do the job effectively, subordinates must have the same tools and information at their disposal that managers had when they were responsible for the same task. In other words, for delegation to work, delegated authority must be commensurate with delegated responsibility. For example, Tom Stendahl, the CEO of Schwinn Cycling & Fitness, said, "[We] purchased Schwinn out of bankruptcy four years ago. We didn't have the luxury of time to set up sophisticated administrative and reporting structures. What we did is split the business into pieces such as bikes, parts/accessories and fitness. Then we hired the best people we could find and said: 'Here it is guys, go out and reshape the world. You have total freedom.'"[10]

The third transfer that occurs with delegation is the transfer of accountability. The subordinate now has the authority and responsibility to do the job, and is then accountable for getting the job done. In other words, managers give subordinates their managerial authority and responsibility

in exchange for results. *Forbes* magazine columnist John Rutledge called delegation "MBB," Managing by Belly Button. He said, "The belly button is the person whose belly you point your finger at when you want to know how the work is proceeding, i.e., the person who will actually be accountable for each step..." "The belly button is not a scapegoat—a person to blame later when things go wrong. He or she is the person who makes sure that things go right."[11] Table 11.1 gives some tips on how to be an effective delegator.

2.4
Degree of Centralization

Companies A and B both sell computers directly to the public via the Internet and free 1-800 sales lines. At Company A, when a customer calls to complain that the computer monitor doesn't work, the customer service representative is not authorized to handle the situation. He must forward the call to his manager, who handles the situation herself. In such instances, the average customer waits on hold an additional 10–20 minutes, because the manager of the customer service department is dealing with other customers' problems, too. By contrast, when the same thing happens at Company B, the customer representative walks the customer through an installation checklist to determine if the monitor is set up correctly. Then, convinced that the monitor is indeed broken, the customer representative immediately instructs the company ordering system to ship a new monitor, overnight, at no cost to the customer. Furthermore, she immediately faxes or e-mails packing instructions and account authorization numbers to the

Table 11.1

How to Be a More Effective Delegator

1. Trust your staff to do a good job. Recognize that others have the talent and ability to complete projects.
2. Avoid seeking perfection. Establish a standard of quality and provide a time frame for reaching it.
3. Give effective job instructions. Make sure employees have enough information to complete the job successfully.
4. Know your true interests. Delegation is difficult for some people who actually prefer doing the work themselves rather than managing it.
5. Follow up on progress. Build in checkpoints to help identify potential problems.
6. Praise the efforts of your staff.
7. Don't wait to the last minute to delegate. Avoid crisis management by routinely delegating work.
8. Ask questions, expect answers, and assist employees to help them complete the work assignments as expected.
9. Provide the resources you would expect if you were doing an assignment yourself.
10. Delegate to the lowest possible level to make the best possible use of organizational resources, energy, and knowledge.

Source: S.B. Wilson, "Are You an Effective Delegator?" *Female Executive,* 1 November 1994, 19.

customer, so that the broken monitor can be picked up, again, at no expense to the customer, when UPS delivers the new one the next morning. Total elapsed time to handle the problem: less than 10 minutes.

The primary difference between Companies A and B is the location of authority in the organization. Company A, where the customer representative must "kick" the customer problem "upstairs" to management, is an example of centralization. **Centralization of authority** is the location of most authority at the upper levels of the organization. In a centralized organization, managers make most decisions, even the relatively small ones. By contrast, the approach used in Company B, where the customer representative handled the entire problem without any input or consultation from company management, is an example of decentralization. **Decentralization** is the location of a significant amount of authority in the lower levels of the organization. An organization is decentralized if it has a high degree of delegation at all levels. In a decentralized organization, workers closest to problems are authorized to make the decisions necessary to solve the problems on their own.

centralization of authority the location of most authority at the upper levels of the organization

decentralization the location of a significant amount of authority in the lower levels of the organization

Decentralization has a number of advantages. It develops employee capabilities throughout the company and leads to faster decision making and more satisfied customers and employees. Furthermore, a study of 1,000 large companies found that companies with a high degree of decentralization outperformed those with a low degree of decentralization in terms of return on assets (6.9 percent versus 4.7 percent), return on investment (14.6 percent versus 9 percent), return on equity (22.8 percent versus 16.6 percent), and return on sales (10.3 percent versus 6.3 percent). Ironically, however, the same study found that few large companies are actually decentralized. Specifically, only 31 percent of employees in these 1,000 companies were responsible for recommending improvements to management. Overall, just 10 percent of employees received the training and information needed to support a truly decentralized approach to management.[12]

With results like these, the key question is no longer whether companies should decentralize, but where they should decentralize. One rule of thumb is to stay centralized where standardization is important and to decentralize where standardization is unimportant. **Standardization** is solving problems by consistently applying the same rules, procedures, and processes. For example, at Verifone, a company that ensures the secure transfer of electronic funds (from bank to bank, or from customer to company, via the Internet), management decided that decisions about the computer network and e-mail systems should be centralized. Why? Because a standard system used by everyone in the company would ensure that all employees could exchange e-mail and computer documents without difficulty. By contrast, Verifone management took a decentralized approach to the administration of the company compensation plan. As long as they meet their performance goals, Verifone's organizational units are free to make whatever changes they want in their workers' compensation packages without asking headquarters for approval.[13]

standardization solving problems by consistently applying the same rules, procedures, and processes

Review 2: *Organizational Authority*

Organizational authority is determined by the chain of command, line versus staff authority, delegation, and the degree of centralization in a company. The chain of command vertically connects every job in the company to higher levels of management and makes clear who reports to whom. Managers have line authority to command employees below them in the chain of command, but have only staff or advisory authority over employees not below them in the chain of command. Managers delegate authority by transferring to subordinates the authority and responsibility needed to do a task, and, in exchange, subordinates become accountable for task completion. In centralized companies, most authority to make decisions lies with managers in the upper levels of the company. In decentralized companies, much of the authority is delegated to the workers closest to problems, who can then make the decisions necessary for solving the problems themselves. Centralization works best for tasks that require standardized decision making. When standardization isn't important, decentralization can lead to faster decisions, greater employee and customer satisfaction, and significantly better financial performance.

3 Job Design

Imagine that McDonald's decided to pay $50,000 a year to its drive-through window cashiers. $50,000 for saying "Welcome to McDonald's. May I have your order please?" Would you take the job? Sure you would. Work a couple of years. Make a hundred grand. Why not? However, let's assume that to get this outrageous salary, you have to be a full-time drive-through McDonald's window cashier for the next 10 years. Would you still take the job? Just imagine, 40 to 60 times an hour, you repeat the same basic process:

1. "Welcome to McDonald's. May I have your order please?"
2. Listen to the order. Repeat it for accuracy. State the total cost. "Please drive to the second window."
3. Take the money. Make change.
4. Give customers drinks, straws, and napkins.
5. Give customers food.
6. "Thank you for coming to McDonald's."

Could you stand to do the same simple tasks an average of 50 times per hour, 400 times per day, 2,000 times per week, or 8,000 times per month? Few can. It's rare for fast-food workers to stay on the job more than six months. Indeed, McDonald's and other fast-food restaurants have well over 100 percent employee turnover each year.[14]

job design
the number, kind, and variety of tasks that individual workers perform in doing their jobs

*In this next section, you will learn about **job design**—the number, kind, and variety of tasks that individual workers perform in doing their jobs. You will learn **3.1** why companies continue to use specialized jobs like the McDonald's drive-through job, and **3.2** how job rotation, job enlargement, job enrichment, and the **3.3** job characteristics model are being used to overcome the problems associated with job specialization.*

3.1 *Job Specialization*

job specialization
a job composed of a small part of a larger task or process

Job specialization is a job composed of a small part of a larger task or process. Specialized jobs are characterized by simple, easy-to-learn steps, low variety, and high repetition, like the McDonald's drive-through window job described above. One of the clear disadvantages of specialized jobs is

Personal Productivity Tip

Signing Bonuses, Not Just for Executives Anymore

You hear about multimillion-dollar signing bonuses for athletes or, in some cases, for top executives at the largest companies. However, with unemployment at record low levels, signing bonuses are becoming a popular recruitment tool. White Castle, the fast-food burger chain, pays employees a $200 bonus if they work for at least six months. Job applicants with in-demand technology skills are getting signing bonuses anywhere from $5,000 to $30,000. In large industries, bonuses worth one-third to one-half a year's salary are also being offered. So next time you're in search of a job, ask about a signing bonus. They're not just for executives anymore.

Source: J.S. Lublin, "Management: Now Butchers, Engineers Get Signing Bonuses," *The Wall Street Journal*, 2 June 1997.

that, being so easy to learn, they quickly become boring. This, in turn, can lead to low job satisfaction and high absenteeism and employee turnover, all of which are very costly to organizations.

Why, then, do companies continue to create and use specialized jobs? The primary reason is that specialized jobs are very economical. Once a job has been specialized, it takes little time to learn and master. Consequently, when experienced workers quit or are absent, the company loses little productivity when replacing them with a new employee. For example, next time you're at McDonald's, notice the pictures of the food on the cash registers. These pictures make it easy for McDonald's trainees to quickly learn to take orders. Likewise, to simplify and speed operations, the drink dispensers behind the counter are set to automatically fill drink cups. Put a medium cup below the dispenser. Punch the medium drink button. The soft drink machine then fills the cup to within a half inch of the top, while that same worker goes to get your fries. At McDonald's, every task has been simplified in this way. Because the work is designed to be simple, wages can remain low, since it isn't necessary to pay high salaries to attract highly experienced, educated, or trained workers.

BLAST FROM THE PAST

From Farms to Factories to Telecommuting

An 8 a.m. to 5 p.m. workday, coffee breaks, lunch hours, crushing rush-hour traffic, and punching a time clock are things we associate with work. However, work hasn't always been this way. In fact, the design of jobs and organizations has changed dramatically over the last 500 years.

For most of humankind's history, people didn't commute to work. In fact, travel of any kind was arduous and extremely rare. Work usually occurred in homes or on farms. For example, in 1720, 4¼ million of the 5½ million people in England lived and worked in the country. As recently as 1870, two-thirds of Americans earned their living from agriculture. However, even most of those who didn't earn their living from agriculture still didn't commute to work. Skilled tradesmen or craftsmen, such as blacksmiths, furniture makers, and leather goods makers, who formed trade guilds (the historical predecessors of labor unions) in England as early as 1093, typically worked out of shops in or next to their homes. Likewise, cottage workers worked with each other out of small homes (i.e., cottages) that were often built in a semicircle. Families in each cottage would complete different production steps, passing work from one cottage to the next until production was complete. For example, textile work was a common "cottage industry." Families in different cottages would sheer the sheep, clean the wool, and then comb, spin, weave, bleach, and dye the wool to turn it into yarn. Cottage work was very different from today's jobs and companies. There was no commute, no bosses (workers determined the amount and pace of their work), and no common building (from the time of the ancient Greeks, Romans, and Egyptians through the middle of the 19th century, it was rare for more than 12 people to actually work together under one roof).

However, during the industrial revolution (1750–1900), jobs and organizations changed dramatically. First, thanks to the availability of power (steam engines and later electricity) and numerous inventions, such as Darby's coke-smelting process and Cort's puddling and rolling process (both for making iron) and Hargreave's Jenny and Arkwright's water frame (both for spinning cotton), low-paid, unskilled laborers running machines began to replace high-paid, skilled craftsmen. Craftsmen hand made entire goods by themselves. This new production system was based on a division of labor in which each worker, interacting with machines, performed separate, highly specialized tasks that were but a small part of all the steps required to make manufactured goods. Mass production was born as rope- and chain-driven assembly lines moved work to stationary workers, who concentrated on performing one small task over and over again. As a result, productivity skyrocketed. At Ford Motor

Company, the time required to assemble a car dropped from 12½ worker-hours to just 93 worker-minutes.

Second, instead of being performed in fields, homes, or small shops, jobs occurred in large, formal organizations in which hundreds if not thousands of people worked under one roof. For example, with just 123 workers in 1849, Chicago Harvester (predecessor of International Harvester) ran the largest factory in the U.S. Yet, by 1913, Henry Ford employed 12,000 employees in his Highland Park, Michigan, factory. Between 1860 and 1890, the number of Americans working in factories quintupled, while the number of people working in cities grew even faster. Chicago's population grew from 109,620 in 1860 to 2.2 million in 1910.

Third, with factories employing so many workers, companies now had a need for disciplinary rules (to impose order and structure) and, for the first time, managers who knew how to organize, work with employees, and make good decisions.

Today, with Internet access, laptop computers, teleconferencing, and telecommuting (15 million Americans now telecommute to their jobs), the beginning of the Information Revolution (1995 to ?) promises to bring even more significant changes to jobs and organizations.

Sources: J. Burke, *The Day the Universe Changed* (Boston: Little, Brown, and Company, 1985). "Current Telecommuting Survey Data Shows Strong Growth," *Telecommuting Review: The Gordon Report*, 1 November 1998. From *Britannica Online*, "History of the Organization of Work: Organization of Work in Preindustrial Times" the following articles: "From the 16th to the 18th Century," (**www.eb.com:180/cgi-bin/g?DocF=macro/5006/66/4.html**); "The Ancient World," (**www.eb.com:180/cgi-bin/g?DocF=macro/5006/66/1.html**); "Medieval Industry," (**www.eb.com:180/cgi-bin/g?DocF=macro/5006/66/3.html**), all available 15 January 1999. R.B. Reich, *The Next American Frontier* (New York: Times Books, 1983). J.B. White, "The Line Starts Here: Mass Production Techniques Changed the Way People Work and Live Throughout the World," *The Wall Street Journal*, 11 January 1999, R25.

3.2

Job Rotation, Enlargement, and Enrichment

Because of the efficiency of specialized jobs, companies are often reluctant to eliminate them. Consequently, job redesign efforts have focused on modifying jobs to keep the benefits of specialized jobs, but to reduce their obvious costs and disadvantages. Three methods, job rotation, job enlargement, and job enrichment, have been used to try to improve specialized jobs.[15]

In factory work or even some office jobs, many workers perform the same task all day long. For example, if you attach side mirrors in an auto factory, you probably complete this task 45–60 times an hour. If you work as the cashier at a grocery store, you check out a different customer every two to three minutes. And if you work as an office receptionist, you may answer and direct phone calls up to 200 times an hour.

job rotation
periodically moving workers from one specialized job to another to give them more variety and the opportunity to use different skills

Job rotation attempts to overcome the disadvantages of job specialization by periodically moving workers from one specialized job to another to give them more variety and the opportunity to use different skills. For example, the office receptionist who does nothing but answer phones could be systematically rotated to a different job, such as typing, filing, or data entry, every day or two. Likewise, the "mirror attacher" in the automobile plant might attach mirrors in the first half of the day's work shift and then install bumpers during the second half. Because employees simply switch from one specialized job to another, job rotation allows companies to retain the economic benefits of specialized work. However, the greater variety of tasks makes the work less boring and more satisfying for workers.

job enlargement
increasing the number of different tasks that a worker performs within one particular job

Another way to counter the disadvantages of specialization is to enlarge the job. **Job enlargement** is increasing the number of different tasks that a worker performs within one particular job. So, instead of having to perform just one task, workers with enlarged jobs would be given several tasks to perform. For example, an enlarged "mirror attacher" job might include attaching the mirror, checking to see that the mirror's power adjustment controls work, and then cleaning the mirror's surface. While job enlargement increases variety, many workers report feeling more stress when their jobs are enlarged. Consequently, many workers view enlarged jobs as simply "more work," especially if they are not given additional time to complete the additional tasks.

job enrichment
increasing the number of tasks in a particular job and giving workers the authority and control to make meaningful decisions about their work

Job enrichment attempts to overcome the deficiencies in specialized work by increasing the number of tasks *and* by giving workers the authority and control to make meaningful decisions about their work.[16] For example, when the Chilean phone company, Cia. de Telecomunicaciones de Chile, was a government-owned monopoly, phone service in Chile was poor quality when it worked and slow to be fixed when it didn't. Customers were dissatisfied and employees were cynical. But now that a job enrichment process is well under way, repairs are being made in days instead of weeks. Formerly cynical lower-level managers and technical workers enthusiastically volunteer to try to bring about improvements now that they have been given full responsibility and authority in their jobs. For instance, employees are combining three previously separate jobs—installation, repair, and complaints—under one title, "customer satisfaction." Said Juan Aqueveque, a phone line technician, "Everyone is bored with having customers mad at the company."[17]

3.3 *Job Characteristics Model*

job characteristics model (JCM)
an approach to job redesign that seeks to formulate jobs in ways that motivate workers and lead to positive work outcomes

internal motivation
motivation that comes from the job itself rather than from outside rewards

By contrast to job rotation, job enlargement, and job enrichment, which focus on providing variety in job tasks, the **job characteristics model (JCM)** is an approach to job redesign that seeks to formulate jobs in ways that motivate workers and lead to positive work outcomes.[18] As shown in Figure 11.9, the primary goal of the model is to create jobs that result in positive personal and work outcomes such as internal work motivation, satisfaction with one's job, and work effectiveness. Of these, the central outcome of the JCM is internal motivation. **Internal motivation** is motivation that comes from the job itself rather than from outside rewards, such as a raise or praise from the boss. If workers feel that performing the job well is itself rewarding, then the job has internal motivation. Statements such as "I get a nice sense of accomplishment" or "I feel good about myself and what I'm producing" are examples of internal motivation.

Moving to the left in Figure 11.9, you can see that the JCM specifies three critical psychological states that must occur for work to be internally motivating. First, workers must *experience the work as meaningful*, that is, they must view their job as being important. Second, they must *experience responsibility for work outcomes*—they must feel personally responsible for the work being done well. Third, workers must have *knowledge of results*, that is, know how well they are performing their jobs. All three critical psychological states must occur for work to be internally motivating.

For example, let's return to our grocery store cashier. Cashiers usually have knowledge of results. When you're slow, your checkout line grows long. If you make a mistake, customers point it out. "No, I think that's on sale for $2.99, not $3.99." Likewise, cashiers experience responsibility for work outcomes. At the end of the day, the register is totaled and the money is counted. Ideally, the money matches the total sales in the register. However, if the money in the till is less than what's recorded in the register, most stores make the cashier pay the difference. Consequently, most cashiers are very careful to avoid being caught "short" at the end of the day. However, despite the presence of knowledge of results and experienced responsibility for work

Figure 11.9 **Job Characteristics Model**

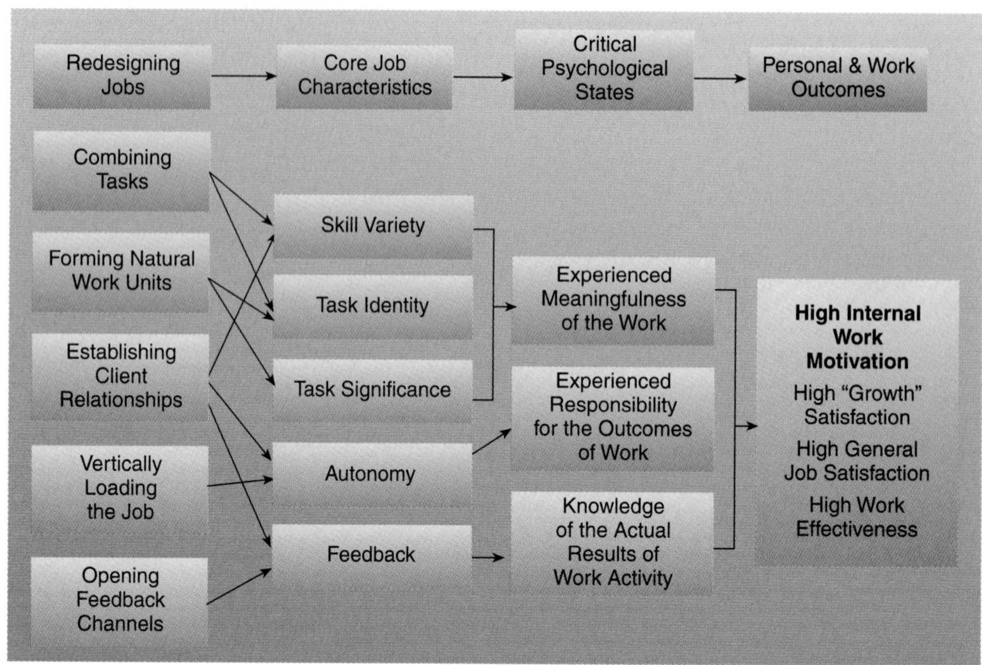

Source: J.R. Hackman and G.R. Oldham, *Work Redesign* (Reading, MA: Addison-Wesley, 1980).

outcomes, most grocery store cashiers (at least where I shop) aren't internally motivated, because they don't experience the work as meaningful. With scanners, it takes little skill to learn or do the job. Anyone can do it. In addition, cashiers have few decisions to make. Plus, the job is highly repetitive.

Of course, this raises the question: What kinds of jobs produce the three critical psychological states? Again, moving to the left in Figure 11.9, the JCM specifies that the three critical psychological states arise from jobs that are strong on five core job characteristics: skill variety, task identity, task significance, autonomy, and feedback. **Skill variety** is the number of different activities performed in a job. **Task identity** is the degree to which a job requires completion of a whole and identifiable piece of work, from beginning to end. **Task significance** is the degree to which a job is perceived to have a substantial impact on others inside or outside the organization. **Autonomy** is the degree to which a job gives workers the discretion, freedom, and independence to decide how and when to accomplish the job. Finally, **feedback** is the amount of information the job provides to workers about their work performance.

skill variety
the number of different activities performed in a job

task identity
the degree to which a job requires, from beginning to end, the completion of a whole and identifiable piece of work

task significance
the degree to which a job is perceived to have a substantial impact on others inside or outside the organization

autonomy
the degree to which a job gives workers the discretion, freedom, and independence to decide how and when to accomplish the job

feedback
the amount of information the job provides to workers about their work performance

To illustrate how the core job characteristics work together, let's use them to more thoroughly assess why the McDonald's drive-through window job is not particularly satisfying or motivating. To start, skill variety is low. Except for the size of an order or special requests (no onions), the process is the same for each customer. At best, task identity is moderate. Although you take the order, handle the money, and deliver the food, others are responsible for a larger part of the process, preparing the food. However, task identity will be even lower if a McDonald's has two drive-through windows. When this is the case, each drive-through window worker has an even more specialized task. The first is limited to taking the order and making change,

Trucking companies sometimes make drivers' jobs more internally motivating by expecting drivers to establish relationships with customers and giving them the authority to resolve customer problems.

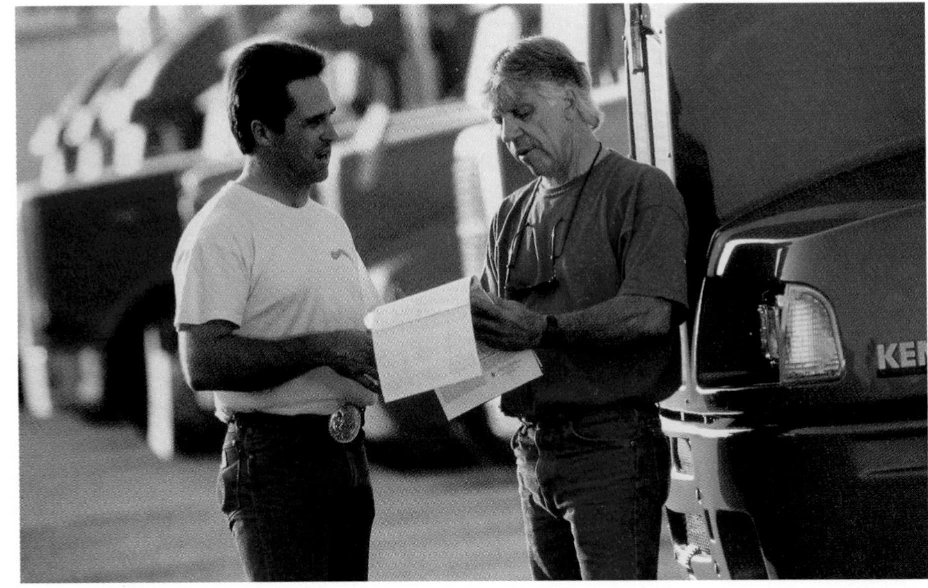

while the second just delivers the food. Task significance, the impact you have on others, is probably low. Autonomy is also very low. McDonald's has strict rules about dress, cleanliness, and procedures. But the job does provide immediate feedback, such as positive and negative customer comments, car horns honking, how long it takes to process orders, and the length of the line of cars in the drive-through. With the exception of feedback, the core job characteristics show why the drive-through window job is not internally motivating for many workers.

So, what can managers do when jobs aren't internally motivating? The far left column of Figure 11.9 lists five job redesign techniques that managers can use to strengthen a job's core characteristics. *Combining tasks* increases skill variety and task identity by joining separate, specialized tasks into larger work modules. For example, some trucking firms are now requiring truck drivers to drive and load their rigs. The hope is that involving drivers in loading will ensure that trucks are properly loaded, thus reducing damage claims.

Work can be formed into *natural work units* by arranging tasks according to logical or meaningful groups. Many trucking companies simply assign any driver to any truck. However, some have begun assigning drivers to particular geographic locations (i.e., the Northeast or Southwest) or to truckloads that require special driving skill when being transported (i.e., oversized loads, chemicals, etc.). Forming natural work units increases task identity and task significance.

Establishing client relationships increases skill variety, autonomy, and feedback by giving employees direct contact with clients and customers. In some companies, truck drivers are expected to establish business relationships with their regular customers. When something goes wrong with a shipment, customers are told to call drivers directly.

Vertical loading means pushing some managerial authority down to workers. For truck drivers, this means that they have the same authority that managers would have to resolve customer problems. In some companies, this means that if a late shipment causes problems for a customer, the driver has the ability to fully refund the cost of that shipment (without first requiring management's approval).

The last job redesign technique offered by the model, *opening feedback channels*, means finding additional ways to give employees direct, frequent feedback about their job performance. For example, with advances in electronics, many truck drivers get instantaneous data as to whether they're on schedule and driving their rigs in a fuel-efficient manner. Likewise, the increased contact with customers also means that many drivers now receive monthly data on customer satisfaction. For additional information on the JCM, see "What Really Works: The Job Characteristics Model."

What Really Works

The Job Characteristics Model: Making Jobs More Interesting and Motivating

Think of the worst job you ever had. Was it factory work in which you repeated the same task every few minutes? Was it an office job requiring a lot of meaningless paperwork? Or was it a job so specialized that it took no effort or thinking whatsoever to do?

The job characteristics model reviewed in this chapter suggests that workers will be more motivated or satisfied with their work if their jobs have greater task identity, task significance, skill variety, autonomy, and feedback. Eighty-four studies, with a combined total of 22,472 study participants, indicated that, on average, these core job characteristics make jobs more satisfying for most workers. However, jobs rich with the five core job characteristics are especially satisfying for workers who possess an individual characteristic called *growth need strength.* Read on to see how well the job characteristics model really increases job satisfaction and reduces workplace absenteeism.

JOB SATISFACTION

Task Identity and Job Satisfaction

There is a 66 percent chance that workers will be more satisfied with their work when their jobs have task identity, the chance to complete an entire job from beginning to end, than when they don't.

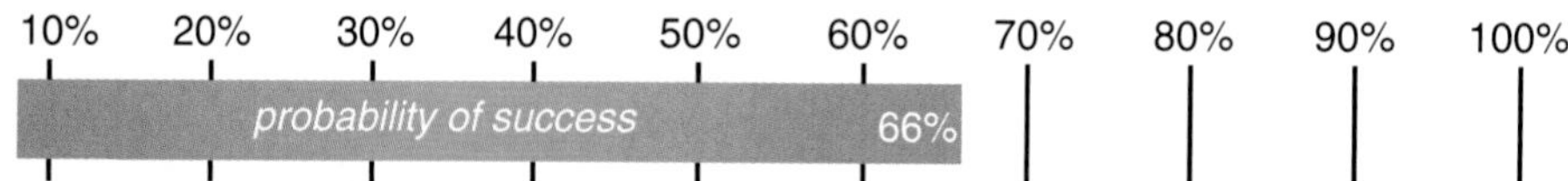

Task Significance and Job Satisfaction

On average, there is a 69 percent chance that workers will be more satisfied with their work when their jobs have task significance, meaning a substantial impact on others, than when they don't.

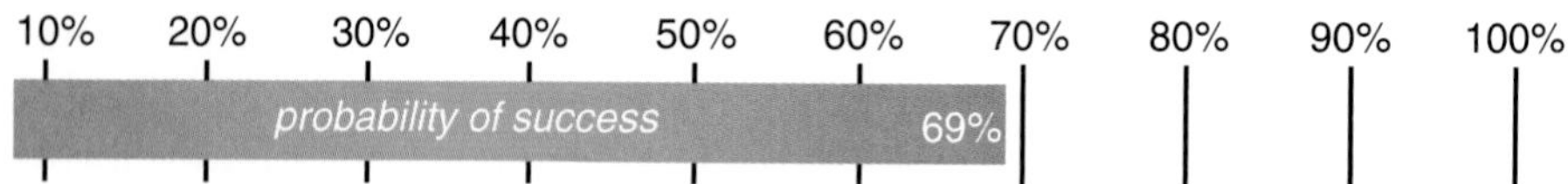

Skill Variety and Job Satisfaction

On average, there is a 70 percent chance that workers will be more satisfied with their work when their jobs have skill variety, meaning a variety of different activities, skills, and talents, than when they don't.

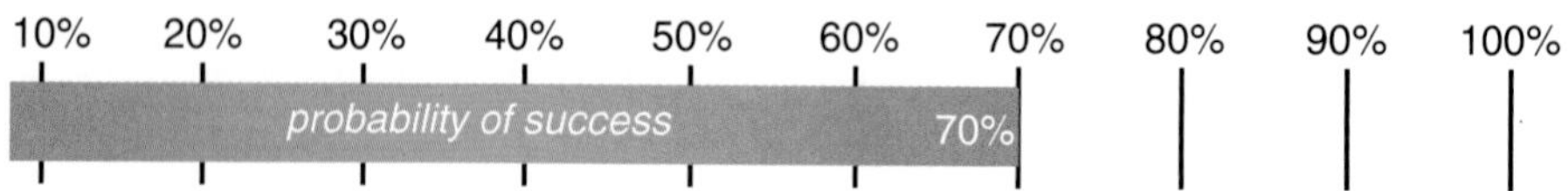

Autonomy and Job Satisfaction

On average, there is a 73 percent chance that workers will be more satisfied with their work when their jobs have autonomy, meaning the discretion to decide how and when to accomplish the jobs, than when they don't.

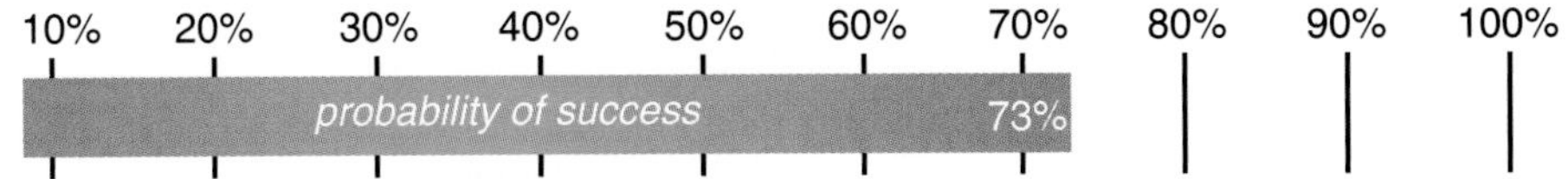

Feedback and Job Satisfaction

On average, there is a 70 percent chance that workers will be more satisfied with their work when their jobs have feedback, meaning knowledge about their work performance, than when they don't.

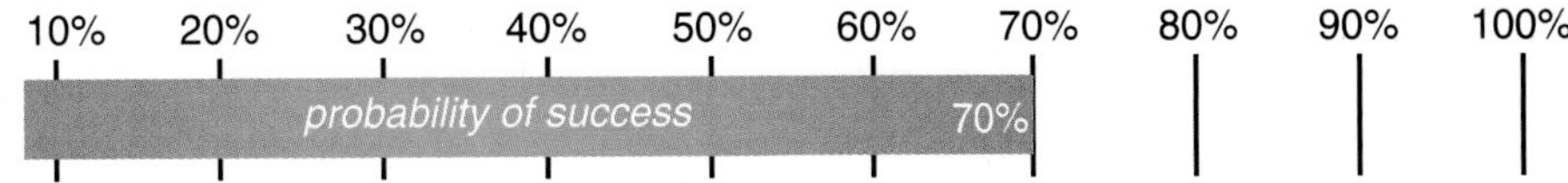

High Growth Need Strength and Job Satisfaction

The statistics presented above indicate that, on average, the job characteristics model has at worst a 66 percent chance of improving workers' job satisfaction. In all, this is impressive evidence that the model works. In general, you can expect these results when redesigning jobs based on the job characteristics model.

However, we can be more accurate about the effects of the job characteristics model if we split workers into two groups, those with high growth need strength and those with low growth need strength. *Growth need strength* is the need or desire to achieve personal growth and development through your job. Workers high in growth need strength respond well to jobs designed according to the job characteristics model, because they enjoy work that challenges them and allows them to learn new skills and knowledge. In fact, there is an 84 percent chance that workers with high growth need strength will be more satisfied with their work when their jobs are redesigned according to the job characteristics model.

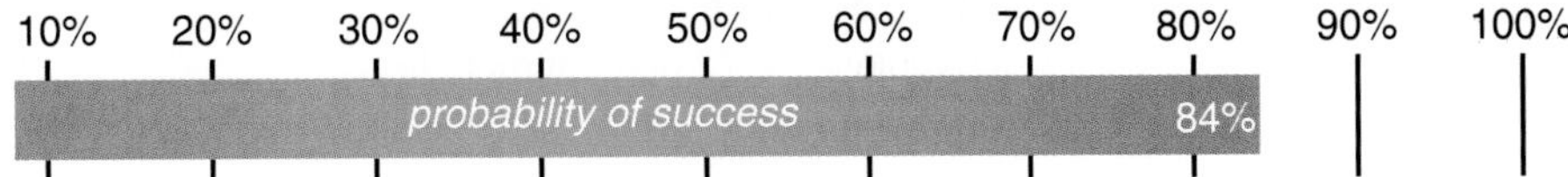

Low Growth Need Strength and Job Satisfaction

By comparison, because they aren't as interested in being challenged or learning new things at work, there is only a 69 percent chance that workers low in growth need strength will be satisfied with jobs that have been redesigned according to the principles of the job characteristics model. This is still a favorable percentage, but weaker than the 84 percent chance of job satisfaction that occurs for workers high in growth need strength.

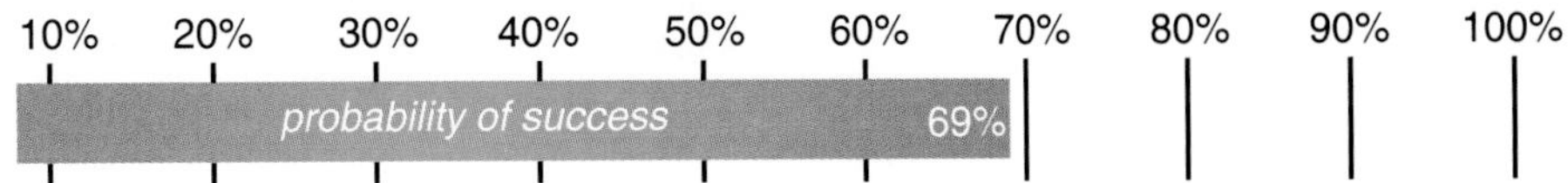

WORKPLACE ABSENTEEISM

Although not shown in the job characteristics model displayed in Figure 11.9, workplace absenteeism is an important personal or work outcome affected by a job's core job characteristics. In general, the "richer" your job is with task identity, task significance, skill variety, autonomy, and feedback, the more likely you are to show up for work every day.

Task Identity and Absenteeism

Workers are 63 percent more likely to attend work when their jobs have task identity, the chance to complete an entire job from beginning to end, than when they don't.

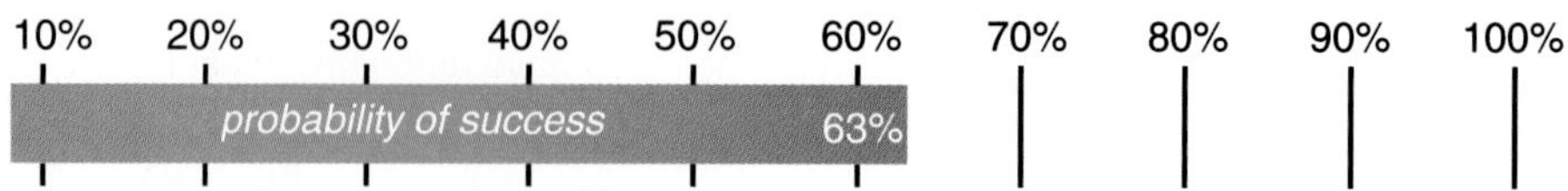

Task Significance and Absenteeism

Workers are 68 percent more likely to attend work when their jobs have task significance, meaning a substantial impact on others, than when they don't.

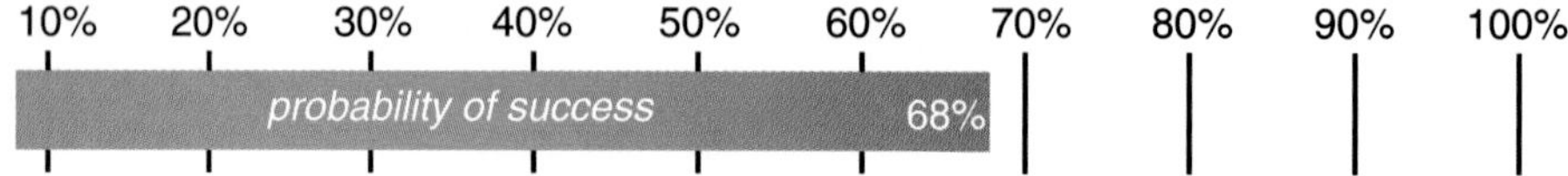

Skill Variety and Absenteeism

Workers are 72 percent more likely to attend work when their jobs have skill variety, meaning a variety of different activities, skills, and talents, than when they don't.

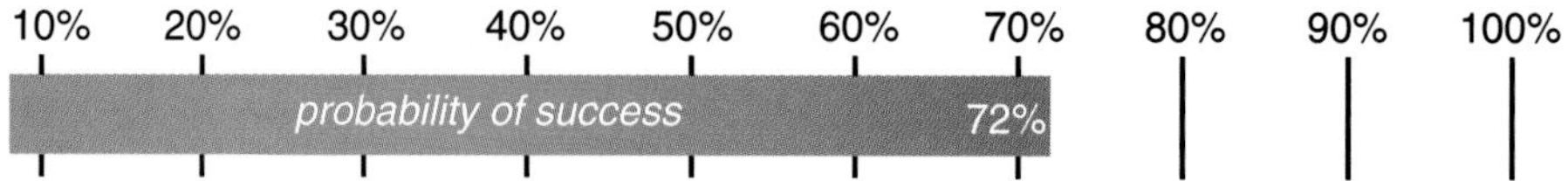

Autonomy and Absenteeism

Workers are 74 percent more likely to attend work when their jobs have autonomy, meaning the discretion to decide how and when to accomplish a job, than when they don't.

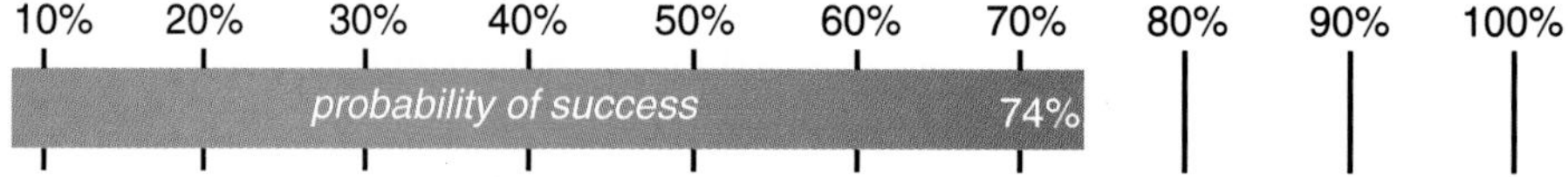

Feedback and Absenteeism

Workers are 72 percent more likely to attend work when their jobs have feedback, meaning knowledge about their work performance, than when they don't.

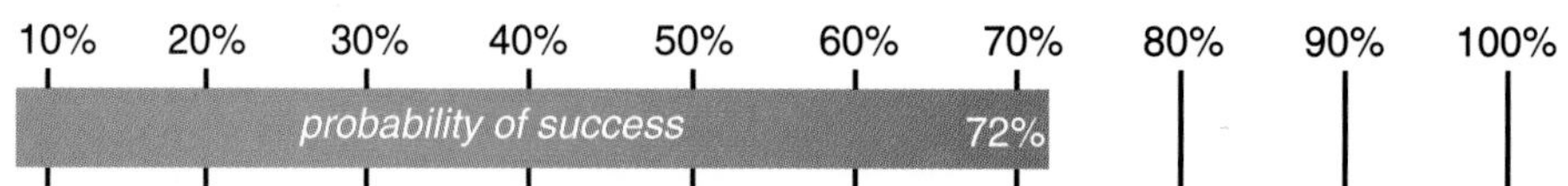

Sources: Y. Fried & G.R. Ferris, "The Validity of the Job Characteristics Model: A Review and Meta-Analysis," *Personnel Psychology* 40 (1987): 287-322. B.T. Loher, R.A. Noe, N.L. Moeller, & M.P. Fitzgerald, "A Meta-Analysis of the Relation of Job Characteristics to Job Satisfaction," *Journal of Applied Psychology* 70 (1985): 280-289.

Review 3: *Job Design*

Companies use specialized jobs because they are economical and easy to learn and don't require highly paid workers. However, specialized jobs aren't motivating or particularly satisfying for employees. Companies have used job rotation, job enlargement, job enrichment, and the job characteristics model to make specialized jobs more interesting and motivating. With job rotation, workers move from one specialized job to another. Job enlargement simply increases the number of different tasks within a particular job. Job enrichment increases the number of tasks in a job and gives workers authority and control over their work. The goal of the job characteristics model is to make jobs intrinsically motivating. For this to happen, jobs must be strong on five core job characteristics (skill variety, task identity, task significance, autonomy, and feedback), and workers must experience three critical psychological states (knowledge of results, responsibility for work outcomes, and meaningful work). If jobs aren't internally motivating, they can be redesigned by combining tasks, forming natural work units, establishing client relationships, vertical loading, and opening feedback channels.

Designing Organizational Processes

mechanistic organization organization characterized by specialized jobs and responsibilities, precisely defined, unchanging roles, and a rigid chain of command based on centralized authority and vertical communication

organic organization organization characterized by broadly defined jobs and responsibility, loosely defined, frequently changing roles, and decentralized authority and horizontal communication based on task knowledge

intraorganizational process the collection of activities that take place within an organization to transform inputs into outputs that customers value

Nearly 40 years ago, Tom Burns and G.M. Stalker described how two kinds of organizational designs, mechanistic and organic, are appropriate for different kinds of organizational environments.[19] **Mechanistic organizations** are characterized by specialized jobs and responsibilities, precisely defined, unchanging roles, and a rigid chain of command based on centralized authority and vertical communication. This type of organization works best in stable, unchanging business environments. By contrast, **organic organizations** are characterized by broadly defined jobs and responsibility, loosely defined, frequently changing roles, and decentralized authority and horizontal communication based on task knowledge. This type of organization works best in dynamic, changing business environments.

The organizational design techniques described in the first half of this chapter, departmentalization, authority, and job design, are methods better suited for mechanistic organizations and the stable business environments that were more prevalent before 1980. However, the organizational design techniques discussed here in the second part of the chapter are more appropriate for organic organizations and the increasingly dynamic environments in which today's businesses compete.

The key difference between these approaches is that while mechanistic organizational designs focus on organizational structure, organic organizational designs are concerned with organizational processes, the collection of activities that transform inputs into outputs valued by customers. After reading these next two sections, you should be able to:

4 explain the methods that companies are using to redesign internal organizational processes (i.e., **intraorganizational processes**).

5 describe the methods that companies are using to redesign external organizational processes (i.e., **interorganizational processes**).

4 Intraorganizational Processes

An **intraorganizational process** is the collection of activities that take place within an organization to transform inputs into outputs that customers value. The steps involved in an automobile insurance claim are a good example of an intraorganizational process:

1. Document the loss (i.e., the accident).
2. Assign an appraiser to determine the dollar amount of damage.
3. Make an appointment to inspect the vehicle.
4. Inspect the vehicle.
5. Write an appraisal and get the repair shop to agree to the damage estimate.
6. Pay for the repair work.
7. Return the repaired car to the customer.

Back to the Future

Designing Tomorrow's Organizations

In the past, organizational design was based on traditional vertical and horizontal dimensions, such as departments, lines of authority, chains of command, and jobs. Today, progressive companies are redesigning their organizational processes by creating modular, virtual, and boundaryless organizations. But what will the design of tomorrow's organizations look like?

Professors Ian Mitroff, Richard Mason, and Christine Pearson believe that they will be radically different. Instead of human resources, accounting, or production departments, Mitroff, Mason, and Pearson believe that tomorrow's organizations will be based on five very different centers: (1) a knowledge/learning center, (2) a recovery/development center, (3) a world service/spiritual center, (4) a world class operations center, and (5) a leadership institute.

The purpose of a knowledge/learning center is to get the right people the right information and knowledge at the right time. In some respects, a knowledge/learning center is similar to managing information (see Chapter 6). However, it goes beyond the traditional management of information in three ways. First, it facilitates improved thinking, decisions, and actions. Second, it helps break down barriers between functions, so decision-makers can think systematically about the entire organizational system. Third, it helps acquire, evaluate, and widely disseminate information, so managers and workers can be better problem-solvers.

The focus of a recovery/development center is to aid the development of healthy employees and a healthy company. In other words, how can the company help employees recover from the personal or emotional dysfunctions (i.e., child abuse, alcoholism, etc.) that they bring to work? The recovery/development center is also responsible for monitoring the "psychological health" of the workplace. Why worry about a company's psychological health? Because the pressures to achieve organizational goals may prompt leaders to unintentionally create highly stressful, psychologically "sick" environments, in which feelings of grandiosity motivate corporate decision-makers to value power and destructiveness in their quest to be victorious over others.

By contrast to the recovery/development center, which is inwardly focused, the goal of a world service/spiritual center is to aid the development of a healthy outside world. One way to do this is to allow workers to work on "world problems" on company time. Another is to acknowledge and correct organizational mistakes and wrong-doings, such as pollution, accidents, or exploitation that have negatively affected those outside the company. A third way is to create meaningful work, so that managers and workers can see that what they do benefits humanity in some way.

The focus of a world class operations center is to be a laboratory for innovation and change. This doesn't mean designing new products and services. Instead, the goal of a world class operations center is to strive for new, innovative, and better ways in which to structure the organization or redesign its manufacturing or service processes. Should work be done in teams or individually? Must workers all work in the same place, or can they work in different places and telecommute? Can new products be brought to market faster by bringing the company's suppliers into the design process before production begins? The job of the world class operations center is to answer questions like these.

Finally, the job of the leadership institute is to bring the other four centers together. The leadership institute is made up of the company's top officers and the heads of each of the four centers mentioned above. Their task is to manage the tensions and tradeoffs between the four centers. Importantly, unlike today's companies in which key individuals often make final decisions, the leadership institute makes collective decisions based on what's best for the company as a whole.

Source: I.I. Mitroff, R.O. Mason, & C.M. Pearson, "Radical Surgery: What Will Tomorrow's Organizations Look Like?" *Academy of Management Executive* 8, no. 2 (1994): 11-21.

Let's take a look at how companies are using **4.1** *reengineering,* **4.2** *empowerment, and* **4.3** *behavioral informality to redesign internal organizational processes like these.*

4.1 *Reengineering*

reengineering
fundamental rethinking and radical redesign of business processes to achieve dramatic improvements in critical measures of performance, such as cost, quality, service, and speed

In their best-selling book *Reengineering the Corporation,* Michael Hammer and James Champy defined **reengineering** as "the *fundamental* rethinking and *radical* redesign of business *processes* to achieve *dramatic* improvements in critical, contemporary measures of performance, such as cost, quality, service and speed."[20] Hammer and Champy further explained the four key words shown in italics in this definition. The first key word is "fundamental." When reengineering organizational designs, managers must ask themselves, "Why do we do what we do?" and "Why do we do it the way we do?" The usual answer is "Because that's the way we've always done it." The second key word is "radical." Reengineering is about significant change, about starting over by throwing out the old ways of getting work done. The third key word is "processes." Hammer and Champy noted that "Most business people are not process oriented; they are focused on tasks, on jobs, on people, on structures, but not on processes." The fourth key word is "dramatic." Reengineering is about achieving "quantum" improvements in company performance.

An example from IBM's Credit operation illustrates how work can be reengineered.[21] IBM Credit loans businesses money to buy IBM computers. Previously, the loan process would begin when an IBM salesperson called needing credit approval for a customer's purchase. The first department involved in the process would take the credit information over the phone from the salesperson and record it on the credit form. Then, the credit form was sent to a separate credit checking department, and then to a separate pricing department (where the interest rate was determined), and so on. In all, it would take five departments six days to approve or deny the customer's loan. Of course, this delay cost IBM business. Some customers got their loans elsewhere. Others, frustrated by the wait, simply canceled their orders.

Finally, two IBM managers decided to walk a loan straight through to each of the five departments involved in the process. At each step, they asked the workers to stop what they were doing to immediately process their loan application. They were shocked by what they found. From start to stop the entire process took just 90 minutes! It turns out that the average time of six days was created by delays that occurred in handing off the work from one department to another. The solution: IBM redesigned the process so that one person, not five in five separate departments, handled the entire loan approval process by themselves without any handoffs. The results were "dramatic." Reengineering the credit process reduced approval time from six days to four hours and allowed IBM Credit to increase the number of loans it handled by a factor of 100!

Reengineering changes an organization's orientation from vertical to horizontal. Instead of "taking orders" from upper management, lower- and middle-level managers and workers "take orders" from a customer who is at the beginning and end of each process. Instead of running independent functional departments, managers and workers in different departments take ownership of cross-functional processes. Instead of simplifying work so that

task interdependence the extent to which collective action is required to complete an entire piece of work

pooled interdependence work completed by having each job or department independently contribute to the whole

sequential interdependence work completed in succession, with one group or job's outputs becoming the inputs for the next group or job

it becomes increasingly specialized, reengineering complicates work by giving workers increased autonomy and responsibility for complete processes.

In essence, reengineering changes work by changing **task interdependence**, the extent to which collective action is required to complete an entire piece of work. As shown in Figure 11.10, there are three kinds of task interdependence.[22] In **pooled interdependence**, each job or department independently contributes to the whole. In **sequential interdependence**, work must be performed in succession, as one group's or job's outputs become the inputs for the next group or job. Finally, in **reciprocal interdependence**, different jobs or groups work together in a back-and-forth manner to complete the process. By reducing the handoffs between different jobs or groups, reengineering decreases sequential interdependence. Likewise, reengineering decreases pooled interdependence by redesigning work so that formerly independent jobs or departments now work together to complete

Figure 11.10 **Reengineering and Task Interdependence**

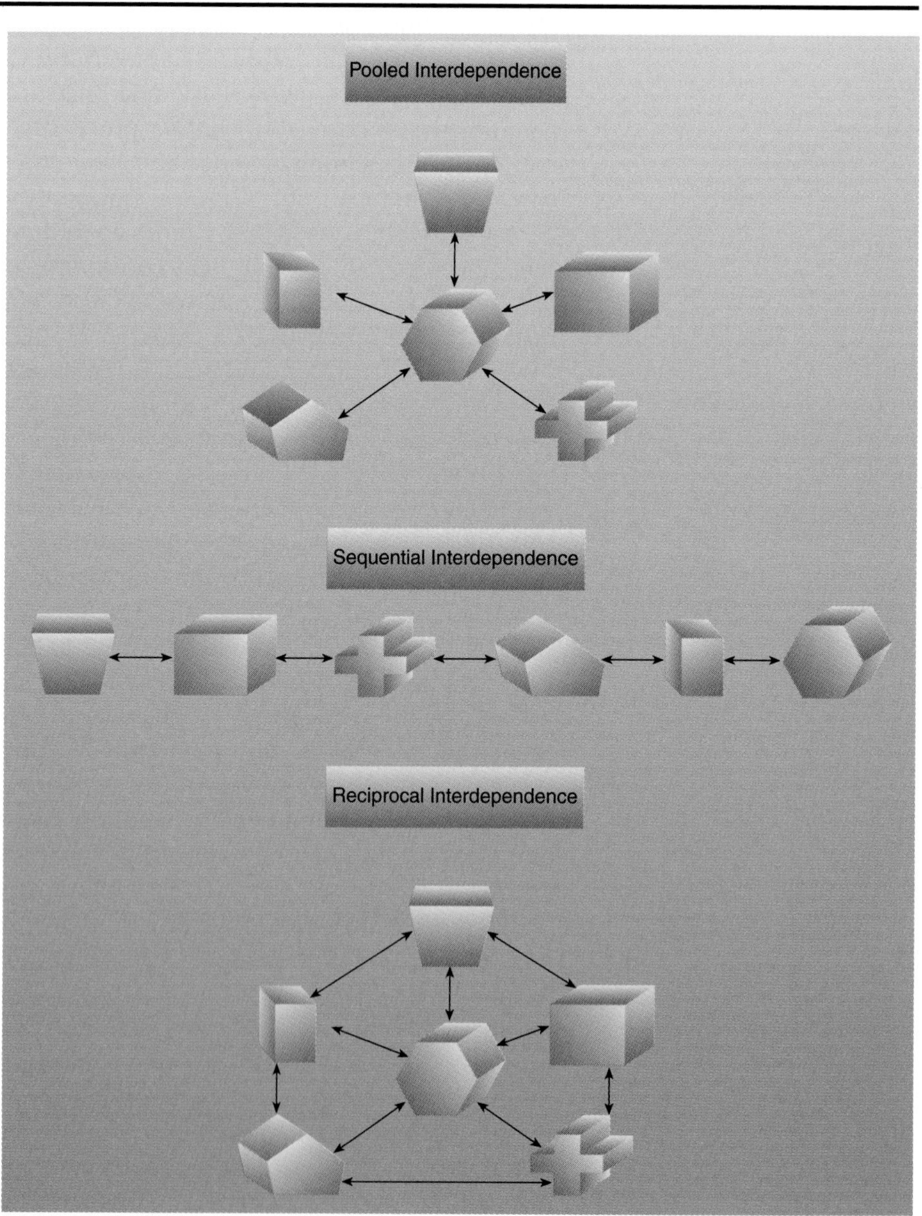

reciprocal interdependence
work completed by different jobs or groups working together in a back-and-forth manner

processes. Finally, reengineering increases reciprocal interdependence by making groups or individuals responsible for larger, more complete processes in which several steps may be accomplished at the same time.

As an organizational design tool, reengineering promises big rewards. However, it has come under severe criticism, too. The most serious complaint is that since it allows a few workers to do the work formerly done by many, reengineering is simply a corporate code word for cost cutting and worker layoffs. Likewise, for that reason, detractors claim that reengineering hurts morale and performance. For example, despite reducing ordering times from three weeks to three days, Levi Strauss ended an $850 million reengineering project because of the fear and turmoil it created in its work force. One of the low points occurred when Levi management, encouraged by its reengineering consultants, told 4,000 workers that they would have to "reapply for their jobs" as the company shifted from its traditional vertical structure to a process-based form of organizing. Thomas Kasten, Levi's vice president for reengineering and customer service, said, "We felt the pressure building up [over reengineering efforts], and we were worried about the business."[23] Today, even reengineering gurus Hammer and Champy admit that roughly 70 percent of all reengineering projects fail because of the effects on people in the workplace. Said Hammer, "I wasn't smart enough about that [the people issues]. I was reflecting my engineering background and was insufficiently appreciative of the human dimension. I've learned [now] that's critical."[24]

4.2 *Empowerment*

empowering workers
permanently passing decision-making authority and responsibility from managers to workers by giving them the information and resources they need to make and carry out good decisions

Another way of redesigning interorganizational processes is through empowerment. **Empowering workers** means permanently passing decision-making authority and responsibility from managers to workers. However, for workers to be fully empowered, companies must give them the information and resources they need to make and carry out good decisions, and then reward them for taking individual initiative.[25] For example, Bill Armstrong owns Armstrong Ambulance in Arlington, Massachusetts. In a time when national ambulance companies dominate the business, this small, family-owned business is thriving because Bill Armstrong empowers the emergency medical technicians (EMTs) who operate his ambulances. He does it by sparing no expense when buying the most advanced life-saving equipment and then training his EMTs to use it. His EMTs have access to the latest life-saving drugs, computerized defibrillators to restart hearts, and an electrocardiogram that transmits 12 graphs of information about a patient's heart to emergency room physicians while the ambulance is en route to the hospital. Says EMT Michael Forget, "We want for nothing."[26]

empowerment
feelings of intrinsic motivation, in which workers perceive their work to have impact and meaning, and perceive themselves to be competent and capable of self-determination

When workers like Armstrong Ambulance's EMTs are rewarded for taking initiative and given the proper information and resources to make good decisions, they experience strong feelings of empowerment. **Empowerment** is a feeling of intrinsic motivation, in which workers perceive their work to have meaning, and perceive themselves to be competent, having an impact, and capable of self-determination.[27] Work has meaning when it is consistent with personal standards and beliefs. Workers feel competent when they believe they can perform an activity with skill. The belief that they are having an impact comes from a feeling that they can affect work outcomes. A feeling of self-determination arises from workers' belief that they have the autonomy to choose how best to do their work.

Empowerment can lead to changes in organizational processes, because meaning, competence, impact, and self-determination produce empowered employees who take active rather than passive roles in their work. For example, after computer programmer Beat Poltera reserved a room for $200 per night at the San Francisco Fairmont Hotel, he arrived to find all the rooms filled. Because of an employee empowerment program instituted earlier that year, the Fairmont's front desk clerk didn't hesitate to book him in a $250-a-night room at the nearby Sheraton. The clerk also paid for his taxi ride to the Sheraton and tossed in a free meal at the Fairmont's expensive Crown Room restaurant. Said Mr. Poltera, "I was in a state of shock. It wasn't the money, but the fact that the decision was made on the spot." Mr. Poltera was so impressed that he has returned to the Fairmont several times since this happened.[28]

4.3 *Behavioral Informality*

behavioral informality workplace atmosphere characterized by spontaneity, casualness, and interpersonal familiarity

behavioral formality workplace atmosphere characterized by routine and regimen, specific rules about how to behave, and interpersonal detachment

How would you describe the atmosphere in the office in which you last worked? Was it a formal, by-the-book, follow-the-rules, address-each-other-by-last-names atmosphere? Or was it more informal, with an emphasis on results rather than rules, casual business dress rather than suits, and first names rather than last names and titles? Or was it somewhere in between?

Behavioral informality (or formality) is a third influence on intraorganizational processes. **Behavioral informality** refers to workplace situations characterized by spontaneity, casualness, and interpersonal familiarity. By contrast, **behavioral formality** refers to workplace situations characterized by routine and regimen, specific rules about how to behave, and impersonal detachment. Table 11.2 shows that behavioral formality and informality are characterized by four factors: language usage, conversational turntaking and topic selection, emotional and proxemic gestures, and physical and contextual cues. Let's examine each in more detail. [29]

Personal Productivity Tip

Singles, Not Home Runs

Reengineering, the radical redesign of business processes, can dramatically improve business performance. However, when you swing for home runs, you strike out a lot (i.e., the 70 percent failure rate of reengineering projects). Dana Corporation, a maker of car parts, swings for singles, not home runs, by focusing on daily continuous improvement. Every day, teams are encouraged to question how things are done. Employees submit two ideas (in writing) each month for improving manufacturing processes. And when small improvements occur, company management celebrates with free barbecue and soft drinks for all. Swing for singles every day, and you're much more likely to get a hit.

Source: T. Petzinger, Jr., "Manager Keeps Reinventing His Plant's Production Line," *The Wall Street Journal Interactive Edition,* 19 September 1997.

Compared to formal work atmospheres, the language in informal workplaces is often slurred ("Whatcha doin'?"), elliptical ("Coffee?" versus "Would you like some coffee?"), and filled with slang terms and vivid descriptions. People use first names and perhaps nicknames to address each other, rather than Mr., Ms., Dr., or formal titles. When it comes to conversations in informal workplaces, people jump right in when they have something to say (i.e., unregulated turntaking), conversations shift from topic to topic, many of which are unrelated to business, and joking and laughter are common. From joy to disappointment, people show much more emotion in informal workplaces. In addition, relaxed expressions, such as putting your feet on your desk, or congregating in hallways for impromptu discussions, are more common, too. In terms of physical and contextual cues, informal workplaces deemphasize differences in hierarchical status or rank to encourage more frequent interaction between organizational members. Consequently, to make their organizations feel less formal, many companies have eliminated what used to be considered "management perks," things like executive dining rooms, reserved parking spaces, and large corner offices separated from most workers because they were located on a higher floor of the company building (the higher the floor, the greater one's status).

Casual dress policies and open office systems are two of the most popular methods for increasing behavioral informality. In fact, a survey con-

Table 11.2

Differences Between Formal and Informal Workplaces

Formal	*Informal*
	Language Usage
Fully articulated speech ("What are you doing?")	Phonological slurring ("Whatcha doin'?")
Grammatically complete phrasing ("Would you like some coffee?")	Use of elliptical expressions ("Coffee?")
Use of formal word choices ("Would you care to dine?")	Use of colloquial and slang expressions ("Wanna grab a bite to eat?")
Use of honorifics ("Ms.," "Sir," "Dr.")	Use of the vivid present ("So I come down the stairs, and she says…")
Elimination of "I" and "you" (It is requested that…")	First name, in-group names ("Mac," "Bud")
	Conversational Turntaking and Topic Selection
Turntaking well regulated	Turntaking relatively unregulated
Few interruptions or overlaps	Many interruptions or overlaps
Few changes of topic	Many shifts of topic possible
Seriousness of topic	Joking or conversational levity possible
	Emotional and Proxemic Gestures
Sober facial demeanor	Greater latitude of emotional expression
Much interpersonal distance	Small interpersonal distance
No touching, postural attention	Touching, postural relaxation allowed
	Physical and Contextual Cues
Formal clothing, shoes, etc.	Informal clothing, shoes, etc.
Central focus of attention	Decentralized, multiple centers of attention possible
Symmetric arrangement of chairs/furniture	Asymmetric arrangement of chairs/furniture
Artifacts related to official status	Informal trappings: flowers, art, food, soft furniture
Hushed atmosphere, little background noise	Background noise acceptable

Source: D.A. Morland, "The Role of Behavioral Formality and Informality in the Enactment of Bureaucratic Versus Organic Organizations," *Academy of Management Review* 20 (1995): 831-872.

ducted by Levi Strauss and the Society for Human Resource Management indicates that casual dress policies (no suits, ties, jackets, dresses, or formal clothing required) are exploding in popularity.[30] Ninety percent of companies today have some form of casual dress code compared to 63 percent three years ago. Forty-two percent of all companies permit casual dress at least one day a week compared to 17 percent three years ago. Moreover, compared to 20 percent three years ago, 33 percent of companies permit casual dress every day of the week. Amazingly, even staid, stuffy IBM, known as "Big Blue," in part for the dark blue suits and white shirts traditionally worn by its employees, has gone business casual. So has AT&T. Burke Stinson, an AT&T spokesperson, explained that "Brainpower is more important than appearance, and brainpower is what makes you productive, not a gray flannel suit."[31] Many managers seem to agree. In fact, 85 percent of human resources directors believe that casual dress can improve office morale. Moreover, nearly two-thirds of them believe that casual dress policies are an important tool for attracting qualified employees in today's tight labor markets. Michael Losey, president of the Society for Human Resource Management, concluded that "for the majority of corporations and industries, allowing casual dress can have clear advantages at virtually no cost."[32]

While casual dress increases behavioral informality by having managers and workers at all levels dress in a more relaxed manner, open office systems increase behavioral informality by significantly increasing the level of communication and interaction among employees. By definition, **open office systems** try to increase interaction by removing physical barriers that separate workers. One characteristic of open office systems is that they have much more shared space than private space. **Shared spaces** are used by and open to all employees. Cubicles with low-to-the-ground partitions, offices with no doors or with glass walls, collections of comfortable furniture that encourage people to congregate, and common areas with tables and chairs that encourage people to meet, work, or eat together are examples of shared space. **Private spaces**, such as a private office with a door, are used by and open to just one employee. Before Steelcase, a leading office furniture manufacturer, switched to open systems, 80 percent of its executive office space was private space used for individual offices, whereas 20 percent was shared space. However, after switching to open offices, 80 percent is shared space and 20 percent is private space. After the change, CEO Jim Hackett went from a private, 700-square-foot office to a 48-square-foot enclosure that sits out in the open of a 22,000-square-foot environment that workers have dubbed "The Leadership Community."[33]

open office systems
offices in which the physical barriers that separate workers have been removed in order to increase communication and interaction

shared spaces
spaces used by and open to all employees

private spaces
spaces used by and open to just one employee

The advantage of this much-shared space in open offices is that it dramatically increases the amount of unplanned, spontaneous, and chance communication between employees.[34] People are much more likely to plan meetings and work together when numerous "collaboration spaces" with conference tables, white boards, and computers are readily available. With no office walls, with inviting common areas, and with different departments mixed together in large open spaces, spontaneous communication occurs more often. Kit Tuveson of Hewlett-Packard said that open environments encourage "more momentary interaction [than private-office plans] because when people are more easily seen, they are perceived to be more accessi-

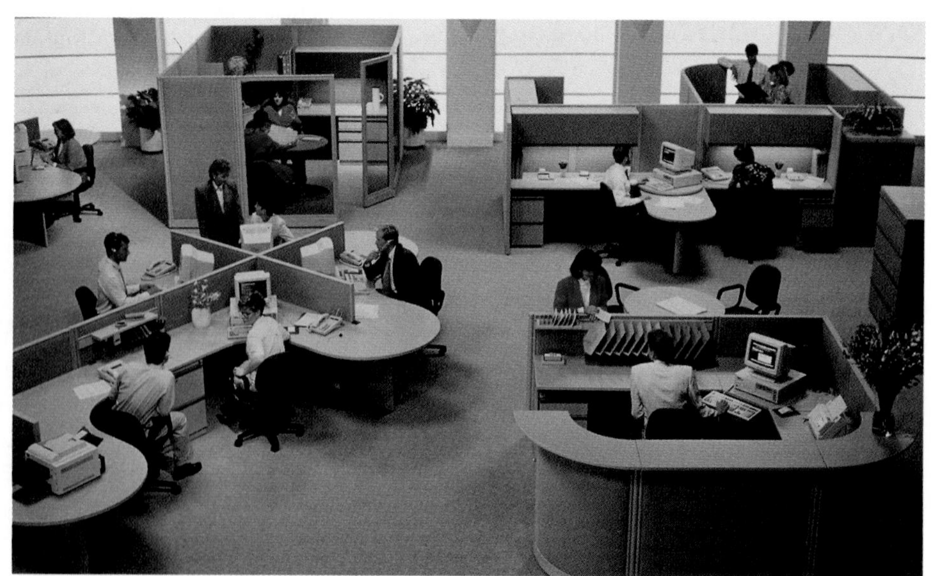

Open office systems offer a large amount of shared space, encouraging interaction among employees.
© Chuck Keeler/Tony Stone

Personal Productivity Tip

Dress for Success the Casual Way

Dressing for success used to be easy. Conservative suits, shirts, blouses, and ties were the norm. Yet, with the popularity of casual dress, many are now unsure what to wear to work. In general, women should not wear denim, leggings, sneakers, tank tops, plunging necklines, or short skirts. Men should not wear jeans, shorts, T-shirts, gym shoes, or sandals. In general, women can wear flat shoes, blazers, and linen slacks or full-skirted dresses. Men can wear pleated pants (i.e., Dockers) with a polo or dress shirt. To be safe, though, always check with co-workers and read your company's casual dress policy.

Sources: L. Halloran, "Make Yourself Comfy, and Get Back to Work," *The Hartford Courant*, 23 July 1996. S.C. Ryan, "Dressing for Success Goes Casual," *Portland Oregonian*, 25 May 1997.

ble."[35] Also, open office systems increase chance communication by making it much more likely that people from different departments or areas will run into each other. John Lewis, Arthur Andersen's chief financial officer, said, "From my personal point of view, it's [the open office] been fantastic. I'm getting visits from people I hardly ever see. It's just a far more interactive environment than what we've had before and exactly what I hoped to achieve."[36]

However, not all companies are enthusiastic about open offices. Microsoft gives employees private offices so they can concentrate on their work. Says Microsoft's John Pinette, "Private offices allow our employees to concentrate on their work and to avoid unnecessary distractions—[which is] obviously critical when you're doing something that requires as much focus as developing software does." Indeed, because there is so much shared space and so little private space, companies with open systems have to take a number of steps to give employees privacy when they need to concentrate on individual work. At Arthur Anderson, the company pipes in white noise through the ceiling to prevent voices and other noises from disrupting others. In contrast to traditional offices, many employees reserve conference rooms when they need private time to work. At Steelcase, employees and managers can put privacy screens around their work stations (the equivalent of shutting your door in a traditional office), display large "do not disturb" signs, or wear brightly colored earplugs.[37]

Review 4: *Intraorganizational Processes*

Today, companies are using reengineering, empowerment, and behavioral informality to change their intraorganizational processes. Through fundamental rethinking and radical redesign of business processes, reengineering changes an organization's orientation from vertical to horizontal. Reengineering changes work processes by decreasing sequential and pooled interdependence, and by increasing reciprocal interdependence. Reengineering promises dramatic increases in productivity and customer satisfaction, but has been criticized as simply an excuse to cut costs and lay off workers. Empowering workers means taking decision-making authority and responsibility from managers and giving it to workers. Empowered workers develop feelings of competence and self-determination and believe their work to have meaning and impact. Workplaces characterized by behavioral informality are spontaneous and casual. The formality or informality of a workplace depends on four factors: language usage, conversational turntaking and topic selection, emotional and proxemic gestures, and physical and contextual cues. Casual dress policies and open office systems are two of the most popular methods for increasing behavioral informality.

5 Interorganizational Processes

What do "Voodoo Lounge," "$100 million," and an "interorganizational process" have in common? "Voodoo Lounge" is the name of a Rolling Stones tour. "$100 million" is the profit the Stones earned from the Voodoo Lounge tour.[38] And an "interorganizational process" is the method the Stones' business manager used to organize the tour.

interorganizational process
a collection of activities that take place among companies to transform inputs into outputs that customers value

An **interorganizational process** is a collection of activities that occur *among companies* to transform inputs into outputs that customers value. In other words, many companies work together to create a product or service that keeps customers happy. For example, in the interorganizational process used to manage the Voodoo Lounge tour, the Stones did one thing, play music. Everything else in the tour—recording, transportation, marketing, and construction—was farmed out to other companies. For example, after 57 trucks transported the materials, it took four days to construct the 92-foot-high Voodoo Lounge stage (with a 924-square-foot Sony Jumbotron) in each stadium in which the Stones played. However, other than the design, the Stones didn't have anything to do with the set. Instead, they hired RZO productions, which employed stagehands, laborers, and lighting and sound technicians to get the stage ready for the Stones each night. Likewise, the Stones didn't own or run the expensive sound equipment needed to blast rock and roll into every corner of huge, 100,000-seat stadiums. Instead, the band contracted that responsibility to a separate sound company which, because it could keep that equipment in use nearly every day, provided the sound system much more cheaply than the Stones could have themselves.

In this section, you'll explore interorganizational processes by learning about **5.1** *modular organizations,* **5.2** *virtual organizations, and* **5.3** *boundaryless organizations.*[39]

5.1
Modular Organizations

modular organization
an organization that outsources noncore business activities to outside companies, suppliers, specialists, or consultants

Except for the core business activities that they can perform better, faster, and cheaper than others, **modular organizations** outsource all remaining business activities to outside companies, suppliers, specialists, or consultants. The term "modular" is used because the business activities purchased from outside companies can be added and dropped as needed, much like adding pieces to a three-dimensional puzzle. Figure 11.11 depicts a modular organization in which the company has chosen to keep training, human resources, sales, research and development, information technology, product design, customer service, and manufacturing as core business activities.

The Rolling Stones used an interorganizational process to organize the Voodoo Lounge tour, freeing the musicians to do what they do best.
© Corbis-Bettmann

Figure 11.11 **Modular Organizations**

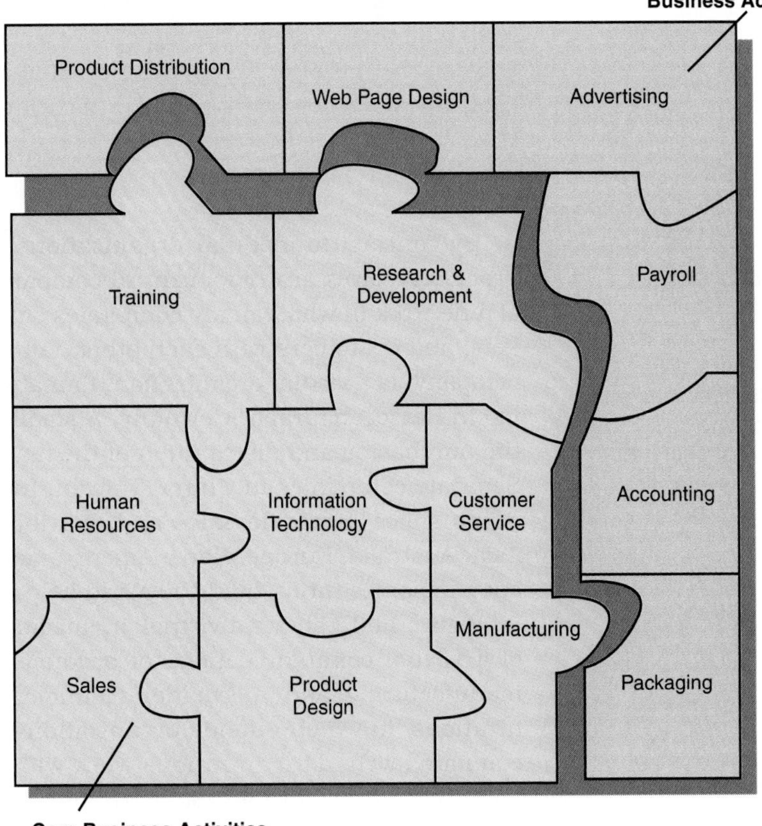

Personal Productivity Tip

Hot Desks and Big Savings?

With "hot desks," workers no longer have permanent offices or desks. Using central storage for personal belongings, networks that permit access to work files from any computer, and phone systems that forward permanent phone numbers to any phone, workers are simply assigned to the next empty desk when they arrive for work. Because you sit next to somebody different each day, "hot desks" improve communication. And, in offices where people spend time with customers or working from home, overall office space can be reduced by 30 percent to 45 percent. Would you be willing to give up your desk to achieve these savings?

Sources: T. Petzinger, Jr., "Cisco Systems' Staff Conquers Anxiety after Losing Desks," *The Wall Street Journal Interactive Edition*, 21 February 1997.

However, it has chosen to outsource noncore activities of product distribution, Web page design, advertising, payroll, accounting, and packaging.

Modular organizations have several advantages. First, because modular organizations pay for outsourced labor, expertise, or manufacturing capabilities only when needed, they can cost significantly less to run than traditional organizations. For example, of the "big three" automakers in the U.S., DaimlerChrysler, which outsources 70 percent of its parts manufacturing to suppliers, has by far the lowest costs. Next lowest is Ford, which outsources 50 percent of parts manufacturing to suppliers, and then General Motors, which outsources only 30 percent of parts manufacturing.[40] Second, outsourcing allows both modular companies, and the companies to whom they outsource, to focus on the core activities they do best.

However, to obtain these advantages, several preconditions must be met. The most important is that modular organizations need to work closely with reliable partners, that is, vendors and suppliers that they can trust. For example, DaimlerChrysler calls its close relationships with outside suppliers an "extended enterprise," where the business activities conducted by DaimlerChrysler's suppliers are literally viewed as an extension of the company.[41] In fact, some of DaimlerChrysler's key suppliers have permanent offices at the company, so they can work with DaimlerChrysler from the beginning of the process, parts design, to the end, parts delivery. DaimlerChrysler's CEO Robert Eaton said, "We do not typically put a design [for parts] out for bids and have a bunch of people bid on it. We really want long-term suppliers and the extended-enterprise concept."[42]

However, modular organizations have disadvantages, too. The primary disadvantage is the loss of control that occurs when key business activities are outsourced to other companies. Also, companies may reduce their competitive advantage in two ways if they mistakenly outsource a core business activity. First, competitive and technological change may produce a situation in which the noncore business activities a company has outsourced suddenly become the basis for competitive advantage. Second, related to that point, companies to whom work is outsourced can sometimes become competitors.

5.2
Virtual Organizations

virtual organization
an organization that is part of a network in which many companies share skills, costs, capabilities, markets, and customers to collectively solve customer problems or provide specific products or services

By contrast to modular organizations in which the interorganizational process revolves around a central company, a **virtual organization** is part of a network in which many companies share skills, costs, capabilities, markets, and customers with each other. For example, Puma, the athletic shoe company, is a virtual organization. Puma takes care of strategy and marketing in Herzogenaurach, Germany. A small network of firms in Asia handles the purchasing and distribution of the materials used to make Puma shoes. Separate companies in China, Taiwan, Indonesia, and Korea manufacture Puma shoes. Separate sales and distribution networks operate in Africa, Asia, Australia, Europe, North America, and South America. In all, 80 different companies throughout the world help make and sell Puma shoes.[43]

Figure 11.12 shows a virtual organization in which, for "today," the parts of a virtual company consist of product design, purchasing, advertising, manufacturing, and information technology. However, unlike modular organizations, in which outside organizations are tightly linked to one central company, virtual organizations work with some companies in the network alliance, but not with all. So, whereas a puzzle with various pieces is a fitting metaphor for modular organizations, a potluck dinner is an appropriate metaphor for virtual organizations. Everyone brings their finest food dish, but only eats what they want.

Another difference is that the working relationships between modular organizations and outside companies tend to be more stable and longer lasting than the shorter, often temporary relationships found among the virtual companies in a network alliance. Thus, the composition of a virtual organization is always changing. The combination of network partners that a virtual corporation has at any one time simply depends on the expertise needed to solve a particular problem or provide a specific product or service. This is why the businessperson in the network organization shown in Figure 11.12 said, "Today, I'll have . . ." Tomorrow, the business could want something completely different. In this sense, the term "virtual organization" means the organization that exists "at the moment." For example, 19 small companies in Pennsylvania have formed a network of virtual organizations that they call the "Agile Web." Together, the companies have expertise in product development and design, machining, metal fabrication, die casting, plastic-injection molding, finishing and coating, and the design and manufacture of electronic components. Tony Nickel, who coordinates business opportunities for the 19 web members, said, "We do have multiple machine shops and multiple sheet-metal shops. If only one is needed, I make the decision based on the nature of the [customer's] request and the areas of specialization of the member firms." He added that ". . . we've already had one occasion where, while negotiating with a customer, we discovered that we

Figure 11.12 **Network Organization**

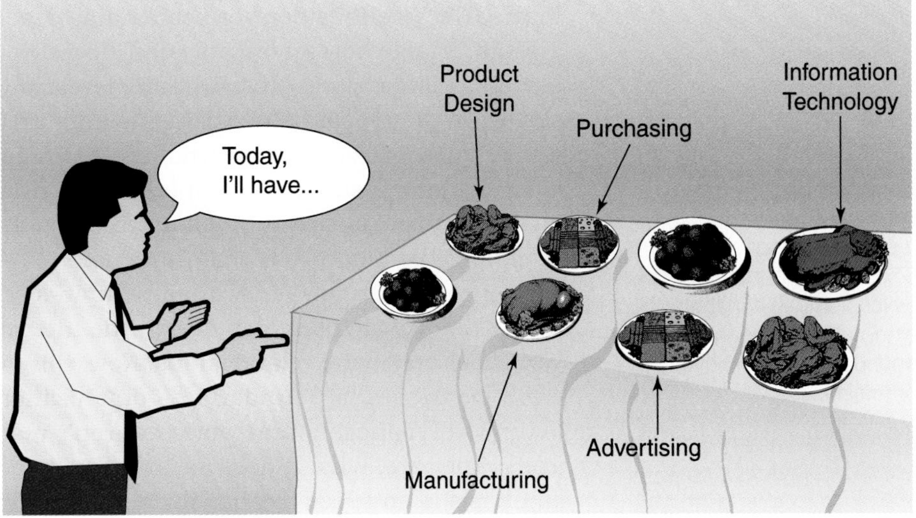

really didn't have the right Web member for a particular part—so we changed members."[44]

Virtual organizations have a number of advantages. They let companies share costs. And, because members can quickly combine their efforts to meet customers' needs, they are fast and flexible. For example, Tony Nickel of the Agile Web said, "Where we think we really can have rapid response is when a customer wants help in the design and building of an assembly or system. Then I can bring members of the Web to the table—or to the customer's facility—right away; the next day, if required. We are able to assemble a team from the Web within 24 hours if that is what the customer wants."[45] Finally, because each member of the network alliance is the "best" at what it does, in theory, virtual organizations should provide better products and services in all respects.

Like modular organizations, a disadvantage of virtual organizations is that once work has been outsourced, it can be difficult to control the quality of work done by network partners. However, the greatest disadvantage is that it requires tremendous managerial skills to make a network of independent organizations work well together, especially since their relationships tend to be shorter and task or project based. However, virtual organizations are using two methods to solve this problem. The first is to use a *broker*, like Tony Nickel. In traditional, hierarchical organizations, managers plan, organize, and control. But with the horizontal, interorganizational processes that characterize virtual organizations, the job of a broker is to create and assemble the knowledge, skills, and resources from different companies for outside parties, such as customers.[46] The second way to make networks of virtual organizations more manageable is to use a *virtual organization agreement* that, somewhat like a contract, specifies the schedules, responsibilities, costs, and payouts to participating organizations.[47]

5.3
Boundaryless Organizations

In 1989, General Electric CEO Jack Welch coined the term "boundaryless organization" in his annual letter to GE shareholders. Welch wrote, "Our dream for the 1990s is a boundaryless company, a company where we knock down the walls that separate us from each other on the inside and from our constituencies on the outside." Why was Welch, arguably one of the most effective CEOs of this decade, so concerned with boundaries? Steve Kerr, GE's Vice President of Leadership Development, explained: "Boundaries determine how an organization operates. There are vertical boundaries like floors and ceilings that separate levels of the organization; there are inside walls that separate departments from each other; and there are outside walls that separate the firm from its environment, from its customers, outside regulators, suppliers, and other constituencies."[48] Thus, a **boundaryless organization** would break down the vertical, horizontal, external, and geographic boundaries in organizations.[49]

boundaryless organization
a speedy, responsive, and flexible organization in which vertical, horizontal, external, and geographic boundaries are removed or minimized

Figure 11.13 shows how a boundaryless organization might work. First, notice that inside the company, in the internal environment, there are no vertical or horizontal relationships. Now, this doesn't mean that there are literally no bosses in boundaryless organizations. It also doesn't mean that lower-level managers and workers aren't responsible to upper-level managers. They are. What it does mean is that in boundaryless organizations the emphasis is on speed, responsiveness, and flexibility rather than to whom you report. GE's Steve Kerr said, "In a hierarchy, you're always asking who is the boss. In a boundaryless company, you don't ask that question. It

Figure 11.13 **Boundaryless Organizations**

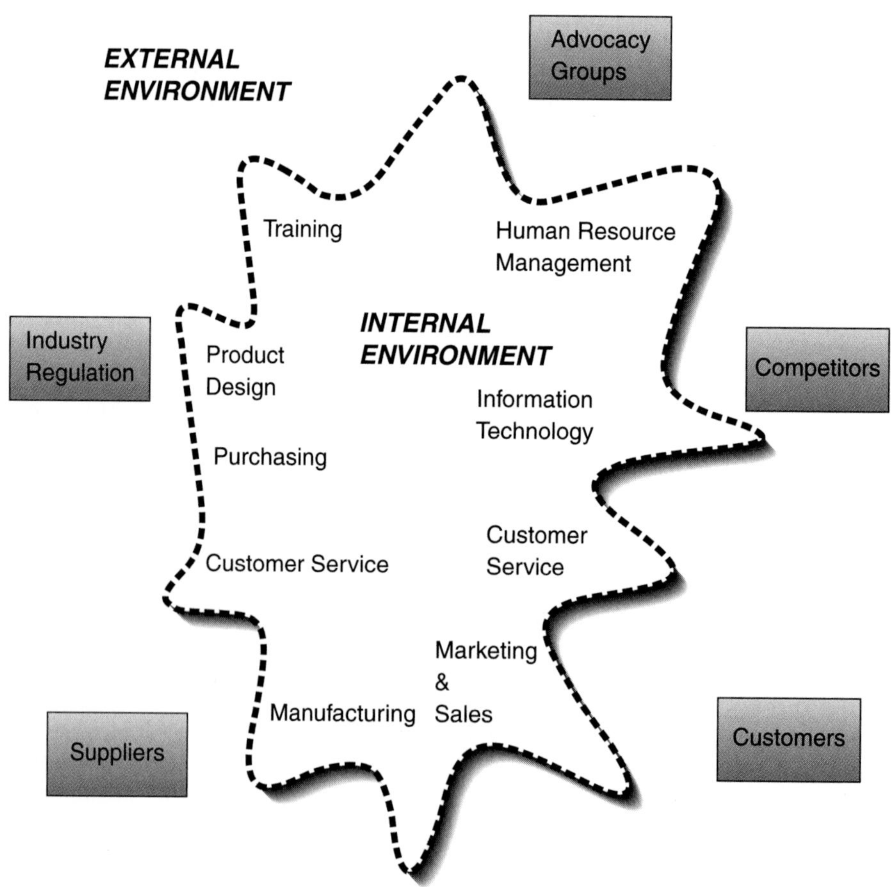

Source: Adapted from G.G. Dess, A.M.A. Rasheed, K.J. McLaughlin, & R.L. Priem, "The New Corporate Architecture," *Academy of Management Executive* 9 (1995): 7-18.

stops being relevant. You ask who has the information that would improve the decision."[50] Second, notice that in Figure 11.13, the organization's external boundary, represented by the dotted line, is permeable. Again, the point here is to remove the boundary separating the organization's internal environment from its external environment (i.e., industry regulation, suppliers, customers, competitors, and advocacy groups).

By focusing on results rather than reporting relationships, one of the advantages of boundaryless organizations is that they make much better use of employee knowledge, skills, and abilities. Instead of asking what department or job is "responsible" for a problem, the question that gets asked is "Who inside or outside the company can best solve this problem?" Another advantage is that they lead to much closer relationships with the components of the company's external environment. For example, one of the ways that GE has made external boundaries more permeable is by putting key managers "on loan" to outside companies. So, instead of reporting to work at a GE office in a GE building, these "on loan" managers report to work at offices that are permanently located in customers' or suppliers' offices or buildings.

However, boundaryless organizations have significant disadvantages as well. To start, managers and employees often find the transition to boundaryless organizations threatening. Managers and workers who are used to the clear accountability and reporting relationships of vertical hierarchies often struggle with the new emphasis on speed and flexibility. However, the biggest disadvantage to boundaryless organizations is that there is no clear way to achieve them. The suggested methods read like a list of ingredients: create interdivisional committees, establish communication flows, create mutually beneficial relationships with suppliers and customers, build trust with employees, etc. Unfortunately, there is little advice on how best to combine and "cook" them.[51]

Review 5: *Interorganizational Processes*

Organizations are using modular, virtual, and boundaryless organizations to change interorganizational processes. Because modular organizations outsource all noncore activities to other businesses, they are less expensive to run than traditional companies. However, modular organizations require extremely close relationships with suppliers, may result in a loss of control, and could create new competitors if the wrong business activities are outsourced. Virtual organizations participate in a network in which they share skills, costs, capabilities, markets, and customers. As customer problems, products, or services change, the combination of virtual organizations that work together changes. Virtual organizations reduce costs, respond quickly, and, if they can successfully coordinate their efforts, can produce outstanding products and service. By breaking down internal and external boundaries, boundaryless organizations try to increase organizational speed, flexibility, and responsiveness. However, boundaryless organizations are threatening to managers and workers and are difficult to create.

What**Really**Happened?

In the opening case, you learned that American Express was hoping to turn around its performance by "reengineering" and "restructuring" its organizational design and processes. Read the following answers to the opening case questions to find out what steps American Express has taken so far to improve company performance.

After a decade of poor performance, American Express has decided that it needs to "reengineer" and "restructure" the way it does business if it wants to return to the success it once had. Of course, the difficult question is "how?" How should the company be organized? Should it be by function, product, customer, or geography?

Companies can be organized in the following ways: functional, product, customer, geographical, and matrix. American Express has organized into separate units that are responsible for different kinds of customers: Cards for credit and charge card customers; Travel for the needs of travelers for travelers' checks, airline tickets, vacation planning services, and worldwide travel offices; Financial Services for investors who need advisors, mutual and money market funds, etc.; Shopping for consumers shopping by catalog or online; and Business Services for the needs of business customers for travel services and corporate cards, plus financing, accounting, planning, and lending for small businesses.

Each form of departmentalization has advantages and disadvantages. For American Express, the primary advantage of customer departmentalization is that it focuses the organization on customer needs, rather than on products or business functions. Furthermore, creating separate departments to serve specific kinds of customers allows American Express companies to specialize and adapt their products and services to customer needs and problems. After all, the customer who uses only the American Express card or American Express travelers' checks is going to have different expectations than the customer who uses the American Express Financial Services division to manage investments.

Second, what changes should be made in who makes what decisions? Should the approach be centralized or highly decentralized?

The issue of who makes what decisions is related to the amount and kind of authority given to company employees. Centralization of authority is the concentration of decision-making authority at the upper levels of the organization. Decentralization is the delegation of decision-making authority down to the workers closest to the problems, so that they can make the decisions necessary to solve the problems themselves. In the 1990s, there has been a clear trend toward decentralization and away from centralization. Indeed, studies show that companies that are highly decentralized outperform those that are highly centralized on a number of important financial measures.

However, there is one exception. When standardization is important, when it's advantageous to consistently apply the same rules, procedures, or processes, then companies can improve performance by centralizing authority. American Express cut expenses by $1.9 billion when it tightened and centralized the different "back offices" that handle its billing and card statements for consumers and retailers. With the American Express Card, the American Express Gold Card, the American Express Platinum Card, and the Optima credit cards, the same kind of work was being done in too many different ways. Consequently, those back-office services that used to be run independently for each American Express card (there are more than 20) have now been centralized and consolidated into one back office that handles all billing statements.

Third, if American Express wants to truly "reengineer" the way it does business, should it focus on reengineering its internal processes, the way it does business internally, or should it reengineer its external processes, the way it does business with other companies?

An intraorganizational process is the collection of activities that take place within an organization to transform inputs into outputs that customers value. By contrast, an interorganizational process is the collection of activities that occur among companies to transform inputs into outputs. Companies use reengineering, empowerment, and behavioral informality to change intraorganizational processes, and modular, virtual, and boundaryless organizations to change interorganizational processes.

Thus far, by becoming a modular organization, American Express has largely focused on changing interorganizational processes. Except for the core business activities that they can perform better, faster, and cheaper than others, modular organizations outsource all remaining business activities to outside companies. At American Express, most of its card business is handled within the company. However, it has now begun outsourcing functions like late collections, the manufacturing of its green, gold, and platinum cards, and its global assistance program (in which travelers call when they need special assistance traveling abroad, such as replacing lost travelers' checks or obtaining a hard-to-get medical prescription).

American Express has also worked hard to redesign its intraorganizational processes, so that it can respond faster to competitors and adapt more quickly for customers. For example, it took American Express more than 18 months to bring to market its Optima True Grace credit card (which has a 25-day interest-free grace period before interest starts accruing). However, it took one of its competitors only seven weeks to bring out an identical card. Said CEO Harvey Golub about American Express's lack of speed, "The process was like giving birth to an elephant." Today, however, because it has reengineered its intraorganizational processes, American Express is bringing out about 15 new cards per year! For example, it now has joint cards with the New York Knicks, a professional basketball team, the New York Rangers, a professional hockey team, ITT Sheraton, a hotel chain that awards points that can be used for discounts on hotel rooms and car rentals, and Delta Airlines, where the American Express Delta Skymiles card can be used to earn free flights or ticket upgrades. Says Phillip Reese, who heads the consumer card group, "We used to spend huge amounts of time and money researching every product that we put into the marketplace. Today we develop products, put them into the market in small test environments and we have a far better idea from real life experience than we could get from research."

There are no long-term guarantees, but thus far, the changes to American Express's organizational structure and intra- and interorganizational processes appear to be working. Purchases on American Express cards are increasing faster than purchases on Visa or MasterCard. Likewise, profits and market share are up. To read the latest information about American Express's current performance, visit its Web site at **www.americanexpress.com**. See the latest annual report and the latest press releases.

Sources: "Amexco 'reengineers'," *Travel Weekly*, 10 February 1997. D. Brady & S.E. Frank, "American Express Recasts Overseas Part of the Travel Unit," *The Wall Street Journal*, 24 May 1996. L. Fickenscher, "Rivals Spurred American Express Revamping," *American Banker*, 12 October 1994. S.E. Frank, "Credit Cards: Amex Strategy on Cards Way to Growth," *The Wall Street Journal*, 28 April 1997. S.E. Frank, "American Express Posts 15% Net Rise on Card Strengths," *The Wall Street Journal Interactive Edition*, 25 April 1997. S.E. Frank, "American Express Stages Its First Gain in Credit-Card Market Share in Decade," *The Wall Street Journal Interactive Edition*, 24 March 1998. D. Jones, "Amexco Cuts Not Lost on the Industry," *Travel Weekly*, 17 February 1997. S. Oliver, "The Battle of the Credit Cards," *Forbes*, 1 July 1996.

Key Terms

authority p. 423

autonomy p. 432

behavioral formality p. 442

behavioral informality p. 442

boundaryless organization p. 450

centralization of authority p. 427

chain of command p. 423

complex matrix p. 422

customer departmentalization p. 416

decentralization p. 427

delegation of authority p. 424

departmentalization p. 413

empowering workers p. 441

empowerment p. 441

feedback p. 432

functional departmentalization p. 413

geographic departmentalization p. 419

internal motivation p. 431

interorganizational process p. 446

intraorganizational process p. 437

job characteristics model (JCM) p. 431

job design p. 428

job enlargement p. 430

job enrichment p. 431

job rotation p. 430

job specialization p. 428

line authority p. 423

line function p. 424

matrix departmentalization p. 419

mechanistic organization p. 437

modular organization p. 446

open office systems p. 444

organic organization p. 437

organizational process p. 410

organizational structure p. 410

pooled interdependence p. 440

private spaces p. 444

product departmentalization p. 414

reciprocal interdependence p. 440

reengineering p. 439

sequential interdependence p. 440

shared spaces p. 444

simple matrix p. 422

skill variety p. 432

staff authority p. 424

staff function p. 424

standardization p. 427

task identity p. 432

task interdependence p. 440

task significance p. 432

unity of command p. 423

virtual organization p. 448

What Would You Do-II?

Morton, Mississippi

"Welcome to McDonald's. Can I take your order please?" "Yeah, I'll have a McChicken Value Meal. Oh, and super-size the drinks and fries. That'll be all. Thanks." A decade ago, most drive-through orders were for beef sandwiches, like a Big Mac or a double-cheeseburger. However, today, health-conscious consumers are just as likely to eat chicken. In fact, with over 11,000,000 metric tons of chicken produced each year, the U.S. produces and consumes twice as much chicken as any other nation.

Because of the huge rise in demand for chicken, a quarter of a million people now work in poultry-processing factories—more than double the number in 1980. Furthermore, since poultry-processing jobs are now the second fastest growing job category in the U.S., wages have climbed from $5 an hour to roughly $8 to $10 an hour for work that requires no skill, experience, or training. However, the basic steps of processing poultry—scalding, eviscerating, de-boning, dripping (for removing blood and bodily fluids), removing feet, and removing giblets—make this an inherently gruesome job. Furthermore, due to intensified competition and increased demand, the job has gotten even worse, as companies have increased the number of chickens they process from around 50 per minute, which was the standard in 1985, to the maximum government-allowed amount of 91 chickens per minute today. The resulting pace is frantic and stressful. Chicken skin, guts, parts, and feathers literally fly as workers struggle to keep up.

With one out of four experiencing job-related injuries, poultry workers suffer one of the highest rates of job injury. Workers wielding sharp knives and scissors frequently cut themselves or others. And since poultry processing involves rapid and repetitive motions, uncomfortable body postures, forceful movements, and no control over the pace of work, repetitive stress injuries, like carpal tunnel syndrome, are common. Repetitive stress injuries comprise one-quarter of all work-related injuries. Of those, two-thirds involve back injuries, while one-third include upper extremities such as fingers, hands, wrists, elbows, necks, and shoulders. Symptoms can include shooting, searing pain in the joints and tendons or an inability to grasp and control ordinary objects.

If the gore, injuries, and frantic pace weren't tough enough, most companies automatically fire workers if they leave the manufacturing line for any reason, including going to the bathroom. With work shifts often lasting 10–12 hours (until the last chicken is processed), and with breaks infrequent and short (one company in Mississippi allows workers only three breaks per week), employees often struggle to make it to the end of their shifts. In some instances, employees who have been unable to get their supervisor's attention (the plants are large and very loud) have wet themselves rather than lose their jobs by leaving the line to go to the bathroom.

Not surprisingly, people don't last very long in these jobs. Since most quit within three to six months, the average annual rate of employee turnover is 100 percent or more. However, companies feel there is little they can do to improve working conditions. Poultry processing is a highly competitive business. Consequently, companies have been more concerned with cutting costs, speeding production, and improving productivity than with improving working conditions. Furthermore, the tough working conditions weren't a problem when unemployment was high. There were always enough job applicants to replace those who left. But today, with unemployment at record lows, poultry companies are having a much more difficult time attracting and keeping workers. But how do you redesign poultry-processing jobs to make them more tolerable (they're never going to be great jobs), to reduce the number of repetitive stress injuries, *and* still address the competitive issues of cost, production, and productivity? **If you were in charge of a poultry-processing plant, what would you do?**

Sources: M. Cooper, "The Heartland's Raw Deal: How Meatpacking Is Creating a New Immigrant Underclass," *The Nation*, 3 February 1997, 11. F. Greve, "OSHA Demands Bathroom Freedom," *The Des Moines Register*, 24 August 1997, 18. T. Horwitz, "9 to Nowhere: These Six Growth Jobs Are Dull, Dead-End, Sometimes Dangerous—They Show How '90s Trends Can Make Work Grimmer for Unskilled Workers—Blues on the Chicken Line," *The Wall Street Journal*, 1 December 1994. "Just the Facts: The Role of the Meat Industry in the U.S. Economy," American Meat Institute Web site. [Online] Available **www.meatami.org/FactBK01.HTM**, 14 September 1997. C.E. Morris & L. Mancini, "No Pain, No Gain," *Chilton's Food Engineering*, 1 May 1996, 53. "Preventing Repetitive Stress Injuries," U.S. Department of Labor, OSHA Web site. [Online] Available **www.osha-slc.gov/ergo/prsi.html**, 10 December 1996.

Critical-Thinking Video Case

Organizational Design: JIAN

JIAN Corporation is a successful software company located in the Silicon Valley area of Northern California. JIAN was created in 1988 by Burt Franklin, an entrepreneur who saw the need for effective, timesaving software. One of its early products was the award-winning BizPlan Builder, which has sold over 300,000 copies. Today, JIAN is recognized as a leader in providing useful software for emerging and established businesses.

Burt Franklin started JIAN as a home business. When JIAN rapidly outgrew his apartment, Burt realized that he had to design an organization that would continue to grow and maintain the speed and flexibility needed to survive in the competitive, fast-changing software business. As you watch the video, consider the following critical-thinking questions.

Critical-Thinking Questions

1. How might JIAN design an organization that will enable the company to grow?
2. How might JIAN and its partners work together to create a successful virtual corporation?
3. What type of relationship should exist to enable the partners in a virtual corporation to succeed?

Management Decisions

Super Bakery

Former Pittsburgh Steelers' running back Franco Harris is best known for the "immaculate reception," an unlikely shoe-top catch of a tipped pass that he ran in from 60 yards out to help the Steelers defeat the Oakland Raiders with just 22 seconds remaining in a 1972 playoff game. Today, Franco Harris is the owner of Super Bakery, Inc., a small Pittsburgh-based bakery with approximately $10 million in annual revenues. Super Bakery's best-selling product is the Super Donut, a nutritional, low-fat, vitamin-enriched donut that actually tastes good. In fact, elementary schools that had eliminated regular donuts from their breakfast and lunch menus are now serving Super Donuts, because they meet the strict nutritional requirements of the federal government's school lunch program.

After buying the company, Harris decided that Super Bakery's organizational structure needed to be reorganized in order to accomplish the following objectives. First, unlike most baked goods that are sold in local markets like Pittsburgh, Harris wanted to sell Super Donuts nationwide. Second, Super Bakery needed to find a way to simultaneously cut costs and increase quality. Third, Super Bakery needed to find a way to reliably deliver its Super Donuts to schools, hospitals, and airlines. Keep these objectives in mind as you answer these questions.

Questions

1. One of the basic decisions in modular, virtual, or boundaryless organizations is deciding which business functions your company should perform itself and which should be done by other companies (i.e., outsourcing). For example, every time a school or hospital orders Super Donuts for its cafeteria, Super Bakery has to complete the following steps:
   1. Sell purchase contracts to customers.
   2. Enter food orders.
   3. Get credit clearance for orders.
   4. Cost the order.
   5. Price the order.
   6. Schedule production.
   7. Buy ingredients.
   8. Manufacture the order.
   9. Ship the order.
   10. Bill the customer.
   11. Collect payment.

   Given Super Bakery's objectives, which of these steps should it keep and which should it let other companies do? Explain why. In other words, what criteria should Super Bakery use for making this decision?

2. Given these objectives, and the advantages and disadvantages of different interorganizational processes, which kind of organization—modular, virtual, or boundaryless—is best for Super Bakery? Explain why.

Sources: T.R.V. Davis & B.L. Darling, "The Super Bakery Case," *Organizational Dynamics*, Summer 1995, 70-75. T.R.V. Davis & B.L. Darling, "Update on Super Bakery, Inc.," *Organizational Dynamics*, Autumn 1996, 86-87. S. Somerville, "Parks' 2nd Chance; Challenge: Franco Harris and Lydell Mitchell, Former Football Teammates at Penn State, Face a Tough Battle to Return Parks Sausage Co. to Prosperity," *Baltimore Sun*, 22 September 1996. E.L. Smith, "The Immaculate Reception of Park Sausage," *Black Enterprise*, 1 September 1996, 58.

Management Decisions

Plush Management Perks: Partaking or Pruning?

"They do, too!" "*They do not!*" "You don't know what you're talking about." "*See, it's attitudes like yours that prove my point!*"

Ah, nothing like watching your top two executives argue during lunch to raise your blood pressure. You knew that Sam, the VP of Sales, was going to get mad when Catherine, the VP of Human Resources, suggested getting rid of executive perks (the private dining room, company cars, first-class air travel, etc.). It took Sam 25 years to become a vice president and nobody, including Sam, wants to see his or her perks and rewards reduced. However, you didn't think it was possible for someone to get that mad that fast. Given the way Sam's face instantly turned beet red when Catherine suggested that the reserved parking spaces be eliminated, it's a good thing she caught him between bites or he might have choked on his shrimp salad.

Well, with executive perks topping the agenda for the annual executive retreat next weekend, Sam and Catherine's argument has given you something to think about. Is Catherine right? Do all executive perks need to be eliminated? Or is Sam right? Do the executive perks need to be left alone? After all, even Catherine got defensive when Sam asked her how happy she'd be if the company closed its on-site daycare. When she responded, "They wouldn't dare do that," Sam barked, "That's exactly the way I feel about your recommendations!"

Well, you need to get your thoughts sorted out. A good place to start is with the list of executive perks currently being offered by the company:

- company cars
- reserved parking spaces
- company cellular phones
- personal financial counseling
- personal liability insurance
- executive dining room
- first-class air travel
- spouse travel on extended business trips
- signing bonuses
- stock options
- country club memberships
- large, expensively furnished private offices
- home security systems
- home computer/office equipment

Questions

1. Of the perks listed above, choose three that your managers are most likely to desire. In other words, which three executive perks would your managers scream the most about if you took them away? Explain why for each of the three perks.

2. Of the perks listed above, which three probably create the most resentment among your work force (i.e., nonmanagers)? In other words, which three executive perks anger your work force the most? Explain why for each of the three perks.

3. Choose the option (a, b, or c) that is likely to benefit the company most in the long run:
   a. eliminate all executive perks
   b. retain all executive perks
   c. selectively eliminate perks

   Explain the reasoning behind your choice. If you choose option c, specify the perks you kept and why you kept them.

Sources: M. Budman, "The Persistence of Perks," *Across the Board*, 1 February 1994. L. Fleeson, "In Today's Efficient, Egalitarian Offices, Plush Perks Are Passe," *The News Tribune*, 10 July 1994. S. Lohr, "Cubicle or Cavern? Egalitarian Work Space Duels with Need for Privacy Among Brainy Folks in High-Tech Firms," *Rocky Mountain News*, 7 September 1997. T. Schellhardt, "Executive Pay (A Special Report)—Passing Of Perks: Company Cars, Country Club Memberships, Executive Dining Rooms; Where Have All the Goodies Gone?" *The Wall Street Journal*, 13 April 1994.

Develop Your Management Potential

"Work" in Someone Else's Shoes

Why is learning to see things from someone else's perspective one of the most difficult things to do in today's workplace? Sometimes, the inability to see things as others see them has to do with the people involved. Inexperience, ignorance, and selfishness can all play a role. However, in most organizations, the inability to see things from someone else's perspective results from the jobs themselves, not the people who do them. Because jobs limit who we talk to, what we talk about, what we think about, and what we care about at work, it should not be a surprise that people who perform different jobs have very different views about each other and the workplace.

For example, at Southwest Airlines the pilots who fly the planes and the ground crews who unload, load, and refuel them had little appreciation for each other. The ground crews felt that the pilots treated them like second-class citizens. The pilots couldn't understand why the ground crews weren't doing more to get their planes out of the gates and in the air as fast as possible. To improve understanding and help them see things from each other's perspective, Southwest created a program called the Cutting Edge, in which the captains and ground crews learned a lot about each other's jobs. For example, the pilots brought the ground crews into their cockpits and showed them the detailed processes they were required to follow to get planes ready for departure. The pilots, on the other hand, gained appreciation and understanding by actually working as members of Southwest's ground crews. After several days of demanding ground crew work, Southwest pilot Captain Mark Boyter said:

> *I remember one time when I was working the ramp [as a member of a ground crew] in Los Angeles. I was dead tired. I had flown that morning and had a couple of legs in, so I got out of my uniform and jumped into my ramp clothes. That afternoon was very hot. It was in the 80s—I can't imagine how they do it on a 120-degree day in Phoenix. I was tired and hungry and hadn't had a break. Then I saw this pilot sitting up there in the cockpit eating his frozen yogurt. I said to myself, "Man, I'd like to be up there now." Then I caught myself. I'm up there every day. Now, I know that pilot has been up since 3:00 in the morning. I know that he's been flying an airplane since 6:00 a.m. I know it's 3:00 in the afternoon and he hasn't had a chance to get off and have a meal yet today. I know all that, and yet, the yogurt still looks really good to me. Then I thought, "How can a ramp agent [on the ground crew] in Los Angeles who works his butt off for two or three years, working double shifts two or three times a week, understand this? It hit me that there's a big gap in understanding here.*

The misunderstandings between Southwest's pilots and ground crews are not unique.

All organizations experience them. Nurses and doctors, teachers and students, and managers and employees all have difficulty seeing things from each other's perspective. However, as Southwest's Cutting Edge program shows, you can minimize differences and build understanding by "working" in someone else's shoes.

Questions

1. Describe the job-related differences or tensions where you work. Who is involved? What jobs do they do? Explain why the job-related differences or tensions exist.

2. Since the best way to see things from someone else's perspective is to "work" in his or her shoes, see if you can spend a day, a morning, or even two hours performing one of these jobs. If that's not possible, spend some time carefully observing the jobs and then interview several people who perform them. Describe your boss's reaction to this request. Was he or she supportive or not? Why?

3. Answer the following questions after you have worked the job or conducted your interviews. What most surprised you about this job? What was easiest? What was hardest? Explain. Now that you've had the chance to see things as others see them, what do you think would happen, good or bad, from letting other people in your organization work in someone else's shoes? Explain.

Sources: K. Freiberg & J. Freiberg, *Nuts! Southwest Airlines' Crazy Recipe for Business and Personal Success* (Austin, TX: Bard Press, 1996).

Part Four

Organizing People, Projects, and Processes

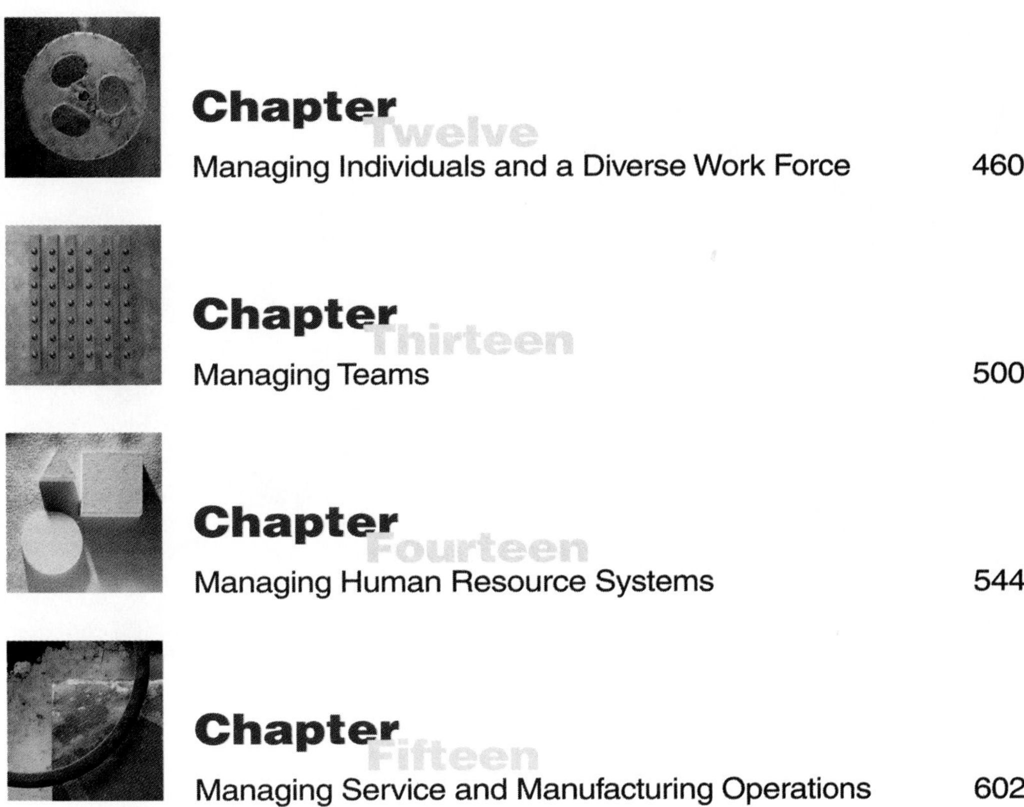

Chapter Twelve

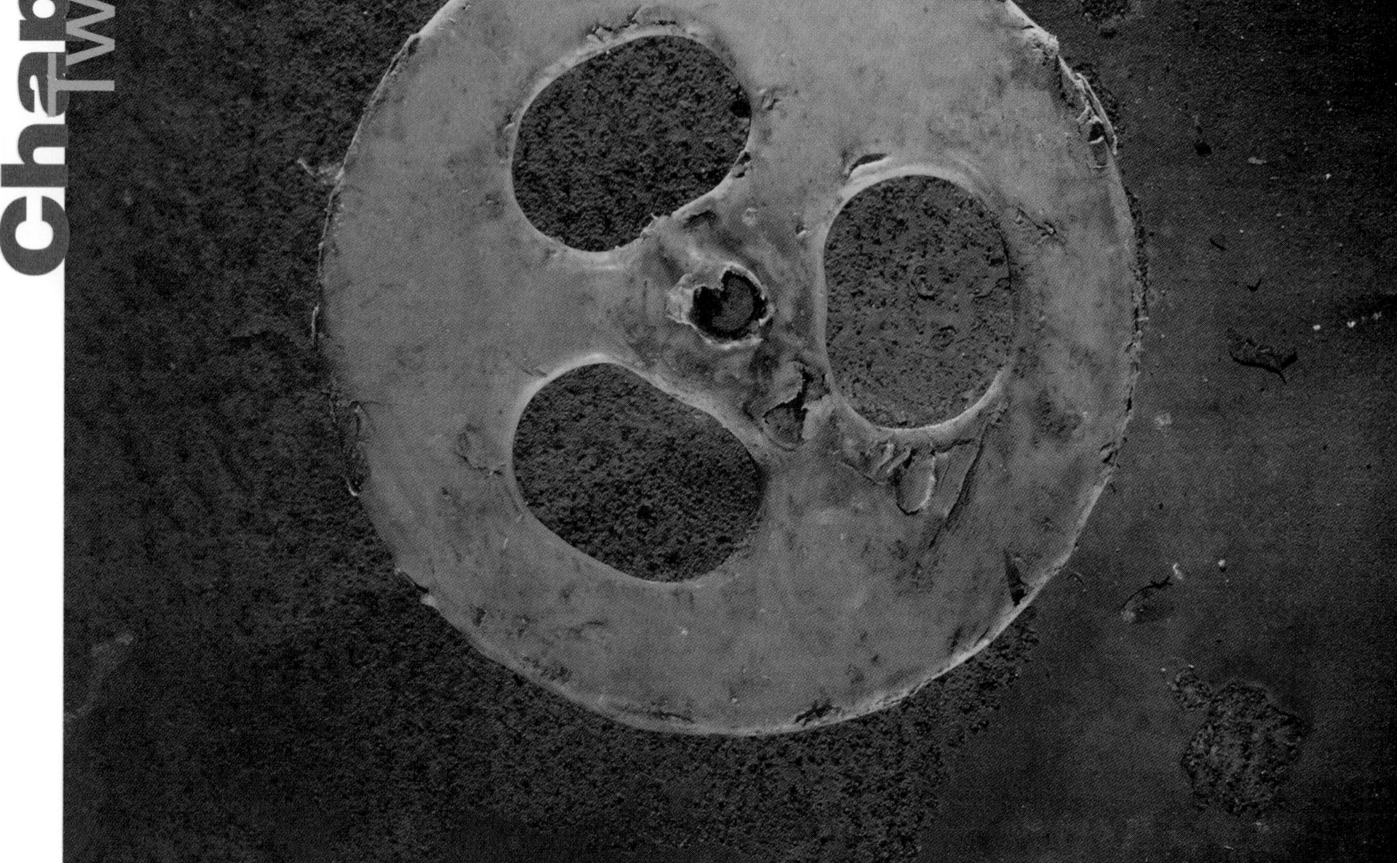

Chapter 12 Outline

Managing Individuals and a Diverse Work Force

What Would **You** Do?

MacTemps, Cambridge, Massachusetts. You couldn't have been happier when the MacTemps job offer arrived in the mail last year. While you had three other offers, MacTemps was the one you wanted. After a decade in business, MacTemps, a staffing firm specializing in the placement of employees with computer skills, was earning $100 million per year by helping employers find the talented workers they needed in 36 locations across the U.S. In short, the opportunities at MacTemps seemed limitless. Further, company founder John Chaung believed that rewards and promotion should be based solely on competence and performance. You had heard John state his beliefs on several occasions: "I think managers should turn a blind eye to race, age and gender and similar characteristics and hire and promote based exclusively on merit. You'll get a diverse work force without imposing any rules or guidelines." And, as an ambitious, hard-charger right out of school, you liked the idea of rewards being based on performance. In all, it looked like a great opportunity, so you snapped up the job the minute it was offered. Your job involves recruiting and hiring employees with computer skills (HTML, computer graphics, relational databases, etc.) for a variety of organizations that contract with MacTemps. You have to develop a pool of candidates based on the client's specifications, interview them, and then send three to five finalists to the client for final interviews. All of the finalists have to be good candidates if you expect any repeat business. You like the challenge and you like making contacts with managers and workers in a variety of industries. Everything seemed to be going quite well.

So when John came over to your desk and asked if you'd seen the newspaper article about the company, you were surprised by what you heard. Instead of describing MacTemps as a successful up-and-coming, minority-owned business, the article described MacTemps as rather typical of firms in the staffing industry—"unbalanced by gender and race." The reporter wrote that she found white males in executive positions and females concentrated in positions traditionally held by women in this industry (i.e., clerical and other nonmanagement jobs). John said, "I can't believe it. I thought by ignoring factors such as race and gender, we'd naturally end up with a diverse work force. This is the kind of publicity a firm in the staffing industry can't tolerate. If we can't achieve diversity, how many companies are going to hire us to help them staff their work forces? I'm pulling you off all of your accounts. I want you to develop a diversity plan for MacTemps, and I need it as soon as possible." "Diversity plan?" Isn't diversity just the result of affirmative action? And why didn't John's philosophy of ignoring race, gender, and age result in an adequately diverse work force? If these factors are irrelevant in hiring and promotion decisions, shouldn't the work force just naturally be diverse? What kinds of things go into a diversity plan? And how do you "manage diversity" without making race and gender more significant factors than merit?

If you were in charge of managing diversity at MacTemps, what would you do?

Sources: MacTemps Home Page, "About MacTemps." [Online] Available **http://www.mactemps.com/about.html,** 1 April 1999. J. Chaung, "On Balance," *Inc.,* July 1995, 25. D.H. Pink, "The Talent Market," *Fast Company*, August 1998, 87.

As we begin a new millennium, predictions abound about advances in medicine and computer technology, the possibility of finding life on other planets, and the chances of another world war. However, one prediction that is already beginning to come true is that workplace diversity will increase dramatically in this new millennium.

For example, Table 12.1 shows estimates from the U.S. Bureau of the Census that indicate that the percentage of white, non-Hispanic Americans in the general population will decline from 73.6 percent in 1995 to 52.8 percent by the year 2050. By contrast, the percentage of African Americans in the general population will increase from 12.0 percent to 13.6 percent over the same period. Also on the increase is the proportion of American Indians (0.7 percent to 0.9 percent) and Asians (3.3 percent to 8.2 percent). The fastest-growing group by far, though, is Hispanics, which will increase from 10.2 percent of the total population in 1995 to an estimated 24.5 percent by 2050.

Other significant changes are expected, too. For example, women will hold half the jobs in the U.S. by 2005, up from 38.2 percent in 1970.[1] Furthermore, the percentage of white males in the work force, who comprised 63.9 percent of all workers in 1950, will drop to just 38.2 percent of the total work force by 2005.[2]

These represent rather dramatic changes in a relatively short time. And, these trends clearly show that the work force of the near future will be more Hispanic, Asian, African-American, and female. However, it will also be older, as the average "baby boomer" approaches the age of 60 around 2010. And, since many of these boomers are likely to postpone retirement and work well into their 70s in order to offset predicted reductions in Social Security and Medicare benefits, the work force may become even older than expected.[3]

This chapter begins with a review of work force diversity—what it is and why it matters. Next, you will learn about two basic dimensions of diversity: surface-level diversity, in which you will explore how age, gender, race/ethnicity, and mental and physical disabilities affect people at work, and deep-level diversity, in which you will learn how core personality differences influence behavior and attitudes. In the last section, you will learn ways to answer the major question posed by John Chaung (founder of MacTemps) in the opening

Table 12.1

Predicted U.S. Population, Distributed by Race, 1995 to 2050

Year	White	Black	American Indian	Asian	Hispanic
1995	73.6%	12.0%	0.7%	3.3%	10.2%
2000	71.8%	12.2%	0.7%	3.9%	11.4%
2005	69.9%	12.4%	0.8%	4.4%	12.6%
2010	68.0%	12.6%	0.8%	4.8%	13.8%
2020	64.3%	12.9%	0.8%	5.7%	16.3%
2030	60.5%	13.1%	0.8%	6.6%	18.9%
2040	56.7%	13.3%	0.9%	7.5%	21.7%
2050	52.8%	13.6%	0.9%	8.2%	24.5%

Source: J.C. Day, *Population Projections of the United States by Age, Sex, Race, and Hispanic Origin: 1995 to 2050*, U.S. Bureau of the Census, Current Population Reports, P25-1130 (Washington, DC: U.S. Government Printing Office, 1996).

case: How can diversity be managed? Here, you'll read about diversity paradigms, principles, and practices that help managers like John Chaung strengthen the diversity *and* the competitiveness of their organizations.

Diversity and Why It Matters

diversity
a variety of demographic, cultural, and personal differences among the people who work in an organization and the customers who do business there

Diversity means variety. Therefore, **diversity** exists in organizations when there is a variety of demographic, cultural, and personal differences among the people who work there and the customers who do business there. For example, step into Longo Toyota in El Monte, California, one of Toyota's top-selling dealerships, and you'll find diversity in the form of salespeople who speak Spanish, Korean, Arabic, Vietnamese, Hebrew, and Mandarin Chinese. In fact, the 60 salespeople at Longo Toyota speak 20 different languages. Surprisingly, this level of diversity was achieved without a formal diversity plan in place.[4]

By contrast, some companies lack diversity, either in their work force or their customers. For example, Advantica, the parent company of Denny's restaurants, paid $54.4 million to settle a class-action lawsuit alleging discriminatory treatment of black customers at Denny's restaurants. Shoney's, another restaurant company, paid $132.8 million for wrongly rejecting job applicants on the basis of race. Edison International, a California-based utility company, paid more than $11 million for the same mistake. And phone company Bell Atlantic paid a whopping $500 million to black employees who were unfairly passed over for promotions.[5]

Today, however, Advantica, Shoney's, Bell Atlantic, and Edison International have made great improvements in their level of diversity. At Advantica, all the company's charitable contributions now go to organizations that benefit minorities. At Shoney's, Bell Atlantic, and Edison International, minorities now comprise 30 percent, 17 percent, and 25 percent, respectively, of all managers. In fact, Advantica, Shoney's, Edison International, and Bell Atlantic have increased their diversity so much that all recently made *Fortune* magazine's list of 50 best companies for blacks, Asians, and Hispanics.[6]

After reading this next section, you should be able to:

1 describe **diversity and why it matters**.

1 Diversity: Differences That Matter

You'll begin your exploration of diversity by learning **1.1** *that diversity is not affirmative action and* **1.1** *how to build a business case for diversity.*

1.1 *Diversity Is Not Affirmative Action*

affirmative action
purposeful steps taken by an organization to create employment opportunities for minorities and women

A common misconception is that workplace diversity and affirmative action are the same. However, diversity and affirmative action are different in several critical ways. To start, **affirmative action** is purposeful steps taken by an organization to create employment opportunities for minorities and women.[7] By contrast, diversity exists in organizations when there is a variety of demographic, cultural, and personal differences among the people who work there and the customers who do business there. So one key

Diversity means variety—demographic, cultural, and personal differences among an organization's workers.
© William Taufic/The Stock Market

difference is that affirmative action is more narrowly focused on demographics such as gender and race, while diversity has a broader focus that includes demographic, cultural, and personal differences. Furthermore, diversity can exist even if organizations don't take purposeful steps to create it. For example, you learned that the 60 salespeople at Longo Toyota speak 20 different languages. However, Longo Toyota achieved this level of diversity without using a formal affirmative action program. Likewise, a local restaurant located near a university in a major city is likely to have a more diverse group of employees than one located in a small town. So, organizations can achieve diversity without affirmative action. Likewise, organizations that take affirmative action to create employment opportunities for women and minorities may not yet have diverse work forces.

Another important difference is that affirmative action is required by law for private employers with 15 or more employees, while diversity is not. Affirmative action originated with the 1964 Civil Rights Act that bans discrimination in voting, public places, federal government programs, federally supported public education, and employment. Title VII of the Civil Rights Act (**http://www.eeoc.gov/laws/vii.html**) requires that workers have equal employment opportunities when being hired or promoted. More specifically, Title VII prohibits companies from discriminating on the basis of race, color, religion, sex, or national origin. Furthermore, Title VII created the Equal Employment Opportunity Commission (**http://www.eeoc.gov**) to administer these laws. By contrast, there is no federal law or agency to oversee diversity. Organizations that pursue diversity goals and programs do so voluntarily. For example, Fannie Mae, an organization that makes it easier and cheaper for lower-income families to purchase mortgages for home ownership, has pursued a diverse work force and customer base because, in the words of its CEO Jim Johnson, it is "morally right."[8]

Another difference is that affirmative action programs and diversity programs have different purposes. The purpose of affirmative action programs is to compensate for past discrimination, which was widespread when legislation was introduced in the 1960s, to prevent ongoing discrimination, and to provide equal opportunities to all, regardless of race, color, religion, gender, or national origin. Organizations that fail to uphold these laws may be required to

- hire, promote, or give back pay to those not hired or promoted;
- reinstate those who were wrongly terminated;
- pay attorneys' fees and court costs for those who brought charges against them; or
- take other actions that make individuals whole by returning them to the condition or place they would have been had it not been for discrimination.[9]

Consequently, affirmative action is basically a punitive approach.[10] By contrast, the general purpose of diversity programs is to create a positive work environment where no one is advantaged or disadvantaged, where "we" is everyone, where everyone can do their best work, where differences are respected and not ignored, and where everyone feels comfortable.[11] So unlike affirmative action, which punishes companies for not achieving specific gender and race differences in their work forces, diversity programs seek to benefit both organizations and their employees by encouraging organizations to value all kinds of differences.

At this time, affirmative action programs are substantially more controversial than diversity programs.[12] Despite their overall success in making workplaces much fairer than they used to be,[13] many people, including the courts (see *Hopwood v. State of Texas*[14]), have viewed some affirmative action programs as offering preferential treatment to females and minorities at the expense of other employees. Nathan Glazer, author of *Ethnic Dilemmas*, said, "The outrage an American feels when he (or she) is deprived of a job or promotion because of his race or ethnic background is no less when that person is white than when he (or she) is black, or yellow, or brown."[15] Furthermore, research clearly shows that people who have gotten a job or promotion as a result of affirmative action are frequently viewed as unqualified, even when clear evidence of their qualifications exists.[16] For example, one woman said, "I won a major prize [in my field], and some of the guys in my lab said it was because I was a woman. I'm certain they didn't choose me because I was a woman. But it gave some disgruntled guys who didn't get the prize a convenient excuse."[17] So, while affirmative action programs have created opportunities for minorities and women, those same minorities and women are frequently presumed to be unqualified when it is believed that their jobs were obtained as a result of affirmative action.

In summary, affirmative action and diversity are not the same thing. Not only are they fundamentally different, but they also differ in purpose, practice, and the reactions they produce.

1.2 *Diversity Makes Good Business Sense*

While most managers would agree that diversity has become much more important in recent years, few believe that diversity actually makes good business sense. Indeed, supporters of diversity often ignore its business aspects altogether, claiming instead that diversity is simply the "right thing to do." However, diversity actually makes good business sense in several ways: cost savings, attracting and retaining talent, and driving business growth.[18]

Diversity helps companies with *cost savings* by reducing turnover, decreasing absenteeism, and avoiding expensive lawsuits. Because of lost productivity and the cost of recruiting and selecting new workers, companies lose substantial money when employees quit their jobs. In fact, turnover costs typically amount to more than 90 percent of employees' salaries. So if an executive who makes $100,000 leaves an organization, it would cost approximately $90,000 to find a replacement. Using the 90 percent estimate, even the lowest-paid hourly workers can cost companies as much as $10,000 when they quit. Since the turnover rates for blacks average 40 percent higher than for whites, and since women quit their jobs at twice the rate men do, companies that manage diverse work forces well can cut costs by reducing the turnover rates of these employees.[19] And, with women absent from work 60 percent more often than men, primarily because of family responsibilities, diversity programs that address the needs of female workers can also reduce the substantial costs of absenteeism.

Been There,

Diversity at 7-Eleven

Jeanne Hitchcock is Southland Corporation's manager of urban affairs. In this interview, she discusses how Southland manages diversity at its headquarters and its thousands of 7-Eleven stores.

Q: Sometimes the whole topic of diversity gets bogged down in a heavy, sociopolitical debate about affirmative action. Is managing diversity as unpleasant as the controversy that sometimes surrounds it?

A: No. We have fun at 7-Eleven. It's a new 7-Eleven. We've been able to capture and profit from the differences of our various constituencies. I'd say to other corporations who are standing on the sidelines: try it, you'll like it!

Q: Is diversity a business imperative?

A: Absolutely. We certainly recognize that at 7-Eleven. If you are a forward-thinking company, if you want to be profitable, if you want growth, if you want efficiency in your operation, if you want an intelligent, skilled work force, then you are going to have to learn to manage a work force and service a consumer base that are becoming increasingly diverse. The question lies not so much in your philosophy regarding race relations or affirmative action and those kinds of principles, but how well can you manage change? How well can you identify it? And how well can you adjust to it? For those who can't, I suggest that they will not be successful entrepreneurs in the 21st century.

Q: Isn't that part of how you came to the Southland Corporation, as an agent of change?

"You must be able to look beyond these physical characteristics and determine their unique skill sets."

A: No. Southland has been profitable over the years because it has always been willing to identify and adjust to change. Everything about our business principles continues to reflect that today. We have a new look, a new merchandising system, and a new distribution system, and we have been a diverse franchise system for a long, long time. Over 40 percent of our franchisees are ethnic minorities and over half are women. So Southland was a pioneer in managing diversity before it became popular to do so. It wasn't a hard sell for me to agree to join the Southland team when I could look around and see diversity as a natural part of the way we do business.

Q: We still hear talk about the corporate glass ceiling, which forces the best women and minorities to leave a company because the environment does not foster or promote their own growth. Can diversity training programs help alleviate these problems? Is that a good place to start?

A: It is, if that's what's needed. Southland did that in the '80s. Everyone from the CEO all the way down through the organization went through diversity training. But diversity training for management has evolved over the years. What we're looking to do now is manage diversity from a skill set. There are varying groups of people coming from different religions and different ethnic persuasions, different ages and genders. You must be able to look beyond these physical characteristics and determine their unique skill sets. Then you can manage toward those skill sets to get the best out of that person, get their best performance, and benefit from their creative thinking. That's the best approach to creating an effective and efficient business environment where people of different cultures, colors and genders work together.

Q: How do the kinds of products and services 7-Eleven offers today differ from the past?

A: One easy example is in our merchandising program. You'll notice the difference in the health and beauty aids category line. We carry stockings, cosmetics and hair products targeted toward women of color. You will also find differences in merchandising in the soft drink category. Individuals in different parts of the country prefer different flavors. You will find a very targeted approach to satisfying what our customers want—as between men and women, as between young and old, as between ethnic groups. It's a function of each franchisee knowing exactly who his or her customers are and adjusting the product selection accordingly.

Source: T. Barnes, "The Art of Diversity at 7-Eleven," *Franchising World* 27 (1995): 14-17. This interview was edited for inclusion in this textbook.

Done That

PersonalProductivityTip

Employment Practices Liability Insurance

If company policy makes clear that discrimination won't be tolerated, and if you train employees to recognize discrimination, designate at least one person to handle complaints, and investigate promptly and fairly, you greatly reduce the chance of being sued for discrimination. You can reduce the threat even more with employment practices liability insurance. EPLI covers claims against sexual harassment and age, sex, race, religion, or disability discrimination. A $10 million policy goes for $75,000 to $160,000. Coverage starts at $1,000 per year for a $500,000 policy. Are you covered by EPLI? With the average lawsuit costing $675,000, can you afford not to be?

Source: J. Hovey, "Company Procedures, Policy Reduce Risk of Discrimination Claims," *The Los Angeles Times,* 24 March 1999, 6. B.J. Wolfson, "Employers Seek Safety Net against Liability Abyss: With Enhanced Worker Protections, Today More Than 30 Percent of Companies Carry Special Insurance," *Orange County Register,* 8 March 1999, d10.

Diversity programs also save companies money by avoiding discrimination lawsuits, which have increased by a factor of 20 since 1970 and quadrupled just since 1995. Indeed, because companies lose two-thirds of all discrimination cases that go to trial, the best strategy from a business perspective is not to be sued for discrimination at all. And when companies lose, the average settlement costs more than $600,000.[20] Of course, this is just an average. Settlement costs can be much larger. For example, Home Depot paid $65 million to settle a sex discrimination lawsuit with 25,000 female employees who were paid less and not promoted because they were women.[21] State Farm Insurance, however, paid $157 million to 814 women who were not given the chance to be hired or promoted into its key sales agent jobs in California between 1974 and 1987.[22]

Diversity also makes business sense by helping companies *attract and retain talented workers*. And in today's red-hot job market, where job seekers have more choice and opportunity than ever before, diversity-friendly companies are attracting better *and* more diverse job applicants. Very simply, diversity begets more diversity. Companies that make *Fortune* magazine's list of 50 best companies for blacks, Asians, and Hispanics already attract a diverse and talented pool of job applicants. But after being recognized by *Fortune* for their efforts, they experience even bigger increases in both the quality and diversity of people who apply for jobs.

Just as important, however, is that these companies also create opportunities that encourage workers to stay. For example, Anne Shen Smith, vice president of support services for Pacific Enterprises, a California-based utility holding company, said that the company created opportunities by replacing the "old boy network," in which only bosses could nominate employees for promotions, with a "Readiness for Management" program, in which employees nominate themselves. Workers begin the process by taking a number of self-assessment tests to determine their strengths and weaknesses. Then, they take training courses to improve their skills and knowledge. The Readiness for Management program works because it gives people who were previously overlooked a chance to move up and because it makes employees responsible for improving their skills and knowledge.[23] Employees who don't take that responsibility don't get promoted.

The third way in which diversity makes business sense is by *driving business growth*. Diversity helps companies grow by improving marketplace understanding. When companies have diverse work forces, they are better able to understand the needs of their increasingly diverse customer bases. Table 12.2 indicates just how diverse customers are becoming. For example, there are 134 million women in the U.S. with total annual purchasing power of $1.1 trillion! Moreover, seven million women own businesses that generate annual business revenues of $2.3 trillion. Similarly impressive numbers appear for gays and lesbians and African, Hispanic, and Asian Americans. Kathleen Lynch, a human resources manager with Nortel Communications Systems, said, "There's no question about it. It's just a very diverse world. By the year 2000, we are going to have an increasingly diverse population, and, as a result, a more diverse work force. And the more diversity you have in your work force, the better you're going to be able to serve your customers and be competitive."[24] William Howell, former chairman of J.C. Penney, said, "If we don't have people of diverse backgrounds in the back, how in the world can we satisfy the diversity of people coming in through the front door?"[25] In fact, a survey of 34 U.S. multinational organizations found that tapping into "diverse customers and markets" was the number one reason managers gave for implementing diversity programs.[26]

Diversity also helps companies grow through higher-quality problem solving. While diverse groups initially have more difficulty working together than homogeneous groups, after several months, diverse groups do a better job of identifying problems and generating alternative solutions, the two most important steps in problem solving.[27] Ernest Drew, former CEO of Hoechst Celanese, a chemical company, recalled a company conference in which the company's top 125 managers, mostly white males, were joined by 50 lower-level minorities and women. Problem-solving teams were formed to discuss how the company's corporate culture affected business and how it could be changed. Half the teams were composed of white males, while the other half were of mixed gender and race. Drew said that "It was so obvious that the diverse teams had the broader solutions. They had ideas I hadn't even thought of. For the first time, we realized that diversity is a strength as it relates to problem solving. Before, we just thought of diversity as the total number of minorities and women in the company, like affirmative action. Now we knew we needed diversity at every level of the company where decisions are made."[28]

Table 12.2

Rising Customer Diversity by Population, Purchasing Power, Business Ownership, and Business Revenue

	U.S. Population	*Purchasing Power*	*Business Owners*	*Annual Business Revenue*
Women	134,000,000	$1,100,000,000,000	7,000,000	2,300,000,000,000
Gays & Lesbians	20,000,000	$514,000,000	2,200,000	37,000,000,000
People with Disabilities	49,000,000	$100,000,000,000	not available	not available
African Americans	34,000,000	$400,000,000,000	621,000	32,000,000,000
Asian Americans	10,000,000	$150,000,000,000	706,000	1,000,000,000,000
Hispanic Americans	28,000,000	$235,000,000,000	1,500,000	200,000,000,000

Source: K. Ellison & N. Bond, "Diversity: The Bottom Line for Small Business," *Inc.*, 19 May 1998, D1.

Review 1
Diversity: Differences That Matter

Diversity exists in organizations when there is a variety of demographic, cultural, and personal differences among the people who work there and the customers who do business there. A common misconception is that workplace diversity and affirmative action are the same. However, affirmative action is more narrowly focused on demographics, is required by law, and is used to punish companies that discriminate on the basis of race, color, religion, gender, or national origin. By contrast, diversity is broader in focus (going beyond demographics), voluntary, more positive in that it encourages companies to value all kinds of differences, and, at this time, substantially less controversial than affirmative action. So, affirmative action and diversity differ in purpose, practice, and the reactions they produce. Diversity also makes good business sense in terms of cost savings (reducing turnover, decreasing absenteeism, and avoiding lawsuits), attracting and retaining talent, and driving business growth (improving marketplace understanding and higher-quality problem solving).

Diversity and Individual Differences

Want a glimpse into the world of diversity? Try the men's bathroom in any American factory. For whatever reason, the bathroom wall remains the broadsheet of the blue-collar male. What a shock the day in March that I checked out our plant's men's room at the urging of a concerned employee. Every imaginable racial and ethnic slur was scrawled across the surface of the largest stall. I asked myself, Is this what people really think? How are they ever going to work together if they feel this way?

Wandering the factory floor, though, you'd never guess the writing on the wall. Anglos bend over machines helping Spanish-speaking workers repair timing belts. Koreans mix inks for African American printing-press operators. Women and men spell one another on the packing lines. Everyone seems to be working together to get the job done at our vegetable-bag printing plant.[29]

Kevin Kelly, a former *Business Week* reporter who now works at Emerald Packaging in Union City, California, wrote this description of diversity. Did you notice that he described his workers in terms of ethnicity (Anglos and African Americans), national origin (Koreans and Spanish-speaking workers) and gender (men and women)? Kelly's description of the diversity of his workers is fairly typical. A survey found that when managers were asked, "What is meant by diversity to decision makers in your organization?" they most frequently mentioned race, culture, gender, national origin, age, religion, and regional origin.[30]

surface-level diversity differences such as age, gender, race/ethnicity, and physical disabilities that are observable, typically unchangeable, and easy to measure

When managers describe workers this way, they are focusing on surface-level diversity. **Surface-level diversity**, as illustrated in Figure 12.1, consists of differences that are immediately observable, typically unchangeable, and easy to measure.[31] In other words, independent observers can usually agree on dimensions of surface-level diversity, such as another person's age, gender, race/ethnicity, or mental or physical disabilities.

Figure 12.1 **Surface- and Deep-Level Diversity**

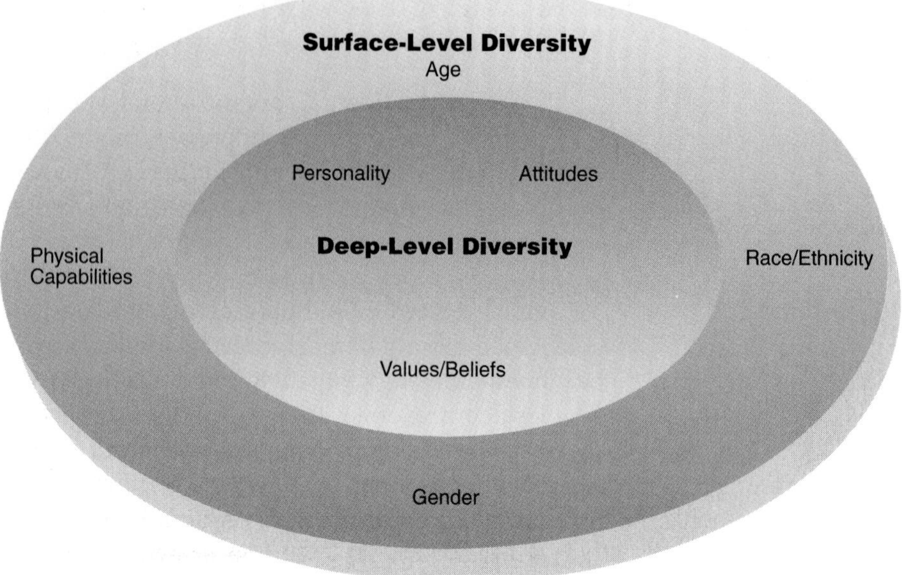

Did you also notice that when Kelly's employees at Emerald Packaging actually worked with each other, the surface-level differences such as race/ethnicity, national origin, and gender didn't seem to matter as much? In fact, Kelly said, "Everyone seems to be *working together to get the job done* at our vegetable-bag printing plant."

This, too, is more typical than you'd think. In fact, the good news is that while most people start by using easily observable characteristics, such as surface-level diversity, to categorize or stereotype other people, those initial, superficial categorizations typically give way to deeper impressions formed from knowledge of others' behavior and psychological characteristics, such as personality or attitudes. When you think of others this way, you are focusing on deep-level diversity. **Deep-level diversity** consists of differences communicated through verbal and nonverbal behaviors that are learned only through extended interaction with others.[32] Examples of deep-level diversity include personality differences, attitudes, beliefs, and values. In other words, as people in diverse workplaces get to know each other, the initial focus on surface-level differences such as age, race/ethnicity, gender, and physical capabilities is replaced by deeper, more accurate knowledge of co-workers.

deep-level diversity
differences communicated through verbal and nonverbal behaviors, such as personality and attitudes, that are learned only through extended interaction with others

If managed properly, the shift from surface- to deep-level diversity can accomplish two things.[33] First, coming to know and understand each other better can result in reduced prejudice and conflict. Second, it can lead to stronger social integration. **Social integration** is the degree to which group members are psychologically attracted to working with each other to accomplish a common objective, or, as Kevin Kelly described it, "working together to get the job done."

social integration
the degree to which group members are psychologically attracted to working with each other to accomplish a common objective

After reading the next two sections, you should be able to:

2 understand the special challenges that the dimensions of **surface-level diversity** pose for managers.

3 explain how the dimensions of **deep-level diversity** affect individual behavior and interactions in the workplace.

2 Surface-Level Diversity

Because age, gender, race/ethnicity, and disabilities are usually immediately observable, many managers and workers use these dimensions of surface-level diversity to form initial impressions and categorizations of co-workers, bosses, customers, or job applicants. Whether intentional or not, sometimes those initial categorizations and impressions lead to decisions or behaviors that discriminate. Consequently, these dimensions of surface-level diversity pose special challenges for managers who are trying to create positive work environments where everyone feels comfortable and no one is advantaged or disadvantaged.

Let's learn more about those challenges and the ways that **2.1** *age,* **2.2** *gender,* **2.3** *race/ethnicity, and* **2.4** *mental or physical disabilities can affect decisions and behaviors in organizations.*

2.1 *Age*

age discrimination treating people differently (e.g., in hiring and firing, promotion, and compensation decisions) because of their age

Age discrimination is treating people differently (e.g., in hiring and firing, promotion, and compensation decisions) because of their age. Since age discrimination almost always occurs against "older" workers, no cliche captures the basic idea behind age discrimination as well as "You can't teach an old dog new tricks." It's commonly believed that older workers are unable to learn how to use computers and technology, are incapable of adapting to change, are sick more often, and, in general, are much more expensive to employ than younger workers. One manager explained his preference for younger workers over older workers this way: "The way I look at it, for $40,000 or $50,000, I can get a smart, raw kid right out of undergrad who's going to work seven days a week for me for the next two years. I'll train him the way I want him, he'll grow with me, and I'll pay him long-term options so I own him, for lack of a better word. He'll do exactly what I want—and if he doesn't, I'll fire him. . . . The alternative is to pay twice as much for some 40-year-old who does half the amount of work, has been trained improperly, and doesn't listen to what I say."[34]

Unfortunately, attitudes like this are all too common. For example, 80 percent of human resource managers surveyed by *Personnel Management* magazine said that age discrimination was a major problem in their organizations and that older employees were not receiving the same training and promotional opportunities as younger workers.[35] Likewise, two-thirds of the 10,000 people surveyed by the American Association for Retired People felt that they had been wrongly discharged from a job because of their age. In fact, a study by the Society for Human Resource Management found that 20 percent of all companies had been sued for age discrimination in the last five years. However, the actual incidence of age discrimination may be even higher, given that 90 percent of age discrimination cases are settled before official complaints are registered with the EEOC and then the courts. And of the cases that have gone to court in the last few years, plaintiffs won more than 90 percent.[36]

So, what's reality and what's myth? Do older employees actually cost more? In some ways, they do. The older people are and the longer they've stayed with a company, the more the company pays for salaries, pension plans, and vacation time. However, older workers cost companies less, too,

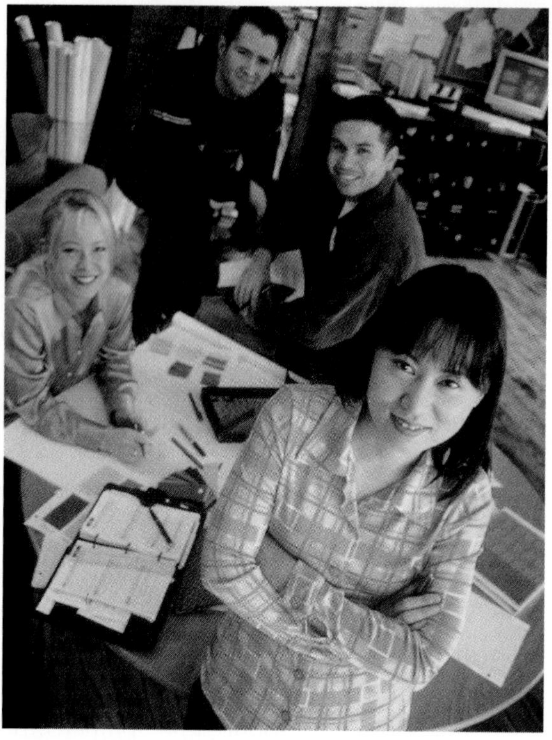

Age discrimination often favors younger workers, because of pervasive stereotypical attitudes toward older workers.

because they show better judgment, care more about the quality of their work, and are less likely to quit, show up late, or be absent, the cost of which can be substantial.[37] A survey by Chicago outplacement firm Challenger, Gray & Christmas found that only 3 percent of employees age 50 or over changed jobs in any given year compared to 10 percent of the entire work force and 12 percent of workers ages 25 to 34. The study also found that while older workers make up about 14 percent of the work force, they suffer only 10 percent of all workplace injuries and use fewer health care benefits than younger workers with school-age children.[38] As for the widespread belief that job performance declines with age, the scientific evidence clearly refutes this stereotype. Performance does not decline with age, regardless of the type of job.[39]

What can companies do to reduce age discrimination?[40] To start, managers need to recognize that age discrimination is much more pervasive than they probably think. While "old" used to mean mid-50s, in today's workplace, "old" is closer to 40. When 773 CEOs were asked, "At what age does a worker's productivity peak?" the average age was 43. So, age discrimination may affect more workers simply because perceptions about age have changed. However, with the aging of baby boomers, age discrimination is more likely simply because there really are millions more older workers than there used to be. And, because studies show that interviewers rate younger job candidates as more qualified (even when they aren't), companies need to train managers and recruiters to make hiring and promotion decisions on the basis of qualifications, not age. Companies also need to monitor the extent to which older workers receive training. The Bureau of Labor Statistics indicates that the number of training courses and number of hours spent in training drops dramatically after employees reach the age of 44. Finally, companies need to ensure that younger and older workers interact with each other. One study found that younger workers generally hold positive views of older workers and that the more time they spent working with older co-workers, the more positive their attitudes became.[41]

2.2 Gender

gender discrimination treating people differently because of their gender

glass ceiling the so-called invisible barrier that prevents women and minorities from advancing to the top jobs in organizations

Gender discrimination means treating people differently because of their gender. Gender discrimination and racial/ethnic discrimination (discussed in the next section) are often associated with the **glass ceiling**, the so-called invisible barrier that prevents women and minorities from advancing to the top jobs in organizations.

To what extent do women face gender discrimination in the workplace? In some ways, there is much less gender discrimination than there used to be. For example, while women held only 17 percent of managerial jobs in 1972, today they hold nearly 43 percent of managerial jobs, a number that nearly parallels the percentage of women (45 percent) in the work force. However, in general, gender discrimination continues to operate via the glass ceiling at higher levels in organizations. For instance, women hold only 5 percent of top-level management jobs, up from 0.5 percent in 1979. Furthermore, out of the 1,000 largest companies in the U.S., only four have women CEOs. Membership on corporate boards of directors is somewhat better, as women hold about 10 percent of all board memberships in the U.S.[42] Unfortunately, contrary to popular opinion, women are actually worse off in Europe than in the U.S. While women make up 41 percent of the European work force, they hold only 29 percent of all management jobs, no more than 2 percent of top management jobs, and just 1 percent of board membership positions, far worse than the 10 percent of board seats held by American women. Furthermore, while 95 percent of the 100 largest U.S. companies have at least one female on their board of directors, the percentage is far less in most European countries. For example, only 41 percent of the 100 largest British companies have at least one female board director.[43]

Is gender discrimination the sole reason for the slow rate at which women have been promoted to mid and upper levels of management and corporate boards? Some studies indicate that it's not. In some instances, the slow progress appears to be due to career and job choices. Unlike men, whose career and job choices are often driven by the search for higher pay and advancement, women are more likely to choose jobs or careers that also give them a greater sense of accomplishment, more control over their work schedules, and easier movement in and out of the workplace.[44] Furthermore, women are historically much more likely than men to prioritize family over work at some time in their careers. Gilberte Beaux, CEO of Paris-based Basic Petroleum International and one France's most accomplished women managers who managed to have both a successful career and a family, said, "It's hard to drop out for a family if you want to get to the top." As to why so many women choose families over careers, she said, "Women should be able to do what they want in life . . . just like men."[45]

However, beyond these reasons, it's likely that gender discrimination plays a major role in the slow advancement of women into higher levels of management. And even if you don't think so, a clear majority of the women you work with probably do. Indeed, one study found that more than 90 percent of executive women believed that the glass ceiling had hurt their careers.[46] In another study, 80 percent of women said they left their last organization because the glass ceiling had limited their chances for advancement.[47] A third study indicated that the glass ceiling is prompting more and more women to leave companies to start their own businesses.[48] Anita Borg, a senior researcher at Digital Equipment Corp, summed up the frustrations of many professional women when she said, "You run into subtle sexism every day. It's like water torture. It wears you down."[49]

What can companies do to make sure that women have the same opportunities for development and advancement as men? One strategy is mentoring, to pair promising female executives with more senior executives with whom they can talk and seek advice and support. A vice president at a utility company said, "I think it's the single most critical piece to women advancing career-wise. In my experience you need somebody to help guide you and . . . go to bat for you."[50] In fact, 91 percent of female executives had a mentor at some point and felt their mentor was critical to their advancement.

Another strategy is to make sure that a male-dominated activity doesn't unintentionally exclude women. For example, at Avon, the CEO stopped the annual hunting trips, during which top managers would drink and play cards all night.[51] One final strategy is to designate a "go-to person," other than employees' supervisors, that women can talk to if they believe that they are being held back or discriminated against because of their gender. Make sure this person has the knowledge and authority to conduct a fair, confidential internal investigation.[52]

2.3 *Race/Ethnicity*

racial and ethnic discrimination treating people differently because of their race or ethnicity

Racial and ethnic discrimination means treating people differently because of their race or ethnicity. To what extent is racial and ethnic discrimination a factor in the workplace? Thanks to the 1964 Civil Rights Act and Title VII, there is much less racial and ethnic discrimination than there used to be. For example, the number of African Americans and Hispanics in top management positions increased 200 percent in Fortune 1,000 firms between 1979 and 1989.[53] However, strong racial and ethnic disparities still exist. For instance, while about 12 percent of Americans are black, only 6 percent of managers and less than 1 percent of top managers are black. Similarly, while 11 percent of Americans are Hispanic, only 5 percent of all managers are Hispanic.

What accounts for the disparities between the percentages of African, Hispanic, and Asian Americans in the general population and their smaller representation in management positions? Sometimes studies show that the disparities are due to preexisting differences in training, education, and skills and that when African, Hispanic, Asian, and white Americans have similar skills, training, and education, they are much more likely to have similar jobs and salaries.[54]

However, other studies provide increasingly strong direct evidence of racial or ethnic discrimination in the workplace. For example, one study directly tested hiring discrimination by sending pairs of black and white males and pairs of Hispanic and non-Hispanic males to apply for the same jobs. Each pair had resumes with identical qualifications and were trained to present themselves in similar ways to minimize differences during interviews. The researchers found that white males got three times as many job offers as black males and that non-Hispanic males got three times as many job offers as Hispanic males.[55]

Personal Productivity Tip

Form a Friendly Supper Club

Since 1983, blacks and whites have come to the Piccadilly Cafeteria in Montgomery, Alabama, for the monthly meeting of the Friendly Supper Club. The goal is simple: to get people to talk. There are no agendas, no club officers, and no speeches. One member said, "We are people who come to dinner just to enjoy each other." The result is significantly improved race relations in a town once thick with racial tensions. To improve things in your corner of our diverse world, start a Friendly Supper Club and make a habit of inviting someone different to dinner. You might find out how much you have in common.

Source: R. Thurow, "Can Liver and Onions Lead People to Peace and Understanding? Just Ask the Friendlies, Who Have Been Dining for Years on Racial Reconciliation," *The Wall Street Journal,* 17 December 1998, A1.

Another study, which used similar methods to test hiring procedures at 149 different companies, found that whites received 10 percent more interviews than blacks. Of those interviewed, half of whites received job offers as compared to only 11 percent of blacks. And when job offers were made, blacks were much more likely to be offered lower-level positions, while whites were more likely to be offered jobs that were at higher levels than the jobs they had applied for.[56]

Critics of these studies point out that it's nearly impossible to train different applicants to give identical responses in job interviews and that differences in interviewing skills may have somehow accounted for the results. However, British researchers found similar kinds of discrimination just by sending letters of inquiry to prospective employers. As before, the letters sent to employers were identical except for the applicant's race. Employers frequently responded to letters from Afro-Caribbean, Indian, or Pakistani "applicants" by indicating that the positions had been filled. By contrast, they often responded to white, Anglo-Saxon "applicants" by inviting them to face-to-face interviews. Similar results were found with Vietnamese and Greek "applicants" in Australia.[57] In short, the evidence strongly indicates that there is strong and persistent racial and ethnic discrimination in the hiring processes of many organizations.

What can companies do to make sure that people of all racial and ethnic backgrounds have the same opportunities?[58] Start by looking at the numbers. Compare the hiring rates of whites to the hiring rates for different racial and ethnic applicants. Do the same thing for promotions within the company. See if nonwhite workers quit the company at higher rates than white workers. Also, survey employees to compare white and nonwhite employees' satisfaction with jobs, bosses, and the company, as well as perceptions concerning equal treatment. Next, if the numbers indicate racial or ethnic disparities, consider a test of your hiring system by employing a private firm to have applicants of different races with identical qualifications apply for jobs in your company.[59] Although disparities aren't proof of discrimination, it's much better to investigate hiring and promotion disparities yourself than to have the EEOC or a plaintiff's lawyer do it for you, especially since nearly half of the discrimination charges filed with the EEOC in the last six years were related to race and ethnicity (which the EEOC calls "national origin").[60]

Another step is to eliminate unclear selection and promotion criteria. Vague hiring and promotion criteria allow decision makers to focus on non-job-related characteristics that may unintentionally lead to employment discrimination. Instead, selection and promotion criteria should spell out the specific knowledge, skills, abilities, education, and experience needed to perform a job well.

Finally, train managers and decision makers who make hiring and promotion decisions. At Tower Records, the human resources staff assembles on a giant game board that covers a conference room floor. Tower store managers then answer questions about hiring situations. If they answer a question correctly, they move forward on the board. If they answer it incorrectly, they stay in place, and the group discusses what should have been done instead. The number of grievances about hiring procedures has dropped significantly since the training began.[61]

2.4 *Mental or Physical Disabilities*

disability
a mental or physical impairment that substantially limits one or more major life activities

disability discrimination
treating people differently because of their disabilities

Back problems, foot pain, depression, alcoholism, epilepsy, paralysis, AIDS, cancer, learning disabilities, and substantial hearing or visual impairments: What do all these things have in common? Each is a disability. According to the Americans with Disabilities Act (**http://www.usdoj.gov/crt/ada/adahom1.htm**), a **disability** is a mental or physical impairment that substantially limits one or more major life activities.[62] One out of five Americans, or more than 49 million people, have a disability. **Disability discrimination** means treating people differently because of their disabilities.

To what extent is disability discrimination a factor in the workplace? According to the U.S. Census Bureau, 80 percent of able people have jobs, compared to only 77 percent of those with nonsevere disabilities and 26 percent of those with severe disabilities. More specifically, only 64 percent of those who have difficulty hearing, 44 percent of those who have difficulty seeing, 41 percent of those with a mental disability, and 34 percent of those who have difficulty walking have jobs.[63] Furthermore, people with disabilities are disproportionately employed in low-status or part-time jobs, have little chance for advancement, and, on average, have incomes 35 percent smaller than able people.[64] Numerous studies also indicate that managers and the general public believe that discrimination against people with disabilities is common and widespread.[65]

What accounts for the disparities between the employment and income levels of able people and people with disabilities? Contrary to popular opinion, it has nothing to do with the ability of people with disabilities to do their

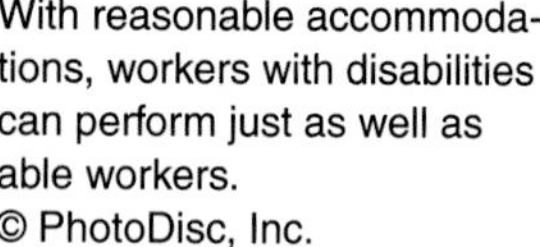

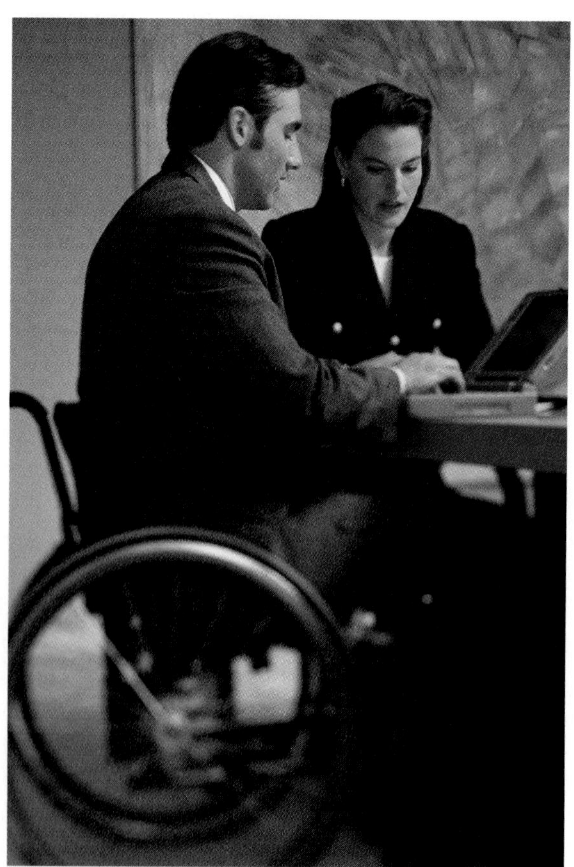

With reasonable accommodations, workers with disabilities can perform just as well as able workers.
© PhotoDisc, Inc.

jobs well. Studies show that as long as companies make reasonable accommodations for disabilities (i.e., changes in procedures or equipment, etc.), people with disabilities perform their jobs just as well as able people. Furthermore, they have better safety records and are not any more likely to be absent or quit their jobs.[66] Plus, most accommodations for disabilities are relatively inexpensive, with half costing $50 or less, and 69 percent costing less than $500.[67] Sears spends an average of just $45 to accommodate employees with disabilities. In fact, 75 percent of the accommodations it makes cost nothing at all. For example, when a saleswoman indicated that she was allergic to nylon, Sears simply waived the requirement that she wear panty hose. Hamilton Davis, Sears' assistant general counsel of employment practices, said, "The bulk of our accommodations are common sense and any company should be able to provide them."[68]

In most cases, whether intentional or not, discrimination toward people with disabilities results from incorrect stereotypes, incorrect expectations, and the emotional responses that people have when interacting with people with disabilities.[69] **Stereotypes** are negative, false, overgeneralized beliefs about people in particular categories.[70] People with disabilities are often thought to be shy, honest, helpless, hypersensitive, depressed, unappealing, bitter, unaggressive, insecure, dependent, or less competent. Inaccurate stereotypes of people with disabilities can lead to inaccurate expectations about on-the-job performance. For example, the stereotypes listed above lead to the expectation that people with disabilities are less qualified and have difficulty interacting with others. Consistent with these expectations, people with disabilities are less likely to be hired or recommended for promotion. Also, it's well established that people react emotionally to others' physical or mental disabilities. Reactions, which range from simple discomfort to negative attitudes to revulsion, can lead organizational decision makers to not hire or promote people with disabilities.

stereotypes
negative, false, overgeneralized beliefs about people in particular categories

What can companies do to make sure that people with disabilities have the same opportunities as everyone else? Beyond educational efforts to address incorrect stereotypes and expectations, a good place to start is to make a commitment to reasonable workplace accommodations. Examples include changing work schedules, reassigning jobs, acquiring or modifying equipment, or providing assistance when needed. Furthermore, as discussed above, accommodations needn't be expensive. For example, rather than rebuild its offices, the U.S. Postal Service used inexpensive ramps to raise wheelchair-bound clerks to counter level, so they could wait on customers. For further information about reasonable accommodations, contact the Job Accommodations Network of the President's Committee on Employment of People with Disabilities (**http://www.pcepd.gov/**), which provides free help and has a database of 26,000 successful accommodations.[71]

Another effective strategy is to provide *assistive technology* that gives workers with disabilities the tools they need to overcome their disabilities. According to the National Council on Disability, 92 percent of workers with disabilities who use assistive technology reported that it helps them work faster and better, 81 percent indicated that it helps them work longer hours, and 67 percent said that it is critical to getting a job.[72] To learn about assistive technologies that can help workers with disabilities, see Abledata (**http://www.abledata.com/**), which lists 25,000 products from 3,000 organizations, or the National Rehabilitation Information Center (**http://207.16.145.11/index.html**), which provides information for specific disabilities.

Personal Productivity Tip

Disabled Doesn't Mean Disqualified

One in five Americans has a disability. The most common disabilities among noninstitutionalized people are arthritis, hearing impairment, hypertensive disease (high blood pressure and strokes), and heart disease. There are four keys to assimilating workers with disabilities into organizations. First, focus on the employee's ability, not the disability. Second, since all employees have strengths and weaknesses, think of disabilities as another kind of weakness rather than a limitation that disqualifies someone from employment. Third, listen. Employees with disabilities know what they need to do their work. Just ask. Finally, educate everyone about disabilities to minimize misconceptions or biases.

Source: E.E. Spragins, "Tapping Workers with Disabilities," *Inc.*, November 1992, 33.

Finally, companies should actively recruit qualified workers with disabilities. Numerous organizations such as Mainstream, Kidder Resources, Just One Break (**http://www.justonebreak.org/**), the American Council of the Blind (**http://www.acb.org/**), the National Federation of the Blind (**http://www.nfb.org/**), the National Association for the Deaf (**http://www.nad.org/**), the Epilepsy Foundation of America (**http://www.efa.org/**), and the National Amputation Foundation (**http://www.va.gov/vso/naf.htm**) actively work with employers to find jobs for qualified people with disabilities. Companies can also place advertisements in publications, such as *Careers and the Disabled*, that specifically target workers with disabilities.[73]

Review 2
Surface-Level Diversity

Age, gender, race/ethnicity, and physical and mental disabilities are dimensions of surface-level diversity. Because those dimensions are (usually) easily observed, managers and workers tend to rely on them to form initial impressions and stereotypes of others. Sometimes, this can lead to age, gender, racial/ethnic, or disability discrimination (i.e., treating people differently) in the workplace. In general, older workers, women, people of color or different national origins, and people with disabilities are much less likely to be hired or promoted than white males. This disparity is often due to incorrect beliefs or stereotypes, such as "job performance declines with age," or "females aren't willing to travel on business," or "workers with disabilities aren't as competent as able workers." To reduce discrimination, companies can determine the hiring and promotion rates for different groups, train managers to make hiring and promotion decisions on the basis of specific criteria, and make sure that everyone has equal access to training, mentors, reasonable work accommodations, and assistive technology. Finally, companies need to designate a "go-to person" that employees can talk to if they believe they have suffered discrimination.

3 Deep-Level Diversity

Have you ever just disliked someone from the minute you met him or her—the way the person talked, acted, or treated you? But then after spending some time working or interacting with this person, you decided that your initial impressions were wrong and that he or she wasn't so bad after all?

If you've had this experience, then you understand the difference between surface- and deep-level diversity. As you just learned, people often use the dimensions of surface-level diversity to form initial impressions about others. However, over time, as people have a chance to get to know each other, initial impressions based on age, gender, race/ethnicity, and mental or physical disabilities give way to deeper impressions based on behavior and psychological characteristics. When we think of others this way, we are focusing on deep-level diversity. *Deep-level diversity* is differences that can only be learned through extended interaction with others. Examples of deep-level diversity include personality differences, attitudes, beliefs, and values. In short, deep-level diversity means getting to know and understand one another better. And that matters, because it can result in less prejudice, discrimination, and conflict in the workplace. These changes can then lead to better *social integration*, the degree to which organizational or group members are psychologically attracted to working with each other to accomplish a common objective.

*Let's examine deep-level diversity by exploring **3.1** the "Big Five" dimensions of personality and **3.2** other significant work-related aspects of personality.*

3.1 *Big Five Dimensions of Personality*

Stop for a second and think about your boss (or the boss you had in your last job). What words would you use to describe him or her? Is your boss introverted or extraverted? Emotionally stable or unstable? Agreeable or disagreeable? Organized or disorganized? Open or closed to new experience? When you describe your boss or others this way, what you're really doing is describing dispositions and personality.

disposition
the tendency to respond to situations and events in a predetermined manner

personality
the relatively stable set of behaviors, attitudes, and emotions displayed over time that makes people different from each other

A **disposition** is the tendency to respond to situations and events in a predetermined manner. **Personality** is the relatively stable set of behaviors, attitudes, and emotions displayed over time that makes people different from each other.[74] For example, think of your closest friends. Among them, is there someone you trust enough to invest your money for you? Chances are, there's not. Why? It could be that this friend doesn't know any more about investing than you do. Or, it could be that he or she just doesn't have the personality or disposition to do this well. In fact, the people who run multibillion dollar investment funds are typically introverted, make decisions on the basis of data rather than intuitive hunches, are swayed by thinking and analysis rather than emotion, and are single-minded in their jobs (i.e., improving fund performance). It makes sense, doesn't it? After all, would you invest in a fund in which the fund manager made decisions on hunches, was swayed more by emotion than analysis, and wasn't solely devoted to improving the return on your investments? People with these personality traits may make great friends, but you probably wouldn't want them to invest your money.[75]

For years, personality researchers studied thousands of different ways to describe people's personalities. However, in the last decade, personality research conducted in different cultures, different settings, and different languages indicated that there are five basic dimensions of personality that account for most of the differences in peoples' behaviors, attitudes, and emotions (or for why your boss is the way he or she is!). The *Big Five personality dimensions* are extraversion, emotional stability, agreeableness, conscientiousness, and openness to experience.[76]

extraversion
the degree to which someone is active, assertive, gregarious, sociable, talkative, and energized by others

Extraversion is the degree to which someone is active, assertive, gregarious, sociable, talkative, and energized by others. In contrast to extraverts, introverts are less active, prefer to be alone, and are shy, quiet, and reserved. For the best results in the workplace, introverts and extraverts should be correctly matched to their jobs. For example, the Peabody Hotel in Memphis, Tennessee, solved one of its problems by having job applicants complete an introversion/extraversion personality measure. Ken Hamko, a manager at the hotel, said, "We had hostesses who wouldn't stay by the door or greet guests or smile. When we gave them the personality profile we found they didn't like being in front of people. So we moved them into other positions and replaced them with extroverts."[77]

emotional stability
the degree to which someone is angry, depressed, anxious, emotional, insecure, and excitable

Emotional stability is the degree to which someone is angry, depressed, anxious, emotional, insecure, and excitable. People who are emotionally stable respond well to stress. In other words, they can maintain a calm, problem-solving attitude in even the toughest situations (i.e., conflict, hostility, dangerous conditions, or extreme time pressures). By contrast, under moderately stressful situations, emotionally unstable people are unable to handle the most basic demands of their jobs and become distraught, tearful, self-doubting, and anxious. Emotional stability is particularly important for high-stress jobs, such as police work, fire fighting, emergency medical treatment, or piloting planes. For instance, the Federal Aviation Administration grounds an average of 2,500 pilots a year for medical reasons. Of those, nearly one in five is grounded for emotional instability related to psychological or psychiatric problems.[78]

As you learned in Chapter 1, emotional stability is also important for managers. Indeed, the number one mistake managers make is intimidating, bullying, and being abrasive to the people who work for them.

agreeableness
the degree to which someone is cooperative, polite, flexible, forgiving, good natured, tolerant, and trusting

Agreeableness is the degree to which someone is cooperative, polite, flexible, forgiving, good natured, tolerant, and trusting. Basically, agreeable people are easy to work with and be around, while disagreeable people are distrusting and difficult to work with and be around. A number of companies have made general attitude or agreeableness the most important factor in their hiring decisions. Hal Rosenbluth, CEO of Rosenbluth International, one of the nation's largest travel companies, said, "We try to attract and hire great human beings with the prerequisite of being nice . . . [because] when nice people work together they're effective and they have fun."[79] Likewise, Southwest Airlines CEO Herb Kelleher said, "At Southwest, we hire attitudes. We can teach someone anything they need to know, but they must start with the right attitude."[80] Sherry Phelps, Southwest's director of corporate employment, explained that attitude (i.e., agreeableness) is a key hiring criterion for pilots, too. Speaking about a pilot who applied for a job, she said, "He came highly recommended, had won several flying awards while in the military and was an excellent candidate in terms of technical skills. But we didn't hire him. Because although he interviewed well with the recruiters, we found out he was rude to the flight attendants and customer-service agents he came in contact with on the way to the interview. We hire people who want to please everyone they meet, not just the audience they think they have to perform for."[81]

conscientiousness
the degree to which someone is organized, hard working, responsible, persevering, thorough, and achievement oriented

Conscientiousness is the degree to which someone is organized, hardworking, responsible, persevering, thorough, and achievement oriented. One management consultant wrote about his experiences with high- and low-conscientiousness employees. He said:

> *Many of the latter were charming individuals; they were often laid back, relaxed and hard to ruffle. One once told me, "I don't sweat the small stuff." He might have added: "even many of the things that you think are critical!" One highly conscientious subordinate was all business. He arrived at our first meeting with a typed copy of his daily schedule, a sheet bearing his home and office phone numbers and addresses and his e-mail address. At his request, we established a timetable for meetings for the next four months. He showed up on time every time, day planner in hand, and carefully listed tasks and due*

dates. He questioned me exhaustively if he didn't understand an assignment and returned on schedule with the completed work or with a clear explanation as to why it wasn't done.[82]

How accurately do measures of conscientiousness categorize employees? The U.S. Department of Defense sponsored a study in which it asked 320 upper-level, white-collar employees (in organizations ranging from banks to government agencies to a state university) and 329 white-collar criminals (in 23 federal prisons) to complete a battery of personality tests to learn what, if any, personality differences existed between the two groups. Of all the personality tests given, conscientiousness was by far the strongest differentiator of the two groups. Only 18 percent of the criminals scored high on the conscientiousness scales compared to 88 percent of the white-collar employees.[83]

What Really Works

Conscientiousness: The Organized, Hard-Working, Responsible Personality

Conscientious people are organized, hardworking, responsible, persevering, thorough, and achievement oriented. Who wouldn't want to hire people with these personality traits? Indeed, 92 studies across five occupational groups (professionals, police, managers, sales, and skilled/semi-skilled) with a combined total of 12,893 study participants indicated that, on average, conscientious people are inherently more motivated and are better at their jobs.

Motivational Effort

There is a 71 percent chance that conscientious workers will be more motivated and will work harder than less conscientious workers.

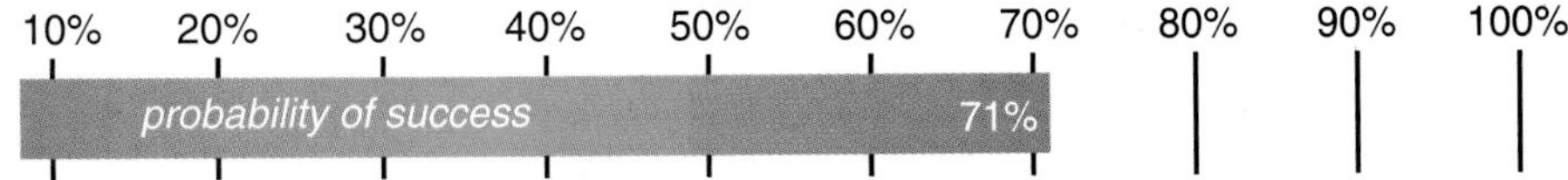

Job Performance

There is a 66 percent chance that conscientious workers will be better at their jobs than less conscientious workers.

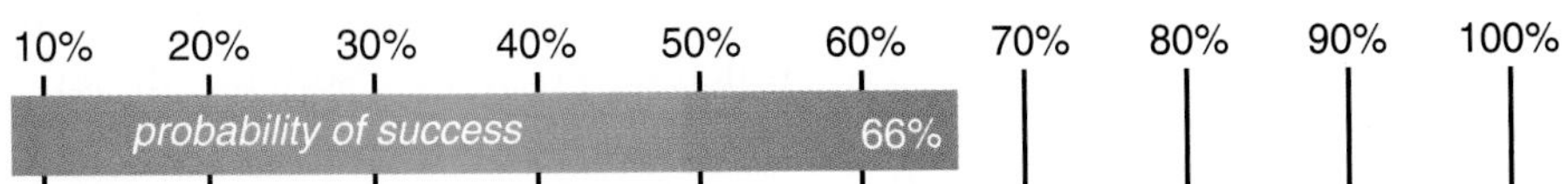

Sources: M.R. Barrick & M.K. Mount, "The Big Five Personality Dimensions and Job Performance," *Personnel Psychology* 44 (1991): 1-26. M.K. Mount & M.R. Barrick, "The Big Five Personality Dimensions: Implications for Research and Practice in Human Resource Management," *Research in Personnel and Human Resources Management* 13 (1995): 153-200. M.K. Mount & M.R. Barrick, "Five Reasons Why the 'Big Five' Article Has Been Frequently Cited," *Personnel Psychology* 51 (1998): 849-857. D.S. Ones, M.K. Mount, M.R. Barrick, & J.E. Hunter, "Personality and Job Performance: A Critique of the Tett, Jackson, and Rothstein (1991) Meta-Analysis," *Personnel Psychology* 47 (1994): 147-156.

Openness to experience is the degree to which someone is curious, broad-minded, and open to new ideas, things, and experiences; is spontaneous; and has a high tolerance for ambiguity. Most companies need people

openness to experience the degree to which someone is curious, broad-minded, and open to new ideas, things, and experiences; is spontaneous; and has a high tolerance for ambiguity

with personalities both strong and weak in terms of openness to experience. People in marketing, advertising, research, or other creative jobs need to be curious, open to new ideas, and spontaneous. By contrast, openness to experience is not particularly important to accountants, who need to consistently apply stringent rules and formulas to makes sense out of complex financial information.

Which of the Big Five personality measures has the largest impact on behavior in organizations? The cumulative results across 117 studies indicate that conscientiousness is related to job performance across five different occupational groups (professionals, police, managers, sales, and skilled or semi-skilled).[84] In short, people "who are dependable, persistent, goal directed and organized tend to be higher performers on virtually any job; viewed negatively, those who are careless, irresponsible, low achievement striving and impulsive tend to be lower performers on virtually any job."[85] However, the results also indicate that extraversion is related to performance in jobs, such as sales and management, in which there is significant interaction with others. In highly people-intensive jobs like these, it helps to be sociable, assertive, and talkative, and to have energy and be able to energize others. Finally, people who are extraverted and open to experience seem to do much better in training. Being curious and open to new experiences, as well as sociable, assertive, talkative, and full of energy, helps people perform better in learning situations.[86]

3.2 *Work-Related Personality Dimensions*

Does the way you keep your desk reveal something about your personality? Lots of people think so. For example, people with ultra-neat desks tend to believe that a desk buried under mounds of paper, food wrappers, and old magazines is a sign that its owner is lazy, disorganized, undependable, and a dreamer. On the other hand, people with messy desks believe that a spotless desk with everything in its place is a sign that its owner is impatient, critical, controlling, analytical, and a perfectionist. Who knows, maybe if your desk is somewhere between "operating-room clean" and the "aftermath of a tornado," it is a sign that you have a good-natured, flexible, and fun-loving personality.[87]

Although studies indicate that extraversion, emotional stability, agreeableness, conscientiousness, and openness to experience are the five basic dimensions of personality in any culture, setting, or language, research has also identified additional personality dimensions that directly affect workplace attitudes, and behaviors. These additional personality dimensions are authoritarianism, Machiavellian tendencies, Type A/B personality, self-monitoring, locus of control, and positive/negative affectivity.

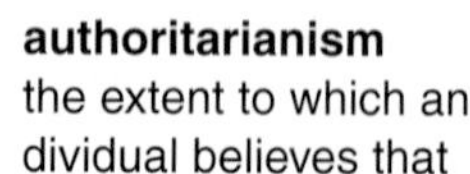

authoritarianism the extent to which an individual believes that there should be power and status differences within organizations

Authoritarianism is the extent to which an individual believes there should be power and status differences within the organization.[88] Authoritarian employees are likely to prefer a direct leadership style, in which the boss tells them exactly what to do. While this sounds desirable, one disadvantage is that even when they know a better solution or are aware of problems, authoritarian employees may simply carry out their boss's orders without question. Also, authoritarian employees may not perform well on ambiguous tasks, or for managers who encourage employees to use their own initiative and judgment.

Authoritarian leaders are highly demanding and expect employees to unquestioningly obey their orders. Don Bibeault is a boss who owns up to his strongly authoritarian personality. Says Bibeault, "I'm not a jolly fellow who's fun to be with. I'm extremely dedicated and determined, and I don't have time to sugarcoat problems. If that's considered abrasive behavior, so be it." What's it like to work for an authoritarian boss like Mr. Bibeault? David Corcoran, who has worked for Bibeault for six years, said, "Well, he yells a lot. Don doesn't believe in wasting time being politically correct. He'll say, 'This is my plan and that's it,' which can be very upsetting to some people. Fortunately, I found his style to be my cup of tea . . . most of the time."[89]

Machiavellianism
the extent to which an individual believes that virtually any type of behavior is acceptable in trying to satisfy their needs or meet their goals

People with **Machiavellian** personalities believe that virtually any type of behavior is acceptable if it helps satisfy needs or accomplish goals.[90] In other words, people with Machiavellian personalities believe that the ends justify the means. For example, "high Machs" are generally more willing to use lies and deceit to get their way than are "low Machs," even in high-pressure situations where the chances of being caught in a lie are high.[91] High Machs believe that most people are gullible and can be manipulated. High Machs also are more effective in persuading others than are low Machs and tend to be resistant to others' efforts to persuade them.[92] One reason high Machs are more effective in persuading others is that low Machs (meaning most people) may be distracted by emotions or issues unrelated to winning. According to *Executive Strategies*, a management newsletter, one high-Mach strategy for influencing low Machs is to "make a visitor stand in front of your desk. . . . Lean back and look at him coldly through a frozen smile. The body language of contempt can cut your opponent like a razor."[93] Another high-Mach persuasion strategy is to throw a tantrum: "Tantrums should be sudden, scary and seemingly irrational. . . . Throwing a tantrum can be fun." By contrast, high Machs are difficult to persuade, because they ignore emotions and secondary issues and focus only on the things that move them closer to their goals.

Also, because they are out for themselves and no one else, high Machs don't do well in work teams. High Machs often cause conflicts within teams and sometimes cause teams to break up. For example, a businessman in Alexandria, Virginia, worked with two of his oldest friends to build a small company that eventually grew into a multimillion dollar business. After his friends actively encouraged him to take a six-week paternity leave following the birth of his baby, they then fired him to reduce his negotiating leverage and force him to take a lower price for his shares of the business! Said the businessman, "I was suddenly fired, broke, humiliated and facing a whole new life with a new baby. These [people] are Machiavellian, but this extreme I never anticipated."[94] Finally, high Machs can have a devastating effect on trust in the workplace. As soon as people realize that a high Mach has used them, there are likely to be interpersonal problems and conflict.[95]

Type A/B personality dimension
the extent to which people tend toward impatience, hurriedness, competitiveness, and hostility

Type A personality
a person who tries to complete as many tasks as possible in the shortest possible time and is hard driving, competitive, impatient, perfectionistic, angry, and unable to relax

The **Type A/B personality dimension** is the extent to which people tend toward impatience, hurriedness, competitiveness, and hostility.[96] **Type A personalities** try to complete as many tasks as possible in the shortest possible time and are hard driving, competitive, impatient, perfectionistic, angry, and unable to relax.[97] Type As are also likely to be aggressive, self-confident, dominant, and extroverted and have a high need for achievement. For example, John Chatwin, a sales representative for EMC, a maker of large-scale computer data storage devices, is a classic Type A personality. John treats nearly all parts of his life as a contest. Each morning, he races up the stairs to see how many he can climb before the office door closes behind him. Chatwin also works incredibly long hours and hasn't missed more than two days of work since he and his wife vacationed in Hawaii three years ago. Even then, Chatwin was so dedicated to succeeding at his sales job that he would get up in the middle of the night while in Hawaii to call customers on the U.S. mainland (where it was morning). Chatwin's monstrous work hours, combined with his penchant for playing ice hockey and softball several evenings a week, leaves little time for his family. Said Chatwin, "I want to win at everything I do."[98]

Type B personality
a person who is relaxed and easygoing and able to engage in leisure activities without worrying about work

By contrast to Chatwin's hurried Type A tendencies, **Type B personalities** are relaxed, easygoing, patient, and able to relax and engage in leisure activities. Unlike Type A personalities, they are neither highly competitive nor excessively driven to accomplishment.

What do we know about the Type A/B personality dimension and the workplace? Contrary to what you'd expect, Type As don't always outperform Type Bs on the job. Type As tend to perform better on tasks that demand quick decisions made at a rapid work pace under time pressure, but Type Bs tend to perform better at tasks requiring well-thought-out decisions in which there is little time pressure. And despite their ambition to succeed, top managers are much more likely to have Type B personalities than Type A personalities.[99] Ironically, the task complexity and psychological challenge inherent in management jobs actually works against many Type A managers by dramatically increasing their stress levels.[100] Type Bs, on the other hand, do a much better job of handling and responding to the stress of managerial jobs. The Type A/B personality dimension is also known for its well-established link to heart attacks.[101] However, it is the hostility and anger of Type A personalities that increase the risk of heart attack, and not impatience, hurriedness, or competitiveness. In fact, a long-term study at Duke University followed a group of lawyers for 25 years and found that those with higher hostility scores were 4.2 times as likely to have died over that period as those with low scores.[102]

self-monitoring
the ability to adjust one's behavior to different situations and environments

Self-monitoring refers to the ability to adjust one's behavior to different situations and environments.[103] High self-monitors have the ability to adapt when situational expectations change, while low self-monitors are more likely to insist on behaving in the same way, regardless of the situation. More specifically, high self-monitors are very sensitive to cues from others concerning appropriate behavior. In other words, they are able to adjust their own behavior to suit the situation. By contrast, low self-monitors are controlled from within by their feelings and attitudes. When interacting with others, high self-monitors ask themselves, "Who does this situation want me to be and how can I be that person?" whereas low self-monitors ask themselves "Who am I and how can I be me in this situation?"[104]

For example, you're in an interview situation and you're asked what your strengths and weaknesses are. How do you respond? If you're a high self-monitor, you sense that the interviewer doesn't want to hire an egomaniac and is looking for a balanced description of your capabilities, so you describe your strengths and a few weaknesses (but nothing that would torpedo your chances of getting the job). If you're a low self-monitor and intent on portraying yourself in the best possible way (to increase your chances of getting the job), you miss this cue and respond by describing your strengths and then declaring, "I don't have any major weaknesses." The result? The high self-monitor gets the job offer and the low self-monitor does not.

Studies also show that high self-monitors do better than low self-monitors at boundary-spanning jobs that require interactions with others across and outside organizations, that they often emerge as leaders in work groups, and that they are more likely to resolve conflicts through compromise or collaboration.[105] Because of their ability to adapt to the demands of different situations and circumstances, high self-monitors are also much more likely to be promoted or to receive job offers from outside companies.[106] And once promoted, high self-monitors are generally better performers. Indeed, a comparison of average and high-performing managers found that high-performing managers were higher self-monitors, more adaptable, and more self-aware than average managers.[107] Of course, one downside of excessive self-monitoring is that people may be seen as unreliable and inconsistent.[108]

locus of control
the degree to which individuals believe that their actions can influence what happens to them

internal locus of control
the belief that what happens to you is largely the result of your own actions

external locus of control
the belief that what happens to you is largely the result of factors beyond your control

Locus of control is the degree to which people believe that their actions influence what happens to them. **Internal locus of control** is the belief that what happens to you is largely under your control. **External locus of control** is the belief that what happens to you is primarily due to factors beyond your control, such as luck, chance, or other powerful people.[109] For example, two decades ago, at the age of 36, James Sweeney came up with the idea for the home healthcare business (in which patients are treated at home rather than in hospitals). McGaw Laboratories, the company he worked for, rejected his idea and fired him. If Sweeney were an "external," he might have given up his dream. However, being an "internal," Sweeney immediately started his home healthcare business. Indeed, Warren Bennis, a leading management author, said that internals, unlike externals, view failures as "false starts, stumbles, or steps to greatness."[110] In fact, eight years later, Sweeney sold his business for nearly $600 million. Ironically, he then used that money to purchase McGaw Labs, the company that had rejected his idea and fired him. Then when the home healthcare business he started and sold began to struggle, he bought it back for half of what he sold it for.[111]

Besides believing that what happens to them is largely under their control, internals have been found to be easier to motivate (especially when rewards are linked to performance), more difficult to lead, more independent, and better able to handle complex information and solve complex problems.[112] On the other hand, externals are more compliant and conforming and therefore are easier to lead than internals. For example, internals may question directives from their managers, while externals are likely to quietly accept them. Finally, internals are likely to perform better on complex tasks that require initiative and independent decision making, whereas externals tend to perform better on simple, repetitive tasks that are well structured.

affectivity
the stable tendency to experience positive or negative moods and to react to things in a generally positive or negative way

positive affectivity
personality trait in which individuals tend to notice and focus on the positive aspects of themselves and their environments

Affectivity is the stable tendency to experience positive or negative moods and to react to things in a generally positive or negative way.[113] People with **positive affectivity** consistently notice and focus on the positive aspects of themselves and their environments. In other words, they seem to be in a good mood most of the time and are predisposed to being optimistic,

negative affectivity
personality trait in which individuals tend to notice and focus on the negative aspects of themselves and their environments

cheerful, and cordial. By contrast, people with **negative affectivity** consistently notice and focus on the negative in themselves and their environments. They are frequently in bad moods, consistently expect the worst to happen, and are often irritated or pessimistic.

How stable are the positive or negative moods associated with positive/negative affectivity? A ten-year study by the National Institute of Aging found that even when people changed jobs or companies, the people who were the happiest at the beginning of the study were still the happiest people ten years later at the end of the study.[114] Likewise, the results of a much longer study found that high school counselors' ratings of student cheerfulness predicted how satisfied these people were with their jobs 30 years later.[115] Since dispositions toward positive or negative affectivity are long lasting and very stable, some companies have begun measuring affectivity during the hiring process. For example, Delta Airlines has applicants for flight attendant jobs engage in role plays designed to simulate interactions with passengers (i.e., boarding, serving food, etc.). Dennis Schmidt, Delta's assistant vice president for training and security, said applicants are more likely to be hired if they have "warmth" and if they are pleased to have the passengers on board.[116]

mood linkage
a phenomenon where one worker's negative affectivity and bad moods can spread to others

Studies also show that employees with positive affectivity are absent less often, report feeling less stress, are less likely to be injured in workplace accidents, and are less likely to retaliate against management and the company when they believe that they have been treated unfairly.[117] Affectivity is also important because of **mood linkage**, a phenomenon where one worker's negative affectivity and bad moods can spread to others. Studies of nurses and accountants show a strong relationship between individual workers' moods and the moods of their co-workers.[118] Finally, people with positive affectivity are better decision makers, are rated as having much higher managerial potential, and are more successful in sales jobs.[119]

Review 3
Deep-Level Diversity

Deep-level diversity matters because it can reduce prejudice, discrimination, and conflict while increasing social integration. It consists of dispositional and personality differences that can be learned only through extended interaction with others. Research conducted in different cultures, settings, and languages indicates that there are five basic dimensions of personality: extraversion, emotional stability, agreeableness, conscientiousness, and openness to experience. Of these, conscientiousness is the perhaps most important, because conscientious workers tend to be higher performers on virtually any job. Extraversion is also related to performance in jobs that require significant interaction with others. Studies also show that the personality dimensions of authoritarianism, Machiavellian tendencies, Type A/B personality, self-monitoring, locus of control, and positive/negative affectivity are important in the workplace. These personality dimensions are related to honesty, trust, teamwork, persuasive abilities, job performance, decision making, stress, heart disease, adaptability, promotions, interpersonal skills, motivation, initiative, job satisfaction, absenteeism, accidents, retaliatory behavior, mood linkage, and management potential.

How Can Diversity Be Managed?

How much should companies change their standard business practices to accommodate the diversity of their workers? For example, at Whirlpool Corporation's Lavergne, Tennessee, appliance factory, 10 percent of the work force is Muslim. Many Muslim men have long beards and wear skullcaps, while Muslim women wear flowing headscarves and modest, loose-fitting, form-hiding clothes. For safety reasons, long hair, hats of any kind, and loose clothing are prohibited on the factory floor. (Imagine any of these getting caught in moving machinery.) How should Whirlpool's managers deal with the obvious conflict between the Muslim religious practices and the company's safety procedures that are designed to prevent injury? Furthermore, at noon on Fridays, all Muslims attend 45- to 90-minute religious services at their mosques. With a typical Monday to Friday workweek and lunch breaks of just 30 minutes, how can Whirlpool's managers accommodate this Friday service without hurting the production schedule and without giving the Muslims special treatment (that may be resented by the 90 percent of workers who aren't Muslim)?[120]

Likewise, what do you do when a talented top executive has a drinking problem that only seems to affect his behavior at company business parties (for entertaining clients), where he made inappropriate advances toward female employees? What do you do when, despite aggressive company policies against racial discrimination, employees continue to tell racial jokes and publicly post cartoons displaying racial humor? And, since many people confuse diversity with affirmative action, what do you do to make sure that your company's diversity practices and policies are viewed as benefiting all workers and not just some workers?

No doubt about it, questions like these make managing diversity one of the toughest challenges that managers face.[121] However, there are steps companies can take to begin to address these issues. After reading this next section, you should be able to:

4 explain the basic principles and practices that can be used to **manage diversity**.

4 Managing Diversity

As discussed earlier, diversity programs try to create a positive work environment where no one is advantaged or disadvantaged, where "we" is everyone, where everyone can do their best work, where differences are respected and not ignored, and where everyone feels comfortable.

Let's begin to address those goals by learning about **4.1** *different diversity paradigms,* **4.2** *diversity principles, and* **4.3** *diversity training and practices.*

4.1 *Diversity Paradigms*

There are several different methods or paradigms for managing diversity: the discrimination and fairness paradigm, the access and legitimacy paradigm, and the learning and effectiveness paradigm.[122] The *discrimination and fairness paradigm*, which is the most common method of approaching diversity, focuses on equal opportunity, fair treatment, recruitment of minorities, and strict compliance with the equal employment opportunity laws. Under this approach, success is usually measured by how well companies achieve recruitment, promotion, and retention goals for women, people of different racial/ethnic backgrounds, or other underrepresented groups. For example, one manager said, ". . . I do know that if you don't measure something, it doesn't count. You measure your market share. You measure your profitability. The same should be true for diversity. There has to be some way of measuring whether you did, in fact, cast your net widely, and whether the company is better off today in terms of the experience of people of color than it was a few years ago. I measure my market share and my profitability. Why not this?"[123] The primary benefit of the discrimination and fairness paradigm is that it generally brings about fairer treatment of employees and increases demographic diversity. The primary limitation is that the focus of diversity remains on the surface-level diversity dimensions of gender, race, and ethnicity.

The *access and legitimacy paradigm* focuses on the acceptance and celebration of differences, so that the diversity within the company matches the diversity found among primary stakeholders, such as customers, suppliers, and local communities. This is similar to the *business growth* advantage of diversity discussed earlier in the chapter. The basic idea behind this approach is: "We are living in an increasingly multicultural country, and new ethnic groups are quickly gaining consumer power. Our company needs a demographically more diverse work force to help us gain access to these differentiated segments."[124] For example, Cheryl Horrigan, a regional staffing manager for Marshall's, a retail store, said, "It's important that we reflect our customer base. If our customers are shopping a store that doesn't reflect the environment, then it's not going to be as inviting. [People] have to relate to the environment in order to be comfortable shopping there."[125] The primary benefit of this approach is that it establishes a clear business reason for diversity. However, like the discrimination and fairness paradigm, it does no more than focus on the surface-level diversity dimensions of gender, race, and ethnicity. Furthermore, employees who are assigned responsibility for customers and stakeholders on the basis of their gender, race, or ethnicity may eventually feel frustrated and exploited.

While the discrimination and fairness paradigm focuses on assimilation (having a demographically representative work force), and the access and legitimacy paradigm focuses on differentiation (where demographic differences inside the company match those of key customers and stakeholders), the *learning and effectiveness paradigm* focuses on integrating deep-level diversity differences such as personality, attitudes, beliefs, and values into the actual work of the organization. Under this approach, people are valued not only on the basis of surface-level diversity (i.e., gender, race/ethnicity), but also for all of their knowledge, skills, abilities, and experiences. In other words, the learning and effectiveness paradigm is consistent with achieving organizational plurality. **Organizational plurality** is a work environment where (1) each member is empowered to contribute in a way that maximizes the benefits to the organization, customers, and themselves, and (2) the individuality of each member is respected by not segmenting or polarizing people on the basis of their membership in a particular group.[126]

organizational plurality
a work environment where (1) each member is empowered to contribute in a way that maximizes the benefits to the organization, customers, and themselves, and (2) the individuality of each member is respected by not segmenting or polarizing people on the basis of their membership in a particular group

There are four benefits to the learning and effectiveness diversity paradigm.[127] First, it values common ground. Dave Thomas of the Harvard Business School said, "Like the fairness paradigm, it promotes equal opportunity for all individuals. And like the access paradigm, it acknowledges cultural differences among people and recognizes the value in those differences. Yet this new model for managing diversity lets the organization internalize differences among employees so that it learns and grows because of them. Indeed, with the model fully in place, members of the organization can say, 'We are all on the same team, with our differences—not despite them.'"[128]

Second, it makes a distinction between individual and group differences. When diversity focuses only on differences between groups, such as females versus white males, large differences within groups are ignored.[129] For example, think of the women you know at work. Now, think for a second about what they have in common. After that, think about how they're different. If your situation is typical, the list of differences should be just as long, if not longer, than the list of commonalties. In short, managers can achieve a greater understanding of diversity and their people by treating them as individuals and by realizing that not all African Americans, Hispanics, women, or white males want the same things at work.[130]

Third, because the focus is on individual differences, the learning and effectiveness paradigm is less likely to encounter the conflict, backlash, and divisiveness sometimes associated with diversity programs that just focus on group differences. Taylor Cox, one of the leading management writers on diversity, said, "We are concerned here with these more destructive forms of conflict which may be present with diverse work forces due to language barriers, cultural clash, or resentment by majority-group members of what they may perceive as preferential and unwarranted treatment of minority-group members."[131] Ray Haines, a consultant who has helped companies deal with the aftermath of diversity programs that became divisive, said, "There's a large amount of backlash related to diversity training. It stirs up a lot of hostility, anguish and resentment but doesn't give people tools to deal with [the backlash]. You have people come in and talk about their specific ax to grind."[132] Certainly, not all diversity programs are divisive or lead to conflict. But, by focusing on individual rather than group differences, the learning and effectiveness paradigm helps to minimize these potential problems.

Finally, unlike the other diversity paradigms that simply focus on the value of being different (primarily in terms of surface-level diversity), there is a focus on bringing different talents and perspectives *together* (i.e., deep-level diversity) to make the best organizational decisions and to produce innovative, competitive products and services.

Table 12.3 shows the necessary preconditions for creating a learning and effectiveness diversity paradigm within an organization.

4.2 *Diversity Principles*

What principles can companies use when managing diversity?[133] In terms of diversity principles, begin by *carefully and faithfully following and enforcing federal and state laws regarding equal employment opportunity*. Diversity programs can't and won't succeed if the company is being sued for discriminatory actions and behavior. Faithfully following the law will also reduce the

Table 12.3

Creating a Learning and Effectiveness Diversity Paradigm in an Organization

1. The leadership must understand that a diverse work force will embody different perspectives and approaches to work, and must truly value variety of opinion and insight.
2. The leadership must recognize both the learning opportunities and the challenges that the expression of different perspectives presents for an organization.
3. The organizational culture must create an expectation of high standards of performance for everyone.
4. The organizational culture must stimulate personal development.
5. The organizational culture must encourage openness, a high tolerance for debate, and support constructive conflict on work-related matters.
6. The culture must make workers feel valued.
7. The organization must have a well-articulated and widely understood mission. This keeps discussions about work differences from degenerating into debates about the validity of people's perspectives.
8. The organization must have a relatively egalitarian, nonbureaucratic structure.

Source: D.A. Thomas & R.J. Ely, "Making Differences Matter: A New Paradigm for Managing Diversity," *Harvard Business Review* 74 (September/October 1996): 79-90.

time and expense associated with EEOC investigations or lawsuits. Start by learning more at the Equal Employment Opportunity Commission Web site (*http://www.eeoc.gov*). Following the law also means strictly and fairly enforcing company policies. Kevin Kelly, the former *Business Week* reporter whose workers were writing racial slurs on the stalls of the company bathroom, said:

> *Last year, at the urging of our labor attorney, we assembled an employee handbook, the first few pages of which spell out tough harassment and equal opportunity policies. We passed out literature on sexual harassment and adopted formal investigation procedures for any bias complaint. Anybody found guilty of breaking the rules is dealt with harshly. This seems to have improved things considerably. Employees on one shift, it turned out, felt they had been putting up with racially insensitive jokes of a foreman. With the new policy, a few men felt free to complain, which prompted an investigation in which the foreman cooperated. We suspended him without pay for two weeks, enrolled him in a class on managing a multicultural work force, and told him if he broke the rules again, he'd be fired. It seems to have worked.*[134]

Treat group differences as important, but not special. Surface-level diversity dimensions such as age, gender, and race/ethnicity should be respected, but should not be treated as more important than other kinds of differences (i.e., deep-level diversity). Remember, the shift from surface- to deep-level diversity helps people know and understand each other better, reduces prejudice and conflict, and leads to stronger social integration where people want to work together and get the job done. Also, *find the common ground.* While respecting differences is important, it's just as important, especially with diverse work forces, to actively find ways for employees to see and share commonalties.

Tailor opportunities to individuals, not groups. Special programs for training, development, mentoring, or promotions should be based on individual strengths and weaknesses, not group status. Instead of making mentoring available just for one group of workers, create mentoring opportunities for everyone who wants to be mentored. For example, at Pacific Enterprises, all programs, including the Career Conversations forums, in which upper-level managers are publicly interviewed about themselves and how they got their jobs, are open to all employees.[135]

Reexamine, but maintain high standards. Companies have a legal and moral obligation to make sure that their hiring and promotion procedures and standards are fair to all. However, in today's competitive markets, companies should not lower standards because of diversity. This not only hurts organizations, but also feeds stereotypes that applicants who are hired or promoted in the name of affirmative action or diversity are less qualified. For example, at the Marriott Marquis Hotel in New York's Times Square, where the hotel's 1,700 employees come from 70 countries and speak 47 different languages, managers are taught to cope with diversity by focusing on job performance. Jessica Brown, a quality-assurance manager who checks the cleanliness of rooms, said, "I don't lower my standards for anybody."[136]

Solicit negative as well as positive feedback. Diversity is one of the most difficult management issues. No company or manager gets it right from the start. Consequently, companies should aggressively seek positive and negative feedback about their diversity programs. For example, Allstate Insurance surveys all 50,000 of its employees on a quarterly basis to compile a "diversity index" that indicates whether customers are receiving bias-free service and managers are showing respect for employees and following the company's diversity policies.[137]

Set high but realistic goals. Just because diversity is difficult doesn't mean that organizations shouldn't try to accomplish as much as possible. The general purpose of diversity programs is to try to create a positive work environment where no one is advantaged or disadvantaged, where "we" is everyone, where everyone can do their best work, where differences are respected and not ignored, and where everyone feels comfortable. Even if progress is slow, companies should not shrink from these goals.

4.3 *Diversity Training and Practices*

awareness training
training that is designed to raise employees' awareness of diversity issues and to challenge the underlying assumptions or stereotypes they may have about others

Organizations use diversity training and several common diversity practices to manage diversity. There are two basic types of diversity training programs. **Awareness training** is designed to raise employees' awareness of diversity issues, such as the dimensions discussed in this chapter, and to get employees to challenge underlying assumptions or stereotypes they may have about others. For example, in Texaco's awareness training, employees "get in touch with their negative assumptions" and learn how their behavior affects others.[138] By contrast, **skills-based diversity training** teaches employees the practical skills they need for managing a diverse work force, such as flexibility and adaptability, negotiation, problem solving, and conflict resolution.[139]

Companies also use these diversity practices to better manage diversity: diversity audits, diversity pairing, and having top executives experience

skills-based diversity training
training that teaches employees the practical skills they need for managing a diverse work force, such as flexibility and adaptability, negotiation, problem solving, and conflict resolution

diversity audits
formal assessments that measure employee and management attitudes, investigate the extent to which people are advantaged or disadvantaged with respect to hiring and promotions, and review companies' diversity-related policies and procedures

diversity pairing
mentoring program in which people of different cultural backgrounds, genders, or races/ethnicities are paired together to get to know each other and change stereotypical beliefs and attitudes

what it is like to be a minority. **Diversity audits** are formal assessments that measure employee and management attitudes, investigate the extent to which people are advantaged or disadvantaged with respect to hiring and promotions, and review companies' diversity-related policies and procedures. For example, the results of a formal diversity audit prompted BRW, an architecture and engineering firm, to increase job advertising in minority publications, set up a diversity committee to provide recommendations to upper management, provide diversity training for all employees, and rewrite the company handbook to make a stronger statement about the company's commitment to a diverse work force.[140]

Earlier in the chapter you learned that *mentoring*, pairing a junior employee with a senior employee, is a common strategy for creating learning and promotional opportunities for women. Diversity pairing is a special kind of mentoring. **Diversity pairing** is pairing people of different cultural backgrounds, genders, or races/ethnicities for mentoring. The hope is that stereotypical beliefs and attitudes will change as people get to know each other as individuals.[141] Procter & Gamble uses diversity pairing in its "Mentor Up" program, which pairs senior men with junior women. But unlike traditional mentoring programs, the Mentor Up program is designed to have the junior women mentor the senior men. The basic idea is to change the culture among P&G's executives one manager at a time. Lisa Gevelber, a 29-year-old detergent brand manager paired with Rob Steele, a 43-year-old vice president and general manager of cleaning products, said, "I provide him a lot of perspective on what issues are hot among young women in the company today."[142]

Finally, because top managers are still overwhelmingly white and male, a number of companies believe that it is worthwhile to *have top executives experience what it is like to be in the minority*. This can be done by having top managers go to places or events in which nearly everyone else there is of a different gender or racial/ethnic background. At Hoechst Celanese, top managers must join two organizations in which they are a minority. For instance, the CEO, who is white and male, joined the board of Hampton University, a historically black college, and Jobs for Progress, a Hispanic organization that helps people prepare for jobs. As a result of his experiences, he said, "The only way to break out of comfort zones is to be exposed to other people. When we are, it becomes clear that all people are similar." A Hoechst VP who joined three organizations in which he was in the minority said, "Joining these organizations has been more helpful to me than two weeks of diversity training."[143]

Review 4
Managing Diversity

The three paradigms for managing diversity are the discrimination and fairness paradigm (equal opportunity, fair treatment, strict compliance with the law), the access and legitimacy paradigm (matching internal diversity to external diversity), and the learning and effectiveness paradigm (achieving organizational plurality by integrating deep-level diversity into the work of the organization). Unlike the other paradigms that focus on surface-level differences, the learning and effectiveness program values common ground, distinguishes between individual and group differences, minimizes conflict and divisiveness, and focuses on bringing different talents and perspectives together. What principles can companies use when managing diversity? Follow and enforce federal and state laws regarding equal employment opportunity. Treat group differences as important, but not special. Find the common ground. Tailor opportunities to individuals, not groups. Reexamine, but maintain high standards. Solicit negative as well as positive feedback. Set high but realistic goals. The two types of diversity training are awareness training and skills-based diversity training. Companies also manage diversity through diversity audits, diversity pairing, and by having top executives experience what it is like to be a minority.

What**Really**Happened?

In the opening case, you learned that MacTemps founder John Chaung was struggling with how his company manages diversity. John thought that by ignoring gender and race the company would naturally end up with a diverse work force, but it didn't happen that way. White males held most of the executive positions while females were concentrated in clerical and other nonmanagement jobs. Read the answers to the opening case to find out what steps John took to address diversity at MacTemps.

Isn't diversity just the result of affirmative action?

Affirmative action occurs when organizations take purposeful steps to create employment opportunities for minorities and women. By contrast, diversity exists in organizations when there is a variety of demographic, cultural, and personal differences among the people who work there and the customers who do business there. So one key difference is that affirmative action is more narrowly focused on demographics such as gender and race, while diversity has a broader focus that includes demographic, cultural, and personal differences. Furthermore, diversity can exist even if organizations don't take purposeful steps to create it. Another important difference is that affirmative action is required by law, while diversity is not. Organizations that pursue diversity goals and programs do so voluntarily. Affirmative action programs and diversity programs also have different purposes. The purpose of affirmative action programs is to compensate for past discrimination, to prevent ongoing discrimination, and to provide equal opportunities to all. By contrast, the general purpose of diversity programs is to create a positive work environment where no one is advantaged or disadvantaged, where "we" is everyone, where everyone can do their best work, where differences are respected and not ignored, and where everyone feels comfortable.

And why didn't John's philosophy of ignoring race, gender, and age result in an adequately diverse work force? If these factors are irrelevant in hiring and promotion decisions, shouldn't the work force just naturally be diverse?

Because age, gender, race/ethnicity, and disabilities are usually immediately observable, many managers and workers use these dimensions of surface-level diversity to form initial impressions and categorizations of co-workers, bosses, customers, or job applicants. Whether intentional or not, sometimes those initial categorizations and impressions lead to decisions or behaviors that discriminate against people of certain ages, genders, race/ethnicity, or mental or physical capabilities.

For example, John's policy, which he thought was quite fair and objective, was to make experience a critical consideration in hiring decisions. However, making experience important in the hiring process may perpetuate previous biases or even previous discrimination. John explained it this way: "The staffing industry has historically been skewed toward secretarial and clerical occupations. Since the traditional labor and middle management forces of the industry have been women—by and large, white women—they're the ones with the best experience. By choosing employees based on experience, I hired a disproportionate number of women in traditional roles—which is fine, but it didn't help my company in terms of true diversity." So, while experience may appear to be race- or gender-neutral, it may unintentionally perpetuate past imbalances and discrimination.

At first, MacTemps also relied on referrals from employees and friends. And like experience, this, too, resulted in unintentional biases. John said, "When you're in the initial startup phase, you're not thinking about diversity for the future; you're thinking about getting sales, and you count on the people you know. The pitfall of hiring friends, of course, is that they tend to be like you in terms of race, socioeconomic status, age, and gender. Before you know it, you've got a lot of the same kind of people hanging around making management decisions."

What kinds of things go into a diversity plan?

Before establishing a diversity plan, companies need to decide which diversity paradigm or model they want to follow. The three paradigms for managing diversity are the discrimination and fairness paradigm (equal opportunity, fair treatment, strict compliance with the law), the access and legitimacy paradigm (matching internal diversity to external diversity), and the learning and effectiveness paradigm (achieving organizational plurality by integrating deep-level diversity into the work of the organization).

The next step is to develop a set of principles to guide the development of the diversity plan. A basic diversity principle is to "follow and enforce federal and state laws regarding equal employment opportunity." Another is to "reexamine, but maintain high standards." For example, John said that "We're making sure our pool of entry-level employees is proportionally balanced in terms of gender, ethnicity, and age. [We] will never promote a less qualified person over a more qualified person."

The last step is to implement specific diversity training and practices. The two types of diversity training are awareness training and skills-based training. Awareness training is designed to get employees to challenge underlying assumptions or stereotypes they may have about others. Skills-based training teaches employees the practical skills they need for managing a diverse work force, such as flexibility and adaptability, negotiation, problem solving, and conflict resolution. Companies also manage diversity through specific practices such as diversity audits, diversity pairing, and by having top executives experience what it is like to be a minority.

How do you "manage diversity" without making race and gender more significant than merit?

There are several ways to do this. One is to treat group differences as important, but not special. Surface-level diversity dimensions such as age, gender, and race/ethnicity should be respected, but should not be treated as more important than other kinds of differences (i.e., deep-level diversity). Remember, the shift from surface- to deep-level diversity helps people know and understand each other better, reduces prejudice and conflict, and leads to stronger social integration in which people want to work together and get the job done.

Another approach is the access and legitimacy paradigm that creates a direct link between diversity and business success by matching internal diversity to external diversity. John believes that as markets are becoming more diverse, companies need a diverse group of managers to better deal with these markets. For example, MacTemps has two publishing clients in Miami that never would have signed a contract if the company hadn't had a Spanish-speaking manager. In Los Angeles and Hollywood, many animation artists come from China and Japan, so MacTemps hired a Chinese manager who is experienced in this work and familiar with both of these cultures.

A third option is to use the learning and effectiveness paradigm, which focuses on integrating deep-level diversity differences such as personality, attitudes, beliefs, and values into the actual work of the organization. Under this approach, people are valued not only on the basis of surface-level diversity (i.e., gender, race/ethnicity), but also for all of their knowledge, skill, abilities, and experiences. For example, John is convinced that a diverse work force helps MacTemps make better decisions. As he put it, "Can a committee of all men create an informed maternity policy?" He also said that "Since we were all the same age, we created advertising materials that we liked but nobody over 45 could read because the typeface was too small. Ageism never occurred to us." In short, a diverse staff will do a better job of making decisions and developing policies for today's (and tomorrow's) increasingly diverse work force.

Sources: MacTemps Home Page, "About MacTemps." [Online] Available **http://www.mactemps.com/about.html,** 1 April 1999. J. Chaung, "On Balance," *Inc.,* July 1995, 25. D.H. Pink, "The Talent Market," *Fast Company*, August 1998, 87.

Key Terms

affectivity p. 485

affirmative action p. 463

age discrimination p. 471

agreeableness p. 480

authoritarianism p. 482

awareness training p. 491

conscientiousness p. 480

deep-level diversity p. 470

disability p. 476

disability discrimination p. 476

disposition p. 479

diversity p. 463

diversity audits p. 492

diversity pairing p. 492

emotional stability p. 480

external locus of control p. 485

extraversion p. 479

gender discrimination p. 473

glass ceiling p. 473

internal locus of control p. 485

locus of control p. 485

Machiavellianism p. 483

mood linkage p. 486

negative affectivity p. 486

openness to experience p. 481

organizational plurality p. 488

personality p. 479

positive affectivity p. 485

racial and ethnic discrimination p. 474

self-monitoring p. 484

skills-based diversity training p. 491

social integration p. 470

stereotypes p. 477

surface-level diversity p. 469

Type A personality p. 483

Type A/B personality dimension p. 483

Type B personality p. 484

What Would You Do-II?

Avon Headquarters, New York City.

In the last decade, Avon has come a long way in terms of its performance and its diversity. It started the decade with a huge amount of debt, a number of badly run businesses that had been acquired (and later sold) in a poorly thought out diversification plan, and a deterioration of its core business—direct selling of makeup and personal products to women. However, it ended the decade in fine fashion, with little debt, strong cash flows, strongly rising profits, and enormous growth of Avon products in emerging markets, such as Mexico, Argentina, Chile, Taiwan, and China. In all, Avon's 2.6 million independent sales representatives serve the needs of women in 135 countries worldwide.

Ironically, in terms of diversity, Avon started the decade as a boy's club. At that time, women could be found in district sales managers' jobs, the lowest level in Avon's corporate hierarchy, but generally not any higher. Further evidence of the boy's club mentality (and remember, this was with a business that made its money by selling products just for women) could be found in the annual hunting trips for executives and expensive season tickets for the New York Knicks basketball team and the New York Yankees baseball team. However, thanks to the progressive leadership of Avon's CEO, Jim Preston, that has all changed. Today, Avon has more women in management positions (86 percent) than any other Fortune 500 company. Furthermore, 17 of Avon's 54 officers (32 percent) are women and four women sit on Avon's board of directors. Also, Avon has been named one of the "100 Best Companies for Working Mothers" six times, has been recognized for providing outstanding opportunities for Hispanic employees, and has been cited as one of the "25 Best Places for Blacks to Work" by *Black Enterprise* magazine. So, in almost every way, women and other minorities don't seem to run into the glass ceiling at Avon.

However, there is one place where the glass ceiling has not been broken at Avon—the CEO's office. Even though it sells primarily to women, Avon has never had a female CEO. But with Jim Preston set to retire, Avon could finally have its very first female CEO. In fact, four of the six leading candidates are women. There's 41-year-old Jose Ferrira, Jr., president of the Asia Pacific region; 49-year-old Alfredo Cuello, head of European operations; Andrea Jung, a 38-year-old Princeton graduate who earned her reputation as an executive at Bloomingdale's, I. Magnin, and Neiman Marcus; 48-year-old Susan Kropf, an NYU MBA who joined Avon as an administrative assistant and worked her way up to head of U.S. operations; 49-year-old Christina Gold who smartly handled a near mutiny among Avon's sales ladies and now heads worldwide strategy development; and 45-year-old Edwina Woodbury, who is the company's chief financial and administrative officer.

As a member of the search committee, you'll be part of this very difficult decision. While all the candidates are highly qualified, Jose Ferrira, Andrea Jung, and Susan Kropf are seen as having more CEO potential than the others.

With women comprising nearly all of its customers, 84 percent of its managers, half of its board of directors, and two of the five slots on the search committee, you know that gender is going to be discussed and considered as the committee makes its decision. Which way will you lean? Should gender be an important criterion for the Avon CEO job? Are there valid business reasons for believing that a woman would do a better job? **If you were a member of Avon's CEO search committee, what would you do?**

Sources: Avon Web site, "A Century in Partnership with Women." [Online] Available **http://www.avon.com/about/women/history/history.html,** 29 April 1999. Avon Web Site, "Backgrounder." [Online] Available **http://www.avon.com/about/financial/company/background.html,** 29 April 1999. G. Brewer, "How Avon's CEO Implements Diversity," *Sales and Marketing Management* 149, no. 1 (January 1997): 37. Y. Gault, "Avon Is Calling on its Women to Fill CEO Post," *Crain's New York Business,* 2 June 1997, 1. B. Morris, "If Women Ran the World It Would Look a Lot Like Avon: In a Beauty Contest Unlike Any Other, Four of the Six Candidates for the Next CEO Are Women," *Fortune,* 21 July 1997, 74.

Critical-Thinking Video Case

Diversity in Business: Hudson's

Dayton Hudson Corporation, located in Minneapolis, Minnesota, is the fourth-largest retailer in the United States. The company owns Target, Mervyns, Dayton's, Hudson's, and Marshall Field's, all department stores. Hudson's is committed to the well-being of the communities in which all 22 of its stores are located. It is especially committed to promoting diversity within all its stores and at corporate headquarters.

As you watch the video, consider the following critical-thinking questions.

Critical-Thinking Questions

1. Why is Hudson's committed to diversity?
2. What can Hudson's do to promote diversity?

Management Decisions

Personality Similarities and Differences

From teamwork to job performance to interpersonal skills to mood, personality differences affect how people behave on the job as well as the type of job for which they are best suited. To learn more about yourself and your classmates, use the Internet to complete the personality inventories listed under Additional Internet Resources. (If you're not sure which inventories you should complete for this assignment, ask your instructor.) Print the results and bring them to class. Also, answer the four questions shown below. Bring those to class, too, and be willing to discuss them with others.

Additional Internet Resources

If these Web sites become inactive, search the Web using keywords to find similar tests. There are many such tests available on the Web.

- **Introversion/Extroversion**
  To determine whether you are an introvert or extrovert, complete the Extraversion/Introversion Inventory at **http://www.queendom.com/extraver.html.**
- **Responding to Stress**
  To determine how well you respond to stress, complete the Coping Skills Inventory at **http://www.queendom.com/coping.html.**
- **Type A/B Personality**
  To determine whether you are Type A or Type B, take the Type A Personality Test at **http://www.queendom.com/typea.html.**
- **Locus of Control**
  To determine your locus of control, complete the Locus of Control and Attributional Style Inventory at **http://www.queendom.com/lc.html.**
- **Affectivity**
  To determine your affectivity, complete the Optimism/Pessimism Inventory at **http://www.queendom.com/optimist.html.**

Questions

1. What is your perfect job? Describe three characteristics your perfect job would have.
2. What do you look for in terms of leadership? Describe three things you want your leaders

to do and three things you never want your leaders to do.

3. When was the last time you woke up in the middle of the night unable to sleep? How often does this happen: almost never, once every six months, once every three months, once a month, once a week, or several or more times per week? Why?

4. You've been on the job only three months and are just beginning to feel like you're getting a handle on things. Then your boss quits, and you're asked to take his job. Would you take it or turn it down? Why or why not?

Management Decisions

Family-Friendly or Discrimination?

Flexible work schedules, a daycare center, extended health coverage for families, and generous parental leaves (when babies are born): When these benefits were announced last year, company management had the people in public relations work their contacts to make sure that there was plenty of coverage from the local press about the "family-friendly" workplace it was creating. At that time, everyone seemed to have praise for these "socially responsible" policies.

However, over the last 18 months, an increasing number of employees have griped about how unfair these policies are to people without kids. One common complaint is that whenever there are critical deadlines, the people without kids seem to be expected to stay, while the people with children get to go home. Likewise, in the factory, the complaint is that people with families are more likely to get the highly prized day shift, while people without kids are more likely to be assigned to the evening and midnight shifts. Another employee complained that she wasn't allowed to leave early one day to take a hurt friend to the hospital but that her boss left at 5:00 *every* day to pick up her children from daycare. Her boss's response was, "Why can't someone else take her?"

At first, you thought these were just isolated complaints, but after some research, you found out that this kind of resentment is much more common than you thought. For example, according to the U.S. Bureau of Labor, only 38 percent of workers have children at home under the age of 18. In other words, a clear majority of workers, 62 percent, do not benefit from these family-friendly policies. In fact, women with children under six comprise only 8 percent of the work force. Not surprisingly, a Conference Board survey found that 56 percent of companies report that childless employees resent the "special treatment" given to workers with children. Leslie Lafayette, founder of the Childfree Network, which has 38 chapters and 5,000 members, said, "To expect other people to, in effect, subsidize you for having your own children, I think is really off the mark." Lafayette went on to say, "I feel that there should be equal treatment for all, whether or not you are a parent. It's not business's place to put a value on parenting, or to judge and reward you because you are a parent, but the workplace is set up to do just that."

Questions

1. Do family-friendly policies discriminate against people who don't have children? Explain.

2. What should the company do with its family-friendly policies: leave them alone, eliminate them, or change them? Explain the reasons behind your choice.

Sources: V. Frazee, "When the Team Takes Advantage of Single Employees," *Personnel Journal* 75 (November 1996): 103. L. Jenner, "Family-Friendly Backlash," *Management Review* 83 (May 1994): 7. M. Picard, "No Kids? Get Back to Work!" *Training* 34 (September 1997): 33-40. D. Seligman, "Who Needs Family-Friendly Companies? A Contrarian View: It Sounds Lovely to Help Out Workers with Families, Except Then You Are Discriminating Against Singles," *Forbes,* 11 January 1999, 72.

Develop Your Management Potential

From Majority to Minority and Back Again

Do you know what it feels like to walk into a room where, because of your gender, race/ethnicity, religion, language, or some other dimension, you are intensely aware of being different from everyone else? Some of you do. Most of you probably don't. And, since most managers are white and male, it's a good bet that they don't know either. It can be unsettling, especially the first time you experience it.

Some companies have begun broadening perspectives and understanding by having their managers join groups or attend events in which they are different from everyone else. For instance, at Hoechst Celanese, the CEO, who is white and male, joined the board of Hampton University, a historically black college, and Jobs for Progress, a Hispanic organization that helps people prepare for jobs.

For more than 30 years, United Parcel Service has required its top managers to participate in community service programs in inner cities or poor rural areas. James Casey, UPS's founder, started the program in 1968 to expose his white male managers to diverse experiences, people, and communities. Casey also hoped that the experience would increase empathy, break down stereotypes, and encourage volunteer and community service. The program works by assigning managers with 10 to 30 years of experience to community service tasks in inner cities or rural areas. Don Wofford, who directs the program, said, "We choose managers on the fast track, people who'll be positioned to influence their work force and the community for years to come." UPS managers spend two weeks doing community service, followed by a weekend at their homes, and then two more weeks of community service. Wofford said, "This format gives them a chance to digest the experience—they tend to come back renewed after the break, with a new focus, sometimes even more bewildered, but still ready to go for it."

Your assignment for this Develop Your Management Potential is to attend an event, meeting, or activity in which your are different from almost everyone else in terms of your gender, race/ethnicity, religion, language, or some other dimension. You can choose a church service, local community group, volunteer organization, or student group on campus. Ask your professor for ideas. You should probably contact the group beforehand to arrange your visit. Answer the following questions after your visit.

Questions

1. Describe the event, meeting, activity, and/or organization you visited.
2. How were you different from others in attendance? Describe what it was like to be different from everyone else.
3. In what ways was this event, meeting, activity, and/or organization actually similar to previous experiences that you've had? In other words, while question 2 focuses on differences, this question focuses on similarities and commonalties.
4. What did you learn from this experience?

Sources: M. Crowe, "UPS Managers Trained in the Real World to Deliver Results," *The Business Journal – San Jose,* 21 September 1998, 26. F. Rice, "How to Make Diversity Pay," *Fortune,* 8 August 1994, 78.

Chapter 13 Outline

Managing Teams

What Would **You** Do?

Cigna's Customer Service Center, Bethlehem, Pennsylvania. Cigna's Customer Service Center is a busy place. Each day, thousands of calls come in from policyholders with billing questions, claims, or an interest in buying more insurance. Your job, as the manager of the Customer Service Division, is to run an efficient operation and maintain a high level of customer service. You know that customers often judge a company by how they are treated when they call with a problem or question. Therefore, you want to make sure that their needs are met in a polite and expedient manner. Unfortunately, system bottlenecks are slowing down response times. The center's three main functions are customer service (including claims), accounting, and new business development. Each is a separate department with its own staff and hierarchy. Unfortunately, this creates complications and communication barriers when employees try to deal with customers. For example, when a policyholder calls with a billing question, the customer service representative has to put the caller on hold, contact the accounting department to retrieve the pertinent information, and then communicate the answer to the customer. This causes delays and frustrates your staff and customers. You have given this problem a lot of thought. What you have tentatively decided to do may strike some people as radical, but the more you think about it, the more you are convinced that it is the right decision. You are thinking about eliminating the separate departments and replacing them with a number of "customer representative" teams. The teams would be made up of one or more members from each of the departments. Each team would be assigned to service a specific group of Cigna customers (for example, all the policyholders in New England). Under this structure, when a customer calls, the customer would be connected to the team assigned to handle all of that customer's business. A handful of support personnel would be needed to handle specific functions, such as underwriting, but would not be needed for most routine calls. You see several benefits to this plan, especially reduced call times, lower costs, and increased customer and employee satisfaction. A few things worry you, however. Some employees may not fit into a team environment. What if these employees quit their jobs, or complain a lot and make everybody's life miserable? There will also be fewer jobs open at the supervisor level. And, the last thing that you want to do is to create the impression that there is no opportunity for top performers to move up in the firm. You also know that despite the outward promise of teamwork, it is difficult to know whether teams will actually work until you try it. What if productivity doesn't go up, and employee morale suffers rather than improves? Will work teams actually improve customer service? Will you be putting your own job on the line? That's a scary thought, particularly with two kids in college. In the background, you can hear your customer service representatives fielding phone calls, and you know that some of your customers will be on hold longer than they like. A decision has to be made soon. **If you were the head of Cigna's Customer Service Center, what would you do?**

Sources: M. Brown, "National Winner: Cigna Services UK," *Management Today*, June 1994, 95. J.R. Caron, S.L. Jarvenpaa, & D.B. Stoddard, "Business Reengineering at CIGNA Corporation: Experiences and Lessons Learned from the First Five Years," *MIS Quarterly* 18, no. 3 (1994): 233. S.E. Gross, *Compensation for Teams* (New York: American Management Association, 1995). T. Hoffman, "Re-engineering Pays Off at Cigna," *Computerworld*, August 1993, 70. "International Healthcare News," *Business Conference and Management Reports*, 1 December 1995, 6.

Like Cigna, a growing number of organizations are significantly improving their effectiveness by establishing work teams. In fact, 91 percent of U.S. companies use teams and groups of one kind or another to solve specific problems.[1] However, Table 13.1 shows that with the exception of Procter & Gamble, which began using teams in 1962, work teams were not established in many companies until the mid- to late 1980s. And since many of the companies shown in Table 13.1 were early adopters, this means that teams really haven't been in place at most companies for more than five to ten years, if that long. In other words, teams are a relatively new phenomenon in companies, and there's still much for organizations to learn about managing them.

We begin this chapter by reviewing the advantages and disadvantages of teams and exploring when companies should use them over more traditional approaches. Next, we discuss the different types of work teams and the characteristics common to all teams. The chapter ends by focusing on the practical steps to managing teams—team goals and priorities and organizing, training, and compensating teams.

Why Work Teams?

work team
a small number of people with complementary skills who hold themselves mutually accountable for pursuing a common purpose, achieving performance goals, and improving interdependent work processes

Work teams consist of a small number of people with complementary skills who hold themselves mutually accountable for pursuing a common purpose, achieving performance goals, and improving interdependent work processes.[2] By this definition, computer programmers working on separate projects in the same department of a company would not be considered a team. To be a team, the programmers would have to be interdependent and share responsibility and accountability for the quality and amount of computer code they produced.[3]

Julia Garcia is a member of a work team in a Frito-Lay snack plant in Lubbock, Texas. Prior to the establishment of teams at the plant, Garcia and her co-workers never paid any attention to the quality and cost data posted on company bulletin boards and rarely concerned themselves with ways to improve the running of the plant. Today, however, Garcia and her teammates receive weekly updates on costs, quality, and performance and take as much responsibility for quality standards and performance as company management does. When products don't meet Frito-Lay's quality standards, Garcia and her teammates reject them. When machines are shut down for maintenance and there are too many workers sitting around with nothing to

Table 13.1 **When Selected Companies Began Using Work Teams**

Company	Year
Boeing	1987
Caterpillar	1986
Champion International	1985
Cummings Engine	1973
Digital Equipment	1982
Ford	1982
General Electric	1985
LTV Steel	1985
Procter & Gamble	1962

Source: J. Hoerr, "The Payoff from Teamwork—The Gains in Quality Are Substantial—So Why Isn't It Spreading Faster?" *Business Week*, 10 July 1989, 56.

do, Garcia and her teammates keep costs down by deciding who should be sent home until the work is done.

Since the move to teams, the number of managers at the Frito-Lay plant has dropped from 38 to 13, while the number of hourly workers (i.e., team members) has increased by 20 percent to more than 220. More importantly, the teams have produced double-digit decreases in costs and such huge improvements in quality that the plant is now ranked sixth out of 48 plants by Frito management, up from the bottom 20 where it was previously ranked. Furthermore, Garcia and her co-workers are thriving in the team atmosphere. She said, "It kind of frightened me at first. I thought, 'I'm not going to be able to decide anything.' [But now] I really enjoy [the team approach] because it gives me a sense of pride. I know my work and what we need to do. . . . It's more fun. It used to be it was just the 'same-ol'-same-ol',' [but] now there are more things happening."[4]

The success that Julia Garcia and Frito-Lay experienced with teams is not uncommon. In many industries, teams are growing in importance because they help organizations respond to specific problems and challenges. For Frito-Lay, the challenges were to increase product quality and lower costs. For a service business, like a restaurant or an airline, the challenge may be to increase customer satisfaction or employee motivation. While work teams are not the answer for every situation or organization, if the right teams are used properly and in the right settings, teams can dramatically improve company performance over more traditional management approaches and instill a sense of vitality in the workplace that is otherwise difficult to achieve.

After reading the next two sections, you should be able to:

1. explain the **good and bad of using teams.**
2. recognize and understand the different **kinds of teams.**

1 The Good and Bad of Using Teams

Let's begin our discussion of teams by learning about **1.1** *the advantages of teams,* **1.2** *the disadvantages of teams, and* **1.3** *when to use and not use teams.*

1.1 *The Advantages of Teams*

Companies are making greater use of teams because teams have been shown to increase customer satisfaction, product and service quality, speed and efficiency in product development, and employee job satisfaction.[5] Teams help businesses increase *customer satisfaction* in several ways. One way is to create work teams that are trained to meet the needs of specific customer groups. When Kodak reengineered its customer service center, it created specific teams to field calls from the general public (based on the geographic location of the caller), scientific users, and corporate users. Under this system, customers were immediately directed to the team trained to meet their needs. Within a year, the work teams doubled the rate at which Kodak solved customer problems on the first phone call.[6]

Businesses also create problem-solving teams and employee-involvement teams to study ways to improve overall customer satisfaction and make

Companies use teams, like the one that developed Windows 95 for Microsoft, to design new products more quickly and efficiently than can traditional departmental structures.

recommendations for improvements. Teams like these typically meet on a weekly or monthly basis. The Published Image, a small publishing company, increased customer satisfaction when it switched from a traditional management hierarchy to separate work teams with their own clients and their own sales, editorial, and production workers. Client Peter Herlihy said, "we [now] have one group of people who know all facets of our job, and we can contact any of them during the process."[7]

Teams also help firms improve *product and service quality* in several ways.[8] Here, in contrast to traditional organizational structures where management is responsible for organizational outcomes and performance, one of the primary advantages is that teams take direct responsibility for the quality of the products and service they produce. At Texas Instruments, production teams are directly responsible for resolving quality issues, and even visit suppliers when necessary to track down quality problems.[9] At Whole Foods, a supermarket chain that sells groceries and health foods, the ten teams that manage each store are not only responsible for store quality and performance, but they are also directly accountable, since the size of their team bonus depends on it.[10] And making teams directly responsible for service and production quality pays off. A survey by *Industry Week* indicates that 42 percent of the companies who use teams report revenues of more than $250,000 per employee compared to only 25 percent of the companies that don't use teams.[11]

As you learned in Chapter 10, companies that are slow to innovate or integrate new features and technologies into their products are at a competitive disadvantage. Therefore, a third reason that teams are increasingly popular is *the need for speed and efficiency when designing and manufacturing products.*[12] Traditional product design proceeds sequentially, meaning that one department has to finish its work on the design of a product before the next department can start. Unfortunately, this is not only slow, but it also encourages departments to work in isolation from one another.[13] For example, with sequential design processes, it's common for different departments, such as manufacturing, to work for months on their part of the product design only to have it rejected by another department, such as marketing, which was never consulted as the work was being done.

As you learned in Chapter 4, *overlapping development phases* is a faster and better way to design products and is often made possible through the use of teams. With overlapping development phases, teams of employees, consisting of members from the different functional areas in a firm (i.e., engineering, manufacturing, and marketing), work on the product design at the same time. Because each of the different functional areas is involved in the design process from the start, the company can avoid most of the delays and frustration associated with sequential development. The Boeing 777, a highly successful commercial aircraft, was designed in this manner. To design the 777 in an expedient and cost-effective manner, Boeing created 238 design teams that worked on separate components of the 777 simultaneously. The design teams were made up of employees from different departments and, in some cases, even Boeing customers and suppliers. Each team was responsible for designing a specific part of the 777 and communicated with other teams through a sophisticated computer network. As a result, the design of this completely new aircraft was completed in just over two years, which is a record for the aircraft industry. The Boeing 777 teams also achieved impressive results in terms of quality and efficiency. In comparison to the design of other Boeing aircraft, the 777 teams reduced changes in design, errors, and rework by 50 percent.[14]

Another reason for using teams is that teamwork often leads to increased job satisfaction.[15] One reason that teamwork can be more satisfying than traditional work is that it gives workers a chance to improve their skills. This is often accomplished through **cross training**, in which team members are taught how to do all or most of the jobs performed by the other team members. When work teams were introduced at Westinghouse's electronics assembly plant in College Station, Texas, workers were trained in robotics, assembly, soldering, and testing—in other words, in all of the basic steps for making electronic products.[16] The advantage for the organization is that cross training allows teams to function normally when one member is absent or a team member quits or is transferred. The advantage for workers is that cross training broadens their skills and makes them more capable while also making their work more varied and interesting.

cross training
training team members how to do all or most of the jobs performed by the other team members

Participation in work teams also increases job satisfaction by providing team members unique opportunities that would otherwise not be available to them. At Chaparral Steel, employee work teams routinely visit customers' production facilities to discuss quality-related issues.

Also, work teams often receive proprietary business information that is only available to managers at most companies. For example, at Whole Foods, the supermarket chain that sells groceries and health foods, team members are given full access to their store's financial information and everyone's salaries, including the store manager and the CEO.[17] Each day, next to the time clock, Whole Foods employees can see the previous day's sales for each team, as well as the sales on the same day from the previous year. Each week, team members can examine the same information, broken down by team, for all of the Whole Foods stores in their regions. And each month, store managers review information on profitability, including sales, product costs, wages, and operating profits, with each team in the store.

Personal Productivity Tip

Learn to Celebrate Success

When athletes celebrate success, they share high fives, low fives, torso bumps, and bash bumps (forearm to forearm). There is impromptu dancing, spiking, stuffing, and jumping into the stands. The emotions are palpable, and fans and athletes share the celebration. Celebration and emotions are also important for work teams. Next time your team does something well or exceeds a goal, start a celebration. Order a pizza, print some T-shirts, or plan a team outing. The energy and emotions that you and your teammates share by celebrating will drive you to higher levels of success.

Source: Donald J. Bodwell, "Combined File Print Out of High Performance Team: Celebration," *High Performance Teams.* [Online] Available **http://rampages.onramp.net/~bodwell/combined.htm**, 16 May 1999.

Since team members decide how much to spend, what to order, what things should cost, and how many team members should work each day, this information is critical to making teams work at Whole Foods.[18]

Team members often gain job satisfaction from unique leadership responsibilities that would typically not be available in traditional organizations. For example, at Colgate-Palmolive work teams are responsible for determining their own work assignments, scheduling overtime, making out vacation schedules, performing preventive equipment maintenance, and assuring quality control. For each work team, the position of team leader rotates, giving different team members the opportunity to build leadership skills.[19]

Teams share many of the advantages of group decision making discussed in Chapter 5. For instance, because team members possess different knowledge, skills, abilities, and experiences, teams will be able to view problems from multiple perspectives. This diversity of viewpoints increases the odds that team decisions will solve the underlying causes of problems rather than simply address the symptoms. The increased knowledge and information available to teams also make it easier for them to generate more alternative solutions, which is a critical part of improving the quality of decisions. Finally, because teams members are involved in decision-making processes, they should be more committed to making those decisions work. In short, teams can do a much better job than individuals in two important steps of the decision-making process: defining the problem and generating alternative solutions.

1.2 *The Disadvantages of Teams*

Although teams can significantly increase customer satisfaction, product and service quality, speed and efficiency in product development, and employee job satisfaction, using teams does not guarantee these positive outcomes. In fact, if you've ever participated in team projects in your classes, you're probably already aware of some of the problems inherent in work teams. So despite all of their promise, teams and teamwork are also prone to these significant disadvantages: initially high turnover, social loafing, self-limiting behavior, and legal risk.

The first disadvantage of work teams is *initially high turnover.* Teams aren't for everyone, and some workers will balk at the responsibility, effort, and learning required in team settings. When General Electric's Salisbury plant switched to teams, the turnover rate, which was near zero, jumped to 14 percent. Plant manager Roger Gasaway said of teams and teamwork, "It's not all wonderful stuff."[20] Other people quit because they object to the way in which team members closely scrutinize each other's job performance, particularly when teams are small. Randy Savage, who works for Eaton Corp., a manufacturer of car and truck parts, said, "They say there are no bosses here, but if you screw up, you find one pretty fast." Beverly Reynolds, who quit Eaton's team-based system after nine months, said her co-workers "weren't standing watching me, but from afar, they were watching me." And even though her teammates were willing to help her improve her job performance, she concluded, "As it turns out, it just wasn't for me at all."[21]

social loafing
behavior in which team members withhold their efforts and fail to perform their share of the work

Social loafing is another disadvantage of work teams. **Social loafing** occurs when workers withhold their efforts and fail to perform their share of the work. A 19th century German scientist named Ringleman first documented social loafing when he found that one person pulling on a rope by himself or herself exerted an average of 63 kg of force on the rope. In groups of three, the average force dropped to 53 kg. In groups of eight, the average dropped to just 31 kg. Ringleman concluded that the larger the team, the smaller the individual effort. In fact, social loafing is more likely to occur in larger groups where it can be difficult to identify and monitor the efforts of individual team members.[22] In other words, social loafers count on being able to blend into the background so that their lack of effort isn't easily spotted. Because of team-based class projects, most students already know about social loafers or "slackers," who contribute poor, little, or no work whatsoever. Not surprisingly, research with 250 student teams clearly shows that the most talented students are typically the least satisfied with teamwork because of having to carry "slackers" and having to do a disproportionate share of their team's work.[23]

self-limiting behavior behavior in which team members choose to limit their involvement in a team's work

Self-limiting behavior is another disadvantage of teams. **Self-limiting behavior** occurs whenever team members choose to limit their involvement in the team's work.[24] Of course, self-limiting behavior, such as daydreaming, doodling, thinking about tasks other than work, withholding opinions, or not participating in meetings, reduces team performance. While similar to social loafing, there is a difference. Social loafers try to make sure that no one detects that they are withholding their efforts. The payoff is that they get away with it. Self-limiters have a different motivation. They reduce their involvement in team activities because they just don't see any payoff to participating. For example, one manager said, "The last time we went through this process it was just an exercise in futility—no one listened to our suggestions. Why fight or argue the point? This is a meaningless exercise anyway."[25] Self-limiters just don't see the point. They give up. They "raise a white flag" and "surrender."

How prevalent is self-limiting behavior? One study found that when team activities were not mandatory, 25 percent of manufacturing workers would volunteer to join problem-solving teams, 70 percent were quiet, passive supporters (i.e., self-limiters), and 5 percent were opposed to these activities.[26] Another study found that self-limiting behavior was somewhat less prevalent among managers. Still, 56 percent of managers, more than half, engaged in self-limiting behavior in management teams. Table 13.2 lists the factors that encourage self-limiting behavior in teams.

Table 13.2

Factors That Encourage Self-Limiting Behavior in Teams

1. *The presence of someone with expertise.* Team members will self-limit when another team member is highly qualified to make a decision or comment on an issue.
2. *The presentation of a compelling argument.* Team members will self-limit if the arguments for a course of action are very persuasive or similar to their own thinking.
3. *Lacking confidence in one's ability to contribute.* Team members will self-limit if they are unsure about their ability to contribute to discussions, activities, or decisions. This is especially so for high profile decisions.
4. *An unimportant or meaningless decision.* Team members will self-limit by mentally withdrawing or adopting a "who cares" attitude if decisions don't affect them or their units, or if they don't see a connection between their efforts and their team's successes or failures.
5. *A dysfunctional decision-making climate.* Team members will self-limit if other team members are frustrated or indifferent or if a team is floundering or disorganized.

Source: P.W. Mulvey, J.F. Veiga, & P.M. Elsass, "When Teammates Raise a White Flag," *Academy of Management Executive* 10, no. 1 (1996): 40-49.

Another disadvantage of teams is that they can present a legal risk to companies that violate the National Labor Relations Act (NLRA), which is the primary law governing relationships between unions and employers in the private sector.[27] With respect to teams, the National Labor Relations Board (NLRB) (**http://www.nlrb.gov/**), which administers the NLRA, looks for two things. First, it determines whether the work teams in a company can be categorized as a *labor organization*, which it defines as "any organization of any kind, or any agency or employee representation committee or plan, in which employees participate and which exists for the purpose . . . of dealing with employers concerning grievances, labor disputes, wages, rates of pay, hours of employment or conditions of work." Since many work teams control or have a large say on these issues, teams in many companies can be categorized as labor organizations. Second, if teams can be categorized as labor organizations, then the NLRA tries to determine if the company controlled or dominated the teams by having management participate on the teams, by financially supporting the teams, or by determining team membership. As we will discuss later in the chapter, management is likely to do all of these things in one way or another to make teams run more efficiently and effectively.

How much of a legal risk does the NLRA represent to companies that use teams? It's hard to say. Thus far, 23 companies, including EFCO, Polaroid, NCR, and Dillon Stores, have violated the NLRA by using teams in these ways. So with teams of some kind in use at more than 80 percent of companies, the absolute risk is relatively low. However, there's no way of knowing how many companies have not used teams or have restricted the way they use teams because of this legal threat.

What scares managers away is that the companies that have violated the NLRA have done so using teams for relatively straightforward business purposes. For example, at EFCO Corporation, participation on teams and committees was completely voluntary. Moreover, the EFCO committees that were disbanded following the NLRB's ruling were the employee policy review committee, the safety committee, the employee suggestion screening committee, and the employee benefit committee.[28] Even more foreboding is that the NLRB has also ruled that employers using teams can violate the NLRA even when employees aren't members of unions and even if the company takes steps to comply with the law. For example, Polaroid changed its teams and participation programs to make sure that they did not violate the NLRA, but was still found in violation because the work teams "represented" the views of other workers and therefore constituted a "labor organization." Like EFCO, the members of Polaroid's Employee Owner Influence Council were picked from a pool of volunteers. The council, which received office space and supplies from the company, served as a sounding board for management by offering opinions on pay, benefits, and other issues.[29] Table 13.3 provides some guidelines for minimizing the legal risks that teams pose for companies at this time.

Finally, teams share many of the disadvantages of group decision making discussed in Chapter 5. This includes *groupthink*, in which, in highly cohesive groups, group members feel intense pressure not to disagree with each other so that the group can approve a solution that has been proposed. Because groupthink restricts discussion and leads to consideration of a limited number of alternative solutions, it usually results in poor decisions. Also, team decision making takes considerable time. Furthermore, it's the rare team that consistently holds productive task-oriented meetings to effectively work

Table 13.3

Minimizing the Legal Risks Associated with Teams and the National Labor Relations Act

1. *Suggestion boxes.* Use suggestion boxes that invite all employees to share their thoughts and feelings with management.
2. *Greater worker control.* Establish teams that give workers greater direct control over their own work.
3. *Don't overrule.* If teams are used to settle workplace grievances or make other decisions concerning workers, don't overrule those decisions or influence the autonomy of the groups making them. Doing so may lead to charges that management is dominating the teams or committees.
4. *Don't turn teams into representative bodies.* One of the key complaints in terms of the NLRA is that teams or committees "represent" the views and opinions of other employees and thus usurp the role of labor unions. So make sure that teams and committees don't speak for all groups or all employees in a representational manner.
5. *Timing is important.* Don't form teams when a labor union is trying to convince your employees to consider union representation. Forming teams at that time could be viewed as illegal management interference.

Source: M.E. Pivec & H.Z. Robbins, "Employee Involvement Remains Controversial," *HRMagazine* 41, no. 11 (1996): 145-150.

through the decision process. Another possible pitfall is that sometimes just one or two people dominate team discussions, restricting consideration of different problem definitions and alternative solutions. Last, team members may not feel accountable for the decisions and actions taken by the "team."

1.3 *When to Use Teams*

The two previous subsections make clear that teams come with significant advantages *and* disadvantages. Therefore, the question is not whether to use teams, but when and where to use teams for maximum benefit and minimum cost. Doug Johnson, associate director at the Center for the Study of Work Teams, said, " Teams are a means to an end, not an end in themselves. You have to ask yourself questions first. Does the work require interdependence? Will the team philosophy fit company strategy? Will management make a long-term commitment to this process?"[30] Table 13.4 provides some additional guidelines on when to use or not use teams.[31]

Table 13.4

When to Use or Not Use Teams

Use Teams When...	*Don't Use Teams When...*
1. There is a clear, engaging reason or purpose.	1. There isn't a clear, engaging reason or purpose.
2. The job can't be done unless people work together.	2. The job can be done by people working independently.
3. Rewards can be provided for teamwork and team performance.	3. Rewards are provided for individual effort and performance.
4. Ample resources are available.	4. The necessary resources are not available.
5. Teams will have clear authority to manage and change how work gets done.	5. Management will continue to monitor and influence how work gets done.

Sources: R. Wageman, "Critical Success Factors for Creating Superb Self-Managing Teams," *Organizational Dynamics* 26, no. 1 (1997): 49-61.

First, teams should be used where there is a clear, engaging reason or purpose for using them. Too many companies use teams because they're popular or because they assume that teams can fix all problems. But teams are much more likely to succeed if they know why they exist and what they are supposed to accomplish. For example, Apache Corporation, which is in the oil and gas industry, has an acquisition team composed of members from accounting, engineering, and product pricing. Their purpose is to review potential oil and gas reserves that are reasonably priced, long lasting, and accessible (meaning that extraordinary costs won't be incurred to extract the oil or gas).[32] Oil and gas reserves that meet these criteria are recommended for purchase.

Second, teams should be used when the job can't be done unless people work together. This typically means that teams are required when tasks are complex, require multiple perspectives, or require repeated interaction with others to complete. For example, contrary to stories of legendary programmers who write software programs by themselves, Microsoft uses teams to write computer code because of the enormous complexity of today's software. Most software simply has too many options and features for one person (or even one team) to complete it all. Likewise, Microsoft uses teams because writing good software requires repeated interaction with others. Microsoft ensures this interaction by having its teams "check in" their computer code every few days. The different pieces of code written by the different teams are then compiled to create an updated working build or prototype of the software. Then, beginning the next day, all the teams and team members begin testing and debugging the new build. Over and over again, the computer code is compiled, then sent back to the teams to be tested and improved, and then compiled and tested again.[33]

However, if tasks are simple and don't require multiple perspectives or repeated interaction with others, teams should not be used. For instance, production levels dropped by 23 percent when Levi Strauss introduced teams in its factories. Levi's mistake was assuming that teams were appropriate for garment work, where workers performed single, specialized tasks, like sewing zippers or belt loops. Because this kind of work does not require interaction with others, Levi's unwittingly pitted the faster workers against the slower workers in each team. Arguments, infighting, insults, and threats were common between faster workers and the slower workers who held back team performance. One seamstress even had to physically restrain an angry co-worker who was about to throw a chair at a faster worker who constantly nagged her about her slow pace.[34]

Third, teams should be used when rewards can be provided for teamwork and team performance. Team rewards that depend on team performance rather than individual performance are the key to rewarding team behaviors and efforts. You'll read more about team rewards later in the chapter, but for now it's enough to know that if the level of rewards (individual vs. team) is not matched to the level of performance (individual vs. team), groups won't work. As discussed above, this was the case with Levi's, where a team structure was superimposed on individual jobs that didn't require interaction between workers. After the switch to teams, faster workers placed tremendous pressure on slower workers to increase their production speed. And since pay was determined by team performance, top individual performers saw their pay drop by several dollars an hour, while slower workers saw their pay increase by several dollars an hour, all while overall productivity dropped in the plant.[35]

Fourth, teams should be used when ample resources are available. The resources that teams need include training (discussed later in the chapter), sufficient time and a place or method to work together, job-specific tools, and consistent information and feedback concerning team work processes and job performance. Susan Cohen, a professor at the University of Southern California's Center for Effective Organizations, said, "People keep doing it [teams] because it is popular, a fad, a thing to do. But then they find that they run into problems because these things do require considerable care and feeding. Companies have to invest some resources in making them succeed."[36] At Levi's, team members complained that there were few resources, such as training, to support the transition from independent, individual-based work to team-based work. They also complained about not being

Back to the Future

Is Your Office Ready for Teamwork?

Have you ever experienced this problem? You are part of a team that is working on an important project. You have just come up with a good idea, so you decide to call an impromptu team meeting. But, as you walk by the conference room, it's being used for a sales meeting. You check with the receptionist upstairs to see if the boardroom is available, but it has already been reserved for the day. So you send an e-mail message to your teammates and ask them to bring their chairs to your office for the meeting. You end up with six people squeezed into your office. Your teammates like your idea, but want to want discuss it in more detail next week when the conference room is available. You think to yourself, "If we're going to emphasize teamwork in this company, we have got to reengineer our physical space."

For many team-based organizations, that is just what is happening. There is a growing awareness among team-based firms that the physical environment in which people work plays a large role in facilitating effective collaboration. For example, in high-rise buildings, typically people get on the elevator and travel directly to their floor. As a result, there is very little opportunity for people on one floor to interact with people on other floors. Unfortunately, the same problem occurs when team members work in different parts of a company. It's hard to get them together. This is one of the reasons that team-based organizations like EDS, 3M, and Microsoft have built corporate headquarters that resemble college campuses rather than skyscrapers. Workers in low-rise settings often have more varied, informal contacts, because they are required to walk from building to building during the course of a day. Building planners call this "functional inconvenience." Efficiency is sacrificed in the hope that by forcing employees to walk through each other's work areas, spontaneous interactions will take place.

Office design and layout is also important. Facility planners have long known that employees unconsciously respond to their environment. For example, traditional office layouts that provide each employee a small private office do not encourage or facilitate teamwork. As a result, many team-based organizations are changing the way they approach office layout and design. NationsBank took a close look at this issue when the company's Business Marketing Group implemented cross-functional teams. Commenting on the importance of office design, Tim Laney, NationsBank Senior Vice President, said, "In my mind we had three primary objectives—We wanted a flexible design that would allow the environment to change as our projects and composition of our teams changed. We wanted a design that would support a high-energy, creative team environment. Finally, we wanted to eliminate the cost and limitations associated with traditional enclosed offices." When he asked his work teams about the type of office layout that they wanted, Mr. Laney indicated that "The feedback we got was 'Put us into an environment where we can exchange ideas on the spot and not have to log out a meeting room somewhere. Let the exchange happen when and where it needs to happen.'" NationsBank responded to this challenge by designing a work environment that allows employees to quickly convert areas so that they can work alone, participate in a meeting, conduct a conference call, or capitalize on chance encounters with teammates.

Poor Dilbert. He may never get out of his cubicle at work. But progressive team-based organizations are designing their buildings and workspaces with the needs of work teams firmly in mind. Next time you are in an office building, ask yourself, "Would this building work well for a team-based organization?" The answer to that question may help explain whether teamwork is flourishing or struggling in that organization.

Source: Herman Miller, "NationsBank Has a New Team on the Field." [Online] Available **http://www.hermanmiller.com/research/case_studies/nationsbank.html**, 15 May 1999.

given enough time to learn how to run the new machines to which they were assigned on the team system.

Another key problem with resources is management resistance. Managers who have been in charge are often reluctant to help teams or turn over resources to them. At Levi's, when team members would ask supervisors for assistance, a common reaction was "Y'all are empowered; y'all decide."[37]

Finally, teams should be used when they have clear authority to manage and change how the work gets done. This means that teams—not managers—decide what problem to tackle next, when to schedule time for maintenance or training, or how to solve customer problems. Research clearly shows that teams with the authority to manage their own work strongly outperform teams that don't.[38] Unfortunately, managers can undermine teams' authority by closely monitoring their work, asking teams to change their decisions, or directly ignoring or overruling team decisions. Jeffrey Pfeffer, a Stanford professor and management consultant/author, said, "The fact is, the people doing the work know better how to do it. Get the managers out of the way and you will do better."[39]

Review 1
The Good and Bad of Using Teams

In many industries, teams are growing in importance because they help organizations respond to specific problems and challenges. Teams have been shown to increase customer satisfaction (specific customer teams), product and service quality (direct responsibility), speed and efficiency in product development (overlapping development phases), and employee job satisfaction (cross training, unique opportunities, and leadership responsibilities). While teams can produce significant improvements in these areas, using teams does not guarantee these positive outcomes. Teams and teamwork have the disadvantages of initially high turnover, social loafing (especially in large groups), self-limiting behavior, and legal risk (National Labor Relations Act). Teams also share many of the advantages (multiple perspectives, generation of more alternatives, and more commitment) and disadvantages (groupthink, time, poorly run meetings, domination by a few team members, and weak accountability) of group decision making. Finally, teams should be used for a clear purpose, when the work requires that people work together, when rewards can be provided for both teamwork and team performance, when ample resources can be provided, and when teams can be given clear authority over their work.

2 Kinds of Teams

In the mid-1980s, Ford Motor Company experienced declining sales, laid off thousands of workers, was billions of dollars in the red, and faced a real possibility of bankruptcy. It turned to teams to turn the company around. Ford formed "Team Taurus," a multifunctional group consisting of car stylists, design engineers, manufacturing managers and workers, and marketers, and gave them complete control over design and manufacture of the then brand new Ford Taurus. In fact, their control over the Taurus was so complete that team members had full authority to stop the production line if quality was not up to standards. And because of their commitment to quality, the team delayed final production several months until all of the quality problems were worked out.[40]

In the mid-1990s, after returning to consistent profitability, Ford still relied on teams for production and development of its cars. This time, though, Ford used design teams to completely redesign its global compact car, the Ford Escort. "Team Escort," based in Dunton, England, was similar to Team Taurus in that it consisted of car stylists, design engineers, manufacturing managers and workers, and marketers. But since Ford wanted the Escort to be manufactured and sold all over the world, it added a twist by making sure that Team Escort was international. In fact, 85 percent of its members were from different European countries, while only 15 percent were Americans.[41]

Today, Ford continues to rely on teams for product development, but it has expanded their role into nearly every corner of the company. Let's continue our discussion of teams by learning about the different kinds of teams that companies like Ford use to make themselves more competitive.

Let's start by looking at **2.1** *how teams differ in terms of autonomy, which is the key dimension that makes one team different from another, and finish by examining* **2.2** *some special kinds of teams.*

2.1 *Autonomy, the Key Dimension*

Teams can be classified in a number of ways, such as whether they are permanent or temporary, or functional or cross-functional. However, studies indicate that the amount of autonomy possessed by a team is the key dimension that makes teams different from each another.[42] *Autonomy* is the degree to which workers have the discretion, freedom, and independence to decide how and when to accomplish their jobs.

Table 13.5 displays an autonomy continuum that shows how five kinds of teams differ in terms of autonomy. Moving left to right at the top of Table 13.5, notice that traditional work groups and employee involvement groups have the lowest levels of autonomy, followed by semi-autonomous work groups, which have a higher level of autonomy, and then self-managing teams and self-designing teams, which have the highest levels of autonomy. Moving from top to bottom along the left side of Table 13.5, note that the number of responsibilities given to each kind of team increases directly with that team's autonomy. Let's review each of these teams and their autonomy and responsibilities in more detail.

traditional work group
group composed of two or more people who work together to achieve a shared goal

The smallest amount of autonomy is found in **traditional work groups**, where two or more people work together to achieve a shared goal. In these groups, workers do not have direct responsibility or control over their work, but are responsible for doing the work or "executing the task." Workers report to managers, who are responsible for their performance and have the authority to hire and fire them, make job assignments, and control resources. For instance, take the situation of an experienced worker who blatantly refuses to do his share of the work, saying, "I've done my time. Let the younger employees do the work." In a team with high autonomy, the responsibility of getting this employee to put forth his fair share of effort would belong to his teammates. But in traditional work groups, the responsibility of telling this employee that his "sitting days are over" belongs to the boss or supervisor. In fact, the supervisor in this situation calmly confronted this employee and told him, "We need

Table 13.5 **Team Autonomy Continuum**

Low Team Autonomy ◄——► *High Team Autonomy*

Responsibilities	***Traditional Work Groups***	***Employee Involvement Groups***	***Semi-Autonomous Work Groups***	***Self-Managing Teams***	***Self-Designing Teams***
Execute Task	√	√	√	√	√
Give Advice/Make Suggestions		√	√	√	√
Information			√	√	√
Major Production/Service Tasks:					
Make Decisions			√	√	√
Solve Problems			√	√	√
All Production/Service Tasks:					
Make Decisions				√	√
Solve Problems				√	√
Control Design:					
Team					√
Tasks					√
Membership					√

Sources: R.D. Banker, J.M. Field, R.G. Schroeder, & K.K. Sinha, "Impact of Work Teams on Manufacturing Performance: A Longitudinal Field Study," *Academy of Management Journal* 39 (1996): 867-890. J.R. Hackman, "The Psychology of Self-Management in Organizations," in *Psychology and Work: Productivity, Change, and Employment*, eds. M.S. Pallak & R. Perloff (Washington, D.C.: American Psychological Association), 85-136.

your talent, [and] your knowledge of these machines. But if you won't work, you'll have to go elsewhere." Within days, the employee's behavior improved.[43]

employee involvement team
team that provides advice or makes suggestions to management concerning specific issues

Employee involvement teams, which have somewhat more autonomy, meet on company time on a weekly or monthly basis to provide advice or make suggestions to management concerning specific issues, such as plant safety, customer relations, or product quality.[44] And while they offer advice and suggestions, they do not have the authority to make decisions. Membership on these teams is often voluntary, but members may be selected because of their expertise. The idea behind employee involvement teams is that the people closest to the problem or situation are best able to recommend solutions. Commercial Casework, a woodworking and cabinetry company in Fremont, California, used an employee involvement team consisting of seven volunteers to research and suggest possibilities for the company bonus plan. Commercial Casework manager Bill Palmer said, "They learned a whole lot more about what it means to give and get a bonus. They saw how difficult it was and wound up really taking ownership of the process."[45]

semi-autonomous work group
group that has the authority to make decisions and solve problems related to the major tasks of producing a product or service

Semi-autonomous work groups not only provide advice and suggestions to management, but they also have the authority to make decisions and solve problems related to the major tasks required to produce a product or service. Semi-autonomous groups regularly receive information about budgets, work quality, and performance, as well as competitors' products. Furthermore, members of semi-autonomous work groups are typically cross trained in a number of different skills and tasks. In short, semi-autonomous work groups give employees the autonomy to make decisions that are typically made by supervisors and managers.

However, that authority is not complete. Managers still play a role, though much reduced compared to traditional work groups, in supporting the work of semi-autonomous work groups. At the Ritz-Carlton, Kansas City, where semi-autonomous work groups were implemented, long-time manager Sandi Shartzer, director of housekeeping, said, "I had attendants who for 22 years had been told where to go, what to do. Now they're being told to do it on their own. Sure, the staff still runs to me occasionally, but they're learning to 'own' their own responsibility. I even had one worker tell me today that she's setting goals for herself." Hotel manager Bob Schrader reinforced Shartzer's view of the Ritz's semi-autonomous work groups. Schrader said, "My role is to be out on the floor, not sit in my office and look at paperwork. I attend team meetings and try to get people comfortable about approaching me on issues, but then a lot of my job is directing people back to their teams for solutions. A lot of what I should be doing now is asking questions instead of dictating methods."[46]

self-managing team
team that manages and controls all of the major tasks of producing a product or service

Self-managing teams are different from semi-autonomous work groups in that team members manage and control *all* of the major tasks directly related to production of a product or service without first getting approval from management. This includes managing and controlling the acquisition of materials, making a product or providing a service, and ensuring timely delivery. For example, when Ford was bringing out its new version of the Ford Escort, "product specialist" Tom Arnold was part of a self-managing team consisting of engineers, car designers, and auto suppliers. Compared to the limited authority he had before, Arnold said, "I've had so many freedoms, it's unbelievable. I never had this experience until I got here. This [self-managing team] has been fantastic." Mike Oblack, a United Auto Workers officer who was part of another self-managing team at Ford, said, "What Ford has discovered is that by allowing us to make mistakes and work through them, the company benefits."[47]

self-designing team
team that has the characteristics of self-managing teams but that also controls team design, work tasks, and team membership

Self-designing teams have all the characteristics of self-managing teams, but they can also control and change the design of the teams themselves, the tasks they do and how they do them, and who belongs to the teams. At Saturn, a division of General Motors, self-designing teams of about ten people each build Saturn cars. Each team determines work schedules, vacation time, and even how assembly jobs are to be performed. Furthermore, the teams determine team membership by conducting the hiring interviews.[48]

2.2 *Special Kinds of Teams*

There are a number of other kinds of teams that can't be easily categorized in terms of autonomy. In other words, depending on how these teams are designed, they can be either low- or high-autonomy teams. Nonetheless, companies are increasingly using these teams. These special kinds of teams are cross-functional teams, virtual teams, and project teams.

cross-functional team
team composed of employees from different functional areas of the organization

Cross-functional teams are purposively composed of employees from different functional areas of the organization.[49] Because their members have different functional backgrounds, education, and experience, cross-functional teams usually attack problems from multiple perspectives and generate more ideas and alternative solutions, all of which are especially important when trying to innovate or do creative problem solving.[50] Cross-functional teams can be used almost anywhere in an organization and are often used in conjunction with matrix and product organizational structures. They can also be used with either part-time or temporary team assignments, or they can be used with full-time, long-term teams. What does a cross-functional team look like in practice? Charles Parnell of Miller Brewing Company explained how a cross-functional team might work at Miller:

> *If Marketing wants to launch a group of new products, they will set up a Task Force and call in someone from Finance, Human Resources and Operations.*
>
> *The Operations people will explain to the Marketing Group the realities of brewing, packaging and shipping more than 40 brands of beer in more than twenty-eight hundred different can, bottle, keg, package and label configurations. This means that if Marketing had been thinking about introducing 10 new brands next year, they will understand that's a virtual impossibility for the Operations people and* they will know why *[emphasis added].*
>
> *Based on these discussions, they mutually agree on just how many new products Miller can introduce in an effective, profitable manner.*[51]

virtual team
team composed of geographically and/or organizationally dispersed co-workers who use telecommunications and information technologies to accomplish an organizational task

Virtual teams are groups of geographically and/or organizationally dispersed co-workers who use a combination of telecommunications and information technologies to accomplish an organizational task.[52] In other words, members of virtual teams rarely meet face to face. The idea of virtual teams is relatively new and has been made possible by advances in communications and technology, such as e-mail, the World Wide Web, videoconferencing, and other products. Virtual teams can be employee involvement teams, self-managing teams, or nearly any kind of team discussed in this chapter. Virtual teams are often (but not necessarily) temporary teams that are set up to accomplish a specific task.[53]

Because the team members don't meet in a physical location, one of the unique qualities of virtual teams is that it is much easier to include other key stakeholders, such as suppliers and customers. The development of the Boeing 777 was largely a virtual team effort. As discussed earlier in the chapter, Boeing developed the 777 through the combined efforts of 238 design teams. The 238 teams used a network of 1,700 individual computer systems, which had links to Japan, Wichita, Kansas, Philadelphia, Boeing's headquarters near Seattle, and other locations. Virtual project teams worked on the 777 in each location and used computer technology to communicate with each other, including airlines that had purchased the 777 and suppliers who provided key expertise and parts.[54]

PersonalProductivityTip

A Picture Is Worth a Thousand Words

As companies make greater use of teams, it has become increasingly common for teammates to work in separate locations. For example, insurance companies have teams with agents in the field and claims processors in the central offices. In virtual teams like these, sometimes teammates never meet. One way for geographically separated teammates to increase team cohesion is to exchange photos and display the photos in their work areas. So if you have teammates whom you've never met, swap photos. It will help you feel more like part of a team.

Source: L. Miller, "What's New?" *HRMagazine*, 1 March 1999, 140.

The principal advantage of virtual teams is that they are very flexible. Employees can work with each other, regardless of physical location, time zone, or organizational affiliation.[55] Plus, virtual teams have certain efficiency advantages over traditional team structures. Because the teammates do not meet face to face, the time commitment involved in participating in a virtual team is typically not as great as for a traditional team. Moreover, employees can fulfill the responsibilities of their virtual team membership from the comfort of their own offices, without the travel time or downtime typically required by "real" face-to-face meetings.[56]

A drawback of virtual teams is that the team members must learn to express themselves in new contexts. For example, the give-and-take that naturally occurs in face-to-face meetings is more difficult to achieve through

Telecommunications and information technology allow geographically dispersed virtual teams to work together to accomplish organizational tasks.

videoconferencing or other methods of virtual teaming. In addition, several studies have shown that physical proximity enhances information processing.[57] Virtual teams have to devise ways to overcome these shortcomings.

project team
team created to complete specific, one-time projects or tasks within a limited time

Project teams are created to complete specific, one-time projects or tasks within a limited time.[58] Project teams are often used to develop new products (i.e., Ford's Team Taurus), to significantly improve existing products (i.e., Ford's Team Escort), to roll out new information systems, or to build new factories or offices. The project team is typically led by a project manager, who has the overall responsibility for planning, staffing, and managing the team.

Because project tasks are often unique, project teams are often staffed by employees from different functional areas and may also include members from the company's suppliers or customers. US Airways, a major airline, used a project team when it decided to start its own low-fare airline. The team included a pilot, the driver of a catering truck (that delivers food to planes), an aircraft cleaner, a ramp supervisor, a mechanic, a flight attendant, a dispatcher, a reservation agent, and others. Relieved of their regular jobs for four months, the members of the project team flew to Virginia each week to plan a low-fare airline to compete with Southwest Airlines, which had begun flying into Baltimore, Providence, Rhode Island, and other East Coast destinations where US Airways flies. Team members made hundreds of flights on other airlines to scout the competition and decided almost everything about the new airline, from whether it would have first class seats (no) to where freezers should be stationed so that food could be quickly loaded onto planes. At the end of the four months, the team disbanded after completing a detailed business plan now being used by MetroJet, US Airways's new low-fare airline.[59]

One advantage of project teams is that drawing employees from different functional areas can reduce or eliminate communication barriers. In turn, free-flowing communication encourages cooperation among separate departments and typically speeds up the design process. In describing Hewlett-Packard's method of designing new products before the company adopted a project team approach, one author wrote, "Once products were developed, they were 'thrown over the wall' to manufacturing and marketing. Manufacturing was then stuck with performing heroic deeds in figuring out how to make the products, and marketing was stuck with finding ways to sell them to the outside world." Hewlett-Packard now relies on project teams to develop new products, especially to avoid these types of problems.[60]

Another advantage of project teams is their flexibility. When projects are finished, project team members either move on to the next project or return to their functional units. For example, the members of US Airways's MetroJet project team returned to their jobs as pilots, flight attendants, baggage handlers, etc., after designing the new low-fare airline. Publication of this book required designers, editors, page makeup artists, and Web designers, among others. When the task was finished, these people applied their skills to other text assignments. Because of this flexibility, project teams are often used with the matrix organizational designs discussed in Chapter 11.

Review 2
Kinds of Teams

Companies use different kinds of teams to make themselves more competitive. Autonomy is the key dimension that makes teams different. Traditional work groups (that execute tasks) and employee involvement groups (that make suggestions) have the lowest levels of autonomy. Semiautonomous work groups (that control major, direct tasks) have more autonomy, followed by self-managing teams (that control all direct tasks) and self-designing teams (that control membership and how tasks are done), which have the highest levels of autonomy. Cross-functional, virtual, and project teams are common, but not easily categorized in terms of autonomy. Cross-functional teams combine employees from different functional areas to help teams attack problems from multiple perspectives and generate more ideas and solutions. Virtual teams use telecommunications and information technologies to bring co-workers "together," regardless of physical location or time zone. Virtual teams reduce travel and work time, but communication may suffer since team members don't work face-to-face. Finally, project teams are used for specific, one-time projects or tasks that must be completed within a limited time. Project teams reduce communication barriers and promote flexibility, as teams and team members are reassigned to their departments or new projects as old projects are completed.

Managing Work Teams

Operations manager: Why did I ever let you talk me into teams? They're nothing but trouble. I have to spend all my time in training and meetings, and we're behind on our production schedule.

Human resources manager: Hey, you were the one who wanted to try teams, remember? We went to visit that car company and you fell in love with their program.

Operations manager: I know, but obviously there's something wrong here. Maybe the car people were giving us a song and dance.

HR manager: I don't know about that. Maybe we ought to look at ourselves. What is it we're doing that's causing the problem?[61]

"Why did I ever let you talk me into teams?" Lots of managers have this reaction after making the move to teams. However, many don't realize that this reaction is normal, both for them and for workers. In fact, such a reaction is characteristic of the storming stage of team development. Managers who are familiar with these stages and with the other important characteristics of teams will be better prepared to manage the predictable changes that occur when companies make the switch to team-based structures. After reading the next two sections, you should be able to:

3 understand the general **characteristics of work teams**.

4 explain how to **enhance work team effectiveness**.

3 Work Team Characteristics

Understanding the characteristics of work teams is a requirement for making teams an effective part of an organization.

Therefore, in this section you'll learn about **3.1** *team norms,* **3.2** *team cohesiveness,* **3.3** *team size,* **3.4** *team conflict, and* **3.5** *stages of team development.*

3.1 *Team Norms*

norms
informally agreed-on standards that regulate team behavior

Over time, teams develop **norms**, informally agreed-on standards that regulate team behavior.[62] Norms are valuable because they let team members know what is expected of them. At Nucor Steel, work groups expect their members to get to work on time. To reinforce this norm, if someone is late to work, he or she cannot receive the team bonus for that day (assuming the team is productive). If the worker is more than 30 minutes late, he or she cannot receive the team bonus for the entire week. At Nucor this matters, since bonuses can double the size of a worker's take-home pay.[63]

Studies indicate that norms are one of the most powerful influences on work behavior. Team norms are often associated with positive outcomes, such as stronger organizational commitment, more trust in management, and stronger job and organizational satisfaction.[64] In general, effective work teams develop norms about the quality and timeliness of job performance, absenteeism, safety, and honest expression of ideas and opinions. The power of norms also comes from the fact that they regulate the everyday kinds of behaviors that allow teams to function effectively. For example, at Cambridge Technology Partners, a project team working on an important product for AT&T established an informal norm that team members were not allowed to play music at their desks before 5:00 p.m. This sounds trivial, but without this rule, it would have been difficult for the 10 project team members to get their work done, especially since they all worked in a small open area without walls between their desks.[65]

However, norms can also influence team behavior in negative ways. For example, most people would agree that "damaging organizational property," "saying or doing something to hurt someone at work," "purposively doing one's work badly, incorrectly, or slowly," "griping about co-workers," "deliberately bending or breaking rules," or "doing something to harm the company or your boss" are negative behaviors. However, a study of workers from 34 teams in 20 different organizations found that teams with negative norms strongly influenced their team members to engage in these negative behaviors. In fact, the longer they were a member of a team with negative norms, and the more frequently they interacted with their teammates, the more likely individual team members were to perform negative behaviors. Since team norms typically develop early in the life of a team, these results indicate how important it is for teams to establish positive norms from the outset.[66]

3.2 *Team Cohesiveness*

cohesiveness
the extent to which team members are attracted to a team and motivated to remain in it

Cohesiveness is another important characteristic of work teams. **Cohesiveness** is the extent to which team members are attracted to a team and motivated to remain in it.[67] Burlington Northern Railroad's intermodal team, which was charged with finding efficient ways to combine transportation through trucks and trains, was a particularly cohesive team. Dave Burns, a member of that team, said, "In my mind, the key word to this team was 'shared.' We shared everything. There was a complete openness among us. And the biggest thing that we shared was an objective and a strategy that we had put together jointly. That was our benchmark every day. Were we doing things in support of *our* plan?"[68]

The level of cohesiveness that exists in a group is important for several reasons. To start, cohesive groups have a better chance of retaining their members. As a result, cohesive groups typically experience lower turnover.[69] In addition, team cohesiveness promotes cooperative behavior, generosity, and a willingness on the part of team members to assist each other.[70] When team cohesiveness is high, team members are more motivated to contribute to the team, because they want to gain the approval of other team members. As a result of these reasons and others, studies have clearly established that cohe-

Team cohesiveness promotes cooperation, generosity, and willingness to assist each other, resulting in better performance. © Corbis/Bettmann

sive teams are consistently better performing teams.[71] Furthermore, cohesive teams quickly achieve high levels of performance. By contrast, it takes teams low in cohesion much longer to reach the same levels of performance.[72]

What can be done to promote team cohesiveness? First, make sure that all team members are present at team meetings and activities. Team cohesiveness suffers when members are allowed to withdraw from the team and miss team meetings and events.[73] Second, create additional opportunities for teammates to work together by rearranging work schedules and creating common workspaces. When task interdependence is high and team members have lots of chances to work together, team cohesiveness tends to increase.[74] Third, engaging in nonwork activities as a team can help build cohesion. At Cambridge Technology Partners, where teams put in extraordinarily long hours coding computer software, the software teams maintained cohesion by doing "fun stuff" together. Team leader Tammy Urban said, "We went on team outings at least once a week. We'd play darts, shoot pool. Teams work best when you get to know each other outside of work—what people's interests are, who they are. Personal connections go a long way when you're developing complex applications in our kind of time frames."[75] Finally, companies build team cohesiveness by making employees feel that they are part of a "special" organization. For example, all the new hires at Disney World in Orlando are required to take a course entitled "Traditions One," in which they learn the traditions and history of the Walt Disney Company (including the names of the seven dwarfs!). The purpose of Traditions One is to instill a sense of pride in working for Disney.

What Really Works

Cohesion and Team Performance

Have you ever worked in a really cohesive group where everyone really liked and enjoyed each other and was glad to be part of the group? It's great. By contrast, have you ever worked in a group where everyone really disliked each other and was unhappy to be a part of the group? It's terrible. Anyone who has had either of these experiences can appreciate how important group cohesion is and the effect it can have on team performance. Indeed, 46 studies based on 1,279 groups confirm that cohesion does matter.

Team Performance

On average, there is a 66 percent chance that cohesive teams will outperform less cohesive teams.

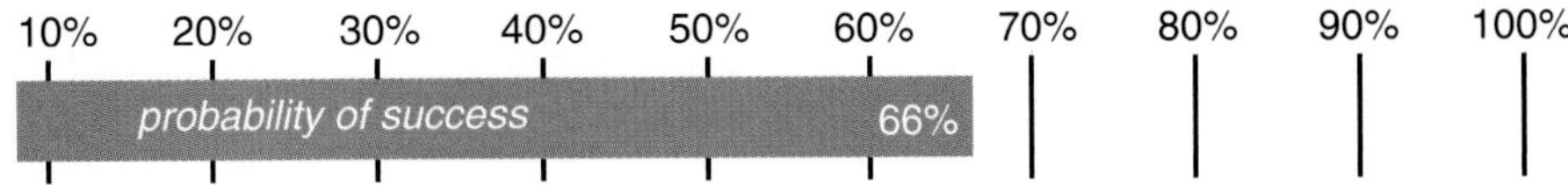

Team Performance with Interdependent Tasks

Teams work best for interdependent tasks that require people to work together to get the job done. When teams perform interdependent tasks, there is a 73 percent chance that cohesive teams will outperform less cohesive teams.

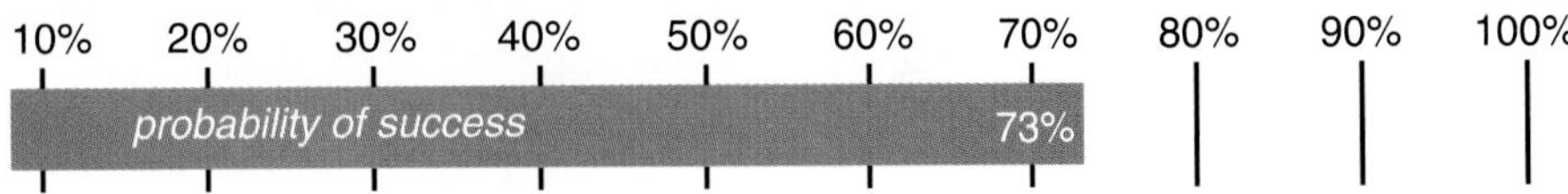

Team Performance with Independent Tasks

Teams are generally not suited for independent tasks in which people can accomplish the job by themselves. When teams perform independent tasks, there is a only a 60 percent chance that cohesive teams will outperform less cohesive teams.

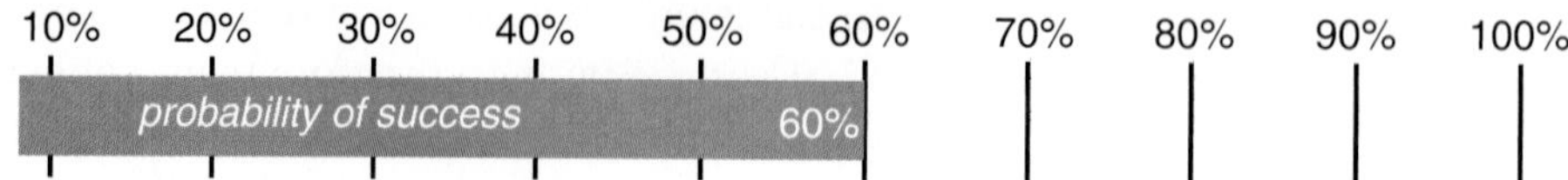

Some caution is warranted in interpreting these results. For example, there is always the possibility that a team could become so cohesive that its team goals become more important than organizational goals. Also, teams sometimes unite around negative goals and norms that are harmful rather than helpful to organizations. However, there is also room for even more optimism about cohesive teams. Teams that are cohesive and committed to the goals they are asked to achieve should have an even higher probability of success than the numbers shown here.

Sources: S.M. Gully, D.S. Devine, and D.J. Whitney, "A Meta-analysis of Cohesion and Performance: Effects of Level of Analysis and Task Interdependence," *Small Group Research* 26, no. 4 (1995): 497-520.

3.3 *Team Size*

There appears to be a curvilinear relationship between team size and performance. In other words, very small or very large teams may not perform as well as moderately sized teams. For most teams, the right size is somewhere between six and nine members.[76] This size is conducive to high team cohesion, which has a positive affect on team performance as discussed above. Teams of this size are small enough for the team members get to know each other, and for each member to have an opportunity to contribute in a meaningful way to the success of the team. However, they're also large enough to take advantage of team members' diverse skills, knowledge, and perspectives. It is also easier to instill a sense of responsibility and mutual accountability in teams of this size.[77]

By contrast, when teams gets too large, team members find it difficult to get to know one another and may splinter into smaller subgroups. When this occurs, subgroups sometimes argue and disagree, weakening overall team cohesion. As teams grow, there is a greater chance of *minority domination*, where just a few team members dominate team discussions. Even if minority domination doesn't occur, there still isn't as much time in larger groups for all team members to share their input. And when team members feel that their contributions are unimportant or not needed, the result is less involvement, effort, and accountability to the team.[78] Large teams also face logistical problems, such as finding an appropriate time or place to meet. Finally, the incidence of social loafing, discussed earlier in the chapter, is much higher in large teams. All of these factors indicate how large teams can have a negative impact on team performance.

While teams should not be too large, it's also important that they not be too small. Teams with just a few people may lack the diversity of skills and knowledge found in larger teams. Also, teams that are too small are unlikely to gain the advantages of team decision making (i.e., multiple perspectives, generating more ideas and alternative solutions, and stronger commitment) found in larger teams.

What signs indicate that a team's size needs to be changed? If decisions are taking too long, if it is difficult for the team to make decisions or take action, if the team is dominated by a few members, or if the commitment or efforts of team members are weak, chances are the team is too big. However, if a team is having difficulty coming up with ideas or generating solutions, or if the team does not have the expertise to address a specific problem, chances are the team is too small.

3.4 Team Conflict

Conflict and disagreement are inevitable in most teams. But this shouldn't surprise anyone. From time to time, people who work together are going to disagree about what and how things get done. What causes conflict in teams? While almost anything can lead to conflict—casual remarks that unintentionally offend a team member or fighting over scarce resources—the primary cause of team conflict is disagreement over team goals and priorities.[79] Other common causes of team conflict include disagreements over task-related issues, interpersonal incompatibilities, and simple fatigue.

While most people view conflict negatively, the key to dealing with team conflict is not avoiding conflict, but making sure that teams experience the right kind of conflict. In Chapter 5, you learned about *c-type conflict*, or cognitive conflict, which focuses on problem-related differences of opinion; and *a-type conflict*, or affective conflict, which refers to the emotional reactions that can occur when disagreements become personal rather than professional.[80] Cognitive conflict is strongly associated with improvements in team performance, while affective conflict is strongly associated with decreases in team performance.[81] Why does this happen? With cognitive conflict, team members disagree because their different experiences and expertise lead them to different views of the problem and solutions. Indeed, managers who participated on teams that emphasized cognitive conflict described their teammates as "smart," "team players," and "best in the business." They described their teams as "open," "fun," and "productive." One manager summed up the positive attitude that team members had about cognitive conflict by saying, "We scream a lot, then laugh, and then resolve the issue."[82] Thus, cognitive conflict is also characterized by a willingness to examine, compare, and reconcile differences to produce the best possible solution.

By contrast, affective conflict often results in hostility, anger, resentment, distrust, cynicism, and apathy. Managers who participated on teams that emphasized affective conflict described their teammates as "manipulative," "secretive," "burned out," and "political."[83] Not surprisingly, affective conflict can make people uncomfortable and cause them to withdraw and decrease their commitment to a team.[84] Affective conflict also lowers the satisfaction of team members, may lead to personal hostility between co-workers, and can decrease team cohesiveness.[85] So, unlike cognitive conflict, affective conflict undermines team effectiveness by preventing teams from engaging in the kinds of activities that are critical to team effectiveness.

So, what can managers do to manage team conflict? First, managers need to realize that emphasizing cognitive conflict alone won't be enough. Studies show that cognitive and affective conflicts often occur together in

Personal Productivity Tip

Relax. It's Just Conflict

Team conflict stresses people, but it shouldn't. Conflict is normal and manageable. When you experience conflict, ask yourself these questions. Is the conflict real? Sometimes, it's just perceptions. What is the conflict? People even disagree over conflicts. Know what the conflict is about. What's causing the conflict? Is it personality, ideas, or scarce resources? Finally, understand the five stages of conflict: the latent stage (where conflict isn't apparent), perceived stage (when conflict is first recognized), felt stage (stress, anxiety, and hostility), manifest stage (conflict is open and observable), and aftermath stage (conflict has been resolved or become latent). So, relax. It's just conflict.

Source: G.H. Johnson, T. Means, & J. Pullis, "Managing Conflict," *The Internal Auditor*, December 1998, 54-59.

the same teams! Therefore, sincere attempts to reach agreement on a difficult issue can quickly deteriorate from cognitive to affective conflict if the discussion turns personal and tempers and emotions flare. So while cognitive conflict is clearly the better approach to take, efforts to engage in cognitive conflict should be approached with caution.

Can teams disagree and still get along? Fortunately, they can. In an attempt to study this issue, researchers examined team conflict in 12 high-tech companies. In 4 of the 12 companies, work teams used cognitive conflict to address work problems but did so in a way that minimized the occurrence of affective conflict. Table 13.6 shows what steps these teams took to be able to have a "good fight."[86]

First, work with more, rather than less, information. If data are plentiful, objective, and up-to-date, teams will focus on issues, not personalities. Second, develop multiple alternatives to enrich debate. Focusing on multiple solutions diffuses conflict by getting teams to keep searching for a better solution. Positions and opinions are naturally more flexible with five alternatives than with just two. Third, establish common goals. Remember, most team conflict arises from disagreements over team goals and priorities. Therefore, common goals encourage collaboration and minimize conflict over a team's purpose. Steve Jobs, CEO of Apple Computer, explains it this way: "It's okay to spend a lot of time arguing about which route to take to San Francisco when everyone wants to end up there, but a lot of time gets wasted in such arguments if one person wants to go to San Francisco and another secretly wants to go to San Diego."[87] Fourth, inject humor into the workplace. Humor relieves tension, builds cohesion, and just makes being in teams fun. Fifth, maintain a balance of power by involving as many people as possible in the decision process. And sixth, resolve issues without forcing a consensus. Consensus means that everyone must agree before decisions are finalized. Effectively, consensus gives everyone on the team veto power. Nothing gets done until everyone agrees, which, of course, is nearly impossible. The result is that consensus usually promotes affective rather than cognitive conflict. If teams can't agree after constructively discussing their options, it's better to have the team leader make the final choice. Most team members can accept the team leader's choice if they've been thoroughly involved in the decision process.

3.5
Stages of Team Development

As teams develop and grow, they pass through four stages of development. As shown in Figure 13.1, those stages are forming, storming, norming, and performing.[88] While not every team passes through each of these

Table 13.6 **How Teams Can Have a Good Fight**

1. Work with more, rather than less, information.
2. Develop multiple alternatives to enrich debate.
3. Establish common goals.
4. Inject humor into the workplace.
5. Maintain a balance of power.
6. Resolve issues without forcing a consensus.

Source: K.M. Eisenhardt, J.L. Kahwajy, & L.J. Bourgeois III, "How Management Teams Can Have a Good Fight," *Harvard Business Review* 75, no. 4 (July/August 1997): 77-87.

Figure 13.1 **Stages of Team Development**

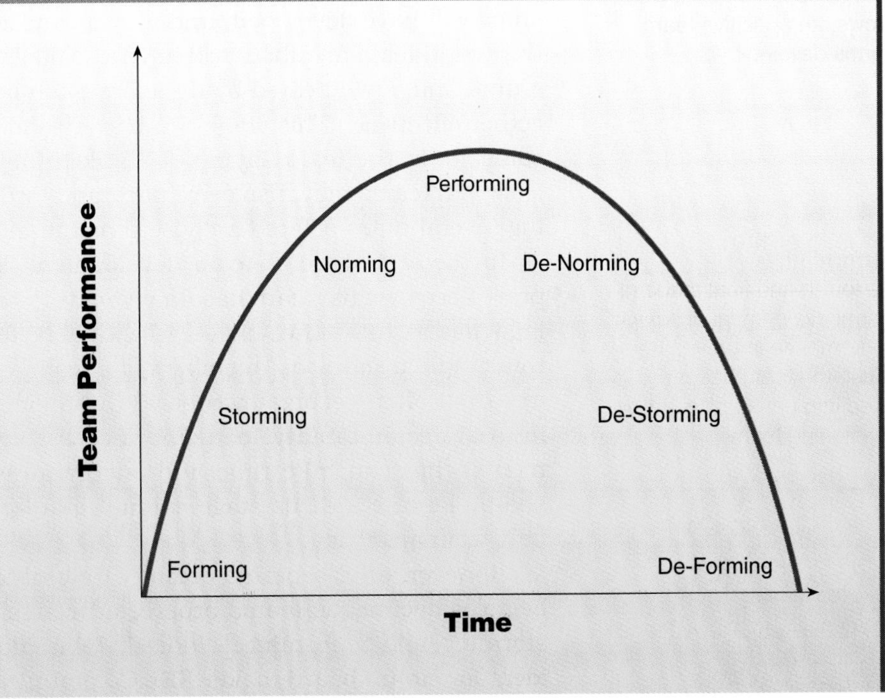

Sources: J.F. McGrew, J.G. Bilotta, & J.M. Deeney, "Software Team Formation and Decay: Extending the Standard Model for Small Groups," *Small Group Research* 30, no. 2 (1999): 209-234. B.W. Tuckman, "Development Sequence in Small Groups," *Psychological Bulletin* 63, no. 6 (1965): 384-399.

stages, teams that do tend to be better performers.[89] This holds true even for teams composed of seasoned executives. However, after a period of time, if not managed well, performance may start to deteriorate as teams begin a process of decline, in which they progress through the stages of de-norming, de-storming, and de-forming.[90]

forming
the first stage of team development in which team members meet each other, form initial impressions, and begin to establish team norms

Forming is the initial stage of team development. This is the getting-acquainted stage, where team members first meet each other, form initial impressions, and try to get a sense of what it will be like to be part of the team. Some of the first team norms will be established during this stage, as team members begin to find out what behaviors will and won't be accepted by the team. Team leaders should allow enough time for team members to get to know each other during this stage and should set early ground rules and begin to set up a preliminary team structure.

storming
the second stage of team development, characterized by conflict and disagreement, in which team members disagree over what the team should do and how it should do it

Conflicts and disagreements often characterize the second stage of team development, **storming**. As team members begin working together, different personalities and work styles may clash. Team members become more assertive at this stage and more willing to state opinions. This is also the stage when team members jockey for position and try to establish a favorable role for themselves in the team. In addition, team members are likely to disagree about what the group should do and how it should do it. Team performance is still relatively low, given that team cohesion is weak and team members are still reluctant to support each other. Since teams that get stuck in the storming stage are almost always ineffective, it is important for team leaders to focus the team on team goals and on improving team performance. Team members need to be particularly patient and tolerant with each other in this stage.

norming
the third stage of team development, in which team members begin to settle into their roles, group cohesion grows, and positive team norms develop

During **norming**, the third stage of team development, team members begin to settle into their roles as team members. Positive team norms will have developed by this stage, and teammates should know what to expect from each other. Petty differences should also have been resolved, friendships will have developed, and group cohesion will be relatively strong. At this point, team members will have accepted team goals, will be operating as a unit, and, as indicated by the increase in performance, will be working together effectively. This stage can be very short and is often characterized by someone in the team saying, "I think things are finally coming together." However, teams may also cycle back and forth between storming and norming several times before finally settling into norming.

performing
the fourth and final stage of team development, in which performance improves because the team has matured into an effective, fully functioning team

In the last stage of team development, **performing**, performance improves because the team has finally matured into an effective, fully functioning team. At this point, members should be fully committed to the team and think of themselves as "members of a team" and not just "employees." Team members often become intensely loyal to one another at this stage and feel mutual accountability for team successes and failures. Trivial disagreements, that can take time and energy away from the work of the team, should be rare. At this stage, teams get a lot of work done, and it is fun to be a team member.

However, after a period of time, if not managed well, performance may begin to decline, as teams progress through the stages of de-norming, de-storming, and de-forming.[91] Indeed, John Puckett, manufacturing vice president for circuit board maker XEL Communications, said, "The books all say you start in this state of chaos and march through these various stages, and you end up in this state of ultimate self-direction, where everything is going just great. They never tell you it can go back in the other direction, sometimes just as quickly."[92]

de-norming
a reversal of the norming stage, in which team performance begins to decline as the size, scope, goal, or members of the team change

In **de-norming**, which is a reversal of the norming stage, team performance begins to decline as the size, scope, goal, or members of the team change. With new members joining the group, older members may become defensive as established ways of doing things are questioned and challenged. Expression of ideas and opinions becomes less open. New members change team norms by actively rejecting or passively neglecting previously established team roles and behaviors.

de-storming
a reversal of the storming phase, in which the team's comfort level decreases, team cohesion weakens, and angry emotions and conflict may flare

In **de-storming**, which is a reversal of the storming phase, the team's comfort level decreases. Team cohesion weakens as more group members resist conforming to team norms and quit participating in team activities. Angry emotions flare as the group explodes in conflict and moves into the final stage of de-forming.

de-forming
a reversal of the forming stage, in which team members position themselves to control pieces of the team, avoid each other, and isolate themselves from team leaders

In **de-forming**, which is a reversal of the forming stage, team members position themselves to gain control of pieces of the team. Team members begin to avoid each other and isolate themselves from team leaders. Team performance rapidly declines as the team quits caring about even minimal requirements of team performance.

If teams are actively managed, decline is not inevitable. However, managers need to recognize that the forces at work in the de-norming, de-storming, and de-forming stages represent a powerful, disruptive, and real threat to teams that have finally made it to the performing stage. Getting to the performing stage is half the battle. Staying there is the second half.

Review 3
Work Team Characteristics

The most important characteristics of work teams are team norms, cohesiveness, size, conflict, and development. Norms let team members know what is expected of them and can influence team behavior in positive and negative ways. Positive team norms are associated with organizational commitment, trust, and job satisfaction. Team cohesiveness helps teams retain members, promotes cooperative behavior, increases motivation, and facilitates team performance. Attending team meetings and activities, creating opportunities to work together, and engaging in nonwork activities can increase cohesiveness. Team size has a curvilinear relationship with team performance, such that very small or very large teams do not perform as well as moderately sized teams of six to nine members. Teams of this size are cohesive and small enough for team members to get to know each other and contribute in a meaningful way, but are large enough to take advantage of team members' diverse skills, knowledge, and perspectives. Conflict and disagreement are inevitable in most teams. The key to dealing with team conflict is to maximize cognitive conflict, which focuses on issue-related differences, and minimize affective conflict, the emotional reactions that occur when disagreements become personal rather than professional. As teams develop and grow, they pass through four stages of development: forming, storming, norming, and performing. However, after a period of time, if not managed well, performance may decline, as teams progress through the stages of de-norming, de-storming, and de-forming.

4 Enhancing Work Team Effectiveness

Making teams work is a challenging and difficult process. However, companies can increase the likelihood that teams will succeed by carefully managing **4.1** *the setting of team goals and priorities and how work team members are* **4.2** *selected,* **4.3** *trained, and* **4.4** *compensated.*[93]

4.1
Setting Team Goals and Priorities

In Chapter 4 you learned that specific, measurable, attainable, realistic, and timely (i.e., S.M.A.R.T.) goals are one of the most effective means for improving individual job performance. Fortunately, team goals also improve team performance. In fact, team goals lead to much higher team performance 93 percent of the time.[94] For example, Nucor Steel sets specific, challenging goals for each of its production teams, which consist of first-line supervisors and production and maintenance workers. Each day these teams are challenged to produce a specific number of tons of high-quality steel.[95] Teams that meet their goals earn daily bonuses that can double their base salaries.

Why is the setting of specific, challenging team goals so critical to team success? One reason is that increasing a team's performance is inherently more complex than just increasing one individual's job performance. For instance, consider that for any team there are likely to be at least four different kinds of goals: each member's goal for the team, each member's goal for himself or herself on the team, the team's goal for each member, and the team's goal for itself.[96] In other words, without a specific, challenging goal for the team itself (the last of the four goals listed), these other goals may encourage team members to head off in twelve different directions at once. Consequently, setting a specific, challenging goal *for the team* clarifies team priorities by providing a clear focus and purpose.

Specific, challenging team goals also regulate how hard team members work. In particular, challenging team goals greatly reduce the incidence of social loafing. When faced with difficult goals, team members simply expect everyone to contribute. Consequently, they are much more likely to notice and complain if a teammate isn't doing his or her share. In fact, when teammates know each other well, when team goals are specific, when team communication is good, and when teams are rewarded for team performance (discussed below), there is only a 1 in 16 chance that teammates will be social loafers.[97]

What can companies and teams do to ensure that team goals lead to superior team performance? One increasingly popular approach is to give teams stretch goals. In Chapter 4, you learned that *stretch goals* are extremely ambitious goals that workers don't know how to reach.[98] The purpose of stretch goals is to achieve extraordinary improvements in performance by forcing managers and workers to throw away old comfortable solutions and adopt radical, never-used solutions. For instance, when Allied Signal bought the Budd Company's wheel and brake division, Allied managers challenged Budd's product development team to cut the development time for new car brake systems in half. The team succeeded, cutting development time from 36 to 18 months.[99]

Four things must occur for stretch goals to effectively motivate teams.[100] First, teams must have a high degree of autonomy or control over how they achieve their goals. At CSX's railroad division, top management challenged the new management team at its Cumberland, Maryland, office to increase productivity by 16 percent. The goal was specific and challenging: ship the same amount of coal each month, but do it with 4,200 rail cars instead of 5,000 rail cars. The local team, consisting of five new managers, quickly figured out that the trains were spending too much time sitting idly in the rail yards. Finance director Peter Mills said, "We'd look out our office windows at the tracks and wonder, 'Why aren't the cars moving?'" The problem? Headquarters wouldn't let the trains run until they had 160 full rail cars to pull, a process that could take nearly a week to complete. But since the local management team had the autonomy to pay for the extra crews to run the trains more frequently, it started running the trains with as few as 78 cars. Now, since coal cars never wait more than a day to be transported to customers, rail productivity has skyrocketed.[101]

Second, teams must be empowered with control resources, such as budgets, workspaces, computers, or whatever they need to do their jobs. Steve Kerr, General Electric's "Chief Learning Officer," said, ". . . we have a moral obligation to try to give people the tools to meet tough goals. I think it's totally wrong if you don't give employees the tools to succeed, then punish them when they fail."[102]

structural accommodation the ability to change organizational structures, policies, and practices

Third, teams need structural accommodation. **Structural accommodation** means giving teams the ability to change organizational structures, policies, and practices if it helps them meet their stretch goals. When Hewlett-Packard imposed tough goals on its customer service teams, one of the unintended consequences was a big increase in work stress from being called to customer sites on weekends and at all hours of the night. As a result, overworked customer service engineers began quitting their jobs, making it unlikely that the teams could achieve their stretch goals. HP responded by giving teams the ability to "reinvent work" in a way that would meet the stretch goals, but reduce worker stress. The teams decided to throw out existing policies on employee work hours and simply asked who would be willing to work Fridays through Mondays and who would be willing to work Tuesdays through Fridays. Stress dropped immediately, and employees stopped quitting their jobs.[103]

bureaucratic immunity the ability to make changes without first getting approval from managers or other parts of an organization

Finally, teams need bureaucratic immunity. **Bureaucratic immunity** means that teams no longer have to go through the frustratingly slow process of multilevel reviews and signoffs to get management approval before making changes. Once granted bureaucratic immunity, teams are immune from the influence of various organizational groups and are only accountable to top management. Therefore teams can act quickly and even experiment with little fear of failure. One of Motorola's computer chip teams found that its division chiefs did not want to support their computer chip designs. However, top management granted the team bureaucratic immunity by agreeing to let the team continue work on the chips without interference. Because of bureaucratic immunity, the team was able to perfect its designs, and today the Motorola 68000 series microprocessor can be found in millions of computers worldwide.[104]

BLASTFROMTHEPAST

Work Teams: Just Horsing Around

The Hawthorne studies were the first large-scale, systematic study of work groups. Conducted by Elton Mayo in the 1920s and 1930s, the Hawthorne studies indicated that work groups form strong "informal" norms and that these norms are not always positive. For example, in one of the factories in Mayo's studies, managers posted the daily output of individual workers for all to see, hoping to stimulate competition and increase production. What happened instead was that the workers used this information to punish the best workers. Their motivation was simple. They punished the best workers because they didn't want management to think that everyone could and should do more work. Mayo and his researchers used this finding to warn managers about the unintended effects that can occur in workplace groups and teams.

Historians believe that the term "work team" was first used in the 15th century to refer to teams of horses that were put together to increase their ability to pull heavy loads. However, Eric Trist was the first to use the term "work team" to describe groups in business organizations. Trist was studying the work processes in British mines when a dramatic change occurred in the way that the miners performed their jobs. An improvement in hydraulic jack technology made it possible for the miners to work in small areas (15 to 150 feet), rather than in tunnels that were several hundred feet long. The new method was called "shortwall" mining, while the old method was called "longwall" mining. The miners responded to this change by asking to be put into small, autonomous groups to work the short mines. Trist found that the miners that worked in small groups were more productive and committed to their work than the miners that did not work in groups.

Finally, the term "skunkworks" entered our vocabulary in the 1970s. "Skunk Works" was the nickname for the group that Lockheed (now Lockheed Martin) used in 1943 to design the U.S. Army's first generation of jet airplanes. The urgency of the war effort in Europe demanded that a prototype aircraft be delivered in 180 days. To accomplish this task, Lockheed formed a team of 23 engineers and 103 shop mechanics and separated them from the rest of the company in a windowless facility in the corner of the Burbank, California, airport. The Skunk Works team completed the XP-80, nicknamed the Lulu-belle, in just 143 days, 37 days ahead of schedule. The initial success of the Skunk Works and its continuing successes have been studied by many team-based organizations. Today, the term "skunkworks" is commonly used to denote a work team that has been "set apart" from a corporation's normal hierarchy to try to accomplish an extraordinary task in a relatively short period of time.

Sources: M.M. Beyerlein, "The History of Work Teams," in *Handbook of Best Practices for Teams,* Volume 1, ed. Glenn M. Parker (Amherst, MA: Irwin, 1996), 13-19. R.A. Guzzo, "Fundamental Considerations about Work Groups," in *Handbook of Work Group Psychology,* ed. Michael A. West (New York: John Wiley & Sons, 1996), 3-21.

4.2
Selecting People for Teamwork

University of Southern California Professor Edward Lawler said, "People are very naive about how easy it is to create a team. Teams are the Ferraris of work design. They're high performance but high maintenance and expensive."[105] It's almost impossible to make effective work teams without carefully selecting people who are suited for teamwork or for working on a particular team. A preference for teamwork, team elevation, and team diversity can help companies choose the right team members.[106]

Are you more comfortable working alone or with others? If you strongly prefer to work alone, you may not be well suited for teamwork. Indeed, studies show that job satisfaction is higher in teams when team members prefer working with others.[107] An indirect way to measure someone's *preference for teamwork* is to assess the person's degree of individualism or collectivism. **Individualism-collectivism** is the degree to which a person believes that people should be self-sufficient and that loyalty to one's self is more important than loyalty to one's team or company.[108] *Individualists*, who put their welfare and interests first, generally prefer independent tasks in which they work alone. On the other hand, *collectivists*, who put group or team interests ahead of self-interests, generally prefer interdependent tasks in which they work with others. Collectivists would also rather cooperate than compete and are fearful of disappointing team members or of being ostracized from teams. Given these differences, it makes sense to select team members who are collectivists rather than individualists. Indeed, many companies use individualism-collectivism as an initial screening device for team members. However, as discussed below, individualists may be appropriate if team diversity is desired. To determine your preference for teamwork, take the Team Player Inventory shown in Table 13.7.

individualism-collectivism the degree to which a person believes that people should be self-sufficient and that loyalty to one's self is more important than loyalty to one's team or company

Team level is the average level of ability, experience, personality, or any other factor on a team. For example, a high level of team experience means that a team has particularly experienced team members. This does not mean that every member of the team has considerable experience, but that enough team members do to significantly raise the average level of experience on the team. Team level is used to guide selection of teammates when teams need a particular set of skills or capabilities to do their jobs well. For instance, in retail sales jobs, teams with high average levels of conscientiousness, agreeableness, and openness to experience have much higher sales than teams with low average levels on these dimensions.[109]

team level the average level of ability, experience, personality, or any other factor on a team

While team level represents the average level or capability on a team, **team diversity** represents the variances or differences in ability, experience, personality, or any other factor on a team. For example, teams with strong team diversity on job experience would have a mix of team members, ranging from seasoned veterans to people with three or four years of experience to rookies with little or no experience. Team diversity is used to guide selection of teammates when teams are asked to complete a wide range of different tasks or when tasks are particularly complex.

team diversity the variances or differences in ability, experience, personality, or any other factor on a team

Delta Dental Plan in Medford, Massachusetts, used the principle of team diversity to select the team members who service its largest account. Tom Raffio, senior vice president, explained that the company wanted a team of people whose strengths complemented each other. The first step was to administer personality inventories to potential team members. Raffio said, "We were looking for a combination of introverts and extroverts, people who

Table 13.7 **The Team Player Inventory**

	Strongly Disagree 1	2	3	4	5 Strongly Agree
1. I enjoy working on team/group projects.	1	2	3	4	5
2. Team/group project work easily allows others to not "pull their weight."	1	2	3	4	5
3. Work that is done as a team/group is better than the work done individually.	1	2	3	4	5
4. I do my best work alone rather than in a team/group.	1	2	3	4	5
5. Team/group work is overrated in terms of the actual results produced.	1	2	3	4	5
6. Working in a team/group gets me to think more creatively.	1	2	3	4	5
7. Team/groups are used too often, when individual work would be more effective.	1	2	3	4	5
8. My own work is enhanced when I am in a team/group situation.	1	2	3	4	5
9. My experiences working in team/group situations have been primarily negative.	1	2	3	4	5
10. More solutions/ideas are generated when working in a team/group situation than when working alone.	1	2	3	4	5

Reverse score items 2, 4, 5, 7, and 9. Then add the scores for items 1–10. Higher scores indicate a preference for teamwork, while lower total scores indicate a preference for individual work.

Source: T.J.B. Kline, "The Team Player Inventory: Reliability and Validity of a Measure of Predisposition toward Organizational Team-Working Environments," *Journal for Specialists in Group Work* 24, no. 1 (1999): 102-112.

reflect on things and people who close on things, and people who could process claims efficiently on a daily basis, as well as those who could keep in mind the long-term vision of the company." The next step was to make sure there was a mixture of language capabilities on the team: English, Spanish, and French. Finally, the company wanted a mix of experience, including seasoned employees who understood the company culture and new employees who brought outside ideas and perspectives. Accordingly, team members were recruited from both inside and outside the company.[110]

4.3 *Team Training*

Organizations that create work teams often underestimate the amount of training required to make teams effective. This mistake occurs frequently in successful organizations, where managers assume that if employees can work effectively on their own, they can work effectively in teams. However, companies that successfully use teams provide thousands of hours of training to make sure that teams work. Ames Rubber provided more than 17,000 hours of training in communication, quality improvement, and problem solving to its 445 team members. As a result, Ames' defect rate fell from 30,000 parts per million to just 11 parts per million. Productivity rose 43 percent and teams' ideas saved the company more than $3 million, or an average of $2,700 per employee. At Saturn, a division of General Motors famous for its use of teams, employees spend 5 percent of their work time each year in training. This amounts to more than 100 hours per person per year learning about things such as quality control, purchasing, budgeting, decision making, and how to recruit and hire new team members.[111]

interpersonal skills skills, such as listening, communicating, questioning, and providing feedback, that enable people to have effective working relationships with others

The most common type of training provided to members of work teams is training in interpersonal skills. **Interpersonal skills**, such as listening, communicating, questioning, and providing feedback, enable people to have effective working relationships with others. When Super Sack, a maker of heavy-duty plastic bags for the food and pharmaceutical industries, first used teams, it failed. David Kellenberger, Super Sack's vice president of manufacturing, said, "One of our greatest mistakes at the beginning was our failure to recognize how important training was. You need to make a huge commitment of time and resources for training people in communication, goal-setting, and general team-building skills to make a successful transition [to teams] . . ."[112] Experiences like these are why Wilson Sporting Goods provides all of its first-year team members 26 hours of training on team interaction skills and how to run meetings.[113]

Because of their autonomy and responsibility, many companies give teams training in decision-making and problem-solving skills to help them do a better job of cutting costs and improving quality and customer service. Stacy Myers, a consultant who helps companies implement teams, said, ". . . when we help companies move to teams, we also require that employees take basic quality and business knowledge classes as well. Teams must know how their work affects the company, and how their success will be measured."[114] Many organizations also teach teams conflict resolution skills. Coldwater Machine Company formed teams but waited several months to provide conflict resolution training. Ken Meyer, Coldwater's coordinator of work groups, said, "People are starting to encounter differences right now, so we're starting conflict resolution training. We think work group members will appreciate the training more now that they're in particular situations and see the relevance."[115]

Firms must also provide team members the technical training they need to do their jobs, particularly if they are expected to perform all of the different jobs on the team (i.e., cross training). Before teams were created at Milwaukee Mutual Insurance, separate employees performed the tasks of rating, underwriting, and processing insurance policies. However, after extensive cross training, each team member can now do all three jobs.[116] Cross training is less appropriate for teams of highly skilled workers. For instance, it is unlikely that a group of engineers, computer programmers, and systems analysts would be cross trained for each other's jobs.

Finally, companies need to provide training for team leaders, who often feel unprepared for their new duties. Table 13.8 shows the top ten problems reported by new team leaders. These range from confusion about their new roles as team leaders (compared to their old jobs as managers or employees) to not knowing where to go for help when their teams have problems. The solution is extensive training for team leaders.

4.4
Team Compensation and Recognition

Compensating teams correctly is very difficult. For instance, one survey found that only 37 percent of companies were satisfied with their team compensation plans and even fewer, just 10 percent, reported being "very positive."[117] One of the problems, according to Monty Mohrman of the Center for Effective Organizations, is that "There is a very strong set of beliefs in most organizations that people should be paid for how well they do. So when

Table 13.8

Top Ten Problems Reported by Team Leaders

1. Confusion about their new roles and about what they should be doing differently.
2. Feeling they've lost control.
3. Not knowing what it means to coach or empower.
4. Having personal doubts about whether the team concept will really work.
5. Uncertainty about how to deal with employees' doubts about the team concept.
6. Confusion about when a team is ready for more responsibility.
7. Confusion about how to share responsibility and accountability with the team.
8. Concern about promotional opportunities, especially about whether the "team leader" title carries any prestige.
9. Uncertainty about the strategic aspects of the leader's role as teams mature.
10. Not knowing where to turn for help with team problems, since few if any of their organization's leaders have led teams.

Source: B. Filipczak, M. Hequet, C. Lee, M. Picard, & D. Stamps, "More Trouble with Teams," *Training*, October 1996, 21.

people first get put into team-based organizations, they really balk at being paid for how well the team does. It sounds illogical to them. It sounds like their individuality and their sense of self-worth are being threatened."[118] Consequently, companies need to carefully choose a team compensation plan and then fully explain how teams will be rewarded. One basic requirement is that the level of rewards (individual vs. team) must match the level of performance (individual vs. team) for team compensation to work.

skill-based pay
compensation system that pays employees for learning additional skills or knowledge

There are three methods of compensating employees for team participation and accomplishments. The first is called skill-based pay. **Skill-based pay** programs pay employees for learning additional skills or knowledge.[119] These programs encourage employees to acquire the additional skills they will need to perform multiple jobs within a team. For example, at XEL Communications, the number of skills each employee has mastered determines his or her individual pay. An employee who takes a class in advanced soldering (XEL makes circuit boards) followed by on-the-job training will earn thirty cents more per hour. Passing a written test or satisfactorily performing a skill or job for a supervisor or trainer certifies mastery of new skills and results in increased pay. Eastman Chemical uses a similar approach with its teams. But in Eastman's case, however, team members also have to demonstrate that they use their new skills at least 10 percent of the time. Otherwise, they lose their pay increase.[120]

gainsharing
compensation system in which companies share the financial value of performance gains, such as productivity, cost savings, or quality, with their workers

The second approach to compensating employees for team participation is through **gainsharing** programs, in which companies share the financial value of performance gains, such as productivity, cost savings, or quality, with their workers.[121] The first month that gainsharing was used at Rogan Corporation, a maker of plastic handles and knobs, employee teams saved the company $23,424, earning an additional $11,712 for themselves. They earned slightly more the second month. Since its inception, gainsharing has added 16 percent to 22 percent to the salaries of Rogan's employees, typically $3,000 to $5,000 per employee per year. But, the company has benefited as well. Before gainsharing, employees produced an average of 95,000 knobs per employee each year. But after gainsharing, employees produced at more than twice that rate, turning out an average of 206,000 knobs per employee per year.[122]

Nonfinancial rewards are another way to reward teams for their performance. These awards, which can range from vacation trips to T-shirts, plaques, and coffee mugs, are especially effective when coupled with management recognition.[123] At Motorola, each year several thousand teams enter a companywide competition in which work teams review their past accomplishments and discuss their future goals. The final 24 teams make presentations to a panel of top managers at company headquarters. Becoming a finalist is quite prestigious and gives those employees unique exposure to Motorola's top managers. Likewise, NCR has a "Great Performance Award" that recognizes its top teams.[124]

Which team plan should your company use? In general, skill-based pay is most effective for self-managing and self-directing teams performing complex tasks. In these situations, the more each team member knows and can do, the better the whole team performs. By contrast, gainsharing works best in relatively stable environments where employees can focus on improving the productivity, cost savings, or quality of their current work system.

Been There,

AAL: A Pioneer in the Use of Self-Managed Teams

The Aid Association for Lutherans (AAL) is the largest fraternal benefit society in the United States in terms of assets ($18.7 billion) and insurance ($82 billion). In this interview, Charles Dull, senior vice president and chief quality officer for AAL, discusses AAL's pioneering use of self-managed teams.

Q: The self-managed team concept at AAL was a very innovative approach, especially for an organization in the financial services industry. Tell me about your involvement in that.

A: During a major corporate transformation, I was asked to provide leadership for the insurance operations of AAL. There were over 500 people in its service operation. We had an interesting challenge in that we were in a downsizing mode, while at the same time we were trying to get closer to our customers. We were able to reduce our layers of management from eight to three. We did it by creating self-managed teams. A group of our employees borrowed this concept from the manufacturing world and challenged us to use it to get closer to our customers and improve our response times.

Q: During this restructuring, were positions eliminated through attrition?

A: Yes. We were able to find places for most of the management and supervisory people that were displaced. They were very good people. After all, we had promoted talented people into those supervisory positions. During a four-year period, we reduced our entire home office work force by 250, or over 15 percent. At the same time, we increased our business volume by about 50 percent.

"Everyone won when the field team won."

Q: Let's go back to these self-managed teams. What were some of the results that they were able to accomplish?

A: We have about 2,400 men and women in our field organization, and each home office business team partnered with a group of those field people. The satisfaction level of the field people with our service just took off after that. We keep track of satisfaction data, and the level dramatically increased—almost overnight. We moved from a controlling and somewhat adversarial relationship to more of a helping, supporting relationship with our colleagues in the field. Everyone won when the field team won.

Response time improved. By having all the work done by one team, we reduced hand-off time. Teams were cross trained so the products and services got out the door much faster. We had one group of people who literally could service a problem immediately after it arrived at the home office.

Q: Do you remember any of the numbers, like productivity improvement?
A: Service time was reduced by 75 percent in some processes. In fact, through downsizing and other factors, the overall productivity of those service teams increased by about 40 percent over a five-year period.

Q: So that had to be good news for the whole corporation, as well as for your board and your members.
A: It was a significant factor that contributed to our recognition as one of the lowest cost providers in the entire financial services industry.

Q: How extensive was the self-managed concept at AAL?
A: We really did transfer this social technology throughout the insurance division. We were the only large group that went that far in our industry during the late '80s. A number of other financial service organizations, here and abroad, are, of course, also adopting some version of self-managed teams.

Q: Now I suppose you have all the other insurers coming up to Appleton, Wisconsin? [Appleton is the location of AAL's headquarters.]
A: We've had over 250 organizations visit us in the past three years. And we were selected as a benchmark organization by General Electric because of our approach to self-managed teams.

Q: That's interesting that General Electric used you, a fraternal insurance organization, as their best practice for self-managed teams.
A: That's correct.

Q: Chuck, we all hear the success stories, including in this case AAL's success. But could you tell me what some of the problems have been?
A: We've certainly had our share of problems. As I mentioned earlier, we moved to self-managed teams to get closer to the customer. We wanted to gain more flexibility in our staff so that we can handle the rise and fall of the business cycle better and build a partnership with our field organization. But what we didn't do right away was change our compensation structure. What we had was a classic individual merit pay system that did not reward people operating in teams. It rewarded people for individual effort and accomplishment. The result was that we were into the team structure for more than a year before we realized our reward system was working at cross purposes with this. Finally, we created a performance-based compensation structure that rewarded people for applied knowledge in a group setting.

Q: Do you feel that, under that team approach, you were able to objectively determine the group reward? Did the groups buy into that?
A: I'd say it was a mixed bag at first. The high performer was feeling dragged down, if you will, by the lower performer, because it was the team totals that triggered the rewards. We went through a period of refining the system to gain the appropriate balance among organization, group, and individual measures.

The way we solved performance-management challenges was quite different from our traditional approach. The teams wanted a manager to come in and fix things. But the new managers were more facilitators than experts in the particular processes under their supervision. So they turned this challenge back to the team for resolution.

Q: In other words, management held fast and said, it's your problem, you resolve it—that's why you're doing self-managed teams.
A: That's right. And some people—not a lot—said, I didn't sign up for this kind of responsibility. I don't mind receiving the compensation of my ex-managers, but I'm not sure I want their managerial responsibility.

Q: Did those people self-select out, or are they still there?
A: A few moved out. It just wasn't a good fit for some employees. Most of the unhappy folks elected to move elsewhere in the organization to an area that wasn't self-managed. In very few cases, they elected to leave the organization. However, except for these few, nearly all our employees soon embraced the concept.

Source: F. Luthans, "A Conversation with Charles Dull," *Organizational Dynamics* 18, no. 7 (1993): 57-70. This interview was edited for inclusion in this textbook.

Done That

Finally, given the level of dissatisfaction with most team compensation systems, what compensation plans would today's managers like to use with the teams in their companies? Forty percent of managers would directly link merit pay increases to team performance, but allow adjustments within teams for differences in individual performance. By contrast, 13.7 percent would link merit-based increases directly to team performance, but would give each team member an equal share of the team's merit-based reward.

Nineteen percent would use gainsharing plans based on quality, delivery, productivity, or cost reduction, and then provide equal payouts to all teams and team members. Fourteen and a half percent would use gainsharing, but would vary the team gainsharing award, depending on how much money the team saved the company. Payouts would still be equally distributed within teams. Finally, 12.2 percent of managers would opt for plantwide profit-sharing plans tied to overall company or division performance. In this case, there would be no payout distinctions between or within teams.

Review 4
Enhancing Work Team Effectiveness

Companies can make teams more effective by setting team goals and managing how work team members are selected, trained, and compensated. Team goals provide a clear focus and purpose, reduce the incidence of social loafing, and lead to higher team performance 93 percent of the time. Extremely difficult stretch goals can be used to motivate teams as long as teams have autonomy, control over resources, structural accommodation, and bureaucratic immunity. Not everyone is suited for teamwork. When selecting team members, companies should select people who have a preference for teamwork (individualism-collectivism) and should consider the importance of team level (average ability on a team) and team diversity (different abilities on a team). Organizations that successfully use teams provide thousands of hours of training to make sure that teams work. The most common types of team training are for interpersonal decision-making and problem-solving skills, conflict resolution, technical training to help team members learn multiple jobs (i.e., cross training), and training for team leaders. There are three methods of compensating employees for team participation and accomplishments: skill-based pay, gainsharing, and nonfinancial rewards.

What**Really**Happened?

In the opening case, you learned that Cigna's Customer Service Center was struggling and the company was considering the use of teams to address its problems. After considering the costs and benefits, Cigna replaced the traditional departments in its Customer Service Center with employee work teams. Read the answers to the opening case to find out how well teams worked at Cigna's Customer Service Center.

A few things worry you, however. Some employees may not fit into a team environment. What if these employees quit their jobs, or complain a lot and make everybody's life miserable?

One of the clear disadvantages of work teams is initially high turnover. Teams aren't for everyone, and some workers will balk at the responsibility, effort, and learning required in team settings. As you read in the chapter, turnover jumped when GE and Eaton Corporation began implementing teams in their factories. The same thing happened at Cigna, as roughly 25 percent of its customer service representatives left after Cigna switched to teams. Most of those who left just felt that they wouldn't fit well in a team environment. According to William Faris, Assistant Vice President of Compensation Design and Education at the time the switch to teams was made, "It was a recognition thing. They felt they wouldn't be as important as they were before." Chances are the workers who left were individualists, that is, people who put their welfare and interests first. Individualists generally prefer independent tasks in which they work alone. By contrast, the employees who stayed at Cigna to work in teams were more likely to have been collectivists, people who put group or team interests ahead of self-interests. Collectivists generally like team work because they prefer interdependent tasks in which they work with others.

There will also be fewer jobs open at the supervisor level. And, the last thing that you want to do is to create the impression that there is no opportunity for top performers to move up in the firm.

Did Cigna's employees believe that self-managed teams would lead to fewer chances for promotion? Some employees genuinely feared that with supervisory jobs being eliminated (due to self-managed teams), there would be less room for advancement. In reality, though, because the teams required a substantial amount of support, Cigna did not reduce the number of upper-level jobs available for promotion. It was difficult, however, to get employees to see it that way.

Despite the outward promise of teamwork, it is difficult to know whether teams will actually work until you try it. What if productivity doesn't go up, and employee morale suffers rather than improves?

While teams are clearly not appropriate for all tasks or all companies, this was not the case at Cigna, where the teams thrived after implementation. The first sign that teamwork was succeeding at Cigna was that employees started liking their jobs. While employee turnover initially jumped to 25 percent soon after the change to teams, it dropped dramatically to just 5 percent within two years. In other words, 95 percent of Cigna's team members were choosing to stay in their jobs and with the company. Productivity increased dramatically as well. Costs dropped 30 percent. Quality rose by 50 percent. The amount of time it took to complete standard tasks, such as delivering price quotes to customers (such as large companies seeking insurance coverage) dropped from 17 days to 3 days, as empowered teams eliminated seven authorization steps and reduced the number of handoffs between departments from 14 to 3. Staff who processed only 35 to 40 claims a day before teams were able to process 75 to 90 claims a day once they became members of self-managed teams.

Will work teams actually improve customer service?

One of the keys to making teams work is to set a specific, challenging goal. Teams work 93 percent of the time when this is done. Accordingly, Cigna made clear that the singular goal of its teams was to "satisfy the customer with one contact," in other words, take care of customers' concerns and problems in one phone call. The teams exceeded this goal, as customer satisfaction rose by more than 50 percent after the implementation of teams. And customer satisfaction levels, measured by periodic surveys, remain high.

Will you be putting your own job on the line? That's a scary thought, particularly with two kids in college.

Could the move to teams have put your job on the line? Most definitely. When teams are appropriate, they can produce incredible improvements in productivity, quality, and employee and customer satisfaction. But when teams aren't appropriate, they can fail miserably. For instance, production levels dropped by 23 percent when Levi

Strauss introduced teams in its factories. Levi's mistake was assuming that teams were appropriate for garment work, where workers performed single, specialized tasks, like sewing zippers or belt loops. Because this kind of work does not require interaction with others, teams failed miserably at Levi's.

So the question is not whether to use teams, but when and where to use teams for maximum benefit and minimum cost. In short, teams should be used for a clear purpose, when the work requires that people work together, when rewards can be provided for both teamwork and team performance, when ample resources can be provided, and when teams can be given clear authority over their work.

Sources: M. Brown, "National Winner: Cigna Services UK," *Management Today*, June 1994, 95. J.R. Caron, S.L. Jarvenpaa, & D.B. Stoddard, "Business Reengineering at CIGNA Corporation: Experiences and Lessons Learned from the First Five Years," *MIS Quarterly* 18, no. 3 (1994): 233. S.E. Gross, *Compensation for Teams* (New York: American Management Association, 1995). T. Hoffman, "Re-engineering Pays Off at Cigna," *Computerworld*, August 1993, 70. "International Healthcare News," *Business Conference and Management Reports*, 1 December 1995, 6.

Key Terms

bureaucratic immunity p. 529

cohesiveness p. 520

cross training p. 505

cross-functional team p. 515

de-forming p. 526

de-norming p. 526

de-storming p. 526

employee involvement team p. 514

forming p. 525

gainsharing p. 533

individualism-collectivism p. 530

interpersonal skills p. 532

norming p. 526

norms p. 519

performing p. 526

project team p. 517

self-designing team p. 515

self-limiting behavior p. 507

self-managing team p. 515

semi-autonomous work group p. 514

skill-based pay p. 533

social loafing p. 506

storming p. 525

structural accommodation p. 528

team diversity p. 530

team level p. 530

traditional work group p. 513

virtual team p. 516

work team p. 502

What Would You Do-II?

Lafayette, Indiana.

Jack Murdock, the CEO of Goldstar Trailers, rubbed his eyes and looked up from his computer screen to collect his thoughts. Ten months ago, he had led an effort to organize his employees into self-managing work teams. The employees seemed to like the new structure, and early on he got good feedback. But lately, he was sensing that no real progress was being made. Productivity in the plant was up slightly, but nothing like he had hoped for. In addition, turnover in the plant was up, not down like the books and videos on teamwork promised. Rubbing his eyes again, Jack turned his office chair toward the window. Gazing outside, he ran through in his mind one more time why he had insisted on teamwork.

Goldstar manufactures three types of horse trailers: a gooseneck, a hitch trailer, and a slant load. Before the creation of work teams, the employees worked in separate departments: metalwork, assembly, painting, and design. Although the company made good trailers, Jack had worried about his employees. They just didn't seem to be excited about their jobs. He had also worried about a decline in quality. One phone call from a dealer had been particularly disturbing. The dealer, located in central Kentucky, said that he had sold nine Goldstar trailers since the first of the year, and five had already come back for repairs. Jack remembered that the call had sent chills down his back.

The idea to implement self-managing work teams came from a book that Jack had read. In fact, Jack reorganized the manufacturing process based on the ideas in the book. The departments were eliminated, and each employee was assigned to a process team. A separate team was set up for each type of trailer that the company made. Jack remembered asking his employees what to call the new teams. He had wanted to call them Team A, Team B, and Team C. The employees would have none of that. They decided to call themselves the Gooseneck Team, the Hitch Trailer Team, and the Slant Load Team, which corresponded to the trailers that each team would be making. Privately, Jack was pleased. He wanted the teams to closely identify with the trailers they made.

The way the new structure worked, each team manufactured only the trailer that corresponded to its name. However, employees on each team were cross trained in the areas of metalwork, assembly, painting, and in some cases, design. Each team had a team leader, and the teams were responsible for their own hiring, budgeting, purchasing, inventory control, and inspection. The teams had weekly meetings to talk about quality improvements, inventory control, absenteeism, and product design. The idea was to get each team member fully involved in making a better product. He also hoped that the employees would gain a sense of pride in "their" trailers. In fact, a small metal plate containing the names of the team members was welded to the inside wall of the trailer just for this purpose.

Although this all sounded good, it hadn't worked, at least not yet. The overall performance of the plant had not improved, and Jack was hearing more and more complaints. Jack remembered thinking a hundred times over the past ten months, "Are we doing something wrong, or is teamwork a bad idea?" One way or another, Jack knew that he had to find an answer to that question.

A truck on the road outside of Jack's window blew its horn at another vehicle and snapped Jack out of his daydream. He turned back to his computer screen and reread the e-mail message that he had just received from the leader of the Gooseneck Team. The message read as follows:

Dear Jack,

We are all behind you on this teamwork thing, but we have got to get better organized. The team meetings are a good idea, but most of the time we just drink coffee and talk about sports. What, specifically, would you like us to accomplish? Also, our team has outperformed the other two teams for the past two months, but that hasn't affected our take-home pay. We have appreciated your letters, but letters of congratulations only go so far. Jack, I don't mean to be critical. Your dad hired me and I am committed to Goldstar Trailers. But teamwork has to be more than an idea. We need your help and support. Think it over and let me know what you decide. I need to go to my people with some concrete ideas.

Bill Waters
Team Leader, Gooseneck Team

Jack turned his chair and looked outside his window again. He asked himself aloud, "What should I do?" **If you were CEO of Goldstar Trailers, what would you do?**

Sources: P. Berman, "The Wabash Way," *Forbes*, 6 April 1998, 78-81. M. Krantz, "Wabash Keeps Work Flowing on Innovative Truck Trailers," *Investor's Business Daily*, 6 May 1994, A4. R.L. Rose, "Hard Driving: A Productivity Push at Wabash National Puts Firm on a Roll—Workers Are Strongly Urged to Improve Their Skills; Teams Offer Many Ideas—But Paternalism Irks Some," *The Wall Street Journal*, 7 September 1995, A1.

Critical-Thinking Video Case

Teamwork: Valassis Communications

Valassis Communications, a leader in sales promotions, puts together more than 55 million coupon booklets that appear in 400 newspapers each Sunday morning. Valassis has developed a unique corporate culture that fosters teamwork, change, and creativity and emphasizes customer satisfaction. Valassis believes that teams are essential to its success. The company's strong commitment to its employees and its outstanding quality of work life have won it the designation as one of the best 100 companies to work for in America.

As you watch the video, consider the following critical thinking questions.

Critical-Thinking Questions

1. Why would an organization such as Valassis use teams?
2. How would an organization such as Valassis create an environment to support effective teamwork?

Management Decisions

A Team Leader's Worst Nightmare

"OK, Ted, tell me one more time what happened." Ted Knight, a new employee just assigned to the Hard Disk Assembly Team, is sitting in your office on a Friday afternoon, and you can't believe what you're hearing.

Each member of the Hard Disk Assembly Team is responsible for assembling and testing hard disks that go into PCs. As a way of creating healthy competition among the team's six members, you've been recording each member's production output each day and posting it near the team's work area. At the end of each week, the team member who has assembled the most hard disks without a quality failure receives a $50 bonus.

You always thought that the competition had worked well. Several different team members had won the $50 bonus, production numbers were inching up, and no one had complained about the availability of extra cash. But Ted's story was making you heartsick. Ted joined the Hard Disk Assembly Team three weeks ago. His first two weeks were primarily training. But this week, Ted had a workstation of his own on the factory floor. Ted is a quick learner, which is one of the reasons you hired him. According to Ted, two of his teammates cornered him in a quiet corner of the snack room during his afternoon break. They told him that under no circumstances was he to assemble more than 30 hard disks during a single day. One of the employees, whom Ted was not willing to identify, told him, "We all work at a comfortable pace around here. If you assemble more than 30 hard disks a day, the team leader will expect us all to." Ted went on to say that the second employee told him, "And by the way, no one gets to win the weekly production award until they've been around for awhile. If you are leading toward the end of the week, I'll let you know so you can slow down some."

You took a deep breath and looked Ted straight in the eye. "Ted, thanks for letting me know what's going on. I honestly had no idea that anything like this was happening. Give me the weekend, and on Monday morning I'll let you know what I am going to do."

Questions

1. If you were the team leader, what would you do? Would you call a team meeting and deal directly with this problem, or would you try a more subtle approach?

2. What about Ted? If you go to Ted's teammates and reveal what he told you, will he ever be accepted as a member of the team? Also, what about the weekly production award? Should you cancel it, allow it to continue as is, or change it in some way?

Sources: J. George, "Extrinsic and Intrinsic Origins of Perceived Social Loafing in Organizations," *Academy of Management Journal* 35 (1992): 191-202. R.E. Kidwell, Jr. & N. Bennett, "Employee Propensity to Withhold Effort: A Conceptual Model to Intersect Three Avenues Research," *Academy of Management Review* 18, no. 3 (1993): 429-456. P.W. Mulvey, J.F. Veiga, & P.M. Elsass, "When Teammates Raise a White Flag," *Academy of Management Executive* 10, no. 1 (1996): 40-49.

Management Decisions

You'd Think that Awarding Bonuses Would Be Easy. Think Again.

You've just reread the fifth e-mail message this month about the new team bonus plan. None of them has been positive. Two years ago, you switched your Credit Card Customer Service Center to a team-based design. Prior to the switch, your employees had been assigned to traditional functional areas. But with the hope of increasing customer service and decreasing costs, you decided to eliminate the traditional departments and put your employees into teams. Now you have five teams to service your credit card customers. The teams are as follows:

- Team 1 Handles routine requests for personal accounts
- Team 2 Handles routine requests for corporate accounts
- Team 3 Investigates requests for credit line increases
- Team 4 Sells credit card protection insurance
- Team 5 Investigates disputed charges

Ever since you created the work teams, your employees have complained about the lack of team incentives. Basically, you were still paying employees an individually based merit increase plus a cost-of-living adjustment. Six months ago you decided to give team incentives a try. You challenged each team to increase its productivity by 5 percent per month. According to the new plan, teams that increased productivity by that amount would receive a $500 bonus to split among its team members.

But it hasn't worked. Here's the problem. Teams 1, 2, and 3 have won the bonus for each of the six months that the bonus has been in existence. Teams 4 and 5 have never won the bonus. You're getting the same complaint from every member of Teams 4 and 5 that you talk to. What they keep telling you is that it is easier for Teams 1, 2, and 3 to increase their productivity than it is for them. Teams 1 and 2 handle hundreds of routine calls every day. To increase productivity, all they have to do is move more quickly through their calls. Team 3 investigates requests for credit line increases. Because interest rates have been going down, they have gotten numerous requests and have been able to approve the majority of them. So these teams have been steadily increasing their productivity and have been awarded the $500 bonus each month.

However, according to members of Teams 4 and 5, it is not as easy for them to increase their productivity. Team 4 sells credit card protection insurance, which is a tough product to sell. Team 5 investigates disputed charges. It can sometimes take weeks to get to the bottom of a disputed charge. It is not a process that is easily rushed. As a result, despite their efforts, Teams 4 and 5 have never won the award. Instead, they continue to complain that the bonus program just isn't fair.

As you look up from your desk, a group of employees from Team 4 is waiting to see you. They had called earlier in the day and asked if they could stop by to talk about the bonus program. You are really tiring of this. You thought that awarding bonuses would be easy. What should you tell them?

Questions

1. Is the bonus compensation program fair? If not, would you scrap the program or revise it in some way?
2. Was the implementation of the bonus compensation plan handled appropriately in the first place? What could have been done initially to create a more equitable plan?

Sources: Anonymous, "AT&T Universal Card Services," *Business America* 113, no. 22 (1992): 12-13. S.E. Gross, *Compensation for Teams* (New York: American Management Association, 1995). P.A. Murphy, "It's No Longer Just Teleservices," *Credit Card Management* 11, no. 1 (1998): 115-119.

Develop Your Management Potential

A Quick Check of Your Team Skills

To be part of an effective team, you have to be a good team member. However, sometimes it's hard to objectively judge our contributions in a team or group effort. Think about one of your most important team experiences. Were you an effective team member? Take the following test to find out. After you take the test, answer the questions below to begin thinking about how you can improve.

Instructions:

Step 1: Answer the following questions the way that you think other members of your team would if they were describing your actions.

Step 2: Total your score for each section. Then transfer all totals to the "Quick Check of My Team Skills" section at the conclusion of the exercise.

Scale: 1 = Almost never
2 = Seldom
3 = Sometimes
4 = Usually
5 = Almost always

I. Honor team values and agreements.

As a team member, I: **Your score:**

a. Show appreciation for other team members' ideas. ______
b. Help other team members cope with change. ______
c. Encourage others to use their strengths. ______
d. Help the team develop a productive relationship with other teams. ______
e. Willingly assume a leadership role when needed. ______
Total: ______

II. Promote team development.

As a team member, I: **Your score:**

a. Volunteer for all types of tasks, including the hard ones. ______
b. Help orient and train new team members. ______
c. Help organize and run effective meetings. ______
d. Help examine how we are doing as a team and make any necessary changes in the way we work together. ______
e. Help identify milestones and mini-successes to celebrate. ______
Total: ______

III. Help make team decisions.

As a team member, I: **Your score:**

a. Analyze what a decision entails. ______
b. Ensure that the team selects and includes the appropriate people in the decision process. ______
c. Clearly state my concerns. ______
d. Search for common ground when team members have different views. ______
e. Actively support the team's decisions. ______
Total: ______

IV. Coordinate and carry out team tasks.

As a team member, I: **Your score:**

a. Help identify the information, skills, and resources necessary to accomplish team tasks. ______
b. Help formulate and agree on a plan to meet performance goals. ______
c. Stay abreast of what is happening in other parts of the organization and bring that information to the team. ______
d. Find innovative ways to meet the needs of the team and of others in the organization. ______
e. Maintain a win-win outlook in all dealings with other teams. ______
Total: ______

V. Handle difficult issues with the team.

As a team member, I: **Your score:**

a. Bring team issues and problems to the team's attention. ______
b. Encourage others on the team to state their views. ______
c. Help build trust among team members by speaking openly about the team's problems. ______

d. Give specific, constructive, and timely feedback to others. ________

e. Admit when I've made a mistake. ________

Total: ________

A Quick Check of My Team Skills

Category	Total Score
Honor team values and agreements.	________
Promote team development.	________
Help make team decisions.	________
Coordinate and carry out team tasks.	________
Handle difficult issues with the team.	________

Interpreting Scores

- A score of 20 or above in any activity indicates an area of strength.
- A score of 19 or below in any activity indicates an area that needs more attention.

Questions to Ask Yourself

Looking at your scores, what areas are strengths? How can you maintain these strengths? What areas are weaknesses? What steps can you take to turn these areas into strengths?

Source: Michael A. West, ed., *Handbook of Work Group Psychology* (Chichester, UK: Wiley, 1996).

Chapter Fourteen

544

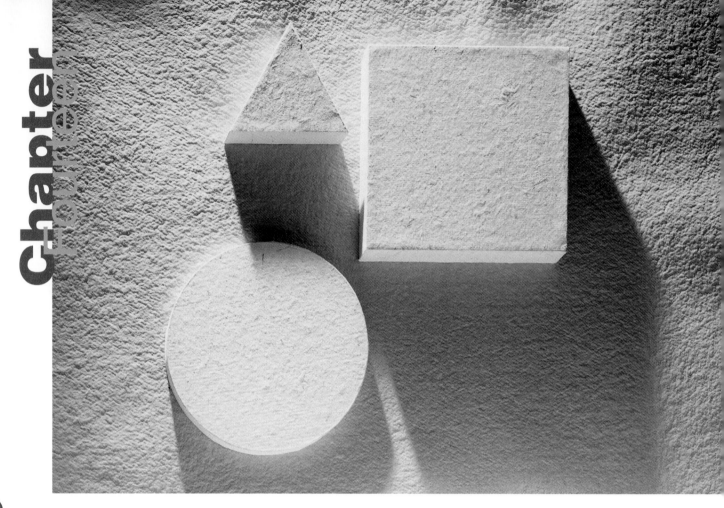

Managing Human Resource Systems

What Would **You** Do?

Magnolia Medical Services, Thomasville, Georgia. The interview had gone well, so you weren't surprised when Magnolia Medical Services, a small private clinic in southwest Georgia, asked you to be their human resource director. Magnolia, which is a medium-sized medical practice, employs 65 people, who work as nurses, lab technicians, secretaries, office managers, receptionists, bookkeepers, and janitors. During the interview, the physicians who owned the practice mentioned that they had "personnel problems," which they didn't have the expertise or time to handle. Whoever they hired would have responsibility for those problems and complete control over Magnolia's human resources. "What an opportunity!" you remember thinking. It's not often that you get to run the entire HRM function in your second job out of college. However, for some reason, you couldn't get the phrase "personnel problems" out of your mind. Nonetheless, the job was too good to pass up, "personnel problems" or not. When you showed up on Monday, Beth, the office manager, was only too happy to give you the details. Christine, Tish, and Donna were the "personnel problems" and had been the talk of the clinic for several months. Christine had been hired as one of the office managers. At first, she seemed perfect for the job, developing a number of new office procedures and rewriting the job descriptions for every position within the clinic. The owners were thrilled with her performance. However, four months after she was hired, employee turnover reached an all-time high. By the time the owners finally figured out that Christine was a control freak (she even demanded that the janitors wipe off the countertops "her way"), they had lost six key employees. Tish was hired as a nurse. While paid fairly well compared to most people in the office, other employees still wondered how Tish could afford such expensive clothes and cars. It turned out that Tish was using some creative accounting to line her pockets. The clinic had a "professional courtesy" policy of not charging doctors, nurses, or clergy for office visits or tests. Purely by chance one afternoon, one of the owners heard a nurse stop in and pay for her last visit to the clinic. Tish had been charging these people, pocketing the cash, and then marking their paperwork "No Charge"! Donna was another office manager who, at first, looked to be an excellent employee. She had a great personality and made friends with everyone, including a number of wealthy patients, several of whom began inviting her to spend weekends on their boats on a nearby lake. Donna also took a lot of Fridays off, supposedly for visits to the dentist or to care for sick relatives. One Friday, when one of the doctors asked where Donna was, one of the other employees, who had tired of covering for her, blurted out, "Probably down on some rich patient's boat. We usually have to stay late on Fridays to finish up her work!" In fact, once the doctors began paying more attention to Donna's work, they found that their office costs had increased dramatically because she had been using clinic stamps, envelopes, and the copying machine to mail out invitations to these weekend parties. Beth made it very clear. The doctors didn't know much about HRM issues and, frankly, they were just too busy with patients to be involved. But they did expect you to clean things up around here. They were really tired of hiring people who turned out to be problems or poor performers. With all of these jobs to fill, she said you'd better make sure that the first few employees you hire turn out to be good ones. How do you go about recruiting qualified applicants? What's the best way to learn something about applicants' work experience before hiring them? What can you do to improve the accuracy of the selection decisions at Magnolia Medical Services? And if employees don't work out, what process should be used to let them go that is fair to them and the company (and decreases chances of a lawsuit)? **If you were the new human resource director for Magnolia Medical Services, what would you do?**

Sources: Anonymous, "Bad Hiring Practices Can Cost You Money," *Agency Sales* 28, no. 9 (September 1998): 40-43. M. Barrier, "Hiring the Right People," *Nation's Business* 84, no. 6 (June 1996): 18. L.D. Dunsmore, "Hiring Tips We Learned the Hard Way," *Medical Economics*, 12 February 1996, 140-146. D. Wiggins, "Hiring Employees Intelligently," *Journal of Environmental Health* 60, no. 10 (June 1998): 46-47.

Unfortunately, "personnel problems" like those at Magnolia Medical Services are all too common. For example, when Erler Industries, a small industrial painting and finishing company, signed a contract for a large amount of work with Dell Computer, it grew from 6 to 175 people almost overnight to meet the increased workload. Co-owner Linda Erler said, "We were so desperate for employees that if we could see the whites of your eyes and it looked as if blood was running through your veins, [you were offered a job]." Linda explained that this approach didn't always translate into successful hiring, like the time that a group of new hires all came to work with "whiskey in their soda cans." And even though new employees could earn bonuses if they stayed for just 30 days, she said, "we had tremendous turnover. Everyone had to be replaced five or six times before we found a person who really wanted to work."[1]

human resource management
the process of finding, developing, and keeping the right people to form a qualified work force

The experiences of Magnolia Medical Services and Erler Industries indicate that **human resource management**, the process of finding, developing, and keeping the right people to form a qualified work force, remains one of the most difficult and important of all management tasks. This chapter is organized around the four parts of the human resource management process shown in Figure 14.1: determining human resource needs and attracting, developing, and keeping a qualified work force.

Accordingly, the chapter begins by reviewing how human resource planning determines human resource needs, such as the kind and number of employees a company requires to meet its strategic plans and objectives. Next, we explore how companies use recruiting and selection techniques to attract and hire qualified employees to fulfill those needs. The third part of the chapter reviews how training and performance appraisal can develop the knowledge, skills, and abilities of the work force. The chapter concludes with a review of compensation and employee separation, that is, how companies can keep their best workers through effective compensation practices, and how they can manage the separation process when employees do leave the organization.

Determining Human Resource Needs

Should we hire more workers? What should we pay our current employees to slow employee turnover? What kinds of training do our new employees need to be prepared to do a good job, and what's the best way to deliver that training? In other words, what are our human resource needs and what's the best way to address them?

Managers often treat these questions as separate issues. However, the human resource process illustrated in Figure 14.1 shows that attracting (recruiting and selecting), developing (orienting, training, appraising performance, and compensating), and keeping or losing employees (separating) are interdependent issues. You can't solve one problem without considering its impact on the others. More specifically, Figure 14.1 indicates that human resource needs affect how the company uses recruiting and selection to attract employees. In turn, the kind and number of employees hired influence the orientation, training, performance appraisal, and compensation strategies the company uses, which then affect who stays and who leaves. Finally, as indicated by the feedback loop, the process comes full circle, as the number and kind of employees who leave the company affect its human resource needs and planning.

Figure 14.1 **The Human Resource Management Process**

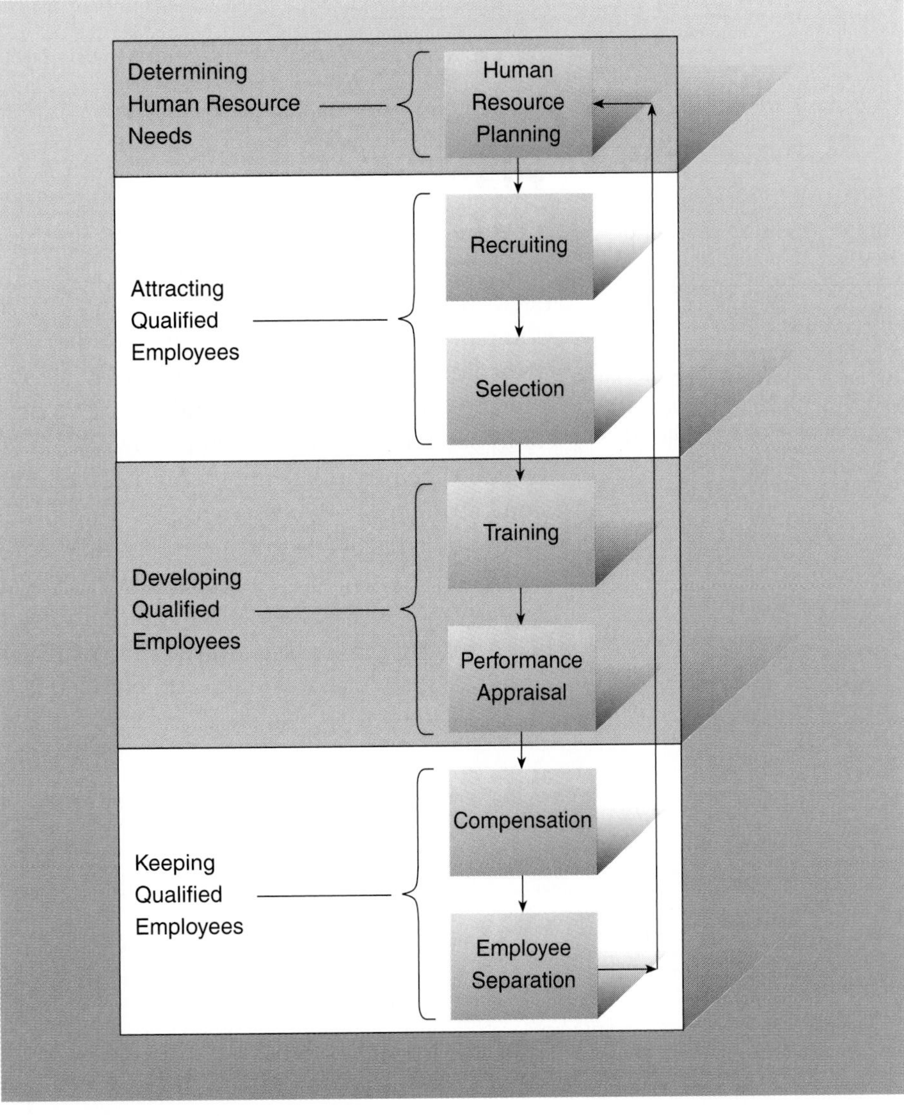

You can see how the HR process works by examining what high-tech companies are doing to deal with the acute shortage of qualified workers in the U.S. For instance, because of the shortage, a number of American software companies have been recruiting software engineers in countries such as Ireland and India.[2] But since the supply of foreign workers wasn't large enough to alleviate the shortage, companies have had to keep increasing compensation packages for IT workers. At the time this chapter was written, entry-level IT workers were earning well over $70,000 per year and were getting $3,000 to $5,000 signing bonuses. They were also being offered phenomenal benefits, such as four-star restaurant quality food in company cafeterias, pool and ping pong tables for recreation, massage therapists, free soft drinks, juice, popcorn, and snacks, dry-cleaning drop-off and pickup, car detailers, dog walkers, and special staffers to run personal errands.[3] Finally, some high-tech companies are dealing with the demand for workers by doing less recruiting, hoping instead that retraining current workers will be an effective way to fill empty jobs.

Fortunately, there are steps that companies can take to begin to address the employee shortfalls experienced in the high-tech industry. After reading the next two sections, you should be able to:

1 describe the basic steps involved in **human resource planning**.

2 explain how different **employment laws** affect human resource practice.

1 Human Resource Planning

human resource planning (HRP)
using an organization's goals and strategy to forecast the organization's human resource needs in terms of attracting, developing, and keeping a qualified work force

Human resource planning (HRP) is the process of using an organization's goals and strategy to forecast the organization's human resource needs in terms of attracting, developing, and keeping a qualified work force.[4] Companies that don't use HRP or that do HRP poorly may end up with either a surplus of employees and have to lay off some to correct the surplus, or a shortage of employees that leads to increased overtime costs and an inability to meet demand for the company's product or service.

The HRP process begins with a consideration of the organization's mission, strategy, and objectives. Therefore, HRP is directly related to and should be considered part of an organization's strategic planning process.[5] Dell Computer makes sure that the HRP process is tied to its mission and strategy by splitting its HR function into two departments. "HR Operations" has a service center that takes care of all "transactional" activities for Dell employees, such as benefits and compensation. HR Operations rarely has

BLASTFROMTHEPAST

The First HR Department

During the late 1800s and early 1900s, the predecessors of today's human resource departments began to emerge from the brand new field of industrial psychology, in which psychologists were beginning to apply their knowledge to factory settings. Hugo Munsterberg (1863-1916), the "Father of Industrial Psychology," established a psychology laboratory at Harvard University in 1892 that became the foundation of the industrial psychology movement. In 1913, he published a book entitled *Psychology and Industrial Efficiency*, in which he discussed the demands that jobs make on people and the importance of matching individuals to jobs. He was also one of the first people to suggest using tests to select workers. And in 1913, Munsterberg met with President Wilson, the Secretary of Commerce, and the Secretary of Labor in an attempt to convince them to establish a government research center that would examine the application of psychology to industrial problems. The center was never established, but Munsterberg continued to conduct research on employee motivation and methods for reducing employee fatigue. His work, and that of his colleagues, resulted in more concern for the human factors in work.

In 1900, the B.F. Goodrich Company established the first human resource department. Goodrich's "employment department" performed a limited number of functions, such as handling employee discipline, keeping performance records, and administering compensation. In 1914, Henry Ford formed one of the earliest personnel departments in his Detroit automobile plant, calling it the "Sociological Department." When a $5-per-day minimum wage was established, Ford hired 100 investigators, called "advisors," who visited employees' homes to make sure the homes were neat and clean and that the employees didn't drink too much. Ford was concerned that with a $5-per-day income, which was enormous for that time, employees might go astray and spend their money irresponsibly. And similar to the wellness benefits offered by many companies today, Ford's Sociological Department also employed social workers to help employees with family or other nonwork problems.

Sources: "Industrial Relations," *Encyclopædia Britannica Online*. [Online] Available **http://www.eb.com:180/bol/topic?eu=115715&sctn=12**, 5 June 1999. H. Munsterberg, *Psychology and Industrial Efficiency* (Boston: Houghton-Mifflin Company, 1913). L. Baritz, *The Servants of Power* (New York: John Wiley & Sons, 1960). D.A. Wren, *The Evolution of Management Thought*, 2d ed. (New York: John Wiley and Sons, 1979).

direct contact with Dell's business units. Its job is to serve Dell's individual employees. By contrast, the HR staffers in Dell's "HR Management" department report directly to the vice president of HR *and* the vice president of a Dell business unit (e.g., procurement, higher education sales, etc.). The HR staffers then attend that business unit's staff meetings, help to develop that unit's leadership team, and then create a specific HR strategy for that part of Dell's business.[6] Dell's HR Management team also helps business units identify personnel needs, assess training needs, and determine the best organizational structure for reporting relationships (i.e., the organizational chart).

Let's explore human resource planning by examining how to **1.1** *forecast the supply and demand of human resources and* **1.2** *use human resource information systems to improve those forecasts.*

1.1 *Forecasting Demand and Supply*

work force forecasting the process of predicting the number and kind of workers with specific skills and abilities that an organization will need in the future

Work force forecasting is the process of predicting the number and kind of workers with specific skills and abilities that an organization will need in the future.[7] There are two kinds of work force forecasts, internal and external forecasts, and three kinds of forecasting methods, direct managerial input, best guess, and statistical/historical ratios.

Internal forecasts are projections about factors within the organization that affect the supply and demand for human resources. These factors include the financial performance of the organization, productivity, the organization's mission, changes in technology or the way the work is performed, and the termination, promotion, transfer, retirement, resignation, and death of current employees. For example, because of productivity increases and advances in technology, Bell South, which provides local phone coverage throughout the southeastern U.S., has decreased the number of employees in its Telecommunications Division from 68,500 to less than 57,000 in the last three years.[8] Table 14.1 provides a more complete list of factors that influence internal forecasts.

Table 14.1

Internal and External Factors That Influence Work force Forecasting

Internal Factors	*External Factors*
• New positions	• Demographics of labor supply
• New equipment and technology	• Geographic population shifts
• Eliminated positions	• Shift from manufacturing- to service- to information-based economy
• Terminations	• General economic conditions
• Retirements	• Unemployment rate
• Resignations	• Labor unions
• Turnover	• Availability of applicants with specific skills and education
• Transfers	• Technological advances
• Deaths	• Strength and number of competitors
• Promotions	• Growth in particular businesses and markets
• Organization's mission	
• Productivity of current employees	
• Skills/education of current employees	

External forecasts are projections about factors outside the organization that affect the supply and demand for human resources. These factors include the labor supply for specific types of workers, the economy (unemployment rate), labor unions, demographics of the labor force (e.g., proportion of labor force in various age groups), geographic movement of the labor force, strength of competitors, and growth in particular businesses and markets. While increased productivity, an internal factor, prompted Bell South to reduce the number of employees in its local telephone division, increased competition, an external factor, resulted in the hiring of hundreds more customer service representatives. Likewise, the increased demand for second phone lines in people's homes led Bell South to hire more service technicians. The dramatic increase in cell phone usage prompted Bell South to greatly expand the number of employees in Bell South Mobility, its cellular phone division.[9] Table 14.1 provides a more complete list of factors that influence external forecasts.

Three kinds of forecasting methods—direct managerial input, best guess, and statistical/historical ratios—are often used to predict the number and kind of workers with specific skills and abilities that an organization will need in the future.[10] The most common forecasting method, *direct managerial input*, is based on straightforward projections of cash flows, expenses, or financial measures, such as return on capital. While financial indicators are relatively quick to calculate and can help managers determine how many workers they might need, they don't help managers decide which critical skills new employees should possess.

The *best guess* forecasting method is based on managers' assessment of current head count, plus a best guess of how internal factors and external factors would affect that head count. Summing these together produces the total projection. Dell Computer, in part, uses a best guess system to forecast the kinds of people it would like to hire. Steve Price, Dell's vice president of human resources for its Public and Americas International Group, said, "We look at the people who have been given the biggest merit increases, the best appraisals and so forth, and then we interview against these competencies."[11]

Finally, the *statistical/historical ratios* forecasting method uses statistical methods, such as multiple regression, in combination with historical data, to predict the number and kind of workers a company should hire. For example, a manager might run a regression analysis using data from the last two years. In that regression equation, the number of employees that need to be hired is the dependent (predicted) variable, and the number of items manufactured, number of clients, or average increase in sales, etc., are the independent (predictor) variables. The regression analysis produces a simple equation that indicates how many more employees should be added for each increase in the independent variables, such as items manufactured or increased sales. This approach takes advantage of existing data and can be much more accurate than best guess predictions, but only if a company's internal and external environments have not changed significantly.

Dell also uses statistical/historical ratios to help predict its work force needs. Andy Esparza, vice president of staffing for Dell's companywide staffing function, said, "One of the things this [HR planning process] maps into is a set of key job openings that we can use to start forecasting and sourcing people in advance. More specifically, Dell's Web-based HR planning process allows managers to play "what if?" with work force predictions. Kathleen Woodhouse, an HR manager who supports Dell's preferred accounts division, said, "Managers use our intranet to complete HR functions, like appraisals; our appraisal system also feeds into the financial system so they can play with figures if they need to."[12]

1.2

Human Resource Information Systems

human resource information systems (HRIS) computerized systems for gathering, analyzing, storing, and disseminating information related to the HRM process

Human resource information systems (HRIS) are computerized systems for gathering, analyzing, storing, and disseminating information related to attracting, developing, and keeping a qualified work force.[13] Table 14.2 shows some of the data that are commonly used in HR information systems, such as personal and educational data, company employment history, performance appraisal information, work history, and promotions.

Human resource information systems can be used for transaction processing, employee self-service, and decision support. As you learned in Chapter 6, *transaction processing* is a centralized computer system, often a mainframe, that records the thousands of routine daily transactions involved in running a business. For HRIS systems, transaction processing usually involves employee payroll checks, taxes, and benefit deductions. Tenet Healthcare Corp. uses an HRIS to keep track of the payroll information for the 100,000 employees who work in its 127 hospitals in 22 states. Tenet switched to a centralized HRIS because lists of employees and their pay and benefits were being kept in 85 different data locations. Regarding its new centralized HRIS, Alan Ewalt, Tenet's senior vice president of human resources, said, "This will combine everything in one automated system. Once we enter the employees' names upon hiring them, the system will continually be updated with each payroll change and know exactly where they're located,

Table 14.2

Common Data Categories in Human Resource Information Systems

Personal Data

- Name
- Address/Telephone Number
- Employee Identification Number
- Social Security Number
- Medical Plan/Coverage
- Retirement/Investment Plan

Company Employment History

- Previous Job Assignments
- Current Position
- Date of Initial Employment
- Seniority Date
- Salary/Pay History
- Current Salary/Pay
- Fringe Benefit Package
- Last Pay Raise

Work History

- Previous Employers
- Previous Positions
- Duties in Previous Positions
- Supervisory Experience

Educational Data

- High School Diploma
- College Degrees
- Special Courses/Training

Performance Appraisal

- Date of Last Performance Appraisal
- Productivity Measures
- Disciplinary Action
- Tardiness
- Absenteeism
- Last Performance Rating
- Quality Measures

Promotion Data

- Geographic Preferences
- Personal Interests
- Awards
- Job Preferences
- Special Skills/Knowledge
- Foreign Language(s)

what department they're in and how many hours they are working."[14] The advantage of this system is that it will quickly provide accurate, up-to-date information about staff compensation in one complete database. HRISs can also reduce administrative costs by preparing certain routine reports, such as the EEOC (Equal Employment Opportunity Commission) or OSHA (Occupational Safety and Health Administration) reports that are required of many companies.

While human resource information systems are typically used to give managers and HR staffers access to human resource data, the flip side of today's Web-based HRISs is that they also give employees immediate, 24-hour *self-service* access to personal data, such as benefits and retirement packages. With secure, Web-based systems, employees need to enter only a user name and password to access and change their medical insurance plan, adjust the mix of investments in their 401(k) retirement plan, or check on the status of medical or childcare reimbursements.[15] According to benefits coordinator Priscilla Craven, the primary advantage of self-service systems is that "You no longer need to call a person when an office is open to get a form or make an enrollment choice." And with access available 24 hours a day, companies have also begun eliminating restricted "open enrollment" periods, in which employees have to make (and then not change) all of their benefit decisions for the entire year at one time. With Web-based systems, employees can make changes whenever they want. Dick Quinn, director of performance and rewards at Public Service Electric & Gas Company of New Jersey, said, "Our intent next year is to have completely eliminated the concept of annual open enrollment. This will eliminate all of the printing and communication costs associated with the annual sign-up period. When employees know they aren't locked into a health-care choice for a full year, it will make all of our managed-care choices more attractive."[16]

Human resource information systems are not only useful for gathering and storing information, but they also help managers by serving as decision support systems for critical human resource decisions.[17] In Chapter 6, you learned that *decision support systems* (DSS) help managers understand problems and potential solutions by acquiring and analyzing information with sophisticated models and tools. For instance, an HRIS can help managers make human resource decisions from the moment that job applicants submit resumes to the company. Those resumes are scanned, turned into text via optimal character recognition software, and then fed into the HRIS, where they are analyzed for the quality of the writing and for key words that match the organization's job database. John Reese, founder of Interactive Search, an Internet recruiting site, said, "Whatever the media—paper, e-mail, the Web or fax—we can scan a resume into a database, re-format it according to our specifications, and then make it available to the hiring manager or HR manager anywhere in a company, anywhere in the world. An applicant can send in an application on Thursday and have an interview by Monday."[18]

An HRIS can even be used to do preemployment testing or background screening. Elaine Daily, marketing director for Qwiz, Inc., which sells computerized employment tests to companies, said, "We can do remote testing through a Web site or through software installed on a PC. This saves the company from having to bring in a candidate to headquarters before deciding whether the person is technically competent."[19]

HRISs can also be used effectively to screen internal applicants on particular qualifications, to match the qualifications of external applicants against those of internal applicants, to compare salaries within and between departments, and to review and change employees' salaries instantaneously without lengthy paperwork. In short, today's HRISs can help managers make any number of critical human resource decisions.

Review 1
Human Resource Planning

Human resource planning (HRP) uses organizational goals and strategies to determine what needs to be done to attract, develop, and keep a qualified work force. Work force forecasts are used to predict the number and kind of workers with specific skills and abilities that an organization needs. Work force forecasts consider both internal and external factors that affect the supply and demand for workers and can be formulated using three kinds of forecasting methods: direct managerial input, best guess, and statistical/historical ratios. Computerized human resource information systems improve human resource planning by gathering, analyzing, storing, and disseminating information (personal, educational, work history, performance, and promotions) related to human resource management activities. Human resource information systems can be used for transaction processing (payroll checks and routine reports), employee self-service (24-hour Web access allowing instant changes to benefit and retirement packages), and decision support for human resource decisions (analyzing resumes, background screening, and preemployment testing).

2 Employment Legislation

Since their inception, Hooters restaurants have hired only female waitresses. Moreover, consistent with the company's marketing theme, it has its attractive, female waitresses wear short nylon shorts and cutoff T-shirts that show their midriffs. The Equal Employment Opportunity Commission (EEOC) began an investigation of Hooters when a Chicago man filed a gender-based discrimination charge. The man alleged that he had applied for a waiter's job at a Hooters restaurant and was rejected because of his gender. The dispute between Hooters and the EEOC quickly gained national attention. One sarcastic letter to the EEOC printed in *Fortune* magazine read as follows:

> *Dear EEOC:*
> *Hi! I just wanted to thank you for investigating those Hooters restaurants, where the waitresses wear those shorty shorts and midriffy T-shirts. I think it's a great idea that you have decided to make Hooters hire men as—how do you say it?—waitpersons. Gee, I never knew so many men wanted to be waitpersons at Hooters. No reason to let them sue on their own either. You're right, the government needs to take the lead on this one.*[20]

This letter characterized public sentiment at the time. With a backlog of 100,000 job discrimination cases, many wondered why the EEOC didn't have better things to do with its scarce resources.

Three years after the initial complaint, the EEOC ruled that Hooters had violated antidiscrimination laws. The EEOC offered Hooters a settlement, which demanded that the company pay $22 million to the EEOC for distribution to male victims of the "Hooters Girl" hiring policy, establish a scholarship fund to enhance opportunities or education for men, and provide sensitivity training to teach Hooters' employees how to be more sensitive to men's needs. Hooters responded with a $1 million publicity campaign, chastising the EEOC for its investigation. Billboards featuring "Vince," a male dressed in a Hooters Girl uniform and blond wig sprang up all over the country. Hooters customers were given postcards to send complaints to the EEOC. Of course, Hooters paid the postage. As a result of the publicity campaign, restaurant sales increased by 10 percent. Soon thereafter, the EEOC announced that it would not pursue discriminatory hiring charges against Hooters.[21] However, the company still ended up paying $3.75 million to settle a class action suit brought by seven men who claimed that not being able to get a job at Hooters violated federal law.[22] The settlement still allowed Hooters to maintain its women-only policy for waitress jobs, but the company was required to create additional support jobs, such as hosts and bartenders, that would also be open to men.

As the Hooters example illustrates, the human resource planning process occurs in a very complicated legal environment. Since the 1960s, a large number of new federal employment laws directly affecting HRM practice have come into existence.

Let's explore employment legislation by reviewing **2.1** *the major federal employment laws that affect human resource practice,* **2.2** *how the concept of adverse impact is related to employment discrimination, and* **2.3** *the laws regarding sexual harassment in the workplace.*

2.1 *Federal Employment Laws*

Table 14.3 lists the major federal employment laws as well as their Web sites, where you can find more detailed information. The general result of this body of law, which is still evolving through court decisions, is that employers may not discriminate in employment decisions on the basis of gender, age, religion, color, national origin, race, or disability. The intent is to make these factors irrelevant in employment decisions. Stated another way, employment decisions should be based on factors that are "job related," "reasonably necessary," or a "business necessity" for successful job performance. The only time that gender, age, religion, etc. can be used to make employment decisions is when they are considered a bona fide occupational qualification (BFOQ).[23] Title VII of the 1964 Civil Rights Act says that it is not unlawful to hire and employ someone on the basis of their gender, religion, or national origin when there is a *bona fide occupational qualification* that is "reasonably necessary to the normal operation of that particular business." For example, a Baptist church hiring a new minister can reasonably specify that being a Baptist rather than a Catholic or Presbyterian is a BFOQ for Baptist ministers. However, it's unlikely that a church could specify race or national origin as a BFOQ. In general, the courts and the EEOC take a hard look when a business claims that gender, age, religion, color, national origin, race, or disability are BFOQs. For instance, the EEOC disagreed with Hooters' claim that it was "in the business of providing vicarious sexual recreation" and that "female sexuality is a bona fide occupational qualification."[24]

Table 14.3

Summary of Major Federal Employment Laws

Equal Pay Act of 1963 *http://www.eeoc.gov/laws/epa.html*	Prohibits unequal pay for males and females doing substantially similar work.
Civil Rights Act of 1964 *http://www.eeoc.gov/laws/vii.html*	Prohibits discrimination on the basis of race, color, religion, gender, or national origin.
Age Discrimination in Employment Act of 1967 *http://www.eeoc.gov/laws/adea.html*	Prohibits discrimination in employment decisions against persons age 40 and over.
Pregnancy Discrimination Act of 1978 *http://www.eeoc.gov/facts/fs-preg.html*	Prohibits discrimination in employment against pregnant women.
Americans with Disabilities Act of 1990 *http://www.eeoc.gov/laws/ada.html*	Prohibits discrimination on the basis of physical or mental disabilities.
Civil Rights Act of 1991 *http://www.eeoc.gov/laws/cra91.html*	Strengthened the provisions of the Civil Rights Act of 1964 by providing for jury trials and punitive compensation.
Family and Medical Leave Act of 1993 *http://www.dol.gov/dol/esa/fmla.htm*	Permits workers to take up to 12 weeks of unpaid leave for pregnancy and/or birth of a new child, adoption or foster care of a new child, illness of an immediate family member, or personal medical leave.

It is important to understand, however, that these laws don't just apply to selection decisions (i.e., hiring and promotion), but rather to the entire HRM process. Thus, these laws cover all training and development activities, performance appraisals, terminations, and compensation decisions.

Except for the Department of Labor (**http://www.dol.gov**), which administers the Family and Medical Leave Act, all of these laws are administered by the EEOC (**http://www.eeoc.gov**). Employers who use gender, age, race, or religion to make employment-related decisions when those factors are unrelated to an applicant's or employee's ability to perform a job may face charges of discrimination from the EEOC. For example, Kimberly Ortega worked as a telephone banker at the Norwest Bank in Phoenix, Arizona. She claimed that being required to work on Sundays interfered with her religious beliefs and her ability to attend religious services. She asked if she could change shifts with other workers, but was refused by company management, who argued that her work unit was too small to permit shift changes. The EEOC brought suit against Norwest on Ortega's behalf, asking for lost wages and benefits, as well as compensatory damages for emotional distress stemming from the bank's discriminatory practices.[25] Norwest eventually settled, offering Ortega her job back (she declined) and an unspecified financial settlement. Norwest also agreed to teach its supervisors about religious sensitivity.[26]

In addition to the laws presented in Table 14.3, there are two other important sets of federal laws. Labor laws regulate the interaction between management and labor unions that represent groups of employees. These laws guarantee employees the right to form and join unions of their own choosing. For more information about labor laws, see the National Labor Relations Board at **http://www.nlrb.gov**. The Occupational Safety and Health Act (OSHA) requires that employers provide employees with a place of employment that is "free from recognized hazards that are causing or are likely to cause death or serious physical harm." OSHA sets safety and health standards for employers and conducts inspections to determine whether those standards are being met. Employers who do not meet OSHA standards may be fined.[27] For more information about OSHA, see **http://www.osha.gov.**

2.2
Adverse Impact and Employment Discrimination

The EEOC has investigatory, enforcement, and informational responsibilities. Therefore, it investigates charges of discrimination, enforces the provisions of these laws in federal court, and publishes guidelines that organizations can use to ensure they are in compliance with the law. One of the most important guidelines jointly issued by the EEOC, the Department of Labor, the U.S. Justice Department, and the federal Office of Personnel Management is the *Uniform Guidelines on Employee Selection Procedures*, which can be read in their entirety at **http://www2.dol.gov/dol/esa/public/regs/cfr/41cfr/toc_Chapt60/60_3_toc.htm.** These guidelines define two important criteria, disparate treatment and adverse impact, that are used in deciding whether companies have participated in discriminatory hiring and promotion practices.

disparate treatment
intentional discrimination that occurs when people are purposively not given the same hiring, promotion, or membership opportunities because of their race, sex, age, ethnic group, national origin, or religious beliefs

Discrimination means treating people differently. **Disparate treatment**, which is intentional discrimination, occurs when people who, because of their race, sex, ethnic group, national origin, religious beliefs, etc., are purposively not given the same hiring, promotion, or membership opportunities as other employees, despite being qualified.[28] For example, Shoney's restaurants paid $132.8 million dollars to settle a class-action disparate treatment lawsuit in which it was accused of purposively not giving black employees a chance to be hired for jobs that entailed frequent customer contact.[29] Legally, one of the key parts of discrimination lawsuits is establishing motive, that the employer intended to discriminate.

adverse impact
unintentional discrimination in which there is a substantially different rate of selection in hiring, promotion, or other employment decisions that works to the disadvantage of members of a particular race, sex, age, ethnicity, or protected group

80% or four-fifths rule
a rule of thumb used by the courts and the EEOC to determine whether there is evidence of disparate impact. A violation of this rule occurs when the selection rate for a protected group is less than 80% or four-fifths of the selection rate for a nonprotected group.

If no motive can be established, then a case of disparate treatment may actually be a case of adverse impact. **Adverse impact**, which is unintentional discrimination, is a substantially different rate of selection in hiring, promotion, or other employment decisions that works to the disadvantage of members of a particular race, sex, or ethnic group. The courts and federal enforcement agencies use the **four-fifths rule** to determine if adverse impact has occurred. Adverse impact occurs if the selection rate for a protected group of people is less than four-fifths (or 80%) of the selection rate for a nonprotected group (usually white males). So, if 100 white applicants and 100 black applicants apply for entry-level jobs, and 60 white applicants are hired (60/100 = 60%), but only 20 black applicants are hired (20/100 = 20%), adverse impact will have been created. (.20/.60 = .33. The criterion for the four-fifths rule in this situation is .48: .60 × .80 = .48. Since .33 is less than .48, then the four-fifths rule has been violated.)

However, violation of the four-fifths rule is not an automatic indication of discrimination. If an employer can demonstrate that a selection procedure or test is valid, meaning that the test accurately predicts job performance or that the test is job related because it assesses applicants on specific tasks actually used in the job, then the organization may continue to use the test. However, if validity cannot be established, then a violation of the four-fifths rule may likely result in a lawsuit brought by employees, job applicants, or the EEOC itself.

2.3
Sexual Harassment

sexual harassment
form of discrimination in which unwelcome sexual advances, requests for sexual favors, or other verbal or physical conduct of a sexual nature occur while performing one's job

quid pro quo sexual harassment
form of sexual harassment in which employment outcomes, such as hiring, promotion, or simply keeping one's job, depend on whether an individual submits to sexual harassment

hostile work environment
form of sexual harassment in which unwelcome and demeaning sexually related behavior creates an intimidating and offensive work environment

According to the EEOC, **sexual harassment** is a form of discrimination in which unwelcome sexual advances, requests for sexual favors, or other verbal or physical conduct of a sexual nature occur. From a legal perspective, there are two kinds of sexual harassment, quid pro quo and hostile work environment.[30]

Quid pro quo sexual harassment occurs when employment outcomes, such as hiring, promotion, or simply keeping one's job, depend on whether an individual submits to being sexually harassed. For example, in a quid pro quo sexual harassment lawsuit against Prudential Insurance, a female employee alleged that she was repeatedly propositioned for sexual favors by her boss, and that when she refused, he said that "she would not amount to anything in this business without his help."[31] By contrast, a **hostile work environment** occurs when unwelcome and demeaning sexually related behavior creates an intimidating, hostile, and offensive work environment. One example of a hostile work environment was a Sears manager who would ask his female subordinates to step into his office to look at close-up photos of women's breasts and bottoms that he had taken while on vacation at a beach.[32] Or at Prudential, the same manager who was alleged to have engaged in quid pro quo harassment was also alleged to have made inappropriate sexual comments about women in front of female workers, to have allowed the display of pornographic material on company computers, and to have permitted the posting of a sign saying, "Sexual harassment will not be tolerated, it will be graded."[33]

What common mistakes do managers make when it comes to sexual harassment laws?[34] First, many assume that the victim and harasser must be of the opposite sex. According to the courts, they do not. Sexual harassment can also occur between people of the same sex. Second, it is assumed that sexual harassment can occur only between co-workers or between supervisors and subordinates. Not so. Sexual harassers can also include agents of employers, such as consultants, and can even include nonemployees. The key is not employee status but whether the harassment takes place while conducting company business. Third, it is often assumed that only people who have themselves been harassed can file complaints or lawsuits. In fact, especially in hostile work environments, anyone affected by offensive conduct can file a complaint or lawsuit.

Finally, what should companies do to make sure that sexual harassment laws are followed and not violated?[35] First, respond immediately when sexual harassment is reported. A quick response encourages victims of sexual harassment to report problems to management rather than to lawyers or the EEOC. Furthermore, a quick and fair investigation may serve as a deterrent to future harassment. A lawyer for the EEOC said, "Worse than having no sexual harassment policy is a policy that is not followed. It's merely window dressing. You wind up with destroyed morale when people who come forward are ignored, ridiculed, retaliated against, or nothing happens to the harasser."[36] Next, take the time to write a clear, understandable sexual harassment policy that is strongly worded, gives specific examples of what constitutes sexual harassment, spells outs sanctions and punishments, and is widely publicized within the company. This lets potential harassers and victims know what will not be tolerated and how the firm will deal with harassment should it occur. Figure 14.2 provides an example of such a sexual harassment policy.

Figure 14.2 **Example of a Sexual Harassment Policy**

Sexual harassment is a form of sexual discrimination. Sexual harassment negatively affects job performance, productivity, morale and employment opportunities. Sexual harassment negatively affects (*your company's*) goodwill, community standing, and profitability. Sexual harassment is offensive, inappropriate, and illegal. (*your company*) prohibits the sexual harassment of its employees by management, co-workers, independent contractors, non-employees, vendors, and visitors. Sexual harassment will not be tolerated. Violators of our sexual harassment policy will be subject to disciplinary action, up to and including discharge.

Sexual harassment includes unwelcome sexual advances, requests for sexual favors, and other verbal and physical conduct of a sexual nature. Sexual harassment includes conduct that is based on a person's sex and alters the terms and conditions of that person's employment. Sexual harassment includes inappropriate conduct irrespective of whether the harasser and the person harassed are of different sexes or are of the same sex. Examples of sexual harassment include:

Employment decisions that are based on the submission to or the rejection of unwelcome sexual advances or requests for sexual favor;

Conduct of a sexual nature that unreasonably interferes with work performance;

Conduct of a sexual nature that creates an intimidating, hostile, or offensive work environment, including: unwelcome verbal comments, jokes, suggestions, or derogatory remarks based on sex; unwelcome leering, whistling, physical touching, pats, squeezes, repeated brushing against, or the impeding or blocking of one's movement; references regarding an individual's sex life or comments about an individual's sexual activities, deficiencies, or prowess; unwelcome visual harassment, sexually suggestive or derogatory pictures, drawings, or cartoons; and unwelcome communications, notes, phone calls, and e-mail.

Employees are encouraged to take action when sexual harassment occurs.

Any employee who believes that he/she is being harassed should take the following action:

1. Where appropriate, express your discomfort to the harasser. Speak to the harasser about his/her conduct or behavior. State firmly and specifically what action you find objectionable and what you want stopped. Please respond immediately to the offending conduct or behavior. Do NOT ignore the problem.

2. Where appropriate, notify your supervisor or manager immediately. We want to respond to and remedy your problem. By notifying us of improper conduct we can respond more quickly.

NOTE: You should always feel free to bypass your supervisor and report instances of sexual harassment to (*name, address, and telephone number of senior management*). This individual is also available to provide information and to answer questions about our sexual harassment policy.

3. If a non-employee harasses you, immediately report the incident to your supervisor. Sexual harassment by non-employees, including visitors, vendors, or customers, will not be tolerated.

4. Keep your supervisor or (*member of management*) informed of any repeat occurrences after the harasser has been notified that his/her conduct is offensive.

The creation of a harassment-free workplace is the responsibility of all managers, supervisors, and employees. You should be aware of how fellow employees react to your comments and actions. If a fellow employee objects to or seems uncomfortable with your conduct, heed the objection and discontinue the conduct that may be objectionable. Remember that what is acceptable behavior to some employees may not be acceptable to others.

Any manager, supervisor, or employee who witnesses or becomes aware of instances of sexual harassment must report such instances to his or her supervisor or to senior management. Violations of this reporting requirement may be grounds for disciplinary action, up to and including discharge.

Retaliation against an individual for reporting an instance of sexual harassment, for cooperating in an investigation, or for helping to achieve the purposes of this policy is prohibited and may be grounds for disciplinary action, up to and including discharge.

All complaints of sexual harassment will be investigated promptly and thoroughly. To the extent practicable under the circumstance, information related to the complaint will be held in confidence and will only be disclosed on a "need-to-know" basis. If an investigation reveals that sexual harassment has occurred, disciplinary action will be taken to stop the harassment and to prevent harassment in the future.

No action will be taken against any individual who makes a good faith complaint, or against any individual participating in the investigation or the enforcement of this policy. However, any individual who knowingly makes a false claim of sexual harassment may be subject to appropriate disciplinary action, up to and including discharge.

If you have any questions or comments, please contact: (*member of management*).

Source: Anonymous, "XYZ Printing Sexual Harassment," *American Printer* 222, no. 1 (1998): 166-167.

Next, clear reporting procedures that indicate how, where, and to whom incidents of sexual harassment can be reported should also be established. The best procedures ensure a quick response, that impartial parties will handle the complaint, and that the privacy of the accused and accusers will be protected. At Du Pont, employees can call a confidential hotline 24 hours a day, 365 days a year.

Finally, managers should also be aware that most states and many cities or local governments have their own employment-related laws and enforcement agencies. So, compliance with federal law is often not enough. In fact, organizations can be in full compliance with federal law, while at the same time violating state or local sexual harassment laws.

Review 2
Employment Legislation

Human resource management is subject to the following major federal employment laws: Equal Pay Act, Civil Rights Acts of 1964 and 1991, Age Discrimination in Employment Act, Pregnancy Discrimination Act, Americans with Disabilities Act, and Family and Medical Leave Act. HR management is also subject to review by these federal agencies: Equal Employment Opportunity Commission, Department of Labor, Occupational Safety and Health Administration, and National Labor Relations Board. In general, these laws indicate that gender, age, religion, color, national origin, race, disability, and pregnancy may not be considered in employment decisions unless these factors reasonably qualify as a BFOQ. Two important criteria, disparate treatment (intentional discrimination) and adverse impact (unintentional discrimination), are used to decide whether companies have wrongly discriminated against someone. While motive is a key part of determining disparate treatment, the courts and federal enforcement agencies use the four-fifths rule to determine if adverse impact has occurred.

The two kinds of sexual harassment are quid pro quo and hostile work environment. Managers often wrongly assume that the victim and harasser must be of the opposite sex, that sexual harassment can only occur between co-workers or between supervisors and their employees, and that only people who have themselves been harassed can file complaints or lawsuits. To make sure that sexual harassment laws are followed, companies should respond immediately when harassment is reported, write a clear, understandable sexual harassment policy, establish clear reporting procedures, and be aware of and follow city and state laws concerning sexual harassment.

Finding Qualified Workers

In Orlando, Florida, home to major attractions such as Walt Disney World, EPCOT center, and Universal Studios Florida, the local unemployment rate was less than 3 percent. Finding qualified workers was so difficult that Moira Oliver, human resources director for the Orlando Hyatt Regency hotel, recruited maids and laundry workers from Poland, Hungary, and the Ukraine. She also traveled to Switzerland and France to visit cooking schools, where she hoped to convince top students to do their cooking internships in the Orlando Hyatt's kitchens.[37] The situation was even more desperate on Wall Street, where Charles Schwab Corp., a stock brokerage firm, paid $94,500 for a full page advertisement in *The Wall Street Journal* to recruit the 1,000 new workers that it needed to meet the incredible growth of its online Internet service and its traditional branch offices. "We do need lots of employees, and we continue to grow on all fronts," said Schwab Co-Chief Executive David S. Pottruck.[38]

As these examples illustrate, finding qualified workers in today's tight labor market is an increasingly difficult task. However, finding qualified applicants is just the first step. Selecting which applicants to hire is the second. CEO John Chambers of Cisco Systems, the leading designer and manufacturer of high-tech equipment that serves as the backbone of the Internet, said, "Cisco has an overall goal of getting the top 10% to 15% of people in our industry. Our philosophy is very simple—if you get the best people in the industry to fit into your culture and you motivate them properly, then you're going to be an industry leader."[39]

After reading the next two sections, you should be able to:

3 explain how companies use **recruiting** to find qualified job applicants.

4 describe the **selection** techniques and procedures that companies use when deciding which applicants should receive job offers.

3 Recruiting

recruiting
the process of developing a pool of qualified job applicants

Recruiting is the process of developing a pool of qualified job applicants.

Let's examine **3.1** *what job analysis is and how it is used in recruiting, and how companies use* **3.2** *internal recruitment and* **3.3** *external recruiting to find qualified job applicants.*

3.1
Job Analysis and Recruiting

Job analysis is a "purposeful, systematic process for collecting information on the important work-related aspects of a job."[40] Typically, a job analysis collects four kinds of information:

job analysis
a purposeful, systematic process for collecting information on the important work-related aspects of a job

job description
a written description of the basic tasks, duties, and responsibilities required of an employee holding a particular job

job specifications
a written summary of the qualifications needed to successfully perform a particular job

- work activities, such as what workers do and how, when, and why they do it,
- the tools and equipment used to do the job,
- the context in which the job is performed, such as the actual working conditions or schedule, and
- the personnel requirements for performing the job, meaning the knowledge, skills, and abilities needed to do a job well.[41]

Job analysis information can be collected by having job incumbents and/or supervisors complete questionnaires about their jobs, by direct observation, by interviews, or by filming employees as they perform their jobs.

Job descriptions and job specifications are two of the most important results of a job analysis. A **job description** is a written description of the basic tasks, duties, and responsibilities required of an employee holding a particular job. **Job specifications**, which are often included as a separate section of a job description, are a summary of the qualifications needed to successfully perform the job. Figure 14.3 shows a job description and the job specifications for a general recreation leader for the City of Seattle's Parks and Recreation Department.

Figure 14.3

Job Description and Job Specifications for a General Recreation Leader for the City of Seattle's Parks and Recreation Department

Job Description for General Recreation Leader (40 hrs/wk):

General recreation leaders are responsible for a broad range of programs including but not limited to indoor/outdoor recreation activities (educational and recreational), athletic skills development and competitions, aquatics, special events and family programs, drop-in activities, seasonal and major community gatherings. Leaders will organize, plan, implement, and lead activities; handle all administrative aspects including registration, financial administration and budgeting, collection of performance measures and other statistics, and evaluation. Leaders will have lead responsibilities for Recreation Attendants, seasonal workers and volunteers assigned. They will maintain personal contacts with the public, including interaction with participants, parents, volunteers, and employees of off-site program locations, and staff at other departments or community agencies to coordinate program activities or facility use. General leaders will be required to meet the performance measures for their program area and support the facility efforts to achieve performance measures.

Job Specifications for General Recreation Leader (40 hrs/wk):

Required Qualifications: The equivalent of one year of experience in a community-based recreation program and an Associate Degree in Recreation, Therapeutic Recreation, or related field (or a combination of education and/or training and/or experience which provides an equivalent background required to perform the work of the class). Washington State Driver's License.

Desired Qualifications: One year of experience in planning and implementing a program budget, developing programmatic timelines, anticipating all aspects of events and programs, collecting fees and registering participants, keeping accurate financial, demographic and programmatic statistics, evaluating programs, and seeking assistance from outside resources. Competitive candidates will be able to demonstrate a history of developing programs to meet the community needs of a diverse, urban population, and possess skills in the following areas: conflict resolution, use of computer programs, customer service, and proficiency in a language other than English. Knowledge of youth development and marketing/publicity is important. Food Handler's Permit, Red Cross First Aid and Community CPR certification.

Source: City of Seattle Parks and Recreation Department, "Recreation Leader." [Online] Available **http://www.ci.seattle.wa.us/jobs/Prks%20Rec%20Leader.htm**, 25 May 1999.

Figure 14.4 **Importance of Job Analysis to Human Resource Management**

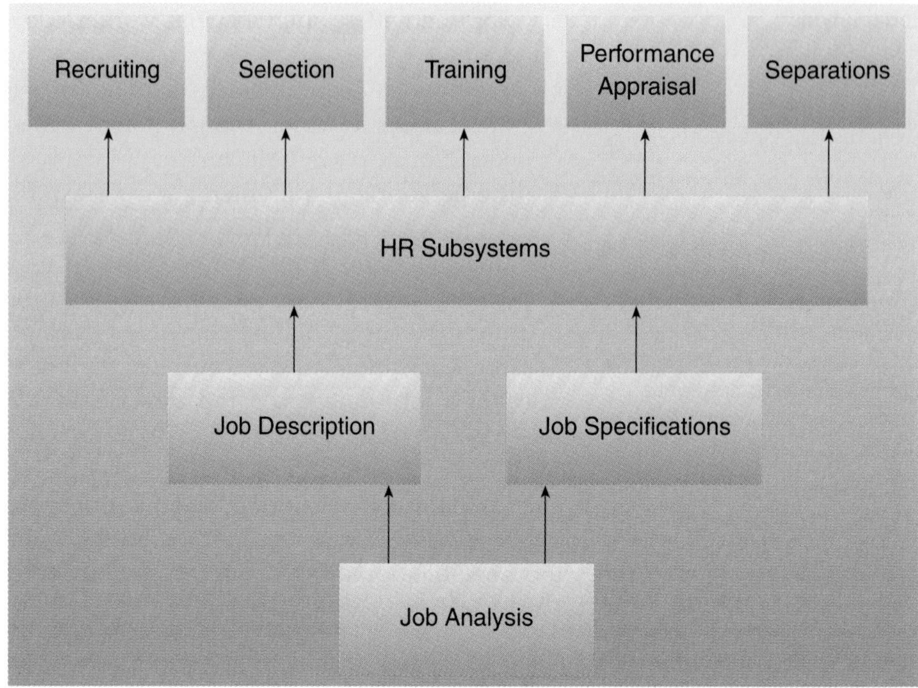

Because a job analysis clearly specifies what a job entails, as well as the knowledge, skills, and ability that are needed to do a job well, companies must complete a job analysis *before* beginning to recruit job applicants. Figure 14.4 shows that job analysis, job descriptions, and job specifications are the foundation on which all critical human resource activities are built. They are used during recruiting and selection to match applicant qualifications with the requirements of the job. They are used throughout the staffing process to ensure that selection devices and the decisions based on these devices are job related. For example, the questions asked in an interview should be based on the most important work activities identified by a job analysis. Likewise, during performance appraisals, employees should be evaluated in areas that a job analysis has identified as the most important in a job.

Job analyses, job descriptions, and job specifications also help companies meet the legal requirement that their human resource decisions be job related. To be judged *job related*, recruitment, selection, training, performance appraisals, and employee separations must be valid and be directly related to the important aspects of the job, as identified by a careful job analysis. In fact, in *Griggs v. Duke Power Co.* and *Albemarle Paper Co. v. Moody*, the U.S. Supreme Court ruled that job analyses should be used to help companies establish the job relatedness of their human resource procedures.[42] The EEOC's *Uniform Guidelines on Employee Selection Procedures* also recommend that companies base their human resource procedures on job analysis.

3.2 *Internal Recruiting*

internal recruiting the process of developing a pool of qualified job applicants from people who already work in the company

Internal recruiting is the process of developing a pool of qualified job applicants from people who already work in the company. Internal recruiting, sometimes called "promotion from within," improves employee commitment, morale, and motivation. Recruiting current employees also reduces recruitment startup time and costs and, because employees are already familiar with the company's culture and procedures, generally increases workers' chances of success in new jobs. Kotak Mahindra Finance, a Japanese company, cuts costs by using internal recruitment first before looking outside the company for qualified applicants. SmithKline Beecham Consumer Healthcare internally recruits 20 first-level managers each year to keep recruiting costs low and to keep talented people in the company.[43] Job posting and career paths are two methods of internal recruiting.

Job posting is a procedure for advertising job openings within the company to existing employees. A job description and requirements are typically posted on a bulletin board, in a company newsletter, or in an internal computerized job bank that is only accessible to employees. Job posting helps organizations discover hidden talent, allows employees to take responsibility for career planning, and makes it easier for companies to retain talented workers who are dissatisfied in their current jobs and would otherwise leave the company.[44] Baxter HealthCare calls its job posting program the "Inside Advantage Program." Baxter employees can access this program via an automated telephone prompting system. To encourage employee retention, Baxter now uses its Inside Advantage Program to highlight its new work flexibility plan, where employees can search for jobs that permit compressed workweeks, job sharing, part-time work, or telecommuting.[45]

A *career path* is a planned sequence of jobs through which employees may advance within an organization. For example, a person who starts as a sales representative may then move up to sales manager, and then to district or regional sales manager. Career paths help employees focus on long-term goals and development while also helping companies do succession or replacement planning. For instance, one of the disadvantages of internal recruitment is that it sets off a domino effect of job changes. When an internal employee changes jobs within a company, this person fills one job opening but automatically creates another. Career paths help companies deal with these changes by quickly identifying possible replacements as job openings ricochet through an organization. Coca-Cola deals with this problem by making sure that all of its managers are developing replacements at least two levels below their current position. Ian Pinto, senior HR manager for Coca-Cola of India, said, "This enables us to cut the costs associated with scrambling for replacements when people leave, or are moved up or sideways."[46]

3.3 *External Recruiting*

external recruiting
the process of developing a pool of qualified job applicants from outside the company

External recruiting is the process of developing a pool of qualified job applicants from outside the company. External recruitment methods include advertising (newspapers, magazines, direct mail, radio, or television), employee referrals (asking current employees to recommend possible job applicants), walk-ins (people who apply on their own), outside organizations (universities, technical/trade schools, professional societies), employment services (state or private employment agencies, temporary agencies, and professional search firms), special events (career conferences or job fairs), and Internet job sites.

Which external recruiting method should you use? Studies show that employee referrals, walk-ins, newspaper advertisements, and state employment agencies tend to be used most frequently for office/clerical and production/service employees. By contrast, newspaper advertisements and college/university recruiting are used most frequently for professional/technical employees. When recruiting managers, organizations tend to rely most heavily on newspaper advertisements, employee referrals, and search firms.[47]

PersonalProductivityTip

Creating an Electronic Resume

Having your resume in an electronic format allows you to quickly apply for a large number of jobs through the Internet. To make your resume universally accessible, use a word processor, but don't format with bold or italic. Instead, use asterisks (*), plus symbols (+), and CAPITAL letters. Set margins to 65 characters, so you can e-mail your resume without reformatting it. Use the "Save As" command to save your resume in ASCII or MS-DOS Text format. Send your resume and cover letter in one file. Use the job title or reference number in the subject line.

Source: Career Builder, "Electronic Resumes." [Online] Available **http://www.careerbuilder.com/gh_res_htg_elec.html**, 9 July 1999.

However, in the last few years the biggest changes in external recruiting have come as a result of the Internet. For example, Cisco Systems no longer runs newspaper help-wanted ads. Instead, it takes out simple newspaper ads that direct recruits to its Web site (**http://www.cisco.com/jobs**), where they can see hundreds of job descriptions, learn in detail about Cisco's highly competitive benefits, and submit an online resume.[48] In addition to extensive job information on corporate Web sites, some companies have begun subscribing to Internet job sites such as The Monster Board (**http://www.monster.com**), Career Mosaic (**http://www.careermosaic.com**), and CareerBuilder (**http://www.careerbuilder.com**). For just $2,000 to $2,500 per month, companies can advertise up to 100 job openings and reach millions of job applicants worldwide. By contrast, a simple, one-day, quarter-page ad in the *Washington Post* would cost about $6,000. According to Rob McGovern of CareerBuilder, the average cost of using the Net to recruit an employee is about $900, compared to the average cost of $8,000 through more traditional external recruitment methods. Said McGovern, "We are one-tenth of the cost of newspaper advertising," plus there are no agency fees or commissions or advertising costs.[49] In addition to greatly reduced costs, the Internet allows companies to quickly reach large numbers of people. For instance, Computer Sciences Corporation listed 200 jobs on its Web site and received over 8,000 resumes.[50]

Despite its promise, there are some disadvantages to Internet recruiting. The main drawback (which some companies consider a plus) is that Internet recruiting is unlikely to reach recruits who don't use or have access to the Internet. And, since it is so easy for applicants to apply, companies may receive hundreds, if not thousands, of applications from unqualified applicants, which increases the importance of proper screening and selection. Furthermore, if the proper security precautions aren't taken, there is also the danger of violating employee/applicant privacy.[51] Still, despite these disadvantages, companies are expected to make even more use of the Internet for external recruiting. It's predicted that 20 percent of all external job recruiting will be done via the Internet by 2005.

Review 3
Recruiting

Recruiting is the process of finding qualified job applicants. The first step in recruiting is to conduct a job analysis to collect information about the important work-related aspects of the job. The job analysis is then used to write a job description of basic tasks, duties, and responsibilities and to write job specifications indicating the knowledge, skills, and abilities needed to perform the job. Job analyses, descriptions, and specifications help companies meet the legal requirement that their human resource decisions be job related. Internal recruiting, finding qualified job applicants from inside the company, can be done through job posting and career paths. External recruiting, finding qualified job applicants from outside the company, is done through advertising, employee referrals, walk-ins, outside organizations, employment services, special events, and Internet job sites. The Internet is a particularly promising method of external recruiting because of its low cost, wide reach, and ability to communicate and receive unlimited information.

4 Selection

Once the recruitment process has produced a pool of qualified applicants, the selection process is used to determine which applicants have the best chance of performing well on the job. Tom Blangiardo, president of Basic Education and Training Associations (BETA group) in Fishers, Indiana, uses a fairly typical selection process to hire telemarketers to sell the company's educational videos. "For every ad we place, we get about 100 applicants. I interview everyone over the phone, because the way you come across on the phone is very important here. I evaluate voice tone, friendliness, and persuasiveness." Around 30 to 40 candidates are then chosen for group interviews. Managers explain BETA Group's philosophy and benefits and show the candidates examples of the videos they'll be selling. After the group interviews, 9 candidates are typically eliminated, 6 receive job offers, and 15 go on to individual interviews with human resource director John Brown. During the individual interview, candidates are asked to role-play a sales call. Another 7 applicants are lost at this stage. The 10 to 15 survivors are hired and put through a one-week orientation program that includes product and technology training, practice taking live calls, and more role playing. "We put people on the hot seat to see how they behave," says Kara O'Connor, BETA Group's employee training manager. After 30 to 60 days, about half of these survivors leave because it's either too intense for them, or they're just not selling enough.[52]

selection
the process of gathering information about job applicants to decide who should be offered a job

validation
the process of determining how well a selection test or procedure predicts future job performance. The better or more accurate the prediction of future job performance, the more valid a test is said to be.

As this example illustrates, **selection** is the process of gathering information about job applicants to decide who should be offered a job. To make sure that selection decisions are accurate and legally defendable, the *Uniform Guidelines on Employee Selection Procedures* recommend that all selection procedures be validated. **Validation** is the process of determining how well a selection test or procedure predicts future job performance. The better or more accurate the prediction of future job performance, the more valid a test is said to be. See the "What Really Works" section of this chapter for more on the validity of common selection tests and procedures.

Let's examine common selection procedures, such as **4.1** *application forms and resumes,* **4.2** *references and background checks,* **4.3** *selection tests, and* **4.4** *interviews.*

4.1 *Application Forms and Resumes*

The first selection devices that most job applicants encounter when they seek a job are application forms and resumes. Both contain similar information about job applicants, such as name, address, job and educational history, etc. While an organization's application form often asks for information already provided by the resume, most organizations prefer to collect this information in their own format for entry into a human resource information system.

Employment-related laws apply to application forms, as they do all selection devices. Application forms may ask applicants about only valid, job-related information. However, application forms commonly ask applicants to report non-job-related information, such as marital status, maiden name, age, or date of high school graduation. Indeed, one study found that 73 percent of organizations have application forms that violate at least one federal or state law.[53] Table 14.4 presents a list of the kinds of information that companies may not request in application forms, during job interviews, or in any other part of the selection process. Attorney Tiberio Trimmer said, "Your objective is to hire someone qualified to perform the requirements of the job. Not asking things that are peripheral to the work itself helps you to stay on the right side of the law."[54] Consequently, most companies should closely examine their application forms for compliance with the law.

Resumes also pose problems for companies, but in a different way. Studies show as many as one out of every three job applicants falsifies some information on his or her resume. The items most frequently falsified are job

Table 14.4

Topics That Employers Should Avoid in Application Blanks, Interviews, or Other Parts of the Selection Process

1. *Children*—Don't ask applicants if they have children, plan to have them, or have or need childcare. Questions about children can unintentionally single out women.
2. *Age*—Because of the Age Discrimination Act, employers cannot ask job applicants their age during the hiring process. Since most people graduate high school at the age of 18, even asking for high school graduation dates could violate the law.
3. *Disabilities*—Don't ask if applicants have physical or mental disabilities. According to the Americans with Disabilities Act, disabilities (and reasonable accommodations for them) cannot be discussed until a job offer has been made.
4. *Physical Characteristics*—Don't ask for information about height, weight, or other physical characteristics. Questions about weight could somehow be construed as leading to discrimination toward overweight people, who studies show are less likely to be hired in general.
5. *Name*—Yes, you can ask people for their name, but you cannot ask female applicants for their maiden name because it indicates marital status. Asking for a maiden name could also lead to charges that the organization was trying to establish a candidate's ethnic background.
6. *Citizenship*—Asking applicants about citizenship could lead to claims of discrimination on the basis of national origin. However, according to the Immigration Reform and Control Act, companies may ask applicants if they have a legal right to work in the U.S.
7. *Lawsuits*—Applicants may not be asked if they have ever filed a lawsuit against an employer. Federal and state laws prevent this so that whistleblowers may be protected from retaliation by future employers.
8. *Arrest Records*—Applicants cannot be asked about their arrest records. Arrests don't have legal standing. However, applicants can be asked whether they have been convicted of a crime.
9. *Smoking*—Applicants cannot be asked if they smoke. Smokers might be able to claim that they weren't hired because of fears of higher absenteeism and medical costs. However, they can be asked if they are aware of company policies which restrict smoking at work.
10. *AIDS/HIV*—Applicants can't be asked about AIDS, HIV, or any other medical condition. Questions of this nature would violate the Americans with Disabilities Act, as well as federal and state civil rights laws.

Source: J.S. Pouliot, "Topics to Avoid with Applicants," *Nation's Business* 80, no. 7 (1992): 57.

employment references sources such as previous employers or co-workers who can provide job-related information about job candidates

background checks procedures used to verify the truthfulness and accuracy of information that applicants provide about themselves and to uncover negative, job-related background information not provided by applicants

responsibilities, job titles, previous salary, and the length of employment on previous jobs. Other frequently falsified information includes educational background, academic degrees, and college majors and minors.[55] Therefore, managers should verify the information collected via resumes and application forms by comparing it with additional information collected during interviews and other stages of the selection process. Another way to check resume information is to hire a private firm to do it. Costs vary but can often be as low as $50 per person. Cynthia Myers, who runs a company that verifies resume information, said that companies can discourage false resumes by including this warning in their application forms and recruiting literature: "All information on this form is checked by a national agency that specializes in checking credentials. If any false claims are uncovered, that applicant will no longer be considered for a position."[56]

4.2 *References and Background Checks*

Nearly all companies ask applicants to provide **employment references,** such as previous employers or co-workers, that they can contact to learn more about job candidates. **Background checks** are used to verify the truthfulness and accuracy of information that applicants provide about themselves and to uncover negative, job-related background information not provided by applicants. Background checks are conducted by contacting "educational institutions, prior employers, court records, police and governmental agencies and other informational sources, either by telephone, mail, remote computer access or through in-person investigations."[57]

Unfortunately, previous employers are increasingly reluctant to provide references or background check information for fear of being sued by previous employees for defamation. If former employers provide unsubstantiated information to potential employers that damages applicants' chances of being hired, applicants can (and do) sue for defamation. As a result, many employers are reluctant to provide information about previous employees. Many provide only dates of employment, positions held, and date of separation.

When previous employers decline to provide meaningful references or background information, they put other employers at risk of *negligent hiring* lawsuits, in which employers are held liable for the actions of employees who should not have been hired had employers conducted thorough reference searches and background checks. For example, a company in Missouri hired an employee who had previously served time in a Missouri prison for a rape and robbery conviction. After being hired, this employee then raped and killed a secretary. The secretary's parents sued the company, claiming that the company either knew or should have known about the employee's previous conviction. A Missouri Court of Appeals ruled that the parents had the right to sue the company for negligence in its hiring practices.[58]

With previous employers generally unwilling to give full, candid references, and with negligent hiring lawsuits awaiting companies that don't get full, candid references and background information, what can companies do? Dig deeper for more information. Ask references to provide references. Voca Corporation, based in Columbus, Ohio, has 2,500 employees in six states, who care for people with mental retardation and developmental disabilities. Hilary Franklin, director of human resources, said she not only checks references, but she also asks the references to provide references,

Personal Productivity Tip

Using a Reference Release Form

Employment references are often reluctant to talk. Encourage them to share information by having applicants sign a reference release form like this.

I have applied for employment with [company name] and have listed you as a reference. Please provide answers to the following questions and return this form to [company contact] in the enclosed envelope. By this authorization, I hereby release you from any liability or action based upon the content of your answers.

Thank you for your cooperation and assistance.

Sincerely yours,

[candidate signature]

[date]

And when references talk, listen carefully to how they answer the questions (e.g., hesitancy, damning with faint praise).

Source: B. Weinstein, "Tips for Getting References to Talk," *Career. WSJ.Com.* [Online] Available **http://public.wsj.com/careers/resources/documents/19980909-weinstein.htm**, 9 July 1999.

and asks those references for still others. She said, "As you get two or three times removed, you get more detailed, honest information."

Next, ask in writing before checking references or running a background check. Before Voca runs a background check, it asks applicants if there is anything they would like the company to know. This, in itself, is often enough to get applicants to share information that they previously withheld. Voca also keeps its findings confidential to minimize the chances of a defamation charge.[59]

Always document all reference and background checks, who was called and what information was obtained. And to reduce the success of negligent hiring lawsuits, it's particularly important to document which companies and people refused to share reference check and background information.

Finally, consider hiring private investigators to conduct background checks. Pinkerton performs more than a million such checks a year and estimates that its background investigation business is growing by 30 percent per year.[60]

4.3
Selection Tests

Why do some people do well on jobs while other people do poorly? If only you could know before deciding who to hire! Selection tests give organizational decision makers a chance to know who will likely do well in a job and who won't. The basic idea behind selection testing is to have applicants take a test that measures something directly or indirectly related to doing well on the job. The selection tests discussed here are specific ability tests, cognitive ability tests, biographical data, personality tests, work sample tests, and assessment centers.

specific ability tests (aptitude tests)
tests that measure the extent to which an applicant possesses the particular kind of ability needed to do a job well

Specific ability tests are tests that measure the extent to which an applicant possesses the particular kind of ability needed to do a job well. Specific ability tests are also called **aptitude tests**, because they measure aptitude for doing a particular task well. For example, if you took the SAT to get into college, then you've taken the aptly named Scholastic Aptitude Test, which is one of the best predictors of how well students will do in college (i.e., scholastic performance). Specific ability tests also exist for mechanical, clerical, sales, and physical work. For example, clerical workers have to be good at accurately reading and scanning numbers as they type or enter data. Table 14.5 shows items similar to the Minnesota Clerical Test, in which applicants have only a short time to determine if the two columns of numbers and letters are identical. Applicants who are good at this would likely be better clerical or data-entry workers.

cognitive ability tests
tests that measure the extent to which applicants have abilities in perceptual speed, verbal comprehension, numerical aptitude, general reasoning, and spatial aptitude

Cognitive ability tests measure the extent to which applicants have abilities in perceptual speed, verbal comprehension, numerical aptitude, general reasoning, and spatial aptitude. In other words, these tests indicate how quickly and how well people understand words, numbers, logic, and spatial dimensions. While specific ability tests predict job performance in only particular types of jobs, cognitive ability tests accurately predict job performance in almost all kinds of jobs.[61] Why is this so? Because people with strong cognitive or mental abilities are usually good at learning new things, processing complex information, and solving problems and making decisions, and these abilities are important in almost all jobs to some extent. And not only do cognitive ability tests predict job performance well in almost all kinds of jobs, but they are almost always the best predictors of job per-

Table 14.5

Example Clerical Test Items, Similar to Those Found on the Minnesota Clerical Test

Numbers/Letters		*Same*	
1. 3468251	3467251	Yes	No
2. 4681371	4681371	Yes	No
3. 7218510	7218520	Yes	No
4. ZXYAZAB	ZXYAZAB	Yes	No
5. ALZYXMN	ALZYXNM	Yes	No
6 PRQZYMN	PRQZYMN	Yes	No

Source: N.W. Schmitt & R.J. Klimoski, *Research Methods in Human Resources Management* (Cincinnati, OH: South-Western Publishing Co., 1991).

formance. Consequently, if you were allowed to use just one selection test, cognitive ability tests would be the one to use. (In practice, though, companies use a battery of different tests, because this leads to much more accurate selection decisions.)

biographical data (biodata)
extensive surveys that ask applicants questions about their personal backgrounds and life experiences

Biographical data, or **biodata**, are extensive surveys that ask applicants questions about their personal backgrounds and life experiences. The basic idea behind biodata is that past behavior (personal background and life experience) is the best predictor of future behavior. For example, during World War II, the U.S. Air Force had to quickly test tens of thousands of men without flying experience to determine who was likely to be a good pilot. Since flight training took several months and was very expensive, selecting the right people for training was important. After examining extensive biodata, it found that one of the best predictors of success in flight school was whether flight students had ever built model airplanes that actually flew. This one biodata item was almost as good a predictor as the entire set of selection tests that the Air Force was using at the time.[62]

Most biodata questionnaires have over 100 items that gather information about habits and attitudes, health, interpersonal relations, money, what it was like growing up in your family (parents, siblings, childhood years, teen years), personal habits, current home (spouse, children), hobbies, education and training, values, preferences, and work.[63] In general, biodata are very good predictors of future job performance, especially in entry-level jobs.

You may have noticed that some of the information requested in biodata surveys also appears in Table 14.4 as topics employers should avoid in application blanks, interviews, or other parts of the selection process. This information can be requested in biodata questionnaires provided that companies can demonstrate that the information is job related (i.e., valid) and does not result in adverse impact against protected groups of job applicants. Biodata surveys should be validated and tested for adverse impact before using them to make selection decisions.[64]

personality tests
tests that measure the extent to which applicants possess different kinds of job-related personality dimensions

Personality is the relatively stable set of behaviors, attitudes, and emotions displayed over time that makes people different from each other. **Personality tests** measure the extent to which applicants possess different kinds of job-related personality dimensions. In Chapter 12, you learned that there are five major personality dimensions (the Big 5)—extraversion, emotional stability, agreeableness, conscientiousness, and openness to experience—that are related to work behavior.[65] Of these, only conscientiousness, the degree to which someone is organized, hardworking, responsible, persevering, thorough, and achievement oriented, predicts job performance across a wide variety of jobs. Conscientiousness works especially well in combination with cognitive ability tests, allowing companies to select applicants who are organized, hard-working, responsible, and smart!

work sample tests
tests that require applicants to perform tasks that are actually done on the job

Work sample tests, also called *performance tests*, require applicants to perform tasks that are actually done on the job. So unlike specific ability, cognitive ability, biographical data, and personality tests, which are indirect predictors of job performance, work sample tests directly measure job applicants' capability to do the job. At Microtraining Plus, a Norwalk, Connecticut, company that does computer training, employee-trainers have to be able to get up in front of people they don't know and present complex information in a clear, interesting way. Therefore, CEO David Knise uses work sample tests by having job candidates make hour-long presentations to his eight-person staff on any topic other than computers. He believes that since they're all computer people, they'd focus too much on content and not on delivery. By asking applicants to give an hour-long presentation, "We see how applicants organize their thoughts, if they've given themselves enough time to cover the material, and if they have overall command of a classroom."[66] These work sample presentations give Microtraining direct evidence of whether job candidates can do the job if they are hired. Work sample tests generally do a very good job of predicting future job performance, however they can be expensive to administer and can be used for only one kind of job. For example, at an auto dealership, a work sample test for mechanics could not be used as a selection test for sales representatives.

assessment centers
a series of managerial simulations, graded by trained observers, that are used to determine applicants' capability for managerial work

Assessment centers use a series of job-specific simulations that are graded by multiple trained observers to determine the extent to which applicants can perform managerial work. So unlike the previously described selection tests commonly used for specific jobs or entry-level jobs, assessment centers are most often used to select applicants who have high potential to be good managers. Assessment centers often last two to five days and require participants to complete a number of tests and exercises that simulate managerial work.

Some of the more common assessment center exercises are in-basket exercises, role plays, small-group presentations, and leaderless group discussion. An *in-basket exercise* is a paper-and-pencil test in which an applicant is given the contents of a manager's "in-basket," which contains memos, phone messages, organizational policies, and other communication normally received by and available to managers. Applicants have a limited time to read through the in-basket, prioritize the items, and decide how to deal with each item. Experienced managers then score applicants' decisions and recommendations. Figure 14.5 shows an item that could be used in an assessment center for assessing applicants for the job of high school principal.

In a *leaderless group discussion*, which is another common assessment center exercise, a group of six applicants is given approximately two hours to solve a problem, but no one is put in charge (hence the name "leaderless" group discussion). Trained observers watch and score each participant on the extent to which he or she facilitates discussion, listens, leads, persuades, and works well with others.

Are tests perfect predictors of job performance? No, they aren't. Some people who do well on selection tests will do poorly in their jobs. Likewise, some people who do poorly on selection tests (and should have been hired, but

Figure 14.5 **In-Basket Item for an Assessment Center for High School Principals**

February 28

R. A. Howard, Principal
Avon High School

Dear Mr. Principal,

I have observed a number of high school students smoking dope on my property during and after school hours.

Yesterday, I was startled to see a group of students amusing themselves by breaking pop bottles in the empty lot adjacent to my home. I went outside and yelled to them to get off of my property.

If you dont' take any action, I'm going to the police. I'm fed up with this!

Sincerely,
Jean Wagner

Source: N.W. Schmitt & R.J. Klimoski, *Research Methods in Human Resources Management* (Cincinnati, OH: South-Western Publishing Co., 1991).

weren't) would have been very good performers. However, valid tests will minimize these selection errors (hiring people who should not have been hired, and not hiring people who should have been hired) while maximizing correct selection decisions (hiring people who should have been hired, and not hiring people who should not have been hired). In short, tests increase the chances that you'll hire the right person for the job, that is, someone who turns out to be a good performer. So while tests aren't perfect, almost nothing predicts future job performance as well as the selection tests discussed here. For more on how well selection tests increase the odds of hiring the right person for the job, see the "What Really Works" section of this chapter.

4.4 *Interviews*

interviews
selection tool in which company representatives ask job applicants job-related questions to determine whether they are qualified for the job

In **interviews**, company representatives ask job applicants job-related questions to determine whether they are qualified for the job. Interviews are probably the most frequently used and relied on selection device. There are several basic kinds of interviews: unstructured, structured, and semi-structured.

In *unstructured interviews*, interviewers are free to ask applicants anything they want, and studies show that they do. For instance, because interviewers often disagree about which questions should be asked during interviews, different interviewers tend to ask applicants very different questions.[67] Furthermore, individual interviewers even seem to have a tough time asking the same questions from one interview to the next. This high level of inconsistency lowers the validity of unstructured interviews as a selection device, because it becomes difficult to compare applicant responses. As a result, unstructured interviews do about half as well as structured interviews in accurately predicting which job applicants should be hired.

structured interviews
interviews in which all applicants are asked the same set of standardized questions, usually including situational, behavioral, background, and job-knowledge questions

By contrast, with **structured interviews**, standardized interview questions are prepared ahead of time, so that all applicants are asked the same job-related questions. Four kinds of questions are typically asked in structured interviews:

Personal Productivity Tip

Preparing for Structured Interviews

Structured interviews assume that past performance predicts future performance. Therefore, structured interview questions often begin with "Tell me about a time when. . . ." or "Give me an example of. . . ." Use the P-A-R (Problem-Action-Result) technique to prepare for structured interviews. Go through the job description and your resume line by line to think up examples and stories. Then write, edit, and rehearse them in the P-A-R format. And for variety, use the R-A-P approach, too. Start by describing your results. Then describe your actions. Finish by describing the problem you solved. You're less likely to be stumped by questions if you prepare in this way.

Source: A. Hirsh, "Tricky Questions Reign in Behavioral Interviews," *National Business Employment Weekly* (posted on **Careers.WSJ.com**). [Online] Available **http://public.wsj.com/careers/resources/documents/19990420-hirsch.htm**, 6 June 1999.

- *situational questions,* which ask applicants how they would respond in a hypothetical situation (e.g., "What would you do if . . . ?").
- *behavioral questions,* which ask applicants what they did in previous jobs that were similar to the job for which they are applying (e.g., "In your previous jobs, tell me about . . . ").
- *background questions,* which ask applicants about their work experience, education, and other qualifications (e.g., "Tell me about the training you received at . . . ").
- *job-knowledge questions,* which ask applicants to demonstrate their job knowledge (e.g., for nurses, "Give me an example of a time when one of your patients had a severe reaction to a medication. How did you handle it?").[68]

The primary advantage of structured interviews is that asking all applicants the same questions makes comparing applicants a much easier process. Structuring interviews also ensures that interviewers only ask for important, job-related information. These advantages not only improve the accuracy, usefulness, and validity of the interview, but also reduce the chances that interviewers will ask questions about topics that violate employment laws (go back to Table 14.4 for a list of these topics).

Semi-structured interviews lie somewhere in between structured and unstructured interviews. A major part of the semi-structured interview (perhaps as much as 80 percent) is based on structured questions. However, some time is set aside for unstructured interviewing to allow interviewers to probe into ambiguous or missing information uncovered during the structured portion of the interview.

How well do interviews predict future job performance? Contrary to what you've probably heard, recent evidence indicates that even unstructured interviews do a fairly good job. However, when conducted properly, structured interviews can lead to much more accurate hiring decisions than unstructured interviews. In some cases, the validity of structured interviews can rival that of cognitive ability tests. But even more important, since interviews are especially good at assessing applicants' interpersonal skills, they work especially well together with cognitive ability tests. The combination (i.e., smart people who work well with others) leads to even better selection decisions than using either alone. Table 14.6 provides a set of guidelines for conducting effective structured employment interviews.

What Really Works

Using Selection Tests to Hire Good Workers

Hiring new employees always seems like a gamble. When you speak the words "We'd like to offer you a job," you never know how it's going to turn out. However, the selection tests discussed in this chapter and reviewed in this section go a long way toward helping employers take the gambling aspect out of the hiring process. Indeed, more than 1,000 studies based on over 100,000 study participants strongly indicate that selection tests can give employers a much better than average (50-50) chance of hiring the right workers. In fact, if you had odds like these working for you in Las Vegas, you'd make so much money the casinos wouldn't let you in the door.

Cognitive Ability Tests

There is a 76 percent chance that workers who did well on cognitive ability tests will be much better performers in their jobs than employees who did not do well on such tests.

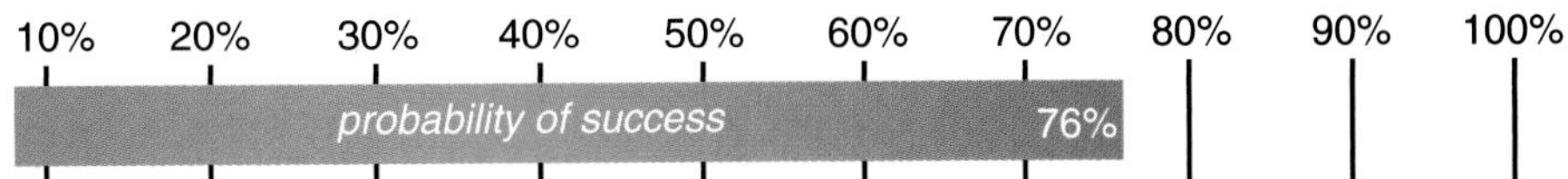

Work Sample Tests

There is a 77 percent chance that workers who did well on work sample tests will be much better performers in their jobs than employees who did not do well on such tests.

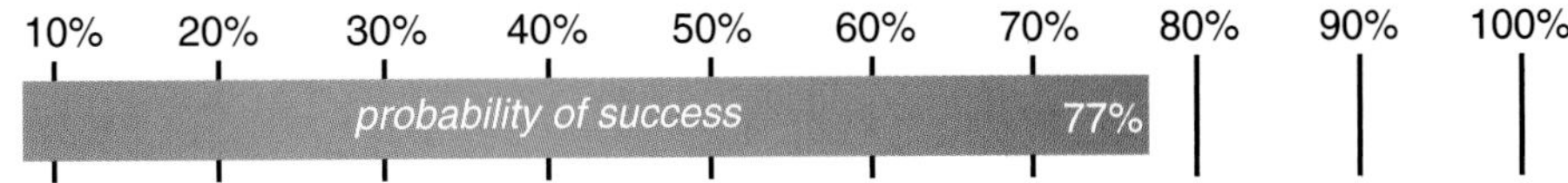

Assessment Centers

There is a 69 percent chance that workers who did well on assessment center exercises will be much better managers than employees who did not do well on such exercises.

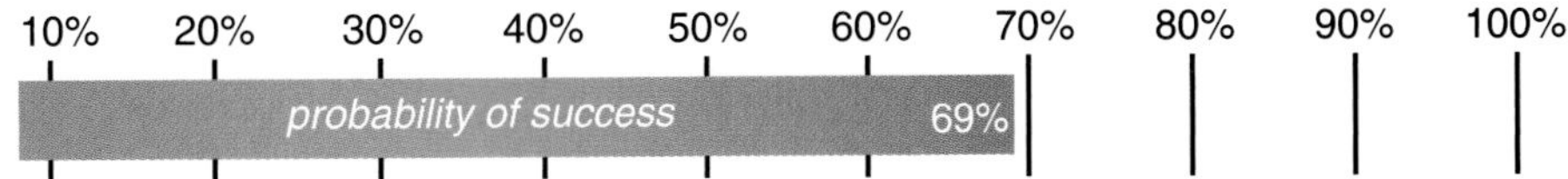

Structured Interviews

There is a 76 percent chance that workers who did well in structured interviews will be much better performers in their jobs than employees who did not do well in structured interviews.

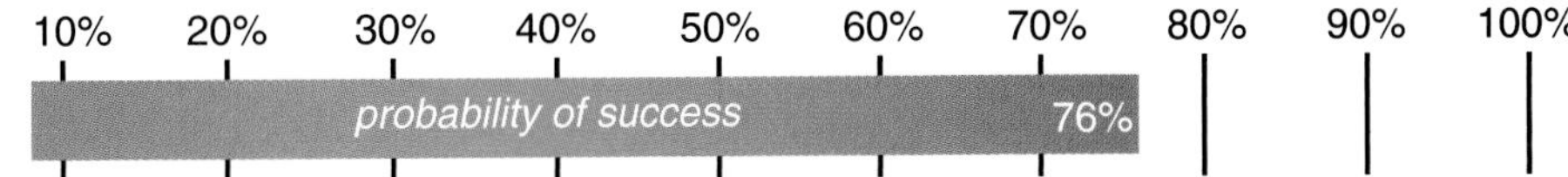

Cognitive Ability + Work Sample Tests

When deciding who to hire, most companies use a number of tests together to make even more accurate selection decisions. There is an 82 percent chance that workers who did well on a combination of cognitive ability tests and work sample tests will be much better performers in their jobs than employees who did not do well on both tests.

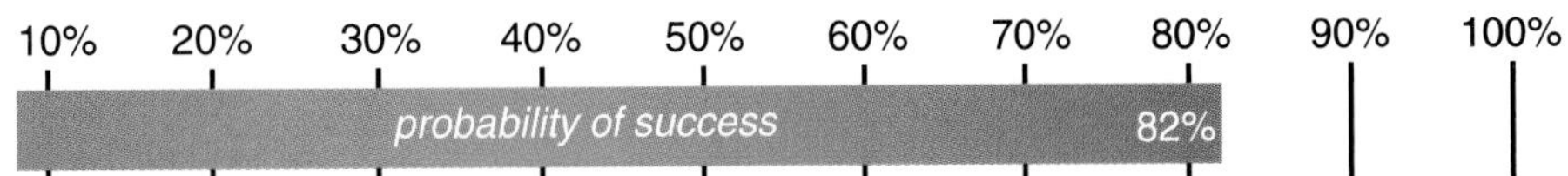

Cognitive Ability + Integrity Tests

There is an 83 percent chance that workers who did well on a combination of cognitive ability tests and integrity tests (see Chapter 3 for a discussion of integrity tests) will be much better performers in their jobs than employees who did not do well on both tests.

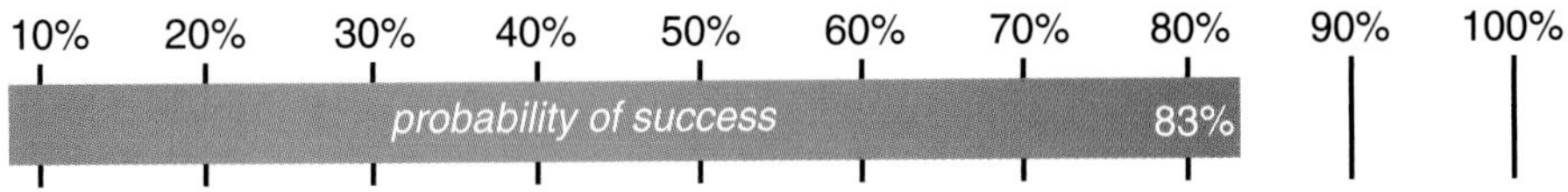

Cognitive Ability + Structured Interviews

There is an 82 percent chance that workers who did well on a combination of cognitive ability tests and structured interviews will be much better performers in their jobs than employees who did not do well on both tests.

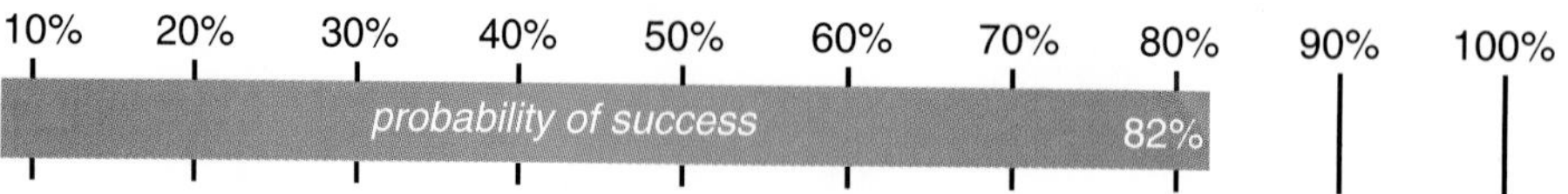

Source: F.L. Schmidt & J.E. Hunter, "The Validity and Utility of Selection Methods in Personnel Psychology: Practical and Theoretical Implications of 85 Years of Research Findings," *Psychological Bulletin* 124, no. 2 (1998): 262-274.

Review 4
Selection

Selection is the process of gathering information about job applicants to decide who should be offered a job. Accurate selection procedures are valid, are legally defendable, and improve organizational performance. Application forms and resumes are the most common selection devices. Because many application forms request illegal, non-job-related information, and because as many as one-third of job applicants falsify information on resumes, these procedures can sometimes be of little value when making hiring decisions. References and background checks can also be problematic, given that previous employers are reluctant to provide such information for fear of being sued for defamation. Unfortunately, the lack of this information puts other employers at risk of negligent hiring lawsuits. Selection tests generally do the best job of predicting applicants' future job performance. In general, cognitive ability tests, work sample tests, biographical data, and assessment cen-

Table 14.6

Guidelines for Conducting Effective Structured Interviews

Planning the Interview

- Identify and define the knowledge, skills, abilities and other (KSAO) characteristics needed for successful job performance.
- For each essential KSAO, develop key behavioral questions that will elicit examples of past accomplishments, activities, and performance.
- For each KSAO, develop a list of things to look for in applicants' responses to key questions.

Conducting the Interview

- Create a relaxed, nonstressful interview atmosphere.
- Review applicants' application blanks, resumes, and other information.
- Allocate enough time to complete the interview without interruption.
- Put the applicant at ease; don't jump right into heavy questioning.
- Tell the applicant what to expect. Explain the interview process.
- Obtain job-related information from the applicant by asking those questions prepared for each KSAO.
- Describe the job and the organization to applicants. Applicants need adequate information to make a selection decision about the organization.

After the Interview

- Immediately after the interview, review your notes and make sure they are complete.
- Evaluate applicants on each essential KSAO.
- Determine each applicant's probability of success and make a hiring decision.

Source: B.M. Farrell, "The Art and Science of Employment Interviews," *Personnel Journal* 65 (1986): 91-94.

ters are the most valid tests, followed by personality tests and specific ability tests, which are still good predictors. Selection tests aren't perfect predictors of job performance, but almost nothing predicts future job performance as well as selection tests. The three kinds of job interviews are unstructured, structured, and semi-structured interviews. Of these, structured interviews work best, because they ensure that all applicants are consistently asked the same situational, behavioral, background, or job-knowledge questions.

Developing Qualified Workers

Harmon Industries, which makes signaling and communications equipment for the railway and transit industries, has a new training center where its employees learn engineering, safety, teamwork, time management, and other workplace skills. Ron Breshears, Harmon's vice president of human resources and safety, said, "Training is an investment, not a cost. Once you see that, you see that you get a good return on your investment."[69] At Sprint, the telecommunications company, 50,000 out of 62,000 employees received training last year. Sprint's University of Excellence has 400 employees, who provide classroom and on-the-job training in 20 cities. Said Brad Harsha, assistant vice president of Sprint's University of Excellence, "Our philosophy is that Sprint supports continuous learning. Our training doesn't stop with orientation to the company. It's a lifelong learning commitment."[70]

Why are Harmon Industries and Sprint spending so much time and money to train their workers? Because, according to the American Society for Training and Development, an investment in training increases productivity by an average of 17 percent, reduces employee turnover, and makes companies more profitable.[71]

However, giving employees the knowledge and skills they need to improve their performance is just the first step in developing employees. The second step is giving employees formal feedback about their actual job performance. For example, at his last performance appraisal, Thomas Loarie, CEO of KeraVision, a company that invented a patented vision correction procedure, learned that he needed to be more realistic about his sales plans and that he needed to hold his subordinates more accountable for their work. Gilbert Amelio, Apple Computer's former CEO, said, "CEOs really want the feedback about how we're doing and what we can be doing to improve what's going on."[72] So, in today's competitive business environment, even CEOs understand the importance of formal performance feedback.

After reading the next two sections, you should be able to:

5 describe how to determine **training** needs and select the appropriate training methods.

6 discuss how to use **performance appraisal** to give meaningful performance feedback.

training
developing the skills, experience, and knowledge employees need to perform their jobs or improve their performance

5 Training

Training means providing opportunities for employees to develop the job-specific skills, experience, and knowledge they need to do their jobs or improve their performance. American companies spend more than $60 billion a year on training.

To make sure those training dollars are well spent, companies need to **5.1** *determine specific training needs,* **5.2** *select appropriate training methods, and* **5.3** *evaluate training.*

5.1 *Determining Training Needs*

needs assessment the process of identifying and prioritizing the learning needs of employees

Needs assessment is the process of identifying and prioritizing the learning needs of employees. Needs assessments can be conducted by identifying performance deficiencies, listening to customer complaints, surveying employees and managers, or formally testing employees' skills and knowledge.

Been There,

Human Resources and Gillette's MACH3 Razor

The Gillette Company spent more than $750 million to set up production of its MACH3 triple-blade razor. Tom Webber is the director of human resources for manufacturing at Gillette. In this interview, he discusses how Gillette hired and trained 400 workers and kept the project secret from its competition.

Q: Gillette spent roughly $750 million to develop machinery and processes to produce 1.2 billion triple-bladed razors. How much effort was spent on hiring and training your workforce?

A: Approximately a year before the product was introduced, we put together a cross-functional team that consisted of manufacturing, engineering and human resources to look at our skilled-labor requirements for mechanics and operators. We conducted an assessment survey and looked at the experience of our current workforce. That gave us a picture of the skills we needed from our technical staff in areas such as sophisticated control systems, automated parts handling systems, pneumatics and hydraulics. Once we realized we needed to increase the skills of our own people in those areas, we looked to enhance the company's technical education and machine-specific training.

We then targeted those radio stations and magazines—ones we typically wouldn't have used, for example, a magazine that targeted Harley-Davidson riders.

Q: How did you analyze the capabilities of your workforce before you decided the number and type of workers to hire?

A: We first looked at our skills requirements, and then we did a needs analysis—not only of what our current employees possessed, but of what our new hires needed to possess. We came up with a list of courses that we needed, like control systems, engineering, drawings and metrics, and even PC fundamentals. Some of the employees hadn't used computers to the level we felt they needed.

Q: What sort of strategies did you use to hire these new workers?

A: We used our own internal bidding processes wherein we looked at our current workforce and provided them an opportunity to submit their names if they were interested in working on this project.

We also used other fairly traditional methods, such as newspaper ads and employee referrals, but we quickly recognized that we needed to step up the process because the skilled-labor market was tight in the Boston area. We polled our current mechanics population and asked them what radio stations they listen to and what magazines they read. We then targeted those radio stations and magazines—ones we typically wouldn't have used, for example, a magazine that targeted Harley-Davidson riders.

This process went on for pretty much the full year. On the final leg we had a two-day job fair in central Massachusetts. We needed to hire mechanics who had a plastics background and were within driving distance. In the end, all three phases of the recruiting campaign added to the success of hiring people.

Q: How did you train workers on equipment that was specifically designed for the project?

A: We operate 24 hours a day, seven days a week, so we needed training that could accommodate employees on different schedules. For example, we had a general mechanics program that included 125 hours of training per person and we had an additional 105 hours of training per person in the plastics arena.

We brought someone on board to manage the process. She juggled all the work schedules, figured out the needs of the production floor, determined who was available for training and who wasn't. She stayed with us for about a year.

Q: Who conducted the training?
A: The training was conducted through a partnership with the University of Massachusetts at Lowell. We selected it because of its plastics engineering program. A portion of the training dealt with mechanics working in a plastics environment. Courses revolved around such topics as injection molding and mold design and maintenance. We contracted with the university and its instructors to teach the programs. All training was done on site.

Employees also got paid during the period they were in classroom instruction. They ended up increasing their general technical knowledge. The machine-specific training was done by our internal staff and engineers. Overall, it was a successful program for everyone.

Q: Secrecy was key to the MACH3 project. How did you develop a "proprietary approach" to hiring and training workers?
A: As part of our normal employment processes, we ask everyone to sign an agreement that concerns inventions, patents and so on. We also had several security measures in place at the South Boston facility. We actually built walls around the equipment that makes cartridges—the biggest competitive issue. Every employee was assigned a badge to have special clearance to get inside the enclosed areas. We also had a security guard present.

During the interview process, we talked with potential candidates in general terms about the sophisticated equipment, but we didn't talk specifics with them. It was a combination of Gillette's reputation as a sophisticated equipment user in the manufacturing process that worked for us. We let everyone know we were going to be using high-speed equipment for the manufacturing process.

Q: What were some of the logistical problems you faced?
A: The recruiting efforts were a challenge because we were looking for a large number of highly specialized people in a short period of time. Developing the training curriculum was less of a challenge in terms of just getting people together.

One of the greatest challenges in the training process was how the equipment evolved and how our needs changed. Machine-specific training needed to evolve because the actual design of the equipment evolved. We design our own equipment. As a result, we may design equipment a certain way and discover later it's not meeting our production needs. During the manufacturing process of the MACH3, the design of the equipment changed and consequently the machine-specific training changed slightly.

Source: S. Hays, "HR Strategies Help Push New Razor to Number One," *Workforce* 78, no. 2 (1999): 92-93. This interview was edited for inclusion in this textbook.

Done That

The Work Keys method created by American College Testing in Iowa City, Iowa (makers of the ACT test used for college admissions) is a needs assessment tool being used by more than 1,400 companies nationwide.[73] Work Keys is a series of tests that determines the knowledge and skill levels that an organization's employees have in communication (listening, reading for information, and writing), problem-solving (applied mathematics, applied technology, locating information, and observation), and interpersonal skills (teamwork). A needs assessment using Work Keys begins with a job analysis (what ACT calls "job profiling") to determine the knowledge and skill levels required to perform a job successfully. For example, Figure 14.6 shows that the job of customer service representative requires strong listening, reading, and writing skills, but only moderate capabilities in locating information, applied technology, and teamwork. Following the job analysis, employees are tested and their skill levels are compared to the requirements for the job. The greater the difference between an employee's skill levels and those required by the job, the greater the need for training. Figure 14.6 shows the

Figure 14.6 **Work Keys Needs Assessment for a Customer Service Representative Job**

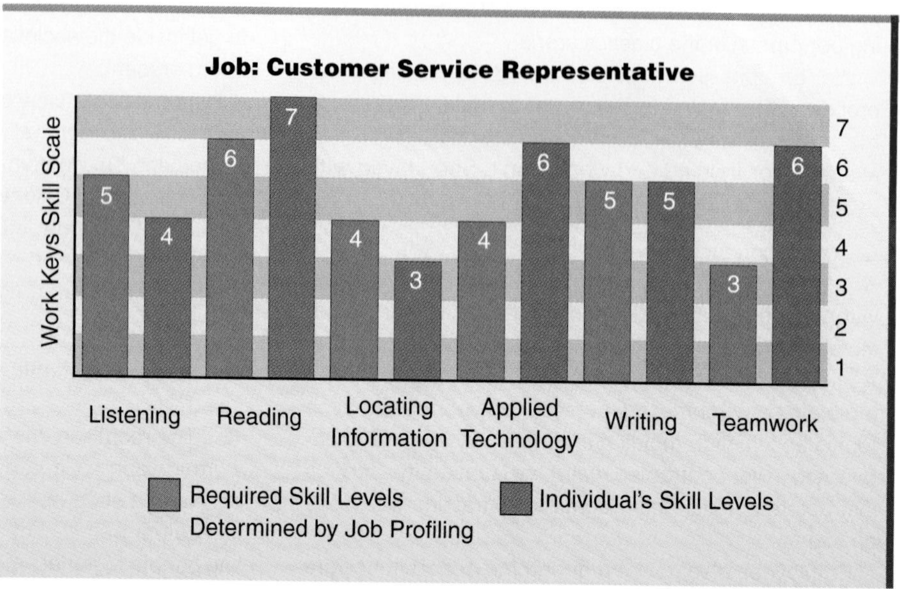

Source: "Work Keys in Action," *Introduction to Work Keys*. [Online] Available **http://www.act.org/workkeys/tour/wktour3.html**, 31 May 1999.

current skill levels in each area for one individual. Based on the Work Keys needs assessment, this employee needs some training in listening and locating information.

Note that training should never be conducted without first performing a needs assessment. Sometimes, training isn't needed at all, or it isn't needed for all employees. Since the needs assessment shown in Figure 14.6 indicates that the customer service representative has reading, applied technology, and teamwork skills that exceed those required for the job, it would be a waste of time and money to send this employee for training in these skills. Unfortunately, however, many organizations simply require all employees to attend training, whether they need to or not. The result is that employees who are not interested or don't need the training may react negatively during or after training. Likewise, employees who should be sent for training but aren't may also react negatively. Consequently, a needs assessment is an important tool for deciding who should or should not attend training. In fact, employment law restricts employers from discriminating on the basis of age, sex, race, color, religion, national origin, or handicap when selecting training participants. Instead, just like hiring decisions, the selection of training participants should be based on job-related information.

5.2 *Training Methods*

Assume that you're a training director for a bank and that you're in charge of making sure that all bank employees know what to do in case of a robbery.[74] Table 14.7 lists a number of training methods you could use: films and videos, lectures, planned readings, case studies, coaching and mentoring, group discussions, on-the-job training, role playing, simulations

Table 14.7

Training Objectives and Methods

Training Objective: Impart information or Knowledge

- *Films and Videos:* Films and videos share information, illustrate problems and solutions, and do a good job of holding trainees' attention.
- *Lecture:* Instructors present oral presentations to trainees.
- *Planned Readings:* Trainees read about concepts or ideas before attending training.

Training Objective: Develop Analytical and Problem-Solving Skills

- *Case Studies:* Cases are analyzed and discussed in small groups. The cases present a specific problem or decision and trainees develop methods for solving the problem or making the decision.
- *Coaching and Mentoring:* Coaching and mentoring of trainees by managers involves informal advice, suggestions, and guidance. This method is helpful for reinforcing other kinds of training and for trainees who benefit from support and personal encouragement.
- *Group Discussions:* Small groups of trainees actively discuss specific topics. Instructor may perform the role of discussion leader.

Training Objective: Practice, Learn, or Change Job Behaviors

- *On-the-Job Training (OJT):* New employees are assigned to experienced employees. The trainee is expected to learn by watching the experienced employee perform the job, and eventually by working alongside the experienced employee. Gradually, the trainee is left on his/her own to perform the job.
- *Role Playing:* Trainees assume job-related roles and practice new behaviors by acting out what they would do in job-related situations.
- *Simulations and Games:* Experiential exercises that place trainees in realistic job-related situations and give them the opportunity to experience a job-related condition in a relatively low-cost setting. The trainee benefits from "hands-on experience" before actually performing the job where mistakes may be more costly.
- *Vestibule Training:* Procedures and equipment similar to those used in the actual job are set up in a special area called a vestibule. The trainee is then taught how to perform the job at his/her own pace without disrupting the actual flow of work, making costly mistakes, or exposing the trainee and others to dangerous conditions.

Training Objective: Impart information or Knowledge; Develop Analytical and Problem-Solving Skills; Practice, Learn, or Change Job Behaviors

- *Computer-Based Learning:* Interactive videos, software, CD-ROMs, personal computers, teleconferencing, and the Internet may be combined to present multimedia-based training.

Source: A. Fowler, "How to Decide on Training Methods," *People Management* 25, no. 1 (1995): 36.

and games, vestibule training, and computer-based learning. Which method would be best?

To choose the best method, you should consider a number of factors, such as the number of people to be trained, the cost of training, and the objectives of the training. For instance, if the training objective is to impart information or knowledge to trainees, then you should use films and videos, lectures, and planned readings. In our robbery training example, trainees would hear, see, or read about what to do in case of a robbery.

If developing analytical and problem-solving skills is the objective, then use case studies, group discussions, and coaching and mentoring. In our

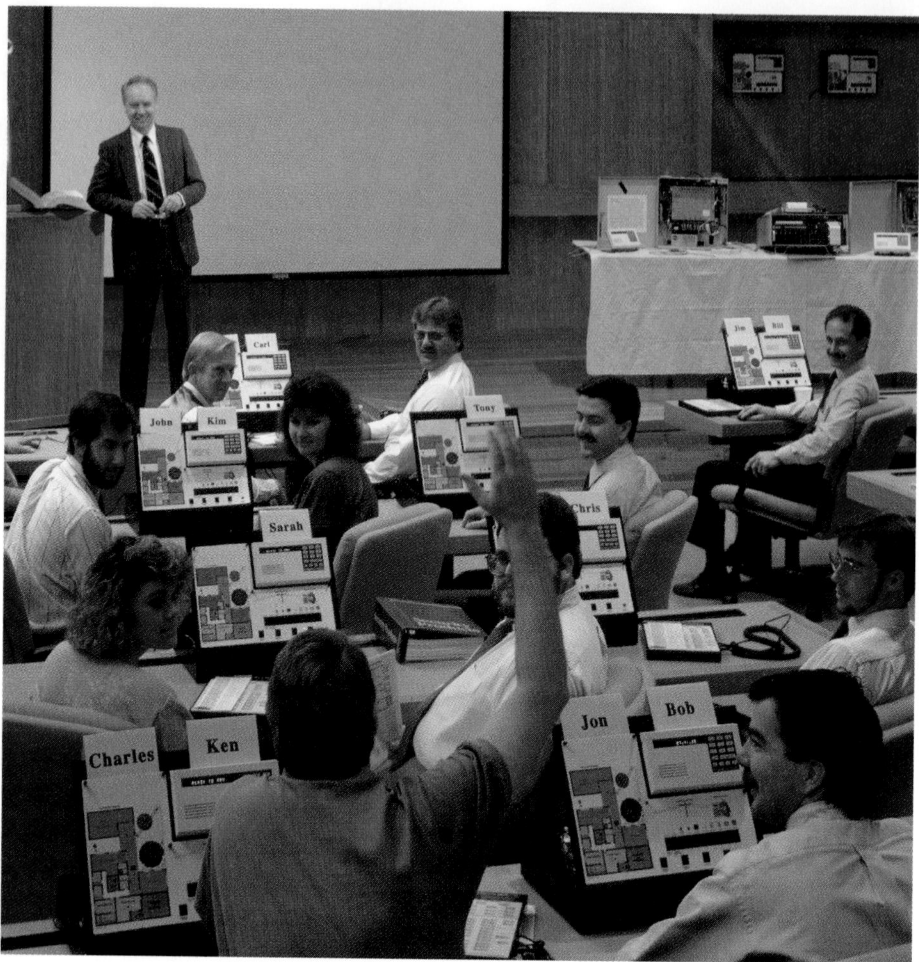

If the training objective is to impart information to a large number of trainees, then lectures and videos are good methods to choose.
© Corbis/Ed Young

example, trainees would read about a real robbery, discuss what to do, and then talk to people who had been through robberies before.

If practicing, learning, or changing job behaviors is the objective, then use on-the-job training, role playing, simulations and games, and vestibule training. In our example, trainees would learn about robbery situations on the job, pretend that they were in a robbery situation, or participate in a highly realistic mock robbery.

If training is supposed to meet more than one of these objectives, then your best choice may be to combine one of the previous methods with computer-based training. Customer service representatives at Aetna Healthcare attend training by logging onto the personal computers in their offices. Aetna's trainees, who learn together from their offices in California, North Carolina, Ohio, and Texas, simply click a computer icon to get a live feed of their training instructor from Aetna's Hartford, Connecticut, headquarters.[75]

5.3 *Evaluating Training*

After selecting a training method and conducting the training, the last step is to evaluate the training. Training can be evaluated in four ways: on *reactions*, how satisfied trainees were with the program; on *learning*, how much employees improved their knowledge or skills; on *behavior*, how much employees actually changed their on-the-job behavior because of training; or on *results*, how much training improved job performance, such as increased sales or quality, or decreased costs.[76] For example, Aetna Healthcare found that its computer-based training led to higher levels of learning and saved the company $5 million a year in travel costs.

Review 5
Training

Training is used to give employees the job-specific skills, experience, and knowledge they need to do their jobs or improve their job performance. To make sure training dollars are well spent, companies need to determine specific training needs, select appropriate training methods, and then evaluate the training. Needs assessments can be conducted by identifying performance deficiencies, listening to customer complaints, surveying employees and managers, or formally testing employees' skills and knowledge. Selection of an appropriate training method depends on a number of factors, such as the number of people to be trained, the cost of training, and the objectives of the training. If the objective is to impart information or knowledge, then films and videos, lectures, and planned readings should be used. If developing analytical and problem-solving skills is the objective, then case studies, group discussions, and coaching and mentoring should be used. If practicing, learning, or changing job behaviors is the objective, then on-the-job training, role playing, simulations and games, and vestibule training would be used. If training is supposed to meet more than one of these objectives, then it may be best to combine one of the previous methods with computer-based training. Training can be evaluated on reactions, learning, behavior, or results.

6 Performance Appraisal

performance appraisal the process of assessing how well employees are doing their jobs

Performance appraisal is the process of assessing how well employees are doing their jobs. Most employees and managers intensely dislike the performance appraisal process. One manager said, "I hate annual performance reviews. I hated them when I used to get them, and I hate them now that I give them. If I had to choose between performance reviews and paper cuts, I'd take paper cuts every time. I'd even take razor burns and the sound of fingernails on a blackboard."[77] Unfortunately, attitudes like this are all too common. In fact, seven out of ten employees are dissatisfied with the performance appraisal process in their companies. Likewise, with 44 percent of companies having changed their performance appraisal processes in the last two years and with 29 percent expecting to do so, approximately seven out of ten companies are dissatisfied with performance appraisals, too.[78]

Because they are used for so many important purposes, companies with poor performance appraisal systems face tremendous problems. For example, performance appraisals are used as a basis for compensation, promotion, and training decisions. In human resource planning, performance appraisals are used for career planning and for making termination decisions.[79]

And because of their key role in so many organizational decisions, performance appraisals are also central to many of the lawsuits that employees (or former employees) file against employers.

Let's explore how companies can avoid some of these problems with performance appraisals by **6.1** *accurately measuring job performance and* **6.2** *effectively sharing performance feedback with employees.*

6.1
Accurately Measuring Job Performance

Workers often have strong doubts about the accuracy of their performance appraisals. And they may be right. For example, it's widely known that assessors are prone to rater errors when rating worker performance. Three of the most common rater errors are central tendency, halo, and leniency. *Central tendency* error occurs when assessors rate all workers as average or in the middle of the scale. *Halo error* occurs when assessors rate all workers as performing at the same level (good, bad, or average) in all parts of their jobs. *Leniency error* occurs when assessors rate all workers as performing particularly well. One of the reasons that managers make these errors is they often don't spend enough time gathering or reviewing performance data. Winston Connor, the former vice president of human resources at Huntsman Chemical, said, "Most of the time, it's just a ritual that managers go through. They pull out last year's review, update it and do it quickly."[80]

What can be done to minimize rater errors and improve the accuracy with which job performance is measured? In general, two approaches have been used: improving performance appraisal measures themselves and training performance raters to be more accurate.

objective performance measures
measures of job performance that are easily and directly counted or quantified

subjective performance measures
measures of job performance that require someone to judge or assess a worker's performance

trait rating scales
a rating scale that indicates the extent to which a worker possesses particular traits or characteristics

behavioral observation scales (BOS)
rating scales that indicate the frequency with which workers perform specific behaviors that are representative of the job dimensions critical to successful job performance

One of the ways in which companies try to improve performance appraisal measures is to use as many objective performance measures as possible. **Objective performance measures** are measures of performance that are easily and directly counted or quantified. Common objective performance measures include output, scrap, waste, sales, customer complaints, or rejection rates.

But when objective performance measures aren't available, and frequently they aren't, subjective performance measures have to be used instead. **Subjective performance measures** require that someone judge or assess a worker's performance. The most common kind of subjective performance appraisal measure is the trait rating scale shown in Table 14.8. **Trait rating scales** ask raters to indicate the extent to which a worker possesses a particular trait or characteristic, such as reliability or honesty. However, trait rating scales, also called *graphic rating scales*, are typically inaccurate measures of performance. To start, managers are notoriously poor judges of employee traits. Second, traits are not related to job performance in any meaningful way.

So instead of using trait rating scales, subjective performance should be measured using behavioral observation scales. **Behavioral observation scales (BOS)** ask raters to rate the frequency with which workers perform specific behaviors representative of the job dimensions that are critical to successful job performance. Table 14.8 shows a BOS for two important job dimensions for a retail salesperson, customer service and handling money. Notice that each dimension lists several specific behaviors characteristic of

Table 14.8 **Subjective Performance Appraisal Scales**

Trait Rating Scale

	Strongly Disagree	*1*	*2*	*3*	*4*	*5*	*Strongly Agree*
1. Employee is a hard worker.		1	2	3	4	5	
2. Employee is reliable.		1	2	3	4	5	
3. Employee is trustworthy.		1	2	3	4	5	

Behavioral Observation Scale

Dimension: Customer Service	*Almost Never*	*1*	*2*	*3*	*4*	*5*	*Almost Always*
1. Greets customers with a smile and a "hello."		1	2	3	4	5	
2. Calls other stores to help customers find merchandise that is not in stock.		1	2	3	4	5	
3. Promptly handles customer concerns and complaints.		1	2	3	4	5	
Dimension: Handling Money	***Almost Never***	***1***	***2***	***3***	***4***	***5***	***Almost Always***
1. Accurately makes change from customer transactions.		1	2	3	4	5	
2. Accounts balance at the end of the day, no shortages or surpluses.		1	2	3	4	5	
3. Accurately records transactions in computer system.		1	2	3	4	5	

a worker who excels in that dimension of job performance. (Normally, the scale would list 7 to 12 items, not 3 as shown in the table.)

Not only do BOSs work well for rating critical dimensions of performance, but studies also show that managers strongly prefer BOSs for giving performance feedback; accurately differentiating between poor, average, and good workers; identifying training needs; and accurately measuring performance. And in response to the statement, "If I were defending a company, this rating format would be an asset to my case," attorneys strongly preferred BOSs over other kinds of subjective performance appraisal scales.[81]

rater training
training performance appraisal raters in how to avoid rating errors and increase rating accuracy

The second approach to improving the measurement of workers' job performance appraisal is rater training. **Rater training** is the process of training performance raters how to avoid rating errors (i.e., central tendency, halo, and leniency) and how to increase rating accuracy. In rater training designed to minimize rating errors, trainees view videotapes of managers observing an employee performing some aspect of a job. Following each video, trainees are asked how they would have rated the worker's performance and how the manager on the tape would have rated it. Each videotape, however, is an example of the different kinds of rating errors. So trainees have a chance to actually observe rating errors being made (by the manager in the videotape), and then discuss how to avoid those errors.

Another common form of rater training stresses rater accuracy (rather than minimizing errors). Here, raters closely examine the key dimensions of job performance (e.g., customer service and handling money for the retail salesperson in our example) and discuss specific behaviors representative of each dimension. Trainees may then be asked to role-play examples of these behaviors or to watch videos containing behavioral examples of each dimension of job performance. Both kinds of rater training are effective.[82]

6.2 *Sharing Performance Feedback*

After gathering accurate performance data, the next step is to share performance feedback with employees. Unfortunately, even when performance appraisal ratings are accurate, the appraisal process often breaks down at the feedback stage. Employees become defensive and dislike hearing any negative assessments of their work, no matter how small. Managers become defensive, too, and dislike giving appraisal feedback as much as employees dislike receiving it. One manager said, "I myself don't go as far as those who say performance reviews are inherently destructive and ought to be abolished, but I agree that the typical annual-review process does nothing but harm. It creates divisions. It undermines morale. It makes people angry, jealous, and cynical. It unleashes a whole lot of negative energy, and the organization gets nothing in return."[83]

So what can be done to overcome the inherent difficulties in performance appraisal feedback sessions? Since performance appraisal ratings have traditionally been the judgments of just one person, the boss, one approach is to use **360-degree feedback**. In this approach, feedback comes from four sources: the boss, subordinates, peers and co-workers, and the employees themselves. The data, which are obtained anonymously (except for the boss), are then compiled into a feedback report comparing the employee's self-ratings to those of the boss, subordinates, and peers and co-workers. Usually, a consultant or human resource specialist discusses the results with the employee. The advantage of 360-degree programs is that negative feedback ("You don't listen.") is often more credible if heard from several people. For example, one boss who received 360-degree feedback thought he was a great writer, so he regularly criticized and corrected his subordinates' reports. Though the subordinates never discussed it among themselves, they all complained about his writing in the 360-degree feedback and mentioned that he should quit rewriting their reports. After receiving the feedback, he apologized and stopped.[84]

360-degree feedback
a performance appraisal process in which feedback is obtained from the boss, subordinates, peers and co-workers, and the employees themselves

A word of caution, though. About half of the companies using 360-degree feedback for performance appraisal now use the feedback only for developmental purposes. They found that sometimes with raises and promotions on the line, peers and subordinates would distort ratings to harm competitors or help people they liked, and that sometimes people would give high ratings in order to get high ratings from others. On the other hand, studies clearly show that ratees prefer to receive feedback from multiple raters, so 360-degree feedback is likely to continue to grow in popularity.[85]

Herbert Meyer, who has been studying performance appraisal feedback for more than 30 years, made the following specific recommendations for sharing performance feedback with employees.[86] First, managers should separate developmental feedback, which is designed to improve future performance, from administrative feedback, which is used as a reward for past performance, such as for raises. When managers give developmental feedback, they're acting as coaches, but when they give administrative feedback, they're acting as judges. These roles, coaches and judges, are clearly incompatible. As coaches, managers are encouraging, pointing out opportunities for growth and improvement, and employees are typically open and receptive to feedback. But as judges, managers are evaluative, and employees are typically defensive and closed to feedback. Jean Gatz, a training expert in Baton Rouge, said, "Most of us don't like to sit down and hear where we're lacking and where we need to improve. It's like sitting down with your mom and dad and they're telling you, 'We know what's best.'"[87]

Second, Meyer suggests that performance appraisal feedback sessions be based on self-appraisals, in which employees carefully assess their own strengths, weaknesses, successes, and failures in writing. Because employees play an active role in the review of their performance, managers can be coaches rather than judges. Also, because the focus is on future goals and development, both employees and managers are likely to be more satisfied with the process and more committed to future plans and changes. See Table 14.9 for the list of topics that Meyer recommends for discussion in performance appraisal feedback sessions.

One concern about self-appraisals is that employees will be overly positive when evaluating their performance. However, when the focus is on development and not administrative assessment, studies show that self-appraisals lead to more candid self-assessments than traditional supervisory reviews.[88]

Third, Meyer suggests eliminating the "grading" aspect of performance appraisal, in which employees are ranked on a 1–5 scale or are scored as below average, average, above average, or exceptional. He says that "Assigning a numerical or adjectival grade, such as "satisfactory," "excellent," "adequate," "outstanding," or "poor," to overall performance or specific performance tends to obstruct rather than facilitate constructive discussion. It treats a mature person like a schoolchild. The administrative action taken, such as the amount of salary increase or a promotion, will communicate an overall appraisal better than will a grade."[89]

Review 6
Performance Appraisal

Most employees and managers intensely dislike the performance appraisal process. However, some of the problems associated with appraisals can be avoided by accurately measuring job performance and effectively sharing performance feedback with employees. Managers are prone to three kinds of rating errors: central tendency, halo, and leniency error. One way to minimize rating errors is to use better appraisal measures, such as objective measures of performance or behavioral observation scales. Another

Table 14.9

What to Discuss in a Performance Appraisal Feedback Session

1. Overall progress—an analysis of accomplishments and shortcomings.
2. Problems encountered in meeting job requirements.
3. Opportunities to improve performance.
4. Long-range plans, opportunities—for the job and for the individual's career.
5. General discussion of possible plans and goals for the coming year.

Source: H.H. Meyer, "A Solution to the Performance Appraisal Feedback Enigma," *Academy of Management Executive* 5, no. 1 (1991): 68-76.

method is to directly train performance raters to minimize errors and more accurately rate the important dimensions of job performance.

After gathering accurate performance data, the next step is to share performance feedback with employees. One way to overcome the inherent difficulties in performance appraisal feedback is to provide 360-degree feedback, in which feedback is obtained from four sources: the boss, subordinates, peers and co-workers, and the employees themselves. Feedback tends to be more credible if heard from several sources. Traditional performance appraisal feedback sessions can be improved by separating developmental and administrative feedback, by basing feedback discussions on employee self-appraisals, and by eliminating the "grading" aspect.

Keeping Qualified Workers

When Toyota built a huge new truck factory in the small town of Princeton, Indiana, and began offering incredible benefits and paying workers $19 an hour, it sent a shockwave through the pay scales of employers in the area. Not surprisingly, more than 50,000 people applied for the 1,300 jobs at Toyota's plant. Of course, many of the highly skilled workers that Toyota hired used to work for other employers for much less pay. As a result, to keep workers from jumping ship to Toyota and other high-paying companies in the area (Alcoa pays $16.50 an hour), companies throughout the Princeton area responded by increasing their pay and benefits.

Gene Weisheit, director of human resources at Evansville Veneer & Lumber Company, said that increasing wages is the only way to not be left "scraping the bottom of the barrel in a strong economy." Accordingly, his company just raised its starting pay by 50 cents to $9 an hour. His more experienced workers now earn more than $11 an hour. However, other companies, like Flanders Electric Motor Service, have focused on increasing benefits to retain workers. While Flanders Electric always sponsored one bowling team, it now sponsors several teams in men's and women's bowling leagues. It also pays for health club memberships at the local YMCA and conducts blood pressure screening during work hours. Flanders co-owner David Patterson said, "We didn't get intense with our wellness and other programs until we started to lose people to Toyota."

Unfortunately, keeping their employees will become even more difficult when Toyota hires another 1,000 workers to build a sports utility vehicle at the same manufacturing plant. And with acute labor shortages occurring nationwide, nearly all employers now understand the effect that compensation has on their ability to keep qualified workers.

After reading the next two sections, you should be able to:

7 describe basic **compensation** strategies and how they affect human resource practice.

8 discuss the four kinds of **employee separations**: termination, downsizing, retirements, and turnover.

compensation
the financial and nonfinancial rewards that organizations give employees in exchange for their work

7 Compensation

Compensation includes both the financial and nonfinancial rewards that organizations give employees in exchange for their work.

Let's learn more about compensation by examining the **7.1** *compensation decisions that managers must make and* **7.2** *the role that employment benefits play in compensating today's employees.*

7.1 Compensation Decisions

There are four basic kinds of compensation decisions: pay level, pay variability, pay structure, and employment benefits. We'll discuss employment benefits in the next subsection.[90]

Pay-level decisions are decisions about whether to pay workers at a level that is below, above, or at current market wages. Companies use job evaluation to set their pay structures. **Job evaluation** determines the worth of each job by determining the market value of the knowledge, skills, and requirements needed to perform it. After conducting a job evaluation, most companies try to pay the "going rate," meaning the current market wage. There are always companies, however, such as Evansville Veneer & Lumber Company and Flanders Electric Motor Service mentioned above, whose financial situation leads them to pay considerably less than current market wages. The childcare industry, for example, has chronic difficulties filling jobs, because it pays well below market wages. Also, because wages are so low ($10,000 to $19,000 a year), the applicants it attracts are increasingly less qualified. Donna Krause, who runs Creative Learning and Child Care in Dundalk, Maryland, lost five childcare teachers one August when all were hired away by higher-paying public school systems. While the teachers who left all had college degrees, none of their replacements did.[91]

job evaluation
a process that determines the worth of each job in a company by evaluating the market value of the knowledge, skills, and requirements needed to perform it

Some companies choose to pay above-average wages to attract and keep employees. Above-market wages can attract a larger, more qualified pool of job applicants, increase the rate of job acceptance, decrease the time it takes to fill positions, and increase how long employees stay.[92] Of course, it's very difficult to attract and keep good employees when your company has to compete with the likes of Toyota that purposively pays above-market wages. Government agencies, which typically pay well below market wages, find that it can take months and sometimes years to fill job openings, as applicants go to the private sector for much more money. Tom Cunningham, senior economist at the Federal Reserve Bank of Atlanta, summed it up when he said, "In a tight labor market, no one wants to inspect pig farms" for the government for poor wages.[93]

Pay-variability decisions are decisions concerning the extent to which employees' pay varies with individual and organizational performance. Linking pay to organizational performance is intended to increase employee motivation, effort, and job performance. Piecework, sales commission, profit sharing, employee stock ownership plans, and stock options are common pay-variability options. For instance, under **piecework** pay plans, employees are paid a set rate for each item produced up to some standard (e.g., $0.35 per item produced for output up to 100 units per day). Once productivity exceeds the standard, employees are paid a set amount for each unit of output over the standard (e.g., $0.45 for each unit above 100 units). Sales **commission** is another kind of pay variability, in which salespeople are paid a percentage of the purchase price of items they sell. The more they sell, the more they earn.

piecework
a compensation system in which employees are paid a set rate for each item they produce

commission
a compensation system in which employees earn a percentage of each sale they make

Because pay plans such as piecework and commissions are based on individual performance, they can reduce the incentive that people have to work together. Therefore, companies also use group incentives (discussed in Chapter 13) and organizational incentives, such as profit sharing, employee stock ownership plans, and stock options, to encourage teamwork and cooperation.

profit sharing
a compensation system in which a percentage of company profits is paid to employees in addition to their regular compensation

Profit sharing is the payment of a portion of the organization's profits to employees over and above their regular compensation. The more profitable the company, the more profit is shared. In 1998, DaimlerChrysler's assembly workers received $7,400 each in profit sharing checks. Ford's assembly workers received $6,100 each. However, General Motors, the least profitable of the three U.S. auto companies, was able to pay its assembly workers profit sharing checks of only $200 each.[94]

employee stock ownership plans (ESOPs)
a compensation system that awards employees shares of company stock in addition to their regular compensation

Employee stock ownership plans (ESOPs) compensate employees by awarding them shares of the company stock in addition to their regular compensation. At McKay Nursery in Waterloo, Wisconsin, Joe Hernandez, a 41-year-old migrant worker, makes $20,000 a year working from April to November. But Joe also gets an additional 20 to 25 percent in company stock. So far, he's accumulated more than $80,000 through the company ESOP.

stock options
a compensation system that gives employees the right to purchase shares of stock at a set price, even if the value of the stock increases above that price

Stock options give employees the right to purchase shares of stock at a set price. It works like this. If you are awarded the right (or option) to 100 shares of stock valued at $5 a share and the stock price rises to $15 a share, you can exercise your options and make $1000 (100 shares which have increased $10 in value, from $5 to $15). Of course, as company profits and share values increase, stock options become even more valuable to employees. To learn more about ESOPs and stock options, see The National Center for Employee Ownership (**http://www.nceo.org**).

Pay-structure decisions are concerned with internal pay distributions, meaning the extent to which people in the company receive very different levels of pay.[95] With *hierarchical pay structures*, there are big differences from one pay level to another. The largest pay levels are for people near the top of the pay distribution. The basic idea behind hierarchical pay structures is that large differences in pay between jobs or organizational levels should motivate people to work harder to obtain those higher-paying jobs.

Many publicly owned companies have hierarchical pay structures by virtue of the huge amounts they pay their top managers and CEOs. For example, in 1998, the average CEO made 419 times more than the average blue-collar worker. This enormous difference in pay occurs because CEOs almost always receive much larger annual pay increases than regular workers. For instance, in 1998, CEO pay rose by 36 percent compared to just 2.7 percent for blue-collar workers and 3.9 percent for white-collar workers.[96]

By contrast, with *compressed pay structures*, there are typically fewer pay levels and smaller differences in pay between pay levels. Pay is less dispersed and more similar across jobs in the company. The basic idea behind compressed pay structures is that similar pay levels should lead to higher levels of cooperation, feelings of fairness and a common purpose, and better group and team performance.

So should companies choose hierarchical or compressed pay structures? The evidence isn't straightforward, but studies seem to indicate that there are significant problems with the hierarchical approach. The most damaging is that there appears to be little link between organizational performance and the pay of top managers.[97] Furthermore, studies of professional athletes indicate that hierarchical pay structures (e.g., paying superstars 40 to 50 times more than the lowest-paid athlete on the team) hurt the performance of teams and individual players.[98] For now, the key seems to be that hierarchical pay structures work best for independent work, where it's easy to determine the contributions of individual performers and where little coordination with others is needed to get the job done. In other words, hierarchical pay structures work best when clear links can be drawn between individual performance and individual rewards. By contrast, compressed pay structures, that is, paying everyone similar amounts of money, seem to work best for interdependent work, in which employees must work with each other. But some companies are pursuing a middle ground, in which they try to balance hierarchical and compressed pay structures by giving ordinary workers the chance to earn more through ESOPs, stock options, and profit sharing.

7.2 *Employment Benefits*

employment benefits a method of rewarding employees that includes virtually any kind of compensation other than wages or salaries

Employment benefits include virtually any kind of compensation other than direct wages paid to employees.[99] Three employee benefits are mandated by law: social security, worker's compensation, and unemployment insurance. However, to attract and retain a good work force, most organizations offer a wide variety of benefits, including retirement plans and pensions, paid holidays, paid vacations, sick leave, health insurance, life insurance, dental care, eye care, daycare facilities, paid personal days, legal assistance, physical fitness facilities, educational assistance, and discounts on company products and services. Currently, benefits cost organizations about 37 percent of their payroll, with an average cost per employee of $4,250 for a basic benefits plan.[100]

cafeteria benefit plans (flexible benefit plans) plans that allow employees to choose which benefits they receive, up to a certain dollar value

Managers should understand that benefits are not likely to improve employee motivation and performance. However, benefits do affect job satisfaction, employee decisions about staying or leaving the company, and the company's attractiveness to job applicants.[101] One way in which organizations make their benefit plans more attractive to employees is through **cafeteria benefit plans** or **flexible benefit plans**, which allow employees to choose which benefits they receive, up to a certain dollar value.[102] Many cafeteria or flexible benefit plans start with a core of benefits, such as health insurance and life insurance that are available to all employees. Then employees are allowed to select other benefits that best fit their needs, up to a predetermined dollar amount. Some organizations provide several packages of benefits from which employees may choose. Each package is of equivalent value; however, the mix of benefits differs. For example, older employees may prefer more benefit dollars spent on retirement plans, while younger employees may prefer additional vacation days.

Payroll deductions are one of the more popular benefits options, especially for small companies. With payroll deductions, organizations pass their buying power on to employees. For example, some employees can save as much as 20 percent on auto insurance if they purchase it through their employer. Furthermore, since the fees are automatically taken out of their checks, employees don't have to worry about setting aside the money to pay their premium every six months. The advantage for employers is that they don't pay for the benefit; employees do. The advantages for employees are low costs and easy payment method via automatic payroll deductions.[103]

The drawback to flexible benefit plans has been the high cost of administering these programs. However, with advances in information processing technology and HRISs, the cost of administering benefits has begun to drop in recent years.

Review 7
Compensation

Compensation includes both the financial and nonfinancial rewards that organizations give employees in exchange for their work. There are four basic kinds of compensation decisions: pay level, pay variability, pay structure, and employment benefits. Pay-level decisions determine whether workers will receive wages below, above, or at current market levels. Pay-variability decisions concern the extent to which pay varies with individual and organizational performance. Piecework, sales commission, profit sharing, employee stock ownership plans, and stock options are common pay-variability options. Pay-structure decisions concern the extent to which people in the company receive very different levels of pay. Hierarchical pay structures work best for independent work, while compressed pay structures work best for interdependent work.

Employee benefits include virtually any kind of compensation other than direct wages paid to employees. Flexible or cafeteria benefit plans, which offer employees a wide variety of benefits, improve job satisfaction, increase the chances that employees will stay with companies, and make organizations more attractive to job applicants. The cost of administering benefits has begun to drop in recent years.

8 Employee Separations

employee separation the voluntary or involuntary loss of an employee

Employee separation is a broad term covering the loss of an employee for any reason. *Involuntary separation* occurs when employers decide to terminate or lay off employees. *Voluntary separation* occurs when employees decide to quit or retire. Because employee separations affect recruiting, selection, training, and compensation, organizations should forecast the number of employees they expect to lose through terminations, layoffs, turnover, or retirements when doing human resource planning.

Let's explore employee separation by examining **8.1** *terminations,* **8.2** *downsizing,* **8.3** *retirements, and* **8.4** *turnover.*

8.1
Terminating Employees

Hopefully, the words "You're fired!" have never been directed at you. Lots of people hear them, however, as more than 400,000 people a year get fired from their jobs. Getting fired is a terrible thing, but many managers make it even worse by bungling the firing process, needlessly provoking the people who were fired, and unintentionally inviting lawsuits. For example, one worker found out he had been fired after a restaurant told him that his company credit card was no longer active. A manager found out that she had been fired when she came back from lunch and found a note on her desk chair. And workers at a high-tech company know that they've been fired when their security codes no longer open their office doors or the front door to their office buildings.[104] How would you feel if you had been fired in one of these ways? While firing is never pleasant (and managers hate firings nearly as much as employees do), there are several things managers can do to minimize the problems inherent in firing employees.

First, in most firing situations, firing should not be the first option. Instead, employees should be given a chance to change their behavior. So when problems arise, employees should have ample warning and must be specifically informed as to the nature and seriousness of the trouble they're in. After being notified, they should be given sufficient time to change. If the problems continue, they should again be counseled about their job performance, what could be done to improve it, and the possible consequences if things don't change (e.g., written reprimand, suspension without pay, or firing). Sometimes, this is enough to solve the problem. Outplacement specialist Laurence Stybel tells the story about a large hospital that was getting ready to fire its director of radiology because of his bad attitude and increasing rudeness to co-workers. Rather than fire him, hospital management put him on probation and hired a consultant to counsel him about working with others. Within weeks, his attitude and behavior changed, and the hospital avoided firing him and the expense of replacing him (which could have included a lawsuit).[105] However, after several rounds of warnings and discussions, if the problem isn't corrected, the employee may be terminated.[106]

Second, employees should be fired for a good reason. Employers used to hire and fire employees under the legal principle of "termination at will," which allowed them to fire employees for a good reason, a bad reason, or no reason at all. However, as employees began contesting their firings in court, the principle of wrongful discharge emerged. **Wrongful discharge** is a legal doctrine that requires employers to have a job-related reason to terminate employees. In other words, just like other major human resource decisions, termination decisions should be made on the basis of job-related factors, such as violating company rules or consistently poor performance. And with former employees winning 68 percent of wrongful discharge cases, managers should record the job-related reasons for the termination, document specific instances of rule violations or continued poor performance, and keep notes and documents from the counseling sessions held with employees.[107]

wrongful discharge
a legal doctrine that requires employers to have a job-related reason to terminate employees

Third, companies need to pay attention to reactions of remaining employees after someone has been fired. Jenai Lane of Respect, Inc., a maker of jewelry and accessories located in San Francisco, believes it is important to consider the employees who remain after someone is terminated. After she fires someone, she holds an "emergency pow-wow" and encourages employees to speak their minds. "It takes a little prodding, but it's good to get people's feelings out in the open."[108] However, managers should be careful not to criticize the employee who has just been fired, as this could lead to a wrongful discharge lawsuit.

8.2 *Downsizing*

downsizing
the planned elimination of jobs in a company

Downsizing is the planned elimination of jobs in a company. Whether it's because of cost cutting, declining market share, or overaggressive hiring and growth, it's estimated that companies eliminate more than three million jobs a year.[109] Two-thirds of companies that downsize will downsize a second time within a year. For example, Applied Materials, based in California's

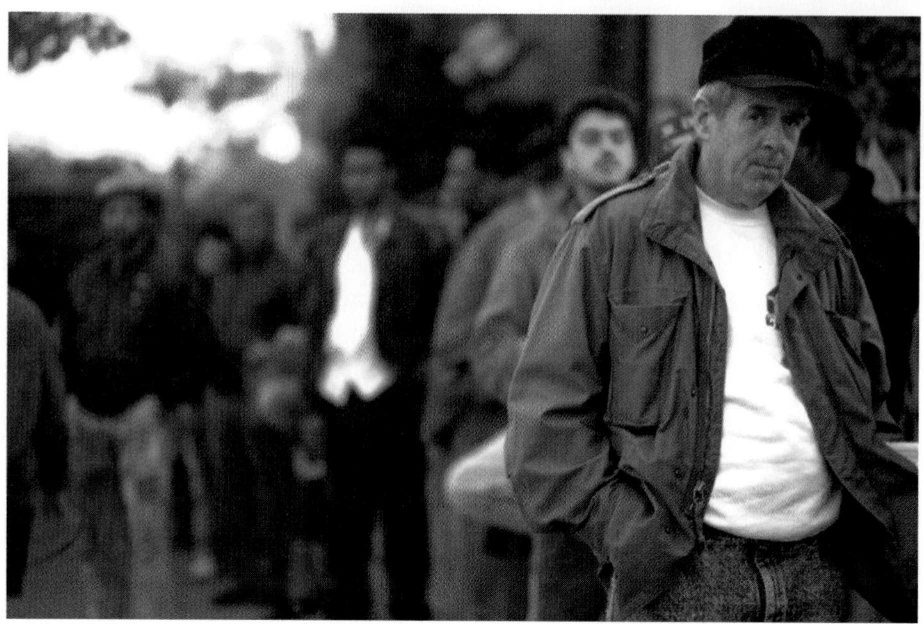

More than three million employees a year lose their jobs through downsizing.

Silicon Valley, downsized 1,500 workers the first time it downsized, followed by another 2,000 workers less than three months later.[110]

Does downsizing work? In theory, downsizing is supposed to lead to higher productivity and profits, better stock performance, and increased organizational flexibility. However, numerous studies demonstrate that it doesn't. For instance, a 15-year study of downsizing found that downsizing 10 percent of a company's work force only produces a 1.5 percent decrease in costs, that firms that downsized increased their stock price by 4.7 percent over three years compared to 34.3 percent for firms that didn't, and that profitability and productivity were generally not improved by downsizing.[111] These results make it clear that the best strategy is to conduct effective human resource planning and avoid downsizing altogether. Indeed, downsizing should always be used as a measure of last resort.

However, if companies do find themselves in financial or strategic situations where downsizing is required for survival, they should train managers how to break the news to downsized employees, have senior managers explain in detail why downsizing is necessary, and time the announcement so employees hear it from the company and not from other sources, such as TV or newspaper reports.[112] Finally, companies should do everything they can to help downsized employees find other jobs. One of the best ways to do this is to use **outplacement services** that provide employment-counseling services for employees faced with downsizing. Outplacement services often include advice and training in preparing resumes and getting ready for job interviews, and even identifying job opportunities in other companies.

outplacement services employment-counseling services offered to employees who are losing their jobs because of downsizing

When faced with sluggish sales, the E.D. Smith manufacturing company decided to close its Byhalia, Mississippi, plant. One hundred and twenty employees, some of whom had worked there for 30 years, found themselves without jobs. Two months before the plant closed, the company brought in a national outplacement firm to help employees find new jobs. A job development center was established within the plant to provide training in job search techniques, interviewing skills, and resume writing. In addition, hundreds of job openings were posted at the center. The company also advertised the availability of its employees by sending letters to prospective employers. The letter stated, in part, "These employees are skilled in such areas as purchasing, quality assurance, shipping and receiving, forklift operations, production, inventory control, process cooks and blenders. These employees are loyal, reliable, and dedicated. They have extensive experience in a fast-paced production environment."[113] Extensive outplacement programs not only help laid-off employees, but also help the company maintain a positive image in the community affected by downsizing. Steps such as these also help employees remain productive during their final days at the company.

8.3
Retirement

early retirement incentive programs (ERIPs)
programs that offer financial benefits to employees to encourage them to retire early

Early retirement incentive programs (ERIPs) offer financial benefits to employees to encourage them to retire early. Companies use ERIPs to reduce the number of employees in the organization, to lower costs by eliminating positions after employees retire, to lower costs by replacing high-paid retirees with lower-paid, less-experienced employees, or to create openings and job opportunities for people inside the company. For example, the state of Wyoming offered its employees a lump-sum bonus, additional insurance benefits, and increased monthly retirement payments to encourage early retirement. Its ERIP must have been fairly attractive, because 56 percent of the state employees eligible for early retirement accepted. Thirty percent of the 437 positions vacated by early retirees remained empty, saving the state $23.2 million over the first 46 months of the program and a projected $65 million over eight years. After accounting for the costs of the increased early retirement benefits, the predicted savings came to more than $148,000 per retiree.[114]

The biggest problem with most ERIPs is accurately predicting who and how many will accept early retirement. The company will likely lose good as well as poor performers, and sometimes more workers than they expect. For example, Ameritech Corporation, the largest telephone company in the Midwest, offered an ERIP consisting of a $5,000 educational assistance program to retrain workers, financial planning counseling, and outplacement advice and guidance. Since most pension benefits are based on a formula including years of service and employee age, the core of Ameritech's program was the "three-plus-three enhancement," which added three years to the employees' age and three years to their years of service to help them qualify for greater retirement benefits. Ameritech carefully identified the number of employees near retirement age and estimated that 5,000 to 6,000 of its 48,000 employees would take advantage of the program. Instead, nearly 22,000 employees accepted the ERIP offer and applied for early retirement![115]

8.4
Employee Turnover

employee turnover
loss of employees who voluntarily choose to leave the company

functional turnover
loss of poor-performing employees who voluntarily choose to leave a company

Employee turnover is the loss of employees who voluntarily choose to leave the company. In general, most companies try to keep the rate of employee turnover low to reduce recruiting, hiring, training, and replacement costs. However, not all kinds of employee turnover are bad for organizations. In fact, some turnover can actually be good. For instance, **functional turnover** is the loss of poor-performing employees who choose to leave the organization.[116] Functional turnover gives the organization a chance to replace poor performers with better replacements. In fact, one study found that simply replacing poor-performing leavers with average replacements would increase the revenues produced by retail salespeople in an upscale department store by $112,000 per person per year.[117] By contrast, **dysfunctional turnover**, the loss of high performers who choose to leave, is a costly loss to the organization.

dysfunctional turnover
loss of high-performing employees who voluntarily choose to leave a company

Employee turnover should be carefully analyzed to determine exactly who is choosing to leave the organization, good or poor performers. If the company is losing too many high performers, managers should determine the reasons and find ways to reduce the loss of valuable employees. The company may have to raise salary levels, offer enhanced benefits, or improve working conditions to retain skilled workers. One of the best ways to influence functional and dysfunctional turnover is to link pay directly to performance. A study of four sales forces found that when pay was strongly linked to performance via sales commissions and bonuses, poor performers were much more likely to leave (i.e. functional turnover). By contrast, poor performers were much more likely to stay when paid large, guaranteed monthly salaries and small sales commissions and bonuses.[118]

Review 8
Employee Separations

Employee separation is the loss of an employee, which can occur voluntarily or involuntarily. Before firing or terminating employees, managers should give employees a chance to improve. If firing becomes necessary, it should be done because of job-related factors, such as violating company rules or consistently poor performance. Downsizing is supposed to lead to higher productivity and profits, better stock performance, and increased organizational flexibility, but studies show that it doesn't. The best strategy is to downsize only as a last resort. Companies that do downsize should offer outplacement services to help employees find other jobs. Companies use early retirement incentive programs to reduce the number of employees in the organization, lower costs, and create openings and job opportunities for people inside the company. The biggest problem with ERIPs is accurately predicting who and how many will accept early retirement. Companies generally try to keep the rate of employee turnover low to reduce costs. However, functional turnover can be good for organizations, because it offers the chance to replace poor performers with better replacements. Managers should analyze employee turnover to determine who is resigning and take steps to reduce the loss of good performers.

What**Really**Happened?

From Christine, the control freak, to Tish, who was pocketing cash, to Donna, who took too many days off and used office supplies for personal use, the opening case introduced you to the hiring problems that Magnolia Medical Services was having. Read the answers to the opening case to learn what steps Magnolia Medical Services took to do a better job of hiring qualified workers.

How do you go about recruiting qualified applicants?

Finding qualified workers in today's job market is an increasingly difficult task. Successful selection decisions begin by using recruiting to develop a pool of qualified job applicants. The first step in recruiting is to conduct a job analysis to collect information about the important work-related aspects of a job. The job analysis is then used to write a job description of basic tasks, duties, and responsibilities and job specifications indicating the knowledge, skills, and abilities needed to perform the job. That information is then used to write recruiting material and advertisements and to determine which applicants meet the basic job qualifications.

For Magnolia Medical Services, internal recruiting, the process of developing a pool of qualified job applicants from people who already work in the company, didn't make sense, since most of the job openings were entry level. Therefore, Magnolia relied exclusively on external recruiting to find qualified job applicants from outside the company. And since many of its job openings were for clerical or office workers, it relied on employee referrals, walk-ins, newspaper ads, and state employment agencies to generate its pool of job applicants. However, given its lack of success in hiring employees, Magnolia needed to reach a larger number of better-qualified applicants. Internet jobs sites are one way to do that cheaply for all of its job openings. Another option is to advertise in professional journals, especially when hiring medical staff, such as nurses.

What's the best way to learn something about applicants' work experience before hiring them?

A basic principle of hiring is that past behavior is one of the best predictors of future behavior. For employers like Magnolia Medical Services, that means it pays to find out something about job applicants' work experiences. The question is, how? One quick and simple step that Magnolia took was to develop two versions of the company's generic application form (which was purchased from a local printing company). One version was for clerical and office jobs, while the other was for medical jobs, such as nurses and medical technicians. Developing separate forms allowed Magnolia to collect information more specific to these particular jobs. Developing new forms also gave Magnolia the chance to remove requests for potentially illegal, non-job-related information (e.g., marital status, maiden name, age, and date of high school graduation).

Magnolia also began doing a much better job of checking applicants' references and background information. This was critical, because the information it was getting from applicants' well-prepared resumes wasn't helping it make good selection decisions. In retrospect, this shouldn't have been a surprise, since nearly one out of three job applicants falsifies information on his or her resume. But for Magnolia, it seemed as if it were three out of three! Accordingly, Magnolia's new HR director thoroughly checked applicants' references to verify the truthfulness and accuracy of information they provided and to possibly uncover negative, job-related background information that they did not share with the company. Because it was located in a small city, Magnolia had good success calling previous employers for information. However, the HR director found that he could pick up even more information by talking to applicants' references in person. People were more willing to share information face-to-face, and it gave him the chance to ask additional questions based on nonverbal feedback not easily detected over the phone.

What can you do to improve the accuracy of the selection decisions at Magnolia Medical Services?

Magnolia's first step was to conduct complete job analyses of each job in the company. Once those were complete, and the job specifications indicated the specific qualifications needed to perform the job, Magnolia was able to more accurately screen job applicants. For example, since Magnolia relied heavily on interviews for selection decisions, the job analyses were used to eliminate interview questions that were not job related and that could put the company in legal jeopardy. Likewise, the job analyses were instrumental in creating a set of job-related questions to be asked of applicants in every job interview. These included situational questions, which asked applicants how they would respond in a hypothetical situation (e.g., "What would you do if . . . ?"); behavioral questions, which asked applicants what they did in previous jobs similar to the job for which they were applying (e.g., "In your previous jobs, tell me about . . . ?"); background questions, which asked applicants about their work experience, education, and other qualifications (e.g., "Tell me about the training you received at . . . "); and job knowledge questions, which asked applicants to demonstrate their job knowledge (e.g., for nurses, "Give me an example of a time when one of your patients had a severe reaction to a medication. How did you handle it?").

In addition to structured interviews, Magnolia could have improved its hiring decisions by using selection tests. Typing tests would have been useful for selecting office workers. However, since the jobs required a great deal of contact with customers, most of whom were stressed or not feeling well, it was important to hire people who exhibited warmth and a sense of humor. Consequently, it would have been useful to select applicants on the basis of some of the Big 5 personality dimensions: extraversion, emotional stability, agreeableness, conscientiousness, and openness to experience.

And if employees don't work out, what process should be used to let them go that is fair to them and the company (and decreases chances of a lawsuit)?

Unfortunately, Magnolia Medical Services was better at firing workers than it was at hiring them. While firing is never pleasant, the company was generally doing a good job of letting employees go. To start, Magnolia usually gave people a chance to change their behavior before firing them. However, after several rounds of warnings and discussions, if the problem wasn't corrected, employees were terminated.

There was one exception to giving employees a "second chance." After hiring Kristin as their new front office secretary (Kristin wasn't discussed in the opening case), the doctors noticed that they were seeing fewer patients each day. At first, they were glad for the break. After several weeks, they figured out what was happening when they overheard Kristin talking to a patient on the phone. She said, "You're short of breath and have chest pain? Well, did you break out in a cold sweat? No? Then you couldn't possibly be having a heart attack, Mr. Grosski." Kristin was fired on the spot. Fortunately, Mr. Grosski made it to the hospital where his heart attack was successfully treated. Firing Kristin on the spot was permissible, because the violation was clearly job related. Doctors' offices can't have secretaries doling out medical advice. (The lawyers would be licking their chops over a case like this, wouldn't they?)

Just like other major human resource decisions, termination decisions should be made on the basis of job-related factors, such as violating company rules or consistently poor performance. Then after firing employees, the company should pay attention to the reactions of the remaining employees. In a small office like Magnolia's, it's especially important to talk to the remaining employees to give them a chance to react and to give managers a chance to listen.

Sources: Anonymous, "Bad Hiring Practices Can Cost You Money," *Agency Sales* 28, no. 9 (September 1998): 40-43. M. Barrier, "Hiring the Right People," *Nation's Business* 84, no. 6 (June 1996): 18. L.D. Dunsmore, "Hiring Tips We Learned the Hard Way," *Medical Economics,* 12 February 1996, 140-146. D. Wiggins, "Hiring Employees Intelligently," *Journal of Environmental Health* 60, no. 10 (June 1998): 46-47.

Key Terms

adverse impact p. 556

assessment centers p. 570

background checks p. 567

behavioral observation scales (BOS) p. 582

biographical data (biodata) p. 569

cafeteria benefit plans (flexible benefit plans) p. 589

cognitive ability tests p. 568

commission p. 587

compensation p. 586

disparate treatment p. 556

downsizing p. 591

dysfunctional turnover p. 594

early retirement incentive programs (ERIPs) p. 593

80% or four-fifths rule p. 556

employee separation p. 590

employee stock ownership plans (ESOPs) p. 588

employee turnover p. 593

employment benefits p. 589

employment references p. 567

external recruiting p. 563

functional turnover p. 593

hostile work environment p. 557

human resource information systems (HRIS) p. 551

human resource management p. 546

human resource planning (HRP) p. 548

internal recruiting p. 562

interviews p. 571

job analysis p. 560

job description p. 561

job evaluation p. 587

job specifications p. 561

needs assessment p. 576

objective performance measures p. 582

outplacement services p. 592

performance appraisal p. 581

personality tests p. 569

piecework p. 587

profit sharing p. 588

quid pro quo sexual harassment p. 557

rater training p. 583

recruiting p. 560

selection p. 565

sexual harassment p. 557

specific ability tests (aptitude tests) p. 568

stock options p. 588

structured interviews p. 571

subjective performance measures p. 582

360-degree feedback p. 584

training p. 575

trait rating scales p. 582

validation p. 565

work sample tests p. 570

work force forecasting p. 549

wrongful discharge p. 591

What Would You Do-II?

Rockford, Illinois.

Three months ago, you accepted a job as a human resource director at Rockford Memorial Hospital in Rockford, Illinois. During the interview process, you were told that your responsibilities would include a variety of standard HRM projects. And since arriving, you've worked on projects related to training, recruiting, and selection. Yesterday, your boss, Mary Wells, the vice president of human resources, gave you another assignment. "The hospital's paid sick leave policy just isn't working as we intended," Mary explained. "See if you can fix it. By the way, here's a report we had done on it last year."

When she left, you pulled out the employee handbook and read the policy:

> *Full-time employees earn 12 sick days and 3 personal days per year. Unused personal days may not be carried over to the next calendar year. However, full-time employees may accumulate and carry over up to 60 sick days. Upon voluntary separation from hospital employment, employees will receive compensation at their hourly wage for up to 30 unused sick days.*

Your next stop was the hospital's human resource information system, which is updated daily and provides current information on all hospital employees. The HRIS indicated that over one-third of the hospital's 2,300 employees had accrued more than 60 days of unused paid sick days. Although unlikely, you calculated that if all of these employees quit today, the hospital would have to pay out more than $1.5 million!

And according to the report that Mary left with you, illness only accounts for 45 percent of the sick days used by hospital employees. Sick days are also used for family issues (27 percent), personal needs (13 percent), entitlement ("because I earned them," 9 percent), and stress

(6 percent). In other words, these data indicate that sick days are being used for their intended purpose only about half of the time (45 percent for sick days and 6 percent for stress).

Ironically, the policy may also be encouraging employees to call in "sick" more frequently than they normally would. In fact, the report Mary left you says that employees in most organizations use only 4 to 7 paid sick days per year at a cost of $212 to $668 per employee per year (much less than what 12 days of sick leave are costing the hospital). Of course, when medical personnel call in at the last minute, this creates additional problems and expenses. Units may be understaffed and critically ill patients may be left without adequate medical care unless other employees, who must now be paid overtime, can be called in to replace them. In fact, you've heard nurses complaining about understaffing since your first day on the job.

You wonder, "If employees received enough paid vacation, would they be less likely to abuse the sick leave policy?" You look up the vacation policy in your handbook:

Full-time employees receive paid vacation based on years of service according to the following schedule:

1–4 years	*10 days*
5–9 years	*15 days*
10+ years	*20 days*

"Wow! Even employees with only one year of service get 10 paid vacation days, 3 personal days, and 12 sick days per year. That's 25 days a year of paid time off! And an employee with ten or more years of service gets 35 days of paid time off per year. That's almost two months! There's got to be a better way to do this." **If you were the human resource specialist at this hospital, what would you do?** (Hint: Develop a new sick leave policy that solves these problems.)

Sources: S. Armour, "Stay Home Sick or Risk the Wrath of Co-Workers," *USA Today*, 11 November 1997, 04B. P. Hermann, "Commissioner Targets Abuse of Sick Leave; City Police Policy Doesn't Limit Days," *Baltimore Sun*, 7 February 1996, 1A. M.M. Markowich & S. Eckberg, "Get Control of the Absentee-Minded," *Personnel Journal* 75, no. 3 (1 March 1991): 115-116. J.P. Vistnes, "Gender Differences in Days Lost from Work Due to Illness," *Industrial & Labor Relations Review* 50, no. 2: 304-323.

Critical-Thinking Video Case

Managing Human Resources: Next Door Food Stores

Next Door Food Stores is a family-run business consisting of 30 convenience stores in two states. The stores sell gasoline and 3,000 different grocery and general merchandise items. Next Door serves a diverse customer base, and each store must adapt to meet the needs of its customers. The company's strategy is to meet the needs of its target market by providing exceptional customer service. Next Door relies heavily on repeat customers.

Dave Johnson, CEO and president of Next Door Food Stores, believes that employee retention is important in achieving repeat business. Senior employees get to know their customers and provide better service. Turnover averages 100 percent per year in the convenience store industry, and Next Door is experiencing the industry average. However, the Human Resources Department is attempting to reduce this number. Another problem being addressed by the Human Resources Department is personnel costs, such as worker's compensation.

Critical-Thinking Questions

1. How can Next Door Food Stores' Human Resources Department help reduce employee turnover?
2. How can Next Door Food Stores' Human Resources Department help control personnel costs?

Management Decisions

Job Analysis

Job analysis is a foundation for many of the HRM subsystems. Even though you may never have to actually conduct a job analysis and write job descriptions, you should be familiar with the process to better understand how to use this information in selection decisions. Pick a relatively simple job that you can observe without interrupting the employee. You should observe this job at least twice at different times (e.g., once in the morning and once in the afternoon) for approximately 30 minutes each time. The goal is to observe a representative performance of this job.

Copy or recreate the form below and use it to perform a job analysis of this job. Remember, your goal is to identify the most important activities, responsibilities, and duties, as well as any special equipment or tools that are used or any significant customer/client/co-worker contact. If you are working in teams, have two or three team members observe the same job. When you've finished, write a job description and job specifications for this job.

On the job analysis form below, the column headings stand for I = Importance of the activity, T = Time spent performing the activity (e.g., percentage of each day on average), and D = Difficulty of this activity. Use the following rating scales for these factors:

Importance of Activity	*Time Spent on Average*	*Difficulty of Activity*
1 Very Unimportant	1 0-19% of each day	1 Extremely Easy
2 Slightly Unimportant	2 20-39% of each day	2 Fairly Easy
3 Slightly Important	3 40-59% of each day	3 Average Difficulty
4 Fairly Important	4 60-79% of each day	4 Above Average Difficulty
5 Very Important	5 80-100% of each day	5 High Difficulty

After rating each activity, add the scores in each column and the total score. These scores can be used to compare relative values of different jobs to the company. If you are working in teams, average the scores from your group members to come up with a total for the job.

Activity	*I*	*T*	*D*	*I + T + D*
______	___	___	___	______
______	___	___	___	______
______	___	___	___	______
______	___	___	___	______
TOTAL				______

Job Description:

Job Specifications:

Management Decisions

A Behavioral Interview for Your Professor?

Interviews are by far the most frequently used selection procedure. In fact, it's rare for people to be hired without first being interviewed. But as you learned in the chapter, most managers conduct unstructured interviews, in which they are free to ask applicants anything they want, and studies show that they do. Indeed, studies show that because interviewers often disagree about which questions should be asked during interviews, different interviewers tend to ask applicants very different questions. However, individual interviewers even seem to have a tough time asking the same questions from one interview to the next. This high level of inconsistency lowers the validity of interviews as a selection device, because it becomes difficult to compare applicant responses. As a result, unstructured interviews do about half as well as structured interviews in accurately predicting which job applicants should be hired.

By contrast, with structured interviews, standardized interview questions are prepared ahead of time, so that all applicants may be asked the same job-related questions. The primary advantage of structured interviews is that asking all applicants the same questions makes comparing applicants a much easier process. Also, structuring interviews ensures that interviewers will ask for only important, job-related information. These advantages significantly improve the accuracy, usefulness, and validity of interviews as a selection procedure. Since you're likely to use interviewing more than any other selection procedure, the purpose of this assignment is to give you some experience creating questions for structured interviews.

You'll be writing questions for the job of college professor, a job with which all of you should be familiar (having observed each of your instructors for an average of 40 hours per college class). Your job is to write 12 questions that you would ask applicants who wanted to teach at your university. Remember, four kinds of questions are typically asked in structured interviews. You'll be writing three questions for each of the four kinds of questions shown below.

- *Situational questions* ask applicants how they would respond in a hypothetical situation (e.g., "What would you do if . . . ?").
- *Behavioral questions* ask applicants what they did in previous jobs that were similar to the job for which they are applying (e.g., "In your previous jobs, can you tell me about . . . ?").
- *Background questions* ask applicants about their work experience, education, and other qualifications (e.g., Tell me about the training you received at . . . ").
- *Job-knowledge questions* ask applicants to demonstrate their job knowledge (e.g., for nurses, "Give me an example of a time in which one of your patients had a severe reaction to a medication. How did you handle it?).

Always ask open-ended questions, not closed-ended questions that can be answered with a "yes" or a "no." The point of the interview is to get applicants to talk about themselves, so that you can make a good hiring decision. Also, make sure your questions are job related. Finally, remember that if you were actually using this interview to hire college instructors, every person interviewing for the job would be asked these 12 questions. So try to pick questions that would help you differentiate good instructors from bad instructors. For example, asking candidates where they received their Ph.D., which is a research degree, would probably not help you determine which candidates are most qualified to teach.

Assignment

Write three questions of each type (situational, behavioral, background, and job-knowledge) that you would like to ask someone who wanted to teach at your university.

Develop Your Management Potential

360-Degree Feedback

While most performance appraisal ratings have traditionally come from just one person, the boss, 360-degree feedback is obtained from four sources: the boss, subordinates, peers and co-workers, and the employees themselves. In this assignment, you will be gathering 360-degree feedback from people that you work with or from a team or group that you're a member of for a class.

Here are some guidelines for obtaining your 360-degree feedback:

- *Carefully select respondents.* One of the keys to good 360-degree feedback is getting feedback from the right people. In general, the people you ask for feedback should interact with you on a regular basis and have the chance to regularly observe your behavior. Also be sure to get a representative sample of opinions from a similar number of co-workers and subordinates (assuming you have some).
- *Get a large enough number of responses.* Except for the boss, you should have a minimum of three respondents to give you feedback in each category (peers and subordinates). Five or six respondents per category is even better.

- *Ensure confidentiality.* Respondents are much more likely to be honest if they know that their comments are confidential and anonymous. So when you ask respondents for feedback, have them return their comments to someone other than yourself. Have this person, we'll call the person your feedback facilitator, remove the names and any other information that would identify who made particular comments.
- *Explain how the 360-degree feedback will be used.* In this case, explain that the feedback is for a class assignment, that the results will be used for your own personal growth and development, and that the feedback they give you will not affect your grade or formal assessment at work.
- *Ask them to make their feedback as specific as possible.* For instance, writing "bad attitude" isn't very good feedback. However, writing "won't listen to others' suggestions" is much better feedback, because it would let you know how to improve your behavior. Have your respondents use the feedback form shown below to provide your feedback.

Here's what you need to turn in for this assignment:

1. The names and relationships (boss, peers, subordinates, classmates, teammates) of those that you've asked for feedback.
2. The name of the person you've asked to be your feedback facilitator.
3. Copies of all written feedback that was returned to you.
4. A one-page summary of the written feedback.
5. A one-page plan in which you describe specific goals and action plans for responding to the feedback you received.

360-Degree Feedback Form

As part of a class assignment, I, __________, am collecting feedback from you about my performance. What you say or write will not affect my grade. The purpose of this assignment is for me to receive honest feedback from the people I work with in order to identify the things I'm doing well and the things that I need to improve. So please be honest and direct in your evaluation.

When you have completed this feedback form, please return it to ________. S/he has been selected as my feedback facilitator and is responsible for ensuring that your confidentiality and anonymity are maintained. After all feedback forms have been returned to _______, s/he will make sure that your particular responses cannot be identified. Only then will the feedback be shared with me.

Please provide the following feedback.

Continue doing . . .

Describe 3 things that __________ is doing that are a positive part of his/her performance and that you want them to continue doing.

1.

2.

3.

Start doing . . .

Describe 3 things that ________ needs to start doing that would significantly improve his/her performance.

1.

2.

3.

Please make your feedback as specific and behavioral as possible. For instance, writing "needs to adjust attitude" isn't very good feedback. However, writing "needs to begin listening to others' suggestions" is much better feedback because the group member now knows exactly how they should change their behavior. So please be specific. Also please write more than one sentence per comment. This will help feedback recipients better understand your comments.

Chapter 15 Outline

Managing Service and Manufacturing Operations

What Would **You** Do?

Long Island, New York. It's 6:00 a.m. on Friday morning. Phone calls from unhappy *Newsday* subscribers are already rolling into the circulation department. *Newsday* is the leading newspaper on Long Island, and the eighth-largest newspaper in the U.S. Callers are complaining, "I just went out in the cold to get my newspaper from the driveway, and it doesn't have all the sports scores!" "I wanted to read about the Knicks-Bulls basketball game, and all you've got is the score through the third quarter! Who cares about that? I want to know who won the game and why!" Newspapers like *Newsday* get complaints like this every time a sports game runs late. In fact, newspapers get complaints whenever a late-breaking story of any kind doesn't appear in the morning edition of the newspaper. When subscribers trudge out to their mailboxes for the newspaper or people pick one up at a newsstand on their way to work, they want it to include the latest news stories and updates. However, to get out a daily paper, news stories usually have to be finalized and filed between 9:00 and 11:00 p.m. the night before the paper ends up in readers' hands. It's a limitation that all newspapers face. At some point, you've got to quit covering new stories and go with the stories you've got. After all, if you waited for all the late stories to come in, you wouldn't be able to get the paper printed and delivered in time for the morning rush hour, which begins when commuters start their morning around 5:30 a.m. However, the problem for *Newsday* is that it competes in one of the most competitive newspaper markets in the U.S. If *Newsday* doesn't run the latest sports scores and stories, then readers may turn to the *New York Times*, the *New York Post*, or the *New York Daily News* instead. Even worse, in this age of instant news, potential newspaper readers may decide that they don't need to buy the morning edition of *Newsday* at all. With 24-hour TV news channels like CNN, 24-hour TV sports and sports news channels like ESPN and ESPN2, and instantly updated Web sites for news (**www.cnn.com, www.msnbc.com, www.abcnews.com**) and sports (**espnet.sportszone.com, www.sportsline.com, www.cnnsi.com**), why pay for a newspaper? Especially if it doesn't have the news you want. The production of a daily newspaper begins when section editors (i.e., sports, lifestyle, politics, etc.) and writers decide what stories to cover and approximately how long those stories should be. Writers then conduct their interviews, check their facts, and write the stories. Layout editors manage the overall look and layout on each page, arranging the advertisements, pictures, and the amount of copy space for articles. Copy editors then edit the stories, double-check facts, rearrange paragraphs, and make sure that stories fit in the allotted layout space. Once pages are completed or "closed," they're sent to the printers, who pull the advertisements, pictures, headlines, and stories together to form each page. When all pages have been "assembled," press operators run the giant printing presses that churn out hundreds of thousands of newspapers per day. Additional machines cut, fold, and bind the newspapers into bundles, which are then loaded onto trucks that drive out to delivery points to drop off the bundles to the carriers, who deliver individual copies of newspapers to subscribers' driveways and mailboxes. Given the production process described above, how can *Newsday* change its writing, editing, production, printing, and delivery processes to include as many late-breaking stories as possible but still deliver newspapers by 5:30 each morning? In other words, how can *Newsday* become more productive during each 24-hour news cycle? While productivity is important to companies, quality is what matters to customers. What can *Newsday* do to improve quality for customers while increasing productivity for itself? As it makes these changes, what should *Newsday's* goals be with respect to this production process? Should it focus on speed or flexibility? Finally, if you think of news stories as unfinished inventory, what techniques for managing inventory might *Newsday* use to address these problems? **If you were the publishing editor in charge of *Newsday*, what would you do?**

Sources: F. Ahrens, "*The Washington Post:* One Day in the Life," *The Washington Post,* 11 February 1998. G.B. Knecht, "*Newsday* Changes Playbook to Offer Later Sports Scores," *The Wall Street Journal Interactive Edition,* 12 March 1997.

The problems that *Newsday* faces in publishing a daily paper are not unique to the newspaper business. Airlines, auto manufacturers, hospitals, restaurants, and many other kinds of businesses also struggle to find ways to efficiently produce quality products and services and then deliver them in a timely manner.

operations management
managing the daily production of goods and services

In this chapter, you will learn about **operations management**—managing the daily production of goods and services. You will begin by learning about the basics of operations management: productivity and quality. Next, you will read about managing operations, beginning with service operations, turning next to manufacturing operations, and finishing with an examination of the types, measures, costs, and methods for managing inventory.

Managing for Productivity and Quality

Brothers Hank and Bucky Kashiwa started Volant, Inc., a manufacturer of skis and snowboards. Combining Hank's experience as an Olympic and professional skier and Bucky's Ph.D. in fluid mechanics, the Kashiwas designed a less-expensive, more-stable, easier-to-turn ski. In contrast to standard skis made of a composite of several materials layered atop each other, the top and sides of Volant skis were made from a single sheet of steel. Ski shops and customers loved the skis, and sales soared. However, despite their superior design and performance, Volant's skis literally started falling apart on the slopes soon after skiers started using them. The company finally fixed this problem, but because of other problems with quality control in its manufacturing facility, it still had to throw away more than 40 percent of the skis it was producing! This led to sky-high costs and an inability to ship product orders on time. So, even though sales were taking off, productivity and quality levels were so bad that Volant was losing money on every pair of skis it sold.[1]

The Kashiwas eventually solved Volant's problems by hiring a manufacturing consultant, who taught company managers and employees how to improve the quality of their products and the productivity of their factory. Today, Volant skis don't fall apart on the slopes, the company ships orders early, and Volant is profitable for the first time in its history.

After reading these next two sections, you should be able to:

1 discuss the kinds of **productivity** and their importance in managing operations.

2 explain the role that **quality** plays in managing operations.

1 Productivity

productivity
a measure of performance that indicates how many inputs it takes to produce or create an output

At their core, organizations are production systems. Companies combine inputs, such as labor, raw materials, capital, and knowledge, to produce outputs in the form of finished products or services. **Productivity** is a measure of performance that indicates how many inputs it takes to produce or create an output.

$$\text{Productivity} = \frac{\text{Outputs}}{\text{Inputs}}$$

The fewer inputs it takes to create an output (or the greater the output from one input), the higher the productivity. For example, a car's gas mileage is a common measure of productivity. A car that gets 35 miles (output) per gallon (input) is more productive and fuel efficient than a car that gets 18 miles per gallon.

Let's examine **1.1** *why productivity matters and* **1.2** *the different kinds of productivity.*

1.1 Why Productivity Matters

Why does productivity matter? For companies, higher productivity, that is, doing more with less, results in lower costs. In turn, lower costs can lead to lower prices, higher market share, and higher profits. For example, U.S. defense contractors, like Lockheed Martin, which produces F-16 fighter jets and the F-117 stealth fighter, have greatly increased productivity in recent years. How did the company do it? First, it reduced the complexity of its products by reducing the number of parts. Now instead of 41 different subassemblies per plane, there are just 27. (Subassemblies are the major parts of the plane, such as landing gear, cockpit controls, dashboard, etc.). By contrast, European defense contractors typically use 64 subassemblies. Fewer inputs or subassemblies mean increased productivity.

Second, in U.S. defense companies, 81 out of 100 workers are directly involved with the assembly or design of products, that is, the most crucial jobs in the company. In European defense companies, only 71 of 100 workers are involved in these core jobs. Because they are 30 percent more productive than European defense contractors, U.S. defense companies have been able to offer better, more sophisticated products at a lower cost. The result? U.S. defense companies have doubled their share of the export market for defense products such as jets and missiles from 25 percent to 57 percent in the last decade.[2]

For countries, productivity matters because it produces a higher standard of living. One way productivity leads to a higher standard of living is through increased wages. When companies can do more with less, they can raise employee wages without increasing prices or sacrificing normal profits. For example, because a Motorola plant in Florida makes 200 percent more

Lockheed Martin was able to increase its productivity in producing the stealth fighter by reducing the number of parts per plane, resulting in higher market share and higher profits.
© 1995 Hans Halberstadt/The Stock Market

Personal Productivity Tip

Tracking Your Personal Productivity

Are you productive at work, or are you a time waster? Chances are, you'd be shocked at how much time you really waste. The first step to improved personal productivity is to keep a detailed time log of daily activities, including your time wasters. Keeping time logs can be tedious, but today, computer shareware makes them easier. To download time log software, go to the ZDNet Software Library, **www.zdnet.com/swlib,** and search for the keyword "time." You'll find a number of software titles that can help you track your time and improve your personal productivity.

Source: W. Fletcher, "Don't Let Wafflers Waste Your Time," *Management Today,* 11 November 1998, 29.

pagers now with only 22 percent more employees, it can give those employees better benefits and wages and still make good profits. Being able to offer higher wages also helps the company by attracting and retaining good workers. And, thanks to long-term increases in business productivity, the average American family today earns 20 percent more than the average family in 1980 and 50 percent more than the average family in 1950.[3]

Rising income stemming from increased productivity creates numerous other benefits. For example, during the productive 1980s, charitable giving increased 5.1 percent per year, compared to an average of 3.5 percent per year during the previous 25 years. Likewise, when productivity increased and incomes rose, medical coverage became more widely available. Today, more than 85 percent of Americans are covered by some form of medical insurance compared to just 70 percent in 1960.

Another way that productivity increases the standard of living is by making products more affordable. For example, while inflation has pushed the average cost of a car to more than $20,000, increases in productivity have actually made cars cheaper. In 1960, the average family needed 26 weeks of income to pay for the average car. Today, the average family needs only 23 weeks of income—and today's car is loaded with accessories, like airbags, power steering and brakes, power windows, cruise control, stereo/CD players, and air conditioning, features that weren't even available in 1960.[4] So, in terms of real purchasing power, productivity gains have actually made the $20,000 car of today cheaper than the $2,000 car of 1960.

1.2 *Kinds of Productivity*

partial productivity a measure of performance that indicates how much of a particular kind of input it takes to produce an output

Two common measures of productivity are partial productivity and multifactor productivity. **Partial productivity** indicates how much of a particular kind of input it takes to produce an output.

$$\text{Partial Productivity} = \frac{\text{Outputs}}{\text{Single Kind of Input}}$$

Labor is one kind of input that is frequently used when determining partial productivity. *Labor productivity* typically indicates the cost or number of hours of labor it takes to produce an output. In other words, the smaller the cost of the labor to produce a unit of output, or the less time it takes to produce a unit of output, the higher the labor productivity. For example, the automobile industry often measures labor productivity by determining the average number of hours of labor it takes to completely assemble a car. The three most productive auto manufacturers can assemble a car with 31 or fewer hours of labor. Nissan assembles a car in only 27 hours of labor. Toyota does it in 29 hours and Honda assembles a car in 31 hours. By comparison, Nissan, Toyota, and Honda have much higher labor productivity than Ford, which needs 38 hours of labor to assemble a car, or Chrysler, which needs 43 hours, or General Motors, which needs 46.[5] In terms of labor costs, this means that Nissan pays $1,332 less for labor per car than does Ford. In turn, Ford pays $507 less for labor per car than does General Motors.[6]

multifactor productivity an overall measure of performance that indicates how much labor, capital, materials, and energy it takes to produce an output

Partial productivity assesses how efficiently companies use only one input, such as labor, when creating outputs. Multifactor productivity is an overall measure of productivity that assesses how efficiently companies use all the inputs it takes to make outputs. More specifically, **multifactor**

productivity indicates how much labor, capital, materials, and energy it takes to produce an output.[7]

$$\text{Multifactor Productivity} = \frac{\text{Outputs}}{\text{Labor} + \text{Capital} + \text{Materials} + \text{Energy}}$$

Figure 15.1 shows the trends in multifactor productivity across a number of different U.S. industries since 1987. The steel and telephone communications industries have easily seen the largest overall increases in multifactor productivity, followed next by electrical utilities and commercial banks, and finally by hotels and motels, air transportation, gas utilities, and motor vehicles and equipment.

An examination of the components of multifactor productivity shows how the steel industry has obtained such large increases in productivity. First, with respect to labor, the number of worker-hours required to produce a ton of steel has decreased from 11 to 4. Second, with respect to capital, multifactor productivity assesses how efficiently a company uses the money it

Figure 15.1 **Multifactor Productivity Growth Across Industries**

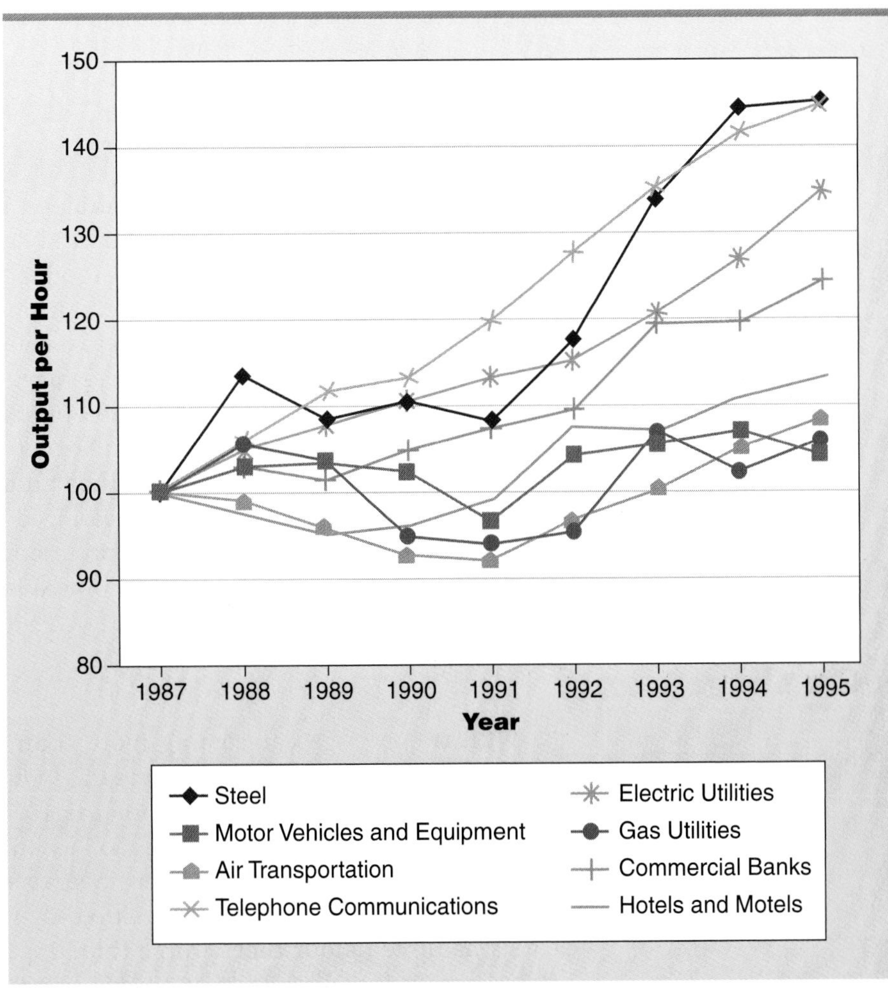

Source: Bureau of Labor Statistics, "Multifactor Productivity: Most Requested Series." [Online] Available **http://146.142.4.24/cgi-bin/surveymost?mp,** 7 March 1998.

spends on equipment, facilities (offices and operating plants), inventories, and land. In this example, steel companies have increased their capacity utilization rate, the extent to which they make use of all of their production facilities, from 60 percent to 90 percent. In other words, now steel companies have only 10 percent excess capacity rather than 40 percent. Third, with respect to materials, steel mills melt iron ore, coke, and limestone into pig iron that is then turned into steel. Today, rather than melting 1.5 tons of pig iron for each ton of finished steel, steel mills have become much more productive and melt only 1.1 tons of pig iron to produce a ton of finished steel. Finally, with respect to energy, steel makers have managed to keep their use of electricity, which is used to run their plants, at a steady 42 billion kilowatt-hours per ton over the last ten years, despite increasing steel production an average of 2.44 percent per year. Together, these improvements in multifactor productivity allow steel companies to sell steel for just a few dollars more per ton than what it sold for in 1984.[8]

Should managers use multiple or partial productivity measures? In general, they should use both. Multifactor productivity indicates a company's overall level of productivity relative to its competitors. In the end, that's what counts most. However, multifactor productivity measures don't indicate the specific contributions that labor, capital, materials, or energy make to overall productivity. To analyze the contributions of these individual components, managers need to use partial productivity measures.

Review 1
Productivity

At their core, companies are production systems that combine inputs, such as labor, raw materials, capital, and knowledge, to produce outputs, such as finished products or services. Productivity is a measure of how many inputs it takes to produce or create an output. The greater the output from one input, or the fewer inputs it takes to create an output, the higher the productivity. Partial productivity measures how much of a single kind of input, such as labor, is needed to produce an output. Multifactor productivity is an overall measure of productivity that indicates how much labor, capital, materials, and energy are needed to produce an output. Increased productivity helps companies lower costs, which can lead to lower prices, higher market share, and higher profits. Increased productivity helps countries by leading to higher wages, lower product prices, and a higher standard of living.

2 Quality

With the average car costing more than $20,000, car buyers want to make sure that they're getting good quality for their money. Fortunately, as indicated by the number of problems per 100 cars (PP100), today's cars are of much higher quality than earlier models. In 1981, Japanese cars averaged 240 PP100. GM averaged 670, Ford averaged 740, and Chrysler averaged 870 PP100! In other words, as measured by PP100, the quality of American cars was three to four times worse than Japanese cars. However, by 1992, U.S. carmakers had made great strides, reducing the number of problems to 155 PP100. Japanese vehicles had improved, too, averaging just 125 PP100. By 1997, overall car quality had improved so much that the average number of problems for all kinds of cars was just 100 PP100. In fact, after three months of ownership, half of new car buyers report no problems whatsoever with their cars![9]

quality
a product or service free of deficiencies, or the characteristics of a product or service that satisfy customer needs

The American Society for Quality gives two meanings for **quality**. First, it can mean a product or service free of deficiencies, such as the number of problems per 100 cars. Second, quality can mean the characteristics of a product or service that satisfy customer needs.[10] In this sense, today's cars are of higher quality because of the additional standard features (power brakes and steering, stereo/CD player, power windows and locks, rear defrosters, cruise control, etc.) they have compared to 20 years ago.

In this part of the chapter, you will learn about **2.1** *quality-related product characteristics,* **2.2** *quality-related service characteristics,* **2.3** *ISO 9000,* **2.4** *the Malcolm Baldrige National Quality Award, and* **2.5** *Total Quality Management.*

2.1
Quality-Related Product Characteristics

Quality products usually possess three characteristics: reliability, serviceability, and durability.[11] A breakdown occurs when a product quits working or doesn't do what it was designed to do. The longer it takes for a product to break down, or the longer the time between breakdowns, the more reliable the product. Consequently, many companies define *product reliability* in terms of the average time between breakdowns. For example, Quantum Corporation sells a computer product called the DLT 7000 tape drive that customers can use to back up 70 gigabytes of data. The DLT 7000 is so reliable that the estimated mean time between breakdowns is 300,000 hours, or more than 35 years![12] Of course, this is just an average. Some DLT 7000 tape drives will break down much sooner. However, some will last even longer than 35 years before breaking down.

Serviceability refers to how easy or difficult it is to fix a product. The easier it is to maintain a working product or fix a broken product, the more serviceable that product is. For example, Ford redesigned its cars to make them easier for mechanics to fix and owners to maintain. On the Ford Escort and Mercury Tracer, if a bulb burns out in the dashboard, the entire instrument cluster (gauges and speedometer) can be accessed by removing a few simple screws. This process now takes minutes instead of hours. Likewise, a two-piece bracket now holds the car's alternator in a spot that is easy for mechanics to reach. Before, mechanics had to empty and remove the car's radiator to reach the alternator. The engine compartments of the Ford Taurus and Mercury Sable were also redesigned so that mechanics could change the engine's spark plugs and air filter without having to disassemble part of the engine. Ford also marked the filler spouts for oil, washer fluid, and power steering in easy-to-see yellow and placed them all in one location, so that customers don't have to search to find them when checking the fluid levels in their cars.[13]

A product breakdown assumes that a product can be repaired. However, some products don't break down—they fail. *Product failure* means these products can't be repaired. They can only be replaced. Thus, durability is a quality characteristic that applies to products that can't be repaired. *Durability* is defined as the mean time to failure. For example, most household light bulbs have an estimated time to failure of between 750 and 1,000 hours. By contrast, the durability of fluorescent light bulbs is as long as 10,000 hours.[14]

Another product for which durability matters is the defibrillation equipment used by emergency medical technicians, doctors, and nurses to restart patients' hearts. Imagine the lost lives (and lawsuits) that would occur if this equipment were prone to frequent failure. Dick Martin, president of Physio-Control, which manufactures 80 percent of the defibrillation units in use today, said, "We know there are people alive today who wouldn't be if we weren't in business. If anybody in the world ought to be preoccupied with quality, it is this company."[15] The mean time between failures for Physio-Control's defibrillation units is 20 years. However, if a Physio-Control "LIFEPAK" does break, the company replaces it within 24 hours.

2.2 Quality-Related Service Characteristics

Reliability, serviceability, and durability characterize high-quality products. However, services and products are different. With services, there's no point in assessing durability. Unlike products, services don't last. Services are consumed the minute they're performed. For example, once a lawn service has mowed your lawn, the job is done until the mowers come back next week to do it again. Likewise, services don't have serviceability. You can't maintain or fix a service. If a service wasn't performed correctly, all you can do is perform the service again. Finally, the quality of service interactions often depends on how the service provider interacts with the customer. Was the service provider friendly, rude, or helpful? Consequently, five characteristics—reliability, tangibles, responsiveness, assurance, and empathy—typically distinguish a quality service.[16]

Service reliability is the ability to consistently perform a service well. Studies clearly show that reliability matters more to customers than anything else when buying services. Also, while services themselves are not tangible (you can't see or touch them), services are provided in tangible places. Thus, *tangibles* refer to the appearance of the offices, equipment, and personnel involved with the delivery of a service. *Responsiveness* is the promptness and willingness with which service providers give good service. *Assurance* is the confidence that service providers are knowledgeable, courteous, and can be trusted. *Empathy* is the extent to which service providers give individual attention and care to customers' concerns and problems.

Newark International Airport is a good example of quality service. If you're thinking to yourself, "Newark Airport and quality?" you're not alone. In the past, Newark was known for dirty terminals, auto theft, and delayed departures and arrivals. However, in the last few years, Newark has improved the quality of the services it provides to the airlines and passengers that use it.[17] For example, with respect to *reliability*, both flight delays and auto thefts have been greatly reduced. As a result, passenger traffic has increased 32 percent in the last six years. James Jarvis, a planner associated with Boston's Logan International Airport, said, "They have turned that airport [Newark] around. You don't even recognize the place anymore."

With respect to *tangibles*, Newark is much cleaner than it used to be. Standards were set and enforced for the cleanliness of the parking lots and the terminals. Airport manager Benjamin Decosta said, "My philosophy is that if the place appears to be well managed, people looking to break the rules will go elsewhere."

As part of improved *responsiveness*, Decosta holds monthly meetings with Newark's airlines, giving them a say on things ranging from snow removal to police staffing. Decosta even asks the airlines how he should spend the airport's money.

To improve *assurance*, Decosta launched a customer-service training program to instill a "customer-first orientation." The mission, now embossed on all airport employees' caps, is "to be the best by putting the customer first."

Decosta also found ways to improve *empathy* in the airport's service. Continental Airlines had long sought space in a building used by airport management. This building overlooked Newark's tarmac, where planes sit before heading to and from the runways. From this location, Continental could direct it's own ground traffic and more easily prevent ground delays, such as a jumbo jet sitting at a gate where its size prevents other planes from getting to and from their terminals. Previously, this request had been denied, because airport managers would have to give up the great view in their cafeteria. Decosta quickly approved the change after taking charge of the airport, deeming Continental's needs much more important than his managers'.[18]

2.3 *ISO 9000*

ISO 9000
a series of five international standards, from ISO 9000 to ISO 9004, for achieving consistency in quality management and quality assurance in companies throughout the world

ISO, pronounced *ice-o*, comes from the Greek word *isos*, meaning *equal, similar, alike,* or *identical*. Thus, **ISO 9000** is series of five international standards, from ISO 9000 to ISO 9004, for achieving consistency in quality management and quality assurance in companies throughout the world. The ISO 9000 standards were created by the International Organization of Standards, which is an international agency that helps set standards for 91 countries. The purpose of this agency is to develop and publish standards that facilitate the international exchange of goods and services.[19]

The ISO 9000 standards publications, which can be purchased from the American National Standards Institute (**http://web.ansi.org/default.htm**) for about $250, are general and can be used for manufacturing any kind of product or delivering any kind of service. Importantly, the ISO 9000 standards don't describe how to make a better-quality car, computer, or widget. Instead, they describe how companies can extensively document (and thus standardize) the steps they take to create and improve the quality of their products.

Why should companies go to the trouble to achieve ISO 9000 certification? Because, increasingly, their customers want them to. Indeed, Du Pont, General Electric, Eastman Kodak, British Telecom, and Philips Electronics are some of the Fortune 500 companies that are telling their suppliers to achieve ISO 9000 certification. John Yates, GE's general manager of global sourcing, said, "There is absolutely no negotiation. If you want to work with us, you have to get it."[20]

Typically, "getting" ISO 9000 means having your company certified for ISO 9000 registration by an accredited third party. The process is similar to having a certified accountant indicate that a company's financial accounts are up-to-date and accurate. But in this case, the certification is for quality, not accounting procedures. To become certified, a process that can take months to prepare for, companies must show that they are following their own procedures for improving production, updating design plans and specifications, keeping machinery in top condition, educating and training workers, and satisfactorily dealing with customer complaints.[21]

Once a company has been certified as ISO 9000 compliant, the accredited third party will issue an ISO 9000 certificate that the company can use in its advertising and publications. This is the quality equivalent of the "Good Housekeeping Seal of Approval." However, ISO 9000 certification is not guaranteed. Accredited third parties typically conduct periodic audits to make sure quality procedures continue to be followed. Companies that don't follow their quality systems have their certifications suspended or canceled.

It's estimated that more than half of mid-sized U.S. manufacturers plan to have achieved ISO 9000 certification. In fact, two-thirds of companies that already have achieved ISO 9000 certification said they did so because it increases customer satisfaction. Most advertise their ISO certification in their advertising and promotional materials. A spokesperson for Hyundai Electronics Americas said, "We always mention our certification when we can."[22] See the American National Standard Institute (**http://web.ansi.org/default.htm**) and the American Society for Quality (**http://www.asqc.org/**) for additional information on ISO 9000 guidelines and procedures.

2.4 *Malcolm Baldrige National Quality Award*

The Malcolm Baldrige National Quality Award was established in 1987 to honor Malcolm Baldrige, a former Secretary of Commerce, who died in a rodeo accident in 1987. The purpose of the award, which is administered by the U.S. government's National Institute for Standards and Technology, is "to recognize U.S. companies for their achievements in quality and business performance and to raise awareness about the importance of quality and performance excellence as a competitive edge."[23] Each year, two awards may be given in three categories: manufacturing, service, and small business. Table 15.1 lists the 1993 to 1997 Baldrige Award winners in these three categories.

Table 15.1	**Malcolm Baldrige National Quality Award Recipients (1993 – 1997)**
Manufacturing	3M Dental Products Division (1997) Solectron Corporation (1997) ADAC Laboratories (1996) Armstrong World Industries Building Products Operations (1995) Corning Incorporated, Telecommunications Products Division (1995) Eastman Chemical Company (1993)
Service	Merrill Lynch Credit Corporation (1997) Xerox Business Services (1997) Dana Commercial Credit Corporation (1996) AT&T Consumer Communications Services (1994) (now part of AT&T Consumer Markets Division) GTE Directories Corporation (1994)
Small Business	Custom Research Inc. (1996) Trident Precision Manufacturing, Inc. (1996) Wainwright Industries, Inc. (1994) Ames Rubber Corporation (1993)

Source: National Institute for Standards and Technology, "1998 Fact Sheet—Part A." [Online] Available **www.quality.nist.gov/98fact-a.htm,** 29 March 1998.

The cost of applying for the Baldrige Award is $4,500 for large businesses and $1,500 for small businesses. At a minimum, each company that applies receives an extensive report based on 300 hours of assessment from at least eight business and quality experts. At $5 an hour for small businesses and $15 an hour for large businesses, the *Journal for Quality and Participation* called the Baldrige feedback report "the best bargain in consulting in America."[24] Roger Milliken, CEO of Milliken & Company, a Baldrige Award winner, said, "Applying for the Baldrige and getting the feedback they give you is of incredible value to a company."[25]

As shown in Table 15.2, companies that apply for the Baldrige Award are judged on a 1,000-point scale based on seven criteria: leadership, strategic planning, customer and market focus, information and analysis, human resource focus, process management, and business results.[26] But with 450 out of 1,000 points, "business results" is clearly the most important. In other words, in addition to the six other criteria, companies must show that

Table 15.2

Criteria for the Malcolm Baldrige National Quality Award

1998 Categories/Items	*Point Values*
1 Leadership	**(110)**
Leadership System	80
Company Responsibility and Citizenship	30
2 Strategic Planning	**(80)**
Strategy Development Process	40
Company Strategy	40
3 Customer and Market Focus	**(80)**
Customer and Market Knowledge	40
Customer Satisfaction and Relationship Enhancement	40
4 Information and Analysis	**(80)**
Selection and Use of Information and Data	25
Selection and Use of Comparative Information and Data	15
Analysis and Review of Company Performance	40
5 Human Resource Focus	**(100)**
Work Systems	40
Employee Education, Training, and Development	30
Employee Well-Being and Satisfaction	30
6 Process Management	**(100)**
Management of Product and Service Processes	60
Management of Support Processes	20
Management of Supplier and Partnering Processes	20
7 Business Results	**(450)**
Customer Satisfaction Results	125
Financial and Market Results	125
Human Resource Results	50
Supplier and Partner Results	25
Company-Specific Results	125
TOTAL POINTS	**1000**

Source: National Institute for Standards and Technology, "1998 Criteria for Performance Excellence." [Online] Available **www.quality.nist.gov/docs/98_crit/itemlist.htm,** 29 March 1998.

they have achieved superior quality when it comes to customer satisfaction, financial performance, market share, treatment of employees, and relationships with suppliers and partners. This emphasis on "results" is what differentiates the Baldrige Award from the ISO 9000 standards. The Baldrige Award indicates the extent to which companies have actually achieved world-class quality. ISO 9000 standards simply indicate whether a company is following the management system it put in place to improve quality. In fact, ISO 9000 certification covers less than 10 percent of the requirements for the Baldrige Award.[27]

Why should companies go to the trouble of applying for the Baldrige Award? Earnest Deavenport, Chairman and CEO of Eastman Chemical, said, "Eastman, like other Baldrige Award winners, didn't apply the concepts of total quality management to win an award. We did it to win customers. We did it to grow. We did it to prosper and to remain competitive in a world marketplace."[28] Furthermore, the companies that have won the Baldrige Award have achieved superior financial returns. Since 1988, an investment in Baldrige Award winners would have outperformed the Standard & Poor's 500 stock index by nearly 3 to 1. The return on investment from the Baldrige Award winners was 394.5 percent compared to 146.9 percent for the Standard & Poor's stock index.[29] For additional information about the Baldrige Award, see the National Institute of Standards and Technology Web site at **www.quality.nist.gov.**

2.5 *Total Quality Management*

total quality management (TQM)
an integrated, principle-based, organization-wide strategy for improving product and service quality

Total quality management (TQM) is an integrated organization-wide strategy for improving product and service quality.[30] TQM is not a specific tool or technique. Rather, TQM is a philosophy or overall approach to management that is characterized by three principles: customer focus and satisfaction, continuous improvement, and teamwork.[31]

customer focus
an organizational goal to concentrate on meeting customers' needs at all levels of the organization

Contrary to most economists, accountants, and financiers, who argue that companies exist to earn profits for shareholders, TQM suggests that customer focus and customer satisfaction should be a company's primary goals. **Customer focus** means the entire organization, from top to bottom, should be focused on meeting customers' needs. For example, Motorola increased the customer focus of its management by having its 250 top executives carry beepers, so that they could always be accessible to their customers. The goal, from the CEO down, was to return all customer calls within five to ten minutes.[32]

customer satisfaction
an organizational goal to provide products or services that meet or exceed customers' expectations

Customer satisfaction is an organizational goal to make products or deliver services that meet or exceed customers' expectations. And at companies where TQM is taken seriously, such as Cisco Systems, a leading provider of the routers used to run the Internet, paychecks depend on keeping customers satisfied. For example, Cisco surveys clients each year about 60 different performance criteria. CEO John Chambers said, "If a manager improves his [customer satisfaction] scores, he can get a fair amount [of a financial bonus]. But if the scores go down, we'll take money out of the manager's pocket."[33] Not surprisingly, this emphasis on quality increased the number of completely satisfied Cisco customers from 81 percent to 85 percent in just one year.

continuous improvement
an organization's ongoing commitment to constantly assess and improve the processes and procedures used to create products and services

Continuous improvement is an ongoing commitment to increase product and service quality by constantly assessing and improving the processes and procedures used to create those products and services. How do companies know whether they're achieving continuous improvement? Besides higher customer satisfaction, continuous improvement is usually associated with a reduction in variation. **Variation** is a deviation in the form, condition, or appearance of a product from the quality standard for that product. The less a product varies from the quality standard, or the more consistently a company's products meet a quality standard, the higher the quality. At Allied Signal Corporation, continuous improvement means shooting for a goal of "six sigma" quality, meaning just 3.4 defective or nonstandard parts per million. Achieving this goal would eliminate almost all product variation. One factor helping Allied Signal make progress toward this goal is the increased quality of the parts it receives from its suppliers. In the last five years, the number of defective parts sent to Allied Signal by its suppliers has shrunk from 35,000 parts per million to just 1,902 parts per million. Besides increasing customer satisfaction, those higher-quality parts will save Allied more than $300 million a year in rework and replacement costs.[34]

variation
a deviation in the form, condition, or appearance of a product from the quality standard for that product

The third principle of TQM is teamwork. **Teamwork** means collaboration between managers and nonmanagers, across business functions, and between the company and its customers and suppliers. In short, quality improves when everyone in the company is given the incentive to work together and the responsibility and authority to make improvements and solve problems. For example, at Johnson Control's auto parts factory in Georgetown, Kentucky, 230 workers provided 631 suggestions last year for improving how the plant is run. In particular, one employee, Jason Moncer, came up with 30 different suggestions. Moncer, who said, "I go on sprees," is now trying to figure out how best to organize the metal parts that are used to make car seats.[35]

teamwork
collaboration between managers and nonmanagers, across business functions, and between the companies, customers, and suppliers

Together, customer focus and satisfaction, continuous improvement, and teamwork mutually reinforce each other to improve quality throughout a company. Customer-focused continuous improvement is necessary to increase customer satisfaction. However, continuous improvement depends on teamwork from different functional and hierarchical parts of the company.

Personal Productivity Tip

Continuous Improvement? Ask for Feedback.

"Continuous improvement" is usually associated with manufacturing operations, but can also be used to improve your job performance and career opportunities. Begin with a candid evaluation of where your job performance needs improvement. Next, after a thorough self-assessment, ask your boss, trusted co-workers, and key customers to identify what they'd like you to do differently. Ask for only a few suggestions per person. The point is to generate specific targets for improvement, not put you into a depression. Then, phase in changes by taking action on only two or three things at time. Finally, repeat this process periodically to ensure continuous improvement.

Source: J.L. Kennedy, "Win Over a Difficult Boss by Practicing the Fine Art of 'Followership,'" *Buffalo News,* 2 August 1997, C10.

Review 2
Quality

Quality can mean a product or service free of deficiencies or the characteristics of a product or service that satisfy customer needs. Quality products usually possess three characteristics: reliability, serviceability, and durability. Quality service means reliability, tangibles, responsiveness, assurance, and empathy. ISO 9000 is a series of five international standards for achieving consistency in quality management and quality assurance. The ISO 9000 standards can be used for any product or service, because they ensure that companies carefully document the steps they take to create and improve quality. ISO 9000 certification is awarded following a quality audit from an accredited third party. The Malcolm Baldrige National Quality Award recognizes U.S. companies for their achievements in quality and business performance. Each year, two Baldrige Awards may be given for manufacturing, service, and small business. Companies that apply for the Baldrige Award are judged on a 1,000-point scale based on leadership, strategic planning, customer and market focus, information and analysis, human resource focus, process management, and business results. Total quality management (TQM) is an integrated organization-wide strategy for improving product and service quality. TQM is based on three mutually reinforcing principles: customer focus and satisfaction, continuous improvement, and teamwork.

Managing Operations

At the start of this chapter, you learned that operations management means managing the daily production of goods and services. Then you learned that to manage production, you must oversee the factors that affect productivity and quality. In this half of the chapter, you will learn about managing operations in service and manufacturing businesses. The chapter ends with a discussion of inventory management, a key factor in a company's profitability.

After reading these next three sections, you should be able to:

3 explain the essentials of managing a **service business**.

4 describe the different kinds of **manufacturing operations**.

5 describe why and how companies should manage **inventory** levels.

3 Service Operations

Imagine that your trusty five-year-old VCR breaks down as you try to record your favorite TV show. You've got two choices. You can run to Wal-Mart and spend about $150 to purchase a new VCR. Or, you can spend somewhere between $50 and $100 (you hope) to have it fixed at a repair shop. With either choice, you end up with the same thing, a working VCR. However, the first choice, getting a new VCR, involves buying a physical product (a "good"), while the second, dealing with a repair shop, involves buying a service.

Services are different from goods in several ways. First, goods are produced or made, but services are performed. In other words, services are almost always labor intensive. Someone typically has to perform the service for you. A repair shop could give you the parts needed to repair your old VCR, but without the technician to perform the repairs, you're still going to have a broken VCR. Second, goods are tangible, but services are intangible. You can touch and see that new VCR from Wal-Mart. But you can't touch or see the service provided by the technician who fixed your old VCR. All you can "see" is that the VCR works. Third, services are perishable and unstorable. If you don't use them when they're available, they're wasted. For example, if your VCR repair shop is backlogged on repair jobs, then you'll just have to wait until next week to get your VCR repaired. You can't store an unused service and use it when you like. By contrast, you can purchase a good, such as motor oil, and store it until you're ready to use it.

Because services are different from goods, managing a service operation is different from managing a manufacturing or production operation. Let's look at **3.1** *the service profit chain and* **3.2** *service recovery and empowerment.*

3.1
The Service-Profit Chain

One of the key assumptions in the service business is that success depends on how well employees, that is, service providers, deliver their services to customers. However, the concept of the service-profit chain, depicted in Figure 15.2, suggests that in service businesses, success begins with how well management treats service employees.[36]

The first step in the service-profit chain is *internal service quality*, meaning the quality of treatment that employees receive from a company's internal service providers, such as management, payroll and benefits, human resources, etc. For example, Southwest Airlines is legendary for its positive culture and treatment of employees. And much of that culture and treatment emanates from Southwest CEO Herb Kelleher. Tom Burnette, president of a local Teamsters Union office in Grapevine, Texas, said, "Let me put it this way. How many CEOs [like Kelleher] do you know who come into the

Figure 15.2 **Service-Profit Chain**

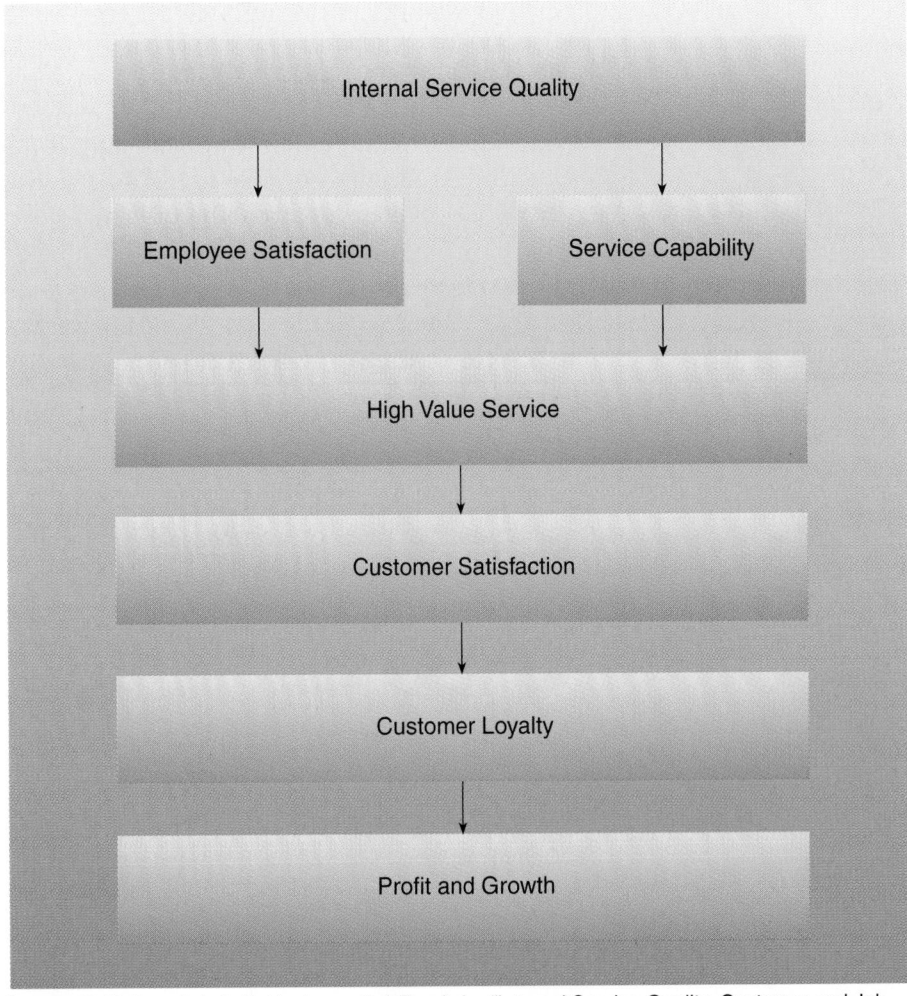

Source: R. Hallowell, L.A. Schlesinger, & J. Zornitsky, "Internal Service Quality, Customer and Job Satisfaction: Linkages and Implications for Management," *Human Resource Planning* 19 (1996): 20-31. J.L. Heskett, T.O. Jones, G.W. Loveman, W.E. Sasser, Jr., & L.A. Schlesinger, "Putting the Service-Profit Chain to Work," *Harvard Business Review,* March-April 1994, 164-174.

cleaners' [the people who clean Southwest's planes] break room at 3:00 a.m. on a Sunday, passing out donuts or putting on a pair of overalls to clean a plane? If employees feel like they are respected and dignified, cared for and loved, then they will take good care of outside customers."[37]

Table 15.3 defines the elements that constitute good internal service quality. For employees to do a good job serving customers, management must implement policies and procedures that support good customer service, provide workers the tools and training they need to do their jobs, and reward, recognize, and communicate the importance of good customer service. For example, at FirstMerit, an Akron-based bank, management has instituted a program to improve and recognize internal service quality. Called "FirstHonors," the program provides every employee with special FirstHonors stationery to write thank you letters to those in the company who have provided exceptional service to others. Employees receiving "FirstHonors" so appreciate being recognized that they often publicly display their letters on the walls of their offices or cubicles.[38]

As depicted in Figure 15.2, good internal service leads to employee satisfaction and service capability. *Employee satisfaction* occurs when companies treat employees in a way that meets or exceeds their expectations. In other words, the better employees are treated, the more satisfied they are, and the more likely they are to give high-value service to satisfy customers.

Service capability is an employee's perception of his or her ability to serve customers well. When an organization serves its employees in ways that help them to do their jobs well, employees, in turn, are more likely to believe that they can and ought to provide high-value service to customers. Again, Southwest Airlines not only treats its employees well, but also takes a number of direct steps to strengthen the service capability of its employees. CEO Herb Kelleher said, "I can't anticipate all of the situations that will arise at the stations [airport terminals] across our system. So what we tell our peo-

Table 15.3

Components of Internal Service Quality

Component	Question
Tools	Has the organization provided service employees the tools they need to serve customers?
Policies and Procedures	Do policies and procedures facilitate serving customers?
Teamwork	Does teamwork occur among individuals and between departments when necessary?
Management Support	Does management aid (versus hinder) employees' ability to serve customers?
Goal Alignment	Are the goals of senior management aligned with the goals of frontline service employees?
Effective Training	Is effective, useful, job-specific training made available in a timely fashion?
Communication	Does necessary communication occur both vertically and horizontally throughout the organization?
Rewards and Recognition	Are individuals rewarded and/or recognized for good performance?

Source: R. Hallowell, L.A. Schlesinger, & J. Zornitsky, "Internal Service Quality, Customer and Job Satisfaction: Linkages and Implications for Management," *Human Resource Planning* 19 (1996): 20-31.

ple is, 'Hey, we can't anticipate all of these things; *you* handle them the best way possible. *You* make a judgment and use *your* discretion; we trust you'll do the right thing. If we think you've done something erroneous, we'll let you know—without criticism, without backbiting.'"[39]

Finally, according to the service-profit chain shown in Figure 15.2, high-value service leads to customer satisfaction and customer loyalty, which, in turn, lead to long-term profits and growth. What's the link between customer satisfaction and loyalty and profits? To start, the average business keeps only 70 percent to 90 percent of its existing customers each year. No big deal, you say? Just replace leaving customers with new customers. Well, there's one significant problem with that solution. It costs five times as much to find a new customer as it does to keep an existing customer. Also, new customers typically buy only 20 percent as much as established customers. In fact, keeping existing customers is so cost-effective that most businesses could double their profits by simply keeping 5 percent more customers per year![40]

One service company that understands the relationship between high-value service, customer loyalty, and profits is USAA, a Texas-based finance/insurance company. When USAA's customers have young children, it sends them booklets on how to save for a college education. When its customers near the age of 50, it contacts them about retirement and estate planning. And when it issues credit cards to college students, it takes the time to teach them how to manage their credit and avoid excessive credit card debt. Says USAA Vice President Phyllis Stahle, "We build loyalty by convincing [customers] we're loyal to them."[41] Indeed, USAA has a 97 percent customer retention rate!

3.2
Service Recovery and Empowerment

Many service businesses organize themselves like manufacturing companies. Tasks and jobs are simplified and separated, creating a clear division of labor. Equipment and technology are substituted for people whenever possible. Strict guidelines and rules take the place of employee authority and discretion. This production-line approach to running a service business is still widely used today in businesses that sell a high-volume, low-cost service in which there is a brief, simple transaction between customers and service providers.[42]

service recovery
restoring customer satisfaction to strongly dissatisfied customers

While the production-line model excels at efficiency and low costs, it doesn't work well when mistakes are made and customers have become dissatisfied with the service they've received. When this occurs, service businesses must switch from the process of service delivery to the process of **service recovery**, that is, restoring customer satisfaction to strongly dissatisfied customers.[43] Sometimes, service recovery requires service employees to not only fix whatever mistake was made, but also perform "heroic" service acts that "delight" highly dissatisfied customers by far surpassing their expectations of fair treatment. For example, at Delta Hotels, if a guest tells a member of the housecleaning staff that there were no towels in the room, that guest will not only receive fresh towels as quickly as possible, but may also receive a complimentary fruit basket. Likewise, if guests complain that they were mistakenly given a room reserved for smokers, the front desk will transfer them to a nonsmoking room and may also arrange for a free night's stay to make up for the inconvenience.[44] In both instances, Delta Hotel's service employees fixed the original problem and then performed service recovery by surpassing guests' expectations with an additional act meant to make up for the poor service.

Unfortunately, when mistakes occur under a production-line system, service employees typically don't have the discretion to resolve customer complaints. Customers who want service employees to correct or make up for poor service are frequently told, "I'm not allowed to do that," "I'm just following company rules," or "I'm sorry, only managers are allowed to make changes of any kind." In other words, the production-line system prevents them from engaging in acts of service recovery meant to turn dissatisfied customers back into satisfied customers. The result is frustration for customers and service employees and lost customers for the company.

Because production-line systems make it difficult for service employees to do service recovery, many companies are now empowering their service employees.[45] In Chapter 11, you learned that *empowering workers* means permanently passing decision-making authority and responsibility from managers to workers. With respect to service recovery, empowering workers means giving service employees the authority and responsibility to make decisions that immediately solve customer problems.[46] For example, at Disney World, if a small child trips and accidentally dumps her popcorn and drink on the ground, Disney "cast members" (Disney's terminology for employees) have the authority to walk to the nearest food stand and replace the spilled food at no cost. Likewise, at Marriott Hotels, doormen like Tony Prsyszlak are now empowered to check in guests if lines are long or solve other problems that guests mention to him. Says Prsyszlak, "I'm a bellman, a doorman, a front-desk clerk, and a concierge all rolled into one. I have more responsibilities. I feel better about my job, and the guest gets better service."[47] In short, the purpose of empowering service employees is zero customer defections, that is, to turn dissatisfied customers back into satisfied customers who continue to do business with the company.

Empowering service workers does entail some costs. Table 15.4 describes some costs and benefits of empowering service workers to act in ways that they believe will accomplish service recovery. The savings to the company of retaining customers usually exceed the costs of empowering workers.

Review 3
Service Operations

Services are different from goods. Goods are produced, tangible, and storable. Services are performed, intangible, and perishable. Likewise, managing service operations is different from managing production operations. The service-profit chain indicates that success begins with internal service quality, meaning how well management treats service employees. Internal service quality leads to employee satisfaction and service capability, which, in turn, lead to high-value service to customers, customer satisfaction, customer loyalty, and long-term profits and growth. Many service businesses are organized like manufacturers. While this "production-line" approach is efficient and inexpensive, its strict rules and guidelines make it difficult for service workers to perform service recovery, restoring customer satisfaction to strongly dissatisfied customers. To resolve this problem, some companies are empowering service employees to perform service recovery by giving

Table 15.4

Costs and Benefits of Empowering Service Workers for Service Recovery

Benefits

1. Quicker responses to customer complaints and problems.
2. Employees feel better about their jobs and themselves.
3. Employee interaction with customers will be warm and enthusiastic.
4. Employees are more likely to offer ideas for improving service or preventing problems.

Costs of Empowering Service Workers

1. Increased cost of selection to find service workers who are capable of solving problems and dealing with upset customers.
2. Increased cost to train service workers how to solve different kinds of problems.
3. Higher wages to attract and keep talented service workers.
4. A focus on service recovery may lead to less emphasis on service reliability, doing it right the first time. Ultimately, this could lead to slower delivery of services.
5. In their quest to please customers, empowered service workers may cost the company money by being too eager to provide "giveaways" to make up for poor or slow service.
6. Empowered service workers may unintentionally treat customers unfairly by occasionally being overly generous to make up for poor or slow service.

Source: D.E. Bowen & E.E. Lawler III, "The Empowerment of Service Workers: What, Why, How, and When," *Sloan Management Review* 33 (Spring 1992): 31-39.

them the authority and responsibility to immediately solve customer problems. The hope is that empowered service recovery will prevent customer defections.

4 Manufacturing Operations

Let's play word association. What do the words "Chicken and Stars," "Chicken Noodle," "Cream of Mushroom," and "Cream of Tomato" make you think of? Well, soup, of course! And, chances are, you thought of Campbell's soup, the world's best-selling soup brand. In fact, Campbell's soup can be found in 93 percent of U.S. households. While Campbell's effective "hmmm-mmmm good" advertisements bring to mind images of home cooking, Campbell's obviously doesn't make its soups in small kitchens. It makes them in large factories, like its 1.4-million-square-foot facility in Maxton, North Carolina, that produces 4.9 million cans of soup per day! Moreover, this factory can make over 200 different kinds of soup, as well as SpaghettiOs, pork and beans, and different kinds of gravy.

In contrast to soup, Americana Foods makes food that you'd want to eat on a hot day. In its 220,000-square-foot facility in Dallas, Americana makes TCBY frozen yogurt, as well as ice cream, frozen yogurt, sorbet, and popsicles for other private label companies. At one million pounds per day, the plant's total capacity is split among three manufacturing lines for hard-pack ice cream, two manufacturing lines for soft-serve frozen yogurt, two manufacturing lines for novelty products (sorbet, popsicles, etc.), and one manufacturing line for flavored syrup.

Like the Campbell's soup and Americana ice cream/frozen yogurt manufacturing plants described above, all *manufacturing operations* produce physical goods. But not all manufacturing operations are the same. And, despite the fact that they both produce food, the Campbell's and Americana factories are actually quite different.

Let's learn how various manufacturing operations differ in terms of **4.1** *the amount of processing that is done to produce and assemble a product, and* **4.2** *the flexibility to change the number, kind, and characteristics of products that are produced.*

4.1
Amount of Processing in Manufacturing Operations

Manufacturing operations can be classified according to the amount of processing or assembly that occurs after receiving an order from customers. For example, at regular-sized Burger King restaurants, Whopper sandwiches are not assembled until a customer makes an order. Only then does the cooking crew put a burger on the grill, begin toasting the hamburger buns, and then prepare the sandwich to customer specifications (i.e., "lettuce, tomatoes, and onion, no pickles"). By contrast, at some of Burger King's largest, busiest restaurants, such as those in airports, museums, schools, and university campuses, cheeseburgers, Whoppers, chicken sandwiches, and fries are prepared ahead of time and left out for customers to retrieve and place on their food trays. In this instance, unless a customer makes a special order, no processing occurs after a customer orders.

make-to-order operation manufacturing operation that does not start processing or assembling products until a customer order is received

The highest degree of processing occurs in **make-to-order operations**. A make-to-order operation does not start processing or assembling products until it receives a customer order. In fact, some make-to-order operations may not even order parts until that customer order is received. Not surprisingly, these practices permit make-to-order operations to produce or assemble highly specialized or customized products for customers.

For example, Dell Computer has one of the most advanced make-to-order operations in the computer business. Dell has no finished-goods inventory—it does not build a computer until someone buys it. Because Dell doesn't order parts from suppliers until machines are purchased, its computers always have the latest, most advanced computer components. No one who buys a Dell computer gets stuck with old technology. Also, because prices of computer components tend to fall, Dell's make-to-order operation can pass on price cuts to customers. Plus, Dell can customize all of its orders, big and small. For example, it took Dell just six weeks to make and ship 2,000 personal computers and 4,000 network servers for Wal-Mart. Furthermore, Dell preloaded each of these 6,000 machines with proprietary software that Wal-Mart uses in its stores and offices.[48]

assemble-to-order operation manufacturing operation that divides manufacturing processes into separate parts or modules that are combined to create semi-customized products

A moderate degree of processing occurs in **assemble-to-order operations**. A company using an assemble-to-order operation divides its manufacturing or assembly process into separate parts or modules. They order parts and assemble modules ahead of customer orders. Then, on the basis of actual customer orders or on research forecasting what customers will want, those modules are then combined to create semi-customized products. For example, when a customer orders a new car, Ford may have already ordered the basic parts or modules it needs from suppliers. In other words, on the basis of sales forecasts, Ford may already have ordered enough tires, air-conditioning compressors, brake systems, and seats from suppli-

Dell does not even order parts to build a computer until someone buys it, giving Dell the flexibility to customize orders and include the latest technology in every machine.
© Robert Daemmrich/Stock, Boston/PNI

ers to accommodate nearly all customer orders on a particular day. However, special orders from customers and car dealers are then used to determine the final assembly checklist for particular cars as they move down the assembly line.

Table 15.5 shows the different package options that come with the Ford Explorer. Each option is different and is the equivalent of a different manufacturing module under an assemble-to-order operation. The table, reading left to right, shows some of the additional options that come with the Explorer as buyers upgrade from the Explorer Sport, to the XL, XLT, Eddie Bauer, and finally to the Limited. For example, all five Explorer models come with air conditioning and the power equipment group, but only the Eddie Bauer and the Limited come with the leather-wrapped steering wheel and running boards.

make-to-stock operation manufacturing operation that orders parts and assembles standardized products before receiving customer orders

The lowest degree of processing occurs in **make-to-stock operations**. A company using a make-to-stock operation starts ordering parts and assembling finished products before receiving customer orders. These standardized products are typically purchased by consumers at retail stores or directly from the manufacturer. Because parts are ordered and products are assembled before customers order the products, make-to-stock operations are highly dependent on the accuracy of sales forecasts. If sales forecasts are incorrect, make-to-stock operations may end up building too many or too few products, or they may make products with the wrong features or lacking the features that customers want.

These disadvantages led Wilkerson Corporation, a manufacturer of pneumatic devices such as air compressors, to switch to a make-to-order assembly operation. Under its old make-to-stock system, Wilkerson would make large batches of its best-selling products and store them on shelves that reached all the way to the ceiling of its manufacturing plant. Storing unsold inventory was not only expensive (costs ran as high as 30 percent of sales), but it also sometimes took 6 to 18 months to sell off the unsold finished inventory. And because the company was spending all of its time producing

Table 15.5

An Example of Assemble-to-Order Operations: Ford Explorer Package Options

Features	*Sport*	*XL*	*XLT*	*Eddie Bauer*	*Limited*
Air conditioning	Yes	Yes	Yes	Yes	Yes
Floor console (unique high series) with dual cupholders, ashtray, armrest, rear audio and rear heater/ AC controls			Yes	Yes	Yes
Power equipment group with power windows/door locks, illuminated controls, "one-touch-down" feature for driver's window, electric mirrors, accessory delay, two-step unlocking system with interior lock/unlock button in cargo area	Yes	Yes	Yes	Yes	Yes
SecuriLock™ passive anti-theft system	Yes	Yes	Yes	Yes	Yes
Childproof rear door locks	Yes	Yes	Yes	Yes	Yes
Front overhead console with deluxe front map/reading lamps, compass and outside temperature. Includes rear reading lamps			Yes	Yes	Yes
Color-keyed leather-wrapped steering wheel with auxiliary audio, climate and speed controls				Yes	Yes
Running boards (illuminated on Eddie Bauer/Limited)				Yes	Yes
Heated electric remote LH/RH mirrors with puddle lamps					Yes

Source: Ford Motor Company Web site, "Ford Explorer: Features and Options." [Online] Available **www.fordvehicles.com/explorer/specs1_fp_middle.html,** 10 February 1999.

large batches of its best-selling products, it was frequently unable to make special, customized products for customers who required them. With a product catalog of more than 50,000 items, it was almost impossible under the make-to-stock system for Wilkerson to have all of its products in stock and ready for delivery.[49]

4.2 *Flexibility of Manufacturing Operations*

manufacturing flexibility degree to which manufacturing operations can easily and quickly change the number, kind, and characteristics of products they produce

A second way to categorize manufacturing operations is by **manufacturing flexibility**, meaning the degree to which manufacturing operations can easily and quickly change the number, kind, and characteristics of products they produce. Flexibility allows companies to respond quicker to changes in the marketplace (i.e., competitors and customers) and to reduce the lead time between ordering and final delivery of products. However, there is often a tradeoff between flexibility and cost, with the most flexible manufacturing operations frequently having higher costs per unit and the least flexible operations having lower costs per unit.[50] As shown in Figure 15.3, the least to most flexible manufacturing operations are continuous-flow production, line-flow production, batch production, job shops, and project manufacturing.

Back to the Future

Software Simplifies Operations Management

Because of their complexity, sophisticated mathematical and statistical models have often been needed to solve the productivity, quality, scheduling, inventory, factory layout, and distribution problems that are at the heart of operations management. Furthermore, these sophisticated mathematical and statistical models often couldn't be used unless companies had access to mainframe or mid-range computers and programmers to write the computer code to run the models. In most cases, this meant that only the largest companies had access to many of these tools. However, with falling prices and exponential increases in computing power, companies can buy a desktop computer with the capability of yesterday's mainframe for under $3,000. Furthermore, thanks to easy-to-use software packages, the sophisticated mathematical and statistical models used in operations management are now available to all businesses regardless of size.

One such product is Rimms software by the Lightstone Group (**www.lightstone.com**). "RIMMS" stands for Resources in Motion Management System. RIMMS uses special routing algorithms and detailed street maps to help companies optimize delivery routes and service calls by minimizing the time and distance traveled by truck drivers or service providers. For example, the *New York Times* uses RIMMS to determine the optimal truck routes for newspaper distribution. Oakwood Medical Labs in Detroit uses RIMMS to determine the best routes when picking up blood samples at 1,000 hospitals and clinics every day.

RIMMS is a practical tool, because it creates full-color maps with precise street-by-street directions for each route. Moreover, the software, which is Windows compatible, easily allows companies to change routes, add stops, accommodate emergency calls, automatically allow for potential runovers (i.e., jobs that are typically difficult to complete on time), and make sure that technicians are assigned to calls they are qualified to handle and that they arrive on time with the right parts and tools. Patrick Malloy, director of operations at Homemakers, a furniture superstore chain, said, "We love it," because before RIMMS, "it would take two days to prepare the schedules and, even though we used to give a four-hour delivery window, maybe we made it in time or maybe not." Lightstone also has a similar program, called Easy Router (**www.easyrouter.com**), that smaller businesses can access via the Internet.

ROBCAD, by Tecnomatix (**www.aesop.de**), is another example of a sophisticated operations management tool that is now available via software. ROBCAD is used for the difficult task of programming the movements of assembly robots. Robots are notoriously difficult to program for assembly-line production. Since every single movement has to be approximated, tried, and perfected (hundreds of movements per robot are not uncommon), it can take as long as 4 months to program a single robot. Furthermore, programming has to take place "on-line" with the robots in place on the assembly line. Consequently, companies could experience months of downtime anytime they added robots or made changes to the assembly line that required the robots to be reprogrammed.

However, with ROBCAD, companies can now do off-line programming of their assembly-line robots. ROBCAD takes the three-dimensional computerized drawings of parts, such as car bodies, and then simulates robot movements and actions around those parts. And once robot movements are optimized on the computer, implementing the changes on the actual production line can take just a few days. For example, an auto manufacturer needed to reprogram over 12,000 movements into the 30 robots it used to paint cars. Before ROBCAD, a trial-and-error process would typically have taken four months of preparation time, one month of downtime for the entire production line, 20 "test trucks" (that would be painted and scrapped), and thousands of gallons of paint to optimize the paint process. But with ROBCAD, it took only four weeks of preparation time, two weeks of production line downtime, and one test truck to get the robots operational. Furthermore, the company estimated that it saved $1 million on the paint it would have otherwise spent testing and optimizing the robots by hand.

So next time your company needs to solve complex operations management problems, don't automatically assume that solutions are beyond your means. Look to widely available operations management software. The solution may be as close as the click of a mouse.

Sources: R. Narisetti, "Waiting for the Cable Guy? Software Can Save the Day," *The Wall Street Journal,* 2 April, 1998. P.E. Ross, "Virtual Robots," *Forbes,* 4 May 1998, 168.

Figure 15.3 **Flexibility of Manufacturing Operations**

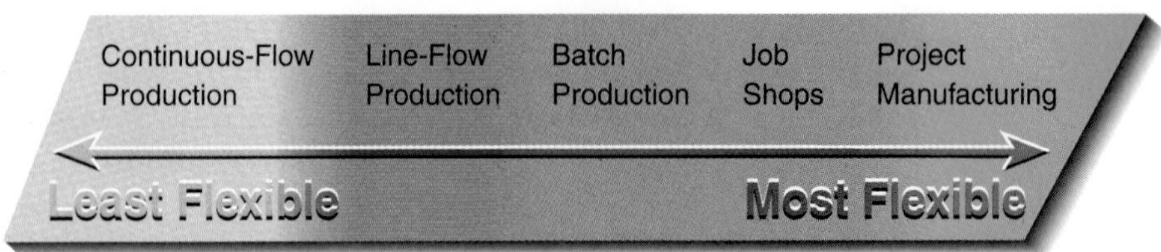

Most production processes generate finished products at a discrete rate. A product is completed, and then, perhaps a few seconds, minutes, or hours later, another is completed, and so on. For instance, if you stood at the end of an automobile assembly line, it would appear as if nothing much was happening for 55 seconds of every minute. However, in that last 5 seconds, a new car would be started and driven off the assembly line, ready for its new owner. By contrast, in **continuous-flow production,** products are produced at a continuous, rather than discrete, rate, in which production of the final product never stops. It's sort of like a water hose that is never turned off. The water (or product) just keeps on flowing. In other words, the product is always and continuously being produced. Liquid chemicals and petroleum products are examples of continuous-flow production. If you're still struggling with this concept (and it can be confusing), think of PlayDoh. Continuous-flow production is similar to squeezing PlayDoh into a toy press and watching the various shapes ooze out of the "PlayDoh Machine." But with continuous-flow production, the PlayDoh machine would never quit oozing or producing rectangle- or triangle-shaped PlayDoh. Because of their complexity, continuous-flow production processes are the most standardized and least flexible manufacturing operations.

continuous-flow production manufacturing operation that produces goods in a continuous, rather than a discrete, rate

Line-flow production processes are preestablished, occur in a serial or linear manner, and are dedicated to making one type of product. In this way, the 10 different steps required to make product X can be completed in a separate manufacturing process (with separate machines, parts, treatments, locations, and workers) from the 12 different steps required to make product Y. Line-flow production processes are inflexible, because they are typically dedicated to the manufacture of one kind of product, like Seattle-based Redhook Ale's new manufacturing plant that can make only beer. Furthermore, the processes or steps in the Redhook plant are serial, meaning they must occur in a particular order. For example, after empty bottles are sterilized, they are filled with beer using a special dispenser that distributes the beer down the inside walls of the bottle. This fills the bottle from the bottom up and displaces the air that was in the bottle. The bottles are then crowned or capped, checked for underfilling and missing caps, labeled, inspected a final time for fill levels and missing labels, and then placed in cases that are shrink-wrapped on pallets and put on trucks for delivery.[51]

line-flow production manufacturing processes that are preestablished, occur in a serial or linear manner, and are dedicated to making one type of product

The next most flexible manufacturing operation is **batch production**, which involves the manufacture of large batches of different products in standard lot sizes. Consequently, a worker in a batch production operation will perform the same manufacturing process on 100 copies of product X, followed by 200 copies of product Y, and then 50 copies of product Q. Furthermore, these "batches" move through each manufacturing department or

batch production manufacturing operation that produces goods in large batches in standard lot sizes

process in identical order. So, if the paint department follows chemical treatment, and chemical treatment is now processing a batch of 50 copies of product Q, then the paint department's next task will be to paint 50 copies of product Q. Batch production is finding increasing use among restaurant chains. To ensure consistency in the taste and quality of their products, many restaurants have central kitchens produce batches of food, such as mashed potatoes, stuffing, macaroni and cheese, rice, quiches, chili, etc, in volumes ranging from 10 to 200 gallons. These batches are then delivered to restaurants, where the food is served to customers.

job shops manufacturing operations that handle custom orders or small batch jobs

The next most flexible manufacturing operation is called a job shop. **Job shops** are typically small manufacturing operations that handle special manufacturing processes or jobs. By contrast to batch production, which handles large batches of different products, job shops typically handle very small batches, some as small as one product or process per "batch." Basically, each "job" in a job shop is different, and once a job is done, the job shop moves on to a completely different job or manufacturing process for, most likely, a different customer. For example, ATI Manufacturing in Orlando, Florida, is a job shop that specializes in assembling products for other firms. ATI's 12 full-time employees have assembled strobe-light electronics, laser light-show equipment, personal air-monitoring devices, speedboat steering wheels, automated chemical dispensers, and hand held barcode readers.[52] Another example of a job shop is Heil Trailer International in Athens, Tennessee. Heil specializes in the production of custom truck trailers that carry petroleum or dry bulk. Heil also makes intermodal trailers that can be pulled by trucks and transported by trains. Steve Slaughter, Heil's general manager, said, "Even when we get orders for multiple trailers, the trailers normally aren't the same. The shape of the tank itself doesn't really change that much. But with all the different weight laws and customer preferences, it's unusual to see two identical trailers going down the same assembly line."[53]

project manufacturing manufacturing operations designed to produce large, expensive, specialized products

The most flexible manufacturing operation is project manufacturing. **Project manufacturing** is an operation designed to produce large, expensive, specialized products like custom homes, defense weapons such as aircraft carriers and submarines, and aerospace products like passenger planes and the space shuttle. Project manufacturing is highly flexible, because each project is usually significantly different from the one before it, even if the projects produce the same type of product, such as a submarine. Because of each project's size and expense and high degree of customization, project manufacturing can take an extremely long time to complete.

For example, in the years leading up to the year 2000, most companies devoted significant resources to fixing the Y2K problem, in which older computers couldn't distinguish between the years 1900 and 2000. Both were coded "00." The Y2K problem mattered, because everything from billing and ordering on large mainframes, to computer-controlled machines and operations in factories, to simple Excel spreadsheets on personal computers could be affected by this problem. The Y2K problem qualified as project manufacturing, because it was a unique problem or project to which most companies devoted a huge amount of time, money, and effort. For instance, because Fidelity Investments thought that the Y2K problem would affect only its mainframe computers, its Y2K project team originally consisted of two people. But within a year, when the company determined that nearly all of its computers were affected, the team had grown to 30 people. Julita Lisowski, who headed Fidelity's Y2K team, said that every day they discovered new applications that required a fix for the Y2K problem.[54]

Review 4
Manufacturing Operations

Manufacturing operations produce physical goods. Manufacturing operations can be classified according to the amount of processing or assembly that occurs after receiving an order from customers. Make-to-order operations have the highest degree of processing, in which assembly doesn't begin until products are ordered. The next-highest degree of processing occurs in assemble-to-order operations, in which preassembled modules are combined after orders are received to produce semi-customized products. The lowest degree of processing occurs in make-to-stock operations, in which, on the basis of sales forecasts, standard parts are ordered and assembled before orders occur.

Manufacturing operations can also be classified in terms of flexibility, the degree to which the number, kind, and characteristics of products can easily and quickly be changed. Flexibility allows companies to respond quickly to competitors and customers and to reduce order lead times, but can also lead to higher unit costs. The least to most flexible manufacturing operations are continuous-flow production, line-flow production, batch production, job shops, and project manufacturing.

5 Inventory

Heinz, the food company, closed a baby food and soup factory for ten weeks to reduce inventories and cut costs. During this time, 400 of the plant's 700 workers were temporarily suspended without pay. A company spokesperson called the temporary closure a "one-time adjustment." Said the spokesperson, "It is not related to sales at all. Right now, the focus of the Heinz Corporation is to control costs. What this represents is an attempt to control costs by managing inventory levels."[55] Likewise, Ford shut down its Wayne, Michigan, assembly plant for two weeks. The plant, which assembles Ford Escorts and Mercury Tracers, laid off 3,500 workers during that time. According to Jim Bright, a Ford spokesperson, the plant was closed to "maintain dealer inventories at reasonable levels." Said Bright, "We have a 117-day supply on Escort and a 103-day supply on Tracer and that's higher than we'd like to have, which is ideally about a 72-day supply."[56]

inventory
the amount and number of raw materials, parts, and finished products that a company has in its possession

Inventory is the amount and number of raw materials, parts, and finished products that a company has in its possession. Both Heinz and Ford made the mistake of having too much inventory on hand and had to close their factories to let existing sales draw down inventory levels to an acceptable and affordable level.

In this section, you will learn about **5.1** *the different types of inventory,* **5.2** *how to measure inventory levels,* **5.3** *the costs of maintaining an inventory, and* **5.4** *the different systems for managing inventory.*

5.1
Types of Inventory

raw material inventories
the basic inputs in a manufacturing process

component parts inventories
the basic parts used in manufacturing that are fabricated from raw materials

Figure 15.4 shows the four kinds of inventory a manufacturer stores: raw materials, component parts, work-in-process, and finished goods. The flow of inventory through a manufacturing plant begins when the purchasing department buys raw materials from vendors. **Raw material inventories** are the basic inputs in the manufacturing process. For example, to begin making a car, automobile manufacturers purchase raw materials like steel, iron, aluminum, copper, rubber, and unprocessed plastic.

Next, raw materials are fabricated or processed into **component parts inventories**, meaning the basic parts used in manufacturing a product. For example, in an automobile plant, steel is fabricated or processed into a car's body panels and steel and iron are melted and shaped into engine parts like pistons or engine blocks. Component parts inventories are sometimes purchased directly from vendors.

Figure 15.4 **Types of Inventory**

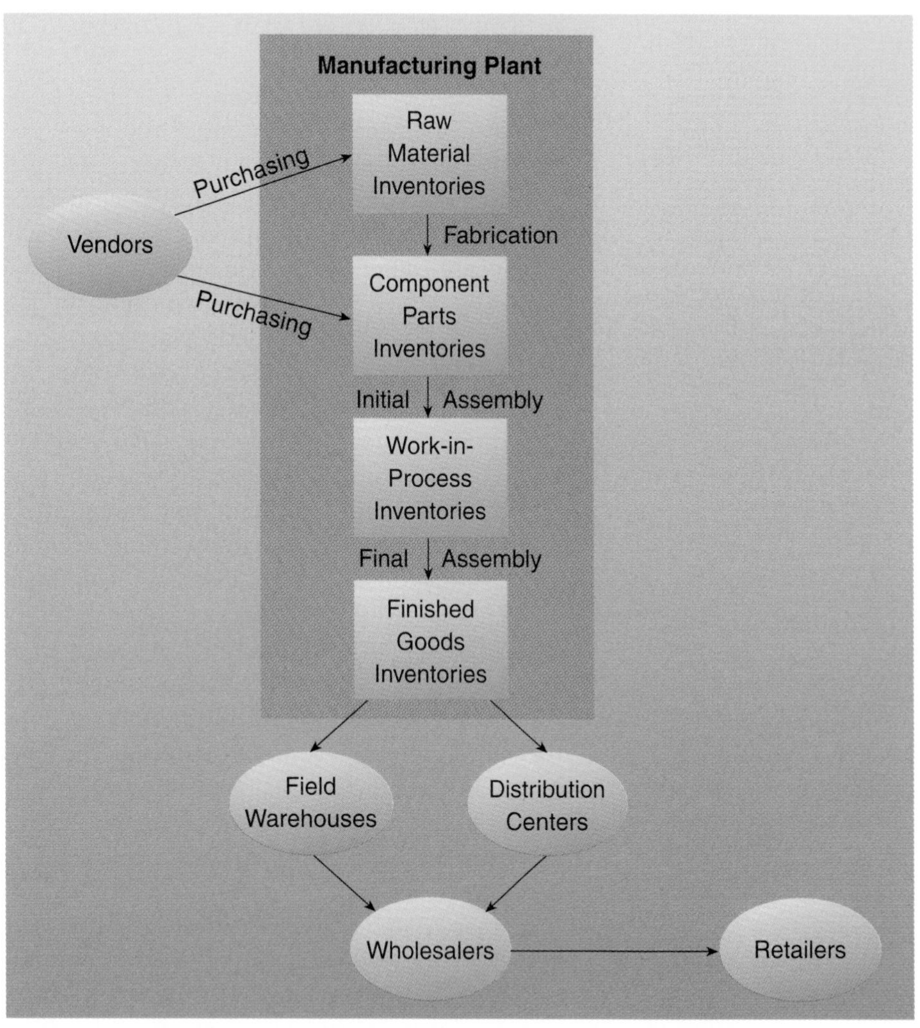

Source: Adapted from R.E. Markland, S.K. Vickery, & R.A. Davis, *Operations Management* (Cincinnati, OH: South-Western College Publishing, 1998).

work-in-process inventories
partially finished goods consisting of assembled component parts

The component parts are then assembled to make unfinished **work-in-process inventories**, which are also known as partially finished goods. This process is also called *initial assembly*. For example, steel body panels are welded to each other and to the frame of the car to make a "unibody," which comprises the unpainted interior frame and exterior structure of the car. Likewise, pistons, camshafts, and other engine parts are inserted into the engine block to create a working engine.

finished goods inventories
the final outputs of manufacturing operations

Next, all the work-in-process inventories are assembled to create **finished goods inventories**, which are the final outputs of the manufacturing process. This process is also called *final assembly*. So, for a car, the engine, wheels, brake system, suspension, interior, and electrical system are assembled into a car's painted unibody to make the working automobile, which is the factory's finished product. In the last step in the process, the finished goods are sent to field warehouses or distribution centers or wholesalers, and then to retailers for final sale to consumers.

5.2 Measuring Inventory

PersonalProductivityTip

Buy High and Sell Low?
Conventional wisdom in investing says to "buy low and sell high." However, with inventory levels, you should *buy high*, because sellers are more likely to cut prices when they have excess inventory. For example, since 60 days of inventory is the norm in the auto industry, car manufacturers will usually cut car prices when they have 90 or more days of inventory. *The Wall Street Journal* regularly publishes this information. Likewise, you should *sell low*, because when inventories are low, buyers will typically pay more to obtain hard-to-get items. So, to make your hard-earned money go further, remember to *buy high and sell low*.

As you'll learn below, uncontrolled inventory can lead to huge costs for a manufacturing operation. Consequently, managers need good measures of inventory to prevent inventory costs from becoming too large. Three basic measures of inventory are average aggregate inventory, weeks of supply, and inventory turnover.

If you've ever worked in a retail store and have had to "take inventory," you probably weren't too excited about the process of counting every item in the store and storeroom. It's an extensive process. Fortunately, "taking inventory" is somewhat easier today because of bar codes that mark items and computers that can count and track them. However, if you took inventory at the beginning of the month, the inventory count would likely be different from the count at the end of the month. Similar differences in inventory count might occur if inventory was taken on a Friday rather than a Monday. Because of day-to-day differences in inventories, companies often measure **average aggregate inventory**, which is the average overall inventory during a particular time period. Average aggregate inventory for a month can be determined by simply averaging the inventory counts at the end of each business day for that month. One way companies know whether they're carrying too much or too little inventory is to compare their average aggregate inventory to the industry average for aggregate inventory. For example, in the automobile industry, 60 to 65 days of inventory is the industry average.

average aggregate inventory
average overall inventory during a particular time period

stockout
situation in which a company runs out of finished product

Inventory is also measured in terms of *weeks of supply*, meaning the number of weeks it would take for a company to run out of its current supply of inventory. In general, there is an acceptable number of weeks of inventory for a particular kind of business. Too few weeks of inventory on the one hand, and a company risks a **stockout**—running out of inventory. Too many weeks of inventory on the other hand, and the business incurs high costs (discussed below). For example, companies that make linerboard used for corrugated cardboard boxes typically have too much inventory when they have more than six weeks' supply on hand and about the right amount of inventory when the level drops to four weeks' supply.[57] Likewise, 3Com, which makes computer modems and network cards, aims for a four- to six-week supply of network cards, a six- to eight-week supply of modems, and a five- to seven-week supply of network hubs and switches. Anything more than that results in excess inventory, which can only be reduced through price cuts or by temporarily stopping production.[58]

inventory turnover the number of times per year that a company sells or "turns over" its average inventory

Another common inventory measure, **inventory turnover**, is the number of times per year that a company sells or "turns over" its average inventory. For example, if a company keeps an average of 100 finished widgets in inventory each month, and it sold 1,000 widgets this year, then it "turned" its inventory 10 times this year.

In general, the higher the number of inventory "turns," the better. In practice, a high turnover means that a company can continue its daily operations with just a small amount of inventory on hand. For example, let's take two companies, A and B, which, over the course of a year, have identical inventory levels (520,000 widget parts and raw materials). If company A turns its inventories 26 times a year, it would completely replenish its inventory every two weeks and have an average inventory of 20,000 widget parts and raw materials. By contrast, if company B turned its inventories only 2 times a year, it would completely replenish its inventory every 26 weeks and have an average inventory of 260,000 widget parts and raw materials. So by turning its inventory more often, company A has 92 percent less inventory on hand at any one time than company B.

Across all kinds of manufacturing plants, the average number of inventory turns is approximately seven per year. However, food manufacturing plants, which have an obvious need for fresh ingredients, average 25 inventory turns per year, while auto and truck makers, which aggressively manage their inventories, can average inventory turns as high as 52 per year![59]

BLASTFROMTHEPAST

Guns, Geometry, and Fire: A Brief History of Manufacturing Operations

Today, we take it for granted that manufactured goods will be made with standardized, interchangeable parts; that the design of those parts will be based on specific, detailed plans; and that manufacturing companies will aggressively manage inventories to keep costs low and increase productivity. Surprisingly, these key elements of modern manufacturing operations have some rather strange origins: guns, geometry, and fire.

Since 1526, in Gardone, Italy, the family of Fabbrica d'Armi Pietro Beretta has been making world-renowned Beretta firearms and gun barrels. Throughout most of the company's history, skilled craftsmen handmade the lock, stock, and barrel of Beretta guns. After each part had been handmade, a skilled gun finisher assembled the parts into a complete gun. However, a gun finisher's job was not simply screwing the different parts of a gun together, as is done today. Instead, each handmade part required extensive finishing and adjusting, so it would fit together with the other handmade gun parts. This was necessary because, even if made by the same skilled craftsman, no two parts were alike. In fact, gun finishers played a role similar to that of fine watchmakers, who meticulously assembled expensive watches—without them, the product simply wouldn't work.

However, this all changed in 1791 when the U.S. government, worried about a possible war with France, ordered 40,000 muskets from private gun contractors. Like Beretta, all but one contractor built handmade muskets assembled by skilled gun finishers who made sure that each part fit together. Thus, each musket was unique. If a part broke, a replacement part would have to be handcrafted. But one contractor, Eli Whitney of New Haven, Connecticut, who is better known for his invention of the cotton gin, determined that if gun parts were made accurately enough, guns could be made with standardized, interchangeable parts. So he designed machine tools that allowed unskilled workers to make each gun part the same as the next. Said Whitney, "The tools which I contemplate to make are similar to an engraving on copper plate from which may be taken a great number of impressions perceptibly alike." Years passed before Whitney delivered his 10,000 muskets to the U.S. government. However, in 1801, he demonstrated the superiority of interchangeable parts to President-elect Thomas Jefferson by quickly and easily assembling complete muskets from randomly picked piles of musket parts.

Today, because of Whitney's ideas, most things, from cars to toasters to space shuttles, are manufactured using standardized, interchangeable parts. But even with this advance, manufacturers still faced the significant limitation of not being able to produce a part that they had not seen or examined firsthand. Yet, thanks to Gaspard Monge, a Frenchmen of modest beginnings, this soon changed.

In Monge's time, maps were crude, often inaccurate, and almost never up-to-date. However, in 1762, as a 16-year-old, Monge drew a large-scale map of the town of Beaune, France. He developed new surveying tools and systematic methods of observation, so that everything on the map was in proportion and correctly placed. Monge's advanced skills as a draftsman led to his appointment to the prestigious École Militaire de Mézières, a military institute, where one of his first assignments was to determine the proper placement of cannons for a military fortress. This task normally involved long, complicated mathematical computations, but using the geometrical principles he developed as a draftsman, Monge calculated his estimates so quickly that, at first, commanders refused to believe they were accurate. However, they soon realized the importance of his breakthrough and protected it as a military secret for more than a decade.

However, the book *Descriptive Geometry* was Monge's greatest achievement. In it, he explained techniques for drawing three-dimensional objects on paper. For the first time, such precise drawings permitted manufacturers to make standardized, interchangeable parts without first examining a prototype. Today, thanks to Monge, manufacturers rely on CAD (computer-aided design) and CAM (computer-aided manufacturing) to take three-dimensional designs straight from the computer to the factory floor.

With standardized, interchangeable parts now the norm, and with parts that could be made from design drawings alone, manufacturers ran into a problem that they had never faced before: too much inventory. In fact, it became common for large factories to have as much as two months' parts inventory on hand. Ironically, a solution to this problem was found in 1905 when the Oldsmobile Motor Works in Detroit burned down. At a time when cars were far too expensive for most Americans, Oldsmobile had become the leading automobile manufacturer in the U.S. by being the first to produce an affordable car. So when the Oldsmobile factory burned down, management rented a new production facility to get production up and running as quickly as possible. However, because the new facility was much smaller (and because the company was short on funds), there was no room to store large stockpiles of inventory, as was the custom of the day. Therefore, the company made do with what it called "hand-to-mouth inventories," in which each production station had only enough parts on hand to do a short production run. Fortunately, since all of its parts suppliers were close by, Oldsmobile could place orders in the morning and receive them in the afternoon (even without telephones), just like today's computerized just-in-time inventory systems. So, contrary to common belief, just-in-time inventory systems were not invented by Japanese manufacturers. Instead, they were invented out of necessity nearly a century ago because of a fire.

Sources: "The Arsenals of Progress," *Economist,* 5 March 1995, 5. C. Behagg, "Mass Production Without the Factory: Craft Producers, Guns and Small Firm Innovation, 1790-1815," *Business History* 40, no. 3 (1 July 1998): 1. The Beretta Museum, "Beretta History." [Online] Available **www.beretta.com/international/museo.htm,** 15 February 1999. *Morning Chronicle,* 11 November 1850. *Household Words* IV (1851/52): 582. Select Committee on Small Arms, QQ. 411-15. M. Schwartz & A. Fish, "Just-in-Time Inventories in Old Detroit," *Business History* 40, no. 3 (July 1998): 48. J.B. White, "The Line Starts Here: Mass Production Techniques Changed the Way People Work and Live Throughout the World. So Whose Idea Was It Anyway?" *The Wall Street Journal,* 11 January 1999, R25. "Whitney, Eli" Britannica Online. [Online] Available **www.eb.com:180/cgi-bin/g?DocF=micro/638/74.html,** 15 February 1999.

5.3
Costs of Maintaining an Inventory

ordering cost
the costs associated with ordering inventory, including the cost of data entry, phone calls, obtaining bids, correcting mistakes, and determining when and how much inventory to order

Maintaining an inventory incurs four kinds of costs: ordering, setup, holding, and stockout. **Ordering cost** is not the cost of the inventory itself, but the costs associated with ordering the inventory. It includes the costs of completing paperwork, manually entering data into a computer, making phone calls, getting competing bids, correcting mistakes, and simply determining when and how much new inventory should be reordered. For example, ordering costs are relatively high in the restaurant business, because 80 percent of food service orders (in which restaurants reorder food supplies) are processed manually. However, it's estimated that the food industry could save $6.6 billion if all restaurants converted to electronic data interchange (see Chapter 6), in which purchase and ordering information from one company's computer system is automatically relayed to another company's computer system. In fact, a number of restaurants and food service trade groups have formed an interest group called Efficient Foodservice Response to encourage restaurants and food suppliers to use EDI and other methods of electronic commerce.[60]

setup cost
the costs of downtime and lost efficiency that occur when changing or adjusting a machine to produce a different kind of inventory

Setup cost is the cost of changing or adjusting a machine so it can produce a different kind of inventory.[61] For example, 3M uses the same production machinery to make several kinds of industrial tape. However, different adjustments have to be made to the machines for each kind of tape. There are two kinds of setup costs, downtime and lost efficiency. *Downtime* occurs anytime a machine is not being used to process inventory. So if it takes five hours to switch a machine from processing one kind of inventory to another, then five hours of downtime have occurred. Downtime is costly, because companies only earn an economic return when machines are actively turning raw materials into parts or parts into finished products. The second setup cost is *lost efficiency*. Typically, after a switchover, it takes some time to recalibrate a machine to its optimal settings. It may take several days of fine tuning before a machine finally produces the number of high-quality parts that it is supposed to.

holding cost
the cost of keeping inventory until it is used or sold, including storage, insurance, taxes, obsolescence, and opportunity costs

Holding cost, also known as *carrying* or *storage cost*, is the cost of keeping inventory until it is used or sold. Holding costs include the cost of storage facilities, insurance to protect inventory from damage or theft, inventory taxes, the cost of obsolescence (holding inventory that is no longer useful to the company), and the opportunity cost of spending money on inventory that could have been spent elsewhere in the company. For example, it's estimated that at any one time, U.S. airlines have a total of $12 billion worth of airplane parts in stock for maintenance, repair, and overhauling their planes. The holding costs for managing, storing, and purchasing these parts is nearly $10 billion—almost as much as the parts themselves![62]

stockout costs
the costs incurred when a company runs out of a product, including transaction costs to replace inventory and the loss of customers' goodwill

Stockout costs are the costs incurred when a company runs out of a product. There are two basic kinds of stockout costs. The first is the transaction costs of overtime work, shipping, etc., that are incurred in trying to quickly replace out-of-stock inventories with new inventories. The second and perhaps most damaging cost is the loss of customers' goodwill when a company cannot deliver the products that it promised. Marc Pritchard, vice president and general manager for Procter & Gamble, said, "Research shows the number-one complaint of mass shoppers is product availability. Twenty-five percent of shoppers walk out of the mass store without a purchase. What's worse is what you'd find in the back of stores and in manufacturers' warehouses—$1.3 billion in inventory, think of that—but we still can't keep the right product in stock."[63]

5.4 *Managing Inventory*

Inventory management has two basic goals. The first is to avoid running out of stock and angering and dissatisfying customers. Consequently, this goal seeks to increase inventory levels to a "safe" level that won't risk stockouts. The second is to efficiently reduce inventory levels and costs as much as possible without impairing daily operations. Thus, this goal seeks a minimum level of inventory. The following inventory management techniques—economic order quantity (EOQ), just-in-time inventory (JIT), and materials requirement planning (MRP)—are different ways of balancing these competing goals.

economic order quantity (EOQ)
a system of formulas that minimizes ordering and holding costs and helps determine how much and how often inventory should be ordered

Economic order quantity (EOQ) is a system of formulas that helps determine how much and how often inventory should be ordered. EOQ takes into account the overall demand (D) for a product while trying to minimize ordering costs (O) and holding costs (H). The formula for EOQ is

$$EOQ = \sqrt{\frac{2DO}{H}}.$$

For example, if a factory uses 40,000 gallons of paint a year (D), and ordering costs (O) are $75 per order, and holding costs (H) are $4 per gallon, then the optimal quantity to order is 1,225 gallons,

$$EOQ = \sqrt{\frac{2(40{,}000)(75)}{4}} = 1{,}225.$$

And, with 40,000 gallons of paint being used per year, the factory uses approximately 110 gallons per day,

$$\left(\frac{40{,}000 \text{ gallons}}{365 \text{ days}} = 110\right)$$

Consequently, the factory would order 1,225 new gallons of paint approximately every 11 days,

$$\left(\frac{1{,}225 \text{ gallons}}{100 \text{ gallons per day}} = 11.1 \text{ days}\right)$$

just-in-time (JIT) inventory system
inventory system in which component parts arrive from suppliers just as they are needed at each stage of production

While EOQ formulas try to minimize holding and ordering costs, the just-in-time (JIT) approach to inventory management attempts to eliminate holding costs by reducing inventory levels to near zero. A **just-in-time (JIT) inventory system** is a system in which component parts arrive from suppliers just as they are needed at each stage of production. By having parts arrive "just in time," the manufacturer has little inventory on hand, avoiding the costs associated with holding inventory. For example, thanks to its JIT inventory system, Toyota's Georgetown, Kentucky, car factory has only 2.8 hours' worth of inventory on hand at any one time. This low level of inventory saves Toyota millions of dollars a year in inventory expenses.[64] When Ford needs more seats at its Taurus plant in Chicago, it uses an electronic system to give its seat supplier two hours' notice to make its next delivery of seats to the factory.[65]

To have just the right amount of inventory arrive at just the right time requires a tremendous amount of coordination between manufacturing operations and suppliers. One way to promote tight coordination under JIT is close proximity. At Toyota's Georgetown, Kentucky, plant, most parts suppliers are located within 200 miles of the plant. Furthermore, parts are picked up from suppliers and delivered to Toyota as often as 16 times a day.[66]

A second way to promote close coordination under JIT is shared information systems. These systems allow manufacturers and their suppliers to know the quantity and kinds of parts inventory the other has in stock. One way to facilitate information sharing is for factories and suppliers to use the same parts numbers and names. Ford's seat supplier accomplishes this by sticking a bar code on each seat. Ford then uses the same bar code in its factories to determine when the seat is needed, which car the seat is in-

Been There,

Mr. Kaizen

Masaaki Imai is an international lecturer and consultant on the concept and application of Kaizen*, which means continuous improvement. He is Chairman of the Kaizen Institute of Japan (**www.kaizen-institute.com**). In Japan, he is known as "Mr. Kaizen."*

Q: You've stated that U.S. companies have not fully embraced Kaizen. Can you elaborate on your views of that situation?

A: Most Western companies have been pursuing quality management. Nobody would argue against quality, and there is no doubt that it should be the first thing on the minds of management. But while quality is the most important objective to pursue, that is not the end in itself. If you don't develop a management system where you address not only quality, but also cost management, then you won't be successful. You have to have a system to develop, produce, and deliver quality products at a good price, or a competitive price. And the best way to do that is to introduce a lean production—or just-in-time—system.

Many American companies talk about quality. You have the Malcolm Baldrige Award, you have the ISO 9000 certification program, you have QS-9000 for the automakers. But there is one important point that is missing, and that's the concept of *muda. Muda* means non-value-adding activity—anything that doesn't add value to what you are doing.

Q: Please explain your concept of just-in-time (JIT).

A: Most people think just-in-time means exactly what it says—that materials arrive just in time to be used. Such a view focuses solely on supply delivery issues. But a just-in-time system must cover the entire value chain, from the origins of the raw material to the end user, and it must be implemented at every step in the value chain. And because just-in-time removes waste, every process in the value chain needs to be flexible and able to respond within the time it takes for a customer to place an order.

Also, just-in-time demands that every process and resource be aligned and responsive to customer fluctuations. It demands that equipment be ready to produce without failure, it demands that every product be of the highest quality, and it means changing the way employees think about their work. Everybody in the company should be seeking a better way of doing their job all the time by constantly eliminating muda and streamlining their work processes, and managers should be establishing a challenging target to motivate employees.

"Go to Gemba."

Q: How can the implementation of JIT affect a company's chances for success?

A: If a company is successful in introducing just-in-time, it can survive in the bad times. This is because just-in-time allows the company to substantially lower its break-even point and, at the same time, meet fluctuating demand. With just-in-time, a company can significantly improve its profits in the good times and manage to stay profitable in the bad times.

Q: What other problems do you see related to quality management today?

A: We must comply with two contradicting customer requirements. One is to improve on quality and the other is to reduce the costs of operations. Still, even to this day, management philosophy has been that in order to improve quality, you've got to spend more money. Managers want to buy more expensive machines and hire more people to do inspection. But those approaches are what I call innovation approaches, and I make a distinction between innovation and Kaizen. Innovation is the kind of improvement you make by spending lots of money, whereas Kaizen is an approach to improve not by spending money but by using common sense and making better use of existing technology.

To eliminate muda, it doesn't cost any money, because you're simply throwing away what you've been doing that doesn't add value. Then you concentrate on what does add value, because you have more time and resources available. And if you pursue this elimination of waste to the extreme, you arrive at just-in-time, or lean production.

Q: Please explain and discuss the concept of *gemba*.
A: The term "gemba" is just as popular as the term "Kaizen" is in Japan. *Gemba* is the real place where value is added for the customer. So in manufacturing, gemba means the shop floor, where machining is being done, where assembly is being done, where products are made to satisfy the customer.

Now, what are managers' jobs? Their jobs are to support gemba, so that gemba people can do their jobs better to satisfy the customer. Unfortunately, most companies don't think that way. Managers think that gemba is a source of failure, so they don't want to go to gemba. Some managers are even proud because they don't know much about gemba. But we have a saying: "Go to gemba." Managers should be familiar with what goes on there, and whatever improvements you want to make should originate there. They must stay very close to what goes on at gemba.

The one place that is not gemba is the manager's desk. When a manager is sitting at the desk, waiting for a report to arrive, he or she is definitely not at gemba. Go to gemba and get to know what is going on—have a good look and get a good understanding of the constraints and opportunities there, and that should be the starting point. This concept is fundamental to Kaizen.

Q: When managers go to the place where work is being done, should they ask the people who are actually doing the work for suggestions on how to make improvements?
A: Management should already have a good idea about what kind of improvements should be made, but yes, they should go to gemba, ask questions, and make observations. Because gemba is a source of all kinds of improvements. If you don't know what is going on there, when abnormalities happen, you won't even recognize them.

Look at what the engineers are doing. At some Japanese companies, engineers are actively working in gemba. They are called "resident engineers." For example, some programs have an enormous amount of red tape to go through. The gemba people have to keep records; they have to make reports. So, suppose you have resident engineers right next to you. If there's a problem, you go right to them and ask the question, and they can make a suggestion, and communication is facilitated.

Source: A. Allnoch, "Q & A: Masaaki Imai," *Industrial Management* 40 (1998): 4-6. This interview was edited for inclusion in this textbook.

Done That

stalled in, and which workstation on the assembly line will install the seat.

kanban
a ticket-based system that indicates when to reorder inventory

Another way to facilitate close coordination between manufacturing operations and their parts suppliers is the Japanese system of kanban. **Kanban**, which is Japanese for "sign," is a simple ticket-based system that indicates when it is time to reorder inventory. Suppliers attach kanban cards to batches of parts. Then when an assembly line worker uses the first part out of a batch, the kanban card is removed. The cards are then collected, sorted, and quickly returned to the supplier, who begins resupplying the factory with parts that match the order information on the kanban cards. Glenn Uminger, manager of production control and logistics at Toyota's Georgetown, Kentucky, plant, said, "We are placing orders for new parts as the first part is used out of a box." And, because prices and batch sizes are typically agreed to ahead of time, kanban tickets greatly reduce paperwork and ordering costs.[67]

materials requirement planning (MRP)
a production and inventory system that determines the production schedule, production batch sizes, and inventory needed to complete final products

A third method for managing inventory is **materials requirement planning (MRP)**. MRP is a production and inventory system that, from beginning to end, precisely determines the production schedule, production batch sizes, and inventories needed to complete final products. The three key parts of MRP systems are the master production schedule, the bill of materials, and inventory records. The *master production schedule* is a detailed schedule that indicates the quantity of each item to be produced, the planned delivery dates for those items, and the time by which each step of the production process must be completed in order to meet those delivery dates. Based on the quantity and kind of products set forth in the master production schedule, the *bill of materials* identifies all the necessary parts and inventory, the quantity or volume of inventory to be ordered, and the order in which the parts and inventory should be assembled. *Inventory records* indicate the kind, quantity, and location of inventory that is on hand or that has been ordered. When inventory records are combined with the bill of materials, the resulting report indicates what to buy, when to buy it, and what it will cost to order. Today, nearly all MRP systems are available in the form of powerful, flexible computer software.[68]

independent demand system
inventory system in which the level of one kind of inventory does not depend on another

dependent demand system
inventory system in which the level of inventory depends on the number of finished units to be produced

Which inventory management system should you use? Economic order quantity (EOQ) formulas are intended for use with **independent demand systems**, in which the level of one kind of inventory does not depend on another. For example, because inventory levels for automobile tires are unrelated to the inventory levels of ladies dresses, Sears could use EOQ formulas to calculate separate optimal order quantities for dresses and tires. By contrast, JIT and MRP are used with **dependent demand systems**, in which the level of inventory depends on the number of finished units to be produced. For example, if Yamaha makes 1,000 motorcycles a day, then it will need 1,000 seats, 1,000 gas tanks, and 2,000 wheels and tires each day. So when optimal inventory levels depend on the number of products to be produced, use a JIT or MRP management system.

Review 5
Inventory

The are four kinds of inventory: raw materials, component parts, work-in-process, and finished goods. Because companies incur ordering, setup, holding, and stockout costs when handling inventory, inventory costs can be enormous. To control those costs, companies measure and track inventory in three ways: average aggregate inventory, weeks of supply, and turnover. Companies meet the basic goals of inventory management (avoiding stockouts and reducing inventory without hurting daily operations) through economic order quantity (EOQ) formulas, just-in-time (JIT) inventory systems, and materials requirement planning (MRP). EOQ formulas minimize holding and ordering costs by determining how much and how often inventory should be ordered. By having parts arrive just when they are needed at each stage of production, JIT systems attempt to minimize inventory levels and holding costs. JIT systems often depend on proximity, shared information, and the Japanese system of kanban. MRP precisely determines the production schedule, production batch sizes, and the ordering of inventories needed to complete final products. The three key parts of MRP systems are the master production schedule, the bill of materials, and inventory records. Use EOQ formulas when inventory levels are independent, and JIT and MRP when inventory levels are dependent on the number of products to be produced.

What**Really**Happened?

At the beginning of this chapter, you read about the problems *Newsday* was having trying to cover more late-breaking news and still deliver newspapers to customers when they want them. Solutions to its problems involve managing productivity and quality, services, operations, and inventory. Find out what really happened at *Newsday* by reading the following answers to the opening case.

How can *Newsday* change its writing, editing, production, printing, and delivery processes to include as many late-breaking stories as possible but still deliver newspapers by 5:30 each morning? In other words, how can *Newsday* become more productive during each 24-hour news cycle?

Organizations are production systems that take inputs, such as labor, raw materials, capital, and knowledge, and turn them into outputs in the form of finished products or services. *Newsday* does this by turning facts and events into the news stories, commentary, and photos that make up a daily newspaper. As production systems, organizations become more efficient and productive when they do more (produce more output) with less (fewer inputs). For *Newsday,* being more productive means adding late sports scores (i.e., doing more) by extending the deadline for sports scores from 11:20 p.m. to 11:55 p.m. and by moving up morning delivery times from 6:00 a.m. to 5:30 a.m. (i.e., with 65 fewer minutes). You'll see below how *Newsday* was able to do this.

Why should *Newsday* or any other company be concerned about productivity? In general, doing more with less results in lower costs, lower prices, higher market share, and higher profits. While it's still too early to determine if these changes will produce the desired results, *Newsday*'s publisher believes that increasing productivity will add "tens of millions of dollars" to its profits.

While productivity is important to companies, quality is what matters to customers. What can *Newsday* do to improve quality for customers while increasing productivity for itself?

Quality means several things. It can mean a product or service free of deficiencies. It can also mean the characteristics of a product or service that satisfy customer needs, such as reliability, serviceability, durability, responsiveness, assurance, and empathy. Of these characteristics, studies clearly show that reliability, the consistent ability to perform a service well, is most important to customers. For *Newsday,* this means delivering papers with complete sports scores and news by 5:30 each morning. *Newsday* gets just one chance each day. If the paper doesn't arrive on time, or if it arrives without the latest news, customers will be dissatisfied. In short, for *Newsday*'s customers, quality simply means that *Newsday* will consistently do what it promises to do—deliver a fact-filled newspaper by 5:30 a.m. To emphasize the importance of quality to its customers and workers, *Newsday* now offers a money-back guarantee for late papers. Whatever the reason, if your paper is late, it costs you nothing.

However, with the last story filed at 11:55 p.m. and delivery trucks scheduled to leave the loading docks by 3:45 a.m., there's little room for mistakes, breakdowns, or delays. So to make sure that it achieves its 5:30 a.m. guaranteed delivery, *Newsday* needs to make sure that its printing machines and processes are well maintained and reliable. For example, *Newsday* has improved quality by reducing the number of "web breaks," or tears in the two-ton rolls of newsprint on which the paper is printed. Each tear shuts down the line for the ten minutes it takes press workers to pull out the torn sheets and then rethread the press to resume printing. Tears used to occur once every 18 rolls. But by closely monitoring the tension on the rolls of newsprint, tears now occur only once every 30 rolls.

As it makes these changes, what should *Newsday*'s goals be with respect to this production process? Should it focus on speed or flexibility?

When it comes to speed and flexibility, most operation managers believe that you can have one or the other. *Newsday,* however, managed to incorporate both when it completely redesigned its daily production process.

Flexibility is the degree to which manufacturing operations can easily and quickly change the number, kind, and characteristics of products they produce. Flexibility allows companies to respond quicker to changes in the marketplace and reduce the lead time between ordering and final delivery of products. *Newsday* took away flexibility in some parts of the production process so it could add it in others. Previously, reporters sent stories to copy editors by 6:30 p.m. The editors would make changes in the stories, wait for photos and updates, and then "release" the stories to production at 10:00 p.m. Now, though, editors have moved up the "closing" time, so that some nights as much as 80 percent of the paper is closed before 7:00 p.m. However, *Newsday* added flexibility in other areas by extending the closing time for sports. Now, 22 sports pages close at 11:30 p.m., while another 9 close at 11:50 p.m.

Similar procedures now give *Newsday*'s advertisers more flexibility. Advertisers now have until 7:00 p.m., 19 more hours than before, to change their advertisements.

To increase speed and reduce the amount of time it took to write, print, and distribute stories, *Newsday* formed an "End to End Committee" that examined every stage of its daily newspaper production. In addition to moving up the closing time for most of the paper, *Newsday* was able to shorten its press run by 45 minutes. Likewise, it speeded up the distribution of its papers in the following ways. First, instead of loading paper bundles (60 papers held together by plastic or metal wire) one at a time onto trucks, bundles are now placed on wooden pallets and shrink-wrapped in plastic, and then the pallets are loaded onto trucks using forklifts. This process cuts the loading and unloading time by half, shortening the distribution process by 30 minutes. Second, the End to End Committee reduced delivery times by adding more newspaper carriers and reducing the number of papers delivered by each carrier.

Finally, if you think of news stories as unfinished inventory, what techniques for managing inventory might *Newsday* use to address these problems?

Inventory is the amount and number of raw materials, parts, and finished products that a company has in its possession. So like the steel used to build cars and the silicon used to make computer chips, unfinished news stories are really a form of inventory. However, unlike many kinds of inventory, news stories are perishable, like food. Newspapers must get the latest news into today's newspaper. Tomorrow, it is "old news," and no one will want to read it.

Maintaining an inventory incurs four kinds of costs: ordering, setup, holding, and stockout. The most serious for newspapers are setup and stockout costs. Setup cost is the cost of changing or adjusting a machine or production process to produce a different kind of inventory. Since today's newspaper has completely different stories, pictures, and advertisements than yesterday's, newspapers incur new setup costs every day. Stockout costs are incurred when a company runs out of a product. For newspapers, this means that stockouts occur when papers are not delivered or are delivered late. Stockouts are costly for newspapers because of the additional cost of delivering papers that were not delivered by the normal delivery system, and because of the loss of customers' goodwill.

Given the significant cost of inventory, even for newspapers, what procedures could *Newsday* use to manage its inventory? The first step, which *Newsday* took, is to recognize that it had a dependent demand system, in which the level of inventory depends on the number of finished units (i.e., newspaper pages) produced. Furthermore, in a newspaper, every step of the production process depends on the one before it. Editors edit reporters' stories. Printers position edited stories, along with advertisements, on pages. Completed pages and papers are printed, folded, and then distributed by trucks and individual paper carriers. Each step is dependent on the other.

Given that *Newsday* has a dependent demand system, it had two choices, just-in-time inventory (JIT) or materials resource planning (MRP). In effect, it used a little of both. JIT systems minimize inventory and speed production by having parts arrive just when they are needed at each stage of production. Newsday used the basic idea behind JIT when it "closed" 80 percent of its daily pages by 7:00 p.m., but left its sports pages "open" until just before midnight. MRP precisely determines production schedules, batch sizes, and the ordering of inventories needed to complete final products. The goal of MRP is to manage inventory and optimize the entire production process. *Newsday* used the basic ideas behind MRP when its End to End Committee critically reexamined how and when stories were filed, advertisements were approved, printing presses were run, trucks were loaded, and papers were distributed.

Sources: F. Ahrens, "*The Washington Post:* One Day in the Life," *The Washington Post,* 11 February 1998. G.B. Knecht, "*Newsday* Changes Playbook to Offer Later Sports Scores," *The Wall Street Journal Interactive Edition,* 12 March 1997.

Key Terms

assemble-to-order operation p. 622

average aggregate inventory p. 630

batch production p. 626

component parts inventories p. 629

continuous-flow production p. 626

continuous improvement p. 614

customer focus p. 614

customer satisfaction p. 614

dependent demand system p. 637

economic order quantity (EOQ) p. 634

finished goods inventories p. 630

holding cost p. 633

independent demand system p. 637

inventory p. 628

inventory turnover p. 631

ISO 9000 p. 611

job shops p. 627

just-in-time (JIT) inventory system p. 634

kanban p. 636

line-flow production p. 626

make-to-order operation p. 622

make-to-stock operation p. 623

manufacturing flexibility p. 624

materials requirement planning (MRP) p. 636

multifactor productivity p. 606

operations management p. 604

ordering cost p. 632

partial productivity p. 606

productivity p. 604

project manufacturing p. 627

quality p. 609

raw material inventories p. 629

service recovery p. 619

setup cost p. 633

stockout p. 630

stockout costs p. 633

teamwork p. 615

total quality management (TQM) p. 614

variation p. 615

work-in-process inventories p. 630

What Would You Do-II?

Pharmacology Department, Methodist Hospital

"...seventeen, eighteen, nineteen, twenty! Thank goodness that's the last pharmaceutical order. I didn't spend all those years in college to get a degree in counting, but you'd never know it if you followed me around."

As head of Pharmacology for Methodist Hospital, one of your primary responsibilities is overseeing the daily filling of prescriptions. Every night at 10:00 p.m., the scramble begins as Pharmacology receives the fill list containing all of the next day's prescriptions for all the patients in each unit of the hospital (critical care, coronary, orthopedic, newborn, etc.). As one of the largest hospitals in the city, this means that 500–600 orders must be filled each night. Typically, it takes four pharmacy technicians eight hours apiece to fill the orders. For each prescription, technicians must retrieve one of 3,000 different medications, count the number of pills, mix the medicine (if needed), make sure the dosage is correct, label the order, and then place it in a bin to be delivered to the appropriate nursing station the next day. Then, in the morning, in accordance with state law, certified pharmacists must check the accuracy of each prescription. With 500–600 orders each day, it usually takes each staff pharmacist two to three hours to check all the orders (or, as you call it, making use of your "counting" degree).

It's not that you're against making sure that the prescriptions are correct. As head of Pharmacology, that's *exactly* what you want. But even with all of these precautions, mistakes sometimes occur in the form of miscounts, inappropriate dosages, or wrong medications. However, a more common problem is unexpected reactions to prescribed medications. In fact, a recent article in the *Journal of the American Medical Association* found that reactions to prescriptions and over-the-counter medicines kill 100,000 Americans a year and seriously injure another 2.1 million. Ironically, if you didn't have to spend so much time checking and counting prescriptions, you and your staff could reduce the number of unexpected reactions to prescription medications by collecting and using information about allergies, reactions to previous medications, and other drugs patients are taking. In other words, preventing problems in one area (making sure patients get their prescribed medications) limits your ability to prevent problems in another (unintended reactions to prescribed medications).

Now the hospital's CEO is pressuring you to cut costs. Because HMOs cut hospital payments by 10 percent in the last four years, the CEO has told you and the other department heads that costs have to drop by the same amount. Well, the cost savings aren't going to come from layoffs. You're already understaffed and would hire two more technicians and one more pharmacist if you could. And, it's not going to come from lower salaries. If you cut salaries, you won't be able to keep the staff you've got. Maybe the cuts should come from inventories, which have increased substantially in the last few years. But will reducing inventory increase the chance of not having critical drugs on hand when patients need them? Is that a reasonable risk to take just to save costs? And, how do you cut costs, reduce inventory, and increase productivity and quality all at the same time? **If you were in charge of the Pharmacology Department at Methodist Hospital, what would you do?**

Sources: L.J. Aron, "Takeout Health Care: New Systems Shorten Supply Chain," *Crain's New York Business,* 26 January 1998, 24. Associated Press, "Drug Side Effects Killing Thousands," *MSNBC.* [Online] Available **http://www.msnbc.com/news/158473.asp,** 15 April 1998. J. Joseph, "Prescription Drugs Save Lives—There's No Question About That," *ABCNEWS.com.* [Online] Available **http://archive.abcnews.com/sections/living/DailyNews/drugreactions980413.html,** 14 April 1998.

Critical-Thinking Video Case

Quality: Wainwright Industries

Wainwright Industries is a family-owned business that manufactures, stamps, and machines parts for U.S. and foreign customers. The company serves the automotive, aerospace, home security, and high-tech industries. In this video, you learn about the changes that Wainwright made to implement quality improvement programs and eventually win the Malcolm Baldrige Quality Award. As you watch the video, consider the following critical-thinking questions.

Critical-Thinking Questions

1. What should a manufacturing company such as Wainwright do to improve its quality?
2. How does Wainwright use empowerment, customer satisfaction, and continuous improvement to improve quality?
3. What could a company such as Wainwright do to increase employee involvement in a continuous improvement process?

Management Decisions

Customer Seriously Steamed at Starbucks

The problems began when Jeremy Dorosin bought a $299 espresso machine from his local Starbucks Coffee shop. Because of the size of his purchase, he did what many Starbucks customers do—he asked for several half-pound bags of coffee to be thrown in for free. However, the clerk refused.

The next problem occurred when his espresso machine leaked and the milk steamer didn't work. When he returned it for repairs, Starbucks tried to make it right by lending him a cheaper, $189 model until his was fixed. He liked the cheaper model so well that he bought one for a friend's wedding gift. However, his friend's espresso machine was rusted and missing parts. When Dorosin tried to return it, the store manager claimed that there was nothing wrong or missing and that the machines sometimes developed a bit of rust when being tested at the factory. According to the manager, the machine only needed cleaning to restore it to its brand new condition.

By this point, Dorosin was angry. He called the Starbucks regional office in San Francisco and then company headquarters in Seattle. Convinced that Starbucks had tried to sell him a used espresso machine, he demanded that the company send a letter of apology to his friend and that it replace his friend's $189 espresso machine with the most expensive machine in the store, one that cost $2,500! A company spokesperson said, "We were certainly willing to send a letter apologizing, but we weren't going to say we sold him used goods, because that is not true." And when Starbucks mailed Dorosin a full refund and his friend a more expensive $269 machine, both immediately returned the unopened packages to Starbucks.

At this point, Dorosin began threatening to take out ads in the newspaper, disparaging Starbucks for its poor customer service. Eventually, he did, spending $5,000 for an ad that appeared four times in the California edition of *The Wall Street Journal*. "They thought I was bluffing," Dorosin said. The ads listed a toll-free number and said, "Had any problems at Starbucks Coffee? You're not alone. Interested? Let's talk." Dorosin received over 3,000 responses, nearly all complaints. Dorosin then escalated his demands, asking Starbucks to pay for a two-page ad in *The Wall Street Journal* in which it would make a personal apology to him. Dorosin told the CBS Evening News, "My pain is not for sale. So what I want is what any decent, normal human being wants, a public apology." He later demanded that Starbucks build a brand new center for runaway kids that he would then run.

Starbucks then issued a statement saying, "It is unfortunate that in this particular case we were unable to please Jeremy Dorosin. We regret that our efforts were not sufficient to meet his needs, but there is nothing more we can do." Barbara Reed, Starbucks' manager of customer relations, said, "We truly believe that we have done everything reasonable to rectify the situation."

Questions

1. What mistakes, if any, did Starbucks make in handling this situation? Explain.
2. What should it have done differently? Be specific and explain why.

Sources: A. Lucas, "Trouble Brews for Starbucks," *Sales & Marketing Management,* 1 August 1995, 15. R. Koury, "Justifiably Steamed, or Just a Drip? Angry Buyer Nags Starbucks," *The News Tribune,* 9 July 1995, D4. J. Blackstone, "Starbucks Customer Stirs Up Controversy over Defective Brewers," *CBS Morning News,* 30 June 1995. E. Knickmeyer, "Unhappy Coffeehouse Patron Steamed: Slow Roast of Firm in Big *Wall Street Journal* Ad Is Brewing," *The Detroit News,* 2 June 1995, B3. J. Flinn, "Steamed at Starbucks: Espresso-Maker Incident Boils Over into One-Man Crusade for Public Apology," *San Francisco Examiner,* 31 May 1995, B1.

Management Decisions

Something Old or Something New?

The last plane you flew on may have been older than you are. In fact, the Federal Aviation Administration estimates that nearly 40 percent of the passenger jets flown by U.S. airlines are 20 years old! As long as airlines perform proper maintenance, most passenger jets can fly for 50 years without harming performance or passenger safety. Ted Lopatkiewitz, a spokesperson for the National Transportation Safety Board, said, "The NTSB has always been more concerned with . . . maintenance, not age itself. The public would rather fly in an aircraft that's 20 years old but well maintained than in one only four years old but poorly maintained." While most airlines don't intend to fly 50-year-old planes (and it's doubtful that many passengers would want to fly in them), the airlines do have to decide whether they should continue to fly and maintain their older jets or replace them with new jets. The choice they make has implications for airline productivity and profits.

Purchasing new jets has a number of advantages. In general, new jets are roughly 25 percent cheaper to operate. For example, by replacing 35 old jets with 35 new ones, TWA will save $2 million in fuel costs for each penny increase in the price of jet fuel. Also, because new jets are more reliable, they're less likely to break down and delay flights. For instance, TWA's 35 new jets helped it move from last place to second place in on-time arrivals in just one year. Another advantage is that pilots and passengers like the new jets and all of their new features (i.e., digital controls, in-seat videos, more room, etc.). However, these advantages come at a cost. For example, a new Boeing 767, which can carry 230 passengers, costs $140 million.

Maintaining old jets has advantages, too. For instance, it can be much cheaper to maintain older jets than to buy and fly new ones. Northwest Airlines, whose fleet of jets is, on average, more than 20 years old, estimates that it has saved over a billion dollars by not buying new planes. Richard Anderson, Northwest's executive vice president of technical and flight operations, said, "From a financial perspective, this is the singular best investment we've ever made." However, spending increases in other areas have offset some of these savings. For example, Northwest spends nearly $1.5 million a year to maintain each plane, while United Airlines, whose jets average 10 years of age, spends just $1 million per year to maintain each plane. And, because its older planes require much more maintenance, Northwest had to hire an additional 1,200 mechanics. It also had to spend millions to expand its maintenance facilities. Finally, while Northwest's planes haven't been involved in a serious accident since 1990, it has seen a sizeable increase in the number of minor problems that its planes experience. For example, service "difficulties" with its older DC-9s resulted in 217 unscheduled landings per year, nearly three times the rate of other airlines. Likewise, landing gear indicators, which show that the wheels are either safely retracted or locked for landing, failed 97 times on Northwest planes last year, a rate that is twice as bad as other airlines.

Additional Internet Resources

- **Northwest Airlines Facts and Figures (http://www.nwa.com/corpinfo/profi/facts.shtml)**. Facts and figures about Northwest's services, cities, facilities, and planes.
- **Fatal Event Rates for Selected Airliner Models (http://airsafe.com/events/models/rate_mod.htm)**. This page ranks airline models by the rate of fatal events they have experienced per one million flights.
- **Fatal Event Rates for Selected Airliner Models (http://airsafe.com/airline.htm#uscan)**. This page ranks airlines based on the rate of fatal events they've had since 1970.

Questions

1. Would purchasing new jets or maintaining older jets be the better way to increase airline productivity? Explain your reasoning.
2. Use the quality-related product and service characteristics to explain the choice you made in question 1.

Sources: S. Carey & S. McCartney, "Northwest's Choice to Upgrade Older Jets Leads to Disruptions," *The Wall Street Journal Interactive Edition,* 12 June 1998. G. Jiminez, "Flying the Aging Skies," *Chicago Sun-Times,* 12 May 1998, 6. K.M. Song, "TWA Continues to Polish Up its Fleet," *St. Louis Post-Dispatch,* 12 April 1998, E1.

Develop Your Management Potential

Take a Factory Tour

Imagine that you're watching the Super Bowl (and that the game was better than the commercials—remember, you're imagining). As it ends, the camera zooms in on the game's most valuable player. The on-air announcer says to the MVP, "You've just won another championship. What are you going to do next?" And the player responds, "I'm going to Spamtown!" Spamtown? Actually, the winning athlete is supposed to say, "I'm going to Disney World," not Spamtown, the museum that Hormel Corporation established for its best-known product, Spam (**www.spam.com**).

Well, Spamtown isn't about to displace Disney World, but 60,000 people actually visit Spamtown each year. Thousands more also visit these corporate facilities:

- The J.C. Penney Museum (**www.jcpenneyinc.com/archive/archive2.htm**), which displays the history and products of James Cash Penney and the company he founded.
- Hershey's Chocolate World in Hershey, Pennsylvania (**www.hersheys.com/chocworld/**), Hershey Food Corporation's free visitor's center with a Disney-like ride through a simulated chocolate factory.
- The Everett Tour Center (**www.boeing.com/companyoffices/aboutus/tours/**), where Boeing makes its 747, 767, and 777 passenger jets.
- Cereal City (**www.kelloggscerealcityusa.com**), which shows how Kellogg makes its best-selling cereals

In fact, visiting factories has become so popular that there are now two books on the subject, *Watch It Made in the U.S.A.: A Visitor's Guide to the Companies That Make Your Favorite Products*, by Karen Axelrod and Bruce Brumberg (John Muir Publications), and *Inside America: The Great American Industrial Tour Guide, 1,000 Free Industrial Tours Open to the Public Covering More Than 300 Different Industries*, by Jack and Eunice Berger (Heritage Publications).

If you've never toured a factory, you might wonder what the fuss is all about. Author Karen Axelrod said, "Everyone's eyes get bigger when they see the way things work. Everyone becomes a 5-year-old." Barbara Bernstein of Annapolis, Maryland, said, "I'm interested in how companies make anything, plastic bags for grocery stores, peanut butter, Formica, anything." There's just something magical about watching the manufacture of familiar products like cereal, cars, or candy.

Your assignment for this Develop Your Management Potential is to take a factory tour. Consult one of the books mentioned above (both are available from **www.amazon.com**), do a quick Web search on the keywords "factory tour," or just ask around about a good factory tour near you. When on your tour, gather some literature and ask about the following issues.

Questions

1. What steps or procedures does the company take to ensure the quality of its products?
2. How does the company measure productivity and how does its productivity compare to others in the industry?
3. Describe the basic steps used to make the finished products in this factory. As you do this, be sure to describe the raw material inventories, component parts inventories, and work-in-process inventories used to create the finished products.
4. What did you find most impressive about the factory or manufacturing processes? Also, using the material from the chapter, describe one thing that the company could do differently to improve quality, increase productivity, or reduce inventory.

Sources: E. Gehrman, "Factory Facts Show Heart, Soul of America," *Boston Herald,* 29 January 1998. E. Perkins, "Factory Tour Can Be Fun, Not to Mention Real Cheap," *Orlando Sentinel,* 1 February, 1998, L6. L. Singhania (Associated Press), "Breakfast for Battle Creek's New Cereal City," *Grand Rapids Press,* 24 May 1998, F2. C. Quintanilla, "Planning a Vacation? Give Some Thought to Spamtown USA," *The Wall Street Journal,* 30 April 1998, A1.

Part Five

Leading

Chapter Sixteen

Chapter 16 Outline

Motivation

What Would **You** Do?

Diamond International Corporation, Palmer, Massachusetts. No one was surprised when the vice president of manufacturing announced that "the entire division must improve its profit picture or face plant closings." Still, finally hearing the actual announcement sent a chill through you, given the impact this would have on your workers' families. The Palmer, Massachusetts, plant, which manufactures molded-pulp egg cartons, has 350 employees, 290 of whom are represented by the United Paperworkers International Union. The plant is experiencing intense competition from another molded-pulp manufacturer (Packaging Corporation of America) and from Styrofoam egg carton producers, such as Mobil Corporation. There has been a round of layoffs every month since the announcement. As a result, employees don't know from one day to the next whether they'll have a job when they go home after their shifts. However, working in the plant hasn't been a picnic either. Management has begun transferring employees to different machines and departments in a frantic attempt to cover the jobs of those who have been laid off. Not surprisingly, both productivity and quality have declined, and the unionized workers have filed more than 150 grievances against management this year alone! The results of an informal employee opinion survey confirm that employee morale is also deteriorating: 65 percent of employees stated they felt that management did not treat them with respect, 56 percent responded that they approached their work pessimistically, and 79 percent said that they felt they were not rewarded for good work. With things so bad, company management unexpectedly turned to you to improve employee morale and motivation. You were sitting in your office looking forward to the weekend when the plant manager stopped by on his way to the parking lot to give you the assignment. "We've got to improve morale and motivation if we're going to remain competitive and survive. And we've got to do it soon. I just came from a meeting where 14 new grievances were being considered. Only three of them were legitimate. Eleven were filed just because workers were unhappy with management. Why is it that we spend most of our time dealing with the 5 percent of the work force that is unproductive and causes problems? Shouldn't we be paying more attention to the 95 percent who do what's expected of them? Take two weeks and develop a program to turn this place around. And, by the way, have a good weekend." "Have a good weekend?! How, with this problem on my mind?" What exactly is it that motivates employees, and is it the same for everyone? What can you do without spending a lot of money to get employees excited about their work again? The fact that there are so many grievances being filed, and that some of them are over trivial matters, suggests that employees don't feel they are being treated fairly. What can you do to change these perceptions? What can you do to get employees to meet their goals? As you thought about it, you realized you didn't have a good answer. Why couldn't you have been out of your office when the boss came around?" **If you were in charge of motivating these employees, what would you do?**

Sources: Anonymous, "Diamond International: Worker Woes? Motivate the Good Ones, Not the Bad," *Incentive Marketing* 157 (October 1983): 104-110. D.C. Boyle, "Employee Motivation That Works," *HR Magazine,* October 1992, 83-89. D.C. Boyle, "Divining the Secrets of a Successful Employee Recognition System," *Security Management* 40 (July 1996): 21-24. D.C. Boyle, "To Employees—'Thanks' Means Millions—Literally," *Supervision* 53 (November 1992): 3-6. Anonymous, "Case History: Employee Recognition Programs," *Small Business Report* 11 (October 1986): 98. D.C. Boyle, "The 100 Club," *Harvard Business Review* 65 (March/April 1987): 26-27. D.C. Boyle, "Recognition That Works," *Incentive Marketing* 161 (December 1987): 32-36.

"Why are they putting forth as little effort as they can get away with?" "What can you do to get employees to meet their goals?" "Would more or different rewards be the answer?" The set of problems that Diamond International is experiencing illustrates that motivating workers is never easy. And, with layoffs occurring, it is hard to imagine a more difficult situation in which to maintain a motivated work force. However, managers face these kinds of questions in these kinds of situations on a daily basis.

This chapter begins by reviewing the basics of motivation—effort, needs, and intrinsic and extrinsic motivation. We will start with a basic model of motivation and add to it as we progress through each section in the chapter. Next, we will explore how employees' equity perceptions and reward expectations affect their motivation. If you're familiar with the phrase "perception is reality," you're off to a good start in understanding the importance of perceptions and expectations in motivation. The third part of the chapter reviews the role that rewards and goals play in motivating employees. You'll see that finding the right combination of goals and rewards is much harder in practice than it looks. The chapter finishes with a summary of practical, theory-based actions that managers can take to motivate their workers.

What Is Motivation?

motivation
the set of forces that initiates, directs, and makes people persist in their efforts to accomplish a goal

Motivation is the set of forces that initiates, directs, and makes people persist in their efforts to accomplish a goal.[1] In terms of this definition, *initiation of effort* is concerned with the choices that people make about how much effort to put forth in their jobs. ("Gosh, I hate writing performance appraisals, so maybe I'll just add a paragraph to last year's appraisals," versus "Performance feedback is important. I'm going to schedule an hour to review each file and an hour to write each appraisal.") *Direction of effort* is concerned with the choices that people make in deciding where to put forth effort in their jobs. ("I'm really excited about the new computer system and can't wait to get started," versus "Yeah, yeah, another new computer system. I'll do what I need to get by with it, but I think my time is better spent working directly with employees and customers.") *Persistence of effort* is concerned with the choices that people make about how long they will put forth effort in their jobs before reducing or eliminating those efforts. ("We're only halfway to our goal with three months to get it done. We'll never make it, so I'm not going to work at this anymore," versus "We're only halfway to our goal with three months to go, but if we all keep working hard, we can do it.")

As shown in Figure 16.1, initiation, direction, and persistence are at the heart of motivation. After reading the next section, you should be able to:

1 explain the **basics of motivation**.

1 Basics of Motivation

Take your right hand and point the palm toward your face. Keep your thumb and pinky finger straight and bend the three middle fingers so the tips are touching your palm. Now rotate your wrist back and forth. If you were in the Regent Square Tavern in Pittsburgh, Pennsylvania, that hand signal would tell waitress Marjorie Landale that you wanted a Yeungling beer. However, Marjorie, who isn't deaf, would not have understood that sign

Figure 16.1 **The Components of Motivation**

a few years ago. But with a state school for the deaf nearby, the tavern always had its share of deaf customers, so she decided on her own to take classes to learn how to sign. She said, "It occurred to me that I could learn their language more easily than they could learn mine." At first, deaf customers would signal for a pen and paper to write out their orders. But after Marjorie signaled that she was learning to sign, she said, "Their eyes [would] light up, and they [would] finger-spell their order and [then] we've made a connection." The tavern's regular deaf customers teased her in a friendly way about her poor signing skills, but word quickly spread as the students started bringing in their friends, classmates, teachers, and hearing friends as well. Said Marjorie, "The deaf customers are patient with my amateur signing. They appreciate the effort."[2]

What would motivate an employee like Marjorie to voluntarily learn a new language like the American Sign Language? (Sign language is every bit as much a language as French or Spanish.) She wasn't paid to take classes in her free time. She chose to do it on her own. And while she undoubtedly makes more tip money with a full bar than with an empty one, it's highly unlikely that she began her classes with the objective of making more money. Just what is it that motivates employees like Marjorie Landale?

Let's learn more about motivation by building a basic model of motivation out of these parts: **1.1** *effort and performance,* **1.2** *need satisfaction, and* **1.3** *intrinsic and extrinsic rewards. This section ends with a brief discussion of* **1.4** *how to motivate people with this basic model of motivation.*

1.1
Effort and Performance

When most people think of work motivation, they think that working hard (effort) should lead to doing a good job (performance). Figure 16.2 shows a basic model of work motivation and performance, displaying this process.

The first thing to notice about Figure 16.2 is that this is a basic model of work motivation *and* performance. In practice, it's almost impossible to talk

Figure 16.2 **A Basic Model of Work Motivation and Performance**

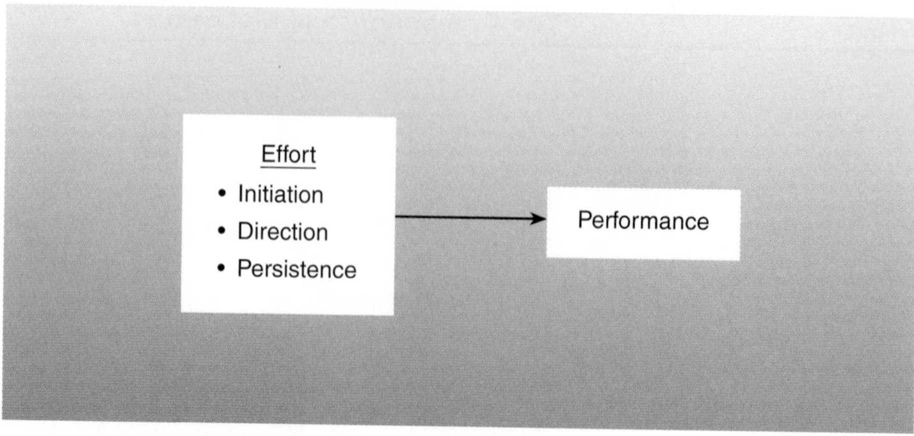

about one without mentioning the other. Not surprisingly, managers often confuse the two, saying things such as "Your performance was really terrible last quarter. What's the matter? Aren't you as motivated as you used to be?" In fact, motivation is just one of three primary determinants of job performance. In industrial psychology, job performance is frequently represented by this equation:

$$\text{Job Performance} = \text{Motivation} \times \text{Ability} \times \text{Situational Constraints}$$

In this formula, *job performance* is how well someone performs the requirements of the job. *Motivation*, as defined above, is effort, the degree to which someone works hard to do the job well. *Ability* is the degree to which workers possess the knowledge, skills, and talent needed to do a job well. And, *situational constraints* are factors beyond the control of individual employees, such as tools, policies, and resources that have an effect on job performance.

Since job performance is a multiplicative function of motivation times ability times situational constraints, job performance will suffer if any one of these components is weak. For example, in 1988, the East German bobsled team was fully funded by the East German government and had state-of-the art coaching and equipment (no situational constraints). It also recruited and selected bobsled team members from a wide pool of highly trained athletes (ability) who had trained year-round for most of their lives (motivation) for a chance to make the highly prestigious East German bobsled team. By contrast, consider the Jamaican bobsled team that Disney made famous in the movie "Cool Runnings." In 1988 at its first winter Olympics, it had limited funding, a coach with bobsledding experience (a five-time U.S. champion) but no coaching experience, and an old bobsled that couldn't compete with the world-class equipment used by the best teams (high situational constraints). It also had a group of drivers and riders raised in tropical Jamaica with almost no bobsledding or winter sports experience (very little ability). However, this group of drivers dreamed of competing in the Olympics and did what little they could to train for several months, considering their limited circumstances (strong motivation).

It's not hard to guess which team did better, is it? With ample motivation, ability, and almost no situational constraints, you'd expect the East Germans to be competitive, and they were—finishing second and third in the two-man competition and second in the four-man competition.[3] By contrast, with strong motivation, little ability, and extremely high situational constraints, the Jamaican two-man team finished in 35th place, while the four-man team crashed spectacularly and had to push the bobsled across the line to complete its final run on the course.

Does this mean that motivation doesn't matter? No, not at all. It just means that all the motivation in the world won't translate into high performance when you have little ability and high situational constraints. In fact, prior to the 1996 Winter Olympics, the Jamaican team spent six weeks working with Sam Bock, who also worked with the elite Canadian team. Bock put the Jamaicans through their paces at a special bobsled training center in Oberhof, Germany. After training for four to eight hours a day in world-class conditions under world-class tutelage, the Jamaican four-man team finished in 14th place, ahead of the Americans, French, Russians, and one of the two Swiss and Italian teams. The two-man team did even better, finishing 10th.[4]

1.2
Need Satisfaction

In Figure 16.2, we started with a very basic model of motivation in which effort leads to job performance. However, managers want to know, "What leads to effort?" And they will try almost anything they can to find the answer to this question. For example, the Illinois Trade Association, a small company of 50 employees that barters everything from advertising to cruises, conducted a survey that revealed that many employees were interested in nontraditional health care. So it revised its health coverage to pay for chiropractic services, herbal therapy, one free massage per month, and other nontraditional forms of health care. Employees at Wilton Connor Packaging Inc. in Charlotte, North Carolina, can take their laundry to work and have it washed, dried, and folded. The company also employs a handyman, who does free minor household repairs for employees while they're at work. At Autodesk in San Rafael, California, employees can take their dogs to work. At Motorola, employees receive $5,000 after they have reached 10 years of service.[5] So which of these techniques will motivate employees and lead to increased effort? The answer is all of them and none of them: It depends on employees' needs.

needs
the physical or psychological requirements that must be met to ensure survival and well-being

Needs are the physical or psychological requirements that must be met to ensure survival and well-being.[6] As shown in the left side of Figure 16.3, a person's unmet need creates an uncomfortable, internal state of tension that must be resolved. For example, if you normally skip breakfast, but then get stuck working through lunch, chances are you'll be so hungry by late afternoon that the only thing you'll be motivated to do is find something to eat. So, according to needs theories, people are motivated by unmet needs. But once a need is met, it no longer motivates. When this occurs, people become satisfied, as illustrated on the right side of Figure 16.3.

Note: Throughout the chapter, as we build on this basic model, the parts of the model that we've already discussed will appear shaded in color. For example, since we've already discussed the effort → performance part of the model, those components are shown with a shaded background. However, when we add new parts to the model, those parts will have a white background. For instance, since we're adding need satisfaction to the model at this step, the need-satisfaction components of unsatisfied need, tension,

Figure 16.3 **Adding Need Satisfaction to the Model**

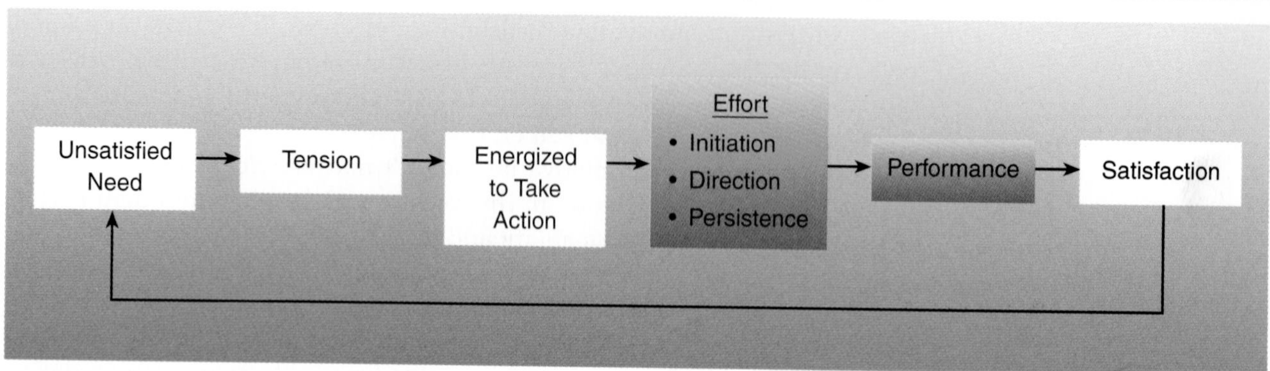

energized to take action, and satisfaction are shown with a white background. This shading convention should make it easier to understand the work motivation model as we add to it in each section of the chapter.

Since people are motivated by unmet needs, managers must learn what those unmet needs are and address them. However, this is not always a straightforward task, since different needs theories suggest different needs categories. Table 16.1 shows needs from three well-known needs theories. Maslow's Hierarchy of Needs suggests that people are motivated by *physiological* (food and water), *safety* (physical and economic), *belongingness* (friendship, love, social interaction), *esteem* (achievement and recognition), and *self-actualization* (realizing your full potential) needs.[7] Alderfer's ERG theory collapses Maslow's five needs into three: *existence* (safety and physiological needs), *relatedness* (belongingness), and *growth* (esteem and self-actualization).[8] McClelland's Learned Needs Theory suggests that people are motivated by the need for *affiliation* (to be liked and accepted), the need for *achievement* (to accomplish challenging goals), or the need for *power* (to influence others).[9]

Things become even more complicated when we consider the different predictions made by these theories. According to Maslow, needs are arranged in a hierarchy from low (physiological) to high (self-actualization). Within this hierarchy, people are motivated by their lowest unsatisfied need. And, as needs are met, they work their way up the hierarchy from physiological to self-actualization needs. By contrast, Alderfer says that people can be motivated by more than one need at a time. Furthermore, he suggests that people are just as likely to move down the needs hierarchy as up, particularly when unable to achieve satisfaction at the next-higher need level. McClelland, on the other hand, argues that the degree to which particular

Table 16.1 **Needs Classification of Different Theories**

	Maslow's Hierarchy	*Alderfer's ERG*	*McClelland's Learned Needs*
Higher-Order Needs	Self-Actualization	Growth	Power
	Esteem		Achievement
	Belongingness	Relatedness	Affiliation
Lower-Order Needs	Safety		
	Physiological	Existence	

needs motivate varies tremendously from person to person, with some people being motivated primarily by achievement, and others by power or affiliation. Moreover, McClelland says that needs are learned, not innate. For instance, studies show that children whose fathers own a small business or hold a managerial position are much more likely to have a high need for achievement.[10]

So with three different sets of needs and three very different ideas about how needs motivate, where does this leave managers who want a practical answer to the question "What leads to effort?" Fortunately, the research evidence simplifies things a bit. To start, studies indicate that there are two basic kinds of needs categories.[11] As shown in Table 16.1, *lower-order needs* are concerned with safety and with physiological and existence requirements. However, *higher-order needs* are concerned with relationships (belongingness, relatedness, and affiliation); challenges and accomplishments (esteem, self-actualization, growth, and achievement); and influence (power). Studies generally show that higher-order needs will not motivate people as long as lower-order needs remain unsatisfied.

For example, imagine that it's six months since you graduated from college and that you're still looking for your first job. With money running short (you're probably living on your credit cards) and the looming possibility of having to move back in with your parents (If this didn't motivate you, what would?), your basic needs for food, shelter, and security drive your thoughts, behavior, and choices at this point. But once you land that job, find a great place (of your own!) to live, and put some money in the bank, these basic needs should decrease in importance as you begin to think about making new friends and taking on challenging work assignments. In fact, once lower-order needs are satisfied, it's difficult for managers to predict which higher-order needs will motivate behavior.[12] Some people will be motivated by affiliation, while others will be motivated by growth or esteem. Also, the relative importance of the various needs may change over time, but not necessarily in any predictable pattern.

So, what leads to effort? In part, needs do. Subsection 1.4 discusses how managers can use what we know from need-satisfaction theories to motivate workers.

1.3 Extrinsic and Intrinsic Rewards

No discussion of motivation would be complete without considering rewards. Let's add two kinds of rewards, extrinsic and intrinsic, to the model, as shown in Figure 16.4.[13]

extrinsic reward
a reward that is tangible, visible to others, and given to employees contingent on the performance of specific tasks or behaviors

Extrinsic rewards are tangible and visible to others and are given to employees contingent on the performance of specific tasks or behaviors.[14] External agents (managers, for example) determine and control the distribution, frequency, and amount of extrinsic rewards, such as pay, company stock, benefits, and promotions. At Ascend Communications, which makes computer equipment that connects millions of people to the Internet, stock options are the key extrinsic reward that attracts and keeps people at the company. New employees are awarded options to buy shares at the price of the stock on the day they are hired. So if the stock was selling for $1 when they were hired, but is now worth $10, employees who exercise their stock

Figure 16.4 **Adding Rewards to the Model**

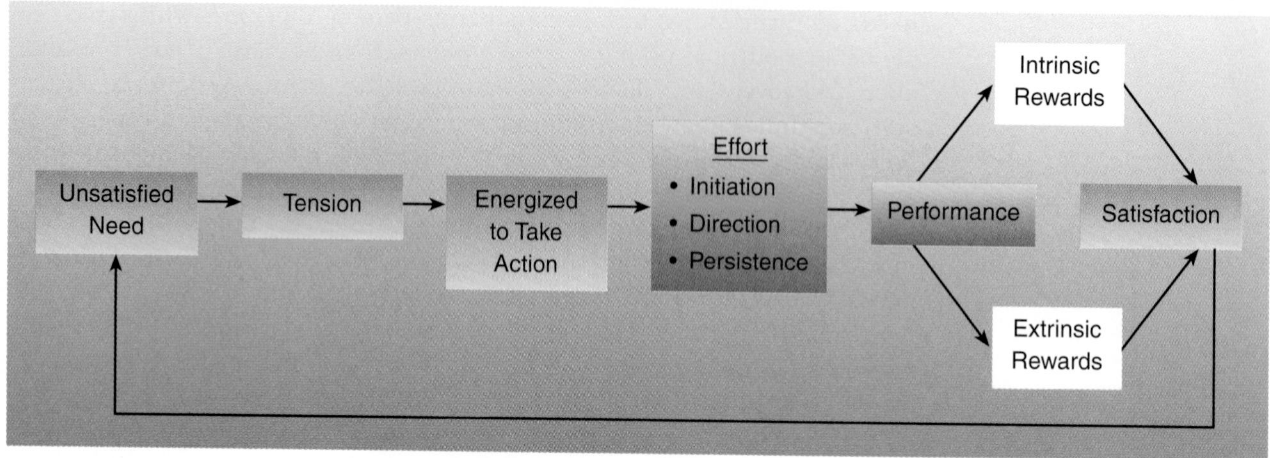

Personal Productivity Tip

Let Employees Have Fun!

Creating fun is a great way to motivate. Some companies have "treat days," when managers serve employees coffee, doughnuts, or ice cream. Others ask their managers to bring in baby pictures, so that people can have fun guessing which baby was which manager. Some companies create a "stress-free zone," with a hammock, an inflatable palm tree, and a "stress-reduction dummy"—a large inflatable punching bag. One manager sends employees "stress support kits," which contain chewing gum, aspirin, a comedy cassette, wind-up toys for employees' desks, and a rubber toy for squeezing during tense moments. So if you want to motivate employees, let them have fun.

Sources: P. Brotherton, "The Company That Plays Together . . . ," *HR Magazine* 41 (December 1996): 76-82. K. Johnson, "Companies Try New Perks to Keep Stressed Workers Happy," *Lawrence Eagle-Tribune*, 26 September 1995, A1. E.W. Hall, "Companies Perk Up Employee Morale," *Cincinnati Enquirer*, 6 September 1991, C5. K. Fehr-Snyder, "Performance Rewards a Double-Edged Sword," *Phoenix Gazette*, 12 April 1995, D1.

options can earn $9 per share. In fact, during a two-year period in which Ascend's stock price rose from $1.63 to $71.25, new employees saw the value of their stock options soar. One new employee, Bruce Ruberg, saw the value of his options increase to $250,000 after one week with the company! Altogether, 650 Ascend employees have stock options worth approximately $525 million.[15]

Why do companies need extrinsic rewards? To get people to do things they wouldn't otherwise do. Companies use rewards to motivate people to perform three basic behaviors: joining the organization, regularly attending their jobs, and performing their jobs well.[16] Think about it. Would you show up to work every day to do the best possible job that you could just out of the goodness of your heart? Very few people would. Take the example of Bill Cecil, an autoworker for DaimlerChrysler. Bill worked 12 hours a day last year without one day off—not one! Bill gets up at 5 a.m., arrives at the plant at 6 a.m., and leaves at 6 p.m., with only one hour in between for breaks. He's home by 7 p.m., eats, sees a little of his family, and then falls asleep in his chair before 10 p.m. Would you be willing to work 12 hours a day every day with no days off? Most people wouldn't. But would you be willing to follow Bill's killer schedule if you could make $125,000 a year? Thousands of other autoworkers do, but they probably wouldn't without those extrinsic rewards.[17]

By contrast, **intrinsic rewards** are the natural rewards associated with performing a task or activity for its own sake. For example, aside from the external rewards management offers for doing something well, employees often experience a sense of interest and enjoyment from the activities or tasks they perform. Examples of intrinsic rewards include a sense of accomplishment or achievement, a feeling of responsibility, the chance to learn something new or interact with others, or simply the fun that comes from performing an interesting, challenging, and engaging task.

intrinsic reward
a natural reward associated with performing a task or activity for its own sake

Which types of rewards are most important to workers in general? A number of surveys suggest that both extrinsic and intrinsic rewards are important. One survey found that the most important rewards were good benefits and health insurance, job security, having a week or more of vacation (all extrinsic rewards) and interesting work, the opportunity to learn new skills, and being able to work independently (all intrinsic rewards). And, employee preferences for intrinsic and extrinsic rewards appear to be relatively stable. In 1973, 52 percent of employees listed "important and meaningful work" as very important, while in 1990, 50 percent of employees did. Similarly, in 1973, 19 percent of employees rated high income as very important. By 1990, this had increased only slightly to 24 percent.[18]

1.4 Motivating with the Basics

So, given the basic model of work motivation in Figure 16.4, what practical things can managers do to motivate employees to increase their effort?

Start by asking people what their needs are. If managers don't know what workers' needs are, they won't be able to provide them the opportunities and rewards that can satisfy those needs. Accordingly, managers at Electronic Data Systems are encouraged to get to know their employees' interests and tastes, so they can individualize rewards and give employees what they desire. One EDS employee was rewarded for her good performance with a new washer and dryer, while another employee returned home from vacation to find that her kitchen had been remodeled (based on her plans and paid for by EDS).[19] And when trainers begin work at Pegasus Personal Fitness Centers in Dallas, President Kirk Malicki simply asks them to make a list of rewards ranging in value from $25 to $200 that they'd like to receive for reaching weekly and monthly goals. Employees have chosen rock-concert tickets, limousine rentals, and half days off. Malicki said, "They know what motivates them better than I do, so I just ask."[20]

Next, satisfy lower-order needs first. Since higher-order needs will not motivate people as long as lower-order needs remain unsatisfied, companies should satisfy lower-order needs first. In practice, this means providing the equipment, training, and knowledge to create a safe workplace free of physical risks, paying employees well enough to provide financial security, and offering a benefits package that will protect employees and their families through good medical coverage and health and disability insurance. Indeed, a survey based on a representative sample of Americans found that when people choose jobs or organizations, three of the four most important factors—starting pay/salary (62 percent), employee benefits (57 percent), and job security (47 percent)—are lower-order needs.[21]

Expect people's needs to change. As other needs are satisfied, or situations change, managers should expect that employees' needs will change. In other words, what motivated people before may not motivate them again. Likewise, what motivates people to accept a job may not necessarily motivate them once they have a job. For instance, David Stum, president of the Loyalty Institute, said, ". . . the [attractive] power of pay and benefits is only [strong] during the recruitment stage. After employees take the job, pay and benefits become entitlements to them. They think: 'Now that I work here, you owe me that.'"[22] Managers should also expect needs to change as people mature. For employees 40 or older, benefits are more important than pay, which is always ranked as most important by younger employees. Also, employees 40 or older rank job security as more important than personal and family time, which is more important to younger employees.[23]

Finally, as needs change and lower-order needs are satisfied, satisfy higher-order needs by looking for ways to allow employees to experience intrinsic rewards. Recall that intrinsic rewards, such as accomplishment, achievement, learning something new, and interacting with others, are the natural rewards associated with performing a task or activity for its own sake. And with the exception of influence (power), intrinsic rewards correspond very closely to higher-order needs that are concerned with relationships (belongingness, relatedness, and affiliation) and challenges and accomplishments (esteem, self-actualization, growth, and achievement). Therefore, one way for managers to meet employees' higher-order needs is to create opportunities for employees to experience intrinsic rewards by providing challenging work, encouraging employees to take greater responsibility for their work, and giving employees the freedom to pursue tasks and projects they find naturally interesting. For example, we began this section by asking, "What would motivate an employee like Marjorie Landale to voluntarily learn the American Sign Language?" Marjorie wasn't paid to do this. In fact, she even spent her own money and free time to learn how to sign. The reason that Marjorie learned how to sign is that doing so met her higher-order needs. It gave her a sense of accomplishment, and it allowed her to interact with deaf customers with whom she had been previously unable to interact. And, Marjorie learned how to sign because her boss was smart enough to realize that there was no downside to giving her the freedom to pursue a task or project that she found naturally interesting.

Review 1
Basics of Motivation

Motivation is the set of forces that initiates, directs, and makes people persist in their efforts over time to accomplish a goal. Managers often confuse motivation and performance. However, since job performance is a multiplicative function of motivation times ability times situational constraints, job performance will suffer if any one of these components is weak. Needs are the physical or psychological requirements that must be met to ensure survival and well-being. When needs are not met, people experience an internal state of tension. But once a particular need is met, it no longer motivates. When this occurs, people become satisfied and are then motivated by other unmet needs. Different motivational theories, such as Maslow's Hierarchy of Needs (physiological, safety, belongingness, esteem, and self-actualization); Alderfer's ERG Theory (existence, relatedness, and growth); and McClelland's Learned Needs Theory (affiliation, achievement, and power), specify a number of different needs. However, studies generally show that there are only two general kinds of needs, lower-order needs and higher-order needs, and that higher-order needs will not motivate people as long as lower-order needs remain unsatisfied. Both extrinsic and intrinsic rewards motivate people. Extrinsic rewards, which include pay, company stock, benefits, and promotions, are used to motivate people to join organizations and attend and perform their jobs. The basic model of motivation suggests that managers can motivate employees by asking them what their needs are, satisfying lower-order needs first, expecting people's needs to change, and satisfying higher-order needs through intrinsic rewards.

How Perceptions and Expectations Affect Motivation

On July 1, 2002, Europe's new currency, the Euro, will replace the currencies of 11 countries (Austria, Belgium, Finland, France, Germany, Ireland, Italy, Luxembourg, Netherlands, Portugal, and Spain). When it does, consumers will be able to easily compare the prices of goods from one country to those of another without having to make cumbersome currency translations. ("Let's see, 100 deutsche marks are worth 335 French francs, and 100 Spanish pesetas are worth 1,164 Italian lira, so that means it's cheaper if I buy it in. . . .") But consumers won't be the only ones making cross-border Euro comparisons. Companies and employees will, too, as they compare salaries and benefits from one country to those of another. For example, salaries tend to be much higher in northern than in southern Europe. In Germany, a sales and marketing director in a medium-sized company would be paid about 160,000 Euros ($185,600) a year. But in Spain, the same job pays about 100,000 Euros ($116,000). Yet even after taxes, which are higher in Germany, the German sales and marketing director takes home 80,000 Euros a year ($92,800), while the Spanish sales and marketing director takes home 55,000 Euros ($63,800). The difference is a whopping 45 percent.[24]

So with much of Europe's work force about to be paid in Euros, companies are expecting a firestorm of salary adjustments, as employees, like the Spanish sales and marketing director, complain loudly about the unfairness of their pay. William Scott, who heads the Paris office of Hewitt Associates, a human resources consulting company, said, "We're doing many more cross-border [pay] comparisons. The need to compete and pay on a European-wide basis is quite significant. There will be a pay extravaganza for some folks." And if companies don't make salary adjustments, they can expect some employees to leave for higher pay in other companies or countries, especially multilingual employees who possess technical skills.

After reading the next two sections, you should be able to:

2 use **equity theory** to explain how employees' perceptions of fairness affect motivation.

3 use **expectancy theory** to describe how workers' expectations about rewards, effort, and the link between rewards and performance influence motivation.

2 Equity Theory

As a kid, do you remember the disagreements you'd have while playing with your friends? "That ball was out." "No, it was in." "Out." "In." "OUT!" "IN!" "Do-Over!" "Yeah, why don't you both shut up and we'll have a do-over." Even as children, we have a strong desire for fairness, for being treated equitably. And when this need isn't met, we are strongly motivated to find a way to restore equity and be fair, hence the "do-over." Not surprisingly, equity is just as important at the office as it is on the playground. For example, a number of organizations, including American Airlines, United Airlines, and United Parcel Service, have experimented with two-tier wage structures in which new employees are paid significantly less than experienced employees. Chris Boschert was hired as a package handler at UPS under a two-tier wage structure. He said, "It makes me mad. I earn $9.68 per hour and the guy working next to me makes $13.99 per hour for exactly the same job!"[25]

equity theory
theory that states that people will be motivated when they perceive that they are being treated fairly

Equity theory says that people will be motivated when they perceive that they are being treated fairly. In particular, equity theory stresses the importance of perceptions. So, regardless of the actual level of rewards people receive, they must also perceive that, relative to others, they are being treated fairly. For instance, by any objective measure, it's hard to make the argument that the best professional athletes, who make upwards of $8 million a year (and no doubt more by the time you read this), are treated unfairly, especially when the average American earns $26,000 a year. But, as is explained below, equity theory doesn't focus on objective equity. Instead, equity, like beauty, is in the eye of the beholder. So, according to equity theory, if people truly perceive that they are being treated unfairly, then inequity exists, regardless of the "objective equity." Witness the inclusion of escalator clauses in top athletes' contracts that specify that if another player at the same position receives a larger contract, then their contract will automatically be revised to that higher amount. So, despite their already enormous paychecks, top athletes still want to be paid as much or more than other top athletes.

Let's learn more about equity theory by examining **2.1** *the components of equity theory,* **2.2** *how people react to perceived inequities, and* **2.3** *how to motivate people using equity theory.*

2.1 *Components of Equity Theory*

inputs
in equity theory, the contributions employees make to the organization

outcomes
in equity theory, the rewards employees receive for their contributions to the organization

referents
in equity theory, others with whom people compare themselves to determine if they have been treated fairly

The basic components of equity theory are inputs, outcomes, and referents. **Inputs** are the contributions employees make to the organization. Inputs include education and training, intelligence, experience, effort, number of hours worked, and ability. **Outcomes** are the rewards employees receive in exchange for their contributions to the organization. Outcomes include pay, fringe benefits, status symbols, job titles and assignments, and even the leadership style of their superiors. And since perceptions of equity depend on how you are being treated compared to others, **referents** are others with whom people compare themselves to determine if they have been treated fairly. Usually, people choose to compare themselves to referents who hold the same or similar jobs, or are otherwise similar to themselves in some way, such as in gender, race, age, or tenure.[26]

outcome/input (O/I) ratio
in equity theory, an employee's perception of the comparison between the rewards received from an organization and the employee's contributions to that organization

underreward
when the referent you compare yourself to is getting more outcomes relative to their inputs than you are

According to the equity theory process shown in Table 16.2, employees compare inputs, their contributions to the organization, to outcomes, the rewards they received from the organization in exchange for those inputs. This comparison of outcomes to inputs is called the **outcome/input (O/I) ratio**. After an internal comparison in which they compare their outcomes to their inputs, employees then make an external comparison in which they compare their O/I ratio with the O/I ratio of a referent.[27] When people perceive that their O/I ratio is equal to the referent's O/I ratio, they conclude that they are being treated fairly. But when people perceive that their O/I ratio is different from their referent's O/I ratio, they conclude that they have been treated inequitably or unfairly.

There are two kinds of inequity, underreward and overreward. **Underreward** occurs when a referent's O/I ratio is better than your O/I ratio. In other words, the referent you compare yourself to is getting more outcomes

Table 16.2

Outcome/Input Ratios

$$\frac{\text{Outcomes}_{self}}{\text{Inputs}_{self}} = \frac{\text{Outcomes}_{others}}{\text{Inputs}_{others}}$$

relative to his or her inputs than you are. When people perceive that they have been underrewarded, they tend to experience anger or frustration. For example, when a manufacturing company received notice that some important contracts had been canceled, management cut employees' pay by 15 percent in one plant but not in another. Just as equity theory predicts, theft doubled in the plant that received the pay cut. Likewise, employee turnover increased from 5 percent to 23 percent.[28]

overreward
when you are getting more outcomes relative to your inputs than the referent to whom you compare yourself

By contrast, **overreward** occurs when a referent's O/I ratio is worse than your O/I ratio. In this case, you are getting more outcomes relative to your inputs than your referent is. In theory, when people perceive that they have been overrewarded, they experience guilt. Not surprisingly, people have a very high tolerance for overreward. It takes a tremendous amount of overpayment before people decide that their pay or benefits are more than they deserve.

2.2 *How People React to Perceived Inequity*

What happens when people perceive that they have been treated inequitably? Figure 16.5 shows that perceived inequity affects satisfaction. In the case of underreward, this usually translates into frustration or anger, while with overreward the reaction is guilt. In turn, these reactions leads to tension and a strong need to take action to restore equity in some way. At first, a slight inequity may not be strong enough to motivate an employee to take immediate action. However, if the inequity continues or there are multiple inequities, tension may build over time until a point of intolerance is reached, and the person is energized to take action.[29]

There are five ways in which people try to restore equity when they perceive that they have been treated unfairly: reducing inputs, increasing outcomes, rationalizing inputs or outcomes, changing the referent, or simply leaving. These will be discussed in terms of the inequity associated with underreward, which is much more common than the inequity associated with overreward.

People who perceive that they have been underrewarded may try to restore equity by decreasing or withholding their inputs (i.e., effort). For example, over the last 15 years, Alaska Air, the tenth-largest U.S. airline, has had tremendous difficulty trying to reach labor agreements with the labor unions representing its pilots, mechanics, and flight attendants. During the last round of negotiations, flight attendants initiated a plan against the company that they dubbed C.H.A.O.S., create havoc around our system, in which flight attendants simply walked off flights because they thought the company was offering an unfair compensation package. Mechanics used a similar strategy, slowing the rate at which they repaired or completed scheduled maintenance work on company planes. Hundreds of flights were delayed as a result.[30]

Increasing outcomes is another way in which people try to restore equity. This might include asking for a raise or pointing out the inequity to the boss

Figure 16.5 **Adding Equity Theory to the Model**

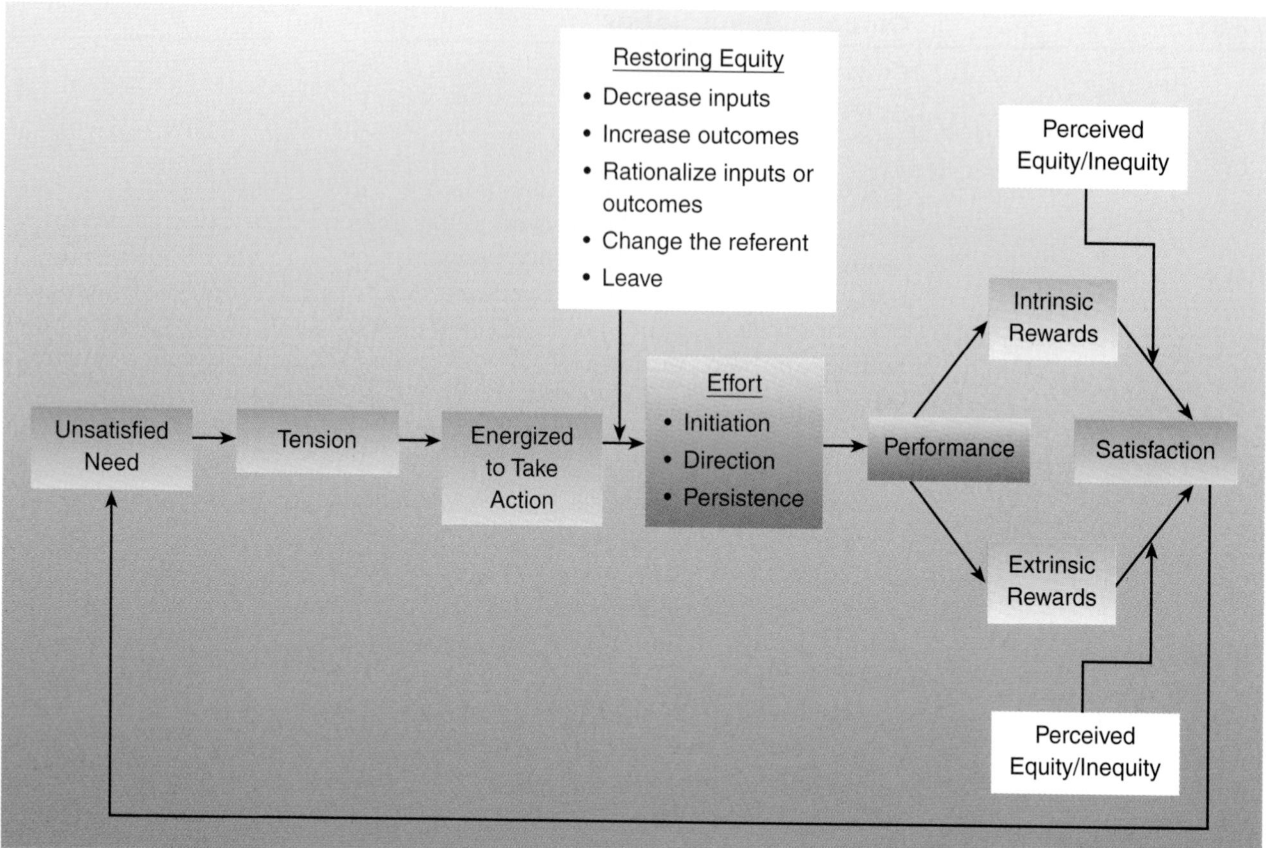

PersonalProductivityTip

Asking for a Raise

Getting a raise can restore equity. What's the best way to ask for one? First, make sure you're worth it. Critically evaluate your contributions and results, not just your efforts. Be ruthlessly honest about this; your boss will be. Drop hints to give your boss time to consider it before officially asking for a raise. Be patient. It usually takes three to six months to get raises approved. Be persistent, but don't issue ultimatums. Bosses sometimes wear down, but not if you make them angry. Is money all you want? Would you take a smaller raise and more vacation time? Be sure before you ask.

Source: A. Fisher & M. O'Malley, "How to Get the Raise You Deserve: They're Given Not for Hard Work but for Adding Economic Value. Even Then, Says Compensation Planner Michael O'Malley, You'll Need to Be Persistent, and Patient," *Fortune*, 7 September 1998, 169.

and hoping that she takes care of it. Sometimes, however, employees may go to external organizations, such as labor unions or federal agencies, to get some help in increasing outcomes to restore equity. For instance, the U.S. Department of Labor estimates that 1 in 10 workers is not getting the extra overtime pay they deserve when they work more than 40 hours a week. In fact, there are nearly 20,000 such cases each year and employees win 90 percent of them. Joining a union is another way to increase outcomes. The workers at the Fisherman's Outlet restaurant in Los Angeles joined a union after not being paid for overtime work despite working 10 hours a day, six days a week. Today, thanks to its union, workers now earn an extra $35 to $60 a week in overtime pay. Employee Miguel Chan said, "Everybody is a lot happier now. We get paid properly for the hours we work."[31]

Another method of restoring equity is to rationalize or distort inputs or outcomes. So instead of actually decreasing inputs or increasing outcomes, employees restore equity by making mental or emotional "adjustments" in their O/I ratios or the O/I ratios of their referents. For example, say a company downsizes 10 percent of its work force. It's likely that the survivors, the people who still have jobs, will be angry or frustrated with company management because of the layoffs. However, if alternative jobs are difficult to find, the employees who are still with the company may rationalize or distort their O/I ratios and conclude, "Well, things could be worse. At least I still have my job." Rationalizing or distorting outcomes may be used when other ways to restore equity aren't available.

Changing the referent is another way of restoring equity. In this case, people compare themselves to someone other than the referent they had been using for previous O/I ratio comparisons. Since people usually choose to compare themselves to others who hold the same or similar jobs or are otherwise similar, they may change referents to restore equity when their personal situations change, such as a decrease in job status or pay.

Finally, when reducing inputs, increasing outcomes, rationalizing inputs or outcomes, or changing referents doesn't restore equity, employees may leave by quitting their jobs, transferring, or increasing absenteeism.[32] For example, Disney Corporation's Internet divisions have had a very difficult time keeping their top talent. While Disney is well managed and pays very well, because it's an established company, it hasn't been able to offer the stock options that Internet startup companies are able to offer their employees. Both former Disney Online President Richard Wolpert and Winney Wechsler, head of Disney.com, left to take jobs with startup companies. Toby Lenk, a former Disney executive, left to help start eToys Inc. and now has eToys stock worth $573 million.[33]

2.3 *Motivating with Equity Theory*

What practical things can managers do to use equity theory to motivate employees?

Start by looking for and correcting major inequities. One of the difficulties that equity theory makes us aware of is that an employee's sense of fairness is based on subjective perceptions. So what one employee considers grossly unfair may not affect another employee's perceptions of equity at all. While this makes it difficult for managers to create conditions that satisfy all employees, it's critical that they do their best to take care of major inequities that can energize employees to take actions, such as decreasing inputs or leaving, that can be extremely disruptive, costly, and harmful. So, whenever possible, managers should look for and correct major inequities. For example, British-based Zurich Financial Services decided to pay its information technology staff a bonus of an extra year's salary if they agree to stay with the company for another three years. The total cost of the bonus plan was £17 million ($27.5 million). The company began offering this retention bonus after one quarter of its staff quit to pursue much higher paying jobs in other companies. Employees who leave before the three years is up will be asked to completely repay the bonus. Corporate affairs manager Wendy May said, "We are doing what it takes to hold on to these staff. We cannot lock our staff in a cupboard to make them stay, so we are offering them a long-term incentive to stick with us. What it is costing is a small price to pay compared to the catastrophe of losing all our in-house expertise."[34]

Reduce employees' inputs. Increasing outcomes is often the first and only strategy that companies use to restore equity. This approach is unfortunate, because reducing employee inputs is just as viable a strategy. In fact, with 50-hour weeks, dual-career couples, and working at work *and* home being more the norm than the exception, more and more employees are looking for ways to reduce stress and restore a balance between work and family. In this context, it makes sense to ask employees to do less, not more, to have them identify and eliminate the 20 percent of their jobs that doesn't increase productivity or add value for customers, and to have managers eliminate company-imposed requirements that really aren't critical to managers', employees', or companies' performance (i.e., unnecessary meetings, reports, etc.). The SAS Institute, maker of the Statistical Analysis Software used by nearly every major company in the U.S., has been reducing employees' inputs with success for years. Unlike most software companies that expect employees to work 12- to 14-hour days, SAS offices close at 6 p.m. every evening. Also, employees receive unlimited sick days each year. And, to encourage employees to spend time with their families, there's an on-site daycare facility, the company cafeteria has plenty of highchairs and baby seats, and the company even has a seven-hour workday. The payoff? With an employee turnover of just 3.7 percent a year (compared to 20 percent and up for most software companies), the company saves $67 million a year in unnecessary costs and expenses.[35]

distributive justice the perceived degree to which outcomes and rewards are fairly distributed or allocated

procedural justice the perceived fairness of the process used to make reward allocation decisions

Make sure decision-making processes are fair. Equity theory focuses on **distributive justice**, the degree to which outcomes and rewards are fairly distributed or allocated. However, **procedural justice**, the fairness of the process used to make reward allocation decisions, is just as important.[36] Procedural justice matters because even when employees are unhappy with their outcomes (i.e., low pay), they're much less likely to be unhappy with company management if they believe that the procedures used to allocate outcomes were fair. For example, employees who are laid off tend to be hostile toward their employer when they perceive that the procedures leading to the layoffs were unfair. By contrast, employees who perceive layoff procedures to be fair tend to continue to support and trust their employers.[37] Also, if employees perceive that their outcomes are unfair (i.e., distributive injustice), but that the decisions and procedures leading to those outcomes were fair (i.e., procedural justice), they are much more likely to seek constructive ways of restoring equity, such as discussing these matters with their manager. In contrast, if employees perceive both distributive and procedural injustice, they may resort to more destructive tactics, such as withholding effort, absenteeism, tardiness, or even sabotage and theft.[38]

Review 2
Equity Theory

The basic components of equity theory are inputs, outcomes, and referents. After an internal comparison in which employees compare their outcomes to their inputs, they then make an external comparison in which they compare their O/I ratio with the O/I ratio of a referent, a person who works in a similar job or is otherwise similar. When their O/I ratio is equal to the referent's O/I ratio, employees perceive that they are being treated fairly. But when their O/I ratio is different from their referent's O/I ratio, they perceive that they have been treated inequitably or unfairly. There are two kinds of inequity, underreward and overreward. Underreward occurs when a referent's O/I ratio is better than the employee's O/I ratio. Underreward leads to anger or frustration. Overreward occurs when a referent's O/I ratio is worse than the employee's O/I ratio. Overreward can lead to guilt, but only when the level of overreward is extreme. When employees perceive that they have been treated inequitably (i.e., underreward), they may try to restore equity by reducing inputs, increasing outcomes, rationalizing inputs or outcomes, changing the referent, or simply leaving. Managers can use equity theory to motivate workers by looking for and correcting major inequities, reducing employees' inputs, and emphasizing procedural as well as distributive justice.

3 Expectancy Theory

How attractive would you find the following rewards? A company concierge service that sends someone to be at your house when the cable guy or repair person shows up, or picks up your car from the mechanic? A "7 to 7" travel policy that stipulates that no one has to leave home for business travel before 7 a.m. on Mondays and that everyone should return home from their business travels by 7 p.m. on Fridays? The opportunity to telecommute, so that you can feed your kids breakfast, pick them up after school, and then tuck them into bed at night? A "circle of excellence" award, in which employees nominate co-workers for outstanding work, and the winners get company-paid trips to Hawaii and the Bahamas? A full-sized basketball court with a real wooden floor? Or a sabbatical program that gives employees the chance to take a paid leave, so they can work for local charities?[39]

If you had kids, you might love the chance to telecommute; but if you didn't, you might not be interested. If you didn't travel much on business, you wouldn't be interested in the "7 to 7" travel policy; but if you did, you'd probably love it. One of the hardest things about motivating people is that rewards that are attractive to some employees are unattractive to others. **Expectancy theory** says that people will be motivated to the extent to which they believe that their efforts will lead to good performance, that good performance will be rewarded, and that they are offered attractive rewards.[40]

expectancy theory
theory that states that people will be motivated to the extent to which they believe that their efforts will lead to good performance, that good performance will be rewarded, and that they will be offered attractive rewards

Let's learn more about expectancy theory by examining **3.1** *the components of expectancy theory and* **3.2** *how to use expectancy theory as a motivational tool.*

3.1
Components of Expectancy Theory

Expectancy theory holds that people make conscious choices about their motivation. The three factors that affect those choices are valence, expectancy, and instrumentality.

Valence is simply the attractiveness or desirability of various rewards or outcomes. Expectancy theory recognizes that the same reward or outcome, say, a promotion, will be highly attractive to some people, highly disliked by others, and for some, may not make much difference one way or the other. Accordingly, when people are deciding how much effort to put forth, expectancy theory says that they will consider the valence of all possible rewards and outcomes that they can receive from their jobs. The greater the sum of those valences, each of which could be positive, negative, or neutral, the more effort people will choose to put forth on the job.

valence
the attractiveness or desirability of a reward or outcome

Expectancy is the perceived relationship between effort and performance. When expectancies are strong, employees believe that their hard work and efforts will result in good performance, so they work harder. By contrast, when expectancies are weak, employees figure that no matter what they do or how hard they work, they won't be able to perform their jobs successfully, so they don't work as hard.

expectancy
the perceived relationship between effort and performance

instrumentality the perceived relationship between performance and rewards

Instrumentality is the perceived relationship between performance and rewards. When instrumentality is strong, employees believe that improved performance will lead to better and more rewards, and they will choose to work harder. When instrumentality is weak, employees don't believe that better performance will result in more or better rewards, so they will choose not to work as hard.

Expectancy theory holds that for people to be highly motivated, all three variables—valence, expectancy, and instrumentality—must be high. Thus, expectancy theory can be represented by the following simple equation:

$$\text{Motivation} = \text{Valence} \times \text{Instrumentality} \times \text{Expectancy}$$

So if any one of these variables (valence, instrumentality, or expectancy) declines, overall motivation will decline, too.

Figure 16.6 incorporates the expectancy theory variables into our motivation model. Valence and instrumentality combine to affect employees' willingness to put forth effort (i.e., the degree to which they are energized to take action), while expectancy transforms intended effort ("I'm really going to work hard in this job") into actual effort. If you're offered rewards that you desire, and you believe that you will in fact receive these rewards for good performance, you're highly likely to be energized to take action. However, you're not likely to actually exert effort unless you also believe that you can do the job (i.e., that your efforts will lead to successful performance).

Caribou Coffee, which has stores in Minnesota, Illinois, Ohio, Georgia, North Carolina, and Michigan, integrates valence, expectancy, and instru-

Figure 16.6 **Adding Expectancy Theory to the Model**

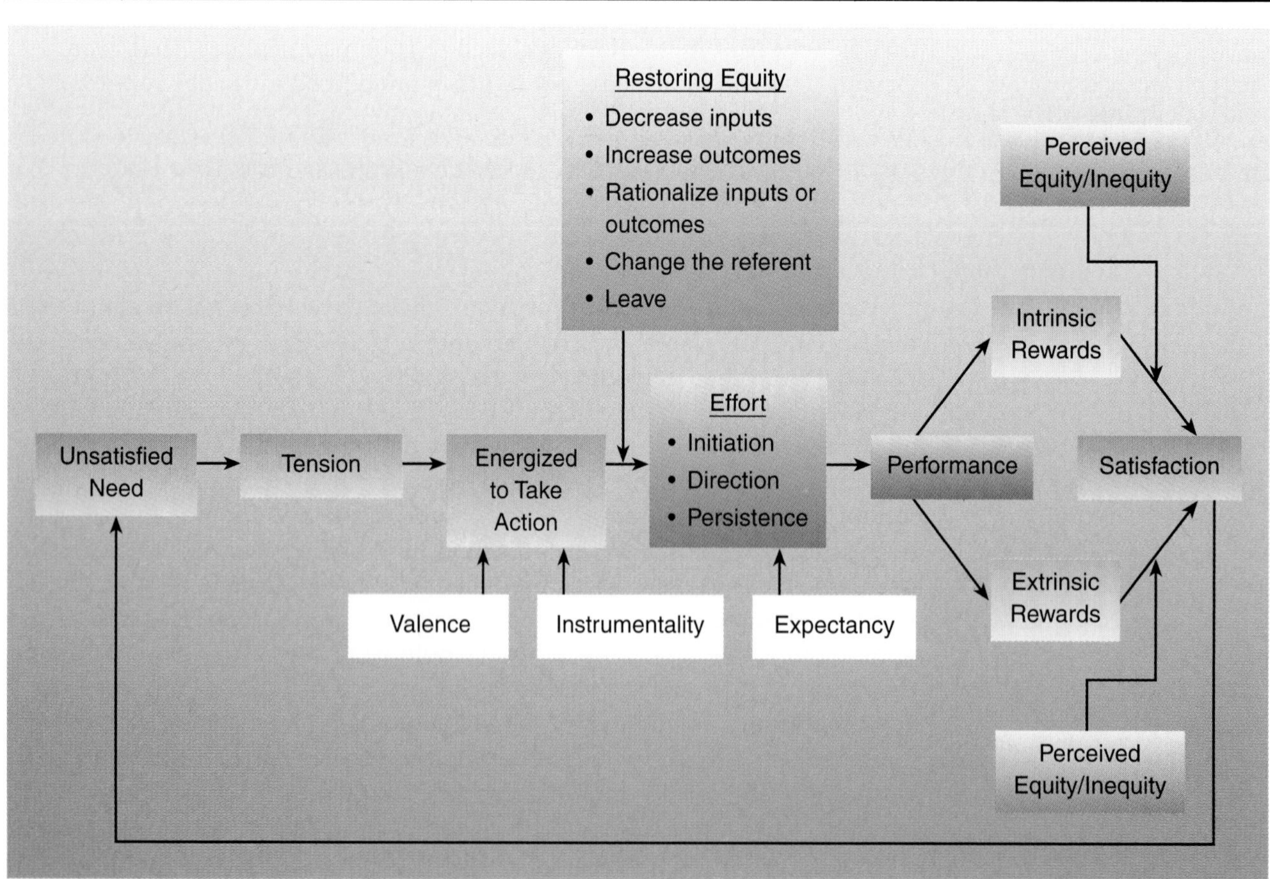

mentality into its employee motivation program. First, Caribou offers a wide variety of rewards, such as employee recognition programs, sales incentives, and company-wide contests, so that all of its employees can receive highly valent rewards that they desire. The company manages employee expectancies by using its "Coffee College" to provide substantial training to new hires and continuing education for long-time employees. Caribou's Director of Training, Annmarie Lofy, said that the program sets new employees up for success from the very beginning. When they start their new job, they're not nervous and unsure, because the training has prepared them to do their jobs well. Finally, Caribou manages instrumentality by linking various rewards to the specific behaviors it wants to reward. In one such program, store employees receive "Bou Bucks" from store managers for performance above and beyond their job descriptions. Bou Bucks are redeemable for merchandise at stores such as Marshall Field's and Foot Locker. One of the reasons that Bou Bucks have had such a strong effect on instrumentality perceptions is that Caribou Coffee managers immediately award them when they see employees performing their jobs well. This strengthens employees' perceptions that performance is instrumental to receiving rewards.[41]

3.2 Motivating with Expectancy Theory

What practical things can managers do to use expectancy theory to motivate employees?

Systematically gather information to find out what employees want from their jobs. In addition to individual managers' directly asking employees what they want from their jobs (see "Motivating with Equity Theory"), companies still need to survey their employees regularly to determine their wants, needs, and dissatisfactions. Since people consider the valence of all the possible rewards and outcomes that they can receive from their jobs, regular identification of wants, needs, and dissatisfaction gives companies the chance to turn negatively valent rewards and outcomes into positively valent rewards and outcomes, thus raising overall motivation and effort. For example, even the most successful companies, like Microsoft, need to keep track of what employees want from their jobs. In the last few years, some of Microsoft's most talented managers and employees have begun to leave. Three vice presidents, the chief technology officer, the president of Microsoft's WebTV unit, and the senior vice president who ran the Windows 95 group as well as Microsoft's charge into Internet software have all left. After years of 14-hour days, these people, now mostly in their mid-30s and early 40s, want to spend more time with their families and on outside interests. As a result of these and other departures, Microsoft increased its compensation packages and doubled the number of steps in its pay scales, so that employees could receive promotions more frequently. However, since most of the top managers who are leaving are multimillionaires thanks to their Microsoft stock, it's unlikely that they'll find these changes attractive. Therefore, Microsoft is also now encouraging workers to go home earlier, take weekend time off, take the company sabbaticals that they've earned, and, ultimately, spend more time with their families.[42]

Take clear steps to link rewards to individual performance in a way that is clear and understandable to employees. Unfortunately, most employees are extremely dissatisfied with the link between pay and performance in their organizations. A study based on a representative sample of Americans found that 80 percent of employees wanted to be paid according to a different kind of pay system! Moreover, only 32 percent of employees were satisfied with how their annual pay raises were determined, while only 22 percent were happy with the way in which companies determined the starting salaries for their jobs.[43] Other than making sure there is a connection between pay and performance in their companies (See Chapter 14 for a discussion of compensation strategies), another way for managers to establish a clearer link between pay and performance is to publicize the way in which pay decisions are made. For example, at Allstate Insurance, the company compensation team wrote a pamphlet called "Tracking the Clues to Your Pay," which explained how Allstate carefully used market value surveys and analyses to determine employee pay. Importantly, this helped counter the widespread belief that employee pay was determined in some random way. When asked "To what extent does the pay system competitively reward you for results?" 27 percent more employees responded "A great deal" or "Quite a bit" after the publication of "Tracking the Clues to Your Pay."[44]

Empower employees to make decisions if you really want them to believe that their hard work and effort will lead to good performance. If valent rewards are linked to good performance, people should be energized to take action. However, this works only if they also believe that their efforts will lead to good performance. One of the ways in which managers destroy the expectancy that hard work and effort will lead to good performance is by restricting what employees can do or by ignoring employees' ideas. In Chapter 11, you learned that *empowerment* is a feeling of intrinsic motivation, in which workers perceive their work to have meaning and perceive themselves to be competent, having an impact, and capable of self-determination.[45] So if managers want workers to have strong expectancies, they should empower them to make decisions. Doing so will motivate employees to take active rather than passive roles in their work. For instance, British billionaire Richard Branson, founder and chief of Virgin Corporation (Virgin Atlantic Airways, Virgin Records, Virgin Rail, etc.), builds strong expectancies in his employees through empowerment. He said:

> *Yes. It all comes down to people. There's nothing that comes close. Motivating people, bringing in the best. The girl who opened what will be the best bridal shop in Europe was flying on the airline [Virgin Air] as an air hostess. She came to me with an idea and I said, "Go to it." She did. Now it's Virgin Bride. By having the freedom to prove herself, she has excelled. . . . Praise people—like plants, they must be nurtured —and make it fun. Value them and give them the opportunity to contribute in ways that excite them.*[46]

Review 3
Expectancy Theory

Expectancy theory holds that three factors affect the conscious choices people make about their motivation: valence, expectancy, and instrumentality. Valence is simply the attractiveness or desirability of various rewards or outcomes. Expectancy is the perceived relationship between effort and performance. Instrumentality is the perceived relationship between performance and rewards. Expectancy theory holds that for people to be highly motivated, all three factors must be high. So if any one of these factors declines, overall motivation will decline, too. Managers can use expectancy theory to motivate workers by systematically gathering information to find out what employees want from their jobs, by linking rewards to individual performance in a way that is clear and understandable to employees, and by empowering employees to make decisions, which will increase their expectancies that hard work and efforts will lead to good performance.

How Rewards and Goals Affect Motivation

No matter what management tried, it couldn't find a way to prevent the mechanics at Monsanto's Pensacola, Florida, plant from accidentally dropping heavy machine parts on their toes or the yarn workers from accidentally cutting their fingers. Regular meetings, accident investigations, safety slogans and posters—nothing seemed to work. Finally, management called in psychologists and statisticians to identify the causes and teach workers how to avoid accidents by reinforcing each other's safe behavior. After identifying dozens of possible causes, workers were given "scorecards" to count the number of times they observed other employees performing safe or potentially unsafe behaviors. Employees looked for things like "shortcuts and deviations," "keeping eyes on hands," "avoiding pinch points," and housekeeping issues such as "clutter." Using the feedback obtained from the scorecards, management set specific safety goals and recognized safe workers at weekly meetings and in quarterly reviews. When an entire division improved its safety behavior, everyone won a free lunch or a coffee mug. Plus, safety records were considered in promotion decisions. As a result, Monsanto's safety record improved from 6.5 to just 1.6 injuries per hundred workers. Overall, injuries dropped by more then 75 percent, all without heavy-handed supervision or punishment.[47]

reinforcement theory theory that states that behavior is a function of its consequences, that behaviors followed by positive consequences will occur more frequently, and that behaviors followed by negative consequences, or not followed by positive consequences, will occur less frequently

After reading the next three sections, you should be able to:

4 explain how **reinforcement theory** works and how it can be used to motivate.

5 describe the components of **goal-setting theory** and how managers can use them to motivate workers.

6 discuss how the entire **motivation model can be used to motivate workers**.

4 Reinforcement Theory

Reinforcement theory says that behavior is a function of its consequences, that behaviors followed by positive consequences (i.e., reinforced) will occur more frequently, and that behaviors followed by negative consequences, or not followed by positive consequences, will occur less frequently.[48] Therefore, Monsanto decided to reinforce safe behaviors. Chuck Davis, a safety consultant, said, "It's better to recognize a guy for success than beat him up for failure. It's amazing how little reward a guy needs so he doesn't stick his arm in a machine."[49] More specifically, **reinforcement** is the process of changing behavior by changing the consequences that

reinforcement the process of changing behavior by changing the consequences that follow behavior

reinforcement contingencies cause-and-effect relationships between the performance of specific behaviors and specific consequences

schedule of reinforcement rules that specify which behaviors will be reinforced, which consequences will follow those behaviors, and the schedule by which those consequences will be delivered

follow behavior.[50] Reinforcement has two parts: reinforcement contingencies and schedules of reinforcement. **Reinforcement contingencies** are the cause-and-effect relationships between the performance of specific behaviors and specific consequences. For example, if you get docked an hour's pay for being late to work, then a reinforcement contingency exists between a behavior, being late to work, and a consequence, losing an hour's pay. A **schedule of reinforcement** is the set of rules regarding reinforcement contingencies, such as which behaviors will be reinforced, which consequences will follow those behaviors, and the schedule by which those consequences will be delivered.[51]

BLASTFROMTHEPAST

Send in the Reinforcements!

With the enormous interest in stock options, profit sharing, and other pay-for-performance plans this decade, you'd think that reinforcement theory was something new. However, reinforcements have been used (though not widely) to motivate workers throughout this century. Here are some classic examples of positive reinforcement.

1972, Michigan Bell Telephone Company. Because of high rates of absenteeism among its telephone operators, the company decided to provide workers more frequent feedback on how often they missed work. So instead of receiving absence reports on a monthly basis, telephone operators received absence reports on a weekly basis. The combination of more frequent feedback and praise for good attendance dropped the rate of absenteeism from 11 percent to 6.5 percent in just six weeks. E.D. Grady, the general manager in charge of operator services, said, "It has been our experience, over the past ten years, that when standards are set and feedback provided in a positive manner, performance will reach very high levels—perhaps in the upper 90th percentile in a very short period of time. . . . We have also found that when positive reinforcement is discontinued, performance returns to levels that existed prior to the establishment of feedback."

1971, Emery Air Freight. Employees in the customer service department believed they were accomplishing the departmental goal of responding to customer inquiries within 90 minutes at least 90 percent of the time. But without careful measurement and charting of the desired behavior (called "establishing a baseline" in reinforcement terminology), employees were basically guessing about how well they were doing. So when the customer service representatives were given tally sheets and asked to keep track of how long it actually took them to respond to each call, they were shocked to find out that they were actually responding within 90 minutes only 30 percent of the time. In addition to having employees generate feedback by keeping track of their response times, Emery also trained supervisors to provide praise and recognition for employees who met the goal or whose performance had improved. Supervisors were also taught that if performance did not improve, they should simply remind employees of the goal in a nonpunitive manner. As a result, performance in one office improved from 30 percent of standard to 95 percent in a single day. And, after three years, the department still met the goal 90 percent to 95 percent of the time.

1911, Frederick W. Taylor and Bethlehem Steel. Frederick W. Taylor is known as the "Father of Scientific Management." In his book *The Principles of Scientific Management*, which was published in 1911, he wrote this about incentives:

> *The writer repeats, therefore, that in order to have any hope of obtaining the initiative of his workmen the manager must give some special incentive to his men beyond that which is given to the average of the trade. This incentive can be given in several different ways, as, for example, the hope of rapid promotion or advancement; higher wages, either in the form of generous piecework prices or of a premium or bonus of some kind for good and rapid work; shorter hours of labor; better surroundings and working conditions than are ordinarily given, etc., and, above all, this special incentive should be accompanied by that personal consideration for, and friendly contact with, his workmen which comes only from a genuine and kindly interest in the welfare of those under him. It is only by giving a special inducement or "incentive" of this kind that the employer can hope even approximately to get the "initiative" of his workmen.*

Taylor then proved the effectiveness of incentives by using them to increase productivity among laborers at the Bethlehem Steel Company. The laborers had the job of picking up and loading 92-pound pieces of pig iron (unprocessed iron) into a railroad car. The job was made more difficult by having to carry the pig iron pieces up a steep plank to load them onto the rail car. The average laborer could load about 12½ tons, or 272 pieces, of pig iron per day. However, through studying the workers and the work process, Taylor determined that the average laborer should be able to load 47 tons, or 1,022 pieces, of pig iron per day. Of course, the question was how to do it. Taylor also wrote, "And it was further our duty to see that this work was done without bringing on a strike among the men, without any quarrel with the men, and to see that the men were happier and better contented when loading at the new rate of 47 tons than they were when loading at the old rate of 12½ tons."

Taylor decided that the best way to accomplish this task was through a combination of rest periods and incentive pay, both of which were unheard of at the time. And to prove his point that any man should be able to move 47 tons of pig iron per day, he selected the smallest worker in the group to test his ideas. Taylor increased this worker's pay by 61 percent, from $1.15 a day to $1.85 a day, contingent on loading 47 tons of pig iron. Taylor explained the results this way:

> *Schmidt [the laborer] started to work, and all day long, and at regular intervals, was told by the man [one of Taylor's associates] who stood over him with a watch, "Now pick up a pig and walk. Now sit down and rest. Now walk—now rest," etc. He worked when he was told to work, and rested when he was told to rest, and at half-past five in the afternoon had his 47½ tons loaded on the car. And he practically never failed to work at this pace and do the task that was set him during the three years that the writer was at Bethlehem. And throughout this time he averaged a little more than $1.85 per day, whereas before he had never received over $1.15 per day, which was the ruling rate of wages at that time in Bethlehem. That is, he received 60 per cent higher wages than were paid to other men who were not working on task work. One man after another was picked out and trained to handle pig iron at the rate of 47½ tons per day until all of the pig iron was handled at this rate, and the men were receiving 60 per cent more wages than other workmen around them.*

Sources: E.J. Feeney, "At Emery Air Freight: Positive Reinforcement Boosts Performance," *Organizational Dynamics* 1, no. 3 (1973): 41-50. W.C. Hamner & E.P. Hamner, "Behavior Modification on the Bottom Line," *Organizational Dynamics* 4, no. 4 (1976): 3-21. B.F. Skinner & W.F. Dowling, "Conversation with B.F. Skinner," *Organizational Dynamics* 1, no. 1 (1973): 31-40. F.W. Taylor, *The Principles of Scientific Management* (New York: Harper, 1911).

Figure 16.7 incorporates reinforcement contingencies and reinforcement schedules into our motivation model. First, notice that extrinsic rewards and the schedules of reinforcement used to deliver them are the primary method for creating reinforcement contingencies in organizations. In turn, those reward contingencies directly affect valences (the attractiveness of rewards), instrumentality (the perceived link between rewards and performance), and effort (how hard employees will work).

Let's learn more about reinforcement theory by examining **4.1** *the components of reinforcement theory,* **4.2** *the different schedules for delivering reinforcement, and* **4.3** *how to motivate with reinforcement theory.*

4.1 Components of Reinforcement Theory

Reinforcement contingencies are the cause-and-effect relationships between the performance of specific behaviors and specific consequences. The four kinds of reinforcement contingencies are positive reinforcement, negative reinforcement, punishment, and extinction.

positive reinforcement reinforcement that strengthens behavior by following behaviors with desirable consequences

Positive reinforcement strengthens behavior (i.e., increases its frequency) by following behaviors with desirable consequences. For example, most people are members of frequent flyer clubs that earn them air miles for flying with a particular airline. In return, those air miles can be used for free first-class upgrades or free airline tickets. So while most people dislike

Figure 16.7 **Adding Reinforcement Theory to the Model**

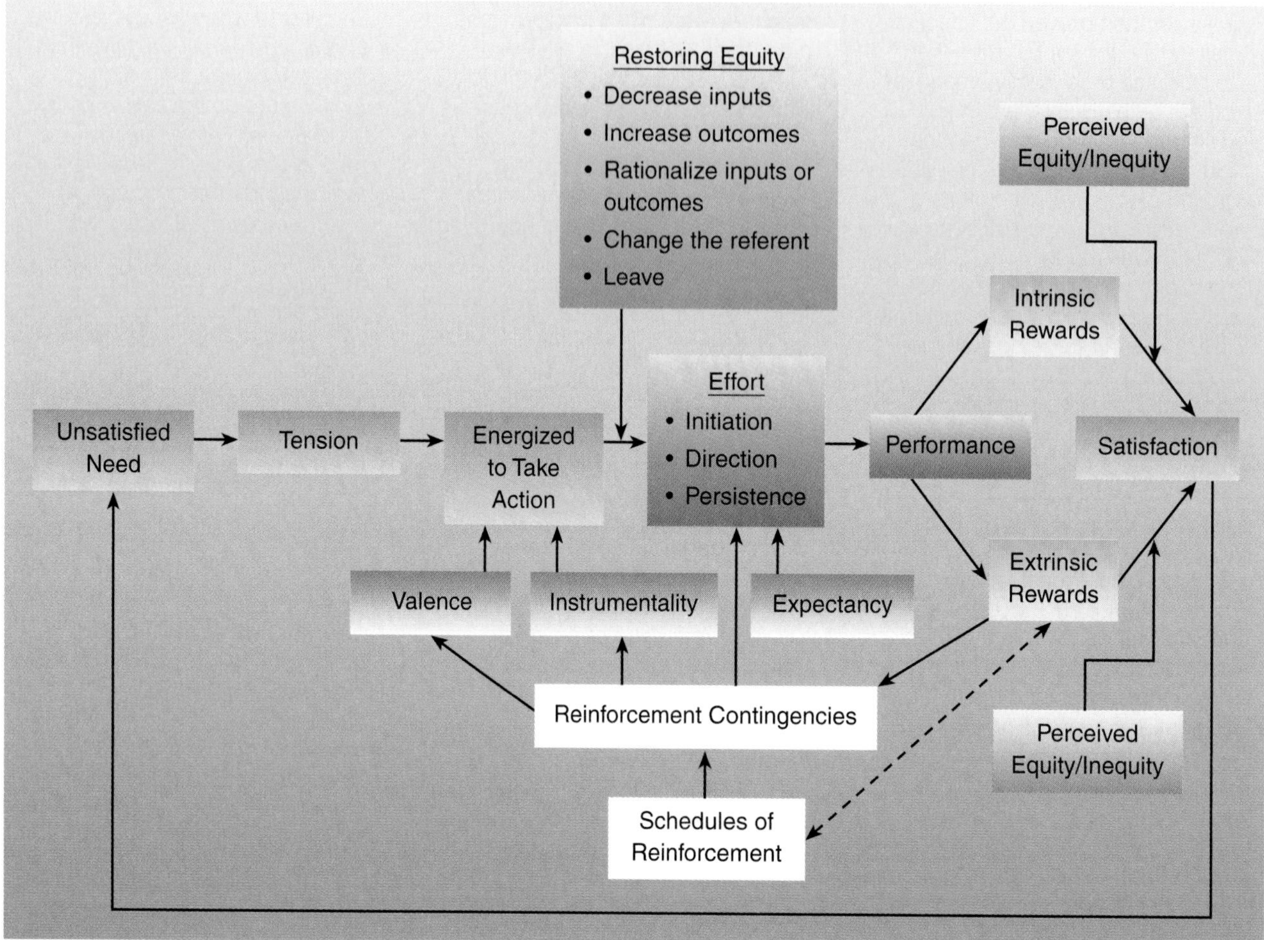

Personal Productivity Tip

Try Praise

Positive reinforcement doesn't have to be costly. In fact, praise and recognition are just as important to employees as financial rewards. However, many managers forget to praise employees or simply don't know how. Until praising employees becomes second nature to you, here are some simple ways to make sure you're praising employees effectively. Put praising employees on your to-do list. Set aside 10 minutes at the end of the day to write notes or e-mails to employees who deserve praise. If you can't be there in person, praise using the telephone, voice mail, or e-mail. Finally, make sure your praise is prompt, sincere, specific, and positive.

Sources: B. Nelson, "Try Praise," *Inc.*, September 1996, 115. B. Nelson, "Rewarding Employees," *Canadian Manager* 20 (1 January 1995): 21.

frequent business travel because it takes them away from their friends and family, one of the reasons they put up with it is that employers typically let them keep the air miles they earn while traveling for the company. So, every time they travel, they earn air miles that can be used for personal trips or family vacations. In fact, company-earned air miles are so valued by employees that many would leave if their companies tried to keep the air miles for themselves. Chuck Collins, a technology and management consultant, said, if a company "tried to nickel-and-dime me for miles I'd get my résumé up to date real fast."[52]

Negative reinforcement strengthens behavior by withholding an unpleasant consequence when employees perform a specific behavior. Negative reinforcement is also called *avoidance learning*, because workers perform a behavior to *avoid* a negative consequence. For example, at Nucor Steel, employees make sure that they get to work on time, because if they are late, they lose their bonus for the day. If they are more than 30 minutes late, they lose their bonus for the week. Since bonuses can exceed hourly wages, Nucor employees make sure to avoid being late for work.

By contrast, **punishment** weakens behavior (i.e., decreases its frequency) by following behaviors with undesirable consequences. For example, the standard disciplinary or punishment process in most companies is an oral warning ("Don't ever do that again."), followed by a written warning ("This let-

negative reinforcement reinforcement that strengthens behavior by withholding an unpleasant consequence when employees perform a specific behavior

punishment reinforcement that weakens behavior by following behaviors with undesirable consequences

extinction reinforcement in which a positive consequence is no longer allowed to follow a previously reinforced behavior, thus weakening the behavior

ter is to discuss the serious problem you're having with . . ."), followed by three days off without pay ("While you're at home not being paid, we want you to think hard about . . ."), followed by being fired ("This was your last chance. You're fired."). While punishment can weaken behavior, managers have to be careful to avoid the backlash that sometimes occurs when employees are punished at work. For example, Frito-Lay began getting complaints from customers that they were finding potato chips with obscene messages written on them. Frito-Lay eventually traced the problem to a potato chip plant where supervisors had fired 58 out of the 210 workers for disciplinary reasons over a nine-month period. The remaining employees were so angry over what they saw as unfair treatment from management that they began writing obscene phrases on potato chips with felt-tipped pens.[53]

Extinction is a reinforcement strategy in which a positive consequence is no longer allowed to follow a previously reinforced behavior. By removing the positive consequence, extinction weakens the behavior, making it less likely to occur. For example, there are a number of unintended consequences that occur when employees are allowed to keep the air miles they earn when traveling on company business. The worst is that employees are likely to choose flights, hotels, restaurants, and car rentals based on air miles rather than price. Companies can stop this behavior by requiring employees to make all of their travel arrangements through a central travel agency. At DaimlerChrysler, employees' flights are tracked and purchased through American Express Travel. And when enough mileage is earned, the free tickets are awarded to the company rather than to employees. This extinguishes the behavior of choosing travel arrangements based on what's best for the employee (maximizing air miles) rather than what's best for the company (low cost).[54]

4.2
Schedules for Delivering Reinforcement

continuous reinforcement schedule schedule that requires a consequence to be administered following every instance of a behavior

intermittent reinforcement schedule schedule in which consequences are delivered after a specified or average time has elapsed or after a specified or average number of behaviors has occurred

A *schedule of reinforcement* is the set of rules regarding reinforcement contingencies, such as which behaviors will be reinforced, which consequences will follow those behaviors, and the schedule by which those consequences will be delivered. There are two categories of reinforcement schedules: continuous and intermittent.

With **continuous reinforcement schedules**, a consequence follows every instance of a behavior. For example, employees working on a piece-rate pay system earn money (consequence) for every part they manufacture (the behavior). The more they produce, they more they earn. By contrast, with **intermittent reinforcement schedules**, consequences are delivered after a specified or average time has elapsed or after a specified or average number of behaviors has occurred. As shown in Table 16.3, there are four types of intermittent reinforcement schedules. Two of these are based on

Table 16.3 **Intermittent Reinforcement Schedules**

Interval Schedules	*Ratio Schedules*
• Fixed Interval Schedules	• Fixed Ratio Schedules
• Variable Interval Schedules	• Variable Ratio Schedules

time and are called *interval reinforcement schedules*, while the other two, known as *ratio schedules*, are based on behaviors.

fixed interval reinforcement schedule intermittent schedule in which consequences follow a behavior only after a fixed time has elapsed

variable interval reinforcement schedule intermittent schedule in which the time between a behavior and the following consequences varies around a specified average

fixed ratio reinforcement schedule intermittent schedule in which consequences are delivered following a specific number of behaviors

variable ratio reinforcement schedule intermittent schedule in which consequences are delivered following a different number of behaviors, sometimes more and sometimes less, that vary around a specified average number of behaviors

With **fixed interval reinforcement schedules**, consequences follow a behavior only after a fixed time has elapsed. For example, most people receive their paychecks on a fixed interval schedule (e.g., once or twice per month). As long as they work (behavior) during a specified pay period (interval), they get a paycheck (consequence). With **variable interval reinforcement schedules**, consequences follow a behavior after different times, some shorter and some longer, that vary around a specified average time. On a 90-day variable interval reinforcement schedule, you might receive a bonus after 80 days or perhaps after 100 days, but the average interval between performing your job well (behavior) and receiving your bonus (consequence) would be 90 days.

With **fixed ratio reinforcement schedules**, consequences are delivered following a specific number of behaviors. For example, a car salesperson might receive a $1,000 bonus after every 10 sales. Therefore, a salesperson with only 9 sales would not receive the bonus until he or she finally sold a tenth car. With **variable ratio reinforcement schedules**, consequences are delivered following a different number of behaviors, sometimes more and sometimes less, that vary around a specified average number of behaviors. With a 10-car variable ratio reinforcement schedule, a salesperson might receive the bonus after 7 car sales, or after 12, 11, or 9 sales, but the average number of cars sold before receiving the bonus would be 10 cars.

Students often have trouble envisioning how these schedules could actually be used in a work setting, so a couple of examples will help. In one study, tree planters working for a forestry and logging company were paid to plant bags of tree seedlings (about 1,000 seedlings per bag) to re-grow trees that had been cut down. Workers were paid under several different conditions: (1) an hourly wage ($3 an hour), (2) continuous reinforcement in which they were paid $2 for every bag of seedlings they planted, (3) variable ratio reinforcement in which they were paid $4 for planting a bag of tree seedlings and then had to correctly guess what color marble their supervisor had in their hand (supervisors had two differently colored marbles, so workers were correct about half the time, which is equivalent to $2 a bag), and (4) another variable ratio reinforcement schedule in which they were paid $8 for planting a bag of tree seedlings and had to correctly guess the color of two marbles (on average, workers were correct about a quarter of the time, which is equivalent to $2 a bag).[55] In another study designed to increase employee attendance, employees who came to work participated in an innovative variable ratio schedule in which they would draw a card from a deck of playing cards. At the end of each week, the employee with the best poker hand from those cards received a $20 bonus.[56]

Which reinforcement schedules work best? In the past, the standard advice was to use continuous reinforcement when employees were learning new behaviors, since reinforcement after each success leads to faster learning. Likewise, the standard advice was to use intermittent reinforcement schedules to maintain behavior after it is learned, since intermittent rewards are supposed to make behavior much less subject to extinction.[57] However, except for interval-based systems, which usually produce weak results, there is little difference between the effectiveness of continuous reinforcement, fixed ratio, or variable ratio schedules.[58] In organizational settings, all three produce consistently large increases over noncontingent reward schedules. So managers should choose whichever of these three is easiest to use in their companies.

4.3 *Motivating with Reinforcement Theory*

What practical things can managers do to use reinforcement theory to motivate employees? Professor Fred Luthans, who has been studying the effects of reinforcement theory in organizations for more than a quarter of a century, says that there are five steps to motivating workers with reinforcement theory: *identify, measure, analyze, intervene,* and *evaluate* critical performance-related behaviors.[59]

Identify means identifying critical, observable, performance-related behaviors. These are the behaviors that are most important to successful job performance. However, they must also be easily observed, so they can be accurately measured. *Measure* means measuring the baseline frequencies of these behaviors. In other words, find out how often workers perform them. *Analyze* means analyzing the causes and consequences of these behaviors. Analyzing the causes helps managers create the conditions that produce these critical behaviors, while analyzing the consequences helps them determine if these behaviors produce the results that they want. *Intervene* means changing the organization by using positive and negative reinforcement to increase the frequency of these critical behaviors. *Evaluate* means evaluating the extent to which the intervention actually changed workers' behavior. This is done by comparing behavior after the intervention to the original baseline of behavior before the intervention. For more on the effectiveness of reinforcement theory, see the "What Really Works?" feature in this chapter.

What Really Works

Financial, Nonfinancial, and Social Rewards

Throughout this chapter, we have been making the point that there is more to motivating people than money. But we haven't yet examined how well financial (money or prizes), nonfinancial (performance feedback), or social (recognition and attention) rewards motivate workers by themselves, or in combination. However, 19 studies based on more than 2,800 people clearly indicate that rewarding and reinforcing employees greatly improves motivation and performance.

Overall Performance and Rewards

On average, there is a 63 percent chance that employees whose behavior is reinforced in some way will outperform employees whose behavior is not reinforced.

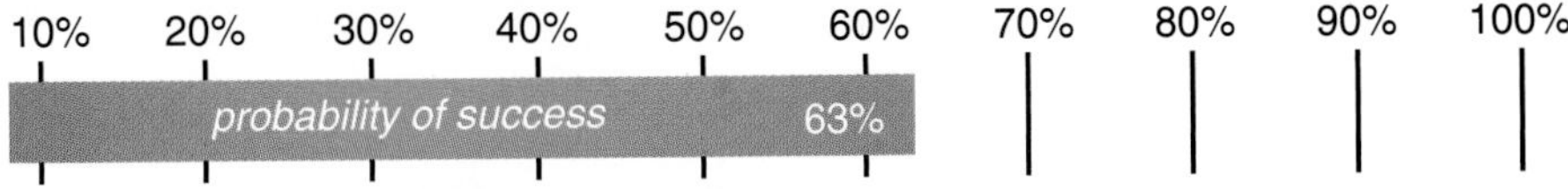

Performance in Manufacturing Organizations

Financial rewards. On average, there is an 84 percent chance that employees in manufacturing organizations whose behavior is reinforced with financial rewards will outperform employees whose behavior is not reinforced.

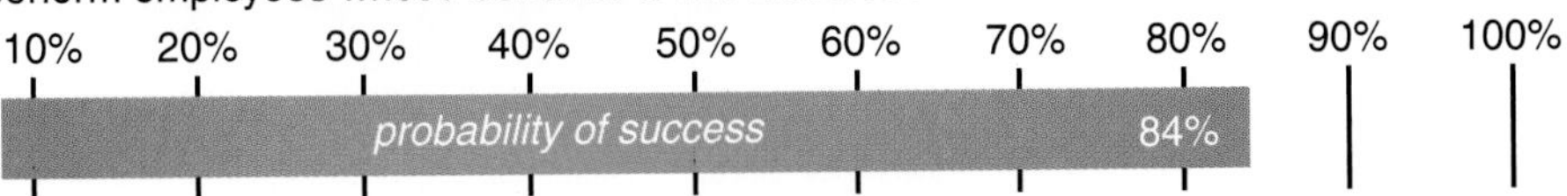

Nonfinancial rewards. On average, there is an 87 percent chance that employees in manufacturing organizations whose behavior is reinforced with nonfinancial rewards will outperform employees whose behavior is not reinforced.

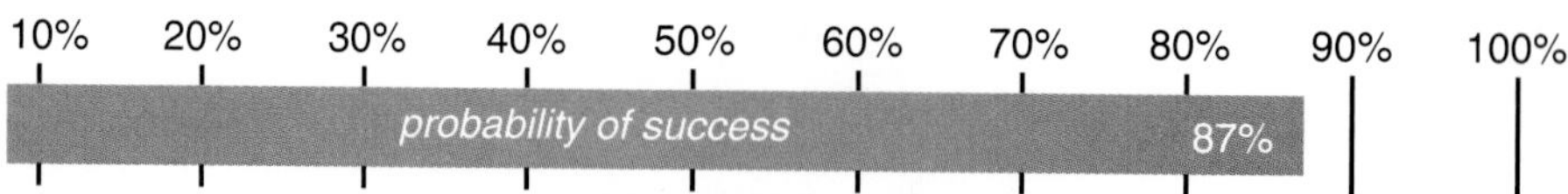

Financial, nonfinancial, and social rewards. On average, there is a 96 percent chance that employees in manufacturing organizations whose behavior is reinforced with a combination of financial, nonfinancial, and social rewards will outperform employees whose behavior is not reinforced.

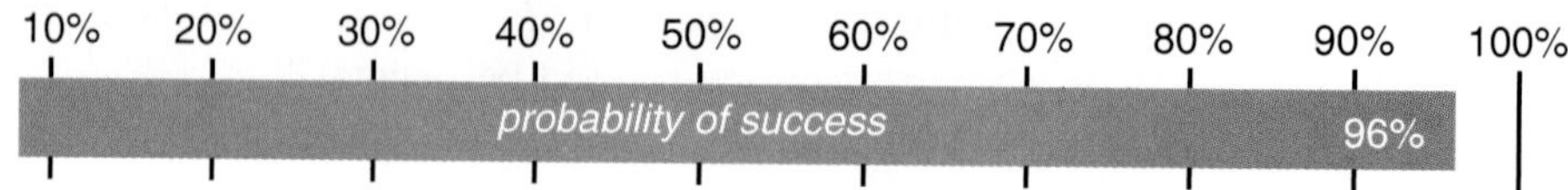

Performance in Service Organizations

Financial rewards. On average, there is a 61 percent chance that employees in service organizations whose behavior is reinforced with financial rewards will outperform employees whose behavior is not reinforced.

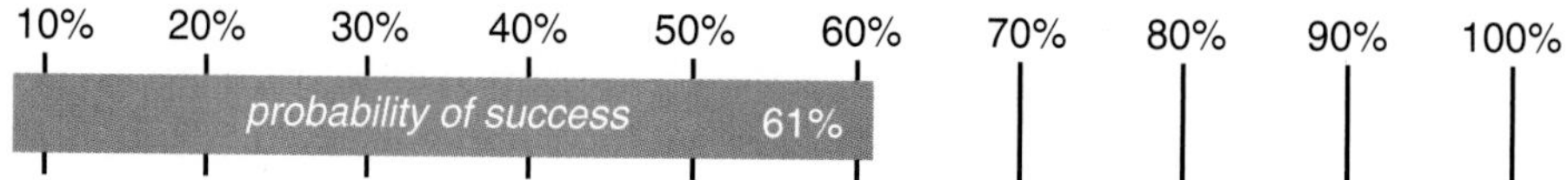

Nonfinancial rewards. On average, there is a 54 percent chance that employees in service organizations whose behavior is reinforced with nonfinancial rewards will outperform employees whose behavior is not reinforced.

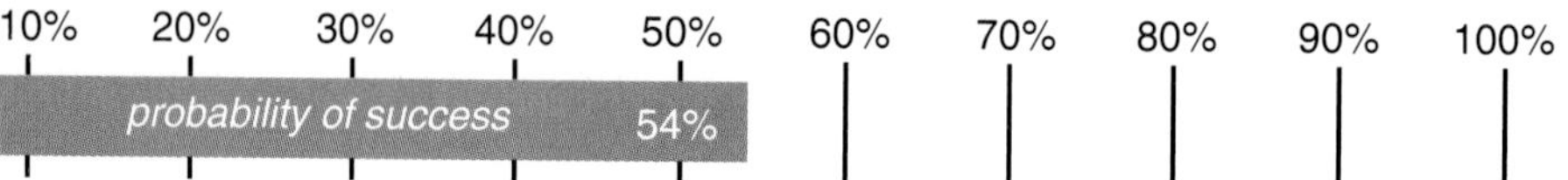

Social rewards. On average, there is a 61 percent chance that employees in service organizations whose behavior is reinforced with social rewards will outperform employees whose behavior is not reinforced.

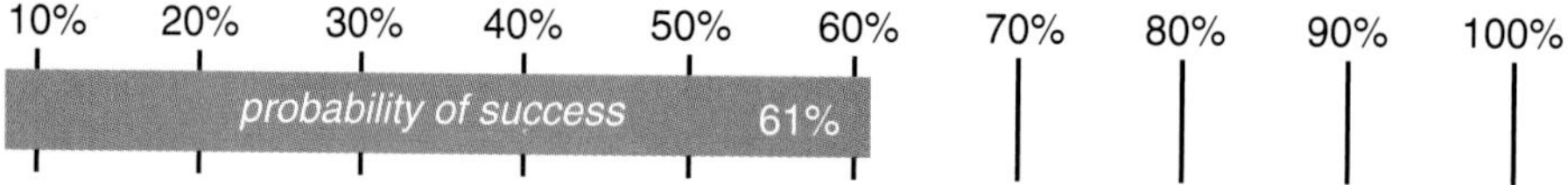

Financial and nonfinancial rewards. On average, there is a 72 percent chance that employees in service organizations whose behavior is reinforced with a combination of financial and nonfinancial rewards will outperform employees whose behavior is not reinforced.

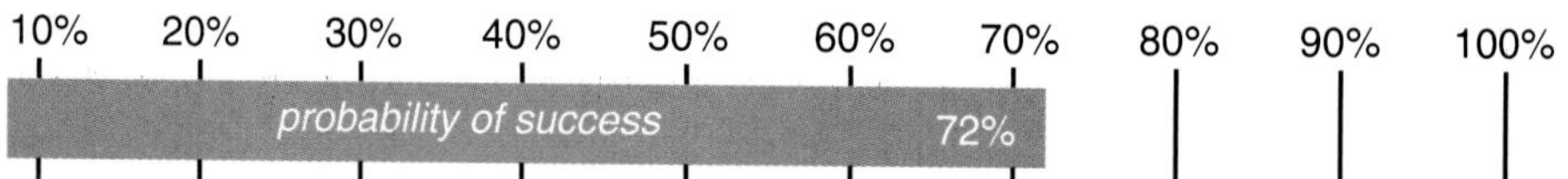

Nonfinancial and social rewards. On average, there is a 73 percent chance that employees in service organizations whose behavior is reinforced with a combination of nonfinancial and social rewards will outperform employees whose behavior is not reinforced.

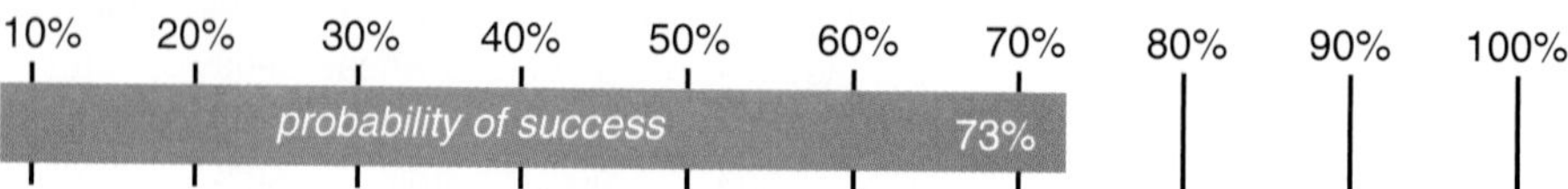

Source: A.D. Stajkovic & F. Luthans, "A Meta-analysis of the Effects of Organizational Behavior Modification on Task Performance, 1975-95," *Academy of Management Journal* 40, no. 5 (1997): 1122-1149.

Don't reinforce the wrong behaviors. While reinforcement theory sounds simple, it's actually very difficult to put into practice. One of the most common mistakes is accidentally reinforcing the wrong behaviors. In fact, sometimes managers reinforce behaviors that they don't want! For example, the Group Health Claims Division of a large insurance company wanted to increase the accuracy with which it paid medical claims. So it began tracking the number of errors made by its insurance claim processors. Since mistakes were measured by the number of returned checks (customers would only return checks when the amount paid was too small) and the number of complaint letters, claims processors decided that the best way to minimize "errors" was to pay for nearly anything that customers wanted. "When in doubt, pay it out!" became their motto. So rather than reinforcing accuracy, the company unwittingly reinforced inaccuracy by reinforcing workers for paying nearly any kind or size of claim.[60]

Correctly administer punishment at the appropriate time. Most managers believe that punishment can change workers' behavior and help them improve their job performance. Furthermore, managers believe that fairly punishing workers also lets other workers know what is or isn't acceptable.[61] However, one of the dangers of using punishment is that it can produce a backlash against managers and companies. However, if it is administered properly, punishment can weaken the frequency of undesirable behaviors without creating a backlash.[62] For punishment to work, the punishment must be strong enough to stop the undesired behavior and must be administered objectively (same rules applied to everyone), impersonally (without emotion or anger), consistently and contingently (each time improper behavior occurs), and quickly (as soon as possible following the undesirable behavior). In addition, managers should clearly explain what the appropriate behavior is and why the employee is being punished. When administered this way, employees typically respond well to punishment.[63]

Choose the simplest and most effective schedule of reinforcement. When choosing a schedule of reinforcement, managers need to balance effectiveness against simplicity. In fact, the more complex the schedule of reinforcement, the more likely it is to be misunderstood and resisted by managers and employees. For example, when the forestry and logging company discussed above first paid tree planters to plant bags of tree seedlings, it didn't have much luck with its initial variable ratio schedule. When planters finished planting a bag of seedlings, they got to flip a coin. If they called the coin flip correctly (heads or tails), they were paid $4, double the hourly rate. If they called the coin flip incorrectly, they got nothing. The company began having problems when a manager, who was a part-time minister, and several workers claimed that the coin flip was a form of gambling. Then, one of the workers found that the company was taking out too much money in taxes from their paychecks. Since workers didn't really understand the reinforcement schedule, they blamed the payment plan associated with it and accused the company of trying to cheat them out of their money. After all of these problems, the researchers who implemented the variable ratio schedule concluded that "the results of this study may not be so much an indication of the relative effectiveness of different schedules of reinforcement as they are an indication of the types of problems that one encounters when applying these concepts in an industrial setting."[64] In short, choose the simplest, most effective schedule of reinforcement. Since there is little difference between the effectiveness of continuous reinforcement, fixed ratio, or variable ratio schedules, continuous reinforcement schedules may be the best choice in many instances by virtue of their simplicity and effectiveness.

Review 4
Reinforcement Theory

Reinforcement theory says that behavior is a function of its consequences. Reinforcement has two parts: reinforcement contingencies and schedules of reinforcement. The four kinds of reinforcement contingencies are positive reinforcement and negative reinforcement, which strengthen behavior, and punishment and extinction, which weaken behavior. There are two kinds of reinforcement schedules, continuous and intermittent, the latter of which can be separated into fixed and variable interval schedules and fixed and variable ratio schedules. Managers can use reinforcement theory to motivate workers by following five steps (identify, measure, analyze, intervene, and evaluate critical performance-related behaviors); not reinforcing the wrong behaviors; correctly administering punishment at the appropriate time; and choosing a reinforcement schedule, such as continuous reinforcement, that balances simplicity and effectiveness.

5 Goal-Setting Theory

Scott Grocki, president of Grocki Magic Studios, believes in the power of setting goals. In his Boca Raton office, he and his performing partner, Jennifer Brown, have more goals than places to put them! Long-term goals ("BROADWAY" and "TELEVISION") are written on the office wall as a constant reminder that they want to appear on television and develop a Broadway show about magic. "ART" is also written on the wall to remind them to strive for "artistic integrity." They keep monthly and six-month goals on file and review them every two weeks. Weekly goals are kept near the office telephone. Every Monday, they set new goals, and Jennifer makes sure that they "match the writing on the wall." In other words, she ensures that each new goal contributes to their long-term goals. Grocki describes the importance of goals in this manner: "When you set a goal, you create something and it becomes real. You write it down. You focus on it, you aspire to it, and that's your motivation."[65]

goal
a target, objective, or result that someone tries to accomplish

goal-setting theory
theory that states that people will be motivated to the extent to which they accept specific, challenging goals and receive feedback that indicates their progress toward goal achievement

The basic model of motivation with which we began this chapter showed that individuals feel tension after becoming aware of an unfulfilled need. Once they experience tension, they search for and select courses of action that they believe will eliminate this tension. In other words, they direct their behavior toward something. This something is a goal. A **goal** is a target, objective, or result that someone tries to accomplish. **Goal-setting theory** says that people will be motivated to the extent to which they accept specific, challenging goals and receive feedback that indicates their progress toward goal achievement.

Let's learn more about goal-setting by examining **5.1** *the components of goal-setting theory and* **5.2** *how to motivate with goal-setting theory.*

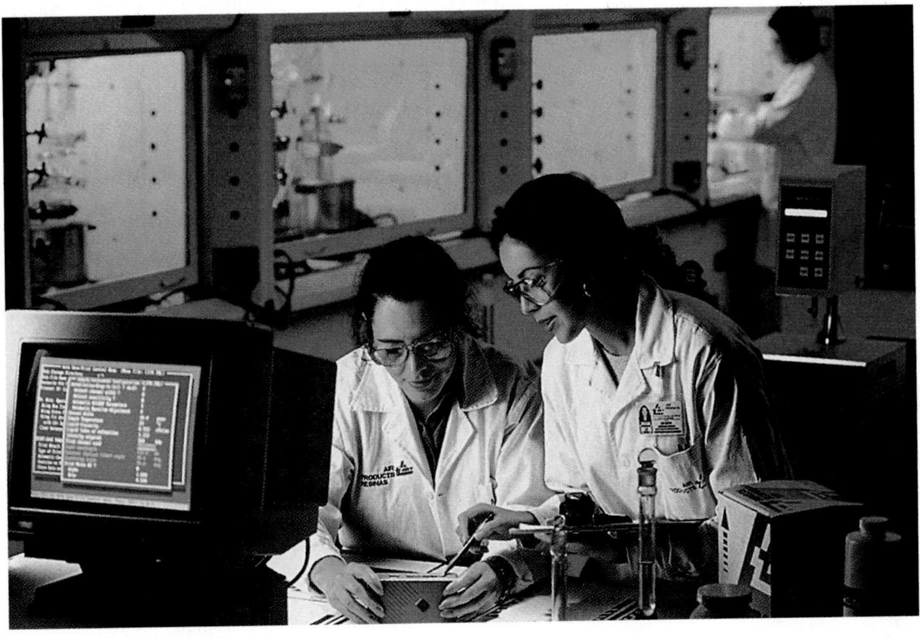

For goals to be motivating, workers must receive performance feedback about progress toward goal achievement.
© William Taufic/The Stock Market

5.1 Components of Goal-Setting Theory

The basic components of goal-setting theory are goal specificity, goal difficulty, goal acceptance, and performance feedback.[66] **Goal specificity** is the extent to which goals are detailed, exact, and unambiguous. Specific goals, such as "I'm going to have a 3.0 average this semester," are more motivating than general goals, such as "I'm going to get better grades this semester."

goal specificity
the extent to which goals are detailed, exact, and unambiguous

Goal difficulty is the extent to which a goal is hard or challenging to accomplish. Difficult goals, such as "I'm going to have a 3.5 average and make Dean's List this semester," are more motivating than easy goals, such as "I'm going to have a 2.0 average this semester."

goal difficulty
the extent to which a goal is hard or challenging to accomplish

Goal acceptance is the extent to which people consciously understand and agree to goals. Accepted goals, such as "I really want to get a 3.5 average this semester to show my parents how much I've improved," are more motivating than unaccepted goals, such as "My parents really want me to get a 3.5 this semester, but there's so much more I'd rather do on campus than study!"

goal acceptance
the extent to which people consciously understand and agree to goals

Performance feedback is information about the quality or quantity of past performance and indicates whether progress is being made toward the accomplishment of a goal. Performance feedback, such as "My prof said I need a 92 on the final to get an A in the class," is more motivating than no feedback, "I have no idea what my grade is in that class." In short, goal-setting theory says that people will be motivated to the extent to which they accept specific, challenging goals and receive feedback that indicates their progress toward goal achievement.

performance feedback
information about the quality or quantity of past performance that indicates whether progress is being made toward the accomplishment of a goal

How does goal-setting work? To start, challenging goals focus employees' attention (i.e., direct effort) on the critical aspects of their jobs and away from unimportant areas. Goals also energize behavior. When faced with unaccomplished goals, employees typically develop plans and strategies to reach those goals. Goals also create a tension between the goal, which is the desired future

Back to the Future

Will the "Virtual Worker" Require "Virtual Motivation"?

Telecommuting and home offices have been with us for awhile. However, rapid improvements in computer and telecommunications technology have lead to a new trend—the "virtual workplace." One version of the virtual workplace is the central office that electronically links permanent and temporary employees who work at home or in the field. For example, Buckman Laboratories is an international company that researches, develops, and markets specialty chemical products for industrial and agricultural uses. The company has more than 1,200 employees in more than 20 countries with distribution outlets in 70 more. Buckman's advanced telecommunications network allows employees in different locations to communicate, share documents, and collaborate on decisions in real time. Journal Graphics, the company that makes transcripts for most news-related shows, like NBC's *Meet the Press*, is another virtual organization. While you can obtain a transcript by mailing a check to Journal Graphics in Denver, Colorado, you wouldn't find many employees there. In fact, most of Journal Graphics' employees work out of their homes. They record TV shows on VCRs and use the videotapes to type up transcripts that are uploaded to the central office within hours of being broadcast. Or, in Boulder, Colorado, a company calling itself The Virtual Office consists of a bank of professional "tele-secretaries," who answer calls for 91 different companies. When the phone rings, the name of the company being called appears on the tele-secretary's computer screen. He or she then takes a message or routes the call to the correct number or person, who can be thousands of miles away. Companies contracting with The Virtual Office reduce their costs by not having to maintain offices and secretarial staff.

Where will the virtual office trend take us? AT&T is experimenting with a "mobile office" that travels with an employee and can be set up anywhere. Another company is working on an "office-in-a-box," a briefcase containing a miniature notebook computer, fax, cellular telephone, modem, scanner, printer, and keyboard. Someday there may even be "virtual reality offices," where you put on special glasses and appear to enter a meeting room filled with other managers. In reality, these managers, who are in different locations throughout the world, are also wearing these special glasses and only appear to be in the same room with you.

By not having to maintain large, expensive offices, companies using virtual workplaces often have lower overhead and fixed costs. They may also hire fewer full-time employees and potentially reduce labor costs by 30 to 40 percent.

But what does it take to motivate a virtual employee? How do you manage an employee you no longer see every day? Clearly it takes more to become a virtual workplace than just technology. For example, when one service company decided to go virtual, it installed a corporate e-mail system and bought laptop computers for all its employees and sent them home. But workers hated it so much that sales dropped like a rock and employee turnover went through the roof. So while virtual offices appear to hold promise, there's no getting around the fact that "virtual workers" may require some sort of "virtual motivation."

For these reasons, goal-setting seems to work quite well when motivating virtual workers. At AT&T, managers meet face-to-face with virtual workers to set objectives. In turn, progress toward those objectives is closely monitored. An AT&T manager said, "Everyone felt better about working away from his supervisor because he knew what he had to do and how it would be measured. These had been laid out in the objectives-setting meeting before the telecommuting began." Another change from traditional organizations is that employees rather than managers monitor this progress. One of AT&T's virtual workers said, "The supervisor is there to guide you, not to structure your workday. It is up to me to keep my supervisor informed of what I do. I send periodic e-mails to him with an update of my activities. I leave voice mail if there is a particular issue on which I need assistance. And I request a meeting every few months to specifically discuss my progress."

Sources: S. Lucas, "Staffing the Virtual Office," *Memphis Business Journal*, 20 November 1995, Section 1, p. 49. S.E. O'Connel, "The Virtual Workplace Moves at Warp Speed," *HR Magazine* 41 (March 1996): 50-53. D. Churbuck & J.S. Young, "The Virtual Workplace," *Forbes* 150 (November 23, 1992):184-190. M.A. Piotrowski, "Virtual Office Arrives Via Jacksonville," *Tampa Bay Business Journal* 14 (24 June 1994): Section 1, p. 3. Anonymous, "Disasters Prompt Drive Toward Virtual Work," *Futurist* 30 (September/October 1996): 48-50. W.R. Pape, "Remote Control," *Inc. Technology*, no. 3 (1996): 25-29. W.R. Pape, "Beyond E-mail," *Inc. Technology*, no. 1 (1995). Anonymous, "Seven Trends Will Change Your Future Worklife," *Managing Office Technology* 39 (February 1994): 64. T.H. Davenport & K. Pearlson, "Two Cheers for the Virtual Office," *Sloan Management Review* 39, no. 4 (1998): 51.

state of affairs, and where the employee or company is now, meaning the current state of affairs. This tension can only be satisfied by eliminating or abandoning the goal. Finally, goals influence persistence. Since goals only "go away" when they are accomplished, employees are more likely to persist in their efforts in the presence of goals. Figure 16.8 incorporates goals into the motivation model by showing how goals directly affect tension, effort, and the extent to which employees are energized to take action.

5.2 *Motivating with Goal-Setting Theory*

What practical things can managers do to use goal-setting theory to motivate employees?

Assign specific, challenging goals. One of the simplest, most effective ways to motivate workers is to give them specific, challenging goals. However, an amazing number of managers never do this with their employees. One manager who does is Jim Schaefer. When Schaefer's top management asked him to increase profits at his oil refinery plant by $7 million, he turned around and promised them profits of $60 million. Then, with this difficult goal on the line, he met with senior managers and union leaders every

Figure 16.8 **Adding Goal-Setting Theory to the Model**

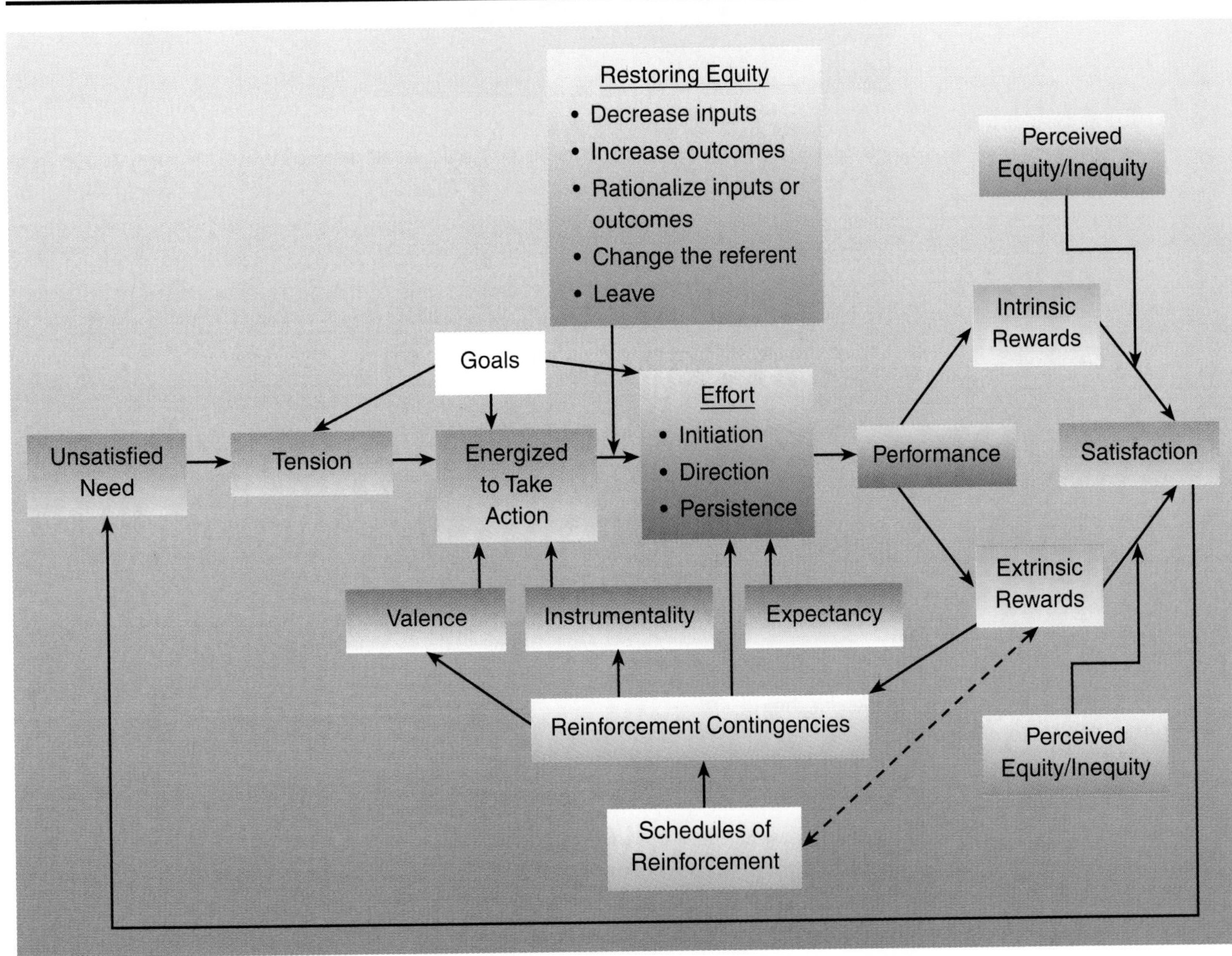

Specific, challenging goals are an effective way to motivate workers.

90 days to set specific goals for overall improvement in the plant. He also met with first-level supervisors every 30 days to get them to develop specific goals for improvement in their departments. The result? While most oil refineries scratch and claw to find ways to produce 1 percent more oil, thanks to specific challenging goals Schaefer's oil refinery increased its production by 20 percent.[67] For more information on assigning specific, challenging goals see the discussion in Chapter 4 on S.M.A.R.T. goals.

Been There,

Goal *for It!*

Zig Ziglar is the author of nine books, seven of which have made the bestseller list, including See You at the Top*, and is one of the most popular motivational speakers in the business world. In this interview, he discusses the importance of goal setting.*

Q: So goal-setting works?

A: That's right. Absolutely. It works for the person, it works for the family, it works for the business, it works for the nation.

Q: So what is the best way to set goals?

A: To get started setting goals, we have to look at the whole picture. Step number one is I write down everything I want to be, do or have. I then ask myself why I want to be or do or have each of my goals. I go right down the list of everything I have written down and if I cannot articulate in one sentence why I want to achieve that goal, then I scratch it off the list for the time being. That will reduce the size of my list dramatically.

"... if you don't have direction in your life, you are what we call a wandering generality. ..."

Q: Okay.

A: Then I do a quick rundown to identify the category that each goal fits in—is it a social goal, a career goal, a family goal, a physical goal, a mental goal, a spiritual goal, a career goal? Then I take another quick look at the list to see whether I have a balance. Are all of them mental goals or are all of them financial goals? Do I have my family and social goals in there as well? The average person will have well over 100 things on that list. As a general rule, you can almost universally say if it ain't planned, it don't happen.

Once I have done that, then I ask myself five questions. The purpose of all of this is to get everything on the table; it's just like going down a cafeteria line. Since you can't eat some of everything on the line, you choose what you really want. That's what we are doing here. (1) Is this really my goal? In other words, maybe I have set a goal to write $10 million in premiums this year. Well now, is that really my goal or was that my manager's goal for me? Do I want a Lexus or am I saying I want one because my buddy's got one? (2) Is this goal morally fair to everyone involved? (3) Will reaching this goal take me closer to or farther from my major objectives in life? (4) Can I emotionally commit myself to reaching this goal? (5) Do I believe I have a legitimate chance of reaching this goal? Answering these five questions will reduce my list.

Q: How long should a session like this take?
A: To properly do your goal planning, it is going to take a couple of days. Once you have reduced your list dramatically with the five questions, you still might have 20 things there, and you just can't work on 20 things. So there are seven steps that I take to cut that list down to an absolutely manageable size.

Step number one is to specifically write your goals down. In other words, now I've got my list down to let's say 20. Write down exactly what the goal is. The second thing I write is the benefits I'll get from reaching this goal. Third, I list the obstacles I've got to overcome to reach this goal. Then, what do I need to know to reach this goal? Then, who are the individuals, groups and organizations that I need to work with to reach this goal? Number six, what is my specific plan of action to reach this goal? And then finally, number seven, what is the date of completion of this goal?

Q: You mentioned the seven steps to get your list of goals down to a manageable size, somewhere around 20. Is that a reasonable amount of goals to be working on?
A: No, it is not. Twenty goals are not reasonable to work on every day. Let me give an example. Being a writer, I generally start working on my next book about three years before I expect the book to be published. Now I might go a month without doing anything on that particular goal, but I review that goal and when I see articles or publications or something that specifically has to do with the subject matter of the book, I simply take it and put it in a file for future reference. So about 10 to 12 months out, I move the book to my daily agenda, and I set my weekly goals. Then each day I record how much time I spend working on that goal. Some days I don't do anything. Other days, I might spend five or six hours on it.

Q: Many people set goals for the year, but few people actually follow through with them. How do you keep on target?
A: We have what we call a Performance Planner that our company sells, and it provides a look at the coming week and month. The goal planner has spaces to record specifically what I do each day so far as my activities are concerned, then it shows that amount of effort and what I did on each of my specific goals. I work on four goals daily.

Q: How did you settle on four?
A: Well, I found out that's about the maximum number I could count on doing something on every day. Now for the week I might end up working on 10 goals. More likely, it would be closer to seven. But on some of those, I might work just one day, others I might work three days, but there are some things I do every day.

Q: What do you do when you reach a goal?
A: You better set another one real quick. If you reach a significant goal and you don't set another goal, there will be an emotional letdown and you will do a lot of drifting. When I finish writing one book, for example, I immediately start the next. When I say immediately, I mean within the month I start another one.

Q: You talk about goals and figuring out the time frames to reach them, but how should your goals be grouped? Should you set a few goals for today, a few goals for this week, a few for this month and then some reaching goals?
A: Actually, some of your goals won't have a completion date. For example, building a better relationship with your family, or getting a better education or raising morally sound, positive children. Those don't have completion dates.

Q: Why are goals important, Zig?
A: Well, you know, if you don't have direction in your life, you are what we call a wandering generality and in order to utilize your maximum potential, you've got to be a meaningful specific, and I can give you any number of illustrations of what happens when people set goals; the financial goals we are talking about that are being tracked by David Jensen of UCLA would just be one example.

Source: D.J. Nahorney, "You Need Goals: An Interview with Zig Ziglar," *Managers Magazine* 67, no. 9 (1992): 6-11. This interview was edited for inclusion in this textbook.

Make sure workers truly accept organizational goals. Specific, challenging goals won't motivate workers unless they really accept, understand, and agree to the organization's goals. For this to occur, people must see the goals as fair and reasonable. Plus, they must trust management and believe that managers are using goals to clarify what is expected from them rather than to exploit or threaten them ("If you don't achieve these goals . . ."). However, participative goal-setting, in which managers and employees generate goals together, can help increase trust and understanding and thus acceptance of goals. Furthermore, providing workers with training can help increase goal acceptance, particularly when workers don't believe they are capable of reaching the organization's goals.[68]

Provide frequent, specific performance-related feedback. In addition to accepting specific, challenging goals, goal-setting theory also specifies that employees should receive frequent performance-related feedback so they can track progress toward goal completion. Feedback leads to stronger motivation and effort in three ways.[69] First, receiving specific performance feedback that indicates how well you're performing can encourage employees who don't have specific, challenging goals to actually set goals to improve their performance. Second, once people meet goals, performance feedback often encourages them to set higher, more difficult goals. Third, feedback lets people know whether they need to increase their efforts or change strategies in order to accomplish their goals.

For example, Figure 16.9 shows the checklist that was used to gather performance feedback for the banquet staff at a large conference hotel. The banquet staff was responsible for setting up the tables, dishes, silverware, and cups for coffee breaks, breakfasts, lunches, dinners, and receptions that were held at the hotel. Supervisors used this checklist to assess the room setup 15 minutes before each event. After gathering data for a month, supervisors determined that the banquet staff was completing these tasks only 69 percent of the time. Consequently, supervisors began using a graph to display setup completion percentages on a daily basis. When employees reported for work, the setup completion graph was one of the first things they'd see. Supervisors also chose an 85 percent setup completion percentage as their goal and promised a small $10 reward to employees who met this goal each month. Introducing the goal and daily performance feedback immediately increased the setup completion rate to 100 percent. However, after a successful four-month period, a new banquet manager was hired, and the hotel quit posting feedback and offering the $10 reward. As a result, setup completion rates dropped to 82 percent. However, when banquet management subsequently reintroduced goals, daily feedback, and the $10 reward, setup completion rates immediately rose again to 100 percent and then averaged 98 percent.[70] So, to motivate employees with goal-setting theory, make sure they receive frequent performance-related feedback so they can track progress toward goal completion.

Review 5
Goal-Setting Theory

A goal is a target, objective, or result that someone tries to accomplish. Goal-setting theory says that people will be motivated to the extent to which they accept specific, challenging goals and receive feedback that indicates

Figure 16.9 **Checklist Used to Gather Performance Feedback for Lunch Buffet Setups**

LUNCH BUFFET

Checklist used for lunch buffet setups. Columns at right contain boxes for employee and supervisor initials that are used to sign off for task completion.

All Buffet Lunch Setups Will Include the Following:	**Employee Initials**	**Supervisor Initials**
1. Plates	|___|	|___|
2. Elevation/Ruffled Cloths	|___|	|___|
3. Chafing Dishes/Sternos	|___|	|___|
4. Silverware	|___|	|___|
5. Iced Tea Glasses	|___|	|___|
6. Serving Utensils	|___|	|___|
7. Sugar/Salt/Peper/Condiments	|___|	|___|
8. Napkins	|___|	|___|
9. Decorations	|___|	|___|
10. Cream	|___|	|___|
11. Covered Tray/Tray Stand	|___|	|___|
12. Breakdown Station	|___|	|___|
13. Centerpieces	|___|	|___|
14. Coffee Cups	|___|	|___|

Source: T. LaFleur & C. Hyten, "Improving the Quality of Hotel Banquet Staff Performance," *Journal of Organizational Behavior Management* 15, no. 1 (1995): 69-93.

their progress toward goal achievement. The basic components of goal-setting theory are goal specificity, goal difficulty, goal acceptance, and performance feedback. Goal specificity is the extent to which goals are detailed, exact, and unambiguous. Goal difficulty is the extent to which a goal is hard or challenging to accomplish. Goal acceptance is the extent to which people consciously understand and agree to goals. Performance feedback is information about the quality or quantity of past performance and indicates whether progress is being made toward the accomplishment of a goal. Managers can use goal-setting theory to motivate workers by assigning specific, challenging goals, making sure workers truly accept organizational goals, and providing frequent, specific performance-related feedback.

6 Motivating with the Integrated Model

We began this chapter by defining motivation as the set of forces that initiates, directs, and makes people persist in their efforts to accomplish a goal. We also asked the basic question that managers ask when they try to figure out how to motivate their workers: "What leads to effort?" While the answer

Table 16.4	Motivating with the Integrated Model
Motivating with the Basics	• Ask people what their needs are. • Satisfy lower-order needs first. • Expect people's needs to change. • As needs change and lower-order needs are satisfied, satisfy higher order needs by looking for ways to allow employees to experience intrinsic rewards.
Motivating with Equity Theory	• Look for and correct major inequities. • Reduce employees' inputs. • Make sure decision-making processes are fair.
Motivating with Expectancy Theory	• Systematically gather information to find out what employees want from their jobs. • Take clear steps to link rewards to individual performance in a way that is clear and understandable to employees. • Empower employees to make decisions if you really want them to believe that their hard work and efforts will lead to good performance.
Motivating with Reinforcement Theory	• Identify, measure, analyze, intervene, and evaluate critical performance-related behaviors. • Don't reinforce the wrong behaviors. • Correctly administer punishment at the appropriate time. • Choose the simplest and most effective schedules of reinforcement.
Motivating with Goal-Setting Theory	• Assign specific, challenging goals. • Make sure workers truly accept organizational goals. • Provide frequent, specific performance-related feedback.

to that question is likely to be somewhat different for each employee, Table 16.4 helps you begin to answer it by consolidating the practical advice from the theories reviewed in this chapter into one convenient location. So if you're having difficulty figuring out why people aren't motivated where you work, Table 16.4 provides a useful, theory-based starting point.

What**Really**Happened?

At the beginning of this chapter, you read about the problems Diamond International was having motivating its employees. And, with layoffs occurring, it is hard to imagine a more difficult situation in which to maintain a motivated work force. However, Diamond came up with a solution that motivated its employees and returned the company to profitability. Read the answers to the opening case to find out what really happened.

What exactly is it that motivates employees, and is it the same for everyone?

One of the things we know about motivation is that what motivates one employee may not motivate another. Expectancy theory calls this *valence*, which is simply the attractiveness or desirability of various rewards or outcomes. Diamond International tried to make sure that all employees had valent rewards by using a point system, explained below, to reward employees for good performance. When employees earned 150 points, they could "spend" those points to "buy" themselves a gift. Employees with 600 or more points could "buy" gifts such as luggage, cameras, etc.

Another reason for differences in motivation is that employees may have different needs: physiological, safety, belongingness, esteem, and self-actualization needs (Maslow's Hierarchy); existence, relatedness, and growth needs (Alderfer's ERG Theory); or affiliation, achievement, and power needs (McClelland's Learned Needs Theory).

What can you do without spending a lot of money to get employees excited about their work again?

Daniel Boyle was one of the managers at Diamond International who was instrumental in finding ways to motivate Diamond's employees. He wrote, "As a supervisor, when was the last time you, personally, thanked every one of your employees for doing a good job? For such things as: Reporting to work when scheduled and on time? For working safely? For working cooperatively? For being quality conscious? For accurate paperwork? When was the last time you made a conscious effort to go around and personally thank every employee for doing a good job? Was it yesterday? Last week? Last month? Or last year?" Boyle believes that recognition is one of the most important and powerful motivators that managers have at their disposal. But, he says, few managers actually recognize employees for their work.

As a result of his beliefs, he created Diamond International's "100 Club." "100" stands for the number of points employees need to earn in order to become members of the 100 Club. Employees earn points for positive work-related behavior, such as attendance, punctuality, work quality, a good safety record, meeting goals, accurate paperwork, and participating on company committees. When they reach 100 points, they receive a jacket with a "100 Club" insignia on it. And, as explained above, the more points they earn, they more stuff they can "buy" for themselves. Boyle said, "For too long, the people who have got the majority of [our managers'] attention have been those who cause problems. The [100 Club] program's primary focus is the recognition of good employees."

Should Diamond's recognition program work? According to reinforcement theory, it should. Reinforcement theory says that behavior is a function of its consequences, that behaviors followed by positive consequences will occur more frequently, and that behaviors followed by negative consequences, or not followed by positive consequences, will occur less frequently. In fact, while management had hoped for first-year savings of between $14,000 and $15,000, it actually realized savings of more than $1,600,000 at its Palmer, Massachusetts, plant! Attendance improvements alone saved the manufacturing plant over $90,000. Further, productivity increased by 14.2 percent, and quality mistakes decreased by 40 percent. The 100 Club plan was then implemented in other Diamond International manufacturing plants located in Natchez, Mississippi, Red Bluff, California, and Plattsburgh, New York. Similar results occurred in these locations. In total, the 100 Club saved Diamond International over $15,200,000 in its first 18 months of existence! Plus, employees truly valued the recognition. Boyle said that one of Diamond's employees told a friend, "My employer gave me this (a 100 Club jacket) for doing a good job. It's the first time in the 18 years I have been there that they've recognized the things I do every day."

The fact that there are so many grievances being filed, and that some of them are over trivial matters, suggests that employees don't feel they are being treated fairly. What can you do to change these perceptions?

Equity theory says that people will be motivated when they perceive that they are being treated fairly. So with layoffs occurring nearly every month and employees being rotated into jobs that they had never performed before, it shouldn't have surprised anyone that the unionized workers at Diamond's

Palmer, Massachusetts, plant were angry and frustrated. In fact, they retaliated by filing 150 grievances against the company. However, even with all of these grievances, the managers at the Palmer plant didn't really begin to appreciate the importance of employee perceptions until the employee survey results indicated that 65 percent of employees felt that management did not treat them with respect, that 56 percent of employees approached their work pessimistically, and that 79 percent felt they were not rewarded for good work. Only then did management appreciate that they needed to address employees' perceptions. The Palmer plant manager, who was surprised by these results, said, "We must do whatever's possible to change the way our employees view management. We must create a team spirit—all of our jobs depend on it."

The 100 Club program was the primary way in which Diamond's managers tried to change employees' perceptions. However, the key was not to change employees' perceptions of managers, but to change their perceptions concerning whether they were being treated fairly by those managers. According to equity theory, when workers feel underrewarded, they get angry or frustrated, just like the workers at the Palmer plant. Therefore, the 100 Club program restored workers' perceptions of equity by increasing the outcomes that employees received for their efforts. When employees showed up for work on time, went to training, and otherwise did a good job, they earned points via the 100 Club that could be used to purchase whatever the workers wanted. How well did the 100 Club restore equity? Survey results indicated that 86 percent of the employees said they felt the company and supervisors now believed them to be "very important" or "important," that 81 percent said their work now provided them with "recognition by the company," and that 73 percent said their supervisors showed "concern for them as people." Other indications of its success in restoring equity were that the number of grievances dropped 72 percent and the issuance of disciplinary actions declined by 48 percent.

What can you do to get employees to meet their goals?

The most obvious way in which Diamond encouraged employees to meet their goals was by allowing them to earn points in the 100 Club for accomplishing specific goals. For instance, a year's worth of perfect attendance was worth 25 points, while going a year without having an accident was worth 20 points. Likewise, maintenance employees also earned points for reducing the amount of unscheduled downtime (i.e., breakdowns) on the machines that made cardboard egg cartons. Also, management made sure that the behaviors for which employees earned points were observable and measurable. This made it easier for employees to see what behaviors were earning rewards for their co-workers.

However, Diamond also encouraged employees to meet their goals by giving them frequent performance-related feedback. Feedback leads to stronger motivation and effort in three ways. First, because receiving specific performance feedback indicates how well they are performing, it can encourage employees who don't have specific, challenging goals to actually set goals to improve their performance. In fact, because of the feedback employees received as a result of the points they earned through the 100 Club, employees would often skip scheduled breaks so they could continue earning points. Second, once people meet goals, performance feedback often encourages them to set higher, more difficult goals. One manager said, "It's made my job a lot easier. When a machine breaks down, maintenance workers are here in a hurry to get it back on line." Third, feedback lets people know whether they need to increase their efforts or change strategies in order to accomplish their goals. Another supervisor said, "Machine operators are working better together as a team. Morale has improved tremendously! It's hard to imagine the gains we've received just by giving people points for doing the same things as they've always done."

Sources: Anonymous, "Diamond International: Worker Woes? Motivate the Good Ones, Not the Bad," *Incentive Marketing* 157 (October 1983): 104-110. D.C. Boyle, "Employee Motivation That Works," *HR Magazine,* October 1992, 83-89. D.C. Boyle, "Divining the Secrets of a Successful Employee Recognition System," *Security Management* 40 (July 1996): 21-24. D.C. Boyle, "To Employees—'Thanks' Means Millions—Literally," *Supervision* 53 (November 1992): 3-6. Anonymous, "Case History: Employee Recognition Programs," *Small Business Report* 11 (October 1986): 98. D.C. Boyle, "The 100 Club," *Harvard Business Review* 65 (March/April 1987): 26-27. D.C. Boyle, "Recognition That Works," *Incentive Marketing* 161 (December 1987): 32-36.

continuous reinforcement schedule p. 671

distributive justice p. 662

equity theory p. 658

expectancy p. 663

expectancy theory p. 663

extinction p. 671

extrinsic reward p. 653

fixed interval reinforcement schedule p. 672

fixed ratio reinforcement schedule p. 672

goal p. 676

goal acceptance p. 677

goal difficulty p. 677

goal specificity p. 677

goal-setting theory p. 676

inputs p. 658

instrumentality p. 664

intermittent reinforcement schedule p. 671

intrinsic reward p. 654

motivation p. 648

needs p. 651

negative reinforcement p. 670

outcome/input (O/I) ratio p. 658

outcomes p. 658

overreward p. 659

performance feedback p. 677

positive reinforcement p. 669

procedural justice p. 662

punishment p. 670

referents p. 658

reinforcement p. 667

reinforcement contingencies p. 668

reinforcement theory p. 667

schedule of reinforcement p. 668

underreward p. 658

valence p. 663

variable interval reinforcement schedule p. 672

variable ratio reinforcement schedule p. 672

What Would You Do-II?

JBS Restaurants, St. Louis, Missouri

JBS Restaurants, which owns and operates 12 fast-food restaurants in the St. Louis area, just hired you as a consultant. Turnover at its restaurants has averaged 100 percent per year over the past three years. In other words, almost no one who begins the year working at a JBS restaurant is still employed there at the end of the year. Furthermore, customer service questionnaires show that customers are increasingly dissatisfied with the service they're receiving. A recent employee questionnaire produced even worse results. More than 90 percent of employees said they "were only working here until they could find a better job." Some employees even wrote on their questionnaires that they hoped their friends didn't find out they were working in a fast-food restaurant. It would be too embarrassing. JBS's top manager put it this way: "We know these jobs are boring and repetitive, and, during busy times, the pace is hectic. But there has to be something that we can do to reduce turnover and motivate employees. The average wage at the six restaurants is around $7.00 per hour, but we don't think just paying higher salaries is the answer. We'll listen to whatever suggestions you have to make. When do you think you can have a proposal ready for us?" You responded, "Well, let me visit a couple of your restaurants as a customer and get familiar with your operation and the kinds of jobs you have. I'll get back to you in a couple of weeks."

After doing some research, you found that the service industry is the fastest growing sector of the U.S. economy. The U.S. Bureau of Labor Statistics said that in the next few years employment opportunities for food preparation and food service will grow by 37 percent, adding 2.6 million jobs to the economy. However, at the same time, the labor force that is available to fill those jobs will grow by only about 15 percent. In the past, applicants for fast-food restaurant jobs were plentiful, and JBS's store managers could treat employees as if they were expendable. And, to some extent they were, since managers didn't have any difficulty finding and hiring new workers. However, in today's job market, it has already become difficult to attract and retain quality employees in these jobs. Your research indicates that in the future it will become even more difficult.

"Wow. This is going to be tough. How can I make flipping hamburgers interesting and motivating? How can I get these employees, many of whom are temporary and part-time, to care about customer service? How can I get them to stay on the job, much less come to work on time?" **If you were helping JBS Restaurants, what would you do?**

Sources: H. Acland, "Motivating Staff Can Improve Productivity and Customer Service," *Marketing*, 24 September 1998, 36. J. Barlow, "How to Motivate Without Much Cash," *Houston Chronicle*, 11 May 1999, Business, p. 1. M. Barrier, "Develop Workers—And Your Business," *Nation's Business*, 1 December 1998. C. Benini, "The Commitment: Earning Part-Timers' Full-Time Loyalty," *Meetings & Conventions*, 1 October 1997, S22. K.M. Song, "Low Unemployment Means Businesses 'Can't Be Selective': Finding and Keeping Employees a Full-Time Challenge for Many," *The Courier-Journal*, 11 August 1996, 01E.

Critical-Thinking Video Case

Motivation: Self-Directed Work Teams at Next Door Food Stores

Next Door Food Stores is a chain of 30 convenience stores and gas stations. A major problem for Next Door Food Stores and the convenience store industry in general is an extremely high turnover rate. In an attempt to increase employee motivation and improve customer service, Next Door has begun to empower employees by creating self-directed work teams. The first self-directed work teams were implemented in the DGIT Department, which is the internal auditing department at Next Door headquarters. The DGIT Department is responsible for checking all the invoices from each of Next Door's 30 convenience stores for accuracy before sending them on to the Accounts Payable Department. This video shows how employee empowerment, in the form of self-directed work teams, affects employee motivation.

Critical-Thinking Questions

1. What concerns would interfere with DGIT team members' motivation and ability to create a successful self-directed work team?
2. How would being a part of a self-directed work team, such as the DGIT team, increase motivation?
3. What would motivate DGIT team members to eliminate their own jobs?

Management Decisions

Laid Off at Levi Strauss

Levi Strauss, maker of Levi's jeans, had just experienced 10 straight years of record sales. And, to reward its employees, it announced an extremely generous incentive plan that would have given every Levi's employee up to a year's pay if the company met its financial goals over the next four years. Therefore, everyone was shocked when just a few months later the company announced that it was cutting up to 35 percent of its work force worldwide. The announcement stated that both management and hourly workers would be included in the cutbacks. Company management cited increased competition from designer and private-label brands, along with weaker demand for jeans, as reasons for the layoffs.

Questions

1. What would you do to maintain the commitment and motivation of your work force in light of the layoffs?
2. Most of the employees, including yourself, had already mentally lined their pockets with the one-year bonus. Every employee knew just what he or she was going to do with that money. But now, one-third of them are going to lose their jobs. So what will you do to restore a sense of equity for the employees who are not laid off?

Sources: W. Bounds, "Inside Levi's Race to Restore a Tarnished Brand," *The Wall Street Journal*, 4 August 1998, B1. W. Bounds, "Levi Strauss to Cut 1,000 Jobs in U.S., Propose Closing Four European Plants," *The Wall Street Journal*, 29 September 1998, B2. L. Himelstein, "Ain't That a Kick in the Pants," *Business Week*, 10 March 1997, 6.

Management Decisions

Employee of the Month!

As you get back to your desk with your third cup of coffee this morning, your boss stops at your desk in the middle of his morning rounds. He says, "Hey, you've got a degree in management, don't you? Heck, even if you don't, you're probably more up to date on all these new motivational theories and ideas than I am. Here's what I want. We need an employee-of-the-month award for our clerical employees. I want to boost their morale and motivate them to work harder and do their jobs better! So take a couple of weeks and design a basic employee award program, but make sure that it's got an employee-of-the-month award in it. That's the key. Have it on my desk two weeks from Friday." Before you can say yes, he's off to another co-worker's desk, to give them some other assignment that he brainstormed last night. You're not even sure he heard you say, "Sure, Mr. Smith, no problem."

However, what you really wanted to say was, "I don't know, Mr. Smith. I've never seen an employee-of-the-month award motivate anyone." In fact, no one really seemed to care about being employee-of-the-month in the places you had worked before, even when there was a small amount of cash involved. You think to yourself, "Well, if he wants an employee of the month award, I'll make sure that's in there. But there have got to be better ways to motivate the clerical staff. I'm just going to have to figure out what those are."

Questions

1. What is wrong with many employee-of-the-month award programs? Why wouldn't they be particularly effective at motivating employees?
2. Describe the three most important steps you'd take to motivate the clerical staff in your office. Explain what the steps are, the reasoning behind them, and what they're meant to accomplish. Be specific.

Develop Your Management Potential

Show Me the Noncash Rewards?

"Show me the money! Show me the money!" Lots of managers mistakenly assume that money is the primary motivator for most employees. However, studies regularly show that while money affects people's decisions to take or leave jobs, it is not one of the primary motivators once someone has a job.

New managers also assume that they'll have access to the money they need to "really motivate" their workers. This is wrong in two ways. First, most managers are given a pool of money to allocate among all employees as raises. So if they give one employee a large raise, they have less money for other raises. Second, psychological studies show that pay increases must be at least 15–20 percent before employees really feel that they've gotten a substantial increase in pay. In other words, with most annual pay raises between 2 and 4 percent, most managers simply aren't given the money they need to create the wow-what-a-great-raise reaction they want from their employees.

As a result of these factors, more and more managers are turning to noncash rewards to motivate their employees.

Questions

1. Develop a list of 10 creative, noncash rewards that would be effective in motivating employees. If you're not sure what would be effective, think of the things that motivate you and your friends. You also might want to ask two or three managers about the noncash rewards they offer their employees.
2. Describe how you would administer each of these rewards. In other words, explain when and why you would give employees these particular rewards. Be specific.

Chapter Seventeen

Chapter 17 Outline

Leadership

What Would **You** Do?

Microsoft Headquarters, Redmond, Washington. As president of Microsoft, you've worked for CEO Bill Gates since 1981. You went to Harvard together, and you have served him and Microsoft by performing important jobs in nearly every part of the company. And with profits rising 30 percent a year, income levels at an incredible $257,000 per employee (compared to an average of $17,000 per employee for most businesses), $22 billion in cash on hand (even after buying 92 companies in the last five years), and a total stock market valuation of $414 billion, no one would argue if you claimed that Microsoft was the biggest business success of the last two decades. So if things are so great, why are you losing sleep? It all started about the time you became Microsoft's president, second in command to Bill Gates. One of your first tasks was to get a feel for the thoughts and concerns of Microsoft employees. So you conducted interviews with a cross section of 100 Microsoft workers. Despite record financial success, the interviews identified several key problems that could prove troublesome if not addressed. First, as Microsoft grew in size (now 30,000 employees), it became slow and bureaucratic. One top manager quit as a result of the maddeningly slow pace at which decisions were made. For example, he suggested that the company write some simple software code that would allow users of Microsoft's free e-mail service, HotMail, to quickly and easily link to Microsoft's MSN Web sites, such as CarPoint (new and used cars), Expedia (travel), and MoneyCentral (personal finance). The code itself was simple—no more than 30 minutes to write and test it. But, because Microsoft insisted on gaining consensus from everyone affected by the decision, it took three months and ten meetings to gain its approval. Second, it was clear that employees did not understand the company's long-term vision and strategic plans. But with over 183 products across several different operating systems (Windows NT for servers and high-end work stations, Windows 95 and Windows 98 for personal PCs, and Windows CE for computing devices such as palm PCs), dozens of different Internet sites, and acquisition of cable TV providers, computer device manufacturers, and other software companies (nearly 100 different companies in all), this shouldn't have been surprising. Microsoft seemed to be heading off into 50 different directions, and even its employees weren't sure where it was going. The irony, of course, was that Microsoft's advertising slogan was "Where do you want to go today?" Apparently, even Microsoft's own employees didn't know. The third problem was that top managers didn't feel they had the discretion and control to run their divisions and departments as they saw fit. Unfortunately, this was your fault, as well as Bill's. Nearly all decisions and reviews were being bumped up to the two of you, from basic features in software to how long it took Microsoft customer support to answer their phones and solve customer problems. These decisions should have been made by the managers responsible for them, but you and Bill had been making decisions like these, big and small, since Microsoft's inception, and habits like these were hard to break. Finally, though you didn't hear this directly from your interviews, a few of your trusted friends in the company recently told you that some managers and employees were uncomfortable with your leadership style. While friendly and outgoing, you're also known for your hot temper and big voice, having shouted yourself hoarse several times while yelling at managers and employees who weren't keeping up. Smacking a baseball bat into your open palm during these outbursts didn't earn you any friends, either. Of course, it was all for effect. You certainly didn't intend to hurt anybody. But it didn't come across that way to the people on the receiving end of your outbursts. You click open the latest version of Microsoft Word and start writing down your thoughts. Just what makes a good leader, and do I have whatever that is? What do good leaders do? When do leaders need to adapt their behavior? I've been leading this way for years, but now it seems I need to change. Why? And how can I lead people to produce in the short term, while at the same time helping them understand where we're headed in the long term? **If you were the president of Microsoft, what would you do?**

Sources: S. Hamm, "'I'm Trying to Let Other People Dive In Before I Do.'" *Business Week,* 17 May 1999, 110. S. Hamm & T.J. Mullaney, "Remaking Microsoft: Why America's Most Successful Company Needed an Overhaul," *Business Week,* 17 May 1999, 106. B. Japsen, "Amid Settlement Talks, Microsoft Plans Major Reorganization," *Chicago Tribune,* 30 March 1999, Business 3. Times Wire Services, "Microsoft Plans Customer-Based Changes, Seeks Silverberg's Return: Software Firm Will Restructure into Four Groups and Hopes to Bring Back Programming Whiz to Lead One," *Los Angeles Times,* 8 February 1999, C1.

"Leadership problems at Microsoft, how can that be? They're so successful." But as the opening case illustrates, even successful companies like Microsoft can have leadership problems. In fact, leadership problems may be more likely to take root after companies have been successful.

We begin this chapter by discussing what leadership is, who leaders are, meaning their traits and characteristics, and what leaders do that makes them different from people who aren't leaders. Next we examine four major contingency theories of leadership that specify which leaders are best suited for which situations or how leaders should change their behavior to lead different people in different circumstances. The chapter ends with a review of strategic leadership issues, such as charismatic and transformational leadership, that are concerned with working with others to meet long-term goals and creating a viable future for an organization.

What Is Leadership?

When Cynthia Danaher became general manager of Hewlett-Packard's Medical Products Group, she told her 5,300 employees, "I want to do this job, but it's scary and I need your help." And you finally have a boss who "knows how to make coffee." After three years of experience as a leader, she now regrets that choice of words. If she had a chance to hold that meeting again, she says that she would emphasize goals and challenge her people to find ways to meet them. She said, "People say they want a leader to be vulnerable just like them, but deep down they want to believe you have the skill to move and fix things they can't. And while anyone who starts something new is bound to feel some anxiety, you don't need to bare your soul." Moreover, she says that for leaders, setting a direction is more important than making employees feel comfortable.[1]

leadership
the process of influencing others to achieve group or organizational goals

As H-P's Cynthia Danaher discovered, **leadership** is the process of influencing others to achieve group or organizational goals. After reading the next two sections, you should be able to:

1 explain what **leadership** is.

2 describe **who leaders are and what effective leaders do.**

1 Leadership

Southwest Airlines flies two- to- three times as many passengers per employee as other airlines at a cost 25 percent to 40 percent below its competitors.[2] A key part of Southwest's performance is that it empties its planes, refills them with passengers, crews, fuel, and food (peanuts and soft drinks), and has them back on the runway in 20 minutes, compared to an hour for most airlines. This allows Southwest to keep each of its planes filled with paying passengers about three more hours a day. Why is Southwest able to achieve such incredible results? Herb Kelleher, Southwest's CEO and cofounder, answered the question this way: "We pay just as good wages and benefits as other airlines, but our costs are lower because our productivity is higher, which is achieved through the dedicated energy of our people. It's sheer willpower—no mechanical tricks. We've got exactly the same equipment. The difference is, when a plane pulls into a gate, our people run to meet it. Ponce de León was looking for the Fountain of Youth in the wrong place—he should have come to Southwest Airlines." In other words, the people of Southwest Airlines have been successfully influenced to achieve company goals (i.e., leadership).

Let's learn more about leadership by exploring **1.1** *the differences between leaders and managers and* **1.2** *substitutes for leadership.*

1.1 Leaders versus Managers

In Chapter 1, we defined *management* as getting work done through others. In other words, managers don't do the work themselves. Managers help others do their jobs better. By contrast, *leadership* is the process of influencing others to achieve group or organizational goals. So what are the key differences between leadership and management?

According to Professor Warren Bennis, the primary difference, as shown in Figure 17.1, is that leaders are concerned with doing the right thing, while managers are concerned with doing things right.[3] In other words, leaders will begin with the question "What should we be doing?" while managers start with "How can we do what already we're doing better?" Leaders focus on visions, missions, goals, and objectives, while managers focus solely on productivity and efficiency. Managers see themselves as preservers of the status quo, while leaders see themselves as promoters of change, as challengers of the status quo in that they encourage creativity and risk taking. Carol Bartz, CEO of Autodesk, Inc, a software company, said managers "know how to write business plans, while leaders get companies—and people—to change." She went on to say that "Human nature says cling to what you have, whether that's an old coat, a boyfriend, or a way of doing business," but that leaders have to "leave that behind." And since Bartz took over six years ago, Autodesk has doubled its revenues to more than $600 million a year.[4] Managers have a relatively short-term perspective, while leaders take a long-term view. Managers are more concerned with *means*, how to get things done, while leaders are more concerned with *ends*, what gets done. Managers are concerned with control and limiting the choices of others, while leaders are more concerned with expanding peoples' choices and options.[5] Finally, managers solve problems so that others can do their work, while leaders and managers inspire and motivate others to find their own solutions.

Let's illustrate the difference between managers and leaders by taking another look at Southwest Airlines. After the federal government deregulated the airline industry, giving airlines the right to determine how many flights they would have and where those flights would go (previously, this was determined by the government), one of the first things Southwest did was reassess its strategic plan and objectives. Howard Putnam, Southwest's CEO at the time, told his top managers, "We aren't going to leave this room until we can write up on the wall, in a hundred words or less, what we are going to be when we grow up." And then, unlike other airlines, which simply tried to improve what they were already doing (i.e., management), Southwest critically examined what it was doing, why it was doing what it was doing, and whether it should continue to do what it had been doing. For instance, unlike most airlines, which have long-haul flights to major airport hubs (Chicago for United Airlines, Dallas-Fort Worth for American Airlines),

Figure 17.1 **Managers versus leaders**

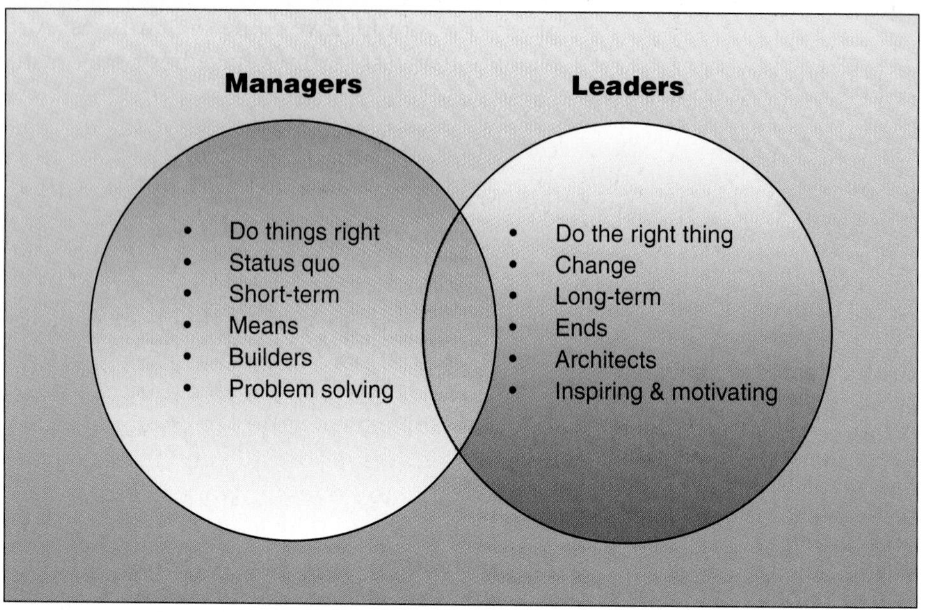

Southwest flies short flights to smaller city airports so that it can cater to higher-paying business travelers. And while most airlines fly a number of different airplanes—for example, American Airlines flies the Airbus A300, the Boeing 727, 737, 757, 767, and 777, and the McDonnell Douglas DC-10, MD-11, and MD-80—Southwest flies only one plane, the Boeing 737. This saves millions of dollars because pilots, flight attendants, and mechanics have to learn only one kind of airplane. Plus, Southwest saves millions by needing only one kind of parts inventory.[6] Finally, instead of paying its competitors to be part of their reservation systems (for example, the Apollo, Amadeus, and SABRE travel reservation systems used by travel agents to book tickets worldwide for dozens of different airlines), Southwest set up its own ticket reservation system and office.[7]

While leaders are different from managers, in practice, organizations need them both. Managers are critical to getting out the day-to-day work, and leaders are critical to inspiring employees and setting the organization's long-term direction. The key issue is the extent to which organizations are properly led or properly managed. Warren Bennis summed up the difference between leaders and managers by noting that "American organizations (and probably those in much of the rest of the industrialized world) are underled and overmanaged. They do not pay enough attention to doing the right thing, while they pay too much attention to doing things right."[8]

1.2
Substitutes for Leadership: Do Leaders Always Matter?

One of the basic assumptions about leadership is that leaders always matter. The thinking goes that without sound leadership, organizations are sure to fail. In fact, when companies struggle, their leaders are almost always blamed for their poor performance. When Lockheed Martin, an aerospace company, struggled, *The Wall Street Journal* wrote this about Vance Coffman, its chairman and CEO:

As head of Lockheed Martin Corp.'s classified government space business over the years, Vance Coffman was known for his engineering savvy and secretive management style.

But now, as chairman and chief executive of the struggling aerospace company, Mr. Coffman's same penchant for secrecy, combined with a string of serious setbacks afflicting some of the programs he once ran directly, has put his leadership into question. Increasingly, many investors, senior Pentagon officials and even some of his own managers fault Mr. Coffman for failing to promptly disclose, or follow, a consistent strategy in facing the problems that have recently bedeviled the world's largest defense contractor.[9]

However, there are situations and circumstances in which leadership isn't necessary, or is unlikely to make much of a difference, or where leaders aren't to blame for poor performance. These are known as leadership substitutes and leadership neutralizers.[10] Table 17.1 lists a number of subordinate, task, or organizational characteristics that can act as leadership substitutes or neutralizers for either task-related or people-related leader behaviors.

leadership substitutes subordinate, task, or organizational characteristics that make leaders redundant or unnecessary

Leadership substitutes are subordinate, task, or organizational characteristics that make leaders redundant or unnecessary. For instance, when leadership substitutes such as ability and performance feedback are present, task-related leader behavior that specifies goals, task assignments, and

Table 17.1

Leadership Substitutes and Neutralizers

Characteristic	People-Related Leadership Behaviors	Task-Related Leadership Behaviors
Subordinate Characteristics		
• Ability, experience, training, knowledge	Neutralize	Substitute, Neutralize
• Need for independence	Neutralize	Neutralize
• Professional orientation	Substitute, Neutralize	Substitute, Neutralize
• Indifference toward organizational rewards	Neutralize	Neutralize
Task Characteristics		
• Unambiguous and routine tasks	No effect	Substitute, Neutralize
• Performance feedback provided by the work itself	No effect	Substitute, Neutralize
• Intrinsically satisfying work	Substitute, Neutralize	Neutralize
Organizational Characteristics		
• Formalization, meaning specific plans, goals, and areas of responsibility	No effect	Neutralize
• Inflexibility, meaning rigid, unbending rules and procedures	No effect	Neutralize
• Highly specified staff functions	No effect	Neutralize
• Cohesive work groups	Substitute, Neutralize	Substitute, Neutralize
• Organizational rewards beyond a leader's control	Neutralize	Neutralize
• Spatial distance between supervisors and subordinates	Neutralize	Neutralize

Source: S. Kerr & J.M. Jermier, "Substitutes for Leadership: Their Meaning and Measurement," *Organizational Behavior and Human Performance* 22 (1978): 375-403.

how to do the job aren't likely to improve a subordinate's work performance. Think about it. Workers already have the capability to do their jobs. And, the job itself provides enough information to let them know how well they're doing their jobs or what they might do to correct performance problems. In situations like this, where leadership substitutes are strong, leaders don't need to tell workers what to do or how to do their jobs.

leadership neutralizers subordinate, task, or organizational characteristics that can interfere with a leader's actions or make it impossible for a leader to influence followers' performance

Leadership neutralizers are subordinate, task, or organizational characteristics that can interfere with a leader's actions or make it impossible for a leader to influence followers' performance. Unlike substitutes, which simply take the place of leaders, leadership neutralizers create an "influence vacuum." In other words, leadership neutralizers create a need for leadership by ironically preventing leadership from working. For example, when a subordinate is indifferent toward organizational rewards, there may be nothing that a leader can do to reward them for good performance. Likewise, union contracts that specify that all employees be paid the same, organizational policies that reward employees by seniority, and salary and raise processes that don't give leaders enough money to substantially reward good performers effectively neutralize the ability of leaders to reward workers. Spatial distance (an organizational characteristic) can also neutralize leadership. *Spatial distance* is a situation in which supervisors and subordinates don't work in the same place, such as with telecommuters or people working thousands of miles away in overseas offices. Spatial distance typically means infrequent feedback, little or no face-to-face contact, and being "out of sight and out of mind," all of which make it very difficult for leaders to lead. In fact, some companies find telecommuting to be so disruptive to leadership processes that they require their telecommuters to come into the office at least once or twice a week.

So do leaders *always* matter? Leadership substitutes and neutralizers indicate that sometimes they don't. However, this doesn't mean that leaders don't matter at all. Quite the opposite. Leaders do matter, but they're not superhuman. They can't do it all by themselves. And they can't fix every situation. In short, leadership is very important. But poor leadership isn't the cause of every organizational crisis, and changing leaders isn't the solution to every company problem.

Review 1
Leadership

Leadership is the process of influencing others to achieve group or organizational goals. Leaders are different from managers. The primary difference is that leaders are concerned with doing the right thing, while managers are concerned with doing things right. Furthermore, managers have a short-term focus and are concerned with the status quo, with means rather than ends, and with solving others' problems. By contrast, leaders have a long-term focus, are concerned with change, with ends rather than means, and with inspiring and motivating others to solve their own problems. Organizations need both managers and leaders. But, in general, companies are overmanaged and underled. While leadership is important, leadership substitutes and neutralizers create situations in which leadership isn't necessary or is unlikely to make much of a difference. Leadership substitutes are subordinate, task, or organizational characteristics that make leaders redundant or unnecessary. By contrast, leadership neutralizers are subordinate, task, or organizational characteristics that interfere with a leader's actions or make it impossible for a leader to influence followers' performance.

2 Who Leaders Are and What Leaders Do

Every year, *Fortune* magazine conducts a survey to determine corporate America's "most admired" companies. And, every year, as part of that study, it takes a look at the leaders of those companies. However, the last time it did this, it found that the CEOs of its ten most admired companies were surprisingly different. In fact, *Fortune* wrote that "Every conceivable leadership style is represented by these CEOs."[11] General Electric's Jack Welch was described as "combative," as someone who "tilts his head, and thrusts out his chin as if to say, 'Go ahead, take your best shot'—and is never happier than when you do." Southwest Airline's Herb Kelleher was described as "a prankster and a kisser so unabashedly affectionate that his company's ticker symbol is LUV, so hands-on he has loaded baggage and served peanuts to passengers." In fact, Kelleher admitted that he is terrible at understanding the financial side of business, something that no regular CEO would ever admit. Finally, Coke's CEO, Douglas Ivester, could be Kelleher's mirror image. *Fortune* described Ivester as "undemonstrative and a 'financial wizard.'"

So if the CEOs of Fortune*'s "most admired" corporations are all different, just what makes a good leader? Let's learn more about who leaders are by investigating* **2.1** *leadership traits and* **2.2** *leadership behavior.*

2.1 *Leadership Traits*

trait theory
leadership theory that holds that effective leaders possess a similar set of traits or characteristics

traits
relatively stable characteristics, such as abilities, psychological motives, or consistent patterns of behavior

Trait theory is one way to describe who leaders are. **Trait theory** says that effective leaders possess a similar set of traits or characteristics. **Traits** are relatively stable characteristics, such as abilities, psychological motives, or consistent patterns of behavior. For example, according to trait theory, leaders were commonly thought to be taller, more confident, and have greater physical stamina (i.e., higher energy levels). Trait theory is also known as the "great person" theory, because early versions of trait theory stated that leaders were born, not made. In other words, you either had the "right stuff" to be a leader, or you didn't. And if you didn't, there was no way to get "it."

Until recently, studies indicated that trait theory was wrong, that there were no consistent trait differences between leaders and nonleaders, or between effective and ineffective leaders. However, more recent evidence shows that "successful leaders are not like other people," that successful leaders are indeed different from the rest of us.[12] More specifically, leaders are different from nonleaders on the following traits: drive, the desire to lead, honesty/integrity, self-confidence, emotional stability, cognitive ability, and knowledge of the business.[13]

Leadership Traits Do Make a Difference

For decades, researchers assumed that leadership traits, such as drive, emotional stability, cognitive ability, and charisma were *not* related to effective leadership. However, more recent evidence shows that there are reliable trait differences between leaders and nonleaders. In fact, 54 studies based on more than 6,000 people clearly indicate that in terms of leadership traits, "successful leaders are not like other people."

TRAITS AND PERCEPTIONS OF LEADERSHIP EFFECTIVENESS

Several leadership models argue that successful leaders will be viewed by their followers as good leaders. (This is completely different from determining whether leaders actually improve organizational performance.) Consequently, one test of trait theory is whether leaders with particular traits are viewed as more or less effective leaders by their followers.

Intelligence

On average, there is a 75 percent chance that intelligent leaders will be seen as better leaders than less intelligent leaders.

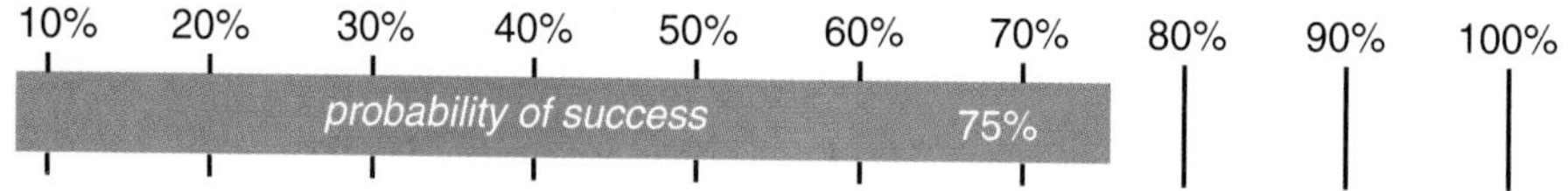

Dominance

On average, there is only a 57 percent chance that leaders with highly dominant personalities will be seen as better leaders than those with less dominant personalities.

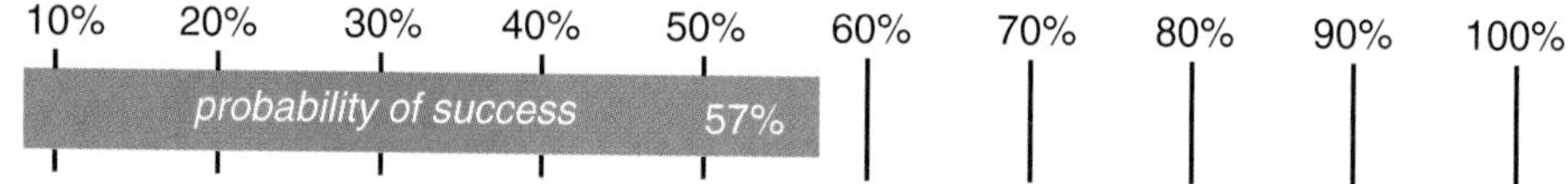

Extroversion

On average, there is a 63 percent chance that extroverts will be seen as better leaders than introverts.

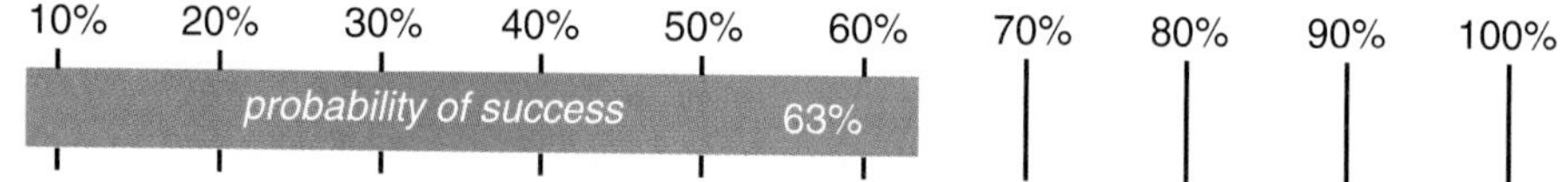

CHARISMA AND LEADERSHIP EFFECTIVENESS

As discussed at the end of the chapter, *charismatic leadership* is the set of behavioral tendencies and personal characteristics of leaders that creates an exceptionally strong relationship between leaders and their followers. More specifically, charismatic leaders articulate a clear vision for the future that is based on strongly held values or morals, model those values by acting in a way consistent with the vision, communicate high performance expectations to followers, and display confidence in followers' abilities to achieve the vision.

Performance and Charisma

On average, there is a 72 percent chance that charismatic leaders will have better performing followers and organizations than less charismatic leaders.

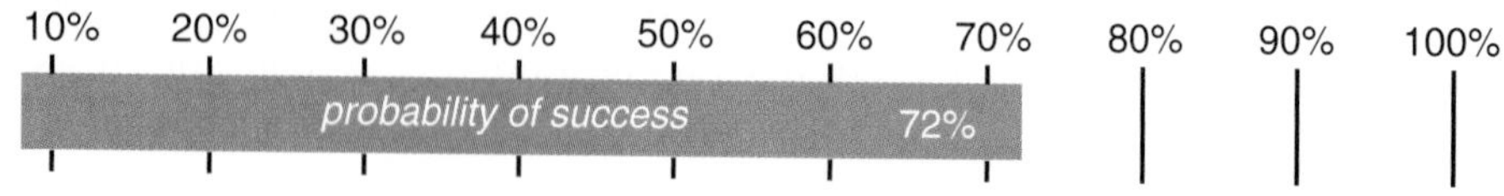

Charisma and Perceived Leader Effectiveness

On average, there is a 89 percent chance that charismatic leaders will be perceived as more effective leaders than less charismatic leaders.

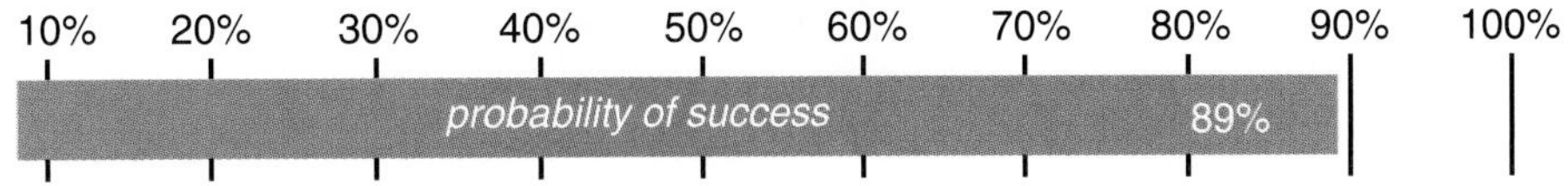

Charisma and Leader Satisfaction

On average, there is a 90 percent chance that the followers of charismatic leaders will be more satisfied with their leaders than the followers of less charismatic leaders.

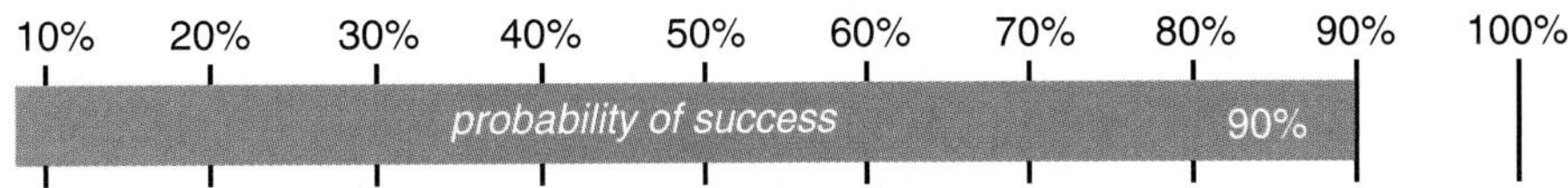

Sources: J.B. Fuller, C.E.P. Patterson, K. Hester, & D. Stringer, "A Quantitative Review of Research on Charismatic Leadership," *Psychological Reports* 78 (1996): 271-287. R.G. Lord, C.L. De Vader, & G.M. Alliger, "A Meta-Analysis of the Relation Between Personality Traits and Leadership Perceptions: An Application of Validity Generalization Procedures," *Journal of Applied Psychology* 71, no. 3 (1986): 402–410.

Drive refers to high levels of effort and is characterized by achievement, motivation, ambition, energy, tenacity, and initiative. In terms of achievement and ambition, leaders always try to make improvements or achieve success in what they're doing and have strong desires to "get ahead." Leaders typically have more energy, and they have to, given the long hours they put in year after year. Furthermore, leaders don't have the luxury of being "down." Since we tend to take our cues from leaders, we expect them to be positive and "up." Thus, leaders must have physical, mental, and emotional vitality. Leaders are also more tenacious than nonleaders and are better at overcoming obstacles and problems that would deter most of us. Most change takes place slowly, and leaders need to have a "stick-to-it-iveness" to see changes through. Leaders also show more initiative. For example, GE's CEO Jack Welch said, "Some CEOs think the day they become CEO is the high point of their careers. They ought to feel they're just beginning." Indeed, legendary investor Warren Buffet said, "Jack feels there's more to do at GE than when he started," more than 15 years ago.[14] So rather than waiting for others to take action, leaders move forward quickly to promote change or solve problems.

Successful leaders also have a stronger *desire to lead.* They want to be in charge and think about ways to influence or convince others about what should or shouldn't be done. *Honesty/integrity* is also important to leaders. *Honesty,* that is, being truthful with others, is a cornerstone of leadership. Without honesty, leaders won't be trusted. But with it, subordinates are willing to overlook other flaws. For example, one follower said this about the leadership qualities of his manager: "I don't like a lot of the things he does, but he's basically honest. He's a genuine article and you'll forgive a lot of things because of that. That goes a long way in how much I trust him."[15] *Integrity* is the extent to which leaders do what they said they would do. Leaders may be honest and have good intentions, but if they don't consistently deliver on what they promise, they won't be trusted.

Self-confidence, believing in one's abilities, also distinguishes leaders from nonleaders. Self-confidence is critical to leadership. Leaders make risky, long-term decisions and must convince others of the correctness of those decisions. Self-confident leaders are more decisive and assertive and more likely to gain others' confidence. Moreover, self-confident leaders will admit mistakes, because they view them as learning opportunities rather than a refutation of their leadership capabilities. This also means that leaders have *emotional stability.* Even when things go wrong, they remain even-tempered and consistent in their outlook and the way in which they treat others. Leaders who can't control their emotions, who anger quickly or attack and blame others for mistakes are unlikely to be trusted. For example, Steve Jobs, CEO and cofounder of Apple Computers, is well known for his temper and for being an extremely demanding boss. When one of his assistants was late installing a high-speed, T-1 Internet connection, Jobs marched out to his cubicle and said, "No T-1. You're fired." The assistant went home, not sure whether Jobs was serious. Jobs apologized the next morning, but the assistant resigned soon after the incident.[16]

Leaders are also smart. Leaders typically have strong cognitive abilities. This doesn't mean that leaders are geniuses—far from it. But it does mean that leaders have the capacity to analyze large amounts of seemingly unrelated, complex information and can see patterns or opportunities or threats where others might not see them. Finally, leaders also "know their stuff," which means they have superior technical knowledge about the businesses they run. Leaders who have a good *knowledge of the business* understand the key technological decisions and concerns facing their companies. More often than not, studies indicate that effective leaders have long, extensive experience in their industries.

2.2
Leadership Behaviors

Thus far, you've read about who leaders are. However, traits alone are not enough to be a successful leader. Traits are a precondition for success. After all, it's hard to imagine a truly successful leader who lacks all of these qualities. Leaders who have these traits (or many of them) must then take actions that encourage people to achieve group or organizational goals.[17] Accordingly, we now examine what leaders do, meaning the behaviors they perform or the actions they take to influence others to achieve group or organizational goals.

Research at the University of Michigan, Ohio State University, and the University of Texas examined the specific behaviors that leaders use to improve subordinate satisfaction and performance. Hundreds of studies were conducted and hundreds of leader behaviors were examined. At all three universities, two basic leader behaviors emerged as central to successful leadership: initiating structure (called *job-centered leadership* at the University of Michigan and *concern for production* at the University of Texas) and considerate leader behavior (called *employee-centered leadership* at the University of Michigan and *concern for people* at the University of Texas).[18] In fact, these two leader behaviors form the basis for many of the leadership theories discussed in this chapter.

initiating structure
the degree to which a leader structures the roles of followers by setting goals, giving directions, setting deadlines, and assigning tasks

Initiating structure is the degree to which a leader structures the roles of followers by setting goals, giving directions, setting deadlines, and assigning tasks. A leader's ability to initiate structure primarily affects subordinates' job performance. Indeed, in an article entitled "Why CEOs Fail," *Fortune* magazine indicated that CEOs who do initiate structure are likely to succeed, while those who don't are likely to fail and often lose their jobs. *Fortune* wrote, "Watch the likes of [Jack] Welch [GE's CEO] or EDS's [CEO] Richard Brown or [Lawrence] Bossidy [CEO of Allied Signal] or any other proven implementer in a meeting. Near the end he'll grab a pen and start writing: He's noting exactly what is supposed to be done by whom, by when. He'll go over this with everyone before the meeting closes, and he'll probably send each one a reminder afterward." That, in a nutshell, is initiating structure.[19]

consideration
the extent to which a leader is friendly, approachable, supportive, and shows concern for employees

Consideration is the extent to which a leader is friendly, approachable, supportive, and shows concern for employees. Consideration primarily affects subordinates' job satisfaction. Specific leader consideration behaviors include listening to employees' problems and concerns, consulting with employees before making decisions, and treating employees as equals. With the average workweek increasing in length, and with people in many top companies putting in 60+ hours a week, one kind of considerate leader behavior is finding ways to do ordinary tasks that employees don't have time to do because they put in so much time at work. For example, it may not seem like much, but for the average Intel employee who puts in 60+ hours a week, it's a tremendous convenience to simply hand over the keys and have the car cleaned and detailed for them while they are at work. Intel spokesperson Tracy Koon said, "People work hard here. These [perks] bring respite for short periods of time to people who are pretty much nose-to-the-grindstone." Likewise, at Netscape, employees can drop their laundry off near the corporate cafeteria. The next day, it's delivered freshly washed and dried to their cubicles.[20] When most people think of leadership, they don't think of car washing and laundry. But, because these activities address employees' problems and concerns, they qualify as considerate leader behavior.

Personal Productivity Tip

Monitor These Signs of Failing Leadership

Successful leaders seem to have a "sixth sense" that helps them monitor how followers feel about them and their ideas. You can develop your own sixth sense by monitoring these signs of failed leadership: (1) performance—not meeting your numbers and goals, (2) execution—not meeting commitments to direct reports, (3) isolation—bad news and problems aren't coming to you, (4) turnover—talented subordinates start leaving because of you or organizational problems, and (5) people problems—not having the emotional strength to confront or replace poor-performing key subordinates. So develop your sixth sense and monitor these signs of failed leadership.

Source: R. Charan & G. Colvin, "Why CEOs Fail," *Fortune,* 21 June 1999, 69-78.

While researchers at all three universities generally agreed on the two kinds of basic leader behaviors, initiating structure and consideration, they differed on the interaction and effectiveness of these behaviors. The University of Michigan studies indicated that initiating structure and consideration were mutually exclusive behaviors on opposite ends of the same continuum. In other words, leaders who wanted to be more considerate would have to do less initiating of structure (and vice versa). The University of Michigan studies also indicated that only considerate leader behaviors (i.e., employee-centered) were associated with successful leadership. By contrast, researchers at Ohio State University and the University of Texas found that initiating structure and consideration were independent behaviors, meaning that leaders can be considerate and initiate structure at the same time. Additional evidence confirms this finding.[21] The same researchers also concluded that the most effective leaders were strong on both initiating structure and considerate leader behaviors.

This "high-high" approach can be seen in the upper right corner of the Blake and Mouton Leadership Grid shown in Figure 17.2. Blake and Mouton used two leadership behaviors, concern for people (i.e. consideration) and concern for production (i.e., initiating structure), to categorize five

Figure 17.2 **Blake/Mouton Leadership Grid**

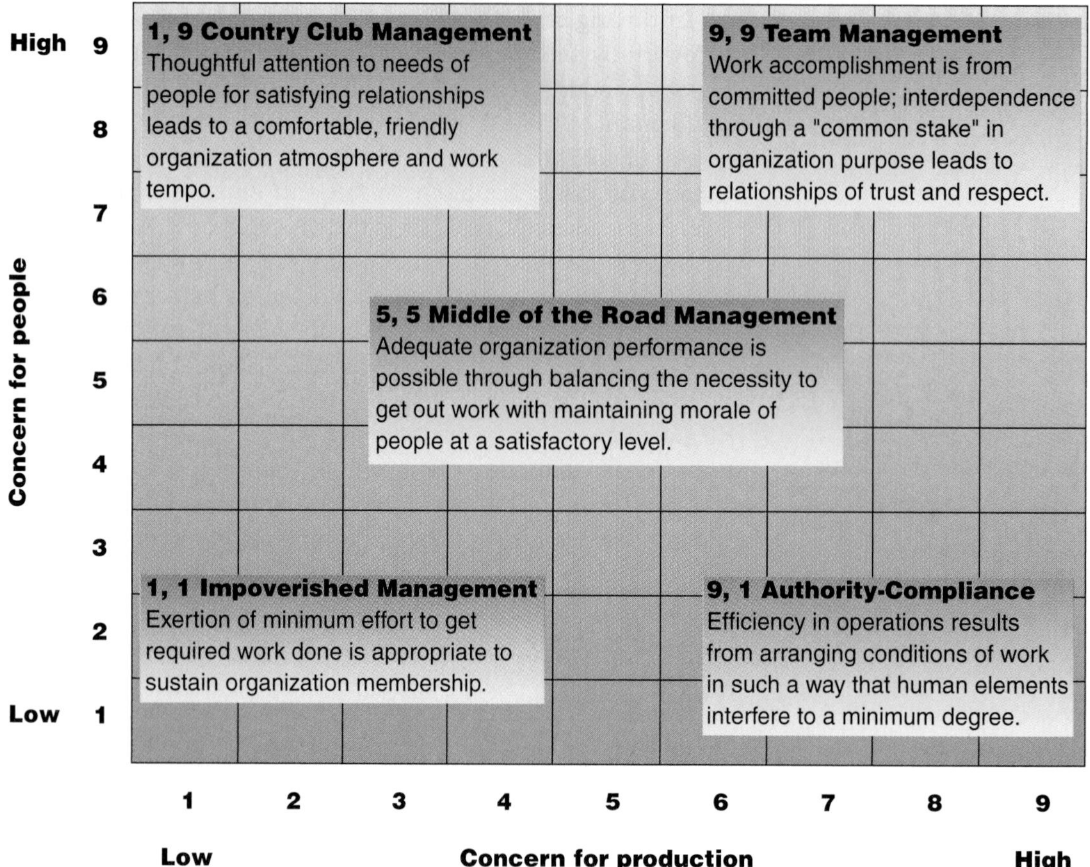

Source: R.R. Blake & A.A. McCanse, "The Leadership Grid®," *Leadership Dilemmas—Grid Solutions* (Houston: Gulf Publishing Company), 29. Copyright © 1991, by Scientific Methods, Inc. Reproduced by permission of the owners.

different leadership styles. Both behaviors are rated on a 9-point scale, with 1 representing "low" and 9 representing "high." Blake and Mouton suggest that a "high-high" or 9-9 leadership style is the best. They call this style *team management,* because leaders who use it display a high concern for people (9) and a high concern for production (9). By contrast, leaders use a 9-1 *authority-compliance* leadership style when they have a high concern for production and a low concern for people. A 1-9 *country club* style occurs when leaders really care about producing a friendly and enjoyable work environment but don't really pay much attention to production or performance. The worst leadership style, according to the grid, is the 1-1 *impoverished* leader, who shows little concern for people or production and does the bare minimum needed to keep his or her job. Finally, the 5-5 *middle-of-the-road* style occurs when leaders show a moderate amount of concern for people and production.

Is the team management style, with a high concern for production and a high concern for people, the "best" leadership style? Logically, it would seem so. Why wouldn't you want to show high concern for both people and production? However, nearly 50 years' worth of research indicates that there isn't one "best" leadership style. The "best" leadership style depends on the situation. In other words, no one leadership behavior by itself and no one combination of leadership behaviors works well across all situations and employees.

Review 2
Who Leaders Are and What Leaders Do

Trait theory says that effective leaders possess traits or characteristics that differentiate them from nonleaders. Those traits are drive, the desire to lead, honesty/integrity, self-confidence, emotional stability, cognitive ability, and knowledge of the business. However, traits aren't enough for successful leadership. Leaders who have these traits (or many of them) must behave in ways that encourage people to achieve group or organizational goals. Two key leader behaviors are initiating structure, which improves subordinate performance, and consideration, which improves subordinate satisfaction. There is no "best" combination of these behaviors. The "best" leadership style depends on the situation.

Situational Leadership

Imagine that you're the Director of Emergency Medicine at a major hospital and that you've just learned that one of your doctors broke hospital policy by ordering a series of expensive tests for an emergency room patient without first getting approval from the hospital's cardiologist. The tests were for an extremely rare heart condition that could prove fatal if not detected. In fact, you were incensed when you learned that the doctor who broke the policy was a new intern with just two months of job experience. Why would he order an expensive test like this when hospital treatment policies and protocols make clear that this test cannot be ordered without a consulting cardiologist's approval? What a waste of money! This doctor obviously didn't know what he was doing! However, what if the physician who ordered the series of expensive tests was your most experienced emergency room physician? Instead of being angry and doubting the diagnosis, you probably would have thought to yourself, "I wonder what condition or mannerism tipped her off? Something had to be symptomatic of this rare condition or else she wouldn't have ordered this expensive test without first consulting the hospital cardiologist." In other words, you would have reacted differently depending on the situation and the person you were dealing with.

After leader traits and behaviors, situational leadership is the third major approach to the study of leadership. The four major situational leadership theories—Fiedler's contingency theory, path-goal theory, Hersey and Blanchard's situational theory, and Vroom and Yetton's normative decision model—all assume that the effectiveness of any **leadership style,** the way a leader generally behaves toward followers, depends on the situation.[22] Accordingly, there is no one "best" leadership style. However, these theories differ in one significant way. Fiedler's contingency theory assumes that leadership styles are consistent and difficult to change. Therefore, leaders must be placed in or "matched" to a situation that fits their leadership style. However, the other three situational theories all assume that leaders are capable

leadership style
the way a leader generally behaves toward followers

of adapting and adjusting their leadership styles to fit the demands of different situations.

After reading the next four sections, you should be able to:

3 explain **Fiedler's contingency theory.**

4 describe how **path-goal theory** works.

5 discuss **Hersey and Blanchard's situational theory.**

6 use the **normative decision model** when deciding how you will make decisions as a leader.

3 Putting Leaders in the Right Situation: Fiedler's Contingency Theory

contingency theory leadership theory that states that in order to maximize work group performance, leaders must be matched to the situation that best fits their leadership style

Fiedler's **contingency theory** states that in order to maximize work group performance, leaders must be matched to the right leadership situation.[23] More specifically, as shown in Figure 17.3, the first basic assumption of Fiedler's theory is that leaders are effective when the work groups they lead perform well. So instead of judging leader effectiveness by what a leader does (i.e., initiating structure and consideration) or who the leader is (i.e., trait theory), Fiedler assesses leaders by the conduct and performance of the people they supervise. Second, Fiedler assumes that leaders are generally unable to change their leadership styles and that leaders will be more effective when their leadership styles are matched to the proper situation. The third assumption is that the favorableness of a situation for a leader depends on the degree to which the situation permits the leader to influence the behavior of group members. Thus, Fiedler's third assumption is consistent with our definition of leadership, which is the process of influencing others to achieve group or organizational goals

Let's learn more about Fiedler's contingency theory by examining **3.1** *the least preferred co-worker and leadership styles,* **3.2** *situational favorableness, and* **3.3** *how to match leadership styles to situations.*

Figure 17.3 **Fiedler's Contingency Theory**

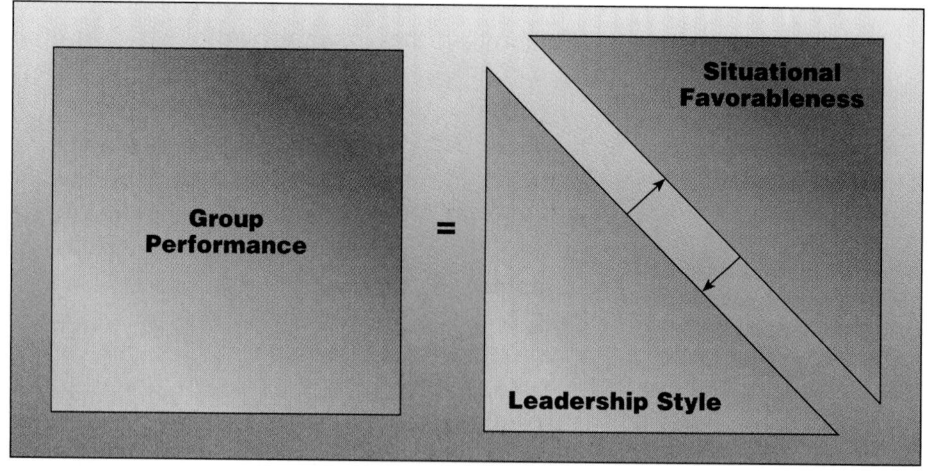

3.1
Leadership Style: Least Preferred Co-worker

When Fiedler uses the term *leadership style*, he means the way in which a leader generally behaves toward followers. However, Fiedler also assumes that leadership styles are tied to leaders' underlying needs and personality. And since personality and needs are relatively stable, he assumes that leaders are generally incapable of changing their leadership styles. For example, earlier in the chapter you read about the hot temper of Apple CEO Steve Jobs and how he fired one of his assistants when a high-speed Internet connection was installed late. However, stories about Jobs's temper have been around for more than 20 years. In fact, his temper is one of the reasons that he was fired from Apple in the 1980s (before returning in the last few years). In other words, over the last two decades, Jobs's leadership style and personality have been remarkably consistent.[24]

Fiedler uses a questionnaire called the Least Preferred Co-worker scale (LPC) to measure leadership style. When completing the LPC scale, people are instructed to consider all of the people with whom they have ever worked and then to choose the one person with whom they "least preferred" to work. Take a second yourself to identify your LPC. It's usually someone you had a big disagreement with, or, for whatever reason, you couldn't get along with or didn't like. After identifying their LPC, people use the LPC scale shown in Figure 17.4 to "describe" their LPC.

Complete the LPC yourself. Did you describe your LPC as pleasant, friendly, helpful, supportive, interesting and cheerful? Or did you describe the person as unpleasant, unfriendly, frustrating, hostile, boring, and gloomy? People who describe their LPC in a positive way (scoring 64 and above) have *relationship-oriented* leadership styles. After all, if they can still be positive about their least preferred co-worker, they must be people-oriented. By contrast, people who describe their LPC in a negative way (scoring 57 or below) have *task-oriented* leadership styles. Given a choice, they'll focus first on getting the job done and second on making sure everyone gets along. Finally, there is a third group with moderate scores (from 58 to 63) who are somewhat more flexible in their leadership style and can be somewhat relationship-oriented or somewhat task-oriented.

3.2
Situational Favorableness

situational favorableness
the degree to which a particular situation either permits or denies a leader the chance to influence the behavior of group members

leader-member relations
the degree to which followers respect, trust, and like their leaders

task structure
the degree to which the requirements of a subordinate's tasks are clearly specified

Fiedler assumes that leaders will be more effective when their leadership styles are matched to the proper situation. More specifically, Fiedler defines **situational favorableness** as the degree to which a particular situation either permits or denies a leader the chance to influence the behavior of group members.[25] In highly favorable situations, leaders find that their actions influence followers. However, in highly unfavorable situations, leaders have little or no success influencing them.

Three situational factors determine the favorability of a situation: leader-member relations, task structure, and position power. **Leader-member relations,** which is the most important situational factor, is how well followers respect, trust, and like their leaders. When leader-member relations are good, followers trust the leader and there is a friendly work atmosphere. **Task structure** is the degree to which the requirements of a subordinate's

Figure 17.4 **Least Preferred Co-worker Scale**

Pleasant	8	7	6	5	4	3	2	1	Unpleasant
Friendly	8	7	6	5	4	3	2	1	Unfriendly
Rejecting	1	2	3	4	5	6	7	8	Accepting
Helpful	8	7	6	5	4	3	2	1	Frustrating
Unenthusiastic	1	2	3	4	5	6	7	8	Enthusiastic
Tense	1	2	3	4	5	6	7	8	Relaxed
Distant	1	2	3	4	5	6	7	8	Close
Cold	1	2	3	4	5	6	7	8	Warm
Cooperative	8	7	6	5	4	3	2	1	Uncooperative
Supportive	8	7	6	5	4	3	2	1	Hostile
Boring	1	2	3	4	5	6	7	8	Interesting
Quarrelsome	1	2	3	4	5	6	7	8	Harmonious
Self-assured	8	7	6	5	4	3	2	1	Hesitant
Efficient	8	7	6	5	4	3	2	1	Inefficient
Gloomy	1	2	3	4	5	6	7	8	Cheerful
Open	8	7	6	5	4	3	2	1	Guarded

Source: F.E. Fiedler & M.M. Chemers, *Leadership and Effective Management* (Glenview, IL: Scott, Foresman, 1974). Reprinted by permission of authors.

position power
the degree to which leaders are able to hire, fire, reward, and punish workers

tasks are clearly specified. With highly structured tasks, employees have clear job responsibilities, goals, and procedures. **Position power** is the degree to which leaders are able to hire, fire, reward, and punish workers. The more influence leaders have over hiring, firing, rewards, and punishments, the greater their power.

Figure 17.5 shows how leader-member relations, task structure, and position power can be combined into eight different situations that differ in their favorability to leaders. In general, Situation I is the most favorable leader situation. Followers like and trust their leaders and know what to do because their tasks are highly structured. Also, the leader has the formal power to influence workers through hiring, firing, rewarding, and punishing them. Therefore, in Situation I it's relatively easy for a leader to influence followers. By contrast, Situation VIII is the least favorable situation for leaders. Followers don't like or trust their leaders. Plus, followers are not sure what they're supposed to be doing, given that their tasks or jobs are highly unstructured. Finally, leaders find it difficult to influence followers since they don't have the ability to hire, fire, reward, or punish the people who work for them. In short, it's very difficult to influence followers given the conditions found in Situation VIII.

Figure 17.5 **Situational Favorableness**

Leader-Member Relations	Good	Good	Good	Good	Poor	Poor	Poor	Poor
Task Structure	High	High	Low	Low	High	High	Low	Low
Position Power	Strong	Weak	Strong	Weak	Strong	Weak	Strong	Weak
Situation	I	II	III	IV	V	VI	VII	VIII

Favorable — Moderately Favorable — Unfavorable

3.3
Matching Leadership Styles to Situations

After studying thousands of leaders and followers in hundreds of different situations, Fiedler found that the performance of relationship- and task-oriented leaders followed the pattern displayed in Figure 17.6. Relationship-oriented leaders with high LPC scores were better leaders (i.e., their groups performed more effectively) under moderately favorable situations. In moderately favorable situations, the leader may be liked somewhat, tasks may be somewhat structured, and the leader may have some position power. In this situation, a relationship-oriented leader improves leader-member relations, which is the most important of the three situational factors. In turn, morale and performance improve. By contrast, task-oriented leaders with low LPC scores were better leaders in highly favorable and unfavorable situations. Task-oriented leaders do well in favorable situations where leaders are liked, tasks are structured, and the leader has the power to hire, fire, reward, and punish. In these favorable situations, task-oriented leaders effectively step on the gas of a highly tuned car that's in perfect running condition. Their focus on performance sets the goal for the group, which then charges forward to meet it. But task-oriented leaders also do well in unfavorable situations where leaders are disliked, tasks are unstructured, and the leader doesn't have the power to hire, fire, reward, and punish. In these unfavorable situations, the task-oriented leader sets goals, which focuses attention on performance, and clarifies what needs to be done, thus overcoming low task structure. This is enough to jump-start performance, even if workers don't like or trust the leader.

Recall, however, that Fiedler assumes that leaders are incapable of changing their leadership styles. Accordingly, the key to making Fiedler's

Figure 17.6 **Matching Leadership Styles to Situations**

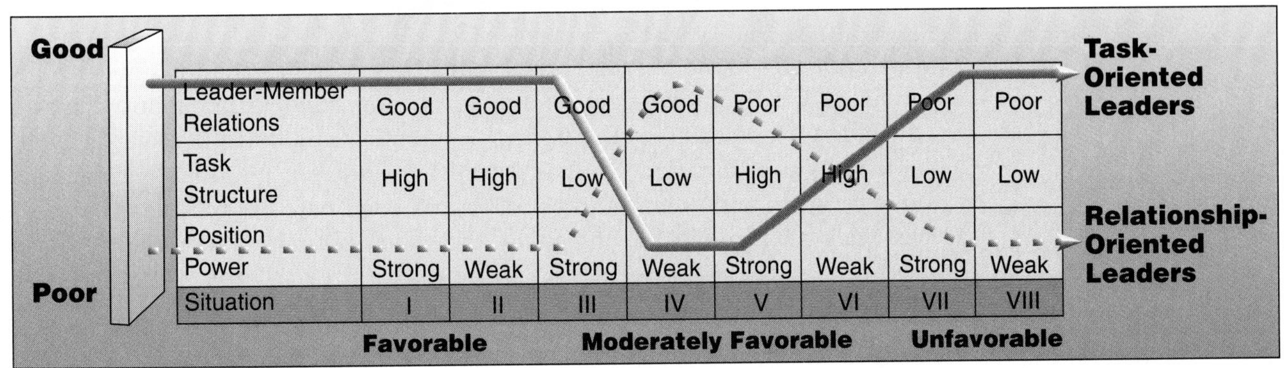

contingency theory practical in the workplace is to accurately measure and match leaders to situations or to teach leaders how to change situational favorableness by changing leader-member relations, task structure, or position power. While matching or placing leaders in appropriate situations works particularly well, practicing managers have had little luck with "reengineering situations" to fit their leadership styles. The primary problem, as you've no doubt realized, is the complexity of the theory. In a study designed to teach leaders how to reengineer their situations to fit their leadership styles, Fiedler found that most of the leaders simply did not understand what they were supposed to do to change their leadership situations. Furthermore, if they didn't like their LPC profile (perhaps they felt they were more relationship-oriented than their scores indicated), they arbitrarily changed it to better suit their view of themselves. Of course, the theory won't work as well if leaders are attempting to change situational factors to fit their perceived leadership style rather than their real leadership style.[26]

Review 3
Putting Leaders in the Right Situation: Fiedler's Contingency Theory

Fiedler's theory assumes that leaders are effective when their work groups perform well, that leaders are unable to change their leadership styles, that leadership styles must be matched to the proper situation, and that favorable situations permit leaders to influence group members. According to the Least Preferred Co-worker (LPC) scale, there are two basic leader styles. People who describe their LPC in a positive way have relationship-oriented leadership styles. By contrast, people who describe their LPC in a negative way have task-oriented leadership styles. Situational favorableness occurs when leaders can influence followers and is determined by leader-member relations, task structure, and position power. In general, relationship-oriented leaders with high LPC scores are better leaders under moderately favorable situations, while task-oriented leaders with low LPC scores are better leaders in highly favorable and unfavorable situations. Since Fiedler assumes that leaders are incapable of changing their leadership styles, the key is to accurately measure and match leaders to situations or to teach leaders how to change situational factors. While matching or placing leaders in appropriate situations has worked well, "reengineering situations" to fit leadership styles hasn't because of the complexity of the model, which people find difficult to understand.

4 Adapting Leader Behavior: Path-Goal Theory

Just as its name suggests, **path-goal theory** states that leaders can increase subordinate satisfaction and performance by clarifying and clearing the paths to goals and by increasing the number and kinds of rewards available for goal attainment. Said another way, leaders need to make clear how followers can achieve organizational goals, take care of problems that prevent followers from achieving goals, and then find more and varied rewards to motivate followers who achieve those goals.[27]

path-goal theory
leadership theory that states that leaders can increase subordinate satisfaction and performance by clarifying and clearing the paths to goals and by increasing the number and kinds of rewards available for goal attainment

However, leaders must meet two conditions in order for path clarification, path clearing, and rewards to increase followers' motivation and effort. First, leader behavior must be an immediate or future source of satisfaction for followers. Therefore, the things you do as a leader must please your followers today or lead to future activities or rewards that will satisfy them in the future. For example, Susie Burkhart, a product manager for J.M. Smucker Company, doesn't return the calls of recruitment headhunters who are trying to lure her away to higher-paying jobs. She doesn't want to leave Smucker's where, in the last seven years, she's earned an M.B.A. at company expense and has been promoted three times. Furthermore, she says, "I'm growing in this position," and "the fact that people come to me for answers and decisions and I don't have to go to my superior is very empowering."[28]

Second, while providing the coaching, guidance, support, and rewards necessary for effective work performance, leader behaviors must complement and not duplicate the characteristics of followers' work environments. Thus, leader behaviors must offer something unique and valuable to followers beyond what they're already experiencing as they do their jobs or beyond that which they can already do for themselves. Table 17.2 summarizes these basic assumptions of path-goal theory.

In contrast to Fiedler's contingency theory, path-goal theory assumes that leaders can change and adapt their leadership styles. Figure 17.7 illustrates this process, showing that leaders change and adapt their leadership styles contingent on the subordinate they are leading or the environment in which that subordinate works.

Let's learn more about path-goal theory by examining **4.1** *the four kinds of leadership styles that leaders use and* **4.2** *the environmental and subordinate contingency factors that determine when different leader styles are effective.*

4.1
Leadership Styles

directive leadership
leadership style in which the leader lets employees know precisely what is expected of them, gives them specific guidelines for performing tasks, schedules work, sets standards of performance, and makes sure that people follow standard rules and regulations

According to path-goal theory, illustrated in Figure 17.7, the four leadership styles are directive, supportive, participative, and achievement oriented.[29] **Directive leadership** involves letting employees know precisely what is expected of them, giving them specific guidelines for performing tasks, scheduling work, setting standards of performance, and making sure that people follow standard rules and regulations. T.J. Rodgers, the CEO of Cypress Semiconductor, has developed computer software that actually stops work on computer chips if something goes wrong. It's a tremendous help in quality control. The same program, however, is also used to keep

Table 17.2 **Basic Assumptions of Path-Goal Theory**

To Increase Subordinate Satisfaction and Performance, Leaders Need to:

- clarify paths to goals.
- clear paths to goals by solving problems and removing roadblocks.
- increase the number and kinds of rewards available for goal attainment.
- do things that satisfy followers today or will lead to future rewards or satisfaction.
- offer followers something unique and valuable beyond what they're experiencing or can already do for themselves.

Source: R.J. House & T.R. Mitchell, "Path-Goal Theory of Leadership," *Journal of Contemporary Business* 3 (1974): 81-97.

Figure 17.7 **Path-Goal Theory**

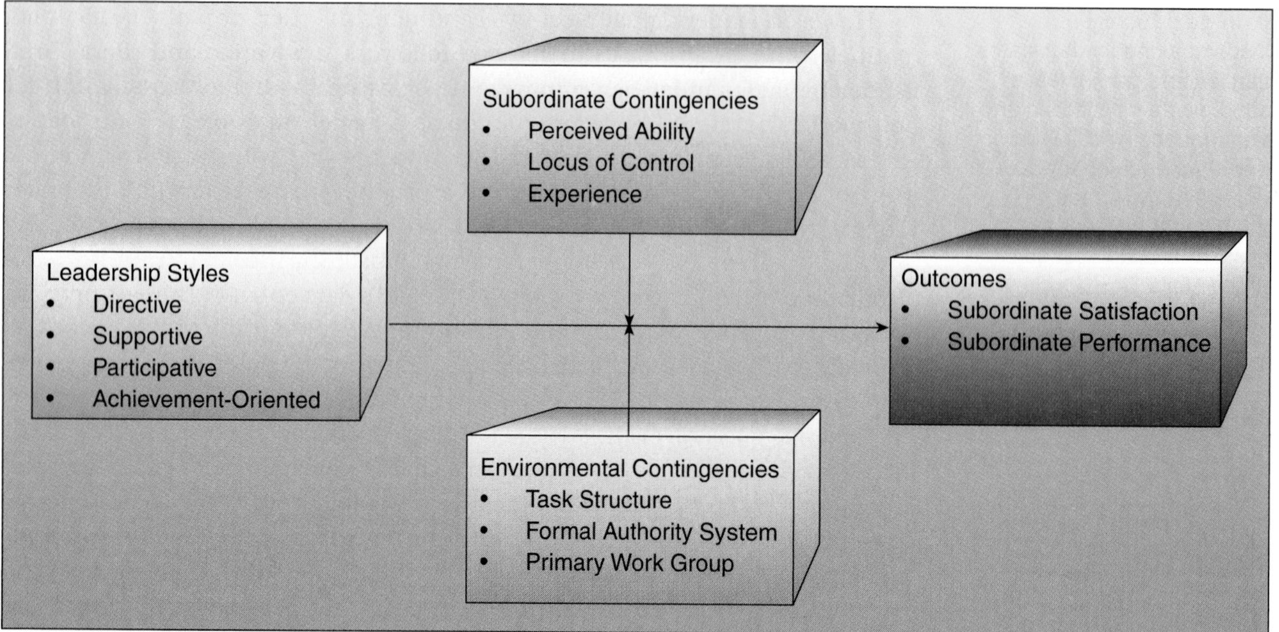

track of who meets and follows company standards and regulations. For instance, when one of Cypress's vice presidents didn't turn in his annual employee evaluations on time, the system put a stop on his paycheck. When he asked Rodgers where his paycheck was, Rodgers told him that he wouldn't get it until the evaluations were done. To no one's surprise, the vice president turned them in the very next day. However, when Rodgers was late with some of his own work, the system stopped his paycheck, too. In fact, he had to sell some Cypress stock until he caught up with his work and his paycheck was released.[30]

supportive leadership leadership style in which the leader is friendly and approachable to employees, shows concern for them and their welfare, treats them as equals, and creates a friendly climate

Supportive leadership involves being friendly and approachable to employees, showing concern for them and their welfare, treating them as equals, and creating a friendly climate. Supportive leadership is very similar to considerate leader behavior. Supportive leadership often results in employee job satisfaction and satisfaction with leaders. This leadership style may also result in improved performance when it increases employee confidence, lowers employee job stress, or improves relations and trust between employees and leaders.[31] Southwest Airlines, Harley-Davidson, and Federal Express are practicing supportive leadership via their official, recently adopted no-layoff policies. That is, no matter the company's circumstances, employees at these companies are guaranteed a job. According to Fred Reichheld, a management consultant and author of *The Loyalty Effect*, "Their employees are much more likely to dig in and commit, even in tough times."[32]

participative leadership leadership style in which the leader consults employees for their suggestions and input before making decisions

Participative leadership involves consulting employees for their suggestions and input before making decisions. Participation in decision making should help followers understand which goals are most important and clarify the paths to accomplishing them. Furthermore, when people participate in decisions, they become more committed to making them work.

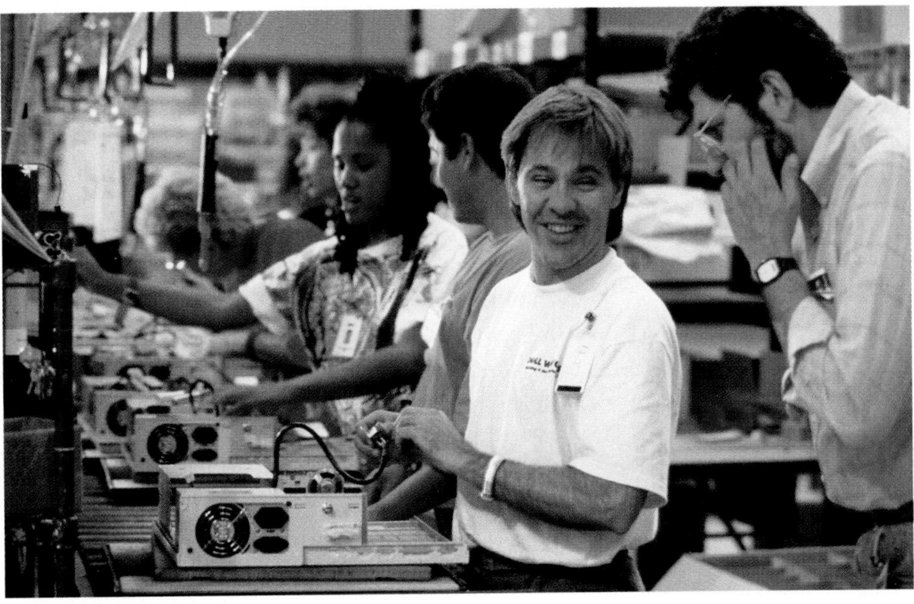

Supportive leaders create a friendly workplace climate. © Andrew Sacks/Tony Stone Images.

achievement-oriented leadership
leadership style in which the leader sets challenging goals, has high expectations of employees, and displays confidence that employees will assume responsibility and put forth extraordinary effort

Achievement-oriented leadership means setting challenging goals, having high expectations of employees, and displaying confidence that employees will assume responsibility and put forth extraordinary effort. Retired general Norman Schwarzkopf believes that leaders generally don't ask enough of their people. Early in his career, Schwarzkopf was placed in charge of helicopter maintenance at a military base, something that he knew little about. Since readiness is always a key factor in military operations, he asked what percentage of the helicopter fleet was available for flight operations on any given day. The answer was "roughly 75 percent." Schwarzkopf recalls telling workers, "I don't know anything about helicopter maintenance, but I'm establishing a new standard—85 percent." Within a short

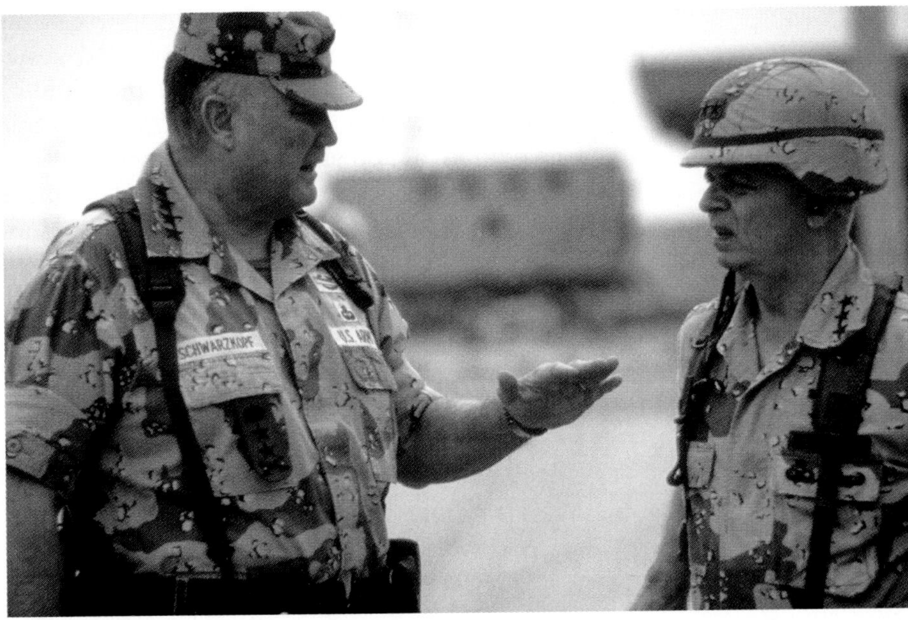

Achievement-oriented leaders like Norman Schwarzkopf set challenging goals but have confidence that employees will work hard to achieve these goals. © Corbis.

time, 85 percent of the helicopter fleet was available for daily flight operations. The moral, according to the general, is that employees will usually not perform above your expectations, so it's important to expect a lot.[33]

4.2 Subordinate and Environmental Contingencies

As shown in Figure 17.7, path-goal theory specifies that leader behaviors should be fitted to subordinate characteristics. The theory identifies three kinds of subordinate contingencies: perceived ability, experience, and locus of control. *Perceived ability* is simply how much ability subordinates believe they have for doing their jobs well. Subordinates who perceive that they have a great deal of ability will be dissatisfied with directive leader behaviors. Experienced employees are likely to react in a similar way. Since they already know how to do their jobs (or perceive that they do), they don't need or want close supervision. By contrast, subordinates with little experience or little perceived ability will welcome directive leadership.

Locus of control is a personality measure that indicates the extent to which people believe that they have control over what happens to them in life. *Internals* believe that what happens to them, good or bad, is largely a result of their choices and actions. *Externals,* on the other hand, believe that what happens to them is caused by external forces outside of their control. Accordingly, externals are much more comfortable with a directive leadership style, while internals greatly prefer a participative leadership style, because they like to have a say in what goes on at work.

Path-goal theory specifies that leader behaviors should complement rather than duplicate the characteristics of followers' work environments. There are three kinds of environmental contingencies: task structure, the formal authority system, and the primary work group. As in Fiedler's contingency theory, *task structure* is the degree to which the requirements of a subordinate's tasks are clearly specified. When task structure is low and tasks are unclear, directive leadership should be used, because it complements the work environment. However, when task structure is high and tasks are clear, directive leadership duplicates what task structure provides and is not needed. Alternatively, when tasks are stressful, frustrating, or dissatisfying, leaders should respond with supportive leadership.

The *formal authority system* is an organization's set of procedures, rules, and policies. When the formal authority system is unclear, directive leadership complements the situation by reducing uncertainty and increasing clarity. But when the formal authority system is clear, directive leadership is redundant and should not be used.

Primary work group refers to the amount of work-oriented participation or emotional support that is provided by an employee's immediate work group. Participative leadership should be used when tasks are complex and there is little existing work-oriented participation in the primary work group. Likewise, when performing complex tasks, leaders should use participative leadership. When tasks are stressful, frustrating, or repetitive, supportive leadership is called for.

Finally, since keeping track of all of these subordinate and environmental contingencies can get a bit confusing, Table 17.3 provides a summary of when directive, supportive, participative, or achievement-oriented leadership styles should be used.

Table 17.3	Path-Goal Theory: When to Use Directive, Supportive, Participative, or Achievement-Oriented Leadership

Directive Leadership

- Unstructured tasks
- Inexperienced workers
- Workers with low perceived ability
- Workers with external locus of control
- Unclear formal authority system

Supportive Leadership

- Structured, simple, repetitive tasks
- Stressful, frustrating tasks
- When workers lack confidence
- Clear formal authority system

Participative Leadership

- Experienced workers
- Workers with high perceived ability
- Workers with internal locus of control
- Workers not satisfied with rewards
- Complex tasks

Achievement-Oriented Leadership

- Unchallenging tasks

Review 4
Adapting Leader Behavior: Path-Goal Theory

Path-goal theory states that leaders can increase subordinate satisfaction and performance by clarifying and clearing the paths to goals and by increasing the number and kinds of rewards available for goal attainment. However, for this to work, leader behavior must be an immediate or future source of satisfaction for followers and must complement and not duplicate the characteristics of followers' work environments. In contrast to Fiedler's contingency theory, path-goal theory assumes that leaders can change and adapt their leadership styles (directive, supportive, participative, and achievement oriented) depending on the subordinate they are leading (experience, perceived ability, internal or external) or the environment in which that subordinate works (task structure, formal authority system, or primary work group).

5 Adapting Leader Behavior: Hersey & Blanchard's Situational Theory

Have you ever had a new job that you didn't know how to do and the boss wasn't around to help you learn it? Or, have you been in the other situation where you knew exactly how to do your job but your boss kept treating you like you didn't? Hersey and Blanchard's situational leadership theory is based on the idea of follower readiness or maturity. Hersey and Blanchard argue that just like children at different stages of maturity, employees have different levels of readiness for handling different jobs, responsibilities, and work assignments. Accordingly, Hersey and Blanchard's **situational theory** states that leaders need to adjust their leadership styles to match followers' maturity.[34]

situational theory leadership theory that states that leaders need to adjust their leadership styles to match followers' maturity

Let's learn more about the Hersey & Blanchard situational theory by examining **5.1** *worker maturity and* **5.2** *different leadership styles.*

5.1
Worker Maturity

worker maturity
the ability and willingness to take responsibility for directing one's behavior at work

Worker maturity is the ability and willingness to take responsibility for directing one's behavior at work. Maturity is made up of two components. *Job maturity* consists of the amount of knowledge, skill, ability, and experience people have to perform their jobs. As you would expect, people with greater skill, ability, and experience do a better job of supervising their own work. *Psychological maturity*, on the other hand, is a feeling of self-confidence or self-respect. Likewise, confident people do a better job of guiding their own work than do insecure people.

The bottom of Figure 17.8 shows how job maturity and psychological maturity are combined to produce four different levels of maturity in Hersey and Blanchard's situational theory. The lowest level, M1, represents insecure people who are neither willing nor able to take responsibility for guiding their own work. M2 represents people who are confident and are willing but not able to take responsibility for guiding their own work. M3 represents people who are insecure and are able but not willing to take responsibility for guiding their own work. And M4 represents people who are confident and willing and able to take responsibility for guiding their own work. It's important to note that a follower's maturity is usually task specific. For example, you may be highly confident and capable when it comes to personal computers but know nothing about setting up budgets for planning purposes. Thus, you would be mature (M4) with computers and immature (M1) with budgets.

5.2
Leadership Styles

Similar to Blake and Mouton's managerial grid, situational theory defines leadership styles in terms of task behavior (i.e., concern for production) and relationship behavior (i.e., concern for people). Figure 17.8 shows that these two behaviors can be combined to form four different leadership styles: telling, selling, participating, and delegating. Leaders choose one of these styles depending on the maturity a follower has for a specific task.

A *telling* leadership style (high task behavior and low relationship behavior) is based on one-way communication, in which followers are told what, how, when, and where to do particular tasks. Telling is used when people are insecure and neither willing nor able to take responsibility for guiding their own work (M1). For instance, someone using a telling leadership style might say, "We're going to start a company newsletter. I want you to contact three printers for cost estimates. Then get together with each manager and get a one-page update with the latest activities from each department. Don't write these yourself. Have the managers write them and we'll edit them as we see fit. Also, call the CEO's assistant to remind her that we need her comments. Finally, have this all assembled in a three-ring notebook for me next Friday."

A *selling* leadership style (high task behavior and high relationship behavior) involves two-way communication and psychological support to encourage followers to "own" or "buy into" particular ways of doing things. Selling is used when confident people are willing but not able to take responsibility for guiding their own work (M2). For instance, someone using a selling leadership style might say, "We're going to start a company newsletter. I really think that's a great idea, don't you? We're going to need some cost estimates from printers and some comments from each of the managers. But that's pretty

Figure 17.8 **Hersey & Blanchard Situational Theory**

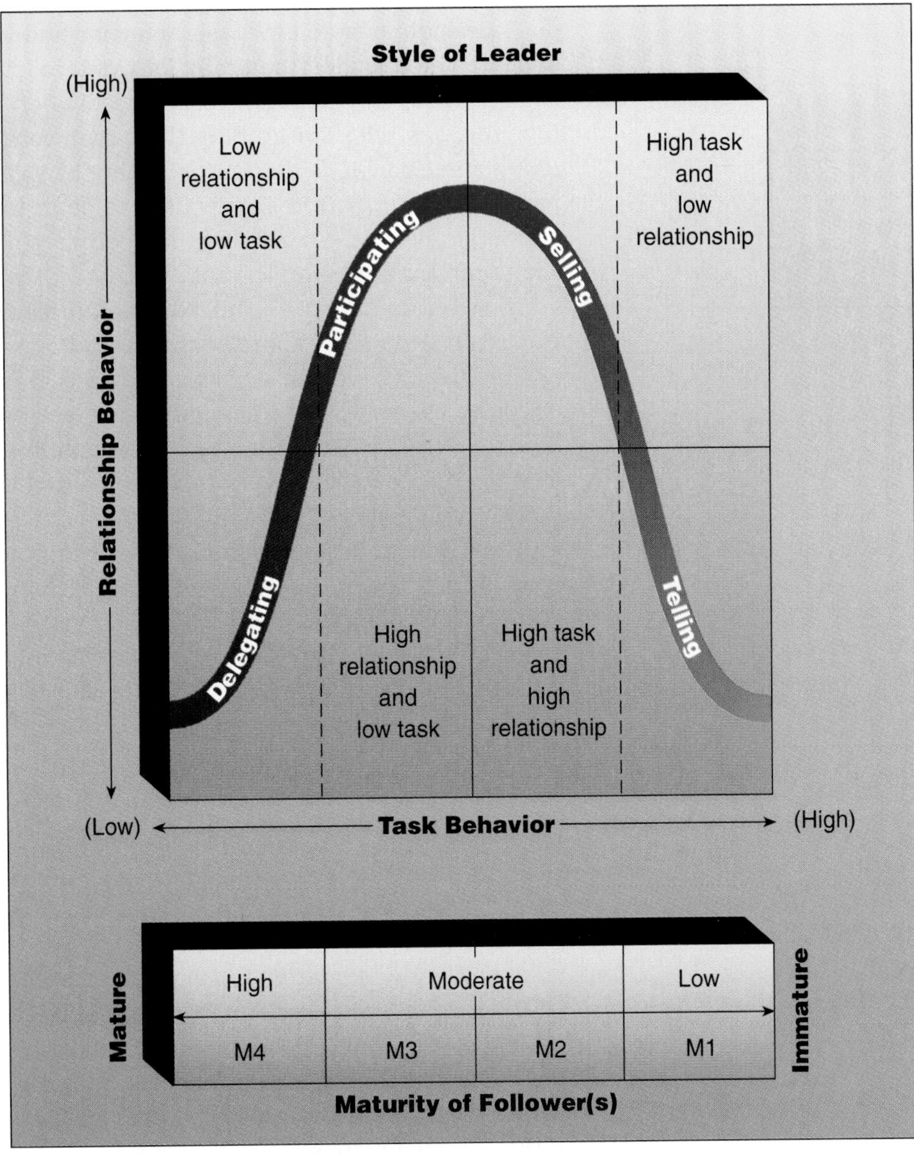

Source: Adapted from P. Hersey and K. Blanchard, *Management of Organizational Behavior: Utilizing Human Resources,* 4th ed. (Englewood Cliffs, NJ: Prentice-Hall, 1982), 152.

straightforward. Oh, don't forget that we need the CEO's comments, too. She's expecting you to call. I know that you'll do a great job on this. We'll meet next Tuesday to see if you have any questions once you've dug into this. By the way, we need to have this done by next Friday."

A *participating* style (low task behavior and high relationship behavior) is based on two-way communication and shared decision making. Participating is used when insecure people are able but not willing to take responsibility for guiding their own work (M3). Since the problem is with motivation and not ability, someone using a participating leadership style might say, "What do you think about starting a company newsletter? Uh-huh, uh-huh (listening)? Ok, I think so, too. What kind of stuff do you hate in company newsletters? Uh-huh (listening). Ok, I agree. That stuff drives me nuts, too. Well, what do you think we should put in our company newsletter. Uh-huh (listening). Those are great ideas. I'd like to see you implement them. We've got about 10 days to put it together. Why don't you put together a first draft, based on what we talked about here today, and we can meet on Tuesday to review those ideas. Great!"

A *delegating* style (low task behavior and low relationship behavior) is a style in which leaders basically let workers "run their own show" and make their own decisions. Delegating is used when people are willing and able to take responsibility for guiding their own work (M4). For instance, someone using a delegating leadership style might say, "We're going to start a company newsletter. You've got 10 days to do it. Run with it. Let me know when you've got it done. I'll e-mail you a couple of ideas, but other than that, do what you think is best. Thanks."

In general, Figure 17.8 shows that at first, as people become more mature, and thus increasingly willing and capable of guiding their own behavior, leaders should become less task oriented and more relationship oriented. However, after people mature even more, leaders should become both less task-oriented and less relationship-oriented as people eventually manage their own work with little input from their leaders.

How well does Hersey & Blanchard's situational theory work? Despite its intuitive appeal (managers and consultants tend to prefer it over Fiedler's contingency theory because of its underlying logic and simplicity), most studies don't support situational theory.[35] While managers generally do a good job of judging followers' maturity levels, the theory doesn't seem to work well, except at lower levels, where a telling style is recommended for people who are insecure and neither willing nor able to take responsibility for guiding their own work.[36]

Review 5
Adapting Leader Behavior: Hersey & Blanchard's Situational Theory

According to situational theory, leaders need to adjust their leadership styles to match follower's maturity, which is the ability (job maturity) and willingness (psychological maturity) to take responsibility for directing one's work. Job maturity and psychological maturity combine to produce four different levels of maturity (M1–M4) in which people vary in their confidence, ability, and willingness to guide their own work. Situational theory combines task and relationship behavior to create four leadership styles: telling (M1), selling (M2), participating (M3), and delegating (M4), that are used with employees at different maturity levels.

6 Adapting Leader Behavior: Normative Decision Theory

For years, your company has insisted on formal business attire for men and women. However, you want to make a change to casual wear. Do you make the decision yourself and announce it, or do you consult your employees first before making a decision?

Your sales divisions are organized geographically into West Coast, East Coast, Midwest, and Southwest regions. The Southwest region has seen exponential growth in the last five years, and its sales representatives and managers make double the income of people in other regions. Out of fairness and out of concern that your current staff won't be able to keep up with the growth, you're going to cut the Southwest region in half, add staff, and effectively reduce the earnings of its sales representatives and managers. Do you make the decision yourself, announce it, and then live with the backlash? Do you consult all of your regional managers before making this decision? Or do you take your concerns straight to the people in the Southwest region to let them know what your concerns are?

Many people believe that making tough decisions is at the heart of leadership. However, experienced leaders will tell you that deciding how to make decisions is just as important. The **normative decision theory** (also known as the *Vroom-Yetton-Jago Model*) helps leaders decide how much employee participation (from none to letting employees make the entire decision) should be used when making decisions.[37]

normative decision theory theory that suggests how leaders can determine the appropriate amount of employee participation when making decisions

Let's learn more about normative decision theory by investigating **6.1** *decision styles and* **6.2** *decision quality and acceptance.*

6.1
Decision Styles

While nearly all of the other leadership theories in this chapter have specified leadership styles—that is, the way a leader generally behaves toward followers—the normative decision theory instead specifies five different decision styles or ways of making decisions. As shown in Table 17.4, those styles vary from *autocratic decisions* (AI or AII), in which leaders make the decisions by themselves, to *consultative decisions* (CI or CII), in which leaders share problems with subordinates but still make the decisions themselves, to *group decisions* (GII), in which leaders share the problems with subordinates and then have the group make the decisions.

6.2
Decision Quality and Acceptance

According to the normative decision theory, using the right degree of employee participation improves the quality of decisions and the extent to which

Table 17.4

Decision Styles and Levels of Employee Participation

AI: Using information available at the time, the leader solves the problem or makes the decision.

AII: The leader obtains necessary information from employees and then selects a solution to the problem. When being asked to share information, employees may or may not be told what the problem is.

CI: The leader shares the problem and gets ideas and suggestions from relevant employees on an individual basis. Individuals are not brought together as a group. Then the leader makes the decision, which may or may not reflect their input.

CII: The leader shares the problem with employees as a group, obtains their ideas and suggestions, and then makes the decision, which may or may not reflect their input.

GII: The leader shares the problem with employees as a group. Together, the leader and employees generate and evaluate alternatives and try to reach an agreement on a solution. The leader acts as a facilitator and does not try to influence the group. The leader is willing to accept and implement any solution that has the support of the entire group.

Source: Adapted from V.H. Vroom & P. W. Yetton, *Leadership and Decision Making* (Pittsburgh: University of Pittsburgh Press, 1973), 13.

employees accept and are committed to decisions. Table 17.5 lists the decision rules that normative decision theory uses to increase decision quality and employee acceptance and commitment. The quality, leader information, subordinate information, goal congruence, and problem structure rules are used to increase decision quality. For example, the leader information rule states that if a leader doesn't have enough information to make a decision on his or her own, then the leader should not use an autocratic decision style.

The commitment probability, subordinate conflict, and commitment requirement rules shown in Table 17.5 are used to increase employee acceptance and commitment to decisions. For example, the commitment requirement rule says that if decision acceptance and commitment are important, and the subordinates being led share the organization's goals, then don't use an autocratic or consultative style. In other words, if followers want to do what's best for the company and you need their acceptance and commitment to make a decision work, then use a group decision style and let them make the decision.

As you can see, these decision rules help leaders improve decision quality and follower acceptance and commitment by eliminating decision styles that don't fit the decision or situation they're facing. Normative decision theory then operationalizes these decision rules in the form of yes/no questions, which are shown in the decision tree displayed in Figure 17.9. You start at the left side of the model and answer the first question, "How important is the technical quality of this decision?" by choosing "high" or "low." Then answer the next question and so forth as you branch to the right along the decision tree until you get to the end and a recommended decision style.

Let's use the model by returning to the problem of whether to change from a formal business attire policy to a casual wear policy. The decision sounds simple, but working through the decision tree indicates that it is more complex than you'd think.

Table 17.5 **Normative Theory Decision Rules**

	Decision Rules to Increase Decision Quality
Quality Rule.	If the quality of the decision is important, then don't use an autocratic decision style.
Leader Information Rule.	If the quality of the decision is important and if the leader doesn't have enough information to make the decision on his or her own, then don't use an autocratic decision style.
Subordinate Information Rule.	If the quality of the decision is important and if the subordinates don't have enough information to make the decision themselves, then don't use a group decision style.
Goal Congruence Rule.	If the quality of the decision is important and subordinates' goals are different from the organization's goals, then don't use a group decision style.
Problem Structure Rule.	If the quality of the decision is important, the leader doesn't have enough information to make the decision on his or her own, and the problem is unstructured, then don't use an autocratic decision style.
	Decision Rules to Increase Decision Acceptance
Commitment Probability Rule.	If having subordinates accept and commit to the decision is important, then don't use an autocratic decision style.
Subordinate Conflict Rule.	If having subordinates accept the decision is important and critical to successful implementation and subordinates are likely to disagree or end up in conflict over the decision, then don't use an autocratic or consultative decision style.
Commitment Requirement Rule.	If having subordinates accept the decision is absolutely required for successful implementation and subordinates share the organization's goals, then don't use an autocratic or consultative style.

Source: Adapted from V.H. Vroom, "Leadership," in *Handbook of Industrial and Organizational Psychology,* ed. M.D. Dunnette (Chicago: Rand McNally, 1976). V.H. Vroom & A.G. Jago, *The New Leadership: Managing Participation in Organizations* (Englewood Cliffs, NJ: Prentice Hall, 1988).

Figure 17.9 **Normative Decision Theory Tree for Determining the Level of Participation in Decision Making**

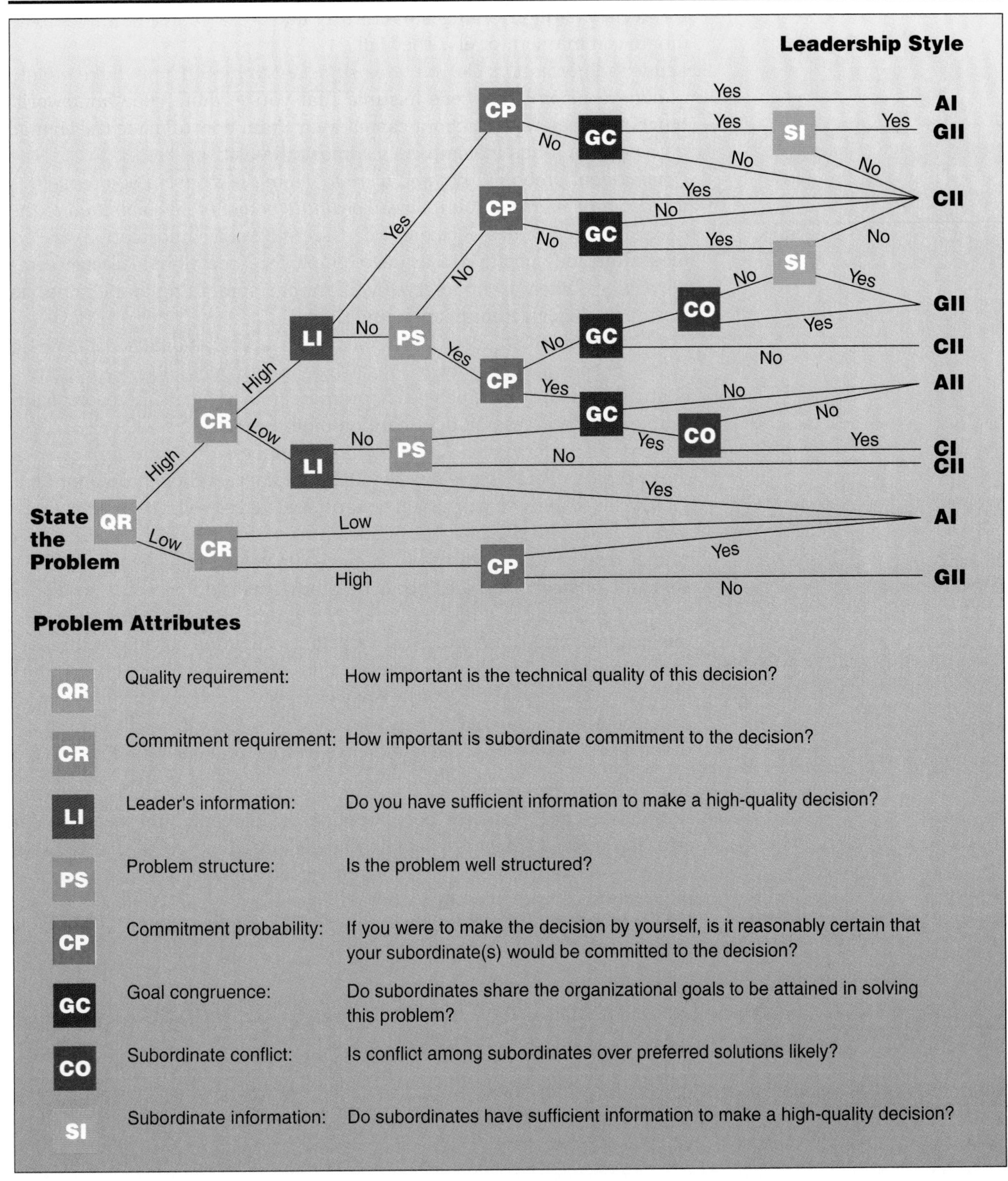

Leadership Style
State the Problem
QR
High
Low
CR
High
Low
LI
No
Yes
PS
CP
GC
CO
SI
Yes
No
AI
GII
CII
GII
CII
AII
CI
CII
AI
GII
Problem Attributes
QR Quality requirement: How important is the technical quality of this decision?
CR Commitment requirement: How important is subordinate commitment to the decision?
LI Leader's information: Do you have sufficient information to make a high-quality decision?
PS Problem structure: Is the problem well structured?
CP Commitment probability: If you were to make the decision by yourself, is it reasonably certain that your subordinate(s) would be committed to the decision?
GC Goal congruence: Do subordinates share the organizational goals to be attained in solving this problem?
CO Subordinate conflict: Is conflict among subordinates over preferred solutions likely?
SI Subordinate information: Do subordinates have sufficient information to make a high-quality decision?

Source: V.H. Vroom & A.G. Jago, *The New Leadership: Managing Participation in Organizations* (Englewood Cliffs, NJ: Prentice Hall, 1988).

Problem: Change to Casual Wear?

1. *Quality requirement: How important is the technical quality of this decision?* High. This question has to do with whether there are quality differences in the alternatives and whether those quality differences

matter. While most people would assume that quality really isn't an issue here, it really is, given the overall positive changes that generally accompany changes to casual wear.

2. *Commitment requirement: How important is subordinate commitment to the decision?* High. Changes in culture, like dress codes, require subordinate commitment or else they fail.
3. *Leader's information: Do you have sufficient information to make a high-quality decision?* Yes. Let's assume that you've done your homework. Much has been written about casual wear, from how to make the change to the effects it has in companies (almost all positive).
4. *Commitment probability: If you were to make the decision by yourself, is it reasonably certain that your subordinate(s) would be committed to the decision?* No. Studies of casual wear (see #3, leader information) are almost uniformly positive in terms of employees' reactions. However, employees are likely to be angry if you change something as personal as clothing policies without consulting them.
5. *Goal congruence: Do subordinates share the organizational goals to be attained in solving this problem?* Yes. The goals that usually accompany a change to casual dress policies are a more informal culture, better communication, and less money spent on business attire.
6. *Subordinate information: Do subordinates have sufficient information to make a high-quality decision?* No. Most employees know little about casual wear policies or what even constitutes casual wear in most companies. Consequently, most companies have to educate employees about casual wear practices and policies even before making a decision.
7. *CII is the answer:* With a CII, or consultative decision process, the leader shares the problem with employees as a group, obtains their ideas and suggestions, and then makes the decision, which may or may not reflect their input. So, given the answers to these questions (remember, different managers won't necessarily answer these questions the same way), the normative theory recommends that leaders consult with their subordinates first before deciding whether to change to a casual wear policy.

How well does the normative decision theory work? A leading leadership scholar has described it as the best supported of all leadership theories.[38] In general, the more managers violate the decision rules discussed in Table 17.5, the less effective their decisions are, especially with respect to subordinate acceptance and commitment.[39]

Review 6
Adapting Leader Behavior: Normative Decision Theory

The normative decision theory helps leaders decide how much employee participation should be used when making decisions. Using the right degree of employee participation improves the quality of decisions and the extent to which employees accept and are committed to decisions. The theory specifies five different decision styles or ways of making decisions: autocratic decisions (AI or AII), consultative decisions (CI or CII), and group decisions (GII). The theory improves decision quality via the quality, leader information, subordinate information, goal congruence, and unstructured problem decision rules. The theory improves employee commitment and acceptance via the commitment probability, subordinate conflict, and commitment requirement decision rules. These decision rules help leaders improve decision quality and follower acceptance and commitment by eliminating decision styles that don't fit the decision or situation they're facing. Normative decision theory then operationalizes these decision rules in the form of yes/no questions, which were shown in the decision tree displayed in Figure 17.9.

Strategic Leadership

Thus far, you have read about three major leadership ideas: traits, behaviors, and situational theories. Leader *traits* are relatively stable characteristics, such as abilities or psychological motives. Traits capture who effective leaders are. Leader *behaviors* are the actions leaders takes to influence others to achieve group or organizational goals. Behaviors capture what effective leaders do (i.e., initiate structure and consideration). And *situational theories* indicate that the effectiveness of a leadership style, the way a leader generally behaves toward followers, depends on the situation. Situational theories capture what leaders need to do or not do in particular situations or circumstances. This final part of the chapter introduces a fourth major leadership idea—strategic leadership—and its components: visionary, charismatic, and transformational leadership.

strategic leadership the ability to anticipate, envision, maintain flexibility, think strategically, and work with others to initiate changes that will create a positive future for an organization

Strategic leadership is the ability to anticipate, envision, maintain flexibility, think strategically, and work with others to initiate changes that will create a positive future for an organization.[40] For example, General Electric's CEO, Jack Welch, is one of the most successful CEOs ever, having increased GE's stock market value from $12 billion when he took over in 1981 to more than $300 billion today. From the start, Welch imparted strategic leadership by making it clear that every GE business (there are more than a dozen) needed to be "#1 or #2 in its industry." For two decades, he has reinforced GE's strategic leadership by holding half-day "classes" with more than 15,000 GE managers and executives at GE's executive center in Crotonville, New York. Every week, Welch also uses surprise visits to GE plants and offices to maintain connections with GE's lower- and middle-level managers. Brian Nailor, a GE marketing manager, said, "We're pebbles in an ocean, but he knows about us."[41]

visionary leadership leadership that creates a positive image of the future that motivates organizational members and provides direction for future planning and goal setting

Thus, strategic leadership captures how leaders inspire their followers to change and to give extraordinary effort to accomplish organizational goals. After reading this next section, you should be able to:

7 explain how **visionary leadership** (i.e., charismatic and transformational leadership) helps leaders achieve strategic leadership.

7 Visionary Leadership

In Chapter 4, we defined a *vision* as a statement of a company's purpose or reason for existing. Similarly, **visionary leadership** creates a positive image of the future that motivates organizational members and provides direction for future planning and goal setting.[42]

Two kinds of visionary leadership are **7.1** *charismatic leadership and* **7.2** *transformational leadership.*

7.1
Charismatic Leadership

Charisma is a Greek word meaning "gift from God." The Greeks saw people with charisma as divinely inspired and capable of incredible accomplishments. German sociologist Max Weber viewed charisma as a special bond between leaders and followers.[43] Weber wrote that the special qualities of charismatic leaders enable them to strongly influence followers. Weber also noted that charismatic leaders tended to emerge in times of crisis and that the radical solutions they propose enhance the admiration that followers feel for them. Indeed, charismatic leaders tend to have incredible influence over their followers, who become zealously inspired by and attracted to their leaders. From this perspective, charismatic leaders are often seen as bigger-than-life or uniquely special.

Charismatic leaders have strong, confident, dynamic personalities that attract followers and enable them to create strong bonds between themselves and their followers. Followers trust charismatic leaders, are loyal to them, and are inspired to work toward the accomplishment of the leader's vision. Because of these qualities, followers become devoted to charismatic leaders and may go to extraordinary lengths to please them. Therefore, we can define **charismatic leadership** as the behavioral tendencies and personal characteristics of leaders that create an exceptionally strong relationship between them and their followers. Charismatic leaders also:

- articulate a clear vision for the future that is based on strongly held values or morals,
- model those values by acting in a way consistent with the vision,
- communicate high performance expectations to followers, and
- display confidence in followers' abilities to achieve the vision.[44]

Personal Productivity Tip

Develop Your Charisma

It's often assumed that charisma is an unchangeable trait. However, several simple steps can develop your charisma:

1. Use symbols, metaphors, and stories to refine complex ideas into simple, powerful messages.
2. Embrace risk. Charismatics long to accomplish what hasn't been done before.
3. Defy the status quo. Fight convention. Question why things are done the way they are.
4. Step into others' shoes. Be empathetic and see things from the perspective of customers and employees.
5. Poke, prod, and challenge others to think and act differently and quickly.

Follow these steps, and you'll be more charismatic and develop a stronger relationship with your followers.

Source: P. Sellers, "What Exactly Is Charisma?" *Fortune,* 15 January 1996, 68.

charismatic leadership
the behavioral tendencies and personal characteristics of leaders that create an exceptionally strong relationship between them and their followers

Orit Gadiesh, chairman of Bain & Co., a management consulting firm, is an example of charismatic leadership. Gadiesh led Bain out of serious financial problems, expanded the company from 990 to 1,400 employees, and increased revenues by 25 percent a year. Gadiesh dresses with flair and is described as complex, intense, driven, painfully direct, and a lot of fun. Founder Bill Bain recalls interviewing Gadiesh for the job: "The way she listened made my energy level go up. She asked the most thoughtful, original questions. There was nothing boilerplate about her." Bain managing director Tom Tierney says, "Her style comes from this intense passion about being true to herself and the client." Says James Morgan, CEO of Philip Morris USA, one of Bain's clients, "Orit has that talent for making you feel you're the most important person in the room."[45]

Does charismatic leadership work? Studies indicate that it often does. In general, the followers of charismatic leaders are more committed and satisfied, are better performers, are more likely to trust their leaders, and simply work harder.[46] However, the risks associated with charismatic leadership are at least as large as its benefits, particularly if ego-driven leaders take advantage of fanatical followers.

ethical charismatics
charismatic leaders that provide developmental opportunities for followers, are open to positive and negative feedback, recognize others' contributions, share information, and have moral standards that emphasize the larger interests of the group, organization, or society

In general, there are two kinds of charismatic leaders, ethical charismatics and unethical charismatics.[47] **Ethical charismatics** provide developmental opportunities for followers, are open to positive and negative feedback, recognize others' contributions, share information, and have moral standards that emphasize the larger interests of the group, organization, or society. Ethical charismatics produce stronger commitment, higher satisfaction, more effort, better performance, and greater trust.

Been There,

Richard Branson: Charisma without Hot Air

Richard Branson, CEO and founder of the Virgin Group, which owns Virgin Atlantic Airways, Virgin Cola, and Virgin Mega stores, as well as hotels, video game and book publishing, and radio and television production, is one of the most charismatic business leaders of our time. Besides his highly publicized attempts at flying a hot-air balloon around the world, Branson is known for his sense of humor, his openness to ideas, and the large amount of freedom that he grants to the people who run various parts of the Virgin "empire." In this interview with Manfred Kets de Vries, he discusses his views on business and leadership.

Q: What do you see as Virgin's key success factors? What makes your company different from others?

A: I'm absolutely certain that it's a question of the kind of people you have, and the way you motivate them. I'm sure that's what makes any company successful. If you can motivate your people, use their creative potential, you can get through bad times and you can enjoy the good times together. If you fail to motivate your people, your company is doomed....If your employees are happy and smiling and enjoying their work, they will perform well. Consequently, the customers will enjoy their experience with your company. If your employees are sad and miserable and not having a good time, the customers will be equally miserable.

"I admire anyone who takes on either the establishment of something like a mountain and succeeds or fails."

Q: Could you say something about the way you design your organization, its architecture?

A: Well, our record company [now divested], I suppose, would have been the best example. My philosophy was always that if there were 50 people in a building, I would go there and ask to see the deputy managing director, the deputy sales manager, and the deputy marketing manager. I would say: "You are now the managing director, the sales manager, the marketing manager, or the press officer of a new company." And I would put them into a new building. Then again, when that company got to a certain size, say 50 people, I would do the same thing again. So we actually set up about 25 or 30 small record companies. Cumulatively, they became the biggest independent record company in the world.

Q: What can you say about your reward systems? You once said that you were in the business of making millionaires.

A: Yes, I suppose that we have made maybe 15 or 20 multimillionaires through this structure. We like to reward our key performers for their creative contribution.

Q: When you look at creative, high-performing organizations, they seem to have a number of characteristics in common. What do you think they are?

A: Obviously, speed is something that we are better at than most other companies. We don't have formal board meetings, committees, etc. If someone has an idea, they can pick up the phone and talk to me. I can vote "done, let's do it." Or better still, they can just go ahead and do it. They know that they are not going to get a mouthful from me if they make a mistake. Rules and regulations are not our forte. Analyzing things to death is not our kind of thing. We very rarely sit back and analyze what we do.

Q: Some people argue that the way you run your company is almost like a venture capital firm. Basically, anybody with a crazy idea gets a hearing.

A: I hope that "crazy idea" part is not too true. But to an extent, the statement is valid. . . . It's a fair comment.

Q: What do you see as your weaknesses? Do you have any characteristics that get in the way of your work?

A: I suspect not being able to say no. Hopefully, I am getting better at it now. But there are so many wonderful ideas. I do love new projects; I love new ideas. We are in a position where almost anybody and everybody who has got an idea likes to bring it to us. There aren't many companies like us, who have got, in a sense, a certain amount of entrepreneurial flair, companies that seem accessible to the public. Therefore, in any one day we receive hundreds of requests of all sorts. And some of them are very good ones.

My weaknesses really go back to the fact that I have spread myself too thin. In a purely business sense, I suspect that if I just wanted to maximize profits, I should have stayed more focused on one area and really concentrated on that one area. That's the conventional way, and I'm sure that's what most business schools teach. Perhaps it's right. But it wouldn't have been half as much fun.

I must admit that I feel very much alive when I set out to achieve something. On reflection, it's really more the fight than the actual achieving. I love people and I just love new creative challenges. Some people ask, why keep battling on when you can take it easy? My reason, basically, is that I'm very fortunate to be in the position I am. I've learned a great deal and I've had great fun doing so. I'm in a unique position of being able to do almost anything I like and achieve almost anything I wish. I don't want to waste the position that I find myself in. I know that at age 80 or 90 I would kick myself if I just frittered away this second half of my life. I really do believe that fighting competition is exciting. And it's good for business. I think that Virgin can get in there and it can compete with the biggest and improve them—and hopefully survive alongside them, have fun, and pay the bills at the same time. Basically, I admire anyone who takes on either the establishment or something like a mountain and succeeds or fails.

I sometimes wake up at night and lie there and think, "Is it all a dream?" Because it has been pretty good to date. It just seems almost too much for one man in one lifetime. So, if I am to reflect, I have been very fortunate to have so many wonderful experiences. Every day is fascinating. Every day, I am learning something new.

Q: When you leave Virgin, what kind of enduring mark do you want to leave behind? How do you want to be remembered?

A: I think that it would be nice if Virgin can be remembered as a company that challenged the established way of doing things, and that built up a number of companies that were world leaders in their own fields. That doesn't necessarily mean being the biggest companies, but the best in that particular field. I also would like that the staff of Virgin would have very happy memories of the time that they spent working here.

Source: M. Kets de Vries, "Charisma in Action: The Transformational Abilities of Virgin's Richard Branson and ABB's Percy Barnevik [includes interview with Virgin Group's CEO and ABB's chairman]," *Organizational Dynamics* 26, no. 3 (1 January 1998).

Done That

unethical charismatics charismatic leaders that control and manipulate followers, do what is best for themselves instead of their organizations, only want to hear positive feedback, only share information that is beneficial to themselves, and have moral standards that put their interests before everyone else's

By contrast, unethical charismatics pose a tremendous risk for companies. Followers can be just as supportive and committed to unethical charismatics as they are to ethical charismatics. However, **unethical charismatics** control and manipulate followers, do what is best for themselves instead of their organizations, only want to hear positive feedback, only share information that is beneficial to themselves, and have moral standards that put their interests before everyone else's. John Thompson, a management consultant, said, "Often what begins as a mission becomes an obsession. Leaders can cut corners on values and become driven by self-interest. Then they may abuse anyone who makes a mistake."[48]

For example, a former bank CEO, whom we will call "William," was probably an unethical charismatic. His workers followed and feared him, never knowing when he would "attack" those around him. At times, he was such a tyrant that he became known as WWW, "Whatever William Wants." His top managers were terrified of him, especially during monthly meetings when he would fire questions at a randomly chosen "victim." For instance, a bank officer at the meeting might say, "Deposits are up 10 percent, and we're really pleased because it's the second month in a row," and then William would say "Why are you pleased? Do you think 10 percent is enough? Why do you jump to conclusions? Are we running a bank where 10 percent is enough?" One of the bank managers commented that "Once Walter was riled up, people would end up *yessing* him to death."[49]

Table 17.6 shows the stark differences between ethical and unethical charismatics on several leader behaviors: exercising power, creating the vision, communicating with followers, accepting feedback, stimulating followers intellectually, developing followers, and moral standards. For example, in terms of creating the vision, ethical charismatics include followers' concerns and wishes by having them participate in the development of the company vision. By contrast, unethical charismatics develop the vision by themselves solely to meet their personal agendas. One unethical charismatic said, "The key thing is that it is my idea; and I am going to win with it at all costs."[50]

So, what can companies do to reduce the risks associated with unethical charismatics?[51] To start, they need a clearly written code of conduct that is

Table 17.6 **Ethical and Unethical Charismatics**

Charismatic Leader Behaviors	*Ethical Charismatics*	*Unethical Charismatics*
Exercising power	Power is used to serve others.	Power is used to dominate or manipulate others for personal gain.
Creating the vision	Followers help develop the vision.	Vision comes solely from leader and serves his/her personal agenda.
Communicating with followers	Two-way communication: Seek out viewpoints on critical issues.	One-way communication: Not open to input and suggestions from others.
Accepting feedback	Open to feedback. Willing to learn from criticism.	Inflated ego thrives on attention and admiration of yes-men. Avoid or punish candid feedback.
Stimulating followers intellectually	Want followers to think and question status quo as well as leader's views.	Don't want followers to think. Want uncritical, unquestioning acceptance of leader's ideas.
Developing followers	Focus on developing people with whom they interact. Express confidence in them and share recognition with others.	Insensitive and unresponsive to followers' needs and aspirations.
Moral standards	Follow self-guided principles that may go against popular opinion. Have three virtues: courage, a sense of fairness or justice, and integrity.	Follow standards only if they satisfy immediate self-interests. Manipulate impressions so that others think they are "doing the right thing." Use communication skills to manipulate others to support their personal agenda.

Source: J.M. Howell & B.J. Avolio, "The Ethics of Charismatic Leadership: Submission or Liberation?" *Academy of Management Executive* 6, no. 2 (1992): 43-54.

fairly and consistently enforced for all managers. Next, companies should recruit, select, and promote managers with high ethical standards. Also, companies need to train leaders how to value, seek, and use diverse points of view. Leaders and subordinates also need training regarding ethical leader behaviors so abuses can be recognized and corrected. Finally, companies should celebrate and reward people who exhibit ethical behaviors, especially ethical leader behaviors.[52]

7.2 *Transformational Leadership*

transformational leadership leadership that generates awareness and acceptance of a group's purpose and mission and gets employees to see beyond their own needs and self-interest for the good of the group

While charismatic leaders are able to articulate a clear vision, model values consistent with that vision, communicate high performance expectations, and establish very strong relationships between themselves and their followers, **transformational leadership** goes further by generating awareness and acceptance of a group's purpose and mission and by getting employees to see beyond their own needs and self-interest for the good of the group.[53] Transformational leaders, like charismatic leaders, are visionary. However, transformational leaders transform their organizations by getting their followers to accomplish more than they intended and even more than they thought possible. Transformational leaders are able to make their followers feel as if they are a vital part of the organization and can help them see how their jobs fit with the organization's vision. By linking individual and organizational interests, transformational leaders encourage followers to make sacrifices for the organization, because they know that they will prosper when the organization prospers. There are four components of transformational leadership: charismatic leadership or idealized influence, inspirational motivation, intellectual stimulation, and individualized consideration.[54]

Charismatic leadership or idealized influence means that transformational leaders act as role models for their followers. Because transformational leaders put others' needs ahead of their own and share risks with followers, they are admired, respected, and trusted, and followers want to emulate them. Thus, in contrast to purely charismatic leaders (especially unethical charismatics), transformational leaders can be counted on to do the right thing and maintain high standards for ethical and personal conduct. For example, GE's CEO, Jack Welch, acts as a role model for his employees (three vice presidents and the heads of GE's 12 businesses) by setting and monitoring specific performance targets for each of them. Each of these top managers also receives a detailed, handwritten, two-page performance evaluation from Welch each year. Said Welch, "I do the evaluations on Sunday nights in my library at home. It gives me a chance to reflect on each business." Modeling their behavior after Welch, these top managers do the same with their direct reports. Thomas E. Dunham of GE's Medical Systems said, "Welch preaches it from the top, and people see it at the bottom."[55] Accordingly, Welch serves as a role model for all of GE's managers.

Personal Productivity Tip

Be a Good Follower

David Ogilvy, founder of Olgilvy & Mather, told this story about the importance of being a good follower. He wrote:

> *On the night before a major battle, the first Duke of Marlborough was reconnoitering the terrain. He and his staff were on horseback. Marlborough dropped his glove. Cadogan, his chief of staff, dismounted, picked up the glove and handed it to Marlborough. . . . Later that evening, Marlborough issued his final order: "Cadogan, put a battery of guns where I dropped my glove." "I have already done so," replied Cadogan. He had read Marlborough's mind, and anticipated his order. Cadogan was the kind of follower who makes leadership easy.*

Source: D. Ogilvy, "Leadership," in *The Book of Business Wisdom*, ed. P. Krass (New York: Wiley, 1997).

Inspirational motivation means that transformational leaders motivate and inspire followers by providing meaning and challenge to their work. By clearly communicating expectations and demonstrating commitment to goals, transformational leaders help followers envision future states, such as the organizational vision. In turn, this leads to greater enthusiasm and optimism about the future. For GE's Jack Welch, inspirational motivation is rooted in his belief that everyone at GE can make a difference. Said Welch, "The idea flow from the human spirit is absolutely unlimited. All you have to do is tap into that well. I don't like to use the word efficiency. It's creativity. It's a belief that every person counts."[56] Furthermore, Welch reinforces his beliefs by spreading organizational rewards to all levels. Stock options, which used to be reserved for top managers, have been given to 27,000 GE employees. Of those, more than 1,200 (800 below senior management) have options worth more than $1 million. And Welch loves spreading those rewards around. Welch said, "It means that everyone is getting the rewards, not just a few of us. That's a big deal. We're changing their game and their lives. They've got their kids' tuition or they've got a second house. That's a real kick."

Intellectual stimulation means that transformational leaders encourage followers to be creative and innovative, to question assumptions, and to look at problems and situations in new ways, even if they are different from the leader's ideas. For example, at General Electric's Corporate Executive Council sessions, where GE's top 30 managers meet before the end of each financial quarter, CEO Welch presses top managers by insisting on candid, unfiltered discussions and opinions from everyone. His executives describe these sessions as "food fights" and "free-for-alls." The intent is not to bruise egos or shame poor performers, but to realistically face up to problems that need solving. Welch also brings managers and employees from GE's 12 businesses together each January in Boca Raton, Florida, to communicate ideas and successes so that best practices are shared across all parts of GE. The point, again, is to look for good solutions wherever they can be found.

Individualized consideration means that transformational leaders pay special attention to followers' individual needs by creating learning opportunities, accepting and tolerating individual differences, encouraging two-way communication, and being a good listener. One of the ways in which Jack Welch shows individualized consideration is through the personal, spontaneous handwritten notes that he sends to people throughout GE. When William Woodburn, who manages GE's industrial diamonds business, turned down a promotion because he didn't want to uproot his teenage daughter, Welch wrote to him, saying, "Bill, we like you for a lot of reasons—one of them is that you are a very special person. You proved it again this morning. Good for you and your lucky family. Make Diamonds a great business and keep your priorities straight." Woodburn responded that this gesture ". . . showed me he cared about me not as a manager but as a person," and "that means a lot."[57]

transactional leadership leadership based on an exchange process, in which followers are rewarded for good performance and punished for poor performance

Finally, a distinction needs to be drawn between transformational leadership and transactional leadership. While transformational leaders use visionary and inspirational appeals to influence followers, **transactional leadership** is based on an exchange process, in which followers are rewarded for good performance and punished for poor performance. When leaders administer rewards fairly and offer followers the rewards that they want, followers will often reciprocate with effort. However, transactional leaders often over-rely on discipline or threats to bring performance up to standards. While this may work in the short run, it's much less effective in the long run. Also, as discussed in Chapters 12 and 16, many leaders and organizations have difficulty successfully linking pay practices to individual performance. The result is that studies consistently show that transformational leadership is much more effective on average than transactional leadership. In the U.S., Canada, Japan, and India, and at all organizational levels, from first-level supervisors to upper level executives, followers view transformational leaders as much better leaders and are much more satisfied when working for them. Furthermore, companies with transformational leaders have significantly better financial performance.[58]

Review 7
Visionary Leadership

Strategic leadership requires visionary, charismatic, and transformational leadership. Visionary leadership creates a positive image of the future that motivates organizational members and provides direction for future planning and goal setting. Charismatic leaders have strong, confident, dynamic personalities that attract followers, enable them to create strong bonds, and inspire followers to accomplish the leader's vision. Followers of ethical charismatic leaders work harder, are more committed and satisfied, are better performers, are more likely to trust their leaders. Followers can be just as supportive and committed to unethical charismatics, but these leaders can pose a tremendous risk for companies. Unethical charismatics control and manipulate followers and do what is best for themselves instead of their organizations. To reduce the risks associated with unethical charismatics, companies need to enforce a clearly written code of conduct; recruit, select, and promote managers with high ethical standards; train leaders how to value, seek, and use diverse points of view; teach everyone in the company to recognize unethical leader behaviors; and celebrate and reward people who exhibit ethical behaviors. Transformational leadership goes beyond charismatic leadership by generating awareness and acceptance of a group's purpose and mission and by getting employees to see beyond their own needs and self-interest for the good of the group. The four components of transformational leadership are charisma or idealized influence, inspirational motivation, intellectual stimulation, and individualized consideration.

What**Really**Happened?

In the opening case, you learned that Microsoft, one of the most successful companies of the last two decades, was encountering leadership problems. Microsoft had become slow and bureaucratic. Employees did not understand the company's long-term vision and strategic plans. Top managers didn't feel they had the discretion and control to run their divisions and departments as they saw fit. And, employees were not comfortable with the leadership styles of several top managers. Read the answers to the opening case to find out what Microsoft did to address these leadership issues.

Just what makes a good leader, and do I have whatever that is? What do good leaders do?

What makes a good leader? In general, trait theory indicates that leaders have more drive, a greater desire to lead, honesty/integrity, self-confidence, emotional stability, cognitive ability, and knowledge of the business. Throughout his career at Microsoft, Steven Ballmer has had all but one of these traits, emotional stability. Ballmer was known for his explosive temper and for his loud voice, shouting himself hoarse on numerous occasions. He once screamed at a group of engineers while smacking a baseball bat into his hand. However, since becoming president of Microsoft, second only to Bill Gates, Ballmer has worked on his emotional stability. Said Ballmer, "I'm trying to temper myself. I don't think I've mellowed. But I try to redirect my energy." Indeed, Jon Shirley, a member of Microsoft's board, said, "He's certainly changed. He's calmer." A former Microsoft executive said of Ballmer, "Of the upper management at Microsoft, Steve's the one that gets it."

What do good leaders do? Two key leader behaviors are initiating structure and consideration. Initiating structure has its primary effect on subordinates' job performance and is the degree to which a leader structures the roles of followers by setting goals, giving directions, setting deadlines, and assigning tasks to employees. Initiating structure is something at which Microsoft's leaders have always excelled. From its inception, Microsoft has always closely tracked productivity and focused its employees on beating its original competitors, such as IBM and Apple, and today's competitors, such as Sun Microsystems (Java), Red Hat Software (Linux), and America Online. Today, however, Steve Ballmer and other Microsoft managers have begun to emphasize considerate leader behavior, too. For example, now that he has "calmed down," Ballmer is much more likely to listen to what people have to say before speaking himself. General manager Bill Veghte said, "I see him coaching more than in the past—as opposed to pushing." Ballmer admits to the change, too, saying, "I'm used to diving in deeply. [But] Now I'm trying to let other people dive in before I do." Finally, while he still gets upset, Ballmer's commitment to considerate leader behavior is serious—he has even given up his baseball bat, turning it over to a marketing vice president who reports to him.

When do leaders need to adapt their behavior? I've been leading this way for years, but now it seems I need to change. Why?

The four major situational leadership theories, Fiedler's contingency theory, path-goal theory, Hersey and Blanchard's situational theory, and Vroom and Yetton's normative decision model, all assume that the effectiveness of any leadership style, the way a leader generally behaves toward followers, depends on the situation. Accordingly, there is no one "best" leadership style. Instead, there are better or worse leadership styles for particular situations. With the exception of Fiedler's contingency theory, situational leadership theories assume that leaders are capable of adapting and adjusting their leadership styles to fit the demands of different situations.

In terms of Hersey and Blanchard's situational theory, Steve Ballmer seems to have changed from a *telling* leadership style, in which followers are told what, how, when, and where to do particular tasks, to a *delegating* style, in which leaders basically let workers "run their own show" and make their own decisions. For instance, Microsoft's decision making slowed to a crawl as decisions large and small were sent up the hierarchy to Ballmer and Gates. Chris Williams, Microsoft's vice president of human resources, said that as a result of this *telling* style, "Senior executives didn't feel like they were in control of their own destiny." However, now that Ballmer has changed to a *delegating* style, Microsoft's top managers can make whatever decisions they want as long as they make their revenue and profit goals. Likewise, while Ballmer is glad to attend "kickoff" meetings to help get new project and product groups off to a good start, he now leaves subsequent meetings and decisions to his managers. "I have to grow from being a leader to being a leader of leaders," he said. The early results are positive. Decisions are being made faster, and Microsoft's top managers are comfortable with the change. Robbie Bach, who runs

Microsoft's Home and Retail Division, said that he "feels like I am running my own little company."

And how can I lead people to produce in the short term, while at the same time helping them understand where we're headed in the long term?

Strategic leadership is the ability to anticipate, envision, maintain flexibility, think strategically, and work with others to initiate changes that will create a positive future for an organization. Similarly, visionary leadership creates a positive image of the future that motivates organizational members and provides direction for future planning and goal setting. But with over 183 products for several different operating systems, dozens of different Internet sites, and acquisitions of cable TV providers, computer device manufacturers, and other software, Microsoft seemed to be heading off into 50 different directions. The irony was that even Microsoft's employees weren't sure where it was going.

Ballmer is trying to reassert strategic and visionary leadership through what Microsoft calls "Vision, Version 2." Microsoft's previous vision was a personal computer on every desk and every home. The point of this vision was to encourage Microsoft's marketers and software writers to produce as many Windows-related software products as possible. However, "Vision, Version 2" changes that by emphasizing the importance of doing what customers want. Ballmer said, "Follow the customer. That's the No. 1 thing you do if you are lost." Accordingly, with customers needing software for their palm PCs, for digital cable-TV set-top boxes, and for numerous other devices that increasingly contain computer chips and other kinds of software, Microsoft's "Vision, Version 2" now frees Microsoft employees and divisions to produce software for products and platforms other than for Windows and personal computers. Founder and CEO Bill Gates called it "a very big deal."

Sources: S. Hamm, "'I'm Trying to Let Other People Dive In Before I Do.'" *Business Week,* 17 May 1999, 110. S. Hamm & T.J. Mullaney, "Remaking Microsoft: Why America's Most Successful Company Needed an Overhaul," *Business Week,* 17 May 1999, 106. B. Japsen, "Amid Settlement Talks, Microsoft Plans Major Reorganization," *Chicago Tribune,* 30 March 1999, Business 3. Times Wire Services, "Microsoft Plans Customer-Based Changes, Seeks Silverberg's Return: Software Firm Will Restructure into Four Groups and Hopes to Bring Back Programming Whiz to Lead One," *Los Angeles Times,* 8 February 1999, C1.

Key Terms

What Would You Do-II?

American Airlines Headquarters, Fort Worth, Texas. With major hubs in Dallas/Fort Worth, Chicago, New York, and Miami, and with direct flights to Europe, Latin America, South America, and the Orient, American Airlines can take passengers almost anywhere in the world. However, because of recent company problems, American's passengers have been very unhappy and have filed thousands of complaints with the U.S. Department of Transportation about rude and unhelpful employees. Passengers are also angry about being late. With only two-thirds of American's flights arriving on time, American ranks last on the Department of Transportation's list for on-time performance.

While American's CEO, Donald Carty, blames the Federal Aviation Administration for the late arrivals (because it installed new air traffic computer systems in American's major hubs, Chicago, New York, and Fort Worth), there is little doubt that poor service and negative employee attitudes are largely the result of a long, adversarial relationship between American Airlines and its employees. For instance, the Allied Pilots Association, which represents American's pilots, became unhappy when American purchased Reno Air so it could continue to expand its routes to the West Coast. American's pilots wanted the company to immediately double the salaries of Reno Air's pilots (who made about half what American paid). The company refused, because it was planning to increase the pay of Reno Air's Pilots over an 18-month period as they became certified to fly American's planes. Consequently, the Allied Pilots Association called for a two-week "sick-out," in which as many as half of American's pilots did not report to work, thus forcing American to cancel up to half of its flights. The sick-out cost the company well over $200 million. Relations between American and the pilot's union became even more strained when the courts subsequently ruled that the sick-out violated the labor union's contract with the company. And when pilots ignored the court order to return to work, the judge fined the union $45 million to pay for the losses incurred by the company.

American's pilots, however, aren't the only employees upset with company management. Gate agents and flight attendants have been dissatisfied, too. While American's senior gate agents earn as much as $20 an hour, those hired since 1996 are limited to no more than $13 an hour. When people working side by side earn such different wages, the resentment toward management can be strong. Said gate agent Sally Fowlkes, "There is so little trust." Likewise, American has a history of strained relationships with its flight attendants. Several years ago, American's flight attendants went on strike right before the Thanksgiving holiday, one of the busiest flying seasons of the year. While a presidential order ended the strike by requiring both parties to enter into binding arbitration, that forced settlement did little to improve relations between flight attendants and the company. Today, flight attendants are not any more excited about American's most recent contract offer. In fact, many flight attendants have started wearing buttons saying, "Just Say No," or "No WAAy AA." Jennifer, a 12-year flight attendant, said, "I'm a team player, and I really try to look at these things to see what's best for everybody overall. . . . This benefits the company far more than it benefits us." Laura, a 9-year veteran, said, "Not only is this not that great a contract, my [union] leadership is trying to tell me that it's an industry-leading contract. And, I'm sorry, it's just not."

Ironically, when Donald Carty replaced notorious tough-guy Robert Crandall as CEO, everyone was optimistic that he would be able to improve relationships with employees. And Carty has certainly tried. Travel benefits have been improved. A relaxed summer dress code was instituted for employees. And, in nearly every speech he gave, Carty stressed the importance of a positive work culture that "involves and excites" employees. Indeed, after the pilots' sick-out, Carty told employees, "Like all families, we're not always going to agree. I hope as our pilots return to work you will assume that any pilot you see is one of the pilots who chose to come to work."

Yet, significant problems remain despite his efforts. Carty summarized his feelings this way: "There have probably been a few more frustrations than I would have expected."

If you were helping Don Carty and American Airlines with its leadership problems, what would you do?

Sources: S. McCartney, "On Carty's Watch, American Hits Turbulence," *The Wall Street Journal,* 23 July 1999, B1. S. McCartney, "At American Airlines, Pilots Trace Grievances to Deals in Lean Years—With Carriers Flush, Unions Get Tougher; Industry Braces for More Disputes—But Judge Orders Fliers Back," *The Wall Street Journal,* 11 February 1999, A1. S. McCartney, "Tension at AMR Outlasts Fading Sick-out—Union Remains Hard-Line; Near-Normal Schedule Is Promised for Today," *The Wall Street Journal,* 16 February 1999, A3. D. Reed, "American Airlines and Pilots Deeply Divided: Both Sides Want a Negotiated Peace, But Stakes Are High," *Fort Worth Star-Telegram,* 17 April 1999, Business 1. D. Reed, "American Proposal Drawing Criticism: Some Attendants Say Contract Falls Short," *Fort Worth Star-Telegram,* 2 July 1999, Business 1. W. Zellner, "Gliding Toward a Labor Union? American's Ticket Agents Are Set to Vote on Joining the CWA," *Business Week,* 26 October 1998, 42.

Critical-Thinking Video Case

Leadership: Sunshine Cleaning Systems

Sunshine Cleaning Systems is a privately held company, located in Florida, with about 1,000 employees and roughly $10 million per year in sales. The company provides janitorial service, pressure cleaning, and window cleaning. Some of Sunshine's customers include the Miami Dolphin Training Center, the Orlando Arena (home of the Orlando Magic basketball team), the Florida Citrus Bowl, the Ft. Lauderdale Airport, the Florida Turnpike, the Orange County Convention Center, and banks, restaurants, and office buildings throughout Florida. Sunshine recently expanded outside Florida and now cleans all the windows of the 14 buildings of the Smithsonian Institute.

Founder Larry Calufetti has instilled his own "coaching" leadership style throughout the company. A former catcher for the New York Mets, Calufetti believes his baseball experiences helped him develop his leadership style.

Critical-Thinking Questions

1. How does coaching differ from managing?
2. What are the characteristics of a coaching leadership style at Sunshine?

Management Decisions

Unhealthy Hideaway Hospital

As the new manager of the local hospital, you knew that there were problems to be solved, but you never thought they were this bad. With the hospital located in a vacation town, you knew there would be seasonal swings in the amount of care that the hospital needed to provide. But you didn't realize that the hospital had to be able to provide care for as many as 100,000 people in July and August and as few as 15,000 in December, January, and February. You knew it would be difficult to attract staff to work at the hospital. With small hotel rooms costing as much as $200 a night during high season, and with apartment rentals going for $1,000 a week, living expenses can be extraordinary. But you didn't think that your medical staff would leave their jobs to make $25 an hour cleaning houses and waiting on tables.

You knew that the building needed work, but you didn't expect basics like the roof and air conditioning to need major repairs. And, you never figured that all medical records and lab reports would be handwritten—not in this day and age. With annual costs running three-quarters of a million dollars, you knew that the emergency room needed to be staffed with doctors 24 hours a day. But you didn't realize that the emergency room would only see a couple of patients a day between Labor Day and Memorial Day each year.

You knew that the hospital was struggling financially, having just come out of bankruptcy.

But you didn't know that it had lost nearly a million and a half dollars through the first six months of the year. And you knew that the hospital needed new leadership. That's why they hired you. But you didn't know that the previous leader interfered with doctors' decisions, that six of the hospital's board members resigned to protest his poor leadership, and that other wealthy board members promised to pull the hospital out of financial trouble if only he would resign. (He didn't and was later fired.)

Questions

1. As leader of this resort hospital, what would be your four top priorities, and why?
2. Which leadership theories or ideas seem most relevant to you in this situation? Why?
3. Using the leadership theories or ideas you think most relevant, what actions would you take to begin to address the priorities you identified in Question 1?

Source: C. Gentry, "Battle at Island Hospital Pits the Elite vs. the Elite," *The Wall Street Journal,* 18 September 1999, NE1.

Management Decisions

"To Name or Not to Name, That Is the Question"

Herb Kelleher, chairman, CEO, and president of Southwest Airlines, and Jack Welch, chairman and CEO of General Electric, are two of the best corporate leaders around, having led their companies to unparalleled long-term success in their industries. However, contrary to Kelleher's jovial claims that he is "immortal," neither will lead their companies forever. In fact, Kelleher, who is 68, has first-stage prostate cancer for which he is receiving radiation treatment and from which he expects a full recovery. Kelleher said, ". . . I was diagnosed as having a rather mundane, routine and fairly insignificant case of prostate cancer. I don't intend to make any change in my lifestyle." Welch, on the other hand, who is 64, is a year away from GE's mandatory retirement age of 65.

Kelleher and Welch, however, have taken very different approaches to the issue of CEO succession, that is, deciding who will follow them as chairman and CEO. Kelleher steadfastly refuses to name a possible successor or even discuss the company's succession plan. After his cancer was made public, he said, "There is no need to update any succession plan. The board discusses it on a regular basis and has for many years." Plus, Southwest's board of directors does not have a succession committee to identify potential candidates. And, Southwest's senior managers apparently have little contact with or exposure to its board of directors. One of Southwest's board members said, "If Herb were to contract a terminal illness and knew he had six months to live, I'm sure when the time came that he thought he needed to step down, we'd probably accept his judgment as to who should succeed him. He knows better than we."

By contrast, at GE, there are at least a half dozen people who have been clearly identified as potential successors to Welch, though no clear favorite has been indicated. Furthermore, Welch makes sure that GE's board of directors has contact with these people, having them make frequent presentations to the board and having his board members spend time with them as they do their jobs.

However, other companies, such as Coca-Cola, Wal-Mart, and Intel, have taken the approach of naming their successors while previous CEOs were still in office. For instance, David Glass, who is currently Wal-Mart's CEO, was identified as Sam Walton's replacement long before Sam Walton stepped down as Wal-Mart's CEO. Likewise, the late Roberto C. Goizueta, Coca-Cola's CEO, named Douglas Ivester as his replacement several years before stepping down.

So, these examples show three approaches to leadership succession: not naming any potential candidates, naming a collection of potential candidates but not identifying a favorite, and clearly identifying the CEO replacement long before the previous CEO steps down.

Questions

1. Describe two disadvantages of each approach.

2. Describe two advantages of each approach.

3. If you were a CEO, which succession approach would you favor? Why?

Sources: J.A. Byrne, J. Reingold, & R.A. Melcher, "Wanted: A Few Good CEOs; Why Managing Succession Is Such a Problem—And What Companies Ought to Do about It," *Business Week,* 11 August 1997, 64. S. McCartney, "Who's News: Southwest Airlines Chief to Be Treated for Prostate Cancer but Stay on Job," *The Wall Street Journal,* 12 August 1999, B11. M. Murrary, "Your Career Matters: GE's Next Generation Prepares for Life Without 'Jack," *The Wall Street Journal,* 3 August 1999, B1. W. Zellner, "Earth to Herb: Pick a Co-Pilot," *Business Week,* 16 August 1999, 70.

Develop Your Management Potential

Fear Not—Volunteer to Take Charge!

You can learn something about leadership from reading books. But until you're actually in charge, you won't be able to test those ideas for yourself. You can learn a tremendous amount about leadership by studying and observing the people who lead you, but until you're the leader, you won't know if their leadership practices and styles will work for you. In short, when learning about leadership, there is no substitute for leadership experience. So the next time there is an opportunity to lead, and someone asks, "Alright, who wants to take charge of this?" step forward and volunteer to take charge!

Then, once you're in charge, record your thoughts, feelings, and observations in a daily diary for one week. Turn in the diary and answer the questions shown below.

Questions

1. Describe what you were "in charge" of and where and how you were "in charge."

2. What surprised you most about being in charge? Explain.

3. Many people are fearful about assuming leadership roles. Author Peter McWilliams says that fear is short for "False Expectations Appearing Real." Was there something about being a leader that you feared or expected to be difficult that was much easier than you expected?

4. What was the most difficult thing about being a leader? Explain.

5. What do you know now about leadership that you wish you had known when you were first put in charge?

Chapter Eighteen

Chapter 18 Outline

Managing Communication

What Would **You** Do?

Buckman Laboratories, Memphis, Tennessee. Buckman Labs is a maker of a variety of specialty chemicals used to treat pulp and paper for recycling and publishing, to keep mechanical equipment corrosion free, to preserve and cure animal hides into fine leather, to slow or prevent fires through the use of fire retardants, dispersants, and defoamers, and to enhance wood products by preventing staining and rotting. As sales director for Buckman labs, you spend nearly half of your time helping Buckman's U.S. and international sales representatives solve problems for existing customers. For example, when a client, Manistique Papers, was unable to remove the ink from the old magazine paper it was recycling, your local sales representatives called wanting you to put the company in touch with people at Buckman who could solve the problem. Traditionally, the solution has been to hire more Ph.D.-trained chemists and fly them to customers who needed their help and expertise. This worked well when the company was small. But with significant growth and overseas expansion, there just aren't enough company chemists to go around anymore. And, even if there were, with customers in Africa, Europe, the Pacific Rim, and South America, it would take too long to fly technical support to every customer that needed immediate help. Not surprisingly, sales representatives have been frustrated by how long it takes to get answers to customers' questions. Indeed, since questions were typically routed to you and then out to the appropriate technical experts, it usually took three to five days to begin addressing customer problems—an eternity for sales representatives who are being pressured by customers for solutions. You thought that the corporate e-mail would speed things up and encourage faster, better communication. But it hasn't. While e-mail is great for quickly identifying problems ("Hey, one of my customers is having some problems with rotting wood and we can't figure out why. Here's the situation . . ."), it still has to be routed to the right people. And, here's the critical part, those people have to be willing to share their expertise with customers and sales representatives. In fact, what surprised you the most was that people in different parts of the company weren't always willing to share their knowledge with others. Well, with customer satisfaction on the line, you've got to find a way to improve communication within and outside the company. The first thing you need to figure out is why people in different parts of the company are so reluctant to communicate with each other. Is it perception, culture, or simply poor communication techniques? Next, anything's got to be better than having you, the sales manager, as the first point of contact for expert help, but what? How can you match sales representatives with the right technical experts without having to serve as the go-between? There's got to be a reasonable technological solution. But if e-mail wasn't the technological solution, and everybody uses e-mail, what's the answer? **If you were the sales director at Buckman Labs and wanted to improve company communications, what would you do?**

Sources: Buckman Laboratories. [Online] Available http://www.buckman.com/home.html, 5 September 1999. J. Eckhouse, "Get Creative with Knowledge Sharing—In Today's Culture, Businesses Must Rebuild Their Processes to Take Advantage of Their Knowledge Base," *Information Week*, 8 February 1999, ER19. D.J. Knight, "Strategy in Practice: Making It Happen," *Strategy & Leadership* 26, No. 3 (1 July 1998): 29. M.N. Martinez, "The Collective Power of Employee Knowledge," *HR Magazine* 43, No. 2 (1 February 1998): 88. S. Thurm, "What Do You Know? Getting Employees to Share Their Knowledge Isn't as Simple as Installing New Software; Just Ask Buckman Labs," *The Wall Street Journal*, 21 June 1999, R10.

Like Buckman Lab's sales director, it's estimated that managers spend over 80 percent of their day communicating with others.[1] Indeed, much of the basic management process—making things happen, meeting the competition, organizing people, projects, and processes, and leading—cannot be performed without effective communication. If this weren't reason enough to study communication, consider that oral communication, such as listening, following instructions, conversing, and giving feedback, is the most important skill for college graduates who are entering the work force.[2] Furthermore, across all industries, poor communication skill is the single most important reason that people do not advance in their careers.[3] Finally, communication is especially important for top managers. Mark DeMichele, president of Arizona Public Service Company, says that "communication is the key to success. A CEO can have good ideas, a vision, and a plan. But they also have to be able to communicate those plans to people who work for them."[4]

This chapter begins by examining the role of perception in communication and how perception can make it difficult for managers to achieve effective communication. Next, you'll read about the communication process and the various kinds of communication found in most organizations. In the last half of the chapter, the focus is on improving communication in organizations. You'll learn about the significant barriers to effective one-on-one communication and organization-wide communication. But, more importantly, you'll learn ways to overcome those barriers, too.

Communication

When Grand Metropolitan PLC, a British-based firm, purchased Pillsbury Corporation, the new management sensed that Pillsbury's top managers had become isolated and that they weren't receiving the information, good or bad, that they needed to run the company well. And, they were right. Pillsbury employees generally ignored the company's highly promoted suggestion box system, refused to call its in-house whistleblower hotline (to report problems), and had little, if any, contact with top management.

To change this situation, Pillsbury hired InTouch, a neutral outside firm that uses voice mail technology to anonymously record employees' comments, which are then transcribed and forwarded straight to Pillsbury's new CEO. And to encourage employees to call, Pillsbury distributed the InTouch phone number on stickers, wallet cards, and even refrigerator magnets. Karen Gustafson, director of employee communications, said, "We wanted people to call whenever a thought hit them." And, because callers knew the system was completely anonymous (transcripts don't even identify a caller's gender), the calls started flooding in. As a result, management began learning about problems (an inaccurate time clock and slow methods of reimbursing employees for travel expenses) and opportunities (employees identified stores that didn't carry Pillsbury food products) that it wasn't otherwise hearing from its employees.[5]

communication
the process of transmitting information from one person or place to another

Communication is the process of transmitting information from one person or place to another. When Pillsbury's employees began calling InTouch, information was transmitted from them directly to Pillsbury's CEO. Why didn't Pillsbury's employees simply share this information with top management? Why did it take the InTouch phone system to get employees to communicate? Because it was widely perceived that employees would be punished if they came forward with negative information about the company or its managers. After reading the next two sections, you should be able to:

1 explain the role that **perception** plays in communication and **communication problems**.

2 describe the communication process and the various **kinds of communication in organizations**.

1 Perception and Communication Problems

One study showed that when asked whether their supervisor gives recognition for good work, 13 percent of employees said that their supervisor gives a pat on the back, while 14 percent said that their supervisor gives sincere and thorough praise. But when the supervisors of these employees were asked if they give recognition for good work, 82 percent said they gave pats on the back, while 80 percent said that they give sincere and thorough praise.[6] Given that these managers and employees worked closely together, how could they have had such different perceptions of something as simple as praise?

Let's learn more about perception and communication problems by examining **1.1** *the basic perception process,* **1.2** *perception problems, how we* **1.3** *perceive others and* **1.4** *ourselves, and how all of these factors make it difficult for managers to achieve effective communication.*

1.1
Basic Perception Process

perception
the process by which individuals attend to, organize, interpret, and retain information from their environments

As shown in Figure 18.1, **perception** is the process by which individuals attend to, organize, interpret, and retain information from their environments. And since communication is the process of transmitting information from one person or place to another, perception is obviously a key part of communication. However, perception can be a key obstacle to communication, as well.

perceptual filters
the personality-, psychology-, or experience-based differences that influence people to ignore or pay attention to particular stimuli

As people perform their jobs, they are exposed to a wide variety of informational stimuli, such as e-mails, direct conversations with the boss or coworkers, rumors heard over lunch, stories about the company in the press, or a video broadcast of a speech from the CEO to all employees. However, exposure to an informational stimulus is no guarantee that an individual will pay attention or attend to that stimulus. People experience stimuli through their own **perceptual filters**—the personality-, psychology-, or experience-based differences that influence them to ignore or pay attention to particular stimuli. Because of filtering, people exposed to the same information will often disagree about what they saw or heard. For example, every major stadium in the National Football League has a huge TV monitor on which fans can watch replays. As the slow-motion videotape is replayed on the stadium monitor, you can often hear cheers *and* boos, as fans of both teams perceive the same replay in completely different ways. This happens because sports fans' perceptual filters predispose them to attend to stimuli that support their teams and not their opponents.

Been There, Done That

Deborah Tannen, author and socio-linguist, believes that men tend to view conversations as "negotiations" in which they try to achieve status and power and maintain independence. In contrast, women view conversations as a way to connect with people, to find commonality and build networks of connection and intimacy. In this interview with Richard Koonce, she discusses the different ways that men and women communicate in the workplace.

Q: How much do you think current communication problems in the workplace are related to gender?

A: Gender cross-cuts everything else. You could say that all workplace problems are about power differentials. You tell one of your staff what to do and he or she doesn't do it. Or you think your boss makes unreasonable demands. All of those things are filtered through gender. The way you expect a male boss to talk is different from how you expect a female boss to talk. You might not realize that if your boss were the other sex and talking to you in the same way, you would have a different reaction.

> "... if your boss were the other sex and talking to you the same way, you would have a different reaction."

Q: You also say that no one conversational style is best and that men and women can learn important things from each other's styles.

A: To say that one conversational style is better than another is like saying Spanish is better than French. In most organizations, a style, usually a predominantly male one, was established as the norm before women arrived in great numbers and positions of authority. Women weren't there when the rules were set so, in that sense, women's and men's styles aren't considered equally valid.

Q: Given that male imprint on many corporate cultures, should women adopt male styles of communication if they want to get ahead?

A: There is no one right way to communicate. Women bring many styles to the workplace that are effective, sometimes more effective than the norm. They tend to make people feel included, ask for their input, and give praise—things that all people seem to like. You don't find men complaining that their bosses praise them too much. There are women who adopt typically male styles, and that works great. They're happy that way. Other women find that if they adopt male styles, they get negative responses. So, they don't feel comfortable doing that. And there are women who say, "I stick with my style and do a good job. The people I work with learn that's me." What matters is the specific situation—what a woman feels comfortable doing and how people around her react.

Q: How do you counsel men who want to be more effective at managing women?

A: If you're managing people, it's important to remember that not everyone has the same style. What's right for one person may not be right for other people. I recall someone whom I interviewed and observed who thought he had the right style at work. Once a day, every day, he checked in with everyone who worked for him. Some people, generally men, thought that was too much. They felt that he was looking over their shoulders and didn't trust them to do a good job. They asked, "Why are you always coming in here to check on me?" For other staff members, generally women, it wasn't enough. They said, "You're not interested. You don't spend any time. Why should I be interested if you're not?" And for some people, his style was just right.

So, developing awareness that people have different styles is important. Try to raise your own sensitivity to the kind of responses you get so that you can gauge: This seems to be working well with this person, I'm okay. Or, this person isn't reacting well; what can I do differently? In some cases, you need to meta-communicate—in other words, talk to people about what you're doing.

Q: Are there differences in managing men and women that managers should be aware of?

A: There are things women have to watch out for in managing men and things men have to watch out for in managing women. When I was doing research for 9-5, I found that women expect more feedback from male bosses than they sometimes get. So, it's important for male bosses to tell women staff members when they're doing a good job and praise them if things are going well. In comparison, a lot of men told me that the best thing to do is hire good people and get out of their way. But not every man or woman is going to fit into these profiles.

Q: So, don't take a cookie-cutter approach to managing people based on gender?

A: Right. Treating all women the same is just as bad as treating women as men. You need to see individual differences in people. Women who manage men, however, probably do want to be aware that many men are sensitive to being told what to do by women. Women managers have to find a way to deal with that. Some women find a way to tell people what to do without actually giving orders.

Source: R. Koonce, "Language, Sex, and Power: Women and Men in the Workplace," *Training & Development* 51 (1997): 34–39.

Figure 18.1 **Basic Perception Process**

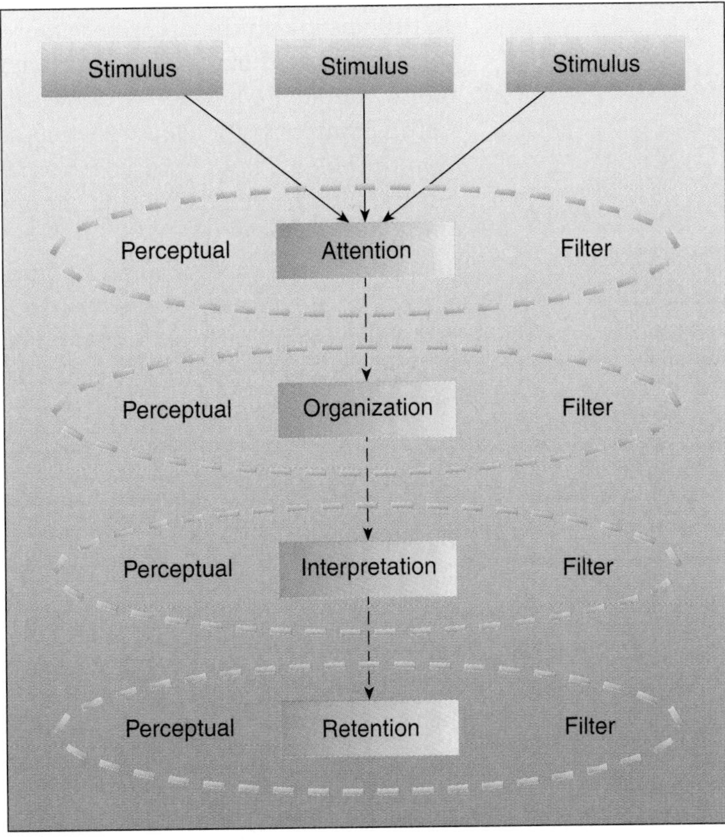

And the same perceptual filters that affect whether we believe our favorite teams were "robbed" by the referees also affect communication, that is, the transmitting of information from one person or place to another. As shown in Figure 18.1, perceptual filters affect each part of the *perception process*: attention, organization, interpretation, and retention.

Attention is the process of noticing or becoming aware of particular stimuli. Because of perceptual filters, we attend to some stimuli and not others. *Organization* is the process of incorporating new information (from the stimuli that you notice) into your existing knowledge. Because of perceptual filters, we are more likely to incorporate new knowledge that is consistent with what we already know or believe. *Interpretation* is the process of attaching meaning to new knowledge. Because of perceptual filters, our preferences and beliefs strongly influence the meaning we attach to new information (e.g., "This must mean that top management supports our project."). Finally, *retention* is the process of remembering interpreted information. In other words, retention is what we recall and commit to memory after we have perceived something. Of course, perceptual filters also affect retention, that is, what we're likely to remember in the end.

For instance, imagine that you missed the first ten minutes of a TV show and that you turned on your TV to a scene in which two people were talking to each other in a living room. As they talked, they walked around the room and picked up and then put down various items, some of which were valuable, such as a ring, a watch, and a credit card, and some of which appeared to be drug related, such as a water pipe for smoking marijuana. In fact, this situation was depicted on videotape in a well-known study that manipulated people's perceptual filters.[7] One-third of the study participants were told that these people were there to rob the apartment. Another third of the participants were told that police were on their way to conduct a drug raid and that the people in the apartment were getting rid of incriminating evidence. The remaining third of study participants were told that these people were simply waiting for a friend to show up.

After watching the video, participants were asked to list all of the objects from the video that they could remember. Not surprisingly, the different perceptual filters (theft, drug raid, and waiting for a friend) affected what the study participants attended to, how they organized the information, how they interpreted the information, and ultimately what objects they remembered from the video. People who thought a theft was in process were more likely to remember the valuable objects in the video. Those who thought a drug raid was imminent were more likely to remember drug-related objects. There was no discernable pattern to the items remembers by those who thought that the people in the video were simply waiting for a friend.

In short, because of perception and perceptual filters, people are likely to pay attention to different things, organize and interpret what they pay attention to differently, and finally remember things differently. Consequently, even when people are exposed to the same communications (e.g., organizational memos, customers, discussions with managers, etc.), they can end up with very different perceptions and understandings. This is why communication can be so difficult and frustrating for managers. Let's review some of the communication problems created by perception and perceptual filters.

1.2 *Perception Problems*

Perception creates communication problems for organizations, because people exposed to the same communication and information can end up with completely different ideas and understandings. Two of the most common perception problems in organizations are selective perception and closure.

At work, we are constantly bombarded with sensory stimuli—the phone ringing, people talking in the background, the sounds of our computers dinging as new e-mail arrives, people calling our names, etc. As limited processors of information, we cannot possibly notice, receive, and interpret all of this information. As a result, we attend to and accept some stimuli but screen out and reject others. However, this isn't a random process. **Selective perception** is the tendency to notice and accept objects and information consistent with our values, beliefs, and expectations, while ignoring or screening out or not accepting inconsistent information.

selective perception
the tendency to notice and accept objects and information consistent with our values, beliefs, and expectations, while ignoring or screening out or not accepting inconsistent information

For example, United Airlines sometimes shows a video of swimming fish as its passengers board its planes. Bob Williams, United's manager of in-flight entertainment, said, "We picked the fish because some psychological research says it's soothing." However, because of selective perception, passengers haven't viewed it that way. Kyle MacLean, who regularly flies United, said, "The first time I saw it, I thought it was really odd. And the more you fly, the more irritating it gets." Furthermore, passengers hated the "soothing" music, too. Frequent United customer John Goldwater said that on one flight, "There must have been 20 people coming back up the aisle asking them to turn it off. At first, the flight attendants were reluctant, but when it became obvious that the flight was going to be delayed, they turned it off."[8]

Since we cannot attend to all the stimuli in our environment, we selectively notice some and not others. Something out of the ordinary tends to grab our attention. © Tim Davis/Tony Stone Images

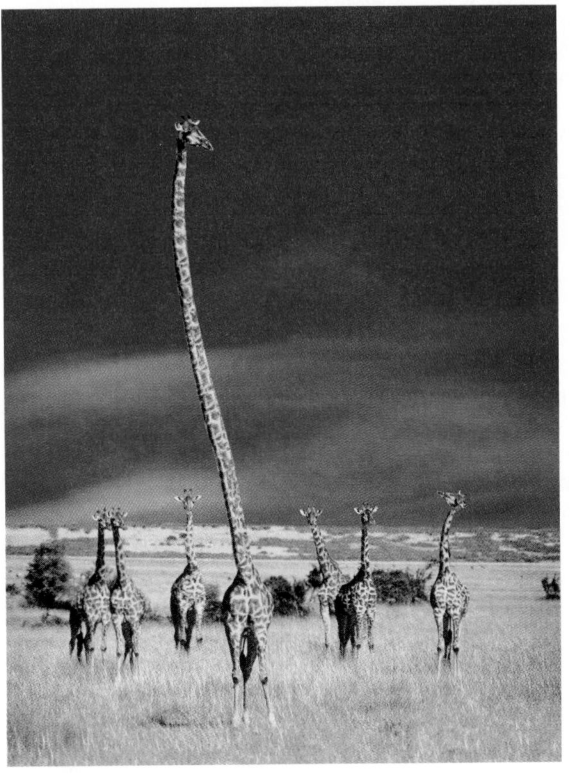

closure
the tendency to fill in gaps of missing information by assuming that what we don't know is consistent with what we already know

Once we have initial information about a person, event, or process, **closure** is the tendency to fill in the gaps where information is missing, that is, to assume that what we don't know is consistent with what we already know. If employees are told that budgets must be cut by 10 percent, they may automatically assume that 10 percent of employees will lose their jobs, too, even if that isn't the case. Not surprisingly, when closure occurs, people sometimes "fill in the gaps" with inaccurate information, and this can create problems for organizations.

For example, J.B. Hunt is one of the largest trucking firms in the nation. Historically, because of its driving school (to teach people how to drive semi-trucks), because it limits its drivers to a top speed of 59 MPH (to increase gas mileage and reduce accidents), and because its drivers drive underpowered, "cab-over" trucks (where the truck has a flat front, like a bus), the company has been perceived as one that only hires inexperienced drivers. Truck driver Carl Jackson said, "On the CB, you would hear all kinds of jokes about J.B. Hunt drivers. These guys don't want to work for someone who is the brunt of so many jokes. It's a little dumb, but I believe that is the problem of recruiting drivers." He also said, "If they would snaz up the trucks, they would be able to overcome the stigma associated with driving for them." And while the company disputes this, it recognized that this negative perception was widespread among experienced truckers, and that it was preventing the company from hiring all of the truck drivers it needed. So, to dispel these perceptions, it closed its truck driving school to discourage brand new truck drivers from applying and then raised driver pay by 33 percent to attract experienced truck drivers.[9]

1.3 Perceptions of Others

attribution theory
theory that states that we all have a basic need to understand and explain the causes of other people's behavior

Attribution theory says that we all have a basic need to understand and explain the causes of other people's behavior.[10] In other words, we need to know why people do what they do. And, according to attribution theory, we use two general reasons or attributions to explain people's behavior: an *internal attribution*, in which behavior is thought to be voluntary or under the control of the individual, and an *external attribution*, in which behavior is thought to be involuntary and outside of the control of the individual.

defensive bias
the tendency for people to perceive themselves as personally and situationally similar to someone who is having difficulty or trouble

For example, have you ever seen anyone changing a flat tire on the side of the road and thought to yourself, "What rotten luck—somebody's having a bad day"? If you did, you perceived the person through an external attribution known as the defensive bias. The **defensive bias** is the tendency for people to perceive themselves as personally and situationally similar to someone who is having difficulty or trouble.[11] And when we identify with the person in a situation, we tend to use external attributions (i.e., the situation) to explain the person's behavior. For instance, since flat tires are fairly common, it's easy to perceive ourselves in that same situation and put the blame on external causes, such as running over a nail.

Now, let's assume a different situation, this time in the workplace:

> *A utility company worker puts a ladder on a utility pole and then climbs up to do his work. As he's doing his work, he falls from the ladder and seriously injures himself.*[12]

Answer this question: Who or what caused the accident? If you thought, "It's not the worker's fault. Anybody could fall from a tall ladder," then you're still operating from a defensive bias in which you see yourself as personally and situationally similar to someone who is having difficulty or trouble. In other words, you made an external attribution and attributed the accident to an external cause, meaning the situation.

fundamental attribution error
the tendency to ignore external causes of behavior and to attribute other people's actions to internal causes

However, most accident investigations end up blaming the worker (i.e., an internal attribution) and not the situation (i.e., an external attribution) in which people do their jobs. Typically, 60 percent to 80 percent of the 5,000 or so workplace accidents that occur each year are blamed on "operator error," that is, the employees themselves. However, more complete investigations usually show that workers are really only responsible for 30 percent to 40 percent of all workplace accidents.[13] Why would accident investigators be so quick to blame workers? Because they are committing the **fundamental attribution error**, which is the tendency to ignore external causes of behavior and to attribute other people's actions to internal causes.[14] In other words, when investigators examine the possible causes of an accident, they're much more likely to assume that the accident is a function of the person and not the situation.

Which attribution, the defensive bias or the fundamental attribution error, are workers likely to make when something goes wrong? In general, workers are more likely to perceive events and explain behavior from a defensive bias. Because they do the work themselves, and because they see themselves as similar to others who make mistakes, have accidents, or are otherwise held responsible for things that go wrong at work, workers are likely to attribute problems to external causes, such as failed machinery, poor support, or inadequate training. By contrast, because they are typically observers (who don't do the work themselves), and see themselves as situationally and personally different from workers, managers tend to commit the fundamental attribution error and blame mistakes, accidents, and other things that go wrong on workers (i.e., an internal attribution).

Consequently, in most workplaces, when things go wrong, the natural response is one in which workers and managers can be expected to take completely opposite views. Therefore, together, the defensive bias, which is typically used by workers, and the fundamental attribution error, which is typically made by managers, represent a significant challenge to effective communication and understanding in organizations.

1.4 *Self-Perception*

A manager at Exxon Corporation decided that he wanted to find a way to help his poor-performing employees improve their performance. So he sat down with each one of them and, in a positive, nonconfrontational way, explained that "I'm here to help you improve." Most of his employees took his offer in the spirit it was meant and accepted his help. However, one employee burst into tears, because no one had ever told her that her performance needed improvement. In fact, her hour-long outburst was so emotional that her manager decided that he would never "criticize" her again.[15]

self-serving bias the tendency to overestimate our value by attributing successes to ourselves (internal causes) and attributing failures to others or the environment (external causes)

The **self-serving bias** is the tendency to overestimate our value by attributing successes to ourselves (internal causes) and attributing failures to others or the environment (external causes).[16] As the example with the upset Exxon employee illustrates, the self-serving bias can make it especially difficult for managers to talk to employees about performance problems. In general, people have a need to maintain a positive self-image. This need is so strong that when people seek feedback at work, they typically want verification of their worth (rather than information about performance deficiencies) or assurance that mistakes or problems haven't been their fault.[17] And when managerial communication threatens people's positive self-image, they can become defensive and emotional. In turn, they quit listening, and communication becomes ineffective. In the second half of the chapter, which focuses on improving communication, we'll explain ways in which managers can minimize this self-serving bias and improve effective one-on-one communication with employees.

Review 1
Perception and Communication Problems

Perception is the process by which people attend to, organize, interpret, and retain information from their environments. However, perception is not a straightforward process. Because of perceptual filters, such as selective perception and closure, people exposed to the same information stimuli often end up with very different perceptions and understandings. Perception-based differences can also lead to differences in the attributions (internal or external) that managers and workers make when explaining workplace behavior. In general, workers are more likely to explain behavior from a defensive bias, in which they attribute problems to external causes (i.e., the situation). Managers, on the other hand, tend to commit the fundamental attribution error, attributing problems to internal causes (i.e., the worker associated with a mistake or error). Consequently, when things go wrong, it's common for managers to blame workers and for workers to blame the situation or context in which they do their jobs. Finally, this problem is compounded by a self-serving bias that leads people to attribute successes to internal causes and failures to external causes. So when workers receive negative feedback from managers, they can become defensive and emotional and not hear what their managers have to say. In short, perceptions and attributions represent a significant challenge to effective communication and understanding in organizations.

2 Kinds of Communication

In Oviedo, Florida, the city stopped construction of a 24-unit apartment complex when workers accidentally cut down ten trees. The trees were marked with ribbons. However, the work crew misunderstood and thought that the ribbons meant the trees *should* be cut down. David Materna, president of the apartment complex, said, "Obviously, the errors were made in our chain of command," and that they were caused by "a very unfortunate misunderstanding and miscommunication" between his supervisors and his employees.[18] Likewise, 80 Tampa Bay area McDonald's restaurants were participating in a "Halloween at Sea" promotion, in which they gave away discount coupons and used paper tray liners to promote the Tampa Bay Aquarium. When an employee noticed that the coupons and the tray liners smelled "funny," local managers panicked that the printers had not used nontoxic ink, so they destroyed thousands of dollars' worth of coupons and tray liners. However, several days later, McDonald's regional marketing chief, Cheryl Smith, said, "It's not toxic; it's not hazardous. There was a miscommunication. It's very unfortunate."[19]

In both of these situations, the communication process between senders and receivers broke down at some point. The trees were accidentally cut down because of a misunderstanding about the meaning of the ribbons tied around them. McDonald's mistakenly destroyed paper coupons and tray liners because of a miscommunication between store managers, the local advertising agency that created the "Halloween at Sea" promotion, and the local printer who printed the coupons and tray liners. Miscommunication is possible with every kind of communication.

Let's learn more about the different kinds of communication by examining **2.1** *the communication process,* **2.2** *formal communication channels,* **2.3** *informal communication channels,* **2.4** *coaching and counseling: one-on-one communication, and* **2.5** *nonverbal communication.*

2.1 *The Communication Process*

Earlier in the chapter, we defined *communication* as the process of transmitting information from one person or place to another. Figure 18.2 displays a model of the communication process and its major components: the sender (message to be conveyed, encoding the message, transmitting the message), the receiver (received message, decoded message, and the message that was understood), and noise, which interferes with the communication process.

Figure 18.2 **The Interpersonal Communication Process**

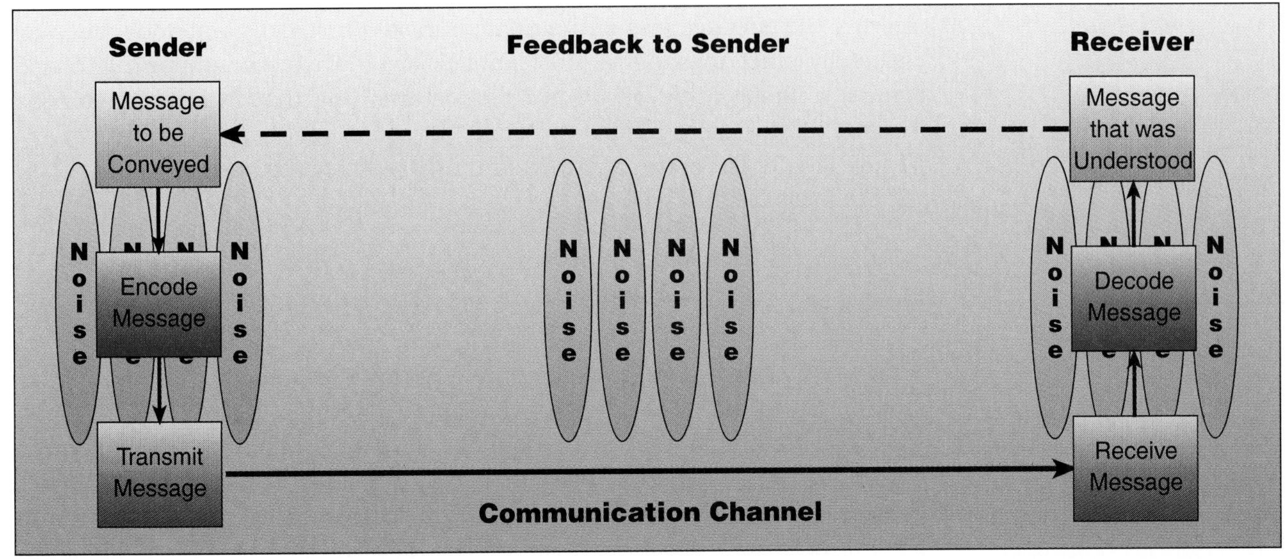

The communication process begins when a sender thinks of a message he or she wants to convey to another person. This could be what the sender wants someone else to know ("The meeting has been changed to 3:00 p.m.), to do ("Make sure to include last quarter's financial information in the proposal."), or not to do ("Sorry, the budget is tight. You'll have to fly coach rather than business class."). The next step is to encode the message. **Encoding** means putting a message into a written, oral, or symbolic form that can be recognized and understood by the receiver. The sender then transmits the message via *communication channels*, such as the telephone or face-to-face communication, which allow the sender to receive immediate feedback; or e-mail (text messages and file attachments), fax, beepers, voice mail, memos, and letters, in which senders must wait for receivers to respond.

encoding
putting a message into a written, oral, or symbolic form that can be recognized and understood by the receiver

If the message is received—and because of technical difficulties (e.g., fax down, dead battery on the mobile phone, inability to read e-mail attachments) or people-based transmission problems (e.g., forgetting to pass on the message), messages often aren't received—the next step is for the receiver to decode the message. **Decoding** is the process by which the receiver translates the written, oral, or symbolic form of the message into an understood message. However, the message, as understood by the receiver, isn't always the same message that was intended by the sender. Because of different experiences or perceptual filters, receivers may attach a completely different meaning to a message than was intended.

decoding
the process by which the receiver translates the written, oral, or symbolic form of a message into an understood message

The last step of the communication process occurs when the receiver gives the sender feedback. **Feedback** is a return message to the sender that indicates the receiver's understanding of the message (of what the receiver was supposed to know, to do, or not to do). Feedback makes senders aware of possible miscommunications and enables them to continue communicating until the receiver understands the intended message.

feedback
in the communication process, a return message to the sender that indicates the receiver's understanding of the message

noise
anything that interferes with the transmission of the intended message

conduit metaphor
the mistaken assumption that senders can pipe their intended messages directly into the heads of receivers with perfect clarity and without noise or perceptual filters interfering with the receivers' understanding of the message

Unfortunately, feedback doesn't always occur in the communication process. Complacency and overconfidence about the ease and simplicity of communication can lead senders and receivers to simply assume that they share a common understanding of the message and to not use feedback to improve the effectiveness of their communication. This is a serious mistake, especially since messages and feedback are always transmitted with and against a background of noise. **Noise** is anything that interferes with the transmission of the intended message. Noise can occur if:

1. the sender isn't sure about what message to communicate.
2. the message is not clearly encoded.
3. the wrong communication channel is chosen.
4. the message is not received or decoded properly.
5. the receiver doesn't have the experience or time to understand the message.

When managers wrongly assume that communication is easy, they reduce communication to something called the "conduit metaphor."[20] Strictly speaking, conduit is a pipe or tube that protects electrical wire. The **conduit metaphor** refers to the mistaken assumption that senders can pipe their intended messages directly into the heads of receivers with perfect clarity and without noise or perceptual filters interfering with the receivers' understanding of the message. However, this just isn't possible. Even if managers could telepathically direct their thoughts straight into receivers' heads, there would still be misunderstandings and communication problems because, depending on how they're used, words and symbols typically have multiple meanings. For example, Table 18.1 shows several meanings of an extremely common word, "fine." Depending on how you use it, "fine" can mean a penalty, a good job, or that something is delicate, small, pure, or flimsy.

In summary, the conduit metaphor causes problems in communication by making managers too complacent and confident in their ability to easily and accurately transfer messages to receivers. Managers who want to be effective communicators need to carefully choose words and symbols that will help receivers derive the intended meaning of a message. Furthermore, they need to be aware of all of the steps of the communication process, beginning with the sender (message to be conveyed, encoding the message, transmitting the message) and ending with the receiver (received message, decoded message, understanding the message, and using feedback to communicate what was understood).

Table 18.1

Meanings of the Word "Fine"

1. If you exceed the 55-mph speed limit, you may have to pay a fine (meaning a penalty).
2. During the playoffs, Michael Jordan turned in a fine performance (meaning excellent).
3. The machine has to run at a slow speed, because the tolerance is extremely fine (meaning delicate).
4. It is difficult to put this puzzle together, since many of the pieces are so fine (meaning small).
5. Recently, experiments have been conducted on manufacturing certain drugs in space. It is hoped that these drugs, as compared to those manufactured on Earth, will be extremely fine (meaning pure).
6. Be careful when you handle that antique book. Its pages are extremely fine (meaning flimsy).

2.2 *Formal Communication Channels*

formal communication channel
the system of official channels that carry organizationally approved messages and information

The **formal communication channel** is the system of official channels that carry organizationally approved messages and information. Organizational objectives, rules, policies, procedures, instructions, commands, and requests for information are all transmitted via the formal communication system or "channel." There are three formal communication channels: downward communication, upward communication, and horizontal communication.[21]

downward communication
communication that flows from higher to lower levels in an organization

Downward communication flows from higher to lower levels in an organization. Downward communication is used to issue orders down the organizational hierarchy, to give organizational members job-related information, to give managers and workers performance reviews from upper managers, and to make clear organizational objectives and goals.[22] Sometimes, however, downward communication is used to put out rumors of impending change. For example, after a two-day board or directors meeting, Phil Condit, chairman and CEO of Boeing, the aircraft manufacturer, took the unusual step of sending an e-mail to all of Boeing's managers. The purpose of the e-mail was to dispel rumors that he was about to be fired after several years of bad company performance. Said Condit to his managers, "Many, if not all of you, have heard or read media speculation about senior management changes. Rumors do not contribute to doing the job that we have before us, so let me put them to rest. I expect every Boeing person to contribute to these tasks by doing what we do best—focusing on our customers and working to find solutions to the problems that face us. Enough of the rumors and speculation; let's prove how good we are."[23]

upward communication
communication that flows from lower to higher levels in an organization

Upward communication flows from lower levels to higher levels in an organization. Upward communication is used to give higher-level managers feedback about operations, issues, and problems; to help higher-level managers assess organizational performance and effectiveness; to encourage lower-level managers and employees to participate in organizational decision making; and to give those at lower levels the chance to share their concerns with higher-level authorities. For example, in the mid-1990s, after several billion dollars in losses, Delta Airlines chairman Ronald W. Allen announced a strategic goal of "Leadership 7.5." This goal was concerned with getting Delta's costs down from 9.26 cents per seat-mile (the cost of flying one passenger one mile) to 7.5 cents per seat-mile. Eventually, this cost cutting strategy returned Delta to profitability. However, in an interview, when he was asked whether his cost-cutting program had upset and angered long-time Delta employees (many of whom had been laid off to cut costs), he responded, "But so be it." Delta's pilots, flight attendants, and mechanics responded angrily by sporting "So Be It" buttons to let Delta's board members, all of whom regularly flew the airline, know that they resented his cavalier attitude. In fact, Delta's board became so worried about the anger that its employees had toward Allen that they forced him into early retirement at the age of 55.[24]

horizontal communication
communication that flows among managers and workers who are at the same organizational level

Horizontal communication flows among managers and workers who are at the same organizational level. For instance, horizontal communication occurs when the day-shift supervisor comes in at 7:30 a.m. for a half-hour discussion with the midnight-shift supervisor who leaves at 8:00 a.m, or when the regional marketing director meets with the regional accounting director to discuss costs and plans for a new marketing campaign. Horizontal communication helps facilitate coordination and cooperation between different parts of a company and allows co-workers to share relevant information. It also helps people at the same level resolve conflicts and solve problems without involving high levels of management. At Oracle Software, Ray Lane implemented a program called "Vision and Values" that structured company rules regarding interpersonal communication. Because the company had grown to more than 20,000 employees, it had to stop employees from taking problems straight to founder and CEO Larry Ellison. This worked well while the company was small, but produced bottlenecks and slow decisions now that it was large. So, according to "Vision and Values," horizontal communication became the first step in problem solving. In fact, employees were not allowed to elevate problems and issues to higher levels unless they communicated first with managers and workers at their organizational level.[25]

In general, what can managers do to improve formal communication? First, decrease reliance on downward communication. Second, increase chances for upward communication by increasing personal contact with lower-level managers and workers. Third, like at Oracle software, encourage much greater use of horizontal communication. Finally, be aware of the problems associated with downward, upward, and horizontal communication, some of which are listed in Table 18.2.

2.3 *Informal Communication Channels*

The **informal communication channel**, sometimes called the "**grapevine**," is the transmission of messages from employee to employee outside of formal communication channels. The grapevine arises out of curiosity, that is, the need to know what is going on in an organization and how it might affect you or others. And to satisfy this curiosity, employees need a consistent supply of

Table 18.2

Common Problems with Downward, Upward, and Horizontal Communication

Common Problems with Downward Communication

- Overusing downward communication by sending too many messages.
- Issuing contradictory messages.
- Hurriedly communicating vague, unclear messages.
- Issuing messages that indicate management's low regard for lower-level workers.

Common Problems with Upward Communication

- Risky to tell upper management about problems (i.e., fear of retribution).
- Managers react angrily and defensively when workers report problems.
- Not enough opportunities or channels for lower-level workers to contact upper levels of management.

Common Problems with Horizontal Communication

- Management discourages or punishes horizontal communication, viewing it as small talk.
- Managers and workers are not given the time or opportunity for horizontal communization.
- Not enough opportunities or channels for lower-level workers to engage in horizontal communication

Source: G.L. Kreps, *Organizational Communication: Theory and Practice* (New York: Longman, 1990).

informal communication channel ("grapevine") the transmission of messages from employee to employee outside of formal communication channels

relevant, accurate, in-depth information about "who is doing what and what changes are occurring within the organization."[26] For example, when top AT&T managers told Wall Street security analysts that it was planning to eliminate thousands of jobs, the analysts blabbed the news to reporters, and AT&T's employees learned about the job cuts in the newspapers. As a result, work in AT&T offices practically stopped as employees worked the corporate grapevine to find out what was going to happen next. A former AT&T manager said, "No one in top management stepped forward and said the rumors weren't true. Nobody told us anything official at all, in fact. So the grapevine went berserk."[27]

Grapevines arise out of informal communication networks, such as the gossip or cluster chains shown in Figure 18.3. In the *gossip chain*, one "highly connected" individual shares information with many other managers and workers. By contrast, in the *cluster chain*, numerous people simply tell a few of their friends. The result in both cases is that information flows freely and quickly through the organization. Some believe that grapevines are a waste of employees' time, that they promote gossip and rumors that fuel political speculation, and that they are sources of highly unreliable, inaccurate information. Yet studies clearly show that grapevines are highly accurate sources of information for a number of reasons.[28] First, because grapevines typically carry "juicy" information that is interesting and timely, information spreads rapidly. Second, since information is typically spread by face-to-face conversation, senders can seek feedback to make sure they understand the message that is being communicated. This reduces misunderstandings and increases accuracy. Third, since most of the information in a company moves along the grapevine, as opposed to formal communication channels, people can usually verify the accuracy of information by "checking it out" with others.

Figure 18.3 **Grapevine Communication Networks**

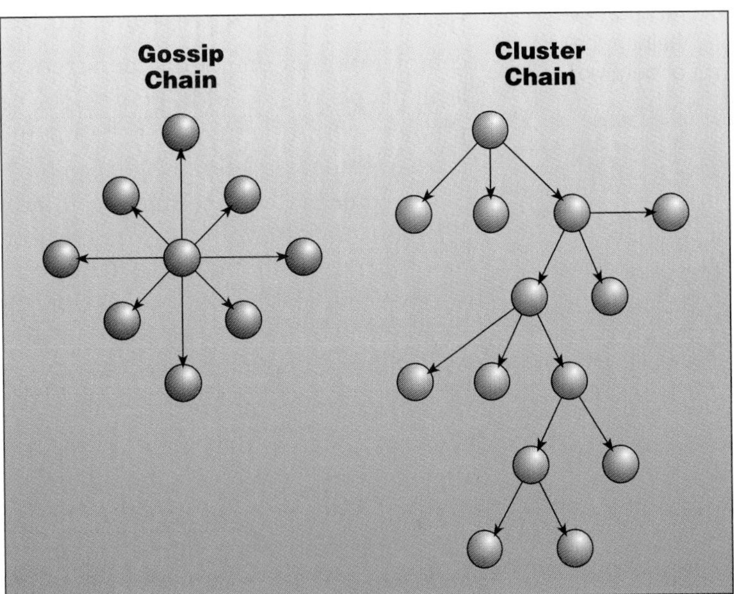

Source: K. Davis & J.W. Newstrom, *Human Behavior at Work: Organizational Behavior,* 8th ed. (New York: McGraw-Hill, 1989).

What can managers do to "manage" organizational grapevines? The very worst thing managers can do is withhold information or try to punish those who share information with others. The grapevine abhors a vacuum, and in the absence of information from company management, rumors and anxiety will flourish. A former CBS employee said, "There were a couple of months [when layoff rumors were prevalent] where we sat around and worried all day. Then we started to worry that we were worrying too much, so we went back to work for ten minutes. Then somebody would call up and say, 'Did you see the papers this morning? Are you getting laid off?' So we'd go back to worrying again."[29]

A better strategy is to embrace the grapevine to keep employees informed about possible changes and strategies. Management consultant Arnold Brown said managers should "identify the key people in your company's grapevine and, instead of punishing them, feed them information. When a company issues a press release it knows what newspapers to contact, so why not know your internal media?"[30]

Finally, in addition to using the grapevine to communicate with others, managers should not overlook the fact that the grapevine can be a tremendous source of valuable information and feedback. In fact, information flowing through organizational grapevines is estimated to be 75 percent to 95 percent accurate.[31]

2.4
Coaching and Counseling: One-on-One Communication

The Wyatt Company surveyed 531 U.S. companies undergoing major changes and restructuring. CEOs were asked, "If you could go back and change one thing, what would it be." The answer? "The way we communicated with our employees." CEOs stated that instead of flashy videos, printed materials, or formal meetings, they would make greater use of one-to-one communication, especially with employees' immediate supervisors, and not higher-level executives that employees didn't know.[32]

coaching
communicating with someone for the direct purpose of improving their on-the-job performance or behavior

counseling
communicating with someone about non-job-related issues that may be affecting or interfering with their performance

There are two kinds of one-on-one communication: coaching and counseling. **Coaching** is communicating with someone for the direct purpose of improving the person's on-the-job performance or behavior.[33] For example, David Prosser, CEO of RTW, a worker's compensation firm, began getting complaints that one of his managers would become angry and yell at lower-level people who wouldn't dare fight back. When others tried to discuss the problem with this manager, he maintained that he didn't have a problem. Prosser said that "I finally went to him and said, 'You need some help.'"[34]

By contrast, **counseling** is communicating with someone about non-job-related issues that may be affecting or interfering with the person's performance. For example, after a top-performing employee was repeatedly late and absent from work, he was asked if he had some personal problems that he needed to discuss. It turned out that he had gone through a divorce and that his teenage son, who was in trouble for truancy and stealing, was now his sole responsibility. Marina London, who counseled this manager, said, "It's very common that the personal problem is coming from somewhere else, that someone is dragging him (the employee) down with them."[35]

While we'll discuss a number of specific steps for effective one-on-one communication later in the chapter, you should know that, in general, openness is one of the most important factors in effective one-on-one communication. Consistent with our discussion of the communication model, *openness in message sending* is the candid disclosure of information. *Openness in message receiving* is encouraging employees to respond with candid, forthright opinions, even when they disagree.[36]

What value does open communications provide? George "Rusty" Childress, the 34-year-old president of Childress Buick/Kia Company of Phoenix, Arizona, said that "by maintaining open communications with customers and employees, not only will you learn exactly what customers need and expect, but employees' job satisfaction will increase as well. . . ." Indeed, numerous studies show that open communications between employees and managers leads to increased employee job satisfaction and job performance.[37] Childress Buick/Kia encourages openness in communication through e-mail, bulletin boards, hot lines, questionnaires, town hall meetings, focus groups, a monthly newsletter called "Squeaks and Rattles," questionnaires, and a suggestion system where employee suggestions are computerized and analyzed by a committee of managers and employees. How effective has open communication been for Childress and his auto dealership? The dealership ranks near the top in the customer service index most automobile dealers use to rank customer satisfaction.[38]

2.5 Nonverbal Communication

nonverbal communication any communication that doesn't involve words

kinesics movements of the body and face

When people talk, they send verbal and nonverbal messages. Verbal messages are sent and received through the words we speak. "That was a great presentation." By contrast, nonverbal messages are sent through body language, facial expressions, or tone of voice. For instance, hearing "THAT was a GREAT presentation!" is very different from hearing "ahem (clearing throat), that was, ahem, ahem, a great presentation."

More specifically, **nonverbal communication** is any communication that doesn't involve words. Nonverbal communication and messages almost always accompany verbal communication and may support and reinforce the verbal message or contradict it. The importance of nonverbal communication is well established. Researchers have estimated that as much as 93 percent of any message is transmitted nonverbally, with 55 percent coming from body language and facial expressions and 38 percent coming from tone and pitch of voice.[39] And since many nonverbal cues are unintentional, receivers often consider nonverbal communication to be a more accurate representation of what senders are really thinking and feeling. If you have ever asked someone out on a date and been told "yes," but realized that the real answer was "no," then you understand the importance of paying attention to nonverbal communication.

PersonalProductivityTip

Study *Your* Nonverbal Behavior

As much as 93 percent of any message is transmitted nonverbally. While we're often good students of others' nonverbal behavior, we're often woefully ignorant of our own. To gain some insight into your nonverbal behavior, have someone videotape you when you are speaking, preferably in two or three different situations. Then study this tape and analyze your speaking style and your nonverbal messages and mannerisms. Look for anything that might distract a receiver from the content of your message. Also assess whether your nonverbal messages support or contradict your verbal messages. If you see something you don't like, change it. You'll become a more effective communicator.

Kinesics and paralanguage are two kinds of nonverbal communication.[40] **Kinesics** are movements of the body and face.[41] These movements include arm and hand gestures, facial expressions, eye contact, folding arms, crossing legs, and leaning toward or away from another person. For example, people tend to avoid eye contact when they are embarrassed or unsure of the message they are sending. Crossed arms and/or legs usually indicate defensiveness or that the person is not receptive to the message or the sender. Also, people tend to smile frequently when they are seeking someone's approval. Lawyers frequently use body language and facial movements to communicate nonverbal messages to jurors. Attorney and trial consultant Lisa Blue said, "If you want to show that the cross-examination of your witness was ridiculous or boring, you could start looking at your watch." Likewise, while suing Dow Chemical, attorney Thomas Pirtle would express his disbelief by shaking his head "no," or show his disgust by waving his arms while Dow's attorneys addressed the jury. However, because of its power to sway jurors' opinions, some judges have begun tightly regulating attorneys' nonverbal behavior. U.S. District Judge Samuel Kent said, "Facial gestures, nods of the head, audible sighs, anything along those lines is strictly prohibited."[42]

paralanguage
the pitch, rate, tone, volume, and speaking pattern (i.e., use of silences, pauses, or hesitations) of one's voice

Paralanguage includes the pitch, rate, tone, volume, and speaking pattern (i.e., use of silences, pauses, or hesitations) of one's voice. For example, when people are unsure what to say, they tend to decrease their communication effectiveness by speaking softly. By contrast, when people are nervous, they tend to talk faster and louder. These characteristics have a tremendous influence on whether listeners are receptive to what speakers are saying. Again, lawyers have long used the power of their voices to influence whether jurors were receptive to arguments that supported their clients. For instance, tobacco company lawyers complained about the dramatic way in which plaintiffs' attorney Stanley Rosenblatt would read secret company documents aloud to jurors. Rosenblatt, who would vary his voice from a slow whisper to a fast, loud voice that filled the entire courtroom, said that opposing attorneys always complained that ". . . I should read in a very flat monotone."[43]

In short, since nonverbal communication is so informative, especially when it contradicts verbal communication, managers need to learn how to monitor and control their nonverbal behavior.

Review 2
Kinds of Communication

Organizational communication depends on the communication process, formal and informal communication channels, one-on-one communication, and nonverbal communication. The major components of the communication process are the sender, the receiver, noise, and feedback. The conduit metaphor refers to the mistaken assumption that senders can pipe their intended messages directly into receivers' heads with perfect clarity. However, with noise, perceptual filters, and little feedback, this just isn't possible. Formal communication channels, such as downward, upward, and horizontal communication, carry organizationally approved messages and information. By contrast, the informal communication channel, called the "grapevine," arises out of curiosity and is carried out through gossip or cluster chains. Managers should use the grapevine to keep employees informed and to obtain better, clearer information for themselves. Effective one-on-one communication, such as coaching and counseling, depends on openness in message receiving and message sending. Nonverbal communication, such as kinesics and paralanguage, account for as much as 93 percent of a message's content and understanding. Since nonverbal communication is so informative, managers need to learn how to monitor and control their nonverbal behavior.

Improving Communication

An employee comes in late every day, takes long lunches, and leaves early. His co-workers resent his tardiness and having to do his share of the work. Another employee makes as many as ten personal phone calls a day on company time. Another employee has seen her job performance drop significantly in the last three months. How do you communicate with these employees to begin solving these problems? On the other hand, if you supervise a division of 50 or 100, or even 1,000 people, how can you communicate effectively with everyone in that division? Moreover, how can top managers communicate effectively with everyone in the company when employees work in different offices, states, countries, and time zones? Turning that around, how can managers make themselves accessible so that they can hear what employees feel and think throughout the organization?

When it comes to improving communication, managers face two primary tasks, managing one-on-one communication and managing organization wide communication. After reading the next two sections, you should be able to:

3 explain how managers can **manage effective one-on-one communication.**

4 describe how managers can **manage effective organization-wide communication.**

3 Managing One-on-One Communication

In Chapter 1, you learned that, on average, first-line managers spend 57 percent of their time with people, middle managers spend 63 percent of their time directly with people, and top managers spend as much as 78 percent of their time dealing with people.[44] These numbers make it clear that managers spend a great deal of time in one-on-one communication with others.

Learn more about managing one-on-one communication by reading how to **3.1** *choose the right communication medium,* **3.2** *be a good listener,* **3.3** *give effective feedback, and* **3.4** *improve cross-cultural communication.*

3.1
Choosing the Right Communication Medium

communication medium the method used to deliver an oral or written message

Sometimes messages are poorly communicated simply because they are delivered using the wrong **communication medium**, which is the method used to deliver a message. For example, the wrong communication medium is being used when an employee returns from lunch, picks up the note left on her office chair, and learns she has been fired. Or, the wrong communication medium is being used when an employee pops into your office every ten minutes with a simple request.

There are two general kinds of communication media: oral and written communication. *Oral communication* includes face-to-face and group meetings, as well as telephone calls or other ways, such as videoconferencing, in which spoken messages are sent and received. Studies show that managers generally prefer oral communication, because it provides the opportunity to ask questions about parts of the message that they don't understand. Oral communication is also a rich communication medium, because it allows managers to receive and assess the nonverbal communication that accompanies spoken messages (i.e., body language, facial expressions, or the voice characteristics associated with paralanguage). Furthermore, you don't need a personal computer and an Internet connection to conduct oral communication. Simply schedule an appointment, track someone down in the hall, or catch someone on the phone. In fact, management consultant Tom Durel worries that with voice mail and e-mail, managers are not as willing to engage in meaningful face-to-face, oral communication as they once were. He said, "Why is it that the first thing people do in the morning is turn on their computer and send e-mail to a colleague in the office next door? What's wrong with getting up, walking over there, and actually *talking* to that person?"[45] However, oral communication should not be used for all communication. In general, when messages are simple, such as a quick request or presentation of straightforward information, memos or e-mail are often the better communication medium.

Personal Productivity Tip

Writing Memos

Memos often create misperceptions and send unintended messages. Yet, they are sometimes necessary to create a record of decisions or responsibilities. To write good memos: (1) Don't use accusatory or autocratic language, such as "I am appalled by your decision" or "I don't like your attitude." (2) Avoid absolutes, such as "never," "cannot," and "must not." (3) Keep them short and to the point—use bullet points for structure. (4) Never write anything in a memo that you don't want everyone else to see. (5) Always consider whether a phone call or personal conversation would be more effective than a memo.

Source: R. Davidhizar and S. Erdel, "Send Me a Memo on It, or Better Yet, Don't," *Health Care Supervisor* 15 (1997): 42–47.

Written communication includes letters, e-mail, and memos. While most managers like and use oral communication, they are generally less receptive to using written communication. They may avoid written communication for a number of reasons, such as poor writing skills, being a poor typist, or not knowing (or refusing to learn) how to use Internet or corporate e-mail systems. However, written communication is well suited for delivering straightforward messages and information. Furthermore, with e-mail access available at the office, at home, and on the road (by laptop computer or Web-based e-mail), managers can use e-mail to stay in touch from anywhere at almost any time. And, since e-mail and other written communications don't have to be sent and received simultaneously, messages can be sent and stored for reading at any time. This allows managers to send and receive many more messages using e-mail than with oral communication, which requires people to get together in person or by phone or videoconference.

However, written communication is not well suited to ambiguous or emotionally laden topics, which are better delivered through oral communication. Management consultant Tom Durel said, "Don't assume that you did your part just because you sent out a bunch of memos. If you really want to communicate, you need to take the time to get real-time feedback."[46]

3.2 *Listening*

Are you a good listener? You probably think so. But, in fact, most people, including managers, are terrible listeners, retaining only about 25 percent of what they hear.[47] You qualify as a poor listener if you frequently interrupt others, jump to conclusions about what people will say before they've said it, hurry the speaker to finish his or her point, are a passive listener (not actively working at your listening), and simply don't pay attention to what people are saying.[48] On this last point, attentiveness, college students were periodically asked to record their thoughts during a psychology course. On average, 20 percent of the students were paying attention (only 12 percent were actively working at being good listeners), 20 percent were thinking about sex, 20 percent were thinking about things they had done before, and the remaining 40 percent thought about a number of things

Active listeners clarify responses, paraphrase, and summarize to show interest and assure the speaker that they have derived the intended meaning. © Corbis/R.W. Jones

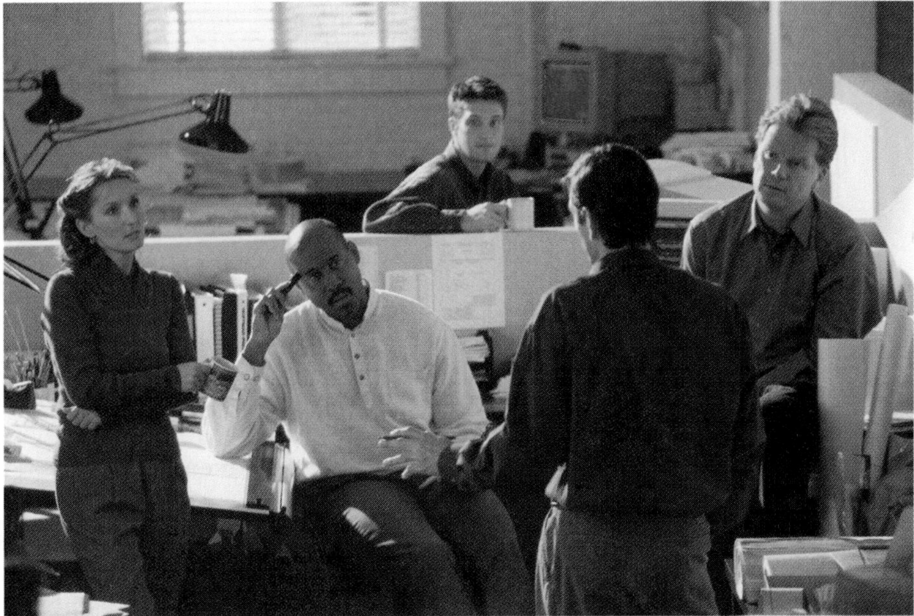

PersonalProductivityTip

Listen Up!

To be a better listener: (1) Listen to more than the first few words or phrases of each sentence. (2) Let the speaker complete the message before forming a conclusion. (3) Listen for intent as well as content. (4) Nonverbally encourage the speaker (with body language, eye contact, and facial expression). (5) Don't analyze or evaluate a message until you are sure it is complete. (6) Focus on what the person is saying, verbally and nonverbally. (7) Check your understanding by asking questions, paraphrasing, and summarizing. (8) Listen for what is *not* said.

Sources: P. Slizewski, "Tips for Active Listening," *HR Focus*, May 1995. R.B. Cousins, "Active Listening Is More than Just Hearing," *Supervision*, December 1996. P.C. Blodgett, "Six Ways To Be a Better Listener," *Training and Development* 5 (1997): 11–12.

(worries, religion, lunch, daydreaming, etc.), none of which were related to class.[49]

How important is it to be a good listener? In general, about 45 percent of the total time you spend communicating with others is spent listening. Furthermore, listening is particularly important for managerial success. Neil Kadisha, CEO of HPM, an Ohio manufacturer, said, "No one has a thing to fear about coming to me and lodging a complaint or making a suggestion. In all of my companies, janitors to the highest level of management can come to me. . . . We manage by respect, not by fear. We respect our employees' opinions and suggestions. They have the right to get upset and angry, and they have the right to be *heard*."[50] In fact, managers with better listening skills are rated as better managers by their employees and are much more likely to be promoted.[51]

hearing
the act or process of perceiving sounds

listening
making a conscious effort to hear

So, what can you do to improve your listening ability? First, understand the difference between hearing and listening. According to *Webster's New World Dictionary*, **hearing** is the "act or process of perceiving sounds," whereas **listening** is "making a conscious effort to hear." In other words, we react to sounds, such as bottles breaking or music being played too loud, because hearing is an involuntary physiological process. By contrast, listening is a voluntary behavior. So if you want to be a good listener, you have to choose to be a good listener. Typically, that means choosing to be an active, empathetic listener.[52]

active listening
assuming half the responsibility for successful communication by actively giving the speaker nonjudgmental feedback that shows you've accurately heard what he or she said

Active listening means assuming half the responsibility for successful communication by actively giving the speaker nonjudgmental feedback that shows you've accurately heard what he or she said. Active listeners make it clear from this behavior that they are listening carefully to what the speaker has to say. Active listeners put the speaker at ease, maintain eye contact, and show the speaker that they are attentively listening by nodding and making short statements.

Several specific strategies can help you be a better active listener. First, *clarify responses* by asking the speaker to explain confusing or ambiguous statements. Second, when there are natural breaks in the speaker's delivery, use this time to paraphrase or summarize what has been said. *Paraphrasing* is restating what has been said in your own words. *Summarizing* is reviewing the speaker's main points or emotions. Paraphrasing and summarizing give the speaker the chance to correct the message if the active listener has attached the wrong meaning to it. Paraphrasing and summarizing also show the speaker that the active listener is interested in the speaker's message. Table 18.3 lists specific statements that listeners can use to clarify responses, paraphrase, or summarize what has been said.

Active listeners also avoid evaluating the message or being critical until the message is complete. They recognize that their only responsibility during the transmission of a message is to accurately receive it and derive the intended meaning from it. Evaluation and criticism can take place after the message is accurately received. Finally, active listeners also recognize that a large portion of any message is transmitted nonverbally and thus pay very careful attention to the nonverbal cues transmitted by the speaker.

empathetic listening understanding the speaker's perspective and personal frame of reference and giving feedback that conveys that understanding to the speaker

Empathetic listening means understanding the speaker's perspective and personal frame of reference and giving feedback that conveys that understanding to the speaker. Empathetic listening goes beyond active listening, because it depends on our ability to set aside our own attitudes or relationships to be able to see and understand things through someone else's eyes. Empathetic listening is just as important as active listening, especially for managers, because it helps build rapport and trust with others.

The key to being a more empathetic listener is to show your desire to understand and to reflect people's feelings. You can *show your desire to understand* by listening first, that is, asking people to talk about what's most important to them and then giving them sufficient time to talk before responding or interrupting. Management consultant Neil Grammer said, "One of the best sales meetings I've ever had taught me a valuable lesson about the importance of listening. The meeting was with an investment bank's managing director. The appointment lasted 30 minutes—28 of those min-

Table 18.3

Clarifying, Paraphrasing, and Summarizing Responses for Active Listeners

Clarifying Responses

- Could you explain that again?
- I don't understand what you mean.
- I'm confused, would you run though that again?
- I'm not sure how . . . .

Paraphrasing Responses

- What you're really saying is . . . .
- If I understand you correctly . . . .
- So your perspective is that . . . .
- In other words . . . .
- Tell me if I'm wrong, but what you're saying is . . . .

Summarizing Responses

- Let me summarize . . . .
- Ok, your main concerns are . . . .
- Thus far, you've discussed . . . .
- To recap what you've said . . . .

Source: E. Atwater, *I Hear You,* revised ed. (New York: Walker, 1992).

utes were spent by the director telling me everything about his business and personnel. I told him nothing more about my company and its services than I had in our initial phone conversation. As the meeting concluded, he enthusiastically shook my hand and proclaimed how much he was looking forward to working with me—someone who understood his business."[53]

Reflecting feelings is also an important part of empathetic listening, because it demonstrates that you understand the speaker's emotions. But unlike active listening, in which you would restate or summarize the informational content of what had been said, the focus is on the affective part of the message. As an empathetic listener, you can use the following statements to reflect the speaker's emotions:

- So, right now you're feeling . . .
- You seem as if you're . . .
- Do you feel a bit . . . ?
- I could be wrong, but I'm sensing that you're feeling . . .

3.3 Giving Feedback

In Chapter 14, you learned that performance appraisal feedback (i.e., judging) should be separated from developmental feedback (i.e., coaching).[54] At this point, we now focus on the steps needed to communicate feedback one-on-one to employees.

destructive feedback feedback that disapproves without any intention of being helpful and almost always causes a negative or defensive reaction in the recipient

To start, managers need to recognize that feedback can be constructive or destructive. **Destructive feedback** is disapproving without any intention of being helpful and almost always causes a negative or defensive reaction in the recipient. In fact, one study found that 98 percent of employees responded to destructive feedback from their bosses with either verbal aggression (two-thirds) or physical aggression (one-third).[55] Surprisingly, some managers don't realize that they're giving people destructive feedback. For example, at a management seminar on "How to Deal with Difficult People," every time the management trainer discussed a different type of difficult person, a manager named Henry would raise his hand and say, "Just fire them." People who are late for work? "Just fire them." People who argue with others? "Just fire them." When the seminar was over, the trainer asked Henry why he had even bothered to attend the seminar. Henry replied that his boss had sent him so he could learn how to be more sensitive when dealing with employees.[56]

constructive feedback feedback intended to be helpful, corrective, and/or encouraging

By contrast, **constructive feedback** is intended to be helpful, corrective, and/or encouraging. It is aimed at correcting performance deficiencies and motivating employees. However, even when they want to give constructive rather than destructive feedback, managers still get nervous about discussing problems with employees. Frank Sharp, an employment manager at Carondelet Health Network in Tucson, Arizona, said, "I didn't like the way I was evaluated [by my managers] and vowed to do it differently." But, "I often wonder, 'Am I doing this right or wrong?'"[57]

In order for feedback to be constructive rather than destructive, it must be immediate, focused on specific behaviors, and problem oriented. Because the mistake or incident can be recalled more accurately and discussed in detail by the manager and the worker, *immediate feedback* is much more effective than delayed feedback. For example, if a worker is rude to a customer and the customer immediately reports the incident to management, and the manager, in turn, immediately discusses the issue with the employee, there should be little disagreement over what was said or done. By contrast, if the manager waits several weeks to discuss the incident, it's unlikely that either the manager or the worker will be able to accurately remember the specifics of what occurred. When that happens, it's usually too late to have a meaningful conversation.

Specific feedback focuses on particular acts or incidents that are clearly under the control of the employee. For instance, instead of telling an employee that he or she is "always late for work," it's much more constructive to say, "In the last three weeks, you have been 30 minutes late on four occasions and more than an hour late on two others." Furthermore, specific feedback isn't very helpful unless employees have control over the problems that the feedback addresses. Indeed, giving negative feedback about behaviors beyond someone's control is likely to be seen as unfair. Similarly, giving positive feedback about behaviors beyond someone's control may be viewed as insincere.

Last, *problem-oriented feedback* focuses on the problems or incidents associated with the poor performance rather than on the worker or the worker's personality. Giving feedback does not give managers the right to personally attack workers. While managers may be frustrated by a worker's poor performance, the point of problem-oriented feedback is to draw attention to the problem in a nonjudgmental way, so that the employee has enough information to correct it. So, rather than telling people that they're "idiots," focus on the problem. For instance, a shipping clerk at A&S Restaurant had a bad case of body odor. Rather than telling him "You stink" or "You're doing a lousy job because you stink," the manager explained the specific ways in which his body odor was "getting in the way of doing his job." Because the manager's feedback was specific and problem oriented and didn't attack or blame the employee, the employee didn't get defensive and took steps to take care of his body odor.[58]

3.4
Improving Cross-Cultural Communication

cross-cultural communication
transmitting information from a person in one country or culture to a person from another country or culture

As you know by now, effective communication is very difficult to accomplish. However, **cross-cultural communication**, which involves transmitting information from a person in one country or culture to a person from another country or culture, is much more difficult. But there are a number of things you can do to increase your chances for successful cross-cultural communication: familiarize yourself with that culture's work norms, address terms, and attitudes toward time.[59]

In Chapter 8, you learned that expatriates who receive predeparture language and cross-cultural training make faster adjustments to foreign cultures and perform better on their international assignments.[60] Therefore, *familiarizing yourself with cultural work norms* is the first step for successful cross-cultural communication. For instance, when Mercedes built a manufacturing plant in Vance, Alabama, the management team, consisting primarily of Germans and Americans, spent six months deciding how Mercedes would blend German and American management philosophies and work practices. The biggest disagreements were over image and decorum. Consistent with its hierarchical work norms, the Germans preferred private offices along narrow hallways, whereas the Americans, who are generally more egalitarian, preferred open offices in which people of all ranks could easily find and talk to each other. Likewise, the German managers preferred formal business attire because it emphasized status differences (i.e., hierarchy), whereas the Americans pushed for casual wear, such as dress slacks with polo shirts and sweaters bearing the Mercedes logo. Because the plant is in Alabama, the team eventually opted for the open office and casual dress.[61]

address terms
cultural norms that establish whether you should address businesspeople by their first names, family names, or titles

Next, *know the address terms* that people in that culture use to address each other in the workplace. **Address terms** are the cultural norms that establish whether you address businesspeople by their first names, family names, or titles. When meeting for the first time, Americans and Australians tend to be informal and address each other by first names, even nicknames. However, such immediate informality is not accepted in many cultures. For instance, an American manager working in one of his company's British subsidiaries introduced himself as "Chuck" to his British employees and coworkers. However, even after six months on the job, his British counterparts still referred to him as Charles. And the more he insisted they call him "Chuck," the more they seemed to dig in their heels and call him "Charles."[62] So, to decrease defensiveness, know your address terms before addressing your international business counterparts.

appointment time
cultural norm for how punctual you must be when showing up for scheduled appointments or meetings

schedule time
cultural norm for the time by which scheduled projects or jobs should actually be completed

discussion time
cultural norm for how much time should be spent in discussion with others

acquaintance time
cultural norm for how much time you must spend getting to know someone before the person is prepared to do business with you

Understanding cultural attitudes toward time is another major consideration for effective one-on-communication when conducting international business. Four important temporal concepts affect cross-cultural communication: appointment time, schedule time, discussion time, and acquaintance time.[63] **Appointment time** is concerned with how punctual you must be when showing up for scheduled appointments or meetings. In the U.S., any amount beyond 5 minutes late is considered "late." However, Swedes don't even allow 5 minutes, expecting others to arrive by their appointment time. By contrast, in Latin countries, people can arrive 20 to 30 minutes after a scheduled appointment and still not be considered late.

Schedule time is the time by which scheduled projects or jobs should actually be completed. In the U.S. and other Anglo cultures, a premium is placed on completing things on time. By contrast, more relaxed attitudes toward schedule time can be found throughout Asia and Latin America.

Discussion time concerns how much time should be spent in discussion with others. In the U.S., we carefully manage discussion time to avoid "wasting" time on nonbusiness topics. In Brazil, though, because of the emphasis on building relationships, as much as two hours of general discussion on nonbusiness topics can be required before moving on to business issues.

Finally, **acquaintance time** is how much time you must spend getting to know someone before the person is prepared to do business with you. Again, in the U.S., people are quick to get down to business and are willing to strike a deal on the same day if the terms are good and initial impressions are positive. In the Middle East, however, it may take two or three weeks of meetings before reaching this comfort level. The French also have a different attitude toward acquaintance time. Polly Platt, author of *French or Foe*, a book that explains French culture and its people for travelers and businesspeople, says, "Know that things are going to take longer and don't resent it. Realize that the time system is different. Time is not a quantity for them. We save time, we spend time, we waste time; all this comes from money. The French don't. They pass time. It's a totally different concept."[64]

Review 3
Managing One-on-One Communication

One-on-one communication can be managed by choosing the right communication medium, being a good listener, giving effective feedback, and understanding cross-cultural communication. Managers generally prefer oral communication, because it provides the opportunity to ask questions and assess nonverbal communication. Oral communication is best suited to complex, ambiguous, or emotionally laden topics. Written communication is best suited for delivering straightforward messages and information. Listening is important for managerial success, but most people are terrible listeners. To improve your listening skills, choose to be an active listener (clarifying responses, paraphrasing, and summarizing) and an empathetic listener (show your desire to understand, reflect feelings). Feedback can be constructive or destructive. To be constructive, feedback must be immediate, focused on specific behaviors, and problem oriented. Finally, to increase chances for successful cross-cultural communication, familiarize yourself with the culture's work norms, address terms, and attitudes toward time (appointment time, schedule time, discussion time, and acquaintance time).

4 Managing Organization-Wide Communication

While managing one-on-one communication is important, managers must also know how to effectively communicate to a larger number of people throughout an organization. For instance, Barry Salzman, president of DoubleClick International, the Internet advertising firm, spends 75 percent of his time traveling to 14 international offices. And every Monday, no matter where he is, he conducts a conference call with DoubleClick managers in Canada, Europe, and Asia. Says Salzman, "We try to maintain voice contact. We lose that with computers and e-mail."[65] While this is an effective method of managing a small group of geographically dispersed people, managers can't hold a conference call with everyone in the company. Thus, managers need additional methods for organization-wide communication and for making themselves accessible, so they can hear what employees throughout their organizations are feeling and thinking.

Learn more about organization-wide communication by reading the following sections about **4.1** *improving transmission by getting the message out and* **4.2** *improving reception by finding ways to hear what others feel and think.*

4.1
Improving Transmission: Getting the Message Out

Several methods of electronic communication—e-mail, online discussion forums, televised/videotaped speeches and conferences, corporate talk shows, and broadcast voice mail—now make it easier for managers to communicate with people throughout the organization and "get the message out." Although we normally think of *e-mail*, the transmission of messages via computers, as a means of one-on-one communication, it also plays an important role in organization-wide communication. For example:

> *Perot Systems Corporation, based in Dallas, publishes three online newsletters via e-mail. The internal communication department pro-*

Personal Productivity Tip

The Dangers of Corporate E-mail

E-mail is fast and convenient but has serious pitfalls. It can be easily saved, duplicated, forwarded, and printed. The original sender has no control over who sees it. And while senders delete e-mail on their machines, most likely other copies can be found on the company's mail server or backup tapes, which most companies run every night. E-mail also allows disgruntled employees to easily send out sensitive or fraudulent information to competitors or outsiders. Finally, many employees use easily guessed passwords or don't log off their computers, making it easy for outsiders to e-mail while posing as members of your company.

Sources: B. Mattson, "E-mail Message Carry Legal Pitfalls," *Minneapolis/St. Paul City Business*, 23 December 1996. F.S. Manitzas, "Employers Should Formulate Rules Governing Use of E-mail," *San Antonio Business Journal*, 16 June 1997.

duces one every week and writes the others on an as-needed basis. Perot Systems chose this "low frills" approach for its simplicity and affordability. The department spends 15 hours a week collecting information. Copy approvals are completed within 24 hours, and the newsletters are distributed to its 2,400 associates (employees). The newsletters are typically no longer than three pages and include briefs about the latest company news.[66]

Also, with the click of a button, managers can send e-mail to everyone in the company via e-mail distribution lists. Many CEOs now use this capability regularly to keep employees up to date on changes and developments in the company. Also, many CEOs and top executives make their e-mail addresses public and encourage employees to contact them directly.

Another way to electronically promote organization-wide communication is through discussion forums. **Online discussion forums**, which are the in-house equivalent of Internet newsgroups, are Web- or software-based discussion tools that are available across the company to permit employees to easily ask questions and share knowledge with each other. The point is to share expertise and not duplicate solutions already "discovered" by others in the company. Furthermore, because online discussion forums remain online, they provide a historical database for people who are dealing with particular problems for the first time.

online discussion forums the in-house equivalent of Internet newsgroups; Web- or software-based discussion tools available across the company to permit employees to easily ask questions and share knowledge with each other

Online discussion forums are typically organized by topic. For example, at Ernst & Young, a major accounting and management-consulting corporation, consultants who have questions about multinational tax analysis can simply log on to the E & Y tax forum (or dozens of other forums, too). They can either post new questions and get help from others who respond with answers, or read previously posted questions and answers to see if the information they need has already been discussed. If either of those options fails, they can at least come away with the names of people in the organization that they can contact for help.[67] British Petroleum Amoco has taken this a step farther by creating "Connect," which is essentially a company Yellow Pages where more than 12,000 managers and workers have entered their contact information and listed their expertise to make it easier for others to find expert help for their problems.[68] Table 18.4 lists the steps companies need to take to establish successful online discussion forums.

Televised/videotaped speeches and meetings are a third electronic method of organization-wide communication. **Televised/videotaped speeches and meetings** are simply speeches and meetings originally made to a smaller

Table 18.4

Establishing Online Discussion Forums

1. *Perform a "Knowledge" Audit*—to pinpoint your company's top intellectual assets; then spread that knowledge throughout the organization.
2. *Create an Online Directory*—detailing the expertise of individual workers, and make it available to all employees.
3. *Set Up Discussion Groups on the Net*—so that managers and workers can collaborate on problem-solving.
4. *Reward Information Sharing*—make sharing knowledge online a key part of performance ratings.

Source: G. McWilliams & M. Stepanek, "Knowledge Management: Taming the Info Monster," *Business Week*, 22 June 1998, 170.

televised/videotaped speeches and meetings speeches and meetings originally made to a smaller audience that are either simultaneously broadcast to other locations in the company or videotaped for subsequent distribution and viewing

corporate talk shows televised company meetings that allow remote audiences (employees) to pose questions to the show's host and guests

audience that are either simultaneously broadcast to other locations in the company or videotaped for subsequent distribution and viewing. For example, when Nationwide Insurance changed its logo and marketing strategy, it rented 33 movie theaters around the country so that its employees could watch a live 90-minute satellite broadcast from company headquarters in Columbus, Ohio. Thanks to the live satellite broadcast, CEO Dimon McFersen and other top managers were able to explain to every Nationwide employee why those changes were being made. Said McFersen, "Companies that don't change, don't survive."[69]

Corporate talk shows are a variant on televised/videotaped speeches and meetings. But instead of simply watching a televised/videotaped speech or meeting, **corporate talk shows** allow remote audience members, all of whom are typically workers or managers, to pose questions to the show's host and guests. For example, once a month, Emma Carasco, vice president of marketing and communication, and Dan Hunt, president of Caribbean and Latin American operations, host the Virtual Leadership Academy, which is a corporate talk show for Nortel Networks. A typical broadcast is seen live by 2,000 employees in 46 countries, who call in with questions about Nortel and its competitors. Why a corporate talk show? Carrasco said, "We're always looking for ways to break down barriers in the company, and people are comfortable with the talk-show format. People watch talk shows in every country in the region, and they've learned that it's okay to say what's on their mind. In fact, it's expected."

In Chapter 6, you learned that *voice messaging*, or "voice mail," is a telephone answering system that records audio messages. Eighty-nine percent of respondents believe that voice messaging is critical to business communication, 78 percent believe that it improves productivity, and 58 percent would rather leave a message on a voice messaging system than with a receptionist.[70] Coke CEO Doug Ivester is a dedicated user of voice mail and uses it every night to leave messages for Coke's senior managers in Europe, Asia, the U.S., and Latin America to listen to when they come in each morning. Said Ivester, "Neville's [Head of Coke's European Offices] in Europe this morning, but I've already left him five voice mails. I've dealt with Spain, Italy, France and a personnel issue in Eastern Europe. And I didn't even need to talk to him once."[71] However, most people are unfamiliar with the ability to *broadcast voice mail* by sending a recorded message to everyone in the company. Broadcast voice mail gives top managers a quick, convenient way to address their work forces via oral communication. Ivester regularly sends two-minute voice mails to Coke's entire work force, updating them on company performance, and even using it to inform managers and employees about the death of Roberto Goizueta, Coke's previous CEO.[72]

4.2 *Improving Reception: Hearing What Others Feel and Think*

When people think of "organization-wide" communication, they think of the CEO and top managers getting their message out to people in the company. However, organization-wide communication also means finding ways to communicate and stay in touch with people throughout the organization. Company hotlines, survey feedback, frequent informal meetings, and surprise visits are ways of accomplishing this.

We began this chapter with a story about how Pillsbury employees could call a phone number and use voice mail technology to anonymously record their comments, which were then transcribed and forwarded straight to Pillsbury's CEO. **Company hot lines** are phone numbers that anyone in the company can anonymously call to leave information for upper management. Like Pillsbury, some companies hire outside firms to run their hot lines, so as to maintain the complete anonymity of callers. For example, Pillsbury's hot line, which is run by InTouch Corporation, doesn't even reveal callers' gender. Companies then publicize these precautions in hopes that more people will be willing to call. For instance, Toyota's employee handbook says, "Don't spend time worrying about something. Speak up!" The Toyota hot line is anonymous and available 24 hours a day, seven days a week. Every message is reviewed and fully investigated by Toyota's top human resources manager. Moreover, if the questions or statements left on the hot line would be of interest to others in the company, they are then posted on company bulletin boards (without sacrificing callers' anonymity).[73]

company hot lines
phone numbers that anyone in the company can anonymously call to leave information for upper management

Survey feedback is information collected by survey from organizational members that is then compiled, disseminated, and used to develop action plans for improvement. Many organizations make use of survey feedback by surveying their managers and employees several times a year. FedEx, for example, runs its own Survey Feedback Action program. The survey, which is administered online and is completely anonymous, includes sections for employees to evaluate their managers, as well as the overall environment at FedEx, including benefits, incentives, working conditions, etc. After the surveys are completed, the results are compiled, fed back, and made public to each FedEx work group. Each group then uses the results to decide where changes and improvements need to be made and to develop specific action plans to address those problems. The final step is to look for improvements in subsequent employee surveys to see if those plans worked.[74]

survey feedback
information collected by survey from organizational members that is then compiled, disseminated, and used to develop action plans for improvement

Frequent, *informal meetings* between top managers and lower-level employees are one of the best ways for top managers to hear what others feel and think. Many people assume that top managers are at the center of everything that goes on in organizations. However, it's common for top managers to feel isolated from most of the managers and employees in their companies. Consequently, more and more top managers are scheduling frequent, informal meetings with people throughout their companies. For instance, every week, GE's Jack Welch schedules lunches with managers several levels below him. At Nucor Corporation, a steel company, plant managers have dinner at least once a year with each employee. After dinner, employees may ask questions or make comments about company practices.

Have you ever been around supervisors when they found out that upper management was going to be paying a visit? First, there's shock. Next, there's anxiety. And then there's panic, as everyone is told to drop what they're doing to polish, shine, and spruce up the workplace, so it looks perfect for top management's visit. Of course, when visits are conducted under these conditions, top managers don't get a realistic look at what's going on in the company. Consequently, one of the ways to get an accurate picture is to pay *surprise visits* to various parts of the organization. However, surprise visits should not be surprise inspections, which is what Volkswagen's CEO, Ferdinand Piech, uses them for. Piech likes to keep his people nervous by making surprise visits to VW's technical center or its huge Wolfsburg factory.[75] Instead, surprise visits should be used as an opportunity to increase the chances for meaningful upward communication from those who normally don't get a chance to work with upper management. Indeed, surprise visits like these are part of the culture at Enterprise Rent-a-Car. Fred Sorino, who manages an Enterprise office in Eatontown, New Jersey, said, "Once I was working at a branch in Cranbury, New Jersey, and a corporate vice president and a regional president showed up for a surprise visit. I was outside washing cars in 20-degree weather, and we were very busy. These two executives offered to help me clean the cars. I felt so awkward that I said I didn't need help, but they did it anyway." Enterprise's CEO, Andy Taylor, tells a similar story, saying, "We were visiting an office in Berkeley and it was mobbed, so I started cleaning cars. As it was happening, I wondered if it was a good use of my time, but the effect on morale was tremendous."[76]

Review 4
Managing Organization-Wide Communication

Managers need methods for organization-wide communication and for making themselves accessible, so they can hear what employees throughout their organizations are feeling and thinking. E-mail, online discussion forums, televised/videotaped speeches and conferences, corporate talk shows, and broadcast voice mail make it much easier for managers to improve message transmission and "get the message out." By contrast, anonymous company hot lines, survey feedback, frequent informal meetings, and surprise visits help managers improve reception by hearing what others in the organization feel and think.

What**Really**Happened?

In the opening case, you learned that Buckman Laboratories was having communication problems. As sales director, you were frustrated because sales representatives would contact you looking for answers to their clients' technical questions. In turn, you would send those messages to technical experts in the company, who weren't very fast or reliable about getting back in touch with sales representatives. Any way you looked at it, organizational communication was not very good. Read the answers to the opening case to find out what Buckman Labs did to address these communication issues.

The first thing you need to figure out is why people in different parts of the company are so reluctant to communicate with each other. Is it perception, culture, or simply poor communication techniques?

Perception is the process by which individuals attend to, organize, interpret, and retain information from their environments. As people perform their jobs, they are exposed to a wide variety of informational stimuli, such as e-mails, direct conversations with the boss or co-workers, rumors heard over lunch, stories about the company in the press, or a video broadcast of a speech from the CEO to all employees. However, because of perceptual filters, exposure to an informational stimulus is no guarantee that an individual will pay attention or attend to that stimulus. Indeed, since sales representatives had frequent face-to-face contact with customers and technical experts did not, it's not surprising that sales representatives wanted customer problems to be solved immediately. However, because of their Ph.D. training, technical experts were much more interested in figuring the problem out right than in figuring it out quickly.

Next, anything's got to be better than having you, the sales manager, as the first point of contact for expert help, but what? How can you match sales representatives with the right technical experts without having to serve as the go-between? There's got to be a reasonable technological solution.
But if e-mail wasn't the technological solution, and everybody uses e-mail, what's the answer?

One way to promote organization-wide communication is through discussion forums. Online discussion forums, which are the in-house equivalent of Internet newsgroups, are Web- or software-based discussion tools that are available across the company to permit people to easily ask questions and share knowledge with each other. Buckman solved its problems by creating online discussion forums, called K'Netix, for its customers, sales representatives, technical experts, and everyone else in the company. K'Netix allows Buckman's 1,300 employees, who work all over the world, to come together to share knowledge via voice or video conferences, text chats, or document sharing. For example, a sales representative in Indonesia needed help in quickly writing a client proposal. He obtained the marketing information he needed from existing information on K'Netix and then was able to obtain answers to detailed technical questions from technical experts who regularly log on to the K'Netix system. In fact, technical answers were obtained from people at headquarters in six hours, from people in Europe in eight hours, and from six other Buckman people at various places around the globe in forty-eight hours. All of this timely information helped him create a successful sales proposal in just three days, the result of which was a new $6 million contract.

K'netix was also important as a communication system because it had as much appeal for Buckman's technical experts as it did for Buckman's clients and sales representatives. Buckman's vice president of human resources, Mark Koskiniemi, said, "We have Ph.D.s in our lab who know everything about everything. If they don't share their knowledge, they are not valuable." In contrast to the previous system in which requests were routed through the sales director, the K'netix network encourages open, unrestricted communication among Buckman's experts and the free exchange of ideas. This helps Buckman to find innovative solutions to customer challenges, as well as to develop products in anticipation of future needs. And, it makes the application of innovation easier.

For more on Buckman's K'netix network, go to **http://www.buckman.com/** and click on the "Knowledge Nurture Website."

Sources: Buckman Laboratories. [Online] Available http://www.buckman.com/home.html, 5 September 1999. J. Eckhouse, "Get Creative with Knowledge Sharing—In Today's Culture, Businesses Must Rebuild Their Processes to Take Advantage of Their Knowledge Base," *Information Week*, 8 February 1999, ER19. D.J. Knight, "Strategy in Practice: Making It Happen," *Strategy & Leadership* 26, No. 3 (1 July 1998): 29. M.N. Martinez, "The Collective Power of Employee Knowledge," *HR Magazine* 43, No. 2 (1 February 1998): 88. S. Thurm, "What Do You Know? Getting Employees to Share Their Knowledge Isn't as Simple as Installing New Software; Just Ask Buckman Labs," *The Wall Street Journal*, 21 June 1999, R10.

Key Terms

acquaintance time p. 759

active listening p. 755

address terms p. 759

appointment time p. 759

attribution theory p. 742

closure p. 741

coaching p. 750

communication p. 736

communication medium p. 753

company hot lines p. 763

conduit metaphor p. 746

constructive feedback p. 757

corporate talk shows p. 762

counseling p. 750

cross-cultural communication p. 758

decoding p. 745

defensive bias p. 742

destructive feedback p. 757

discussion time p. 759

downward communication p. 747

empathetic listening p. 756

encoding p. 745

feedback p. 745

formal communication channel p. 747

fundamental attribution error p. 742

hearing p. 755

horizontal communication p. 747

informal communication channel ("grapevine") p. 748

kinesics p. 751

listening p. 755

noise p. 746

nonverbal communication p. 751

online discussion forums p. 761

paralanguage p. 752

perception p. 737

perceptual filters p. 737

schedule time p. 759

selective perception p. 740

self-serving bias p. 743

survey feedback p. 763

televised/videotaped speeches and meetings p. 761

upward communication p. 747

What Would You Do-II?

Stuttgart, Germany, and Auburn Hills, Michigan

At 9 a.m. each day at a Mercedes-Benz plant, the workers take their *first* beer break of the day. When they've finished their beers, the workers light up cigarettes and return to the manufacturing line. At 10:00 a.m. each day in a Chrysler plant, the workers take their first coffee break, have cigarettes outside (because smoking isn't permitted inside the plant), and then return to the manufacturing line. Stuttgart, Germany, and Auburn Hills, Michigan. Mercedes-Benz and Chrysler. These two very different places and two very different companies are now one, having merged into the fourth-largest auto company in the world, DaimlerChrysler.

And while, legally, the merger is now final—officially, DaimlerChrysler is a German-registered company—in management terms, the merger has barely started. To facilitate the merger of these two different languages and two different business cultures, the company bought an Airbus A320 jet, which normally seats 150 people. The plane, which now comfortably sleeps 53 people, makes four round-trip flights a week, shuttling Germans and Americans between the Stuttgart and Detroit international airports.

But despite significant efforts to make the merger run smoothly, significant cultural and communication differences keep getting in the way. For instance, there were arguments over whether new automobile plants should be highly automated (the German preference) or streamlined to increase efficiencies and reduce inventories (the American preference). Furthermore, freewheeling Chrysler managers bristled under the strict planning-oriented approach used by their German counterparts. Steve Harris, formerly Chrysler's chief of communications (now with General Motors), said, "You'd go into a meeting and have to turn to Volume 7, Section 42, page 597" of the planning book. He went on to say that "the Germans pride themselves on analytical research that produces a plan, while the American way is to try for the impossible and keep coming up with new ideas to make it happen."

While some differences were expected—after all, these were both very successful companies with their own ways of doing things—it's obvious that the two sides aren't communicating very well, especially when you consider the silly disagreements they continue to have. For example, just as the new company, DaimlerChrysler, was about to be listed on the New York Stock Exchange, the merger almost fell apart over whether to use American-sized business cards, which are smaller, or the European-sized business cards, which are larger. Tom Stallkamp, Chrysler's president, said, "It got all the way up to me, and I said, 'What the hell, they're only business cards,'" so he chose the slightly larger European-sized cards because they were unique. Likewise, the German emphasis on hierarchy and titles became a point of contention, especially when German managers insisted on their customary title of "Doctor" (the way in which Germans address upper management).

The question, of course, is what to do to handle all of these cultural and communication difficulties. It certainly won't be easy, especially since Daimler's own research indicates that 70 percent of such mergers fail within the first three years. In the end, it comes down to communication and people. One financial analyst said, "The biggest challenge in a merger like this is on the [production] floor. The chairmen and boards of directors can be all for it, but it eventually comes down to the work forces." **If you were in charge of the DaimlerChrysler merger, what would you do?**

Sources: D.A. Blackman, "Autos: A Factory in Alabama Is the Merger in Microcosm," *The Wall Street Journal*, 8 May 1998, B1. F. Gibney, Jr. & J.R. Szczesny, "Worldwide Fender Blender Billed as a 'Merger of Equals,' the Union of Chrysler with Daimler-Benz Has Been Anything But. Yet Amid Crashed Marriages and Careers, a Transglobal Company Is Emerging," *Time*, 24 May 1999, 58. C.J. Williams, "Steering Around Culture Clashes Autos: An Integration Team at Daimler-Chrysler Is Trying to Cope with Cross-Border Differences—Everything from Labor-Management Relations to Germany's 9 A.M. Beer Breaks," *Los Angeles Times*, 17 January 1999, C1.

Critical-Thinking Video Case

Organizational Communication: Valassis Communications

Valassis Communications has been a leader in the sales promotion industry for 27 years. Its flagship product, the freestanding insert, is a colorful booklet containing coupons from some of America's largest companies, such as Kellogg and General Mills. These inserts are distributed through newspapers to over 57 million households each Sunday. Valassis has a reputation as an excellent employer, having twice been recognized as one of the best 100 companies to work for. This video shows how Valassis uses communication to create an extremely good working environment.

Critical-Thinking Questions

1. What factors might influence the organizational communication at Valassis?
2. How might the emphasis on organizational communication have influenced management decisions at Valassis?
3. How might Valassis use technology to improve its organizational communication?

Management Decisions

Is Upward Communication Worth the Risk?

It's been 18 months now since the new CEO was hired, and what a breath of fresh air he's been. He's exciting and visionary, but also friendly and approachable, and has gone out of his way to meet as many people as possible, holding quarterly town hall meetings and doing lunch with lower-level managers and workers at least once a week. And, every time you've heard him speak, he's announced his e-mail address and encouraged anyone who wanted to contact him directly.

In fact, people throughout the organization have been energized by his leadership and the changes he's made to bring about a more open, innovative culture. Of course, not everything can change at once. In fact, things haven't changed much in your division at all. Your division head, Tim Howard, hasn't really embraced the new leadership style. You might even say he's rejected it. Tim is short with subordinates, prone to yelling when things aren't done to his satisfaction, and, in the last year or so, incredibly indecisive. Each week, dozens of big and little decisions that need to be made aren't being made. The whole division just sits there with no direction and no momentum. And, if you come up with an idea that might make the division more competitive and are brave enough to discuss it with Tim, you find out that he's not completely indecisive. Indeed, Tim has a bad case of "not invented here" syndrome, so if it's not his idea, the automatic answer is "no."

It's obvious to you and everyone else that Tim is burned out and that you need a new division head. You're tempted to e-mail the new CEO about the situation—after all, he's open to communication from anyone in the company. However, you worry about going around Tim to top management. And, what if the CEO isn't quite as open as he makes himself out to be?

Questions

1. What risks do you incur if you e-mail the CEO about Tim's leadership of your division?
2. If you were going to e-mail the CEO, what would your opening paragraph say?
3. Would you e-mail the CEO about Tim? Yes or no? Explain your decision.

Management Decisions

"He's Such a Jerk!"

"Diane, where are the antacids? My stomach is killing me!" You've just come back from lunch with four of the ten people in your department. You thought it was going to be one of your regular, friendly lunches that everyone in the office calls the "lunch bunch." Except today, it wasn't fun at all. It started as soon as everyone got in the car to go the restaurant. "Bill," they said, "Mike is driving everyone in the office nuts. We know he's a big producer—after all, he tells us on an hourly basis—but he's also a huge pain in everyone's side. He's arrogant, throws temper tantrums, and is rude to all of us. Basically, he's such a jerk! And we want to know what you're going to do about it."

Of course, you didn't say what you were going to do. In fact, you're not sure. So you spent your lunch hour eating crow, gathering as much information as you could, and wishing you had grabbed a sandwich in your office, locked the door, and read the *Interactive Wall Street Journal* on the Web while you ate. What you didn't tell the "lunch bunch" is that Mike had approached you a few days ago with his own complaints about them, namely, that they weren't cooperative and would often ignore his comments or requests. What are you going to do?

Questions

1. Explain your plan for handling this situation. What is your basic plan for handling Mike? What is your basic plan for handling the lunch bunch?
2. Giving employees feedback can sometimes be difficult. Outline the four or five points you would make if you were to give Mike feedback based on what you've heard.

Source: P. Carbonara, "Fire Me. I Dare You! Sane Strategies for Managing the Prima Donna in Your Life," *Inc.*, 1 March 1997, 58.

Develop Your Management Potential

I Don't Agree, but I'm Listening.

Being a good listener is a critical part of effective communication. Without it, you're unlikely to be a good manager. Therefore, the purpose of this assignment is to help you develop your listening skills. And, there's no better way to do that than to talk to someone whose views are quite different from yours.

In the best of situations, being a good listener is difficult. Because of perceptual filters, distractions, or daydreams, you retain only about 25 percent of what you hear. However, it can be almost impossible to be a good listener when you're talking to someone who has very different views and opinions. When you talk to people with different views, it's easy to interrupt, jump to conclusions about what they'll say, and hurry them to finish their points (which you don't want to listen to anyway), so you can "correct" their thinking with your opinions.

To complete this assignment, you'll have to find someone who has different views or opinions on some topic (handgun control, abortion, capital punishment, and euthanasia are just some of the topics on which you can always find someone with a different viewpoint). Once you've found someone, conduct a ten-minute listening session, following this simple rule: Before stating your opinion, you must first accurately reflect or paraphrase the statement that your listening partner just made (be sure to reread section 3.2 on listening). So if your listening partner said, "Women shouldn't have to ask anyone for permission for what they do to their bodies. If they decide they want an abortion, they should go ahead and have it," you would have to accurately paraphrase that statement in your own words before being allowed to make your point or disagree with your partner's. If you don't paraphrase it correctly, your listening partner will tell you. If you or your partner have difficulty accurately paraphrasing a statement, then ask the other person to repeat the statement, and try again. Also, don't parrot the response by repeating it word for word. Good listening isn't mimicry. It's capturing the essence of what others have said in your own words. And, before your listening partner responds, he or she, too, has to accurately paraphrase what you say. Continue this listening-based discussion for ten minutes.

Questions

1. Was this different from the way in which you normally discuss contentious topics with other people? Why or why not?
2. Was it difficult to reflect or paraphrase your listening partner's perspectives? Explain and give an example.
3. What led to more effective listening for you, active listening techniques or empathetic listening techniques? Explain.

End Notes

Chapter 1

1. Laurent, "Management Magicians," *Government Executive*, 1 February 1998.
2. J. A. Byrne, "The Craze for Consultants," *Business Week*, 25 July 1994, 60–66.
3. T. Peters, "The Leadership Alliance" (Pat Carrigan excerpt), *In Search of Excellence* (Northbrook, IL: Video Arts, distributor,1985), videocassette.
4. R. Stagner, "Corporate Decision Making," *Journal of Applied Psychology* 53 (1969): 1–13.
5. D. W. Bray, R.J. Campbell, & D.L. Grant, Formative Years in Business: A Long-Term AT&T Study of Managerial Lives (New York: Wiley, 1993).
6. Dumaine, "The New Non-Manager Managers," *Fortune*, 22 February 1993, 80–84.
7. Ibid.
8. G. A. Patterson, "Bad Fit: Lands' End Kicks Out Modern New Managers, Rejecting a Makeover," *The Wall Street Journal*, 3 April 1995, A1.
9. S. B. Garland, S.Hamm, & M. France. "The Cops Converge on Microsoft," *Business Week*, 18 May 1998, 34–37.
10. Fisher, "Making Change Stick," *Fortune*, 17 April 1995, 121–127.
11. M. Carter, "Back from the Dead (Ford Revitalizes Jaguar Cars)," *The European*, 6 April 1998, 22–23.
12. Staff Reporter, "Entrepreneur Mary Kay Ash: Unflagging Faith Lifted Her to Top of Cosmetics World," *Investor's Business Daily*," 5 May 1998, A1.
13. Farnham, "Mary Kay's Lessons in Leadership," *Fortune*, 20 September 1993, 68–77.
14. G. Colvin. "The Changing Art of Becoming Unbeatable" *Fortune*, 24 November 1997, 299–300.
15. K. Labich, "Is Herb Kelleher America's Best CEO?" *Fortune*, 2 May 1994, 44–52.
16. H. S. Jonas, III, R.E. Fry, & S. Srivastva, "The Office of the CEO: Understanding the Executive Experience," *Academy of Management Executive* 4 (1990): 36–47.
17. K. Labich, "Is Herb Kelleher America's Best CEO?" *Fortune*, 2 May 1994, 44–52.
18. H. S. Jonas, III, R.E. Fry, & S. Srivastva, "The Office of the CEO: Understanding the Executive Experience," *Academy of Management Executive* 4 (1990): 36–47.
19. Saporito, "David Glass Won't Crack under Fire," *Fortune*, 3 February 1991, 75–80.
20. L. Jones Townsel, "David E. Jackson: Wal-Mart's $11 Billion Executive," *Ebony*, 1 June 1997.
21. Saporito, "David Glass Won't Crack under Fire," *Fortune*, 3 February 1991, 75–80.
22. Ibid.
23. Ibid.
24. Milbank, "'New-Collar' Work: Telephone Sales Reps Do Unrewarding Jobs that Few Can Abide," *The Wall Street Journal*, 9 September 1993, A1.
25. Ibid.
26. B. M. Bass, *Stogdill's Handbook of Leadership* (New York: Free Press, 1981).
27. J. Vrba, "The 'Grass Roots' Training of a Young Administrator," *Nursing Homes*, 1 April 1995.
28. S. Tully, "What Team Leaders Need to Know," *Fortune*, 20 February 1995.
29. Ibid.
30. K. Hultman, "The 10 Commandments of Team Leadership," *Training & Development*, 1 February 1998, 12–13.
31. S. Tully, "What Team Leaders Need to Know," *Fortune*, 20 February 1995.
32. N. Steckler & N. Fondas, "Building Team Leader Effectiveness: A Diagnostic Tool," *Organizational Dynamics*, Winter 1995, 20–34.
33. J. S. Case, "What the Experts Forgot to Mention," *Inc.*, 1 September 1993, 66.
34. S. Tully, "What Team Leaders Need to Know," *Fortune*, 20 February 1995.
35. H. Mintzberg, *The Nature of Managerial Work* (New York: Harper & Row, 1973).
36. C. P. Hales, "What Do Managers Do? A Critical Review of the Evidence," *Journal of Management Studies* 23, no. 1 (1986): 88–115.
37. J. Huey, "The World's Best Brand," *Fortune*, 31 May 1993, 44.
38. M. Boyd, "Motivating on a Dime," *Sales & Marketing Management*, 1 March 1995.
39. Ashley, S. "Keys to Chrysler's Comeback," *Mechanical Engineering*, 1 November 1997. L. Brooke, "Chrysler's 1996 Minivan," *Automotive Industries*, 1 January 1995.
40. Hauss, "Technology Gives Early Warning of News Breaks," *Public Relations Journal*, 1 May 1995.
41. Deutschman, "The Managing Wisdom of High-Tech Superstars," *Fortune*, 17 October 1994, 197–206.
42. R. Gibson, "McDonald's Makes Changes in Top Management," *The Wall Street Journal*, 1 May 1998, A3.
43. J. Bailey, "Waste Management to Scrap 1,200 Jobs in Effort to Rein in Costs, Bureaucracy," *The Wall Street Journal*, 11 November 1997, A6.
44. Fisher, "Making Change Stick," *Fortune*, 17 April 1995.
45. J. S. Lublin & A. Markels, "How Three CEOs Achieved Fast Turnarounds," *TheWall Street Journal*, 21 July 1995, B1.
46. D. W. Linden, "You Want Somebody to Like You, Get a Dog." *Forbes*, 28 August 1995, 44–46.
47. O. Suris & N.M. Christian, "UAW Bet on a Peacemaker When Leadership Chose Ford," *TheWall Street Journal Interactive Edition*, 5 September 1996.
48. N. M. Christian, O. Suris, & G. Stern, "UAW and Ford Convene to Negotiate Auto Pact," *The Wall Street Journal Interactive Edition*, 9 September 1996.
49. L. A. Hill, *Becoming a Manager: Mastery of a New Identity* (Boston, MA: Harvard Business School Press, 1992).
50. R. L. Katz, "Skills of an Effective Administrator," *Harvard Business Review*, September–October 1974, 90–102.
51. C. A. Bartlett & S. Ghoshal, "Changing the Role of Top Management: Beyond Systems to People," *Harvard Business Review*, May–June 1995, 132–142.
52. F. L. Schmidt & J.E. Hunter, "Development of a Causal Model of Process Determining Job Performance," *Current Directions in Psychological Science* 1 (1992): 89–92.
53. J. B. Miner, "Sentence Completion Measures in Personnel Research: The Development and Validation of the Miner Sentence Completion Scales," in *Personality Assessment in Organizations*, eds. H. J. Bernardin & D.A. Bownas (New York: Praeger, 1986), 147–146.
54. M. W. McCall, Jr. & M.M. Lombardo, "What Makes a Top Executive?" *Psychology Today*, February 1983, 26–31. E. van Velsor & J. Brittain, "Why Executives Derail: Perspectives across Time and Cultures," *Academy of Management Executive*, November 1995, 62–72.
55. M. W. McCall, Jr. & M.M. Lombardo, "What Makes a Top Executive?" *Psychology Today*, February 1983, 26–31.
56. S. N. Chakravarty, "The Best-Laid Plans . . . ," *Forbes*, 3 January 1994, 44–45.
57. T. E. Ricks, "The New Brass Get in Touch With Their 'Inner Jerks," *The Wall Street Journal Interactive Edition*, 19 January 1998.
58. A.K. Naj, "Corporate Therapy: The Latest Addition to Executive Suite Is Psychologist's Couch," *The Wall Street Journal*, 29 August 1994, A1.
59. S. Stecklow, "Chief Prerequisite for College President's Job: Stamina," *The Wall Street Journal*, 1 December 1994, B1.
60. J. Pfeffer, "Producing Sustainable Competitive Advantage through the Effective Management of People," *Academy of Management Executive* 9 (1995): 55–72.
61. Ibid.
62. M.A. Huselid, "The Impact of Human Resource Management Practices on Turnover, Productivity, and Corporate Financial Performance," *Academy of Management Journal* 38 (1995): 635–672.
63. McDonald & A. Smith, "A Proven Connection: Performance Management and Business Results," *Compensation & Benefits Review* 27, no. 6 (1 January 1995): 59.
64. Schneider & D.E. Bowen, "Employee and Customer Perceptions of Service in Banks: Replication and Extension," *Journal of Applied Psychology* 70 (1985): 423–33. B. Schneider, J.J. Parkington, & V.M. Buxton, "Employee and Customer Perceptions of Service in Banks," *Administrative Science Quarterly* 25 (1980): 252–67.

Chapter 2

1. S. Ginsberg, "CEO's Aggressive, No-Nonsense Style Leads EA to Victory," *San Francisco Business Times*, 26 September 1997.

2. E. Romanelli & M.L. Tushman, "Organizational Transformation as Punctuated Equilibrium: An Empirical Test," *Academy of Management Journal* 37 (1994): 1141–1166.
3. H. Banks, "A Sixties Industry in a Nineties Economy," *Forbes*, 9 May 1994, 107–112.
4. L. Cowan, "Cheap Fuel Should Carry Many Airlines to More Record Profits for 1st Quarter," *The Wall Street Journal*, 4 April 1998, B17A.
5. G. Morgenson, "Denial in Battle Creek," *Forbes*, 7 October 1996, 44–46.
6. J. B. White & J.S. Lublin, "Some Concerns Try to Rebuild Loyalty among Employees," *The Wall Street Journal Interactive Edition*, 27 September 1996.
7. K. A. Dolan, "Help Wanted: Urgent!" *Forbes*, 7 October 1996, 18–20.
8. S. McGee, "Continued Boom in U.S. Economy Upsets Timing on Cyclical Stocks," *The Wall Street Journal*, 30 March 1998, C1.
9. G. Eisenstodt, "Job Shokku," *Forbes*, 31 July 1995, 42–43.
10. D. P. Hamilton, "Asia's Deflation Rattles Economists World-Wide," *The Interactive Wall Street Journal*, 27 January 1998.
11. R. Norton, "Where Is this Economy Really Heading?" *Fortune*, 7 August 1995, 54–56.
12. T. Grillo, "Trying to Turn Over a New Leaf: With Sales Sagging, Encyclopedia Britannica Looks to Go On Line," *Boston Globe*, 16 June 1995.
13. A. Shanley, C. Crabb, & T. Kamiva, "More Than a Concession, Family Friendly Policy Is Becoming a Competitive Tool," *Chemical Engineering*, 1 March 1998.
14. S. Crampton, J. Hodge, & J. Mishra, "Transition—Ready or Not: The Aging of America's Work Force," *Public Personnel Management* 25 (Summer 1996): 243.
15. E. Graham, "Working Parents' Torment: Teens after School," *The Wall Street Journal*, 9 May 1995, B1.
16. D. Frum, "Speed Brake," *Forbes*, 11 October 1993,162.
17. D. Lohse, "Family Leave Act Offers a Wide Range of Benefits," *The Wall Street Journal*, 28 April 1995, C1.
18. A. Caffrey, "Bay State's Enforcement of 'Rideshare' Draws Fire," *The Wall Street Journal*, 18 March 1998, NE1.
19. R. J. Bies & T.R. Tyler, "The Litigation Mentality in Organizations: A Test of Alternative Psychological Explanations," *Organization Science* 4 (1993): 352–366.
20. D. Jones, "Fired Workers Fight Back . . . and Win: Laws, Juries Shift Protection to Terminated Employees," *USA Today*, 2 April 1998, B1.
21. Ibid.
22. J. Semas, "Companies Want to Recall Defective Product Liability Laws," *San Francisco Business Times*, 18 August 1995.
23. J. Semas, "Companies Want to Recall Defective Product Liability Laws," *San Francisco Business Times*, 18 August 1995.
24. J. Flanigan, "Selling Used Cars the Blockbuster Video Way," *Indianapolis Business Journal*, 15 July 1996, 0B.
25. D. Smart & C. Martin, "Manufacturer Responsiveness to Consumer Correspondence: An Empirical Investigation of Consumer Perceptions," *Journal of Consumer Affairs* 26 (1992): 104.
26. Cotton Incorporated, What's New in Cotton: Lifestyle Monitor. [Online] Available http://www.cottoninc.com/lifemon2a.htm, October 4, 1996.
27. S.G. Maycumber, "Cotton Inc.'s Lifestyle Monitor Puts Together a Year's Data; Price Looms Large in Apparel Purchases," *Daily News Record*, 4 January 1996, 11.
28. S.A. Zahra & S.S. Chaples, "Blind Spots in Competitive Analysis," *Academy of Management Executive* 7 (1993): 7–28.
29. C. Haddad, "BellSouth Wields the Knife to Fend Off Predators," *Atlanta Constitution*, 20 May 1995.
30. J.M. Moran, "Getting Closer Together—Videophones Don't Deliver TV Quality Sound, Visuals, But They're Improving," *The Seattle Times*, 15 March 1998.
31. T. Shurley, "Internet Phone System Could Revolutionize Long Distance," *Springfield Business Journal*, 29 May 1995.
32. K.G. Provan, "Embeddedness, Interdependence, and Opportunism in Organizational Supplier-Buyer Networks, *Journal of Management* 19 (1993): 841–856.
33. D. Takahashi, "How the Competition Got Ahead of Intel in Making Cheap Chips," *The Wall Street Journal*, 12 February 1998, A1.
34. F. Shalom, "Clothing Firms Fight Wal-Mart Price Rollbacks," *Montreal Gazette*, 6 July 1995.
35. C. Duff, "Big Stores' Outlandish Demands Alienate Small Suppliers," *The Wall Street Journal*, 27 October 1995, B1.
36. B.K. Pilling, L.A. Crosby, & D.W. Jackson, "Relational Bonds in Industrial Exchange: An Experimental Test of the Transaction Cost Economic Framework," *Journal of Business Research* 30 (1994): 237–251.
37. W. Tucker, "Overregulation and the Black Market,"*Consumers' Research Magazine* 74 (1 October1991): 32.
38. S. Kazman, "Large Vehicles Are the Solution, Not the Problem," *The Wall Street Journal*, 12 March 1998, A18.
39. R. Spencer, "Final Standards Issued on Care at Nation's Nursing Homes," *Los Angeles Times*, 11 November 1994, D-2.
40. B. Menninger & D. Margolies, "Business Groans under Weight of Regulations," *Puget Sound Business Journal*, 3 March 1995, 16.
41. A. Paine-Andrews, K.J. Harris, S.B. Fawcett, K.P. Richter, R.K. Lewis, V.T. Francisco, J.S. Johnston, "Evaluating a Statewide Partnership for Reducing Risks for Chronic Diseases," *Journal of Community Health*, 1 October 1997, 343–359.
42. R. Adams & K. Jennings, "Media Advocacy: A Case Study of Philip Sokolof's Cholesterol Awareness Campaigns," *Journal of Consumer Affairs* 27 (1993): 145–165.
43. A. Oyog, "France: Businesses Wary of Boycott Backlash from Nuclear Tests," *Inter Press Service English News Wire*, 29 July 1995.
44. M. Hertsgaard, "Are the French Headed for a Meltdown? A Motley Flotilla and Consumer Boycotts Could Give Paris Fits over Nuclear Testing," *Washington Post*, 3 September 1995.
45. "Technology Weighs Heavily on Minds of Hoteliers," *Hotel & Motel Management*, 6 November 1995.
46. N. Wingfield, "UPS Strike Proves a Mixed Bag for Merchants in Cyberspace," *The Wall Street Journal Interactive Edition*, 15 August 1997.
47. D.F. Jennings & J.R. Lumpkin, "Insights Between Environmental Scanning Activities and Porter's Generic Strategies: An Empirical Analysis," *Journal of Management* 4 (1992): 791–803.
48. B. Ettore, "Managing Competitive Intelligence," *Management Review*, October 1995, 15–19.
49. S.E. Jackson & J.E. Dutton, "Discerning Threats and Opportunities," *Administrative Science Quarterly* 33 (1988): 370–387.
50. J.B. Thomas, S.M. Clark, & D.A. Gioia, "Strategic Sensemaking and Organizational Performance: Linkages among Scanning, Interpretation, Action, and Outcomes," *Academy of Management Journal* 36 (1993): 239–270.
51. R. Daft, J. Sormunen, & D. Parks, "Chief Executive Scanning, Environmental Characteristics, and Company Performance: An Empirical Study," *Strategic Management Journal* 9 (1988): 123–139. D. Miller & P.H. Friesen, "Strategy-Making and Environment: The Third Link," *Strategic Management Journal* 4 (1983): 221–235.
52. S. Kraft, "Tradition under Siege/ Supermarkets? Sacre Bleu!/A Shopping Revolution Imperils French Merchants," *Los Angeles Times*, 5 May 1996, D10.
53. R. Frank, "Corporate Focus: Frito-Lay Devours Snack-Food Business," *The Wall Street Journal*, 27 October 1995.
54. L. Hays, "Gerstner Is Struggling as He Tries to Change Ingrained IBM Culture," *The Wall Street Journal*, 13 May 1994, A1.
55. P. Elmer-DeWitt, "Mine, All Mine; Bill Gates Wants a Piece of Everybody's Action. But Can He Get It?" *Time*, 5 June 1995.
56. D.M. Boje, "The Storytelling Organization: A Study of Story Performance in an Office-Supply Firm," *Administrative Science Quarterly* 36 (1991): 106–126.
57. M.H. McCormack, *What They Don't Teach You at Harvard Business School* (New York: Bantam, 1984).
58. T.K. McCraw, "Henry Ford and Alfred Sloan," Case 26 in *Management: Past and Present, A Casebook on the History of American Business*, by A.D. Chandler, Jr., T.K. McCraw, & R.S. Tedlow (Cincinnati, OH: South-Western College Publishing, 1996).
59. A.L. Wilkins & N.J. Bristow, "For Successful Organization Culture, Honor Your Past," *Academy of Management Executive* 1 (1987): 221–229.
60. D.R. Denison & A.K. Mishra, "Toward a Theory of Organizational Culture and Effectiveness," *Organization Science* 6 (1995): 204–223.

61. L. Hays, "Gerstner Is Struggling as He Tries to Change Ingrained IBM Culture," *The Wall Street Journal*, 13 May 1994, A1.
62. A. Deutschman, "How H-P Continues to Grow and Grow," *Fortune*, 2 May 1994, 90–100.
63. T.A. Stewart, "Company Values that Add Value," *Fortune*, 8 July 1996, 145–147.
64. P.E. Bierly, III. & J.C. Spender, "Culture and High Reliability Organizations: The Case of the Nuclear Submarine," *Journal of Management* 21 (1995): 639–656.
65. D.Q. Mills, "The Decline and Rise of IBM," *Sloan Management Review* 37 (1 June 1996).
66. S. Albert & D.A. Whetten, "Organizational Identity," *Research in Organizational Behavior* 7 (1985): 263–295. C.M. Fiol, "Managing Culture as a Competitive Resource: An Identity-Based View of Sustainable Competitive Advantage," *Journal of Management* 17 (1991): 191–211.
67. J. Fuquay, "Exploring New Territory: CEO Jack Messman Is Bucking Tradition as He Transforms Union Pacific," *Fort Worth Star-Telegram*, 1 July 1996, 14.
68. R. Heaster, "A Shift in Direction: Yellow Corp. Seeks Return to Strength with New Leader," *Kansas City Star*, 24 July 1996, B1.

Chapter 3

1. J. L. Badaracco, Jr. & A.P. Webb, "Business Ethics: A View from the Trenches," *California Management Review* 37 (1995): 8–28.
2. M. Jackson (Associated Press), "Workplace Cheating Rampant, Half of Employees Surveyed Admit They Take Unethical Actions," *Peoria Journal Star*, 5 April 1997.
3. G. Stern & J.S. Lublin, "New GM Rules Curb Wining, Dining by Suppliers," *The Wall Street Journal Interactive Edition*, 5 June 1996.
4. M. Maremont, "Blind Ambition: How the Pursuit of Results Got Out of Hand at Bausch & Lomb," *Business Week*, 23 October 1995.
5. M. Bordwin, "Don't Ask Employees to Do Your Dirty Work," *Management Review*, 1 October 1995.
6. L. S. Paine, Managing for Organizational Integrity," *Harvard Business Review*, March-April 1994, 106–117.
7. M. Maremont, "Blind Ambition: How the Pursuit of Results Got Out of Hand at Bausch & Lomb," *Business Week*, 23 October 1995.
8. E. Nelson, "Bausch & Lomb Will Disburse up to $68 Million to Settle Suit," *The Wall Street Journal Interactive Edition*, 2 August 1996.
9. S. L. Robinson & R.J. Bennett, "A Typology of Deviant Workplace Behaviors: A Multidimensional Scaling Study," *Academy of Management Journal* 38 (1995): 555–572.
10. Ibid.
11. R. Wright, "Under Siege: Cons, Fraud, Theft, Vandalism, and Shoplifting . . . It's Not What They Teach in Business School, But Maybe They Should," *Profit-Toronto*, 1 December 1995.
12. J. Fox, "Canadian Retailers Take Bite out of Crime," *Discount Store News*, 17 July 1995.
13. R. Mathews, "Loss Prevention: It's Later Than You Think," *Progressive Grocer*, February 1997, 70.
14. M. P. Coco, Jr., "The New War Zone: The Workplace," *SAM Advanced Management Journal* 63, no. 1 (1998): 15. M.G. Harvey & R.A. Cosier, "Homicides in the Workplace: Crisis or False Alarm?" *Business Horizons* 38, no. 10 (1995): 11.
15. D. Yawn, "New Rules Increase Manager Liability, UM Expert Warns," *Memphis Business Journal*, 16 October 1995.
16. D. R. Dalton, M.B. Metzger, & J.W. Hill, "The "New" U.S. Sentencing Commission Guidelines: A Wake-Up Call for Corporate America," *Academy of Management Executive* 8 (1994): 7–16.
17. B. Ettore, "Crime and Punishment: A Hard Look at White-Collar Crime," *Management Review* 83 (1994): 10–16.
18. F. Robinson & C.C. Pauze, "What Is a Board's Liability for Not Adopting a Compliance Program?" *Healthcare Financial Management* 51, no. 9 (1997): 64.
19. Ibid.
20. L.A. Hays, "A Matter of Time: Widow Sues IBM over Death Benefits," *The Wall Street Journal*, 6 July 1995.
21. T.M. Jones, "Ethical Decision Making by Individuals in Organizations: An Issue-Contingent Model," *Academy of Management Review* 16 (1991): 366–395.
22. B. Mook, "Group Gets Tough on 'Software Piracy,'" *Denver Business Journal*, 6 March 1998, 19A.
23. L. Kohlberg, "Stage and Sequence: The Cognitive-Developmental Approach to Socialization," in *Handbook of Socialization Theory and Research*, ed. D.A. Goslin (Chicago: Rand McNally, 1969). L. Trevino, "Moral Reasoning and Business Ethics: Implications for Research, Education, and Management," *Journal of Business Ethics* 11 (1992): 445–459.
24. L.T. Hosmer, "Trust: The Connecting Link Between Organizational Theory and Philosophical Ethics," *Academy of Management Review* 20 (1995): 379–403.
25. R. K. Bennett, "How Honest Are We?" *Reader's Digest*, December 1995, 49–55.
26. M. R. Cunningham, D.T. Wong, & A.P. Barbee, "Self-Presentation Dynamics on Overt Integrity Tests: Experimental Studies of the Reid Report," *Journal of Applied Psychology* 79 (1994): 643–658.
27. H. J. Bernardin, "Validity of an Honest Test in Predicting Theft among Convenience Store Employees," *Academy of Management Journal* 36 (1993): 1097–1108.
28. J. M. Collins & F.L. Schmidt, "Personality, Integrity, and White Collar Crime: A Construct Validity Study," *Personnel Psychology* (1993): 295–311.
29. W. C. Borman, M.A. Hanson, & J.W. Hedge, "Personnel Selection," *Annual Review of Psychology* 48 (1997).
30. P. E. Murphy, "Corporate Ethics Statements: Current Status and Future Prospects," *Journal of Business Ethics* 14 (1995): 727–740.
31. S. J. Harrington, "What Corporate America Is Teaching about Ethics," *Academy of Management Executive* 5 (1991): 21–30.
32. L. A. Berger, "Train All Employees to Solve Ethical Dilemmas," *Best's Review—Life-Health Insurance Edition* 95 (1995): 70–80.
33. R. McGarver, "Doing the Right Thing," *Training* 30 (1993): 35–38.
34. B. Ettore, Crime and Punishment: A Hard Look at White-Collar Crime," *Management Review* 83 (1994): 10–16.
35. M. Schwartz, "Business Ethics: Time to Blow the Whistle?" *Globe and Mail*, 5 March 1998, B2.
36. M. P. Miceli & J.P Near, "Whistleblowing: Reaping the Benefits," *Academy of Management Executive* 8 (1994): 65–72.
37. H. R. Bower, *Social Responsibilities of the Businessman* (New York: Harper & Row, 1953).
38. B. Carton, "Animal Instincts: Gillette Faces Wrath of Children in Testing on Rats and Rabbits," *The Wall Street Journal*, 5 September 1995.
39. M. Zetlin, "Companies Find Profit in Corporate Giving," *Management Review* 79 (1990): 10–15.
40. S. L. Wartick & P.L. Cochran, "The Evolution of the Corporate Social Performance Model," *Academy of Management Review* 10 (1985): 758–769.
41. T. Donaldson & L.E. Preston, "The Stakeholder Theory of the Corporation: Concepts, Evidence, and Implications," *Academy of Management Review* 20 (1995): 65–91.
42. M. B. E. Clarkson, "A Stakeholder Framework for Analyzing and Evaluating Corporate Social Performance," *Academy of Management Review* 20 (1995): 92–117.
43. G. White, "Some Suppliers of Kmart Want Payment Up Front," *Los Angeles Times*, 19 December 1995.
44. M. Silver, "Doing Your Bit to Save the Earth," *U.S. News & World Report*, 2 April 1990, 61–62.
45. L. E. Preston, "Stakeholder Management and Corporate Performance," *Journal of Behavioral Economics* 19 (1990): 361–375.
46. E. W. Orts, "Beyond Shareholders: Interpreting Corporate Constituency Statutes," *The George Washington Law Review* 61 (1992): 14–135.
47. A. B. Carroll, "A Three-Dimensional Conceptual Model of Corporate Performance," *Academy of Management Review* 4 (1979): 497–505.
48. A. B. Carroll, "A Three-Dimensional Conceptual Model of Corporate Performance," *Academy of Management Review*, 4 (1979): 497–505.
49. J. Carlton & J.E. Rigdon, "After an Apple Buyout, Sun Could Be Mighty in Internet Computers," *The Wall Street Journal*, 24 January 1996, A1.
50. C. Bowman, "Success of Capital Area's War on Smog Challenged," *Sacremento Bee*, 7 February 1998, A1.
51. B. O'Brian, "An Illegal Pleasure: The Smell in the Air of Bread Being Baked," *The Wall Street Journal*, 13 April 1994, A7.
52. A. Gerlin, "A Matter of Degree: How a Jury Decided That a Coffee Spill Is Worth $2.9 Million," *The Wall Street Journal*, 1 September 1994, A1.

53. L. Wozniak, "Spilled Coffee Burns Customer, Who Sues," *St. Petersberg Times*, 19 May 1995, 1E.
54. M. Jackson (Associated Press), "Sales Promotions Tied to Charity Deserve Scrutiny," *Peoria Journal Star*, 30 December 1997, B2.
55. M. Sharfman, "Changing Institutional Rules: The Evolution of Corporate Philanthropy: 1883–1953," *Business and Society* 33, no. 34 (1994): 236.
56. "T. Bryant, "Judge Rejects New Trial in Case of Woman Paralyzed in Suzuki Samurai Accident," *St. Louis Post-Dispatch*, 2 February 1998, C4. "Inclined to Roll, Suzuki Samurai Car Gets Unfavorable Rating Because of Tipping Tendency," *Time*, 13 June 1988, 51.
57. K. R. Sheets, "Annals of Enterprise, Sidekick: Successor to Suzuki Samurai 4-Wheel Drive Vehicle," *U.S. News & World Report*, 25 July 1988, 48.
58. N. Templin, "Nissan Recalls and Destroys Some Minivans," *The Wall Street Journal*, 9 December 1993, B1.
59. P. Romeo, "McDonald's Battles Critics with $160M Recycling Plan," *Nation's Restaurant News*, 30 April 1990, 18-19. S. Shundich, "Green in Green: Beyond the Three Rs: There's a Whole New Set of Expectations When Food Service Operations Talk about Profiting from Environmental Initiatives," *Restaurants & Institutions*, 15 September 1995.
60. H. Haines, "Noah Joins Ranks of Socially Responsible Funds," *Dow Jones News Service*, 13 October 1995.
61. M. B. Meznar, D. Nigh, & C.Y. Kwok, "Effect of Announcements of Withdrawal from South Africa on Stockholder Wealth," *Academy of Management Journal* 37 (1994): 1633–1648.
62. D. Kadlec & B. Van Voorst, "The New World of Giving: Companies Are Doing More Good, and Demanding More Back," *Time*, 5 May 1997.
63 P. Carlin, "Will Rapid Growth Stunt Corporate Do-Gooders?" *Business and Society Review*, Spring 1995, 36–43.
64. B. Finley, "Critics of Starbucks: Gifts Don't Amount to a Hill of Beans," *Denver Post*, 17 April 1998, A23. M. Scott, "An Interview with Howard Schultz, CEO of Starbucks Coffee," *Business Ethics Magazine*, November/December 1995.

Chapter 4

1. J. Fallows, "The Cutting Edge; Alas, Poor Kaypro . . . A Requiem for PCs Past," *Los Angeles Times*, 11 April 1994, 31.
2. S. Tully, "Why Go for Stretch Targets," *Fortune*, 14 November 1994, 145.
3. E. A. Locke & G. P. Latham, *A Theory of Goal Setting & Task Performance* (Englewood Cliffs, NJ: Prentice Hall, 1990).
4. M. E. Tubbs, "Goal-Setting: A Meta-Analytic Examination of the Empirical Evidence," *Journal of Applied Psychology* 71 (1986): 474-83.
5. G. P. Latham & S.B. Kinne, "Improving Job Performance Through Training in Goal Setting," *Journal of Applied Psychology* 59 (1974): 187–191.
6. J. Bavelas & E. S. Lee, "Effect of Goal Level on Performance: A Trade-Off of Quantity and Quality," *Canadian Journal of Psychology* 32 (1978): 219–240.
7. A. Farnham, "Mary Kay's Lessons in Leadership," *Fortune*, 20 September 1993.
8. D. Greising, P. Dwyer, & W. Zeller, "A Destination, but No Flight Plan," *Business Week*, 16 May 1994, 74–75.
9. M. Henterly, "Delta Will Move Cargo into Separate Division," *Cincinnati Enquirer*, 8 November 1995.
10. C. C. Miller, "Strategic Planning and Firm Performance: A Synthesis of More Than Two Decades of Research," *Academy of Management Performance* 37 (1994): 1649–1665.
11. H. Mintzberg, "Rethinking Strategic Planning," Part I: Pitfalls and Fallacies, *Long Range Planning* 27 (1994): 12–21; Part II: New Roles for Planners: 22–30. H. Mintzberg, "The Pitfalls of Strategic Planning," *California Management Review* 36 (1993): 32–47.
12. S. Branch, "What's Eating McDonald's?" *Fortune*, 13 October 1997, 122–125.
13. K. Pope, "International: Runaway Growth at Phone Giant Nokia Humbles Newcomer after Early Success," *The Wall Street Journal*, 12 March 1996.
14. H. Mintzberg, "The Pitfalls of Strategic Planning," *California Management Review* 36 (1993): 32–47.
15. S. Cummings, "Pericles of Athens—Drawing from the Essence of Strategic Leadership," *Business Horizons* 38, no. 6 (1995): 22.
16. C. Rollin, "Rollin's Ancient History: History of the Persians and Grecians," Sections XII–XIV and VIII–XI, *History of the World*, 1 January 1992.
17. E. A. Locke & G. P. Latham, *A Theory of Goal Setting & Task Performance* (Englewood Cliffs, NJ: Prentice Hall, 1990).
18. A. King, B. Oliver, B. Sloop, & K. Vaverek, *Planning and Goal Setting for Improved Performance, Participant's Guide* (Cincinnati, OH: Thomson Executive Press, 1995).
19. E. A. Locke & G. P. Latham, *A Theory of Goal Setting & Task Performance* (Englewood Cliffs, NJ: Prentice Hall, 1990).
20. J. R. Hollenbeck, C.R. Williams, & H.J. Klein, "An Empirical Examination of the Antecedents of Commitment to Difficult Goals," *Journal of Applied Psychology* 74 (1989): 18–23.
21. A. Harmon, "Teamwork: Chrysler Builds a Concept as Well as a Car," *Los Angeles Times*, 26 April 1992, Business p. 1.
22. S. Creedy, "USAir Flies New Route to Financial Survival," *Pittsburgh Post-Gazette*, 7 January 1996.
23. Ibid.
24. A. Bandura & D. H. Schunk, "Cultivating Competence, Self-Efficacy, and Intrinsic Interest through Proximal Self-Motivation," *Journal of Personality and Social Psychology* 41 (1981): 586–598.
25. T. Incantalupo, "Week in Wheels Road Test: Buick Falls Just Shy of Grand," *Newsday*, 7 April 1995, C06.
26. E. A. Locke & G. P. Latham, *A Theory of Goal Setting & Task Performance*. (Englewood Cliffs, NJ: Prentice Hall, 1990).
27. D. A. Blackmon, "FedEx Plans to Establish a Marketplace in Cyberspace—Shipper Aims to Deliver the Goods as it Moves into Internet Commerce," *The Wall Street Journal*, 9 October 1996.
28. E. H. Bowman & D. Hurry, "Strategy through the Option Lens: An Integrated View of Resource Investments and the Incremental-Choice Process," *Academy of Management Review* 18 (1993): 760–782.
29. N. A. Wishart, J. J. Elam, & D. Robey, "Redrawing the Portrait of a Learning Organization: Inside Knight-Ridder, Inc.," *Academy of Management Executive* 10 (1996): 7–20.
30. Ibid.
31. J. Samuelson, "The Geeky Garbageman," *Forbes*, 8 April 1996.
32. J. C. Collins & J. I. Porras, "Organizational Vision and Visionary Organizations," *California Management Review*, Fall 1991, 30–52.
33. Ibid.
34. Ibid.
35. Ibid.
36. M. Keller, "Corporate Vision." *Automotive Industries* 172 (1992): 11.
37. J. C. Collins & J. I. Porras, "Organizational Vision and Visionary Organizations," *California Management Review*, Fall 1991, 30–52.
38. M. Larson, "Ford Puts Quality Data in Human Hands," *Quality Online*. [Online] Available http://www.qualitymag.com/1297f3.html, 5 November 1997.
39. J. A. Pearce & F. David, "Corporate Mission Statements: The Bottom Line," *Academy of Management Executive* 1 (1987): 109–116.
40. S. Kraft, "Disney Magic Is Finally Starting to Work at French Theme Park," *Los Angeles Times*, 4 February 1996, Business p. 1.
41. L. Iococca, with W. Novak, *Iococca* (New York: Bantom, 1984).
42. Ibid.
43. E. Marlow & R. Schilhavy, "Expectation Issues in Management by Objectives Programs," *Industrial Management* 33, no. 4 (1991): 29.
44. M. Peitz, "Breaking Up Is Tempting to Do," *Institutional Investor*, 1 January 1996.
45. N. Templin & R. Blumenstein, "GM to Receive $500 Million Dividend as Part of Plan to Spin Off EDS Unit," *The Wall Street Journal*, 2 April 1996.
46. "Morrision Disclosure Focuses Attention on Policy," *USA Today*, 13 February 1996.
47. R. Johnson, "Developing a Refrigerant Policy," *Engineered Systems*, 1 October 1995, 53.
48. N. Humphrey, "References a Tricky Issue for Both Sides," *Nashville Business Journal* 11 (8 May 1995): 1A.
49. M. Seminerio, "Nielsen: Penthouse Web Site Popular with PC Companies," *PC Week Online*, 2 April 1996.
50. S. Sherman, "Stretch Goals: The Dark Side of Asking for Miracles," *Fortune*, 13 November 1995.
51. Ibid.
52. C. O'Dell, "Out-of-the-Box Benchmarking," *Management Review* 83 (1 January 1994): 63.

53. R. Vartabedian, "Chrysler Board Cuts Bonuses of Top Execs, Cites Lag in Quality," *Los Angeles Times*, 29 March 1996, D-1.
54. A. B. Henderson, "Cars: U-Turn on Caddy Truck Detours GM Strategy," *The Wall Street Journal*, 26 March 1988, B1.
55. D. Martell, "PC Market Up 15%; Compaq, IBM Lead," *Bloomberg News*, [Online] Available http://www.bloomberg.com, 28 July 1997.
56. G. Robbins, "Scenario Planning," *Public Management*, 1 March 1995, 4.
57. P. J. Schoemaker, "Scenario Planning: A Tool for Strategic Thinking," *Sloan Management Review* 36 (1995): 25.
58. T. Carlson, "The Race Is On (Need for Speed in Getting a New Product to Market)," *Brandweek* 35 (9 May 1994): 22.
59. S. C. Wheelwright & K. B. Clark, "Creating Project Plans to Focus Product Development," *Harvard Business Review*, March–April 1992, 70.
60. D. Dimancescu & K. Dwenger, "Smoothing the Product Development Plan," *Management Review* 85, no. 6 (1996): 36.
61. S. L. Brown, "Product Development: Past Research, Present Findings, and Future Directions," *Academy of Management Review* 20 (1995): 343–378.
62. J. Martin, "Ignore Your Customer," *Fortune*, 1 May 1995, 121.
63. M. Iansiti, "Shooting the Rapids: Managing Product Development in Turbulent Environments," *California Management Review* 38 (1995): 36–58.
64. D. Dimancescu & K. Dwenger, "Smoothing the Product Development Plan," *Management Review* 85, no. 6 (1996): 36.

Chapter 5

1. L. A. Hill, *Becoming a Manager: Mastery of a New Identity* (Boston: Harvard Business School Press, 1992).
2. K. R. MacCrimmon, R.N. Taylor, & E.A. Locke, "Decision Making and Problem Solving" in *Handbook of Industrial and Organizational Psychology*, ed. M.D. Dunnette (Chicago: Rand McNally, 1976), pp. 1397–1453.
3. Ben Franklin, in a letter to Joseph Priestly, 1772. Reprinted in B. Franklin, *The Benjamin Franklin Sampler* (New York: Harper Bros., 1911).
4. Frederick W. Taylor, *The Principles of Scientific Management* (New York: Harper Bros., 1911).
5. J. A. Trachtenberg & E. Shapiro, "Record-Store Shakeout Rocks Music Industry," *The Wall Street Journal*, 26 February 1996.
6. K. R. MacCrimmon, R. N. Taylor, & E. A. Locke, "Decision Making and Problem Solving" in *Handbook of Industrial and Organizational Psychology*, ed. M.D. Dunnette (Chicago: Rand McNally, 1976), pp. 1397–1453.
7. G. Kress, "The Role of Interpretation in the Decision Process," *Industrial Management* 37 (1995): 10–14.
8. D. Milbrank, "We Feel Your Pain, Congress Is Saying, with Real Empathy," *The Wall Street Journal*, 1 April 1996.
9. "2001: Computing in the New Millenium," *PC Magazine*, 9 June 1998, p. 101.
10. J. Koblenz, "How a Car Earns a Best Buy," *Consumers Digest*, 1 January 1993, 54.
11. P. Djang, "Selecting Personal Computers," *Journal of Research on Computing in Education*, 25 (1993): 327.
12. K. Galloway, "America's Best Insurance Cities," *Best's Review/Property-Casualty Insurance Edition*, 1 November 1994, 38.
13. J. G. March, *A Primer on Decision Making: How Decisions Happen* (New York: Free Press, 1994).
14. A. Swardson, "Tide of Asian Crisis Rippling: Europe only Beginning to Feel Repercussions," *Washington Post*, 20 January 1998, A16.
15. M. H. Bazerman, *Judgment in Managerial Decision Making* (New York: John Wiley & Sons, 1994).
16. B. Silverman, "Unconventional Wisdom: Twelve Remarkable Innovators Tell How Intuition Can Revolutionize Decision Making," *Sales & Marketing Management* 146 (1994): 106–107.
17. P. J. Hoffman, P. Slovic, & L. G. Rorer, "An Analysis-of-Variance Model for Assessment of Configural Cue Utilization in Clinical Judgment," *Psychological Bulletin* 69 (1968): 338–349.
18. K. Barron, "Your Money or Your Life?" *Forbes*, 17 November 1997, 66–70.
19. K. C. Cole, "Brain's Use of Shortcuts Can Be a Route to Bias," *Los Angeles Times*, 1 May 1995, A1.
20. J. Orbell, "Hamlet and the Psychology of Rational Choice under Uncertainty," *Rationality and Society* 5 (1993): 127–140.
21. A. Kupfer, "Craig McCaw Sees an Internet in the Sky," *Fortune*, 27 May 1996, 62–72.
22. P. J. Schoemaker & J. E. Russo, "A Pyramid of Decision Approaches," *California Management Review*, Fall 1993, 9–33.
23. I. G. Stiell, G. H. Greenberg, R. D. McKnight, R. C. Nair, I. McDowell, M. Reardon, J. P. Stewart, & J. Maloney, "Decision Rules for the Use of Radiography in Acute Ankle Injuries: Refinement and Prospective Validation," *JAMA, The Journal of the American Medical Association* 269 (1993): 1127–1132.
24. R. Koselka, "The New Mantra: MVT," *Forbes*, 11 March 1996, 114–118.
25. Ibid.
26. Ibid.
27. B. Dumaine, "The Trouble with Teams," *Fortune*, 5 September 1994, 86–92.
28. R. L. Rose, "Hard Driving: A Productivity Push at Wabash National Puts Firm on a Roll," *The Wall Street Journal*, 7 September 1995.
29. R. Frank, "Seeing Red Abroad: Pepsi Rolls Out a New Blue Can," *The Wall Street Journal*, 2 April 1996.
30. "How to Form Hiring Teams," *Personnel Journal* 73, no. 3 (August 1994): S14.
31. I. L. Janis, *Groupthink* (Boston: Houghton Mifflin, 1983).
32. C. P. Neck & C. C. Manz, "From Groupthink to Teamthink: Toward the Creation of Constructive Thought Patterns in Self-Managing Work Teams," *Human Relations* 47 (1994): 929–952.
33. G. Moorhead, R. Ference, & C. P. Neck, "Group Decision Fiascoes Continue: Space Shuttle Challenger and a Revised Framework," *Human Relations* 44 (1991): 539–550.
34. C. Dressler, "Keeping Minutes While You Waste Hours," *Los Angeles Times*, 14 January 1996, D-18.
35. A. Mason, W. A. Hochwarter, K. R. Thompson, "Conflict: An Important Dimension in Successful Management Teams," *Organizational Dynamics* 24 (1995): 20.
36. Ibid.
37. R. Cosier & C.R. Schwenk, "Agreement and Thinking Alike: Ingredients for Poor Decisions," *Academy of Management Executive* 4 (1990): 69–74.
38. Ibid.
39. R. L. Priem, D. A. Harrison, & N. K. Muir, "Structured Conflict and Consensus Outcomes in Group Decision Making," *Journal of Management* 21 (1995): 691–710.
40. A. Van De Ven & A. L. Delbecq, "Nominal Versus Interacting Group Processes for Committee Decision Making Effectiveness," *Academy of Management Journal* 14 (1971): 203–212.
41. A. R. Dennis & J. S. Valicich, "Group, Sub-Group, and Nominal Group Idea Generation: New Rules for a New Media?" *Journal of Management* 20 (1994): 723–736.
42. R. B. Gallupe, W. H. Cooper, M. L. Grise, & L. M. Bastianutti, "Blocking Electronic Brainstorms," *Journal of Applied Psychology* 79 (1994): 77–86.
43. R. B. Gallupe & W. H. Cooper, "Brainstorming Electronically," *Sloan Management Review*, Fall 1993, 27–36.
44. Ibid.
45. G. Kay, "Effective Meetings through Electronic Brainstorming," *Management Quarterly* 35 (1995): 15.
46. A. LaPlante, "90s Style Brainstorming," *Forbes ASAP*, 25 October 1993, p. 44.

Chapter 6

1. R. Lenzner, "The Reluctant Entrepreneur," *Forbes*, 11 September 1995, 162–166.
2. U. Tosi, "Commercial Aircraft Are Fast Becoming Flying Computer Systems: Their Downlinked Bitstreams Can Be Critical to High Profits and Happy Landings," *Forbes ASAP*, 4 December 1995, 100–102.
3. Ibid.
4. Ibid.
5. Ibid.
6. J. Novack, "The Data Miners," *Forbes*, 12 February 1996.
7. M. Halper, "Setting Up Is Hard To Do: Data Warehouses Do Not Grow on Trees," *Forbes ASAP*, 8 April 1996, 50–51.
8. J. Novack, "The Data Miners," *Forbes*, 12 February 1996.
9. N. Hutheesing, "Get the Bugs Out," *Forbes*, 8 April 1996.
10. T. Mack & T. Ewing, "In the Real World, Meanwhile . . . ." *Forbes*, 18 December 1995, 284.
11. G. B. Knecht, "How Wall Street Whiz Found a Niche Selling Books on the Internet," *The The Wall Street Journal*, 11 May 1996.

12. R. D. Buzzell & B. T. Gale, *The PIMS Principles: Linking Strategy to Performance* (New York: Free Press, 1987); M. Lambkin, "Order of Entry and Performance in New Markets," *Strategic Management Journal* 9 (1988): 127–40.
13. N. Deogun, "Banks Introduce New ATMs That Deliver Host of Services," *The Wall Street Journal Interactive Edition*, 5 June 1996.
14. G. L. Urban, T. Carter, S. Gaskin, & Z. Mucha, "Market Share Rewards to Pioneering Brands: An Empirical Analysis and Strategic Implications," *Management Science* 32 (1986): 645–659.
15. Steven D. Lubar, *Infoculture* (Boston: Houghton Mifflin, 1993).
16. L. Finnegan, "WinWedge 32 May Be Too Good; Easy-To-Use Software Collects Data So Well It's Overloading Federal Systems," *Government Computer News* 15 (15 April 1996): 35.
17. Steven D. Lubar, *Infoculture* (Boston: Houghton Mifflin, 1993).
18. W. Kawamato, "CD Recording Gets a Second Chance," *PC Computing*, 1 March 1998, 110.
19. Poor, "Stepping Up to DVD (Part One)," *PC Magazine*, 18 November 1997, 183.
20. M. D. Stone, "Endless Storage," *PC Magazine*, 12 March 1996.
21. "iomegazine™—BuyIt Online—Ditto," Iomega Web Site. [Online] Available www.iomega.com/product/prodguide/ditguide/index.html, 15 June 1998.
22. "A-List: Top 200 Steals & Deals," *PC Computing*, 1 June 1998, 116.
23. R. Adhikari, "Hard Drives Crashing? Try RAID for Protection," *Information Week*, 5 Feb 1996, 65–66.
24. Pang, "Riot of RAID Solutions Arises," *Computer Reseller News*, 27 May 1996, 109–110. J. Pournelle, "Jerry Believes in Backups, and Chaos Manor's Multiple Redundancy System Has Just Entered a New Age," *Byte*, 1 May 1998, 131.
25. Ibid.
26. M. Halper, A World of Servers Great and Small," *Forbes ASAP*, 3 June 1995.
27. S. R. Gordon & J. R. Gordon, *Information Systems: A Management Approach* (Fort Worth, TX: Dryden Press, 1996).
28. R. Knee, "Carter Hawley Hale," *American Shipper* 36 (May 1994): 57–60.
29. J. Bigness, "More Hotels Get Impersonal, Automate Front-Desk Functions," *The Wall Street Journal Interactive Edition*, 18 June 1996.
30. "Transportation Solutions: Don't Keep the Customer Waiting," IBM Corporation System/390 Web site. [Online] Available www1.ibmlink.ibm.com/HTML/SPEC/gk202765.html, 20 June 1996.
31. P. J. Aitch, "Taking Charge. Desktop Management: Untying the Knots," *Chief Executive*, November 1995, 10–13.
32. "When Seconds Count," IBM Corporation System/390 Web site. [Online] Available http://www1.ibmlink.ibm.com/HTML/SPEC/gk202842.html, 20 June 1996. "American Airlines SABRE Group Soars On IBM's New System/390 Parallel Enterprise Server," IBM Corporation System/390 Web Site. [Online] Available http://www1.s390.hosting.ibm.com/stories/aairlines.html, 20 June 1996.
33. Laplante, "Invitation to Customers: Come into Our Database," *Forbes ASAP*, 28 August 1995, 124–130.
34. B. Z. Gottesman, "Take Control of Your E-Mail," *PC Magazine*, 5 May 1998, 101.
35. Ey, "E-Mail Saves Companies Time, Money and Effort," *Dallas Business Journal*, 17 Nov 1995, C13–14.
36. M. A. Verespej, "The E-Mail Monster: Can One Manager Handle 250 E-Mail Messages a Day, Plus 15 Voicemails an Hour?" *Industry Week*, 19 June 1995, 52–53.
37. M. Campanelli & N. Friedman, "Welcome to Voice Mail Hell: The New Technology Has Become a Barrier Between Salespeople and Customers. Here's How Smart Sellers Are Breaking Through," *Sales & Marketing Management* 147 (May 1995): 98–101.
38. "The Joys of Voice Mail," *Inc.*, November 1995, 102.
39. "The Joys of Voice Mail," *Inc.*, November 1995, 102.
40. T. Andrews, "E-Mail Empowers, Voice-Mail Enslaves," *PC Week*, 10 April 1995, E11.
41. Hise, "Life after Voice-Mail Hell. Winguth, Donahue and Co., Los Altos, CA Executive Search Firm, Brings Back Human Receptionist Due to Customer Dissatisfaction with Voice Mail Service," *Inc.*, August 1994, 101.
42. O'Malley, "Document Conferencing," *Computer Shopper Online*. [Online] Available www.zdnet.com/cshopper/content/9604/feature3/sub1.html, 23 June 1996. Originally published in the April 1996 issue of *Computer Shopper*.
43. J. Young, "The Transcontinental Blackboard," *Forbes*, 23 October 1995, 322–323.
44. J. van den Hoven, "Executive Support Systems & Decision Making," *Journal of Systems Management* 47, no. 8 (March–April 1996): 48.
45. M. Stevenson, "He Sees All He Knows All," *Canadian Business* 67, no. 5 (Spring 1994): 30.
46. R. C. Kennedy, "Intranets in Action," *PC/Computing*, June 1996, 150.
47. Richards, "Intranet Offers Rewards for Firms Big and Small," *The Wall Street Journal Interactive Edition*, 17 June 1996.
48. V. S. Pasher, "Employee Benefits Info Within a Few Clicks," *National Underwriter Life & Health—Financial Services Edition*, 14 April 1997, S4.
49. R. Ayre, "Intranet How-To: Setting Up Shop," *PC Magazine*, 23 April 1996, 151–158; F.J. Derfler, "The Intranet Platform: A Universal Client?" *PC Magazine*, 23 April 1996, 105–113.
50. R. C. Kennedy, "Intranets in Action," *PC/Computing*, June 1996, 150.
51. Zimmerman, "Report on EDI Tracks Labor Savings," *Supermarket News*, 16 January 1995, S2.
52. Kessler, "Fire Your Purchasing Managers," *Forbes ASAP*, 10 October 1994, 33.
53. Tobey, "Paperless Purchasing," *Hotel & Motel Management* 2, no. 3 (6 November 1995): 104.
54. M. McDonald, "SWA: Ticketless Travel Saved Us Millions in Agent Pay," *Travel Weekly* 2 (20 November 1995): 1.
55. K. C. Laudon & J. P. Laudon, *Management Information Systems: Organization and Technology* (Upper Saddle River, NJ: Prentice-Hall, 1996).
56. S. Oliver, "What Are My Chances, Doc?" *Forbes*, 31 July 1995, 136–137.
57. M. France, "Smart Contracts," *Forbes ASAP* 2 (29 August 1994): 117.

Chapter 7

1. R. Leifer & P. K. Mills, An Information Processing Approach for Deciding upon Control Strategies and Reducing Control Loss in Emerging Organizations," *Journal of Management* 22 (1996): 113–137.
2. "Say Baa-Baa to Bad Driving," *London Times*, 28 July 1996.
3. L. Lee, "Sick of Scams from Shoppers, Retailers Look to Cut Returns," *The Wall Street Journal Interactive Edition*, 18 November 1996.
4. D. Machan, "Polishing the Golden Arches," *Forbes*, 15 June 1998, 42.
5. J. Martin & J. E. Davis, "Are You as Good as You Think You Are? There's Only One Way to Know for Sure," *Fortune*, 30 September 1996, 142.
6. M. Walsh, "Easy on the Popcorn!" *Forbes*, 26 September 1994, 126–127.
7. J. Y. Luchars & T. R. Hinkin, "The Service-Quality Audit: A Hotel Case Study," *Cornell Hotel & Restaurant Administration Quarterly* 37, no. 1 (1996): 34.
8. R. Simons, "Control in an Age of Empowerment," *Harvard Business Review*, March-April 1995, 80–98.
9. H. Koontz & R. W. Bradspies, "Managing Through Feedforward Control: A Future-Directed View," *Business Horizons*, June 1972, 25–36.
10. D. Clark, "Marketing, Performance Earn Windows NT Place in the Sun," *The Wall Street Journal Interactive Edition*, 29 July 1996.
11. R. Leifer & P. K. Mills, "An Information Processing Approach for Deciding upon Control Strategies and Reducing Control Loss in Emerging Organizations," *Journal of Management* 22 (1996): 113–137.
12. C. A. Jaffe, "Magellan's Billion-Dollar 'Oops' Was a Simple Slip of the Hand," *Forth-Worth Star-Telegram*, 11 December 1994, D3.
13. S. G. Green & M. A. Welsh, "Cybernetics and Dependence: Reframing the Control Concept," *Academy of Management Review* 13 (1988): 287–301.
14. T. Eblen, "Airlines Must Try to Fill All Seats, Charge the Highest Possible Fare," *Knight-Ridder/Tribune Business News*, 23 June 1996.
15. E. Allday, "Will Pool Business Evaporate?" *The Wall Street Journal Interactive Edition*, 7 August 1996.
16. J. Stossel, "Protect Us from Legal Vultures," *The Wall Street Journal*, 2 January 1996.
17. S. Joyce, "Tort Wars: Curb Frivolous Lawsuits, Unjust Awards," *San Diego Union-Tribune*, 19 November 1995.
18. M. Brannigan & E. de Lisser, "Ground Control: Cost Cutting at Delta Raises the Stock Price but Lowers the Service," *The Wall Street Journal*, 20 June 1996, A1.
19. L. Miller, "Business Fliers Make Use of On-Line Travel Services," *The Wall Street Journal Interactive Edition*, 2 August 1996.
20. N. Deogun, "Pepsi Has Had Its Fill of Pizza, Tacos, Chicken," *The Wall Street Journal*, 24 January 1997, B1.

21. S. Carey, "Frustrated Firms Buy Planes to Streamline Travel Plans," *The Wall Street Journal Interactive Edition*, 11 October 1996.
22. P. Davis, "Outrageous Perks: Coffee Breaks Are Becoming Coffee Escapes," *The Wall Street Journal Interactive Edition*, 8 August 1996.
23. D. Biers, M. Rose, M. Schumann, & N. Cho, "Labor Complaints Could Prompt International Strife for Korea," *The Wall Street Journal Interactive Edition*, 18 July 1996.
24. "Fifty Cents, Please," *When Winners Work for Losers*. [Online] Available http://www.myboss.com/stories.html, 10 August 1996.
25. M. Weber, *The Protestant Ethic and the Spirit of Capitalism* (New York: Scribner's, 1958).
26. L. Criner, "Politicians Come and Go, Bureaucracies Stay and Grow," *Washington Times*, 11 March 1996, 33.
27. A. C. Greenberg, "Memos from the Chairman," *Fortune*, 29 April 1996, 173–175.
28. H. Gleckman, S. Atchison, T. Smart, & J.A. Byrne, "Bonus Pay: Buzzword or Bonanza?" *Business Week*, 14 November 1994, 62–64.
29. R. Turner, "Disney's Eisner Got No Bonus in '93, Reflecting Firm's Financial Problems," *The Wall Street Journal*, 4 January 1994, A2.
30. S. Williford, "Nordstrom Sets the Standard for Customer Service," *Memphis Business Journal*, 1 July 1996, 21.
31. R. T. Pascale, "Nordstrom: Respond to Unreasonable Customer Requests!" *Planning Review* 2 (May–June 1994): 17.
32. Ibid.
33. Ibid.
34. J. R. Barker, "Tightening the Iron Cage: Concertive Control in Self-Managing Teams," *Administrative Science Quarterly* 38 (1993): 408-437.
35. Ibid.
36. Ibid.
37. Ibid.
38. Ibid.
39. C. Manz & H. Sims, "Leading Workers to Lead Themselves: The External Leadership of Self-Managed Work Teams," *Administrative Science Quarterly* 32 (1987): 106–128.
40. J. Slocum & H. A. Sims, "Typology for Integrating Technology, Organization and Job Design," *Human Relations* 33 (1980): 193–212.
41. C. C. Manz & H. P. Sims, Jr., "Self-Management as a Substitute for Leadership: A Social Learning Perspective," *Academy of Management Review* 5 (1980): 361–367.
42. S. Levy, "Strip Mining the Corporate Life," *Newsweek*, 12 August 1996, 54–55.
43. W. M. Stern, "Lumpy Mashed Potatoes, Yuck!" *Forbes*, 28 March 1994, 63–66.
44. B. McWilliams, "The Measure of Success," *Across the Board*, 1 February 1996, 16.
45. R. S. Kaplan & D. P. Norton, "Using the Balanced Scorecard as a Strategic Management System," *Harvard Business Review*, January–February 1996, 75–85. R. S. Kaplan & D. P. Norton, "The Balanced Scorecard: Measures that Drive Performance," *Harvard Business Review*, January–February 1992, 71–79.
46. Ibid.
47. S. L. Fawcett, "Fear of Accounts: Improving Managers' Competence and Confidence Through Simulation Exercises," *Journal of European Industrial Training*, February 1996, 17.
48. M. H. Stocks & A. Harrell, "The Impact of an Increase in Accounting Information Level on the Judgment Quality of Individuals and Groups," *Accounting, Organizations and Society*, October–November 1995, 685–700.
49. B. Morris, "Roberto Goizueta and Jack Welch: The Wealth Builders," *Fortune*, 11 December 1995, 80–94.
50. B. Morris, "A Conversation with Roberto Goizueta and Jack Welch," *Fortune*, 11 December 1995, 96–102.
51. B. Morris, "Roberto Goizueta and Jack Welch: The Wealth Builders," *Fortune*, 11 December 1995, 80–94.
52. S. Tully, "The Real Key to Creating Wealth," *Fortune*, 20 September 1993, 38-50.
53. F. F. Reichheld, "Learning from Customer Defections," *Harvard Business Review*, March–April 1996, 56–69.
54. P. Hepworth, "Connecting Customer Loyalty to the Bottom Line," *Canadian Business Review*, 1 January 1994, 40.
55. F. F. Reichheld, "Learning from Customer Defections," *Harvard Business Review*, March–April 1996, 56–69.
56. C. B. Furlong, "12 Rules for Customer Retention," *Bank Marketing* 5 (January 1993): 14.
57. P. Hepworth, "Connecting Customer Loyalty to the Bottom Line," *Canadian Business Review*, 1 January 1994, 40.
58. F. F. Reichheld, "Learning from Customer Defections," *Harvard Business Review*, March–April 1996, 56–69.
59. T. K. Gilliam, "Closing the Customer Retention Gap," *Bank Marketing* 3 (December 1994): 51.
60. Orr, "After the Order . . . . (Customer Retention Strategies)," *Target Marketing* 3 (July 1996): 20.
61. C. A. Reeves & D. A. Bednar, "Defining Quality: Alternatives and Implications," *Academy of Management Review* 19 (1994): 419–445.
62. "Readers' Choice Poll 1997: International Airline Rankings," *Conde Nast Traveler*. [Online] Available ttp://travel.epicurious.com/travel/g_cnt/05_poll97/air/inter_intro.html, 26 June 1998.
63. "Airline Way Above Rest in Rankings," *South China Morning Post*, 9 August 1996.
64. D. R. May & B. L. Flannery, "Cutting Waste with Employee Involvement Teams," *Business Horizons*, September–October 1995, 28–38.
65. M. A. Verespej, "Trash to Cash: The Bottom Line, The Environment, and Companies Can Profit from Waste Reduction," *Industry Week*, 5 December 1995, 53–55.
66. Ibid.
67. J. C. Ruthenburg, "Waste Minimization Pays Big Dividends at Red Spot Painting Co." *American Paint & Coatings Journal* 4 (31 May 1993): 42.
68. T. Minahan, "Manufacturers Take Aim at End of the Supply Chain," *Purchasing*, 23 April 1998, 111. T. Moran, "Life-Cycle Managers Show Real Vehicle Costs," *Automotive News Europe*, 25 May 1997, 8.
69. J. Szekely & G. Trapaga, "From Villain to Hero (Materials Industry's Waste Recovery Efforts)," *Technology Review*, 1 January 1995.
70. M. Keller, "Many in Dark about Disposal of Fluorescents," *Minneapolis-St. Paul City Business*, 14 January 1994, 11.
71. C. A. Reeves & D. A. Bednar, "Defining Quality: Alternatives and Implications," *Academy of Management Review* 19 (1994): 419-445.

Chapter 8

1. J. Calmes, "American Opinion (A Special Report): Despite Buoyant Economic Times Americans Don't Buy Free Trade," *The Wall Street Journal*, 10 December 1998, A10. *USA Today*, 25 February 1992. *Lou Harris Survey*, March 1990; March 1992.
2. Ibid.
3. Ibid.
4. International Accounts Data, Bureau of Economic Analysis. [Online] Available *www.bea.doc.gov/bea/di1.htm*, 9 January 1999. F.R. Bleakley, "Foreign Investment by Multinationals Rebounds, Benefiting China, U.N. Says," *The Wall Street Journal*, 31 August 1994, A2.
5. Department of Commerce, National Trade Data Bank.
6. P. Tooher, "Hello, Euro Currency Opens New Era for Continent," *Arizona Republic*, 3 January 1999, E14.
7. B. Emmott, "Multinational: Back in Fashion," *The Economist*, 27 March 1993, 58.
8. "Japan: Annual Fresh Deciduous Fruit Report," *U.S. Department of Agriculture Reports*, 17 September 1997.
9. J. Urquhart, "Canada Seeks to Protect Its Magazines from Losing Ad Revenue to Foreigners," *The Wall Street Journal*, 30 September 1998, B12.
10. M. du Bois, "EC Car Sales Plunged 11% in September," *The Wall Street Journal*, 8 October 1993, B4B.
11. World Trade Organization, "The Agreements: Anti-Dumping, Subsidies, Safeguards, Contingencies, etc." [Online] Available *www.wto.orgabout /agmnts7.htm#subsidies*, 24 January 1999.
12. Associated Press, "U.S. Takes Aim at Chinese Beetle in Trade Battle," *The Plain Dealer*, 12 September 1998, 2c.
13. C. Goldsmith, "After Trailing Boeing for Years, Airbus Aims for 50% of the Market," *The Wall Street Journal*, 16 March 1998, A1.
14. J. Bovard, "The Customs Service's Fickle Philosophers," *The Wall Street Journal*, 7 July 1991, A10.
15. Tanzer, "Here's One Asian Industry That Isn't Declining: Software Piracy. It Is Costing American Companies Billions of Dollars in Lost Revenues," *Forbes*, 7 September 1998, 162.
16. Links to National Parliaments' Web sites, *www.europarl.eu.int/natparl/en/Linkspem.htm*.
17. G. Smith & E. Malkin, "Mexico's Makeover," Business Week, 21 December 1998, 28. D. Blount, "Canada Favors Life after NAFTA," *Denver Post*, 22 November 1998, A10.
18. P. Behr, "NAFTAmath: A Texas-Sized Surge in Trade; Six Months after Treaty's Enactment, Booming Sales to Mexico Overshadow U.S. Job Losses," *Washington Post*, 21 August 1994, H1.

19. Declaration of Principles, Summit of the Americas, "Free Trade Area of the Americas." [Online] Available *www.ftaa-alca.org/EnglishVersion/miami_e.htm*, 27 January 1999.
20. G. P. Goad, "Follow? An Asian Monetary Union Is Unlikely Anytime Soon," *The Wall Street Journal*, 28 September 1998, R23.
21. The Associated Press, "Americans Get More for Money," 29 December 1994.
22. J. Schoolman, "Gauging Currency by Way of Big Macs," *The Orange County Register* (Reuters), 10 May 1998, K1.
23. Howard Banks (ed.), "What's Ahead for Business: An Income Gap that Does Matter," *Forbes*, 29 August 1994, 35.
24. The Associated Press, "Japanese Trade Barriers Cost Consumers," 14 December 1994. "Japan's Protection Racket: How Much Do Barriers to Imports Cost Japanese Consumers?" *The Economist*, 7 January 1995, 58.
25. E. Thornton, "Revolution in Japanese Retailing," *Fortune* 3 (7 February 1994): 143.
26. P. Dwyler, P. Engardio, Z. Schiller, & S. Reed, "Tearing Up Today's Organization Chart," *Business Week*, 18 November 1994, 80–83.
27. Ibid.
28. Sundaram & J. S. Black, "The Environment and Internal-Organization of Multinational Enterprises," *Academy of Management Review* 17 (1992): 729–757.
29. H. S. James, Jr., & M. Weidenbaum, *When Businesses Cross International Borders: Strategic Alliances and Their Alternatives* (Westport, CT: Praeger Publishers, 1993).
30. P. Fuhrman & M. Schuman, "Now We Are Our Own Masters," *Forbes*, 23 May 1994, 128–138.
31. Ibid.
32. L. Luxner, "Getting a Slice of the Onion Market," *The Atlanta Journal Constitution*, 30 December 1994, C1.
33. McDonald's Corporation, "Outside the U.S. Franchising Requirements." [Online] Available *www.mcdonalds.com/corporate/franchise/outside/require/require.html*, 18 January 1999.
34. A.E. Serwer, "Trouble in Franchise Nation," *Fortune*, 6 March 1995, 115.
35. McDonald's Corporation, "McDonald's Reports Global Results (Part 2 of 2)." [Online] Available *www.mcdonalds.com/whatsnew/pressrelease/Press_Release15880642.html*, 17 April 1998. B. McDowall, "The Global Market Challenge," *Restaurants & Institutions*, 1 November 1994, 52.
36. Xerox Corporation, "Fuji Xerox-A Worldwide Franchise # 1 in Competitors' Home Market." [Online] Available *www.xerox.com/investor/irconf/1998/bdr/tsld009.htm*, 26 January 1999.
37. W. Andrews, "Toshiba Joins 64-Meg DRAM Team," *Electronic News*, 30 May 1994, 1.
38. Choi, "International: GM Seeds Grow Nicely in Eastern Europe, Strategy of Starting Small and Expanding Pays Off," *The Wall Street Journal*, 3 May 1995, A11.
39. D. P. Hamilton, "Fuji Xerox Is a Rarity in World Business: A Joint Venture That Works," *The Wall Street Journal*, 26 September 1996, R19. E. Terazono & C. Lorenz, "Fuji Xerox Marriage Successful: Growing Pains with Parent Easing," The Financial Post, 24 September 1994, 55.
40. B. R. Schlender, "How Toshiba Makes Alliances Work," *Fortune*, 4 October 1993, 116–120.
41. B. A. Walters, S. Peters, & G. G. Dess, "Strategic Alliances and Joint Ventures: Making Them Work," *Business Horizons*, July–August 1994, 5–10.
42. W. Beaver, "Volkswagen's American Assembly Plant: Fahrvernugen Was Not Enough," *Business Horizons*, 11 November 1992, 19.
43. Ibid.
44. M. W. Hordes, J. A. Clancy, & J. Baddaley, "A Primer for Global Start-Ups," *Academy of Management Executive*, May 1995, 7–11.
45. B. M. Oviatt & P. P. McDougall, "Toward a Theory of International New Ventures," *Journal of International Business Studies*, Spring 1994, 45–64.
46. B. M. Oviatt, P. P. McDougall, "Global Start-Ups: Entrepreneurs on a Worldwide Stage," *Academy of Management Executive*, May 1995, 30–44.
47. L. Brokaw, "Foreign Affairs: Start-Ups such as National Gyp-Chipper Are Proving That, When You Move from Doing Business Next Door to Doing Business Around the World, the Same Basic Rules Still Apply," *Inc.*, 1 November 1990, 92.
48. J. Huey, "The World's Best Brand," *Fortune*, 31 May 1993, 44.
49. R. Jacob, "The Big Rise: Middle Classes Explode Around the Globe, Bringing New Markets and New Prosperity," *Fortune*, 30 May 1994, 74.
50. R. Tomkins, "Coca-Cola Strives to Rival Tap Water: Despite 48% of Global Market, Coke Chafes at Fact It Supplies only 3% of Every Human's Required Daily Liquid Intake," *Financial Post*, 30 October 1997, 77. J. Huey, "The World's Best Brand," *Fortune*, 31 May 1993, 44.
51. Ortega, "Foreign Forays: Penney Pushes Abroad in Unusually Big Way as It Pursues Growth," *The Wall Street Journal*, 1 February 1994, A1.
52. Snyder, "European Expansion: How to Shop Around," *Management Review*, 1 November 1993, 16.
53. Ibid.
54. K. D. Miller, "A Framework for Integrated Risk Management in International Business," *Journal of International Business Studies*, 2nd Quarter 1992, 311.
55. M. Farley, "Foreign Investors in China Feel Cold Slap of Reality," *Los Angeles Times*, 27 December 1994, A-1.
56. G. Anping, "Old Contract Laws Need Repair to Fit into New Reality," *China Daily*, 7 May 1994, 4–1.
57. F. Bleakley, "High School Seniors Mind Their Business and Even Profit by It: Teens Learn by Their Goofs in Import-Export World; Racy Towels Go Too Far," *The Wall Street Journal*, 20 June 1995, A1.
58. P. Waldman, "Your Lingerie in Iran, Even If It's for Sale: Censors Decide Many Topics Are Unmentionable in Ads," *The Wall Street Journal*, 21 June 1995, A1.
59. G. Hofstede, The Cultural Relativity of the Quality of Life Concept," *Academy of Management Review* 9 (1984): 389–398. G. Hofstede, "The Cultural Relativity of Organizational Practices and Theories, *Journal of International Business Studies*, Fall 1983, 75–89. G. Hofstede, "The Interaction Between National and Organizational Value Systems," *Journal of Management Studies*, July 1985, 347–357.
60. R. Hodgetts, "A Conversation with Geert Hofstede," *Organizational Dynamics*, Spring 1993, 53–61.
61. M. Janssens, J. M. Brett, F.J. Smith, "Confirmatory Cross-Cultural Research: Testing the Viability of a Corporation-Wide Safety Policy," *Academy of Management Journal* 38 (1995): 364–382.
62. R. G. Linowes, "The Japanese Manager's Traumatic Entry into the United States: Understanding the American-Japanese Cultural Divide," *Academy of Management Executive* 7 (1993): 21–40.
63. J. S. Black, M. Mendenhall, & G. Oddou, "Toward a Comprehensive Model of International Adjustment: An Integration of Multiple Theoretical Perspectives," *Academy of Management Journal* 16 (1991): 291–317. R. L. Tung, "American Expatriates Abroad: From Neophytes to Cosmopolitans, *Columbia Journal of World Business*, 22 June 1998, 125.
64. L. Copeland & L. Griggs, *Going International* (New York: Random House, 1985).
65. R. A. Swaak, "Expatriate Failures: Too Many, Too Much Cost, Too Little Planning," *Compensation and Benefits Review* 27, no. 6 (21 November 1995): 47.
66. J. S. Black & M. Mendenhall, "Cross-Cultural Training Effectiveness: A Review and Theoretical Framework for Future Research," *Academy of Management Review* 15 (1990): 113–136.
67. R. L. Thornton & M.K. Thornton, "Personnel Problems in 'Carry the Flag' Missions in Foreign Assignments," *Business Horizons*, 1 January 1995, 59.
68. W. Arthur, Jr., & W. Bennett, Jr., "The International Assignee: The Relative Importance of Factors Perceived to Contribute to Success," *Personnel Psychology* 48 (1995): 99–114.
69. R. Donkin, "Recruitment: Overseas Gravy Train May Be Running Out of Steam-Preparing Expatriate Packages Is Challenging the Expertise of Human Resource Management, *The Financial Times*, 30 November 1994, 10.
70. R. G. Linowes, "The Japanese Manager's Traumatic Entry into the United States: Understanding the American-Japanese Cultural Divide," *Academy of Management Executive* 7 (1993): 21–40.

Chapter 9

1. L. Gornstein, "StarText, Other Providers Gaining Support as Options to an Overwhelmed America Online," *Fort Worth Star-Telegram*, 25 January 1997, C1.
2. Ibid.
3. J. Barney, "Firm Resources and Sustained Competitive Advantage," *Journal of Management* 17 (1991): 99–120. J. Barney, "Looking Inside for Competitive Advantage," *Academy of Management Executive* 9 (1995): 49–61.
4. J. Sandberg & J. P. Miller, "CompuServe Post Big Quarterly Loss—Online Pioneer to Retreat from Con-

sumer Market and End Family Service," *The Wall Street Journal*, 22 November 1996.

5. P. Boyle, "Editor's Choice: America Online," *PC Magazine*, 11 June 1996.
6. M. Perrault, "AOL's Woes Bring Wave of Success Locally: Impatient AOL Surfers Flocking to KC Internet Service Providers," *Kansas City Business Journal*, 17 January 1997.
7. S. Hart & C. Banbury, "How Strategy-Making Processes Can Make a Difference," *Strategic Management Journal* 15 (1994): 251–269.
8. R. A. Burgelman, "Fading Memories: A Process Theory of Strategic Business Exit in Dynamic Environments," *Administrative Science Quarterly*, 39 (1994): 24–56. R. A. Burgelman & A. S. Grove, "Strategic Dissonance," *California Management Review* 38 (1996): 8–28.
9. M. Robichaux, "The Pizza-Pan-Size Dishes Fly Off the Shelves; Prices Plunge," *The Wall Street Journal Interactive Edition*, 7 November 1996.
10. R. A. Burgelman, "Fading Memories: A Process Theory of Strategic Business Exit in Dynamic Environments," *Administrative Science Quarterly* 39 (1994): 24–56.
11. Fiegenbaum, S. Hart, & D. Schendel, "Strategic Reference Point Theory," *Strategic Management Journal* 17 (1996): 219–235.
12. S. Alsop, "Apple's Next Move Misses the Mark," *Fortune*, 3 February 1997.
13. K. Freiberg & J. Freiberg, *Nuts! Southwest Airlines' Crazy Recipe for Business and Personal Success* (Austin, TX: Bard Press, 1996).
14. D. J. Collis, "Research Note: How Valuable Are Organizational Capabilities?" *Strategic Management Journal* 15 (1994): 143–152.
15. K. Freiberg & J. Freiberg, *Nuts! Southwest Airlines' Crazy Recipe for Business and Personal Success* (Austin, TX: Bard Press, 1996).
16. Fiegenbaum & H. Thomas, "Strategic Groups as Reference Groups: Theory, Modeling and Empirical Examination of Industry and Competitive Strategy," *Strategic Management Journal* 16 (1995): 461–476.
17. R. K. Reger & A. S. Huff, "Strategic Groups: A Cognitive Perspective," *Strategic Management Journal* 14 (1993): 103–124.
18. Gannett Web Site, "Company History." [Online] Available *www.gannett.com/map/history.htm*, 30 July 1998.
19. W. B. Werther, Jr. & J. L. Kerr, "The Shifting Sands of Competitive Advantage," *Business Horizons*, May–June 1995, 11–17.
20. Ibid.
21. J. Samuelson, "Tough Guy Billionaire," *Forbes*, 24 February 1997, 64–66.
22. Ibid.
23. H. Rudnitsky, "What Business Are We In?" *Forbes*, 10 March 1997, 68–70.
24. L. Miller & G. Stern, "Ford Will Sell Budget Rental to Licensees for $350 Million," *The Wall Street Journal Interactive Edition*, 8 January 1997. R.L. Simison, "Hertz Offer Is Unlikely to Aid Ford's Stock Price," *The Wall Street Journal Interactive Edition*, 3 March 1997.
25. M. Lubatkin, "Value-Creating Mergers: Fact or Folklore?" *Academy of Management Executive*, 2 (1988): 295–302. M. Lubatkin & S. Chatterjee, "Extending Modern Portfolio Theory into the Domain of Corporate Diversification: Does It Apply?" *Academy of Management Journal*, 37 (1994): 109–136. M.H. Lubatkin & P.J. Lane, "Psst . . . . The Merger Mavens Still Have It Wrong!" *Academy of Management Executive* 10 (1996): 21–39.
26. Morris & J. McGowan, "Roberto Goizueta and Jack Welch: The Wealth Builders," *Fortune*, 11 December 1995, 80–87.
27. J.A. Pearce, II, "Selecting Among Alternative Grand Strategies," *California Management Review*, Spring 1982, 23–31.
28. S. Puri, "Deals of the Year," *Fortune*, 17 February 1997, 102-103.
29. J. Hayes, "Acquisition Is Fine, but Organic Growth Is Better," *Forbes*, 30 December 1996, 52–55.
30. P. Damas, "Danzas Refines 'Core Carriers' Policy," *American Shipper*, August 1996, 39–40.
31. J. A. Pearce, II, "Retrenchment Remains the Foundation of Business Turnaround" *Strategic Management Journal* 15 (1994): 407–417.
32. R. Blumenstein, "GM Plant Closes in New York: Workers Scatter Across Country," *The Wall Street Journal Interactive Edition*, 26 June 1996.
33. Dow Jones News Services, "AT&T Wins Some Respect, but Its Shares Keep Falling," *The Wall Street Journal Interactive Edition*, 4 March 1997.
34. K. Dolan, "Compassion Pays," *Forbes*, 24 February 1997, 86–90.
35. Autobytel Web site, "Customer Endorsements." [Online] Available *www.autobytel.com*, 8 March 1997.
36. S. Kichen, "Cruising the Internet (Car-Shopping on the Internet)," *Forbes*, 24 March 1997, 198.
37. S. Muto, "Firms Battle for On-Line Car Buyers," *The Wall Street Journal*, 25 February 1998, A1.
38. E. Tanouye & R. Langreth, "Top Firms Must Prepare for Onslaught of Generics," *The Wall Street Journal Interactive Edition*, 12 August 1997.
39. Takahashi, "How the Competition Got Ahead of Intel in Making Cheap Chips," *The Wall Street Journal*, 12 February 1998, A1.
40. R. Trigaux, "Selling Cars: 8 Trends Changing the Business," *St. Petersburg Times*, 3 June 1996.
41. R. B. Lieber, "Turns Out This Critter Can Fly," *Fortune*, 27 November 1995, 110–112.
42. R. La Franco, "My Megaplex Is Bigger Than Your Megaplex," *Forbes*, 24 February 1997, 50–52.
43. M. Conlin, "Love Those Logs," *Forbes*, 10 August 1998, 89–90.
44. R. E. Miles & C. C. Snow, *Organizational Strategy, Structure, and Process* (New York: McGraw Hill, 1978). S. Zahra & J.A. Pearce, "Research Evidence on the Miles-Snow Typology," *Journal of Management* 16 (1990): 751–768. W. L. James & K. J. Hatten, "Further Evidence on the Validity of the Self Typing Paragraph Approach: Miles and Snow Strategic Archetypes in Banking," *Strategic Management Journal* 16 (1995): 161–168.
45. Darlin, "Innovate or Die," *Forbes*, 24 February 1997,108–112.
46. G. G. Knecht, "Small Book Publisher Turns Controversies into Best Sellers," *The Wall Street Journal Interactive Edition*, 6 March 1997.
47. Ramstad, "Using a Personal Approach, Many Tiny PC Firms Thrive," *The Wall Street Journal Interactive Edition*, 8 January 1997.
48. R. Ho, "Do You Want to Dance? Head to the Bowling Alley," *The Wall Street Journal Interactive Edition*, 24 January 1997.
49. R. Gibson & C. Y. Coleman, "How Burger King Emerged as a Threat to McDonald's," *The Wall Street Journal Interactive Edition*, 27 February 1997.
50. Ibid.
51. M. Chen, "Competitor Analysis and Interfirm Rivalry: Toward a Theoretical Integration," *Academy of Management Review* 21 (1996): 100–134. J.C. Baum & H.J. Korn, "Competitive Dynamics of Interfirm Rivalry," *Academy of Management Journal* 39 (1996): 255–291.
52. M. Chen, "Competitor Analysis and Interfirm Rivalry: Toward a Theoretical Integration," *Academy of Management Review* 21 (1996): 100–134.
53. M. Stopa, "Wendy's NewFashioned Growth: Buy Hardee's," *Crain's Detroit Business*, 21 October 1996.
54. L. Lavelle, "The Chickens Come Home to Roost, and Boston Market Is Prepared to Expand," *The Record*, 6 October 1996.
55. N. Shirouzu, "Though Japan Nears Saturation, Burger King Turns Up the Heat," *The Wall Street Journal Interactive Edition*, 31 January 1997.
56. R. Narisetti, "P&G Diaper-Patent Trial Expected to Begin Monday," *The Wall Street Journal Interactive Edition*, 3 February 1997.
57. Ibid.
58. J. C. Baum & H. J. Korn, "Competitive Dynamics of Interfirm Rivalry," *Academy of Management Journal* 39 (1996): 255–291.
59. L. Gomes, "Apple May Sell Key Units to Further Reduce Costs," *The Wall Street Journal Interactive Edition*, 3 February 1997.
60. J. G. Auerbach, "CVS Chain Grows Rapidly as Smaller Rivals Cry Foul," *The Wall Street Journal Interactive Edition*, 24 February 1997.
61. P. Lenzner & B. Upbin, "Monsanto v. Malthus," *Forbes*, 10 March 1997, 58–64.
62. G. T. Lumpkin & G. G. Dess, "Clarifying the Entrepreneurial Orientation Construct and Linking It to Performance," *Academy of Management Review* 21 (1996): 135–172.
63. R. B. Lieber, "Beating the Odds," *Fortune*, 31 March 1997, 82–90.
64. D. Miller & P. Friesen, "Archetypes of Strategy Formulation," *Management Science* 24 (1978): 921–933.
65. D. Machan, "Ziti for Dogs," *Forbes*, 24 February 1997, 95–95.
66. N. Venkatraman, "Strategic Orientation of Business Enterprises: The Construct, Dimensionality, and Measurement," *Management Science*, 35 (1989): 942–962.
67. Z. Moukheiber, "Cybercops," *Forbes*, 10 March 1997, 170–172.
68. P. Newcomb, "Peanut Butter and Pearl Jam," *Forbes*, 10 February 1997, 152.

Chapter 10

1. T. M. Amabile, R. Conti, H. Coon, J. Lazenby, & M. Herron, "Assessing the Work Environment for Creativity," *Academy of Management Journal* 39 (1996): 1154–1184.
2. Ibid.
3. B. Ziegler, "IBM's Research Cutbacks Now Seem to Be Brilliant," *The Wall Street Journal*, 6 October 1997.
4. A. H. Van de Ven & M. S. Poole, "Explaining Development and Change in Organizations" *Academy of Management Review* 20 (1995): 510–540.
5. B. Richards, "Ad Business for Blimps Rises Because of One Bright Idea," *The Wall Street Journal Interactive*, 14 October 1997.
6. T. M. Amabile, R. Conti, H. Coon, J. Lazenby, & M. Herron, "Assessing the Work Environment for Creativity," *Academy of Management Journal* 39 (1996): 1154–1184.
7. P. Anderson & M. L. Tushman, "Managing Through Cycles of Technological Change," *Research/Technology Management*, May/June 1991, 26–31.
8. R. N. Foster, *Innovation: The Attacker' Advantage* (New York: Summitt, 1986).
9. iComp Index 2.0. Intel Corporation Web Site. [Online] Available *www.intel.com/procs/performance/icomp/index.htm*, 5 December 1997.
10. J. Burke, *The Day the Universe Changed* (Boston: Little, Brown, and Company, 1985).
11. R. N. Foster, *Innovation: The Attacker' Advantage* (New York: Summitt, 1986).
12. M. L. Tushman, P. C. Anderson, & C. O'Reilly, "Technology Cycles, Innovation Streams, and Ambidextrous Organizations: Organization Renewal Through Innovation Streams and Strategic Change," in *Managing Strategic Innovation and Change*, eds. M. L. Tushman & P. Anderson (1997), 3–23.
13. G. Cowley & A. Underwood, "Surgeon, Drop That Scalpel," *Newsweek Special Issue: The Power of Invention*, Winter 1997-1998, 77–78.
14. "Pony Express," *Encyclopædia Britannica Online*. [Online] Available *www.eb.com:180/bol/topic?eu=62367&sctn=1*, 6 March 1999.
15. J. R. Aldern, "The Victorian Internet: The Remarkable Story of the Telegraph and the Nineteenth Century's On-Line Pioneers (Review)," *Smithsonian*, 1 January 1999.
16. E. Schlossberg, *Interactive Excellence: Defining and Developing New Standards for the Twenty-First Century* (New York: Ballatine, 1998).
17. W. Abernathy & J. Utterback, "Patterns of Industrial Innovation," *Technology Review*, 2 (1978): 40–47.
18. T. M. Amabile, R. Conti, H. Coon, J. Lazenby, & M. Herron, "Assessing the Work Environment for Creativity," *Academy of Management Journal* 39 (1996): 1154–1184.
19. Ibid.
20. M. Csikszentmihalyi, *Flow: The Psychology of Optimal Experience* (New York: Harper & Row, 1990).
21. B. Dumaine, "Closing the Innovation Gap," *Fortune*, 2 December 1991.
22. Ibid.
23. S. Begley & B. Sigesmund, "The Houses of Invention," *Newsweek Special Issue: The Power of Invention*, Winter 1997–1998, 26.
24. K. M. Eisenhardt, "Accelerating Adaptive Processes: Product Innovation in the Global Computer Industry," *Administrative Science Quarterly* 40 (1995): 84–110.
25. Ibid.
26. R. Gibson, "Starbucks Plans to Test a Paper Cup that Insulates Hands from Hot Coffee," *The Interactive Wall Street Journal*, 22 February 1999. S. Kravetz, "These People Search for a Cup that Suits the Coffee it Holds," *The Wall Street Journal*, 24 March 1998, A1.
27. R. Winslow, "Atomic Speed: Utility Cuts Red Tape, Builds Nuclear Plant Almost on Schedule," *The Wall Street Journal*, 22 February 1984.
28. N. M. Christian, "Chrysler Is Driven to Change," *The Interactive Wall Street Journal*, 29 October 997.
29. L. Kraar, "25 Who Help the U.S. Win: Innovators Everywhere Are Generating Ideas to Make America a Stronger Competitor. They Range from a Boss Who Demands the Impossible to a Mathematician with a Mop," *Fortune*, 22 March 1991.
30. Ibid.
31. M. W. Lawless & P. C. Anderson, "Generational Technological Change: Effects of Innovation and Local Rivalry on Performance," *Academy of Management Journal* 39 (1996): 1185–1217.
32. S. Anderson & M. Uzumeri, "Managing Product Families: The Case of the Sony Walkman," *Research Policy* 24 (1995): 761–782.
33. "Solutions Through Partnerships," *Appliance*, 1 September 1996.
34. P. Ponticel, "Integrated Product Process Development," *Automotive Engineering*, 1 October 1996.
35. Taylor, III & J. Kahn, "How Toyota Defies Gravity: Its Secret Is Its Legendary Production System," *Fortune*, 8 December 1997.
36. T. Parker, "Avon's Retooling to Include Fewer Products, Retail Stores," *The Wall Street Journal*, 27 October 1997.
37. P. Strebel, "Choosing the Right Change Path," *California Management Review*, Winter 1994, 29–51.
38. K. Lewin, *Field Theory in Social Science: Selected Theoretical Papers* (New York: Harper & Brothers, 1951).
39. J. Guyon & J. Saddler, "The AT&T Breakup—One Year Later," *The Wall Street Journal*, 17 December 1984.
40. Upbin, "Bit Paramedics," *Forbes*, 3 November 1997, 154–156.
41. J. Schofield, "Intel Chips in with Improvements," *Computer Weekly*, 26 November 1998.
42. G. P. Zachary, "High Tech Is Forming a Role as an Indicator," *The Wall Street Journal*, 30 September 1996.
43. J. Guyon & J. Saddler, "The AT&T Breakup—One Year Later," *The Wall Street Journal*, 17 December 1984.
44. W. Weitzel & E. Jonsson, "Reversing the Downward Spiral: Lessons from W.T. Grant and Sears Roebuck," *Academy of Management Executive* 5 (1991): 7-22.
45. Ibid.
46. T. Agins, L. Bird, & L. Jereski, "Overdoing It: A Thirst for Glitter and a Pliant Partner Got Barney's in a Bind," *The Wall Street Journal*, 19 January 1996.
47. "The Rise and Fall of the House of Barneys: A Family Tale of Chutzpah, Glory, and Greed (Review)," *Publishers Weekly*, 22 February 1999.
48. Ibid.
49. Moin, V.M. Young, & A. Friedman, "Dickson Pool Sees Barney's IPO," *Women's Wear Daily*, 5 August 1997.
50. L. Bird, "Barney's to Close Original Store and Three Others," *The Asian Wall Street Journal*, 19 June 1997.
51. Moin, "Barney's New Owners Plan to Retain Company, Grow Business: Strategy Calls for Boosting Sales, Increasing Cash Flow This Year," *Daily News Record*, 15 February 1999.
52. L. Chang & D. Brady, "China Air Is on Course to Repeat Mistakes: Taiwan Carrier's Safety Record Scares Off Passengers," *The Wall Street Journal*, 29 April 1998, A19.
53. K. Lewin, *Field Theory in Social Science: Selected Theoretical Papers* (New York: Harper & Brothers, 1951).
54. A. B. Fisher, "Making Change Stick," *Fortune*, 17 April 1995.
55. J. P. Kotter & L. A. Schlesinger, "Choosing Strategies for Change," *Harvard Business Review*, March–April 1979, 106–114.
56. A. B. Fisher, "Making Change Stick," *Fortune*, 17 April 1995.
57. R. L. Rose & E. Norton, "ESOP Fables: UAL Worker-Owners May Face Bumpy Ride if the Past Is a Guide—Pay and Management Snags Can Hamper Such Firms, as Weirton Steel Found—But Avis's Switch Pays Off," *The Wall Street Journal*, 23 December 1993.
58. T. Petzinger, Jr., "Bovis Team Helps Builders Construct a Solid Foundation." *The Wall Street Journal Interactive Edition*, 21 March 1997.
59. T. Petzinger, Jr., "Forget Empowerment, This Job Requires Constant Brainpower," *The Wall Street Journal Interactive Edition*, 17 October 1997.
60. R. H. Schaffer & H. A. Thomson, J.D, "Successful Change Programs Begin with Results," *Harvard Business Review on Change* (Boston: Harvard Business School Publishing, 1998), 189–213.
61. T. Petzinger, Jr., "Forget Empowerment, This Job Requires Constant Brainpower," *The Wall Street Journal Interactive Edition*, 17 October 1997.
62. R. N. Ashkenas & T. D. Jick, "From Dialogue to Action in GE Work-Out: Developmental Learning in a Change Process," in *Research in Organizational Change and Development*, Vol. 6, eds. W. A. Pasmore & R. W. Woodman (Greenwhich, CT: JAI Press, 1992) 267–287.
63. T. Stewart, "GE Keeps Those Ideas Coming," *Fortune*, 12 August 1991, 40.
64. J. D. Duck, "Managing Change: The Art of Balancing," *Harvard Business Review on Change* (Boston: Harvard Business School Publishing, 1998), 55–81.
65. L. Landro, "Viacom Names Team to Consolidate Assets of Paramount and Blockbuster," *The Wall Street Journal*, 16 March 1994, B4.
66. W. J. Rothwell, R. Sullivan, & G. M. McLean, *Practicing Organizational Development: A Guide For Consultants* (San Diego, CA: Pfeiffer & Company, 1995).

67. Ibid.
68. R. N. Ashkenas & T. D. Jick, "From Dialogue to Action in GE Work-Out: Developmental Learning in a Change Process," in *Research in Organizational Change and Development*, Vol. 6, eds. W. A. Pasmore & R. W. Woodman (Greenwhich, CT: JAI Press, 1992), 267–287.
69. J. Ford & L. W. Ford, "The Role of Conversations in Producing Intentional Change in Organizations," *Academy of Management Review* 20 (1995): 541–570
70. K. Freiberg & J. Freiberg, *Nuts! Southwest Airlines' Crazy Recipe for Business and Personal Success* (Austin, TX: Bard Press, 1996).
71. J. P. Kotter, "Leading Change: Why Transformation Efforts Fail," *Harvard Business Review*, 73, no. 2 (March–April 1995): 59.
72. W. Zellner, "The Right Place, The Right Time: CEO Bethune Has Continental Climbing," *Business Week*, 27 May 1996, 74.
73. G. Bailey, "Manager's Journal: Fear Is Nothing to Be Afraid Of," *The Wall Street Journal Interactive Edition*, 27 January 1997.
74. M. Hammer & S. A. Stanton, "The Pioneering Consultants Who Touched Off the Reengineering Movement Are Urging a New Imperative: Getting Top Managers to Stop and Reassess Where Their Companies Are Headed," *Fortune*, 24 November 1997, 291–296.
75. G. Bethune, "From Worst to First: Continental Airlines Has Achieved One of the Most Dramatic Business Turnarounds of the Nineties," *Fortune*, 25 May 1998, 185–190.
76. Ibid.
77. Ibid.
78. Ibid.

Chapter 11

1. M. Hammer & J. Champy, *Reengineering the Corporation : A Manifesto for Business Revolution* (New York: Harper & Row, Publishers, 1993).
2. "Reynolds Metals Announces Organizational and Management Changes," Reynolds Metals Press Release. [Online] Available *www.rmc.com/pressrel/reorg0397.html*, 27 March 1997.
3. J. G. March & H. A. Simon, *Organizations* (New York: John Wiley & Sons, 1958).
4. "Management's Discussion of Operations," General Electric's 1997 Annual Report. [Online] Available *www.ge.com/annual97/finsec/f6.htm*, 11 January 1999.
5. L. R. Burns, "Adoption and Abandonment of Matrix Management Programs: Effects of Organizational Characteristics and Interorganizational Networks," *Academy of Management Journal*, 36 (1993): 106–138.
6. H. Fayol, *General and Industrial Management*, translated by Constance Storrs (London: Pitman Publishing, 1949).
7. M. Weber, *The Theory of Social and Economic Organization*, translated and edited by A. M. Henderson & T. Parsons (New York: The Free Press, 1947).
8. H. Fayol, *General and Industrial Management*, translated by Constance Storrs (London: Pitman Publishing, 1949).
9. S. Bistayi, "Delegate—or Not?" *Forbes*, 21 April 1997, 20–21.
10. Ibid.
11. J. Rutledge, "Management by Belly Button," *Forbes*, 4 November 1996, 64.
12. E. E. Lawler, S. A. Mohrman, and G. E. Ledford, *Creating High Performance Organizations: Practices and Results of Employee Involvement and Quality Management in Fortune 1000 Companies* (San Francisco: Jossey-Bass, 1995).
13. W. R. Pape, "Divide and Conquer: Even Small Companies Need to Decentralize. The Key Is Knowing When to Split What," *Inc.*, 18 June 1996.
14. C. Quintanilla, "Food: Come and Get It! Drive-Throughs Upgrade Services," *The Wall Street Journal*, 5 May 1994.
15. R.W. Griffin, *Task Design* (Glenview, IL: Scott, Foresman, 1982).
16. F. Herzberg, *Work and the Nature of Man* (Cleveland, OH: World Press, 1966).
17. T. Petzinger, Jr., "Commitment Creates Change at this Chilean Telecom Firm," *The Wall Street Journal Interactive Edition*, 30 May 1997.
18. J. R. Hackman & G. R. Oldham, *Work Redesign* (Reading, MA: Addison-Wesley, 1980).
19. T. Burns & G. M. Stalker, *The Management of Innovation* (London: Tavistock, 1961).
20. M. Hammer & J. Champy, *Reengineering the Corporation: A Manifesto for Business Revolution* (New York: HarperBusiness, 1993).
21. Ibid.
22. J. D. Thompson, *Organizations in Action* (New York: McGraw-Hill, 1967).
23. J. B. White, "'Next Big Thing': Re-Engineering Gurus Take Steps to Remodel Their Stalling Vehicles," *The Wall Street Journal Interactive Edition*, 26 November 1996.
24. Ibid.
25. G. M. Spreitzer, "Individual Empowerment in the Workplace: Dimensions, Measurement, and Validation," *Academy of Management Journal* 38 (1995): 1442–1465.
26. T. Petzinger, "Frontlines: In Lifesaving Field, Tools of the Trade Earn Loyalty," *The Wall Street Journal Interactive Edition*, 25 October 1996.
27. K. W. Thomas & B.A. Velthouse, "Cognitive Elements of Empowerment," Academy of Management Review 15 (1990): 666–681.
28. J. S. Hirsch, "Travel: Now Hotel Clerks Provide More Than Keys," *The Wall Street Journal*, 5 March 1993.
29. D. A. Morand, "The Role of Behavioral Formality and Informality in the Enactment of Bureaucratic Versus Organic Organizations," *Academy of Management Journal*, 20 (1995): 831–872.
30. F. Swoboda, "Casual Dress Becomes the Rule," *The Las Vegas Review-Journal*, 3 March 1996.
31. K. McCullough, "Analysis: More Companies Allowing Employees to Dress Down, Which Makes-Productivity Go Up," *The Money Club*, 26 March 1996.
32. Ibid.
33. K. A. Edelman, "Take Down the Walls!" *Across the Board* 34 (1 March 1997).
34. "Designing the Ever-Changing Workplace," *Architectural Record*, September 1995, 32–37.
35. K. A. Edelman, "Take Down the Walls!" *Across the Board* 34 (1 March 1997).
36. C. Edwards, "Open Office Policy Workstation Design Aimed at Interaction," *The Fort Worth Star-Telegram*, 27 December 1996.
37. K. A. Edelman, "Take Down the Walls!" *Across the Board* 34 (1 March 1997).
38. R. Nilson, "Virtual Corporations: From the Rolling Stones to IBM to Start-ups, 'Outsourcing' Is the Way to Go," *Sunday Telegram*, 30 July 1995.
39. G. G. Dess, A. M. A. Rasheed, K. J. McLaughlin, & R. L. Priem, "The New Corporate Architecture," *Academy of Management Executive* 9 (1995): 7–18.
40. "Building the CEO: Robert Eaton Has Parlayed Teamwork and Technology to Turn a Troubled Auto," *Industry Week*, 16 September 1996, 10–14.
41. "Ford Setting Agenda in Vehicle Manufacturer/Supplier Relationships," *Automotive Components Analyst*, 1 December 1995.
42. "Building the CEO: Robert Eaton Has Parlayed Teamwork and Technology to Turn a Troubled Auto," *Industry Week*, 16 September 1996, 10–14.
43. H. Voss, "Virtual Organizations: The Future Is Now," *Strategy & Leadership*, 17 July 1996.
44. J. H. Sheridan, "The Agile Web: A Model for the Future?" *Industry Week*, 4 March 1996.
45. Ibid.
46. C. C. Snow, R. E. Miles, & H. J. Coleman, Jr., "Managing 21st Century Network Organizations," *Organizational Dynamics*, Winter 1992, 5–20.
47. J. H. Sheridan, "The Agile Web: A Model for the Future?" *Industry Week*, 4 March 1996.
48. D. Ulrich & S. Kerr, "Creating the *Boundaryless Organization*: The Radical Reconstruction of Organization Capabilities," *Planning Review*, September–October 1995, 41–45.
49. R. Ashkenas, D. Ulrich, T. Jick, & S. Kerr, *The* Boundaryless Organization: *Breaking the Chains of Organizational Structure* (San Francisco: Jossey-Bass, 1995).
50. D. Ulrich & S. Kerr, "Creating the Boundaryless Organization: The Radical Reconstruction of Organization Capabilities," *Planning Review*, September–October 1995, 41–45.
51. G. G. Dess, A. M. A. Rasheed, K. J. McLaughlin, & R. L. Priem, "The New Corporate Architecture," *Academy of Management Executive* 9 (1995): 7–18.

Chapter 12

1. J. H. Boyett & J. T. Boyett, *Beyond Workforce 2000* (New York: Dutton, 1995).
2. Ibid.
3. R. Stodghill, "The Coming Job Bottleneck," *Business Week*, 24 March 1997, 184–185.
4. K. Wallsten, "Diversity Pays Off in Big Sales for Toyota Dealership," *Workforce*, September 1998, 91–92.
5. R. S. Johnson, "The 50 Best Companies for Asians, Blacks, & Hispanics: Talent Comes in All Colors," *Fortune*, 3 August 1999, 94.
6. Ibid.

7. Equal Employment Opportunity Commission, "Affirmative Action Appropriate under Title VII of the Civil Rights Act of 1964, As Amended. Chapter XIV—Equal Employment Opportunity Commission, Part 1608." [Online] Available *http://fr-webgate.access.gpo.gov/cgi-bin/get-cfr.cgi?TITLE=29&PART=1608&SECTION=1&TYPE=TEXT*, 3 April 1999.
8. J. H. Birnbaum, "Fannie Mae: Spinning Idealism into Gold by Building a Diverse Work Force and Lending to More Minority Homebuyers," *Fortune*, 3 August 1998, 101.
9. Equal Employment Opportunity Commission, Federal Laws Prohibiting Job Discrimination: Questions and Answers." [Online] Available *http://www.eeoc.gov/facts/qanda.html*, 4 April 1999.
10. A. P. Carnevale & S. C. Stone, *The American Mosaic: An In-Depth Report on the Future of Diversity at Work* (New York: McGraw-Hill, 1995).
11. T. Roosevelt, "From Affirmative Action to Affirming Diversity," *Harvard Business Review* 68, no. 2 (1990): 107–117.
12. R. Morin & S. Warden, "Americans Vent Anger at Affirmative Action," *Washington Post*, 25 March 1995, A1.
13. A. M. Konrad & F. Linnehan, "Formalized HRM Structures: Coordinating Equal Employment Opportunity or Concealing Organizational Practices?" *Academy of Management Journal* 38, no. 3 (1995): 787–820.
14. *Hopwood v. State of Tex.*, 78 F.3d 932, 64 USLW 2591, 107 Ed. Law Rep. 552 (5th Cir.[Tex.], 18 Mar 1996) (NO. 94-50569, 94-50664).
15. N. Glazer, *Ethnic Dilemmas, 1964–1982* (Cambridge: Harvard University Press, 1983).
16. M. E. Heilman, C. J. Block, & P. Stathatos, "The Affirmative Action Stigma of Incompetence: Effects of Performance Information Ambiguity," *Academy of Management Journal* 40, no. 3 (1997): 603–625.
17. K. C. Cole, "Jury Out on Whether Affirmative Action Beneficiaries Face Stigma: Research Studies Arrive at Conflicting Conclusions," *The Los Angeles Times*, 1 May 1995, 18.
18. G. Robinson & K. Dechant, "Building a Business Case for Diversity," *Academy of Management Executive* 11, no. 3 (1997): 21–31.
19. Ibid.
20. Ibid.
21. B. Egelko, "Home Depot Bias Suit Settled for $87 Million," *The Sacramento Bee* (Associated Press), 21 September 1997, A3.
22. R. R. Schmitt, "State Farm Pays $157 Million in Sex Discrimination Case," *The Wall Street Journal Europe*, 30 April 1992, 15.
23. R. B. Lieber & L. Urresta, "Pacific Enterprises: Keeping Talent after Being Encouraged to Explore Jobs Elsewhere, Most Employees Stay Put," *Fortune*, 3 August 1998, 96.
24. S. P. Jones, "Careers Mirroring the Market: A Diverse Staff Is a Business Plus," *Boston Herald*, 8 April 1996, 37.
25. L. Himelstein & S.A. Forest, "How Much Progress Have Women Made in Corporate America?" Business Week, 17 February 1997, 64.
26. L. E. Wynter, "Business & Race: Advocates Try to Tie Diversity to Profit," *The Wall Street Journal*, 7 February 1996, B1.
27. W. W. Watson, K. Kumar, L.K. Michaelsen, "Cultural Diversity's Impact on Interaction Process and Performance: Comparing Homogeneous and Diverse Task Groups," *Academy of Management Journal* 36 (1993): 590–602.
28. F. Rice, "How to Make Diversity Pay," *Fortune*, 8 August 1994, 78.
29. K. Kelly, "Diversity Rules: It's No Easy Task for a Business Owner to Keep the Melting Pot from Boiling Over," *Business Week*, 1 September 1997, ENT22.
30. M. R. Carrell & E.E. Mann, "Defining Workplace Diversity Programs and Practices in Organizations," *The Labor Law Journal* 44 (1993): 744–764.
31. D. A. Harrison, K.H. Price, & M.P. Bell, "Beyond Relational Demography: Time and the Effects of Surface-and Deep-Level Diversity on Work Group Cohesion," *Academy of Management Journal* 41 (1998): 96–107.
32. Ibid.
33. Ibid.
34. N. Munk, "Finished at Forty: In the New Economy, the Skills that Come with Age Count for Less and Less. Suddenly, 40 Is Starting to Look and Feel Old," *Fortune*, 1 February 1999, 50.
35. S. E. Sullivan & E. A. Duplaga, "Recruiting and Retaining Older Workers for the Millenium," *Business Horizons* 40 (12 November 1997): 65.
36. N. Munk, "Finished at Forty: In the New Economy, the Skills that Come with Age Count for Less and Less. Suddenly, 40 Is Starting to Look and Feel Old," *Fortune*, 1 February 1999, 50.
37. S. R. Rhodes, "Age-Related Differences in Work Attitudes and Behavior," *Psychological Bulletin* 92 (1983): 328–367.
38. Fisher, "Wanted: Aging Baby-Boomers," *Fortune*, 30 September 1996, 204.
39. G. M. McEvoy & W. F. Cascio, "Cumulative Evidence of the Relationship Between Employee Age and Job Performance," *Journal of Applied Psychology* 74 (1989): 11–17.
40. S. E. Sullivan & E. A. Duplaga, "Recruiting and Retaining Older Workers for the Millenium," *Business Horizons* 40 (12 November 1997): 65.
41. B. L. Hassell & P. L. Perrewe, "An Examination of Beliefs about Older Workers: Do Stereotypes Still Exist?" *Journal of Organizational Behavior* 16 (1995): 457–468.
42. B. R. Ragins, B. Townsend, & M. Mattis, "Gender Gap in the Executive Suite: CEOs and Female Executives Report on Breaking the Glass Ceiling," *Academy of Management Executive* 12 (1998): 28–42.
43. P. Dwyer, M. Johnston, & K. L. Miller, "Europe's Corporate Women: Their Progress into Boardrooms and Executive Suites Is Glacial. What's the Likelihood of Change?" *Business Week*, 15 April 1996, 40.
44. J. R. Hollenbeck, D. R. Ilgen, C. Ostroff, & J. B. Vancouver, "Sex Differences in Occupational Choice, Pay, and Worth: A Supply-Side Approach to Understanding the Male-Female Wage Gap," *Personnel Psychology* 40 (1987): 715–744.
45. L. Bernier, "Out of the Typing Pool into Career Limbo in 1985, These Women Vowed to Smash the Glass Ceiling, Few Did," *Business Week*, 15 April 1996, 43.
46. Korn-Ferry International, 1993.
47. Department of Industry, Labor and Human Relations, *Report of the Governor's Task Force on the Glass Ceiling Commission* (Madison, WI: State of Wisconsin, 1993).
48. E.H. Buttner & D.P. Moore, "Women's Organizational Exodus to Entrepreneurship: Self-Reported Motivations and Correlates with Success," *Journal of Small Business Management* 35 (1997): 34–46.
49. S. Hamm, "Why Are Women So Invisible?" *Business Week*, 25 August 1997, 136.
50. B. R. Ragins, B. Townsend, & M. Mattis, "Gender Gap in the Executive Suite: CEOs and Female Executives Report on Breaking the Glass Ceiling," *Academy of Management Executive* 12 (1998): 28–42.
51. Morris, "If Women Ran the World, It Would Look a Lot Like Avon: In a Beauty Contest Unlike Any Other, Four of the Six Candidates for the Next CEO Are Women," *Fortune*, 21 July 1997, 74.
52. T.B. Foley, "Discrimination Lawsuits Are a Small-Business Nightmare: A Guide to Minimizing the Potential Damage," *The Wall Street Journal*, 28 September 1998, 15.
53. D. A. Thomas & S. Wetlaufer, "A Question of Color: A Debate on Race in the U.S. Workplace," *Harvard Business Review* 75 (September/October 1997): 118–132.
54. D. A. Neal & W. R. Johnson, "The Role of Premarket Factors in Black-White Wage Differences," *Journal of Political Economy* 104, no. 5 (1996): 869-895.
55. M. Fix, G. C. Galster, & R. J. Struyk, "An Overview of Auditing for Discrimination," in *Clear and Convincing Evidence: Measurement of Discrimination in America*, eds. Michael Fix and Raymond Struyk (Washington, DC: The Urban Institute Press, 1993), 1–68.
56. M. Bendick, Jr., C. W. Jackson, & V. A. Reinoso, "Measuring Employment Discrimination through Controlled Experiments," in *African-Americans and Post-Industrial Labor Markets*, ed. James B. Stewart (New Brunswick: Transaction Publishers, 1997), 77–100
57. P. B. Riach & J. Rich, "Measuring Discrimination by Direct Experimental Methods: Seeking Gunsmoke," *Journal of PostKeynesian Economics* 14, no. 2 (Winter 1991–1992): 143–50.
58. A. P. Brief, R. T. Buttram, R. M. Reizenstein, & S. D. Pugh, "Beyond Good Intentions: The Next Steps toward Racial Equality in the American Workplace," *Academy of Management Executive* 11 (1997): 59–72.
59. L. E. Wynter, "Business & Race: Federal Agencies, Spurred On by Nonprofit Groups, Are Increasingly Embracing the Use of Undercover Investigators to Identify Discrimination in the Marketplace," *The Wall Street Journal*, 1 July 1998, B1.
60. Equal Employment Opportunity Commission, "Charge Statistics: FY 1992 through FY 1998." [Online] Available *http://www.eeoc.gov/stats/charges.html*, 17 April 1999.

61. S. J. Well, "When the Bias Is in the Hiring," *Journal Record* (Oklahoma City), 26 March 1998, 1.
62. U. S. Department of Justice, "The Americans with Disabilities Act: Questions and Answers." [Online] Available *http://www.usdoj.gov/crt/ada/ada.html*, 19 April 1999.
63. U. S. Bureau of the Census, "Census Brief: Disabilities Affect One-Fifth of All Americans." [Online] Available *http://www.census.gov/prod/3/97pubs/cenbr975.pdf*, 19 April 1999.
64. F. Bowe, "Adults with Disabilities: A Portrait," *President's Committee on Employment of People with Disabilities* (Washington, DC: GPO, 1992). D. Braddock & L. Bachelder, *The Glass Ceiling and Persons with Disabilities*, Glass Ceiling Commission, U.S. Department of Labor (Washington, DC: GPO, 1994).
65. Louis Harris and Associates, Inc., *Public Attitudes toward People with Disabilities* (Washington DC: National Organization on Disability, 1991). Louis Harris and Associates, Inc., *The ICD Survey II: Employing Disabled Americans* (New York: Author, 1987).
66. R. Greenwood & V. A. Johnson, "Employer Perspectives on Workers with Disabilities," *Journal of Rehabilitation* 53 (1987): 37–45.
67. Braddock & L. Bachelder, *The Glass Ceiling and Persons with Disabilities*, Glass Ceiling Commission, U. S. Department of Labor (Washington, DC: GPO, 1994).
68. F. Schwadel, "Sears Sets Model for Compliance with Disabilities Act, Study Says," *The Wall Street Journal*, 4 March 1996, B5.
69. D. L. Stone & A. A. Colella, "Model of Factors Affecting the Treatment of Disabled Individuals in Organizations," *Academy of Management Review* 2 (1996): 352–401.
70. R. D. Ashmore & F. K. Del Boca, "Conceptual Approaches to Stereotypes and Stereotyping, in *Cognitive Processes In Stereotyping And Intergroup Behavior*, ed. D.L. Hamilton (Hillsdale, NJ: Erlbaum, 1981), 1–35.
71. Braddock & L. Bachelder, *The Glass Ceiling and Persons with Disabilities*, Glass Ceiling Commission, U.S. Department of Labor (Washington, DC: GPO, 1994).
72. Ibid.
73. Ibid.
74. R. B. Cattell, "Personality Pinned Down," *Psychology Today* 7 (1973): 40–46. C. S. Carver & M. F. Scheier, *Perspectives on Personality* (Boston: Allyn & Bacon, 1992).
75. B. O'Reilly & K. A. Kelly, "Does Your Fund Manager Play the Piano? How about Bridge? And How Does He Feel about Baseball? The Surprising Personality Traits of the People Who Manage America's Money," *Fortune*, 29 December 1997, 139.
76. J. M. Digman, "Personality Structure: Emergence of the Five-Factor Model," *Annual Review of Psychology* 41 (1990): 417–440. M. P. Barrick & M. K. Mount, "The Big Five Personality Dimensions and Job Performance: A Meta-Analysis," *Personnel Psychology* 44 (1991): 1–26.
77. C. Wolff, "Peabody Enhances Employee Relations," *Lodging Hospitality*, October 1996, 9.
78. M. Brannigan, "Captain WOW: When Is Mental State of a Pilot Grounds for Grounding Him? Delta Is Sued after Benching Flier Who Got into Spats at Home and in Cockpit—Running a Gantlet of Shrinks," *The Wall Street Journal*, 7 March 1996, A1.
79. P. LaBarre, "Lighten Up! Blurring the Line Between Fun and Work Not Only Humanizes Organizations but Strengthens the Bottom Line," *Industry Week* 2 (5 February 1996): 53.
80. "Southwest Air's Leader Takes 'Radical' Approach," *Tucson Citizen*, 22 Oct 1993, B1.
81. S. Caudron, "Hire for Attitude: It's Who They Are that Counts," *Workforce*, August 1997, 20–26.
82. O. Behling, "Employee Selection: Will Intelligence and Conscientiousness Do the Job?" *Academy of Management Executive* 12 (1998): 77–86.
83. J. M. Collins & F. L. Schmidt, "Personality, Integrity, and White Collar Crime: A Construct Validity Study," *Personnel Psychology* 46 (1993): 295–311.
84. M. R. Barrick & M. K. Mount, "The Big Five Personality Dimensions and Job Performance: A Meta-Analysis," *Personnel Psychology* 44 (1991): 1–26.
85. M. K. Mount & M. R. Barrick, "Five Reasons Why the 'Big Five' Article Has Been Frequently Cited," *Personnel Psychology* 4 (1998): 849–857.
86. Ibid.
87. J. A. Lopez, "Talking Desks: Personality Types Revealed in State Workstations," *Arizona Republic*, 7 January 1996, Section D, 1.
88. T. W. Adorno, E. Frenkel-Brunswik, D. J. Levinson, & R. N. Stanford, *The Authoritarian Personality* (New York: Harper & Row, 1950).
89. T. Lee, "Are You More of a Street Fighter or a Jekyll and Hyde?" *The Wall Street Journal*, 11 June 1996, B1.
90. R. G. Vleeming, "Machiavellianism: A Preliminary Review," *Psychological Reports* 53 (1979): 295–310.
91. F. L. Geis & T. H. Moon, "Machiavellianism and Deception," *Journal of Personality and Social Psychology* 41 (1981): 766–775.
92. R. Christie & R. L. Geis, *Studies in Machiavellianism* (New York: Academic Press, 1970), 312.
93. B. Bowers, "How to Get Ahead as a Middle Manager by Being Ruthless—Executive Strategies Monthly Offers Tips, but its Editor Truly Is a Kindhearted Soul," *The Wall Street Journal*, 23 March 1993, A1.
94. K. D. Grimsley, "Warriors in the Workplace: As Readers' Dispatches Attest, the Enemy Is Often the Next Cubicle," *Washington Post*, 25 January 1998, H1.
95. L. H. Primavera & M. Higgins, "Non-Verbal Rigidity and its Relationship to Dogmatism and Machiavellianism," *Perceptual and Motor Skills* 36 (1973): 356–358. T.J. Prociuk & L.J. Breen, "Machiavellianism and Locus of Control," *Journal of Social Psychology* 98 (1976): 141–142. G.W. Russell, "Machiavellianism, Locus of Control, Aggression, Performance and Precautionary Behavior in Ice Hockey," *Human Relations* 27 (1974): 825–837.
96. K. A. Matthews, "Psychological Perspectives on the Type A Behavior Pattern," *Psychological Bulletin* 91 (1982): 293–323.
97. M. Friedman & R. H. Rosenman, *Type A Behavior and Your Heart* (New York: Fawcett Crest, 1974).
98. J. G. Auerbach, "A Will to Win: An EMC Salesman Who Never Eases Up Helps Data Firm—Even on a Rare Vacation, John Chatwin Pursues Storage-System—Athletes' Competitive Edge," *The Wall Street Journal*, 8 July 1998, A1.
99. M. Lee & R. Kanungo, *Management of Work and Personal Life* (New York: Praeger, 1984).
100. J. Schaubroeck, D. C. Ganster, & B. E. Kemmerer, "Job Complexity, 'Type A' Behavior, and Cardiovascular Disorders," *Academy of Management Journal* 37 (1994): 37.
101. M. T. Matteson & J. M. Ivancevich, "The Coronary-Prone Behavior Pattern: A Review and Appraisal," *Social Science and Medicine* 14 (1980): 337–351.
102. J. E. Bishop, "Health: Hostility, Distrust May Put Type A's at Coronary Risk," *The Wall Street Journal*, 17 January 1989.
103. M. Snyder, "The Self-Monitoring of Expressive Behavior," *Journal of Personality and Social Psychology* 30 (1974): 526–537.
104. M. Snyder, "Self-Monitoring Processes," in *Advances in Experimental Social Psychology* 12, ed. L. Berkowitz (New York: Academic Press, 1979), 85–128.
105. D. F. Caldwell & C. A. O'Reilly, "Boundary Spanning and Individual Performance: The Impact of Self-Monitoring," *Journal of Applied Psychology* 67 (1982): 124–127. S. J. Zaccaro, R. J. Foti, & D. A. Kenny, "Self- Monitoring and Trait-Based Variance in Leadership: An Investigation of Leader Flexibility across Multiple Group Situations," *Journal of Applied Psychology* 76 (1991): 308–315. R.A. Baron, "Personality and Organizational Conflict: Effects of the Type A Behavior Pattern and Self-Monitoring," *Organizational Behavior and Human Decision Process* 44 (1989): 281–296.
106. M. Kilduff & D. V. Day, "Do Chameleons Get Ahead? The Effects of Self-Monitoring on Managerial Careers," *Academy of Management Journal* 37 (1994): 1047–1060.
107. A. H. Church, "Managerial Self-Awareness in High-Performing Individuals in Organizations," *Journal of Applied Psychology* 82 (1997): 281–292.
108. D. F. Caldwell & C. A. O'Reilly, III, "Boundary Spanning and Individual Performance: The Impact of Self-Monitoring," *Journal of Applied Psychology* 67 (1982): 124–127. M. Kilduff & D. V. Day, "Do Chameleons Get Ahead? The Effects of Self-Monitoring on Managerial Careers," *Academy of Management Journal* 37 (1994): 1047–1060. H. S. Friedman & T. Miller-Herringer, "Nonverbal Display of Emotion in Public and Private: Self-Monitoring, Personality and Expressive Cues," *Journal of Personality and Social Psychology* 62 (1991): 766–775.
109. B. Rotter, "Generalized Expectancies for Internal versus External Control of Reinforcement," *Psychological Monographs* 80 (1966): Whole No. 609. J. B. Rotter, "Some Problems and Misconceptions Related to the Construct of Internal versus External

Control of Reinforcement," *Journal of Consulting and Clinical Psychology* 43 (1975): 56–67.
110. P. Sellers, "So You Fail. Now Bounce Back!" *Fortune*, 1 May 1995, 48.
111. T.M. Burton, "Visionary's Reward: Combine 'Simple Ideas' and Some Failures; Result: James Sweeney Bought Back His Old Company Cheap; Never Give Up, He Says—Father's Lesson: Take Risks," *The Wall Street Journal*, 3 February 1995, A1.
112. P. E. Spector, "Behavior in Organizations as a Function of Employee's Locus of Control," *Psychological Bulletin* 91 (1982): 482–497.
113. Richard S. Lazarus, *Emotion and Adaptation* (New York: Oxford University Press, 1991).
114. "The Secrets of Happiness," *Psychology Today* 25 (July 1992): 38.
115. B. M. Staw, N. E. Bell, and J. A. Clausen, "The Dispositional Approach to Job Attitudes: A Lifetime Longitudinal Test," *Administrative Science Quarterly* 31 (1986): 56–77.
116. J. Solomon, "Trying To Be Nice Is No Labor of—Customer Service—Challenge for the '90s: Forced Courtesy Strains Workers, Irks Customers," *The Wall Street Journal*, 29 November 1990, B1.
117. A. M. Isen & R. A. Baron, "Positive Affect and Organizational Behavior," in *Research in Organizational Behavior* 12, eds. B. M. Staw & L. L. Cummings (Greenwich, CT: JAI Press, 1990). J. M. George & A. P. Brief, "Feeling Good-Doing Good: A Conceptual Analysis of the Mood at Work—Organizational Spontaneity Relationships," *Psychological Bulletin* 112 (1992): 310–329. R.D. Iverson & P.J. Erwin, "Predicting Occupational Injury: The Role of Affectivity," *Journal of Occupational and Organizational Psychology* 70 (1997): 113–128. D. P. Skarlicki, R. Folger, & P. Tesluk, "Personality as a Moderator in the Relationship Between Fairness and Retaliation," *Academy of Management Journal* 42 (1999): 100–108.
118. P. Totterdell, S. Kellett, K. Teuchmann, & R. B. Briner, "Evidence of Mood Linkage in Work Groups," *Journal of Personality and Social Psychology* 74 (1998): 1504–1515.
119. M. E. P. Seligman & S. Schulman, "Explanatory Style as a Predictor of Productivity and uitting among Life Insurance Sales Agents," *Journal of Personality and Social sychology* 50 (1986): 832–838.
120. T. D. Schellhardt, "In a Tight Factory Schedule, Where Does Religion Fit In?" *The Wall Street Journal Interactive Edition*, 4 March 1999.
121. Staff, "The Diverse Work Force," *Inc.*, January 1993, 33.
122. D. A. Thomas & R. J. Ely, "Making Differences Matter: A New Paradigm for Managing Diversity," *Harvard Business Review* 74 (September/October 1996): 79–90.
123. D. A. Thomas & S. Wetlaufer, "A Question of Color: A Debate on Race in the U.S. Workplace," *Harvard Business Review* 75 (September/October 1997): 118–132.
124. D. A. Thomas & R. J. Ely, "Making Differences Matter: A New Paradigm for Managing Diversity," *Harvard Business Review* 74 (September/October 1996): 79–90.
125. S. P. Jones, "Careers Mirroring the Market: A Diverse Staff Is a Business Plus," *Boston Herald*, 8 April 1996, 37.
126. J. R. Norton & R. E. Fox, *The Change Equation: Capitalizing on Diversity for Effective Organizational Change* (Washington, DC: American Psychological Association, 1997).
127. Ibid.
128. D. A. Thomas & R. J. Ely, "Making Differences Matter: A New Paradigm for Managing Diversity," *Harvard Business Review* 74 (September/October 1996): 79–90.
129. R. R. Thomas, Jr., *Beyond Race and Gender: Unleashing the Power of Your Total Workforce by Managing Diversity* (New York: AMACOM, 1991).
130. Ibid.
131. T. Cox, Jr., "The Multicultural Organization," *Academy of Management Executive* 5 (1991): 34–47.
132. S. Lubove, "Damned If You Do, Damned If You Don't: Preference Programs Are on the Defensive in the Public Sector, but Plaintiffs' Attorneys and Bureaucrats Keep Diversity Inc. Thriving in Corporate America," *Forbes*, 15 December 1997, 122.
133. L. S. Gottfredson, "Dilemmas in Developing Diversity Programs," in *Diversity in the Workplace*, eds. S. E. Jackson and Associates (New York: Guildford Press, 1992).
134. K. Kelly, "Diversity Rules: It's No Easy Task for a Business Owner to Keep the Melting Pot from Boiling Over," *Business Week*, 1 September 1997, 22.
135. R. B. Lieber & L. Urresta, "Pacific Enterprises: Keeping Talent after Being Encouraged to Explore Jobs Elsewhere, Most Employees Stay Put," *Fortune*, 3 August 1998, 96.
136. Markels, "Management: How One Hotel Manages Staff's Diversity," *The Wall Street Journal*, 20 November 1996, B1.
137. L. E. Wynter, "Business & Race: Allstate Rates Managers on Handling Diversity," *The Wall Street Journal*, 1 October 1997, B1.
138. H. Rosin, "Texaco Takes the Diversity Tiger by the Tail: In a Holy Crusade against Racism, the Oil Giant Is Bombarding Employees with Orwellian Admonishments to 'Respect the Individual,'" *Toronto Globe & Mail*, 14 February 1998, D4.
139. A. P. Carnevale & S. C. Stone, *The American Mosaic* (New York: McGraw-Hill, 1995).
140. Fenn, "Diversity: More than just Affirmative Action," *Inc.*, July 1995, 93.
141. J. R. Joplin & C. S. Daus, "Challenges of Leading a Diverse Workforce," *Academy of Management Executive* 11 (1997): 32–47.
142. T. Parker-Pope, "P&G Makes Strong Pitch to Keep Its Women Employees," *The Asian Wall Street Journal*, 15 September 1998, 12.
143. Rice, "How to Make Diversity Pay," *Fortune*, 8 August 1994, 78.

Chapter 13

1. B. Dumaine, "The Trouble with Teams," *Fortune*, 5 September 1994, 86–92.
2. J. R. Katzenback & D. K. Smith, *The Wisdom of Teams* (Boston: Harvard Business School Press, 1993).
3. S. G. Cohen & D. E. Bailey, "What Makes Teams Work: Group Effectiveness Research from the Shop Floor to the Executive Suite," *Journal of Management* 23, no. 3 (1997): 239–290.
4. W. Zellner, "TEAM PLAYER: No More 'Same-Ol'-Same-Ol,'" *Business Week*, 17 October 1994, 95.
5. S. E. Gross, *Compensation for Teams* (New York: American Management Association, 1995). B. L. Kirkman & B. Rosen, "Beyond Self-Management: Antecedents and Consequences of Team Empowerment," *Academy of Management Journal* 42 (1999): 58–74. G. Stock & T. M. Hout, *Competing Against Time* (New York: Free Press, 1990). S. C. Wheelwright & K. B. Clark, *Revolutionizing New Product Development* (New York: Free Press, 1992).
6. R. S. Wellins, W. C. Byham, & G. R. Dixon, *Inside Teams* (San Francisco: Jossey-Bass Publishers, 1994).
7. M. Selz, "Testing Self-Managed Teams, Entrepreneur Hopes to Lose Job," *The Wall Street Journal*, 11 January 1994, B1.
8. R. D. Banker, J. M. Field, R. G. Schroeder, & K. K. Sinha, "Impact of Work Teams on Manufacturing Performance: A Longitudinal Field Study," *Academy of Management Journal* 39 (1996): 867–890.
9. R. S. Wellins, W. C. Byham, & G. R. Dixon, *Inside Teams* (San Francisco: Jossey-Bass Publishers, 1994).
10. C. Fishman, "Whole Foods Is All Teams," *Fast Company*, April 1996, 103.
11. "Beating the Joneses (Learning What the Competition Is Doing)," *Industry Week* 1 (7 December 1998): 27.
12. G. Stalk & T. M. Hout, *Competing Against Time: How Time-Based Competition Is Reshaping Global Markets* (New York: The Free Press, 1990).
13. H. K Bowen, K. B. Clark, C. A. Holloway, & S. C. Wheelwright, *The Perpetual Enterprise Machine* (New York: Oxford Press, 1994).
14. B. Filipczak, "Concurrent Engineering: A Team by Any Other Name?" *Training* 33 (August 1996): 54. B. Marvel, "Group Effort Put 777 Aloft Boeing Came from Behind with a Winner in the Race," *Dallas Morning News*, 31 March 1996, 8J.
15. J. L. Cordery, W. S. Mueller, & L. M. Smith, "Attitudinal and Behavioral Effects of Autonomous Group Working: A Longitudinal Field Study," *Academy of Management Journal* 34 (1991): 464–476. T.D. Wall, N.J. Kemp, P.R. Jackson, & C.W. Clegg, "Outcomes of Autonomous Workgroups: A Longterm Field Experiment," *Academy of Management Journal* 29 (1986): 280–304.
16. R. S. Wellins, W. C. Byham, & G. R. Dixon, *Inside Teams* (San Francisco: Jossey-Bass Publishers, 1994).
17. R. S. Wellins, W. C. Byham, & G. R. Dixon, *Inside Teams* (San Francisco: Jossey-Bass Publishers, 1994).
18. C. Fishman, "Whole Foods Is All Teams," *Fast Company*, April 1996, 103.
19. R. S. Wellins, W. C. Byham, & G. R. Dixon, *Inside Teams* (San Francisco: Jossey-Bass Publishers, 1994).
20. J. Hoerr, "The Payoff from Teamwork—The Gains in Quality Are Substantial—So Why Isn't It Spreading Faster?" *Business Week*, 10 July 1989, 56.
21. T. Aeppel, "Missing the Boss: Not All Workers Find Idea of Empowerment as Neat as It Sounds—Some Hate Fix-

ing Machines, Apologizing for Errors, Disciplining Teammates—Rah-Rah Types Do the Best," *The Wall Street Journal*, 8 September 1997, A1.

22. J. George, "Extrinsic and Intrinsic Origins of Perceived Social Loafing in Organizations," *Academy of Management Journal* 35 (1992): 191–202.
23. T. T. Baldwin, M. D. Bedell, & J. L. Johnson, "The Social Fabric of a Team-Based M.B.A. Program: Network Effects on Student Satisfaction and Performance," *Academy of Management Journal* 40 (1997): 1369–1397.
24. P.W. Mulvey, J.F. Veiga, & P.M. Elsass, "When Teammates Raise a White Flag," *Academy of Management Executive* 10, no. 1 (1996): 40–49.
25. Ibid.
26. J. Hoerr, "The Payoff from Teamwork—The Gains in Quality Are Substantial—So Why Isn't It Spreading Faster?" *Business Week*, 10 July 1989, 56.
27. National Labor Relations Board, *Fact Sheet on the National Labor Relations Board*. [Online] Available *http://www.nlrb.gov/facts.html*, 6 May 1999.
28. K. Hein, "Is Teamwork Against the Law?" *Incentive* 170, no. 8 (August 1996): 7.
29. G. Burkins, "Senate Debates Right to Set Up Worker Teams," *The Wall Street Journal*, 10 July 1996, B1.
30. C. Joinson, "Teams at Work," *HRMagazine*, 1 May 1999, 30.
31. R. Wageman, "Critical Success Factors for Creating Superb Self-Managing Teams," *Organizational Dynamics* 26, no. 1 (1997): 49–61.
32. L. M. Sixel, "Does the Team Scheme Work?" *Houston Chronicle*, 8 November 1996, Business, 1.
33. M. A. Cusumano, "How Microsoft Makes Large Teams Work Like Small Teams," *Sloan Management Review* 39, no. 1 (Fall 1997): 9–20.
34. R. T. King, Jr., "Jeans Therapy: Levi's Factory Workers Are Assigned to Teams, and Morale Takes a Hit—Infighting Rises, Productivity Falls as Employees Miss the Piecework System— 'It's Not the Same Company,'" *The Wall Street Journal*, 20 May 1998, A1.
35. Ibid.
36. M. Curtius, "There Is No 'I' in 'Team'—And Maybe No Point, Either: The Trend Continues but Doesn't Always Succeed. Finding the Proper Structure, Motivating Employees and Getting Managers Out of the Way Can Sometimes Help," *Los Angeles Times*, 24 February 1997, D25.
37. R. T. King, Jr., "Jeans Therapy: Levi's Factory Workers Are Assigned to Teams, and Morale Takes a Hit—Infighting Rises, Productivity Falls as Employees Miss the Piecework System—'It's Not the Same Company,'" *The Wall Street Journal*, 20 May 1998, A1.
38. B. L. Kirkman & B. Rosen, "Beyond Self-Management: Antecedents and Consequences of Team Empowerment," *Academy of Management Journal* 42 (1999): 58–74.
39. M. Curtius, "There Is No 'I' in 'Team'—And Maybe No Point, Either: The Trend Continues but Doesn't Always Succeed. Finding the Proper Structure, Motivating Employees and Getting Managers Out of the Way Can Sometimes Help," *Los Angeles Times*, 24 February 1997, D25.
40. R. A. Melcher, C. Debes, N. Gross, J. Templeman, & Benway, "Can Ford Stay on Top? The World's Hottest Carmaker Has Set its Strategy for the 21st Century," *Business Week*, 28 September 1987, 78.
41. J. B. Treece, K. Kerwin, & H. Dawley, "Alex Trotman's Daring Global Strategy," *Business Week*, 3 April 1995, 94.
42. B. L. Kirkman & B. Rosen, "Beyond Self-Management: Antecedents and Consequences of Team Empowerment," *Academy of Management Journal* 42 (1999): 58–74.
43. K. Kelly, "Managing Workers Is Tough Enough in Theory. When Human Nature Enters the Picture, It's Worse," *Business Week*, 21 October 1996, 32.
44. S. Easton & G. Porter, "Selecting the Right Team Structure to Work in Your Organization," in *Handbook of Best Practices for Teams*, Volume 1, ed. Glenn M. Parker (Amherst, MA: Irwin, 1996).
45. C. Caggiano, "Worker, Rule Thyself," *Inc.*, February 1999, 89–90.
46. D. Stafford, "Hotel Lets Its Workers 'Own' Their Duties: Ritz-Carlton, Kansas City, Tries a Program That Emphasizes Teamwork, Self-Direction," *The Kansas City Star*, 6 February 1996, D1.
47. Knight-Ridder, "Electrician Gets with the Team at Ford Plant," *Chicago Tribune*, 7 April 1996, 8.
48. M. Maynard, "Saturn Workers May Dump Unique Contract," *USA Today*, 17 February 1998, 03B.
49. R. J. Recardo, D. Wade, C. A. Mention, & J. Jolly, *Teams* (Houston: Gulf Publishing Company, 1996).
50. D. R. Denison, S. L. Hart, & J. A. Kahn, "From Chimneys to Cross-Functional Teams: Developing and Validating a Diagnostic Model," *Academy of Management Journal* 39, no. 4 (1996): 1005–1023.
51. C. Parnell, "Teamwork: Not a New Idea, But It's Transforming the Workplace" (Transcript), *Vital Speeches*, 1 November 1996, 46.
52. A. M. Townsend, S. M. DeMarie, & A. R. Hendrickson, "Virtual Teams: Technology and the Workplace of the Future," *Academy of Management Executive* 13, no. 3 (1998): 17–29.
53. A. M. Townsend, S. M. DeMarie, & A. R. Henfrickson, "Are You Ready for Virtual Teams?" *HRMagazine* 41, no.9 (1996): 122–126.
54. Selah School District Website, "The Boeing 777." [Online] Available *http://www.selah.wednet.edu*, 9 September 1998.
55. R. S. Wellins, W. C. Byham, & G. R. Dixon, *Inside Teams* (San Francisco: Jossey-Bass Publishers, 1994).
56. A. M. Townsend, S. M. DeMarie, & A. R. Hendrickson, "Virtual Teams: Technology and the Workplace of the Future," *Academy of Management Executive* 13, no. 3 (1998): 17–29.
57. R. Katz, "The Effects of Group Longevity on Project Communication and Performance," *Administrative Science Quarterly* 27 (1982): 245-282.
58. D. Mankin, S. G. Cohen, & T. K. Bikson, *Teams and Technology: Fulfilling the Promise of the New Organization* (Boston: Harvard Business School Press, 1996).
59. S. Carey, "USAir 'Peon' Team Pilots Start-Up of Low-Fare Airline," *The Wall Street Journal*, 24 March 1998, B1.
60. J. L. Lundy, *Teams* (Chicago: Dartnell, 1992).
61. L. Holpp & H. P. Phillips, "When Is a Team Its Own Worst Enemy?" *Training*, 1 September 1995, 71.
62. S. Asche, "Opinions and Social Pressure," *Scientific America* 193 (1995): 31–35.
63. Nucor Homepage, "The Nucor Story." [Online] Available *http://www.nucor.com/story.htm*, 10 May 1999.
64. S. G. Cohen, G. E. Ledford, & G. M. Spreitzer, "A Predictive Model of Self-Managing Work Team Effectiveness," *Human Relations* 49, no. 5 (1996): 643–676.
65. E. Matson, "Four Rules for Fast Teams," *Fast Company*, August 1996, 87.
66. K. Bettenhausen & J. K. Murnighan, "The Emergence of Norms in Competitive Decision-Making Groups," *Administrative Science Quarterly* 30 (1985): 350–372.
67. M. E. Shaw, *Group Dynamics* (New York: McGraw Hill, 1981).
68. J. R. Katzenback & D. K. Smith, *The Wisdom of Teams* (Boston: Harvard Business School Press, 1993).
69. S. E. Jackson, "The Consequences of Diversity in Multidisciplinary Work Teams," in *Handbook of Work Group Psychology*, ed. Michael A. West (Chichester, UK: Wiley, 1996).
70. A. M. Isen & R. A. Baron, "Positive Affect as a Factor in Organizational Behavior," in *Research in Organizational Behavior* 13, eds. L. L. Cummings & B. M. Staw (Greenwich, CT: JAI Press, 1991), 1–53.
71. C. R. Evans & K. L. Dion, "Group Cohesion and Performance: A Meta Analysis," *Small Group Research* 22, no. 2 (1991): 175–186.
72. R. Stankiewicsz, "The Effectiveness of Research Groups in Six Countries," in *Scientific Productivity*, ed. F.M. Andrews (Cambridge: Cambridge University Press, 1979), 191–221.
73. F. Rees, *Teamwork from Start to Finish* (San Francisco: Jossey-Bass, 1997).
74. S. M. Gully, D. S. Devine, & D. J. Whitney, "A Meta-Analysis of Cohesion and Performance: Effects of Level of Analysis and Task Interdependence," *Small Group Research* 26, no. 4 (1995): 497–520.
75. E. Matson, "Four Rules for Fast Teams," *Fast Company*, August 1996, 87.
76. F. Tschan & M. V. Cranach, "Group Task Structure, Processes and Outcomes," in *Handbook of Work Group Psychology*, ed. Michael A. West (Chichester, UK: Wiley, 1996).
77. D. E. Yeatts & C. Hyten, *High Performance Self Managed Teams* (Thousand Oaks, CA: Sage Publications, 1998).
78. Ibid.
79. D. S. Kezsbom, "Re-Opening Pandora's Box: Sources of Project Team Conflict in the '90s," *Industrial Engineering* 24, no. 5 (1992): 54–59.

80. A. C. Amason, W. A. Hochwarter, K. R. Thompson, "Conflict: An Important Dimension in Successful Management Teams," *Organizational Dynamics* 24 (1995): 20.
81. A. C. Amason, "Distinguishing the Effects of Functional and Dysfunctional Conflict on Strategic Decision Making: Resolving a Paradox for Top Management Teams," *Academy of Management Journal* 39, no. 1 (1996): 123–148.
82. K. M. Eisenhardt, J. L. Kahwajy, & L. J. Bourgeois, "How Management Teams Can Have a Good Fight," *Harvard Business Review*, July–August 1997, 77–85.
83. Ibid.
84. C. Nemeth & Owens, "Making Work Groups More Effective: The Value of Minority Dissent," in *Handbook of Work Group Psychology*, ed. Michael A. West (Chichester, UK: Wiley, 1996).
85. J. M. Levin & R. L. Moreland, "Progress in Small Group Research," *Annual Review of Psychology* 9 (1990): 72–78. S.E. Jackson, "Team Composition in Organizational Settings: Issues in Managing a Diverse Work Force," in *Group Processes and Productivity*, eds. S. Worchel, W. Wood, & J. Simpson (Beverly Hills, CA: Sage, 1992).
86. K. M. Eisenhardt, J. L. Kahwajy, & L. . Bourgeois, III, "How Management Teams Can Have a Good Fight," *Harvard Business Review* 75, no. 4 (July–August 1997): 77–87.
87. Ibid.
88. B. W. Tuckman, "Development Sequence in Small Groups," *Psychological Bulletin* 63, no. 6 (1965): 384–399.
89. S. E. Gross, *Compensation for Teams* (New York: American Management Association, 1995).
90. J. F. McGrew, J. G. Bilotta, & J. M. Deeney, "Software Team Formation and Decay: Extending the Standard Model for Small Groups," *Small Group Research* 30, no. 2 (1999): 209–234.
91. J. F. McGrew, J. G. Bilotta, & J. M. Deeney, "Software Team Formation and Decay: Extending the Standard Model for Small Groups," *Small Group Research* 30, no. 2 (1999): 209–234.
92. J. Case, "What the Experts Forgot to Mention: Management Teams Create New Difficulties, But Succeed for Xel Communication," *Inc.*, 1 September 1993, 66.
93. J. R. Hackman, "The Psychology of Self-Management in Organizations," in *Psychology and Work: Productivity, Change, and Employment*, eds. M. S. Pallak, & R. Perloff (Washington DC: American Psychological Association), 85–136).
94. O Leary-Kelly, J. J. Martocchio, D. D. Frink, "A Review of the Influence of Group Goals on Group Performance," *Academy of Management Journal* 37, no. 5 (1994): 1285–1301.
95. Nucor Homepage, "The Nucor Story." [Online] Available *http://www.nucor.com/story.htm*, 10 May 1999.
96. Zander, "The Origins and Consequences of Group Goals," in *Retrospections on Social Psychology*, ed. L. Festinger (New York: Oxford University Press, 1980), 205–235.
97. M. Erez & A. Somech, "Is Group Productivity Loss the Rule or the Exception? Effects of Culture and Group-Based Motivation," *Academy of Management Journal* 39, no. 6 (1996): 1513–1537.
98. S. Sherman, "Stretch Goals: The Dark Side of Asking for Miracles," *Fortune*, 13 November 1995.
99. S. Tully, "So, Mr. Bossidy, We Know You Can Cut. Now Show Us How to Grow," *Fortune*, 21 August 1995, 70.
100. K. R. Thompson, W. A. Hochwarter, & N. J. Mathys, "Stretch Targets: What Makes Them Effective?" *Academy of Management Executive* 11, no. 3 (1997): 48–60.
101. S. Tully, "Why to Go for Stretch Targets," *Fortune*, 14 November 1994, 145.
102. S. Sherman, "Stretch Goals: The Dark Side of Asking for Miracles," *Fortune*, 13 November 1995.
103. S. Shellenbarger, "Are Saner Workloads the Unexpected Key to More Productivity?" *The Wall Street Journal*, 10 March 1999, B1.
104. G. C. Hill & K. Yamada, "Taming the Monster—How Big Companies Can Change—Staying Power: Motorola Illustrates How an Aged Giant Can Remain Vibrant—Endless Self-Criticism Keeps Walkie-Talkie Creator Thriving," *The Wall Street Journal*, 9 December 1992, A1.
105. Dumaine, "The Trouble with Teams," *Fortune*, 5 September 1994, 86–92.
106. G. A. Neuman, S. H. Wagner, N. D. Christiansen, "The Relationship Between Work-Team Personality Composition and the Job Performance of Teams," *Group & Organization Management* 24, no. 1 (1999): 28–45.
107. M. A. Campion, G. J. Medsker, & A. C. Higgs, "Relations Between Work Group Characteristics and Effectiveness: Implications for Designing Effective Work Groups," *Personnel Psychology* 46, no. 4 (1993): 823–850.
108. B. L. Kirkman & D. L. Shapiro, "The Impact of Cultural Values on Employee Resistance to Teams: Toward a Model of Globalized Self-Managing Work Team Effectiveness," *Academy of Management Review* 22, no. 3 (1997): 730–757.
109. M. A. Campion, G. J. Medsker, & A.C. Higgs, "Relations Between Work Group Characteristics and Effectiveness: Implications for Designing Effective Work Groups," *Personnel Psychology* 46, no. 4 (1993): 823–850.
110. S. Caudron, "Team Staffing Requires New HR Role," *Personnel Journal* 73, no. 5 (1994): 88.
111. T. R. Tudor, R. R. Trumble, & J. J. Diaz, "Work-Teams: Why Do They Often Fail?" *S.A.M. Advanced Management Journal* 61, no. 4 (Autumn 1996): 31.
112. M. A. Verespej, "Super Sack," *Industry Week*, 16 October 1995, 53.
113. R. S. Wellins, W. C. Byham, & G. R. Dixon, *Inside Teams* (San Francisco: Jossey-Bass Publishers, 1994).
114. Joinson, "Teams at Work," *HRMagazine*, 1 May 1999, 30.
115. Ibid.
116. R. S. Wellins, W. C. Byham, & G. R. Dixon, *Inside Teams* (San Francisco: Jossey-Bass Publishers, 1994).
117. S. Caudron, "Tie Individual Pay to Team Success," *Personnel Journal* 73, no. 10 (October 1994): 40.
118. Ibid.
119. S. E. Gross, *Compensation for Teams* (New York: American Management Association, 1995).
120. R. S. Wellins, W. C. Byham, & G. R. Dixon, *Inside Teams* (San Francisco: Jossey-Bass Publishers, 1994).
121. J. R. Schuster & P. K. Zingheim, *The New Pay: Linking Employee and Organizational Performance* (New York: Lexington Books, 1992).
122. R. E. Yates, "Molding a New Future for Manufacturer, Keys Are Planning, People—and Plastics," *Chicago Tribune*, 2 January 1994.
123. S. G. Cohen & D. E. Bailey, "What Makes Teams Work: Group Effectiveness Research from the Shop Floor to the Executive Suite," *Journal of Management* 23, no. 3 (1997): 239–290.
124. Anonymous, "How NCR Uses Compensation to Support Teams," *ACA Journal* 5, no. 4 (Winter 1996): 74–75.
125. J. H. Sheridan, "'Yes' to Team Incentives," *Industry Week*, 4 March 1996, 63.

Chapter 14

1. M. Barrier, "Hiring the Right People," *Nation's Business* 84, no. 6 (June 1996): 18.
2. R. Rapaport, "When Irish IT is Smiling," *Forbes ASAP*, 31 May 1999, 114–124.
3. G. A. Poole, "Silicon Valley Serves Up Worker Perks: Find Dining, Fitness Rooms, Concerts Are Used to Keep Top Talent," *Houston Chronicle*, 14 February 1999, 8.
4. B. Schneider & N. Schmitt, *Staffing Organizations*, 2d ed. (Glenview, IL: Scott, Foresman and ompany, 1986).
5. M. Jones, "Four Trends to Reckon with," *HR Focus* 73 (1996): 22–24.
6. C. Joinson, "Moving at the Speed of Dell," *HRMagazine* 44, no. 4 (1 April 1999): 50.
7. D. M. Atwater, "Workforce Forecasting," *Human Resource Planning* 18, no. 4 (1995): 50.
8. M. E. Kanell, "Bellsouth Adds Jobs as it Hones Downsizing Knife: Eager to Expand its Telecom Realm, the Behemoth Is Quietly Hiring," *The Atlanta Journal*, 17 June 1997, 7.
9. Ibid.
10. D. M. Atwater, "Workforce Forecasting," *Human Resource Planning* 18, no. 4 (1995): 50. D. Ward, "Workforce Demand Forecasting Techniques," *Human Resource Planning* 19, no. 1 (1996): 54.
11. C. Joinson, "Moving at the Speed of Dell," *HRMagazine* 44, no. 4 (1 April 1999): 50.
12. Ibid.
13. A. J. Walker, "The Analytical Element Is Important to an HRIS," *Personnel Administrator* 28 (1983): 33–35, 85.
14. M. A. Cross, "Software Becomes a Strategic Tool for Human Resources Departments," *Health Data Management*, 19 July 1997.
15. L. Asinof, "Click & Shift: Workers Control Their Benefits On-Line," *The Wall Street Journal*, 21 November 1997, C1.
16. Ibid.
17. T. Jolls, "Technology Continues to Redefine HR's Role," *Personnel Journal* 76, no. 7 (July 1997): 46.
18. Ibid.
19. Ibid.
20. S. Bing, "The Feds Make a Pass at Hooters," *Fortune*, 15 January 1996, 82.

21. C. Roush & J. Cummings, "Hooters Wins EEOC Skirmish in Sexual Bias Battle," *Atlanta Constitution*, 2 May 1996, F1. J. Malone & C. Roush, "Restaurant Chain Goes to Battle," *Atlanta Constitution*, 16 November 1995, Section F, p. 3. D. Cardinal, "Hooters Girls on Endangered Species List," *Business Record (Des Moines, Iowa)*, 11 December 1995, 19. K. D. Grimsley, "Hooters Plays Hardball with the EEOC," *Washington Post*, 12 December 1995, Section H, p. 1. Anonymous, "EEOC's Politically Correct Crusade against Hooters a Wasted Effort," *Nation's Restaurant News*, 4 December 1995, 19. S. Keating, "Feds Press Equal-Opportunity Ogling: Hooters Says EEOC Effort to Force Male Waiters Is Absurd," *Denver Post*, 16 November 1995, Section C, p. 1. J. Hayes, "Hooters Comes Out against EEOC Sex-Bias Suit," *Nation's Restaurant News*, 27 November 1995, 3.
22. Associated Press, "Hooters Settles Suit, Won't Hire Waiters," *Denver Post*, 1 October 1997, A11.
23. P. S. Greenlaw & J. P. Kohl, "Employer 'Business' and 'Job' Defenses in Civil Rights Actions," *Public Personnel Management* 23, no. 4 (1994): 573.
24. Associated Press, "Hooters Settles Suit, Won't Hire Waiters," *Denver Post*, 1 October 1997, A11.
25. M. Jarman, "EEOC Accuses Norwest of Religious Discrimination," *Arizona Business Gazette*, 16 November 1995, Section 1, p. 2.
26. K. Ettenborough, "America Debates Religion's Place in Business World," *The Arizona Republic*, 5 April 1997, R1.
27. J. L. Ledvinka, *Federal Regulation of Personnel and Human Resource Management* (Boston: Kent Publishing Company, 1982), 137–198.
28. P. S. Greenlaw & J. P. Kohl, "Employer 'Business' and 'Job' Defenses in Civil Rights Actions," *Public Personnel Management* 23, no. 4 (1994): 573.
29. Faircloth, "Guess Who's Coming to Denny's and Shoney's. Remember When Both Companies Were Pariahs, Charged with Mistreating Minority Customers and Employees? In a Surprising Act of Redemption, They're Now High on Fortune's List," *Fortune*, 3 August 1998, 108.
30. E. Peirce, C. A. Smolinski, & B. Rosen, "Why Sexual Harassment Complaints Fall on Deaf Ears," *Academy of Management Executive* 12, no. 3 (1998): 41–54.
31. Levin, "Prudential Hit with 10 Discrimination Suits," *National Underwriter* 103, no. 4 (1999): 2.
32. W. Peirce, C. A. Smolinski, & B. Rosen, "Why Sexual Harassment Complaints Fall on Deaf Ears," *Academy of Management Executive* 12, no. 3 (1998): 41–54.
33. Ibid.
34. U. S. Equal Employment Opportunity Commission, "Facts about Sexual Harassment." [Online] Available *http://www.eeoc.gov/facts/fs-sex.html*, 23 May 1999.
35. W. Peirce, C. A. Smolinski, & B. Rosen, "Why Sexual Harassment Complaints Fall on Deaf Ears," *Academy of Management Executive* 12, no. 3 (1998): 41–54.
36. Ibid.
37. G. DeGeorge, "Sign of the Times: Help Wanted, All Across the U.S., Employers Are Strapped for Workers," *Business Week*, 11 November 1997, 60.
38. R. Buckman, "Help Wanted: Wall Street Hiring Now," *The Wall Street Journal*, 14 April 1999, C1.
39. P. Nakache, "Cisco's Recruiting Edge Find 'Em, Lure 'Em, Keep 'Em Happy: Devising New Ways to Steal Top Talent from Competitors Has Given This Silicon Valley Standout an Important Advantage," *Fortune*, 29 September 1997, 275.
40. R. D. Gatewood & H. S. Field, *Human Resource Selection* (Fort Worth, TX: Dryden Press, 1998).
41. Ibid.
42. *Griggs v. Duke Co.*, 401 US 424, 436 (1971). *Albemarle Paper Co. v. Moody*, 422 US 405 (1975).
43. P. R. Chowdhury, "Human Resources: Beyond Downsizing, Growing the TCM Manager," *Business Today*, 7 January 1999, 172.
44. J. A. Breaugh, *Recruitment: Science and Practice* (Boston: PWS-Kent, 1992).
45. Campbell, "Baxter Healthcare Gets to the Root of the Issue," *HR Focus* 75, no. 8 (1998): S9.
46. P. R. Chowdhury, "Human Resources: Beyond Downsizing, Growing the TCM Manager," *Business Today*, 7 January 1999, 172.
47. Bureau of National Affairs, Personnel Policies Forum, *Recruiting and Selection Procedures*, survey number 146 (Washington, D.C., 1988, 1993).
48. P. Nakache, "Cisco's Recruiting Edge Find 'Em, Lure 'Em, Keep 'Em Happy: Devising New Ways to Steal Top Talent from Competitors Has Given This Silicon Valley Standout an Important Advantage," *Fortune*, 29 September 1997, 275.
49. "Life on the Web for Matters of Life, Liberty, and the Pursuit of a Nicer Job, There's Help on the Internet," *Fortune*, Special Issue, Technology Buyer's Guide (Winter 1999).
50. L. J. S. Vohra, "Online Recruiting Fills Positions," *Denver Business Journal*, 9 August 1996, 27A.
51. J. King, "Who's in the Online Pool?" *Computerworld*, 10 February 1997, 24. L.J.S. Vohra, "Online Recruiting Fills Positions," *Denver Business Journal*, 9 August 1996, 27A.
52. D. Fenn, "Hiring: Searching for the Chosen Few," *Inc.*, March 1996, 96.
53. Camden & B. Wallace, "Job Application Forms: A Hazardous Employment Practice," *Personnel Administrator* 28 (1983): 31–32.
54. J. S. Pouliot, "Topics to Avoid with Applicants," *Nation's Business* 80, no. 7 (1992): 57.
55. R. D. Broussard & D. E. Brannen, "Credential Distortions: Personnel Practitioners Give Their Views," *Personnel Administrator* 31 (1986): 129–146. K.A. Edelman, "Fiction 101: Resume Writing," *Across the Board*, February 1997, 62.
56. M. Mandell, "The High Cost of Hiring Fakers," *World Trade* 11, no. 3 (1998): 56.
57. S. Adler, "Verifying a Job Candidate's Background: The State of Practice in a Vital Human Resources Activity," *Review of Business* 15, no. 2 (1993/1994): 3–8.
58. S. Baley, "The Legalities of Hiring in the 80s," *Personnel Journal* 64 (1985): 112–115.
59. M. P. Cronin, "This Is a Test," *Inc.*, August 1993, 64-69.
60. J. L. Tyson, "As Lawsuits Rise, Companies Use Detectives to Cull Job Applicants," *Christian Science Monitor*, 12 February 1997, 1.
61. J. Hunter, "Cognitive Ability, Cognitive Aptitudes, Job Knowledge, and Job Performance," *Journal of Vocational Behavior* 29 (1986): 340–362.
62. E. E. Cureton, "Comment," in Edwin R. Henry, *Research Conference on the Use of Autobiographical Data as Psychological Predictors* (Greensboro, NC: The Richardson Foundation, 1965), 13.
63. J. R. Glennon, L. E. Albright, & W. A. Owens, *A Catalog of Life History Items* (Greensboro, NC: The Richardson Foundation, 1966).
64. R. D. Gatewood & H. S. Field, *Human Resource Selection* (Fort Worth, TX: Dryden Press, 1998).
65. J. M. Digman, "Personality Structure: Emergence of the Five-Factor Model," *Annual Review of Psychology* 41 (1990): 417–440. M. R. Barrick & M. K. Mount, "The Big Five Personality Dimensions and Job Performance: A Meta-Analysis," *Personnel Psychology* 44 (1991): 1–26.
66. Fenn, "Hiring: Employee Auditions," *Inc.*, June 1996, 116.
67. M. S. Taylor & J. A. Sniezek, "The College Recruitment Interview: Topical Content and Applicant Reactions," *Journal of Occupational Psychology* 57 (1984): 157–168.
68. M. A. Campion, D. K. Palmer, & J. E. Campion, "A Review of Structure in the Selection Interview," *Personnel Psychology* 50, no. 3 (1997): 655–702.
69. Stafford, "Workers Train, Companies Gain: Harmon Industries, Sprint, Others Make a Big Commitment," *Kansas City Star*, 16 February 1999, D1.
70. Ibid.
71. S. Livingston, T. W. Gerdel, M. Hill, B. Yerak, C. Melvin, & B. Lubinger, "Ohio's Strongest Companies All Agree that Training Is Vital to Their Success," *Plain Dealer*, 21 May 1997, 30S.
72. T. D. Schellhardt, "Management: Behind the Scenes at One CEO's Performance Review," *The Wall Street Journal*, 27 April 1998, B1.
73. T. Dixon Murray, "Setting Standards: Work Keys Is a Relatively New Process Used to Pre-Screen Job Applicants, Evaluate Training Needs and Determine Raises," *Plain Dealer*, 18 October 1998, 1H.
74. J. D. Moore & R. L. Gehrig, "Rehearsing for a Robbery," *Security Management* 35, no. 8 (1991): 51.
75. L. Kroll, "At Work: Good Morning, HAL: Aetna Jumped over a Lot of Hurdles When It Cut Back Face-to-Face Training in Favor of Cyberclasses. Was It Worth It?" *Forbes*, 8 March 1999, 118.
76. D. L. Kirkpatrick, "Four Steps to Measuring Training Effectiveness," *Personnel Administrator* 28 (1983): 19–25.
77. J. Stack, "The Curse of the Annual Performance Review," *Inc.*, 1 March 1997, 39.
78. T. D. Schellhardt, "Annual Agony: It's Time to Evaluate Your Work, and All Involved Are Groaning—Employees Dislike Reviews, Even If Favorable; Bosses Wonder How to Do

Them, Some Prefer Frequent Talks," *The Wall Street Journal*, 19 November 1996, A1.

79. J. Yankovic, "Are the Reviews In?" *Pittsburgh Business Times* 16 (28 October 1996): 7.
80. T. D. Schellhardt, "Annual Agony: It's Time to Evaluate Your Work, and All Involved Are Groaning—Employees Dislike Reviews, Even If Favorable; Bosses Wonder How to Do Them, Some Prefer Frequent Talks," *The Wall Street Journal*, 19 November 1996, A1.
81. U. J. Wiersma & G. P. Latham, "The Practicality of Behavioral Observation Scales, Behavioral Expectation Scales, and Trait Scales," *Personnel Psychology* 39 (1986): 619–628. U. J. Wiersma, P. T. Van Den Berg, & G. P. Latham, "Dutch Reactions to Behavioral Observation, Behavioral Expectation, and Trait Scales," *Group & Organization Management* 20 (1995): 297–309.
82. D. J. Woehr & A. I. Huffcutt, "Rater Training for Performance Appraisal: A Quantitative Review," *Journal of Occupational and Organizational Psychology* 67, no. 3 (1994): 189–205.
83. J. Stack, "The Curse of the Annual Performance Review," *Inc.*, 1 March 1997, 39.
84. O'Reilly, "360-Degree Feedback Can Change Your Life," *Fortune*, 17 October 1994, 93.
85. D.A. Waldman, L.E. Atwater, & D. Antonioni, "Has 360 Feedback Gone Amok?" *Academy of Management Executive* 12, no. 2 (1998): 86-94.
86. H. H. Meyer, "A Solution to the Performance Appraisal Feedback Enigma," *Academy of Management Executive* 5, no. 1 (1991): 68–76.
87. T. D. Schellhardt, "Annual Agony: It's Time to Evaluate Your Work, and All Involved Are Groaning—Employees Dislike Reviews, Even If Favorable; Bosses Wonder How to Do Them, Some Prefer Frequent Talks," *The Wall Street Journal*, 19 November 1996, A1.
88. G. C. Thornton, "Psychometric Properties of Self-Appraisals of Job Performance," *Personnel Psychology* 33 (1980): 263–271.
89. H. H. Meyer, "A Solution to the Performance Appraisal Feedback Enigma," *Academy of Management Executive* 5, no. 1 (1991): 68–76.
90. G. T. Milkovich & J. M. Newman, *Compensation*, 4th ed. (Homewood. IL: Irwin, 1993).
91. S. Shellenbarger, "Tight Labor Market Is Putting Squeeze on Quality Day Care," *The Wall Street Journal*, 21 October 1998, B1.
92. M. L. Williams & G. F. Dreher, "Compensation System Attributes and Applicant Pool Characteristics," *Academy of Management Journal* 35, no. 3 (1992): 571–595.
93. M. Rich, "To Serve and Defect: Governments Struggle to Keep Key Jobs Filled," *The Wall Street Journal*, 16 September 1998, S1.
94. Coleman, "Operating Profit at DaimlerChrysler Jumped 29% in '98 on 12% Sales Rise," *The Wall Street Journal*, 26 February 1999, A4.
95. M. Bloom, "The Performance Effects of Pay Dispersion on Individuals and Organizations," *Academy of Management Journal* 42, no. 1 (1999): 25–40.
96. J. Reingold & R. Grover, "Executive Pay: The Numbers Are Staggering, But So Is the Performance of American Business. So How Closely Are They Linked?" *Business Week*, 19 April 1999, 72.
97. W. Grossman & R. E. Hoskisson, "CEO Pay at the Crossroads of Wall Street and Main: Toward the Strategic Design of Executive Compensation," *Academy of Management Executive* 12, no. 1 (1998): 43–57.
98. M. Bloom, "The Performance Effects of Pay Dispersion on Individuals and Organizations," *Academy of Management Journal* 42, no. 1 (1999): 25–40.
99. J. S. Rosenbloom, "The Environment of Employee Benefit Plans," in *The Handbook of Employee Benefits*, ed. J. S. Rosenbloom (Chicago: Irwin, 1996), 3–13.
100. "401(K)s and Beyond: A Growing Company's Guide to Employee Benefits," *Inc.*, 1 February 1998, 99.
101. A. E. Barber, R. B. Dunham, & R. A. Formisano, "The Impact of Flexible Benefits on Employee Satisfaction: A Field Study," *Personnel Psychology* 45 (1992): 55–75. B. Heshizer, "The Impact of Flexible Benefits on Job Satisfaction and Turnover Intentions," *Benefits Quarterly* 4 (1994): 84-90. D. M. Cable & T. A. Judge, "Pay Preferences and Job Search Decisions: A Person-Organization Fit Perspective," *Personnel Psychology* 47 (1994): 317–348.
102. B. T. Beam & J. J. McFadden, *Employee Benefits* (Chicago: Dearborn Financial Publishing, 1996).
103. J. A. Tannenbaum, "Small Companies Find New Way to Retain Employees—Payroll-Deduction Plans Springing Up to Pay for Things Like Car Insurance," *The Wall Street Journal*, 12 January 1999, B3.
104. K. Labich & E. M. Davies, "How to Fire People and Still Sleep at Night. Shedding Employees Is Something almost Every Manager Dreads. But If You Don't Think Hard about the Process, You and Your Company Could Be Headed Straight for a World of Woes," *Fortune*, 10 June 1996, 64.
105. Ibid.
106. P. Michal-Johnson, *Saying Good-Bye: A Manager's Guide to Employee Dismissal* (Glenview, IL: Scott, Foresman and Company, 1985).
107. M. Bordwin, "Employment Law: Beware of Time Bombs and Shark-Infested Waters," *HR Focus*, 1 April 1995, 19.
108. S. Gruner, "Hot Tip," *Inc.*, December 1996, 121.
109. J. R. Morris, W. F. Cascio, & C. E. Young, "Downsizing after All These Years: Questions and Answers about Who Did It, How Many Did It, and Who Benefited from It," *Organizational Dynamics* 27, no. 3 (1999): 78–87.
110. "Los Angeles Times. Layoffs Rise as Firms Find It's Profitable; 523,000 Are Fired as of Oct., 200,000 More than in 1997; Pink Slips in Golden Times; Study Shows Strategy May Ultimately Lower Earnings, Stock Prices," *Baltimore Sun*, 30 November 1998, 5C.
111. J. R. Morris, W. F. Cascio, & C. E. Young, "Downsizing after All These Years: Questions and Answers about Who Did It, How Many Did It, and Who Benefited from It," *Organizational Dynamics* 27, no. 3 (1999): 78–87.
112. K. E. Mishra, G. M. Spreitzer, & A. K. Mishra, "Preserving Employee Morale during Downsizing," *Sloan Management Review* 39, no. 2 (1998): 83–95.
113. J.E.D. Scott, "Smith Tries to Soothe the Pain of Closing Its Plant," *Memphis Business Journal*, 29 July 1996, 11.
114. Ferrari, "Designing and Evaluating Early Retirement Programs: The State of Wyoming Experience," *Government Finance Review* 15, no. 1 (1999): 29–31
115. R. Mullins, "Early Retirement Programs Can End Up Being Costly," *Business Journal-Milwaukee*, 20 January 1996, Section 1, p. 25.
116. D. R. Dalton, W. D. Todor, & D. M. Krackhardt, "Turnover Overstated: The Functional Taxonomy," *Academy of Management Review* 7 (1982): 117–123.
117. J. R. Hollenbeck & C. R. Williams, "Turnover Functionality versus Turnover Frequency: A Note on Work Attitudes and Organizational Effectiveness," *Journal of Applied Psychology* 71 (1986): 606–611.
118. C. R. Williams, "Reward Contingency, Unemployment, and Functional Turnover," *Human Resource Management Review*, in-press.

Chapter 15

1. T. Petzinger, Jr., "How a Ski Maker Recovered from a Potential Fatal Spill," *The Wall Street Journal Interactive Edition*, 3 October 1997.
2. J. J. Dowdy, "The Productivity Imperative," *Interavia Business & Technology*, 1 September 1997.
3. W. M. Cox & R. Alm, *The Myths of Rich & Poor* (New York: Basic Books, 1999). R. L. Bartley, "The Seven Fat Years," *The Wall Street Journal*, 30 April 1992. S. Nasar & L. Smith, "Do We Live as Well as We Used To?" *Fortune*, 14 September 1987.
4. Ibid.
5. O. Suris, "Chrysler Leads Big Three in Efficiency of Car Factories, But All Trail Japanese," *The Wall Street Journal*, 30 May 1996.
6. J. B. White, "Wide Gap Exists Between GM, Rivals in Labor Productivity," *The Wall Street Journal*, 16 July 1998, A4.
7. Bureau of Labor Statistics, "Multifactor Productivity: Frequently Asked Questions." [Online] Available *http://stats.bls.gov/mprfaq.htm*, 7 March 1998.
8. K. Brister, "Minimills Compete with Integrated Plants," *The Knoxville News-Sentinel*, 18 February 1998. S. Lubove & J. R. Norman, "New Lease on Life (Steel Industry)," *Forbes*, 9 May 1994. "Improving the Efficiency of Electricity Use at EAF Mills," *New Steel*, 1 December 1997.
9. E. Peters, "Dawn of the Trouble-Free Automobile?" *Consumers' Research Magazine*, 1 January 1998.
10. American Society for Quality, "ASQ Glossary of Terms Search." [Online] Available *http://www.asq.org/abtquality/glossary.cgi*, 24 March 1998.
11. R.E. Markland, S.K. Vickery, & R.A. Davis, "Managing Quality" (Chapter 7), *Operations Management: Concepts in Manufacturing and Services* (Cincinnati, OH: South-Western College Publishing, 1998).

12. "Quantum: DLT 7000 Drives Bring High Capacity, High Speed Tape Storage to IBM & Digital Servers," *M2 Presswire*, 3 October 1997.
13. B. Weber, "Quicker Fixes: Big 3 Innovations Make 1997 Cars Easier to Repair," *Chicago Tribune*, 3 November 1996.
14. Lightsource.com. [Online] Available *http://www.light-source.com/incandescent.html*, 28 March 1998.
15. J. H. Sheridan, "At a Glance: Physio-Control Corp." *Industry Week*, 21 October 1996.
16. L. L. Berry & A. Parasuraman, *Marketing Services* (New York: Free Press, 1991).
17. S. McCartney, "A Service-Minded Manager Is Improving Newark Airport," *The Wall Street Journal Interactive Edition*, 9 June 1997.
18. Ibid.
19. American Society for Quality, "ANSI ASC Z-1 Committee on Quality Assurance Answers the Most requently Asked Questions about the ISO 9000 (ANSI/ASQ Q9000) Series." [Online] Available *http://www.asq.org/standcert/iso.html*, 29 March 1998.
20. R. Henkoff, "The Not New Seal of Quality (ISO 9000 Standard of Quality Management)," *Fortune*, 28 June 1993.
21. Ibid.
22. P. Sebastian, "Business Bulletin: A Special Background Report on Trends in Industry and Finance," *The Wall Street Journal*, 14 November 1996, A1.
23. National Institute for Standards and Technology, "Frequently Asked Questions and Answers about the Malcolm Baldrige National Quality Award." [Online] Available *http://www.quality.nist. gov/faq9704.htm*, 29 March 1998.
24. Ibid.
25. J. Main, "How to Win the Baldrige Award," *Fortune*, 23 April 1990.
26. National Institute for Standards and Technology, "Frequently Asked Questions and Answers about the Malcolm Baldrige National Quality Award." [Online] Available *http://www.quality. nist.gov/faq9704.htm*, 29 March 1998.
27. Ibid.
28. Ibid.
29. National Institute for Standards and Technology, "'Baldrige Index' Outperforms S&P 500 for Fourth Year." [Online] Available *http://www.nist.gov/public_affairs/releases/n98-07.htm*, 9 February 1998.
30. J. W. Dean, Jr. & J. Evans, *Total Quality: Management, Organization, and Strategy* (St. Paul, MN: West Publishing Co., 1994).
31. J. W. Dean, Jr & D. E. Bowen, "Management Theory and Total Quality: Improving Research and Practice through Theory Development," *Academy of Management Review* 19 (1994): 392–418.
32. Bennett, C. Hymowitz, "For Customers, More than Lip Service? Firms Say They Put New Stress on Client Needs," *The Wall Street Journal*, 6 October 1989.
33. G. Baum, "The Dynamic 100 Cisco's CEO John Chambers: If You Can't Beat 'Em, Buy 'Em," *Forbes ASAP*, 23 February 1998.
34. T. Minahan, "AlliedSignal Soars by Building Up Suppliers," *Purchasing*, 18 September 1997.
35. R. L. Rose, "Kentucky Plant Workers Are Cranking Out Good Ideas," *The Wall Street Journal*, 13 August 1996.
36. R. Hallowell, L. A. Schlesinger, & J. Zornitsky, "Internal Service Quality, Customer and Job Satisfaction: Linkages and Implications for Management," *Human Resource Planning* 19 (1996): 20–31. J. L. Heskett, T.O. Jones, G.W. Loveman, W.E. Sasser, Jr., & L. A. Schlesinger, "Putting the Service-Profit Chain to Work," *Harvard Business Review*, March–April 1994, 164–174.
37. K. L. Freiberg & J. A. Freiberg, *NUTS! Southwest Airlines' Crazy Recipe for Business and Personal Success* (Austin, TX: Bard Press, 1996), 274.
38. M. McEnaney, "Thank-You Notes Turn into Presents," *Star-Ledger*, 26 September 1996, F4.
39. Ibid, 289.
40. G. Brewer, "The Ultimate Guide to Winning Customers: The Customer Stops Here," *Sales & Marketing Management* 150 (March 1998): 30.
41. Ibid.
42. T. Levitt, "Production-Line Approach to Service," *Harvard Business Review*, September–October 1972, 41–52. T. Levitt, "Industrialization of Service," *Harvard Business Review*, September–October 1976, 63–74.
43. L. L. Berry & A. Parasuraman, "Listening to the Customer—The Concept of a Service-Quality Information System," *Sloan Management Review* 38, no. 3 (Spring 1997): 65. C. W. L. Hart, J. L. Heskett, & W. E. Sasser, Jr., "The Profitable Art of Service Recovery," *Harvard Business Review*, July–August 1990, 148–156.
44. Gladstone, "Trusting in the Power of People," *Toronto Globe and Mail*, 21 October 1997.
45. D. E. Bowen & E. E. Lawler, III, "The Empowerment of Service Workers: What, Why, How, and When," *Sloan Management Review* 33 (Spring 1992): 31–39. D. E. Bowen & E. E. Lawler, III, "Empowering Service Employees," *Sloan Management Review* 36 (Summer 1995): 73–84.
46. D. E. Bowen & E. E. Lawler, III, "The Empowerment of Service Workers: What, Why, How, and When," *Sloan Management Review* 33 (Spring 1992): 31–39.
47. R. Henkoff, "Finding Training and Keeping the Best Service Workers," *Fortune*, 3 October 1994.
48. Serwer, L. Smith, & P. de Llosa, "Michael Dell Rocks," *Fortune*, 11 May 1998, 58.
49. J. Leib, "Wilkerson's Breath of Fresh Air: Pneumatics Firm Re-Engineers Its Production Ways," 9 June 1997, E1.
50. G. V. Frazier & M. T. Spiggs, "Achieving Competitive Advantage through Group Technology," *Business Horizons* 39 (1996): 83–88.
51. "Bottling Line Catapults Beermaker Beyond Microbrewing," *Packaging Digest*, 1 September 1995, 8.
52. J. Kunerth, "Manufacturing Finds Foothold: Companies Praise the Area's Diverse Labor Pool, But Some Smaller Firms Say Finding Financing Can Be Difficult," *Orlando Sentinel*, 23 September 1996, 14.
53. Bruce, "Heil 'Automated Job Shop' Produces Custom Trailers on Assembly Lines," *Trailer/Body Builders*, 30 December 1998.
54. Caldwell & H. Alakhun El, "Beyond the Mainframe—PCs and Servers Are Vulnerable to Year 2000, Too," *Information Week*, 25 May 1998, 50.
55. "Heinz to Temporarily Suspend 400 Jobs at Pittsburgh Plant," *Eurofood*, 1 November 1995, 15.
56. Staff Reporter, "Ford to Close Plant for 2 Weeks, Adjust Levels of Its Inventory," *The Wall Street Journal Interactive Edition*, 20 February 1998.
57. Marshall, "Linerboard: Market Recovery Will Continue; Price Hikes Predicted for 1998," *Pulp & Paper*, 1 January 1998, 13.
58. Alpert, "3Com Says Inventory Glut, Asian Slump Depress Profits," *Barrons*, 8 December 1997, 5.
59. G. Taninecz, "Best Practices & Performances, Part 2," *Industry Week*, 1 December 1997, 28.
60. F. Zappa, "The End of Paperwork? Electronic Commerce Promises to Save Billions of Dollars and Millions of Hours," *Nation's Restaurant News*, 3 November 1997, S10.
61. J. R. Henry, "Minimized Setup Will Make Your Packaging Line S.M.I.L.E.," *Packaging Technology & Engineering*, 1 February 1998, 24.
62. D. W. Nelms, "The Path Best Taken; As the Airline Industry Refines the Purchasing Process, the Question Becomes Which Direction Will Produce Optimum Results," *Air Transport World*, 1 November 1996, 81.
63. F. Brookman, "Managing Inventory (EDI)," *Women's Wear*, 19 September 1997, 20.
64. T. Minahan, "JIT: A Process with Many Faces," *Purchasing*, 4 September 1997, 42.
65. "Fully Automated System Achieves True JIT," *Modern Materials Handling*, 1 April 1998, DPI22.
66. T. Minahan, "JIT: A Process with Many Faces," *Purchasing*, 4 September 1997, 42.
67. Ibid.
68. Crowell, "Seeing the Big Picture through Software (Manufacturing Resource Planning Computer Programs)," *American Metal Market*, 22 July 1997, 12.

Chapter 16

1. J. P. Campbell & R. D. Pritchard, "Motivation Theory in Industrial and Organizational Psychology," *Handbook of Industrial and Organizational Psychology*, ed. M. D. Dunnette (Chicago: Rand McNally, 1976).
2. P. Thomas, "Waitress Makes the Difference in Bringing Deaf to Pittsburgh," *The Wall Street Journal Interactive Edition*, 2 March 1999.
3. ESPN, "Winter Olympics, Bobsled, Past Results." [Online] Available *http://espn.go.com/olympics98/bobsled/almanac.html*, 9 June 1999.
4. Team Jamaica.com, "Jamaica Bobsleigh History." [Online] Available *http://www.bobsledcity.org/Jamaicabobsleigh/services.htm*, 9 June 1999.
5. K. A. Dolan, "When Money Isn't Enough," *Forbes*, 18 November 1996, 164–170.
6. E. A. Locke, "The Nature and Causes of Job Satisfaction," *Handbook of Industrial and Organizational Psychology*, ed. M.D. Dunnette (Chicago: Rand McNally, 1976).
7. A. H. Maslow, "A Theory of Human Motivation," *Psychological Review* 50 (1943): 370–396.

8. C. P. Alderfer, *Existence, Relatedness, and Growth: Human Needs in Organizational Settings* (New York: Free Press, 1972).
9. D. C. McClelland, "Toward a Theory of Motive Acquisition," *American Psychologist* 20 (1965): 321–333. D.C. McClelland & D.H. Burnham, "Power is the Great Motivator," *Harvard Business Review* 54, no. 2 (1976): 100–110.
10. J. H. Turner, "Entrepreneurial Environments and the Emergence of Achievement Motivation in Adolescent Males," *Sociometry* 33 (1970): 147–165.
11. L. W. Porter, E.E. Lawler, III, & J. R. Hackman, *Behavior in Organizations* (New York: McGraw-Hill, 1975).
12. M. A. Wahba & L. B. Birdwell, "Maslow Reconsidered: A Review of Research on the Need Hierarchy Theory," *Organizational Behavior and Human Performance* 15 (1976): 212–240. J. Rauschenberger, N. Schmitt, & J.E. Hunter, "A Test of the Need Hierarchy Concept by a Markov Model of Change in Need Strength," *Administrative Science Quarterly* 25 (1980): 654–670.
13. E. E. Lawler, III & L. W. Porter, "The Effect of Performance on Job Satisfaction," *Industrial Relations* 7 (1967): 20–28.
14. L. W. Porter, E. E. Lawler, III, & J. R. Hackman, *Behavior in Organizations* (New York: McGraw-Hill, 1975).
15. L. Jereski, "Ascend's Generous Options Are (Usually) Beloved by Workers," *The Wall Street Journal Interactive Edition*, 10 September 1996.
16. L. W. Porter, E. E. Lawler, III, & J. R. Hackman, *Behavior in Organizations* (New York: McGraw-Hill, 1975).
17. Lucchetti, "Working Lots of Overtime, Bill Can Afford Good Life," *The Wall Street Journal Interactive Edition*, 1 August 1996.
18. Caggiano, "What Do Workers Want?" *Inc.*, November 1992, 101–104.
19. K. A. Dolan, "When Money Isn't Enough," *Forbes*, 18 November 1996, 164–170.
20. "Tailor-Made Rewards," *Inc.*, February 1991, 76.
21. Aon Consulting, "America@Work: A Focus on Benefits and Compensation." [Online] Available *http://www.aon.com/pdf/america/awork2.pdf*, 12 June 1999.
22. J. Laabs, "Satisfy Them with More Than Money," *Personnel Journal* 77, no. 11 (1998): 40.
23. Aon Consulting, "America@Work: A Focus on Benefits and Compensation." [Online] Available *http://www.aon.com/pdf/america/awork2.pdf*, 12 June 1999.
24. Woodruff, "Salary Spread in Euroland May Force Firms to Compete More for Top Workers," *The Wall Street Journal*, 20 January 1999, B9B.
25. "The Double Standard That's Setting Worker against Worker," *Business Week*, 8 April 1985, 70–71.
26. C. T. Kulik & M. L. Ambrose, "Personal and Situational Determinants of Referent Choice," *Academy of Management Review* 17 (1992): 212–237.
27. J. S. Adams, "Toward an Understanding of Inequity," *Journal of Abnormal Social Psychology* 67 (1963): 422–436.
28. J. Greenberg, "Employee Theft as a Reaction to Underpayment Inequity: The Hidden Costs of Pay Cuts," *Journal of Applied Psychology* 75 (1990): 561–568.
29. R. A. Cosier & D. R. Dalton, "Equity Theory and Time: A Reformulation," *Academy of Management Review* 8 (1983): 311–319. M. R. Carrell & J. E. Dittrich, "Equity Theory: The Recent Literature, Methodological Considerations, and New Directions," *Academy of Management Review* 3 (1978): 202–209.
30. J. D. Opdyke, "Alaska Air, Union Soften Tough Talk in Bargaining," *The Wall Street Journal*, 2 June 1999, NW1.
31. G. P. Zachary, "Some Companies Claim Workers Are Exempt or Raise Output Goals," *The Wall Street Journal Interactive Edition*, 24 June 1996.
32. K. Aquino, R. W. Griffeth, D. G. Allen, & P. W. Hom, "Integrating Justice Constructs into the Turnover Process: A Test of a Referent Cognitions Model," *Academy of Management Journal* 40, no. 5 (1997): 1208–1227.
33. B. Orwall & K. Swisher, "Of Mouse and Men: As Web Riches Beckon, Disney Ranks Become a Poacher's Paradise—Media Giant Can't Compete in Giving Stock Options, and Isn't 'Freewheeling'—Eisner Flames the Techies," *The Wall Street Journal*, 9 June 1999, A1.
34. S. De Bruxelles, "Computer Firm Pays Out £17m to Keep its Staff," *The Times*. [Online] Available *http://www.the-times.co.uk/news/pages/tim/99/06/12/timnwsnws01033*, 12 June 1999.
35. Fishman, "Sanity, Inc.," *Fast Company*, January 1999, 85–96.
36. R. Folger & M. A. Konovsky, "Effects of Procedural and Distributive Justice on Reactions to Pay Raise Decisions," *Academy of Management Journal* 32 (1989): 115–130.
37. Barret-Howard & T. R. Tyler, "Procedural Justice as a Criterion in Allocation Decisions," *Journal of Personality and Social Psychology* 50 (1986): 296–305. R. Folger & M. A. Konovsky, "Effect of Procedural and Distributive Justice on Reactions to Pay Raise Decisions," *Academy of Management Journal* 32 (1989): 115–130.
38. R. Folger & J. Greenberg, "Procedural Justice: An Interpretive Analysis of Personnel Systems," in *Research in Personnel and Human Resources Management*, Volume 3, eds. K. Rowland & G. Ferris (Greenwich, CT: JAI Press, 1985). R. Folger, D. Rosenfield, J. Grove, & L. Corkran, "Effects of 'Voice' and Peer Opinions on Responses to Inequity," *Journal of Personality and Social Psychology* 37 (1979): 2253–2261. E. A. Lind & T. R. Tyler, *The Social Psychology of Procedural Justice* (New York: Plenum Press, 1988).
39. K. A. Dolan, "When Money Isn't Enough," *Forbes*, 18 November 1996, 164–170.
40. V. H. Vroom, *Work and Motivation* (New York: John Wiley & Sons, 1964). L. W. Porter & E. E. Lawler, III, *Managerial Attitudes and Performance* (Homewood, IL: Dorsey Press & Richard D. Irwin, 1968).
41. N. Wood, "Caribou Coffee," *Incentive* 17 (January 1997): 28–29.
42. D. Bank, "As Microsoft Matures, Some Top Talent Is Opting to Leave, at Least Temporarily," *The Wall Street Journal Interactive Edition*, 16 June 1999.
43. P. V. LeBlanc & P. W. Mulvey, "How American Workers See the Rewards of Work," *Compensation & Benefits Review* 30, no. 1 & 24, no. 5 (1998).
44. S. Scholl, "Allstate Pay for Performance Methodology Rewards Excellence," *ACANEWS* 41, no. 8 (1998): 24.
45. K. W. Thomas & B. A. Velthouse, "Cognitive Elements of Empowerment," *Academy of Management Review* 15 (1990): 666–681.
46. D. Sheff, "Richard Branson: The Interview," *Forbes ASAP*, 24 February 1997, 95–102.
47. D. Milbank, "Workplace: Companies Turn to Peer Pressure to Cut Injuries as Psychologists Join the Battle," *The Wall Street Journal*, 29 March 1991, B1.
48. E. L. Thorndike, *Animal Intelligence* (New York: MacMillan, 1911).
49. D. Milbank, "Workplace: Companies Turn to Peer Pressure to Cut Injuries as Psychologists Join the Battle," *The Wall Street Journal*, 29 March 1991, B1.
50. B. F. Skinner, *Science and Human Behavior* (New York: MacMillan, 1954). B. F. Skinner, *Beyond Freedom and Dignity* (New York: Bantam Books, 1971). B.F. Skinner, *A Matter of Consequences* (New York: New York University Press, 1984).
51. A. M. Dickinson & A. D. Poling, "Schedules of Monetary Reinforcement in Organizational Behavior Management: Latham and Huber Revisited," *Journal of Organizational Behavior Management* 16, no. 1 (1992): 71–91.
52. B. Boydston, "Frequent-Flier Miles: Worker Entitlement or Company Asset? Corporations Find Tracking Award Difficult," *Star Tribune*, 29 March 1999, 5D.
53. D. Grote, "Manager's Journal: Discipline Without Punishment," *The Wall Street Journal*, 23 May 1994, A14.
54. B. Boydston, "Frequent-Flier Miles: Worker Entitlement or Company Asset? Corporations Find Tracking Award Difficult," *Star Tribune*, 29 March 1999, 5D.
55. G. A. Yukl, G. P. Latham, & E. D. Pursell, "The Effectiveness of Performance Incentives under Continuous and Variable Ratio Schedules of Reinforcement," *Personnel Psychology* 29 (1976): 221–231.
56. Pedalino & V. U. Gamboa, "Behavior Modification and Absenteeism: Intervention in One Industrial Setting," *Journal of Applied Psychology* 59 (1974): 694–698.
57. J. B. Miner, *Theories of Organizational Behavior* (Hinsdale, IL: Dryden, 1980).
58. A. M. Dickinson & A. D. Poling, "Schedules of Monetary Reinforcement in Organizational Behavior Management: Latham and Huber Revisited," *Journal of Organizational Behavior Management* 16, no. 1, (1992): 71–91.
59. Luthans & A. D. Stajkovic, "Reinforce for Performance: The Need to Go Beyond Pay and Even Rewards," *Academy of Management Executive* 13, no. 2 (1999): 49–57.
60. S. Kerr, "On the Folly of Rewarding A, While Hoping for B," *Academy of*

Management Journal 18 (1975) 769–783
61. K. D. Butterfield, L. K. Trevino, & G. A. Ball, "Punishment from the Manager's Perspective: A Grounded Investigation and Inductive Model," *Academy of Management Journal* 39 (1996): 1479–1512.
62. R. D. Arvey & J. M. Ivancevich, "Punishment in Organizations: A Review, Propositions, and Research Suggestions," *Academy of Management Review* 5 (1980): 123–132.
63. R. D. Arvey, G. A. Davis, & S. M. Nelson, "Use of Discipline in an Organization: A Field Study," *Journal of Applied Psychology* 69 (1984): 448–460. M E. Schnake, "Vicarious Punishment in a Work Setting," *Journal of Applied Psychology* 71 (1986): 343–345.
64. G. A. Yuki & G. P. Latham, "Consequences of Reinforcement Schedules and Incentive Magnitudes for Employee Performance: Problems Encountered in a Field Setting," *Journal of Applied Psychology* 60 (1975): 294–298
65. R. Maynard, "Harboring No Illusions about How to Grow," *Nation's Business* 85 (1 February 1997): 10.
66. E. A. Locke & G. P. Latham, *Goal Setting: A Motivational Technique That Works* (Englewood Cliffs, NJ: Prentice-Hall, 1984). E. A. Locke & G. P. Latham, *A Theory of Goal Setting and Task Performance* (Englewood Cliffs, NJ: Prentice-Hall, 1990).
67. T. Petzinger, Jr., "Competent Works and a Complex Leader Keep Big Oil in Check," *The Wall Street Journal*, 4 December 1998, B1.
68. G. P. Latham & E. A. Locke, "Goal Setting—A Motivational Techniques That Works," *Organizational Dynamics* 8, no. 2 (1979): 68.
69. Ibid.
70. T. LaFleur & C. Hyten, "Improving the Quality of Hotel Banquet Staff Performance," *Journal of Organizational Behavior Management* 15, no. 1 (1995): 69–93.

Chapter 17

1. C. Hymowitz, "In the Lead: How Cynthia Danaher Learned to Stop Sharing and Start Leading," *The Wall Street Journal*, 16 March 1999, B1.
2. G. Colvin, "The Changing Art of Becoming Unbeatable," *Fortune*, 24 November 1997, 299–300.
3. W. Bennis, "Why Leaders Can't Lead," *Training & Development Journal* 43, no. 4 (1989).
4. C. Hymowitz, "In the Lead: Some Managers Are More than Bosses—They're Leaders, Too." *The Wall Street Journal*, 8 December 1998, B1.
5. Zaleznik, "Managers and Leaders: Are They Different?" *Harvard Business Review* 55 (1977): 76–78. A. Zaleznik, "The Leadership Gap," *The Washington Quarterly* 6 (1983): 32–39.
6. K. Freiberg & J. Freiberg, *Nuts! Southwest Airlines' Crazy Recipe for Business and Personal Success* (Austin, TX: Bard Press, 1996).
7. R. Rogoski, "Agent of Change," *Triangle Business Journal* 21 May 1999, 21.
8. W. Bennis, "Why Leaders Can't Lead," *Training & Development Journal* 43, no. 4 (1989).
9. J. Cole, "Lockheed CEO Faces Criticism for Secrecy, Setbacks—Unmet Cost Targets, Failed Rocket Launches Bedevil Defense Contractor," *The Wall Street Journal*, 17 June 1999, B4.
10. J. P. Howell, D. E. Bowen, P. W. Dorfman, S. Kerr, & P. M. Podsakoff, "Substitutes for Leadership: Effective Alternatives to Ineffective Leadership," *Organizational Dynamics*, 22 June 1990, 20. S. Kerr & J. M. Jermier, "Substitutes for Leadership: Their Meaning and Measurement," *Organizational Behavior and Human Performance* 22 (1978): 375–403.
11. T. A. Stewart, A. Harrington, & M. G. Solovar, "America's Most Admired Companies: Why Leadership Matters," *Fortune*, 2 March 1998, 70.
12. S. A. Kirkpatrick & E. A. Locke, "Leadership: Do Traits Matter?" *Academy of Management Executive* 5, no. 2 (1991): 48–60.
13. Ibid.
14. T. A. Stewart, A. Harrington, & M. G. Solovar, "America's Most Admired Companies: Why Leadership Matters," *Fortune*, 2 March 1998, 70.
15. J. J. Gabarro, *The Dynamics of Taking Charge* (Boston: Harvard Business School Press, 1987).
16. J. Carlton, "Thinking Different: At Apple, a Fiery Jobs Often Makes Headway and Sometimes a Mess—He Knows How to Market but Clashes with Cloners and Belittles His Foes—Skewered on the Gil-O-Meter," *The Wall Street Journal*, 14 April 1998, A1.
17. S. A. Kirkpatrick & E. A. Locke, "Leadership: Do Traits Matter?" *Academy of Management Executive* 5, no. 2 (1991): 48–60.
18. E. A. Fleishman, "The Description of Supervisory Behavior," *Personnel Psychology* 37 (1953): 1–6. L. R. Katz, *New Patterns of Management* (New York: McGraw-Hill, 1961).
19. R. Charan & G. Colvin, "Why CEOs Fail," *Fortune*, 21 June 1999, 69–78.
20. L. Fernandes, "Workers Massaged with Handy Perks," *The Business Journal*, 22 September 1997, 1.
21. P. Weissenberg & M. H. Kavanagh, "The Independence of Initiating Structure and Consideration: A Review of the Evidence," *Personnel Psychology* 25 (1972): 119–130.
22. R. J. House & T. R. Mitchell, "Path-Goal Theory of Leadership," *Journal of Contemporary Business* 3 (1974): 81–97. F. E. Fiedler, "A Contingency Model of Leadership Effectiveness," in ed. L. Berkowitz, *Advances in Experimental Social Psychology* (New York: Academic Press, 1964). V. H. Vroom & P. W. Yetton, *Leadership and Decision Making* (Pittsburgh: University of Pittsburgh Press, 1973). P. Hersey & K. H. Blanchard, *The Management of Organizational Behavior*, 4th ed. (Englewood Cliffs, NJ: Prentice-Hall, 1984). S. Kerr & J. M. Jermier, "Substitutes for Leadership: Their Meaning and Measurement," *Organizational Behavior and Human Performance* 22 (1978): 375–403.
23. F. E. Fiedler & M. M. Chemers, *Leadership and Effective Management* (Glenview, IL: Scott, Foresman, 1974).
24. J. Carlton, "Thinking Different: At Apple, a Fiery Jobs Often Makes Headway and Sometimes a Mess—He Knows How to Market but Clashes with Cloners and Belittles His Foes—Skewered on the Gil-O-Meter," *The Wall Street Journal*, 14 April 1998, A1.
25. F. E. Fiedler, "The Effects of Leadership Training and Experience: A Contingency Model Interpretation," *Administrative Science Quarterly* 17, no. 4 (1972): 455. F. E. Fiedler, *A Theory of Leadership Effectiveness* (New York: McGraw-Hill, 1967).
26. L. S. Csoka & F. W. Fiedler, "The Effect of Military Leadership Training: A Test of the Contingency Model," *Organizational Behavior and Human Performance* 8 (1972): 395–407.
27. R. J. House & T. R. Mitchell, "Path-Goal Theory of Leadership," *Journal of Contemporary Business* 3 (1974): 81–97.
28. S. Branch, M. Borden, T. Maroney, & N. Tarpley, "The 100 Best Companies to Work for in America," *Fortune*, 11 January 1999, 118.
29. R. J. House & T. R. Mitchell, "Path-Goal Theory of Leadership," *Journal of Contemporary Business* 3 (1974): 81-97.
30. "Corporate America's Toughest Bosses," *Fortune*, 18 October 1993, 38.
31. B. M. Fisher & J. E. Edwards, "Consideration and Initiating Structure and Their Relationships with Leader Effectiveness: A Meta-analysis," *Proceedings of the Academy of Management*, August 1988, 201–205.
32. S. Branch, M. Borden, T. Maroney, & N. Tarpley, "The 100 Best Companies to Work for in America," *Fortune*, 11 January 1999, 118.
33. G. Gendron, "Schwarzkopf on Leadership," *Inc.*, January 1992, 11.
34. P. Hersey & K. Blanchard, *Management of Organizational Behavior: Utilizing Human Resources*, 4th ed. (Englewood Cliffs, NJ: Prentice-Hall, 1982).
35. W. Blank, J. R. Weitzel, & S. G. Green, "A Test of the Situational Leadership Theory," *Personnel Psychology* 43, no. 3 (1990): 579–597. W. R. Norris & R. P. Vecchio, "Situational Leadership Theory: A Replication," *Group & Organization Management* 17, no. 3 (1992): 331–342.
36. Ibid.
37. V. H. Vroom & A. G. Jago, *The New Theory of Leadership: Managing Participation in Organizations* (Englewood Cliffs, NJ: Prentice Hall, 1988).
38. G. A. Yukl, *Leadership in Organizations*, 3rd ed. (Englewood Cliffs, NJ: Prentice-Hall, 1995).
39. B. M. Bass, *Bass & Stogdill's Handbook of Leadership: Theory, Research, and Managerial Applications* (New York: The Free Press, 1990).
40. R. D. Ireland & M. A. Hitt, "Achieving and Maintaining Strategic Competitiveness in the 21st Century: The Role of Strategic Leadership," *Academy of Management Executive* 13, no. 1 (1999): 43–57.
41. J. A. Byrne, "A Close-up Look at How America's #1 Manager Runs GE," *Business Week*, 8 June 1998, 90.

42. P. Thoms & D. B. Greenberger, "Training Business Leaders to Create Positive Organizational Visions of the Future: Is It Successful?" *Academy of Management Journal* [Best Papers & Proceedings], 1995, 212–216.
43. M. Weber, *The Theory of Social and Economic Organizations*, trans. R.A. Henderson & T. Parsons (New York: Free Press, 1947).
44. D. A. Waldman & F. J. Yammarino, "CEO Charismatic Leadership: Levels-of-Management and Levels-of-Analysis Effects," *Academy of Management Review* 24, no. 2 (1999): 266–285.
45. P. Sellers, "What Exactly Is Charisma?" *Fortune*, 15 January 1996, 68.
46. K. B. Lowe, K. G. Kroeck, & N. Sivasubramaniam, "Effectiveness Correlates of Transformational and Transactional Leadership: A Meta-analytic Review of the MLQ Literature," *Leadership Quarterly* 7 (1996): 385–425.
47. J. M. Howell & B. J. Avolio, "The Ethics of Charismatic Leadership: Submission or Liberation?" *Academy of Management Executive* 6, no. 2 (1992): 43–54.
48. P. Sellers, "What Exactly Is Charisma?" *Fortune*, 15 January 1996, 68.
49. J. A. Byrne, W. C. Symonds, & J. F. Siler, "Ceo Disease—Egotism Can Breed Corporate Disaster—And the Malady Is Spreading," *Business Week*, 1 April 1991, 52.
50. J. M. Howell & B. J. Avolio, "The Ethics of Charismatic Leadership: Submission or Liberation?" *Academy of Management Executive* 6, no. 2 (1992): 43–54.
51. Ibid.
52. J. M. Burns, *Leadership* (New York: Harper & Row, 1978). B. M. Bass, "From Transactional to Transformational Leadership: Learning to Share the Vision," *Organizational Dynamics* 18 (1990): 19–36.
53. B. M. Bass, "From Transactional to Transformational Leadership: Learning to Share the Vision," *Organizational Dynamics* 18 (1990): 19–36.
54. B. M. Bass, *A New Paradigm of Leadership: An Inquiry into Transformational Leadership* (Alexandra, VA: U.S. Army Research Institute for the Behavioral and Social Sciences, 1996).
55. J. A. Byrne, "A Close-up Look at How America's #1 Manager Runs GE," *Business Week*, 8 June 1998, 90.
56. Ibid.
57. Ibid.
58. B. M. Bass, "From Transactional to Transformational Leadership: Learning to Share the Vision," *Organizational Dynamics* 18 (1990): 19–36.

Chapter 18

1. E. E. Lawler, III, L. W. Porter, & A. Tannenbaum, "Manager's Attitudes toward Interaction Episodes," *Journal of Applied Psychology* 52 (1968): 423–439. H. Mintzberg, *The Nature of Managerial Work* (New York: Harper & Row, Publishers, 1973).
2. J. D. Maes, T. G. Weldy, & M. L. Icenogle, "A Managerial Perspective: Oral Communication Competency Is Most Important for Business Students in the Workplace," *Journal of Business Communication* 34 (1997): 67–80.
3. R. Lepsinger & A. D. Lucia, *The Art and Science of 360 Degree Feedback* (San Francisco: Pfeiffer, 1997).
4. I. M. Botero, "Good Communication Skills Needed Today," *The Business Journal: Serving Phoenix and the Valley of the Sun*, 21 October 1996.
5. T. Petzinger, Jr., "Two Executives Cook Up Ways to Make Pillsbury Listen," *The Wall Street Journal*, 27 September 1996, B1.
6. E. E. Jones & K. E. Davis, "From Acts to Dispositions: The Attribution Process in Person Perception," in *Advances in Experimental and Social Psychology*, Volume 2, ed. L. Berkowitz (New York: Academic Press, 1965), 219–266. R. G. Lord & J. E. Smith, "Theoretical, Information-Processing, and Situational Factors Affecting Attribution Theory Models of Organizational Behavior," *Academy of Management Review* 8 (1983): 50–60.
7. J. Zadney & H. B. Gerard, "Attributed Intentions and Informational Selectivity," *Journal of Experimental Social Psychology* 10 (1974): 34–52.
8. J. Costello, "The Latest Entry in Growing List of Travel Irritations: Flying Fish," *The Wall Street Journal Interactive Edition*, 22 June 1999.
9. L. Cowan, "J. B. Hunt's Drive to Improve its Image among Truckers May Be Paying Off," *The Wall Street Journal*, 20 February 1998.
10. H. H. Kelly, *Attribution in Social Interaction* (Morristown, NJ: General Learning Press, 1971).
11. J. M. Burger, "Motivational Biases in the Attribution of Responsibility for an Accident: A Meta-Analysis of the Defensive-Attribution Hypothesis," *Psychological Bulletin* 90 (1981): 496–512.
12. D. A. Hofmann & A. Stetzer, "The Role of Safety Climate and Communication in Accident Interpretation: Implications for Learning from Negative Events," *Academy of Management Journal* 41, No. 6 (1998): 644–657.
13. C. Perrow, *Normal Accidents: Living with High-Risk Technologies* (New York: Basic Books, 1984).
14. A. G. Miller & T. Lawson, "The Effect of an Informational Opinion on the Fundamental Attribution Error," *Journal of Personality and Social Psychology* 47 (1989): 873–896. J. M. Burger, "Changes in Attribution Errors over Time: The Ephemeral Fundamental Attribution Error," *Social Cognition* 9 (1991): 182–193.
15. E. Bernstein, "The Stagnant, Uncriticized Employee—But Those Open to Feedback Seen as Approachable, Primed for Success," *San Antonio Express-News*, 20 February 1997, 1F.
16. F. Heider, *The Psychology of Interpersonal Relations* (New York: Wiley, 1958). D. T. Miller & M. Ross, "Self-Serving Biases in Attribution of Causality: Fact or Fiction?" *Psychological Bulletin* 82 (1975): 213–225.
17. J. R. Larson, Jr., "The Dynamic Interplay between Employees' Feedback-Seeking Strategies and Supervisors' Delivery of Performance Feedback," *Academy of Management Review* 14, No. 3 (1989): 408–422.
18. J. Edwards, "Oviedo Builders Cut Down Conservation Trees: The Owner of the Under-Construction Oviedo Grove Apartments Admitted There Was Miscommunication with Workers," *Orlando Sentinel*, 12 January 1999, D1.
19. S. Huettel, "Mcdonald's Tanks Aquarium Tie-In," *The Tampa Tribune*, 30 October 1996, 1.
20. M. Reddy, "The Conduit Metaphor—A Case of Frame Conflict in Our Language about Our Language," in *Metaphor and Thought*, ed. A. Ortony (Cambridge, England: Cambridge University Press, 1979), 284–324.
21. G. L. Kreps, *Organizational Communication: Theory and Practice* (New York: Longman, 1990).
22. Ibid.
23. Associated Press and Bloomberg News, "Boeing Chairman Says He Won't Resign," *Portland Oregonian*, 16 December 1998, E2.
24. M. Brannigan & J. B. White, "'So Be It': Why Delta Air Lines Decided It Was Time for CEO to Take Off—Issue Was Morale, Not Profit, as a Once-Split Board Came to a Consensus," *The Wall Street Journal*, 30 May 1997, A1.
25. J. Martin & A. Kover, "Meet Six Hot Young Managers Who Have What It Takes to Lead in the 21st Century," *Fortune*, 26 June 1996, 76.
26. G. L. Kreps, *Organizational Communication: Theory and Practice* (New York: Longman, 1990).
27. A. B. Fisher, "The Downside of Downsizing," *Fortune*, 23 May 1988, 42.
28. W. Davis & J. R. O'Connor, "Serial Transmission of Information: A Study of the Grapevine," *Journal of Applied Communication Research* 5 (1977): 61–72.
29. A. B. Fisher, "The Downside of Downsizing," *Fortune*, 23 May 1988, 42.
30. C. Hymowitz, "Managing: Spread the Word, Gossip is Good," *The Wall Street Journal*, 4 October 1988.
31. W. Davis & J. R. O'Connor, "Serial Transmission of Information: A Study of the Grapevine," *Journal of Applied Communication Research* 5 (1977): 61–72. C. Hymowitz, "Managing: Spread the Word, Gossip is Good," *The Wall Street Journal*, 4 October 1988.
32. W. C. Redding, *Communication within the Organization: An Interpretive View of Theory and Research* (New York: Industrial communication Council, 1972).
33. D. T. Hall, K. L. Otazo, & G. P. Hollenbeck, "Behind Closed Doors: What Really Happens in Executive Coaching," *Organizational Dynamics* 27, No. 3 (1999): 39–53.
34. P. Capell, "Salvaging the Careers of Talented Managers Who Behave Badly," *The Wall Street Journal*, 24 December 1996, B1.
35. Anonymous, "Surviving a Work-Life Crisis: Troubles at Home Can Make It Hard for Workers to Do Their Best Job," *Buffalo News*, 24 August 1999, D1.
36. M. McWhorter, "Energen CEO Believes Open Communication Is the Key to Successful Management," *Business First—Birmingham*, Volume 6, Section 1 (1992): 8.

37. R. J. Burke & D. S. Wilcox, "Effects of Different Patterns and Degrees of Openness in Superior-Subordinate Communication on Subordinate Job Satisfaction," *Academy of Management Journal* 12 (1969): 319–326. B. P. Indik, B. S. Georgopoulos, & S. E. Seashore, "Superior-Subordinate Relationships and Performance," *Personnel Psychology* 14 (1961): 357–374.
38. D. M. Herold & M. M. Greller, "Feedback: Definition of a Construct," *Academy of Management Journal* 20 (1977): 142–147.
39. Mehrabian, "Communication without Words," *Psychology Today* 3 (1968): 53. A. Mehrabian, *Silent Messages* (Belmont, CA: Wadsworth, 1971). R. Harrison, *Beyond Words: An Introduction to Nonverbal Communication* (1974). A. Mehrabian, *Non-Verbal Communication* (Chicago, IL: Aldine, 1972).
40. M. L. Knapp, *Nonverbal Communication in Human Interaction*, 2nd ed. (New York: Holt, Reinhart & Winston, 1978).
41. H. M. Rosenfeld, "Instrumental Affiliative Functions of Facial and Gestural Expressions," *Journal of Personality and Social Psychology* 24 (1966): 65–72. P. Ekman, "Differential Communication of Affect by Head and Body Cues," *Journal of Personality and Social Psychology* 2 (1965): 726–735. A. Mehrabian, "Significance of Posture and Position in the Communication of Attitude and Status Relationships," *Psychological Bulletin* 71 (1969): 359–372.
42. R. B. Schmitt, "Judges Try Curbing Lawyers' Body-Language Antics," *The Wall Street Journal*, 9 September 1997, B1.
43. R. B. Schmitt, "Judges Try Curbing Lawyers' Body-Language Antics," *The Wall Street Journal*, 9 September 1997, B1.
44. C. A. Bartlett & S. Ghoshal, "Changing the Role of Top Management: Beyond Systems to People," *Harvard Business Review*, May–June 1995, 132–142.
45. P. Roberts, "Homestyle Talkshows," *Fast Company*, October 1999, 162.
46. Ibid.
47. R. G. Nichols, "Do We Know How to Listen? Practical Helps in a Modern Age," in *Communication Concepts and Processes*, ed. J. DeVitor (Englewood Cliffs, NJ: Prentice-Hall, 1971). P. V. Lewis, *Organizational Communication: The Essence of Effective Management* (Columbus, OH: Grid Publishing Company, 1975).
48. E. Atwater, *I Hear You*, revised ed. (New York: Walker, 1992).
49. R. Adler & N. Towne, *Looking Out/Looking In* (San Francisco: Rinehart Press, 1975).
50. T. D. Zweifel, "Be Still and Hear: The Art and Science of Listening Is Good Business," *Christian Science Monitor*, 22 September 1998, 11.
51. B. D. Seyber, R. N. Bostrom, & J. H. Seibert, "Listening, Communication Abilities, and Success at Work," *Journal of Business Communication* 26 (1989): 293–303.
52. E. Atwater, *I Hear You*, revised ed. (New York: Walker, 1992).
53. N. Grammer, "The Art—and Importance—of Listening," *Toronto Globe & Mail*, 25 June 1999, B11.
54. H. H. Meyer, "A Solution to the Performance Appraisal Feedback Enigma," *Academy of Management Executive* 5, No. 1 (1991): 68–76.
55. T. D. Schellhardt, "Annual Agony: It's Time to Evaluate Your Work, and All Involved Are Groaning—Employees Dislike Reviews, Even if Favorable; Bosses Wonder How to Do Them—Some Prefer Frequent Talks," *The Wall Street Journal*, 19 November 1996, A1.
56. M. J. McCarthy, "What to Do About Difficult Colleagues? Seminars Offer Crash Lessons in Psychic Judo," *The Wall Street Journal*, 6 May 1988.
57. T. D. Schellhardt, "Annual Agony: It's Time to Evaluate Your Work, and All Involved Are Groaning—Employees Dislike Reviews, Even if Favorable; Bosses Wonder How to Do Them—Some Prefer Frequent Talks," *The Wall Street Journal*, 19 November 1996, A1.
58. L. Reibstein, "What to Do When an Employee Is Talented and a Pain in the Neck," *The Wall Street Journal*, 8 August 1986.
59. R. Mead, *Cross-Cultural Management* (New York: Wiley, 1990).
60. J. S. Black & M. Mendenhall, "Cross-Cultural Training Effectiveness: A Review and Theoretical Framework for Future Research," *Academy of Management Review* 15 (1990): 113–136.
61. D. A. Blackmon, "A Factory in Alabama Is the Merger in Microcosm," *The Wall Street Journal*, 8 May 1998, B1.
62. R. Mead, *Cross-Cultural Management* (New York: Wiley, 1990).
63. E. T. Hall & W. F. Whyte, "Intercultural Communication: A Guide to Men of Action," *Human Organization* 19, No. 1 (1961): 5–12.
64. N. Libman, "French Tip: Just Walk the Walk and Talk the Talk, but Not Too Loud," *Chicago Tribune*, 17 March 1996.
65. H. Lancaster, "Global Managers Need Boundless Sensitivity, Rugged Constitutions," *The Wall Street Journal*, 13 October 1998, B1.
66. R. Miller, "Going Inside with the Internet," *IABC Communication World*, November 1995.
67. H. Lancaster, "Contributors to Pools of Company Know-How Are Valued Employees," *The Wall Street Journal*, 9 December 1997, B1.
68. T. A. Stewart, "Telling Tales at BP Amoco: Knowledge Management at Work," *Fortune*, 7 June 1999, 220.
69. "Fortune 500 Company Steals Screen Time & Spotlight from Star Wars," *PR Newswire*, 20 May 1999.
70. M. Campanelli & N. Friedman, "Welcome to Voice Mail Hell: The New Technology Has Become a Barrier Between Salespeople and Customers. Here's How Smart Sellers Are Breaking Through," *Sales & Marketing Management* 147 (May 1995): 98–101.
71. N. Deogun, "Advice to Coke People from Their New Boss: Don't Get Too Cocky—Goizueta's Successor Puts His Stamp on the Firm in a Lot of Small Ways—Soda for the Buffett Crowd," *The Wall Street Journal*, 9 March 1998, A1.
72. Morris, "Doug Is It," *Fortune*, 25 May 1998, p. 70.
73. Toyota Motor Manufacturing, USA, *Team Member Handbook*, February 1988, 52–53. G. Dessler, "How to Earn Your Employees' Commitment," *Academy of Management Review* 13, No. 2 (1999): 58–67.
74. R. V. Lindahl, "Automation Breaks the Language Barrier" (Federal Express Inc.'s Survey-Feedback-Action Program), *HRMagazine*, 1 March 1996, 79.
75. Woodruff & K. Naughton, "Hard-Driving Boss: Ferdinand Piech Is Determined to Make Volkswagen into a Global Force," *Business Week*, 5 October 1998, 82.
76. B. O'Reilly, "Forget Hertz and Avis: Enterprise's Quiet Invasion of Small-Town America—Along with Quirky Hiring Practices and a Generous Supply of Doughnuts—Has Made It the Nation's Biggest Rental Car," *Fortune*, 28 October 1996, 125.

Photo Credits

Chapter 1: Opener: © PhotoDisc, Inc. 1.1: © David Joel/Tony Stone Images. 1.2: © Corbis/Judy Griesedieck. 1.3: © Corbis/Museum of Flight.

Chapter 2: Opener © PhotoDisc, Inc. 2.1: © PhotoDisc, Inc. 2.2: ©Alan Levenson/Tony Stone Images. 2.3: © SWCP/Cary Benbow. 2.4: © Corbis-Bettmann.

Chapter 3: Opener: © PhotoDisc, Inc. 3.1: © 1997 James Marvy/The Stock Market. 3.2: © Corbis/AFP. 3.3: © Corbis/Wolfgang Kaehler.

Chapter 4: Opener: © PhotoDisc, Inc. 4.1: © Matthew McVay/Tony Stone Images. 4.2: © Corbis/Dave G. Hauser. 4.3: © John Feingersh/The Stock Market. 4.4: © Ted Wood/Tony Stone Images.

Chapter 5: Opener: © PhotoDisc, Inc. 5.1: © Hulton Getty. 5.2 © PhotoDisc, Inc. 5.3: © PhotoDisc, Inc.

Chapter 6: Opener: © PhotoDisc, Inc. 6.1: © Paul Chesley/Tony Stone Images. 6.2: © PhotoDisc, Inc. 6.3: © PhotoDisc, Inc. 6.4: © Corbis/R.W. Jones.

Chapter 7: Opener: © PhotoDisc, Inc. 7.1: © Corbis/Patrick Ward. 7.2: © Klaus Lahnstein/Tony Stone Images. 7.3: © Dennis O'Clair/Tony Stone Images. 7.4: © Jeff Zaruba/Tony Stone Images.

Chapter 8: Opener: © PhotoDisc, Inc. 8.1: © 1995 Bill Stormont/The Stock Market. 8.2: © PhotoDisc, Inc. 8.3: © Corbis/Kevin R. Morris. 8.4: © Alan Levenson/Tony Stone Images.

Chapter 9: Opener: © PhotoDisc, Inc. 9.1: © Andy Sacks/Tony Stone Images. 9.2: © Corbis/AFP. 9.3: © PhotoDisc, Inc. 9.4: © Jeff Zaruba/The Stock Market.

Chapter 10: Opener: © PhotoDisc, Inc. 10.1: © PhotoDisc, Inc. 10.2: © Brownie Harris/The Stock Market. 10.3: © Corbis/Lynn Goldsmith. 10.4: © Corbis/Adamsmith Productions.

Chapter 11: Opener: © PhotoDisc, Inc. 11.1: © Corbis/Warren Morgan. 11.2: © Walter Hodges/Tony Stone Images. 11.3: © Chuck Keeler/Tony Stone Images. 11.4: © Corbis-Bettmann.

Chapter 12: Opener: © PhotoDisc, Inc. 12.1: © William Taufic/The Stock Market. .2: © Jose Luis Pelaez Inc./The Stock Market. 12.3: © PhotoDisc, Inc.

Chapter 13: Opener: © PhotoDisc, Inc. 13.1: © Corbis/Dan Lamont. 13.2: © Wayne R. Bilenduke/Tony Stone Images. 13.3: © Corbis/Bettmann.

Chapter 14: Opener: © PhotoDisc, Inc. 14.1: © Corbis/Ed Young. 14.2: © Robert Fox/Impact Visuals/PNI.

Chapter 15: Opener: © PhotoDisc, Inc. 15.1: © 1995 Hans Halberstadt/The Stock Market. 15.2: © Robert Daemmrich/Stock, Boston/PNI.

Chapter 16: Opener: © PhotoDisc, Inc. 16.1: © William Taufic/The Stock Market. 16.2: © Corbis/Adamsmith Productions.

Chapter 17: Opener: © PhotoDisc, Inc. 17.1: © Andrew Sacks/Tony Stone Images. 17.2: © Corbis.

Chapter 18: Opener: © PhotoDisc, Inc. 18.1: © Tim Davis/Tony Stone Images. 18.2: © Corbis/R.W. Jones.

Glossary

360-degree feedback a performance appraisal process in which feedback is obtained from the boss, subordinates, peers and co-workers, and the employees themselves

80% or four-fifths rule a rule of thumb used by the courts and the EEOC to determine whether there is evidence of disparate impact. A violation of this rule occurs when the selection rate for a protected group is less than 80% or four-fifths of the selection rate for a nonprotected group.

absolute comparisons a process in which each decision criterion is compared to a standard or ranked on its own merits

accommodative strategy a social responsiveness strategy where a company chooses to accept responsibility for a problem and do all that society expects to solve problems

achievement-oriented leadership leadership style in which the leader sets challenging goals, has high expectations of employees, and displays confidence that employees will assume responsibility and put forth extraordinary effort

acquaintance time cultural norm for how much time you must spend getting to know someone before the person is prepared to do business with you

acquisition cost the expense of obtaining data that you don't have

acquisition purchase of a company by another company

action plan the specific steps, people, and resources needed to accomplish a goal

active listening assuming half the responsibility for successful communication by actively giving the speaker nonjudgmental feedback that shows you've accurately heard what he or she said

address terms cultural norms that establish whether you should address businesspeople by their first names, family names, or titles

adverse impact unintentional discrimination in which there is a substantially different rate of selection in hiring, promotion, or other employment decisions that works to the disadvantage of members of a particular race, sex, age, ethnicity, or protected group

advocacy groups groups of concerned citizens who band together to try to influence the business practices of specific industries, businesses, and professions

affectivity the stable tendency to experience positive or negative moods and to react to things in a generally positive or negative way

affirmative action purposeful steps taken by an organization to create employment opportunities for minorities and women

age discrimination treating people differently (e.g., in hiring and firing, promotion, and compensation decisions) because of their age

aggregate product plans plans developed to manage and monitor all new products in development at any one time

agreeableness the degree to which someone is cooperative, polite, flexible, forgiving, good natured, tolerant, and trusting

analyzers an adaptive strategy that seeks to minimize risk and maximize profits by following or imitating the proven successes of prospectors

anchoring and adjustment bias unrecognized tendency of decision makers to use an initial value or experience as a basis of comparison throughout the decision process

APEC (Asia-Pacific Economic Cooperation) regional trade agreement between the US, Canada, Japan, South Korea, Australia, New Zealand, China, Taiwan, Hong Kong, and members of ASEAN

application sharing communications system that allows two or more people in different locations to make changes in a document by sharing control of the software application running on one computer

appointment time cultural norm for how punctual you must be when showing up for scheduled appointments or meetings

archived data data kept in long-term storage in separate off-site locations

ASEAN (Association of South East Nations) regional trade agreement between Indonesia, Thailand, Philippines, Malaysia, Singapore, and Brunei

assemble-to-order operation manufacturing operation that divides manufacturing processes into separate parts or modules that are combined to create semi-customized products

assessment centers a series of managerial simulations, graded by trained observers, that are used to determine applicants' capability for managerial work

attack a competitive move designed to reduce a rival's market share or profits

attribution theory theory that states that we all have a basic need to understand and explain the causes of other people's behavior

a-type conflict disagreement that focuses on individual- or personally oriented issues

authoritarianism the extent to which an individual believes that there should be power and status differences within organizations

authority the right to give commands, take action, and make decisions to achieve organizational objectives

automated processing using mainframe systems to automatically collect and process data into useful information

autonomous work groups groups that operate without managers and are completely responsible for controlling work group processes, outputs, and behavior

autonomy the degree to which a job gives workers the discretion, freedom, and independence to decide how and when to accomplish the job

availability bias unrecognized tendency of decision makers to give preference to recent information, vivid images that evoke emotions, and specific acts and behaviors that they personally observed

average aggregate inventory average overall inventory during a particular time period

awareness training training that is designed to raise employees' awareness of diversity issues and to challenge the underlying assumptions or stereotypes they may have about others

background checks procedures used to verify the truthfulness and accuracy of information that applicants provide about themselves and to uncover negative, job-related background information not provided by applicants

balanced scorecard measurement of organizational performance in four equally important areas: finances, customers, internal operations, and innovation and learning

bar code a visual pattern that represents numerical data by varying the thickness and pattern of vertical bars

bargaining power of buyers a measure of the influence that customers have on a firm's prices

bargaining power of suppliers a measure of the influence that suppliers of parts, materials, and services to firms in an industry have on the prices of these inputs

batch production manufacturing operation that produces goods in large batches in standard lot sizes

BCG matrix A portfolio strategy, developed by the Boston Consulting Group, that managers use to categorize the corporation's businesses by growth rate and relative market share, helping them decide how to invest corporate funds

behavior control regulation of the behaviors and actions that workers perform on the job

behavioral addition the process of having managers and employees perform new behaviors that are central to and symbolic of the new organizational culture that a company wants to create

behavioral formality workplace atmosphere characterized by routine and regimen, specific rules about how to behave, and interpersonal detachment

behavioral informality workplace atmosphere characterized by spontaneity, casualness, and interpersonal familiarity

behavioral observation scales (BOS) rating scales that indicate the frequency with which workers perform specific behaviors that are representative of the job dimensions critical to successful job performance

behavioral substitution the process of having managers and employees perform new behaviors central to the "new" organizational culture in place of behaviors that were central to the "old" organizational culture

benchmarking the process of identifying outstanding practices, processes, and standards in other companies and adapting them to your company.

biographical data (biodata) extensive surveys that ask applicants questions about their personal backgrounds and life experiences

boundaryless organization a speedy, responsive, and flexible organization in which vertical, horizontal, external, and geographic boundaries are removed or minimized

bounded rationality decision-making process restricted in the real world by limited resources, incomplete and imperfect information, and managers' limited decision-making capabilities

brainstorming a decision-making method in which group members build on each others' ideas to generate as many alternative solutions as possible

budgeting quantitative planning through which managers decide how to allocate available money to best accomplish company goals

bureaucratic control use of hierarchical authority to influence employee behavior by rewarding or punishing employees for compliance or noncompliance with organizational policies, rules, and procedures

bureaucratic immunity the ability to make changes without first getting approval from managers or other parts of an organization

business confidence indices indices that show managers' level of confidence about future business growth

buyer dependence degree to which a supplier relies on a buyer because of the importance of that buyer to the supplier and the difficulty of selling its products to other buyers

cafeteria benefit plans (flexible benefit plans) plans that allow employees to choose which benefits they receive, up to a certain dollar value

cash cow a company with a large share of a slow-growing market

CD-ROM (compact disk read only memory) a 5 1/4" compact disk that holds up to 650 megabytes of text, sound, or graphic data

centralization of authority the location of most authority at the upper levels of the organization

centralized processing processing and storing data from individual computer terminals on mainframe computers, which have gigabytes of memory and terabytes of hard drive storage space

chain of command the vertical line of authority that clarifies who reports to whom throughout the organization

change agent the person formally in charge of guiding a change effort

change forces forces that produce differences in the form, quality, or condition of an organization over time

change intervention the process used to get workers and managers to change their behavior and work practices

character of the rivalry a measure of the intensity of competitive behavior between companies in an industry

charismatic leadership the behavioral tendencies and personal characteristics of leaders that create an exceptionally strong relationship between them and their followers

client a desktop computer connected to a network through a server

client/server network individual computers connected together through a server computer, so that they can share data and software stored on the server

closure tendency to fill in gaps of missing information by assuming that what we don't know is consistent with what we already know

coaching communicating with someone for the direct purpose of improving the person's on-the-job performance or behavior

coercion use of formal power and authority to force others to change

cognitive ability tests tests that measure the extent to which applicants have abilities in perceptual speed, verbal comprehension, numerical aptitude, general reasoning, and spatial aptitude

cognitive maps graphic depictions of how managers believe environmental factors relate to possible organizational actions

cohesiveness the extent to which team members are attracted to a team and motivated to remain in it

commission a compensation system in which employees earn a percentage of each sale they make

common-enemy mission company goal of defeating a corporate rival

communication cost the expense of transmitting information from one place to another

communication medium the method used to deliver an oral or written message

communication the process of transmitting information from one person or place to another

company hotlines phone numbers that anyone in the company can anonymously call to leave information for upper management

company vision a company's purpose or reason for existence

compensation the financial and nonfinancial rewards that organizations give employees in exchange for their work

competitive advantage providing greater value for customers than competitors can

competitive analysis a process for monitoring competitors that involves identifying competitors, anticipating their moves, and determining their strengths and weaknesses

competitive inertia a reluctance to change strategies or competitive practices that have been successful in the past

competitors companies in the same industry that sell similar products or services to customers

complex environment an environment with many environmental factors

complex matrix a form of matrix departmentalization in which project and functional managers report to matrix managers, who help them sort out conflicts and problems

component parts inventories the basic parts used in manufacturing that are fabricated from raw materials

compression approach to innovation an approach to innovation that assumes that incremental innovation can be planned using a series of steps, and that compressing those steps can speed innovation

concentration of effect the total harm or benefit that an act produces on the average person

conceptual skill the ability to see the organization as a whole, how the different parts affect each other, and how the company fits into or is affected by its environment

concertive control regulation of workers' behavior and decisions through work group values and beliefs

Concurrent control a mechanism for gathering information about performance deficiencies as they occur, eliminating or shortening the delay between performance and feedback

conditions of certainty conditions in which decision makers have complete information and knowledge of all possible outcomes

conditions of risk conditions in which decision makers face a very real possibility of making the wrong decision

conditions of satisfaction a statement of the specific, measurable, and observable conditions that must be met in order for change to be successful

conditions of uncertainty conditions in which decision makers don't know the odds of winning or losing

conduit metaphor the mistaken assumption that senders can pipe their intended messages directly into the heads of receivers with perfect clarity and without noise or perceptual filters interfering with the receivers' understanding of the message

conferencing system communications system that lets two or more users in different locations see and talk to each other as if they were in the same room

conscientiousness the degree to which someone is organized, hard working, responsible, persevering, thorough, and achievement oriented

consideration the extent to which a leader is friendly, approachable, supportive, and shows concern for employees

constructive feedback feedback intended to be helpful, corrective, and/or encouraging

contingency theory leadership theory that states that in order to maximize work group performance, leaders must be matched to the situation that best fits their leadership style

continuous improvement an organization's ongoing commitment to constantly assess and improve the processes and procedures used to create products and services

continuous reinforcement schedule schedule that requires a consequence to be administered following every instance of a behavior

continuous-flow production manufacturing operation that produces goods in a continuous, rather than a discrete, rate

control loss situation in which behavior and work procedures do not conform to standards

control a regulatory process of establishing standards to achieve organizational goals, comparing actual performance against the standards, and taking corrective action, when necessary

controlling monitoring progress toward goal achievement and taking corrective action when needed

conventional level of moral development second level of moral development in which people make decisions that conform to societal expectations

conversations for closure conversations that end the change process by indicating that the work is done and the change process is complete

conversations for performance conversations about action plans, in which managers and workers make specific requests and promise specific results

conversations for understanding conversations that generate a deeper understanding of why change is needed, what problems have been occurring, and what might be done to solve those problems

cooperative contract an agreement in which a foreign business owner pays a company a fee for the right to conduct that business in his or her country

core capabilities the internal decision-making routines, problem-solving processes, and organizational cultures that determine how efficiently inputs can be turned into outputs

core firms the central companies in a strategic group

corporate talk shows televised company meetings that allow remote audiences (employees) to pose questions to the show's host and guests

corporate-level strategy the overall organizational strategy that addresses the question "What business or businesses are we in or should we be in?"

cost leadership the positioning strategy of producing a product or service of acceptable quality at consistently lower production costs than competitors can, so that the firm can offer the product or service at the lowest price in the industry

counseling communicating with someone about non-job-related issues that may be affecting or interfering with the person's performance

country of manufacture country where product is made and assembled

country of origin the home country for a company, where its headquarters is located

creative work environments workplace cultures in which workers perceive that new ideas are welcomed, valued, and encouraged

creativity the production of novel and useful ideas

cross training training team members how to do all or most of the jobs performed by the other team members

cross-cultural communication transmitting information from a person in one country or culture to a person from another country or culture

cross-functional team team composed of employees from different functional areas of the organization

c-type conflict disagreement that focuses on problem- and issue-related differences of opinion

customer defections performance assessment in which companies identify which customers are leaving and measure the rate at which they are leaving

customer departmentalization organizing work and workers into separate units responsible for particular kinds of customers

customer focus an organizational goal to concentrate on meeting customers' needs at all levels of the organization

customer satisfaction an organizational goal to provide products or services that meet or exceed customers' expectations

cybernetic feasibility the extent to which it is possible to implement each step in the control process

data mining the process of discovering unknown patterns and relationships in large amounts of data

data storage tape a magnetic tape used to record and store data

decentralization the location of a significant amount of authority in the lower levels of the organization

decision criteria the standards used to guide judgments and decisions

decision making the process of choosing a solution from available alternatives

decision rule set of criteria that alternative solutions must meet to be acceptable to the decision maker

decision support system (DSS) an information system that helps managers understand specific kinds of problems and potential solutions and to analyze the impact of different decision options using "what if" scenarios

decoding the process by which the receiver translates the written, verbal, or symbolic form of a message into an understood message

deep-level diversity differences communicated through verbal and nonverbal behaviors, such as personality and attitudes, that are learned only through extended interaction with others

defenders an adaptive strategy aimed at defending strategic positions by seeking moderate, steady growth and by offering a limited range of high-quality products and services to a well-defined set of customers

defensive bias the tendency for people to perceive themselves as personally and situationally similar to someone who is having difficulty or trouble

defensive strategy a social responsiveness strategy where a company chooses to admit responsibility for a problem but do the least required to meet societal expectations

de-forming a reversal of the forming stage, in which team members position themselves to control pieces of the team, avoid each other, and isolate themselves from team leaders

degree of dependence the extent to which a company needs a particular resource to accomplish its goals

delegation of authority the assignment of direct authority and responsibility to a subordinate to complete tasks for which the manager is normally responsible

Delphi technique a decision-making method in which a panel of experts respond to questions and to each other until reaching agreement on an issue

de-norming a reversal of the norming stage, in which team performance begins to decline as the size, scope, goal, or members of the team change

departmentalization subdividing work and workers into separate organizational units responsible for completing particular tasks

dependent demand systems inventory system in which the level of inventory depends on the number of finished units to be produced

design competition competition between old and new technologies to establish a new technological standard or dominant design

design iteration a cycle of repetition in which a company tests a prototype of a new product or service, improves on that design, and then builds and tests the improved prototype

desktop videoconferencing communications system that allows two or more people in different locations to use video cameras and computer monitors to see and hear each other and share documents

de-storming a reversal of the storming phase, in which the team's comfort level decreases, team cohesion weakens, and angry emotions and conflict may flare

destructive feedback feedback that disapproves without any intention of being helpful and almost always causes a negative or defensive reaction in the recipient

devil's advocacy a decision-making method in which an individual or a subgroup is assigned the role of a critic

dialectical inquiry a decision-making method in which decision makers state the assumptions of a proposed solution (a thesis) and generate a solution that is the opposite (antithesis) of that solution

dictionary rule decision rule that requires decision makers to rank criteria in order of importance and then test alternative solutions against those criteria in rank order, so that alternatives that meet the most important criterion must then meet the second most important criterion, and so on

differentiation the positioning strategy of providing a product or service that is sufficiently different from competitors' offerings that such customers are willing to pay a premium price for it

direct competition the rivalry between two companies that offer similar products and services, acknowledge each other as rivals, and act and react to each other's strategic actions

direct foreign investment a method of investment in which a company builds a new business or buys an existing business in a foreign county

directive leadership leadership style in which the leader lets employees know precisely what is expected of them, gives them specific guidelines for performing tasks, schedules work, sets standards of performance, and makes sure that people follow standard rules and regulations

disability discrimination treating people differently because of their disabilities

disability a mental or physical impairment that substantially limits one or more major life activities

discretionary responsibilities the expectation that a company will voluntarily serve a social role beyond its economic, legal, and ethical responsibilities

discussion time cultural norm for how much time should be spent in discussion with others

disparate treatment intentional discrimination that occurs when people are purposively not given the same hiring, promotion, or membership opportunities because of their race, sex, age, ethnic group, national origin, or religious beliefs

disposition the tendency to respond to situations and events in a predetermined manner

disseminator role the informational role managers play when they share information with others in their departments or companies

distal goals long-term or primary goals

distinctive competence what a company can make, do, or perform better than its competitors

distributed processing processing and storing data in desktop computers

distributive justice the perceived degree to which outcomes and rewards are fairly distributed or allocated

disturbance handler role the decisional role managers play when they respond to severe problems that demand immediate action

diversification a strategy for reducing risk by buying a variety of items (stocks or, in the case of a corporation, types of businesses), so that the failure of one stock or one business does not doom the entire portfolio

diversity audits formal assessments that measure employee and management attitudes, investigate the extent to which people are advantaged or disadvantaged with respect to hiring and promotions, and review companies' diversity-related policies and procedures

diversity pairing mentoring program in which people of different cultural backgrounds, genders, or races/ethnicities are paired together to get to know each other and change stereotypical beliefs and attitudes

diversity a variety of demographic, cultural, and personal differences among the people who work in an organization and the customers who do business there

document conferencing communications system that allows two or more people in different locations to simultaneously view and make comments about a document

dog a company with a small share of a slow-growing market

dominant design a new technological design or process that becomes the accepted market standard

downsizing the planned elimination of jobs in a company

downward communication communication that flows from higher to lower levels in an organization

DVD (digital video disk) a 51⁄4" compact disk that holds up to 17 gigabytes of text, sound, or graphic data

dynamic environment environment in which the rate of change is fast

dysfunctional turnover loss of high-performing employees who voluntarily choose to leave a company

early retirement incentive programs (ERIPs) programs that offer financial benefits to employees to encourage them to retire early

economic order quantity (EOQ) a system of formulas that minimizes ordering and holding costs and helps determine how much and how often inventory should be ordered

economic responsibility the expectation that a company will make a profit by producing a valued product or service

economic value added (EVA) the amount by which company profits (revenues minus expenses minus taxes) exceed the cost of capital in a given year

effectiveness accomplishing tasks that help fulfill organizational objectives

efficiency getting work done with a minimum of effort, expense, or waste

electronic brainstorming a decision-making method in which group members use computers to build on each others' ideas and generate many alternative solutions

electronic data interchange (EDI) the direct electronic transmission of purchase and ordering information from one company's computer system to another company's computer system

electronic scanner an electronic device that converts printed text and pictures into digital images

e-mail the transmission of messages via computers

emotional stability the degree to which someone is angry, depressed, anxious, emotional, insecure, and excitable

empathetic listening understanding the speaker's perspective and personal frame of reference and giving feedback that conveys that understanding to the speaker

employee involvement team team that provides advice or makes suggestions to management concerning specific issues

employee separation the voluntary or involuntary loss of an employee

employee stock ownership plans (ESOPs) a compensation system that awards employees shares of company stock in addition to their regular compensation

employee turnover loss of employees who voluntarily choose to leave the company

employment benefits a method of rewarding employees that includes virtually any kind of compensation other than wages or salaries

employment references sources such as previous employers or co-workers who can provide job-related information about job candidates

empowering workers permanently passing decision-making authority and responsibility from managers to workers by giving them the information and resources they need to make and carry out good decisions

empowerment feelings of intrinsic motivation, in which workers perceive their work to have impact and meaning, and perceive themselves to be competent and capable of self-determination

encoding putting a message into a written, verbal, or symbolic form that can be recognized and understood by the receiver

entrepreneur role the decisional role managers play when they adapt themselves, their subordinates, and their units to incremental change

entrepreneurial orientation the set of processes, practices, and decision-making activities that lead to new entry, characterized by five dimensions: autonomy, innovativeness, risk-taking, proactiveness, and competitive aggressiveness

entrepreneurship the process of entering new or established markets with new goods or services

environmental change the rate at which a company's general and specific environments change

environmental complexity the number of external

factors in the environment that affect organizations

environmental munificence degree to which an organization's external environment has an abundance or scarcity of critical organizational resources

environmental scanning searching the environment for important events or issues that might affect an organization

equity theory theory that states that people will be motivated when they perceive that they are being treated fairly

era of ferment phase of a technology cycle characterized by technological substitution and design competition

ethical behavior behavior that conforms to a society's accepted principles of right and wrong

ethical charismatics charismatic leaders that provide developmental opportunities for followers, are open to positive and negative feedback, recognize others' contributions, share information, and have moral standards that emphasize the larger interests of the group, organization, or society

ethical intensity the degree of concern people have about an ethical issue

ethical responsibility the expectation that a company will not violate accepted principles of right and wrong when conducting its business

ethics the set of moral principles or values that defines right and wrong for a person or group

evaluation apprehension fear of what others will think of your ideas

executive information system (EIS) data processing system that uses internal and external data sources to provide the information needed to monitor and analyze organizational performance

expatriate someone who lives outside his or her native country

expectancy theory theory that states that people will be motivated to the extent to which they believe that their efforts will lead to good performance, that good performance will be rewarded, and that they will be offered attractive rewards

expectancy the perceived relationship between effort and performance

experiential approach to innovation an approach to innovation that assumes a highly uncertain environment, and uses intuition, flexible options, and hands-on experience to reduce uncertainty and accelerate learning and understanding

expert system information system that contains the specialized knowledge and decision rules used by experts and experienced decision makers, so that nonexperts can draw on this knowledge base to make decisions

exporting selling domestically produced products to customers in foreign countries

external environments all events outside a company that have the potential to influence or affect it

external locus of control the belief that what happens to you is largely the result of factors beyond your control

external recruiting the process of developing a pool of qualified job applicants from outside the company

extinction reinforcement in which a positive consequence is no longer allowed to follow a previously reinforced behavior, thus weakening the behavior

extraversion the degree to which someone is active, assertive, gregarious, sociable, talkative, and energized by others

extrinsic reward a reward that is tangible, visible to others, and given to employees contingent on the performance of specific tasks or behaviors

feedback control a mechanism for gathering information about performance deficiencies after they occur

feedback in the communication process, a return message to the sender that indicates the receiver's understanding of the message

feedback the amount of information the job provides to workers about their work performance

feedforward control a mechanism for monitoring performance inputs rather than outputs to prevent or minimize performance deficiencies before they occur

figurehead role the interpersonal role managers play when they perform ceremonial duties

finished goods inventories the final outputs of manufacturing operations

firm-level strategy corporate strategy that addresses the question "How should we compete against a particular firm?"

first-line managers managers who train and supervise performance of nonmanagerial employees and who are directly responsible for producing the company's products or services

first-mover advantage the strategic advantage that companies earn by being the first to use new information technology to substantially lower costs or to make a product or service different from competitors

fixed interval reinforcement schedule intermittent schedule in which consequences follow a behavior only after a fixed time has elapsed

fixed ratio reinforcement schedule intermittent schedule in which consequences are delivered following a specific number of behaviors

flow a psychological state of effortlessness, in which you become completely absorbed in what you're doing and time seems to pass quickly

focus strategy the positioning strategy of using cost leadership or differentiation to produce a specialized product or service for a limited, specially targeted group of customers in a particular geographic region or market segment

formal communication channel the system of official channels that carry organizationally approved messages and information

forming the first stage of team development in which team members meet each other, form initial impressions, and begin to establish team norms

franchise a collection of networked firms in which the manufacturer or marketer of a product or service, the franchisor, licenses the entire business to another person or organization, the franchisee

freeware computer software that is free to whoever wants it

FTAA (Free Trade Area of the Americas) regional trade agreement that, when signed, will create a regional trading zone encompassing 36 countries in North and South America

functional departmentalization organizing work and workers into separate units responsible for particular business functions or areas of expertise

functional turnover loss of poor-performing employees who voluntarily choose to leave a company

fundamental attribution error the tendency to ignore external causes of behavior and to attribute other people's actions to internal causes

gainsharing compensation system in which companies share the financial value of performance gains, such as productivity, cost savings, or quality, with their workers

GATT (General Agreement on Tariffs and Trade) worldwide trade agreement that will reduce and eliminate tariffs, limit government subsidies, and protect intellectual property

gender discrimination treating people differently because of their gender

General Electric Workout a three-day meeting in which managers and employees from different levels and parts of an organization quickly generate and act on solutions to specific business problems

general environment the economic, technological, sociocultural, and political trends that indirectly affect all organizations

generational change change based on incremental improvements to a dominant technological design such that the improved technology is fully backward compatible with the older technology

geographic departmentalization organizing work and workers into separate units responsible for doing business in particular geographical areas

glass ceiling the so-called invisible barrier that prevents women and minorities from advancing to the top jobs in organizations

global business the buying and selling of goods and services by people from different countries

global new ventures new companies with sales, employees, and financing in different countries that are founded with an active global strategy

goal acceptance the extent to which people consciously understand and agree to goals

goal commitment the determination to achieve a goal

goal difficulty the extent to which a goal is hard or challenging to accomplish

goal specificity the extent to which goals are detailed, exact, and unambiguous

goal a target, objective, or result that someone tries to accomplish

goal-setting theory theory that states that people will be motivated to the extent to which they accept specific, challenging goals and receive feedback that indicates their progress toward goal achievement

grand strategy a broad corporate-level strategic plan used to achieve strategic goals and guide the strategic alternatives that managers of individual businesses or subunits may use

groupthink a barrier to good decision making caused by pressure within the group for members to not disagree with each other

growth strategy strategy that focuses on increasing profits, revenues, market share, or the number of places in which the company does business

hard drive a magnetic disk, usually mounted inside a computer, that allows users to read its stored data and write data to it

hearing the act or process of perceiving sounds

holding cost the cost of keeping inventory until it is used or sold, including storage, insurance, taxes, obsolescence, and opportunity costs

horizontal communication communication that flows among managers and workers who are at the same organizational level

hostile work environment form of sexual harassment in which unwelcome and demeaning sexually related behavior creates an intimidating and offensive work environment

human resource information systems (HRIS) computerized systems for gathering, analyzing, storing, and disseminating information related to the HRM process

human resource management the process of finding, developing, and keeping the right people to form a qualified work force

human resource planning (HRP) using an organization's goals and strategy to forecast the organization's human resource needs in terms of attracting, developing, and keeping a qualified work force

human skill the ability to work well with others

imperfectly imitable resource a resource that is impossible or extremely costly or difficult for other firms to duplicate

incremental change the phase of a technology cycle in which companies innovate by lowering costs and improving the functioning and performance of the dominant technological design

independent demand system inventory system in which the level of one kind of inventory does not depend on another

individualism-collectivism the degree to which a person believes that people should be self-sufficient and that loyalty to one's self is more important than loyalty to one's team or company

industry regulation regulations and rules that govern the business practices and procedures of specific industries, businesses, and professions

industry-level strategy corporate strategy that addresses the question "How should we compete in this industry?"

informal communication channel ("grapevine") the transmission of messages from employee to employee outside of formal communication channels

information overload situation in which decision makers have too much information to attend to

information useful data that can influence peoples' choices and behavior

initiating structure the degree to which a leader structures the roles of followers by setting goals, giving directions, setting deadlines, and assigning tasks

initiative conversations conversations that start the change process by discussing what should or needs to be done to bring about change

innovation streams patterns of innovation over time that can create sustainable competitive advantage

inputs in equity theory, the contributions employees make to the organization

instrumentality the perceived relationship between performance and rewards

intermittent reinforcement schedule schedule in which consequences are delivered after a specified or average time has elapsed or after a specified or average number of behaviors has occurred

internal environment the events and trends inside an organization that affect management, employees, and organizational culture

internal locus of control the belief that what happens to you is largely the result of your own actions

internal motivation motivation that comes from the job itself rather than from outside rewards

internal recruiting the process of developing a pool of qualified job applicants from people who already work in the company

internal-transformation mission company goal of remaining competitive by making dramatic changes in the company

Internet a global network of networks that allows users to send and retrieve data from anywhere in the world

interorganizational process a collection of activities that take place among companies to transform inputs into outputs that customers value

interpersonal skills skills, such as listening, communicating, questioning, and providing feedback, that enable people to have effective working relationships with others

interviews selection tool in which company representatives ask job applicants job-related questions to determine whether they are qualified for the job

intranets private company networks that allow employees to easily access, share, and publish information using Internet software

intraorganizational process the collection of activities that take place within an organization to transform inputs into outputs that customers value

intrinsic reward a natural reward associated with performing a task or activity for its own sake

inventory turnover the number of times per year that a company sells or "turns over" its average inventory

inventory the amount and number of raw materials, parts, and finished products that a company has in its possession

ISO 9000 a series of five international standards, from ISO 9000 to ISO 9004, for achieving consistency in quality management and quality assurance in companies throughout the world

job analysis a purposeful, systematic process for collecting information on the important work-related aspects of a job

job characteristics model (JCM) an approach to job redesign that seeks to formulate jobs in ways that motivate workers and lead to positive work outcomes

job description a written description of the basic tasks, duties, and responsibilities required of an employee holding a particular job

job design the number, kind, and variety of tasks that individual workers perform in doing their jobs

job enlargement increasing the number of different tasks that a worker performs within one particular job

job enrichment increasing the number of tasks in a particular job and giving workers the authority and control to make meaningful decisions about their work

job evaluation a process that determines the worth of each job in a company by evaluating the market value of the knowledge, skills, and requirements needed to perform it

job rotation periodically moving workers from one specialized job to another to give them more variety and the opportunity to use different skills

job shops manufacturing operations that handle custom orders or small batch jobs

job specialization a job composed of a small part of a larger task or process

job specifications a written summary of the qualifications needed to successfully perform a particular job

joint venture a strategic alliance in which two existing companies collaborate to form a third, independent company

just-in-time (JIT) inventory system inventory system in which component parts arrive from suppliers just as they are needed at each stage of production

kanban a ticket-based system that indicates when to reorder inventory

kinesics movements of the body and face

knowledge the understanding that one gains from information

leader role the interpersonal role managers play when they motivate and encourage workers to accomplish organizational objectives

leader-member relations the degree to which followers respect, trust, and like their leaders

leadership the process of influencing others to achieve group or organizational goals

leadership neutralizers subordinate, task, or organizational characteristics that can interfere with a leader's actions or make it impossible for a leader to influence followers' performance

leadership style the way a leader generally behaves toward followers

leadership substitutes subordinate, task, or organizational characteristics that make leaders redundant or unnecessary

leading inspiring and motivating workers to work hard to achieve organizational goals

learning-based planning learning better ways of achieving goals by continually testing, changing, and improving plans and strategies

legal responsibility the expectation that a company will obey society's laws and regulations

liaison role the interpersonal role managers play when they deal with people outside their units

licensing agreement in which a domestic company, the licensor, receives royalty payments for allowing another company, the licensee, to produce its product, sell its service, or use its brand name in a specified foreign market

line authority the right to command immediate subordinates in the chain of command

line function an activity that contributes directly to creating or selling the company's products

line-flow production manufacturing processes that are pre-established, occur in a serial or linear manner, and are dedicated to making one type of product

listening making a conscious effort to hear

locus of control the degree to which individuals believe that their actions can influence what happens to them

Maastricht Treaty of Europe regional trade agreement between most European countries

Machiavellianism the extent to which an individual believes that virtually any type of behavior is acceptable in trying to satisfy their needs or meet their goals

magnitude of consequences the total harm or benefit derived from an ethical decision

make-to-order operation manufacturing operation that does not start processing or assembling products until a customer order is received

make-to-stock operation manufacturing operation that orders parts and assembles standardized products before receiving customer orders

management by objectives a four-step process in which managers and employees discuss and select goals, develop tactical plans, and meet regularly to review progress toward goal accomplishment

management getting work done through others

manufacturing flexibility degree to which manufacturing operations can easily and quickly change the number, kind, and characteristics of products they produce

market commonality the degree to which two companies have overlapping products, services, or customers in multiple markets

materials requirement planning (MRP) a production and inventory system that determines the production schedule, production batch sizes, and inventory needed to complete final products

matrix departmentalization a hybrid organizational structure in which two or more forms of departmentalization, most often product and functional, are used together

maximizing choosing the best alternative

mechanistic organization organization characterized by specialized jobs and responsibilities, precisely defined, unchanging roles, and a rigid chain of command based on centralized authority and vertical communication

media advocacy an advocacy group tactic of framing issues as public issues, exposing questionable, exploitative, or unethical practices, and forcing media coverage by buying media time or creating controversy that is likely to receive extensive news coverage

meta-analysis a study of studies, a statistical approach that provides the best scientific estimate of how well management theories and practices work

microfilm small photographic slides used to store data. A reel of microfilm can store hundreds of pages of data.

middle managers managers responsible for setting objectives consistent with top management's goals, and planning and implementing subunit strategies for achieving these objectives

milestones formal project review points used to assess progress and performance

minimum threshold rule decision rule that requires alternative solutions to meet all the established minimum decision criteria

mission statement of a company's overall goal that unifies company-wide efforts toward its vision, stretches and challenges the organization, and possesses a finish line and a time frame

modular organization an organization that outsources noncore business activities to outside companies, suppliers, specialists, or consultants

monitor role the informational role managers play when they scan their environment for information

mood linkage a phenomenon where one worker's negative affectivity and bad moods can spread to others

Moore's law Prediction that every 18 months, the cost of computing will drop by 50 percent as computer-processing power doubles

motivation to manage an assessment of how enthusiastic employees are about managing the work of others

motivation the set of forces that initiates, directs, and makes people persist in their efforts to accomplish a goal

multifactor productivity an overall measure of performance that indicates how much labor, capital, materials, and energy it takes to produce an output

multifunctional teams work teams composed of people from different departments

multinational corporation corporation that owns businesses in two or more countries

multivariable testing a systematic approach of experimentation used to analyze and evaluate potential solutions

NAFTA (North American Free Trade Agreement) regional trade agreement between the United States, Canada, and Mexico

national culture the set of shared values and beliefs that affects the perceptions, decisions, and behavior of the people from a particular country

needs assessment the process of identifying and prioritizing the learning needs of employees

needs the physical or psychological requirements that must be met to ensure survival and well being

negative affectivity personality trait in which individuals tend to notice and focus on the negative aspects of themselves and their environments

negative frame couching a problem in terms of a loss, thus influencing decision makers toward becoming risk-seeking

negative reinforcement reinforcement that strengthens behavior by withholding an unpleasant consequence when employees perform a specific behavior

negotiator role the decisional role managers play when they negotiate schedules, projects, goals, outcomes, resources, and employee raises

network a system of cable wires or optic fibers that connect computers and allow them to send data to and receive data from each other

noise anything that interferes with the transmission of the intended message

nominal group technique a decision-making method that begins and ends by having group members quietly write down and evaluate ideas to be shared with the group

nonsubstitutable resource a resource, without equivalent substitutes or replacements, that produces value or competitive advantage

nontariff barriers nontax methods of increasing the cost or reducing the volume of imported goods

nonverbal communication any communication that doesn't involve words

normative control regulation of workers'behavior and decisions through widely shared organizational values and beliefs

normative decision theory theory that suggests how leaders can determine an appropriate amount of employee participation to include when making decisions

norming the third stage of team development, in which team members begin to settle into their roles, group cohesion grows, and positive team norms develop

norms informally agreed-on standards that regulate team behavior

objective control use of observable measures of worker behavior or outputs to assess performance and influence behavior

objective performance measures measures of job performance that are easily and directly counted or quantified

online discussion forums the in-house equivalent of Internet newsgroups; Web- or software-based discussion tools available across the company to permit employees to easily ask questions and share knowledge with each other

open office systems offices in which the physical barriers that separate workers have been removed in order to increase communication and interaction

openness to experience the degree to which someone is curious, broad-minded, and open to new ideas, things, and experiences; is spontaneous; and has a high tolerance for ambiguity

operational plans day-to-day plans, developed and implemented by lower-level managers, for producing or delivering the organization's products and services over a 30-day to 6-month period

operations management managing the daily production of goods and services

opportunistic behavior transaction in which one party in the relationship benefits at the expense of the other

optical character recognition software to convert digitized documents into ASCII text (American Standard Code for Information Interchange) that can be searched, read, and edited by word processing and other kinds of software

options-based planning maintaining planning flexibility by making small, simultaneous investments in many alternative plans

ordering cost the costs associated with ordering inventory, including the cost of data entry, phone calls, obtaining bids, correcting mistakes, and determining when and how much inventory to order

organic organization organization characterized by broadly defined jobs and responsibility, loosely defined, frequently changing roles, and decentralized authority and horizontal communication based on task knowledge

organization decline a large decrease in organizational performance that occurs when companies don't anticipate, recognize, neutralize, or adapt to the internal or external pressures that threaten their survival

organizational change a difference in the form, quality, or condition of an organization over time

organizational culture the values, beliefs, and attitudes shared by organizational members

organizational development a philosophy and collection of planned change interventions designed to improve an organization's long-term health and performance

organizational dialogue the process by which people in an organization learn to talk effectively and constructively with each other

organizational heroes people celebrated for their qualities and achievements within an organization

organizational innovation the successful implementation of creative ideas in organizations

organizational plurality a work environment where (1) each member is empowered to contribute in a way that maximizes the benefits to the organization, customers, and themselves, and (2) the individuality of each member is respected by not segmenting or polarizing people on the basis of their membership in a particular group

organizational process the collection of activities that transforms inputs into outputs that customers value

organizational stories stories told by organizational members to make sense of organizational events and changes, and to emphasize culturally consistent assumptions, decisions, and actions

organizational structure the vertical and horizontal configuration of departments, authority, and jobs within a company

organizing deciding where decisions will be made, who will do what jobs and tasks, and who will work for whom

outcome/input (O/I) ratio in equity theory, an employee's perception of the comparison between the rewards received from an organization and the employee's contributions to that organization

outcomes in equity theory, the rewards employees receive for their contributions to the organization

outplacement services employment-counseling services offered to employees who are losing their jobs because of downsizing

output control regulation of worker results or outputs through rewards and incentives

overreward when you are getting more outcomes relative to your inputs than the referent to whom you compare yourself

overt integrity test written test that estimates employee honesty by directly asking job applicants what they think or feel about theft or about punishment of unethical behaviors

paralanguage the pitch, rate, tone, volume, and speaking pattern (i.e., use of silences, pauses, or hesitations) of one's voice

partial productivity a measure of performance that indicates how much of a particular kind of input it takes to produce an output

participative leadership leadership style in which the leader consults employees for their suggestions and input before making decisions

path-goal theory leadership theory that states that leaders can increase subordinate satisfaction and performance by clarifying and clearing the paths to goals and by increasing the number and kinds of rewards available for goal attainment

perception the process by which individuals attend to, organize, interpret, and retain information from their environments

perceptual filters the personality-, psychology-, or experience-based differences that influence people to ignore or pay attention to particular stimuli

performance appraisal the process of assessing how well employees are doing their jobs

performance feedback information about the quality or quantity of past performance that indicates whether progress is being made toward the accomplishment of a goal

performing the fourth and final stage of team development, in which performance improves because the team has matured into an effective, fully functioning team

personal aggression hostile or aggressive behavior toward others

personality tests tests that measure the extent to which applicants possess different kinds of job-related personality dimensions

personality the relatively stable set of behaviors, attitudes, and emotions displayed over time that makes people different from each other

personality-based integrity test written test that indirectly estimates employee honesty by measuring psychological traits such as dependability and conscientiousness

piecework a compensation system in which employees are paid a set rate for each item they produce

planning choosing a goal and developing a strategy to achieve that goal

planning determining organizational goals and the means for achieving them

policy uncertainty the risk associated with changes in laws and government policies that directly affect the way foreign companies conduct business

policy standing plan that indicates the general course of action that should be taken in response to a particular event or situation

political deviance using one's influence to harm others in the company

political uncertainty the risk of major changes in political regimes that can result from war, revolution, death of political leaders, social unrest, or other influential events

pooled interdependence work completed by having each job or department independently contribute to the whole

portfolio strategy corporate-level strategy that minimizes risk by diversifying investment among various businesses or product lines

position power the degree to which leaders are able to hire, fire, reward, and punish workers

positive affectivity personality trait in which individuals tend to notice and focus on the positive aspects of themselves and their environments

positive frame couching a problem in terms of a gain, thus influencing decision makers toward becoming risk-averse

positive reinforcement reinforcement that strengthens behavior by following behaviors with desirable consequences

post conventional level of moral development third level of moral development in which people make decisions based on internalized principles

preconventional level of moral development first level of moral development in which people make decisions based on selfish reasons

primary stakeholder any group on which an organization relies for its long-term survival

primary storage stored data that workers and managers use most often in performing their jobs

principle of distributive justice ethical principle that holds that you should never take any action that harms the least among us: the poor, the uneducated, the unemployed

principle of government requirements ethical principle that holds that you should never take any action that violates the law, for the law represents the minimal moral standard

principle of individual rights ethical principle that holds that you should never take any action that infringes on others' agreed-on rights

principle of long-term self-interest ethical principle that holds that you should never take any action that is not in your or your organization's long-term self-interest

principle of personal virtue ethical principle that holds that you should never do anything that is not honest, open, and truthful, and which you would not be glad to see reported in the newspapers or on TV

principle of religious injunctions ethical principle that holds that you should never take any action that is not kind and that does not build a sense of community, a sense of everyone working together for a commonly accepted goal

principle of utilitarian benefits ethical principle that holds that you should never take any action that does not result in greater good for society. Instead, do whatever creates the greatest good for the greatest number

private spaces spaces used by and open to just one employee

proactive strategy a social responsiveness strategy where a company anticipates responsibility for a problem before it occurs and would do more than society expects to address the problem

probability of effect the chance that something will happen and then result in harm to others

problem a gap between a desired state and an existing state

procedural justice the perceived fairness of the process used to make reward allocation decisions

procedure standing plan that indicates the specific steps that should be taken in response to a particular event

processing cost the expense of turning raw data into usable information

processing information transforming raw data into meaningful information

product boycott an advocacy group tactic of protesting a company's actions by convincing consumers not to purchase its product or service

product departmentalization organizing work and workers into separate units responsible for producing particular products or services

product prototype a full-scale, working model of a final product that is being tested for design, function, and reliability

production blocking a disadvantage of face-to-face brainstorming in which a group member must wait to share an idea because another member is presenting an idea

production deviance unethical behavior that hurts the quality and quantity of work produced

productivity a measure of performance that indicates how many inputs it takes to produce or create an output

profit sharing a compensation system in which a percentage of company profits is paid to employees in addition to their regular compensation

project manufacturing manufacturing operations designed to produce large, expensive, specialized products

project team team created to complete specific, one-time projects or tasks within a limited time

property deviance unethical behavior aimed at the organization's property

prospectors an adaptive strategy that seeks fast growth by searching for new market opportunities, encouraging risk taking, and being the first to bring innovative new products to market

protectionism a government's use of trade barriers to shield domestic companies and their workers from foreign competition

proximal goals short-term goals or subgoals

proximity of effect the social, psychological, cultural, or physical distance between a decision maker and those affected by his or her decisions

public communications an advocacy group tactic that relies on voluntary participation by the news media and the advertising industry to get an advocacy group's message out

punctuated equilibrium theory theory that holds that companies go through long, simple periods of stability (equilibrium), followed by short periods of dynamic, fundamental change (revolution), and ending with a return to stability (new equilibrium)

punishment reinforcement that weakens behavior by following behaviors with undesirable consequences

purchasing power a comparison of the relative cost of a standard set of goods and services in different countries

quality a product or service free of deficiencies, or the characteristics of a product or service that satisfy customer needs

quasi-control reducing dependence or restructuring dependence when control is necessary but not possible

question mark a company with a small share of a fast-growing market

quid pro quo sexual harassment form of sexual harassment in which employment outcomes, such as hiring, promotion, or simply keeping one's job, depend on whether an individual submits to sexual harassment

quota limit on the number or volume of imported products

racial and ethnic discrimination treating people differently because of their race or ethnicity

RAID (redundant array inexpensive disk) a collection of hard drives connected together so that they perform as if they were one large hard drive, to protect data from hard drive failure

rare resource a resource that is not controlled or possessed by many competing firms

rater training training performance appraisal raters in how to avoid rating errors and increase rating accuracy

rational decision making a systematic process of defining problems, evaluating alternatives, and choosing optimal solutions

raw data facts and figures

raw material inventories the basic inputs in a manufacturing process

reactive strategy a social responsiveness strategy where a company chooses to do less than society expects and to deny responsibility for problems

reactors an adaptive strategy of not following a consistent strategy, but instead reacting to changes in the external environment after they occur

reciprocal interdependence work completed by different jobs or groups working together in a back-and-forth manner

recovery the strategic actions taken after retrenchment to return to a growth strategy

recruiting the process of developing a pool of qualified job applicants

reducing dependence abandoning or changing organizational goals to reduce dependence on critical resources

reengineering fundamental rethinking and radical redesign of business processes to achieve dramatic improvements in critical measures of performance, such as cost, quality, service, and speed

referent in equity theory, others with whom people compare themselves to determine if they have been treated fairly

refreezing supporting and reinforcing the new changes so they "stick"

regional trading zones areas in which tariff and nontariff barriers on trade between countries are reduced or eliminated

reinforcement contingencies cause-and-effect relationships between the performance of specific behaviors and specific consequences

reinforcement theory theory that states that behavior is a function of its consequences, that behaviors followed by positive consequences will occur more frequently, and that behaviors followed by negative consequences, or not followed by positive consequences, will occur less frequently

reinforcement the process of changing behavior by changing the consequences that follow behavior

related diversification creating or acquiring companies that share similar products, manufacturing, marketing, technology, or cultures

relationship behavior mutually beneficial, long-term exchanges between buyers and suppliers

relative comparisons a process in which each decision criterion is compared directly to every other criterion

representative bias unrecognized tendency of decision makers to judge the likelihood of an event's occurrence based on its similarity to previous events

resistance forces forces that support the existing state of conditions in organizations

resistance to change opposition to change resulting from self-interest, misunderstanding and distrust, or a general intolerance for change

resource allocator role the decisional role managers play when they decide who gets what resources

resource flow the extent to which companies have access to critical resources

resource similarity the extent to which a competitor has similar amounts and kinds of resources

resources the assets, capabilities, processes, information, and knowledge that an organization uses to improve its effectiveness and efficiency, to create and sustain competitive advantage, and to fulfill a need or solve a problem

response a competitive countermove, prompted by a rival's attack, to defend or improve a company's market share or profit

restructuring dependence exchanging dependence on one critical resource for dependence on another

results-driven change change created quickly by focusing on the measurement and improvement of results

retrenchment strategy strategy that focuses on turning around very poor company performance by shrinking the size or scope of the business

retrieval cost the expense of accessing already-stored and processed information

risk propensity a person's tendency to take or avoid risks

role-model mission company goal of imitating the characteristics and practices of a successful company

rules and regulations standing plans that describe how a particular action should be performed, or what must happen or not happen in response to a particular event

S.M.A.R.T. goals goals that are specific, measurable, attainable, realistic, and timely

satisficing choosing a "good enough" alternative

scenario planning the process of developing plans to deal with several possible future events and trends that might affect the business

schedule of reinforcement rules that specify which behaviors will be reinforced, which consequences will follow those behaviors, and the schedule by which those consequences will be delivered

schedule time cultural norm for the time by which scheduled projects or jobs should actually be completed

S-curve pattern of innovation a pattern of technological innovation characterized by slow initial progress, then rapid progress, and then again by slow progress as a technology matures and reaches its limits

secondary firms the firms in a strategic group that follow related, but somewhat different strategies than do the core firms

secondary stakeholder any group that can influence or be influenced by the company and can affect public perceptions about its socially responsible behavior

secondary storage stored data that are regularly, but infrequently used onsite by workers to do their jobs

selection the process of gathering information about job applicants to decide who should be offered a job

selective perception the tendency to notice and accept objects and information consistent with our values, beliefs, and expectations, while ignoring or screening out or not accepting inconsistent information

self-control (self-management) control system in which managers and workers control their own behavior by setting their own goals, monitoring their own progress, and rewarding themselves for goal achievement

self-designing team team that has the characteristics of self-managing teams but that also controls team design, work tasks, and team membership

self-limiting behavior behavior in which team members choose to limit their involvement in a team's work

self-managing team team that manages and controls all of the major tasks of producing a product or service

self-monitoring the ability to adjust one's behavior to different situations and environments

self-serving bias the tendency to over-estimate our value by attributing successes to ourselves (internal causes) and attributing failures to others or the environment (external causes)

semi-autonomous work group group that has the authority to make decisions and solve problems related to the major tasks of producing a product or service

sequential interdependence work completed in succession, with one group or job's outputs becoming the inputs for the next group or job

server a larger, more powerful computer than client computers that stores data and software requested by clients on a network; also called a file server

service recovery restoring customer satisfaction to strongly dissatisfied customers

setup cost the costs of downtime and lost efficiency that occur when changing or adjusting a machine to produce a different kind of inventory

sexual harassment form of discrimination in which unwelcome sexual advances, requests for sexual favors, or other verbal or physical conduct of a sexual nature occur while performing one's job

shadow-strategy task force a committee within the company that analyzes the company's own weaknesses to determine how competitors could exploit them for competitive advantage

shared processing information processing that is shared by two kinds of computers, clients and servers, across a client/server network

shared spaces spaces used by and open to all employees

shareholder model view of social responsibility which

holds that an organization's overriding goal should be profit maximization for the benefit of shareholders

shareware computer software that you can try before you buy, but, if you keep it beyond the trial period, usually 30 days, you must buy it

shrinkage employee theft of company merchandise

simple environment an environment with few environmental factors

simple matrix a form of matrix departmentalization in which project and functional managers negotiate conflicts and resources

single-use plans plans that cover unique, one-time-only events

situational (SWOT) analysis an assessment of the strengths and weaknesses in an organization's internal environment and the opportunities and threats in its external environment

situational favorableness the degree to which a particular situation either permits or denies a leader the chance to influence the behavior of group members

situational theory leadership theory that states that leaders need to adjust their leadership styles to match followers' maturity

skill variety the number of different activities performed in a job

skill-based pay compensation system that pays employees for learning additional skills or knowledge

skills-based diversity training training that teaches employees the practical skills they need for managing a diverse work force, such as flexibility and adaptability, negotiation, problem solving, and conflict resolution

social consensus agreement on whether behavior is bad or good

social integration the degree to which group members are psychologically attracted to working with each other to accomplish a common objective

social loafing behavior in which team members withhold their efforts and fail to perform their share of the work

social responsibility a business's obligation to pursue policies, make decisions, and take actions that benefit society

social responsiveness the strategy chosen by a company to respond to stakeholders' economic, legal, ethical, or discretionary expectations concerning social responsibility

specific ability tests (aptitude tests) tests that measure the extent to which an applicant possesses the particular kind of ability needed to do a job well

specific environment the customer, competitor, supplier, industry regulation, and public pressure group trends that are unique to an industry and which directly affect how a company does business

spokesman role the informational role managers play when they share information with people outside their departments or companies

stability strategy strategy that focuses on improving the way in which the company sells the same products or services to the same customers

stable environment environment in which the rate of change is slow

staff authority the right to advise but not command others who are not subordinates in the chain of command

staff function an activity that does not contribute directly to creating or selling the company's products, but instead supports line activities

stakeholder model theory of corporate responsibility which holds that management's most important responsibility, long-term survival, is achieved by satisfying the interests of multiple corporate stakeholders

stakeholders persons or groups with a "stake" or legitimate interest in a company's actions

standardization solving problems by consistently applying the same rules, procedures, and processes

standards a basis of comparison when measuring the extent to which various kinds of organizational performance are satisfactory or unsatisfactory

standing plans plans used repeatedly to handle frequently recurring events

star a company with a large share of a fast-growing market

stereotypes negative, false, overgeneralized beliefs about people in particular categories

stock options a compensation system that gives employees the right to purchase shares of stock at a set price, even if the value of the stock increases above that price

stockout costs the costs incurred when a company runs out of a product, including transaction costs to replace inventory and the loss of customers' goodwill

stockout situation in which a company runs out of finished product

storage cost the expense of physically or electronically archiving information for later use and retrieval

storming the second stage of team development, characterized by conflict and disagreement, in which team members disagree over what the team should do and how it should do it

strategic alliance agreement in which companies combine key resources, costs, risk, technology, and people

strategic dissonance a discrepancy between upper management's intended strategy and the strategy actually implemented by lower levels of management

strategic group a group of companies within an industry that top managers choose to compare, evaluate, and benchmark strategic threats and opportunities

strategic leadership the ability to anticipate, envision, maintain flexibility, think strategically, and work with others to initiate changes that will create a positive future for an organization

strategic plans overall company plans that clarify how the company will serve customers and position itself against competitors over the next two to five years

strategic reference points the strategic targets managers use to measure whether a firm has developed the core competencies it needs to achieve a sustainable competitive advantage

stretch goals extremely ambitious goals that, initially, employees don't know how to accomplish

structural accommodation the ability to change organizational structures, policies, and practices

structured interviews interviews in which all applicants are asked the same set of standardized questions, usually including situational, behavioral, background, and job-knowledge questions

subjective performance measures measures of job performance that require someone to judge or assess a worker's performance

suboptimization performance improvement in one part of an organization but only at the expense of decreased performance in another part

subsidies government loans, grants, and tax deferments given to domestic companies to protect them from foreign competition

supplier dependence degree to which a company relies on a supplier because of the importance of the supplier's product to the company and the difficulty of finding other sources of that product

suppliers companies that provide material, human, financial, and informational resources to other companies

supportive leadership leadership style in which the leader is friendly and approachable to employees, shows concern for them and their welfare, treats them as equals, and creates a friendly climate

surface-level diversity differences such as age, gender, race/ethnicity, and physical disabilities that are observable, typically unchangeable, and easy to measure

survey feedback information collected by surveys from organizational members that is then compiled, disseminated, and used to develop action plans for improvement

sustainable competitive advantage a competitive advantage that other companies have tried unsuccessfully to duplicate and have, for the moment, stopped trying to duplicate

tactical plans plans created and implemented by middle managers that specify how the company will use resources, budgets, and people over the next six months to two years to accomplish specific goals within its mission

targeting mission mission stated as a clear, specific company goal

tariff a direct tax on imported goods

task identity the degree to which a job requires, from beginning to end, the completion of a whole and identifiable piece of work

task interdependence the extent to which collective action is required to complete an entire piece of work

task significance the degree to which a job is perceived to have a substantial impact on others inside or outside the organization

task structure the degree to which the requirements of a subordinate's tasks are clearly specified

team diversity the variances or differences in ability, experience, personality, or any other factor on a team

team leaders managers responsible for facilitating team activities toward goal accomplishment

team level the average level of ability, experience, personality, or any other factor on a team

teamwork collaboration between managers and nonmanagers, across business functions, and between companies, customers, and suppliers

technical skills the ability to apply the specialized procedures, techniques, and knowledge required to get the job done

technological discontinuity scientific advance or unique combination of existing technologies that creates a significant breakthrough in performance or function

technological substitution purchase of new technologies to replace older ones

technology cycle cycle that begins with the "birth" of a new technology and ends when that technology reaches its limits and is replaced by a newer, substantially better technology

technology knowledge, tools, and techniques used to transform inputs (raw materials) into outputs (finished products or services)

televised/videotaped speeches and meetings speeches and meetings originally made to a smaller audience that are either simultaneously broadcast to other locations in the company or videotaped for subsequent distribution and viewing

temporal immediacy the time between an act and the consequences the act produces

testing systematic comparison of different product designs or design iterations

threat of new entrants a measure of the degree to which barriers to entry make it easy or difficult for new companies to get started in an industry

threat of substitute products or services a measure of the ease with which customers can find substitutes for an industry's products or services

top managers executives responsible for the overall direction of the organization

total quality management (TQM) an integrated, principle-based, organization-wide strategy for improving product and service quality

trade barriers government-imposed regulations that increase the cost and restrict the number of imported goods

traditional work group group composed of two or more people who work together to achieve a shared goal

training developing the skills, experience, and knowledge employees need to perform their jobs or improve their performance

trait rating scales a rating scale that indicates the extent to which a worker possesses particular traits or characteristics

trait theory leadership theory that holds that effective leaders possess a similar set of traits or characteristics

traits relatively stable characteristics, such as abilities, psychological motives, or consistent patterns of behavior

transaction processing systems centralized mainframe systems that record the thousands of routine, daily transactions involved in running a business

transactional leadership leadership based on an exchange process, in which followers are rewarded for good performance and punished for poor performance

transformational leadership leadership that generates awareness and acceptance of a group's purpose and mission and gets employees to see beyond their own needs and self-interest for the good of the group

transient firms the firms in a strategic group whose strategies are changing from one strategic position to another

transition management team (TMT) a team of 8 to 12 people whose full-time job is to completely manage and coordinate a company's change process

Type A personality a person who tries to complete as many tasks as possible in the shortest possible time and is hard driving, competitive, impatient, perfectionistic, angry, and unable to relax

Type A/B personality dimension the extent to which people tend toward impatience, hurriedness, competitiveness, and hostility

Type B personality a person who is relaxed and easygoing and able to engage in leisure activities without worrying about work

uncertainty extent to which managers can understand or predict which environmental changes and trends will affect their businesses

underreward when the referent you compare yourself to is getting more outcomes relative to their inputs than you are

unethical charismatics charismatic leaders that control and manipulate followers, do what is best for themselves instead of their organizations, only want to hear positive feedback, only share information that is beneficial to themselves, and have moral standards that put their interests before everyone else's

unfreezing getting the people affected by change to believe that change is needed

unity of command a management principle that workers should report to just one boss

unrelated diversification creating or acquiring companies in completely unrelated businesses

upward communication communication that flows from lower to higher levels in an organization

valence the attractiveness or desirability of a reward or outcome

validation the process of determining how well a selection test or procedure predicts future job performance. The better or more accurate the prediction of future job performance, the more valid a test is said to be.

valuable resource a resource that allows companies to improve efficiency and effectiveness

value customer perception that the product quality is excellent for the price offered

variable interval reinforcement schedule intermittent schedule in which the time between a behavior and the following consequences varies around a specified average

variable ratio reinforcement schedule intermittent schedule in which consequences are delivered following a different number of behaviors, sometimes more and sometimes less, that vary around a specified average number of behaviors

variation a deviation in the form, condition, or appearance of a product from the quality standard for that product

virtual organization an organization that is part of a network in which many companies share skills, costs, capabilities, markets, and customers to collectively solve customer problems or provide specific products or services

virtual team team composed of geographically and/or organizationally dispersed co-workers who use telecommunications and information technologies to accomplish an organizational task

visible artifacts visible signs of an organization's culture, such as the office design and layout, company dress codes, and company benefits and perks like stock options, personal parking spaces, or the private company dining room

vision inspirational statement of an organization's enduring purpose

visionary leadership leadership that creates a positive image of the future that motivates organizational members and provides direction for future planning and goal setting

voice messaging telephone answering system that records audio messages

voluntary export restraints voluntarily imposed limits on the number or volume of products exported to a particular country

whistleblowing reporting others' ethics violations to management or legal authorities

wholly owned affiliates foreign offices, facilities, and manufacturing plants that are 100 percent owned by the parent company

work force forecasting the process of predicting the number and kind of workers with specific skills and abilities that an organization will need in the future

work sample tests tests that require applicants to perform tasks that are actually done on the job

work team a small number of people with complementary skills who hold themselves mutually accountable for pursuing a common purpose, achieving performance goals, and improving interdependent work processes

worker maturity the ability and willingness to take responsibility for directing one's behavior at work

work-in-process inventories partially finished goods consisting of assembled component parts

workplace deviance unethical behavior that violates organizational norms about right and wrong

world gross national product the value of all the goods and services produced annually worldwide

wrongful discharge a legal doctrine that requires employers to have a job-related reason to terminate employees

Name and Organization Index

Subject Index